The Psychology of GENDER

FOURTH EDITION

VICKI S. HELGESON

CARNEGIE MELLON UNIVERSITY

PEARSON

Boston   Columbus   Indianapolis   New York   San Francisco   Upper Saddle River
Amsterdam   Cape Town   Dubai   London   Madrid   Milan   Munich   Paris   Montreal   Toronto
Delhi   Mexico City   São Paulo   Sydney   Hong Kong   Seoul   Singapore   Taipei   Tokyo

Executive Acquisitions Editor: Susan Hartman
Editorial Assistant: Alexandra Mitton
Marketing Manager: Nicole Kunzmann
Marketing Assistant: Jessica Warren
Production Assistant: Caitlin Smith
Production Manager: Fran Russello

Cover Administrator: Jayne Conte
Cover Designer: Suzanne Behnke
Cover Image Credit: Kudryashka/Fotolia
Editorial Production and Composition Service:
 Nithya Kuppuraj/PreMediaGlobal
Printer: Courier Companies, Inc.

Credits and acknowledgments borrowed from other sources and reproduced, with permission, in this textbook appear on appropriate page within text.

Many of the designations by manufacturers and seller to distinguish their products are claimed as trademarks. Where those designations appear in this book, and the publisher was aware of a trademark claim, the designations have been printed in initial caps or all caps.

Library of Congress Cataloging-in-Publication Data

Helgeson, Vicki S.
 The psychology of gender / Vicki S. Helgeson. — 4th ed.
 p. cm.
 Includes bibliographical references and index.
 ISBN-13: 978-0-205-05018-5 (alk. paper)
 ISBN-10: 0-205-05018-2 (alk. paper)
 1. Sex role. 2. Sex differences (Psychology) I. Title.
 HQ1075.H45 2012
 305.3—dc23
                          2011024121

ISBN 13: 978-0-205-05018-5
ISBN 10:   0-205-05018-2

To Mark and Katja

BRIEF CONTENTS

CONTENTS

PREFACE

The purpose of this text is to provide a review of the empirical research and conceptual discussions surrounding gender and to examine the implications of gender for relationships and health. The focus of this book goes beyond sex alone—whether one is biologically male or female—to explore the roles that society has assigned to women and men and the other variables that co-occur with sex, such as status and gender-related traits. The implications of social roles, status, and gender-related traits for relationships and health are examined. This is why the book is entitled *The Psychology of Gender* rather than *The Psychology of Sex*. *Gender* is a term that represents the social and cultural forces that influence men and women in our society. The book discusses the "psychology" of gender because the focus is on the individual in the social context. The primary focus is not on biology and anthropology, although their contributions to the study of gender are included.

Rather than review every topic related to gender, I examine the implications of gender for two broad domains of research: relationships and health. These domains are chosen, first, because they are central to our lives. Friendships, romantic relationships, and relationships at work have a great impact on our day-to-day functioning. Psychological well-being and physical health are important outcomes in their own right. A second reason for the focus on relationships and health is that these are domains in which clear sex differences have been documented. These sex differences cannot be attributed to biology alone; thus, relationships and health are domains for which gender, the social category, plays a role.

The book is divided into three sections, with each section building on the previous one. First, the nature of gender and the development of gender roles are presented. In the first chapter, I provide a brief overview of the field of gender, including how gender is construed across cultures and some of the philosophical and political controversies in the area. In Chapter 2, I review the scientific method that is used to study gender, including the unique difficulties that arise in this field, as well as provide a brief history of the psychology of gender, which includes a review of the various instruments used to study gender. In Chapter 3, I present research on attitudes toward gender and gender roles, focusing largely on gender-role stereotypes. Then I turn to the research literature to provide the current data (Chapter 4) and theory (Chapter 5) on sex differences in cognitive, social, and emotional domains. In Chapter 5, I discuss different theories of gender-role development, such as evolutionary theory, social learning theory, social role theory, and gender schema theory. In Chapter 6, I discuss the implications of gender and gender roles for achievement. Thus in the first section of this book, I provide important information on the similarities and differences between women and men and the theories that explain any observed differences. The data and the theories are important for understanding the subsequent sections of this book that address the implications of gender for relationships and health.

The second section of this book begins with a discussion of women's and men's communication and interaction styles (Chapter 7). These findings have implications for the specific relationships discussed: friendship (Chapter 8) and romantic relationships (Chapter 9). Research on cross-sex friendship, relationships among sexual minorities, and friendships at work are included in these chapters. The role of gender in relationships is critical to understanding the third section of the book, how gender influences health.

The third section begins with a chapter that provides an overview of sex differences in health and theories as to their origins (Chapter 10). Health is broadly construed in this book to reflect physical health problems, such as coronary artery disease, as well as mental health problems, such as depression and eating disorders. In Chapter 11, I investigate how gender affects the association of relationships to health. The effects of marriage and parenting on health are reviewed in Chapter 11 as are the effects of relationships gone awry, specifically domestic abuse and rape. Chapter 12 presents an examination of how gender affects the association of work to health, which includes a substantive discussion of pay disparity and sexual harassment. The final chapter focuses on the implications of gender for mental health, specifically, depression, eating disorders, and suicide.

For those of you who are familiar with the previous editions, I would like to highlight some changes that I have made. The basic structure of the book is the same, but the information has been substantially updated—not only in terms of more recent statistics on relationships and health but in terms of more cutting edge research, such as work on implicit gender attitudes and brain imaging studies. I have updated research on people of different cultures, races, and ethnicities and expanded my coverage of gay, lesbian, bisexual and transgendered (GLBT) persons. I have also integrated the research on GLBT persons into the text rather than having separate sections devoted to GLBT persons or GLBT relationships, which only served to accentuate differences. I have not made any major structural changes to the text. I have streamlined the chapters a bit, reorganized some topics to provide a more consistent flow of discussion, and tightened some lengthy discussions so that the primary points of an issue are more easily conveyed. For example, I integrated the leadership and influenceability sections in Chapter 7, and integrated the social support discussion in Chapter 7 with the support and health discussion in Chapter 11. I tried to break down complicated theories with visual aids that highlight key points of the theories. I also made a semantic change in the language used throughout the text. I am embarrassed to reveal that a reviewer pointed out the inconsistency in educating people about the use of sexist language and my consistent use of the phrase "men and women" instead of "women and men."

Multiple perspectives on the development of differences between men and women are offered, but the primary perspective that I emphasize is a social-psychological one. I examine gender as an individual difference variable but focus on the influence of the context—the situation, the environment, the culture—on gender. I have drawn from research in the areas of psychology, biology, sociology, anthropology, medicine, and public health.

I do not merely itemize sex differences in this text. In many domains, sex differences are more elusive than people believe. I highlight both similarities and differences and remind the reader about the magnitude of differences throughout the chapters. I also point out methodological flaws or difficulties that may bear on the observance of sex differences. The focus of the book is on the *explanations* for women's and men's thoughts, feelings, and behavior—not simply a summary statement of the similarities and differences between men and women.

Gender is a topic with which all of us are familiar, regardless of the scientific literature. Thus it is sometimes difficult to mesh personal experiences with the research literature. To help students integrate the two, each of the chapters includes mini-experiments (entitled "Do Gender") for students to test some of the research ideas presented. The results of these experiments will not always work out as intended, partly because the sample sizes will be small, partly because the samples will not be representative, and partly because the best ideas do not always translate into the best research designs. The purpose of the exercises is to allow students to gain experience with some of the methods used to study gender and to learn firsthand about how people experience gender in their lives. When topics of special interest arise—or what would be referred to as "going off on a tangent" in class—I included sidebars in each chapter, such as "How to Raise a Gender-Aschematic Child," "Family Supportive Work Environments," or "Does Abstinence Only Work?" Other aids to learning include key terms in boldface throughout the chapters and a summary of key terms and definitions at the end of the chapter; summaries of the main points at the end of the chapter; a list of thought-provoking discussion questions; and a list of suggested readings accompanying each chapter. To make the text more user friendly for students, I have added a section entitled "Take Home Points" at the end of each section of a chapter. Here, I summarize the major points in bullet-point form.

This text can be used for an undergraduate course on the psychology of gender, preferably for more advanced students. This text could also be supplemented with empirical readings for a graduate-level course. The book should have widespread appeal to students in the sciences and humanities. Students do not have to be psychology majors to read this text, but some knowledge of research methods would be helpful. Because social-psychological theories are so widely discussed in this text, a student who has taken such a course will find the book especially appealing and be able to grasp many of the concepts quite quickly. However, theories are explained in sufficient detail that students without a background in social psychology or psychology should understand the material. I welcome students from other disciplines into my course and find that the diversity in student backgrounds leads to more interesting discussions of the issues brought forth by the text.

VICKI S. HELGESON

SUPPLEMENTS

Pearson Education is pleased to offer the following supplements to qualified adopters.

Instructor's Manual with tests (0205050212) Prepared by Nancy Rogers and Jerry Jordan (University of Cincinnati), the instructor's manual is a wonderful tool for classroom preparation and management. Corresponding to the chapters in the text, each of the manual's 13 chapters contains a brief overview of the chapter with suggestions on how to present the material, sample lecture outlines, classrooms activities and discussion topics, ideas for in-class and out-of-class projects, recommended outside readings and related films and videos.

The test bank contains over 1,300 multiple choice, short answer and essay questions, each referencing the relevant page in the text.

Pearson MyTest Computerized Test Bank MyTest™ (www.pearsonmytest.com): The Test Bank comes with Pearson MyTest, a powerful assessment-generation program that helps instructors easily create and print quizzes and exams. You can do this online, allowing flexibility and the ability to efficiently manage assessments at any time. You can easily access existing questions and edit, create, and store questions using the simple drag-and-drop and Wordlike controls. Each question comes with information on its level of difficulty and related page number in the text. For more information, go to **www.PearsonMyTest.com**.

PowerPoint Presentation (0205050204) Prepared by Wendy Goldberg (UC Irvine), the PowerPoint Presentation is an exciting interactive tool for use in the classroom. Each chapter pairs key concepts with images from the textbook to reinforce student learning.

MySearchLab (0205225578) MySearchLab is the easiest way to master a writing or research project. Features include round-the-clock access to reliable content for Internet research from a variety of databases, Pearson SourceCheck™, and Autocite. Learning resources such as step-by-step tutorials and an exclusive online grammar and usage handbook to guide students through the research and writing process. **www.pearsonhighered.com**

ACKNOWLEDGMENTS

I would like to thank the anonymous reviewers of the previous editions of this book as well as the people who gave so generously of their time to read and comment on chapters of the first edition: Rosalind Barnett, Kay Deaux, Alice Eagly, Barbara Gutek, Judith Hall, Susan Sprecher, and Ingrid Waldron. I will always be indebted to Letitia Anne Peplau who read the entire first edition of this book, provided detailed feedback, and asked thought-provoking questions. These people's comments and suggestions have greatly enhanced this book.

I owe a great deal of gratitude to the many staff members and students at Carnegie Mellon University who have helped me with each edition of the book. I especially appreciate the efforts of Abby Kunz Vaughn who spent countless hours helping me to find references and statistics to update this book. I am eternally grateful to Jamie Vance for entering and organizing all the references into the book, and appreciate Emily Chao's work in revising and creating some of the "visuals" for this edition. I will always be indebted to Denise Janicki, who went through every page of the first volume of this book with a fine-toothed comb, asked questions about statements that were less than sensible, and provided creative ideas to bring the book to life. I also want to thank the students in the Psychology of Gender classes that I have taught over the last 20 years for inspiring me to write this book.

I would like to thank Susan Hartman from Prentice Hall for obtaining such helpful reviews and for lending her assistance with the creation of the fourth edition. I also wish to acknowledge the Prentice Hall reviewers: Mary Fraser, DeAnza College; Wendy Goldberg, UC Irvine; Rosemary Hornak, Meredith College; March Losch, University of Northern Iowa; Jeanne Maracek, Swarthmore College; Tiffany Marra, University of Michigan; Lynda Marshall, University of North Texas; Nancy Rogers, University of Cinncinnati; Aurora Sherman, Oregon State University; and Ashlyn Swartout, University of North Carolina at Greensboro.

Finally, I would like to thank my family: my mother and father for all their love and support over the years; my husband Mark for keeping me in touch with the "real world" outside of academia and for challenging me to think about gender in different ways; and my daughter Katja for teaching me about myself and for providing me with vivid examples of gender-role socialization.

V. S. H.

CHAPTER 1

Introduction

In 1998, my daughter was born and so was my own personal experience with the psychology of gender. As an advocate of equal opportunities and equal treatment for men and women, I thought this practice should begin with infancy. To start, my husband and I tried not to let gender be the overriding principle by which we chose Katja's toys and clothes. This proved to be far more difficult than we thought. In infancy, there are a fair number of "gender-neutral" clothes and toys. But by 1 year of age, the boys' toys and clothes are in one section, the girls' in another, and there is little common ground. I finally figured out why there are gender-neutral clothes for infants: Many parents-to-be and gift givers make purchases before the baby is born and don't know the sex of the newborn. By age 1, everyone knows.

By dressing Katja in gender-neutral clothes, I learned that the default assumption of others was she must be a boy. Any infant girl in her right mind (or her parents' right mind) would wear pink or ruffles or have bows in her hair (see Figure 1.1) or have her ears pierced!

Because I personally dislike pink (probably not a coincidence), Katja had a lot of blue, yellow, purple, and red. (This did come back to haunt me around age 4 when pink emerged as her favorite color! However, it lasted only a year and now she detests pink. It must be genetic.) When we carried her around as an infant, people in the grocery store or the shopping mall would comment on what a cute boy we had. When we mentioned he was a she, people often subtly reprimanded us for not providing the appropriate cues: the pink, the ruffles, the hair bows. Some people remarked that of course she was a girl because she had so much hair. I know of no evidence that girls are born with more hair than boys. I found it an interesting paradox that the biological default is female (i.e., at conception, the embryo is destined to become female unless exposed to male hormones), but the social default is male. When in doubt, assume the baby is a boy—unless there are strong social cues indicating the baby is a girl. It is not nearly

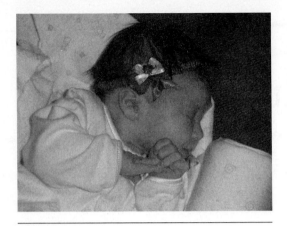

FIGURE 1.1   This infant has a bow in her hair to signal to society that she is a female.

The point I am trying to convey is that sex is a very important category to us as a society. In fact, sex is one of the first categories learned by children because (a) sex has only two categories, (b) the categories are mutually exclusive, and (c) we are immediately exposed to members of both categories (Zemore, Fiske, & Kim, 2000). An infant's sex is one of the first things you try to figure out about her or him and one of the first things you notice about a child or an adult. Have you ever found yourself in a situation where you didn't know the sex of a person, or mistook someone for the wrong sex? I remember being with my father-in-law once while a young man with a ponytail changed the oil in my car. My father-in-law was sure that the person was female. I was hushing him as best I could for fear the man would overhear the conversation and replace my oil with wiper fluid. Why are we bothered so much by these situations? Why do you need to know the person's sex to interact with her—or him? A person's sex—really, a person's gender (I explain the distinction in the next section)—has implications for our feelings, our beliefs, and our behavior toward the person. Your own gender has implications for how others feel about you, what others think about you, and how others behave toward you.

as offensive to assume a girl is a boy as to assume a boy is a girl. But people do expect you to be offended. When someone did mistake Katja for a boy, I wasn't surprised. How can you tell at that age? But the person who made the remark was always extremely apologetic, as if she had insulted me by assuming Katja was of the other sex.

By age 1, girls' and boys' clothes have little in common. Blue jeans that are plain in the boys' section are decorated with flowers, ruffles, or sequins in the girls' section. A simple pair of shorts in the boys' department is elaborated with a flap in the girls' department so it looks like a skirt. Girls' clothes are covered with an amazing assortment of flowers. Girls also are expected to wear dresses. How practical is it to play in the sand, climb a tree, and run around in a dress? You can't even buy socks that are for both boys and girls; there are boy socks and girl socks. Guess which ones have ruffles?

Gender has been the subject of scientific scrutiny for over a century. Scientists have debated the similarities as well as the differences between women and men: Are men better at math than women? Are women more emotional than men? Are men more aggressive than women? Do men and women have the same capacities to be engineers, nurses, and lawyers? Scientists have also examined the implications of being female and male for one's relationships and one's health: Are women's relationships closer than those of men? Does marriage provide more health benefits for men compared to women? Are women more depressed than men? Are men less willing than women to seek help for health problems?

You have probably thought about some of these questions. You may be fairly confident you know the answers to some of them. Gender is a topic with which we are all intimately familiar. What woman doubts that men are less likely than women to ask for directions? What man doubts that women are more likely than men to dwell on their problems? We have many experiences we bring to bear on these issues, but our anecdotal observations are not the same as observations gained from well-established scientific methods. In fact, our anecdotal observations may be biased in favor of sex differences when differences do not really exist. When evaluating the literature, you will see the answer to the question of sex differences is usually fairly complicated. The appearance of sex differences depends on myriad factors: the place, time, person, audience, and characteristics of the one making the observation.

In this text, I evaluate the literature on the psychology of gender, paying special attention to the implications that gender has for our relationships and our health. I begin this first chapter by defining the terminology used in the study of gender. Next, I comment on how gender is construed in other cultures. Finally, I conclude the chapter by providing an overview of the various political and philosophical viewpoints that many researchers have taken when studying gender.

DEFINITION OF TERMS

This textbook is called *Psychology of Gender.* Why not *Psychology of Sex?* What is the difference between sex and gender? Is *gender* just the more politically correct term? One of our first tasks is to define these terms and other sex-related and gender-related ideas.

The first distinction to make is between sex and gender. **Sex** refers to the biological categories of female and male, categories distinguished by genes, chromosomes, and hormones. Culture has no influence on one's sex. Sex is a relatively stable category that is not easily changed, although recent technology has allowed people to change their biological sex. **Gender**, by contrast, is a much more fluid category. It refers to the social categories of male and female. These categories are distinguished from one another by a set of psychological features and role attributes that society has assigned to the biological category of sex. What are some of the psychological features we assign to sex in the United States? Emotionality is a trait we ascribe to women, and competitiveness is a trait we ascribe to men. These traits are features of gender rather than sex. Whereas sex is defined in the same way across cultures, gender differs because each society has its own prescriptions for how women and men ought to behave. A feature of the male sex category includes the Y chromosome; regardless of whether a male wears a baseball cap or barrettes, or is competitive or empathetic, he is of the male sex because he possesses the Y chromosome. Personality and appearance are related to the gender category. In the United States, a feature of the female gender category is nurturance; a person who is nurturant is behaving in a way consistent with the social category for women. Another feature of the female gender category in the United States is to wear a skirt; typically, if you encounter someone in this country wearing a skirt, you can assume the person is psychologically female as well as biologically female. However, in other countries, such as Scotland, wearing a skirt or a kilt is quite normal for a person of the biological male sex; thus we would not want to use wearing a skirt as a feature of the female or male gender category in Scotland. It is American culture that views a kilt as a skirt; a person from Scotland does not view a kilt as feminine attire. The content of gender categories—but not sex categories—is influenced by society, culture, and time.

Now that this important distinction has been made, I must point out the distinction is rarely employed in practice. Laypersons as well as scientists often use the terms interchangeably; articles in the newspaper as well as articles in scientific journals do not use the terms consistently. Even the American Psychological Association is not consistent in its employment of these terms. For example, when submitting an article to be published in a scientific journal, the editor often replaces the phrase *sex differences* with *gender differences*. There is a good chance that the author is simply referring to differences between people who are biologically male versus biologically female without any thought to their psychological attributes; that being the case, the correct term would be sex differences. However, some people believe that the phrase *sex differences* implies the basis of the difference is biological. Yet, if you conduct a study of women and men and find that women have better recall on a memory task than men or that men outperform women on a video game, do you have any evidence that the difference is biological? No. A better term to describe these differences is **sex-related behavior**. This term implies the behavior corresponds to sex, but it does not say anything about the cause or the etiology of the difference.

A term that better captures society's influence on the biologically based categories of female and male is **gender role** rather than *gender*. A **role** is a social position accompanied by a set of norms or expectations. For example, one role you most certainly possess is the role of student. What are some of the expectations that go along with this role? One expectation is that you study for class; another might be that you socialize and stay up late at night with friends. In this instance, a conflict may exist between the expectations within a given role.

Gender role refers to the expectations that go along with being male versus female. We typically expect men to be strong, independent, and competitive, and to keep their emotions hidden. These are features of the male gender role. By contrast, we typically expect women to be caring, emotionally expressive, polite, and helpful: features of the female gender role. In other words, we expect men to be **masculine** and we expect women to be **feminine**. Masculinity includes the traits, behaviors, and interests that society has assigned to the male gender role. A masculine trait is self-confidence; a masculine behavior is aggression; and a masculine interest is watching sports. Femininity includes the traits, behaviors, and interests assigned to the female gender role. A feminine trait is emotional; a feminine behavior is helping someone; and a feminine interest is cooking. In Chapter 2, we discuss the content of femininity and masculinity in more detail.

When expectations within a role conflict, such as in my example of the student, we experience **intrarole conflict**. How might women experience intrarole conflict within their gender role? Women are expected to be emotional and express their feelings but also to be sensitive to the needs of others. So, should a woman who is unhappy with her marriage express those feelings to her husband? If she expresses her feelings, she is adhering to the expectancy that she express emotion, but she is contradicting the expectancy that she not hurt someone's feelings. How might men experience intrarole conflict within their gender role? One expectation of the male gender role is to achieve; another is to be independent and not ask for help. What should a man who desires to adhere to his gender role do if he can't figure out how to put something together by himself? If he asks for help, he will further his achievement goal but at the expense of another goal: appearing independent. Just because a given role has a set of guidelines does not mean those guidelines might not conflict with one another from time to time. Gender roles are no exception.

When the expectations of one role conflict with the expectations of another role, we experience **interrole conflict**. You possess other roles besides your gender role. What roles conflict with your gender role? At times the expectations of the role of student may conflict with both the female gender role and the male gender role. In a large lecture class, the expectation of a student is to sit quietly in the class and listen, a passive role that may conflict with the active aspects of the male gender role. In a small seminar, the expectation of

a student is to participate actively in class discussion, which may include some debate; this active, possibly argumentative role may conflict with the female gender role. Think about some of your relationship roles. Does your role as a friend, son or daughter, boyfriend or girlfriend ever conflict with your gender role? A male student involved in a group project may experience conflict between the male gender role norm to be independent and the student role norm to work together with classmates on group projects. The difficulty here is that the norms for the two different roles clash.

Sometimes we violate the norms associated with our roles, partly due to role conflict. What are the consequences of behaving in ways that violate norms? The consequences could be minor or severe; it will depend on how central that norm is to the role and how strongly the situation calls for adherence to the role. The consequences for a male asking for help are probably minor. However, the consequences for a male wearing a dress—unless it is a costume party—are likely to be severe. A central feature of the male gender role is to not appear feminine. What are the consequences for a female not being emotional? It will depend on the situation. A female who fails to express feelings at an emotional event, such as a funeral, may be judged quite harshly, whereas a female who fails to express emotions in the context of the classroom will not suffer any negative repercussions.

Think about the consequences for violating the norms that go along with your gender role. Examine the effects of norm violation in Do Gender 1.1.

Who do you think suffers more for violating gender role norms, women or men? Many people maintain it is men who suffer more. Today, women who behave "like men" are often accepted and even applauded. It is

---

DO GENDER 1.1
Engaging in Gender-Role Incongruent Behavior

Try adopting some behavior that does not fit your gender role and see how people respond—verbally and nonverbally.

For example, if you are male, try

> Wearing a dress.
> Wearing makeup.
> Calling for an escort service when you walk across campus in the dark.
> Going into a salon and having your fingernails painted.

If you are female, try

> Chewing tobacco in public.
> Joining a group of guys to play football or basketball.
> Working on your car with a man standing by (changing the oil or changing a tire).
> Going into a barbershop and getting your hair cut.

How did you feel?

How did others respond?

FIGURE 1.2   More girls play soccer today than any other sport.

---

acceptable for women to dress like men by wearing pants, suits, and even ties; it is acceptable for women to have jobs that were traditionally held by men, such as doctor, lawyer, even construction worker. And, it is more acceptable for women to participate in sports (see Figure 1.2).

But is it acceptable for men to dress like women by wearing a dress or tights? Are men who possess jobs traditionally held by women, such as nurse or secretary, encouraged or applauded? It is interesting that a little girl who behaves like a boy is called a tomboy, but a little boy who behaves like a girl is called a sissy. *Sissy* has more negative connotations than *tomboy*. Today, parents have no problem giving their little girls trucks to play with and encouraging girls to play sports. But how do parents feel about giving their little boys dolls and encouraging them to play "dress-up"?

Most scientists believe men suffer more negative consequences for gender-role violations than women. The reason? Status. Women who take on characteristics of the male gender role are moving toward a higher status, whereas men who take on characteristics of the female gender role are moving toward a lower status. We applaud the move up but not the move down. The relation of gender to status is elaborated on later in this chapter.

The term *gender role* is used interchangeably with the term *sex role*. Personally, I do not know what to make of the latter term. *Sex role* really does not make sense because it confuses a biological category, sex, with a social category, role. Thus it is peculiar that one of the leading scientific journals in this area is called *Sex Roles* instead of "Gender Roles." I prefer to use the term *sex* when referring to the biological categories of male and female, and to use the terms *gender* and *gender role* when referring to the psychological attributes and expectations we have for those categories.

Now we can ask whether people accept the psychological category that accompanies their biological sex. **Gender identity** or **gender-role identity** is our perception of the self as psychologically female or male. You have probably heard of people who are biologically male but feel as if they are female and wish they were female, or vice versa. **Transgendered individuals** are people who live with a gender identity that does not correspond to their biological sex. That is, their biological sex is incongruent with their psychological sex. A transgendered person may be biologically female but feel psychologically like a male and choose to live life as a male. This transgendered individual may dress and behave like a man, that is, take on the male gender role. **Transsexuals** also have a gender identity that does not correspond to their biological sex but they have hormonal or surgical treatment to change their sex to correspond with their gender identity. There are about two to three times as many male to female transsexuals as female to male transsexuals (Lawrence, 2008). **Intersex** persons are those who are born with ambiguous genitals; these persons typically have surgery to alter their genitals so that they can be consistent biologically.

There is a classification of psychopathology in the *Diagnostic and Statistical Manual of Mental Disorders* (*DSM-IV-TR*) called Gender Identity Disorder, which refers to people who are uncomfortable with the biological sex to which they have been assigned. As noted earlier, one treatment option is to have surgery to change their biological sex to fit their psychological gender. More recently, researchers have called into question whether Gender Identity Disorder should be pathologized—especially in children. See Sidebar 1.1 for a discussion of this issue.

Do not confuse *gender identity* with **sexual orientation**, which refers to whether people prefer to have other-sex or same-sex persons as partners for love, affection, and sex. **Heterosexuals** prefer other-sex partners; **homosexuals** prefer same-sex partners; and **bisexuals** are accepting of other-sex and same-sex partners.

Sex typing (which really should be referred to as gender typing) is the process by which sex-appropriate preferences, behaviors, skills, and self-concept are acquired. How does a girl become feminine? A boy masculine? We review the different theories of sex typing in Chapter 5. People who adhere to the gender role that society assigned them are sex-typed. A male who thinks, feels, and behaves in masculine ways and a female who thinks, feels, and behaves in feminine ways are each **sex-typed**. A male who acts feminine and a female who acts masculine are each said to be **cross-sex-typed**. Someone who incorporates both masculine and feminine qualities is not sex-typed and is often referred to as **androgynous**. Androgyny is discussed in more detail in Chapters 2 and 5.

Thus far, we have been discussing attributes that define a person's sense of self. Gender also comes into play when we think about other people. Our own personal view about how women and men should behave is called a **gender-role attitude**. You might believe women should be caring, be nurturant, and have primary responsibility for raising children, whereas men should be independent, be assertive, and have primary responsibility for earning money to take care of the family—regardless of whether you possess these characteristics. If you hold these beliefs,

SIDEBAR 1.1: *Should Gender Identity Disorder Be Classified as a Mental Illness?*

According to the *Diagnostic and Statistical Manual of Mental Disorders* (*DSM-IV-TR*), Gender Identity Disorder involves the following four characteristics:

a. Identification with the other sex (as indicated by four of the following five):

 1. Desire to be the other sex

 2. Preference to dress as the other sex

 3. Preference to behave as the other sex

 4. Desire to play games and activities associated with the other sex

 5. Preference for other-sex playmates

b. Discomfort with own sex

c. Disturbance causes significant distress and impairs functioning

d. Does not have an intersex condition

Gender Identity Disorder is one of the most controversial disorders in the *DSM-IV-TR* (Manners, 2009). Some people have called for the removal of Gender Identity Disorder from the *DSM-V* that is due to be published in 2013 (Ault & Brzuzy, 2009). Some liken the debate over whether it should be included in the future edition of the *DSM-IV* to the debate that occurred several decades ago over homosexuality, which ultimately led to its removal in 1980. Gender Identity Disorder is especially controversial as a diagnosis in childhood for several reasons. First, characteristic a (listed above) requires only four of the five features, which means that the most critical feature (desire to be the other sex) need not be present. Second, the other four features revolve around gender stereotypical behavior, and what is deemed gender stereotypical today may change with time and does change with culture. This diagnosis suggests that gender nonconformity is evidence of a disorder and justifies the treatment of children who do not conform to stereotypical gender roles. Some have questioned whether the diagnosis in children comes from a discomfort with the behavior among parents rather than the children themselves (Hill et al., 2007). Interestingly, boys are more likely to be referred for Gender Identity Disorder than girls, which may reflect society's greater intolerance of other-sex behavior in boys than girls (Zucker & Cohen-Kettenis, 2008). Furthermore, follow-up studies of children with Gender Identity Disorder show that only a minority persist into adolescence and adulthood (Zucker, 2010). By contrast, there is a higher rate of persistence among adolescents. Even among adults, however, there is debate as to whether the desire to be the other sex should be labeled as a disorder. This diagnosis pathologizes transgendered people and transsexuals, despite the fact that many of these individuals are well functioning. The inclusion of Gender Identity Disorder as a mental illness increases the stigma and subsequent discrimination associated with gender noncomformity.

you have a traditional gender-role attitude. That is, your view fits the traditional expectations that society has for how women and men should behave. Alternatively, you might believe that both women and men should be assertive and caring and that both should be equally responsible for working inside and outside the home. In this case, you have an egalitarian gender-role attitude. Many people hold what Hochschild (1989) refers to as a "transitional attitude," which fits somewhere between traditional and egalitarian gender-role attitudes. You may believe that both men and women should participate in work inside the home and outside the home, but that women should give the home their primary attention and men should give work their primary attention. This person is striving for an egalitarian philosophy, but some residual traditional gender-role attitudes remain.

Three other terms reflect one's attitude toward the category of sex. Each term maps onto one of the three components of an attitude: affect, cognition, and behavior. The affective (feeling) component of our attitude toward the sex category is called **sexism**, or prejudice toward people based on their sex. Typically, we think of sexism as involving a negative attitude or negative affect, but it could entail positive affect. If you dislike the person your wife hired to take care of your children because the person is male, you are showing sexism. Likewise, if you like the person your wife hired merely because she is female, you are again showing sexism. The cognitive component of our attitude toward sex is a **sex stereotype** or **gender-role stereotype**. These terms refer to our beliefs about the features of the biological or psychological categories of male and female. If you believe the male nanny would not be competent because he lacks the required nurturant qualities, you are engaging in gender-role

stereotyping. The behavioral component of our attitude toward men and women is **sex discrimination**, which involves the differential treatment of people based on their biological sex. If you fire the male nanny because you dislike men as nannies and you doubt his competence because he is a man, you are engaging in sex discrimination. Sex discrimination is often a result of both sexism and gender-role stereotyping. These attitudes toward sex are the focus of Chapter 3.

Finally, one last term to discuss is **feminism**. What image did that term conjure up for you? The definitions of *feminism* are vast and varied. At the most fundamental level, a feminist is someone who believes women and men should be treated equally. You are probably thinking, "Is that all there is to feminism? If so, I must be a feminist." In fact, over the years, I have had many students in class tell me they did not realize they were feminists until taking my class. And several students have told me that their parents did not realize they were feminists until the students took my course. A study of college women showed that three-fourths of the women endorsed some or most of the goals of feminism but only 11% identified themselves as feminists (Liss, Crawford, & Popp, 2004). In a more recent study, 17% of women and 7% of men self-identified as feminists (Anderson, Kanner, & Elsayegh, 2009).

Younger people appear to be more supportive of feminism—although it is not always clear that they understand what it means. When a group of Latina high school students were asked whether they were feminist, slightly over half of the eleventh and twelfth graders endorsed feminism and three-fourths of the ninth and tenth graders endorsed feminism (Manago, Brown, & Leaper, 2009). However, some of the younger students confused feminism with femininity. When asked to define feminism, the prevailing theme was equality for women—especially among the older students. Other themes were female empowerment, celebrating women, and encouraging women's aspirations. A minority of students said that feminists favored women and did not like men, which is not a defining characteristic of feminism.

A defining feature of feminism is a high regard for women. Most people in our society would agree women should be valued. However, even when people have a positive attitude toward women, they are typically reluctant to identify themselves as feminists (Suter & Toller, 2006). Why? First, *feminism* has negative connotations. Some people perceive feminists as women who hate men, like some of the Latina adolescents discussed earlier (a stereotype that has been refuted as described in Chapter 3). Second, feminism often includes the belief that society needs to make changes for equality to occur and can include the impetus to take action to make these changes. It is these latter ideas that are more controversial. When feminism is equated with activism, the term becomes less appealing. However, activism can take many forms, ranging from volunteering at a women's shelter to participating in a prochoice rally. See Table 1.1 for examples of feminist activities. Do you participate in similar activities? If so, do you identify yourself as a feminist?

A majority of college women believe that community effort is needed to promote equality for women but that their own achievements depend upon themselves rather than group effort. In other words, the typical college female believes that women as a group need societal help but she, herself, doesn't need any help. This set of beliefs is similar to the "denial of disadvantage" (Crosby, 1984) discussed in Chapter 12—the idea that most women perceive that other

TABLE 1.1   EXAMPLES OF FEMINIST ACTIVISM

Volunteering at a women's shelter.
Helping set up a day care program.
Volunteering at a rape crisis center.
Assisting with a women's study course.
Participating in a women's conference.
Donating money to a female political candidate.
Supporting a female-owned business.
Attending a women's sporting event.
Using nonsexist language.
Buying a baby gender-neutral toys and clothes.

women suffer from discrimination but that they have not been victims of discrimination.

Thus it appears the belief in gender equality is the central feature of feminism, but activism is an important feature of feminism for some individuals. Conduct Do Gender 1.2 to find out how feminism is viewed at your institution.

TAKE HOME POINTS

- *Sex* refers to the biological category; *gender* the psychological category.

- Intrarole conflict is conflict between expectations within a role; interrole conflict is conflict between expectations of different roles.

- Attitudes toward sex can be divided into the affective component (sexism), the cognitive component (gender-role stereotype), and the behavioral component (discrimination).

- The defining feature of feminism is the belief in equality for women and men. Although most people endorse this belief, feminism is perceived negatively. Women typically believe that equality for women as a group should be promoted (probably by someone else), but they do not need any group efforts to aid their own achievements.

DO GENDER 1.2
Defining a Feminist

Ask 10 women and 10 men to describe the first things that come to mind when they think of the term *feminist*. This will tell you a couple of things: First, you will learn whether people view the term favorably or unfavorably; second, you will learn the content of this category. Construct a frequency distribution of the features listed. The features most often listed by these people are those central to the feminist category; the features listed least are often peripheral to the category and probably more reflective of that particular individual. What percentage of features is negative versus positive? Do men or women view a feminist in more positive or negative terms? To address this question, calculate the number of positive and negative features identified by the group of men and the group of women.

Ask these same 20 people two more questions. Ask whether they believe women and men should be treated equally, the defining feature of a feminist. You could ask people to respond on a five-point scale: 1 = Definitely not, 2 = Probably not, 3 = Unsure, 4 = Probably should, 5 = Definitely should. Then ask whether each person is a feminist. Do answers to these two questions correspond?

CULTURAL DIFFERENCES IN THE CONSTRUAL OF GENDER

I have defined the terminology used in the psychology of gender. All these terms, however, are construed at least somewhat differently by people of different ethnic backgrounds in the United States and by people from other cultures. Ramet (1996) proposes the idea of a **gender culture**, which reflects "society's understanding of what is possible, proper, and perverse in gender-linked behavior" (p. 2). In other words, each society generates its own standards for gender-linked behavior.

Because the majority of research that has been conducted and examined in this book interprets gender—the roles of women and men in society—in similar terms, it might be interesting to step outside our cultural view and consider how gender is construed in a few different cultures around the world.

Cultures with Multiple Genders

One assumption about gender shared by many cultures is that there are only two of them: male and female. Did it ever occur to you that there could be more than two genders? In several Native American cultures, there are four genders. One example of multiple genders among Native Americans is the *Berdache* (Tafoya, 2007; Williams, 1993). Berdache is a term that was institutionalized among the Lakota Indians, who currently reside in South Dakota (Medicine, 2002). The male Berdache and female Berdache are third and fourth genders. Of the two, the male Berdache is much more common. The male Berdache is biologically male but takes on characteristics of both women and men in appearance and manner. These are men who prefer not to be warriors but to take care of children and make clothing. Historically, the Berdache was highly respected and viewed as sacred. The Berdache was believed to be endowed with spiritual powers and had the highest status among the genders. Today, however, the status and respect ascribed to the Berdache have waned. Although Berdache is a social identity rather than a sexual orientation, non-Natives infer sexual orientation from the role. This is the result of Western culture imposing its rigid gender categories on a person who does not easily fit into them.

The appearance of multiple genders also occurs in the Balkans (Ramet, 1996). In this case, people primarily take on the other gender role to serve society's needs. For example, some biological females are raised as males when the society is in need of those functions best served by men. In the Balkans, these women assume a male social identity and perform the work of men. They are not allowed to marry and are sworn to virginity. These people are highly respected.

In the city of Juchitan, Mexico, the highest status is conferred to a third gender, the *muxe*—biological males who dress like females and take on women's roles in the community (Sevcik, 2007). They are highly regarded for their excellent design and artistic skills. They rarely marry, often take care of their mothers, and typically make more money than males or females. People in this region are undecided as to whether this gender is genetically or socially determined. It is certainly the case that people could be accused of encouraging a biologically male child to become a muxe, as muxes bring economic prosperity and high status to a family.

In Western cultures, gender is defined by our genitals. We have no culturally defined category for people who are uncomfortable with their sex or who would like to combine elements of both female and male gender roles. We are very uncomfortable when we cannot determine someone's sex, and we are very uncomfortable with people who try to create new gender categories (e.g., transsexuals).

Morocco

In Morocco, there are only two genders, but the two are very distinct (Hessini, 1994). The distinction between the female gender role and the male gender role manifests itself in terms of physical space. Private space, the space reserved for the family inside a home, is female space. Public space, basically everything outside of the home, is male space. The duties of men and women are distinct and take place in their separate physical spaces. The women fulfill their roles in female space, inside the home, and the men fulfill their roles in male space, outside the home. It is clear that public space is men's space because only men are found in coffee shops and theaters or other public places. If women are in public, they are usually scurrying from one place to the next.

The distinct roles of men and women are not questioned in Morocco (Hessini, 1994). The man is the leader of the family and works outside the home to provide for the family; the woman is responsible for the household, which includes the education and religious training of children. Even in modern Morocco, women are not concerned with equality. The Moroccan people believe the two sexes complement one another. Although the cultural code is for men to support the family financially, economic necessity has led to an increase in the number of women working outside the home. This is creating some tension because both women and men believe that women's primary responsibility lies inside the home and that women should not work outside the home.

One way in which women are able to work and enter into public spaces is by wearing the hijab and djellaba when they go out in public (Hessini, 1994). The hijab is a large scarf that covers a woman's head, neck, and shoulders so only her face is seen (see Figure 1.3).

The hijab provides a sense of Muslim identity and security for women. The djellaba is a long, loose-fitting gown that hides the shape of the body. Women believe these

FIGURE 1.3   In this picture, a Muslim woman is dressed in the traditional hijab.

articles of clothing protect them from men and help preserve the social order. A woman who does not wear the hijab and djellaba is viewed as naked. The thought is that other clothing shows the outline of the female body, which provokes and attracts men, leading to adultery. Women are held more responsible for adultery than men; thus, in a sense, the hijab and djellaba are viewed as avenues to freedom for women in that they allow them to go out in public.

The hijab is hardly viewed as liberating by American women. Americans view the hijab as a sign of women's oppression and male domination and as perpetuating the stereotype of women as sexual temptresses whom men are unable to resist. However, a group of educated American Muslim women told a very different story when asked about why they wore the hijab in the United States (Droogsma, 2007). These women said that the hijab defined their Muslim identity, connecting them to other Muslims, and was a constant reminder to follow their religious values. The women also said that wearing the hijab allowed them to resist sexual objectification and freed them from the emphasis placed on appearance in America.

The Agta Negrito

Some people maintain that women's and men's distinct social roles are rooted in biology. As evidence, they cite the distinct roles of women and men in hunter-gatherer societies. Women are biologically predisposed to gather, and men are biologically predisposed to hunt. Women cannot hunt because hunting would reduce their ability to bear and take care of children. In most hunter-gatherer societies, the division of labor is as predicted: Men hunt and women gather.

The Agta Negrito is a society in the Philipines that challenges this idea (Goodman et al., 1985). In this society, women hunt and are as successful as men. Hunting does not impair women's fertility. Women who hunt do not differ from women who do not hunt in age at menarche, age at first pregnancy, or age of the youngest child. Women who hunt are also able to take care of children.

How are women able to hunt in this society? There are two reasons. One is physical, having to do with the Agta terrain: Women can hunt close to home. The second is social: Other people help with child care. Women hunters either take nursing infants with them or leave toddlers at home where they are cared for by other family members. The structure of this culture shows that (1) there is no biological reason that women cannot hunt and (2) the division of labor between the two sexes is not carved in stone.

Tahiti

Evidence indicates that men's and women's roles can be similar. Tahiti is an example of a truly androgynous society (Gilmore, 1990). The social roles of women and men are very much the same. Women have the same status as men and have the same opportunities as men in domestic, occupational, and recreational spheres. Not only are women's and men's roles similar, but women and men share similar personalities. There is no pressure on men and women to behave differently or to behave in accordance with traditional gender roles. Men are not worried about proving their masculinity, for example, and do not feel the need to take risks. This similarity of women and men is even reflected in their language; there is no word for gender in the language and there are no female or male pronouns. The society is based on cooperation rather than competition. Perhaps because resources are available to people, there is no economic reason to compete. There is little aggression, no war, and no hunting; that is, there is nothing for men to defend. Thus there is no basis for an ideology of masculinity to have evolved. The people in this society truly seem to function without thinking about gender.

Status and Culture

With the exception of Tahiti and probably a few other cultures, one commonality in the way gender is construed around the world is that men have higher status than women (Chisholm, 2000). How is this status difference manifested?

There are a number of indices of gender inequality. The higher illiteracy rates of women, less access to medical care for women, a lower earnings ratio of women compared to men, and the legitimization of physical abuse of women in some countries are all manifestations of men's higher status relative to women's (Chisholm, 2000). In India and China, some female fetuses are aborted because they are less valued than males. The one-child policy in China has led to the abortion of female fetuses even though sex-selective abortion is prohibited by the government. Between 1985 and 1989,

there were 108 males born for every 100 females; in 2010, the sex ratio was 123 to 100 ("The Worldwide," 2010). In Korea, there is a greater likelihood of abortion among married women if they have sons than if they have daughters (Chung, 2007). If a family had two sons, there was an 80% chance of abortion; if the family had two daughters, there was a 41% chance of abortion.

In the United States, Gallup Polls have shown a slight preference for boys over girls that has remained over time. Respondents are asked in these surveys which sex they would prefer if they could have only one child. In 2007, a Gallup Poll of 1,000 adults in the United States showed that women slightly preferred a girl to a boy (35% vs. 31%), but men strongly preferred a boy to a girl (45% vs. 21%). One-third had no preference. As shown in Figure 1.4, the preference has remained fairly stable over time.

Most studies conclude that parents desire one child of each sex. In Australia, there is an equal preference for boys and girls,

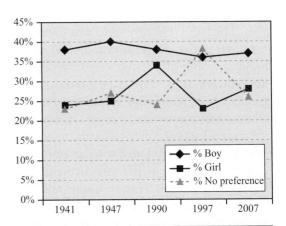

FIGURE 1.4   Gallup Polls conducted from 1941 to 2007 show that a slight preference for a boy compared to a girl persists but that a sizeable number of respondents have no preference. *Source:* Adapted from Newport (2007).

and parents are just as likely to have a third child if they have two sons or two daughters (Kippen, Evans, & Gray, 2007).

Other evidence that males are more highly regarded than females comes from the effect of a child's sex on the structure of the family. In an analysis of census data from the last half of the 20th century, Dahl and Moretti (2008) found that firstborn females are less likely to live with their fathers than firstborn males. Several factors accounted for this difference. First, women whose firstborn child was female were less likely to marry the father than women whose firstborn child was male. Second, women whose firstborn child was female were more likely to divorce than women whose firstborn child was male. Finally, upon divorce, fathers were less likely to have custody of firstborn females than males. The investigators noted that families with firstborn females also ended up with a greater number of children than families with firstborn males. Because the research is archival, one cannot discern cause and effect. However, these data provide circumstantial evidence that people—especially fathers—prefer sons over daughters.

The dominant group in a society has rights and privileges not available to the subordinate group. In our society, we can talk about male privilege, White privilege, heterosexual privilege, class privilege, and even attractiveness privilege. People who have the privilege are often unaware of it; those who lack the privilege are aware. For example, heterosexual privilege entails the right to marry, to have a public ceremony that entails celebration and gifts from family and friends, and to have children without being questioned. Heterosexuals do not view this as a privilege because it has come to be expected. Most homosexuals in the United States, however, do not have

these privileges and certainly recognize heterosexual privilege.

What is male privilege? Historically, women were not allowed to vote or own property. At one time, only men were allowed to serve in the military. Today, men have greater access than women to certain jobs and to political office. Until 1972, only men could run the Boston Marathon. The first two women who ran the marathon, in 1966 and 1967, disguised themselves, one by dress and one by name; upon recognition, their completion of the race was dismissed, questioned, and not officially recognized (Rosenbloom, 2000). It was not until the early 1990s that women were allowed to enter the Citadel and the Virginia Military Institute, all-male military schools. In 1993, Shannon Faulkner applied to the Citadel by omitting any reference to her gender; she was admitted, but on learning of her gender, the Citadel withdrew its offer of admission. Today, women are still not allowed membership in the Augusta National Golf Club, the club that hosts the premier golfing event, the Masters. Annika Sorenstam, however, did compete in the Colonial, one of the PGA tours in 2003, becoming the first woman to do so in 58 years and causing some men to withdraw from the tournament.

Today, great strides have been made in the United States toward gender equality. Obviously, women can vote, run for political office and win elections, and have gained in occupational status. However, women are not nearly as prevalent in government as men, and women are rarely found in the highest occupational statuses, such as chief executive officers of industry. It was not until 2007 that we saw the first female Speaker of the U.S. House of Representatives, Nancy Pelosi. In 2009, we saw the first female contender for president of the United States supported by a major political party, Hillary Clinton (see Figure 1.5). In 1984, Geraldine Ferraro became the first female vice presidential nominee to appear on the ballot, which was then followed by Sarah Palin in 2009.

Another way to examine status is to ask people to imagine what it would be like to wake up one day as the other sex. In my psychology of gender courses, I often ask students to write essays on this question. Women and men identify positives and negatives in considering the transformation. Women note several advantages: They would be less afraid, more adventurous, and more independent; but also note several disadvantages: They would have more difficulty receiving support, and they would have less meaningful conversations. Some aspects of life were considered to have mixed effects. Women said having to work would be a negative, but this would be offset by more opportunities for advancement. On the positive side, women said they would be taken more seriously as men, but on the negative side, this meant more would be expected of them. Men note primarily negatives in their hypothetical transformations to women: becoming more nervous, self-conscious, and concerned about appearance; worrying about men coming on to them; and worrying about walking alone at night. One advantage men note was similar to the disadvantage women noted: As women, the men said they would have more friends and be more sociable. Conduct your own experiment on this issue with Do Gender 1.3.

The similarities and differences in the treatment and behavior of men and women appear in numerous chapters throughout this book. The important point to keep in mind is whether a sex difference in behavior is due to something inherent about being female or male or to something about status.

FIGURE 1.5 In 2008, Hillary Clinton became the first serious female candidate for President of the United States.

DO GENDER 1.3
Life as the Other Sex

Select an age group. Ask 10 males and 10 females to answer the following question: "Imagine that you woke up tomorrow and were the other sex. Go through your entire day and describe how your life would be different."

Read through the stories and identify themes. Construct a frequency distribution of those themes.

PHILOSOPHICAL AND POLITICAL ISSUES SURROUNDING GENDER

The last important issue to address in this introductory chapter is the philosophical and political debates that have taken place with respect to gender. The study of gender, in particular the study of sex differences, is a politically charged topic. With gender, scientists are often in one of two camps: those who believe there are important differences between the sexes and those who believe the two sexes are fundamentally the same. There are also investigators who believe we should or should not compare women and men. I address each of these debates and then turn to the political movements that have influenced the study of gender: the women's movements and the men's movements. Finally, I conclude with a note about nonsexist language.

The Sex Difference Debate

People who believe the two sexes are fundamentally the same are known as the **minimalists**. The minimalists believe there are very few differences between women and men, and if the context was held constant, differences would vanish. That is, any differences in behavior observed between men and women might be due to the roles they hold or the situations in which they find themselves.

By contrast, the **maximalists** believe there are fundamental differences between men and women. However, they argue that "difference" does not mean "deficit." Theorists such as Carol Gilligan and Nancy Chodorow point out that women's views of the world and ways of relating to the world are different from but not inferior to those of men. In 1982, Gilligan published *In a Different Voice*, in which she claimed that women and men have fundamentally different ways of viewing morality, but that women's view of morality is equally valuable to the view held by men. Maximalists argue there are two very different and equally valuable ways of relating to the world.

Whether someone is a minimalist or a maximalist also has implications for whether gender is worth studying. A maximalist would certainly find gender worth studying, whereas not all minimalists would agree. In a literature review that summarized research on sex differences in 46 domains, Hyde (2005a) concluded that women and men are similar on most psychological variables. She raised the concern that our focus on differences ends up reifying stereotypes that have implications for men's and women's behavior and how people respond to their behavior. For example, as shown in Chapter 6, parents have different expectations about females' and males' abilities, which then influence the actual abilities of girls and boys. What is the source of parental expectations—our focus on differences!

You may be wondering, "Why should I care about these debates?" The reason you should care is that our political philosophy determines how we interpret a research finding. Take the sex difference in math. There is a sex difference, and the difference is statistically significant. The difference is also small. One group of researchers emphasizes that the size of the effect is small, that most women and men have similar aptitudes in math, and that only a small percentage of highly gifted men account for this difference. These people might also argue we should ignore the difference. Another group of researchers emphasizes the fact that the difference is real and that even small differences can have large effects. These investigators devote time and economic resources to understanding the cause of the difference and how to eliminate the difference.

Social Construction of Gender

Constructionists argue that it is fruitless to study gender because gender cannot be divorced from its context (Baker, 2006; Marecek, Crawford, & Popp, 2004). Constructionists maintain that gender is created by the perceiver: Facts about gender do not exist, only interpretations do. Constructionists challenge the use of the scientific method to study gender because they maintain you cannot view the world objectively; our history, experiences, and beliefs affect what we observe. Constructivists argue that the empirical method is not untainted by social forces and that science is not as value free as some expect.

Constructionists argue that psychologists should not make sex comparisons because such studies assume gender is a static quality of an individual. They maintain that gender is a dynamic social construct that is ever changing, a social category created by society. Researchers who make sex comparisons might describe women as more empathic than men. Constructionists would focus on the empathy involved in the interaction, the factors that contributed to the empathy, and how empathy becomes linked to women more than men. Constructionists would examine the explanations as to why empathy was illustrated more in women in this particular situation.

Constructionists are concerned that the study of sex comparisons ignores the variability within women and within men. The study of sex comparisons also ignores the situations and circumstances that influence men's and women's behavior. Constructionists argue that whether women and men are similar or different is the wrong question to ask. Questions that ought to be asked revolve around how social institutions, culture, and language contribute to gender and to gendered interactions.

In Chapter 4, I review the literature that compares men and women, being careful to point out the size of the effects, the variability within sexes, and the extent to which the situation or context influences sex differences. Many of the concerns raised by the constructionists are addressed in that chapter. As will be described in Chapter 2, there is also a host of research biases that can influence the domain of sex comparisons.

Women's Movements

It is a common misconception that the women's movement in the United States first began in the 1960s. Women's movements first emerged in the 1800s (Murstein, 1974). The issues these women confronted, however, were different from those of contemporary women. These women believed men and women were fundamentally different, and they did not seek to equalize the roles of men and women. Instead, women aimed for greater respect for their domestic role. Women in the 1800s and early 1900s were concerned with abolition, temperance, and child labor laws. These issues became "women's issues" because women were the ones to raise them. But these women discovered that their low-status position in society kept their voices from being heard. By gaining the right to vote in 1920, women could promote their causes. After that time, the women's movement remained fairly silent until the 1960s.

In 1963, Betty Friedan published *The Feminine Mystique*, in which she discussed "the problem that has no name." The problem was that women's delegation to the domestic sphere of life inhibited their opportunities for personal development. Women were not active in the workforce or in the political community. Friedan organized the National Organization for Women, or NOW, in 1966. The goal of this women's movement differed from the earlier movements. Here, women were concerned with their subordinate position in society and sought to establish equal rights for women. The purpose of NOW was to "take action to bring women into full participation in the mainstream of American society now, exercising all the privileges and responsibilities thereof, in truly equal partnership with men" (Friedan, 1963, p. 384). In the epilogue to *The Feminine Mystique*, Friedan explains that NOW stood for the National Organization *for* Women rather than the National Organization *of* Women because men must be included to accomplish these goals.

NOW is the largest women's rights organization in the United States. To date, it includes more than a half million members and is represented in all states. NOW's goal is to take action to ensure equality for women. Since its formation, NOW has successfully challenged protective labor laws that kept women from high-paying jobs as well as the sex classification of job advertisements in newspapers.

Did you know that job advertisements in the newspaper used to feature a "Help Wanted—Men" column and a "Help Wanted—Women" column? See Table 1.2 for some sample advertisements.

Can you imagine an advertisement for a receptionist today that requested an "attractive young lady"? Can you imagine an accountant position available only to men? In recognition of the work that women perform inside the home, NOW popularized the phrase "women who work outside the home."

TABLE 1.2   Job Advertisements

Help Wanted—Female
Assistant to Executive:
Girl Friday.
Assistant Bookkeeper-Biller:
Young, some steno preferred, but not essential; bright beginner considered.
Assistant Bookkeeper-Typist:
Expd. all-around girl.
Secty-Steno:
Age 25–35 Girl Friday for busy treasurer's office.
Receptionist, 5-day wk:
Attractive young lady, good typist, knowledge of monitor board.

Help Wanted—Male
Pharmacist:
To manage large chain-type indep. drug store.
Refrigeration:
Shop servicemen, experienced.
Maintenance:
Foreman, mach. shop exp.
Accountant-Sr.:
For medium-sized firm, heavy experience, auditing, audit program preparation, report writing, and federal and state income tax.

Source: New York Times, June 11, 1953.

Most of us feel rightly embarrassed when we ask a woman if she works and she says, "Yes, I work at home all day taking care of two kids, a cat, a dog, and a husband." In 1967, NOW endorsed the Equal Rights Amendment (ERA), which was proposed in 1923 and passed by Congress in 1972 but fell 3 states short of the 38 (three-fourths) needed for ratification in 1982. The ERA was reintroduced to Congress in 2009 by Congresswoman Carolyn Maloney (D-NY) and Congresswoman Judy Biggert (R-IL), but Congress still has not voted on the bill. (The late Senator Edward Kennedy (D-MA) was a lead sponsor of the amendment.) In 1992, NOW organized a campaign to elect women and feminist persons to political office, which helped send a record-breaking number of women to Congress and to state governments.

NOW also has organized marches to reduce violence against women and to promote reproductive rights. In 2004, NOW organized the largest mass action in U.S. history, the March for Women's Lives, which brought a record 1.15 million people to Washington, D.C. to advocate for women's reproductive health options, including access to abortion clinics, effective birth control, emergency contraception, and reproductive health services (Reuss & Erickson, 2006). See Sidebar 1.2: "The Morning After" for NOW's advocacy on behalf of Plan B. NOW has been working to get the United States to ratify the United Nations' Convention on the Elimination of All Forms of Discrimination against Women (CEDAW), an international treaty that would ensure human rights for women around the world. The United States is the only industrialized country in the world not to have ratified CEDAW.

The women's movement is not limited to the United States, but the U.S. women's movement serves a larger portion of women compared to the movements in other countries, which are less cohesive. In other countries, the women's movements could pose a threat to people's national identity when

SIDEBAR 1.2: *The Morning After*

Levonorgestrel, or Plan B, is a contraceptive that is commonly known as the "morning after pill." It is widely misconstrued as an abortifacient (American Congress of Obstetricians and Gynecologists, 2009; Reznik, 2010). It is most effective in preventing pregnancy when taken within 24 hours of intercourse. Plan B stops or delays ovulation to prevent fertilization. It does not work once the egg is fertilized, which explains why it rapidly loses its effectiveness with the passage of time. Thus Plan B is similar to a high-dose birth control pill and operates in the same way. People often confuse Plan B with Mifeprex (RU-486), an abortifacient that was widely publicized in the 1990s and approved by the Federal Drug Administration (FDA) in 2000. Plan B was approved by the FDA in 1999 with a prescription. In 2009, a federal court ordered the FDA to make Plan B available to women age 17 and older without a prescription. However, it is not clear how accessible Plan B is. The lack of knowledge about what Plan B is and what Plan B does may make women wary of taking it. A 2009 study of pharmacy students showed that one-third mistakenly thought Plan B disrupted an implanted ovum (Ragland & West, 2009). In addition, some pharmacists and emergency rooms fail to stock the drug—again, in part due to the failure to understand how Plan B operates.

traditional roles are so grounded in culture. Yet, there is a core of commonality to women's movements around the world: They are focused on improving the position of women in society.

Men's Movements

Since the women's movement of the 1960s, several men's movements have appeared. None of these movements, to date, has had the cohesion or impact on society of the women's movement. Some men's movements endorse the women's movement and share some of the concerns the women's movement raised about the harmful aspects of the male gender role. One such movement is the National Organization for Men Against Sexism (NOMAS; see Figure 1.6).

This movement developed in the 1970s as the National Organization for Changing Men, but changed its name to NOMAS in 1983. It supports changing the traditional male role to reduce competitiveness, homophobia, and emotional inhibition. These men are feminists, are antiracists, support equal rights for women, want to end patriarchy, and embrace heterosexual, homosexual, and transgendered individuals.

Other men's movements are a reaction against the women's movement and seek to restore traditional female and male roles. These have attracted more men than the profeminist movements. Two such movements are the mythopoetic movement and the Promise Keepers. Both of these movements view men and women as fundamentally different. Both encourage men to rediscover their masculinity and to reject what they have referred to as "the feminization of men." The movements are referred to as promasculinist.

The mythopoetic movement was organized by Robert Bly (1990), who wrote the national best-selling nonfiction book *Iron John: A Book about Men*. The concern of the mythopoetic movement is that the modernization of society has stripped men of the rituals of tribal society that bound men together. The movement involves rituals, ceremonies, and retreats, with the goal of reconnecting men with one another. To promote the movement, in 1992, Bly started the ManKind Project for men to get in touch with their emotions to live a more fulfilling life. The ManKind Project involves weekend retreats for men to connect with their feelings, bond with one another, and embrace a more mature masculinity centered on leadership, compassion, and multiculturalism. Today, Bly's movement is really more of an experience than a movement, which may have contributed to the waning interest among men.

The Promise Keepers is a Christian fundamentalist movement. Worship, prayer, and evangelism are central to the movement. The Bible is used to justify the differences between women and men and the natural state of men's superior position over women. The traditional nuclear family is endorsed; homosexuality and homosexual households

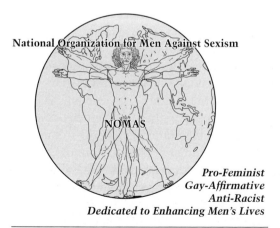

National Organization for Men Against Sexism

NOMAS

Pro-Feminist
Gay-Affirmative
Anti-Racist
Dedicated to Enhancing Men's Lives

FIGURE 1.6 Logo for National Organization for Changing Men.

are rejected. This organization is viewed as antifeminist because men and women are not viewed as equals. One of the promises men are to uphold is to "become warriors who honor women" (keep this in mind when we discuss benevolent sexism in Chapter 3). The first meeting of the Promise Keepers was held in 1990, and 72 men attended. Attendance peaked in 1996 with 1.1 million men participating in 22 cities nationwide. Since that time, participation has declined. In 2008, meetings were held in 7 cities and 25,000 men attended. In more recent years, the Promise Keepers has involved more community service efforts, such as collecting food for faith-based charities and donating blood.

A NOTE ON SEXIST LANGUAGE

In 1972, an article appeared in *Ms.* magazine that began with the following story:

> On the television screen, a teacher of first-graders who had just won a national award is describing her way of teaching. "You take each child where you find him," she says. "You watch to see what he's interested in, and then you build on his interests." A five-year-old looking at the program asks her mother, "Do only boys go to that school?" "No," her mother begins, "she's talking about girls too, but. ..." (Miller, Swift, & Maggio, 1997, p. 50)

But what? Is it acceptable to use the male pronoun to imply male and female? Another indication of men's status in our culture is the use of the generic *he* to imply both women and men. In 1983, the American Psychological Association proclaimed that scientists must refrain from using sexist language in their writing. This means that we cannot use the generic *he* to mean both men and women in our scientific writing. The statement was issued nearly 30 years ago. Even today, it is common to find the use of the generic *he* in books in other disciplines. I find that many college students use *he* to refer to men and women in their writing. When I correct students' papers (changing *he* to *he/she* or *they*), some are quite offended and cast me as an extremist. Many people will say that everyone knows *he* refers to "he and she," so what's the harm? *He* is more efficient. When you write the word *he* or *him*, do you think of both women and men? The answer is clear: No. The concern with sexist language is that people do not really perceive *he* as representing "he or she." There is now clear evidence that the use of masculine generics leads both speakers and listeners to visualize male names, male persons, and more masculine images (Stahlberg et al., 2007).

One study showed that sexist language may have implications for women's opportunities. In a study of four-year colleges and universities in nine southern states, institutions that had basketball teams with sexist names were shown to have less equal opportunities for female athletes (Pelak, 2008). A sexist name of an athletic team typically takes one of two forms. Either the name implies maleness (e.g., Rams or Knights) or there is a female qualifier to the team name (e.g., men = Panthers; women = Lady Panthers). In the latter case, the implication is that male is the standard. Just over two-thirds of schools had sexist team names. This is a correlational study—names could have led to fewer opportunities for women, fewer opportunities for women could have led to these names, or names are a symptom of unequal opportunities for women. The take home point is that the name *does* make a difference.

There is no language in which being female is indicated with less complex or shorter language or in which female is the standard in language. See Sidebar 1.3 for a discussion of gender in other languages.

SIDEBAR 1.3: *A Note on Language in Other Cultures*

When studying Spanish, I always wondered if there were effects of having masculine and feminine pronouns for objects. The word "the" takes one of two forms in Spanish depending on whether the object is masculine (*el*) or feminine (*la*). Many other languages employ masculine and feminine articles. Although I did not really visualize a book as male (*el libro*) or a window as female (*la ventana*), it seemed that the use of these terms must have implications for gender. In 2009, a study supported my hunch (Wasserman & Weseley, 2009). Native English speakers taking advanced Spanish classes in high school completed a survey of sexist attitudes after being randomly assigned to read a *Harry Potter* passage in either English or Spanish. Amazingly, those reading the Spanish passage scored higher on the sexism scale than those reading the English passage—with the difference being especially pronounced among women (see Figure 1.7).

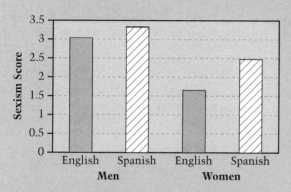

FIGURE 1.7   College men and women scored higher on a sexism scale after reading a passage in Spanish than in English but the difference was only significant for women.
Source: Adapted from Wasserman & Weseley (2009).

The study was replicated with French. Similar but somewhat weaker effects were found with bilingual students. Wasserman and Weseley (2009) suggested that grammatical gender increases one's awareness and attention to differences between women and men.

One way that sexist language was addressed in the 1970s was with the introduction of the term *Ms*. Ms was supposed to reduce the problem of distinguishing women by their marital status. However, *Ms* conjures up images of unique groups of women (e.g., divorced or feminist). When college students were randomly assigned to read a description of a 25-year-old full-time employee who was addressed as Ms, Miss, Mrs., or Mr., Ms led to the perception of the most masculine/agentic traits (see Figure 1.8; Malcolmson & Sinclair, 2007).

Is there any reason to believe the climate is changing, that nonsexist language is

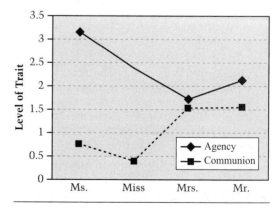

FIGURE 1.8   College students perceived employees addressed as "Ms." to be more agentic and less communal than those addressed as "Mrs.," or "Mr."
Source: Adapted from Malcolmson & Sinclair (2007).

becoming more acceptable and sexist language is becoming more maligned? A study of 18- through 87-year-olds showed that people are fairly undecided about the issue (Parks & Roberton, 2008). Interestingly, there were no age differences in views of nonsexist language, with the exception that the youngest cohort (ages 18–22) held the least favorable views. See how language influences perception at your school with Do Gender 1.4.

In recent years, the issue has been taken up by state legislatures because some states, such as California, Florida, Hawaii, Massachusetts, New York, Rhode Island, and Vermont, have passed legislation to change their state constitutions to use gender-neutral language. Other states are considering the issue, and several states, such as Nebraska, have rejected the change (K. Murphy, 2003).

DO GENDER 1.4
Effects of Sexist Language on Female and Male Images

Ask 10 people to read one of two sentences. The sentences must be identical, with the exception that one version uses sexist language (e.g., "A student should place his homework in a notebook") and one version uses gender-neutral language (e.g., "Students should place their homework in a notebook" or "A student should place his or her homework in a notebook"). You could also compare these two gender-neutral conditions. Ask readers to visualize the sentence while reading it. Then ask them to write a paragraph describing their visual image. Have two people unrelated to the study read the paragraphs and record whether the image was male, female, or unclear.

How should one avoid sexist language? The easiest way to get around the *he/she* issue is to use the plural *they*. Other tips are shown in Table 1.3.

TAKE HOME POINTS

- The minimalists believe that men and women are essentially the same, that differences are small, and that those that do exist are likely to be due to social forces.

- The maximalists believe that women and men are fundamentally different in important ways, but that "different" does not mean that one is better than the other.

- Social constructionists argue that science cannot be applied to the study of gender because gender is not a static quality of a person but is a product of society. As the context changes, so does gender.

- Today's women's movements have as their common thread a concern with improving the position of women in society and ensuring equal opportunities for women and men.

- Today's men's movements are varied, some endorsing feminist positions and others advocating a return to traditional male and female roles.

- Research has shown that sexist language, such as the use of the generic *he* to imply both women and men, activates male images and is not perceived as gender neutral.

THIS BOOK'S APPROACH TO THE STUDY OF GENDER

According to Deaux (1984), there are three approaches to the study of gender. First, sex is used as a subject variable. This is the most traditional approach to research and is

TABLE 1.3   **TIPS FOR NONSEXIST WRITING**

1. Replace pronouns (he, his, him) with he or she.
   The student should raise his hand.   The student should raise his or her hand.

2. Delete pronouns (he, his, him) by rewriting sentence in the plural.
   The student sits quietly at his desk.   Students sit quietly at their desks.

3. Delete pronouns entirely from the sentence.
   The teacher read the folder on his desk.   The teacher read the folder on the desk.

4. Change pronouns to "you."
   A person should wash his own clothes.   You should wash your own clothes.

5. Change pronouns to "one."
   Tell the student that he can write a letter.   Tell the student that one can write a letter.

6. Replace "man" with "someone" or "no one."
   No man is an island.   No one is an island.

7. Replace "mankind" or "ancient man" with "our ancestors" or "men and women" or "humanity."
   This is a giant step for mankind.   This is a giant step for men and women.
                                                     This is a giant step for humanity.

   Ancient man developed the . . .   Our ancestors developed the . . .

8. Replace "men" with "humans."
   Men have always . . .   Humans have always . . .

9. Replace "man-made" with "artificial."
   It is a man-made reservoir.   It is an artificial reservoir.

10. Replace "spokesman" with "spokesperson" or "representative."
    The spokesman for the client's family   The representative for the client's family has
    has arrived.   arrived.

11. Replace "chairman" with "chairperson" or "chair."
    The chairman called the meeting to order.   The chair called the meeting to order.

12. Replace "Englishmen" or "Frenchmen" with "the English" or "the French."
    Englishmen always serve tea with scones.   The English always serve tea with scones.

13. Replace "steward" and "stewardess" with "flight attendant."
    The stewardess served the meal.   The flight attendant served the meal.

14. Replace "salesman" with "salesperson," "salespeople," "sales representative," or "sales clerks."

    Mary is a traveling salesman.   Mary is a traveling salesperson.

Source: Adapted from Miller and Swift (1980).

represented in the studies of sex comparisons. The idea here is that sex is an attribute of a person; investigators compare the thoughts, feelings, and behaviors of men and women. Deaux (1984) concludes that this approach has shown that most sex differences are qualified by interactions with context; for example, sex differences in conformity appear in some situations (e.g., public) but not in others (e.g., private).

A second approach has been to study the psychological differences between women and men: femininity and masculinity. This second approach is still an individual differences approach, but the subject is the social category of gender roles rather than the biological category of sex. Here, we examine how gender roles influence people's thoughts, feelings, and behaviors. Is being female associated with providing help, or is being empathic a better predictor of helping behavior? If the latter is true, both men and women who are high in empathy will be helpful. Third, sex is examined as a stimulus or target variable. Researchers examine how people respond to the categories of female and male. An example of this approach is finding that people rate pictures of infants as more attractive when the infant is thought to be a female and stronger when the infant is thought to be a male. Only with this latter approach can sex be randomly assigned.

All three of these approaches are represented in this text. I examine gender as an individual difference variable but am careful to note how the context influences behavior. I highlight both similarities and differences between women and men. Most important, I focus on the explanations for the source of any observed sex differences, for example, whether other variables that co-occur with sex, such as status or gender-related personality traits, are the causal source of the behavior.

I begin this book by addressing fundamental issues in the psychology of gender, such as sexism, stereotypes, sex comparisons in cognitive and social behavior and theories thereof, and achievement. The rest of the book applies this fundamental material to two domains of behavior: relationships and health. Relationships are an important subject in their own right. Relationships contribute to the quality of our life as well as to our mental and physical health. The impact of relationships on our psychological and physical well-being, the prevalence of violence in relationships, and the high rate of relationship dissolution in the form of divorce in the United States are reasons that relationships require our attention. Health also is an important subject in and of itself. Over the past century, we have extended our life span by decades but now are more likely to live with health problems for longer periods of time. We have been made increasingly aware of the role that psychological and social factors play in our health. Gender has implications for those psychological and social forces.

SUMMARY

First, we reviewed some important terms in the psychological study of gender. Sex, the biological category, was distinguished from gender, the psychological category. An important term is *gender role*, which refers to the expectations that society has for being female or male; we expect men to be masculine and women to be feminine—in other words, to act in accordance with their gender role. Other terms defined include *gender identity, sexual orientation, sex* or *gender typing, sexism, gender-role stereotype,* and *sex discrimination*. I discussed the multiple meanings of feminism, concluding that equality for men and women was the most central component of the definition. Because each society has its own definitions of gender and ways of defining female and male roles, I also described several cultures that have alternative ways of constructing gender.

Next, I presented various political and philosophical issues in the study of gender. The minimalists, who emphasize the similarities between men and women, were distinguished from the maximalists, who emphasize the differences. A brief history of the women's movements was provided along with a description of the more recent men's movements. The chapter concluded with a discussion of sexist language.

DISCUSSION QUESTIONS

1. What is the distinction between *sex* and *gender*? How do you think this distinction should be employed in practice?
2. Describe a personal experience of intrarole or interrole conflict with respect to gender.
3. What are some of the advantages and disadvantages of the way that gender is portrayed in other cultures?
4. How can we determine whether men have higher status than women in a given culture?
5. Do you think we should be comparing women and men? Why or why not?
6. Why hasn't any one men's movement gained the strength of the women's movement?
7. How can the use of sexist language be harmful?

SUGGESTED READING

Eagly, A. (1995). The science and politics of comparing women and men. *American Psychologist, 50*, 145–158.

Hyde, J. S. (2005). The gender similarities hypothesis. *American Psychologist, 60*, 581–592.

Marecek, J., Crawford, M., & Popp, D. (2004). On the construction of gender, sex, and sexualities. In A. Eagly, A. E. Beall, & R. J. Sternberg (Eds.), *The psychology of gender* (2nd ed.), pp. 192–216. New York: Guilford Press.

KEY TERMS

Androgynous—Term describing one who incorporates both masculine and feminine qualities.

Bisexuals—Individuals who accept other-sex and same-sex individuals as sexual partners.

Constructionists—People with the perspective that gender cannot be divorced from its context.

Cross-sex-typed—Condition of possessing the biological traits of one sex but exhibiting the psychological traits that correspond with the other sex.

Feminine—Description of trait, behavior, or interest assigned to the female gender role.

Feminism—Belief that men and women should be treated equally.

Gender—Term used to refer to the social categories of male and female.

Gender culture—Each society's or culture's conceptualization of gender roles.

Gender identity/gender-role identity—One's perception of oneself as psychologically male or female.

Gender role—Expectations that go along with being male or female.

Gender-role attitude—One's personal view about how men and women should behave.

Heterosexuals—Individuals who prefer other-sex sexual partners.

Homosexuals—Individuals who prefer same-sex sexual partners.

Interrole conflict—Experience of conflict between expectations of two or more roles that are assumed simultaneously.

Intersex—A person who is born with ambiguous genitalia.

Intrarole conflict—Experience of conflict between expectations within a given role.

Masculine—Description of a trait, behavior, or interest assigned to the male gender role.

Maximalists—Persons who maintain there are important differences between the two sexes.

Minimalists—Persons who maintain the two sexes are fundamentally the same.

Role—Social position accompanied by a set of norms or expectations.

Sex—Term used to refer to the biological categories of male and female.

Sex discrimination—Behavioral component of one's attitude toward men and women that involves differential treatment of people based on their biological sex.

Sexism—Affective component of one's attitude toward sex characterized by demonstration of prejudice toward people based on their sex.

Sex-related behavior—Behavior that corresponds to sex but is not necessarily caused by sex.

Sex stereotype/gender-role stereotype—Cognitive component of one's attitude toward sex.

Sex-typed—Condition of possessing the biological traits of one sex and exhibiting the psychological traits that correspond with that sex.

Sex typing—Acquisition of sex-appropriate preferences, behaviors, skills, and self-concept (i.e., the acquisition of gender roles).

Sexual orientation—Preference to have other-sex or same-sex persons as sexual partners.

Transgender—Descriptive term referring to an individual whose psychological sex is not congruent with biological sex.

Transsexuals—Persons whose biological sex have been changed surgically to reflect their psychological sex.

CHAPTER 2

Methods and History of Gender Research

"Poverty after Divorce" (Mann, 1985a)

"Disastrous Divorce Results" (Mann, 1985b)

"Victims of Reform" (Williamson, 1985)

These were some headlines following the publication of Lenore J. Weitzman's (1985) book *The Divorce Revolution: The Unexpected Social and Economic Consequences for Women and Children in America.* Weitzman cited statistics that showed women's standard of living drops 73% after divorce, whereas men's standard of living increases by 42%. The study received a great deal of media attention, making headlines of newspapers across the nation. A social scientist and an economist were shocked by these statistics because the statistics did not match their longitudinal data from a representative sample of couples who had divorced in the United States. Their data showed that women's standard of living fell by only 30% during the first year following divorce, and even men's standard of living declined by 7% (Duncan & Hoffman, 1985). These statistics were subsequently confirmed by the U.S. Bureau of the Census (1991).

Why the discrepancy? Weitzman's data were based on a very small sample—114 men and 114 women who became divorced—and the sample was not representative. The response rate in that study was low, less than 50%. And, standard of living was calculated from a fairly unreliable source: respondents' self-reports of their finances before and after divorce. The tragedy in all of this is not so much that a methodologically weak study was conducted but that the methodologically weak study attracted so much attention and the methodologically strong refutations received hardly any.

In this text, I review the scientific literature on gender and its implications for relationships and health. I also make reference to some of the more popular literature on gender, which is more likely to make newspaper headlines. You may already be familiar with books such as Deborah Tannen's (1990) *You Just Don't Understand: Women and Men in Conversation* and Carol Gilligan's (1982) *In a Different Voice.* You will read about sex differences in the newspaper and on the Internet and hear about sex differences on television, especially on news shows such as *60 Minutes* and *20/20.* In this text, we evaluate these popularized notions about gender and sex differences from the point of view of the scientific literature. You will be able to judge which differences are real and which are not, which differences are exaggerated, and which comparisons between men and women have not been studied adequately. You will also know what questions to ask when faced with the results of a sex comparison study. In order to do so, you need to be familiar with the scientific method. Thus, in the first section of this chapter, I review the scientific method on which the majority of the research presented in this text is based. Then I examine the unique difficulties that researchers face when studying gender. In the second half of this chapter, I provide an overview of the history of the psychology of gender. In reviewing the history of the field, I examine the different ways that people conceptualize and measure gender roles.

THE SCIENTIFIC METHOD

If you have taken a research methods course, you are familiar with the scientific method and you know that it is difficult to conduct good research. Here I introduce a number of terms; they are summarized in Table 2.3, which is provided later in this chapter.

The scientific method rests on **empiricism**. Empiricism means information is collected via one of our major senses, usually sight. One can touch, feel, hear, or see the information. This information, referred to as **data**, usually takes the form of thoughts, feelings, or behaviors. For example, I examine the way in which men and women think about themselves and the world, the way men and women experience and express emotions, the way men and women interact with other people, and the way men's and women's bodies respond to stress. Statements about these observations, or data, are called **facts**. A collection of facts can be used to generate a **theory**, or an abstract generalization that provides an explanation for the set of facts.

For a theory to be scientific, it must be falsifiable, meaning there must be the possibility it can be disproved. Creationism, for example, is not a scientific theory because there is no way to disprove it. *Intelligent design* is a new term that has been applied to the study of religion as a way to explain the origin of humankind. Although the term was developed to sound scientific, it also is not a scientific theory because it is not testable—that is, there is no observation or experiment that can be performed to support or refute religion.

A theory is used to generate a **hypothesis**, a prediction that a certain outcome will occur under a specific set of conditions. A hypothesis is tested by creating those conditions and then collecting data. The statements made from the data, or facts, may either support the hypothesis, and thus the theory, or suggest the theory needs to be modified. Each of these steps in the research process is shown in Figure 2.1.

Let's take an example. One theory of the origin of sex differences is social role theory. According to social role theory, any differences in behavior we observe between men

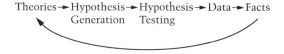

Theories→Hypothesis→Hypothesis→Data→Facts
　　　　　Generation　Testing

FIGURE 2.1　Steps in the research process.

and women are due to the different social roles they hold in society. We can apply this theory to the behavior of nurturance. One hypothesis would be that women are more nurturant than men because their social roles of mother and caretaker require more nurturant behavior than the social roles men possess. This hypothesis suggests that men and women who are in the same social roles will show similar levels of nurturance. We could test this hypothesis in two ways. We could compare the levels of nurturance among women and men who have similar roles in society—stay-at-home moms and stay-at-home dads. We could measure their level of nurturance by how they interact with babies in a nursery. These observations would be the data. Let's say we find that stay-at-home moms and dads spend the same amount of time holding the babies, talking to the babies, and playing with the babies. These are facts, and they would support our hypothesis that men and women who possess the same social roles behave in similar ways.

Another way we could test our hypothesis would be to assign females and males to one of two social roles in the laboratory, a caretaker or a noncaretaker role, and observe their nurturant behavior. In the caretaker condition, we would ask participants to play with and take care of a puppy; in the noncaretaker condition, we would ask participants to teach the puppy some tricks. If both men and women show the same high level of nurturant behavior in the caretaker condition and the same low level of nurturant behavior

in the noncaretaker condition, our hypothesis that social role rather than sex leads to differences in nurturance would be supported, and our theory would be supported. If women are observed to show greater levels of nurturance than men in both conditions, regardless of the instructions received on how to interact with the puppy, we would have to revise our theory. This observation would suggest there is something about being female, aside from the social role, that leads to nurturance.

The two studies just described are quite different in design. The first is a correlational study and the second an experimental study. Most of the studies in this text are either correlational or experimental. Let's examine the differences.

Correlational Study

A **correlational study** is one in which you observe the relation between two variables, usually at a single point in time. For example, we could correlate job characteristics with nurturant behavior. We would probably observe that people who held more people-oriented jobs displayed more nurturance. The problem would be that we would not know if the job caused nurturance or if nurturant people were attracted to those jobs. Does being a social worker lead to nurturance, or do more nurturant people choose social work? We also could correlate sex with job characteristics. We would probably find that women are more likely than men to hold people-oriented jobs. The problem here isn't exactly the same as the one just identified. Here, we know that job characteristics do not cause someone's sex. However, we do not know if someone's sex caused him or her to have a certain kind of job. And, there may be a third variable responsible for the relation between sex and people-oriented jobs. That third variable could be salary. Perhaps the pay of people-oriented jobs is lower than that of other jobs and women are more likely to be hired into low-salary positions. Thus the primary weakness of correlational research is that a number of explanations can account for the relation between two variables.

The value of a correlation can range from −1 to +1. Both −1 and +1 are referred to as perfect correlations, which means you can perfectly predict one variable from the other variable. In the examples just cited, there will not be perfect correlations. It will not be the case that all nurturant people are in people-oriented jobs or all women are in people-oriented jobs. An example of a perfect correlation can be found in physics. There is a perfect correlation between how fast you are driving and how far your car takes you. If you drive 60 mph, you will travel 60 miles in one hour or 120 miles in two hours. For every 1 mph increase in speed, you will travel 1 mile farther in an hour. That is, you can perfectly predict distance from speed. As you might guess, we cannot perfectly predict one variable from another in psychological

research. Most correlations reported in psychology will fall in the +.3 to +.4 range.

A **positive correlation** is one in which the levels of both variables increase or decrease at the same time. For example, you might find that women who hold more traditional gender-role attitudes are more likely to perform the majority of household chores; that is, as women's gender-role attitudes become more traditional, the amount of household chores performed increases. The left half of Figure 2.2 depicts a hypothetical plot of these two variables. The regression line drawn through the scatterplot shows that the relation is positive.

A **negative correlation** occurs when the level of one variable increases as the level of the other decreases. An example of a negative correlation would be the amount of household chores performed by a man with traditional gender-role attitudes: The more traditional his attitude, the fewer household chores he performs. A hypothetical scatterplot of those data is depicted in the right half of Figure 2.2. Here you can see the negative slope of the regression line, indicating a

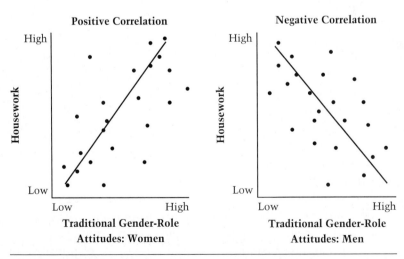

FIGURE 2.2   Examples of a positive and negative correlation.

negative correlation. As shown in Figure 2.2, a negative correlation is not weaker than a positive correlation; it simply reflects a difference in the direction of the relation.

Correlational studies are often conducted with surveys or by making observations of behavior. It is important how you choose the people to complete your survey or to be the subject of observation; they need to be representative of the population to whom you wish to generalize your findings. I once had a student in my class conduct an observational study to see if sex is related to touching. She conducted the study on the bus and concluded that touching is rare. This study suffered from a **selection bias**; people on the bus are not a representative sample, especially during the crowded morning commute to work. To ensure a representative sample, the researcher should **randomly select** or **randomly sample** the participants from the population of interest. Random selection ensures that each member of the population has an equal chance of being a participant in the study. You could randomly select a sample by putting the names of all the people in the population in a hat and drawing out a sample of names. That would be cumbersome. It would be more feasible to assign every member of the population an identification number and randomly select a set of numbers. Imagine you want a representative sample of 100 adults in your community. If every phone number in your community begins with the same first three digits, you could have a computer generate a series of four-digit random sequences and call those phone numbers with those sequences. Would this procedure result in a random sample? Close—but the sample would be biased in one way: You would not be representing the people in your area who do not have telephones. This kind of research is more difficult to conduct today because so many people have caller ID, fail to answer the phone, or have given up land lines for cell phones.

Although random selection is important for the validity of correlational research, it is difficult to achieve and is rarely employed. Often, we want to make inferences that generalize to the entire population, or at least the population of our country. It would be difficult to place 250 million names in a hat. Instead, we approximate and randomly select from a community we believe is fairly representative of the population. The important point to keep in mind is that we should generalize our findings only to the population that the findings represent. This is particularly important in the study of gender because the vast majority of research has been conducted on White middle-class Americans, and findings may not generalize to people of other races, other classes, or other cultures.

You are probably wondering how a research participant pool at a university fits into the random selection process. The answer is, not very well. Do you have a research participant pool at your institution in which you are asked to participate in experiments for credit? Or, are there postings that request volunteers to participate in research? In either case, you are choosing to participate in a particular experiment; that is, you were not randomly selected from the entire population of college students. Worse yet, the kinds of people who choose to participate in a certain experiment may not be representative of the entire population of students. We must keep this research limitation in mind when generalizing from the results of our studies.

Experimental Study

A second research method is the **experimental method**. In an experiment, the investigator manipulates one variable, called the

independent variable, and observes its effect on another variable, called the **dependent variable**. To keep these two concepts straight, remember that the dependent variable "depends on" the independent variable. In the experiment described previously, the instructions on how to interact with the puppy were the independent variable (caretaker vs. noncaretaker condition) and the behavior of nurturance was the dependent variable. Table 2.1 lists more examples of independent variables and dependent variables.

How do we know that other variables besides the independent variable—the instructions—aren't responsible for the effect on nurturance? Maybe the students in the caretaker condition were more nurturant with the animals than students in the noncaretaker condition because they had pets in their homes when they were growing up. This is possible, but unlikely, because participants are randomly assigned to each condition in an experiment. **Random assignment** means each participant has an equal chance of being assigned to each condition. Because of random assignment, on average, the people in one condition will be comparable to the people in the other condition, with the exception of how they are treated with regard to the independent variable. Random assignment is the key feature of the experimental method.

Random assignment can be accomplished by flipping a coin or drawing numbers out of a hat. Random assignment means there is no systematic way of assigning people to conditions. Dividing the classroom in half so people on the right are in one group and people on the left are in another group would not be random. Theoretically, there could be differences between the kinds of people who sit on the right versus the left side of the classroom. In the classroom in which I teach, students who sit on the left side of the seminar table can look out the window, whereas

TABLE 2.1 EXAMPLES OF INDEPENDENT AND DEPENDENT VARIABLES

Research Question	Independent Variable	Dependent Variable
Is employment harmful to women's health?	Employment	Health
Does testosterone increase aggression?	Testosterone	Aggression
Do African Americans have more traditional gender-role attitudes than Caucasians?	Race	Gender-role attitudes
Which relationships are closer—same sex or other sex?	Relationship type	Closeness
Are men or women smarter?	Sex	Intelligence
Does commitment in a relationship decrease power?	Commitment	Power
Are lesbians more masculine than heterosexual women?	Sexual orientation	Gender role
Is touching a function of status?	Status	Touching
Is housework divided more evenly among egalitarian couples?	Egalitarian vs. traditional	Division of labor
Do we smile more at male infants or at female infants?	Infant sex	Smiling

students who sit on the right side have a view of the wall, so they might as well look at me. Imagine you had asked participants to decide whether they wanted to play with the puppy or teach it tricks. If you let people choose their condition, the people in the two conditions would be different; nurturant people are likely to choose to play with the puppy. Differences in nurturant behavior between the two conditions would be due to a selection bias because people selected their own groups and were not randomly assigned to condition.

In a true experiment, one must be able to manipulate the independent variable to study its effects. Notice that some of the independent variables in Table 2.1 are changeable and some are not; that is, one can manipulate employment, testosterone, and status to study their effects. Other independent variables are not changeable, such as sex, race, and ethnicity. When sex is a characteristic of a person, as in the research question "Are men or women smarter?" sex is referred to as a **subject variable**. Studies in which sex is a subject variable are not true experiments because someone cannot be randomly assigned to be female or male. The majority of research that compares men and women—evaluating similarities and differences between men's and women's behavior—is not experimental for this reason. We observe in the laboratory or in the real world how women and men think, feel, and behave. This research is correlational because we cannot manipulate a person's sex.

Is there any way we can use an experiment to make sex comparisons? We can make sex a **stimulus** or **target variable**, meaning it is the characteristic of something to which people respond. Let's take the research question "Do we smile more at male or female infants?" One way to answer that question is to compare how often adults smile at male and female infants. However, this would be a correlational study; we would be correlating infant sex with smiling, and sex would be a subject variable. We would not know if infant sex caused the smiling or something else about the infant caused the smiling; for example, infant girls are more likely to wear pink and perhaps pink causes smiling. A better way to address this research question is by conducting an experimental study in which infant sex is a target variable. We could show people pictures of the same child dressed in gender neutral clothes and randomly tell one group the infant is Sam and the other group the infant is Samantha. Then we can look to see if people smile more at infants they perceive to be female compared to those they perceive to be male. When sex is a target variable, random assignment can take place and a true experiment can be conducted.

There are advantages and disadvantages of both correlational and experimental methods. The major ones are identified in Table 2.2.

The advantage of the experimental method is that cause and effect can be determined because all other variables in the experiment are held constant except for the independent variable (the cause). Thus, any differences in the dependent variable (the effect) can be attributed to the independent

TABLE 2.2   EXPERIMENTAL METHOD VERSUS CORRELATIONAL METHOD

	Experimental	*Correlational*
Strength	Internal validity	External validity
Weakness	External validity	Internal validity

variable. One point on which philosophers of science agree about causality is that the cause must precede the effect. In an experiment, the cause, by definition, precedes the effect. The cause cannot always be determined in a correlational study. Thus, the strength of the experimental method is **internal validity**, that is, being confident you are measuring the true cause of the effect.

The disadvantage of the experimental method is that experiments are usually conducted in an artificial setting, such as a laboratory, so the experimenter can have control over the environment. Recall the experiment in which people were interacting with a puppy. The experiment was set up to observe nurturant behavior. Do interactions with a puppy in a laboratory where people are told how to behave generalize to how adults interact with their own pets? Or to how they interact with their children? Results from experiments conducted in the laboratory may be less likely to generalize to the real world; that is, they are low in **external validity**. In the real world, men and women may be given very different messages about how to interact with puppies, babies, and adults. In addition, in the real world, people do not think their behavior is being observed by an experimenter.

By contrast, external validity is a strength of the correlational method, and internal validity is the major weakness. With correlational research, you are often observing behavior in a real-world setting. You could unobtrusively observe nurturant behavior by studying mothers and fathers with their children at school or during a doctor's visit, or you could administer a survey in which people report their nurturant behavior. The major disadvantage of the correlational method is that one cannot determine cause and effect because the variables are measured simultaneously. If I find that mothers behave

in a more nurturant way toward their children than fathers, I do not know if parent sex caused the difference in behavior or if something else associated with being a mother or a father is responsible for the difference—such as the way children themselves respond to mothers and fathers. The correlational method lacks internal validity.

Field Experiment

On rare occasions, the experimental method is taken into the real world, or the *field* where the behavior under investigation naturally occurs. These are **field experiments**, which attempt to maximize both internal and external validity. An example of a field experiment on gender and nurturance is randomly assigning men and women managers in a business organization to interact with their employees in one of two ways: either to teach them new information and technology (noncaretaker condition), or to make sure they all get along with one another and are happy (caretaker condition). The experiment has internal validity because people are randomly assigned to condition. On average, the only difference between the two groups of managers is the instructions they received. The experiment has external validity because we are observing actual nurturant behavior in a real-world setting: the organization. We could measure nurturant behavior in terms of offers to help the employee or time spent with the employee talking about likes and dislikes about the job. Now, imagine how likely an organization would be to let you randomly assign its managers to have different kinds of interactions with their employees. In addition, imagine how difficult it would be to ensure that only the independent variable differs between the two groups. Many other variables could influence managers' behavior that would be difficult to control: the way the manager is treated by his or her own boss, the nature of the manager's job (whether it involves working with others or whether it involves technology), and the number of employees a single manager has. Would you be able to randomly assign a manager to focus on technology with one employee but focus on relationships with the other employee? Because field experiments do not have the same kind of controls over behavior that laboratory experiments do, they are more difficult to conduct and more likely to pose threats to internal validity.

Cross-Sectional Versus Longitudinal Designs

Aside from conducting a field study, there is another way to enhance the internal validity of correlational studies. Recall that a correlational study usually measures the relation between two variables at a single point in time. This is not always the case. When a single time point is used, we say the study is **cross sectional**. However, we may measure the independent variable at one time and the dependent variable later; this is a **longitudinal study**. In a longitudinal study, there are multiple time points of study. Can we discern cause and effect with a longitudinal study? Remember, a key principle to establishing causality is that the cause precedes the effect. A longitudinal study helps establish causality but does not ensure it. Let's take an example.

We could survey a group of women from the community to see if employment is related to health. If we conduct one survey at a single point in time, we are conducting a cross-sectional study. Let's say we find a correlation: Employment is associated with better health. The problem is that we do not know if employment leads to better health or if healthier people

are more likely to be employed. A longitudinal study may help to solve this problem. We could measure both employment and health at one time (Time 1) and then six months later (Time 2), as shown in Figure 2.3. If employment at Time 1 is associated with a change in health between Time 1 and Time 2 (depicted by line a), employment is likely to have caused better health. We can be even more confident of this relation if health at Time 1 does not predict change in employment between Time 1 and Time 2 (depicted by line b).

Longitudinal studies help establish causality and also help distinguish **age effects** from **cohort effects**. A *cohort* refers to a group of people of similar age, such as a generation. Let's say that we conduct a cross-sectional study of adult women in which we find that age is negatively associated with hours worked outside the home. Can we conclude that women decrease the amount of hours they spend in paid employment as they get older? If so, this would be an age effect. Or, is it the case that older women work fewer hours outside the home because they have more traditional gender-role attitudes than younger women? If so, this finding is a cohort effect, an effect due to the generation of the people. In a cross-sectional design, we

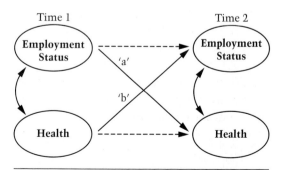

FIGURE 2.3 Depiction of a longitudinal design in which one can disentangle the causal relation between employment and health.

cannot distinguish age effects from cohort effects. With a longitudinal design, we would take a single cohort of women (ages 20 to 25) and follow them for many years to see if they reduce the number of hours they work outside the home over time.

Meta-Analysis

Because the question of whether one sex differs from the other sex on a host of variables is so interesting to people and such an easy question to ask in research, there are hundreds and hundreds of sex comparison studies. In the 1980s, a statistical tool called meta-analysis was applied to these studies to help researchers synthesize the findings. **Meta-analysis** quantifies the results of a group of studies. In a meta-analysis, we take into consideration not only whether a significant difference is found in a study but also the size of the difference. In this way, a meta-analysis can average across the studies and produce an overall effect that can be judged in terms of its significance as well as its magnitude. Meta-analysis will be reviewed in more depth in Chapter 4 when the results of sex comparison studies are presented.

TAKE HOME POINTS

- The scientific method rests on empiricism, and a key determinant of whether a theory is scientific is whether it is falsifiable.

- The key feature of the experimental method is random assignment, which helps to isolate the independent variable as the true cause of the effect.

- Correlational research is often easier to conduct than experimental research and has high external validity but low internal validity.

- Experiments are often high in internal validity but may lack external validity if conducted in the laboratory.

- Most research in the area of sex comparisons is correlational because sex is a subject variable rather than a target variable.

- Field experiments — though difficult to conduct — maximize both internal and external validity.

- Longitudinal studies can help to enhance the internal validity of correlational research.

- Meta-analysis is a statistical tool that was developed to summarize the results of studies. In the area of gender, meta-analyses have been conducted on sex comparison studies in a wide variety of domains.

DIFFICULTIES IN CONDUCTING RESEARCH ON GENDER

Now that you understand the basic components of the research process, we can examine the difficulties that arise when applying this process to the study of gender. The study of gender has some unique difficulties that other research domains do not face. Other difficulties inherent in scientific research are particularly problematic in the study of gender. At each stage of the research process, the researcher, who is sometimes the experimenter, can intentionally or unintentionally influence the outcome. Biases may be detected in the question asked, the way the study is designed, how the data are collected, how the data are interpreted, and how the results are communicated. Participants in experiments also can influence the outcome by their awareness of gender-role stereotypes, their desire to fit or reject gender-role norms, and their concerns with self-presentation. That is, participants care about how they appear to the experimenter and to other participants. In this section, I review the ways the experimenter and the participant can influence study outcomes.

TABLE 2.3   KEY TERMS USED IN SCIENTIFIC METHOD

Age effect: Effect due to the age of the respondent.

Cohort effect: Effect due to the cohort or generation of the respondent.

Correlational study: Study in which one observes the relation between two variables, often at a single point in time.

Cross-sectional study: Study in which the data are collected at one point in time, usually from a cross section of different age groups.

Data: Information (e.g., thoughts, feelings, behaviors) collected for the purpose of scientific examination.

Demand characteristics: The ways participants of an experiment can influence the outcome of a study.

Dependent variable: Variable that is expected to be influenced by manipulation of the independent variable; the effect.

Empiricism: Basis of scientific method that involves the collection of information via one of the major senses (usually sight).

Experimenter effects: Ways in which the experimenter can intentionally or unintentionally influence the results of a study.

Experimental method: Research method in which the investigator manipulates one variable and observes its effect on another variable.

External validity: The confidence that the results from an experiment generalize to the real world.

Facts: Statements made about data.

Field experiments: Experiments in which the investigation is taken into the environment where the behavior to be studied naturally occurs.

Hypothesis: Prediction that a certain outcome will occur under a specific set of conditions.

Independent variable: Variable manipulated during an experiment; the cause.

Internal validity: The confidence that the true cause of the effect is being studied.

Longitudinal study: Study in which data are collected at multiple time points.

Meta-analysis: A statistical tool used to synthesize the results of studies.

Negative correlation: Correlation in which the level of one variable increases and the level of the other variable decreases.

Positive correlation: Correlation in which the levels of both variables increase or the levels of both variables decrease at the same time.

Random assignment: Method of assignment in which each participant has an equal chance of being exposed to each condition.

Random selection/random sampling: Method of selecting a sample in which each member of the population has an equal chance of being a participant in the study.

Replication: Repetition of a study, often with different measures of the independent variable and the dependent variable.

Selection bias: Result of participants not being randomly sampled or not being randomly assigned to condition.

Social desirability response bias: A demand characteristic; ways in which participants behave in experiments to give socially desirable answers.

Stimulus/target variable: Variable that can be manipulated in an experiment.

Subject variable: Variable that is a permanent characteristic of the person (subject) and may affect the person's response to another variable.

Theory: Abstract generalization that provides an explanation for a set of facts.

Experimenter Effects

Experimenter effects refer to the ways the experimenter, or the person conducting the research, can influence the results of a study. A review of studies on sex differences in leadership style showed that the sex of the author influenced the results (van Engen & Willemsen, 2004). It turned out that male authors were more likely than female authors to report that women used a more conventional style of leadership that involved monitoring subordinates and rewarding behavior. How can this be? One explanation is that people published studies that fit their expectations. Another explanation is that women experimenters and men experimenters designed different kinds of studies, with one design showing a sex difference and one not.

The experimenter can influence the outcome of a study at many levels. Each of these is described next and shown in Figure 2.4.

Question Asked and Study Design.   First, the experimenter can influence the outcome of a study by the nature of the question asked and the subsequent design of the study. For example, a researcher could be interested in determining the effects of women's paid employment on children's well-being. One researcher may believe it is harmful for women to work outside the home while they have small children. To test this hypothesis, the researcher could design a study in which children in day care are compared to children at home in terms of the number of days they are sick in a year. Because the children at day care will be exposed to more germs, they will experience more sick days the first year than children at home. In this case, the experimenter's theory about mothers' paid employment being harmful to children will be supported. However, another experimenter may believe mothers' paid employment is beneficial to children. This experimenter examines the reading level of kindergartners and finds that children whose mothers worked outside the home have higher reading levels than children whose mothers did not work outside the home. The problem here: The mothers who worked outside the home were more highly educated than the mothers who worked inside the home, and this education may have been transmitted to the children. In both cases, the experimenter's preexisting beliefs influenced the way the study was designed to answer the question.

Most scientists are very interested in the phenomenon they study and have expectations about the results of their work. In an area as controversial as gender, it is difficult to find a scientist who does not have a belief about the outcome of the study. It is all right to have an expectation, or hypothesis, based on scientific theory, but we must be cautious

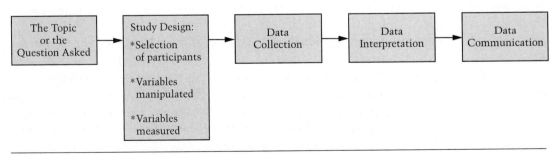

FIGURE 2.4   Stages of the research process that can be influenced by the experimenter.

about hunches based on personal experiences and desires. The best situation is one in which the scientist conducting the research does not care about the outcome of the study and has little invested in it. Perhaps scientists should be randomly assigned to topics! Most of us do care about the outcomes of studies and are invested in those outcomes. As a mother who works outside the home, what would I do if I conducted a study and found that children whose mothers worked outside the home suffered? The task that the scientist must confront is to set aside preexisting beliefs and biases to conduct a study in as objective of a way as possible. **Replication**, or the repeating of a study, by different investigators with different measures of the independent variable and the dependent variable helps enhance our confidence in a finding.

Study Design: Participants. The experimenter can influence the outcome of the study by the participants who are chosen. Obviously, experimenters who limit their studies to all males or all females should question whether their findings generalize to the other sex. Experimenters who study both women and men should also be sensitive to other variables besides sex that could distinguish the two groups. For example, several decades ago, an experimenter who compared the mental health of men and women might have compared employed men to nonemployed women because most men worked outside the home and most women did not. If such a study showed women to be more depressed than men, we might wonder whether this finding was attributable to being female or to not having a job outside the home. Today, any studies conducted of men and women would take into consideration employment status. There are other variables that may co-occur with sex and influence the results of sex comparisons, such as income, occupational status, and even health. Investigators should make sure they are studying comparable groups of men and women.

Study Design: Variables Manipulated and Measured. The experimenter can influence the outcome of a study by the variables that are manipulated and measured. Dependent measures can be biased in favor of males or females. A study that compares female and male mathematical ability by asking children to make calculations of baseball averages is biased against females to the extent that girls and boys have different experiences with baseball. A study that compares women's and men's helping behavior by measuring how quickly a person responds to an infant's cries is biased against men to the extent that men and women have different experiences with children. A helping situation biased in the direction of males is assisting someone with a flat tire on the side of the road. Here, you may find that men are more likely than women to provide assistance because men may have more experience changing tires than women. It is unlikely that men have a "tire-changing" gene and that women have a "diaper-changing" gene that the other sex does not possess. Men are provided with more opportunities to change tires just as women are provided with more opportunities to console a crying infant. Thus, in generalizing across studies, we have to ensure that the different ways a dependent variable is measured do not account for the findings.

Data Collection. The experimenter can influence the outcome of a study by how the data are collected. The experimenter may treat women and men differently in a way that supports the hypothesis. In a now classic study, Rosenthal (1966) found that male and female experimenters smiled more and glanced more at same-sex participants than other-sex participants while giving the experimental instructions. He concluded that men and women are not in the same experiment when the experimenter is aware of their sex. More recently, researchers found that the sex of the target influenced how an emotion is interpreted. When preschoolers were shown a picture of a face that was ambiguous with respect to its emotion, children thought the target was angry if male but sad if female (Parmley & Cunningham, 2008).

The experimenter can influence participants' behavior by giving subtle cues like nodding of the head to indicate the correct response is being given. An experimenter who believes that women self-disclose more than men might unintentionally elicit differences in self-disclosure by revealing more personal information to female than to male participants. The experimenter might provide subtle nonverbal cues that encourage female disclosure (e.g., head nodding, smiling) and subtle cues that discourage male disclosure (e.g., looking bored, not paying attention, shifting around anxiously in one's seat).

The experimenter's beliefs can influence her or his own behavior, which then encourages participants to respond in a way that confirms the experimenter's beliefs. That is, the experimenter's beliefs lead to a **self-fulfilling prophecy**. In these cases, experimenters are probably not intentionally influencing the outcome, but their beliefs are subtly influencing their own behavior and, consequently, the participant's behavior. It may be difficult for experimenters to treat female and male participants equally because most experimenters are aware of gender-role stereotypes and the norms for female and male behavior. One way to minimize this bias is for the investigator to hire an experimenter who is blind to the purpose of the study, especially the hypotheses. In this situation, your only concern is that the experimenter brings to the study her or his lay perceptions of how women and men differ. A better solution is to have the experimenter blind to the participant's sex. One way to accomplish this, although not always feasible, is to provide standardized instructions or questions to participants via an audiotape or intercom, so the experimenter cannot see the participant.

Data Interpretation.   The experimenter can influence the outcome of the study by the way he or she interprets the data. One problem in the area of gender is that we might interpret the same behavior differently depending on whether the person is male or female. In one study, college students rated a professor's written lecture on sex discrimination at work differently depending on whether they thought the professor was male or female (Abel & Meltzer, 2007). The lecture was viewed as more sexist if female than male, and more accurate and of a higher quality if male than female. In many cases, it is difficult to be blind to the participant's sex, especially if you are observing a behavior. Imagine that you observe someone screaming. If the person screaming is female, you may interpret the behavior as hysteria; if the person screaming is male, you may interpret the behavior as anger. Recall the study of preschoolers that showed they were more likely to infer sadness in a female and anger in a male (Parmley & Cunningham, 2008). Imagine how you might respond differently to someone who is sad versus angry!

Communication of Results.   Finally, the experimenter can influence the impact of a study by how the findings are communicated. Experimenters may report only results that support their hypotheses. That is, experimenters who believe there are sex differences may conduct a dozen studies until a difference appears and then report that one difference. Experimenters who believe there are no differences between men and women may conduct a dozen studies, slightly altering the situation in each one, until no difference appears and then report that study. This is a problem for the study of gender because, as noted in Chapter 1, there are different political philosophies about whether there are a few small sex differences or major sex differences that pervade our lives.

Another problem with the communication of results is that sex differences are inherently more interesting than sex similarities; therefore, studies of differences are more likely to be published. A researcher who designs a study that does not involve issues of gender may routinely compare men's and women's behavior in the hope that no differences are found. In this case, the investigator considers sex to be a nuisance variable. If no differences are found, gender is not mentioned in the article or buried in a single sentence in the method section, so there is no record of the similarity! If differences are found, gender may become the focus of the study. The scientific bias of publishing differences is perpetuated by the media, which are not likely to pick up a story on a study that shows sex similarities. A study that shows differences is going to gather the attention of the media and will be placed in a prominent place in the newspaper.

This problem was highlighted in Susan Faludi's (1991) book, *Backlash: The Undeclared War against American Women*. She describes somewhat questionable research findings that are published by the media even when refuted by other scientific research. (The divorce statistic example at the beginning of this chapter was discussed in her book.) According to Faludi, the results of studies that support the culture of the time are more likely to attract headlines. For example, in 1986, a story in the newspaper showed that the chance of a single college-educated woman getting married was 20% at age 30, 5% at age 35, and 1.3% at age 40. The study made front-page news, despite questionable methods and a small sample size. A follow-up study that used actual census data showed quite different statistics: at age 30, 58% to 66%; at age 35, 32% to 41%, and at age 40, 17% to 23%. The follow-up study, however, was not picked up by the media. Faludi reports another example having to do with age and infertility. A 1982 study of infertility widely noted in newspapers and on radio and television talk shows showed that women between the ages of 31 and 35 had a 40% chance of becoming infertile. Reporters did not note, however, that this study was based on a very unique sample: women receiving artificial insemination because their husbands were sterile. A subsequent study based on a more representative sample showed that the infertility rate for women between the ages of 30 and 34 was 14%, only 3% more than women in their early 20s.

Faludi's position is that research findings showing adverse effects of the women's movement on women's economics, fertility, and relationships were being highlighted in the 1980s, whereas research findings showing positive effects of the women's movement were stifled. These examples show that the media are more likely to sensationalize the more outrageous research findings and are less likely to highlight findings of sex similarities. Sex differences are interesting; sex similarities are not. The media can also distort the explanations for findings of differences between men and women. One study showed that the political orientation of a newspaper (as defined by the most recent presidential candidate endorsed) was associated with the explanations provided for sex differences (Brescoll & LaFrance, 2004). More conservative newspapers were more likely to emphasize biological explanations. One of the skills you will gain from reading this text is being able to evaluate reports about sex differences you read in the popular press. Start now with Do Gender 2.1.

In summary, we need to be alert to how experimenter expectancies can shape studies.

DO GENDER 2.1
Comparing Media Reports
to Scientific Reports

Find a news article on gender, most likely on sex differences, in a newspaper or a news magazine. Find one that refers to the original source of the study; that is, it gives the reference to a scientific journal. Compare the news version of the study to the scientific report of the study. Answer the following questions:

1. Did the news article accurately reflect the findings of the scientific study?

2. What did the news article leave out, if anything?

3. What did the news article exaggerate, if anything?

4. Was there anything in the news article that was misleading?

5. What did you learn by reading the scientific article that you would not have learned by reading the news article?

6. Why did this particular study appear in the news? Was it important? Was the finding "catchy"?

One remedy is to have a team of scientists with opposing beliefs conduct research on a topic. Why do you think this does not happen very often? Social psychologists have shown that we are attracted to people who share our beliefs and values—people who are like us. Therefore, it is more likely that we will find ourselves collaborating with people who share our beliefs about the outcome of a study. Replication is one strategy we have built into science as a check on the influence experimenters have on research findings. Before taking a finding seriously, we have to make sure it has been repeated with different samples, with different measures of both the independent and dependent variables, and by different investigators. We can be more confident of similarities or differences between male and female behavior when we see them emerge repeatedly and across a wide variety of contexts. As shown in Chapter 5, however, changing the context usually alters how men and women behave.

Participant Effects

The ways in which participants of an experiment can influence the outcome of a study are referred to as **demand characteristics**. There are certain demands or expectations about how to behave as a participant in an experiment. Participants often conform to or react against these demands. The **social desirability response bias** is one example of a demand characteristic. That is, people want to behave in socially desirable ways, ways in which they appear normal and likable. In our society, it is socially desirable for men to appear masculine and women to appear feminine. On self-report inventories of masculinity and femininity, men typically rate themselves as high on masculinity and women rate themselves as high on femininity regardless of how they really score on traits that define those concepts. That is, regardless of whether a man rates himself as independent or self-confident (traits we ascribe to masculinity), most men rate themselves as masculine. Thus, participants may behave in ways that fit their gender role, especially if they realize the purpose of the experiment.

If I asked the students in my class for a show of hands as to who is emotional, more women than men would raise their hands. If I asked the students for a show of hands as to who is aggressive, more men than women would raise their hands. Does this mean men are more aggressive than women and women more emotional than men? Certainly not—on the basis of that showing of hands. It is socially desirable for men to say they are aggressive and women to say they are emotional. The design of the study is poor because the public behavior increases the chance of introducing a social desirability response bias.

An example of demand characteristics occurred in a study of sexual behavior. College men reported more sexual partners when the experimenter was a female than a male (Fisher, 2007). One precaution that you can take to guard against demand characteristics is to have responses be private—anonymous and confidential—rather than public. However, the students in the previous experimenter were led to believe just that. Another precaution is to disguise the purpose of the experiment.

In a review of the literature on parents' treatment of children, the review concluded that parents treat sons and daughters the same (Lytton & Romney, 1991). However, a closer inspection of the studies revealed that parents *said* they treated sons and daughters the same, but observational studies showed differences.

One remedy to the problem of participant effects is to have multiple measures of a behavior. For example, if you want to know how women and men compare in terms of

assertiveness, you could examine self-reports of assertiveness, you could set up an experiment to elicit assertive behavior, and you could obtain other people's reports of participants' assertive behavior. In studies of aggression among children, a frequently used measure of other people's reports is peer nomination. All the children in the class nominate the most aggressive child, the child most difficult to get along with, or the child who makes them afraid. When one person is named by the majority of the children, we can have a great deal of confidence that the child is exhibiting some kind of behavioral problem.

The Setting: Laboratory Versus Field

Much of our research on gender is conducted in the laboratory rather than the field, or the real world. A number of problems emerge in applying the conclusions from research on gender conducted in the laboratory to our everyday lives, specifically problems with external validity. In the laboratory, everything is held constant except the independent variable, which is usually participant's sex. Thus men and women come into the laboratory and face equal treatment and equal conditions. The problem is that women and men do not face equal conditions in the real world. Thus we might be more likely to find similar behavior in the laboratory than in the real world. If that is the case, the differences in behavior observed in the real world might be due to the different situations in which women and men find themselves.

For example, if you bring men and women into the laboratory and provoke them, they may display similar levels of anger. However, in the real world, women are more likely than men to hold low-status positions where displays of anger are inappropriate and often punished. In addition, in the real world, men are more often provoked than women. Thus men may display more anger than women in the real world because men are more likely to be provoked and women are more likely to be punished for displays of anger.

Another difficulty with laboratory research is that it is often conducted on college students. College students differ from the general population in a number of ways. They are more likely to be White, upper to middle class, higher in education, and homogeneous on a number of dimensions. The college experience is one in which the roles of men and women and the statuses of men and women are more similar compared to their situations after college. Thus it is questionable whether we can generalize the similarities observed among college students to the general population.

Variables Confounded with Sex

A fundamental problem for the study of gender is that we cannot randomly assign a person to be male or female. As mentioned earlier, sex is usually a subject variable rather than a true independent variable that can be manipulated. You can manipulate sex when you are leading respondents to believe a target person is female or male. Here, sex is a target variable. However, when comparing men's and women's feelings, thoughts, and behavior, we cannot be certain any differences found are due to sex alone; men and women come into the laboratory with their own values, histories, and experiences. Most important, sex is confounded with status.

We cannot separate the effects of sex from status. Do women smile more than men, or do low-status people smile more than high-status people? We will see in Chapter 7 that many of the sex differences observed in verbal and nonverbal communication seem to be due to status. When men and women are randomly assigned to a high-status or low-status position in the laboratory, high-status persons of both sexes typically display so-called male behavior and low-status persons of both sexes typically display so-called female behavior.

Another variable besides status that is confounded with sex is gender role. When we observe a sex difference in a behavior, is it due to the biological category of male or female, or is it due to the psychological category of gender? Too often, we fail to examine whether the difference is due to sex or to gender role. One area of research where there is substantial agreement as to whether a sex difference exists is aggression. Even aggression, however, may be partly due to biological sex and partly due to gender role, that is, our encouragement of aggression among males and discouragement of aggression among females. Features of the male gender role have been linked to aggression. Throughout this book, I have been very attentive to the impact that gender roles have in areas of sex differences.

Situational Influences

Even if we examine personality traits in addition to participants' sex, we often find that in some situations we observe a difference and in some situations we do not observe a difference. Some situations are high in behavioral constraints, meaning the behavior required in the situation is clear and not very flexible; in this case, sex may have little to do with behavior. A graduation ceremony is such a situation. Men and women are usually dressed alike in robes, march into the ceremony together, and sit throughout the ceremony quietly until their name is called to receive their diplomas. The behavior in this situation is determined more by the situation than by characteristics of the people, including their sex. Other situations low in behavioral constraints would allow the opportunity for men and women to display different behaviors; informal social gatherings are an example of such a situation.

Certain situations make gender especially salient. As shown in Figure 2.5, a heterosexual wedding is such a situation.

Traditions make sex salient. Here, the norms for men's and women's attire are very different; no one expects men and women to dress the same at a wedding. The dress is formal; it would be highly unusual for a man to attend a wedding in a dress or a woman to attend a wedding in a tuxedo. The bride does

not throw the bouquet to the entire crowd, only to eligible women; likewise, the groom throws the garter to eligible men. This is an occasion that may make differences in the behavior of women and men more likely to appear.

There also may be specific situational pressures to behave in accordance with or in opposition to one's gender role. Being raised in a traditional family, I have often found myself behaving in ways more consistent with the female gender role when I am with my family than when I am at home. When I was growing up, it was customary during large family gatherings for women to tend to the dishes and men to tend to football. Did I help with the dishes? Of course. It would be rude not to. Besides, I don't really like football. Would my dad help with the dishes? Probably not. He likes football and would be chased out of the kitchen.

There may be other situations in which behaving in opposition to gender roles is attractive. I remember the first time I went to look for a car by myself. The salesperson guided me to the cars with automatic transmissions and made some remark about women not being able to drive cars with a manual transmission. The worst part was he was right; I had tried and could not drive a stick shift. But that incident inspired me. I was determined to learn to drive a stick shift and to buy a car with a manual transmission—to do my part in disconfirming the stereotype. To this day, I continue to drive a car with a manual transmission (despite such cars' increasingly limited availability) because of that salesperson's remark. In this case, the situation made gender roles salient, but the effect was to create behavior inconsistent with gender roles.

FIGURE 2.5 Wedding picture, illustrating a situation with high behavioral constraints and a situation in which gender and gender-based norms are salient.

The situational forces that shape behavior are a dominant theme in this book. We cannot study gender outside of the context in which it occurs, the situations in which men and women find themselves, and the people with whom they interact. This is the social-psychological perspective, which is emphasized throughout this book.

TAKE HOME POINTS

- The experimenter can influence the outcome of a study by the way it is designed and by the way the data are collected, interpreted, and reported. This is one reason that we are more confident in findings that have been replicated by a number of researchers who have used different methods and different measures.

- Participants can influence the outcome of the study. Especially when the behavior is public, demand characteristics are likely to operate. Ensuring confidentiality and disguising the nature of the research will minimize demand characteristics.

- Differences between men and women are less likely to be found in the laboratory, where men and women face equal conditions, than in the real world, where they do not.

- When finding that women and men differ on some outcome, one must be careful to determine whether the difference is due to sex, status, gender role, or something else.

HISTORY OF THE PSYCHOLOGY OF GENDER

In Chapter 1, I provided a very abstract definition of gender roles. Where did this concept come from? What did it mean 100 years ago, and what does it mean today? Is it better to be masculine or feminine? Or does it depend on whether you are male or female? Here, I provide a brief review of the history of the psychology of gender. I examine the different ways that people conceptualized and measured gender roles. I have divided the history of the field into four periods that approximate those identified by Richard Ashmore (1990). Each time period is marked by one or more key figures in the field.

1894–1936: Sex Differences in Intelligence

The first period focused on the differences between men and women and was marked by the publication of a book by Ellis (1894) entitled *Man and Woman*, which called for a scientific approach to the study of the similarities and differences between men and women. No consideration was yet given to personality traits or roles associated with sex. Thus, gender roles were not part of the picture. The primary goal of this era was to examine if (really, to establish that) men were intellectually superior to women. To accomplish this goal, scientists turned to the anatomy of the brain (Shields, 1975).

First, scientists focused on the size of the human brain. Because women's heads and brains are smaller than those of men, there seemed to be conclusive evidence that women were intellectually inferior. However, men were also taller and weighed more than women; when body size was taken into account, the evidence for sex differences in intelligence became less clear. If one computed a ratio of the weight of the brain to the weight of the body, women appeared to have relatively larger brains. If one computed the ratio of the surface area of the brain to the surface area of the body, men appeared to have relatively larger brains. Thus brain size alone could not settle the question of sex differences in intelligence.

Next, researchers turned to specific areas of the brain that could be responsible for higher levels of intellectual functioning.

The frontal cortex was first thought to control higher levels of mental functioning, and men were observed to have larger frontal lobes than women. Then it appeared men did not have larger frontal lobes; instead, men had larger parietal lobes. Thus, thinking shifted to the parietal lobe as the seat of intellectual functioning. All this research came under sharp methodological criticism because the scientists observing the anatomy of the brain were not blind to the sex associated with the particular brain; that is, the people evaluating the brain knew whether it belonged to a male or a female! This situation was ripe for the kinds of experimenter biases described earlier in the chapter.

The period ended with the seminal work of *Sex and Personality* published by Lewis Terman and Catherine Cox Miles in 1936. They concluded there are no sex differences in intellect: "Intelligence tests, for example, have demonstrated for all time the falsity of the once widely prevalent belief that women as a class are appreciably or at all inferior to men in the major aspects of intellect" (p. 1).

TAKE HOME POINTS

- Initial research in the area of gender focused on trying to establish that men were smarter than women by examining the size of the brain.

- The research was unsuccessful. It was not clear that one could link brain size to intellect.

1936–1954: Masculinity–Femininity as a Global Personality Trait

During this next period, researchers shifted their focus from sex differences alone to consider the notion of gender roles. The construct of masculinity–femininity, or M/F,

was introduced during this period. Because men and women did not differ in intelligence, Terman concluded that the real mental differences between men and women could be captured by measuring masculinity and femininity.

Researchers developed a 456-item instrument to measure M/F. It was called the Attitude Interest Analysis Survey (AIAS; Terman & Miles, 1936) to disguise the true purpose of the test. The AIAS was the first published M/F scale. The items chosen were based on statistical sex differences observed in elementary, junior high, and high school children. This meant that items on which the average female scored higher than the average male were labeled feminine, and items on which the average male scored higher than the average female were labeled masculine, regardless of the content of those items. The M/F scale was also bipolar, which meant that masculinity and femininity were viewed as opposite ends of a single continuum. The sum of the feminine items was subtracted from the sum of the masculine items to yield a total M/F score.

The instrument was composed of seven subject areas: (1) word association, (2) inkblot interpretation, (3) information, (4) emotional and ethical response, (5) interests (likes and dislikes), (6) admired persons and opinions, and (7) introversion–extroversion, which really measured superiority–subordination. Sample items from each subject area are shown in Table 2.4.

Several of these subscales are quite interesting. The information scale was based on the assumption that men have greater knowledge than women about some areas of life, such as sports and politics, and women have greater knowledge about other areas of life, such as gardening and sewing. Thus, giving a correct response to an item about which

TABLE 2.4   SAMPLE ITEMS FROM THE ATTITUDE INTEREST ANALYSIS SURVEY

Responses with a (+) are indicative of masculinity; responses with a (–) are indicative of femininity; responses with a 0 are neutral and not scored as either.

Word Association

Look at the word in capital letters, then look at the four words that follow it. Draw a line under the word that goes best or most naturally with the one in capitals; the word it tends most to make you think of.

1. POLE	barber (0)	cat (+)	North (–)	telephone (+)
2. DATE	appointment (–)	dance (+)	fruit (+)	history (+)

Inkblot Association

Here are some drawings, a little like inkblots. They are not pictures of anything in particular but might suggest almost anything to you, just as shapes in the clouds sometimes do. Beside each drawing four things are mentioned. Underline the one word that tells what the drawing makes you think of most.

1. bush (0)
   lady (+)
   shadow (+)
   mushroom (–)

2. flame (–)
   flower (+)
   snake (–)
   worm (–)

Information

In each sentence, draw a line under the word that makes the sentence true.

1. Marigold is a kind of	fabric (+)	flower (–)	grain (–)	stone (+)
2. Tokyo is a city of	China (–)	India (–)	Japan (+)	Russia (0)
3. A loom is used for	cooking (+)	embroidering (+)	sewing (+)	weaving (–)
4. The number of players on a baseball team is	7 (–)	9 (+)	11 (–)	13 (0)

Emotional and Ethical Response

Below is a list of things that sometimes cause anger. After each thing mentioned, draw a circle around VM, M, L, or N to show how much anger it causes you.

     VM means VERY MUCH; M means MUCH; L means A LITTLE; N means NONE.

1. Seeing people disfigure library books	VM (–)	M (–)	L (+)	N (+)
2. Seeing someone trying to discredit you with your employer	VM (+)	M (0)	L (+)	N (–)

Below is a list of things that sometimes cause disgust. After each thing mentioned, draw a circle around VM, M, L, or N to indicate how much disgust it causes you.

     VM means VERY MUCH; M means MUCH; L means A LITTLE; N means NONE.

1. An unshaven man	VM (–)	M (–)	L (+)	N (+)
2. Gum chewing	VM (–)	M (–)	L (+)	N (+)

Below is a list of acts of various degrees of wickedness or badness. After each thing mentioned, draw a circle around 3, 2, 1, or 0 to show how wicked or bad you think it is.

     3 means EXTREMELY WICKED; 2 means DECIDEDLY BAD; 1 means SOMEWHAT BAD; 0 means NOT REALLY BAD.

1. Using slang	3 (–)	2 (–)	1 (+)	0 (+)
2. Excessive drinking	3 (–)	2 (+)	1 (+)	0 (0)

TABLE 2.4 (*Continued*)

Interests

For each occupation below, ask yourself: Would I like that work or not? If you would like it, draw a circle around L. If you would dislike it, draw a circle around D. If you would neither like nor dislike it, draw a circle around N. In deciding on your answer, think only of the kind of work. Don't consider the pay. Imagine that you have the ability to do the work, that you are the right age for it, and that it is equally open to men and women.
    L means LIKE; D means DISLIKE; N means NEITHER LIKE NOR DISLIKE

1. Forest ranger	L (+)	D (–)	N (0)
2. Florist	L (–)	D (+)	N (+)

Personalities and Opinion

Below is a list of famous characters. After each name draw a circle around L, D, or N to indicate whether you like that character.
    L means LIKE; D means DISLIKE; N means NEITHER LIKE NOR DISLIKE.

1. Daniel Boone	L (+)	D (–)	N (–)
2. Christopher Columbus	L (–)	D (+)	N (+)
3. Florence Nightingale	L (–)	D (+)	N (+)

Read each statement and consider whether it is mostly true or mostly false. If it is mostly TRUE, draw a circle around T. If it is mostly FALSE, draw a circle around F.

1. The world was created in 6 days of 24 hours each.	T (+)	F (0)
2. Love "at first sight" is usually the truest love.	T (+)	F (–)

Introvertive Response

Answer each question as truthfully as you can by drawing a line under YES or NO.

1. Did you ever have imaginary companions?	YES (–)	NO (+)
2. Do you worry much over possible misfortunes?	YES (–)	NO (+)
3. As a child were you extremely disobedient?	YES (+)	NO (–)
4. Do people ever say that you talk too much?	YES (+)	NO (–)

Source: Terman and Miles (1936).

women are supposed to know more than men would be scored as feminine; conversely, giving a correct response to an item about which men are supposed to know more than women would be scored as masculine. For example, consider the first item on the information subscale shown in Table 2.4. Answering that a marigold is a flower would be scored as feminine, whereas answering that a marigold is a stone would be scored as masculine. The emotional and ethical response subscale was scored such that being feminine meant getting angry when seeing others treated unfairly and being masculine meant getting angry when being disturbed at work.

There were no assumptions about the basis of these sex differences. Terman and Miles (1936) left the cause of the sex differences—biological, psychological, or cultural—unspecified.

A few years later, Hathaway and McKinley (1940) developed the Minnesota Multiphasic Personality Inventory (MMPI). It eventually included an M/F scale that consisted of items reflecting altruism, emotional sensitivity, sexual preference, preference for certain occupations, and gender identity questions. The most notable feature in the development of this scale is that the femininity items were validated on 13 homosexuals. Homosexual men were compared to heterosexual male soldiers; at that time, heterosexual male soldiers epitomized masculinity and homosexual men were considered feminine. In fact, feminine traits were considered to be a predisposing factor to homosexuality in men (Terman & Miles, 1936). Women were not even involved in research to evaluate femininity. Thus we can see at least two major problems with this instrument: First, women were not involved in the conceptualization of the female gender role; second, only 13 homosexual men were involved in the study, which is hardly sufficient to validate an instrument even if they had been the appropriate population.

Some researchers became concerned about the self-report methodology used to assess M/F. The purpose of the tests might have been obvious, which could lead men and women to give socially desirable rather than truthful responses. The concern focused on demand characteristics. Thus several projective tests of M/F were developed, including one by Franck and Rosen (1949). They developed a test that consisted of incomplete drawings, like the stimuli shown in the first column of Figure 2.6.

Franck and Rosen began with 60 stimuli, asked men and women to complete the drawings, and found sex differences in the way that 36 of the 60 were completed. These 36 stimuli then comprised the test. How did men and women differ in their drawings? Men were found to be more likely to close off the stimuli, make sharper edges, include angles, and focus on unifying objects rather

than keeping them separate. Women were found to leave a stimulus open, to make round or blunt edges, and to make lines that pointed inward. The content of the objects men and women drew also was found to differ: Men drew nude women, skyscrapers, and dynamic objects, whereas women drew animals, flowers, houses, and static objects.

Interestingly, Franck and Rosen (1949) did not conclude that a male and a female who receive the same score on the test are the same in terms of masculinity and femininity. In fact, they argued that the drawings of a male who receives a feminine score are quite bizarre and very different from the drawings of a female who receives a feminine

Sample Stimulus Masculine Scored Feminine Scored

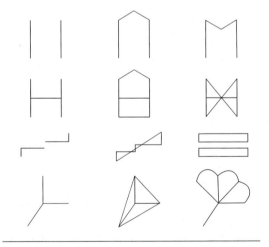

FIGURE 2.6 Examples of the kinds of incomplete drawings that appeared on Franck and Rosen's (1949) projective test of masculinity/femininity. How the drawings were completed was taken as an indication of masculinity or femininity. The second column represents masculine ways of completing the drawings and the third column represents feminine ways of completing the drawings. *Source:* Adapted from Franck and Rosen (1949).

score. They applied the same logic to a female who receives a masculine score. If the instrument does not measure psychological masculinity and femininity among both men and women, we have to wonder about the purpose of the test. Franck and Rosen suggested their instrument measures acceptance of one's gender role rather than the degree of masculinity and femininity. Males who scored masculine and females who scored feminine were considered to have accepted their gender roles.

TAKE HOME POINTS

- During this period, the concept of M/F was introduced. However, it was defined merely by sex differences.

- Because women were rarely included in research, one scale of femininity, from the MMPI, was validated on homosexual men. Homosexuality was thought to be equivalent to femininity.

- Projective tests of M/F were developed to reduce demand characteristics. However, these tests were flawed in that sex differences in drawings were taken to be evidence of masculinity and femininity.

- All the M/F scales developed during this period suffered from a number of conceptual weaknesses:
  - The tests did not distinguish between more or less masculine people, nor did they distinguish between more or less feminine people.
  - They merely distinguished men from women, a distinction that did not need to be made.
  - Any item that revealed sex differences was taken as evidence of masculinity and femininity, regardless of its relevance to these constructs (e.g., thinking Tokyo is a city in India is an indicator of femininity).
  - All the scales were bipolar, such that masculinity represented one end and femininity represented the other.
  - Gay men were equated with feminine women.

- There seemed to be some confusion among masculinity, femininity, and sexual orientation. An assumption at the time was that psychologically healthy men were masculine and psychologically healthy women were feminine.

1954–1982: Sex Typing and Androgyny

This period was marked by Eleanor Maccoby's (1966) publication of *The Development of Sex Differences*, which reviewed important theories of sex typing, that is, how boys and girls developed sex-appropriate preferences, personality traits, and behaviors. Many of these theories are reviewed in detail in Chapter 5.

In addition, in 1973, Anne Constantinople published a major critique of the existing M/F instruments. She questioned the use of sex differences as the basis for defining masculinity and femininity; she also questioned whether M/F was really a unidimensional construct that could be captured by a single bipolar scale. The latter assumption, in particular, was addressed during this period by the publication of instruments that distinguished masculinity and femininity as independent constructs.

Instrumental Versus Expressive Distinction. A distinction brought to the study of gender roles that helped conceptualize masculinity and femininity as separate dimensions was the distinction between an instrumental and an expressive orientation. In 1955, Parsons, a sociologist, and Bales, a social psychologist, distinguished between instrumental or goal-oriented behavior and expressive or emotional behavior in their studies of male group interactions. The instrumental leader focuses on getting the job done and the expressive leader focuses on maintaining group harmony.

Parsons and Bales (1955) extended the instrumental/expressive distinction to gender. They saw a relation between superior power and instrumentality and a relation between inferior power and expressivity. They believed the distinction between the husband role and the wife role was both an instrumental/expressive distinction as well as a superior/inferior power distinction. The instrumental orientation became linked to the male gender role and the expressive orientation became linked to the female gender role.

Two instruments were developed during this period that linked the instrumental versus expressive orientation to gender role. In 1974, Sandra Bem published the Bem Sex Role Inventory (BSRI) and Spence, Helmreich, and Stapp published the Personal Attributes Questionnaire (PAQ). The BSRI and the PAQ are still the most commonly used inventories to measure masculinity and femininity today. The innovative feature of both instruments is that masculinity and femininity are conceptualized as two independent dimensions rather than a single bipolar scale; thus, a person receives a masculinity score and a femininity score. Masculinity and femininity were no longer viewed as opposites.

The BSRI (Bem, 1974) was developed by having undergraduates rate how desirable it is for a man and a woman to possess each of 400 attributes. Items that students rated as more desirable for a male to possess were indicators of masculinity, and items that students rated as more desirable for a female were indicators of femininity. Items were not based on respondents' views of how likely men and women are to have these traits but on their views of how *desirable* it is for men and women to have the traits. The final BSRI consisted of 60 items: 20 masculine, 20 feminine, and 20 neutral items. The neutral items are included in the instrument to disguise the purpose of the scale.

In contrast to the BSRI, the PAQ (Spence, Helmreich, & Stapp, 1974) was developed by focusing on the perception of how *likely* men and women are to possess certain traits. College students were asked to rate the typical adult male and female, the typical college male and female, and the ideal male and female. The items on this instrument are shown in the top half of Table 2.5.

The masculinity scale included items that students viewed as more characteristic of men than women but also as ideal for both men and women to possess. "Independence" was a masculinity item; the typical college male was viewed as more independent than the typical college female, but independence was perceived as equally desirable in both men and women. The femininity scale included items that were more characteristic of women than men but viewed as ideal in both women and men. "Understanding of others" was a femininity item; the typical college female was rated as more understanding of others than the typical college male, but respondents viewed being understanding of others as a socially desirable trait for both women and men. Spence and colleagues (1974) also created a third scale, called the M/F scale, that was bipolar. That is, one end represented masculinity and the other end represented femininity. These were items on which college students believed the typical college male and the typical college female differed, but they also were items that students viewed as socially desirable for one sex to possess but not the other. For example, the typical college male was viewed as worldly, whereas the typical college female was viewed as home oriented. And, respondents viewed it as more socially desirable for men than women to be worldly and for women than men to be home oriented. This scale is seldom used in research.

The items on the masculinity scales of the BSRI and PAQ were thought to reflect an

TABLE 2.5   Personal Attributes Questionnaire

Masculinity (M+)	Femininity (F+)	Masculinity–Femininity (M/F)
Independent	Emotional	Aggressive
Active	Able to devote self to others	Dominant
Competitive	Gentle	Excitable in major crisis
Can make decisions	Helpful to others	Worldly (vs. home-oriented)
Never gives up	Kind	Indifferent to others' approval
Self-confident	Aware of others' feelings	Feelings not easily hurt
Feels superior	Understanding of others	Never cries
Stands up well under pressure	Warm in relations to others	Little need for security

Source: Spence, Helmreich, and Stapp (1974).

Extension of Personal Attributes Questionnaire
Unmitigated Agency (M–)

Arrogant	Dictatorial	
Boastful	Cynical	
Egotistical	Looks out for self	
Greedy	Hostile	

Source: Spence, Helmreich, and Holahan (1979).

instrumental or agentic orientation, and the items on the femininity scales were thought to reflect an expressive or communal orientation. Scores on the masculinity and femininity scales are generally uncorrelated, reflecting the fact that they are two independent dimensions. When these scales were developed, consistent sex differences appeared. Men scored higher than women on the masculinity scales, and women scored higher than men on the femininity scales. But the scales were developed 35 years ago. Do sex differences still appear today? People still have different views of what is desirable in a woman and in a man, although the differences are stronger among some subgroups of Americans (e.g., European American men in the Northeast and African American men in the South) than others (e.g., European American woman in the Northeast; Konrad & Harris, 2002). Sex differences in masculinity and femininity scores have appeared from the 1970s to the late 1990s (Lueptow, Garovich-Szabo, & Lueptow, 2001; Spence & Buckner, 2000). However, women's masculinity scores have increased over time, which has reduced the size of that sex difference (Spence & Buckner, 2000). People view masculine characteristics as more desirable in women today than they did in 1972 (Auster & Ohm, 2000). People's views of what is desirable in men have not changed. These findings reflect the greater changes in the female than the male gender role over the past several decades. There has been more encouragement for women to become agentic than for men to become communal.

Because reports of femininity and masculinity could be influenced by demand characteristics, implicit measures of masculinity and femininity have been developed, the most popular of which is the Implicit Association Test (IAT; Greenwald & Farnham, 2000). The IAT is based on reaction times. Individuals see a series of agentic and communal attributes flashed on a screen, one at a time, and have to indicate whether the attribute reflects a self-related term or an other-related term as well as whether the attribute characterizes themselves or not. The measure correlates with self-report measures of agency and communion and reveals larger sex differences, perhaps because the implicit measure reduces demand characteristics. To date, it is not known whether these measures predict behavior (Wood & Eagly, 2009).

Androgyny.   One outgrowth of these two M/F inventories (the BSRI and the PAQ) was the conceptualization of and research on **androgyny**. Androgyny emerged from the operationalization of masculinity and femininity as unipolar, independent dimensions. The androgynous person was someone who displayed both masculine and feminine traits. Androgyny was first measured with the BSRI by subtracting the masculinity score from the femininity score. Positive difference scores reflected femininity, and negative difference scores reflected masculinity. Scores near zero reflected androgyny, signifying that people had a relatively equal amount of both traits. A male who scored masculine and a female who scored feminine were referred to as **sex-typed**. A masculine female and a feminine male were referred to as **cross-sex-typed**. One problem with this measurement of androgyny is that the score did not distinguish between people who endorsed many masculine and feminine qualities from people who endorsed only a few masculine and feminine qualities. Someone who endorsed 10 masculine and 10 feminine traits received the same score (0) as someone who endorsed 2 masculine and 2 feminine traits; both were viewed as androgynous.

Spence and colleagues (1974) had an alternative system for scoring androgyny. They divided scores on the masculinity and femininity scales in half to create the four groups shown in Figure 2.7.

Someone who possessed a high number of masculine features and a low number of feminine features was designated masculine; someone who possessed a high number of feminine and a low number of masculine features was designated feminine. These people were referred to as sex-typed if their sex corresponded to their gender role. The androgynous person was someone who possessed a high number of both masculine and feminine features. A person who had few masculine or feminine traits was referred to as undifferentiated. To this day, most researchers still do not know the meaning of this last category, yet they often create these four categories when using either the PAQ or the BSRI.

Androgyny was put forth by Bem (1974, 1975) as an ideal: The androgynous person was one who embodied the socially desirable features of both masculinity and femininity. It was no longer believed the most psychologically healthy people were masculine men and feminine women; instead, the healthiest people were thought to be those who possessed both attributes. Androgynous people were supposed to have the best of both worlds and to demonstrate the greatest behavioral flexibility and the best psychological adjustment. Unfortunately, subsequent research revealed that the masculinity scale alone predicts behavioral flexibility and

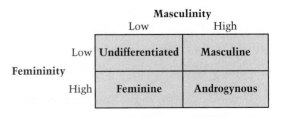

FIGURE 2.7   This is a sex-typing typology based on people's scores on masculinity and femininity.

psychological adjustment as well as, and sometimes better than, the androgyny score (e.g., Woo & Oei, 2006). In hindsight, this finding is not so surprising because the traits included on the BSRI and PAQ masculinity scales are those valued by American society. Bem actually conceptualized androgyny to be much more than the sum of masculine and feminine traits. Androgyny had implications for how one thought about the world. This is elaborated on in Chapter 5 in the discussion of gender-schema theory.

Undesirable Aspects of Masculinity and Femininity. One criticism of the PAQ and the BSRI is that a majority of attributes are socially desirable. In 1979, Spence, Helmreich, and Holahan set out to develop scales that paralleled the original M/F scales in content but differed in social desirability. Conceptually, the masculinity scale, which they referred to as M+, was thought to reflect a positive instrumental or agentic orientation, whereas the femininity scale, which they referred to as F+, was thought to reflect a positive expressive or communal orientation. Spence and colleagues were looking to develop scales that measured socially undesirable aspects of agentic and communal orientations.

Spence and colleagues turned to the work of David Bakan (1966), who richly developed the ideas of agency and communion. Bakan argued there are two principles of human existence: an agentic one that focuses on the self and separation, and a communal one that focuses on others and connection. Bakan also suggested that agency is the male principle and communion the female. Bakan argued that it is important for agency to be mitigated by communion and that **unmitigated agency** would be destructive to the self and society. Unmitigated agency reflected a focus on the self to the neglect of others.

Drawing on this work, Spence and colleagues (1979) developed a negative masculinity scale that reflected unmitigated agency; the scale included in the Extended Personal Attributes Questionnaire (EPAQ) is shown in the bottom of Table 2.5.

The unmitigated agency scale is agentic like the earlier positive masculinity scale, more common in men than women, and socially undesirable in both men and women. Most important, it conceptually reflects the construct of unmitigated agency: a focus on the self to the exclusion of others. It includes a hostile attitude toward others and self-absorption. The scale is positively correlated with the M+ scale, reflecting the focus on the self, and negatively correlated with the F+ scale, reflecting the absence of a focus on others (Helgeson & Fritz, 1999).

Spence and colleagues (1979) also wanted to capture socially undesirable aspects of the female gender role. Turning to Bakan (1966) again, they noted that communion also ought to be mitigated by agency. Although Bakan never used the term **unmitigated communion**, he noted it would be unhealthy to focus on others to the exclusion of the self. Spence and colleagues had more difficulty coming up with traits that conceptually reflected unmitigated communion. They developed two negative femininity scales, but neither conceptually captured the construct of unmitigated communion (Spence et al., 1979). Later, I developed an unmitigated communion scale (Helgeson, 1993; Helgeson & Fritz, 1998), shown in Table 2.6.

The unmitigated communion scale has two components: overinvolvement with others and neglect of the self. It is positively correlated with F+, reflecting the focus on others, and negatively correlated with M+, reflecting the absence of a focus on the self (Helgeson & Fritz, 1999).

TABLE 2.6   UNMITIGATED COMMUNION SCALE

Instructions: Using the following scale, place a number in the blank beside each statement that indicates the extent to which you agree or disagree. Think of the people close to you—friends or family—in responding to each statement.

Strongly Disagree	Slightly Disagree	Neither Agree nor Disagree	Slightly Agree	Strongly Agree
1	2	3	4	5

1. I always place the needs of others above my own.
2. I never find myself getting overly involved in others' problems.*
3. For me to be happy, I need others to be happy.
4. I worry about how other people get along without me when I am not there.
5. I have no trouble getting to sleep at night when other people are upset.*
6. It is impossible for me to satisfy my own needs when they interfere with the needs of others.
7. I can't say no when someone asks me for help.
8. Even when exhausted, I will always help other people.
9. I often worry about others' problems.

*Items are reverse scored.
Source: Helgeson and Fritz (1998).

Both unmitigated communion and unmitigated agency have been shown to be important constructs in the area of gender and health and account for a number of sex differences in health. This research is discussed in later chapters of this book that focus on health.

TAKE HOME POINTS

■ The period between 1954 and 1982 brought with it major innovations in the conceptualization and measurement of gender roles.

■ The distinction between the instrumental and expressive orientation was made and then linked to gender. This led to the development of two instruments, the PAQ and the BSRI, which are the most widely used instruments to measure psychological masculinity and femininity today.

■ These two instruments differed from previous instruments in that masculinity and femininity were established as two independent dimensions rather than bipolar ends of a single continuum.

■ The use of independent M/F scales led to the development of the androgyny construct. Initially, androgyny was captured by similar scores on masculinity and femininity and later by high scores on masculinity and femininity.

■ The most recent advance during this period was the idea that there are socially undesirable aspects of gender roles that ought to be considered and measured. This led to the concepts of unmitigated agency and unmitigated communion.

1982–Present: Gender as a Social Category

Over the past three decades, research on sex and gender has proliferated. There have been two recent trends. The first has been to view gender as a multifaceted or multidimensional construct, meaning that the two-dimensional view of masculinity and femininity is not sufficient to capture gender roles. The development of the unmitigated agency and unmitigated communion scales was a first step in this direction. The second research direction has been to emphasize the social context in which gender occurs. The research on gender diagnosticity addresses this issue. Emphasis on the social context led to research on gender-role constraints, the difficulties people face due to the limits a society places on gender-role-appropriate behavior. I examine each of these research directions in the following sections.

Gender Role as Multifaceted.   In 1985, Spence and Sawin called for the renaming of the PAQ masculinity and femininity scales. They stated that these scales reflect only one aspect of masculinity and femininity—instrumentality or agency and expressiveness or communion—and that the names of the scales should reflect these aspects. They argued that masculinity and femininity are multidimensional constructs that cannot be captured by a single trait instrument.

What else is involved in masculinity and femininity besides the traits that appear on the BSRI and the PAQ? Researchers began to realize that lay conceptions of masculinity and femininity included more diverse content, such as physical characteristics and role behaviors, in addition to personality traits. In 1994, I adopted a different approach to identify the content of masculinity and femininity (Helgeson, 1994b). I asked college students and their parents to describe one of four targets: a masculine man, a masculine woman, a feminine man, or a feminine woman (Helgeson, 1994b). Slightly less than half of the sample was Caucasian; thus, the sample was diverse in terms of age as well as ethnicity. The features of masculinity and femininity fell into one of three categories: personality traits, interests, or physical appearance. The average person identified five personality traits, two interests, and three physical appearance

features for each target. In addition, many of the identified personality traits were reflected on conventional M/F inventories, suggesting that lay conceptions of M/F fit the scientific literature. Whether the target's sex fit society's prescribed gender role influenced people's beliefs. For example, features unique to the masculine male were socially desirable (e.g., well dressed), but features unique to the masculine female were socially undesirable (e.g., uncaring, ugly, hostile). Among the distinct features of the feminine male, some were positive (e.g., talkative, emotional, creative) and some were negative (e.g., insecure, weak).

One limitation of most of this research is that conceptions of masculinity and femininity are limited to the people who have been studied: typically, White, middle-class American men and women. It would be interesting to know more about conceptions of masculinity and femininity across people of different races, classes, religions, and more diverse age groups, such as children and the elderly. Try Do Gender 2.2 to see if you can broaden your understanding of people's views of masculinity and femininity.

The Social Context Surrounding Gender.   An emphasis during this period, and today, is on how the social context influences the nature of gender. Social psychologists, in particular Kay Deaux and Brenda Major (1987), examined gender as a social category by emphasizing the situational forces that influence whether sex differences in behavior are observed. Their model of sex differences is discussed in more detail in Chapter 5. Another approach has been the movement by the **social constructionists**, who argue that gender does not reside inside a person but resides in our interactions with people—an approach that was described in Chapter 1. Social constructionists emphasize

DO GENDER 2.2
Conceptions of Masculinity
and Femininity

Construct your own categories of masculinity and femininity by asking 20 people, 10 women and 10 men, to describe a masculine person and a feminine person and consider the following questions in their descriptions.

1. What does a masculine (feminine) man (woman) look like?

2. What personality traits does a masculine (feminine) man (woman) possess?

3. How does a masculine (feminine) man (woman) behave?

4. What is a masculine (feminine) man (woman) interested in?

5. What does a masculine (feminine) man (woman) think about?

List all the features mentioned, and construct a frequency distribution for each feature. Identify the most frequently named features and indicate what percentage of your respondents named each feature.

To make your study more interesting, focus on a specific group of people you think are underrepresented in this research. You might choose children, the elderly, people of a minority race such as Asian Americans, Hispanic Americans, or African Americans, or people of a unique occupation. Then compare the responses you receive to those described in the text. Use only one target sex, female or male, so you can compare the responses you receive to those in this text.

perceivers, create gender by our expectations, by our behavior, and by what we decide to include in this category. As you will see, there is support for the social constructionist viewpoint. The studies reviewed in Chapter 4 that compare men and women on a number of domains lead to the conclusion that the situation, the context, has a large influence on the size of any differences that appear between women and men.

Gender-Role Strain.   By viewing gender as a social category, researchers paid greater attention to the influence of society on the nature of gender roles. One outgrowth of this recognition was research on **gender-role strain,** a phenomenon that occurs when gender-role expectations have negative consequences for the individual. Gender-role strain is likely to occur when gender-role expectations conflict with naturally occurring tendencies or personal desires. An uncoordinated male or an athletic female may experience gender-role strain in physical education classes. A male who wants to pursue dance or a woman who does not want to have children also may suffer some gender-role strain.

Joseph Pleck (1995) describes two theories of gender-role strain. **Self-role discrepancy theory** suggests that strain arises when you fail to live up to the gender role that society has constructed. This describes the man who is not athletic, the man who is unemployed, the woman who is not attractive, and the woman who does not have children. **Socialized dysfunctional characteristic theory** states that strain arises because the gender roles that society instills contain inherently dysfunctional personality characteristics. For example, the male gender role includes the inhibition of emotional expression, which is not healthy; similarly, the female gender role includes dependency, which also may

the diversity of human experience and view gender as the effect of an interaction rather than the cause of the interaction. We, the not be adaptive. Examine sources of gender-role strain at your college in Do Gender 2.3. The first four questions assess self-role discrepancies, and the last four questions assess socialized dysfunctional characteristics. See Sidebar 2.1 for another view of male gender-role strain in the form of hegemonic masculinity.

The concept of gender-role strain has largely been applied to men. The ideas were inspired by popular books on men that appeared in the 1970s and the 1980s, such as Goldberg's (1976) *The Hazards of Being Male*, Nichols's (1975) *Men's Liberation: A New Definition of Masculinity*, and Naifeh and Smith's (1984) *Why Can't Men Open Up?*, and in the late 1990s by Pollack's (1998) *Real boys: Rescuing Our Sons from the Myths of Boyhood*. These books, based largely on anecdotal evidence collected by men interviewing men or men observing boys, outline how some of the features of the male gender role limit men's relationships and are potentially harmful to men's health. In his examination of young boys, Pollack (1998, 2006) suggests that gender roles are much more rigid for boys than girls in our society. He describes a *male code* by which boys are not to express any form of vulnerability for fear it will be perceived as feminine, and femininity is equated with being gay, which is strongly derogated by boys. More recently, gender-role strain was explored in an interview study about friendship with 15- to 16-year-old (largely Caucasian) boys (Oransky & Maracek, 2009). The major theme that emerged from these interviews is that boys avoid self-disclosure and displays of emotion or physical pain, for fear of being viewed as gay, of lacking masculinity, and of being taunted by peers. Even when friends share emotions or disclose feelings, boys feel that the best thing they can do as a friend is to

DO GENDER 2.3
Gender-Role Strain

Interview 10 women and 10 men at your college. Identify common sources of gender-role strain.

1. Think about how men (women) are expected to behave. How does your behavior differ from how men (women) are expected to behave?

2. Think about how men (women) are expected to look. How does your appearance differ from how men (women) are expected to look?

3. Think about the personality characteristics that men (women) are expected to have. How does your personality differ from the personality men (women) are expected to have?

4. Think about the things that are supposed to interest men (women). How do your interests differ from the interests that men (women) are expected to have?

5. Think about the ways in which your behavior matches the behavior that society expects of men (women). Do you feel any of these behaviors are harmful?

6. Think about the ways in which your physical appearance matches the way society expects men (women) to look. Do you feel any of these expectations are harmful?

7. Think about the ways in which your personality matches the personality society expects men (women) to have. Do you feel any of these personality traits are harmful?

8. Think about the interests you have that correspond to the interests society expects men (women) to have. Do you feel it is harmful to have any of these interests?

SIDEBAR 2.1: *Multiple Masculinities*

Robert Connell argues that there are multiple versions of masculinity—a masculinity for men of color, a masculinity for gay men, and a masculinity for working-class men. The dominant form of masculinity, however, is aggressive, not emotional, heterosexual, and *not* feminine. This is referred to as hegemonic masculinity (Connell & Messerschmidt, 2005; Peralta, 2007). The main goal of hegemonic masculinity is to legitimize male dominance or patriarchy. Hegemonic masculinity may not be the most common masculinity, but it is still depicted as the ideal masculinity in our culture. It involves physical and intellectual strength and supremacy and denigrates any masculinity that does not conform to these standards. Evidence of hegemonic masculinity can be found among white-collar crime involving men, the media's representation of men in sports, the military, male risk-taking behavior, excessive alcohol use, and the gender-based hierarchy of most organizations. In each of these cases, hegemonic masculinity appears to be advantageous to men but is linked to mental and physical health hazards.

ignore or avoid the disclosure to help the friend keep his masculinity in tact. Making fun of friends was another strategy boys used not only to demonstrate their own masculinity but to help other boys learn to assert their masculinity by standing up for themselves.

A variety of instruments measure sources of male gender-role strain, one of which is the Male Role Norms Inventory (Levant & Fischer, 1998). It measures strain from seven male role norms: avoidance of appearing feminine, homophobia, self-reliance, aggression, seeking achievement and status, restrictive emotionality, and interest in sex. Part of the social constructionist view of gender is that different social forces affect different groups of men— not only men in different cultures, but also men of different age groups and men of different racial backgrounds. Thus the nature of gender-role strain will differ. African American men score higher on this inventory than White men, with Latino men falling between the two groups (Levant & Richmond, 2007). Men from other cultures such as China, Japan, Pakistan, and Russia score higher than American men. Scores on this gender-role strain measure are

associated with less relationship satisfaction, less involvement with children, more sexual aggression, more negative attitudes to racial diversity, and less positive attitudes toward using a condom (Levant & Richmond, 2007).

One ethnic group that faces some unique gender-role strains in the United States is African American men. African American men face a dilemma because the male gender role is associated with high power and high status in the United States, but the African American race is associated with a lack of power and low status in the United States. American culture does not provide African American men with legitimate pathways to validate their masculinity. The central features of the masculine gender role are achievement and success, but racism and poverty make it difficult for African American men to be economically successful. African American men are more likely to be unemployed and are less educated than Caucasian men. Compared to White males, African American males are more likely to get in trouble for the same misbehavior at school, more likely to have overall negative experiences in school, less likely to graduate from high school, less likely to achieve every level of education, and less likely to be hired with the same criminal record (Royster, 2007). Thus gender-role strain arises among African American men in part due to self-role discrepancy theory, the idea that African American men are not given the opportunity to achieve the male gender-role ideal as articulated by American culture.

One avenue that African American men are encouraged to pursue to validate masculinity is athletics. A focus on athletics can be healthy, but African American men might neglect their education to spent time on athletics. The reality is that few people will be able to make a living as successful athletes. However, participating in sports can validate masculinity in other ways. Basketball, in particular, is a strong component of African American culture—especially for males (Atencio & Wright, 2008). African American males see basketball not as a means to become famous but as a means to connect with other males, to do well in school, and to avoid gangs.

Female Gender-Role Strain. Gender-role strain rarely has been studied in women. In 1992, Gillespie and Eisler identified five areas of strain for women: (1) fear of unemotional relationships (e.g., feeling pressured to engage in sexual activity); (2) fear of physical unattractiveness (e.g., being perceived by others as overweight); (3) fear of victimization (e.g., having your car break down on the road); (4) fear of behaving assertively (e.g., bargaining with a salesperson when buying a car); and (5) fear of not being nurturant (e.g., a very close friend stops speaking to you). This female gender-role strain scale was associated with depression and was independent from the PAQ femininity scale.

One instance in which gender-role strain may be prevalent among women is when they find themselves in traditionally male settings, such as medical school or law school. McIntosh and colleagues (1994) found that women experienced greater strains than men during law school. Over the course of the first year of law school, women's health declined and levels of depression increased relative to those of men. The investigators identified two major sources of strain among women: (1) the women felt they were treated differently from men, and (2) the women were affected by a lack of free time and a lack of time with one's partner or spouse. The latter source of strain may reflect a conflict that women face between pursuing achievement and tending to relationships. Partners may be less supportive of women than men putting their personal lives on hold to pursue a career.

The main points of each historical period are summarized in Table 2.7.

TAKE HOME POINTS

- Two shifts occurred in the most recent thinking about gender roles: (1) the realization that gender roles are multifaceted constructs that cannot be fully captured by single trait measures of agency and communion and (2) the idea that gender roles are influenced by the social context, time, place, and culture.

- Masculinity and femininity are now conceptualized as broad categories that include personality traits, physical appearance, occupational interests, and role behaviors.

- One outgrowth of the emphasis on the social context in studying gender has been to consider the strains people face from the gender roles society imposes. Strains arise when our behavior is discrepant from the role that society has set forth, and when the behaviors required of the role are not compatible with mental and physical health.

TABLE 2.7 Key Features of Each Historical Period

	1894–1936	1936–1954	1954–1982	1982 to date
Themes	Show men are more intelligent than women	Introduction of gender-role concept	Instrumental-expressive distinction	Masculine personality = agency Feminine personality = communion
		Gender-role = sex differences	Sex-typing	Gender roles are multifaceted
		Masculine/ feminine bipolar		Consider social context
		Homosexuality = feminine		Role strain
Key figures	Terman & Miles	Terman & Miles Franck & Rosen	Maccoby, Parson & Bales, Bem, Spence	Spence, Deaux & Major, Pleck
Measures		456-Item Attitude Interest Analysis Survey	Bem Sex Role Inventory	Male Role Norms Inventory
		Projective tests	Personal Attributes Questionnaire (and Extended Version)	
Conclusions	No sex difference in intelligence	Masculine men and feminine women are healthy	Androgynous healthy	Norms associated with gender roles are associated with strain

- Gender-role strain among men includes homophobia, competitiveness, emotional inhibition, aggression, and a reluctance to seek help.

- Gender-role strain among women, less studied, includes fear of physical unattractiveness, fear of victimization, difficulties with assertion, and uncertainty about how to behave in traditionally masculine settings.

- The nature of gender-role strain differs across race, ethnicity, and culture.

SUMMARY

In the first half of the chapter, the scientific method that is used to study gender was reviewed. The scientific method rests on empiricism; it includes the collection of data that are then used to make statements, develop theories, and generate hypotheses. The correlational method, the experimental method, and field experiments were presented. The advantage of the experimental method is internal validity, and the advantage of the correlational method is external validity. The importance of random selection and random assignment was explained. I also described the differences between cross-sectional and longitudinal studies; longitudinal designs may provide stronger tests of causality and are able to distinguish cohort effects from age effects.

We face a number of difficulties in the scientific study of gender. The experimenter can be a source of bias by influencing the question asked, the way a study is designed (including the participants chosen and the way variables are manipulated and measured), the way the data are collected, how the data are interpreted, and whether the data are reported. Participants also can influence the outcome of a study, in particular by demand characteristics and concerns with self-presentation. Other difficulties that researchers encounter when studying gender include the problem of generalizing from the laboratory to the real world, isolating the effects of participant's sex from variables that are confounded with sex such as status and gender role, and considering how the context influences behavior.

In the second half of the chapter, I reviewed the history of the psychology of gender. The field began by addressing the question of whether women were intellectually inferior to men. When there was insufficient evidence to support this claim, the field shifted to focus on the mental or psychological differences between men and women, that is, masculinity and femininity. The first

comprehensive measure of masculinity and femininity was the AIAS, but numerous other inventories soon followed. A major shift in the conceptualization and measurement of masculinity and femininity occurred in 1974 with the development of the BSRI and the PAQ. These two instruments challenged the bipolar assumption that masculinity and femininity are opposites and the view that the healthiest people are masculine men and feminine women. Instead, the model of mental health was embodied in the androgynous person, someone who incorporates both feminine and masculine traits.

The most recent approaches to the conceptualization of femininity and masculinity have emphasized their multiple components. We now realize that femininity and masculinity consist of behaviors, roles, and physical characteristics as well as personality traits. Researchers have also emphasized how the social context influences the display of sex differences and the meaning of gender. An area of research that emphasizes the role society plays in shaping gender-role norms is gender-role strain. Gender-role strain is experienced when the norms for our gender role conflict with our naturally occurring tendencies or with what would be psychologically adaptive. This area of research has largely been applied to men.

DISCUSSION QUESTIONS

1. Describe a scientific theory with which you are familiar. It does not have to be from psychology; it could be from biology or physics, for example. Go through the stages of the research process shown in Figure 2.1.
2. What is the difference between random assignment and random

   sampling? How is each related to internal and external validity?
3. Identify behaviors you think might be interpreted differently when displayed by a female versus a male. For each one, explain why.
4. If you have ever been in an experiment, discuss some of the ways that just knowing you were

in an experiment influenced your behavior.

5. Describe the greatest difficulty you believe researchers face when studying gender. What is the best precaution to take against this difficulty?

6. What are some of the weaknesses and strengths of the instruments

that have been used to measure masculinity and femininity?

7. Discuss the concepts of agency, communion, unmitigated agency, and unmitigated communion. How would you expect these constructs to be related to one another?

8. What are some areas of gender-role strain for men and women today?

SUGGESTED READING

Ashmore, R. D. (1990). Sex, gender, and the individual. In L. A. Pervin (Ed.), *Handbook of personality: Theory and research* (pp. 486–526). New York: Guilford Press.

Bakan, D. (1966). *The duality of human existence*. Chicago, IL: Rand McNally.

Pollack, W. S. (1998). *Real boys: Rescuing our sons from the myths of boyhood*. New York: Random House.

Spence, J. T., & Sawin, L. L. (1985). Images of masculinity and femininity: A reconceptualization. In V. E. O'Leary, R. K. Unger, and B. S. Wallston (Eds.), *Women, gender, and social psychology* (pp. 35–66). Hillsdale, NJ: Lawrence Erlbaum.

KEY TERMS

Androgyny—Displaying both masculine and feminine traits.

Cross-sex-typed—Exhibiting gender-role characteristics that correspond with the other sex.

Gender-role strain—Tension that develops when the expectations that accompany one's gender role have negative consequences for the individual.

Self-fulfilling prophecy—When people's beliefs influence their actions toward a target in a way such that the target comes to confirm their beliefs.

Self-role discrepancy theory—The strain that arises when we fail to live up to the gender role society has constructed.

Sex-typed—Exhibiting the gender-role characteristics that correspond with our sex.

Social constructionists—People who believe that masculinity and femininity are categories constructed by society and that each society may have a different definition of masculinity and femininity.

Socialized dysfunctional characteristics theory—Inherently dysfunctional personality characteristics that are fundamental to the gender roles instilled by society.

Unmitigated agency—Personality orientation characterized by a focus on the self to the exclusion of others.

Unmitigated communion—Personality orientation characterized by a focus on others to the exclusion of the self.

CHAPTER 3

Gender-Role Attitudes

In 1977, a group of college men were induced to talk on the phone to either an attractive female or an unattractive female. Not surprisingly, men liked the attractive female more than the unattractive female. However, there's a twist—all of the men were talking to the same female—only half were shown a picture of an attractive person and half were shown a picture of an unattractive person. Clearly, the idea that "attractive people are nicer and more likeable" was operating here. The fact that these men's beliefs were influenced by the picture is not surprising. What may be more surprising is the fact that the woman behaved differently toward the men who thought she was attractive versus unattractive. When a set of judges who were blind to condition (i.e., did not know which picture the men saw) listened to the audiotaped phone calls, they rated the woman as warmer and friendlier when she was talking to a male who *thought* she was attractive than unattractive (Snyder, Tanke, & Berscheid, 1977).

The woman's behavior is an example of the self-fulfilling prophecy. That is, she came to fulfill the expectations that the men had—that attractive women are nicer than unattractive women. This study illustrates the dangers of our expectancies. It is not only that our expectations influence our own behavior, but they also influence the behavior of others so that they confirm our expectancy. Now, imagine what could happen in the case of gender. We have strong expectancies about the differences between men and women. There is clearly an opportunity for those expectations to affect our behavior toward men and women so that they produce the stereotypes we hold.

In Chapter 2, I provided a brief history of how gender roles have been conceptualized and measured. This research was devoted to identifying the features of gender roles. In this chapter, I investigate people's attitudes toward gender roles. Do you have favorable attitudes toward someone with traditional gender roles? How do you behave when confronted with people who do not conform to gender-role expectations?

First, I examine research on attitudes toward women's and men's roles, that is, whether you believe women and men should have distinct and separate roles or whether you believe they should have similar and equal roles. Then I review the literature on the three components of attitudes toward the category gender: affect (feelings), cognition (beliefs), and behavior. People's feelings toward gender are described by the term *sexism*; people's beliefs about gender are referred to as *sex-role* or *gender-role stereotypes*; and people's behavior toward others based on gender is known as *sex discrimination*.

ATTITUDES TOWARD MEN'S AND WOMEN'S ROLES

Do you find it acceptable for women to work outside the home? To be construction workers (see Figure 3.1)? To serve in the military? Is it acceptable for men to take the same amount of time off from work as women when a child is born? To stay home and take care of children? If you find all these ideas

FIGURE 3.1   A woman is using a compound miter saw to cut wood for the interior of a house.

acceptable, then you have an egalitarian view of gender roles. Most people find they agree with some of these ideas, but not all, or they only agree in part with each of the ideas. For example, most people find it acceptable for women to work outside the home—which is a good thing, because most women do. Fewer people find it acceptable for a woman to work outside the home when she has a 3-month-old child and there is no financial need for her to work.

Attitudes toward men's and women's roles have been referred to as **gender ideologies** (Hochschild, 1989). A **traditional gender ideology** maintains that men's sphere is work and women's sphere is the home. The implicit assumption is that men have greater power than women. An **egalitarian gender ideology** maintains that power is distributed equally between women and men, and women and men identify equally with the same spheres. There could be an equal emphasis on home, on work, or on some combination of the two. Most people's attitudes toward men's and women's roles lie somewhere between traditional and egalitarian. Thus, Hochschild identified a third gender ideology, **transitional**. A typical transitional attitude toward gender roles is that it is acceptable for women to devote energy to both work and family domains, but women should hold proportionally more responsibility for the home, and men should focus proportionally more of their energy on work.

The most widely used instrument to measure attitudes toward gender roles is the Attitudes Toward Women Scale (ATWS; Spence & Helmreich, 1972). The ATWS was developed during the women's movement of the 1960s and assessed beliefs about the behavior of women and men in domains that have traditionally been divided between them, such as raising children, education, and paid employment. Although the scale's title specifies attitudes toward women, many of the items really measure attitudes toward both women's and men's roles. Here are some sample items from the 15-item scale (Spence & Helmreich, 1972):

■ Swearing and obscenity are more repulsive in the speech of a woman than a man.

■ Women should worry less about their rights and more about becoming good wives and mothers.

■ It is ridiculous for a woman to run a locomotive and for a man to darn socks.

■ Sons in a family should be given more encouragement to go to college than daughters.

■ There are many jobs in which men should be given preference over women in being hired or promoted.

You probably noticed that these items are quite outdated. Today, it is more than common for daughters to go to college and "run a locomotive." Not surprisingly, attitudes toward men's and women's roles using the ATWS have become more liberal over time (Twenge, 1997). Although women's attitudes have always been more egalitarian than men's across a variety of cultures, the size of the sex difference seems to be getting smaller over time. Today, most people appear to have egalitarian attitudes using the ATWS.

However, the ATWS is not a good measure of contemporary gender-role attitudes. First, there are demand characteristics in responding to this scale. Who wouldn't agree at least on a self-report instrument that women and men should have similar

job opportunities? Second, the ATWS fails to capture some of the contemporary concerns about men's and women's roles, such as whether women should serve in the military, whether women and men should participate equally in child care, whether women have the right to an abortion, and whether women should take their husband's last name upon marriage. See if you can come up with some other domains that reflect contemporary gender-role attitudes in Do Gender 3.1.

There are ethnic and cultural differences in attitudes toward men's and women's roles. Black women seem to have less traditional gender-role attitudes than Black men

DO GENDER 3.1
Creating a Contemporary Gender-Role Attitudes Scale

Decide on some ways in which women and men are not treated equally—at your institution, in your town, in your culture. Create a scale to assess people's beliefs about whether the treatment should be equal. Identify more subtle ways in which differential treatment exists and is often accepted (e.g., If there were a draft, women should be just as likely to men to serve in the military; Mothers are better than fathers at caring for a sick child.)

After you have created the scale, decide on some variables—both personality and situational—that you believe might be related to scores on your scale. What personality characteristics do you think might be associated with more liberal gender-role attitudes? What situational variables (perhaps features of the home environment in which the participant was raised) might contribute to more liberal gender-role attitudes?

or White women and men (Carter, Corra, & Carter, 2009). Whereas Black and White men have similar attitudes toward women's involvement in politics, Black men have a more favorable view than White men toward women working outside the home. The fact that Black women have been employed outside the home for a longer period of time than White women due to economic necessity may account for some of these differences.

Attitudes toward gender roles are more traditional in other cultures compared to the United States. For example, historically, women and men in China have held very traditional roles. The Confucian doctrine of the Chinese culture emphasizes the lower status of women compared to men; one doctrine is "The virtue of a woman lies in three obediences: obedience to the father, husband, and son" (cited in Chia, Allred, & Jerzak, 1997, p. 138). In a study comparing students from Taipei, Taiwan, to students in North Carolina, it was found that Chinese students had more conservative attitudes toward marital roles in terms of who should make the decisions within the family (Chia et al., 1994). In addition, Chinese male students thought it more inappropriate for men to express emotion than did American students. Even when Asian women work outside the home, this is not necessarily evidence of what Western cultures would perceive as nontraditional attitudes toward gender. A study of Asian immigrant women showed that those who worked outside the home did not perceive employment as a distinct role but as an extension of their domestic role, which is to place the family's welfare above that of the individual (Suh, 2007). Even though education is greatly valued in Asian cultures, the value for women and men is not the same. The value of education for women is to make them suitable partners and mothers (Hall, 2009).

TAKE HOME POINTS

- One's attitudes toward gender can be classified as traditional, egalitarian, or transitional.

- Although gender-role attitudes have become less traditional over time, most people fit into the transitional category, not fully embracing equality for women and men across all domains.

- To understand cultural differences in gender-role attitudes, one needs to understand what the expectations for men and women are in the particular culture.

- Compared to Caucasians, African Americans have less traditional attitudes about women working outside the home.

AFFECTIVE COMPONENT: SEXISM

Sexism is one's attitude or feeling toward people based on their sex alone. Disliking a doctor because she is female or a nurse because he is male are examples of sexism. Instruments that measure sexism often consist of people's beliefs about men and women but contain an affective component to these beliefs. That is, the beliefs reflect either a high or low regard for someone because of his or her sex.

Traditional Versus Modern Sexism

You might expect that sexism has declined over the past several decades, and perhaps it has. But today, there is a more subtle version of sexism. Swim and colleagues (1995) distinguished between traditional and modern sexism. Traditional sexism includes endorsement of traditional roles for women and men, differential treatment of women and men, and the belief that women are less competent than men. Traditional sexism reflects an open disregard for the value of women. Few people today would publicly express such feelings. Modern sexism, by contrast, includes the denial of any existing discrimination toward women, an antagonism to women's demands, and a resentment of any preferential treatment for women. In short, modern sexism implies that one is not sympathetic to women's issues and indirectly endorses the unequal treatment of men and women. The two sexism scales are positively correlated, meaning that people who score high on one scale are likely to score high on the other scale.

Modern sexism is associated with underestimating women's difficulties in obtaining jobs traditionally held by men. Swim and colleagues (1995) found that modern sexism was correlated with overestimating the percentage of women who hold male-dominated jobs. Modern sexism is also associated with the use of sexist language and with the inability (or unwillingness) to detect sexist language when asked to do so (Swim, Mallett, & Stangor, 2004). As shown in Figure 3.2, when people were divided into three groups on the modern sexism scale, those who scored highest used the most sexist language and the least nonsexist language when writing a response to a moral dilemma.

Hostile Versus Benevolent Sexism

You are probably thinking of sexism as a *negative* feeling toward women. But sexism, like any other affective attitude, can consist of negative or positive feelings. This is reflected in the distinction that Glick and Fiske (1996) made between hostile sexism and benevolent sexism in their Ambivalent Sexism Inventory. **Hostile sexism** is just as it sounds: feelings of hostility toward women. It is a negative attitude toward women, in particular those who challenge the traditional female role. **Benevolent sexism**, by contrast, reflects positive feelings toward

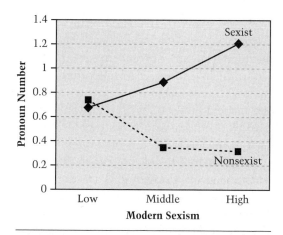

FIGURE 3.2   Students who scored in the upper third of the modern sexism scale used the most pronouns reflecting sexist language and the fewest pronouns reflecting nonsexist language.
Source: Adapted from Swim, Mallett, and Stangor (2004).

women, including a prosocial orientation toward women (e.g., the desire to help women). Both hostile sexism and benevolent sexism are rooted in patriarchy (i.e., justifying the superiority of the dominant group), gender differentiation (i.e., exaggerating the differences between men and women), and sexual reproduction, as indicated by the items shown in Table 3.1 (Glick & Fiske, 2001).

Although there are some commonalities that underlie hostile and benevolent sexism, there also are some differences (Sibley, Wilson, & Duckitt, 2007). Hostile sexism, but not benevolent sexism, is associated with a social dominance orientation—maintaining a position of dominance and superiority over others. Hostile sexism is also associated with the endorsement of rape myths (e.g., women can resist rape if they want to; Chapleau, Oswald, & Russell, 2007). Thus, men who score high on hostile sexism view women as challenging their superiority, which is why they endorse the negative attitudes toward women shown in Table 3.1. By contrast, benevolent sexism is associated with right-wing authoritarianism—preserving social cohesion and maintaining social order. Thus, men who score high on benevolent sexism are more concerned with maintaining the traditional male and female roles, which include men as protectors of women.

Compared to hostile sexism, the items on the benevolent sexism scale are more palatable to people. People who endorse benevolent sexism are viewed more favorably than those who endorse hostile sexism and are less likely to be viewed as sexist (Barreto & Ellemers, 2005). However, the negative implications of benevolent sexism are clear. Benevolent sexism is a harmful attitude because it is rooted in the belief that women are less competent than men and are in need of men's help.

Benevolent sexism provides a powerful justification for the high-status group to exploit the low-status group. According to Jackman (1994), "the agenda for dominant groups is to create an ideological cocoon whereby they can define their discriminatory actions as benevolent" (p. 14). That is, dominant groups need to develop an ideology that justifies their superior position and is supported by the subordinant group. Benevolent sexism fills this prescription. Benevolent sexism justifies the behavior of the high-status group by casting it in positive terms that the low-status group can endorse: Women need men to take care of them. According to Jackman (1994), benevolence is more effective than hostility in exploiting someone. In addition, benevolent sexism among women seems to lead to greater endorsement of hostile sexism over

TABLE 3.1   Sample Items from Ambivalent Sexism Inventory

Hostile Sexism

Patriarchy
      Women seek to gain power by getting control over men.
      Many women are actually seeking special favors, such as hiring policies that favor them over men, under the guise of asking for "equality."
Gender Differentiation
      Women are too easily offended.
Sexual Reproduction
      Many women get a kick out of teasing men by seeming sexually available and then refusing male advances.

Benevolent Sexism

Patriarchy
      In a disaster, women ought to be rescued before men.
      Women should be cherished and protected by men.
Gender Differentiation
      Many women have a quality of purity that few men possess.
      Women, as compared to men, tend to have a more refined sense of culture and good taste.
Sexual Reproduction
      Every man ought to have a woman he adores.
      No matter how accomplished he is, a man is not truly complete as a person unless he has the love of a woman.

Source: Glick and Fiske (1996, 2001).

time, especially among those who endorse right-wing authoritarianism (Sibley, Overall, & Duckitt, 2007).

Not surprisingly, men score higher than women on hostile sexism around the world (Glick et al., 2000). The sex difference in benevolent sexism is less reliable. In four countries, women scored higher than men on benevolent sexism—Cuba, Nigeria, South Africa, and Botswana. These four countries were also the most sexist. A study that compared college students in China and the United States showed that Chinese women scored higher than United States women and higher than Chinese men on benevolent sexism (Chen, Fiske, & Lee, 2009). Why would women in these countries support benevolent sexism? In general, women support benevolent sexism because (1) it does not seem like prejudice because of the "appearance" of positive attributes and (2) women receive rewards from benevolent sexism (i.e., male protection). These rewards may be especially important in sexist countries, where women are most likely to be victims of violence. As stated by Glick and Fiske (2001), "The irony is that women are forced to seek protection from members of the very group that threatens them, and the greater the threat, the stronger the incentive to accept benevolent sexism's protective ideology" (p. 115).

Benevolent sexism is viewed most favorably under circumstances when it appears that women need protection. Vulnerability to crime is one such situation. Women are more afraid than men are of becoming a victim of crime, and these fears are associated with benevolent sexism among women (Phelan, Sanchez, & Broccoli, 2010). When undergraduate women were randomly assigned to a condition in which crime on campus was made salient or not, the crime salience group was more likely to endorse benevolent

sexism. There are other circumstances in which women endorse benevolent sexism. A study of women college students showed that they were more likely to endorse benevolent sexism when told that men held negative rather than positive attitudes toward women (Fischer, 2006). Women are also more likely to endorse benevolent sexism when a protective rather than a hostile justification is provided for limiting women's opportunities. In a community sample of women living in Spain, women reacted more positively to a scenario in which a husband did all the driving on a trip when the reason was that driving a long way could be tiring (protective justification) than when the reason was that women don't drive as well as men (hostile justification)—but only when the women scored high on benevolent sexism (Moya et al., 2007).

A related construct is **benevolent discrimination**, or men providing more help to women than men (Glick & Fiske, 1999b). What is the harm in men holding a door open for a woman? Paying for dinner at a restaurant? Again, the implicit message is that women need help and protection. The behavior appears prosocial but really legitimizes women's inferior position. It is difficult to reject benevolent discrimination because (1) the behavior provides a direct benefit to the recipient, (2) the help provider will be insulted, (3) social norms dictate that one should accept help graciously, and (4) it is difficult to explain why help is being rejected. If you are male on a date with a female, try offering benevolent discrimination as a reason for splitting the bill. If you are female on a date with a male, try remarking that your date paying the bill is an act of discrimination. Neither situation will be comfortable. See Sidebar 3.1 for a discussion of benevolent sexism toward women in the criminal justice system.

Sidebar 3.1: *Benevolent Sexism and Female Criminals*

Are women and men treated equally within the criminal justice system? Some believe that women are treated more leniently than men partly because women are viewed as less of a threat to society than men (weaker) and partly because of a paternalistic need to help and care for women. However, when women commit crimes that violate the female stereotype, they could be treated more harshly. In a study of a local newspaper in Bloomington, Indiana, women who committed violent crimes were treated more harshly than men by the media, whereas women who committed nonviolent crimes were treated more leniently by the media (Grabe et al., 2006). In another study where registered voters posed as mock jurors, women received a lighter sentence than men for a heinous crime unless there was testimony from the victim's family—in which case, the female received a more severe sentence than the male (Forsterlee et al., 2004). Forsterlee and colleagues argue that the testimony made the incongruence between such extreme violence and the female gender role salient.

One example of an extreme violation of the female gender role is killing children. In 1966, Myra Hindley tortured and murdered five children. She was not declared mentally ill and was sentenced to life in prison. When a group of young adults, mostly college students, were presented with this information, those who scored high on benevolent sexism judged Myra more harshly than those who scored lower on the scale (Viki, Massey, & Masser, 2005). Those who scored higher on benevolent sexism also were more likely to say that Myra violated the female gender role, and this gender-role violation explained the link between benevolent sexism and the negative evaluation of Myra. Neither sex nor hostile sexism was related to evaluations of Myra. Thus in this case, benevolent sexism was related to a negative judgment rather than a positive judgment of a woman.

Although the benevolent and hostile sexism scales reflect two very different affective states in regard to women, the two are positively correlated, meaning that people who endorse items on one scale also endorse items on the other. Perceiving women in both negative and positive terms seems contradictory. The ambivalence in attitudes toward women stems from the paradox that women hold a lower status than men, but that the female stereotype is more positive than the male stereotype. This positive correlation underscores the idea that both hostile sexism and benevolent sexism are based on a belief that women are inferior to men. The positive correlation of the benevolent and hostile sexism scales has been shown to exist in 19 countries (Glick et al., 2000). Among those countries, nations that scored higher in hostile and benevolent sexism also scored higher in gender inequality, as measured by the presence of women in politics, the number of women in the workforce, and female literacy rates.

Sexism Toward Men

Although sexism can be exhibited toward both women and men, it is typically studied and measured as feelings toward women. Jokes about female drivers and "dumb blondes" are regularly perceived as examples of sexism. But aren't jokes about men's incompetence at being fathers or men not asking for directions also examples of sexism? I came across the following cartoon in the *New Yorker* (June 5, 2000; see Figure 3.3). Now, imagine that the sex of the characters was reversed: The joke wouldn't be funny, and the cartoon wouldn't be published.

Feelings toward the male sex have been explored in the Ambivalence Toward Men Inventory, which was developed to distinguish feelings of hostility and benevolence toward men (Glick & Fiske, 1999a). This ambivalence also is rooted in patriarchy, gender differentiation, and sexual reproduction. Sample items are shown in Table 3.2. The hostility toward men scale consists of negative attitudes surrounding the resentment of patriarchy, a perception of negative attributes in men, and beliefs that men are sexually aggressive. The benevolence scale reflects positive views of men, including the

TABLE 3.2   SAMPLE ITEMS FROM AMBIVALENCE TOWARD MEN INVENTORY

Hostile Sexism
Patriarchy
Men will always fight for greater control in society.
Gender Differentiation
Most men are really like children.
Sexual Reproduction
Men have no morals in what they will do to get sex.
Benevolent Sexism
Patriarchy
Even if both work, the woman should take care of the man at home.
Gender Differentiation
Men are less likely to fall apart in emergencies.
Sexual Reproduction
Every woman ought to have a man she adores.

Source: Glick and Fiske (1999a).

"There's an article in here that explains why you're such an idiot."

FIGURE 3.3   People do not always recognize this kind of cartoon as sexism, but if the sexes were reversed, it would easily be labeled as sexism.
Source: © The New Yorker collection, 2000, William Haefeli from cartoonbank.com.

benefits of patriarchy, the positive attributes of men, and women's fulfillment through connections with men.

The Ambivalence Toward Men Inventory was examined in a study of 16 nations (Glick et al., 2004). Like the sexism toward women scales, the benevolent and hostile scales are positively correlated. In addition, hostile and benevolent sexism toward men were higher among nations with less gender equality, as assessed by women's education and the representation of women in government and high-status occupations. In 15 of the 16 nations, women scored higher than men on hostile sexism toward men. This sex difference was larger in nations where men endorsed more hostile sexism toward women. Thus it appears that women are more hostile toward men in situations where men are hostile toward women.

However, men scored higher than women on benevolent sexism toward men in 11 of the 16 nations. Why would men endorse benevolent sexism toward men? Benevolent sexism toward men portrays a positive view of men while maintaining their higher status over women. This is unlike women's endorsement of benevolent sexism toward women, which is mixed in its effects—on the one hand, it reflects a positive view of women, but on the other hand, it promotes the idea that women have lower status than men.

Attitudes Toward Lesbians, Gay, Bisexual, and Transgendered Persons

Homophobia is not an attitude toward someone based on sex (i.e., sexism); it is an attitude toward someone based on sexual orientation. **Homophobia** is a fear of homosexuals or a fear of associating with homosexuals. In terms of demographic variables, males and non-Whites score higher on homophobia than females and Whites (Osborne & Wagner, 2007). Men are prejudiced against homosexuals because homosexuality is a threat to the norm of heterosexual relationships in which men are dominant over women (Hamilton, 2007). Homophobia is most prominent among men during the teen years.

Gender-related traits and gender-role attitudes are associated with attitudes toward homosexuality. People who score high on instrumental traits have more favorable attitudes toward homosexuality, whereas people who scored high on hypermasculinity (extreme masculinity) have more negative attitudes toward homosexuality (Whitley, 2001). People who have traditional gender-role attitudes and score high on modern sexism and benevolent sexism possess the most negative attitudes toward homosexuality. Again, this is not surprising because homosexual behavior is a threat to traditional beliefs about women's and men's roles. Men also are less tolerant of homosexuality compared to women because the male gender role is more narrowly defined than the female gender role. Violation of the male gender role has more negative consequences because it has a higher status in our society, so there is more to lose by violating it (Kite & Whitley, 2003).

Social dominance orientation is also linked to negative attitudes toward homosexuals (Whitley & Egisdottir, 2000). Social dominance orientation reflects the desire for the in-group to dominate and be superior to the out-group (e.g., It's okay if some groups have more of a chance in life than others). As shown in Figure 3.4, men are higher than women in social dominance orientation; social dominance orientation is related to having more traditional gender-role beliefs; and traditional gender-role

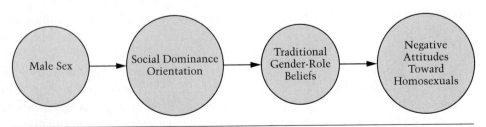

FIGURE 3.4 A pathway by which male sex leads to negative attitudes toward homosexuality.

beliefs are associated with negative attitudes toward homosexuals.

Participation in sports also has been connected to homophobia, but the connection differs for females and males. Male athletes might be expected to be the most homophobic because athletics is viewed as a way to validate masculinity and homosexuals are viewed as a threat to masculinity. For females, however, participation in athletics is sometimes stigmatized by its connection to lesbianism. One study examined the connection between sports participation and homophobia among high school students (Osborne & Wagner, 2007). For males, participation in core sports (i.e., the sports most strongly connected to masculinity like football, basketball, and soccer) was strongly related to homophobia but participation in sports in general was not. For females, sports participation was unrelated to homophobia.

Homophobic attitudes can manifest themselves in terms of behavior—specifically, what are known as *heterosexual hassles*—that is, jokes, insults, and antigay comments or behaviors by others. Heterosexual hassles are particular potent during middle school and high school (Tharinger, 2008). One reason LGBT (lesbians, gay, bisexual, and transgendered) high school students may receive poorer grades than heterosexuals is that they skip school to avoid heterosexual hassles and threats to safety (Stader & Graca, 2007). In 2009, a special issue of the *Journal of Youth and Adolescence* was devoted to studying the lives of LGBT youth (Horn, Kosciw, & Russell, 2009). The authors of the articles note the high prevalence of harassment and victimization in schools and the lack of a response on the part of schools to address this problem. One study of LGBT high school students showed that those students had more depressive symptoms and suicidal ideation than

their heterosexual peers and that perceptions of discrimination accounted for these differences (Almeida et al., 2009). In a study of seventh and eighth graders, LGBT youth had more depressive symptoms and greater drug usage than their heterosexual counterparts, *only* when they perceived the school as unsupportive and only when they were teased about being gay (Birkett, Espelage, & Koenig, 2009). National survey data of LGBT youth show that males face more harassment than females and younger youth face more harassment than older youth (Kosciw, Greytak, & Diaz, 2009). LGBTs who live in rural areas and in communities with lower levels of education achievement also face more hostility. International data has connected homophobic attitudes and behavior with suicide and alcohol abuse among LGBT youth (McDermott, Roen, & Scourfield, 2008).

LGBT adults, too, face victimization. In a one-week daily diary study of LGBT adults, heterosexual hassles were associated with anger and anxiety on a daily basis and with depressed mood and lowered self-esteem for those who most strongly identified with their sexual orientation (Swim, Johnston, & Pearson, 2009). More severe than heterosexual hassles are heterosexual hate crimes. Homosexuals and bisexuals comprise 17% of the victims of hate crime (U.S. Department of Justice, 2008).

Transphobia is defined as a revulsion and irrational fear of transgendered and transsexual persons, cross-dressers, and feminine men and masculine women. Although transphobia is positively correlated with homophobia (Nagoshi et al., 2008), it is a negative attitude toward a broader group of people based on gender concerns rather than only sexual orientation. A scale to measure transphobia is shown in Table 3.3. Men score higher than women on transphobia,

TABLE 3.3   TRANSPHOBIA SCALE

1. I don't like it when someone is flirting with me, and I can't tell if that person is a man or a woman.
2. I think there is something wrong with a person who says that he or she is neither a man nor a woman.
3. I would be upset if someone I'd known a long time revealed to me that he or she used to be another gender.
4. I avoid people on the street whose gender is unclear to me.
5. When I meet someone, it is important for me to be able to identify that person as a man or as a woman.
6. I believe that the male/female dichotomy is natural.
7. I am uncomfortable around people who don't conform to traditional gender roles (e.g., aggressive women or emotional men).
8. I believe that a person can never change his or her gender.

Source: Nagoshi et al. (2008).

and transphobia is associated with aggression proneness in men.

Negative attitudes toward transgender people are higher than negative attitudes toward gay men, lesbians, and bisexuals (Kosciw et al., 2009). Thus, not surprisingly, transgender people face high rates of physical assault, sexual assault, and harassment—and not only from strangers but from people they know (Stotzer, 2009). Male-to-female transgendered persons are much more likely to be victims of crime than female-to-male transgendered persons. The psychological and physical abuse received by transgendered persons is associated with depression and suicide, the relation being stronger during adolescence and young adulthood than later years (Nuttbrock et al., 2010). Conduct Do Gender 3.2 to examine transphobia and its correlates at your school.

DO GENDER 3.2
Transphobia among
College Students

Administer the Transphobia scale shown in Table 3.3 to a group of female and male college students. Do males score higher than females? Consider some of the correlates of transphobia and examine those relations. Some possibilities might be demographic variables such as parent education and income, or personality characteristics such as the gender-related traits you studied in Chapter 2, a measure of conservative/liberal ideology, or a measure of cognitive complexity.

TAKE HOME POINTS

- Traditional sexism is a blatant disregard for women, whereas modern sexism is a more subtle indicator of devaluing women, for example, by denying that women have any disadvantages in society compared to men.

- Hostile sexism reflects a negative feeling toward women, whereas benevolent sexism reflects a positive feeling toward women based on their sex.

- Benevolent sexism is less likely to be regarded as sexist because it focuses on positive beliefs about women and results in prosocial behavior (i.e., men helping women).

- Hostile and benevolent sexism are positively correlated, however, reflecting the fact that both are rooted in the belief that women are less competent than men.

- Women in countries that are more sexist are more likely to endorse benevolent sexism toward women.

- Sexism toward men is less well studied compared to sexism toward women and is more accepted in some sense. Women score higher than men on hostile sexism toward men, whereas men score higher than women on benevolent sexism toward men.

- Homophobia and transphobia reflect negative attitudes toward LGBT persons. These negative feelings are particularly potent for LGBT youth. When negative attitudes are translated into heterosexual hassles and possibly hate crimes, results include poor grades in school, missed school, psychological distress, alcohol and drug problems, and increased risk of suicide.

COGNITIVE COMPONENT: GENDER-ROLE STEREOTYPING

The following is a description of a famous person:

> This powerful figure is an Ivy-league trained lawyer, often referred to as the enforcer—because the person can get the job done. This person is principled, candid, and opinionated. This person was the mentor to the future United States president.

Who do you think this person is? Can you picture the person? Now read the next description of a famous person:

> This parent of two children put the spouse's career first, worked at a nonprofit organization training leaders, and is said to be very protective of family. This person has a personal trainer and a stylist.

Who do you think this person is? Can you picture the person? Does this description bring to mind a different image than the first one? Are the traits described in the second passage incompatible with those described in the first passage? You might be surprised

to know that both passages refer to the same person—the person depicted in Figure 3.5, the First Lady of the United States, Michelle Obama. Gender-role stereotypes probably led you to picture the first person as a man and the second person as a woman.

What Is a Gender-Role Stereotype?

A stereotype is a schema or a set of beliefs about a certain group of people. **Gender-role stereotypes** are the features we assign to women and men in our society, features not assigned due to biological sex but due to the social roles that men and women hold. Thus I refer to these stereotypes as gender-role stereotypes rather than sex stereotypes. One reason that it may not have occurred to you that the descriptions in the previous paragraph were of

FIGURE 3.5 First Lady of the United States, Michelle Obama.
Source: dreamstime.com

the same person is that the first description fits our male gender-role stereotype and the second fits our female gender-role stereotype.

Stereotypes have descriptive and prescriptive components (Fiske & Stevens, 1993). The descriptive component identifies the features of the stereotype. The trait features of the female and male stereotypes are likely to be those found on the PAQ (Personal Attributes Questionnaire) and BSRI (Bem Sex Role Inventory) femininity and masculinity inventories. The descriptive aspect of stereotypes is limiting, as we judge feminine women as less competent for leadership positions and masculine men as less capable of nurturing children.

The prescriptive component of a stereotype is how we think people *ought* to behave due to their sex. The prescriptive component of gender-role stereotypes says that men should be masculine and women should be feminine. Other people enforce the prescriptive component of a stereotype. If you are a man who does not want a career but would prefer to stay home and take care of a family, how will other people react? If you are a female who wants a career and does not want to have children, how will others react? There is a great deal of pressure from other people to adhere to gender roles.

Gender-role stereotypes differ from many other stereotypes because gender is a category that is activated immediately upon meeting someone. One of the first things that you notice about a person is her or his sex. Imagine you see a baby, such as the one in Figure 3.6. The baby has long hair, so it must be a she. If the baby is dressed in blue (as the caption says), it must be a he. You might become extremely uncomfortable because you do not know which pronoun to use. Most people are greatly concerned about referring to a baby by the wrong sex.

However, once you acquire information about a person other than his or her sex, you

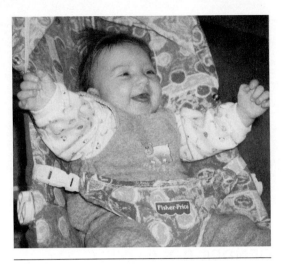

FIGURE 3.6 Photograph of a baby dressed in blue with a lot of hair. Is it a boy or a girl?

may rely more on this individuating information than the gender-role stereotype. That is, **category-based expectancies** occur when you do not know much about a person except the category to which he or she belongs—in this case, sex. In the absence of any other information aside from sex, you might assume sex-related traits and sex-related preferences. **Target-based expectancies** are the perceptions you have about a person based on individuating information. Once you acquire more information about a specific target, besides the person's sex, you will use that information to make judgments. As evidence of this, Chang and Hitchon (2004) had college students read about either a male or a female political candidate in which information on competence about traditionally masculine issues (e.g., economy, national security) or traditionally feminine issues (e.g., education, health care) was present or absent. In the absence of information, people relied on category-based expectancies and judged the female candidate as more competent on feminine issues and the male candidate as more competent on masculine issues. However, when information was provided, target-based expectancies took over; female and male candidates were judged as equally competent on all issues regardless of whether they were feminine or masculine.

Components of Gender-Role Stereotypes

What are the features of the male and female gender-role stereotypes? In 1972, Broverman and colleagues developed a questionnaire to assess people's perceptions of masculine and feminine behavior. They administered this questionnaire to over 1,000 people, and concluded there was a strong consensus as to the characteristics of women and men across age, sex, religion, marital status, and education.

Broverman and colleagues defined a stereotypical feature as one in which 75% of both females and males agreed the trait described one sex more than the other. This definition rule led to the 41 items shown in Table 3.4. The male characteristics (listed in the right column) focused on competence, rationality, and assertion. The female characteristics (listed in the left column) focused on warmth and expressiveness. These traits are similar to the ones found on conventional M/F (masculinity–femininity) inventories.

Broverman and colleagues (1972) also found that the male characteristics were more highly valued than the female characteristics. You can see in Table 3.4 that more masculine characteristics are socially desirable (right column in the top half) than feminine characteristics (left column in the bottom half). When the investigators asked women and men to indicate which of these traits are most desirable in an adult, without specifying the adult's sex, more masculine than feminine items were endorsed. Mental health professionals also rated the masculine items as healthier than the feminine items for an adult to possess. In fact, when

mental health professionals were asked to identify which items fit a healthy female, a healthy male, and a healthy adult, their ratings of the healthy adult and the healthy male did not significantly differ, but their ratings of the healthy adult and healthy female did. That is, the stereotype of the healthy adult more closely approximated the stereotype of an adult male than an adult female. These findings suggest that characteristics of the male gender role are more highly valued than characteristics of the female gender role. Is this still true today? Answer this question by conducting the experiment in Do Gender 3.3.

DO GENDER 3.3
Comparisons of Ideal Adult with Ideal Male and Ideal Female

List the stereotypical sex-role items in Table 3.4. Place each feature on a five-point scale, such as:

Not at   1 2 3 4 5 Very
all caring   caring

Ask a sample of your friends to rate the ideal person on each of these features. On the next page, ask the same friends to rate the ideal male on each of these features. On the third page, ask the same friends to rate the ideal female on each of these features. Always make sure the "ideal person" is the first page so as to disguise the nature of the research. Counterbalance the order of the second and third pages. That is, ask half of your participants to rate the ideal male second and the other half to rate the ideal female second.

For each item, examine the mean response for the ideal person, the ideal male, and the ideal female. Does the ideal person more closely resemble the ideal male, the ideal female, or both equally?

TABLE 3.4 STEREOTYPIC SEX-ROLE ITEMS

Competency Cluster: Masculine Pole Is More Desirable

Feminine	Masculine
Not at all aggressive	Very aggressive
Not at all independent	Very independent
Very emotional	Not at all emotional
Does not hide emotions at all	Almost always hides emotions
Very subjective	Very objective
Very easily influenced	Not at all easily influenced
Very submissive	Very dominant
Dislikes math and science very much	Likes math and science very much
Very excitable in a minor crisis	Not at all excitable in a minor crisis
Very passive	Very active
Not at all competitive	Very competitive
Very illogical	Very logical
Very home-oriented	Very worldly
Not at all skilled in business	Very skilled in business
Very sneaky	Very direct
Does not know the way of the world	Knows the way of the world
Feelings easily hurt	Feelings not easily hurt
Not at all adventurous	Very adventurous
Has difficulty making decisions	Can make decisions easily
Cries very easily	Never cries
Almost never acts as a leader	Almost always acts as a leader
Not at all self-confident	Very self-confident
Very uncomfortable about being aggressive	Not at all uncomfortable about being aggressive
Not at all ambitious	Very ambitious
Unable to separate feelings from ideas	Easily able to separate feelings from ideas
Very dependent	Not at all dependent
Very conceited about appearance	Never conceited about appearance
Thinks women are always superior to men	Thinks men are always superior to women
Does not talk freely about sex with men	Talks freely about sex with men

Warmth-Expressiveness Cluster: Feminine Pole Is More Desirable

Feminine	Masculine
Doesn't use harsh language at all	Uses very harsh language
Very talkative	Not at all talkative
Very tactful	Very blunt
Very gentle	Very rough
Very aware of feelings of others	Not at all aware of feelings of others
Very religious	Not at all religious
Very interested in own appearance	Not at all interested in own appearance
Very neat in habits	Very sloppy in habits
Very quiet	Very loud
Very strong need for security	Very little need for security
Enjoys art and literature	Does not enjoy art and literature at all
Easily expresses tender feelings	Does not express tender feelings at all easily

Source: Broverman et al. (1972).

Gender-role Stereotypes of Older People.   Gender stereotype research often focuses on younger adults, typically college students. Stereotypes of older women and men may differ. Depiction of men and women in the media suggests that we have more negative views of older women than older men, at least when it comes to physical appearance. A meta-analysis of the relation of age to gender stereotypes showed that younger adults are rated more favorably than older adults but that the effect of age differs for men and women (Kite et al., 2005). Increased age was more strongly associated with negative evaluations of women than men. However, age was also related to the perception of a decline in competence, and this relation was stronger for men than women. Because competence is such an integral part of the male gender role, it is interesting that people perceive men to decline more than women on this dimension.

Gender-role Stereotypes of People Who Vary in Ethnicity or Culture.   People's gender-role stereotypes partly depend on the ethnic group to which the person belongs, although there is not a lot of research on this issue. In a study of college students (mostly Caucasian) conducted 15 years ago, perceptions of Anglo American, African American, Asian American, and Mexican American women and men were examined (Niemann et al., 1994). The most frequently generated descriptors for each racial group are shown in Table 3.5.

We can see that race certainly influences the content of female and male stereotypes. Anglo and African American males as well as African American females are described as athletic, whereas Asian American and Mexican American males are not. Anglo and African American men are described as tall, but

Asian American and Mexican American men and women are described as short. Sociable is an attribute used to describe all groups of women except Asian American, but sociable also is used to describe Anglo and African American men. Caring is an attribute shared by all four groups of women, but also Anglo American and Asian American men.

We can also find contradictory features within a given gender-role stereotype, which likely reflect individual differences in perceptions. Mexican American women are viewed as attractive yet overweight. Anglo American men are viewed as hard workers yet ambitionless. African American women and men and Mexican American women and men are viewed as antagonistic yet pleasant.

There are several stereotypes of African American women that pervade our culture, one of which is the matriarch who is aggressive, dominant, and a threat to men's masculinity, and one of which is the jezebel, which is the sexually promiscuous woman. One study examined whether African American men endorsed these negative stereotypes or held a positive perception of African American women (Gillum, 2007). When asked about each stereotype, nearly half of the men indicated some endorsement of the jezebel stereotype, 71% indicated some endorsement of the matriarch stereotype, but 94% endorsed some positive perceptions of African American women. Men without a college education and men who had no committed relationships were more likely to endorse the jezebel stereotype.

Gender stereotypes of men and women in Eastern cultures, such as China, differ from those in Western cultures in a number of ways. Communal traits that are typically viewed as feminine traits in Western cultures are part of both male and female stereotypes in China (Yu & Xie, 2008). Whereas the traditional

TABLE 3.5   MOST FREQUENT FEATURES OF EACH CATEGORY

Anglo-American Males	African American Males	Asian American Males	Mexican American Males
Intelligent	Athletic	Intelligent	Lower class
Egotistical	Antagonistic	Short	Hard worker
Upper class	Dark skin	Achievement oriented	Antagonistic
Light skin	Muscular	Speak softly	Dark skin
Pleasant	Criminal	Hard worker	Noncollege
Racist	Speak loudly	Pleasant	Pleasant
Achievement oriented	Tall	Dark hair	Dark hair
Caring	Intelligent	Good student	Ambitionless
Attractive	Unmannerly	Small build	Family oriented
Athletic	Pleasant	Caring	Short
Sociable	Lower class	Slender	Criminal
Blond hair	Ambitionless	Family oriented	Poorly groomed
Tall	Noncollege	Upper class	Unmannerly
Hard worker	Racist	Shy	Intelligent
Ambitionless	Sociable	Speak with accent	Alcohol user

Anglo-American Females	African American Females	Asian American Females	Mexican American Females
Attractive	Speak loudly	Intelligent	Dark hair
Intelligent	Dark skin	Speak softly	Attractive
Egotistical	Antagonistic	Pleasant	Pleasant
Pleasant	Athletic	Short	Dark skin
Blonde hair	Pleasant	Attractive	Overweight
Sociable	Unmannerly	Small build	Baby makers
Upper class	Sociable	Achievement oriented	Family oriented
Caring	Intelligent	Caring	Caring
Light skin	Attractive	Shy	Intelligent
Achievement oriented	Lower class	Dark hair	Sociable
Fashion conscious	Egotistical	Slender	Noncollege
Light eyes	Ambitionless	Hard worker	Ambitionless
Independent	Caring	Passive	Passive
Passive	Humorous	Good student	Short
	Honest	Well mannered	Antagonistic

Source: Adapted from Niemann et al. (1994).

male in the United States is viewed as independent and athletic, the traditional male in China is viewed as valuing poetry, rituals, music, interdependence, and cooperation (Chia et al., 1994). The Westerner's stereotype of the Asian male is of one who lacks masculine traits—passive and ineffectual (Iwamoto & Liu, 2009),

and the stereotype of the Asian female ranges from the exotic to the subservient (Hall, 2009).

Stereotypes of Homosexuals.   The primary stereotype of homosexuals is that they possess gender-role characteristics associated with the other sex. This stereotype has not changed over the past 20 years (Blashill & Powlishta, 2009). As shown in Figure 3.7, gay men and heterosexual women are perceived to be more feminine than lesbians and heterosexual men; and heterosexual men and lesbians are perceived to be more masculine than gay men and heterosexual women. People associate homosexuality with a variety of emotional difficulties and gender identity problems—especially in the case of men (Boysen et al., 2006). Those who have more negative attitudes toward homosexuality are most likely to endorse these stereotypes.

The media is one source of information about prevailing stereotypes. The media depiction of homosexuals has changed dramatically in the past 10 years. Whereas homosexual characters in television shows were almost nonexistent a decade ago, homosexual characters are fairly common today. The first prominent examples of homosexuals in television were Ellen

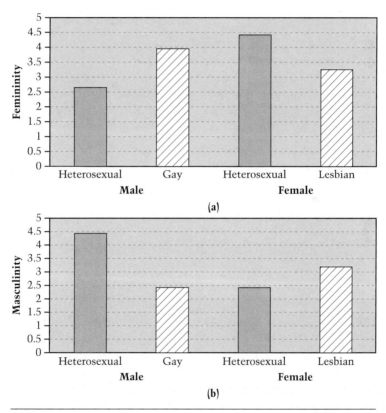

FIGURE 3.7   (a) College men and women viewed gay men and heterosexual women as more feminine than heterosexual men and lesbians; (b) College men and women viewed heterosexual men and lesbians as more masculine than gay men and heterosexual women. *Source*: Adapted from Blashill and Powlishta (2009).

DeGeneres from the show *Ellen* and the two gay men on *Will & Grace*. Many television shows today have gay characters but they typically play a minor role. Consider Oscar on *Office* or the Rachael's two gay dads who are never shown on *Glee*.

The increased exposure to homosexuals on television has the potential to reduce negative stereotypes. In one study, college students were asked to recall a positive gay character from television or movies, a negative gay character, or did not recall a character (control condition) and then completed a homosexual attitudes scale (Bonds-Raacke et al., 2007). The recalled image affected students' attitudes, such that attitudes were more positive if they recalled a positive gay character compared to a negative gay character or no character. There was no difference in people's attitudes between the negative gay character and control conditions, suggesting that people's attitudes toward homosexuals are negative from the start. However, the results of this kind of study suggest that positive images of homosexuals have the potential to alter people's attitudes.

Children's Stereotypes

There appear to be three phases of stereotype development in children (Trautner et al., 2005). First, prior to age 5, children acquire information about gender-related characteristics. There is some evidence that by 18 months of age, children show a greater preference for gender-stereotyped toys (Serbin et al., 2001). By 18 to 24 months, girls are able to link masculine toys and activities with males and feminine toys and activities with females, whereas boys do not make these associations until 31 months of age (Poulin-Dubois et al., 2002; Serbin et al., 2001). Three-year-old girls are

more knowledgeable about stereotypes than same-age boys (O'Brien et al., 2000).

Second, by ages 5–6, children consolidate the information that they have acquired and apply it rigidly to sex. Young children are more likely than adults to rely on target sex than individuating information when making a judgment about a person. That is, children learn that girls play with dolls and girls play with cooking sets, but girls do not yet understand that if someone plays with dolls, the person might also enjoy cooking sets. Martin and Ruble (2009) refer to these as vertical rather than horizontal associations stemming from biological sex. That is, children rely more on category-based expectancies than target-based expectancies in comparison with adults. Attention to individuating information appears to increase with age.

Third, by ages 7–8, children utilize the individuating information rather than sex alone. This may make it seem that increased age leads to a decrease in the use of gender-role stereotypes. However, the use of individuating information can also be viewed as utilizing gender-role stereotypes. That is, older children will infer that Karen would like to climb trees rather than play with dolls because they see that Karen dresses in jeans and a t-shirt. That is, older children may be less likely to rely on target sex to infer behavior, but they use their knowledge of gender-role stereotypes to generalize from one aspect of gender-role behavior to another. Older students take into consideration the individuating information but that individuating information comes from gender-role stereotypes. Beliefs about gender roles—masculinity and femininity—may be more rigid than beliefs about sex.

When the nature of children's gender stereotypes were examined among elementary school children, descriptors of boys and girls fell into three categories: activity/toy, appearance, and trait (Miller et al., 2009). More appearance descriptors emerged for female targets than activity or trait descriptors. By contrast, more activity and trait descriptors emerged for male targets than appearance descriptors. The authors concluded that girls are viewed in terms of how they look and boys are viewed in terms of what they do.

Subcategories of Gender-Role Stereotypes

As women's and men's roles have changed, we have created multiple categories for women and men. That is, there are subcategories of gender-role stereotypes. For example, our stereotype of a male businessman is not the same as our stereotype of a male construction worker; likewise, our stereotype of a female homemaker is not the same as our stereotype of a female doctor. Is having subcategories within one general stereotype helpful? It may seem that subtyping is beneficial because it detracts from the power of the overall stereotype. However, subtyping is merely a way to create an exception and leave the overall stereotype intact (Fiske & Stevens, 1993). How many of you know someone who is prejudiced against African Americans but manages to adore Michael Jordan or Serena and Venus Williams? They are viewed as exceptions to the African American stereotype and members of the subtype "successful African American athlete" or "successful athlete." Thus, subtyping does not necessarily reduce the power of stereotypes.

One subtype of the female stereotype is that of feminist. One of the reasons that few women identify themselves as feminists is that there are a number of negative stereotypes surrounding this group of women. One such stereotype is that feminists hate men. This stereotype was refuted in a study of college women

who completed the Ambivalence Toward Men Inventory previously described (Anderson, Sankis, & Widiger, 2009). Women who proclaimed that they were feminists (the minority—only 17%) scored lower on the hostility toward men scale than women who were not feminists. Another stereotype is that feminists are perceived to have problems in relationships, but there is no evidence that this is the case either (Rudman & Phelan, 2007). Having a feminist partner has been related to healthier relationships and greater relationship stability.

Two other feminist stereotypes are that feminists are unattractive and are likely to be lesbian. And, those two stereotypes are related. When college women were shown four attractive and four plain high school graduation pictures, the attractive female targets were rated by both males and females as less likely to be feminist and less likely to be lesbian than the plain female targets as shown in Figure 3.8 (Rudman & Fairchild, 2007). The study also showed that the relation between unattractiveness and feminism was accounted for by perceived lesbianism. That is, the reason that unattractive targets were perceived to be feminists is that they were perceived to be lesbian.

Feminists seem to be aware of the unattractiveness stereotype—and also influenced by it! One study showed that feminist college women were more influenced by a woman with a feminine appearance delivering a profeminist message than a woman with a masculine appearance (see Figure 3.9; Bullock & Fernald, 2003). Ironically, the appearance of the speaker did not affect nonfeminist women. The authors of the study termed this "feminism lite."

Effects of Gender-Role Stereotypes

A stereotype is a belief about someone based on her or his membership in a category. Categorizing people and objects simplifies

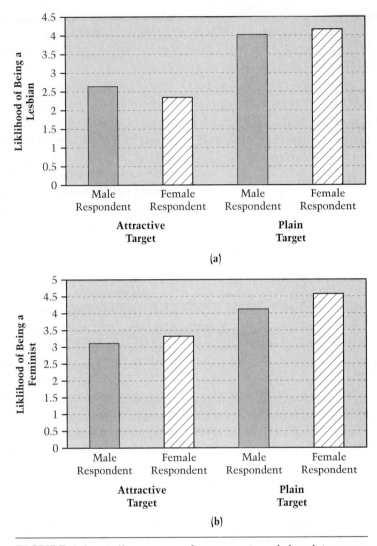

FIGURE 3.8   College men and women viewed the plain target as more likely than the attractive target to be (a) a lesbian and (b) a feminist.
Source: Adapted from Rudman and Fairchild (2007).

our world. Think about when you first meet someone. You place that person into a number of categories, each of which leads you to draw a number of inferences. You notice whether the person is male or female, a student or a professor, Catholic or atheist, athletic or nonathletic. You then use these categories to make certain inferences. For example, you might feel more comfortable swearing in front of an atheist than a Catholic because expletives often have religious connotations. But who is to say the atheist would not be offended or the Catholic does not have a foul mouth? You may assume the

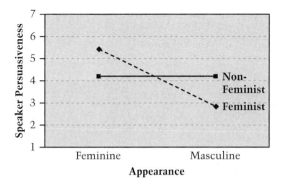

FIGURE 3.9 Paradoxically, feminist women were more influenced by a feminine-appearing speaker than a masculine-appearing speaker delivering a feminist message. The appearance of the speaker did not influence non-feminist women.

Source: Adapted from Bullock and Fernald (2003).

student is about 20 years old and the professor about 50. There are exceptions here, too, as you may find a 50-year-old return-to-school student and a 30-year-old professor. Although there are exceptions, categories generally simplify information processing.

The danger of stereotyping is that it influences our perceptions of and behavior toward others. Stereotyping can influence our behavior toward others in such a way that others confirm the stereotype. This is known as a **self-fulfilling prophecy**. For example, if you believe boys are not good at reading and do not like to read, you might not give your male preschooler as many books to read as your female preschooler. If he doesn't have the same opportunities to read as his sister, will it be a surprise that he has more difficulty reading than she does? No, your stereotype will have created a situation that then confirms the stereotype.

An example of this self-fulfilling prophecy was demonstrated with respect to females' performance on a math test. Female high school students were randomly assigned to a condition in which they were told male students performed better than female students on the test in the past (i.e., activation of negative stereotype) or a condition in which no information was given about others' performance (control condition; Keller, 2002). As shown in Figure 3.10, females performed worse when the negative stereotype was activated compared to the control condition, whereas male students' performance was unaffected by the manipulation. The idea that the activation of a stereotype interfered with performance is referred to as stereotype threat, a concept that will be elaborated on in Chapter 6.

On a global level, the self-fulfilling prophecy was supported by a study of 34 nations that linked stereotypes about women and science with women's test scores in science (Nosek et al., 2009). In this study, people's "implicit" attitudes toward women and science were measured because few people will explicitly endorse the stereotype that women have less aptitude than men for science. Implicit attitudes toward sensitive subjects are measured through the Implicit Association Test (IAT). With the IAT, respondents are shown a set of words and asked to assign the words to a category. On some trials, the categories are connected in a stereotypical way (i.e., men and science) and on some trials, the categories are connected in a counterstereotypical way (i.e., men and liberal arts). Attitudes are measured in terms of response times, with the inference being that respondents will be quicker to categorize words that reflect their beliefs. (See Figure 3.11 for an example and try this yourself by going to https://implicit.harvard.edu/implicit/.)

Using a Web-based IAT, the investigators found that stronger implicit connections of men to science were associated with

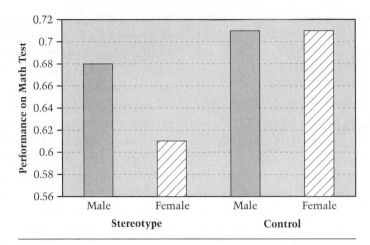

FIGURE 3.10 Females performed worse on a math test after they had received information consistent with the negative stereotype surrounding women and math (experimental condition). Male performance was unaffected by this information. *Source*: Adapted from Keller (2002).

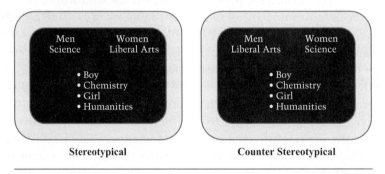

FIGURE 3.11 Example of the Implicit Association Test. The target words (shown in the center of the screen) are flashed one at a time and the respondent is to choose the correct category from the right or left on the top of the screen. The respondent is said to hold stereotypical beliefs when their response times to the stereotype screen are shorter than their response times to the counter-stereotype screen.

sex differences in eighth grade science scores across 34 nations. Respondents' explicit stereotypes—endorsement of men as better than women at science—also were associated with sex differences in math and science scores but the relation was substantially smaller than the relation to implicit attitudes. That is, countries in which people had the strongest implicit stereotypes about sex differences in science were the countries in which the sex differences in test scores were largest.

The IAT has become a useful instrument in the field of gender stereotyping because people are less likely to express gender stereotypes today. The IAT has been applied to the stereotype concerning gender and wealth—specifically, the idea that men make higher salaries than women in the same job (Williams, Paluck, & Spencer-Rodgers, 2010). Respondents whose scores on a wealth IAT showed that they connected being male to high income also rated males as having higher incomes than females. Implicit stereotypes about wealth not only could lead employers to offer women lower salaries than men but also could lead women employees to expect and be satisfied with lower wages.

Up to this point, the impact of the self-fulfilling prophecy on stereotypes has sounded mostly negative. Can the self-fulfilling prophecy ever help performance? If I believe boys are quite skilled at reading and give a boy a lot of books to read, will he develop superior reading skills? Quite possibly. Shih, Pittinsky, and Ambady (1999) investigated whether stereotypes can help as well as hinder performance. They studied quantitative skills among Asian women because these women face contradictory stereotypes: Females are depicted as having inferior quantitative skills, whereas Asians are depicted as having superior quantitative skills. The investigators found that Asian women's performance on a math test improved when their racial identity was made salient but deteriorated when their gender identity was made salient. Thus it appears that stereotypes can influence performance in both positive and negative ways.

Stereotypes can also be harmful in that they restrict our behavior. We feel pressurized to conform to society's gender-role stereotypes. It appears that boys—White, Black, Hispanic, and Chinese—feel greater pressure than girls (Corby, Hodges, & Perry,

2007; Yu & Xie, 2010). Stereotypes also can be internalized in a way that restricts opportunities for both women and men. One study showed that when young adult (ages 20–30) men and women were asked to identify their career preferences, men identified masculine careers and women identified feminine careers (Gadassi & Gati, 2009). In essence, they relied on gender-role stereotypes. However, when stereotypes were made less salient by providing men and women with a list of career possibilities, men's career preferences were slightly less masculine and women's career preferences were much less feminine.

Altering Gender-Role Stereotypes

If we make exceptions for cases that do not fit our stereotypes and treat people in ways that will confirm our stereotypes, how can stereotypes ever be altered? Stereotypes are difficult to change. We tend to notice information that confirms our stereotype and ignore information that disconfirms it, or we create a special subtype for those disconfirming instances. People with strong stereotypes tend to have poorer recall for stereotype-inconsistent information and tend to misremember inconsistent information as consistent with the stereotype (Rudman, Glick, & Phelan, 2008). We also make dispositional or trait attributions for behavior that confirms the stereotype but situational attributions for behavior that disconfirms the stereotype. Let's take an example. We expect women to show an interest in children. Therefore, if we see a woman playing with a baby, we are likely to make the dispositional attribution that she is nurturant rather than the situational attribution that she is bored and looking for a way to distract herself. Conversely, if we see a man playing with a baby, we are more likely to decide that situational forces constrained his behavior (e.g., someone told him to play with the baby) because attentiveness to children is not consistent with the male gender-role stereotype. Test this idea yourself in Do Gender 3.4 by coming up with stereotype-consistent and stereotype-inconsistent behaviors and asking people to make attributions for those behaviors.

Sometimes, when we cannot ignore stereotype-inconsistent information, we instead view the behavior as more extreme. For example, assertiveness may be viewed as more extreme when displayed by a woman than by a man. **Correspondent inference theory** (Jones & Davis, 1965) can explain why this happens. According to this theory, we are more likely to make dispositional attributions

---

DO GENDER 3.4
Attributions for
Stereotype-Consistent and
Stereotype-Inconsistent Behavior

Identify a set of five behaviors that are stereotype consistent for men and five behaviors that are stereotype inconsistent for men. An example of a stereotype-consistent behavior is "Joe watches football on television." An example of a stereotype-inconsistent behavior is "Joe is washing the dishes." Now, do the same for women. An example of a stereotype-consistent behavior is "Maria is sewing a shirt." An example of a stereotype-inconsistent behavior is "Maria is changing the oil in her car."

Ask 10 men and 10 women to explain each of the behaviors. Categorize each explanation as dispositional (due to something about the person; a trait) or situational (due to something about the environment, such as luck, chance, or the force of an external agent). It is best to be blind to the sex of the person who gave you the response.

---

for behavior that is not normative, but unique. For example, we are more likely to infer that a person is emotional if he or she cries during a comedy than during a sad movie. Because many people cry during sad movies, this behavior is considered normative, so crying during a sad movie does not say anything about an individual's personality. Crying during a comedy, however, is not normative and leads to stronger trait attributions for behavior. Thus, we are also more likely to infer aggression in a woman who uses power in her speech than in a man who uses power in his speech because the woman's behavior is more unique.

Another reason that it is difficult to alter stereotypes is the **backlash effect**. When people display counterstereotypical behavior, they may be penalized. In a laboratory study, college students competed against a confederate who either outperformed them in a stereotypical domain (e.g., women categorizing pictures of toddlers) or a counterstereotypical domain (e.g., women categorizing pictures of football players; Rudman & Fairchild, 2004). When losing to someone who succeeded in a counterstereotypical domain, both female and male participants sabotaged the confederate's future performance by providing unhelpful assistance. When losing to someone who succeeded in a stereotypical domain, there was no sabotage. It appears that people are well aware of the backlash effect, as a subsequent experiment showed that participants who succeeded in a counterstereotypical domain tried to conceal their performance. Thus, the backlash effect serves to maintain stereotypes by penalizing people for counterstereotypical behavior, dissuading people from publicizing counterstereotypical behavior, and by undermining performance in counterstereotypical domains.

There are circumstances in which stereotypes can be changed. First, it is easier to disconfirm stereotypical traits when the behavior that reflects the trait is clear rather than ambiguous (Rothbart & John, 1985). For example, it would be easier to disconfirm the stereotype that a woman is talkative rather than the stereotype that a woman is emotional, because it is easier to observe talking or not talking than emotionality. It is also easier to disconfirm positive traits than negative traits (Rothbart & John, 1985). Thus your favorable impressions of people are more easily changed than your unfavorable impressions; it is easier to change people's beliefs that a woman is kind than to change people's beliefs that a woman nags. Rothbart and John (1985) remark, "Favorable traits are difficult to acquire but easy to lose, whereas unfavorable traits are easy to acquire but difficult to lose" (p. 85).

The prototype approach has been applied to stereotyping to understand how stereotypes can be altered (Rothbart & John, 1985). The likelihood of a target being associated with a category depends on how well the target fits the category overall. When faced with a target person, we try to find the closest match between the target person's features and the features of a specific category, or stereotype. How good the match is depends on how prototypical, or how good an example, the target is of the category. Disconfirmation of a feature of a stereotype is more likely to occur if the target person otherwise closely matches the category. That is, we are more likely to change a feature of a stereotype if the disconfirming behavior is in the context of other behavior that fits the stereotype. Let's take an example. The feature "not emotional" is part of the male stereotype. How might we decide that being emotional is acceptable for men? We will be more persuaded by an emotional male who watches football than by an emotional male who reads poetry; similarly, we will be more persuaded by a successful competitive businessman who is emotional

than an emotional male hair stylist. What would have to happen for us to view the traditionally masculine occupations, such as lawyer and doctor, as acceptable for women? We will be more convinced by a female doctor who is married and has a family than by a single female doctor with no family in the area. We are more likely to view disconfirming behavior as acceptable if it is displayed by someone who otherwise fits the gender-role stereotype.

There is some evidence that exposure to counterstereotypes can affect our thinking. When college women were exposed to positive, negative, or no stereotypes about feminists, twice as many women in the positive stereotype condition as the other two conditions identified themselves as feminists (Roy, Weibust, & Miller, 2007).

Sometimes, we do not have to alter our stereotype because a target person calls to mind more than one stereotype; then, we can choose which stereotype to invoke. When thinking of Ellen DeGeneres, do you apply the category "lesbian" or "comedian"? People who like DeGeneres, but have a negative stereotype of lesbians, recall the stereotype of successful comedian. For those people, she does not represent a disconfirming instance of the stereotype of lesbians; instead, she is an example of the stereotype for "successful comedian."

Do Stereotypes Reflect Reality?

Stereotypes reflect society's beliefs about the features that men and women possess, about which there is widespread agreement. But do stereotypes reflect reality? Gender-role stereotypes are an exaggeration in that they do not take into consideration any overlap between women and men. It is certainly not the case that all men are independent and all women are emotional. Some women are more independent than the average man, and some men are more emotional than the average woman.

Some research suggests that our gender-role stereotypes are accurate. Hall and Carter (1999) conducted a study examining 77 traits and behaviors among five samples of college students. Students' perceptions of the magnitude of sex differences were compared to the research findings. On the whole, students were quite accurate. However, there was some variability in accuracy—the students who viewed themselves as more stereotypical were less accurate in their beliefs about women and men.

One problem with this area of research is that it is difficult to test the accuracy of many components of gender-role stereotypes because we do not have objective measures of many traits and behavior. For example, we can determine objectively that men, on average, are taller than women, but how would we determine whether men are more independent than women? This is a difficult task because of the **shifting standard** (Biernat, 2003). The shifting standard is the idea that we might have one standard for defining a behavior for one group, but another standard for defining the behavior in another group. Have you ever heard the phrase (or, dare I say, used the phrase) "she hits well, *for a girl*"? The idea is that you hold the same behavior to different standards for females and males. A certain level of skill at baseball may be regarded as good if the person with the bat is female but only average if the person with the bat is male. Just as the standards for female and male athletes may not be the same, the standards for female and male nurturance may not be the same. You might have regarded a man as a "great dad" because he spends some of his leisure time playing with his kids and taking them shopping. That same behavior may not signify a "great mom," however. Thus it is very difficult to compare men and women on a dimension if different standards are used.

Research supports the shifting standard. In one study, college students were shown the same favorable letter of recommendation ("good student") written by a male physics professor and were told (a) nothing about the professor, (b) that the professor was sexist, or (c) that the professor was antisexist (i.e., promotes women; Biernat & Eidelman, 2007). Students were asked to indicate what they think the letter writer *really* thinks of the student's academic ability. In the sexist and control conditions, students rated the male's ability higher than the female's ability, whereas there were no differences in the nonsexist condition. The authors concluded that "good" means less good for females than males in the absence of information and when the person was explicitly stated to be sexist. In this case, females are held to a lower standard than males.

The shifting standard makes it difficult to compare women's and men's behavior because we have different standards for defining a behavior displayed by a man versus a woman. Behavior that is similar may appear to be different because of shifting standards, as in the study just described. A real-life example of the shifting standard is the media attention that was devoted to a couple of cases of aggressive behavior in women's sports. In 2009, Serena Williams's angry outburst with a lineswoman led to a penalty at match point, causing her to lose the semifinals at the U. S. Open tennis tournament (*Telegraph*, 2009). In 2010, Elizabeth Lambert, a soccer player from the University of New Mexico, was suspended indefinitely for shoving, punching, tripping, and pulling an opponent down to the ground by her ponytail (Longman, 2009). It is not that these aggressive behaviors should go unpunished. The point is that they were viewed as especially aggressive because they were displayed by women and inconsistent with the female gender role. The former coach of the U.S. men's national soccer team, Bruce Arena, seemed to recognize this. He said,

"Let's be fair, there have been worse incidents in games than that. I think we are somewhat sexist in our opinion of the sport. I think maybe people are alarmed to see a woman do that, but men do a hell of a lot worse things. Was it good behavior? No, but because it's coming from a woman, they made it a headline."

Behavior that actually differs between women and men also may appear similar because of shifting standards. For example, you might believe men are helpful because they stop and help someone with a flat tire. You might also believe women are helpful because people are more likely to seek support from a woman than a man. But the behaviors are different and not necessarily comparable.

Taken collectively, these studies show it is difficult to assess the accuracy of stereotypes. We may perceive men and women to behave differently because sex differences in behavior truly exist. Or it may be that our stereotypes about men and women affect our interpretation of the behavior.

What Is the Status of Stereotypes Today?

Have stereotypes changed over time? Lueptow, Garovich-Szabo, and Lueptow (2001) examined college students' perceptions of the typical female and typical male from seven separate samples collected over 23 years—1974 through 1997. They found little evidence that stereotyping of women and men had decreased over time and even found some evidence of an increase. A study of adolescents showed that the vast majority assumed that men and women were clearly different from one another and specified traits of the typical woman and typical man that are consistent with gender-role stereotypes (Nunner-Winkler, Meyer-Nikele, & Wohlrab, 2007). A study of young adults from the United States, Brazil, and Chile showed that stereotypes of women became more masculine and less feminine over time—especially so in the case of Brazil and Chile (Diekman et al., 2005). Diekman and colleagues concluded that the political changes that had taken place in Brazil and Chile in the past decade had led to greater participation of women in the public spheres, which accounts for the greater increase in masculine traits. There was little change in stereotypes of men. All in all, there has been little change in the content of gender-role stereotypes.

There is also evidence that the differential status between men and women can account for gender-role stereotypes (Gerber, 2009). If status accounts for gender-role stereotypes, then the stereotype that men are agentic and women are communal ought to disappear when men and women are in the same status. Studies show that high-status people (men and women) are perceived as more instrumental and assertive, and that low-status people (men and women) are perceived as more expressive and submissive. Status also affects men's and women's perceptions of themselves. When men and women hold the same high-status positions in organizations, they rate their own behavior as more instrumental and assertive than their low-status counterparts; men and women in low-status positions rate their behavior as more expressive.

Another way to learn about whether society's stereotypes of women and men have changed is to examine depictions of women and men on television. Three of the most popular sitcoms in the 1980s reflected the emphasis on androgyny: *Family Ties, Growing Pains*, and *The Cosby Show*. All three depicted feminine-looking, dedicated mothers who were professionals in male-dominated fields (architect, writer, and lawyer). The shows also featured devoted fathers who were professionals in fields that required sensitivity and concern for others (educational program producer for a PBS station, psychiatrist, and obstetrician). By contrast, more recent television shows reflect a range of roles. The popular cartoon *Family Guy* portrays traditional male/female roles in which the father works outside the home and the mother stays home with the baby, whereas *Desperate Housewives* portrays a range of roles for women in the form of a woman who owns her own business, a teacher, and a stay-at-home mom. The influence of the media on gender roles is discussed in Chapter 5 when we review gender-role socialization theories of sex differences. Conduct Do Gender 3.5 to see if you think stereotypes have changed.

DO GENDER 3.5
Stereotypes Obtained from Media Portrayals of Men and Women

Examine a set of television shows to see if and how the stereotypes of women and men have changed. You may focus on a particular type of program or sample across a variety of programs (e.g., drama, comedy, cartoon). Then, examine one episode of 10 different programs and record the following for each character:

1. Character's sex.

2. Character's appearance.

3. Character's role (housewife, doctor, detective).

4. Character's personality traits.

5. Character's behavior.

If you are really energetic, conduct the same kind of experiment on a similar set of shows that appeared on television 20 or 30 years ago. Then compare the two sets of stereotypes. A variation of this experiment is to review television commercials or magazine advertisements.

TAKE HOME POINTS

■ Gender-role stereotypes are the beliefs that we hold about female and male social roles.

■ The descriptive aspects of gender-role stereotypes represent how we believe men and women *are* in our society; the prescriptive aspects of gender-role stereotypes represent how we believe men and women *ought to be* in our society.

■ Stereotypes can be thought of as category-based expectancies. We rely on category-based expectancies, in this case gender-role stereotypes, when we have little information about a person. When provided with more information, we rely on target-based expectancies — meaning that we use what we know about the person (target) to draw inferences.

■ People tend to see a greater correspondence between the mentally healthy person and the mentally healthy male than between the mentally healthy person and the mentally healthy female. This suggests that we attach greater value to the male than the female gender-role stereotype.

■ Gender-role stereotypes are influenced by the age, race, class, and sexual orientation of the target person.

■ In one sense, stereotypes are helpful; they simplify information processing.

■ In another sense, stereotypes are harmful. Our expectations about people can influence how we behave toward them in such a way that they confirm our initial expectancies. This is called a self-fulfilling prophecy.

■ Stereotypes are difficult to alter. When confronted with information that disconfirms a stereotype, we typically ignore the information, fail to recall it, make a situational attribution for it, or create a subtype. In other cases, we view the behavior as more extreme.

■ The best way to change a specific aspect of people's gender-role stereotypes is to present them with an example of someone who disconfirms the stereotype on one dimension but otherwise fits the stereotype. This example will be more compelling than someone who departs from the stereotype on a lot of dimensions.

■ It is difficult to determine whether our stereotypes of women and men are accurate because of the shifting standard. The shifting standard represents the idea that we view the exact same behavior differently when displayed by a female and a male.

BEHAVIORAL COMPONENT: SEX DISCRIMINATION

In 2004, David Schroer applied for a government position as a terrorism specialist (Grossman, 2008). He was extremely well qualified and had been involved with counterterrorism at the Pentagon since 9/11. After receiving the job offer, he revealed that he had been cross-dressing privately for years and had decided to have sex-reassignment surgery so that he could live fully as a female. The job offer was rescinded. A lawsuit ensued. Although the government tried to argue that being a transsexual raised security concerns and that the process of sex reassignment would make it difficult to focus on work, a federal court ruled that Schroer was the victim of sex stereotyping and sex discrimination. This was a landmark ruling for transsexuals.

Discrimination is the differential treatment of individuals based on their membership in a category. Sex discrimination, the subject of the case just cited, is the differential treatment of persons based on their sex. In this case, the question the court faced was if sex discrimination applied to transsexuals.

Both women and men can be victims of sex discrimination. In an archival analysis of new hires in U.S. law firms during the 1990s, Gorman (2005) found that job criteria that were more masculine (e.g., ambitious, independent, logical) were associated with hiring fewer women, and job criteria that were more feminine (e.g., cooperative, friendly, verbally oriented) were associated with hiring fewer men. In a study of letters of recommendation for junior faculty positions, females were described as more communal and males were described as more agentic, controlling for number of years in graduate school, number of publications, number of honors, and number of postdoctoral years (Madera, Hebl, & Martin, 2009). When blind to sex, six psychology professors rated applicants with communal characteristics as less hirable, which accounted for part of why females were viewed as less hirable than males.

One of the most widely publicized cases of sex discrimination resulted from differential evaluation of men and women in the same job. The case is noteworthy because social psychological testimony on gender-role stereotyping played an instrumental role in the Supreme Court decision. The case involved Ann Hopkins, who was denied partnership at Price Waterhouse, one of the top eight accounting firms in the United States. Hopkins maintained she was denied partnership because of her sex. Price Waterhouse maintained that she had some "interpersonal skills" difficulties: "According to some evaluators, this 'lady partner candidate' was 'macho,' she 'overcompensated' for being a woman, and she needed a 'course at charm school.' A sympathetic colleague advised that Hopkins would improve her chances if she would 'walk more femininely, wear make-up, have her hair styled, and wear jewelry'" (*Hopkins v. Price Waterhouse,* 1985, p. 1117, cited in Fiske et al., 1991).

Susan Fiske, a social psychologist and an expert on stereotyping, presented the conditions that foster stereotyping to the Supreme Court. One condition is when an individual is unique in his or her membership in a given category. A single man in a class of 30 women or a single Asian person in a class of 20 Caucasians is more likely to become a victim of stereotyping. Only 1% of the partners (7 of 662) at Price Waterhouse were female at the time (Fiske & Stevens, 1993). Another condition that fosters stereotyping is when the group to which an individual belongs is incongruent with the person's role, in this case, the person's occupation. For example, male nurses are more likely to be viewed in terms of gender-role stereotypes than female nurses. In the 1980s, Ann Hopkins was in a nontraditional occupation for women, as there were few women who were managers of a Big 8 accounting firm. This is a case in which stereotype-inconsistent behavior that could not be ignored was viewed as more extreme; thus, assertive behavior on the part of Hopkins was likely to have been viewed as aggressive. Although some of her clients viewed her aggressive behavior in positive terms—behavior that implied she could get the job done—the partners viewed her aggressive behavior in negative terms— as that of someone who was difficult to get along with. Citing the literature on gender-role stereotyping, Fiske and colleagues (1991) maintained that Hopkins's behavior may have been viewed differently because she was female. Recall the research on the shifting standard.

The Supreme Court took the scientific literature on gender-role stereotyping seriously and found in favor of Hopkins. The Court noted that the situation presented to Hopkins by Price Waterhouse was a no-win situation: The job required the trait of "aggressiveness" in order to succeed, yet the partners objected to women possessing this trait. The Court responded:

> Indeed, we are tempted to say that Dr. Fiske's expert testimony was merely icing on Hopkins's cake. It takes no special training to discern sex stereotyping in a description of an aggressive female employee as requiring "a course in charm school." Nor...does it require expertise in psychology to know that, if an employee's flawed "interpersonal skills" can be corrected by a soft-hued suit or a new shade of lipstick, perhaps it is the employee's sex and not her interpersonal skills that has drawn the criticism. (*Price Waterhouse v. Hopkins,* 1989, p. 1793, cited in Fiske et al., 1991)

It is sometimes difficult to evaluate the equal treatment of men and women when they do not have the same positions in society. See Sidebar 3.2 for a controversial case of sex discrimination. When people think of sex discrimination, they typically think of women as being treated unfairly compared to men, especially in regard to employment situations. This topic is reviewed in more depth in Chapter 12. Can you think of any ways we treat men unfairly? When the military draft was still in effect and only men were chosen, was that sex discrimination? When two working parents divorce and custody is automatically awarded to the mother, is that sex discrimination? Remember that sex discrimination refers to the differential treatment of either men or women due to their sex.

SIDEBAR **3.2:** *A 50–50 Relationship, the Case of Wendt vs. Wendt (Strober, 2002)*

Lorna and Gary Wendt met in high school and married after college. While Gary completed his M.B.A. at Harvard, Lorna Wendt worked as a music teacher. After they had their first child, Lorna Wendt stopped working outside the home and Gary Wendt rose through the corporate ranks to become chairman and CEO of General Electric Capital Services. After 30 years of marriage, in 1995, Gary Wendt asked his wife for a divorce and offered her $10 million. While Gary Wendt considered this sum of money more than enough for his wife to be "comfortable," Lorna Wendt said that the offer was not equitable. Because their estate was worth $100 million, Lorna Wendt argued that she was entitled to $50 million or half the assets.

In cases where the estate is less than $10–$12 million, most courts divide the assets in half upon divorce. However, when the estate exceeds that figure, women often do not receive half the assets. This is when the court tries to figure out how much each party contributed to the marriage. In cases where the husband worked and the wife was a homemaker, it becomes very difficult to identify the value of the unpaid homemaker role. Lorna Wendt started out with the responsibilities of managing the household and taking care of children, but as her husband moved up the career ladder, she took on the added responsibilities of entertaining clients and planning social events. In the end, the court awarded Lorna Wendt $20 million and an additional $250,000 per year in alimony for life.

In 2001, Lorna Wendt was interviewed on National Public Radio Morning Edition (2001). When asked why she contested her husband's initial offer of $10 million, Lorna Wendt said: "My thinking was that I was an equal partner. When I entered this marriage, at that time, we were equal. We were partners in everything we did, every plan we made, even down to the finances. We worked very hard together to get where we were in a position that afforded us this money, and he could not devalue what I had brought to our relationship by putting a number such as that."

Since the divorce and settlement, Lorna Wendt has founded the Institute for Equality of Marriage to provide people with information about managing finances before, during, and after marriage. Lorna Wendt strongly advocates for prenuptial agreements, advising both partners to ask each other before marriage if they are equal partners. She says, "Can you imagine if Gary had said to me, you know, 35 years, ago 'No, I think you're about 10 percent.'"

SUMMARY

In this chapter, I moved beyond conceptions of gender roles to the study of attitudes toward gender roles and to the category of gender. Attitudes consist of three components: affective, cognitive, and behavioral. With respect to gender, the affective component is sexism, the cognitive component is gender-role stereotyping, and the behavioral component is sex discrimination. I reviewed

instruments that measure traditional and modern sexism as well as distinguished between benevolent sexism (positive view of gender category) and hostile sexism (negative view of gender category). Despite the difference in valence, benevolent and hostile sexism are positively correlated, both rooted in the belief that women are less competent than men. I also discussed unfavorable attitudes toward LGBT persons, in the form of homophobia and transphobia. I presented the components of gender-role stereotypes and how those components are influenced by race and ethnicity, sexual orientation, and age. I presented data on the problems with gender-role stereotypes, including how they affect perception and behavior. There are difficulties in changing gender-role stereotypes, in particular because stereotype-inconsistent behavior is often unnoticed, attributed to situational causes, or viewed as more extreme. Sexism and gender-role stereotyping are antecedents to sex discrimination, which I discussed in the context of a Supreme Court ruling that utilized data on gender-role stereotyping in reaching its decision.

DISCUSSION QUESTIONS

1. In what areas have attitudes toward men's and women's roles become less traditional over time, and in what areas have they remained unchanged?
2. What is the difference between hostile and benevolent sexism?
3. Who is most likely to hold benevolent sexist beliefs?
4. What demographic and personality variables would you expect to be related to homophobia and transphobia?
5. How do gender-role stereotypes relate to self-perceptions of gender role discussed in Chapter 2?
6. Why is it difficult to change gender-role stereotypes? How would you go about trying to change someone's gender-role stereotype?
7. A majority of studies on gender-role stereotypes have been conducted on Caucasian, middle-class adults, typically college students. In what ways have these samples limited our research?
8. In what ways does it seem that stereotypes of women and men have changed? In what ways, are they the same?
9. How can gender-role stereotypes be harmful? Can they ever be helpful?

SUGGESTED READING

Biernat, M. (2003). Toward a broader view of social stereotyping. *American Psychologist, 58,* 1019–1027.

Fiske, S. T., Bersoff, D. N., Borgida, E., Deaux, K., & Heilman, M. E. (1991). Social science research on trial: Use of sex stereotyping research in *Price Waterhouse v. Hopkins. American Psychologist, 46,* 1049–1060.

Glick, P., & Fiske, S. T. (2001). An ambivalent alliance: Hostile and benevolent sexism as complementary justifications for gender inequality. *American Psychologist, 56,* 109–118.

Horn, S. S., Kosciw, J. G., & Russell, S. T. (2009). Special issue introduction: New research on lesbian, gay, bisexual, and transgender youth: Studying lives in context. *Journal of Youth and Adolescence, 38,* 863–866.

Martin, C. L., & Ruble, D. N. (2010). Patterns of gender development. *Annual Review of Psychology, 61,* 353–381.

KEY TERMS

Backlash effect—The penalty that is imposed on people for counterstereotypical behavior.

Benevolent discrimination—Providing more help to women than men with the notion that women are less competent than men and are in need of men's help.

Benevolent sexism—Positive feelings toward women coupled with the notion that women are less competent than men and are in need of men's help.

Category-based expectancies—Assumptions about individuals based on characteristics of general categories to which they belong.

Correspondent inference theory—Idea that people are more likely to make dispositional attributions for behavior that is unique or extreme rather than normative.

Egalitarian gender ideology—Maintains that power is distributed equally between men and women and that men and women identify equally with the same spheres.

Gender ideologies—Attitudes toward men's and women's roles.

Gender-role stereotypes—Features that individuals assign to men and women in their society; features not assigned due to one's biological sex, but due to the social roles men and women hold.

Homophobia—A negative attitude toward homosexuals.

Hostile sexism—Feelings of hostility toward women reflected by negative assumptions about women.

Self-fulfilling prophecy—Situation in which expectations influence behavior toward someone so that the person behaves in a way to confirm our expectations.

Sexism—Feeling toward people based on their sex alone.

Shifting standard—Idea that there is one standard for defining the behavior of one group, but another standard for defining the behavior of another group.

Target-based expectancies—Perceptions of a person based on individual information about that person.

Traditional gender ideology—Maintains that men's sphere is work and women's sphere is home.

Transitional gender ideology—Maintains that it is acceptable for women and men to identify with the same spheres, but women should devote proportionately more time to matters at home and men should devote proportionately more time to work.

Transphobia—Negative attitude toward transgendered people.

CHAPTER 4

Sex-Related Comparisons: Observations

"How Different Are Male and Female Brains?" (Radford, *DiscoveryNews,* May 20, 2010)

"Why Do Women Chat More Than Men? (Haworth, *The Scotsman,* November 20, 2008)

"Men Are Better Than Women at Parking" (Harper, London Sunday Paper, December 20, 2009)

"The Boys Have Fallen Behind" (Kristof, New York Times, March 28, 2010)

These are the headlines of stories that you commonly find about sex comparisons. Differences are interesting. Differences are eye-catching. And, as you will see in this chapter, differences are often exaggerated and overinterpreted.

As mentioned in Chapter 1, the subject of sex comparisons is controversial. Scientists continue to debate whether sex comparisons should be made. Regardless of our philosophy on this issue, we cannot ignore the fact that a vast literature exists on this topic. Many sex comparisons have been made in cognitive abilities: Who has better spatial abilities? Who has greater aptitude in math? Are women or men better with language? Sex comparisons have also been made in social domains: Is one sex more empathic? Who helps more? Are men really more aggressive than women? The sexes are also compared in terms of moral and social development. The primary goal of this chapter is to review and evaluate the results of research on sex comparisons in a set of cognitive and social domains. There are other areas of research in which sex comparisons have been made having to do with relationships and health which are addressed in later chapters.

Before embarking on this review, you should realize that there are more similarities than differences between men and women. However, there are some obvious, incontestable differences. For example, men, on average, are taller than women; men, on average, are stronger than women; women, by contrast, have a higher proportion of body fat than men. These are biological facts. However, even within the realm of biology, a great number of similarities exist between women and men. Most women and men have two eyes, two arms, and two legs; most women and men have a heart, lungs, and vocal cords with which they can speak. The same logic applies to the cognitive and social domains. Although there may be some differences, by far, women and men have more in common in the way they think and in the way they behave.

If there are so many similarities between women and men, why do we focus on differences? Belle (1985) suggests that we tend to focus on differences when we are confronted with two of anything. For example, parents with two children are more likely than parents of three or more children to emphasize the differences between the children: "Jennifer is better in math than Matthew; Matthew is better in geography than Jennifer." Parents with three children, however, are more likely to describe each child individually without making a comparison to the other children: "Mary is good in math, Johnny is good in geography, Paul is good in English." Belle also reported that the same phenomenon occurs among anthropologists studying two kinds of cultures. Whereas two cultures are often described in comparison to one another, anthropologists who study more than two cultures emphasize the diversity of human nature. Thus we would be less likely to emphasize sex differences if there were at least three sexes!

If there are more similarities than differences between women and men, why does it seem that women and men are so different? Why do books like John Gray's (1992) *Men Are from Mars, Women Are from Venus* become best sellers if men and women are not opposites? Why did my father respond to the publication of this textbook by saying, "If you can figure out why men and women are so different, that would become a best seller!" One reason is that differences are more salient and more provocative than similarities. I mentioned in Chapter 1 that sex is a very salient attribute of a person. Thus when two people perform differently on a task and we look for an explanation, we can easily draw the inference that sex must be the distinguishing factor. Second, we have stereotypes about men's and women's behavior that are quite strong and quite distinct. We often recall information that confirms our stereotypes and disregard information that disconfirms our stereotypes. This is called **confirmatory hypothesis testing**. We are most likely to do this when we have strong expectations, when the stereotype is about a group, and when the stereotype is about a trait (Stangor & McMillan, 1992). For example, one stereotype about babies is that males are more active than females. Several years ago, my husband and I were visiting some neighbors. There was a male infant and a female infant, both of whom seemed intent on tearing up the house! The mother of the male infant remarked, "Isn't it true about how much more active boys are than girls? Look at Justin compared to

Emily." My husband, who thankfully was oblivious to this gender stereotype, disappointed the mother by failing to confirm her hypothesis. He said, "They both seem pretty active to me!" The mother was clearly disappointed in this response. If a female and a male take a math test and the male outperforms the female, most people will remember this incident. But if the female outperforms the male, as discussed in Chapter 3, we will either forget the incident, decide the female or male was "different" and not representative of the group, or make a situational attribution (e.g., Maria had seen the test before; Matthew didn't get much sleep last night).

As you will see, sex differences have been documented in some domains. Unfortunately, a significant difference in performance between females and males is often misunderstood to mean all males are better at task X than all females, or all females are better at task Y than all males. An example of a significant difference in performance is shown in Figure 4.1. You can see the mean score for men is slightly (and could be significantly) higher than that for women. But you should also notice a great deal of overlap in the distributions of men's and women's scores. Only a small number of men are performing better than all of the women, and only a small number of women are performing worse than all of the men. Thus even though a sex difference exists, most women and men are performing about the same. Keep this in mind when you read about a sex difference in this chapter. Remember that a

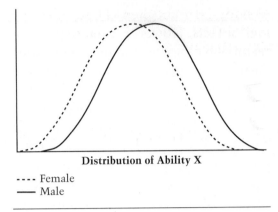

Distribution of Ability X

- - - - Female
——— Male

FIGURE 4.1   Sample distribution of a hypothetical ability (ability X) for males and females. You can see a great deal of overlap between the two distributions. Yet the average of ability X is slightly higher for males than females. This illustrates the fact that a sex difference in an ability does not mean all men differ from all women. In fact, a statistically significant sex difference can exist even when most of the men and women are similar in their ability level.

sex difference does not imply all women differ from all men, which may explain why you will have some personal experiences that do not fit with the research literature.

I begin my review of sex comparison research by discussing the early work of Maccoby and Jacklin, who published the first comprehensive review of sex differences in 1974. Although this book was written a long time ago, it had a great impact on the field. As you will see, it also was subjected to serious criticism. Then I review the more recent work on sex comparisons that have been made in several important cognitive and social domains.

MACCOBY AND JACKLIN'S PSYCHOLOGY OF SEX DIFFERENCES

Maccoby and Jacklin's (1974) *Psychology of Sex Differences* entailed a comprehensive review of the ways men and women differ psychologically. They examined intellectual or cognitive domains as well as social abilities. Their conclusions were surprising to many people: They found that sex differences existed in only a few domains and that many stereotypes had no basis in fact. They identified sex differences in only four domains: verbal ability (advantage girls), visual-spatial ability (advantage boys), mathematical ability (advantage boys), and aggression (greater in boys). They found no sex differences in self-esteem, sociability, analytic ability, or achievement motivation, and it was unclear whether there were sex differences in activity level, competitiveness, dominance, or nurturance.

One limitation of Maccoby and Jacklin's (1974) work is that it was a **narrative review**. In a narrative review, authors decide which studies are included and come to their own conclusions about whether the majority of studies provide evidence for or against a sex difference; basically, a tally is made of the number of studies that reports a difference versus no difference. This kind of review presents several difficulties. One problem is that the authors decide how many studies are enough to show a difference does or does not exist. If 12 of 12 studies show a difference, a difference must exist. But what about 10 of 12? Or 8 of 12? Or even 6 of 12? How many is enough? A second difficulty with narrative reviews is that the pattern of results may be disproportionately influenced by findings from small samples. Perhaps the majority of studies show men and women have equal verbal ability, but all of these "no difference" studies

have sample sizes under 30, and the few studies that report women have greater verbal skills than men are based on sample sizes of over 100. Should we still conclude there is no sex difference in verbal ability? The power to detect a significant difference between women and men when one truly exists is limited in small samples. Thus a narrative review of an area of research that contains many small sample studies may lead to faulty conclusions.

In 1976, Jeanne Block wrote a response to Maccoby and Jacklin's (1974) review of sex differences that was virtually ignored. Block reviewed the same literature and arrived at conclusions very different from the ones reached by Maccoby and Jacklin. First, she noted that Maccoby and Jacklin did not censor the studies they included; that is, they averaged across all studies, whether methodologically sound or not. A number of studies had very small samples, a problem just noted. Some studies used unreliable instruments; other studies used instruments that lacked **construct validity**, meaning there was not sufficient evidence that the instruments measured what they were supposed to measure.

Second, Block (1976) noted tremendous age bias in the studies reviewed. She found that 75% of the reviewed studies were limited to people age 12 and under; 40% used preschool children. The reason so many studies were conducted with children is that comparisons between males and females first became popular in developmental psychology. Developmental psychologists compared females and males in their studies, hoping no differences would be found so they could combine girls and boys when analyzing their data. Why is it a problem that Maccoby and Jacklin's (1974) review focused so heavily on children? The problem is that they did not take into consideration the fact that some sex differences might not appear until adolescence and later; in fact, the three cognitive differences that Maccoby and Jacklin noted did not appear until adolescence. Adolescence is sometimes referred to as a time of **gender intensification**, a time when girls and boys are concerned with adhering to gender roles. Thus sex differences that arise as a result of socialization pressures might not appear until adolescence. Even sex differences thought to be influenced by hormones might not appear until puberty. When Block categorized the studies into three age groups (under 4, between 5 and 12, and over 12), she found that sex differences in many domains became larger with increasing age.

In the end, Block agreed with the sex differences that Maccoby and Jacklin found but also found evidence of other sex differences. She concluded that boys, compared to girls, were better on insight problems, showed greater dominance, had a stronger self-concept, were more active, and were more impulsive. Girls, in comparison to boys, expressed more fear, showed more anxiety, had less confidence on tasks, maintained closer contact with friends, sought more help, scored higher on social desirability, and were more compliant with adults.

The conclusions of Maccoby and Jacklin (1974) and of Block (1976) were obviously not the same. Both, however, relied on narrative reviews of the literature. In the 1980s, a new method was developed to review the literature that led to more objective conclusions: meta-analysis. Much of the recent literature on sex comparisons, which is described in this chapter, has relied on meta-analysis.

Meta-Analysis

Meta-analysis is a statistical tool that quantifies the results of a group of studies. In a meta-analysis, we take into consideration not

only whether a significant difference is found in a study but also the size of the difference, or the **effect size**. The effect size, calculated in terms of the "d statistic," is calculated by taking the difference between the means [M] of the two groups (in this case, women and men), and dividing this difference by the variability in the scores of the members of these two groups (i.e., the standard deviation [SD]), as shown in Figure 4.2. As the size of the sample increases, the estimate of the mean becomes more reliable. This means the variability around the mean, the standard deviation, becomes smaller in larger samples. A small difference between the means of two large groups will result in a larger effect size than a small difference between the means of two small groups. Hence a study that shows men score 10 points higher than women on the math SAT will result in a larger effect size if there are 100 women and men in the study than if there are 20 women and men in the study. The rule of thumb used to interpret the d statistic is that .2 is a small effect, .5 is a medium effect, and .8 is a large effect (Cohen, 1977). A .2 effect size means that sex accounts for less than 1% of the variance in the outcome; a .5 effect means that sex accounts for 6% of the variance; a .8 effect means that sex accounts for 14% of the variance (Cohen, 1977).

If a large effect accounts for only 14% of the variance, is a small effect even worth discussing? As you will discover in this chapter,

$$d = \frac{M_{males} - M_{females}}{\sqrt{\dfrac{SD^2_{males} + SD^2_{females}}{2}}}$$

Note: SD = Standard Deviation

FIGURE 4.2 The d statistic, as calculated by this formula, is used to determine the size of a sex difference.

many sex differences are small. Whether small means trivial depends on the domain you are investigating. The finding that sex accounts for 1% of the variance in an outcome does not appear to be earth-shattering. However, 1% can be quite meaningful (Rosenthal, 1994): It depends on the outcome. For example, small effects in medical studies can have enormous implications. In a study to determine whether aspirin could prevent heart attacks, participants were randomly assigned to receive aspirin or a placebo. The study was called to a halt before it ended because the effects of aspirin were so dramatic (Steering Committee, 1988). The investigators deemed it unethical to withhold aspirin from people. In that study, aspirin accounted for less than 1% of the variance in heart attacks.

What about outcomes that are relevant to gender? Bringing the issue closer to home, Martell, Lane, and Emrich (1996) used computer simulations to examine the implications of a small amount of sex discrimination on promotions within an organization. They showed that if 1% of the variance in performance ratings were due to employee sex, an equal number of men and women at entry-level positions would result in 65% of men holding the highest-level positions over time—assuming promotions were based on performance evaluations. So here, a very small bias had large consequences. However, there are other times when 1% of the variance is trivial and does not translate into larger real-world effects. Keep these ideas in mind when considering the sizes of the effects in this chapter.

Using meta-analysis rather than narrative reviews to understand an area of research has several advantages. As mentioned previously, meta-analysis takes into consideration the size of the effects; thus all studies showing a significant difference will not be weighed

similarly. Another advantage of meta-analysis is that researchers can examine how other variables influence, or moderate, the size of the effect. A **moderating variable** is one that alters the relation between the independent and the dependent variable. I often refer to a moderating variable as an "it depends on" variable. When sex comparisons are made, a difference may "depend on" the age of the respondents, the gender role of the respondents, or the year the study was published. Recall that Block (1976) found that many sex differences were apparent only among older participants; thus age was a moderator variable. Another potential moderating variable is the year of publication. If a sex difference existed in the 1980s but disappeared by the 2000s, perhaps women's and men's behavior became more similar over time. We can even ask if the results of a sex comparison depend on the sex of the author; men or women may be more likely to publish a certain result. Age, gender role, author sex, and year of publication are frequently tested as moderator variables in the following meta-analyses.

In one way, meta-analysis is limited in the same way narrative reviews are: Researchers still make subjective decisions about what studies to include in the review. Researchers conducting a meta-analysis often come up with a set of criteria to decide whether a study is included in the review. Criteria may be based on sample characteristics (e.g., restrict to English-speaking samples) or on methodological requirements (e.g., participants must be randomly assigned to condition). One difficulty with any kind of review, meta-analytic or narrative, is that studies failing to detect a difference are less likely to be published. In meta-analysis, this is referred to as the **file-drawer problem** (Hyde & McKinley, 1997): Studies that do not find sex differences are not published and end up in investigators' file drawers. Thus the published studies represent a biased sample of the studies that have been conducted. More recent meta-analyses have ways of addressing the file-drawer problem, either by reporting the number of studies in file drawers that would be needed to negate the results or by making attempts to include unpublished studies in the meta-analysis. The file-drawer problem may not be as significant in studies of sex comparisons as in other research because some of the sex comparison data come from studies whose primary purpose was not to evaluate sex. Investigators may be studying aggression, empathy, or math ability for other reasons aside from sex but report the results of sex comparisons as a matter of routine.

There have been so many sex comparison meta-analyses published in the 1980s and 1990s that Janet Hyde (2005a) published a paper called "The Gender Similarities Hypothesis," in which she reviewed the results of 46 meta-analyses, many of which are discussed in this chapter. She concluded that 30% of the effects were in the close to zero range ($d < .10$) and that 48% were small ($d < .35$). She noted three exceptions—large effect sizes in throwing velocity (males faster than females), attitudes toward sex (males more liberal than females), and physical aggression (males greater than females). Let's see what some of the meta-analyses have to say.

TAKE HOME POINTS

- Men and women are more similar than different, as shown by the overlapping distributions in Figure 4.1.

- The first comprehensive review of sex differences was published by Maccoby and Jacklin and revealed that there were sex differences in only four domains: verbal, spatial, math, aggression.

- That review was a narrative review, which is limited by the fact that it doesn't take into consideration the size of the differences.

- Meta-analysis provides a way to quantitatively review studies, taking into consideration sample size and effect sizes (*d*s).

- Meta-analysis also allows one to consider whether certain variables, known as moderator variables, influence the size of the sex difference.

- A disadvantage of both narrative and meta-analytic reviews is that studies finding no differences are less likely to be published, a weakness known as the file-drawer problem.

SEX COMPARISONS IN COGNITIVE ABILITIES

Many people assume men have greater spatial and math abilities than women. People also assume women have greater verbal skills than men. As the literature here shows, these statements are overly simplistic. This area of research is highly controversial because a sex difference in an area of cognition could lead people to assume one sex is more suitable for a career requiring that ability. This could ultimately lead to sex discrimination. Thus it is important that we evaluate this research carefully. For each cognitive ability I discuss, one or more meta-analyses exist. I report the effect size, the *d*, in parentheses for the major findings. To be consistent throughout the chapter, a *d* that is positive will indicate men outperform women, and a *d* that is negative will indicate women outperform men (see Figure 4.3).

Spatial Ability

Spatial skills involve the ability to think about and reason using mental pictures rather than words. However, spatial ability is

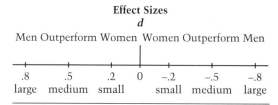

FIGURE 4.3 Indication of the strength of effect sizes (*d*).

not a single construct. Think of all the activities that involve spatial skills: reading maps, doing jigsaw puzzles, trying to pack all your belongings from school into the trunk of a car, and finding where you put your keys. Given the diversity of tasks that involve spatial skills, it is no surprise that the results of sex comparisons depend on the type of spatial skill.

Voyer, Voyer, and Bryden (1995) conducted a meta-analysis on the three distinct spatial skills shown in Figure 4.4. They found moderate sex differences for spatial perception (*d* = +.44) and mental rotation (*d* = +.56), but only a small difference for spatial visualization (*d* = +.19). Thus the size of the sex difference in spatial skills ranged from very small to medium, depending on the particular skill. Since the publication of this meta-analysis, more recent studies have confirmed this finding. For example, a study of 16- to 18-year-olds in the United Kingdom showed large sex differences in mental rotation (*d* = 1.01) and moderate sex differences in spatial visualization (*d* = +.42; Kaufman, 2007). A study of college students in Norway showed large sex differences in mental rotation (*d* = +.85) and moderate sex differences in spatial visualization (*d* = +.48; Nordvik & Amponsah, 1998). These sex differences held even when female and male technology students with a similar high school background in math and physics

were compared. Thus, sex differences in spatial abilities do not appear to be disappearing with time (Halpern & Collaer, 2005).

The meta-analysis showed that the size of the sex difference increased with age (Voyer et al., 1995). Averaging across spatial abilities, sex differences ranged from zero to small in children under 13 but ranged from small to large in children over 18. Research seems to suggest that the sex difference in visual-spatial skills emerges around kindergarten or first grade (Halpern et al., 2007). However, one study showed that sex differences in mental rotation may already be apparent among 3- to 4-month-old infants (Quinn & Liben, 2008).

Of the three spatial abilities discussed, the sex difference in mental rotation is largest and stable over time, causing it to receive the most research attention. Investigators have wondered whether part of this sex difference is due to women and men using different strategies to manipulate objects. There is some evidence from fMRI studies that men use a more holistic strategy by rotating the whole object at one time, whereas women use a more analytic strategy that involves comparing specific features of the object (Jordan et al., 2002). The latter strategy would take more time. It also appears that men use what has been called a leaping strategy, whereas women use a conservative strategy. To understand these strategies, look at the mental rotation task shown in the middle of Figure 4.4. The respondent is asked to find which of the four response stimuli correspond to the standard stimulus. The idea is that men find the two matching stimuli and then move on to the next item on the test, whereas women examine all four stimuli to ensure that they have found the correct matches which takes more time. To test this possibility, Hirnstein, Bayer, and Hausmann (2009) modified the mental rotation task for college

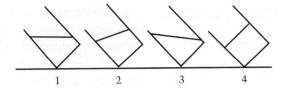

A spatial perception item. Respondents are asked to indicate
which tilted bottle has a horizontal water line.

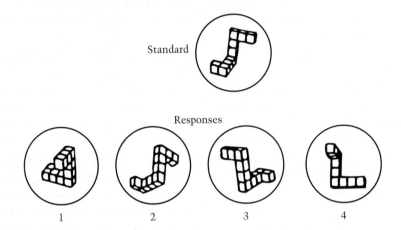

A mental rotation item. Respondents are asked to identify the two responses
that show the standard in a different orientation.

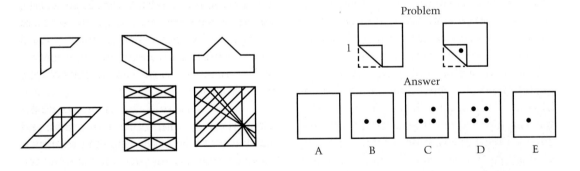

Spatial visualization items. Left, Embedded Figures: Respondents are asked to find the simple
shape shown on the top in the complex shape shown on the bottom. Right, Paper Folding:
Respondents are asked to indicate how the paper would look when unfolded after a hole is punched.

FIGURE 4.4 Sample items from tests that measure spatial perception, mental rotation, and spatial visualization.

Source: M. C. Linn and A. C. Petersen (1985). Emergence and characterization of sex differences in spatial ability: A meta-analysis. Child Development, 56, 1479–1498. © 1985 Society for Research in Child Development.

students by varying the number of correct matches from 1 to 4, which requires respondents to use the conservative strategy. The results, shown in Figure 4.5, show that modifying the task hurt everyone's performance but did not completely eliminate the sex difference—which remained large ($d = +.95$).

A very consistent and sizable sex difference exists in one skill that requires spatial ability: aiming at a target (Kimura, 1999). Men are consistently better than women in their accuracy at hitting a target, whether shooting or throwing darts. Physical factors such as reaction time, height, and weight do not account for this sex difference. Differences in experiences with target shooting also do not account for the sex difference (Kimura, 1999). The sex difference can be observed in children as young as 3 years old. Performance on this task seems to be unrelated to performance on other spatial ability tasks, such as mental rotation (Kimura, 1999).

Up to this point, the size of the sex difference in spatial skills has been variable, but the effects always have been in the direction of men. Can we conclude that the direction of the

effect is consistent across spatial tasks? No. The direction of the sex difference in spatial skills is not consistent across all tasks. A spatial domain in which women appear to have greater aptitude than men is object location memory. A meta-analysis of 36 studies on object identity memory and object location memory showed that women outperform men on both (object identity $d = +.23$; object location $d = +.27$; Voyer et al., 2007). With object identity memory, the experimenter presents the respondent with a set of objects, such as those shown in Figure 4.6a, removes them, and then presents a new set of objects, some of which are old and some of which are new, as shown in Figure 4.6b. The task of the respondent is to identify which objects are old and which are new. For object location memory, the objects are not changed but their location is moved, as shown in Figure 4.6c. Here the task of the respondent is to identify which objects have been moved. Sex differences in object location seemed to depend on participant age and the type of object. That is, sex differences were larger among participants over 13 years of age compared to younger participants. Women outperformed men when objects were feminine or neutral, but men outperformed women when objects were masculine.

One conclusion is that men are better at manipulating objects in space, and women are better at locating objects. If true, these differences could lead men and women to give directions differently. Two studies have found that women are more likely to use landmarks, and men are more likely to use distances and north/south/east/west terminology when giving directions (Dabbs et al., 1998; Lawton, 2001). Look at Figure 4.7. How would you get from the Town Hall to Katja Park? Conduct your own survey on how women and men give directions in Do Gender 4.1 to see if this is true.

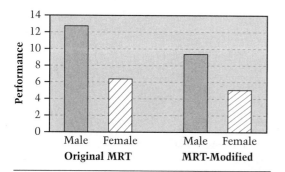

FIGURE 4.5 Men's and women's performance is impaired on the modified mental rotation task (MRT). The overall sex difference is reduced but remains even with the modification.
Source: Adapted from Hirnstein, Bayer, and Hausmann (2009).

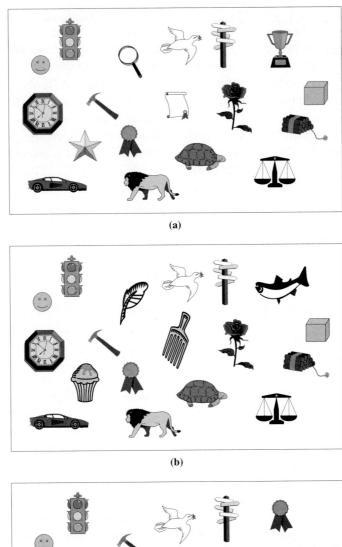

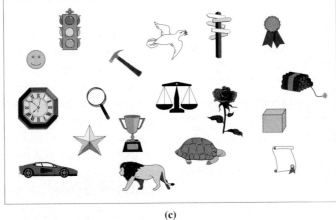

FIGURE 4.6   Example of a test used to measure spatial identity and object location memory. Study Figure 4.6a and then cover it up. Look at Figure 4.6b, which objects are new and which are old? Look at Figure 4.6c, which objects have been moved?

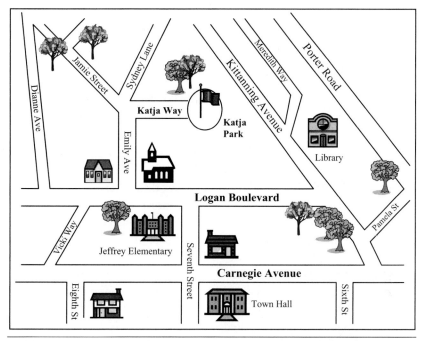

FIGURE 4.7 Research has suggested that men and women give directions differently: Men use north/south/east/west terminology and women use land-marks. How would you get from the Town Hall to Katja Park?

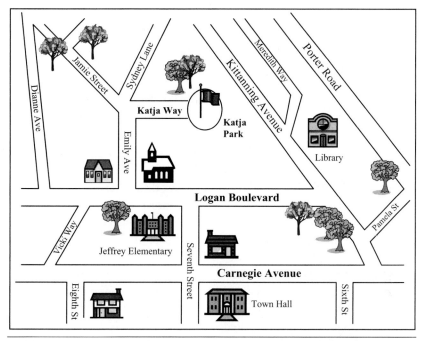

DO GENDER 4.1
Sex Comparisons in Directions

Choose one location that is across the town or city where you live and one location that is not very far away. Ask 10 women and 10 men to give you directions to each of these locations. Then have them write out the directions. Record use of landmarks, esti-mates of distance, use of street names, and north/south/east/west terminology to see if there are sex differences.

the completion of advanced degrees and the entering of Science/Technology/Engineering/ Math (STEM) careers (Wai, Lubinski, & Benbow, 2009). Yet, there is virtually no emphasis on spatial skill development in the U.S. education system. Perhaps because men and women are socialized to pursue different fields, spatial skills end up being related to artistic pursuits in women and engineering careers in men.

TAKE HOME POINTS

■ The direction and magnitude of sex differences in spatial abilities depend on the specific task.

■ Of all the spatial abilities, the sex difference in mental rotation is the largest, in favor of men.

Despite the importance of spatial skills, the educational system and educational test-ing in the United States is oriented toward math and verbal skills. Spatial skills predict

- Although the sex difference in spatial skills does not appear to be changing over time, sex differences are more likely to appear among older than younger children.

- One domain in which women have better spatial skills than men is object location.

Mathematical Ability

Of all the cognitive domains, math is one in which people seem to be confident of sex differences. Two older meta-analytic reviews from the 1990s concluded there was a small sex difference in math ability favoring males. In a meta-analysis of 100 studies on math skills, Hyde, Fennema, and Lamon (1990) found an overall effect size of $d = +.15$, favoring males over females but noted that sex differences were decreasing with time. The effect size in studies published before 1974 was $+.31$, whereas the effect size in studies published from 1974 onward was $+.14$. In a meta-analysis of large samples of high school students, Hedges and Nowell (1995) found an average effect size of $d = +.16$. Thus both reviews concluded that there was an overall sex difference in math in favor of males but that the difference was small.

More recent data suggest that sex differences in math aptitude have approached zero. In an examination of statewide testing in over 7 million students from 10 different states, the overall d was .0065, ranging from $-.02$ to $+.06$ across grades 2 through 11, leading the authors to conclude that sex differences in math aptitude have disappeared (Hyde et al., 2008). Research that has examined women's and men's math performance across 49 countries has shown many effect sizes near zero (Else-quest, Hyde, & Linn, 2010). This research also showed that

the extent to which women had fewer educational and economic opportunities in a country was associated with larger sex differences in math scores in favor of males.

By contrast, higher-stakes testing, such as SAT data, shows that there is a small difference in math scores in favor of males (about 35 points) that has remained the same over the past 35 years (Halpern et al., 2007). This finding is interesting because it suggests that the sex difference has persisted despite the fact that more women are taking advanced math courses in high school today than ever before. However, it also is the case that more women are taking the SAT today than ever before.

When sex differences in math are found, researchers often point to the fact that part of this overall effect is due to men being more likely than women to have really high math scores. Men are more likely than women to be in the very upper end of the math distribution. However, Halpern and colleagues (2007) caution that even this statistic is changing. Among those who scored above 700 on the SAT math exam, the ratio of male to female was 13:1 20 years ago, but it is 2.8:1 today. There also is evidence that men's math scores are more variable than women's math scores (Halpern et al., 2007; Hyde et al., 2008), and the reason for this is not clear.

There is a paradox when it comes to gender and math. Males perform better than females on math achievement tests, such as the SAT, but females receive better math grades in school (Royer & Garofoli, 2005). Why do women perform better than men in school? One reason may be that girls and boys approach their schoolwork differently (Kenney-Benson et al., 2006). Girls have a more mastery-oriented style (I do math to improve my skills), whereas boys have a more performance-oriented style (I do math to show my teacher I'm smarter than the other students). In a study of fifth-graders, sex differences in orientation predicted math grades 2 years later. They also found that girls were less likely than boys to be disruptive in class. The combination of having a mastery orientation and being less disruptive in the classroom was linked to girls' higher math grades.

Regardless of whether there are sex differences in math aptitude, there is a clear sex difference in attitudes toward math. Cross-cultural research has shown that eighth-grade males have more positive attitudes toward math than females across 49 different countries (Else-Quest et al., 2010). Males are more self-confident ($d = +.15$) than females and value math more than females ($d = +.10$). In the United States the effect sizes were .26 and .05. It is not clear whether attitudes toward math have changed much over time. In a U.S. Gallup Poll (2005), similar numbers of male and female teens (aged 13 to 17) said math is their favorite subject (29%) but more girls than boys said that math is their most difficult subject (44% versus 31%).

It is possible that math ability is linked to spatial ability, especially among those who are highly talented in math. Math achievement scores have been linked to mental rotation ability (Nuttall, Casey, & Pezaris, 2005). Math ability is an interesting cognitive ability because it includes both spatial and verbal skills. One study showed that males performed better on math problems that required spatial solutions, whereas females performed better on problems that required verbal solutions and memory from textbooks (Gallagher, Levin, & Cahalan, 2002).

TAKE HOME POINTS

- Sex differences in math for the general population range between small and zero and are decreasing over time.

- Regardless of whether sex differences in math appear on achievement tests, females outperform males in school. Explanations for this paradox have to do with the different orientations girls and boys have toward schoolwork.

- Sex differences in math ability among the highly talented are substantial; these differences may relate to men's advantage in spatial skills, in particular mental rotation.

Verbal Ability

Sex differences in verbal ability are among the first cognitive abilities to be noticed (Halpern, 2000). On average, girls talk earlier than boys and develop larger vocabularies and better grammar than boys. Fourth-grade girls have been shown to be better at reading than boys across 33 countries (Mullis et al., 2003).

In an older meta-analysis of 165 studies that evaluated verbal ability, a very small effect emerged ($d = -.11$), in the direction of women outperforming men (Hyde & Linn, 1988). The investigators examined several types of verbal ability, including vocabulary, analogies, reading comprehension, and essay writing. All the effect sizes were small, except for speech production; in that case, there was a moderate effect of female superior performance ($d = -.33$). There was a trend for articles whose first author was male to report smaller effect sizes than articles whose first author was female; this reminds us of the potential for experimenter bias.

Sex differences were consistent across age groups, from 5-year-olds to adults over age 26, but appeared to be decreasing over time. In studies published before 1974, the effect size was $d = -.23$; in studies published in 1974 and after, the effect size was $d = -.10$. A second meta-analysis of studies of high school students showed that all effects for verbal ability were near zero (Hedges & Nowell, 1995).

There is one verbal ability in which a large sex difference exists: writing (Halpern et al., 2007). Until recently, standardized tests did not include a writing component because it is difficult to score. The 2006 SAT Writing Test showed that females outperformed males on both the multiple-choice and essay sections (SAT Data Tables, 2010).

Like math ability, the size of the sex difference in verbal skills depends on the population studied. Sex differences are larger when people with verbal difficulties are examined (Hyde & McKinley, 1997). Boys are more likely than girls to have dyslexia, which generally involves difficulties with reading, writing, and spelling (Chan et al., 2007), and boys are more likely than girls to stutter (McKinnon, McLeod, & Reilly, 2007; Proctor et al., 2008). Several people question whether boys have more verbal difficulties than girls or whether boys are more likely to be referred for special services than girls. Shaywitz and colleagues (1990) followed 445 kindergartners in the state of Connecticut through third grade. They evaluated the prevalence of reading disabilities among children in the second and third grades in two different ways. First, they identified reading-disabled children by using objective performance criteria; these children were referred to as "research-identified" disabled students. Second, they noted whether teachers referred students for special education services for reading disability; these children were

referred to as "school-identified" disabled students. As shown in Figure 4.8, schools were two to four times more likely to identify second-grade boys as reading-disabled compared to girls—a significant difference, but researchers identified similar percentages of boys and girls as reading-disabled using objective criteria. Why the discrepancy? Specifically, why are boys who are not objectively determined to have a reading disability labeled so by teachers? Investigators also had teachers rate students on a host of other characteristics. Teachers viewed reading-disabled boys as overactive and having more behavioral problems compared to non-reading-disabled boys. Teachers' views of boys' behavior may have influenced their judgments of the boys' reading ability.

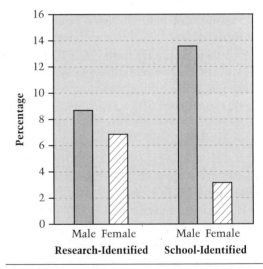

FIGURE 4.8   Identification of reading disability in second-grade boys and girls. Researchers were equally likely to identify boys and girls as having a reading disability using objective criteria. Teachers at the school, however, were more likely to refer boys than girls for a reading disability using their own subjective criteria.

Source: Adapted from Shaywitz et al. (1990).

Again, researchers have concluded that sex differences in verbal ability depend on the specific domain. Most differences are small, but some, such as differences in writing ability, are more substantive. The sex difference may be larger when people with verbal difficulties are considered.

TAKE HOME POINTS

- There is a small sex difference in verbal ability, favoring females.

- The size of the sex difference depends on the specific verbal ability; the sex difference is large in the case of writing.

- One reason for the sex difference in verbal ability has to do with the fact that a larger proportion of males than females have verbal difficulties.

Comprehensive Assessment of Cognitive Abilities

Regardless of the magnitude of sex differences, one thing upon which researchers agree is that males have more variability in their distribution of scores on cognitive abilities than females (see Figure 4.9). Thus slightly more males than females are at both the higher and lower ends of the distribution. The explanation for this finding is not clear, but it has implications for studies in which select populations are evaluated, such as talented children or children with difficulties.

One theory of general intelligence suggests that there are two dimensions of intelligence, one being an image-rotation versus verbal dimension and one being a focus of attention versus diffusion of attention dimension (Johnson & Bouchard, 2007), as shown in Figure 4.10. The first dimension ranges

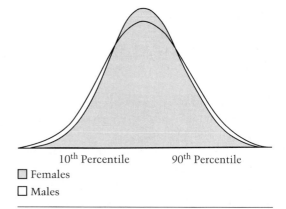

10th Percentile   90th Percentile

☐ Females
☐ Males

FIGURE 4.9 Score distributions. On many tests of academic ability, males have more variability in their scores than females, meaning more males are at the high end and low end of the distribution.

from image rotation skills that involve shape manipulation such as the mental rotation task to verbal abilities. The attention dimension ranges from abilities that require a focus of attention to abilities that require attention to a variety of stimuli simultaneously. A study of 18- to 79-year-old adult twins who were reared apart showed that women are more likely to be located in the verbal diffuse quadrant, whereas men are more likely to be located in the image focus quadrant—although you can see from the figure that there also is great overlap.

Taken collectively, sex differences in most cognitive domains have decreased over time. It is not clear whether one sex is improving, another sex is deteriorating, or more recent studies are more methodologically sound. Standardized tests may be less biased today than they were 30 years ago. It is also possible that the political climate has contributed to the decrease in sex differences. The atmosphere has shifted from emphasizing to minimizing sex differences. The political climate may be a reaction to a true decline in differences, or this

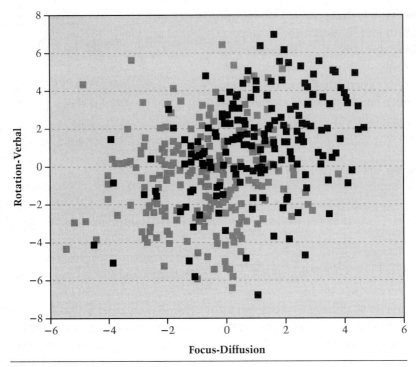

FIGURE 4.10   Women (indicated by the darker dots) score higher than men on abilities that are verbal and require diffuse attention, whereas men (indicated by the lighter dots) score higher than women on abilities that require spatial rotation and focused attention.
Source: Johnson and Bouchard (2007).

climate may contribute to a greater publication of studies that show no differences.

TAKE HOME POINTS

- In many cognitive domains, males' scores are more variable than females' scores.

- One way cognitive sex comparisons have been captured is that women are better at tasks that involve verbal abilities and diffuse attention, whereas men are better at tasks that require rotating objects and focused attention.

SEX COMPARISONS IN SOCIAL DOMAINS

Cognitive abilities are assessed by standardized tests and measures. Social abilities are a little trickier. How do we judge which sex is more helpful, more sexual, more empathic, or more aggressive? Should we rely on self-report measures? Do people know their own abilities, or will they distort their abilities in the direction of the ability they ought to have? Perhaps observing behavior is a better method to assess social abilities. But observers could be biased in their perceptions and interpretations of a behavior.

Each method has its advantages and disadvantages; thus in social domains, we look for consistency in findings across methodologies.

Empathy

Crying at a sad film, saying *I understand* to a friend who has disclosed a problem, and putting yourself in someone else's shoes are all different ways of empathizing. **Empathy** is defined in many ways, but at its core, it seems to involve feeling the same emotion as another person or feeling sympathy or compassion for another person. Sex differences in empathy, like sex differences in cognition, depend on how empathy is measured.

The one meta-analysis that has been conducted on empathy was conducted quite some time ago, and showed across 259 studies a sex difference in empathy, favoring females ($d = -18$; Eisenberg & Fabes, 1998). Despite the fact that the meta-analysis is dated, there are some lessons we can learn from it in regard to moderator variables. First, the sex difference was greater when empathy was measured by self-report than by observation. When measures that were less under the conscious control of the participant were used, such as facial expressions or parent/teacher observations, sex differences appeared in the same direction but of a much smaller magnitude. One concern with self-report measures is demand characteristics. Undoubtedly, men and women realize that women are supposed to be more empathic than men. Thus women and men may distort their self-reports of behavior in the direction of gender-role norms. See if you can find evidence of this problem in Do Gender 4.2.

When physiological measures of empathy are used (e.g., heart rate or skin conductance), there are no clear sex differences. However, it is not clear whether there is a unique physiological response associated with empathy. If your heart starts racing

DO GENDER 4.2
The Effect of Demand Characteristics on Reports of Empathy

Find a standardized empathy self-report scale. Develop two forms of the scale. Name one form "Empathy." Give the second form a title that would be more consistent with the male gender role or at least neutral with respect to gender, like "Environment Accuracy." Randomly distribute one of the two forms to 20 women and 20 men. Do women report more empathy than men on both forms?

when you watch a film of a woman getting attacked, what does this mean? Is it empathy, the actual experiencing of another person's distress? Is it compassion? Or is it discomfort at witnessing such a violent act?

A second moderator variable in the meta-analysis was how empathy was operationalized. Sex differences were larger when measures of kindness and consideration were used rather than measures of instrumental help. (This will help to clarify the finding in the next section on helping.) Third, the sex difference was larger in correlational and naturalistic than experimental studies. Finally, the sex difference was larger if the empathy target was an adult rather than a child, indicating that women and men respond more similarly to children.

At first glance, it appeared that the sex difference in empathy increased with age. However, when the aforementioned moderator variables were taken into consideration, there was no age effect. Age was confounded with study design. Studies of older children and young adults are more likely to be conducted in naturalistic settings where the sex difference is larger. Thus, the apparent age effect was really a study design effect.

Helping Behavior

Although I have shown you that the evidence women are more empathic than men is weaker than you might have assumed, you probably have every confidence that women are more helpful than men. Is this true? It is not true according to an older meta-analysis of helping behavior (Eagly & Crowley, 1986). The effect was in the direction of males helping more than females ($d = +.34$). The 172 studies in this review measured actual helping behavior or the self-report of a commitment to engage in a helping behavior; in other words, self-reports of general helpfulness were not included. The direction of this sex difference may seem surprising because helping is central to the female gender role. The sex difference was limited to a certain kind of help, however. That is, the situation was a moderator variable: Males were more likely than females to help in situations of danger. These early studies relied on experimental research that examined helping in the context of strangers. In the real world, most helping behavior occurs in the context of relationships.

Since this early meta-analysis, more recent literature concludes that men are more likely than women to help in situations of danger or emergencies, but that women are more likely than men to help within the context of relationships (Dovidio & Penner, 2001) and in nonthreatening situations such as volunteering (U.S. Department of Labor, 2009a). Thus, women and men are more likely to help in situations congruent with their gender roles. Women's help is communal (caring for an individual), and men's help is agentic (caring to gain status, heroic helping, and helping the group; Eagly, 2009). It may be that

the costs and rewards of helping differ across context for men and women. For example, women may perceive the cost of not helping to be greater in a situation that threatens relationships, such as a friend in distress, whereas men may perceive the cost of not helping to be greater in a situation that challenges masculinity, such as saving someone from drowning. As you will see in Chapters 8 and 9, both women and men are likely to turn to women for help in friendships and romantic relationships.

An important moderator variable in the early meta-analysis was the sex of the person in need of help. The sex of the recipient influenced whether a male helped but not whether a female helped. Males were more likely to help females than males, whereas females were equally likely to help females and males. There also was a sex difference in receipt of help. Women were more likely than men to receive help in general ($d = -.46$). In addition, women were more likely to receive help from men than women, whereas men were equally likely to receive help from men or women. Thus men helping women seems to be an especially prevalent kind of helping. Again, these results may be limited to situations involving strangers.

Several other moderators emerged in the meta-analysis. Sex differences were stronger under public conditions, where others could view the behavior, than under private conditions, where the behavior was anonymous. Females and males may behave differently in the presence of others because they are concerned with adhering to gender-role norms. In situations of danger, we expect men to provide help and women to receive help. The publication year was inversely correlated with the size of the effect, indicating the sex difference was getting smaller over time. Perhaps our expectations of men's and women's roles in situations of danger have changed over the years.

Aggression

- On November 6, 2009, in Fort Hood, Texas, Major Nidal Malik Hasan, a U.S. army officer, opened fire on soldiers who were having medical check-ups before deployment to Afghanistan, killing 13 and injuring 30 others (Allen & Bloxham, 2009).

- On August 5, 2009, a man walked into an LA Fitness Center dance class and opened fire, killing four and wounding eight others, before turning the gun on himself. Police found a log in which the gunman had planned the mass killing for months ("Four Dead," 2009).

- On April 16, 2007, Cho Seung-Hui killed a woman and a man at 7:15 a.m. in a dormitory at Virginia Poly-technic Institute. Two hours later he proceeded into an academic building and killed another 30 students in offices and classrooms, and then killed himself. Between the first killing and second massacre, he took time to stop at a mailbox and send a news station writings filled with anger and photographs of himself engaging in aggressive behavior.

- On October 2, 2006, Charles Carl Roberts IV, a 32-year-old truck-driver, carried a shotgun, a semi-automatic pistol, a rifle, two knives, and 600 rounds of ammunition into an Amish schoolhouse in Lancaster, Pennsylvania. He told the 15 boys to leave and then lined up the 6 girls before the blackboard and shot them before shooting himself ("Fifth girl dies," 2006).

- On April 20, 1999, Eric Harris and Dylan Klebold, two teenagers, killed 12 classmates and wounded 23 others within 16 minutes and then killed themselves at Columbine High School in Littleton, Colorado. They had intended to kill 488 people in the cafeteria with two bombs. Cho Seung-Hui had referred to Eric and Dylan as martyrs ("Sheriff Releases," 2000).

- And, of course, on September 11, 2001, 19 men on suicide missions hijacked four American planes in the United States, resulting in the collapse of the World Trade Center, an attack on the Pentagon, and the loss of thousands of lives.

- Finally, in the small town where I grew up (Bradley, Illinois), Timothy Buss at age 13 murdered and then mutilated the body of a 5-year-old girl in 1981. Fourteen years later, in 1995, after being released from prison on parole, Buss returned to the area and brutally murdered a 10-year-old boy (Cotliar, 1996).

What do all of these atrocities have in common? They were horrendous acts of violence that received a great deal of media attention, causing us, as a nation, to question the sources of such behavior. They also all involved male perpetrators. The public has taken note of such incidents, especially the Virginia Tech and Columbine massacres, because the perpetrators were so young. In the past decade, books that address the subject of troubled boys who become involved in violence have been best sellers, such as *Lost Boys: Why Our Sons*

Turn Violent and How We Can Save Them by James Garbarino (1999), *The Minds of Boys: Saving Our Sons from Falling Behind in School and Life* by Michael Gurian and Kathy Stevens (2007), and *The Purpose of Boys: Helping Our Sons Find Meaning, Significance, and Direction in Their Lives* by Michael Gurian (2009).

Sex of Perpetrator.   Observational studies of children confirm sex differences in aggression at an early age, and these differences generalize across cultures (Munroe et al., 2000). Boys are more likely than girls to use weapons and are more likely than girls to carry a weapon to school (Cao, Zhang, & He, 2008). A national survey of high school students showed that 27% of boys compared to 7% of girls had carried a weapon, such as a gun or a knife, in the past 30 days (Centers for Disease Control and Prevention, 2010a). These figures were roughly similar for White, Black, and Hispanic students, although White males were most likely to have carried any weapon (29%) and Black male students were most likely to have carried a gun (13%). Adolescent boys report a greater acceptance of aggression compared to girls and are more likely to use aggression to solve problems (Garaigordobil et al., 2009).

A meta-analytic review of sex comparisons showed that men were more aggressive than women (Bettencourt & Miller, 1996). Sex differences in verbal aggression were less consistent than sex differences in physical aggression. There were no sex differences in verbal aggression in the field ($d = +.03$) and only a small sex difference in the laboratory ($d = +.13$; Bettencourt & Miller, 1996). When more indirect forms of aggression, such as relational aggression, are examined (as discussed in Chapter 7), sex differences may disappear. Sex differences in aggression also seem to appear early in life. In a study of 17-month-olds, parents reported that boys were more likely than girls to kick, hit, and bite (Baillargeon et al., 2007). Boys were also 2.5 times more likely than girls to be classified as highly aggressive. The sex difference in aggression remained the same when these children were followed for 1 year.

Like the other domains in which women and men are compared, aggression is influenced by a variety of situational variables. One important situational factor is provocation, which may release women from the constraints the female gender role places on aggressive behavior. The Bettencourt and Miller (1996) meta-analysis showed that provocation led to greater aggression than nonprovocation, and that provocation altered the size of the sex difference in aggression. The sex difference was smaller under provocation conditions ($d = +.17$) than under neutral conditions ($d = +.33$). In addition, a judge's rating of the intensity of a provocation was negatively correlated with sex differences in aggression; in other words, the stronger the provocation, the smaller the sex difference.

Another situational variable that has been investigated is the emotional arousal generated by the situation. Because males may be more easily aroused than females and less able to regulate their emotions, Knight and colleagues (2002) predicted that sex differences in aggression would be minimal in situations of no/low or very high emotional arousal and maximal in situations of medium emotional arousal. As shown in Figure 4.11, at very low levels of arousal, one would expect sex differences to be small because both men and women can control their behavior. At very high levels of arousal, sex differences also would be small because emotion regulation is disrupted in both males and females.

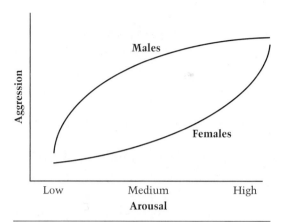

FIGURE 4.11 At low and high levels of arousal, sex differences in aggression are small. At medium levels of arousal, sex differences in aggression are largest.

However, at a moderate level of arousal, one would predict larger sex differences because males will experience the arousal more intensely, and males will be less able to regulate the arousal than females. Their results supported this hypothesis. Sex differences in aggression were significant when there was no arousal ($d = +.30$) but larger when there was a small or medium amount of arousal (both $ds = +.51$) and not significant when there was high arousal ($d = -.15$). The idea that men are less able to regulate their emotions is consistent with research that shows men are more impulsive than women and less able to delay gratification than women (Campbell, 2006).

Other features of the situation may contribute to sex differences in aggression. The meta-analysis showed that sex differences in aggression were larger when women had greater fears of retaliation (Bettencourt & Miller, 1996). Thus fears of retaliation are stronger deterrents of aggression for women than for men, whereas provocation is more likely to release women's inhibitions to behave aggressively.

Are sex differences in aggression getting smaller over time? As men's and women's roles have become more similar, have rates of aggression become more similar? One meta-analysis concluded that sex differences in aggression have not changed over time (Knight, Fabes, & Higgins, 1996). In terms of recent crime statistics, the arrest rate for girls has increased at a faster pace than that for boys. The increase in violence among girls may be more "apparent" than real, however. See Sidebar 4.1 for a discussion of this issue.

Measuring aggression is not as easy as you might think. The limitations of self-report methods are obvious. Are observations of behavior any more objective? We know from previous chapters that the same behavior may be construed differently when it is observed in a man or a woman. We may have a lower threshold for labeling a behavior as aggressive when the perpetrator is female compared to male. Examine how sex influences the perception of aggressive behavior with Do Gender 4.3.

Sex of Victim. Men are not only more likely than women to be the perpetrators of aggression, but they are also more likely than women to be the victims of aggression. We often lose sight of this latter fact. Men are more likely than women to report being victims of physical aggression. In a study of college students, men were twice as likely to report having been kicked, bitten, hit by a fist, and hit by another object (Harris, 1996). Men were three times as likely to report being threatened with a gun or knife. In a survey of over 15,000 sixth- through tenth-graders, more boys than girls reported being bullied in school (16% versus 11%; Nansel et al., 2003).

The sex of the perpetrator and the sex of the victim may be interrelated. A study of elementary school children found that boys

SIDEBAR 4.1: *Is Violence Increasing Among Women?*

In their book *The Female Offender*, Chesney-Lind and Pasko (2004) argue that the media sensationalize female violence in part because it is the exception rather than the rule, but that violent crime among women has not increased in recent years. As shown in Figure 4.12, arrests for violent crime have increased somewhat over the past few years for boys but have remained the same for girls—and arrests have remained substantially lower for girls than boys. The overall arrest rate has increased for both males and females—but the rate of increase has been greater for adolescent and adult women. These arrests, however, are for less serious crimes, such as larceny (shoplifting) and status offenses (e.g., running away from home and curfew violation). When one compares youths' self-report of these crimes to rates of arrest, it appears that girls are more likely than boys to be arrested for the crime. The same pertains to drug offenses. Although boys are much more likely than girls to be arrested for drugs, the rate of arrest has increased much more for girls than boys—despite the fact that the sex difference in usage has remained the same. Among adults there is an increasing number of women in prisons, but this increase is not due to an increase in violent crime among women but to an increase in less severe crimes, such as drugs and shoplifting. Even among white-collar crime, the typical female perpetrator differs from the typical male perpetrator. With the exception of Martha Stewart, the male who embezzles money is more likely to be a manager or an officer of the company, whereas the female who embezzles money is more likely to be a clerical worker or bank teller.

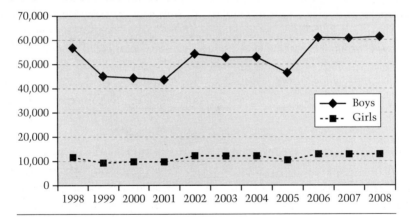

FIGURE 4.12   Total violent crime arrests (murder, forcible rape, robbery, and aggravated assault) for boys and girls under age 18.
Source: Adapted from Federal Bureau of Investigation, Uniform Crime Reports (1998–2008).

were more aggressive toward other boys than girls, but that girls were equally aggressive to boys and girls (Russell & Owens, 1999). However, the kind of aggression that girls used with boys and girls differed; girls tended to be physically aggressive with boys but used verbal and indirect aggression with girls.

Laboratory research shows that who aggresses against whom depends on the characteristics of the perpetrator and the victim. In

DO GENDER 4.3
Perceptions of Aggressive Behavior

Create two different scenarios of aggressive behavior, one a more mild display of aggression and one a more severe or moderate display. For each scenario, manipulate the sex of the perpetrator and the sex of the victim. You will have four different versions of each of the two scenarios. Ask a group of men and women to rate the aggressive behavior in terms of severity. Does the sex of the perpetrator, sex of the victim, or sex of the respondent influence perceptions? Does it depend on the severity of the aggression?

laboratory studies in which women and men compete with a confederate, men who subscribe to male gender-role norms are more aggressive to women who violate the female gender role than women who do not (Reidy et al., 2009) and to gay men than heterosexual men (Parrott, 2009). Women and men also respond differentially to others based on status. A laboratory study showed that women were more aggressive toward a low-status than a high-status person, whereas men were more aggressive toward a high status than a low-status person (Terrell, Hill, & Nagoshi, 2008)—but this held only for men and women who were evaluated as aggression-prone.

Sexuality

Are men the more "sexual" sex, or did the sexual revolution and the women's movement place women and men on more equal ground in the sexual arena? Again, the answer depends on how sexuality is defined. Petersen and Hyde (2010) conducted two meta-analyses on sexual attitudes and sexual

behaviors, one on 834 independent samples and one on 7 large national surveys conducted between 1993 and 2007. Most of these studies were conducted in the United States and Europe. This research addressed the file-drawer problem by including unpublished dissertations in the first meta-analysis and using national surveys in the second meta-analysis, regardless of their publication status.

The first meta-analysis showed sex differences for 26 of the 30 attitudes and behaviors, most of which were small. Results from both meta-analyses showed that men, compared to women, report more sexual partners (study 1: $d = +.36$; study 2: $d = +.15$), more casual sex ($d = +.38$; $d = +.18$), more frequent masturbation ($d = +.53$; $d = +.58$), and greater use of pornography ($d = +.63$; $d = +.46$). Small differences appeared for the sex difference in sexual satisfaction ($d = +.17$; $d = +.19$), condom use ($d = +.15$; $d = +.15$), oral sex ($d = +.06$; $d = +.16$), and attitudes toward premarital sex ($d = +.17$; $d = +.10$)—all in the direction of sexual behavior being greater in men than women. The one exception was the frequency of same-sex sexual behavior which was small but in the direction of females more than males ($d = -.05$; $d = -.03$). The sex difference in attitudes toward extramarital sex was small ($d = +.01$; $d = +.04$), but the sex difference in extramarital sex experiences was larger, in the direction of men ($d = +.33$; $d = +.12$).

In terms of attitudes, one area in which sex differences are found is attitudes toward homosexuality. Women reported more favorable attitudes than men toward gay men (study 1: $d = -.18$; study 2: $d = -.14$), but there were no sex differences in attitudes toward lesbians ($d = -.02$; $d = +.06$). Gender role and gender-role attitudes may be more strongly linked to attitudes toward homosexuality than sex per se. People who score high on hypermasculinity (extreme masculinity), have traditional gender-role attitudes, have a greater desire for dominance, and score high on benevolent or modern sexism have the most negative attitudes toward homosexuality (Kite & Whitley, 2003; Whitley & Egisdottir, 2000). This is not surprising because homosexual behavior is a threat to traditional beliefs about men's and women's roles. Men are less tolerant than women of homosexuality because violation of the male gender role has more negative consequences. Because the male gender role has a higher status in our society, there is more to lose by violating the role.

Are sex differences in sexual behavior limited to young people, or do they persist across the lifespan? Petersen and Hyde (2010) examined age as a moderator variable but noted it was difficult to evaluate because most studies were of adolescents or young adults (i.e., college students). Sex differences in the incidence of intercourse, attitudes toward extramarital sex, and attitudes toward lesbians decreased with age. Year of publication was an important moderator of these sex differences. Sex differences in incidence of intercourse, casual sex, attitudes toward casual sex, and attitudes toward lesbians became smaller with time.

Because the meta-analysis included data from several countries, the authors examined whether the gender equity of the country influenced the size of the sex differences. A gender equity measure was constructed based on the percentage of women in parliament, the percentage of women legislators, and women's income relative to men. Countries that scored higher on the gender empowerment measure revealed smaller sex differences in incidence of intercourse, oral sex, casual sex, masturbation, and attitudes toward gay marriage.

The authors were unable to examine ethnicity as a moderator variable for most of the sexual attitudes and behaviors because studies in the United States typically had mixed ethnicities; studies outside the United States typically examined European Americans leaving little variability in ethnicity. Yet, a few differences appeared. There were larger sex differences for incidence of intercourse among African Americans and smaller differences among Asian Americans compared to European Americans. There were smaller sex differences in masturbation among African Americans compared to European Americans.

One problem with research on sexuality is that the data, for obvious reasons, are gathered via self-report rather than observation. Thus the conclusion we reach is that women and men report differences in sexual attitudes and behaviors. We must be cautious in interpreting these findings because demand characteristics (i.e., men's and women's desire to adhere to their gender roles) may influence the reports. One study demonstrated the influence of demand characteristics on sexual behavior with the use of a bogus pipeline (Alexander & Fisher, 2003). With a bogus pipeline, the respondent is hooked up to a nonfunctioning polygraph and led to believe that the machine can detect false answers. When college students were randomly assigned to a bogus pipeline condition compared to an anonymous condition (answers confidential) or a threatening condition (experimenter may see responses), the sex difference in reports of some sexual behaviors disappeared. As shown in Figure 4.13, reports of sexual behaviors for which there are gender-related expectations (i.e., masturbation and viewing pornography) were similar for males across the three conditions but differed for females. Females admitted to more of these kinds of sexual behaviors when their responses were anonymous and even more of these behaviors in the bogus pipeline condition.

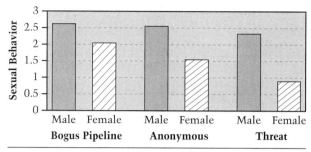

FIGURE 4.13   Men's reports of sexual behavior were not affected by condition. However, women reported more sexual behavior when responses were anonymous and when led to believe that false answers could be detected by a polygraph (i.e., bogus pipeline).
Source: Adapted from Alexander and Fisher (2003).

General Personality Attributes

A review of sex differences in personality traits across 26 cultures showed that sex differences in personality were small but consistent in the direction of men being more assertive, women being more submissive, women being more nurturant, and women having more negative affect (Costa, Terracciano, & McCrae, 2001). In a study of 55 countries, sex differences in the BIG 5 personality traits were examined (Schmitt et al., 2008). Women scored higher than men on neuroticism ($d = +.40$), extraversion ($d = +.10$), agreeableness ($d = +.15$), and conscientiousness ($d = +.12$), but there was no sex difference in openness to experience ($d = -.05$).

Interestingly, in both studies, sex differences were *smaller* among more traditional cultures. This is opposite to what we might have predicted. We would expect women's and men's behavior and thus their personality traits to differ the most in traditional cultures where female and male roles are most distinct. Costa and colleagues (2001) suggested that traditional cultures may link sex differences in behavior to "roles" rather

than "traits." That is, in traditional cultures, men and women are viewed as behaving differently due to their distinct social roles; no personality traits are inferred from behavior. Indeed, other research has shown that Western cultures are more likely than other cultures to link behavior to traits (Church, 2000), a bias referred to as the *fundamental attribution error*.

Sex differences in personality also may be more strongly linked to gender roles rather than sex. For example, empathy is associated with being female and with psychological femininity, or communion. The sex difference in empathy is completely accounted for by empathy's association with communion (Karniol et al., 1998).

TAKE HOME POINTS

- There is a sex difference in empathy, favoring females. The size of the effect depends on how empathy is measured, with larger differences appearing on self-report measures and smaller differences appearing on observational and behavioral measures.

- A meta-analysis on helping behavior showed that men help more than women, contrary to expectations. However, this sex difference is limited to situations of danger. In the context of relationships, women help more than men.

- Men are more likely than women to be the perpetrators and victims of aggression.

- Sex differences in aggression (male more than female) are smaller under conditions of provocation and very low or very high arousal.

- Compared to women, men have more permissive attitudes toward sex, engage in more casual sex, have more sexual partners, and engage in more masturbation. Women have more favorable attitudes toward homosexuality than men.

- There are sex differences in some personality traits. Sex differences seem to be larger in more egalitarian cultures where behavior is more strongly linked to traits.

- For all the domains of social behavior, measurement is an important moderator. Self-report measures are influenced by demand characteristics as men and women try to behave in ways that fit their gender roles (e.g., empathy). Consistent with this idea, sex differences for some behaviors are larger under public than private conditions (e.g., helping).

SEX COMPARISONS IN MORAL DEVELOPMENT

Imagine the following dilemma: Heinz has a wife who is dying, and he is unable to get a drug that would save her life. The only pharmacist who sells the drug is asking an exorbitant amount of money for it, and Heinz is poor.

This is the famous "Heinz dilemma." The question we are faced with is this: Should Heinz steal the drug? It is not the answer to the question that determines the extent of someone's moral development. Rather, it is the reasoning that is used to arrive at an answer.

This dilemma was used by Lawrence Kohlberg (1981) in his creation of a six-stage theory of moral development (see Table 4.1). Kohlberg evaluated people's stages of moral development by presenting them with a series of hypothetical moral dilemmas and coding their responses. The first two stages of moral development are called *preconventional* and emphasize the physical consequences of behavior. In other words, people decide for or against a behavior out of a fear of punishment or a desire to be rewarded. The third and fourth stages are called the *conventional* stages and emphasize the importance of rules and laws; the third stage emphasizes conformity to rules and others' expectations, whereas the fourth stage emphasizes the importance of maintaining law and order. The fifth and sixth stages are referred to as *postconventional* and involve developing one's own internal standards, separate from those of society.

Kohlberg (1981) based his theory on a longitudinal study of boys, following them from elementary school through adulthood. Because Kohlberg's study excluded females, people began to question whether his theory applied to girls. Carol Gilligan was one such person. In 1982, she criticized Kohlberg's work, arguing that his stages did not fairly represent women's views of moral reasoning. Gilligan said that women often ended up being classified as having a lower stage of moral development than men when using the Kohlberg scheme. Girls often were classified at the third stage of development, which emphasizes how others feel about the situation, pleasing others, and gaining approval from others. Boys, by contrast, were more likely to be classified at the

TABLE 4.1 KOHLBERG'S STAGES OF MORAL DEVELOPMENT

1.	Preconventional	Concern for consequences; focus on punishment; obedience
2.		Concern for consequences; motivated by rewards
3.	Conventional	Conformity to others' expectations; concern with disapproval
4.		Adhere to legitimate authority; emphasize rules and justice
5.	Postconventional	Concern with community respect; focus on law
6.		Developing internal standards; moral principles

Source: Kohlberg (1963).

fourth stage, which emphasizes rules and duties, or the postconventional stage, which emphasizes individual rights and personal standards.

Gilligan (1982) argued that women do not have a moral orientation that is inferior to men's but an orientation that is different from men's. She argued that women have a **morality of responsibility** that emphasizes their connection to others, whereas men have a **morality of rights** that emphasizes their separation from others. Women are concerned with their responsibilities to others, others' feelings, and the effect their behavior has on relationships, whereas men are concerned with rights, rules, and standards of justice. Gilligan stated, "While she places herself in relation to the world . . . he places the world in relation to himself" (p. 35). Kohlberg's stages of moral development emphasize the importance of developing a sense of justice, whereas Gilligan emphasizes the importance of a responsibility or care orientation.

Do women and men really think about morality differently? A meta-analysis of 160 independent samples showed a small sex difference in moral reasoning (Jaffe & Hyde, 2000). Women scored higher than men on a care orientation ($d = -.28$), and men scored higher than women on a justice orientation

($d = +.19$). However, a number of variables moderated these effects. One important moderator was the procedure used to elicit moral reasoning. Sex differences were larger when participants were asked to describe their own personal dilemmas (the procedure used by Gilligan) than when participants responded to standard dilemmas (the procedure used by Kohlberg). Thus it may not be that men and women reason about morality differently; instead, men and women may be faced with different kinds of moral dilemmas. Women face those that require a care orientation, and men face those that require a justice orientation.

Reactions to a real-life moral dilemma were examined in a web-based survey administered across the United States within a couple of months after 9/11 (Mainiero, Gibson, & Sullivan, 2008). Reactions were examined in terms of a care or justice orientation. Women scored higher than men on both care orientation reactions (e.g., I have a greater need to connect with others) and justice orientation reactions (e.g., I am concerned about the resolution of this conflict and achieving justice), although the sex difference in the care orientation was larger. Thus, women may have had a stronger response overall than men but did not differ so much from men in their relative response.

Thus, when women and men are faced with a similar moral issue, they may respond in similar ways.

Sex differences in morality also are likely to be influenced by ethnicity and culture. In a study of 600 middle schoolers, White females, Black males, and Black females viewed moral behavior in terms of its effects on an individual's well-being, similar to a care orientation, whereas White males viewed moral behavior more from a rule-based perspective, similar to a justice orientation (Jackson et al., 2009).

Morality can be construed in other ways besides Kohlberg's theory. If one views morality in terms of attitudes toward extramarital affairs, divorce, or legalizing marijuana, for example, women hold more traditional views than men (Eagly et al., 2004). Women also score higher on an index of social compassion, which reflects issues such as gun control, racial discrimination, decrease in the income differential between rich and poor, and the death penalty. These sex differences have remained the same over 25 years.

One reason for some of these sex differences in morality is that women are more religious than men, and religiosity underlies attitudes toward some of these social issues. A 2007 study from Pew Research showed that 77% of women compared to 65% of men believe in God, 63% of women compared to 49% of men say that religion is very important to them, and 44% of women compared to 34% of men attend weekly services (Pew, 2009a).

TAKE HOME POINTS

- Kohlberg's (1981) theory of moral development was criticized for excluding women during its creation; the concern was that women emerged as morally inferior to men.

- The controversy sparked the concept of two different views of morality, one emphasizing individual rights (justice) and the other emphasizing responsibility to others (care). The former was said to characterize men, and the latter was said to characterize women.

- However, research has shown that it is not so much that men and women view morality differently as that men and women face different kinds of moral dilemmas. Men seem to face moral dilemmas that focus on justice, and women seem to face moral dilemmas that focus on relationships.

SEX COMPARISONS IN SOCIAL DEVELOPMENT

List 10 responses to the following question: "Who am I?" Your responses to this question indicate how you define yourself, that is, your identity. The achievement of an identity is one of several stages of Erikson's (1950) stages of social development. According to his theory, social development proceeds through a set of stages; the issues of one stage of development must be resolved successfully before proceeding to the next stage. The identity stage precedes the intimacy stage. That is, one must have established a firm identity before one can establish a truly intimate relationship.

People who study gender have taken issue with the sequence set forth by Erikson. If the achievement of an identity precedes the achievement of intimacy, how do we explain the person who achieves his or her identity in part by connection to others? Some researchers have argued that Erikson's sequence may describe men's social development better than women's social development (Gilligan, 1982; Marcia, 1993) because women are more likely to experience identity and intimacy simultaneously. That is, part of women's identity is their relationship with others.

Early research on adolescents supported this theory (Douvan & Adelson, 1966). Boys formed their identities by making concrete occupational plans, whereas girls' future plans were unclear—their identity would be shaped by whom they married. Thus girls' identities were a consequence rather than an antecedent of intimacy. Did this mean boys had reached a higher level of social development than girls? No. At that time, boys and girls were socialized in ways that made for very different identity formations.

Even today, women's and men's social development may follow different courses. Studies have shown a stronger relation between identity and intimacy development in men than in women because intimacy is as likely to precede as to follow identity development in women (Orlofsky, 1993). A study of high school students showed that identity issues were more salient than intimacy issues in both male and female decision making (Lacombe & Gay, 1998). However, female students were more likely than male students to merge the two concerns. A study of early adolescents showed that males had a stronger identity development than females, but that identity development increased more with age among females (Montgomery, 2005). Thus we may socialize males to focus on identity development earlier than females, and it may take females longer than males to fully develop their identity.

TAKE HOME POINTS

- According to Erikson's theory of social development, identity achievement precedes intimacy achievement.

- Some research suggests that this theory may apply more to men than to women, as women are more likely to work on the two tasks simultaneously. That is, women are more likely than men to define themselves in part through intimate relationships.

SEX SIMILARITIES HYPOTHESIS REVISITED

Having reviewed all the sex differences in this chapter, you may feel a bit overwhelmed. Are there sex differences in cognitive and social abilities or not? Hopefully, you have reached two conclusions: (1) there are few sizable sex differences, and (2) among the ones that do exist, there is a host of moderator variables. These points have been driven home by a review article of 46 meta-analyses on sex differences, many of which were discussed in this chapter. From this review, Hyde (2005a) concludes that it is not the case that "men are from Mars and women are from Venus." As shown in Figure 4.14, the vast majority of effect sizes are quite small.

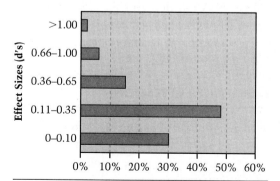

FIGURE 4.14 Effect sizes for sex differences in cognition, communication, social and personality variables, self-esteem, motor skills, activity, and moral reasoning.
Source: Adapted from Hyde (2005a).

SUMMARY

I reviewed the evidence for sex differences in cognitive abilities, specifically spatial skills, math skills, and verbal skills. Overall, most of the differences are small. For each domain, the size of the sex difference varies with how the ability is assessed. For example, in the spatial skills domain, there is a more substantial sex difference favoring males for one particular skill, the mental rotation task, but negligible differences for the other spatial skills. Sex differences in math skills seem to have disappeared with time, although a sex difference in SAT scores persists. In terms of verbal skills, many differences are small, but the female advantage in writing is an exception. The size of many sex differences depends on the nature of the population. For example, sex differences in verbal skills are influenced by the population studied; among children with verbal difficulties, there is a preponderance of boys over girls. For many of these areas of cognition, the differences seem to be getting smaller with time.

I also reviewed the evidence for sex differences in a number of social behaviors. Many domains show larger sex differences when self-report methods are used compared to more objective measures of behavior. For example, self-reports of empathy demonstrate a substantial sex difference favoring women, but observational measures are less clear. Other sex differences in social behavior are influenced by the environment; for example, sex differences in aggression are reduced under conditions of provocation. One limitation of much of this research is a lack of external validity because social behavior is often studied in the laboratory, where the natural context is removed.

Two stage theories of development, moral development and social development, may differ for women and men. Men may define morality in terms of justice and women in terms of responsibility or connection to others. If true, previous theories of moral development may unfairly represent women as inferior. However, it appears that women and men have similar views of morality but face different moral dilemmas that call for construing morality differently. The problem with previous theories of social development is that the sequence of establishing an identity before achieving intimacy may describe men's experiences more than women's.

DISCUSSION QUESTIONS

1. After reading one of the meta-analytic reviews cited in this chapter, what are some of the details on the procedures used and what are some more specific findings?
2. For which of the cognitive domains is there the most evidence of sex differences? Sex similarities?
3. What are some common moderator variables of sex differences in math, verbal, and spatial skills?
4. Among the cognitive domains examined, which sex differences seem to be disappearing with time, and which seem to have persisted?
5. To What does the sex difference in *variability* refer?

6. Which cognitive differences between women and men seem most likely due to environmental factors, and which seem most likely due to biological factors?
7. What are some of the methodological problems in making sex comparisons in social behavior?
8. What are some moderator variables of sex differences in aggression?
9. Do women and men define morality differently?
10. How are identity and intimacy related for men and women today? Should Erikson's theory be modified?

SUGGESTED READING

Gilligan, C. (1982). *In a different voice: Psychological theory and women's development.* Cambridge, MA: Harvard University Press.

Halpern, D. F., Benbow, C. P., Geary, D. C., Gur, R. C., Shibley Hyde, J., & Gernsbacher, M. A. (2007). The science of sex differences in science and mathematics. *Psychological Science in the Public Interest, 8,* 1–51.

Hyde, J. S. (2005a). The gender similarities hypothesis. *American Psychologist, 60,* 581–592.

(Classic) Maccoby, E. E., & Jacklin, C. N. (1974). *The psychology of sex differences.* Stanford, CA: Stanford University Press.

KEY TERMS

Confirmatory hypothesis testing—Process of noticing information that confirms stereotypes and disregarding information that disconfirms stereotypes.

Construct validity—Evidence that a scientific instrument measures what it was intended to measure.

Effect size—Size of a difference that has been found in a study.

Empathy—Ability to experience the same emotion as another person or feel sympathy or compassion for another person.

File-drawer problem—Difficulty encountered when compiling a review of scientific literature because studies showing null results are unlikely to be published.

Gender intensification—Concern on the part of girls and boys with adherence to gender roles; applies to adolescence.

Meta-analysis—Statistical tool that quantifies the results of a group of studies.

Moderating variable—Variable that alters the relation between the independent variable and the dependent variable.

Morality of responsibility (care orientation)—Moral reasoning that emphasizes connections to others, responsibilities, and others' feelings.

Morality of rights (justice orientation)—Moral reasoning that emphasizes separation from others, rights, rules, and standards of justice.

Narrative review—Review of scientific literature in which the authors reach their own conclusions about whether the majority of studies provide evidence for or against the topic of the review (e.g., sex differences).

CHAPTER 5

Sex-Related Comparisons: Theory

Now the opposite of the male is the female. … In human beings the male is much hotter in its nature than the female. On that account, male embryos tend to move about more than female ones, and owing to their moving about they get broken more, since a young creature can easily be destroyed owing to its weakness. And it is due to this self-same cause that the perfecting of female embryos is inferior to that of male ones. … We should look upon the female state as being as it were a deformity, though one which occurs in the ordinary course of nature. (Aristotle, 1963; pp. 391, 459, 461)

Aristotle had one theory of sex differences. Somewhat later, John Gray (1992) set forth another in *Men Are from Mars, Women Are from Venus*:

One day long ago the Martians, looking through their telescopes, discovered the Venusians. Just glimpsing the Venusians awakened feelings they had never known. They fell in love and quickly invented space travel and flew to Venus. The Venusians welcomed the Martians with open arms. … The love between the Venusians and the Martians was magical. They delighted in being together, doing things together, and sharing together. Though from different worlds, they reveled in their differences. … Then they decided to fly to Earth. In the beginning everything was wonderful and beautiful. But the effects of Earth's atmosphere took hold, and one morning everyone woke up with a peculiar kind of amnesia. … Both the Martians and Venusians forgot that they were from different planets and were supposed to be different. … And since that day men and women have been in conflict. (pp. 9–10)

These two theories about the origin of sex differences are quite different and hardly comparable. The first was developed by a famous world-renowned philosopher, the second by a person with a questionable educational background. But both theories share the idea: Men and women are opposites.

In Chapter 4, I reported a number of sex-related differences. In this chapter, I address the explanation of those differences. These theories are applicable to the origin of sex differences in cognition and social behavior, as well as to the development of gender roles. I discuss biology, including the role of genes, hormones, and brain anatomy, and evolutionary theory, a field that applies biological principles to the understanding of social behavior. I examine psychoanalytic theory, social learning theory, cognitive development theory, and a bridge of the latter two theories—gender schema theory. I discuss at length gender-role socialization and a related theory, social role theory. I end the chapter by presenting a premier social psychological theory of sex differences that emphasizes the more immediate (i.e., situational) factors (Deaux & Major, 1987).

As you will see, there is no one correct theory. The answer is not either nature (e.g., genes) or nurture (e.g., socialization) but a combination of the two. Each has something to contribute to discussions of the origin of sex differences and the development of gender roles.

BIOLOGY

Biological theories of sex differences identify genes and hormones, as well as the structure and function of the brain, as the causes of observed differences in cognition, behavior, and even gender roles.

Genes

Could gender roles be hardwired? Are there specific genes linked to masculinity and femininity? The contribution of genes to femininity and masculinity has been examined by comparing monozygotic twins (also known as identical twins) who share 100% of their genes to dizygotic twins (fraternal twins) who share 50% of their genes. The theory behind these twin studies is that genes explain the greater similarity in behavior between identical twins compared to fraternal twins because the environment for both sets of twins is the same, but the genes differ. One such study of 3- and 4-year-old twins examined the genetic and environmental contribution to sex-typed behavior (Iervolino et al., 2005). There was greater correspondence in behavior among monozygotic than dizygotic twins, and greater correspondence between dizygotic twins than siblings. In the end, the authors concluded that both genetics and environment made significant contributions to sex-typed behavior, but that the genetic contribution was stronger for girls than boys. The same twins were examined to determine the genetic and environmental contribution to gender atypical behavior (Knafo, Iervolino, & Plomin, 2005). Genes were said to account for a moderate amount of the variability, but environment was said to account for a substantial portion of variability. Again, the genetic component was stronger for girls than boys.

Twin studies also have been used to examine the heritability of homosexuality. The concordance of homosexuality is considerably higher among monozygotic twins than dizygotic twins—20% to 24% compared to 10% or less (Hyde, 2005b). This difference applies to both gay men and lesbians. However, if one identical twin is homosexual, the chance that the other identical twin is homosexual is far from 100%.

One question to raise about twin studies is whether the environment of identical twins is really the same as the environment of fraternal twins. I have twin nephews who are identical. One of people's first responses to them when they were born was to look for similarities. In fact, people sent them all sorts of newspaper stories depicting bizarre twin coincidences, which encouraged them to look for similarities. Thus, I wonder if there is more environmental similarity for identical than fraternal twins because people create more similar environments.

Aggression is one social behavior for which there are clear-cut sex differences, and some of this difference has been attributed to biology. Twin studies find a much stronger correlation of aggressive behavior between monozygotic than dizygotic twins. A meta-analysis of 51 twin and adoption studies showed that genetics accounted for about 40% of antisocial behavior, including criminal behavior, delinquency, and behavioral aggression (Rhee & Waldman, 2002). Adoption studies are used to establish the contribution of genes to behavior by comparing the similarity in behavior between adopted siblings to the similarity in behavior between biological siblings who have been reared apart. One such study showed that there was a greater correspondence between parents' reports of family functioning and the rate of antisocial behavior in biological than in adopted children (Sharma, McGue, & Benson, 1996).

Sex-related chromosomal abnormalities also have been linked to aggression. An early genetic theory of aggression focused on the role of an extra Y chromosome in men (Manning, 1989). Some studies found a higher than average proportion of men with the XYY configuration in prison than in the normal population. However, more recent studies have called this finding into question. Even if the XYY pattern is linked to aggression, the vast majority of the criminal population does not have this extra Y chromosome, and a vast majority of people with the extra Y chromosome are not prisoners. Studies have shown that boys with the XYY pattern are more irritable and have more temper tantrums than boys without that

configuration. However, it also is the case that parents of these children are aware of the extra Y chromosome and the potential link to aggression. These parents may respond to their child's behavior differently, which may further encourage aggressive behavior.

Hormones

Hormones are chemicals produced by the endocrine system that circulate throughout the body. There are two classes of sex-related hormones: **estrogens** and **androgens**. The female sex hormones are estrogens, and the male sex hormones are androgens (e.g., testosterone). This does not mean, however, that females have only estrogens and males have only androgens; women and men have both classes of hormones, but in different amounts. Sex hormones affect the brain, the immune system, and overall health. Undoubtedly, hormones also influence behavior. The question is, to what extent?

How can we evaluate the effects of hormones on women's and men's behavior? It is not easy to manipulate people's hormone levels. One avenue of research that has enabled us to study the influence of hormones on behavior is the study of **intersex conditions**. Intersex conditions are ones in which there is some inconsistency between the individual's chromosomal sex and phenotypical sex. Either the person's physical appearance with respect to sex organs is inconsistent with the chromosomal sex or the person's physical appearance is ambiguous. One of the most common intersex conditions is congenital adrenal hyperplasia (CAH), a genetic disorder resulting from a malfunction in the adrenal gland that results in prenatal exposure to high levels of male hormones and a lack of cortisol. Girls with CAH may be mistaken for boys because their genitals are somewhat masculinized (e.g., enlarged clitoris); boys do not have any adverse effects on their genitals but may suffer other ill effects from an excess of androgen.

What is the consequence of exposure to an excess of androgens in utero? In terms of cognition, a meta-analytic review of the literature showed that girls with CAH have superior spatial skills compared to girls without CAH (Puts et al., 2008). The link of testosterone to spatial skills is not a simple one, however, because boys with CAH had inferior spatial skills compared to boys without CAH (Puts et al., 2008). Puts and colleagues suggested a curvilinear relation between androgens and spatial abilities, as shown in Figure 5.1, which would explain why exposure to androgens increases spatial abilities in girls but decreases

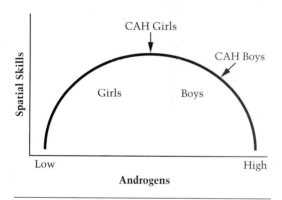

FIGURE 5.1 Hypothetical relation of androgen exposure to the development of spatial skills. Both low and high levels of exposure to androgens are related to lower levels of spatial skills. Because girls have lower levels of androgens than boys, increased exposure to androgens in utero (CAH) increases their spatial ability. By contrast, additional exposure to androgens among boys leads to decreased spatial ability. Thus, very low levels of androgens (non-CAH girls) and very high levels of androgens (CAH-boys) are associated with lower levels of spatial ability.
Source: Adapted from Puts et al. (2008).

spatial abilities in boys. There is also evidence that CAH females are similar to nonaffected males in terms of brain structure. In a study of brain activation in response to facial emotions, amygdala activation in CAH females was stronger than that observed among non-CAH females and similar to that observed among males (Ernst et al., 2007).

Is there any evidence that hormones are related to social behavior? Again, we can turn to the studies on CAH. In a study that compared 3- to 11-year-old CAH girls and boys to their unaffected siblings, CAH girls were more active and aggressive than non-CAH girls, similar to levels of non-CAH boys (Pasterski et al., 2007). There were no differences in activity or aggression between CAH and non-CAH boys. Similar findings have been shown with respect to play behavior. CAH girls are less likely to play with female toys and more likely to play with male toys, whereas play behavior in boys is unaffected by CAH (Hines, Brook, & Conway, 2004).

Researchers also have investigated whether exposure to prenatal androgens is linked to sexual orientation or gender identity problems. There may be a link between CAH and homosexuality or bisexuality in women (Hines et al., 2004). However, the size of this effect is small, meaning a majority of CAH women are heterosexual. In addition, it is the degree of prenatal exposure to androgens that seems to be related to a greater likelihood of homosexuality or bisexuality in CAH women (Meyer-Bahlburg et al., 2008). CAH does not seem to be associated with gender identity problems. In an examination of 250 individuals with CAH reared as females, only 13 reported any gender identity problems, 4 of whom wished to be male (Dessens, Slijper, & Drop, 2005).

There are three potential explanations for the link of CAH to spatial skills, masculine social behavior, and homosexuality (Puts et al., 2008). First, androgens could affect areas of the brain that are linked to spatial skills, masculine social behavior, and sexual orientation. Second, androgens could affect the tendency to engage in activities that affect cognition and behavior. For example, androgens make children more active, which then lead them to more masculine-type behavior. A specific social behavior that has been linked to activity and male hormones is aggression. See Sidebar 5.1 for a discussion of this issue. Third, the masculinization of appearance could somehow

influence behavior. Girls with CAH are often born with male genitalia, a condition usually altered with surgery. Thus the parents and the children are aware of prenatal exposure to androgens. Parents might expect the CAH child to exhibit more masculine behavior, provide the child with more masculine toys and masculine activities, and respond more favorably to masculine behavior displayed by the child. The child herself also might be more comfortable engaging in masculine activities because of her own awareness of the exposure to male hormones. It is difficult to disentangle this issue from the research.

SIDEBAR 5.1: *Does Testosterone Cause Aggression?*

Hormonal explanations for male violence often center on the male hormone, testosterone, which has been linked to frustration, impatience, impulsivity, high levels of physical activity, and sensation-seeking (Harris, 1999). But, is there any evidence that testosterone is linked to violence? A meta-analysis of 54 samples showed a weak but positive relation of testosterone to aggression ($d = +.28$; Book, Starzyk, & Quinsey, 2001). For males, the relation decreased with age such that the largest effect was observed among 13- to 20-year-olds ($d = +.58$). The most aggressive behavior seems to be linked to a combination of high testosterone and low cortisol (Terburg, Morgan, & van Honk, 2009). Studies of male prisoners have found that testosterone levels are higher among men who committed personal crimes of sex and violence than those who committed property crimes of burglary, theft, or drugs (Dabbs et al., 1995) and among men who committed more ruthless crimes (i.e., premeditated; Dabbs, Riad, & Chance, 2001). In addition, prisoners with high testosterone levels were more likely to have violated prison rules.

Thus a relation exists between aggression and testosterone, but the evidence is far from clear that testosterone plays any causal role in aggression. This area of research is largely correlational. Does testosterone cause aggression, or does behaving aggressively lead to a rise in testosterone? Or is there a third variable responsible for both? Competitive situations may be one such variable. In a study of college students, testosterone was measured prior to playing a competitive game (McDermott et al., 2007). Men made higher unprovoked attacks during the game than women, as did people who had higher levels of testosterone. Thus, testosterone appeared to account for the sex differences in aggressive behavior. Hormones also interact with situational factors, such as a threat to status or competition, to produce aggressive behavior (McAndrew, 2009). Some situational factors, such as noise or alcohol, could exacerbate the effects of hormones on aggression, whereas other situational factors, such as the knowledge the behavior is inappropriate for a specific situation, could inhibit the effect of hormones on aggression. See Figure 5.2 for a plausible model of how situational factors interact with biology to influence aggressive behavior.

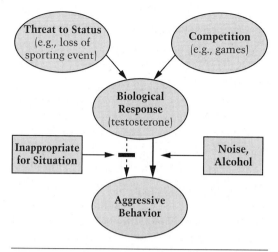

FIGURE 5.2 Factors such as competition and threat to social status may evoke a biological response which could increase aggressive behavior. Some factors, such as noise and alcohol, could magnify that response, whereas other factors, such as the knowledge the behavior is inappropriate for the situation, could inhibit the aggressive response. *Source:* Adapted from McAndrew (2009).

Another way to examine the effect of hormones on cognition and behavior is to examine the relation of different levels of hormones across women and men to a behavior. This kind of correlational design has been used by researchers who sample the amniotic fluid of pregnant women to measure prenatal exposure to testosterone. Higher levels of testosterone have been associated with more male-typical play behavior in 6- to 10-year-old girls and boys (Auyeung et al., 2009), greater **lateralization** of language at age 6 in girls and boys (Lust et al., 2010), and less empathy in 4-year-old girls and boys (Knickmeyer et al., 2006).

Some studies have begun to manipulate hormones to examine their effects on behavior. In one such experiment, testosterone was administered to healthy women and was found to improve their performance on the mental rotation task (Aleman et al., 2004). In a study of male college students, testosterone versus a placebo was administered prior to playing an economics game (Zak et al., 2009). The men who received the testosterone were less generous than the control group, and higher testosterone levels were associated with greater punishment of the competitor.

The relation of male hormones to gender-related behavior also has been studied among people who are genetically male (XY chromosome) but have an insensitivity to androgens. These individuals have what is known as *complete androgen insensitivity syndrome* (CAIS) and are born with testes instead of a uterus but have female genitalia. Recall that all fetuses begin with female genitalia but masculinizing hormones alter the genitals to become male; this does not occur in CAIS. The testes are typically surgically removed, and children are reared as females. One study compared 22 girls with CAIS to healthy girls and found no differences in gender-related behavior or personality traits (Hines, Ahmed, & Hughes, 2003). Here is a case where hormones seemed to override genetics. Historically, many people in the medical community believed hormones (and the social environment) could override genes in determining gender-role behavior. See Sidebar 5.2 for a discussion of a noteworthy case that challenged this perception.

If androgens have a "masculinizing" effect on girls, do estrogens have a "feminizing" effect? Most of the research addressing this question has come from exposure to a synthetic estrogen, diethylstilbestrol (DES), prescribed for pregnant women in the 1960s to prevent miscarriage. Its use was discontinued when it was linked to cancer. In a sample of over 8,000 men and women exposed to DES, there was no evidence that exposure

SIDEBAR 5.2: *Raising a Boy as a Girl—Nature Versus Nurture*

Twin boys, Brian and Bruce Reimer, were born to a couple in Canada in 1965. When Bruce was circumcised at 8 months, the penis was accidentally destroyed. Distraught, the parents turned to Dr. John Money, a noteworthy sex researcher from Johns Hopkins whom they saw on television. Dr. Money had said that you could change a child into a boy or a girl with surgery and hormones, and the child's genetics did not matter. The Reimers visited Dr. Money in 1967. Dr. Money suggested that the Reimers castrate Bruce and raise him as a girl. The parents followed Dr. Money's advice. They changed Bruce's name to Brenda, dressed him in girls' clothes, and gave him girl toys. Dr. Money published numerous articles about this study, citing it as a spectacular example of how a child's sex could be changed. The scientific reports claimed the entire family had adjusted easily to the situation. These results trickled down to the lay community, as evidenced by a *Time* magazine report: "This dramatic case...provides strong support...that conventional patterns of masculine and feminine behavior can be altered. It also casts doubt on the theory that major sex differences, psychological as well as anatomical, are immutably set by the genes at conception" (*Time*, January 8, 1973, p. 34).

However, a later report published by Diamond and Sigmundson (1997) in the *Archives of Pediatrics & Adolescent Medicine* and a biography of Bruce/Brenda written by John Colapinto (2000) suggested differently. Brenda rejected feminine toys, feminine clothing, and feminine interests right from the start. She had no friends, was socially isolated, and was constantly teased and bullied by peers. She perceived herself as a freak and believed early on she was a boy. When she expressed these concerns to Dr. Money during the family's annual visits to Johns Hopkins, they were ignored. During adolescence, Brenda was given hormones to develop breasts. She strongly objected to taking the hormones and often refused. By age 14, she had decided to become a boy and adopt the lifestyle of a boy. Finally, Mr. Reimer broke down and confessed to Brenda what had happened. In the biography, the teenager recalls feelings of anger and disbelief but mostly relief at his dad's revelation. Brenda started taking male hormones, had surgery to remove the breasts, and became David. At age 25, he married.

A short time later, David revealed the full story of his life to John Colapinto who wrote his biography, *As Nature Made Him* (Colapinto, 2000). Unfortunately, the past could not be erased for David. Facing the death of his twin two years earlier, marital difficulties, clinical depression, and unemployment, he took his own life on May 5, 2004. The author of his biography, John Colapinto, said that he was shocked but not surprised by the suicide and lamented that "the real mystery was how he managed to stay alive for 38 years, given the physical and mental torments he suffered in childhood that haunted him the rest of his life" (Colapinto, 2004).

was related to sexual orientation and little evidence that it was related to other psychosexual characteristics (Titus-Ernstoff et al., 2003).

A complicating factor in all of these studies is that prenatal exposure to hormones is not an all or none process. Within each of the conditions described earlier, there are different levels of exposure. The largest effects seem to appear at maximum levels of exposure. There also may be critical periods for exposure, and these critical periods may differ across domains of cognition and behavior (Hines et al., 2003). The evidence presented here suggests that the effects of prenatal hormones on gender-role behavior are stronger among girls than boys. It may be that gender-role behavior is more fluid in society for girls than for boys. Boys may feel stronger pressures to adhere to the male role, overcoming the impact of any prenatal hormone exposure.

The Brain

Perhaps the brain can explain sex differences in cognition by simply showing that women are "right-brained" and men are "left-brained"—or, is it the reverse? Spatial abilities are located in the right hemisphere, and verbal abilities are located in the left hemisphere. Aha! So it must be that males are right-hemisphere-dominant, and females are left-hemisphere-dominant. Unfortunately, this theory does not hold up for long. The left hemisphere is also responsible for analytical skills, those required in math; thus, if females are left-hemisphere-dominant, they should be better than males at math.

One possibility that researchers have entertained for decades is that women's brains are more bilateral than those of men; that is, women are more likely than men to use either hemisphere of their brain for a specific function. Men, by contrast, are said to be more lateralized, meaning the two hemispheres of the brain have more distinct functions. In support of this theory, researchers have tried to argue that women have a larger corpus callosum than men—the corpus callosum being the structure that connects the right and left hemispheres allowing for greater communication. However, there is controversy over whether there are sex differences in the size of the corpus callosum. To many people's surprise, a meta-analytic review of the literature showed no sex differences in the shape or size of the corpus callosum (Bishop & Wahlsten, 1997).

Thus, not surprisingly, there is not a lot of evidence for sex differences in lateralization.

In a meta-analytic review of sex comparisons of the lateralization of language, the overall effect size was not significant (Sommer et al., 2004). In a narrative review of the literature on sex comparisons of brain lateralization for a variety of cognitive tasks, sex seemed to account for between 1% and 2% of the variability in brain lateralization (Hiscock et al., 1995). However, in a meta-analytic review of sex differences in lateralization of spatial skills, men had a right hemisphere advantage and women were bilateral (Vogel, Bowers, & Vogel, 2003). Thus, most studies do not find a sex difference in brain lateralization, but among the ones that do, men appear to be more lateralized than women.

Research on the brain has proliferated in recent years, perhaps as a result of the 1990s being the "decade of the brain." In the area of gender, research has examined whether there are sex differences in the way the brain is structured and functions. One approach that researchers have taken is to see if different areas of the brain are activated for women and men when performing cognitive tasks. If true, this could explain sex differences in cognitive abilities. However, among adolescents, it appears that different areas of the brain are activated even when performance is the same (Lenroot & Giedd, 2010). Thus, differential activation does not always translate into differential performance. Females and males may use different strategies—which activate different parts of the brain—to achieve the same outcome. A study of adults showed that there was the same amount of brain activation among women and men during an object-naming task, but that different objects activated different regions in men and women, suggesting that the brain activation mechanism is very complicated (Garn, Allen, & Larsen, 2009).

There are literally thousands of studies that show sex differences in some aspects of the brain. However, a sex difference in a brain structure does not translate into a sex difference in a brain function (de Vries & Sodersten, 2009). As indicated earlier, a sex difference in an area of the brain does not always lead to a sex difference in behavior. Different structures or differential brain activation can lead to the same behavior. In addition, the brain is not constant, as behavior can alter the brain, as indicated by the following study of juggling. One group of young adults was taught how to juggle over a three-month period, and one group was not. Despite the fact that brain scans showed no differences between the two groups prior to the study, differences in brain structure related to motion processing emerged after three months for the juggling group (Draganski et al., 2004). However, the brain structure difference disappeared when juggling ceased. Thus, the meaning of sex differences in brain structure is not yet fully understood.

Not surprisingly, researchers also have examined whether different areas of the brain can be linked to gender identity. A study of male to female transsexuals on autopsy showed that one area of the brain—the hypothalamic uncinate nucleus—appeared more similar to that area of the brain in women than men (Garcia-Falgueras & Swaab, 2008), suggesting a biological basis for gender identity.

Psychobiosocial Models

A common objection to biological theories of sex differences and gender-related behavior is that any biological differences found between women and men will be used to justify the inferior status of women in society. However, ignoring biological differences between men and women will not help to understand cognition and behavior—nor will

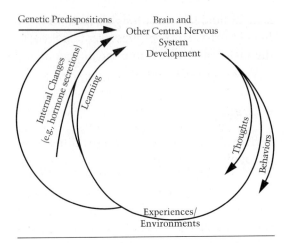

FIGURE 5.3   Psychobiosocial model showing the interrelation between biological, psychological, and social influences.
Source: Halpern, Wai, and Saw (2005).

it help to remedy any deficits found in one sex compared to the other (Halpern, Wai, & Saw, 2005). Halpern and colleagues propose an alternative theory to the traditional nature versus nurture model of sex differences—the psychobiosocial model. They argue that nature and nurture are not two mutually exclusive categories, but categories that interact with one another. As shown in Figure 5.3, biological factors operate within a social context. Even if biological differences exist, the environment can still exert an influence, and an important one at that!

TAKE HOME POINTS

- Twin and adoption studies conclude that genes play a role in sex differences in cognition and social behavior as well as gender-related behavior, but that role is far from 100%.

- The strongest evidence for links of sex hormones to cognition and behavior is in research that has shown prenatal exposure to male hormones (androgens) is associated with enhanced spatial skills and male gender-role behavior in women.

■ The major problem with most studies of the relations of hormones to behavior is that they are correlational; thus cause and effect cannot be established. Some recent studies have begun to manipulate hormones, specifically testosterone.

■ Studies of the brain reveal some sex differences in structure, but the meaning of those differences is unclear.

■ In sum, biological theories leave open to explanation much variability in the behavior of women and men.

EVOLUTIONARY THEORY AND SOCIOBIOLOGY

We typically think of evolution as explaining how humans developed from simpler organisms, not why men behave in masculine ways and women in feminine ways. Evolutionary psychology applies the principles of evolution to the study of cognition and behavior. Sociobiology examines the biological origins of social behavior—in other words, how social behavior evolved over time to perpetuate the species. Both evolutionary psychology and sociobiology are extensions of Darwin's theory of evolution, which states that we behave in ways to ensure the survival of our genes. The idea is that different behaviors may have evolved in women and men because the differences were adaptive for survival.

People often confuse the fields of sociobiology and evolutionary psychology. Although there is a great deal of overlap, there are some distinctions. One is that evolutionary psychology is not limited to the study of social behavior, as is sociobiology. Thus *evolutionary psychology* might be the more

appropriate term to use in the study of gender. There are other, more philosophical distinctions, such as whether the replication of genes is a goal that motivates behavior (sociobiology, yes; evolutionary psychology, no). These distinctions are beyond the scope of this text, but see David Buss's (2007) textbook *Evolutionary Psychology* for an elaboration of these issues.

Evolutionary theory can be applied to several domains of social behavior. Here, I discuss sexual behavior and aggression as examples (mate selection is discussed in Chapter 9). Evolutionary theory is also linked to the development of the hunter-gatherer society, which shaped women's and men's roles.

Sexual Behavior

Buss (1995) argues that we can observe sex differences in behaviors that historically presented men and women with different challenges. One such domain is sexual behavior. First, men and women face different challenges during pregnancy. Because conception takes place inside of the female, males face the challenge of establishing paternity. The challenge that females face is to safely get through nine months of pregnancy and the period of lactation. Thus males will behave in ways to increase their chances of paternity and females in ways to ensure the survival of themselves and their infants. Second, women and men face different challenges to successful reproduction. For women to reproduce successfully, it is in their best interests to be selective in choosing a man who has the resources to help ensure the survival of their children. For men to reproduce successfully, it is in their best interests to have sexual intercourse with as many women as possible and to mate with women who are more likely to be fertile (i.e., young).

This theory can explain some differences in sexual behavior, for example, why men have more favorable attitudes toward casual sex and a lower threshold for interpreting an ambiguous behavior by a female in sexual terms. The theory conflicts, however, with the finding that the sex difference in number of sexual partners is small and that the vast majority of both men and women prefer a long-term relationship over a short-term sexual relationship (Pedersen et al., 2002).

Cultural factors may have overridden the influence of evolutionary theory on sexual behavior. Due to the introduction of effective contraceptives, sexual behavior does not always lead to reproduction. The fact that contraceptives are so commonly used suggests that reproduction is often not the intention of sex. The sociobiological view of sex differences in sexual behavior assumes that sexual intercourse will lead—or is intended to lead—to reproduction. Today, I doubt that the majority of men are thinking about establishing paternity and the majority of women are thinking about their partners' ability to support a child when deciding whether or not to engage in sex.

Aggression

Evolutionary theory has been suggested as an explanation of sex differences in aggression, in part because sex differences emerge early in life (Archer, 2009). A meta-analysis of five studies of toddlers showed that sex differences in aggression are already substantial ($d = +.44$; Archer & Cote, 2005). In addition, sex differences in aggression are consistent over childhood (ages 6–11; $d = +.56$) and puberty (ages 12–17; $d = +.46$; Archer, 2004). Aggression peaks in young adulthood, at a time when men are in competition with each other for women and for the opportunity to reproduce. Consistent with this theory, crime statistics show same-sex homicide is highest between the ages of 18 and 30. A large number of same-sex homicides, in which the victim and the killer are unrelated, occur in the context of men trying to establish dominance or compete for status (Daly & Wilson, 2001). The question is whether competition over women is the precipitating factor. Evidence to support this proposition comes from research that shows married men have the lowest level of homicide rates, but formerly married men—that is, divorced and widowed men—have homicide rates that are similar to single men (Daly & Wilson, 2001).

Evolutionary theory also can be used to explain violence in families (Daly & Wilson, 1999). At first glance, familial violence would seem to violate the basic principles of evolutionary theory. However, a majority of homicides within families occur between spouses who are genetically unrelated to each other rather than between blood relatives. Women, but not men, are at greatest risk for being murdered when they try to end the relationship. Consistent with evolutionary theory, the primary motive men have for killing their spouses is sexual jealousy. Also consistent with evolutionary theory is the fact that young wives are most likely to be murdered, perhaps because youth is a sign of fertility, and fertility would make a woman more attractive to male rivals. Although young men are the individuals most likely to commit murder, the wife's age is a better predictor than the husband's age. Evolutionary theory also has been applied to the study of violence toward children. Among parents who abuse or kill their children, the incidence is much higher among stepparents than biological parents (Daly & Wilson, 1999). In sum, some patterns of violence are consistent with evolutionary principles.

The Hunter-Gatherer Society

Evolutionary theory suggests that the hunter-gatherer society developed from women's stronger investment in children compared to men. With women caring for children, men were left to hunt. The hunter-gatherer society has been linked to sex differences in both social behavior and cognition (Ecuyer-Dab & Robert, 2004). In terms of social behavior, men behave aggressively because aggression was required to hunt and feed the family; women evidence nurturance because nurturance was required to take care of children. Women became emotionally expressive and sensitive to the emotions in others because they were the primary caretakers of children. Men learned to conceal their emotions because a successful hunter needed to be quiet and maintain a stoic demeanor to avoid being detected by prey. In terms of cognition, men's greater spatial skills and geographic knowledge could have stemmed from their venturing farther from the home than women when hunting. Women's greater ability to locate objects could be linked to their having to keep track of objects close to home; foraging for food, in particular, required women to remember the location of objects.

A Final Note

Some people find sociobiology and evolutionary theory distasteful as an explanation for sex-related differences in cognitive and social behavior, in part because these theories make sex-related differences seem unchangeable and view traditional roles as "natural." The concern is that women's and men's different roles must have been—and still are—desirable if they led to survival. However, others suggest that evolutionary theory is not deterministic but interactionistic (Confer et al., 2010). The environment influences the mechanisms that evolve. All evolved mechanisms require some kind of environmental input. Behavior that evolved for survival reasons can be influenced by the culture, such as the example of the influence of birth control pills on sexual behavior. The goal of evolutionary theory is to understand the evolutionary forces that shape behavior. One limitation of evolutionary theory is the inability to explain behaviors that do not maximize reproductive success, such as homosexuality, adoption of children, and suicide. A second limitation is that evolutionary theory does not account for individual differences or cultural differences in behavior.

TAKE HOME POINTS

- Because males and females face different challenges in ensuring the survival of their genes, sex differences in sexual behavior have evolved. Males prefer to have sex with as many fertile women as possible, and females prefer to have sex with a male who can provide economic resources to ensure the survival of their children.

- Because men are in competition with one another over women, men behave in aggressive ways especially when trying to establish dominance or when competing with rivals.

- Women's greater investment in children could be one explanation for the evolution of the hunter-gatherer society. The structure of that society has been linked to some sex differences in social behavior and cognition.

- Evolutionary theory has a deterministic tone but is really interactionistic, as evidenced by the fact that cultural factors can override earlier evolved tendencies.

PSYCHOANALYTIC THEORY

The first name that comes to mind in response to psychoanalytic theory is Sigmund Freud (see Figure 5.4). Freud (1924, 1925) was a physician and a psychoanalyst who developed a theory of personality, most notable for its emphasis on the unconscious. Although his emphasis on the effects of the unconscious on behavior is one of the most noteworthy tenets of his theory, his reliance on unconscious processes also makes his theory very difficult to test.

Freud articulated a series of psychosexual stages of development, the third of which focused on the development of gender roles. According to Freud, stage 3, the phallic stage, develops between 3 and 6 years of age. It is during this stage of development that boys and girls discover their genitals and become aware that only boys have a penis. This realization leads girls and boys to view girls as inferior. It is also during this time that boys are sexually attracted to their mothers, view their fathers as rivals for their mothers' affections, and fear castration by their fathers because of their attraction to their mothers. Boys resolve this castration anxiety, and thus the Oedipal complex, by repressing their feelings toward their mothers, shifting their identification to their fathers, and perceiving women as inferior. This is the basis for the formation of masculine identity.

Girls experience penis envy and thus feel inferior to boys. Girls are sexually attracted to their fathers, jealous of their mothers, and blame their mothers for their lack of a penis. Girls' eventual awareness that they cannot have their fathers leads to a link between pain and pleasure in women, or masochism. Females handle their conflict, known as the Electra complex, by identifying with their mothers and focusing their energies on making themselves sexually attractive to men. Thus self-esteem in women becomes tied to their physical appearance and sexual attractiveness. According to Freud, the Electra complex is not completely resolved in the same way that the Oedipal complex is resolved—partly due to the clearer threat for boys than girls (fear of castration) and partly due to girls having to face a lasting inferior status. According to Freud, how boys and girls resolve all of these issues has implications for their sexuality and future interpersonal relationships.

Several difficulties are inherent in this theory of gender-role acquisition. Most important, there is no way for it to be evaluated from a scientific standpoint because the ideas behind it are unconscious. We must be even more cautious in taking this theory seriously when we realize Freud developed it by studying people who sought him out for therapy.

FIGURE 5.4   Sigmund Freud, the father of psychoanalytic theory.

Freud had many critics. A notable one was Karen Horney (1926, 1973), a feminist psychoanalyst and physician. Like Freud, she placed a great deal of emphasis on the unconscious and the importance of sexual feelings and childhood experiences in personality development. However, Horney believed social forces rather than biology influenced the development of gender identity. She said girls' penis envy did not reflect a literal desire for a penis but reflected a desire for men's power and status in society. She argued that men also experience envy—envy of women's breasts and ability to bear children. She believed men perceive women as inferior as a way to elevate their own status. In fact, she argued that men's feelings of inferiority are responsible for men's need to prove their masculinity through sexual intercourse.

A more modern version of psychoanalytic theory, referred to as object-relations theory, was applied to the acquisition of gender roles by Nancy Chodorow (1978) in her book *The Reproduction of Mothering*. Chodorow's theory emphasizes the importance of early relationships in establishing gender identity. Like other psychoanalytic theorists, she stresses the importance of sexuality, but she believes the family structure and the child's early social experiences, rather than unconscious processes, determine sexuality. She believes that the fact that women are the primary caretakers of children is responsible for the development of distinct gender roles. Both boys' and girls' first primary relationship is with their mothers, a relationship that affects boys' and girls' sense of self, future relationships, and attitudes toward women.

According to Chodorow (1978), girls acquire their gender identity by connecting with the one person with whom they are already attached: their mother. This explains why females focus on relationships and define themselves through their connection to others. In later years, girls have difficulty finding the same intimate attachment to men. Boys, by contrast, acquire their gender identity by rejecting the one person with whom they have become attached, by separating or individuating themselves from their mothers. Thus males learn to repress relationships and define themselves through separation from others. With whom do boys identify? Because fathers are less of a presence than mothers in children's lives, fewer models are available to boys; thus boys come to define masculinity as "not being feminine" or not being like their mothers. Whereas girls learn the feminine role by observing their mothers on a day-to-day basis, boys may find themselves identifying with cultural images of masculinity to learn their gender role.

Because girls identify with their mothers, their tendency to mother "reproduces" itself. Chodorow (1978) argues that women have a greater desire than men to be parents because they are more likely to have identified with a parenting role. According to Chodorow, the fact that women are the primary caretakers of children in our society leads directly to the division of labor (i.e., men working outside the home and women working inside the home) and the subsequent devaluation of women in society. The only way these roles can change, according to Chodorow, is for men to become more involved in raising children. Given the decline of the nuclear family and the greater diversity of family structures today, it is possible to test Chodorow's theory. Conduct Do Gender 5.1 to determine if children have more traditional gender roles when they are raised in a traditional family structure compared to a nontraditional family structure. Like Freud's theory, Chodorow's theory also lacks empirical data.

TAKE HOME POINTS

- Freud's psychoanalytic theory of gender development rested on unconscious processes that emphasized the role of penis envy, the Oedipal complex, and the Electra complex in girls' and boys' relationships and sexuality.

- Karen Horney, a critic of Freud, also emphasized unconscious processes but believed the issues outlined by Freud were due to social forces rather than biology.

- A more modern version of psychoanalytic theory was developed by Nancy Chodorow who emphasized the role of women as primary caretakers in the family on the development of girls' and boys' gender identities.

DO GENDER 5.1
Testing Chodorow's Theory

According to Chodorow, female and male gender roles are grounded in the fact that girls and boys are raised by mothers. This leads to the prediction that children's gender roles will be more traditional when they are raised in two-parent families where the father works outside the home and the mother works inside the home. What would you predict if both parents worked? What would you predict in single-parent families—mother only? Father only? What would you predict in families where the father stays at home and the mother works outside the home?

Answer one of these questions by comparing two kinds of families: the traditional nuclear family (two parents, father works outside the home, mother works inside the home) and a nontraditional family (your choice).

Have the children in each family complete a measure of gender roles or gender-related attitudes from Chapter 2. Record the child's sex. See if children's gender roles are more traditional when raised in traditional than nontraditional families.

SOCIAL LEARNING THEORY

Most people recognize that the social environment plays a role in women's and men's behavior but could the social environment contribute to sex differences in cognition? There are several reasons to believe that social factors play a role here, too (Spelke, 2005). First, sex differences in math and science achievement vary across cultures. Second, some domains of sex differences, such as math, have decreased over time. Thus, biology alone cannot account for observed differences between females and males in cognition. The remaining theories in this chapter are variants on the idea that the social environment plays a role in how women and men think and behave.

The most basic social factors theory is social learning theory (Bandura & Walters, 1963; Mischel, 1966), which states that we learn behavior in two ways. First, we learn behavior that is modeled; second, we learn behavior that is reinforced. These are the primary principles of social learning theory, and they apply to the acquisition of gender-role behavior as they do to any other domain of behavior (Mischel, 1966).

Observational Learning or Modeling

Children develop gender roles by patterning their behavior after models in the social environment. Modeling, or observational learning, is "the tendency for a person to reproduce the actions, attitudes, and emotional responses exhibited by real-life or symbolic models" (Mischel, 1966, p. 57). Observational learning may occur from exposure to television, books, or people. Gender roles are constructed and altered by exposure to new and different models.

Whom will children imitate? At first, children may not be very discriminating and may model anyone's behavior. Eventually, they pay attention to the way others respond to their imitative behavior. If others reward the behavior, it is likely to be repeated. Thus modeling and reinforcement interact with each other to influence behavior. If a little boy sees someone on television punching another person, he may try out this behavior by punching his sibling or a toy. Although the parent may show disapproval when the boy punches his sibling, the parent may respond to punching the toy with mixed reactions. If everyone in the room laughs because they think the boy's imitation of the television figure is cute, the boy will respond to this reinforcement by repeating the behavior. Observational learning is more likely to occur if the consequences of the model's behavior are positive rather than negative. Children should be more likely to imitate an aggressor on television who is glorified rather than punished. And many television aggressors are glorified, in cartoons such as *The Simpsons* and *Family Guy*, for example. Some of the conditions that influence observational learning are shown in Table 5.1.

Initially, social learning theory suggested that one way children become sex-typed is by imitating the same sex. But children do not always imitate the same sex (Maccoby & Jacklin, 1974). They are more likely to imitate same-sex behavior that is perceived as typical for the person's sex (Jacklin, 1989; Perry & Bussey, 1979). Children can easily figure out

TABLE 5.1   CONDITIONS THAT INFLUENCE OBSERVATIONAL LEARNING

Observational learning increases

If there is a positive relationship between the observer and the model.

If the consequences of model's behavior are positive rather than negative.

If the model is in a position of power.

If the model is of the same sex and behaves in a gender-role congruent way.

that women are more likely than men to be nurses and men are more likely than women to be construction workers. This explains why a girl is more likely to imitate a mother who is a nurse rather than a mother who is a construction worker. A girl whose mother is a construction worker may still perceive that only men are construction workers because the majority of people in this field are male.

One sex-related behavior that has been examined extensively in terms of social learning theory is aggression. Models of aggression for males abound. Think of the movies *The Dark Knight, Iron Man, Watchmen, The Departed, Scream, 300,* and *Natural Born Killers.* There have been numerous reports of copycat killings based on these movies. There was a Showtime television series about a serial killer, *Dexter,* that involved a killer pretending to be a woman on a dating Web site, attracting a male and then beheading him. Oddly enough, a filmmaker was accused of copycat killings based on the movie. *Scream* is a slasher film about a woman harassed with phone calls and attacked by a man in a Halloween mask. There are a slew of copycat killings based on this movie, with the Halloween mask left as the insignia.

Aggression is also modeled in television and video games. A content analysis of popular video games revealed that 83% of male characters and 62% of female characters are portrayed as aggressive (Dill & Thill, 2007). Even toy commercials provide models of aggression, and this modeling is aimed at boys. In one study, 69% of the toy commercials depicting only boys showed physical aggression, verbal aggression, or both (Sobieraj, 1998). Not one of the toy commercials featuring only girls involved either physical or verbal aggression.

Why do examples of aggressive behavior lead people to imitate them? Witnessing another's behavior not only teaches us how to perform the behavior but suggests the behavior is appropriate. It also makes aggressive behavior a cognitively available response to provocation. Thus, when faced with a conflict, aggressive behavior may be more likely because it is a learned response and a response that is cognitively accessible.

The application of social learning theory to sex-related differences suggests that as the norms change and the role models of a culture (e.g., in the media) change, sex differences also will change. Think of how the traditional male gender role has been influenced by different models. In the 1950s, a model of the male gender role was John Wayne, a cowboy who smoked cigarettes. It is unlikely this is the aspiration of most young men today. In the 1970s, the macho male gave way to sensitive and caring images like those portrayed by Alan Alda in *M*A*S*H* and Michael Landon in *Little House on the Prairie*. In the 1980s, a model was Detective Sonny Crockett (played by Don Johnson) of the television show *Miami Vice*, whose unshaven face became the decade's symbol of masculinity. Today, images of masculinity that come to mind are the slightly chauvinistic physician Dr. House of *House* and the macho mob boss Tony Soprano of *The Sopranos*.

Social learning theory can explain why some sex differences in cognition and behavior have diminished over time. As nontraditional roles for women and men have gained increased acceptance, the models for female and male roles have become more varied. A longitudinal study of 10-year-olds showed that those who were involved in counterstereotypical activities had less traditional attitudes toward gender and better grades in subjects deemed more appropriate for the other sex (e.g., math for girls) two years later (McHale et al., 2004). These findings were stronger for females than males, however. As men become more involved in child care and more models of men as parents appear, sex differences in empathy and nurturance also

may be reduced. As women become more involved in sports, sex differences in spatial skills could become smaller.

There is already some support for the role of social learning theory in the development of spatial skills. A meta-analysis revealed that experience with spatial activities is related to spatial ability (Baenninger & Newcombe, 1989). Thus one reason that men have superior spatial skills compared to women might be that boys are more likely than girls to be given toys that require spatial abilities. For example, building blocks, math toys, and sports all require spatial skills, and these activities are encouraged more in boys. The meta-analysis also showed that experimental studies of spatial training improved spatial skills. Spatial training typically involved repeated exposure to a spatial skills task or specific instructions on how to perform spatial tasks. The effects of training were similar for women and men, meaning women and men were equally likely to benefit from spatial skills training. This meta-analysis pointed a strong finger at the role of the environment in sex differences in spatial skills. Some researchers have called for spatial instructions in the education system because we know it is teachable and we know it is linked to cognitive skills, including math (Halpern & Collaer, 2005).

Reinforcement

Reinforcement theory no doubt sparks images of Pavlov's dog salivating at the bell, the cue that signifies a reward is coming. With respect to gender-role acquisition, the nature of the bell is different for girls and boys. We reward girls and boys for different behaviors, and the consequences of a behavior determine whether the child performs it again. The cartoon "Jump Start" (Figure 5.5) illustrates how parents reinforce behavior. Imagine a girl playing with a doll; a parent may smile, play with her, or buy her another doll. Now

FIGURE 5.5   Cartoon illustrating parents reinforcing toughness in boys.
Source: JUMP START © Robb Armstrong. Distributed by Universal Uclick for UFS.
Reprinted with permission. All rights reserved.

imagine a boy playing with a doll; a parent may ignore the behavior, take the doll away, frown, or even scold the boy and say, "Only girls play with dolls!" Consequences, however, do not actually have to occur to influence behavior; the child may infer that a consequence is likely to occur. For example, boys do not have to wear eye shadow and lipstick to learn that the consequences will be negative.

We are less tolerant of and more likely to punish cross-sex behavior among boys than among girls. We do not mind if women wear ties or suits, but we mind if men wear dresses; we do not mind if daughters are athletic, but we are less enthusiastic about sons who are graceful; we are even less tolerant of attraction to a member of the same sex in men than in women. Homosexuality is viewed as a greater violation of the male gender role than the female gender

role; that is, men are more likely than women to be punished for being homosexual.

Aggression is a behavior that is more likely to be reinforced in males than females—by parents, teachers, and peers (Feshbach, 1989). Parents may overtly encourage aggression by telling their sons it is okay to fight with other children as a way to settle arguments. Some parents encourage aggression in subtle ways; they verbally declare that fighting is not appropriate, but at the same time, they beam with pride when their child emerges as the victor of a fight. Teachers inadvertently encourage aggression in boys more than girls by reacting more strongly to aggressive behavior in boys than girls. This attention—whether positive or negative—is reinforcing in and of itself. Aggressive behavior is more likely to decrease when it is ignored by teachers and peers.

- Social learning theory states that we acquire gender-related behavior through modeling and reinforcement.

- We are more likely to imitate same-sex models, especially when they display gender-congruent behavior; models who are reinforced for their behavior; and models we like.

- Society is filled with models of male aggression — in movies, on television, and in video games — who are reinforced for their behavior. Boys are more likely to be rewarded by parents, teachers, and peers for aggression.

- As models of appropriate behavior for females and males change, the behavior of females and males may change.

- Girls and boys are rewarded for gender-congruent behavior. Boys are more likely than girls to be punished for gender-incongruent behavior, further supporting the rigidity of the male compared to the female role.

GENDER-ROLE SOCIALIZATION

Social learning theory is believed to be the basis for gender-role socialization theory. According to social learning theory, behavior is a function of rewards and observational learning. According to gender-role socialization, different people and objects in a child's environment provide rewards and models that shape behavior to fit gender-role norms. Agents in the environment encourage women to be communal and men to be agentic, to take on the female and male gender roles. Boys are taught to be assertive and to control their expression of feelings, whereas girls are taught to express concern for others and to control their assertiveness. This encouragement may take the direct form of reinforcement or the indirect form of modeling. See Sidebar 5.3 for an in-depth examination of

SIDEBAR 5.3: *The "Masculine Mystique"*

Suicide and homicide account for one-third of the deaths of male youths between the ages of 10 and 24 (Centers for Disease Control and Prevention, 2010b). We socialize boys to be tough, aggressive, and dominant, and to restrict their emotions. Pollack (2000, 2006) refers to the "boy code" when describing the pressure boys face to keep their emotions to themselves and maintain an emotional distance from others. These aspects of male gender-role socialization have been linked to aggression—aggression toward others and aggression toward one's self (Feder, Levant, & Dean, 2007). The movie *Tough Guise* elaborates on the way that society socializes males to be aggressive. Myriam Miedzian (1991) published a book, *Boys Will Be Boys: Breaking the Link between Masculinity and Violence*, in which she linked the **masculine mystique** to aggression, criminal behavior, and domestic violence. The masculine mystique consists of toughness, dominance, emotional detachment, callousness toward women, eagerness to seek out danger, and competition.

Miedzian argues that we not only tolerate violence in males, but also encourage it. War is an example: We associate war with maleness and we associate avoiding war with a lack of masculinity; we glorify war with toys, books, television, and movies; political leaders affirm their masculinity by engaging in war. Miedzian points out that the media claimed former President George H. Bush proved his manhood and overcame his image as a wimp by going to war with Iraq; Bush's approval ratings hit an all-time high during the Persian Gulf War and plummeted after the war was over. Similar claims were made about President George W. Bush's 2003 invasion of Iraq.

Miedzian (1991) also argues that men grow up in a culture of violence. Hollywood offers an abundance of models of men committing violent acts, and some of these models become heroes (e.g., Sylvester Stallone, Arnold Schwarzenegger). Themes of violence pervade music, sports, video games, and toys geared toward boys. Miedzian says, "He is learning to sacrifice his body unnecessarily and to hide all feelings of fear and vulnerability, however warranted they may be. He is also being taught to sacrifice the bodies of others" (p. 201).

The masculine mystique is more dangerous for lower-class than upper-class boys. Upper-class boys are provided with legitimate pathways to validate their masculinity through achievement; lower-class boys have more difficulty attaining achievement levels that will garner dominance and respect. Black males, in particular, are denied legitimate opportunities to validate their masculinity through achievement and economic success; thus Black men may resort to other means. Staples (1995) argues that higher rates of violence in Black communities may stem from "relative deprivation." In fact, the highest rates of violence occur in communities where the income gap between Blacks and Whites is largest.

An alternative way to view aggression from a gender-role perspective is to consider the facets of the female gender role that might inhibit aggression, such as empathy and nurturance. Empathy involves taking another person's perspective and being able to experience vicariously another person's feelings. Caretaking of children is one way to promote both empathy and nurturance, both of which could reduce aggression. Miedzian describes innovative programs whereby girls and boys receive child care training in elementary school that extends through high school as a way to reduce violence, delinquency, and teenage pregnancy. Some schools today provide life skills training in middle school that includes child care. I find it interesting that this is one lifetime duty for which neither women nor men are adequately prepared; women are expected to know how to take care of and raise children (the maternal instinct), and men are excused for not knowing how to do these things.

how gender-role socialization of males in our culture contributes to aggression.

Gender-role socialization may not only contribute to actual sex differences in behavior but could also contribute to the appearance of sex differences. The issue is one of response bias. Women and men may distort their behavior in ways to make them appear more consistent with traditional gender roles. This may explain why sex differences in empathy are larger for self-report measures than more objective measures. However, evidence also exists for a response bias in spatial ability. When the embedded figures test (a measure of spatial ability) was described as measuring empathy, feminine females performed better than masculine females, as shown in Figure 5.6 (Massa, Mayer, & Bohon, 2005). However, when the task was described as a measure of spatial skills, masculine females performed better than feminine females. Neither gender role nor task

instructions influenced men's performance. To the extent that women and men view a task as one in which they are expected to excel, they may respond in a way to confirm this expectation. Test this idea yourself in Do Gender 5.2.

Gender-role socialization may explain sex-related differences in the expression of emotion. Women's concerns with relationships may lead them to express emotions that strengthen relationships and inhibit emotions that could harm relationships (Timmers, Fischer, & Manstead, 1998). Thus women may express sadness to another person because they believe sharing such an experience will increase the closeness of the relationship. Women may be reluctant to express anger directly toward another person because of the potential damage to the relationship. Men, by contrast, are motivated to express emotions that yield power and control and reluctant to express emotions that suggest low power and

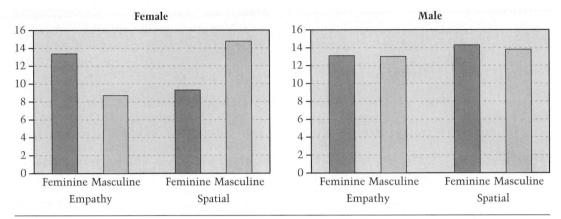

FIGURE 5.6 Score on the embedded figures test. Feminine women performed better than masculine women when the test was presented as a measure of empathy, whereas masculine women performed better than feminine women when the test was presented as a measure of spatial ability. Gender role and test instructions did not affect men's scores.
Source: Adapted from Massa, Mayer, and Bohon (2005).

vulnerability. Sadness and fear are *low-power* emotions, whereas anger and pride are *high-power* emotions.

There is evidence that cultural factors can override gender roles in terms of emotional expression. In a study of college students from 37 countries spanning five continents, sex differences in emotional expression were larger in countries with less traditional gender roles (Fischer & Manstead, 2000). Fischer and Manstead argue that less traditional countries, such as the United States, have an individualistic orientation; the emphasis is on individual expression of feelings. In an individualistic country, individual differences in terms of gender roles may appear. In collectivist countries such as China or India, which are often more traditional, behavior, including the expression of emotion, is determined more by the environment: the norms of the culture and the other people in the situation. Thus women and men behave more similarly in terms of emotional expression in collectivist cultures.

Now we turn to the question of who or what in the environment is the socializing agent for gender roles.

The Influence of Parents

Differential Treatment of Boys and Girls. Parents are prime candidates for contributing to gender-role socialization. Lytton and Romney (1991) conducted a meta-analytic review of 172 studies that evaluated parents' socialization practices with children, and concluded that parents' overall treatment of girls and boys was similar. In only one way were parents found to treat girls and boys differently: Parents encouraged sex-typed toys ($d = +.34$). There were trends that showed parents encouraged achievement, were more restrictive, and were more strict with boys; and that parents encouraged dependence and were warmer with girls. But, these effects were small and did not reach statistical significance. They also found that fathers were more likely than mothers to treat sons and daughters

DO GENDER 5.2
Can Perceptions Alter
Sex Differences?

1. Ask 20 people to complete two tasks, one being a test of spatial skills and one being a test of verbal skills. Come up with your own two tasks.

2. Before asking people to complete the tasks, randomly assign them to one of the following two conditions:

Condition 1: This is the control group. Give no particular instructions.
Condition 2: This is the experimental group. Manipulate respondents into perceiving that the spatial task is one in which females excel and the verbal task is one in which males excel. Think about what information you can provide to alter people's perceptions. You might provide false statistics that show one sex performs better than the other sex. You might describe the type of person who excels on the task in masculine versus feminine terms.

3. After people have completed the task, have them rate how they view each task on a number of scales, two of which are:

Not at all
masculine 1 2 3 4 5 Very masculine
Not at all
feminine 1 2 3 4 5 Very feminine

You may include other rating scales so that respondents will not detect the items of interest. You also could use other terms besides *masculine* and *feminine,* such as those that appear on the masculinity and femininity scales.

4. Compare male and female performance on the two tasks in the two different conditions.

differently. Today, there is still evidence that parents encourage sex-typed toys, although parents may deny it. In a study of 3- to 5-year-old children, parents said that they encouraged both sex-typed and cross-sex typed toys equally among their girls and boys (Freeman, 2007). However, the children had different perceptions of their parents' reactions. When the children were asked how their parents would react to them playing with specific toys, a majority indicated that parents would approve of sex-typed toys (90%) and only a small minority indicated that parents would approve of cross-sex typed toys (26%).

An important moderator of the meta-analysis (Lytton & Romney, 1991) was methodology. Studies that included more objective methods, such as experiments and observational studies, showed larger differences in the way parents treated boys and girls than studies that used more subjective methods, such as questionnaires and interviews. In other words, parents did not report treating daughters and sons differently, but their behavior suggested otherwise. In general, the higher-quality studies showed larger differences in the way parents treated daughters and sons.

More recent studies suggest other ways in which parents may treat girls and boys differently. For example, boys are more likely to be physically punished than girls (Zahn-Waxler & Polanichka, 2004). Other behaviors may be more subtle. One observational study showed that mothers spent more time watching boys and more time actively involved with girls (Clearfield & Nelson, 2006). Clearfield and Nelson concluded that parents could be sending the message that it is okay for boys to be independent whereas girls require assistance.

Lytton and Romney's (1991) meta-analysis also showed that parents' differential treatment of children seemed to decline with the child's age. This is not surprising because parents gain more target-based information as children grow older; thus they are less likely to rely on category-based (stereotypical) information. The question remains as to the impact of these very early differences in boys' and girls' environments and interactions with parents. Exposure to certain classes of toys could lead to later preferences for those toys. Does exposure to some kinds of toys foster particular skills that might advantage one sex over the other? If you think the toys that boys and girls have today are similar, visit a nearby toy store: The aisles of girls' toys are noticeable from 50 feet away because of the blinding pink packaging. Examine girls' and boys' toys by visiting a toy store with Do Gender 5.3.

Emotion.   One area in which parents may treat children differently is emotion. Two studies showed that there are differences between mothers' and fathers' responses to emotion. One study of adolescents showed that mothers were more emotionally expressive to preadolescents than fathers when recalling a past family event (Bohanek, Marin, & Fivush, 2008). Another study showed that

mothers were more likely to reward displays of emotion and magnify emotional responses among adolescents, whereas fathers were more likely to ignore, distract from, or dismiss emotional displays (Klimes-Dougan et al., 2007). To the extent children model same-sex parent behavior, girls learn to be more comfortable expressing emotion than boys do. In general, females are socialized to express their emotions, whereas males are socialized to conceal their emotions. The one exception is anger. Parents are more accepting of boys' than girls' expressions of anger (Zahn-Waxler & Polanichka, 2004).

Gender-Role Beliefs.   Are parents with nontraditional gender roles more likely to have children with nontraditional gender-role attitudes? A meta-analytic review of the literature showed there was a small effect of parents' gender-role beliefs on children's gender-related cognitions ($d = +.33$; Tenenbaum & Lemper, 2002). The correspondence was greater between parents' beliefs and children's beliefs about others (i.e., stereotypes) rather than parents' beliefs and children's perceptions of their own masculine and feminine traits. Aside from parents, siblings may influence gender-role behavior. One study showed that boys with older brothers and girls with older sisters were more sex-typed than only children (Rust et al., 2000). In addition, boys with older sisters and girls with older brothers were the least sex-typed and most androgynous of all.

The Influence of Other People

If parents treat boys and girls in a fairly similar way, who treats them differently? One possibility is that it is other people, such as relatives, teachers, friends, and neighbors. Recall that we are more likely to stereotype people we do not know very well. Thus

DO GENDER 5.3
Toy Store Visit

Visit a toy store or the children's section of a department store. Take notes on what you see. Can you tell which are the girls' toys and which are the boys' toys? If so, how? Pay attention to location in the store, packaging, color, and the nature of the toy. How are the toys different? How are the toys similar? Compare these toys to the ones you had during your childhood. Observe the shoppers, particularly their behavior relating to gender.

parents may be less likely than friends or relatives to use category-based information when interacting with their children.

This line of thinking is similar to that of Judith Harris (1998), who concluded that parents have largely no effect on the development of a child's personality. (This was a great relief to me, as the book appeared shortly after my daughter was born.) She wrote a controversial book entitled *The Nurture Assumption: Why Children Turn Out the Way They Do: Parents Matter Less Than You Think and Peers Matter More*. The title says it all. Harris argues that the source of influence on children comes from outside the home, in particular, from the peer group. Her conclusion is partly based on the fact that children raised by the same parents in the same environment often turn out to have very different personalities. However, we can debate whether the same home and the same parents constitute the same environment for each child. Harris's theory is called *group socialization* and emphasizes the child's experience outside the home. According to her theory, children learn behavior inside the home but then test it on others outside the home to see if it is going to be accepted or rejected. Others' reactions determine if the behavior is repeated.

Is there evidence that peers influence sex differences? The prominence of same-sex play in childhood (discussed in depth in Chapter 7) is thought to reinforce sex-typed behavior (Golombok et al., 2008). The differences in girls' and boys' early peer groups could certainly lead to differences in behavior. Boys play in larger groups, which have the potential for conflict and aggression. In boys' groups, the potential for the expression of anger is high, but the potential for the expression of emotions that make us vulnerable, such as fear and sadness, is low.

Girls play in small groups, which minimize conflict and emphasize cooperation. In girls' groups, the potential for the expression of emotions that foster relationships, such as sadness and fear, is high.

Peers also contribute to aggression through modeling and reinforcement. Whereas aggression in younger children is associated with being rejected by peers, there is some evidence that aggression can confer status among preadolescents and adolescents. Some social cliques are based on aggression. Aggressive behavior may come to be viewed as powerful and attractive. The aggressive adolescents who become more popular may be characterized by what has been referred to as **proactive aggression** compared to **reactive aggression** (Poulin & Boivin, 2000a). Reactive aggression is an angry, impulsive response to threat or provocation more clearly tied to the frustration-aggression hypothesis. Proactive aggression, by contrast, is unprovoked, planned, goal directed, and socially motivated. Reactive aggression has been associated with peer rejection and peer victimization, but proactive aggression has not (Hubbard et al., 2010). Proactive aggressive groups may gang up on and target a specific individual. These children expect to be rewarded for their behavior. Reactive aggression is associated with anger and physiological arousal, but proactive aggression is associated with a noticeable lack of physiological arousal—making it all the more disturbing (Hubbard et al., 2010).

So, is there anything that parents can do, according to Harris (1998)? Yes: Parents should choose to live in a good neighborhood. This is because it is the peers in the neighborhood who are going to influence the child. But we wonder: What is the cause of the neighborhood children's behavior?

Other Features of the Environment

Toys. When my daughter returned to school from one Christmas vacation, the teacher naturally asked each of the third-graders to name their favorite Christmas present. The most popular gifts were the Nintendo DS and iPods—named by both girls and boys. After that, for the girls it was the American Girl doll. My daughter, however, proudly announced that her favorite gift was a giant stuffed triceratops. Although a stuffed animal is a conventional toy for a girl, one that is a dinosaur is not (see Figure 5.7).

Boys and girls play with different toys: Boys overwhelmingly play with vehicles, machines, and construction sets (e.g., building blocks), whereas girls play with dolls, domestic toys, and dress-up clothes, as shown in Figure 5.8. Toys also are marketed to a specific sex by the color and the packaging. Consider the Little Tikes Push and Ride toy shown in Figure 5.9. It is marketed to boys as the Push and Ride Racer in bold primary colors and marketed to girls as the Push and Ride Doll Walker in pink and blue pastel colors. The advertisement for boys reads: "The high spoiler on this sporty toddler-mobile

FIGURE 5.8 Girls are shown in one of their favorite pastimes, playing in dress-up clothes.

FIGURE 5.9 This is the Little Tikes Push and Ride. The toy is marketed to boys as the Push and Ride Racer and to girls as the Push and Ride Doll Walker.

FIGURE 5.7 A girl surrounded by dinosaurs—far from a stereotypical feminine toy.

provides a sturdy handle for a child's first steps." The advertisement for girls reads: "The doll seat on this cute toddler-mobile holds a favorite doll or stuffed toy and provides a sturdy handle for a child's first steps." Thomas the Train, which has been around for over 100 years, still features mostly male trains. Dads and Daughters, a nonprofit organization aimed at monitoring the media for advertising that undermines girls, was instrumental in keeping Hasbro Toys from releasing a line of dolls for young girls modeled after a scantily-clad female music group (FOX News, 2006). Unfortunately, a toned-down version of this kind of doll—the wide-eyed, full-lipped, sexy Bratz dolls—is still on the shelves. More recently, a group of sixth graders in Sweden reported about Toys "R" Us to their government agency that regulates marketing for restricting boys' and girls' choices by reinforcing gender roles in their advertisements and packaging of toys (The Local, 2009). The children complained that the store showed girls and boys playing with different types of toys making it difficult for a boy to play with a toy that shows only girls and vice versa. The agency concurred with the children's opinion and publicly reprimanded Toys "R" Us—but the reprimand is without sanctions.

Does it matter if girls and boys play with different toys? The toys children play with may influence sex differences in cognition and behavior. Blakemore and Centers (2005) examined people's perceptions of the educational value of 126 toys that had been categorized as strongly feminine, moderately feminine, neutral, moderately masculine, and strongly masculine (see Figure 5.10). Neutral and moderately masculine toys were rated the highest on overall educational value, scientific attributes, cognitive skill development, and physical skill development. However, studies have not been conducted to see if playing with boys' toys leads to greater spatial ability or playing with girls' toys improves verbal skills. It also is possible that children with better spatial skills are drawn to boys' toys and children with better verbal skills are attracted to girls' toys.

| Feminine Toys | Gender Neutral | Masculine Toys |

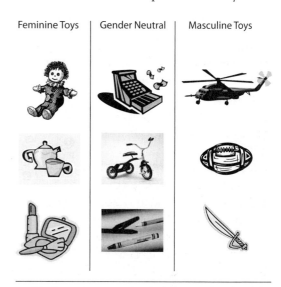

FIGURE 5.10 Examples of toys that were categorized by Blakemore and Centers (2005) as extremely feminine, neutral, or extremely masculine.

Books. Books that children read also may model and encourage gender-role-appropriate behavior. Consider the classic fairy tales and nursery rhymes that are still read to children. Girls and boys alike learn from Cinderella, Sleeping Beauty, and Snow White that "what is beautiful is good" and clearly rewarded. Specifically, men fall in love with beautiful women; good women are obedient, gullible, vulnerable, and—if beautiful—will be rescued by men; other women (stepsisters, stepmothers) are evil, competitors for men; and a woman's ultimate dream is to marry a rich, handsome prince. Nursery rhymes depict females as quiet and sweet, maids, crying, and running away from spiders, whereas males are shown as kings, thieves, butchers, and adventurers. I did not monitor my daughter's first books as carefully as I could have for gender-role stereotypes, but I could not bring myself to read her these nursery rhymes. (She is undoubtedly scarred for life because she is unable to recognize Snow White or Cinderella.) When parents were asked to volunteer at the preschool to read stories, I selected the more egalitarian representation of nursery rhymes to share, some of which are shown in Sidebar 5.4. The teachers politely thanked me, and the children were slightly amused. Since this happened before my daughter was 5, she has no recollection—which is probably a good thing.

Sidebar 5.4: *Mother Goose and Father Gander*

Father Gander alters the traditional *Mother Goose* nursery rhymes to present a more equal representation of men and women and to show men and women in more egalitarian roles. For example, the old woman in the shoe now has a husband to help her take care of the children and Ms. Muffet brings the spider to the garden to catch insects instead of running away from it. Below are listed two classic *Mother Goose* nursery rhymes along with their updated version by *Father Gander* (Larche, 1985).

Mother Goose	*Father Gander*
Peter, Peter, pumpkin eater	Peter, Peter, pumpkin eater
Had a wife and couldn't keep her	Had a wife and wished to keep her
He put her in a pumpkin shell,	Treated her with fair respect,
And then he kept her very well.	She stayed with him and hugged his neck!
Humpty Dumpty sat on a wall	Humpty Dumpty sat on a wall
Humpty Dumpty had a great fall.	Humpty Dumpty had a great fall.
All the king's horses and all the king's men	All of the horses, the women and men
Couldn't put Humpty together again.	Put Humpty Dumpty together again!

In other nursery rhymes, *Father Gander* simply extended the passage to include women. For example,

Mother Goose and Father Gander

Jack be nimble, Jack be quick,
Jack jump over the candlestick!

Father Gander's extension

Jill be nimble, jump it too,
If Jack can do it, so can you!

Father Gander also added some nursery rhymes that depict men and women in more equal roles. For example:

Mandy's Mom stays home to work,
Millie's Mom goes outside.
David's Dad is on the road,
Donald's Dad works inside.

A working Mother's really great,
A working Father, too.
A stay-at-home Mom is first rate,
Or a Dad who stays home with you.

Historically, one problem with children's books is that females were not represented to the extent that males were. More recent studies seem to suggest that females and males are equally likely to be represented as main characters, but that they are still depicted in different roles. In a review of 83 "Notable Books" designated as outstanding by the American Library Association (Gooden & Gooden, 2001), males had more diverse roles than females, female characters held traditional roles, and male characters were seldom depicted as nurturant, as having domestic roles, or as interacting with children—and never depicted performing household chores! Similar findings appeared in a more recent study of children's coloring books. Males were portrayed in more active roles than females, and gender-stereotyped behavior was common (Fitzpatrick & McPherson, 2010). That is, 58% of female characters were depicted in traditional roles, such as cooking or caring for infants, and 44% of male characters were depicted in traditional roles, such as car racing or driving heavy equipment. Cross-sex behavior was extremely rare (6% of female characters, 3% of male characters).

Even among children's books that are designated nonsexist, traditional roles for women persist. In one study, the content of children's books that had been identified as sexist or nonsexist by researchers was examined (Diekman & Murnen, 2004). Although women were more likely to be portrayed as having stereotypically masculine traits and interests in the nonsexist compared to the sexist books, there was no difference in the portrayal of women as having stereotypically feminine traits and interests. Thus the nonsexist books seem to portray an image of women as having masculine traits and interests but also retaining the traditionally feminine traits and interests. This finding seems to suggest that women's entry into nontraditional roles is more acceptable if it takes place in the context of retaining traditional feminine roles. As noted in Chapter 3, we are more accepting of stereotype incongruent behavior if it takes place in the context of a person upholding other aspects of the stereotype. Children's books may portray a woman as a physician but also show her as a nurturant parent. Examine portrayals of gender roles in children's books on your own in Do Gender 5.4.

Television.   Television is also a source of information about gender roles. There seems to be a relation between watching television and holding stereotypical beliefs about gender roles. A study of Latino adolescents found that those who were less acculturated into the United States watched more television, and watching more television was associated with more traditional gender-role attitudes (Rivadeneyra & Ward, 2005). Viewing reality dating programs (RDPs) has been associated with more traditional attitudes toward women and men—in particular, greater sexual double standards, viewing women and men in opposition to one another while dating, viewing men as driven by sex, and viewing dating as a game between men and women (Zurbriggen & Morgan,

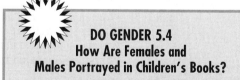

DO GENDER 5.4
**How Are Females and
Males Portrayed in Children's Books?**

Review 10 children's storybooks. Record the sex of all the characters and how the characters are portrayed. What are they doing? Are they good characters or bad characters? What are their personality traits? How do other characters react to them?

2006). The cross-sectional nature of these studies, however, makes it unclear whether viewing television increases sex-role stereotypes or whether those who hold sex-role stereotypes are more likely to be attracted to television or RDPs, in particular.

In some ways, but not all, gender roles are certainly less stereotyped on television today than they were 50 years ago. Although gender roles are somewhat traditional on *Family Guy* and *90201*, they are less so on *Scrubs* and *Modern Family*. Roles are less traditional on the popular show *House*, but a vast majority of doctors are still men and a vast majority of nurses are women. One of the most popular game shows, *Deal or No Deal*, involves viewers choosing briefcases that contain varying amounts of money from a series of scantily clad women. Some shows actually poke fun at the stereotypes and counterstereotypes of men and women, as in the womanizer and the sensitive chiropractor on *Two and a Half Men*.

However, an analysis of men's and women's roles on television in 2005–2006 showed that not much has changed (Lauzen, Dozier, & Horan, 2008). Men are still more likely to be depicted in work-related roles, and women are more likely to be depicted in interpersonal roles. One way in which television reflects gender stereotypes in female–male relationships is the extent to which it displays the **heterosexual script**. The heterosexual script, shown in Table 5.2, reflects three themes: (1) sexual double standards (i.e., it is okay for

TABLE 5.2 HETEROSEXUAL SCRIPT

1. Sexual double standards

a. male:	Sex is a defining component of masculinity. Men always want to have sex and are always thinking about sex. Men are preoccupied by women's bodies.
b. female:	Women are passive in sexual relations. Women are judged by their sexual conduct. Good girls are women who do not have sex. Women set the limits on sex.

2. Courtship

a. male:	Men initiate courtship behavior. Men use dominant and powerful strategies to attract women. Men are valued for their strength, wealth, and power.
b. female:	Women are passive and alluring. Women use indirect strategies to attract men. Women are valued for their appearance. Women use appearance and bodies to attract men.

3. Commitment attitudes

a. male:	Men avoid commitment and emotional attachment. Men want independence. Men prefer sex over emotional commitment.
b. female:	Romantic relationships are a priority for women. Women need a man to be fulfilled.

Source: Adapted from Tolman et al. (2007) and Kim et al. (2007).

men but not women to have sex), (2) court-ship behavior (men initiate, women respond), and (3) commitment (men avoid, women seek). When 25 primetime shows were coded for the heterosexual script, between 15 and 33 such references were noted per hour (Kim et al., 2007). The most frequent reference to the heterosexual script (45%) was the idea that sex was a defining part of masculinity (1a in Table 5.2). Conduct your own analysis of recent television shows in Do Gender 5.5.

One area in which women are under-represented on television is sports. A study that spanned two decades of sports coverage showed that women athletes are taken more seriously today by sports commentators but that overall women's sports receive very little attention. Despite the fact that millions of girls play sports today, only 1.6% of network news was devoted to women's sports compared to 96.3% for men's sports in 2009 (Messner & Cooky, 2010). It also appeared that the cover-age of women's sports in 2009 reached an all time low from a peak of 8.7% coverage in 1999.

DO GENDER 5.5
How Men and Women Are Portrayed on Television

Watch one episode each of the 10 most pop-ular television shows. You may limit your analysis to comedies or dramas or compare the two. What is the sex of the main char-acter/characters? Describe the personality characteristics, behavior, and occupation of the characters in the shows. Are roles tra-ditional or nontraditional? In what ways? What elements of the heterosexual script shown in Table 5.2 did you find?

Advertisements.   Men hold the dominant role in advertisements. In a content analysis of radio ads, 72% of the central characters were male, males were more likely than females to have authority roles, and females were more likely than males to be product users (Monk-Turner et al., 2007). Similar findings emerged from a study of television advertisements in Bulgaria (Ibroscheva, 2007). Advertisements continue to depict women and men in stereo-typical ways (O'Barr, 2006). For babies, pink and blue are the clues to gender. Men are por-trayed as athletic, strong, typically outdoors, and often involved in sports when they are young. As they age, they become financially successful rather than physically successful. Ads emphasize appearance and nurturing qualities for women. Even advertisements that depict girls emphasize appearance. One ad de-picts a girl playing dress-up with the quote "It's never too soon to learn how to accessorize." Whereas females are depicted with big smiles, males are somber—conveying the idea that women are emotionally expressive and men are stoic. There is little sex-role reversal, and when it does occur, it is usually accompanied by humor.

Women also continue to be portrayed as sex objects. In a content analysis of 1988 ad-vertisements from 58 popular U.S. magazines, more than 50% of the ads depicted women as sex objects (i.e., used their sexuality to sell the product; Stankiewicz & Rosselli, 2008). The figures were highest for men's maga-zines (76%) and female adolescent magazines (64%). A group of 24 teenage girls from a variety of backgrounds, races, and neigh-borhoods in Allegheny County, Pennsylva-nia, formed what they called a Girlcott to voice their opposition to such portrayals by Abercrombie & Fitch. Abercrombie & Fitch sold T-shirts that had sexist slogans across the front such as "Do I Make You Look Fat?" and "Who Needs Brains When You Have These?" The girls' advocacy and subsequent media attention (including an appearance on the Today Show) led to a meeting with Abercrombie & Fitch, during which they successfully persuaded the company to remove some of these T-shirts. In 2006, the girls were honored at a conference of the National Organization for Women (Women and Girls Foundation, 2006). I'm sure many of you have had the occasion to hear your parents say "not while you are living under my roof." This phrase came in handy when my daughter asked why we couldn't shop at this store.

Boys and girls are also shown in traditional roles in commercials directed toward children: Boys appear aggressive, dominant, and active, whereas girls appear shy, giggling, and deferent (Browne, 1998). The most sex segregation occurs in children's toy advertisements. In an analysis of such advertisements in the United States and Australia, no commercials depicted girls playing with traditional "boy toys" such as trucks, and no commercials depicted boys playing with traditional "girl toys" such as dolls. This is unfortunate because there is evidence that toy commercials influence how children view toys. In a study of first and second graders, children were shown either a traditional toy commercial (i.e., boy playing with a stereotypical boy toy) or a nontraditional toy commercial (i.e., girl playing with a stereotypical boy toy) and were later asked to sort the toys into those that are for boys, for girls, and for both boys and girls (Pike & Jennings, 2005). Children exposed to the nontraditional commercial were more likely to classify toys as for both boys and girls. In addition, commercials that feature boys or masculine toys are perceived as more aggressive (Klinger, Hamilton, & Cantrell, 2001),

suggesting that the toy industry is targeting boys with aggressive toys.

TAKE HOME POINTS

- Sources of gender-role socialization include parents, teachers, peers, neighbors, and the media.

- Averaging across studies, it appears that parents treat sons and daughters in more similar than different ways.

- One way parents treat girls and boys differently is in providing sex-typed toys. The impact of that behavior is still under investigation.

- Parents also communicate differently with daughters and sons, particularly with respect to emotion.

- Differential treatment of boys and girls is more likely to occur among younger than older children. With age, parents respond to individual characteristics of the child other than sex.

- Because parents have the opportunity to acquire individuating information about their children, it is possible that other people (e.g., neighbors, peers) and other things (e.g., television, books) are stronger social agents in terms of gender-role socialization.

- Girls and boys play with different toys. It is more acceptable for girls to play with stereotypical boy toys than it is for boys to play with stereotypical girl toys. As masculine toys have been found to have more educational value than feminine toys, the question is whether the difference in boys' and girls' toys is related to sex differences in cognition.

- The presence of women has increased in all forms of media—books, television, commercials. Females are increasingly portrayed in nonstereotypical roles on television and in books, but not at the expense of giving up traditional roles.

- Advertisements continue to depict women as sexual objects and often depict women and men in traditional roles.

SOCIAL ROLE THEORY

According to social role theory, differences in women's and men's behavior are a function of the different roles women and men hold in our society (Eagly, Wood, & Diekman, 2000; Wood & Eagly, 2002). This is a variant of gender-role socialization theory. Whereas gender-role socialization theory focuses on the individual and the environmental forces that shape the individual, social role theory focuses on society and how societal role structures shape behavior across groups of people. That is, social role theory focuses on the more abstract social conditions of society rather than on the concrete ways that individuals behave toward women and men. According to social role theory, the way labor is divided between women and men in society accounts for why women become communal and men become agentic. Men are primarily responsible for work outside the home, which leads to an agentic orientation. Women, even when employed, are primarily responsible for domestic labor and taking care of children, which leads to a communal orientation. When the roles that women and men hold are similar, sex differences are minimized. Is there a role for biology? Yes, of course. Social role theory argues that the biological differences between women and men (i.e., women bearing children, men being larger) lead to the assignment of these different roles (Wood & Eagly, 2002).

Social role theory has been used to explain a variety of social behaviors (Eagly, 1987). According to social role theory, women may be more easily influenced or more conforming than men because they want to appear agreeable and maintain group harmony. The nonverbal behaviors in which women engage more than men—smiling, laughing, gazing, and nodding—may reflect women's desire to foster the development of relationships. Finally, women's tendency to be more agreeable in small groups can be construed as behavior that aims to enhance group relations.

Social role theory does not specify that women must be communal and men must be agentic. It simply states that the roles women and men hold in society are responsible for the sex differences in behavior. However, most societies have organized women's and men's roles in a way so that women develop communal characteristics and men develop agentic characteristics. As men's and women's roles have become more similar in Western cultures, sex differences have decreased (Larson & Wilson, 2004). When males and females are provided with equal access to education, males and females take on more similar roles in society—females delay marriage and parenthood and take on the work role. Similar levels of education in females and males, however, do not always mean equal, especially if women are educated and oriented toward domestic roles and men are educated for paid employment roles.

One way to determine the contribution of society to gender roles is to examine practices across cultures. One of the most extensive cross-cultural studies of gender roles was conducted by Whiting and Edwards (1988). They observed the way that children ranging in age from a few months to 10 years from 12 different communities interacted with other children and adults. The investigators' main hypothesis was that the environments of women and men differ and that these different environments contribute to sex differences in behavior. In general, their hypothesis was supported.

Whiting and Edwards (1988) studied several interpersonal behaviors and found sex differences in two of them: nurturance (helping) and egoistic dominance (coercion, competition). In both cases, Whiting and Edwards concluded that differences in behavior were due to the different environments of girls and boys. Different environments provided girls with more practice in nurturance and boys with more practice in egoistic dominance. Specifically, girls interacted more than boys with younger children, and interactions with younger children demanded nurturance. Boys interacted more than girls with peers— especially older same-sex peers, and these interactions were characterized by egoistic dominance. This interpretation of sex differences is consistent with social role theory.

Whiting and Edwards (1988) also observed that parents treated girls and boys differently. Mothers were more likely to assign child care and household chores to girls and to give commands to girls than boys. Why do mothers ask girls rather than boys to take care of children? Is it because mothers believe girls have a greater capacity for caretaking, are more interested in caretaking, or are more suitable for caretaking than boys? Whiting and Edwards remarked, "Girls work while boys play" (p. 125). The differential treatment of boys and girls was greatest in societies where the status of men and women was most unequal. Whiting and Edwards (1988) stated, "The power of mothers to assign girls and boys to different settings may be the single most important factor in shaping gender-specific behaviors in childhood" (p. 86).

There are other social roles that men and women occupy besides work and family roles that influence gender-role behavior. For example, men are more likely than women to occupy military roles and athletic roles. These roles may contribute to sex differences in aggression. Women and men also are likely to hold different occupational roles that may contribute to sex differences in aggression. Women hold service occupations such as nursing and teaching, which require nurturance and are incompatible with aggression, whereas men hold occupations in the business world that require competitiveness.

TAKE HOME POINTS

- Social role theory states that the roles that society assigns women and men are responsible for gender roles. Biological differences between women and men also contribute to these roles.

- Men's role to work outside the home fosters agency, whereas women's role to work inside the home fosters communion.

- Cross-cultural research shows that girls and boys are assigned different roles and that these roles lead to sex-typed behavior. Specifically, girls' time with younger children fosters nurturance, whereas boys' time with older peers fosters egoistic dominance.

COGNITIVE DEVELOPMENT THEORY

Social learning theory, gender-role socialization, and social role theory all emphasize the effect of the environment on the child's skills and behaviors. In contrast, cognitive development theory states that the acquisition of gender roles takes place in the child's head. "It stresses the active nature of the child's thoughts as he organizes his role perceptions and role learnings around his basic conceptions of his body and his world" (Kohlberg, 1966, p. 83). An assumption of cognitive development theory is that the child is an active interpreter of the world. Learning occurs because the child cognitively organizes what she or he sees; learning does not occur from reinforcement or from conditioning. That is, the child is acting on her or his environment; the environment is not acting on the child.

Cognitive development theory suggests there are a series of stages of development that eventually lead to the acquisition of gender roles. First, children develop a **gender identity** (Kohlberg, 1966). By age 2 or 3, children learn the labels *boy* and *girl* and apply these labels to themselves and to other people. The labels are based on superficial characteristics of people rather than biology, however. If someone has long hair, she must be a girl; if someone is wearing a suit, he must be a man; and if you put a dress on the man, he becomes a she. That is, children at this age believe a person's sex can change—including their own sex. A boy may believe he can grow up to be a mother.

Upon recognition that there are two groups—males and females—and that the self belongs to one of those groups, evaluative and motivational consequences follow (Martin & Ruble, 2004). The evaluative consequence is a preference for the group to which one belongs. The motivational consequence is to learn about one's own category and identify ways in which the two categories differ. Even at the age of 18 to 24 months, children's knowledge of these gender categories is linked to sex-typed behavior (Martin & Ruble, 2009). Children who used more gender labels (i.e., man, woman, boy, girl) were found to engage in more sex-typed play. And, sex-typed play at age 2 predicts greater sex-typed play at age 8 (Golombok et al., 2008).

Children do not consistently use the labels *boy* and *girl* correctly until ages 4 and 5.

Children learn **gender constancy** by age 5. That is, they can categorize themselves as female or male and realize they cannot change their category. But even at age 5, children may not use biological distinctions as the basis for categorization. They are more likely to classify people as male or female by their size, strength, or physical appearance. I experienced an example of this confusion one day when I was taking my 2-year-old daughter to day care. Another girl, about 4 or 5 years old, came over and asked, "Is she a boy?" I was a bit surprised because my daughter was wearing a Minnie Mouse outfit. I told the little girl she was a girl. With some frustration, the little girl replied, "Then why is she wearing boy shoes?" My daughter was wearing blue sandals. It is during this stage of development that children's gender-related beliefs are most rigid (Martin & Ruble, 2004). Conduct your own experiment with young children to identify how they decide someone is female versus male (see Do Gender 5.6). By age 5, children also learn the content of gender categories and become aware of the different roles that men and women possess in society.

According to cognitive development theory, gender identity determines gender-role attitudes and values. Once children acquire their gender identity, they have a high internal motivation to behave in ways consistent with their self-concept. The child identifies the self as female or male and wants to behave in ways consistent with this self category. Their self-concept as female or male expands as they take in new information from the environment.

One limitation of Kohlberg's theory is that he states gender constancy must be achieved before children will value and seek out behavior that fits their gender role. Yet studies have shown that children who

DO GENDER 5.6
How Children
Determine Gender

Interview five children: a 2-year-old, a 3-year-old, a 4-year-old, a 5-year-old, and a 6-year-old. If the class is involved in this assignment, each of you can pool the results so that you will have more than five participants. Try to find out how each child determines whether someone is male or female. You can do this through a set of open-ended interview questions. For example, is the teacher female or male? How do you know? Are you female or male? How do you know? Is Santa Claus male or female? How do you know? You can also do this by presenting each child with a series of pictures, perhaps from storybooks, and ask the child to indicate whether the character is female or male and to explain why. Whichever method you choose, be sure to standardize it so you are using the same procedure for each child.

have not achieved gender constancy already choose sex-typed behavior (Bussey & Bandura, 1992). Bussey and Bandura (1999) have advanced the notion of **social cognitive theory**, which states that cognitive development is one factor in gender-role acquisition, but there are social influences as well, such as parents and peers. According to social cognitive theory, external sources have the initial influence on behavior. For example, the promise of a reward or the threat of punishment influences behavior. Later, however, children shift from relying on external sources to internal standards to guide behavior. Social cognitive theory emphasizes the interplay between psychological and social influences.

TAKE HOME POINTS

- Cognitive development theory emphasizes the role that the child plays in interpreting the world. The child is an active agent in gender-role acquisition.

- There is a series of stages that children move through to acquire gender roles, starting with gender identity and proceeding to gender constancy.

- Social cognitive theory combines elements of social learning theory and cognitive development theory by recognizing that the child and the environment interact with one another to produce gender roles.

GENDER SCHEMA THEORY

You are probably familiar with the following puzzle: A little boy and his father get into an automobile accident. The father dies, but the little boy is rushed to the hospital. As soon as the boy gets to the emergency room, the doctor looks down at him and says, "I cannot operate. This boy is my son."

How can this be? Didn't the boy's father die in the accident? The solution, of course, is that the physician is the boy's mother—a concept that was more foreign when I was growing up than it is today. Why is it that people presume the physician is male? Because being male is (or was) part of our schema for the category "physician."

A **schema** is a construct that contains information about the features of a category as well as its associations with other categories. We all have schemas for situations (e.g., parties, funerals), for people at school (e.g., the jocks, the nerds), for objects (e.g., animals, vegetables) and for subjects in school (e.g., chemistry, psychology). The content of a schema varies among people. Those of you who are psychology majors have more elaborate schemas for psychology than those of you who are not psychology majors. You know there are differences among clinical psychology, social psychology, and cognitive psychology; a nonpsychology major may not know all of these distinctions and may think all fields of psychology are alike. Those of you who are avid football fans have more elaborate football schemas, including all the rules of the game, the players on the different teams, and the current status of each team, compared to those of you who are not interested in football.

Schemas can be helpful in processing information. Whenever you encounter the object or the setting for which you have a schema, you do not have to relearn the information. So, those of you who have rich football schemas can use your knowledge of what happened in last week's play-offs to understand the games being played this coming weekend.

A gender schema includes your knowledge of what being female and male means and what behaviors, cognitions, and emotions are associated with these categories. When buying a gift for a newborn, one of the first questions we ask is if the baby is a boy or a girl. This category guides our choice of clothing or toys. When looking over the personnel at the dry cleaners, we presume the person who is sewing is the female clerk and not the male clerk because sewing is consistent with the female gender role, not the male gender role. When hiring a secretary, we presume all applicants are female because *secretary* is part of our female gender-role schema, not our male gender-role schema. In fact, to have male secretaries, we have come up with a new term: *administrative assistant*.

What does it mean to be **gender schematic**? Someone who is gender schematic uses the gender category to make decisions about what to wear, how to behave, what career to pursue, what leisure interests to pursue,

and what emotions to present to others. Someone who is **gender aschematic** does not consider gender when making these decisions.

To understand this more clearly, let's take an example of another variable on which people vary in terms of schematicity: religion. For some of you, religion is central to your identities and one of the first things you notice about a person: whether the person is religious and, if so, to which religion he or she belongs. You notice whether a person observes religious practices and has any religious belongings in the home. And, being religious (or not) influences your behavior. That is, you are religious schematic. For others of you, religion is not central to your self-concept, and you are religious aschematic; you will not notice whether a person engages in religious practices ("Did we say prayers before the meal at Joe's house? I really can't recall"), not notice if religious symbols are in a person's home, and fail to notice religious holidays. Being religious aschematic does not mean you are not religious; it just means religion is not something you think about and not something that influences your behavior. A strong atheist can still be religious schematic; an atheist may be well aware of religious practices and go to great lengths to ignore religion. This person is still letting religion influence behavior.

It is likely that all of us are gender schematic, to some extent. Bem (1981) argues that gender is a pervasive dichotomy in society that guides our thinking about what clothes to wear, what toys to play with, and what occupations to pursue. But there is variability among us in how readily we think of gender when processing information. The person who does not rely on male/female categories as a way of organizing the world is gender aschematic. This person is less likely to be concerned with the gender category when deciding how to think, feel, or behave. It does not occur to the person that a secretary cannot be male, that it is not okay for a male to wear a barrette, or that girls should not play with trucks.

Gender schema theory is a theory about the process by which we acquire gender roles; it is not a theory that describes the content of those roles. The theory simply states that we divide the world into masculine and feminine categories. The culture defines those categories. Gender schema theory combines elements of both social learning theory and cognitive development theory in describing how we acquire gender roles. Social learning theory explains how we acquire the features of the male and female gender categories and what we associate with those categories. Cognitive development theory describes how we begin to encode new information into these cognitive categories to maintain consistency. A child learns to invoke a gender-role category or schema when processing new information.

A construct with which you may be more familiar than gender schema theory is **androgyny**. Recall that the androgynous individual has both feminine and masculine attributes (Bem, 1981). Bem linked gender schematicity to the construct of androgyny. Because the gender aschematic person does not use gender as a guiding principle when thinking about how to behave, Bem suggested this person would incorporate both traditionally feminine and traditionally masculine qualities into her or his self-concept, or be androgynous. Bem presumed the gender aschematic person would have the flexibility to develop both feminine and masculine qualities. By contrast, gender schematic people were thought to be sex-typed, that is, feminine if female and masculine if male. Theoretically, cross-sex-typed people (feminine males, masculine females) are also gender schematic; they would still use gender as an organizing principle but would be

concerned with adhering to behavior consistent with the norms for the other sex.

Bem (1984) advanced her gender schema theory by showing that sex-typed people engage in gender schematic processing. For example, in one study, she flashed the 60 attributes of the Bem Sex Role Inventory on a screen. College students were asked to decide whether the attribute described them. The dependent variable in this experiment was how quickly the student made the judgment. Bem hypothesized that sex-typed respondents, compared to androgynous respondents, would decide more quickly that a sex-appropriate attribute described them and that a sex-inappropriate attribute did not describe them. For example, a feminine female could quickly decide that yes, she is "helpful" and no, she is not "loud." Sex-typed respondents were also expected to take longer to reject a sex-appropriate attribute and to take longer to accept a sex-inappropriate attribute compared to androgynous individuals. So that same feminine female would take longer to admit that no, she does not cook and yes, she is competitive. The results confirmed the hypothesis. The left half of Figure 5.11 indicates how quickly people endorsed terms that were consistent with gender-role schemas compared to terms that were neutral. It appears that sex-typed individuals were faster in making schema-consistent judgments than cross-sex-typed, androgynous, and undifferentiated individuals. The right half of Figure 5.11 indicates how quickly people endorsed terms that were inconsistent with gender-role schemas compared to terms that were neutral. Sex-typed individuals were slower in making schema-inconsistent judgments, especially relative to cross-sex-typed, androgynous, and undifferentiated individuals. In other studies, Bem found that sex-typed individuals were more likely to categorize a list of attributes in

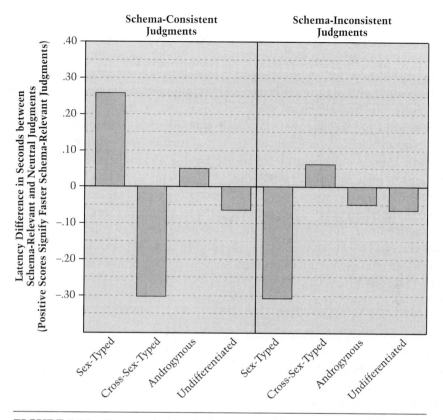

FIGURE 5.11 Sex-typed individuals more quickly endorse information consistent with their gender-role schemas than cross-sex-typed, androgynous, or undifferentiated individuals. Sex-typed individuals are slower to endorse information inconsistent with their gender-role schemas than the other three groups of individuals.

Source: Bem (1981).

terms of gender and more likely to organize groups of others in terms of gender compared to androgynous persons. Bem also found support for her theory by demonstrating that sex-typed individuals prefer to engage in behavior consistent with their gender role and feel more uncomfortable performing gender-role-inconsistent behavior.

One difficulty with gender schema theory is its relation to androgyny. The androgynous person is supposed to be gender aschematic. Being gender aschematic implies

the person does not think of the world in sex-related terms, yet androgyny is defined in terms of gender-related traits. Bem (1981) acknowledges that this measure of androgyny may not imply the flexibility in behavior she had hoped. Androgyny can be restrictive in the sense that the person has two ideals to meet: a masculine one and a feminine one. Androgyny also does not rid society of the two culturally defined gender categories, which was Bem's ultimate aim. Bem really advocated gender aschematicity, not androgyny.

Bem's (1984) gender schema theory obviously has some political overtones. Historically, Bem has advocated the minimization of differences between men and women—basically reducing the differences to biology alone. She has suggested society should rid itself of the social construction of gender associated with biological sex. In such a culture, there would be no need for the terms *masculinity* and *femininity*; the term *androgyny* would also be meaningless. Sex would be viewed as having a very limited influence on us, no more influence then, say, eye color. In fact, Bem encourages the raising of gender aschematic children.

See Sidebar 5.5 for a further discussion of this issue.

Later, Bem (1995) realized her utopian ideals were not reachable. She then suggested an alternative strategy for minimizing sex differences, that is "turning down the volume on sex differences." Her new strategy is to "turn up the volume on sex differences." By this, she means we should have 1,000 categories for sex instead of only 2. She suggests starting with a modest 18 categories, derived from all possible combinations of sex (male, female), gender role (masculine, feminine, androgynous), and sexual orientation (heterosexual, homosexual, bisexual). By having

SIDEBAR 5.5: *How to Raise a Gender Aschematic Child*

Bem (1984) suggests how to raise a gender aschematic child using practices she adopted in raising her son and daughter. These ideas are shown in Table 5.3. Her basic position is that you teach your child that sex is only a biological category, and the only way you can know whether someone is female or male is to see the person naked. Because society associates sex with much more than biology, the parent must go to some lengths to make sure prevailing stereotypes are not instilled in the child. This includes altering storybooks so all men are not viewed as having short hair and all women are not viewed as having long hair; all men are not viewed as heroes and all women are not rescued; all men are not depicted in blue and all women in pink. The parent would provide the child with a range of toys and not let the child's gender influence the choice of toys; both boys and girls would be given blocks, trucks, and dolls. There would be no such thing as "girl clothes" and "boy clothes"; both could wear shirts, pants, dresses, and barrettes.

Boys in dresses! Boys wearing barrettes! When I first present Bem's (1984) ideas in class, these remarks are the most commonly made. Students are all for letting girls wear any clothes and play with any toys, but someone usually draws the line at seeing a boy in a dress. Because I find dresses fairly uncomfortable, my personal response is to remove dresses from the category of clothing for both women and men. Another common reaction from students is that a child should choose who he or she wants to be and how he or she wants to behave—that parents should not force the child to be gender schematic or gender aschematic. Bem would respond that a child is never "free" to behave as she or he pleases because society will provide clear messages about how to behave, and those messages will be sexist. Thus if parents do not inoculate their children against gender schemas, society will impose those schemas. For those of you who are interested in the results of Bem's child-rearing practices, she has published an autobiography describing her egalitarian marriage and her gender aschematic child rearing (Bem, 1998). At the end of her book, her children comment favorably on the way they were raised. And, yes, Bem's grown son still occasionally wears a dress.

TABLE 5.3   BEM'S IDEAS ON HOW TO RAISE A GENDER ASCHEMATIC CHILD

1. Teach what sex is: a biological distinction. (You cannot tell if someone is male or female unless you see the person naked.)
2. Teach what sex is not: get rid of the cultural correlates of sex.
   Provide a child with both male and female toys and clothes.
   Censor books and television for depictions of men and women in traditional roles.
   Eliminate own gender-stereotyped behavior (e.g., only mom washes dishes, only dad washes a car).
3. Counter cultural stereotypes with counterexamples (e.g., Child: "Only men can be doctors." Parent: "But your Aunt Jean is a doctor").
4. Teach that society's view of gender is not only different from the one you are teaching but also incorrect.

so many categories, it would be difficult to have clear-cut boundaries between any two categories. The categories would become fluid and, ultimately, the distinctions among them less important, if not meaningless.

TAKE HOME POINTS

- Gender schema theory combines elements of both social learning theory and cognitive development theory; social learning theory explains how the content of gender schemas is acquired; cognitive development theory suggests that people use those schemas to guide their behavior.

- People who are gender schematic divide the world into feminine and masculine categories and allow the gender category to influence how they dress, behave, and think.

- A person who is gender aschematic relies on other categories besides gender to interpret the world.

- When Bem first put forth her theory of gender aschematicity, she reasoned that someone who is not constrained by the gender category would be likely to develop both feminine and masculine traits — or what is now referred to as *androgyny*.

- However, Bem really advocated a gender-aschematic society rather than an androgynous one.

CONSIDERING THE CONTEXT: DEAUX AND MAJOR'S MODEL

All the theories discussed so far emphasize how biological or social forces alone or in conjunction with one another could have led to sex differences in cognition or behavior or could have shaped the traditional male and female gender roles. Descriptions of each of these theories, as well as their key concepts, are presented in Table 5.4. Instead of focusing on how gender-related behavior is acquired, like the other theories reviewed in this chapter, Deaux and Major (1987) focused on the conditions that create the *display* of gender-related behavior. That is, they emphasized the proximal, or more immediate, causes of whether a sex difference is observed rather than the distal, or more distant, factors such as biology and socialization.

From a social psychological perspective, the theories discussed so far in this chapter are fundamentally flawed because they do not take the situation, the context, into account. Deaux and Major (1987) noted that one reason men's and women's behavior is inconsistent across studies is that the situation has a strong impact on behavior. Thus they incorporated the situation into their model of sex differences.

Deaux and Major's (1987) model emphasizes three determinants of whether a sex

TABLE 5.4   THEORIES OF SEX DIFFERENCES

Theory	Description	Key Terms
Biological	Identifies genes and hormones as well as the structure and function of the brain as the cause of sex differences in cognition, behavior, and gender roles.	androgens, estrogens, corpus collosum, lateralization
Evolutionary	An extension of Darwin's theory of evolution that states different social behaviors may have evolved in men and women because it was adaptive for their survival.	reproductive success, maternal investment, paternity uncertainty, interactionism
Psychoanalytic	Original theory suggested that gender roles are acquired by identification with the same-sex parent. Modern versions emphasize the importance of all early relationships.	Oedipal complex, unconscious processes, identification, object-relations theory
Social learning	Contends that all behaviors—including those specifically related to gender role—are learned through reinforcement and/or modeling.	reinforcement, observational learning
Gender-role socialization	States that people and objects in the child's environment shape behavior to fit gender-role norms.	differential socialization, parental influence, sex typing
Social role	Variant of gender-role socialization theory that suggests differences in women's and men's behavior are a function of the different roles that women and men hold in our society.	agency, communion, nurturance, egoistic dominance
Cognitive development	Assumes the child is an active interpreter of the world, and observational learning occurs because the perceiver cognitively organizes what he or she sees. Social cognitive theory extends this position by suggesting gender-role acquisition is influenced by social as well as cognitive factors.	gender identity, gender constancy, categorization
Gender schema	Contends that children acquire gender roles due to their propensity to process information into sex-linked categories.	gender schema, gender aschematic, androgyny

difference in behavior is displayed: (1) the perceiver's expectancies, (2) the target's (i.e., person who may or may not display the sex difference) self-concept, and (3) the situation. I review how each of these contributes to the display of sex differences.

Perceiver

The perceiver is the person observing the behavior. The perceiver has an expectation about whether a person, the target, will display a behavior. This expectation is likely to be confirmed by either **cognitive confirmation** or **behavioral confirmation**. Cognitive confirmation is the idea that we see what we want to see; it explains how two people can see the same behavior and interpret it differently. Have you ever watched a baseball game with a person rooting for the other team? What happens during those instant replays? You are sure the person on your team is safe and your friend is sure the person is out.

The two of you actually see the same replay but interpret the behavior differently and, not surprisingly, in line with what you hoped to see. Behavior is often subject to multiple interpretations, especially social behavior. Thus the person who believes baby boys are more active than baby girls will probably maintain this belief despite numerous counterexamples because he or she is free to interpret a wide range of behavior as active or inactive.

Behavioral confirmation is the process by which a perceiver's expectation actually alters the target's behavior. The target then confirms the perceiver's expectancy. Imagine that a mother believes girls are more capable than boys of taking care of small children. This mother is likely to give her daughter more opportunities to take care of the new baby in the family. Thus it will not be surprising if the daughter becomes more skilled than the son at feeding and entertaining the baby!

Target

The target in an interaction is the person whose behavior is of interest. The target of an interaction influences whether she or he displays behavior consistent with stereotypes about sex differences by two processes: **self-verification** and **self-presentation**. Self-verification is our concern with behaving in ways consistent with our self-concept. If you are a member of the National Rifle Association (NRA), you may not be able to keep yourself from speaking about the importance of the Second Amendment. If you are a very traditional male, it may be important to you not to express emotions in any situation. Self-presentation is our concern with how our behavior appears to others. The NRA member may find it inappropriate to voice concerns about Second Amendment rights to a mother whose child was accidentally killed by

a gun. The traditional male may realize certain situations call for emotional expression, such as a funeral.

There are individual differences in concerns with self-presentation and self-verification. **Self-monitoring** is an individual difference variable that describes the extent to which one is more concerned with self-presentation or self-verification (Snyder, 1979). A high self-monitor is someone who changes his or her behavior to fit the situation. This person will be outgoing at a party, yet serious during a study session. This person will be both supportive of a woman's right to an abortion when talking to a group of feminists but sympathetic to the plight of the unborn child when talking to a priest. This person is very much concerned with self-presentation. A low self-monitor typically behaves the same from one situation to the next. If this person is serious, he or she will be serious at a party, serious at a study session, and serious at a dinner. If in favor of reducing social security, this person will state his or her beliefs whether talking to a 30-year-old or a 70-year-old. The low self-monitor is most concerned with self-verification. The situation, however, will also influence whether we are more concerned with self-verification or self-presentation.

Situation

In some situations, you may be more concerned with adhering to your principles and values and want to behave in a way that is consistent with them. What will determine this? The strength of your values is one determinant. If the issue is something you care strongly about, you will stand firm in your beliefs no matter what the situation. If I believe hunting is a valuable sport, I will voice this opinion to a group of people whom I expect will disagree with me, such as vegetarians. In other areas, however, I may be less certain about an issue. I may be able to see both the pros and cons of day care for children; thus I will not be outspoken in advocating or rejecting day care in any situation and may tend to agree with both sides of the argument.

In some situations, you will be very much concerned with how you appear to others. These situations include ones in which other people have power over you and situations in which you need something from these other people. If you are a Democrat, and you discover your professor is a Republican, you may decide to conceal your political views. Why? Because you want the professor to like you, especially if you feel grades are going to be subjective. Obviously there are exceptions. If you feel strongly about being a Democrat or are a low self-monitor, you may share your political views with the professor anyway.

The following personal example illustrates how self-verification may operate in some situations and self-presentation may operate in others. In most situations, if someone asked, "Do you mind if I smoke?" I would say yes. I would be behaving true to my self-concept as a nonsmoker and one not very fond of smoke. However, a number of years ago, I was in a situation where I was surrounded by a half dozen male physicians who I was hoping would refer patients to a study I was conducting. The chief among the group, who was sitting next to me in a non-smoking building, started the meeting by turning to me and asking, "Do you mind if I smoke?" I found myself quickly replying, "No, I don't mind at all." In this particular situation, self-presentation won out over self-verification; my goal of behaving in ways consistent with my self-concept was not as strong as my goal of not offending the physician so I would receive patient referrals.

Other aspects of the situation influence behavior. Some situations have high behavioral constraints; they provide strong cues as to how to behave. In these situations, most people will behave in accordance with those cues. For example, church is a situation with high behavioral constraints. Most people, regardless of individual difference variables, will behave in the same way during a church service: sit quietly, listen, try to stay awake, sing when others are singing, and recite passages when others recite passages. There is a set script for behavior. Deviations from these behaviors, such as giggling, are quite noticeable. Other situations are low in behavioral constraints. A party is such a situation. Some people will be loud and mingle with the crowd; others will sit quietly with one other person and talk for hours. Either behavior is acceptable. What situations are high and low in behavioral constraints with respect to gender? A wedding is a situation high in behavioral constraints. Clear guidelines dictate how the bride and groom are to dress and behave, and the guidelines are quite different for the two of them. The classroom is a situation low in behavioral constraints with respect to gender. There are clear guidelines for behavior (sit quietly, take notes, raise hand to answer a question), but these guidelines do not differ for women and men.

Deaux and Major's (1987) model of sex differences, shown in Figure 5.12, shows how these three components—perceiver, target, and situation—interact to determine whether sex differences appear. Let's go through the model, step by step, with an example. In this example, the perceiver is a father, the target is his 3-year-old daughter, and the situation is that they are playing with toys at a day care.

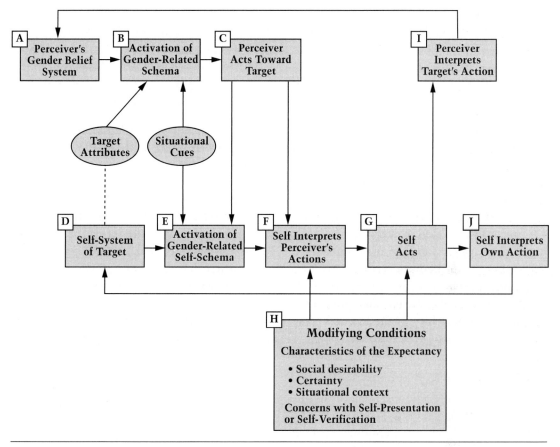

FIGURE 5.12   Deaux and Major's (1987) model of social interaction for gender-related behavior. This model explains how the perceiver, the target, and the situation determine whether sex differences in behavior are displayed in a given situation.
Source: Deaux and Major (1987).

Box A: This box represents the father's beliefs about women and men, that is, whether he is gender schematic and holds gender-role stereotypes, specifically about the toys that are appropriate for a girl to play with. As the father gets to know the daughter more, he will be less likely to rely on gender-role stereotypes (category-based information) and more likely to respond to target-based information (the attributes of his daughter).

Box B: This box represents whether a gender schema is activated in the father's mind. A recent event could activate a gender schema. For example, on the way to the day care, the father could have heard a story on the news about differences in social abilities between boys and girls. Attributes of the daughter or the situation could activate a gender schema. Is his daughter dressed quite differently from the boys at the day care? Is she wearing a pink frilly dress? Or is the daughter wearing a shirt and pants that do not distinguish her from the other children? The day care also may make gender salient if the teacher has the girls on one side of the room and the boys on the other side of the room, or if it appears that children are playing only with members of their same sex.

Box C: Here the father behaves toward his daughter. If he is highly gender schematic and has had gender schemas recently activated, perhaps he will offer his daughter a doll to play with. If he is gender aschematic and has not had gender schemas activated, he might offer his daughter the toy that looks most interesting to him or the toy he knows will be of most interest to her.

Box D: This box represents the target's self-concept, part of which is whether the daughter is gender schematic. In this example, the daughter is likely to know she is a girl and probably has noticed that girls and boys play with different toys. The daughter, however, has her own unique interests in the toys. Let's imagine her favorite toy is a remote-control car and she does not like playing with dolls.

Box E: The same things that activated the father's gender-related schema in Box B can activate the daughter's gender-related schema in Box E. This also includes how the father behaves toward her. Why did he offer her a doll when she never plays with dolls?

Box F: Here the daughter interprets the father's behavior, which is that he has just offered her a doll when she was about to play with the remote-control car. Now she has to decide whether to play with the doll, which would be behavior consistent with self-presentation (pleasing the father), or to play with the car, which would be behavior consistent with self-verification.

Box G: The daughter behaves. The interesting part of this story is that regardless of whether the daughter plays with the doll or the car, the father's gender belief system (Box A) and the daughter's self-system (Box D) are likely to remain intact. If the daughter plays with the car, she will confirm her belief that she likes cars (Box J), which fits with her self-system (Box D). The father is likely to make a situational attribution for the behavior, such as, "The car is novel, but in time she will return to the dolls" (Box I). Thus the father's belief system (Box A) also remains intact. Alternatively, if the daughter plays with the doll, the father naturally sees that the behavior fits his belief system (Box I). The daughter will realize she is playing with the doll so she can play with her dad and discount her aberrant behavior (Box J). She does not have to alter her self-system either.

Box H: This box has to do with the characteristics of the situation that might influence behavior. Is the behavior socially desirable? In our example, playing with a doll or car is socially desirable behavior. But what is socially desirable may differ for females and males. Is it socially desirable for a boy to play with a doll? The certainty of the perceiver's and target's self-concepts will influence the outcome. In our example, the 3-year-old is likely to have a quite malleable concept of what toys are appropriate for girls and boys. If the father has spent little time around the daughter, he, too, might be less certain about the toys she will like. Those who have the strongest stereotypes are most likely to have them confirmed. The situation also determines constraints on behavior. Playtime at day care is likely to be a situation with low behavioral constraints. Finally, the extent to which the target is concerned with self-presentation (i.e., pleasing her father) versus adhering to her self-concept (i.e., playing with what she really likes) will influence behavior.

Although the diagram may seem complicated at first glance, the interaction we just described is actually overly simplified. In every interaction, the perceiver is also a target, and the target is also a perceiver. So we could talk about how the daughter influences her father's behavior. We could also talk about how the other children and the teacher influence the father–daughter interaction. Each person has expectancies for self and others. The point is that in any given situation, many proximal variables determine whether a behavior occurs, specifically whether women and men display differences in behavior.

Numerous studies have supported this model by demonstrating situational influences on behavior. One such study showed that two features of the situation—instructions to cooperate or compete and

the sex of the person with whom one is interacting—influenced how adolescent boys and girls described their personality in terms of masculinity and femininity (Leszczynski & Strough, 2008). Two weeks before the experiment, seventh and eighth grade girls and boys completed a measure of trait masculinity and femininity. During the experiment, they played the game Jenga with a same-sex or other-sex person. Afterward, they were asked to complete state measures of masculinity and femininity. Both girls and boys reported more feminine selves when working with a female than a male and when cooperating than competing. When cooperating, males reported more masculine selves than females, but when competing masculinity scores were equal.

TAKE HOME POINTS

- Unlike the other theories in this chapter, the Deaux and Major (1987) model emphasizes the more proximal causes of sex differences, highlighting the impact of the situation.

- Perceivers influence whether sex differences are observed through cognitive and behavioral confirmation.

- Targets influence whether sex differences are observed through self-verification and self-presentation.

- Features of the situation that influence the observance of sex differences are behavioral constraints, whether the situation calls for self-presentation, and the strength of one's views on the subject of interest.

SUMMARY

I reviewed the different theories that explain the origins of the sex differences discussed in Chapter 4 as well as how gender roles are acquired. Biological theories of sex differences focus largely on the role of hormones and the effects of the structure of the brain on sex differences in cognition and behavior. The evidence for each of these subject areas is fairly controversial. The role of hormones is difficult to study because it is difficult to manipulate hormone levels in humans; thus we are left to rely on correlational research among humans and experimental research on animals. Evolutionary psychology and sociobiology are theories that introduce evolutionary principles to explain cognitive and social behavior. Although a number of social behaviors, such as sexual behavior and aggression, can be explained by sociobiology, it is difficult to test this theory experimentally.

Psychoanalytic theory began with Freud but has been updated by Chodorow. The basis of the theory, whether traditional or modern, is how identifying with the same-sex parent influences the acquisition of gender roles. Social learning theory states that reinforcement and modeling apply to the acquisition of gender-role behavior just as they do to any other behavior. The principles of social learning theory have been applied directly to gender-role acquisition in the form of gender-role socialization theory. Gender-role socialization emphasizes the role that social agents, in particular parents, play in developing children's gender roles. The evidence for parents' differential treatment of daughters and sons is contradictory; put simply, parents treat sons and daughters more similarly than differently, but the few differences may have

a large impact. In particular, parents provide sons and daughters with different toys, ones suitable for their gender. Social role theory is similar to gender-role socialization in that it emphasizes the social forces that shape gender-role behavior. However, social role theory examines those forces at a higher level, for example, by claiming that the division of labor between men and women in society (men working outside the home, women caring for children) fosters agentic and communal behavior. Interesting cross-cultural research confirms the notion that the different opportunities societies present to girls and boys can lead to the development of gender-distinct behavior. By contrast, cognitive development theory emphasizes the child as an active processor of the environment rather than a passive recipient of modeling and reinforcement. Gender schema theory integrates the principles of social learning theory (and gender-role socialization) with cognitive development theory. The principles of social learning theory are responsible for the content of the gender categories in society, and cognitive development theory is responsible for our acting in accordance with those categories. Gender schema theory is really a theory of process, rather than content; people who are gender schematic behave in ways consistent with the gender schema of a given society; people who are gender aschematic do not use gender as a guiding principle for behavior.

Finally, Deaux and Major offer a theory that describes the more proximal determinants of men's and women's behavior. According to Deaux and Major, characteristics of the perceiver, the target, and the situation will determine at any given moment how people behave and whether a sex difference is observed.

Obviously, no one theory is correct in terms of explaining all sex differences or in terms of explaining how men and women come to possess male and female gender roles. Some theories have more evidence than others. Some theories are more easily testable than others. Some theories are more relevant to one aspect of gender than others; for example, hormones may play a greater role in aggression than in verbal ability. Each of these theories appears throughout this text, but the predominant theories discussed are ones that focus on social or environmental contributors to the impact of gender on relationships and health.

DISCUSSION QUESTIONS

1. Discuss the strengths and weaknesses of each theory of gender introduced in this chapter.
2. Which theory of gender is most difficult to test? Easiest to test?
3. For which sex differences in cognition and behavior does biology seem to play the largest role?
4. If you were going to develop a study to determine whether parents treat sons and daughters differently, how would you go about developing this study? In particular, what specific behaviors would you measure?
5. How are gender roles portrayed in the media?
6. Give some specific examples of how our culture models and reinforces violence.
7. What is the masculine mystique?
8. How do the roles women and men hold in society contribute to agentic and communal behavior?
9. Distinguish between social learning theory and cognitive development theory. How does gender schema theory integrate the two?
10. Debate the advantages and disadvantages of raising a gender aschematic child.
11. Apply Deaux and Major's model to a specific behavior. Review each of the steps in the model shown in Figure 5.12.

SUGGESTED READING

Bem, S. L. (1998). *An unconventional family.* New Haven, CT: Yale University Press.

Buss, D. M. (1995). Psychological sex differences: Origins through sexual selection. *American Psychologist, 50*(3), 164–168.

(Classic) Chodorow, N. (1978). *The reproduction of mothering: Psychoanalysis and the sociology of gender.* London: University of California Press.

Deaux, K., & Major, K. (1987). Putting gender into context: An interactive model of gender-related behavior. *Psychological Review, 94,* 369–389.

Spelke, E. S. (2005). Sex differences in intrinsic aptitude for mathematics and science? A critical review. *American Psychologist, 60*, 950–958.

(Classic) Whiting, B. B., & Edwards, C. P. (1988). *Children of different worlds.* Cambridge, MA: Harvard University Press.

Wood, W., & Eagly, A. H. (2002). A cross-cultural analysis of the behavior of women and men: Implications for the origins of sex differences. *Psychological Bulletin, 128*, 699–727.

KEY TERMS

Androgens—Male sex hormones (e.g., testosterone).

Androgyny—Incorporation of both traditionally masculine and traditionally feminine qualities into one's self-concept.

Behavioral confirmation—Process by which a perceiver's expectation actually alters the target's behavior so the target comes to confirm the perceiver's expectancy.

Cognitive confirmation—Idea that individuals see what they want to see.

Estrogens—Female sex hormones.

Gender aschematic—Someone who does not use the gender category as a guiding principle in behavior or as a way of processing information about the world.

Gender constancy—Categorization of the self as male or female and the realization that this category cannot be changed.

Gender identity—Label determined by biological sex that is applied either to the self or other people.

Gender schematic—Someone who uses the gender category as a guiding principle in behavior and as a way of processing information about the world.

Heterosexual script—Stereotypical enactment of male and female roles in romantic relationships.

Intersex conditions—Conditions in which chromosomal sex does not correspond to phenotypic sex or there is an inconsistency within phenotypic sex.

Lateralization—Localization of an ability (e.g., language) in one hemisphere of the brain.

Masculine mystique—Image of masculinity upheld by society that consists of toughness, dominance, emotional detachment, callousness toward women, eagerness to seek out danger, and competition.

Proactive aggression—Aggressive behavior that is planned and generally socially motivated.

Reactive aggression—Aggressive behavior that takes the form of an angry, impulsive response to threat or provocation.

Schema—Category that contains information about the features of the category as well as its associations with other categories.

Self-monitoring—Variable that describes the extent to which one is more concerned with self-presentation or self-verification.

Self-presentation—Concern individuals have with how their behavior appears to others.

Self-verification—Concern individuals have with behaving in ways consistent with their self-concepts.

Social cognitive theory—States that cognitive development is one factor in gender-role acquisition, but there are social influences as well.

CHAPTER 6

Achievement

. . . there is reasonably strong evidence of taste differences between little girls and little boys that are not easy to attribute to socialization. . . . I guess my experience with my two and a half year old twin daughters who were not given dolls and who were given trucks, and found themselves saying to each other, look, daddy truck is carrying the baby truck, tells me something.

Do you recognize this quote? The person who shared this anecdote? This is a story that was told by Larry Summers, at the time president of Harvard University, who was trying to explain to a conference aimed at diversifying the science and engineering workforce why he thought there were gender disparities (Summers, 2005). Summers implied that there was a basic biological difference between men and women that accounted for the disparity, and he dismissed socialization and discrimination as having a minimal impact. He made these remarks in January 2005, tried to clarify them a few days later, and outright apologized one month later. During the intervening month, he was educated about much of the research that you read in Chapters 4 and 5 and some of what you will read in Chapter 6. It was too late, though. He inspired the furor of women's groups all over the country as well as the faculty of Harvard. One year later he resigned. It probably didn't help that the number of women faculty who had received tenure during his five years of administration had declined (Bombardieri, 2005). Yes, this is the same Mr. Summers who was appointed by President Obama in 2008 to be the Assistant to the President for Economic Policy and Director of the National Economic Council.

Is there any truth to Summers's statement? Are sex differences in math and science achievement due to biological differences between women and men? Biology has typically been dismissed as a compelling explanation because sex differences in achievement have changed dramatically over the 20th century, because women's math scores have increased (recall Chapter 4), and because sex differences in math vary across cultures (Ceci, Williams, & Barnett, 2009). The paradox that we are left to explain is why girls receive higher grades than boys in school, even in the traditionally masculine subjects of math and science, yet perform less well than boys on standardized testing of the same domains, such as the SAT. Is there an actual difference in girls' and boys' aptitude, or does the social environment play a role in these differences?

To understand the differences in the levels of women's and men's achievement, let's begin by evaluating the current status of women's and men's educational opportunities. Historically, men were more likely than women to attend college. However, by the early 1990s, women began to exceed men in the rate that they attended college. In 2007, 42% of females and 36% of males between the ages of 18 and 24 were enrolled in college

(National Center for Education Statistics, 2008a). In that same year, 57% of bachelor's degrees were awarded to women (National Center for Education Statistics, 2008b). The sex disparity is even larger among African American and Hispanic persons, with women earning 66% and 61% of the degrees, respectively. Women also receive 61% of master's degrees, and, in recent years, women have achieved parity with men in terms of doctoral degrees earned. In 2007, women received 49% of the degrees in medicine and 48% of the degrees in law (National Center for Education Statistics, 2008c).

Although women have made huge strides in educational achievements, women and men continue to pursue different fields. As shown in Table 6.1, women are more likely than men to receive bachelor's degrees in elementary education and nursing, and men are

TABLE 6.1   PERCENT OF BACHELOR'S DEGREES CONFERRED TO MALES AND FEMALES IN **2007** AND **2008**

Field of Study	Percent Male	Percent Female
Agriculture and natural resources	52.4	47.6
Accounting	43.8	56.2
Biological and biomedical sciences	40.6	59.4
Business administration and management, general	50.5	49.5
Computer and information sciences and support services	82.4	17.6
Education	21.3	78.7
Elementary education and teaching	9.4	90.6
Engineering	81.6	18.4
Nursing/registered nurse training	10.6	89.4
Mathematics, general	55.1	44.9
Physical sciences	59.2	40.8
Psychology	22.9	77.1
Social sciences and history	50.7	49.3

Source: Adapted from National Center for Education of Statistics (2009a).

more likely than women to receive degrees in computer science and engineering. Women are less likely than men to major in what are now known as "STEM" (Science, Technology, Engineering, and Math) fields (Hill, Corbett, & Rose, 2010). There has been little change in these numbers over the last 10 years. In the area of computer science, there was an increase in the number of women who entered the field in the 1980s, but that increase was followed by a decline. In 1986, 35% of all bachelor's degrees in computer science were awarded to women, whereas in 2006 the number was 21%. Women are equally likely as men to receive a science degree, but women tend toward the life sciences whereas men tend toward the physical sciences.

In the first section of the chapter, I describe a number of individual difference explanations for women's and men's choice of different areas of study and levels of achievement. These explanations pertain to characteristics of women and men. Men and women may be motivated to achieve in different domains and may have different beliefs about their abilities, which could influence their motivations. There are a variety of explanations as to why women do not realize their achievement potential, including ideas that women fear success, lack self-confidence, have lower self-esteem, and are faced with stereotype threat.

In the second section of the chapter, I explore social explanations for sex differences in achievement. How do other people's expectations and beliefs—in particular those of parents and teachers—influence women's and men's achievement?

INDIVIDUAL DIFFERENCE FACTORS

The Achievement Motive

Look at the picture of the two acrobats flying through the air depicted in Figure 6.1. What do you see? What kind of story would you write about the two acrobats? If you wrote about how hard the two people had worked to become acrobats, all they had given up for their profession, how successful they were, and the difficult feats they were trying to accomplish, you might be considered to have a high motive for achievement. At least, this is one way the need for achievement has been measured.

David McClelland and colleagues (McClelland et al., 1953) described the **achievement motive** as a stable personality characteristic that reflects the tendency to strive for success. The achievement motive was measured by people's responses to scenes from Thematic Apperception Test (TAT) cards like the one depicted in Figure 6.1. People would view the scene on the card and write a story about it. The content of the story was then coded for themes related to the achievement motive. Mentions of success, striving, challenge, and accomplishment would reflect

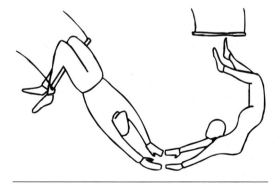

FIGURE 6.1   Adaptation of a Thematic Apperception Test (TAT) card depicting two acrobats flying through the air.

themes of achievement. People who scored high in achievement motivation were found to persist longer at tasks and to reach higher levels of achievement. Those people were men. Achievement motivation did not predict these same outcomes in women. Some people suggested that women did not have as great a desire or need for achievement as men.

There were several problems with this conclusion. First, the domains of achievement studied (or depicted by the TAT cards) may have been more relevant to men than women, especially in the 1950s and 1960s. For example, viewing a TAT card that depicted two scientists in a laboratory may not have aroused the achievement motive in women because few women worked in science laboratories at the time. Women may not have been able to see themselves as scientists in a laboratory, or women may not have had any desire to be scientists in a laboratory. One factor that determines whether someone pursues success in an area is the value the person attaches to success in that area. Women, especially in the 1950s, may not have valued achievement in the sciences.

Another difficulty with the study of achievement motivation in women is that the characteristics that defined the motive (assertiveness, independence, competitiveness) conflicted with the characteristics of the female gender role. Thus another reason women did not fit into the theory of achievement motivation is that women recognized that achievement-related behavior would be inconsistent with their gender role.

What did women do, and what do women do, when they have a high need for achievement but believe achievement conflicts with their gender role? One response is to conceal achievements. Female students may tell their peers they scored lower on an exam than they really did. Another response

is to compensate for the threat to the female gender role that achievement poses by adopting extremely feminine appearance and behavior. Another option is for a woman to master both roles: the role of high achiever and of traditional female wife and mother. Thus high-achievement women may spend enormous amounts of energy both at work and at home to demonstrate that achievement does not conflict with or undermine femininity. One area of research that has addressed how women reconcile a need for achievement with a need to adhere to the female gender role is the fear of achievement or fear of success literature.

Fear of Achievement

Historical Literature.   In the early 1970s, one explanation of why women did not reach high levels of achievement was that they suffered from a "fear of success." Matina Horner (1972) noted that competence, independence, and intellectual achievement were inconsistent with the norms for femininity but consistent with the norms for masculinity. Thus women faced a dilemma when achieving. Women might withdraw from achievement behavior because they are concerned with the threat that achievement poses to their gender role.

Horner (1972) defined the **fear of success** as the association of negative consequences with achievement. For women, the negative consequences were feeling unfeminine and experiencing social rejection. A woman who believes graduating at the top of the class will lead people to dislike, tease, or avoid her may have a fear of success, whereas a woman who believes graduating at the top of the class will bring respect from peers and parents does not have a fear of success (Figure 6.2). In order to have a fear of success, however, the individual must also believe achievement

FIGURE 6.2 The historical "fear of success" literature showed that women associated negative social consequences with high achievements, such as graduating at the top of one's class.

is possible. People who realize they have no way of reaching a goal will not be concerned with the negative consequences of reaching the goal. Thus someone may believe getting an A on an exam will alienate friends but also realize that there is little chance of receiving an A on the exam; this person will not worry about the negative consequences of success. By contrast, the person capable of getting an A and who believes this achievement will lead to rejection by peers is likely to have a fear of success. The person could respond to this fear by either decreasing the amount of effort put into the task (i.e., studying less) or hiding the achievement from peers.

To summarize, there are two requirements for a fear of success: First, the person

must perceive achievement as possible, if not likely; second, the person must associate achievement with negative consequences. A fear of success is not the same as a desire to fail. The person who fears achievement does not seek out failure; instead the person avoids situations that might lead to high achievement and expends less effort so high achievement is not realized.

What was Horner's (1972) evidence for a fear of achievement among women? She used a projective storytelling method. She gave college students the first sentence of a story and asked them to complete it. For example, female students were told "Anne is at the top of her class in medical school," whereas male students were told "John is at the top of his class in medical school." Students were then asked to complete the story. Horner reasoned that anyone who wrote a story that showed conflict about the success, denied credit for the success, or associated negative consequences with the success showed a fear of success. The majority of men (90%) wrote positive stories in response to this cue. A substantial portion of women (65%) wrote troubled stories that showed some conflict or negative consequences associated with Anne's achievement. For example, some women wrote stories about Anne purposely not performing well the next semester or dropping out of medical school. Other women wrote stories about Anne being alienated by friends and family and being very unhappy.

Horner (1972) conducted this first study in 1964 and replicated the findings over the next six years with other samples of college students and with high school and junior high school students. Interestingly, she noted a trend over time for the fear of success to increase among men. Men began to write stories that associated male achievement with selfishness and egoism. Conceptually, the fear of success is the same in men and women: the association of negative consequences with achievement. However, the fear of success was associated with distinct negative consequences for women and men. For women, the major negative consequence was social rejection; for men, the major negative consequence was self-absorption. Both led to unhappiness. Interestingly, these two concerns map onto the two negative gender-related traits discussed in Chapter 2: unmitigated communion and unmitigated agency. Unmitigated communion involves being overly concerned with others and their opinions, whereas unmitigated agency involves being overly absorbed with the self.

Horner (1972) found other indicators of women's fears of success. She noted that high fear of success women performed worse on a task when working with men than with women, admitted they would prefer to tell a male they received a C rather than an A on an exam, and were more likely to switch from nontraditional (e.g., lawyer) to traditional (e.g., teacher) college majors.

Horner's (1972) work has been criticized on many levels. Some have suggested that her projective test actually indicates a discomfort with gender-role-incongruent behavior rather than a fear of success. It turns out that *both* men and women write more negative stories in response to Anne rather than John graduating at the top of the class. Both men and women may be uncomfortable with the idea of women being successful or may realize that successful women face obstacles.

Contemporary Literature.   Most of the studies on fear of success were conducted in the 1960s and the 1970s. Is there any evidence of a residual fear of achievement in women or men today? Do today's college women feel uncomfortable outperforming men? Do women hide their good exam performances from friends, especially male friends? Do women continue to associate

achievement with negative interpersonal consequences?

Some studies have attempted to develop more objective measures of the fear of achievement by asking people directly whether they associate success with negative consequences, including negative peer reactions, social isolation, and pressure to live up to others' expectations. Women tend to score higher than men on these kinds of items (Fried-Buchalter, 1997). Early adolescent girls, in particular, may still associate success with some negative consequences. Bell (1996) held weekly discussions with elementary school girls to identify barriers to their success. She found that girls felt achievement and affiliation were opposites, that one could not do both. She referred to this as the "smart versus social" dilemma. The girls feared that achievement would jeopardize their relationships. Girls also identified a second dilemma, "silence versus bragging." The girls said they often hide their success because talking about it is like bragging and might make other people feel bad. Thus a concern for others and relationships keeps the girls from announcing their achievements. The girls also stated that they felt uncomfortable being singled out by a success because their concerns were with establishing connections to others, not with differentiating themselves from others. The following exchange between the group leader and one of the girls illustrates these ideas (Bell, 1996, p. 422):

JANE: (after receiving a compliment on a science prize): Well, I don't feel that great when you say that to me because I feel like everybody's equal and everybody should have gotten a prize no matter what they did. I think Chris should have gotten it.

MYRA: OK Jane, tell the group why you didn't say "I feel good about winning the prize."

JANE: Well I feel like um, like everybody's looking at me and um saying, "Oh, she shouldn't have won that prize, I should have won" and everybody's gonna be mad at me because um, I won and they didn't.

MYRA: Is there any situation that you could think of where you won an honor that you were deserving of and felt good about?

JANE: If other people won also.

Other studies show that high levels of achievement have negative consequences for girls' self-image. In one study, achievement in math and science predicted an increase in social self-image (i.e., feeling accepted by others) from sixth to seventh grade for both boys and girls, but predicted an increase in social self-image from seventh to eighth grade for boys only (Roberts & Petersen, 1992). Girls' social self-image improved most if they received B's in math rather than C's or even A's. These results especially applied to girls who indicated they valued being popular in school more than they valued getting good grades. Thus the authors concluded that girls feel more accepted if they are not at the top of their math class, especially if they are socially oriented. Conduct Do Gender 6.1 using Horner's (1972) projective method and some objective questions to see if the fear of achievement holds at your school.

Leaving Traditionally Masculine Pursuits.   One facet of the historical literature on women's fear of success is that high-achievement women switch from traditionally masculine pursuits to traditionally feminine ones. In a nationally representative study of eighth graders who aspired to have careers in science and engineering, more females than males changed their minds over the next six years (Mau, 2003). Six years later, 22% of males had pursued careers in these areas compared to 12% of females. Among medical school students, women are as likely as men to start careers in internal medicine and surgery,

**DO GENDER 6.1
Do Women Fear
Achievement, and
Do Men Fear Affiliation?**

Try out Horner's projective test. Ask a group of students to write a story in response to the following sentence: "_____ is at the top of her (his) class in medical school."

You choose the name. You might try a name that can be perceived as either male or female, such as Pat. Or, you might have half of participants respond to a male target and half to a female target. After participants have completed the story, have them respond to a few objective items that could measure fear of success, as discussed in the text.

Decide how you want to code the stories. Do you want to code violent imagery, negative imagery, or threat? Be sure to have clear operational definitions of anything that you code. Ideally, you would find another coder and evaluate the stories independently. Make sure the stories are anonymous with respect to sex when you rate them.

Are there sex differences in fears of success on the projective measure? On the objective measure? How do the objective and projective measures compare?

but over time women are more likely to switch from these fields to gynecology and obstetrics, areas more compatible with the female role (Gjerberg, 2002).

What are women's reasons for switching out of traditionally masculine pursuits? In a study of female twelfth graders who aimed to pursue traditionally masculine fields but switched to neutral or feminine fields seven years later, three reasons were prominent. First, women desired a job with greater flexibility; second, women were unhappy with the high time demands of jobs in traditionally masculine fields; and third, women had low intrinsic interest in the value of physical sciences (Frome et al., 2006). Female engineering students expressed a number of concerns about their future careers, including conflict between work and family, lack of female role models, lack of confidence, and discriminatory attitudes (Hartman & Hartman, 2008). Those who expressed greater concerns in their senior year of college also anticipated that they would be less likely to be working in the field of engineering 10 years later. Find out on your own why women (and possibly men) switch from nontraditional to traditional majors with Do Gender 6.2.

DO GENDER 6.2
Reasons for Switching from Nontraditional to Traditional Majors

Conduct interviews with both women and men who switched from nontraditional to traditional majors and from traditional to nontraditional majors. First, you will have to decide what the traditional majors for men and women are. For example, you might find five women who switched from science, math, or engineering to nursing, and five men who switched from the liberal arts to business. To gather more data on this issue, this could be used as a class project with the interview format standardized.

Ask a series of open-ended questions to find out why people initially chose their major, why they switched, if they had any difficulties switching, and how others reacted to their switch. Then, you might follow up with some closed-ended questions to make sure the issues you are interested in are addressed. For example, you might have some specific statements about negative peer reactions or fears of negative consequences associated with success.

TAKE HOME POINTS

- People who have a fear of success are capable of high achievement but associate negative consequences with achievement.

- The basic concern is that achievement is inconsistent with the female gender role. Females are concerned that attaining high levels of achievement will have social costs.

- The fear of success literature was, and still is, quite controversial. There is concern with the validity of the projective tests that were first used to identify a fear of success in women. However, self-report instruments still show that women more than men associate success with negative consequences.

- Some women who start out in traditionally masculine fields leave those domains for more traditionally feminine pursuits. Further research with these women will tell how much of this change is due to a fear of success versus a concern with the demands and lack of flexibility of a traditionally masculine career.

Self-Confidence

Do women have less confidence in themselves compared to men? Despite the fact that girls do better than boys in school, girls are more worried than boys about their grades in school (Pomerantz, Altermatt, & Saxon, 2002). That is, females earn higher grades in most subjects in school but evaluate their competence in each of those subjects as lower than that of boys—with the exception of language. Interestingly, women will defend other women's abilities but not necessarily their own. Collis (1991) refers to this as the "We can but I can't" paradox. In general, women are more likely than men to underestimate their abilities and less likely to expect success. What are the consequences of a lack of self-confidence?

When we expect not to succeed in a domain, we will give up more easily on a given task, choose an easier task, and pursue activities in other domains.

Nature of Task. Women are not less self-confident than men on all tasks. The nature of the task is an important determinant of sex differences in self-confidence. There are numerous studies that show women are less self-confident than men about their performance on masculine tasks, such as STEM fields (Good, Aronson, & Harder, 2008; Pajares, 2005), despite equal performance. In the field of computer science, women are less self-confident than men despite equal performance (Singh et al., 2007). A study of medical students performing a clinical exam showed that women reported more anxiety and appeared less self-confident to objective observers compared to men—despite the fact that women and men had similar levels of performance (Blanch et al., 2008).

Given the fact that girls' and boys' school performance is the same in traditionally masculine subjects, like math and science, when do sex differences in self-confidence arise? This question was addressed in a study of Italian children (Muzzatti & Agnoli, 2007). As shown in Figure 6.3, there were no sex differences in math self-confidence among the second and third graders, but boys were more confident than girls in the fourth and fifth grades. In addition, stereotypes about math as a male domain emerged with age, as shown in Figure 6.4. Whereas second-grade girls tended to believe that girls were better than boys in math and second-grade boys believed that girls and boys had equal math ability, by fifth-grade, girls shared boys' beliefs that boys were better than girls at math. Other research shows that sex differences in self-confidence appear by middle school (Pajares, 2005).

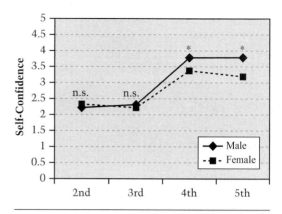

FIGURE 6.3 There were no sex differences in math self-confidence among 2nd and 3rd graders (n.s. = not significant). Among 4th and 5th graders, boys were more confident than girls (* = significant)
Source: Adapted from Muzzatti and Agnoli (2007).

The Appearance of Low Self-Confidence. It is possible that women only *appear* less self-confident than men. Girls might be trying to appear modest because they are concerned about how their superior performance will affect another person's self-esteem. One study showed that women recalled lower grades (12.78) than they received (13.32), whereas men recalled their grades accurately (recall 12.46; actual 12.30; Chatard, Guimond, & Selimbegovic, 2007). One problem with women "appearing" less confident is that behavior often shapes attitudes, as indicated by cognitive dissonance and self-perception theories. That is, women may come to believe the opinions that they express about themselves.

Women's Underconfidence or Men's Overconfidence? The literature on self-confidence has typically been interpreted in terms of a female disadvantage: Women have *less* confidence in themselves compared

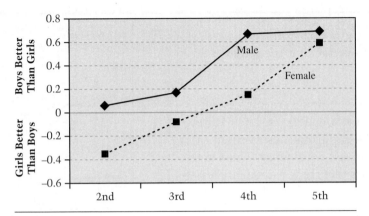

FIGURE 6.4 Among 2nd graders, girls believed that girls were better than boys in math and boys believed boys and girls were about the same; by 4th grade, boys believed that boys were better than girls in math and this belief persisted through 5th grade; 3rd and 4th grade girls thought the two sexes were roughly the same but by 5th grade girls shared boys' beliefs that boys were better than girls at math.
Source: Adapted from Muzzatti and Agnoli (2007).

to men. But, do women underestimate their abilities, or do men overestimate their abilities? One way to address this question is to compare women's and men's confidence to their actual performance. If someone expects to receive a 90 on a test and receives an 80, the person is overconfident. If someone expects to receive an 80 and receives a 90, the person is underconfident. This kind of method was used with college business students who were asked to predict price/equity ratios (Endres, Chowdhury, & Alam, 2008). Men were more confident than women. However, when confidence was compared to accuracy, both men and women were found to be underconfident. In this case, women were more underconfident than men. By contrast, a study that compared exam performance to exam confidence across 25 universities that spanned five countries showed that both women and men were overconfident

(Lundeberg et al., 2000). The nature of the task may moderate these effects. In a study that examined confidence and performance in math, males were overconfident and females were underconfident (Lloyd, Walsh, & Yailagh, 2005).

TAKE HOME POINTS

- The major factor that influences sex differences in self-confidence is the nature of the task. Sex differences in self-confidence seem to be limited to masculine tasks; it is here that women tend to underestimate their performance and lack self-confidence. Thus, lack of self-confidence could be a contributing factor to the underrepresentation of women in masculine areas of achievement, specifically math and science.

- Part of the sex difference in self-confidence is due to women *appearing* less confident. Women are more reluctant than men to display confidence when they have outperformed another person, believing that others' self-esteem would be threatened by such displays.

■ To the extent that a sex difference in self-confidence exists, it appears to be a combination of women being underconfident and men being overconfident.

Response to Evaluative Feedback

I began college with a major in journalism. I took some psychology classes along the way. Two things happened to make me switch from journalism to psychology: First, I discovered all my journalism assignments— news stories, feature stories, editorials, and investigations—were on psychological topics; second, not one of my journalism professors took me aside and told me I was a gifted writer. Receiving A's on papers was not enough to make me think I could be a successful journalist; I was waiting for the tap on my shoulder. Ironically, after I switched my major to psychology in my junior year, a journalism professor did take me aside and told me what I had wanted to hear. By then it was too late. I had already developed a passion for psychology.

While teaching at Carnegie Mellon, a similar experience occurred, but this time I was the one tapping someone else's shoulder. I had taken aside an undergraduate who was torn between art and psychology, and within psychology, torn between clinical work and research. I told her I thought she had all the skills needed to make a fine researcher: clear conceptual thinking, a strong methodological knowledge base, and creativity in experimental design. I did not think twice about this conversation until she told me the following semester that it had influenced her to switch her focus to research. The interesting part of this story— and here is where it becomes relevant to the chapter—is that she shared the experience

with her boyfriend, and he was befuddled. He could not understand why what I had said had made any difference to her.

Women may be more influenced than men by the feedback they receive from others about their performance. This could stem from a lack of self-confidence on the part of women, or it could stem from an openness to others' opinions; the sex difference can easily be cast in a negative or positive light. In either case, when women are told they have performed poorly or lack ability, they may be more likely than men to take the feedback to heart. Grades in math are more strongly correlated with women's than men's perceived competence in math (Correll, 2001), suggesting that others' opinions have a stronger influence on women than men. Women's thoughts about themselves, including beliefs about their abilities, are more influenced by other people's appraisals of their abilities compared to men. The direction of the influence could be positive or negative, depending on whether the feedback is positive or negative.

Females' greater responsiveness to feedback was shown in a study in which college students were asked to give a speech to a group of three other students who were confederates of the experimenter (Roberts & Nolen-Hoeksema, 1994). One of the confederates provided positive feedback, negative feedback, or gave no feedback. Prior to the feedback, women reported higher performance expectancies compared to men, possibly because giving a speech is considered to be a more feminine task. As shown in Figure 6.5, women's evaluations of their speech were more affected by the feedback than those of men. Women's evaluations of their speech became more positive in the positive feedback condition and more negative in the negative feedback condition, whereas men's evaluations were less affected by the

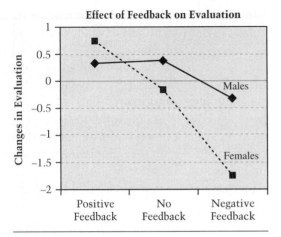

FIGURE 6.5 Effect of feedback on evaluation. Women evaluated their speech as more positive after receiving positive feedback and more negative after receiving negative feedback. Men's evaluations of their speech were relatively unaffected by the nature of the feedback they received. *Source*: Adapted from Roberts and Nolen-Hoeksema (1994, Study 2).

feedback. Women were not more responsive to the feedback because they were less confident than men. Recall that women had higher initial expectancies than men. Women also were not more responsive to the feedback because they wanted to appear agreeable to the confederates; the evaluations were confidential. However, women indicated that the feedback was more accurate than men did. Thus the authors concluded that women are more responsive to feedback than men because they find the feedback to be more informative about their abilities.

One concern about these kinds of studies is that they are conducted with college students, and the feedback is given by peers rather than authority figures. We would expect both women and men to be more responsive to feedback from those judged to be more knowledgeable. An undergraduate and I tested whether there were sex differences

in responsiveness to feedback in a real-world setting (Johnson & Helgeson, 2002). We measured the self-esteem of bank employees before and after they met with their supervisor for their annual performance evaluation. As shown in Figure 6.6, women's self-esteem improved slightly after receiving a positive evaluation and declined substantially after receiving a negative evaluation, whereas men's self-esteem was largely unaffected by the nature of the feedback. Women also took the evaluation process more seriously, regarded the feedback as more accurate, and viewed their supervisors as credible sources. Men who received negative feedback appeared to prepare themselves psychologically for the upcoming evaluation by derogating the source of the feedback ("My supervisor isn't that smart") and the feedback system ("The evaluation process is not fair"). In general, the results of this study supported the laboratory findings.

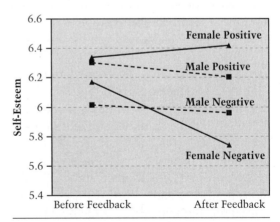

FIGURE 6.6 Women's self-esteem slightly improved after receiving a positive evaluation from their supervisor, and women's self-esteem drastically decreased after receiving a negative evaluation. Men's self-esteem was unaffected by the feedback they received from their supervisor. *Source*: Adapted from Johnson and Helgeson (2002).

TAKE HOME POINTS

- Women are more responsive to evaluative feedback than men — meaning that they use it to make inferences about their abilities.

- One reason that women are more responsive to feedback is that they view the information as more accurate — as more informative of their abilities.

- Men may discount negative feedback in an effort to protect their self-esteem.

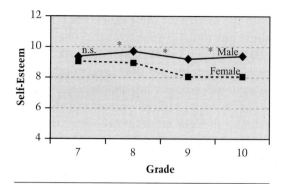

FIGURE 6.7 Sex differences in self-esteem emerge in 8th grade.

Source: Adapted from Heaven and Ciarrochi (2008).

Self-Esteem

Does a lack of self-confidence and a greater responsiveness to evaluative feedback reflect a lower level of self-esteem on the part of women? A meta-analysis of sex comparisons in self-esteem found a small difference in favor of males ($d = +.21$; Kling et al., 1999). However, effect sizes varied greatly by age, with the largest sex difference emerging during adolescence ($d = +.33$ for 15- to 18-year-olds). Effect sizes were smaller for younger and older respondents. A more recent study showed that sex differences in self-esteem emerged in grades 8 through 10, as shown in Figure 6.7 (Heaven & Ciarrochi, 2008).

Is the sex difference in self-esteem among adolescents due to a decrease in females' self-esteem or an increase in males' self-esteem? One review article concluded that both boys' and girls' self-esteem decreases during early adolescence but that boys' self-esteem rebounds and shows a large increase during high school compared to girls (Twenge & Campbell, 2001). The previous study (Figure 6.7) seemed to show some fluctuation in boys' self-esteem and a steady deterioration in girls' self-esteem. A comparison of White and Black girls showed that Black girls' self-esteem is less likely than White girls' self-esteem to decline

over adolescence (Biro et al., 2006), which may explain why the meta-analytic review showed that the sex difference in self-esteem was not significant among Black samples (Kling et al., 1999). A meta-analysis that focused on ethnicity showed that the sex difference in self-esteem is larger for Whites than other ethnic groups (Twenge & Crocker, 2002).

What are some of the reasons that females, especially adolescent White females, have lower self-esteem than males? One reason is that these girls have less favorable attitudes than boys toward their gender role. We saw in Chapter 2 that girls were more likely than boys to want to become the other sex and that boys viewed changing their sex as a negative event, whereas girls viewed changing their sex as more of an opportunity. A second reason for girls' lower self-esteem compared to boys is girls' greater emphasis on popularity and increased contact with the opposite sex. Girls, in particular Caucasian girls, place a greater value on popularity than boys do. Being concerned with how others view oneself leads to a fragile self-esteem, because one's self-worth is dependent on how one is viewed by others at any given moment. In a study of eleventh and twelfth graders, girls' self-esteem was positively correlated with the quality of their other-sex relation-ships but not the quality of their same-sex relationships (Thomas & Daubman, 2001). Boys' self-esteem was unrelated to other-sex or same-sex relationship quality.

There are multiple dimensions of self-esteem. A meta-analytic review of the dif-ferent domains of self-esteem showed that females score higher than males on behav-ioral conduct (i.e., how acceptable your behavior is; $d = -.17$) and moral-ethical self-esteem (i.e., satisfaction with morality, ethics; $d = -.38$), and males score higher than females on appearance ($d = .35$) and athletic self-esteem ($d = .41$; Gentile et al., 2009). Despite the fact that girls do better than boys in school and are more socially skilled, there are no sex differences in academic or social self-esteem.

Interestingly, the sex difference in body satisfaction persists in adulthood, and is apparent among Whites, Asians, and Hispanics (Algars et al., 2009; Frederick et al., 2007). Even among adults over the age of 60, women are less satisfied with their bodies compared to men (Homan & Boyatzis, 2009) and age-related declines in body satisfaction are stronger among women than men (Algars et al., 2009). Women are more anxious than men about the effects of age on their appear-ance. Women's greater investment in their appearance has been supported by brain im-aging. A neural imaging study showed that women show greater brain activation than men when asked to compare their bodies to pictures shown of same-sex bodies in bathing suits (Owens, Allen, & Spangler, 2010).

The relation of gender role to self-esteem is stronger than the relation of sex to self-esteem. Masculinity or agency, as measured with the PAQ or BSRI, is strongly positively related to self-esteem. Femininity or com-munion, by contrast, is not related to one's overall self-regard but may be related to

components of self-esteem (see Helgeson, 1994c, for a review). Communion is often re-lated to the social aspects of self-esteem, such as feeling comfortable and competent in social situations. Communion is correlated with self-esteem in domains reflecting honesty, religion, and parental relationships, whereas agency is correlated with self-esteem in domains reflect-ing physical abilities and problem solving, as well as general self-esteem.

TAKE HOME POINTS

- There is a small sex difference in self-esteem, in the direction of males having a more favorable view of themselves than females.

- Age is an important moderator of sex differences in self-esteem; the difference appears largest among adolescents.

- One dimension of self-esteem particularly relevant to adolescent females is body image. Adolescent girls are more unhappy with their body than adolescent boys, which may partly account for adolescent girls' lower levels of overall self-esteem.

- Gender-related traits, such as agency and communion, seem to show stronger relations to self-esteem than sex per se.

Stereotype Threat

Regardless of women's self-esteem or self-confidence, they are well aware of the ste-reotype that women have less aptitude in traditionally masculine domains, such as math and science, compared to men. The theory of **stereotype threat** suggests that the salience of these kinds of stereotypes may have a negative impact on women's performance. Activating the stereotype increases the pressure on women during performance—a pressure that arises due to fears of confirming the stereotype.

Because some gender stereotypes are so pervasive, they may not need to be made explicit to affect performance. A study of stereotype threat concerning visual-spatial skills showed that college women performed worse than men when the stereotype was explicit (i.e., students told that men perform better than women) and when the stereotype was implicit (i.e., no information was provided; Campbell & Collaer, 2009). Only when the stereotype was nullified (i.e., students told that women and men perform the same on the task) was performance the same for women and men. These results are shown in Figure 6.8.

When do females become vulnerable to stereotype threat in the areas of math and science? It likely emerges as children become aware of the stereotypes. Recall that the study of Italian children showed that perceptions of males as better than females in math emerged around fifth grade (see Figure 6.4; Muzzatti & Agnoli, 2007). That study also showed that stereotype threat affects performance at that time. In their study, second through fifth graders were either shown pictures of famous mathematicians (nine were males and one was female) to activate the stereotype "math = male" or shown pictures of objects (nine were flowers and one was fruit), followed by a math test. There were no sex differences in performance in either condition among second, third, or fourth graders. But, by fifth grade, the stereotype threat condition lowered girls' performance. However, another study conducted in France showed that third-grade girls were vulnerable to stereotype threat (Neuville & Croizet, 2007). When gender was made salient, third-grade girls' math performance deteriorated but boys' did not.

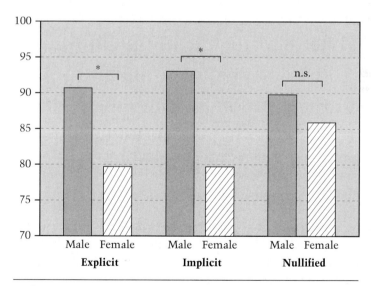

FIGURE 6.8   Men performed better than women on a visual spatial task when the gender stereotype was made explicit or implicit, but men and women performed the same on the task when the stereotype was nullified.
Source: Adapted from Campbell and Collaer (2009).

Stereotype threat is not limited to math and science. The stereotype that men have more political knowledge than women has affected women's performance on a political knowledge survey when made explicit (McGlone, Aronson, & Kobrynowicz, 2006). Men are not invulnerable to stereotype threat. When female and male college students completed a social sensitivity test that involved decoding nonverbal cues, men performed more poorly than women when told the test measured social sensitivity but performed the same as women when told the test measured information processing (Koenig & Eagly, 2005). Thus the theory of stereotype threat generalizes to all groups of people for whom there are stereotypes.

There have been so many studies on this topic in recent years that a meta-analysis of studies across five different countries was conducted (Walton & Spencer, 2009). The finding was that stereotyped groups perform worse than nonstereotyped groups under conditions of threat, but that stereotyped groups' performance improves when the threat is removed. Because standardized tests are threatening, these findings suggest that the academic performance of stereotyped groups—women and ethnic minorities—may be underestimated.

Clearly the activation of a stereotype affects immediate performance, but are there long-term consequences? One study showed that stereotype threat affected ability perception and intentions to pursue the area of ability in the future (Correll, 2004). Stereotype threat was aroused by telling students that males are better than females at an ambiguous task. Despite the fact that all students were given the same score on the test, males perceived that they had greater ability in the task and had greater career aspirations in an area that required competence at this task. However, the long-term effects of stereotype threat may be influenced by people's actual abilities. In one study, stereotype threat was induced by having students take a math test for which past research showed men outperformed women (Lesko & Corpus, 2006). The women in this condition who perceived themselves to be very good at math (strong math identity) discounted their poor performance by saying the test was not accurate and not reflective of their ability. Thus, at least those who identify with a domain may be able to discount poor performance induced by stereotype threat and continue to persist in the area. We should be most concerned about the effects of stereotype threat on people who do not identify with the domain or people who are novices. These people may see poor performance as diagnostic of their abilities and give up the area of pursuit.

More recently, researchers have asked whether there is a specific part of the math stereotype that evokes stereotype threat (Thoman et al., 2008). Female college students were randomly assigned to either read an article that stated males were better than females at math due to innate differences (i.e. genetics), an article that stated males were better than females at math because males exert more effort, or a control condition that did not involve reading an article. Then, students took a math test. The effort group outperformed both the control group and the ability group. There was no difference in performance between the control group and the ability group, consistent with previous research that suggests women are aware of the stereotype without it being explicitly activated. In other words, people in the control group automatically assume that differences in performance are due to differential ability. The effort group also spent more time solving the problems than the ability and control groups. Studies like this suggest that we should be encouraging children to focus on effort rather than ability as an explanation for high achievement. See Sidebar 6.1 for

SIDEBAR 6.1: *Fixed and Growth Mindsets*

Carol Dweck (2008) has been engaged in a program of research that distinguishes a fixed mindset from a growth mindset with respect to achievement. A fixed mindset is one in which performance is assumed to reflect ability that is unchangeable, whereas a growth mindset is one in which performance is assumed to reflect effort that is modifiable. The United States tends to emphasize a fixed mindset, although other cultures (e.g., Asian) are more likely to emphasize a growth mindset. In the United States, we often praise students for their intelligence or aptitude in an area rather than their effort, which leads to a fixed mindset. Those with a fixed mindset are more likely to avoid challenging tasks and to lose confidence when a task becomes difficult. Students with a growth mindset earn higher grades and recover more quickly from receiving a poor grade. A growth mindset also can protect against stereotype threat. Recall the stereotype threat study that showed priming the math stereotype (males perform better than females) did not hinder female performance when the stereotype was based on effort (Thoman et al., 2008)—that is, a growth mindset!

Teachers who adopt a growth mindset might be more successful in helping students to learn. In one study, Dweck and colleagues asked a group of adults to behave as teachers and give feedback to a seventh grader who had received a 65% on a math exam. Half of the participants were told that math performance is due to innate ability (fixed mindset), and half were told that math performance can be learned (growth mindset). Those in the growth mindset condition provided more encouragement and more strategies for improvement to the student, whereas those in the fixed mindset condition gave more comfort to the student and were more likely to tell the student that math isn't for everyone. Thus, parents and teachers ought to praise students for their effort rather than their ability.

Dweck makes several recommendations, including:

1. Teach students about research suggesting the brain is a muscle that gets stronger with exercise (i.e., "brain plasticity") and the view that talent can be developed.

2. Help students to see challenges, efforts, and mistakes as having value.

3. Provide process feedback—that is, feedback about effort and strategies (e.g., that was great that you could come up with a different way of solving the problem than the one you read about)—rather than person feedback (e.g., you are so smart!) or outcome feedback (e.g., the presentation is excellent!).

a discussion of Carol Dweck's work on fixed and growth mindsets consistent with the distinction between ability and effort.

Can the effects of stereotype threat also be nullified if people are educated about the phenomenon? One study suggested that this was the case (Johns, Schmader, & Martens, 2005). College students completed a series of math problems after being randomly assigned to one of three groups. In the first condition, the task was described as a problem-solving task. In the second condition, the task was described as a math test. In the third condition, the task was described as a math test, but students were told that stereotype threat could decrease their performance. Results showed that women performed the same as men in the first condition and worse than men in the second condition—the typical stereotype threat effect. However, women performed the same as men in the third condition—when the task was viewed as a math test but information on stereotype threat was provided.

Finally, researchers also have tried to understand *how* stereotype threat affects performance. One possibility is that stereotype threat provokes anxiety which then interferes with performance (Bosson, Haymovitz, & Pinel, 2004). Others have suggested that stereotype threat interferes with performance by reducing one's cognitive capacity or one's ability to focus on the task (Koenig & Eagly, 2005). Either of these mechanisms is consistent with the findings from a functional magnetic resonance imaging (fMRI) study (Krendl et al., 2008). A group of college women who identified themselves with math (i.e., math was important to them) were asked to complete some math problems while in the scanner after either being told that there are sex differences in math ability (stereotype threat) or not (control). In the control condition, solving math problems was associated with activation of regions in the brain that are linked to math calculations (e.g., angular gyrus). In the stereotype threat condition, those same regions of the brain were *not* activated but regions related to processing emotions (e.g., ventral anterior cingulated cortex) were activated.

TAKE HOME POINTS

- Stereotype threat is the idea that activating a stereotype may create a concern with confirming the stereotype and thereby interfere with performance. In the area of gender, it has most often been applied to women's math performance.

- The effects of stereotype threat on those who strongly identify with a domain may be transient if they discount the validity of a poor performance.

- The effects of stereotype threat may be nullified by discounting the stereotype, indicating that the stereotype is due to effort rather than ability, or educating people about stereotype threat.

- Stereotype threat may interfere with performance by reducing cognitive capacity and/or by increasing anxiety.

Conceptions of the Self

Cross and Madson (1997) argue that many of the sex differences we observe in behavior are due to the different ways men and women define themselves. Men maintain an independent sense of self that is separate from others, or an **independent self-construal**; women, by contrast, maintain an interdependent sense of self in which others are integrated into the self, or a relational-**interdependent self-construal** (Cross & Morris, 2003; Guimond et al., 2006). Men are more likely to describe themselves in terms of their independence from others (e.g., emphasizing personal attributes and skills), and women are more likely to describe themselves in terms of their connection to others (e.g., emphasizing roles and relationships to others). Women think more about other people, pay more attention to others, and have greater recall for information about others.

However, sex differences in self-construal are not universal. Guimond and colleagues (2007) argue that sex differences in self-construal are variable and that social comparison processes influence these sex differences. When women and men make between-group comparisons (i.e., women compare themselves to men and men compare themselves to women), sex differences in self-construal increase. When men and women make within-group comparisons (i.e., men compare themselves to men and women compare themselves to women), sex differences in self-construal decrease. Guimond and colleagues argue that one reason that sex differences in personality and values are stronger in more egalitarian Western countries than less egalitarian Eastern countries is that Western countries promote between-group comparisons. Eastern countries have such a large status difference between men and women that it makes no sense for them to compare themselves to one another. See if there are sex differences in self-construal at your school with Do Gender 6.3.

One problem with suggesting that women have a more interdependent sense of self compared to men has to do with the way interdependence is conceptualized. There are two kinds of interdependence: **relational interdependence** and **collective interdependence** (Baumeister & Sommer, 1997). The relational aspects of the self are those that emphasize close relationships with other people. The collective aspects of the self are those derived from group memberships and affiliations. What appears to be men's desire

for independence and separation may really be their desire to form broader social connections with others, such as those achieved by power and status. Women and men may be equally social but in different spheres: Women invest in a small number of relationships, and men orient themselves toward the broader social structure and embed themselves in larger groups. An example of men's interdependence that Baumeister and Sommer cite comes from the helping literature. Recall that the meta-analysis on helping showed that men were more helpful than women (Eagly & Crowley, 1986), but an important moderator was the relationship to the recipient. Men help people they do not know, which is akin to helping society at large, whereas women help people they do know and with whom they have a relationship, such as family and friends.

How are these different self-definitions related to self-esteem? It is not the case that a relational self-construal is related to low self-esteem (Cross, Bacon, & Morris, 2000). Instead, evidence indicates that agentic self-definitions are related to men's self-esteem, and communal self-definitions are related to women's self-esteem. Men's self-esteem seems to be based on power, differentiating themselves from others, effectiveness, and independent action, whereas women's self-esteem is based on relationships and connections (Miller, 1991).

To this point, I have been emphasizing differences. But there are also similarities in the sources of self-esteem for women and men. For example, feeling accepted by others is associated with feeling good about the self, and feeling rejected by others is associated with feeling bad about the self for both women and men (Leary et al., 1995). However, the associations are stronger for women than men.

It is quite likely that cultural and ethnic factors influence the sources of self-esteem

DO GENDER 6.3
Self-Conceptions

Have a group of students respond to the question "Who am I?" Then, review each of the attributes and categorize them as emphasizing separation from others, connection to others, or neither. Make sure you are blind to the respondent's sex when you categorize the attributes.

Is it true that females define themselves more in terms of connection to others, and males define themselves more in terms of their separation from others?

Administer a measure of gender-related traits and see if agency, communion, unmitigated agency, or unmitigated communion are related to these categories. What would you predict?

for women and men. Although Western cultures emphasize individualism, achievement, and success, there are people whose opportunities to achieve are limited—by poverty or by discrimination. African Americans, in particular, may derive self-esteem from other domains. Because the family is central to the identity of African Americans, partly as a buffer against racism, African Americans may derive more of their self-esteem from relationships. In a study of college students, Black students scored higher on a measure of collectivism than did White students (Oyserman, Gant, & Ager, 1995).

TAKE HOME POINTS

- Men's sense of self is based more on independence, whereas women's sense of self is based more on interdependence.

- *Interdependence* is a broad term, including a relational and a collective component. Women are more likely to emphasize the relational aspect, whereas men are more likely to emphasize the collective aspect.

- These different self-construals have been differentially linked to self-esteem in men and women.

- Sex differences in self-construal may be influenced by ethnic and cultural factors. Western cultures emphasize individualism, which is reflected in the independent self-construal.

Attributions for Performance

Recently, one of my daughter's friends was visiting and explained that she had tried out for a soccer team and did not make it. Was she upset? Did she think that she wasn't good enough for the team? No, she responded by saying that the team had made a mistake and would suffer for not having chosen her. So wise at the age of 13, she continued on by telling us, "I have to tell myself that. That's how I make myself feel better." This girl was demonstrating what is known in social psychology as the **self-serving bias**. The self-serving bias is the tendency to take credit for our successes and blame other people or other things for our failures. In general, self-serving biases are adaptive, in part because self-esteem is protected in the face of failure.

Dimensions of Causality. The self-serving bias has to do with the attributions that we make for performance. An **attribution** is the cause we assign to a behavior. Attributions can be classified along the two dimensions shown in Figure 6.9 (Weiner et al., 1971). The first dimension represents the locus of the cause, internal or external. An **internal attribution** is located within the person, and an **external attribution** is located in the environment. A **stable attribution** is one that does not change across time or situations. An **unstable attribution** is one that does change

Dimensions of Attribution

	Internal	External
Stable	**Ability**	**Task Difficulty**
Unstable	**Effort**	**Luck**

FIGURE 6.9 Two dimensions on which attributions (causes) can be classified: locus (internal vs. external) and stability (stable vs. unstable).

across time and situations. In the context of performance (as shown in Figure 6.9), an internal, stable attribution would be your ability or lack thereof. An internal, unstable attribution would be how much effort you put into the task, presumably by studying. An external, stable attribution would be the difficulty of the test, an unchangeable, inherent characteristic of the task. An external, unstable attribution would be luck or some transient environmental factor, such as the weather.

The locus of causality dimension has implications for self-esteem. An internal attribution for failure (I am stupid) will decrease self-esteem, whereas an internal attribution for success (I am a brain) will increase self-esteem. An external attribution for failure will preserve self-esteem (It wasn't my fault that my computer crashed), whereas an external attribution for success does not confer any self-esteem. (The teacher must not have been paying attention when she graded my essay.)

The stability dimension has implications for persistence. An unstable attribution for failure (I did not study) may lead us to try harder or to try to change the environment. A stable attribution for failure (I do not have the ability) may lead us to give up. A stable attribution for success (The teacher is an easy grader) will encourage us to continue with the behavior or to keep the environment the same (e.g., don't switch teachers). An unstable attribution for success (The teacher didn't have her glasses on) merely tells you that the performance may not be repeated, so you will need to continue to exert the same level of effort or keep the environmental conditions the same (e.g., hide the teacher's glasses).

Sex Comparisons.   Do women and men differ in their attributions for success and failure? In 1984, Kay Deaux developed a model of how people's expectancies about women's and men's performance would influence the attributions made. This model is shown in Figure 6.10. The first part of the model states that we attribute behavior to stable and internal causes if it matches our expectancy (i.e., a person fails whom we expect to fail or a person succeeds whom we expect to succeed; Weiner et al., 1971). Thus, if we expect men to perform well on masculine tasks, we should attribute their success to ability; similarly, if we expect women to perform well on feminine tasks, we should attribute their success to ability. In addition, if we expect women to fail at masculine tasks, we should attribute their failure to lack of ability. The second part of the model states that if a behavior violates our expectations, we attribute it to unstable causes. Thus, if we expect women to fail at a masculine task, we should attribute their success to effort and good luck. If we expect men to succeed at a masculine task, we should attribute their failure to lack of effort and bad luck. This model strongly suggests that the nature of the task should influence the attributions we make for men's and women's performance.

Many of the attribution studies were conducted 25 years ago. Not all of the more recent studies have supported this pattern of sex differences in attributions for performance. A meta-analysis found no sex of perceiver differences in attributions, meaning that women and men tended to make the same attributions for other women's and men's performance (Swim & Sanna, 1996). However, perceivers made different attributions on some tasks, in particular masculine tasks (e.g., those involving math abilities). On masculine tasks, perceivers attributed women's success to effort and men's success to ability. Thus, perceivers are attributing men's success to a stable cause and women's success to an unstable cause, implying that men's success is more likely than women's to

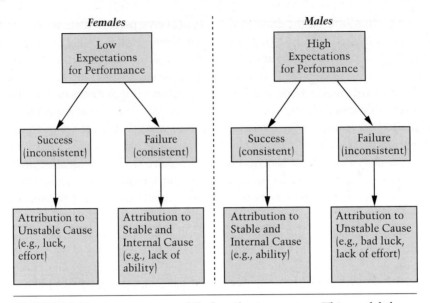

FIGURE 6.10   Expectancy model of attributions: actors. This model shows that when performance fits our expectations (success following high expectations for performance, failure following low expectations for performance), we attribute the cause to stable factors. When performance does not fit our expectations (success following low expectations for performance, failure following high expectations for performance), we attribute the cause to unstable factors.
Source: K. Deaux (1984). From individual differences to social categories: Analysis of a decade's research on gender. American Psychologist, 39, 105–116.

be repeated. On masculine tasks, perceivers attributed men's failure to unstable causes, that is, lack of effort and bad luck, whereas perceivers attributed women's failure to the difficulty of the task. Again, perceivers are attributing men's failure to unstable causes that will not necessarily be repeated but women's failure to a stable cause that implies the failure will be repeated. The meta-analysis showed fewer differences in the attributions made for women's and men's performance on feminine tasks (e.g., those involving verbal abilities). To be fair, most studies examined only masculine tasks, and the majority of studies focused on college students.

A meta-analysis on sex comparisons of the self-serving bias showed that there was

no overall sex difference, but there was a sex by age interaction, meaning that the sex difference depended on the age of the respondents (Mezulis et al., 2004). Among children, girls displayed more of a self-serving bias than boys; among early adolescents, there was no sex difference; and among older adolescents and adults, men displayed more of a self-serving bias than women.

Attributions for performance have been studied among children, in an effort to understand how they perceive their performance. One study of gifted second graders showed that girls were more likely than boys to believe that they had to work hard to get good grades (i.e., attributions to effort), but this sex difference disappeared for the children at the highest end of the gifted spectrum (Nokelainen, Tirri, & Merenti-Valimaki, 2007). A study of 8- to 9-year-olds showed that boys and girls make different attributions for math performance even when their grades are the same. Girls were less likely than boys to attribute math success to ability but more likely than boys to attribute math failure to lack of ability, despite the fact that girls and boys had the same math grades (Dickhauser & Meyer, 2006). These differences are shown in Figure 6.11. Even more worrisome is that these findings were strongest among the high math ability students. If girls and boys have the same grades, why are they assigning different causes to performance? It appeared that boys and girls relied on different information to infer their math abilities. Girls relied on teacher evaluations, whereas boys relied on both teacher evaluations and their objective math performance. Despite no difference in objective math performance, teachers perceived that girls had less math ability than boys. Girls assessed their own abilities in terms of these teacher perceptions.

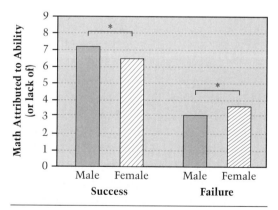

FIGURE 6.11 Boys are more likely than girls to attribute math success to ability, and girls are more likely than boys to attribute math failure to lack of ability.

Source: Adapted from Dickhauser and Meyer (2006).

Implications for Achievement. What are the implications of sex differences in attributions for performance? If you fail an exam because you believe you do not have the ability, what do you do? You might give up on the subject, drop the class, and decide not to pursue other classes in that area. If you fail an exam and believe it was due to lack of effort (i.e., you did not try hard enough), what do you do? The answer is obvious: You try harder next time. Thus the attributions we make for failure can influence whether we persist in an area or give it up completely.

TAKE HOME POINTS

- At least for masculine tasks, which are basically achievement related, males and females make different attributions for their own performance. They also perceive the causes of other males' and females' performance to differ.

- In general, men's success is attributed to internal causes, in particular, ability, and women's success is attributed to internal, unstable causes (e.g., effort) or external causes (e.g., luck). The implications are that men's success will be repeated, but women's will not. By contrast, men's failure is attributed to external causes or internal, unstable causes (e.g., lack of effort), and women's failure is attributed to internal, stable causes (e.g., lack of ability). The implications here are that women's, but not men's, failure will be repeated.

- People's beliefs about the causes of their performance have implications for their future efforts in that area. If we attribute the cause of a failure to lack of ability, such as the case of females in math or males in English, we are less likely to pursue work in that area. If we attribute the cause of a success to an unstable factor, such as females believing they have to put considerable effort into math to do well, we also are less likely to pursue work in that area. We are more likely to pursue areas of interest in which we believe we have the ability to succeed.

SOCIAL FACTORS

Despite the fact that girls either perform better than or equal to boys in areas such as math, girls rate their ability lower and have more negative attitudes toward math compared to boys. What are the reasons for these discrepancies? One answer concerns the beliefs that other people hold about girls' and boys' abilities. Despite the small size of sex differences in most intellectual domains (see Chapter 4), people continue to believe that women and men have different abilities. I begin this next section of the chapter by describing the expectancy/value model of sex differences in achievement. This model rests heavily on gender-role socialization. Then I examine several sources of social influence. First, I examine the role of parents in influencing children's beliefs about their abilities; then I examine the role of teachers in influencing children's beliefs about their abilities. Both parents and teachers may communicate to children that they have different abilities and provide girls and boys with different experiences.

Expectancy/Value Model of Achievement

If girls perform better than boys in math and science at younger ages, why don't more women have careers in math and science? This question puzzled Jacquelynne Eccles and her colleagues, so they developed a theory to account for the discrepancy between men's and women's school performance and career choices. Their **expectancy/value model of achievement** suggests that men's and women's achievement-related choices are a function of their performance expectancies (Will I succeed?) and the value they attach to the area (Is this important?; Do I care about it?; Eccles et al., 1999). The two

are not independent, as performance expectancies influence values. That is, how much ability a child perceives she or he has in an area affects how much value is attached to the area (Denissen & Zarrett, 2007). Performance expectancies and values influence the decision one makes to engage in an activity, the decision to persist in the activity, and ultimately performance in the activity.

Performance expectancies and values are influenced by gender-role socialization. People in children's environments—parents, teachers, peers—influence females and males to value different areas. Performance expectancies and values also are shaped by the experiences children have and by their interpretations of those experiences. For example, girls and boys might have the same math grades but interpret them differently. If girls believe their high grades are due to effort and boys believe their high grades are due to inherent ability, boys will be more likely than girls to believe they will succeed in math in the future. It is the *self-perception* of ability rather than the actual ability that predicts whether students pursue a given domain.

Numerous studies have been conducted in support of this theory. In general, males perceive greater competence in math, science, and team sports, whereas females perceive greater competence in reading (Freedman-Doan et al., 2000; Lupart, Cannon, & Telfer, 2004). The expectancy/value model predicts participation in activities, course selection, and occupational aspirations (Simpkins, Davis-Kean, & Eccles, 2005, 2006). In one study, females' competence beliefs in math predicted whether they enrolled in more math courses the next year (Crombie et al., 2005). Thus, males may be more likely than females to pursue a career in math not because of differences in actual ability but because of differences in "perceived" ability.

One of the features of the expectancy/ value model is that achievement-related behavior is understood as a choice between at least two behaviors (Eccles et al., 1999). In other words, a boy who has equally good grades in all subject areas knows he will pursue a career in only one area. Even if the boy's grades in math and English are the same and he equally values math and English in elementary school, at some point he is likely to choose between the two areas and value one more than the other. Gender-role socialization may lead him to value math over English. Parents, teachers, and counselors all have the opportunity to encourage or discourage pursuits in a given area.

Plenty of research suggests that women and men continue to value different pursuits. In terms of overall career choices, females value whether a job will make the world a better place and are interested in people-oriented jobs, whereas males value the status and money associated with a job (Eccles et al., 1999; Lupart et al., 2004). These divergent interests may explain why girls are underrepresented in computer science. Girls are likely to be attracted to occupations that involve interactions with other people, and the computer scientist often is depicted as a nerd who works in isolation from others. In a series of focus groups with middle school and high school girls from 70 different schools, girls expressed a lack of interest in computer science—not because they lacked the ability but because they lacked the desire (American Association of University Women, 2000). The investigators summarized girls' responses with the phrase "We can, but I don't want to." Girls perceived the computer scientist to be male and antisocial; the career simply did not appeal to them. Today, girls are still less interested in computers than boys (Sainz & Lopez-Saez, 2010).

When comparing the effects of competence beliefs and values on outcomes, it appears that competence beliefs are more strongly linked to performance, and values are more strongly linked to what we pursue (Wigfield & Eccles, 2002). In fact, Wigfield and Eccles argue that the reason there are fewer women in math and sciences has more to do with values than competence. Between the ages of 8 and 17, girls show less intrinsic interest in STEM fields than boys (Hill et al., 2010). One study showed that girls were less interested in math than boys, despite receiving the same grades—and the sex difference was even larger among gifted students (Preckel et al., 2008). This could explain why there are fewer women entering the fields of math and engineering. A recent review of the literature concluded that the number one reason why women are underrepresented in STEM fields is female preference (Ceci et al., 2009). Among those who are proficient in math, women are more likely than men to prefer careers in nonmath intensive fields. In a 20-year follow-up study of gifted math students, women and men were equally likely to have obtained advanced degrees but women were more likely to have pursued other fields besides math, such as law, medicine, administration, and social sciences (Lubinski & Benbow, 2006). Women who are proficient in math are more likely than men to *also* be proficient in verbal skills, providing women with greater flexibility in choosing a profession. Thus, achievement differences between women and men have decreased over time, but the differences in the activities that women and men value have not changed to the same degree.

Girls and boys have also had different interests in sports and athletics, but the size of that difference has been reduced dramatically with the passage of Title IX. See Sidebar 6.2 for a discussion of recent challenges to Title IX.

In the next sections, I will discuss how the social environment can shape females' and males' expectancies and values.

SIDEBAR 6.2: *The Future of Title IX*

Title IX says "No person in the United States shall, on the basis of sex, be excluded from participation in, be denied the benefits of, or be subjected to discrimination under any education program or activity requiring Federal assistance." The law was enacted in 1972 and basically prohibits sex discrimination in educational programs that receive federal assistance. Title IX has made great advances in creating more equal educational opportunities for men and women. The athletic arena is where the greatest strides have been made (U.S. Census Bureau, 2007a). In 1971–1972, less than 300,000 women participated in high school athletics, whereas the figure for 2008–2009 was just over 3 million (4 million for men; National Federation of State High School Associations, 2010).

Institutions can show compliance with Title IX in one of three ways:

1. Provide athletic opportunities to women and men in proportion to their enrollment.

2. Expand programs for the underrepresented sex (i.e., women).

3. Accommodate the interests and abilities of the underrepresented sex (i.e., women).

At several points in time, Title IX has come under attack. One way that Title IX can be achieved is to eliminate teams; that is, if a school has a men's soccer team and no women's soccer team, it can eliminate the men's team rather than add the women's team. In response to several concerns, the secretary of education convened a commission to offer further guidance in regard to Title IX. In 2005, the commission made a number of recommendations, one of which was to use interest surveys to meet the third compliance measure. If a school can show there is less interest in women's soccer than men's soccer, the school would not have to provide a women's soccer team. One problem is that the existence of a team is what generates interest. The current level of men's and women's interest is likely to reflect the opportunities they had in the past. Another problem is that a lack of a survey response (even by email) was considered to reflect lack of interest. We know that people fail to respond to surveys for reasons other than lack of interest. In 2010, the Department of Education repealed this policy. Schools are no longer allowed to rely on surveys to demonstrate interest (or lack of) in a program.

TAKE HOME POINTS

- According to the expectancy/value model of achievement, we pursue areas of achievement in which we expect to succeed and that we value.

- Even when abilities seem to be equal, women and men have different expectancies for success in an area.

- Women and men attach different values to achievement-related pursuits. Women are less interested in STEM careers and more interested in jobs and careers that involve people compared to men.

The Influence of Parents

A great deal of evidence indicates that parents influence children's perceptions of competence, values, and performance. Parents who support their children's studies, monitor their children's schoolwork, and spend time with their children on schoolwork have children who reach higher levels of achievement, partly because those are the girls and boys that expend more effort on academic studies (Kristjansson & Sigfusdottir, 2009). However, parents also have stereotypes about the subject areas in which boys and girls excel, and parents have opinions about the subject areas in which it is important for boys and girls to excel. Specifically, parents rate girls' math ability as lower than that of boys and believe math is more difficult for girls than for boys—despite equal performance by girls and boys in math during elementary school (Herbert & Stipek, 2005). Parents believe girls are more competent in English and boys are more competent in sports (Pomerantz, Ng, & Wang, 2004). Parents also believe that math and athletics are less important for girls than for boys and that English is less important for boys than girls. Parents' general sex stereotypes influence their beliefs about their children's areas of competence. For example, parents who believe girls are better at reading and boys are better at math perceive that their daughter has higher reading ability and their son has higher math ability—even when the children's objective performance on exams is the same (Tenenbaum & Leaper, 2003).

Rather than assume a bias on the part of parents, is it possible their beliefs about their daughters' and sons' different abilities are accurate? It is difficult to assess whether one person has more inherent ability than another. If a sex difference appears on an objective indicator of performance, does this mean one sex has greater natural talent than the other? Not necessarily. Boys and girls may have had different experiences, which led to different performances. For example, women and men may have equal abilities in math, but different experiences provided by teachers, parents, relatives, and peers may lead boys to outperform girls. Even when more objective indicators of performance are taken into consideration (e.g., test scores, teachers' ratings of students, grades), parents still hold sex-differentiated beliefs about their children's abilities that exceed any observed differences in performance. It also turns out that parents who hold stronger stereotypes about women and men are more likely to translate those stereotypes into their beliefs about their individual daughters and sons.

Parents' stereotypes also lead them to make different attributions for girls' and boys' success in different subject areas. Parents are more likely to attribute boys' success in math to talent (an internal, stable attribution) and girls' success in math to effort (an internal, unstable attribution; Räty et al., 2002). Parents also believe that talent is more important than effort for success in math, which would imply that boys should be more successful at math than girls. Parents attribute math failure to lack of effort for both boys and girls, no doubt to preserve a positive image of their children. However, mothers are more likely to attribute girls' failure to the task being too difficult. In summary, parents appear to be less confident about their girls' than their boys' math abilities.

Another way that parents communicate their perceptions of a child's ability is by how they provide help. Helping a child with homework might seem as if it demonstrates parent support. However, it also has the potential to demonstrate to the child that the parent believes the child *needs* help—that is, it can communicate that the child lacks competence in an area. In a study of middle school children, parents who held stereotypes that girls were not as good in math as boys were more likely to intrude on girls' homework, and these were the girls who perceived that they had less math ability (Bhanot & Jovanovic, 2005). In another study, parent help with schoolwork was categorized as either "autonomy-granting" (e.g., emphasizing mastery of content over performance, communicating to children that they can do it on their own) or "controlling" (e.g., rewarding children for schoolwork, emphasizing that performance standards are important, communicating that children are not capable of solving problems on their own; Pomerantz & Ruble, 1998). Parents were found to use both autonomy-facilitating and controlling behavior with sons but controlling behavior alone with daughters. It is the controlling behavior that could undermine children's perceptions of competence.

We know that parents have different beliefs about their children's abilities. The next question is whether those beliefs influence the children's own perceptions of their ability. A study of fourth, sixth, and eighth graders showed that perceptions of adult stereotypes influenced children's beliefs about females and males in general and about their own abilities (Kurtz-Costes et al., 2008). Parents encouraged computer usage in boys more than girls, and boys ended up believing that they were better at computers compared to girls (Vekiri & Chronaki, 2008). Longitudinal research has shown that parents believe that their sons have greater ability in sports, math, and science than their daughters, and that their daughters have greater ability in music than their sons (Fredricks, Simpkins, & Eccles, 2005; Jacobs, Vernon, & Eccles, 2005). And, those beliefs predict children holding these same perceptions of their abilities at a later time. Parents' beliefs translate into children's beliefs about their own abilities even when one controls for the objective grades children receive from teachers (Neuenschwander et al., 2007). Parents' beliefs about their children's abilities may affect how children interpret those grades.

The next question is whether parents' beliefs influence children's actual abilities, not just the children's perceptions of their abilities. In other words, do parents' stereotypes about boys and girls become self-fulfilling prophecies so their sons and daughters differ in their abilities as parents expect? The answer is *yes;* parents' beliefs influence children's actual academic achievements, again independent of actual grades (Neuenschwander et al., 2007). Parents can influence their children's abilities in a myriad of ways. Parents encourage the pursuit of different activities by their emotional reactions to performance (e.g., joy rather than contentment with a child's A on an exam), interest shown in the activity, toys and opportunities provided to pursue an activity, time spent with the child on an activity, and direct advice to pursue an activity (Eccles et al., 2000). For example, parents who believe boys are better than girls at math might buy a son a calculator, play math games with him, or teach him how to calculate baseball averages. They also might work with a son on math homework and express high praise to him for good math performance and great disappointment for poor math performance. These same parents may not provide a daughter with math-related opportunities, not encourage her to spend time on math homework, and show indifference to reports of high or low grades in math. In one study, fathers were found to use more cognitively complex language when talking with sons than daughters about science (e.g., asking more conceptual questions, using more difficult vocabulary), which conveys the importance of science to sons (Tenenbaum & Leaper, 2003). Research has also shown that parents encourage computer usage, math and science, and sports for sons more than daughters by buying sons more items related to those activities and by spending more time with sons than daughters engaged in these activities (Fredricks, Simpkins, & Eccles., 2005; Jacobs et al., 2005; Simpkins et al., 2005). Just the opposite occurs for girls compared to boys in the area of music. These behaviors are subsequently linked to children pursuing the activities that parents encourage. To the extent the child pursues the activities, performance is affected. The theoretical model by which parents may influence children's abilities is shown in Figure 6.12.

Parents' beliefs about their children's abilities are especially likely to influence the

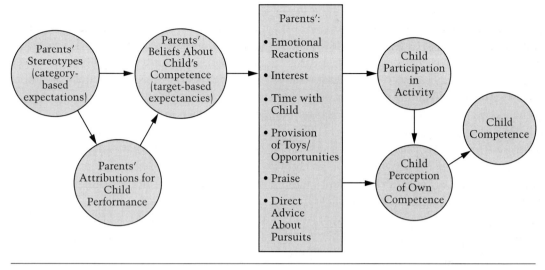

FIGURE 6.12   A model describing how parents' beliefs can influence children's performance.

children's perceptions and the children's actual abilities when parents believe that ability is fixed and not malleable. Pomerantz and Dong (2006) refer to the fixed view of competence as **entity theory**, which is much like Dweck's fixed mindset described in Sidebar 6.1. Self-fulfilling prophecies are more likely to occur when parents endorse the entity theory of competence. In a longitudinal study of fourth through sixth graders, mothers' perceptions of children's competence predicted changes in children's perceptions of competence one year later and changes in children's grades one year later—only among mothers who subscribed to the entity theory of competence.

TAKE HOME POINTS

- Parents have stereotypes that boys are better than girls in math and girls are better than boys in verbal abilities, regardless of actual school performance.

- Parents communicate these stereotypes to children by the activities they encourage, the toys they buy, the time they spend with children, and the attributions they make for performance.

- Parents' communications influence children's ability perceptions and, ultimately, children's performance.

The Influence of Teachers

Teachers can influence children's beliefs about their abilities by the attention and instruction they provide to students and by the nature of the feedback they provide about performance. Some of these effects are due to the stereotypes the teachers, themselves, hold. For example, one study showed that teachers believed a gymnast would perform better after 10 weeks of training when told the video that they had viewed was a male rather than a female (Chalabaev et al., 2009). Teachers' stereotypes that males have more athletic ability than females appear to extend to a female sex-typed domain.

Attention.   In 1994, Sadker and Sadker published a book titled *Failing at Fairness: How*

America's Schools Cheat Girls. In this book, they documented the results of extensive observational studies of teacher-student interactions in rural, urban, and suburban settings across the United States. In 1995, Brady and Eisler reviewed the literature on teacher-student interactions in the classroom, examining both observational and self-report studies. Both sets of investigators reached the same conclusions: From elementary school through graduate school, teachers interact more with boys than girls and give boys better feedback than girls. Teachers call on boys more often than girls, ask boys higher-level questions, and expand on boys' more than girls' comments. In college, professors give men more nonverbal attention than they give women: making greater eye contact with men and waiting longer for men to answer a question. Since those reviews were published, two observational studies of student-teacher interactions showed that teachers initiate more interactions with boys than girls (Altermatt, Jovanovic, & Perry, 1998; Duffy, Warren, & Walsh, 2001). White male students, in particular, seem to be given more "wait time"—time to think and respond to a question (Sadker & Zittleman, 2007). Girls are interrupted more than boys,

and boys receive more criticism from teachers. Teachers, especially male teachers, seem to be reluctant to criticize girls because they fear upsetting girls. This is unfortunate because there are benefits to criticism. Teachers' lack of attention to female students is depicted in the cartoon shown in Figure 6.13.

One reason girls do not receive as much attention as boys is that girls behave well in school and do not demand as much attention as boys do. Part of the sex difference in children's grades has been attributed to the personality factor of agreeableness (Hicks et al., 2008; Steinmayr & Spinath, 2008). That is, girls get better grades than boys because they are more agreeable and teachers perceive them as less disruptive. However, while the girls are behaving themselves, the teachers are spending time with the "difficult" boys. In other words, these girls suffer from benign neglect. Meanwhile, the boys' bad behavior is reinforced because it receives the teacher's attention. Conduct your own observational study of a classroom in Do Gender 6.4 to see if gender bias exists.

Feedback.   The different kinds of attention girls and boys receive for behavior (girls for good behavior and boys for bad behavior)

FIGURE 6.13   Cartoon illustrates how teachers pay more attention to boys than girls, referring to the lack of attention to girls as a "girl's education."
Source: DOONESBURY ©1992 G. B. Trudeau. Reprinted with permission of UNIVERSAL PRESS SYNDICATE. All rights reserved.

DO GENDER 6.4
Classroom Behavior

Conduct your own observational study of classroom behavior. Record some or all of the following, noting whether the interaction involved a female or male student. Are there other features of teacher-student interactions worth observing?

1. Teacher calling on a student.

2. Teacher giving praise to a student.

3. Teacher criticizing a student.

4. Length of time the teacher waits for a response after calling on a student.

5. Nature of the teacher's response to a student's response (praises, criticizes, expands on, ignores the response).

6. Number of times the teacher interrupts a student.

7. Number of times the student interrupts the teacher or another student.

8. Student raising a hand.

9. Student shouting out an answer.

After conducting your observational study, you might also administer a questionnaire to the teacher and the students asking whether they observed different frequencies of behavior with male and female students. You can then compare your observational data to the student and teacher self-report data.

end up affecting how girls and boys respond to the feedback they receive from teachers about their academics. This was shown in an early observational study that has now become a classic in the field (Dweck et al., 1978). Two raters observed instances of evaluative feedback given to children and

noted whether the feedback was positive or negative and whether it pertained to the children's intellectual performance or to nonintellectual aspects of performance. Feedback about nonintellectual aspects often pertained to conduct, as in "Johnny, please settle down and sit in your chair," or appearance: "Mary, you have a lovely outfit on today." The investigators found no difference in the amount of positive or negative feedback given to boys and girls, but an important difference in whether the feedback pertained to intellectual or nonintellectual aspects of the children's performance. For girls, only 30% of the negative feedback pertained to nonintellectual aspects of performance, whereas 70% pertained to intellectual aspects of performance. For boys, 67% of the negative feedback pertained to nonintellectual aspects of performance, whereas only 33% pertained to intellectual aspects of performance. The authors suggested these differences make negative feedback a very salient indicator of poor performance for girls but an unclear indicator of poor performance for boys. When girls receive negative feedback, it is more likely to be related to their schoolwork than work-irrelevant domains, such as conduct or appearance; thus girls take negative feedback seriously. Boys, by contrast, are able to discount negative feedback because it usually has nothing to do with the intellectual aspects of their performance. Thus, when boys receive negative feedback about their work, they can reason, "The teacher doesn't like me. She is always criticizing me. She tells me to dress neater and to be quieter. What does she know about whether or not I can read?"

In the same study, positive feedback typically pertained to intellectual aspects of performance for both boys and girls. However, when compared to the positive feedback boys received, proportionally more of girls' positive feedback concerned nonintellectual aspects of their performance. Thus, positive feedback is a clear indicator of good performance for boys but not as meaningful for girls because it sometimes has to do with nonintellectual aspects of their performance. Girls, then, are unsure whether to take positive feedback about their work seriously because teachers are providing positive feedback about other domains not relevant to work, such as their appearance or behavior. Here, girls may conclude, "The teacher just likes me. She likes how neat I keep my desk and that I don't cause trouble. That's why I received an A on my homework." The investigators also found that teachers made different attributions for boys' and girls' failures: Teachers were more likely to make attributions to motivational factors, such as lack of effort, for boys than for girls.

If these findings hold true today, what are the implications for how teachers and parents should provide feedback to children? Should we start criticizing girls for behavior unrelated to their work so they can discount negative feedback and make external attributions for failure? That would not seem to be an optimal solution. Alternatively, we could make sure we are providing positive feedback to females about areas relevant only to work, so the positive feedback is salient and directly tied to their performance. The idea here is to eliminate the positive feedback about performance-irrelevant domains such as appearance. If we take Dweck and colleagues' (1978) results seriously, the idea of complimenting or praising children about something unrelated to their work to soften the blow before providing negative work-related feedback is doing them a disservice.

The study by Dweck and colleagues is nearly 35 years old. Is there any more recent evidence on this issue? Unfortunately, no one has tried to replicate this study in recent years. Research still shows that boys receive more negative feedback than girls in the classroom—especially about their conduct (Myhill & Jones, 2006). One study showed that this kind of negative feedback affects children's attitudes toward schoolwork and school in general (Morgan, 2001). Boys and girls were randomly assigned to receive positive competence feedback with or without negative feedback about the neatness and organization of their work. Both boys and girls who received the negative behavioral feedback expressed less interest in the project and liked the teacher less than boys and girls who received only the positive competence feedback. In contrast to the Dweck and colleagues' (1978) study, girls and boys who received the negative behavioral feedback also rated their competence on the task as lower. These findings suggest that the effects of negative behavioral feedback in the classroom may be far reaching and may explain why boys have less positive relationships with teachers and less favorable attitudes toward school compared to girls.

Effects on Performance. Teachers' beliefs about students' abilities have been shown to influence student performance. In one study, sixth-grade students were followed over the course of a year to determine the effect of teachers' initial expectations on students' subsequent performance in math (Jussim & Eccles, 1992). The investigators studied 98 teachers and 1,731 students. Although girls and boys performed equally well in math, teachers perceived that girls performed better and tried harder, but that boys had more talent. In other words, the teachers attributed girls' performance to effort and boys' performance to ability. Teachers' attributions to effort appeared to be erroneous because girls did not report expending greater effort on math than boys did. What is important is that teachers' perceptions of students' math ability predicted the change in math achievement from fifth to sixth grades. In other words, a student's math achievement improved between fifth and sixth grade when teachers started out believing the student had high math ability—which was the case for boys more than girls.

Teachers also have different expectations for the performance of different racial groups, which may influence performance. Teachers have especially low expectations for Black males' performance (Simms, Knight, & Dawes, 1993). This is a problem because teachers' expectancies predict students' academic behavior. Thus, one reason Black males have a negative view of school is that teachers' low expectations have been communicated to them. Black males receive more negative feedback and more mixed (positive and negative) feedback than Black females or White students. Although teachers attribute failure to external causes for White males, they attribute failure to internal causes for Black males (Simms et al., 1993). Black males are more likely than Black females to devalue academic success, which accounts for their poorer school performance compared to females (Cokley & Moore, 2007).

Despite the wealth of research on gender biases in the classroom, it is disheartening to learn that the issue is not addressed in the training of teachers. A review of 23 teacher education textbooks showed that only 3% of the space is devoted to gender-related issues (Sadker & Zittleman, 2007). The infusion of technology in the classroom was thought to reduce gender bias but has only served to perpetuate it (Plumm, 2008). Boys have more positive attitudes toward computers and technology and receive greater encouragement to use computers and technology. Boys' greater experience is undoubtedly related to their more positive attitudes. Computer texts and software also are created to be more appealing to boys and often contain stereotypical content, depicting males and females in traditional roles. Some propose single-sex education as a solution to the different experiences that girls and boys have in the classroom. As discussed in Sidebar 6.3, there is no clear evidence that single-sex education provides a solution to the problems discussed in this chapter.

SIDEBAR 6.3: *The Single-Sex Classroom Debate*

Title IX prohibits sex discrimination of federally funded programs. For this reason, public single-sex education was not permitted when Title IX went into effect. However, in 2006, the Department of Education made several amendments to Title IX to permit greater flexibility in single-sex education. These amendments included the permission of single-sex education for extracurricular activities and single-sex schools if equal opportunities are provided to the other sex in another school. Whereas there are about 12 schools that offered single-sex education in 2002, in 2010 there were about 91 single-sex public schools in which all activities were single sex (National Association for Single-Sex Public Education, 2010).

There are several reasons for choosing single-sex education. Some choose single-sex education based on culture or religious reasons (Shah & Conchar, 2009). However, others believe that one sex suffers from being combined with the other sex. For years, people have been concerned with the gender biases in the classroom reviewed in this chapter and thought single-sex education would benefit girls. More recently, there has been a concern that boys also suffer from co-education. Boys are 50% more likely than girls to repeat a grade in school, over twice as likely as girls to be suspended or expelled, and more likely than girls to drop out of high school (National Center for Education Statistics, 2007, 2009b).

Is single-sex education advantageous for either females or males? A review was undertaken for the U.S. Department of Education on single-sex education studies (Mael et al., 2005). They concluded that the results are not clear. For some outcomes, there is the suggestion that single-sex education might be helpful; for many outcomes, there is no evidence. The most common finding is one of "no difference" between single-sex and coeducational schooling. They also cautioned that: (1) few studies examine moderators to determine if there are a certain group of individuals who benefit from single-sex education, such as low socioeconomic status individual, and (2) few studies are methodologically strong. In 2006, Smithers and Robinson published a review that spanned research in Australia, Canada, New Zealand, Ireland, the United Kingdom, and the United States, and concluded that there was little evidence for the benefits of single-sex education. There are no differences in achievement or choices of subjects taken. The primary determinant of students' success seems to be the characteristics of the students rather than single-sex versus coeducation. However, the topic is difficult to study. First, single-sex education can take various forms, ranging from single-sex schools to single-sex classes within a coeducational school, making it difficult to compare findings across studies. Second, there is a selection bias in who attends single-sex schools. A rigorous test of single-sex education would require a control group, but there are few opportunities to randomly assign a student to have a single-sex versus coeducational school experience. Instead, investigators compare the people who attend single-sex schools to the people who attend coeducational schools. But the two groups of students are not the same. Students who attend single-sex schools are often of a higher socioeconomic status, which contributes to higher achievement. Girls who attend single-sex schools have higher achievement aspirations, making them more achievement oriented than girls who attend coeducational schools. Thus, single-sex versus coeducation is confounded with socioeconomic status. Even when single-sex education is successful, investigators suggest that the factors responsible for the positive effects are ones that could be applied to coeducational schools. For example, single-sex schools may have teachers with higher qualifications and smaller classrooms compared to coeducational schools.

Another problem with the study of single-sex education is how to define effectiveness or success. Success is typically defined by grades and by scores on standardized tests. But, there may be other outcomes in which we should be interested, such as how an individual functions as a member of society, subsequent career success, job performance, and leadership. These kinds of outcomes are much more difficult to assess, but they could be outcomes for which single-sex education provides an advantage.

TAKE HOME POINTS

- Teachers give boys more attention than girls in school.

- Teachers are especially more likely to criticize boys than girls in school—but criticism can be helpful as it provides feedback about how to change behavior.

- Teachers provide more negative behavioral feedback to boys than girls which ends up reinforcing the behavior and allowing boys to discount negative feedback about their classwork.

- Teachers provide more positive behavioral feedback to girls than boys, which ends up diluting the positive feedback that girls receive about their classwork and potentially leads females to attribute positive feedback that they receive in the real world to extraneous factors.

- Teachers have different beliefs about girls' and boys' abilities, which translate into how they spend time with girls and boys as well as the nature of the feedback they provide. Like parents, teachers attribute girls' success in math to effort and boys' success in math to ability.

- Teacher expectations have been shown to affect student performance.

Summary

In the first part of the chapter, I examined a number of individual difference variables that might explain differences in the nature of women's and men's achievements. The early work in this area suggested women have a lower need for achievement compared to men. This hypothesis was later dismissed by suggesting that women's lack of achievement compared to men's stems from women's "fear of success." The fear of success literature was and continues to be fairly controversial, in part due to the projective nature of the fear of success measures. Recent studies, however, suggest there is still a concern among some women that success may have negative implications for relationships. Another reason women are thought to achieve less than men is that women have lower levels of self-confidence compared to men or lower levels of general self-esteem. Women's lower self-confidence and lower self-esteem are limited to certain circumstances, specifically when the task is in a masculine domain. Women also seem to take feedback more to heart than men, which means that their self-esteem is affected by others' positive and negative evaluations of their performance. In areas where women are presumed to be inferior to men, making those stereotypes salient adversely affects women's performance. In regard to self-esteem, it is more accurate to say men and women have different beliefs about their strong points and derive their self-esteem from different sources. Evidence suggests that men derive self-esteem more from individuating themselves from others (i.e., feeling unique in comparison to others), whereas women derive self-esteem from their connection to others.

A final individual difference factor that may have implications for women's and men's achievement has to do with the way they explain their successes and failures—at least in the area of masculine endeavors. In those domains, women are more likely than men to attribute success to effort or luck (unstable causes), whereas men are more likely to attribute success to ability (an internal, stable cause). Women are more likely to attribute failure to stable causes, such as lack of ability or task difficulty, whereas men are more likely to attribute failure to unstable causes, such as lack of effort or bad luck. Sex differences in attributions for performance on feminine tasks are less clear. Importantly, the different attributions women and men make for performance may have implications for the decisions they make about how hard to try in an area or even whether to pursue a particular area of achievement.

In the second half of the chapter, I explored social factors that might contribute to women's and men's beliefs about their abilities as well as their attributions for performance. According to the expectancy/value model, people pursue achievement in an area in which they expect to succeed and they regard as important and interesting. Whereas expectancies influence performance, values seem to have a stronger link to areas that women and men pursue. Children's expectancies and values are a function of gender-role socialization. One source of socialization is parents. Parents often have stereotyped views of boys' and girls' abilities, believing boys have greater math ability and girls have greater verbal ability, which they translate into beliefs about their specific sons' and daughters' abilities. Parents seem to hold these sex-differentiated beliefs even when girls and boys receive the same grades in school. Some evidence indicates that parents' beliefs about their children's abilities influence children's own self-perceptions and children's actual abilities. In other words, parents' stereotypes about girls' and boys' abilities may become self-fulfilling prophecies. The feedback and experiences that parents provide to their children may lead the children to develop the different abilities parents initially expected.

A second source of influence on children's beliefs about their abilities is teachers. Teachers pay more attention to boys than girls in the classroom. This may be due, in part, to boys' misbehavior demanding more attention. Teachers are more likely to criticize boys than girls; interestingly, criticism is linked to greater self-confidence. More important, the nature of the feedback that teachers provide to girls and boys differs. Boys seem to receive a great deal of negative feedback about work-irrelevant domains, which then leads boys to discount negative feedback about their work and maintain a belief in their abilities. This type of negative feedback also may undermine boys' interest in school. Girls, by contrast, seem to receive more positive feedback about work-irrelevant domains, which, unfortunately, leads girls to discount positive feedback about their work and make more unstable attributions for success.

DISCUSSION QUESTIONS

1. Discuss the evidence in favor of and against a "fear of success" in women. What would be a good way to examine this issue today?
2. Of all the ideas discussed in this chapter, which do you find to be most convincing as an explanation of why women do not pursue STEM careers to the extent that men do?
3. Which is more adaptive: women's or men's response to evaluative feedback?
4. Under what circumstances would you expect women and men to make similar versus different attributions for their performance?
5. Considering the results from the studies on evaluative feedback and the work by Dweck on teachers' attributions for performance, what is the best way to provide feedback to children? To adults?
6. Given what you have learned about the different ways women and men define their core selves, what would you predict influences women's and men's self-esteem?
7. Consider the expectancy/value model of achievement. In what domains would you predict that women and men would have similar expectancies and values, and in what domains would you predict that women and men would have different expectancies and values?
8. What are some of the specific ways in which parents' beliefs about their children's abilities could influence their children's actual abilities?
9. What do you believe are the major advantages and disadvantages of single-sex classrooms?
10. What could be done to reduce gender bias in the classroom?

Suggested Reading

Cross, S. E., & Madson, L. (1997). Models of the self: Self-construals and gender. *Psychological Bulletin, 122,* 5–37.

(Classic) Dweck, C. S., Davidson, W., Nelson, S., & Enna, B. (1978). Sex differences in learned helplessness: II. The contingencies of evaluative feedback in the classroom; III. An experimental analysis. *Developmental Psychology, 14,* 268–276.

Jacobs, J. E., Davis-Kean, P., Bleeker, M., Eccles, J. S., & Malanchuk, O. (2005). "I can, but I don't want to": The impact of parents, interests, and activities on gender differences in math. In A. M. Gallagher & J. C. Kaufman (Eds.), *Gender differences in mathematics: An integrative psychological approach* (pp. 246–263). New York: Cambridge University Press.

Sadker, M., & Sadker, D. (1994). *Failing at fairness: How America's schools cheat girls.* New York: Scribner's.

Key Terms

Achievement motive—Stable personality characteristic that reflects the tendency to strive for success.

Attribution—Cause assigned to a behavior.

Collective interdependence—Connection to others derived from group membership.

Entity theory (of competence)—Belief that competence is due to fixed ability and cannot be changed.

Expectancy/value model of achievement—Theory that achievement-related choices are a function of our expectancy for success and our value of the area.

External attribution—Cause assigned to a behavior that originates in the environment.

Fear of success—Association of negative consequences with achievement.

Independent self-construal—Sense of self based on independence, individuation, and separation from others.

Interdependent self-construal—Sense of self based on connection to others.

Internal attribution—Cause assigned to a behavior that originates within the person.

Relational interdependence—Emphasis on close relationships.

Self-serving bias—The tendency to assign internal attributions for success and external attributions for failure.

Stable attribution—Cause for a behavior that does not change over time.

Stereotype threat—Theory that activating the female stereotype hinders women's performance.

Unstable attribution—Cause for a behavior that may change with time, day, or place.

CHAPTER 7

Communication

"The 10 Worst Things You Can Say to a Guy" (*Glamour*)

"Why Can't He Hear What You're Saying?" (*Redbook*)

"What It Means When He Clams Up" (*Cosmopolitan*)

"What Women Say and What They Really Mean" (*AskMen.com*)

"Language Lessons: How to Speak Male During a Breakup" (*Marie Claire*)

These are a few of the headlines in recent years that suggest men and women have difficulties communicating with each other. In 1990, Deborah Tannen wrote a popular book entitled *You Just Don't Understand: Women and Men in Conversation.* From this book, it would appear that women and men have completely different styles of conversation, completely different styles of nonverbal communication, and completely different styles of interacting with one another. Indeed, many of the conversational excerpts provided in her book ring true. But the book is largely based on anecdotal evidence of men's and women's interactions. The stories ring true because they are consistent with our schemas about how women and men interact and because it is easier to recall schema-consistent information than schema-inconsistent information. The research evidence, however, shows that women's and men's communication patterns are much more varied. Many more variables than the person's sex influence communication—for example, the sex of the person with whom one is interacting, the situation in which people find themselves, the goal or purpose of the interaction, and the status of the interaction partners. Kathryn Dindia (2006), a gender and communications scholar, concludes that men and women are not from different planets or cultures and do not speak different languages. Rather than men being from Mars and women being from Venus, Dindia (2006) suggests that men are from North Dakota and women are from South Dakota—meaning that there are many more similarities than differences in communication.

This is the first chapter in the section on gender and relationships. Before discussing specific aspects of men's and women's friendships, romantic relationships, and work relationships in the next chapters, here I review the literature on how women and men communicate. This chapter focuses on both verbal and nonverbal communication. I begin by describing the research on men's and women's interaction styles in childhood and adulthood and the variables that influence those styles. I then turn to the literatures on verbal behavior—the language women and men use—and nonverbal behavior—touching, gazing, and smiling. Communication styles have implications for leadership and influence—who becomes a leader, styles of leadership, and how female and male leaders are perceived. The last aspect of communication I examine is emotion—both experiences and expression. I conclude the chapter by reviewing the two most prominent explanations for the sex differences in communication suggested—status theory and social role theory.

INTERACTION STYLES IN CHILDHOOD

Two children are sitting quietly at a table in the family room coloring and talking about being best friends. A group of children are playing soccer in the backyard, shouting at one another to get to the ball. Who are the children at the table? In the backyard? Boys? Girls? Both? Can you tell?

There are certainly some differences in the ways girls and boys play. For example, girls are more likely to play in dyads, and boys are more likely to play in groups. Both girls and boys are also likely to be playing with the same sex. From very early on, children tend to prefer and seek out interactions with same-sex peers. Thus same-sex play, in and of itself, becomes a socializing agent that ultimately leads males and females to have different interaction styles (Maccoby, 1998).

What is the evidence for same-sex play preferences? Do you recall playing with children of the same sex or children of the other sex? At what age? At ages 1 and 2, there are no preferences for same- or other-sex peers, but by age 3, there is a clear same-sex preference in girls (Maccoby, 1998). A year later, boys' same-sex preference emerges. The preference to interact with same-sex peers peaks between the ages of 8 and 11 (Maccoby, 1998). The same-sex play preference also appears across very different cultures (Munroe & Romney, 2006).

Even though girls initiate the same-sex play preference, by age 5, the preference is stronger in boys than girls. Boys' groups are more exclusionary of the other sex than are girls' groups. Boys view other boys who play with girls as feminine, and boys do not tolerate feminine behavior in another boy. It is important for boys' sense of masculinity to demonstrate that they are not feminine and to reject all associations with femininity. Girls, however, do not feel the same need to reject masculinity. Girls are more accepting of masculine behavior in another girl (Maccoby, 1998). Children also believe others like them more if they play with the same sex than with the other sex. In one study, children who said that others approved of other-sex play were more likely to engage in other-sex play (Martin et al., 1999).

Why do children prefer to play with others of the same sex? There are at least three reasons (Maccoby, 1998; Mehta & Strough, 2009). First, girls and boys have different styles of play and communication that are not always compatible. Second, girls find it difficult to influence boys, which makes interactions with boys less desirable for girls. Third, there is institutional support for same-sex play; that is, other people discourage other-sex interactions. In childhood, those other people are parents and peers. In adulthood, those other people are spouses/romantic partners, family, and friends. I discuss the evidence for each of these reasons.

Children's Styles of Play

Boys' play and girls' play are different (Maccoby, 1998; Rose & Rudolph, 2006). Boys play in large groups, whereas girls are more likely to play with only one or two friends. Boys' play is rough, competitive, and emphasizes dominance; girls' play is quiet, often conversational, and involves more structured activities (e.g., drawing or painting; see Figure 7.1). Boys' play is boisterous, activity oriented, and takes up a good deal of space (i.e., the street, the entire yard). Boys are more likely to play outdoors, whereas girls are more likely to play inside the house or stay within their yards. These sex differences

FIGURE 7.1 This is a common form of play among girls—dyadic and quiet, with the opportunity for conversation.

emerge in childhood and persist or increase during middle childhood and adolescence. Even girls' and boys' fantasy play differs. Girls are more likely to pretend to play house or school, where one person enacts the role of teacher or parent and the other enacts the role of student or child; boys, by contrast, are more likely to emulate heroic characters, such as Superman. It is easy to see how these play styles might not be compatible.

Girls and boys also have different conversational styles, which map onto their distinct styles of play (Maccoby, 1998; McCloskey, 1996). Girls' conversation serves to foster connection, whereas boys' conversation is motivated to establish dominance. Girls express agreement with one another, take turns when speaking, acknowledge one another's feeling, and teach younger children how to play games—behavior that has been labeled **prosocial dominance** (Whiting & Edwards, 1988). Boys interrupt each other, threaten each other, refuse to comply with one another, try to top one another's stories, and call each other names—behavior that has been labeled **egoistic dominance**. Girls are more likely to make a polite suggestion ("Could you pick up the ball, please?"), whereas boys are more likely to order someone to do something ("Pick up the ball!"). It is not the case, however, that girls' play is completely free from conflict. See Sidebar 7.1 for a discussion of the different kinds of aggression that characterize children's play.

Yet, there is some evidence that different play styles do not completely account for the same-sex play preference. In one study, children ages 2.5 to 5 who had more and less sex-typed play styles were equally likely to play with the same sex (Hoffmann & Powlishta, 2001). It is also possible that same-sex play leads to different play styles rather than different play styles leading to same-sex play.

SIDEBAR 7.1: *Mean Girls? Relational Aggression*

Spreading rumors, excluding someone, and threatening not to be someone's friend. These are not behaviors that first come to mind when one thinks of aggression. They are not physical aggression but **relational aggression**, also known as *indirect aggression* and *social aggression*. Relational aggression is hurting or threatening to hurt a relationship with another person. Some examples are shown in Table 7.1. Research initially suggested that relational aggression was the "female" form of aggression, the counterpart to boys' physical aggression. In fact, a number of studies have shown that girls are more relationally aggressive than boys (e.g., Lee, 2009) and across a number of cultures (Russia, China, Finland, and Indonesia; Crick et al., 1999; French, Jansen, & Pidada, 2002). However, other research has shown no sex differences in relational aggression (Archer & Coyne, 2005). Finally, a meta-analytic review of the literature was undertaken (Card et al., 2008). It showed a significant sex difference in relational aggression (in the direction of girls) but the size of the effect was very small, suggesting more similarity than difference ($d = -.06$). Age did not moderate these findings, meaning that there was not a particular age group in which girls were substantively more relationally aggressive than boys. A more meaningful way of understanding sex comparisons and relational aggression is to say that boys use physical aggression more than relational aggression, and girls use relational aggression more than physical aggression. Within boys, conflict is more likely to overt, whereas within girls, conflict is more likely to be covert.

Females and males have similar motives for engaging in relational aggression—to gain power, to try to fit in to a group, as a response to jealousy, or in response to some characteristic of the victim, such as lack of confidence (Pronk & Zimmer-Gembeck, 2010). There also is some suggestion that intimacy contributes to relational aggression—at least among girls. Some forms of relational aggression (e.g., rumors, gossiping) require intimate knowledge about the person. In a study of fourth-graders, relationship aggression increased over the year for girls as did intimate disclosure to friends (Murray-Close, Ostrov, & Crick, 2007). The two were related. Because girls have intimate knowledge about their friends, they can use this knowledge in an adverse way.

Both boys and girls view relational aggression as less harmful than physical aggression (Murray-Close, Crick, & Galotti, 2006). The meta-analysis showed that relational aggression is related to subsequent personal difficulties for both girls and boys—both internalizing problems (e.g., depression) and externalizing problems (e.g., acting out, delinquency; Card et al., 2008). The implications of relational aggression for relationships are less clear. The meta-analysis showed that relational aggression was associated with greater rejection by peers but also with greater prosocial behavior (Card et al., 2008). Card and colleagues suggested that relational aggression requires the use of prosocial skills to gain the support of others. Relational aggression has distinct effects on popularity when one distinguishes between sociometric popularity, which is measured by having all the people in the class rate whom they like and dislike, and perceived popularity, which entails having people nominate whom they perceive to be popular. The two are positively correlated but become less strongly related as children grow older. Relational aggression is associated with lower sociometric popularity but greater perceived popularity—especially for girls (Andreou, 2006; Cillessen & Borch, 2006).

What is the source of relational aggression? The environment plays a much larger role than genetics (Brendgen et al., 2005). First, relational aggression may be acquired from modeling, as one study showed that older siblings' relational aggression predicted younger siblings' relational aggression the following year (Ostrov, Crick, & Stauffacher, 2006). Second, to the extent relational aggression is associated with being female, it could be explained by gender-role social-ization. Girls are socialized to conceal their hostility toward others and to express aggression in a more covert way. Third, like physical aggression, relational aggression has been linked to cogni-tive biases in interpreting ambiguous situations (Crick et al., 2004). When the ambiguity occurs in the context of a relationship, children who are relationally aggressive are more likely to make hostile attributions (Leff, Kupersmidt, & Power, 2003).

TABLE 7.1 RELATIONAL AGGRESSION ITEMS

1. When angry, gives others the "silent treatment."
2. When mad, tries to damage others' reputations by passing on negative information.
3. When mad, retaliates by excluding others from activities.
4. Intentionally ignores others until they agree to do something for him or her.
5. Makes it clear to his or her friends that he or she will think less of them unless they do what he or she wants.
6. Threatens to share private information with others in order to get them to comply with his or her wishes.
7. When angry with same-sex peer, tries to steal that person's dating partner.

Source: Werner and Crick (1999).

Greater time in same-sex play predicts more sex-stereotyped play over time (Fabes, Martin, & Hanish, 2004; Martin & Fabes, 2001). Spe-cifically, same-sex play in girls predicted a decrease in activity and aggression over the year, whereas same-sex play in boys pre-dicted an increase in activity, aggression, and rough-and-tumble play over the year.

If same-sex play increases stereotypi-cal play styles, does other-sex play reduce ste-reotypical play styles? There is some evidence that this is the case. Mixed-sex play accounts for about 30% of children's interactions (Fabes et al., 2004) but is typically not dyadic (see Figure 7.2 for an exception; Fabes, Martin, & Hanish, 2003). There is some accommoda-tion of play styles when girls and boys are to-gether. Studies of preschoolers show that boys are less active, less forceful, and more agree-able with females than males, and females are

FIGURE 7.2   A girl and a boy playing together; cross-sex play is not the norm, especially dyadic cross-sex play.

more active, more forceful, more controlling, and less agreeable with males than females (Fabes et al., 2003; Holmes-Lonergan, 2003). Accommodation of interaction styles also has been observed among fifth and sixth graders playing computer games (Calvert et al., 2003). Boys engaged in more fast-moving play and girls engaged in more language-based play, but these differences decreased when interacting with the other sex. Thus same-sex play seems to be the most stereotyped, and other-sex play has the potential to decrease stereotypes.

Girls' Difficulty in Influencing Boys

A second reason children prefer to play with same-sex peers is that girls find it difficult to influence boys. According to Maccoby (1998), girls attempt to influence others by making polite suggestions, whereas boys are more likely to make demands. Boys are not responsive to girls' polite suggestions; thus girls' tactics are effective with other girls and with adults, but not with boys. The question is—why are boys unresponsive to girls?

The differences in interaction styles and influence styles explain why it appears that girls spend more time in close proximity to authority figures (e.g., teachers) than boys do. It was first thought that girls stayed closer to teachers because of their affiliative nature. However, girls stand near teachers only in the presence of boys. Girls likely believe that an adult authority figure will temper boys' dominant behavior.

Institutional Support

Different ways girls and boys play, interact, and attempt to influence one another might explain why girls and boys prefer to play with peers of their own sex. But what is the source of boys' and girls' divergent play styles? Why is boys' play louder and more aggressive than girls' play? One possibility is the *socialization* hypothesis. Children may model same-sex play from parents. Aside from each other, mothers and fathers are typically *friends* with people of the same sex. Parents also treat girls and boys

differently in ways that might influence interaction styles. Parents handle girls more gently, talk more about emotions with girls, are more tolerant of fighting among boys, and are more likely to use physical punishment with boys. In addition, parents give children sex-typed toys and reinforce sex-typed behavior. These *small* differences in behavior could lead girls' play to center more on emotions and boys' play to be rougher. Again, the question is whether parents' differential treatment of girls and boys leads to different play styles, or whether the different play styles of girls and boys lead parents to treat them differently.

Parents, schools, and work environments all encourage same-sex interaction. Parents typically select same-sex playmates for their children. Think about who is invited to a 4- or 5-year-old's birthday party. It is usually the same sex—especially in the case of girls. The question is: Do parents seek out same-sex peers for their children to play with before the children are old enough to have strong preferences?

Schools reinforce the division of girls and boys in a number of ways, ranging from teachers' introductory "Good Morning, boys and girls," to sex segregation of sports. In my daughter's elementary school, girls and boys were not allowed to sit at the same table for lunch. Once I observed a group of 8- to 10-year-olds playing Red Rover at an after-school program. The teachers were distraught because the girls kept losing to the boys. There were about 7 girls on one team and 12 boys on the other. It did not occur to the teachers that boys and girls could be on the same team. Instead, the teachers tried to find ways to give the girls advantages to "even out" the teams.

Again, we can ask the question—do differences in same-sex play styles lead to sex segregated play, or does the encouragement of sex-segregated play lead to same-sex play styles? Regardless, to the extent that there are differences in play styles between girls and boys, more time spent with same-sex peers will reinforce and perpetuate those differences. Little research has tried to distinguish girls and boys who have stronger versus weaker same-sex peer preferences. This may shed some light on the origin of same-sex play preferences. Conduct your own research on the issue with Do Gender 7.1.

DO GENDER 7.1
Which Girls Play with Boys
and Which Boys Play with Girls?

Visit a local day care or preschool. Choose ten children to observe, five girls and five boys. It would be preferable if you could choose these children randomly from a list of the children in the class. Each day observe a different child, recording how much time he or she spends in same-sex play and mixed-sex play.

Now, see if you can distinguish the children who engage in more or less mixed-sex play. Does the type of play differ? How do they speak to one another? If you can find out information about their families, you could determine if they come from different backgrounds, the nature of—parent gender roles, and whether there are siblings in the household. You might also interview the children to measure variables that could distinguish those who play more or less frequently with the same sex, such as the child's gender-role attitudes. Ask Johnny why he plays with Joan, but not Marcus. Ask Tisha why she plays with Hannah, but not Paul.

Unless you follow the children over time, this cross-sectional study will not be able to distinguish cause and effect. That is, you will not know if individual difference variables led the children to become involved in more same-sex play or whether same-sex play shaped the children in some ways.

TAKE HOME POINTS

- Both boys and girls develop a strong preference to play with members of the same sex.

- The same-sex preference appears first among girls but becomes stronger among boys.

- Same-sex play is more gender stereotyped than mixed-sex play, and mixed-sex play has the potential to reduce stereotyped play.

- Reasons for the same-sex play preference include different play styles, girls' difficulty in influencing boys, and institutional support.

INTERACTION STYLES IN ADULTHOOD

There are parallels between the sex differences in interaction styles observed among children and those observed among adults. Much of the research on adult interaction styles comes from studies of how people behave in small groups. This research shows that men's behavior is more directive, dominant, hierarchical, and task focused; by contrast, women's behavior is more supportive, cooperative, and egalitarian. Studies of group interactions show that females engage in more **positive social behavior**, such as agreeing with others, showing group solidarity, encouraging others to talk, and making positive comments (Smith-Lovin & Robinson, 1992; Wood & Rhodes, 1992). Women are also likely to reciprocate positive social acts. In other words, women help escalate positive social behavior. Men talk more in groups compared to women (Smith-Lovin & Robinson, 1992), and men engage in more **task behavior**, such as asking for and offering opinions and suggestions (Wood & Rhodes, 1992). Men also engage in more **negative social behavior**, such as disagreement and antagonism, and help escalate negative social behavior (i.e., respond to negative social behavior with more negative social behavior; Wood & Rhodes, 1992).

Given this brief summary of quite distinct interaction styles, I now must caution you that sex differences in interaction styles are not that clear cut. The way women and men behave with one another is qualified by a host of other variables. As noted by Aries (2006), "we need to move beyond the conception that the interaction styles of men and women reside within individuals." The context is important.

Qualifiers of Sex Differences

One determinant of sex differences in interaction styles is the nature of the task. Men are more task oriented in masculine situations, whereas women are more task oriented in feminine situations. A task orientation includes making suggestions and providing information. Thus a certain degree of confidence in or knowledge of the situation is required before we engage in task behavior. Women and men are likely to be more confident in situations relevant to their own sex, which enables them

to make suggestions and provide information. Because masculine situations are studied more often, it may only appear that men are more task oriented than women.

Another major determinant of women's and men's interaction styles is the sex of the person with whom they are interacting. For example, in a study of dyads, Carli (1989) found that women displayed more positive social behavior (e.g., agreeing with their partners) and men displayed more task-oriented behavior and disagreement when they were interacting with members of the same sex. However, both women and men used more feminine behavior (e.g., agreement) with female partners and more masculine behavior (e.g., disagreement) with male partners. In other words, just as in the studies of children, men and women accommodated to each other. As shown in Figure 7.3, both men and women engaged in more task behavior when they were paired with men than with women (panel a), and both men and women engaged in more positive social behavior when they were paired with women

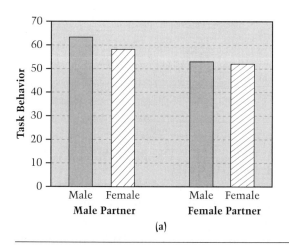

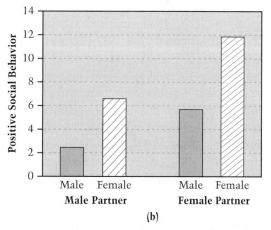

FIGURE 7.3   (a) Both men and women display more task behavior when they interact with a male than a female. (b) Both men and women display more positive social behavior when they interact with a female than a male. Numbers represent the percentage of all behaviors displayed in a particular dyad.
Source: Adapted from Carli (1989).

than men (panel b). Thus men and women behave most differently from each other when they are with members of their same sex.

Sex differences in interaction styles also tend to be greater when the interaction is brief and among strangers (Aries, 2006). This is the typical laboratory study. When we have little information about others besides their sex, we rely more on category-based expectancies (sex stereotypes) when making judgments or deciding how to behave. As people get to know one another and understand each other's abilities, sex becomes a less important determinant of interaction behavior. Is it possible that sex also is a less important determinant of communications in which sex is less visible—that is, online communication? See Sidebar 7.2 for a discussion of this research.

Implications of Interaction Styles for Performance

To the extent that women and men do have different interaction styles, what are the implications for performance? A group's performance may depend on the match between the members' interaction styles and the task with which the group is faced. Groups that have task-oriented goals will perform better when members show task-oriented behavior. Groups focused on a social activity or an activity that requires consensus will perform better if members display more positive social behavior. Consistent with this idea, one study found that male groups outperformed female groups when the task required the generation of ideas, and female groups outperformed male groups when the task required the group to reach consensus (Hutson-Comeaux & Kelly, 1996). One limitation of these studies is that sex—but not sex-specific interaction styles—is being linked to group performance. We assume male groups are performing better

on task outcomes because they are displaying task-oriented behavior and female groups are performing better on social outcomes because they are displaying more positive social behavior. It would be more helpful to know that task behavior contributes to better outcomes in groups where the mission is to solve a problem and that positive social behavior contributes to better outcomes in groups that require members to come to an agreement.

TAKE HOME POINTS

- There are differences in the styles women and men exhibit when interacting in small groups. Women engage in more positive social behavior (e.g., agreement), and men engage in more task behavior (e.g., providing or asking for information) and negative behavior (e.g., disagreement).

- These differences are influenced by whether the group is composed of same-sex or other-sex persons. In the presence of the other sex, men and women accommodate to each other.

- These differences also are a function of the nature of the task. Both women and men exhibit more task-oriented behavior in areas in which they have expertise.

- These differences also are more commonly found in laboratory studies of people who do not know each other. Interaction styles among people in ongoing relationships may be influenced by factors other than sex.

LANGUAGE

Imagine the following interaction:

PERSON A: I haven't talked to you in so long. What's up?

PERSON B: I've been really stressed out lately. Things are kind of weird at home.

SIDEBAR 7.2: *Online Communication*

Today, we have many more forms of communication than face to face or even telephone. We communicate with one another on cell phones via text and on computers via email, instant messaging, and social networking sites. There are some similarities and differences in the ways that females and males communicate. Here, we discuss communication via computer, via phones, and then via social networking sites.

Regarding computers, females and males are equally likely to use the Internet, regardless of whether they are children or adults (Jackson, Zhao, Qiu et al., 2008; Ohannessian, 2009). Nearly three-fourths (74%) of adults use the Internet at least three to five times a week (Pew, 2010). However, there are race differences in usage that interact with sex. Among Caucasians, there is no sex difference in Internet usage but Black women use the Internet more than Black men (Jackson et al., 2010; Jackson, Zhao, Kolenic et al., 2008). Despite the similarities in Internet usage, females and males spend their time on computers somewhat differently. Among both children and adults, females are more likely than males to use computers for writing and for communication by email or instant messaging, whereas males are much more likely than females to play videogames (Jackson, Zhao, Kolenic et al., 2008; Jackson, Zhao, Qiu et al., 2008; Ohannessian, 2009; Rideout, Foehr, & Roberts, 2010). Many of these sex differences extend to other countries such as China, the United Kingdom, and Turkey (Akman & Mishra, 2010; Jackson, Zhao, Qiu et al., 2008; Li & Kirkup, 2007). Although females engage in more online communication than males, the content of those communication are more similar than different. Female online communication contains more references to emotion (Fox et al., 2007) and more nonverbal cues or emotions, such as ☺ (Ledbetter & Larson, 2008). However, these cues have no impact on receiver satisfaction with the message.

Cell phone usage is a form of communication that is increasing exponentially—especially among teens. Whereas 45% of teens ages 12–17 had cell phones in 2004, the figure rose to 71% in 2008 and is projected to be 85% in 2009 (Lenhart, 2009). Females and males are equally likely to use a cell phone. There are no ethnic or racial differences in cell phone ownership but higher socioeconomic status teens are more likely to own phones. Among teens, cell phones are not used for talking as much as they are texting (see Figure 7.4). Today, texting on cell phones is the number one way that teens—girls and boys—communicate with one another (Lenhart et al., 2010). Cell phone texting exceeds email, instant messaging, talking in person, talking on the phone, and social networking sites. Three-quarters of teens between the ages of 12 and 17 have cell phones and one-third of those who do not have had one at one time. A majority (75%) have unlimited text, which is a good thing because one-third send over 100 text messages per day. Females average 80 texts per day, whereas males average 30 texts per day.

A more novel way of communicating is via an online profile on a social networking site, such as Facebook or MySpace. One-third of adults, male and female alike, have an online profile (Pew, 2009b). Among teens of ages 12–17, girls are slightly more likely than boys to use a social networking site (58% vs. 51%; Lenhart & Madden, 2007). Females and males use these sites somewhat differently. Females are more likely to use the sites to communicate with existing friends, whereas males are more likely to use the sites to flirt and make new friends. Females and males present themselves in ways that are consistent with gender-role norms, males emphasizing their power and strength and females emphasizing their sociability and physical attractiveness (Manago et al., 2008).

In the end, technological advances have made it easier for people to communicate with one another. Never before have people been so accessible. It remains to be seen what the impact of this communication is on the nature of relationships, and if the effects vary for males and females.

FIGURE 7.4   Two teenage girls communicating via text.

PERSON A: What's been going on?
PERSON B: It's my brother.
PERSON A: Uh-huh.
PERSON B: It's never anything specific, but he's just really, really annoying me and there's nothing I can do about it. You know?
PERSON A: That sounds tough.
PERSON B: I've even been having dreams where he's doing something really awful.
PERSON A: It's probably a good thing that you don't have to live with him anymore, don't you think? But it seems like it still haunts you. It must still bother you if you have dreams about him a lot and stuff.

Now consider the following interaction:

PERSON A: Pat still hasn't given me back that money I let him borrow.
PERSON B: I wouldn't have given it to him in the first place.
PERSON A: I wouldn't either but he was in a bind and …
PERSON B: Dude, you just don't get it. I told you a long time ago: You never lend money to that guy. Never. I've known him for a long time and you can't trust him.

The two interactions are both same-sex interactions. Can you tell which one is between two women and which is between two men? How? There are aspects of language that distinguish men's and women's speech—but usually only when they interact with the same sex. The language used in mixed-sex interactions is much harder to distinguish. The two same-sex interactions provided are very stereotypical. The first interaction was between two women, and the second was between two men. The speaking styles differed on a number of dimensions discussed in this section.

One of the most common perceptions we have about the differences between women's and men's language is that women use more of it! That is, women talk more than men. In the interactions just described, the women's conversation was longer than the men's. Does this stereotype have a basis in reality? In a meta-analytic review of the literature on children's language, girls were found to talk more than boys (Leaper & Smith, 2004). However, the effect size was small ($d = -.11$), and sex differences were larger among younger children. By contrast, in a meta-analytic review of adult speech, men were more talkative than women ($d = +.14$; Leaper & Ayres, 2007). However, there were several moderators of the latter effect, including the way that language was measured, the nature of the relationship, and the sex composition of the interaction. There were no sex differences in the number of words spoken, but men spoke for longer periods of time and spoke more words per turn, suggesting that men's talkativeness conveyed dominance. To support this theory, men were also found to talk more than women in mixed-sex than same-sex interactions—especially when the dyad examined was a husband and wife.

Aside from general amount of talking, are there specific features of language more characteristic of women or men? Features of

TABLE 7.2 FEATURES OF LANGUAGE

Feature	Example	Sex Difference
Self-reference	"I"	Male
Directive/imperative	"Close the door"	Male
Quantity terms	"Five miles"	Male
Intensive adverb	"so"; "really"	Female
Use emotions	"afraid"; "loved"	Female
Ask questions	"Why?"	Female
Hedges	"sort of"; "kind of"; "maybe"	Female
Exclamation	"wow"	Female
Sentence length	longer sentences	Female
Judgment adjectives	"good"; "stupid"	Male
Offensive language	swear words	Male
Minimal response	"OK"; "uh-huh"	Female
Qualifiers	"unless"	Female

language that have been studied are shown in Table 7.2 (Colley et al., 2004; Guiller & Durndell, 2006; Mulac, 2006; Newman et al., 2008). Men are more likely than women to refer to quantity in language (e.g., "That house is as large as a football field"; "I had to walk four times as far to school as my son does"); to use directives; to make reference to themselves (i.e., use "I"); to use judgment adjectives (e.g., "This is a ridiculous assignment"); and to use offensive language. Women are more likely than men to use intensive adverbs (e.g., I "totally" agree, so, really), refer to emotions in language, use longer sentences, ask questions, use hedges (e.g., sort of, kind of, maybe), use qualifiers, offer the **minimal response** (e.g., uh-huh, okay, nodding), and make exclamations. Men are more likely to talk about sports and to use assertive language, whereas women are more likely to use social words in language and express agreement. Some of these differences can be found in the example interactions I provided. However, I do not want

to overstate the differences. The fact of the matter is that when communications written by women and men are examined, people typically cannot guess the sex of the writer or speaker (Mulac, 2006). Thus again, there must be more similarities than differences in the language used by women and men.

To better understand the language men and women use, we can classify it along three dimensions (Mulac, Bradac & Gibbons, 2001). First, language is direct or indirect. Men's language is more direct because they use directives; women's language is more indirect because they ask questions and use qualifiers and hedges. Second, language can be succinct or elaborative. Women's longer sentences and use of intensive adverbs make their language more elaborative. Third, language can be instrumental or affective. Men's reference to quantity is instrumental, and women's use of emotion words is affective. Thus men's language can be said to be instrumental, succinct, and directive, whereas women's language is affective, elaborative, and indirect. Even among children, girls' language is more affiliative and boys' more assertive (Leaper & Smith, 2004).

Qualifiers of Sex Differences

These conclusions about sex differences in language are overly simplistic. Sex differences in language are not always consistent. One factor that influences the language women and men use is the sex of the person with whom one is talking. The meta-analytic review of children showed that sex differences in talkativeness (girls more than boys) were larger when children interacted with adults compared to peers (Leaper & Smith, 2004). The meta-analytic review of adult language showed that sex differences in talkativeness varied greatly by interaction partner (Leaper & Ayres, 2007). Men were more talkative than women to spouses/partners ($d = -.38$) and strangers ($d = -.17$), but women were more talkative than men to classmates ($d = +.54$) and to their own children ($d = +.42$). In addition, sex differences were larger in mixed-sex interactions ($d = -.28$) than same-sex interactions ($d = -.08$). Thus, among adults, it appears that men's greater talkativeness is limited to contexts in which there is a status difference.

The interaction partner also influences sex differences in the nature of language used. Sex differences in affiliative speech (female more) and assertive speech (male more) are larger when interacting with strangers than when interacting with people who are known (Leaper & Ayres, 2007), underscoring the idea that female and male behavior differs the most when people do not know each other. However, sex differences also were larger for affiliative and assertive behavior in same-sex than mixed-sex interaction patterns, suggesting that women and men accommodate to one another in each other's presence. This

idea was corroborated in a study of an online support group among adults (Mo, Malik, & Coulson, 2009) and a study of email exchanges among college students (Thomson, Murachver, & Green, 2001). It appeared that respondents used the language of their interaction partner, which led to less gendered language during other-sex exchanges.

Another reason for sex differences in language may have to do with the topic of conversation. Women and men speak about different topics that require different language. In one study, titled "Girls Don't Talk About Garages," college students could accurately predict the sex composition of a dyad talking—not because of the language used but because of the differences in topics (Martin, 1997). Male same-sex dyads talked about sports, women, being trapped in relationships, and drinking; female same-sex dyads talked about relationships, men, clothes, and feelings. Recall the interactions described at the beginning of this section. How did you know the first interaction was between two women and the second was between two men? One way you distinguished the conversations may have been the topic. The topic of the first interaction was a relationship problem, and the topic of the second was money. In the study of college students, perceivers were more accurate in identifying same-sex dyads than cross-sex dyads. The greatest confusion was between female-female dyads and cross-sex dyads. The conversations and language used in cross-sex dyads may be more similar to those used in female same-sex dyads. As you will see in Chapter 8, men are more likely than women to change their behavior when interacting with the other sex. Find out for yourself if your classmates can identify the storyteller with Do Gender 7.2.

To make matters more complicated, the nature of the topic and the sex of the

DO GENDER 7.2
Sex Differences in Language Use

Have five female friends and five male friends write stories about a specific topic—but the same topic (current relationship problem, how they feel about school, relationships with parents, or earliest memory). See if your classmates can guess the sex of the writer better than chance (i.e., more than 50%). Ask what information they used to identify the sex of the speaker. Also ask them to rate the stories on the use of the language features shown in Table 7.2. Compare the accurate guesses to the inaccurate guesses to see which information was more diagnostic.

interaction partner may interact to influence language. One study showed that females used more tentative language than males for masculine topics and males used more tentative language than females for feminine topics—but only when communicating with the other sex (Palomares, 2009). There were no differences in tentative language when communicating with the same sex.

The same concern I raised about the brevity of interactions for the study of interaction styles applies to the study of language. Sex differences in language are more likely to be found in shorter interactions. In experimental settings, participants are strangers and interactions are brief. This is the kind of situation in which sex is salient and stereotypes are likely to operate. Sex differences in communication disappear when longer interactions are examined; as men and women become familiar with each other, their speech becomes similar.

One reason that sex differences in language may disappear as people get to know one another is that sex becomes a less salient feature of the interaction. Gender salience has been found to explain sex differences in language and to be a condition that magnifies sex differences in language. The explanatory function of gender salience was demonstrated in a study that showed the extent to which women and men were thinking about being female/male during a communication was associated with greater sex differences in language (Palomares, 2009). The impact of salience also was demonstrated in a study of college students that showed women used more emotion language than men when they were induced to think about themselves in terms of their sex (gender salient) but not in terms of their student status (Palomares, 2008). Another study showed that gender salience only affected the language of gender schematic people—that is, people who are sensitive to gender (Palomares, 2004). Gender schematic women used more feminine language and less masculine language, but only if gender was made salient. The salience manipulation had similar effects on men's language, but the effects were not as strong. The language of gender aschematic men and women was not affected by the salience manipulation.

To the extent that sex differences in language are due to socialization, these differences may not generalize to other cultures with different socialization practices. There is a fairly large literature comparing communication in the United States to communication in Japan (Waldron & DiMare, 1998). Many of the sex differences in language found in this chapter do not generalize to Japan. For example, sex differences in assertive language found in the United States are not found in Japan (Thompson, Klopf, & Ishii, 1991). In general, the language that the Japanese use is more similar to the language used by women in Western cultures (e.g., the United States; Wetzel, 1988). Parallels have been drawn between Japanese versus Western language and female versus male language. The Japanese value language that communicates sensitivity to others' needs, and language that includes empathy and agreement. Whereas people from Western cultures would view this language as powerless language, the Japanese do not. Power, in and of itself, is viewed differently by the two cultures. Americans, for example, view power as an attribute of a person, so a person can use more or less powerful language; the Japanese view power as an attribute of a social role or a position. Thus the position confers power, regardless of the language used. It does not make sense to talk about powerful language in Japan. In fact, language viewed as dominant in the United States—being assertive, interrupting someone, challenging someone—is viewed as childish in Japan.

One gendered interaction that has been studied in terms of language is interactions between patients and physicians. Does a physician's sex affect the interaction? Patient's sex? The combination of the two? See Sidebar 7.3 for a discussion of this research.

TAKE HOME POINTS

- Men's language is more direct, succinct, and instrumental, whereas women's language is more indirect, elaborative, and affective.

- Sex differences in language are moderated by a host of variables, including the sex of the interaction partner and the length of the interaction.

- Women's and men's language becomes more similar in mixed-sex than same-sex dyads, providing some evidence of accommodation.

- The topic more than the language used distinguishes male versus female conversation.

NONVERBAL BEHAVIOR

Recall the two interactions described in the previous section on language. Now, imagine you can see the people talking. What aspects of their behavior—other than their language—provide you with information about the interaction? Is it only people's verbal response that indicates whether they are listening? What about eye contact? What about posture? If someone touches you, does it increase the intimacy of the interaction or make you feel uncomfortable?

A lot more information is contained in an interaction besides the language used. Aspects of communication that do not include words are referred to as *nonverbal behavior*. The domains of nonverbal behavior that scientists have investigated, especially with respect to gender, are smiling, gazing, interpersonal sensitivity (decoding), accuracy in conveying emotion (encoding), and touching.

In 2000, Hall, Carter, and Horgan conducted a meta-analytic review of the literature on nonverbal behavior. They concluded that (1) females smile and gaze more than males; (2) females stand closer to others, face others more directly, and are more likely to touch other people; (3) males have more expansive body movements (i.e., take up more space) than females; (4) females are more accurate in interpreting others' emotional expressions and are better able to convey emotions than males. Interestingly, college students' perceptions of sex differences in nonverbal behavior correspond with the sex differences found in the meta-analytic reviews (Briton & Hall, 1995). Thus people's beliefs about sex differences in nonverbal behavior appear to be

Sidebar 7.3: *Physician–Patient Interactions*

One particularly interesting interaction to study from a gender perspective is the interaction between a patient and a physician. The physician–patient interaction is by definition one of unequal status. When the physician is male and the patient is female, the status difference in roles (physician vs. patient) is congruent with the status difference in sex (male vs. female). But today, it is no longer the case that the physician is always male. Because physician and patient roles are highly structured, with a clearly established hierarchy, female and male physicians might communicate similarly and female and male patients might respond similarly. In other words, the clear-cut demands of these roles may override any sex differences in communication style previously discussed. Research, however, does not support this idea.

A meta-analytic review of patient–physician interaction studies, most of which were observational, showed that female physicians made more active partnership statements (i.e., enlisting patient input, working together on a problem), asked more questions about psychosocial issues, had more emotion-focused conversation, and used more positive talk (i.e., reassurance, agreement, encouragement; Roter, Hall, & Aoki, 2002). In other words, female primary care physicians engaged in more "patient-centered" communication. Visits with female physicians also lasted two minutes longer, which was 10% of the visit. There was no sex difference in the number of general questions asked or the amount of biomedical information provided. Recent studies have confirmed these findings (Bertakis, 2009; Sandhu et al., 2009). A laboratory study demonstrated that female sex more than our expectations about female sex influences physician communication (Nicolai & Demmel, 2007). Adults were asked to evaluate transcripts of female and male physician interactions with patients, half being told the correct physician sex and half being told the wrong physician sex. Respondents rated the communication as more empathic when the physician was actually a female than a male. There was no effect of perceived physician sex on respondent ratings.

There also is some evidence that there is greater patient-centered communication and positive affect expressed in same-sex dyads than other-sex dyads (Bertakis, 2009; Sandhu et al., 2009), and this finding extends to African American patients who have other-race physicians (DiMatteo, Murray, & Williams, 2009). The male physician–female patient dyad seems to be the least patient centered and most formal, and the female physician–male patient dyad seems to be the least comfortable.

What are the implications of the differences between female and male physicians' communications? A meta-analysis of patient responses (Hall & Roter, 2002) showed that patients talk more, make more positive statements, discuss more psychosocial issues, and—most importantly—provide more biomedical information to female than male physicians. In addition, patients of female physicians are more satisfied (Sandhu et al., 2009). Thus female physicians may be more successful than male physicians at making patients feel comfortable and eliciting information. The extent to which these differences influence patient health outcomes, however, is unknown.

fairly accurate. More recently, Hall (2006) concluded that sex differences in nonverbal behavior, in particular smiling and decoding, are larger than most sex differences and larger than most social psychological effects.

Like the other behaviors we have examined in this chapter, sex differences in nonverbal behavior cannot be fully understood without considering the sex of the person with whom one is interacting. Again, women and men accommodate to each other. The sex difference in smiling, gazing, distance, and touch is much larger when comparing same-sex dyads to mixed-sex dyads. For example, the most smiling will be observed between two women, and the least smiling will be observed between two men. Two females will stand closest to one another, two males will stand farthest from one another, and a male–female dyad will fall somewhere in between. Sex comparisons in nonverbal behavior also may be affected by sexual orientation. One study examined the nonverbal behavior of heterosexual, homosexual, and mixed dyads and found that heterosexual dyads displayed the most gender stereotypic behavior (i.e., open posture if male and closed posture if female; Knofler & Imhof, 2007). In addition, heterosexual and homosexual dyads engaged in more direct full-face communication than mixed dyads, and mixed dyads displayed fewer direct gazes and maintained shorter eye contact than heterosexual or homosexual dyads. These findings suggest there was greater discomfort in the mixed dyads. The results are all the more interesting because participants were not made aware of one another's sexual orientation.

Smiling

Several meta-analyses indicate that females smile more than males (Hall et al., 2000; LaFrance & Hecht, 2000; LaFrance, Hecht, & Paluck, 2003). The effect size seems to be moderate, in the $d = -.40$ range. The sex difference appears to be largest among teenagers (LaFrance et al., 2003) and not consistent among children (Kolaric & Galambos, 1995). An interesting study of female and male yearbook pictures spanning kindergarten through college showed that the sex difference in smiling became significant by second grade, peaked in fourth grade, and persisted through college (Dodd, Russell, & Jenkins, 1999).

These findings are cross-sectional, however, making it difficult to determine if the effect is due to age or to differences in smiling across the generations. When a portion of the students were followed over time, the same pattern of results appeared suggesting that the sex difference in smiling emerges over time.

Not all smiles are alike, however. Researchers have distinguished between more genuine smiles (Duchenne smiles) and false smiles (non-Duchenne smiles), which can be observed by the movement of specific facial muscles. When college students role-played the position of job applicant, females engaged in more of both kinds of smiles than males (Woodzicka, 2008). Interestingly, females were aware of non-Duchenne smiles, but were not aware of Duchenne smiles. Women said that they engaged in non-Duchenne smiling to conceal negative emotions, to show enthusiasm, and to take up time so that they could come up with a verbal response to a question.

There are several situational variables that influence the sex difference in smiling. First, the sex difference in smiling seems to be limited to social settings and is especially large when people know they are being observed (LaFrance et al., 2003). Second, there is cross-cultural variation in the sex difference, with the largest sex difference appearing in Canada ($d = -.59$) and the smallest sex difference appearing in Britain ($d = -.13$; LaFrance et al., 2003). Finally, smiling seems to be more strongly correlated with personality variables associated with sex, such as sociability, nurturance, and femininity, rather than sex per se (Hall, 1998).

Gazing

Gazing is a difficult nonverbal behavior to interpret. In general, gazing is thought to convey interest and attention; thus it is not surprising that sex differences in gazing have been found in the direction of women gazing more than men. Furthermore, sex differences in gazing (female more than male) are typically larger when the situation evaluated is a friendly one. Yet, in other situations, gazing can convey a different message, in particular, a message related to status. A high-status person, for example, may gaze intently at the person to whom she or he is speaking. To confuse matters even more, sex differences in gazing do not generalize to all other cultures. For example, in Japan, it appears women make less eye contact than men, especially during interactions with other women. Eye contact here may convey dominance.

Interpersonal Sensitivity

Interpersonal sensitivity (sometimes referred to as *decoding*) is defined as correctly interpreting and assessing others, including their nonverbal behavior and their emotions. Females seem to be more sensitive than males to nonverbal cues, meaning they can more accurately interpret the meaning of nonverbal behavior (Brody & Hall, 2008; Rosip & Hall, 2004). Females are better able to understand the meaning behind nonverbal cues such as facial expression, vocal intonation, and body position. This finding seems to generalize to people in other countries, such as Malaysia, Japan, Hungary, Mexico, New Zealand, Hong Kong, and Israel (Hall et al., 2000). A meta-analytic review of the literature showed that females are better than males at interpreting facial expressions at all age groups examined—infants, children, and adolescents (McClure, 2000). Furthermore, the sex of the target does not make a difference in decoding accuracy; that is, females are more accurate than males in decoding both women's and men's emotions. The female advantage is stronger for nonverbal facial behavior than for nonverbal body movements or auditory cues. Females are also more accurate in recalling information about other people, regardless of

whether the information is female or male stereotypic (Hall & Mast, 2008).

One exception to females' ability to accurately interpret other's feelings and behavior is deception. Females are not more accurate than males at detecting deception unless language is involved, in which case women are better than men at detecting deception (Forrest & Feldman, 2000). If females' decoding ability is related to their orientation toward relationships, it is not a surprise that females are not as good as males at detecting deception. Detecting deception would not necessarily foster relationship development, whereas accurately interpreting another's emotions certainly would.

Encoding

The counterpart to understanding another's emotions is the ability to convey one's own emotions accurately. Encoding reflects the capacity to convey emotions without intentionally doing so. Because emotional expressiveness is central to the female gender role, it is not surprising that women are better at encoding than men (Hall et al., 2000). That is, others are better able to judge the emotions of a woman than of a man. Again, the difference is larger when judging facial expressions than vocal cues. It is not clear whether a sex difference in encoding occurs among children.

Touching

It is difficult to make a generalization about sex comparisons in touch because there are so many moderator variables, including the nature of the touch and the context in which it occurs. The sex composition of the dyad is a strong determinant of touch. In an observational study of touch across a variety of settings, women were significantly more likely than men to receive touching, and there was a trend for men to be more likely than

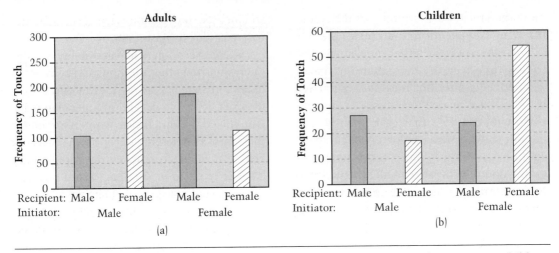

FIGURE 7.5 Among adults, there is greater cross-sex than same-sex touching. Among children, there is greater same-sex than cross-sex touching. Adults are shown in Figure 7.5a and children are shown in Figure 7.5b.
Source: Adapted from Major, Schmidlin, and William (1990).

women to initiate touch (Major, Schmidlin, & Williams, 1990). Both of these findings are misleading, however, because touching was best understood by considering both the sex of the initiator and the sex of the recipient. As shown in Figure 7.5a, there was greater cross-sex than same-sex touch. Within cross-sex dyads, males were more likely to touch females than females were to touch males. Males initiated more touch—but only toward females.

Other contextual factors, such as age and relationship status, have been investigated in regard to touch. In contrast to interactions among adults, interactions among children show greater same-sex than cross-sex touch (see Figure 7.5b). Among children, it appeared that females were more likely to initiate touch, but this was due to the high proportion of touching in the female–female dyad compared to the other three dyads. From preschool through high school, same-sex touch is more common than cross-sex touch—especially for females (Gallace & Spence,

2010). However, from college through adulthood, cross-sex touch is more common than same-sex touch. In cross-sex touch among adults, who initiates the touch may depend on age. In an observational study of touch among teenagers and adults, men initiated touch toward women among the younger group, but women initiated touch toward men among the older group (Hall & Veccia, 1990). In that study, age is confounded with relationship status, such that younger people have less developed relationships than older people. Thus, men may initiate touch among the younger people to indicate their control of a newly formed relationship. Women may initiate touch among the older people as an expression of the intimacy of the more developed relationship. An evolutionary explanation for this behavior is that men use touch to seduce a woman into a sexual relationship during the early stages, and women use touch to preserve the intimacy of the relationship during the later stages.

One interesting arena in which to explore touch is sports. Here it is more acceptable for men to touch one another. When male baseball and female softball teams were observed over 20 games, there were no sex differences for the majority of the 32 kinds of same-sex touch coded (Kneidinger, Maple, & Tross, 2001). Among the sex differences that did appear, they were typically in the direction of females engaging in more touching. Specifically, females were more likely to engage in intimate forms of touch with one another, such as group embraces. The outcome of the event also influenced sex differences in touch. After a positive event, women and men were equally likely to touch. However, after a negative event, women were more likely than men to touch—probably reflective of women conveying greater sympathy for one another.

Conduct your own observational study of touch in Do Gender 7.3 to see what variables influence touch.

DO GENDER 7.3
Observational Study
of Touching

Conduct an observational study of touching. Choose a setting, for example, the cafeteria, an airport, a mall, or a bar. Have the class break into groups so each group can observe a different setting. Record instances of touch. Record the sex of the initiator and of the recipient. Come up with a list of other variables to record that may help you understand touching, such as type of touch, intention of touch, length of touch, age of participants, and relationship status.

TAKE HOME POINTS

- There are fairly robust sex differences in nonverbal behavior.

- Women smile more, gaze more, are better able to express an emotion, and are better able to read another person's emotions.

- The sex difference in touch depends on many factors, including the target of the touch, the age of the participant, and the relationship between the two people. One reason findings are so variable is that touch has many meanings; it can be used to indicate status or to express intimacy.

LEADERSHIP AND INFLUENCEABILITY

An important behavior that occurs in the context of social interactions is interpersonal influence. Recall that one reason children play with members of the same sex is that girls find it difficult to influence boys. Does this difficulty hold up among adults? Are men more influential than women, and thus more likely to become leaders? Who is susceptible to influence? First, I review who is influenced and then who is influential and likely to emerge as a leader in groups. I discuss the different leadership styles and how female and male leaders are perceived.

Who Is Influenced?

It turns out that dispositional characteristics do not predict who is easily influenced as well as situational characteristics. Women may be more easily influenced than men, but it is because they find themselves in different situations than those of men. People interact differently with women than with men, and the interaction style used with women leads to influence.

This idea was shown in a now-classic dyadic interaction study conducted by Carli (1989). Men and women were placed in same-sex or mixed-sex dyads and asked to talk about an issue with which they disagreed. Participants' opinions on lowering the drinking age and providing free day care for working parents were obtained prior to creating the dyads so that disagreement on the issue could be assured. The pair then discussed the topic for 10 minutes. One of the partners in each dyad was randomly assigned to try to persuade the partner to her or his point of view. The discussion was videotaped and later coded for number of task contributions (giving suggestions or opinions), agreements, disagreements, questions, negative social behaviors (showing negative affect), and positive social behaviors (showing positive affect; see Table 7.3 for examples of codes). After the discussion, each member of the dyad indicated privately what his or her opinion was on the topic. The change in opinion from before to after the discussion was the measure of influence.

Neither task behavior nor positive social behavior was related to attitude change. Disagreement was related to *less* attitude change, or less influence. The only interaction style associated with greater influence was agreement. People who interacted with a partner who expressed at least some agreement were more likely to change their attitudes in the direction of the partner than people who interacted with a partner who expressed complete disagreement.

At first glance, this may seem counterintuitive—agreement leads to more influence and disagreement leads to less influence? We are more receptive to the ideas of someone who finds a way to agree with us; disagreement puts us on the defensive. Our intuition is to disagree with someone to try to change the person's mind. When people were randomly assigned to the condition in which they had to persuade their partners, they used more disagreement, less agreement, and more task behavior—but only with males, not with females. Unfortunately, this is exactly opposite of the kind of behavior that is persuasive. Thus, it is not surprising that women and men were more successful in persuading females than males; women and men were more likely to agree with females.

TABLE 7.3 SAMPLE INTERACTION STYLES

Task Behavior
  "You should ask your roommate not to drink in your room."

Agreement
  "I agree that alcoholism is an important problem in our society."

Disagreement
  "I disagree that lowering the drinking age will solve any of our problems."

Questions
  "Why do you think lowering the drinking age would decrease rates of alcoholism?"

Negative Social Behaviors
  "If you think it is OK to drink any alcohol and drive, then you are an idiot."

Positive Social Behavior
  "We all have to figure out how to deal with people who drink and drive."

Thus women are not more easily influenced than men due to some fundamental female trait, but due to the fact that people feel more comfortable in interactions with women and thus display more agreeable behavior. Women are more easily influenced than men because of the way people behave toward women and men. People use ineffective influence strategies with men (e.g., disagreement) but express agreement with women, and agreement leads to influence. Figure 7.6 illustrates the process by which women come to be more easily influenced than men.

Who Emerges as the Leader?

Male and female students view leadership roles in organizations as equally desirable, but women perceive that they are less likely to attain these positions compared to men (Killeen, Lopez-Zafra, & Eagly, 2006). A meta-analysis of group interaction studies evaluated who emerged as the leader in the group (Eagly & Karau, 1991). Leadership was measured by both objective indicators of group participation as well as respondents' reports of who appeared to be the group leader. Across laboratory and field studies and across both measures of leadership, men were more likely than women to emerge as leaders. Men contributed more to the group and were more likely to be perceived and chosen as leaders. The nature of the leadership role influenced

who emerged as a leader. Men were especially likely to emerge as leaders when task leadership was needed ($d = +.41$). When the nature of the task was not specified, men also were more likely to emerge as leaders, but the effect was smaller ($d = +.29$). When social leadership was necessary, there was a small effect for women to be more likely to emerge as leaders ($d = -.18$).

The meta-analytic review also showed that the length of the interaction influenced who emerged as a leader (Eagly & Karau, 1991). Males were more likely to emerge as leaders when the group interaction lasted less than 20 minutes ($d = +.58$), but there was no sex difference if the group lasted longer than one session ($d = +.09$). One reason that men are presumed to be leaders is that being male is associated with dominance, a trait also characteristic of a leader. In an older study, in which the personality trait of dominance was measured, males were chosen to be the leader over females, regardless of who was the dominant personality (Nyquist & Spence, 1986). However, when the study was replicated several years later and people were given an opportunity to interact with one another so that the personality trait of dominance could be revealed, the high-dominant person was chosen to be leader regardless of sex (Davis & Gilbert, 1989). Again, these studies show we are more likely to rely on

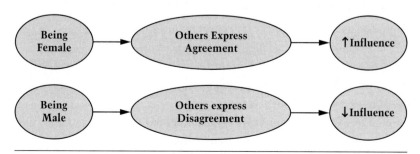

FIGURE 7.6   Model of influence process.

gender-role stereotypes or category-based expectancies in the absence of other information about people. But once we obtain more information, we are likely to use that information when deciding how to behave.

Leadership Styles

Do men and women have different styles of leadership? According to social role theory, women and men should behave similarly when occupying similar roles. However, because gender roles may still be operating on the part of the leader as well as on the part of perceivers, men's and women's behavior is likely to differ when they take on the leadership role (Eagly & Johannesen-Schmidt, 2001). For women, there is a conflict between the characteristics of the leadership role and the female gender role.

Leadership styles have been grouped into three broad categories: transformational, transactional, and laissez-faire. A transformational style involves inspiration, motivation, and being a role model. A transactional style of leadership is a more conventional style that involves monitoring subordinates, rewarding behavior, and intervening. Descriptors of the two are shown in Table 7.4 (Powell & Graves, 2006). A meta-analysis of these three leadership styles showed that women had a more transformational style than men ($d = -.10$; Eagly, Johannesen-Schmidt, & van Engen, 2003). Women also were more likely than men to display the contingent reward aspect of the transactional style ($d = -.13$), whereas men were more likely to display the two other components of the transactional style—active management by exception ($d = +.12$) and passive management by exception ($d = +.27$). Men also were more likely to use laissez-faire leadership than women ($d = +.16$). A second meta-analysis revealed similar results (van Engen & Willemsen, 2004). That meta-analysis showed that the sex difference in the transformational style is larger in more recent than in older studies. Interestingly, studies authored by males (compared to females) were more likely to show that women had a transactional style of leadership. The use of a transformational style of leadership should help women overcome some of the gender-related barriers to leadership because this style combines masculine and feminine behavior. Thus, it is no surprise that when gender-role characteristics are examined, the androgynous person is most likely to use a transformational style of leadership (Ayman & Korabik, 2010).

TABLE 7.4 CONTEMPORARY LEADERSHIP STYLES

Transformational
- **charismatic**—provide role model
- **inspiring**—display optimism and excitement about mission
- **intellectually stimulating**—encourage new perspectives
- **mentoring**—provide individualized attention

Transactional
- **contingent reward**—reward for achieving goals
- **management by exception**—intervening to correct problem
    - **active management by exception**—monitor performance
    - **passive management by exception**—wait for someone to report problem

Which style of leadership is most effective? A meta-analytic review showed that the transformational leadership style was most effective (Judge & Piccolo, 2004). In an experimental study in which college students evaluated a leader named "Pat" (sex purposely ambiguous), he or she was perceived more favorably when using a transformational style of leadership than a transactional style of leadership—regardless of whether Pat was believed to be male or female (Embry, Padgett, & Caldwell, 2008). A study of hospital employees in Australia showed that managers with a transformational style had employees who were more innovative—but the relation was stronger for male than female leaders (Reuvers et al., 2008). Reuvers and colleagues suggested that the gendered setting of the workplace (i.e., hospital where majority of nurses are female) might account for the finding.

Perception of Female and Male Leaders

It is not so much that women and men behave differently as leaders as it is that their behavior is perceived differently. Most difficulties women encounter as leaders occur in male-dominated settings, when women display stereotypical masculine behavior, and when they are evaluated by men (Ayman & Korabik, 2010).

There are two kinds of prejudice against female leaders (Eagly & Karau, 2002). First, due to descriptive stereotypes, people may evaluate a female leader less favorably than a male leader because she lacks the agentic qualities needed for leadership. Second, due to prescriptive stereotypes, people may evaluate a female leader less favorably than a male leader *if* she possesses agentic leadership qualities because those qualities conflict with the female gender role. Numerous studies have shown that female leaders are viewed more negatively than male leaders when they display agentic qualities—especially among males.

Men seem to be more influenced by a woman who behaves in a stereotypical rather than a nonstereotypical way—even though the stereotype for females is lacking credibility (Reid, Keerie, & Palomares, 2003). A study in which college students listened to a speech given by a female or a male who used either masculine (assertive) or feminine (tentative) language showed that female leaders who used masculine language were more influential than those who used feminine language among female students but *less* influential among male students (Carli, 1990). Male leaders had a similar influence on respondents regardless of the style of their speech. Although male respondents rated the female tentative speaker as less competent and less knowledgeable than the female assertive speaker, they were more influenced by her. Why were men influenced by a less competent speaker? Carli (1990) suggests the first thing a person of lower status must convey to a person of higher status is that she or he is not trying to compete for status. Using tentative language communicates this. Thus male respondents may have been more receptive to the female tentative speaker's arguments because they did not have to be concerned with status issues. The female assertive speaker might have been perceived as challenging the men's higher status. Thus women may have to adopt a more stereotypical style to influence men. Women face a dilemma when they are expected to behave in a submissive way but the situation requires assertive skills to succeed.

The problems that women face when trying to influence men are especially salient in the following study of group interactions. In this study, 40 teams of three to five students were assembled to work on a decision-making task (Thomas-Hunt & Phillips, 2004)—a task that was determined to be masculine in nature. Each group contained a female or a male expert; expertise was established by individual performance on the task prior to group discussion. Women and men were equally likely to be defined as experts in these groups, meaning there was no sex difference on individual performance. How did the groups respond when there was a female or a male expert in their midst? First, the female experts were judged as having less knowledge about the task than the male experts. Second, female experts had less influence on the group's overall performance. Finally, groups that contained a female expert had a poorer outcome compared to groups that contained a male expert. How can we explain these findings? When an expert disagrees with the group or offers an opinion that differs from that of the group, it is possible that the consequences are more negative for women than men. To the extent women are aware of this possibility, the female experts may have been less likely to assert themselves. Thus as shown in Figure 7.7, the minimal contribution of the female expert could have accounted for

the poor outcomes. Negative stereotypes of assertive females may lead female experts to be more tentative, to minimize their contributions, and to censor their remarks. The cumulative effect of these behaviors is that the group perceives the female expert to have less expertise than the male expert and the female expert ultimately has less influence on the group outcome. In the end, the group is not able to take advantage of the expertise of the female compared to the male expert.

One reason that women who display agentic qualities face difficulties as leaders is that they are presumed to lack communal qualities. Displays of agency seem to imply a lack of communion. When students viewed a masked person on a video, those who inferred the leader was female rated her as more dominant, more assertive, and less warm compared to those who inferred that the leader was male (Koch, 2004). A study of college students showed that a high-agency man was viewed as more qualified for a job that required social skills than a high-agency woman (Rudman & Glick, 2001), presumably because the high-agency woman is thought to lack social skills. Thus, it is not so much that masculine characteristics harm women as it is that masculine

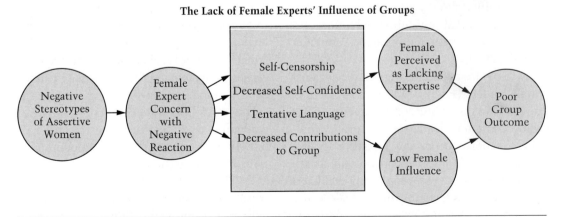

The Lack of Female Experts' Influence of Groups

FIGURE 7.7 Model of how groups are not able to take advantage of female expertise.
Source: Adapted from Thomas-Hunt and Phillips (2004).

characteristics imply a lack of communal characteristics among women—and a lack of communal characteristics is detrimental to women. When Hillary Clinton ran for the Democratic nominee for president of the United States, her strong, decisive, and overall agentic manner was judged harshly. Her ratings became more positive after a brief episode in which she shed a tear in response to an interviewer asking her how she was able to get out of the house everyday to hit the campaign trail. The expression of emotion reminded people of her communal qualities.

To be effective leaders, research suggests that women need to combine agentic qualities with communal qualities (Johnson et al., 2008). One study showed that providing information about a leader's communal traits offset the penalty applied to agentic women (Heilman & Okimoto, 2007). College students read vignettes about a manager

of a finance department (masculine occupation) that either contained communal information (i.e., caring and sensitive), positive noncommunal information (fair minded), or no additional information. The woman was perceived as less desirable as a boss, more hostile, and less likeable than the man in the control and noncommunal conditions, but these biases disappeared in the communal condition, as shown in Figure 7.8.

Another way that women can overcome the bias against female leaders is to establish a "shared identity" with others. This was demonstrated in a study of college students who listened to a recording of a female speaker who used assertive or tentative language and was referred to as either a typical female (sex salient) or a typical college student (student salient; Reid et al., 2009). When her sex was made salient, men were more influenced by the tentative than the assertive speaker,

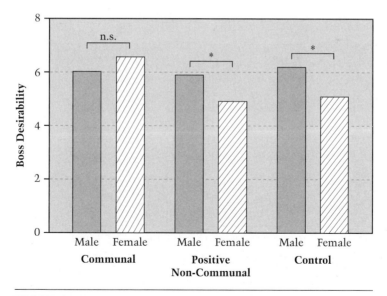

FIGURE 7.8 Women were viewed as less desirable than men as a boss in the control condition and the positive noncommunal information condition but there was no sex difference in desirability when communal information was provided.
Source: Adapted from Heilman and Okimoto (2007).

similar to the earlier study by Carli (1990). However, when her student status was made salient, men were more influenced by the assertive than the tentative speaker. Reid and colleagues (2009) argued that by making her student status salient, they were establishing a shared identity between the female leader and the male respondents. In this condition, men viewed the assertive woman to be more competent and more similar to them than the tentative woman. Female respondents were not influenced by the speech style or the salience condition, most likely because they shared both sex and student status identities. These findings suggest that one way in which strong women can influence men is to emphasize a shared status—that is, to find a way in which men can identify with them.

Outside the laboratory, it appears that women have made some progress in terms of leadership. When women and men are asked whether they would prefer to work for a female or male boss, the preference for a male boss has declined substantially—especially among men (see Figure 7.9; Carroll, 2006). In 2006, 34% of males said they would prefer a male boss, 10% a female boss, but the majority—56%—had no preference. Among females, 40% said they would prefer a male boss, 26% a female boss, and 34% had no preference.

If female leaders are harmed by an assumed lack of communal characteristics, how are lesbian and gay leaders viewed? There is very little research on views of LGBT (lesbians, gay, bisexual, and transgendered) leaders. Whereas sex and race are visible to others, sexual orientation is not. We do know that LGBT leaders who self-disclose are viewed more favorably than those who try to conceal their sexual orientation (Fassinger, Shullman, & Stevenson, 2010). The burden for gay men may be to prove their masculinity, whereas the burden for lesbians may be to prove their femininity. Because lesbians are stereotyped to be

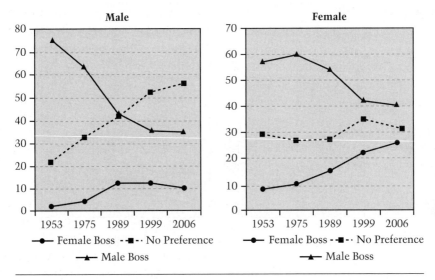

FIGURE 7.9 Preference for a male boss has substantially declined over time and having no preference has substantially increased over time—especially for men. Preference for a female boss has slightly increased, more so for women. *Source*: Adapted from Carroll (2006).

masculine, displays of agency in lesbian leaders may imply a lack of communal characteristics—even more so than among heterosexual women. It is not clear if this lack of communal characteristics will have the same negative repercussions among lesbians, though, because lesbian women may not be held to the same heterosexual expectation to possess communal characteristics.

TAKE HOME POINTS

- Women are more easily influenced than men because people adopt a more agreeable interaction style with women than men. And, agreement leads to influence.

- Men are more likely than women to emerge as leaders in laboratory studies where participants are often strangers and have only a brief opportunity to interact.

- Women are more likely to display a transformational style of leadership, whereas men are more likely to display a transactional style of leadership. The transformational style is most effective.

- Female leaders are judged more harshly than male leaders when they display agentic characteristics — in part because agentic characteristics imply a lack of communion in women (but not men). This finding holds for male rather than for female perceivers.

- Despite the fact that women are more likely than men to use a transformational leadership style, the style that has been shown to be most effective, people still prefer to have men than women as their bosses.

EMOTION

Two people receive news that an accident has caused a neighbor to lose her baby. One cries; the other does not. You probably imagine that the one who cries is female, the more emotional sex. Two people witness some teenagers soaping their car on Halloween. One yells at the teenagers and chases them down the street; the other ignores the incident. You probably imagine the one yelling is male, the more…the more what? Yes, anger, too, is an emotion. So, who is the more emotional sex?

Certainly the stereotype claims women are more emotional than men. In fact, one of the items on the PAQ (Personal Attributes Questionnaire) femininity scale is "very emotional." However, the femininity scale is really a measure of communion or expressiveness rather than emotionality. How should we decide whether women or men are more emotional or whether the sexes are equally emotional? Researchers have examined three primary sources of information to address this issue: people's self-reports of their experience of emotion, people's nonverbal expressions of emotion, and people's physiological responses to emotion stimuli. Unfortunately, there is not a consistent pattern of findings across these three modalities as to whether one sex is more emotional than the other. I review each source of information.

The Experience of Emotion

First, we can ask whether women and men experience emotions similarly. Many investigators argue that men and women have similar emotional experiences. Ekman (1992) points out that there is a universal set of emotions that both men and women experience and common facial expressions that generalize across the two sexes as well as across different cultures.

Do women and men experience emotions with the same frequency? We typically address this question by asking women and men to provide direct reports as to how often they experience a particular emotion. Studies that use this method typically reveal that women report greater emotion than men. Women say that they experience emotions more intensely than men and that they let emotions influence their decisions (van Middendorp et al., 2005). When shown emotionally arousing stimuli in the laboratory, women report more negative emotion than men (Gard & Kring, 2007; Moore, 2007). In a nationally representative sample, participants were asked how often they felt a variety of emotions (Simon & Nath, 2004). Although there was no sex difference in the frequency of emotions experienced, men were more likely than women to report positive emotions and women were more likely than men to report negative emotions. The latter sex difference disappeared when income was statistically controlled, implying that the reason women experience more negative emotions than men is due to their lower status.

One concern about research showing sex differences in the frequency or amount of emotion is that these reports are susceptible to a recall bias (Larson & Pleck, 1999). Much of the data that show women experience more emotion than men come from self-report studies where women and men recall their emotions over a period of time. Possibly women are simply better than men at recalling their emotions. To address this issue, Larson and Pleck (1999) had married couples carry electronic pagers and beeped them periodically throughout the day so they could report their current emotional state. These online reports revealed that men and women experience similar emotions. The frequencies of both positive and negative emotions are shown in Figure 7.10. Other studies have used this same methodology with college students and adults and confirmed the finding (Larson & Pleck, 1999).

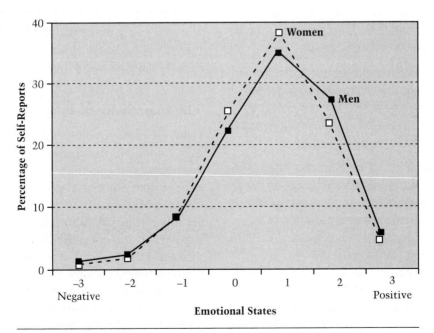

FIGURE 7.10   Men and women report similar frequencies of both positive and negative emotions throughout the day.
Source: Larson and Pleck (1999).

What accounts for the discrepancy in findings between retrospective reports and online measures of emotion? Some suggest that women report more emotion than men on retrospective measures because women encode emotion in greater detail than men. One study showed that women scored higher than men on a test of emotion complexity and differentiation, which suggests that women have more complicated representations of emotion (Feldman, Sussman, & Zigler, 2000).

If true, why would women encode emotion in greater detail than men? It may be that women pay more attention to emotional events than men because emotions occur within the context of relationships, and relationships are more central to women's than men's self-concepts. Richards and Gross (2000) suggested an alternative explanation: Men are more likely than women to suppress emotion, which interferes with the memory for emotional events. In support of their hypotheses, the authors found that people who were randomly assigned to suppress their emotion while watching a film (i.e., told not to let any feelings show that they experience during the film) had poorer memories for the film than those who were simply told to watch the film. As you will see in Chapter 9, among married couples, men are more likely than women to suppress emotion during discussions of relationship conflict.

Cross-cultural research also has examined whether there are sex differences in the experience of emotion. Across 37 countries, there was no sex difference in the experience of the powerful emotions (e.g., anger; Fischer et al., 2004). However, women around the world were more likely than men to report the powerless emotions—namely, fear, sadness, shame, and guilt. Women's status in the particular country did not affect women's reports of emotions but did affect men's reports

of emotions. In countries where women held a higher status, such as the United States, men reported less intense powerless emotions. The authors suggested that power is more strongly associated with the male role in Western than non-Western countries. However, it appears that the higher status of women in Western countries does not translate into men and women experiencing similar emotions.

The Expression of Emotion

Despite men's and women's similar experiences of emotion, considerable evidence supports sex differences in the expression of emotion (Brody & Hall, 2008). Women report they are more emotionally expressive than men. Self-report data are hardly convincing, however, because women and men are clearly aware of the stereotypes that women are emotional and expressive and men are not emotional and inexpressive.

Observational data support the claim that women are more expressive than men, but also are not without limitations. Coders are typically not blind to respondent sex and may rate the same face as more expressive if believed to be female than male. Try Do Gender 7.4 to see how knowledge of sex can influence perceptions of emotion. However, other observational and physiological data are more compelling. For example, both women and men can more easily identify the emotion of a female than of a male (LaFrance & Banaji, 1992), suggesting that women's faces are more emotionally expressive than men's faces. When men and women experience similar emotions, physiological measures reveal greater facial activity in the female face providing evidence of greater expressiveness (Thunberg & Dimberg, 2000).

Gender roles have been related to the expression of emotion and often show

DO GENDER 7.4
Perception of Emotion
in Boys and Girls

Videotape an infant or child playing. Make sure the sex of the child is not obvious. Tell 10 people the child is female and 10 people the child is male. Ask them to rate how emotional the child is, how expressive the child is, and what emotion the child is experiencing. Does the sex of the child influence these reports?

stronger relations than the respondent's sex. Femininity or communion, specifically, has been associated with emotional expression (Brody & Hall, 1993). Two studies have associated androgyny with emotional expression. In a study that compared androgynous, masculine, and feminine persons, androgynous persons were found to be more emotionally expressive than masculine persons, and feminine persons fell between the two groups (Kring & Gordon, 1998). The relation of androgyny to the expression of such a variety of emotions may have to do with the fact that androgyny incorporates both femininity and masculinity, which are each linked to the expression of different emotions: Androgyny includes femininity, which is associated with expressions of love, happiness, and sadness, along with masculinity, which is associated with expressions of anger and hate.

Physiological Measures of Emotion

Given the limitations of self-report methods of measuring emotion, we might hope that physiological methods would provide a more definitive answer to the issue of sex differences in emotions. Unlike the self-report

and observational research, physiological studies either show that men are more physiologically reactive to emotion or that there are no sex differences in physiological reactivity (Brody & Hall, 2008). Unfortunately, physiological indicators of emotionality are controversial. Researchers find it difficult to agree on which physiological measure best taps emotion: heart rate, blood pressure, or galvanic skin response? Even within a given physiological measure, findings are inconsistent across studies. When multiple measures of physiological reactivity are used, findings within a study are often inconsistent across measures. One technique that has been applied to the study of emotion is neuroimaging. A meta-analytic review of neuroimaging studies did not find more frequent activation in one sex compared to another in response to emotion but did show that different regions of the brain are activated in women and men (Wager et al., 2003). For example, one study showed that when negative emotions were induced in men and women via a noxious odor, the more cognitive-related areas were activated in men (e.g., prefrontal cortex) and the more emotion-related areas were activated in women (e.g., amygdala; Koch et al., 2007).

How do we reconcile the different conclusions reached by self-report and physiological data? One answer is that women are more outwardly expressive and men are more internally reactive to emotional stimuli. This idea was supported by a study in which college students viewed a film depicting one of three emotions (sadness, fear, happiness; Kring & Gordon, 1998). There were no sex differences in the self-report of an emotion. However, videotaped documentation showed that women were more emotionally expressive than men, and physiological measures evidenced that men were more reactive to some of the films. The investigators suggested men were more likely to be internalizers with respect to emotions, by experiencing them physiologically but not expressing them, and women were more likely to be externalizers with respect to emotions, by expressing them outwardly but not reacting physiologically.

Attributions for Emotion

Regardless of the data, the stereotype of women as the more emotional sex persists. This is supported by research on the attributions people make for women's and men's emotions. Women's emotions are more likely to be attributed to internal states, whereas men's emotions are more likely to be attributed to situational factors. Even when situational attributions are given for a person's emotional state, people tend to believe that women are "emotional" and men are "having a bad day" (Barrett & Bliss-Moreau, 2009). This is not surprising as being "emotional" is part of the female gender role. These different attributions have implications for how women and men are viewed when expressing an emotion. A laboratory study showed that both women and men view the expression of anger positively when it comes from a male job candidate but negatively when it comes from a female job candidate (Brescoll & Uhlmann, 2008). Respondents granted higher status and higher salary to an angry than a sad male job candidate, but lower status and lower salary to an angry than a sad female job candidate. The findings for salary are shown in Figure 7.11. Differential attributions explained these findings. Again, the female's anger displays were attributed to internal causes (being an emotional person), whereas the male's anger displays were attributed to situational causes (someone made him angry).

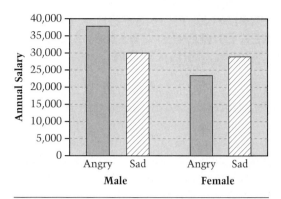

FIGURE 7.11   Male job candidates who were angry were granted higher status and more money than male candidates who were sad. Female job candidates who were angry received lower status and a lower salary compared to female candidates who were sad.
Source: Adapted from Brescoll and Uhlmann (2008).

TAKE HOME POINTS

- Retrospective measures of emotion show that women report more emotion than men, but online measures tend to show no sex differences in the experience of emotion.

- Women may encode emotional events in greater detail than men, which would account for the sex difference in retrospective emotion reports.

- Women are more likely than men to express the majority of emotions; the one exception is anger, which men express more than women.

- Physiological data suggest that either men are more reactive than women or there are no sex differences in physiological reactivity to emotion.

- Women's emotions are attributed to internal causes, whereas men's emotions are attributed to external causes.

EXPLANATIONS FOR SEX DIFFERENCES IN COMMUNICATION

A variety of explanations are available for the differences I have discussed in this chapter on male and female communication. Here I discuss two of them. The first theory, status theory, suggests that any differences in communication between men and women are due to their unequal status. Once one controls for the status or power differential between women and men, sex differences in communication disappear. Second is social role theory, which argues that the roles women and men hold in society are responsible for sex differences in communication. In particular, the female role emphasizes connections to others, whereas the male role emphasizes separation from others. These are not the only theories of sex differences in communication, as biological and evolutionary explanations also have been advanced for sex differences in nonverbal behavior (Andersen, 2006; Ellis, 2006), but they are the two that have received the most attention in the literature.

Status Theory

Sex is inherently confounded with status. Men have a higher status and more power than women. Status theory has been used to explain sex differences in interaction styles, language, and nonverbal behavior.

Interaction Styles.   One theory of how status influences behavior is **expectations states theory**. According to this theory, group members form expectations about their own and others' abilities, which are based on the value they assign to people in the group. We expect the high-status person to contribute more and the low-status person to facilitate the contributions of the

high-status person (Smith-Lovin & Robinson, 1992). Because men have a higher status than women, we have higher expectations of men's abilities compared to women's abilities. This theory suggests that sex differences in interaction styles stem from our more positive evaluation of men's abilities compared to women's. In other words, in the absence of any other information about men's and women's abilities, sex will be interpreted as status during a group interaction.

Status theory was tested in a field study of adults in the community (Moskowitz, Suh, & Desaulniers, 1994). Participants monitored their interactions with their bosses, coworkers, and subordinates over 20 days. For each interaction, respondents rated whether dominant versus submissive behavior and agreeable versus quarrelsome behavior occurred. The former category of behavior was referred to as *agency* and the latter as *communion*. The status of the work role (whether the person was a supervisor or subordinate or coworker) but not sex predicted agentic behaviors. People were more dominant when they were supervisors and more submissive when they were supervisees, regardless of sex. However, sex, but not the status of the work role, predicted communal behavior: Women behaved more communally than men regardless of the status of their interaction partners. Thus this study partly supported status theory and partly supported social role theory, discussed in the next section.

Expectations states theory says we have higher expectations for the contributions of the high-status person. However, the relevance of the task to women and men may alter people's expectations about capabilities. We expect men to be more competent than women on masculine tasks, and we expect women to be more competent than men on feminine tasks. Yet the sex difference in interaction styles does not necessarily disappear or reverse itself when feminine tasks are studied. Thus status based on expectations states theory alone cannot explain sex differences in interaction styles.

Language.   Parallels can be drawn between powerful language and male communication and powerless language and female communication (Kalbfleisch & Herold, 2006). If a male talks more and uses fewer hedges and qualifiers in an interaction with a female, we cannot discern whether the difference is due to sex or status. The more powerful person is more likely to interrupt, to give directives, to talk more in groups, and to show anger—language often attributed to men. The less powerful person inhibits, uses tentative and deferential language, uses other-directed language, displays sadness, and censors one's remarks—language often attributed to women. The meta-analytic review that showed men's talkativeness is due to longer durations of talking during a conversation suggests that dominance or status might be explanations (Leaper & Ayres, 2007). The fact that the sex difference in talkativeness and the sex difference in tentative language are magnified in other-sex compared to same-sex interactions

suggests that status plays a role in this aspect of language. One interesting way in which status is tied to language has to do with the way in which men and women are addressed. See Sidebar 7.4 for a discussion of this issue with respect to your professors.

Nonverbal Behavior.   Henley (1977) was one of the first to argue that differences in nonverbal behavior imply power or status. She argued that the greater social sensitivity of women was due to their low status. She suggested that women would have better decoding skills than men and engage in some nonverbal behaviors more frequently than men (e.g., smiling) because women are in a lower-status position in society. It is important for low-status people to monitor the environment because other people have influence over them.

Status theory has been tested as an explanation of women's greater interpersonal sensitivity compared to men. One study randomly assigned college students to a high-status (leader) or a low-status (leader's assistant) position in same-sex dyads and found that high-status people were more accurate in guessing their partner's feelings

SIDEBAR 7.4: *Is It Dr. X? Professor X? Or Janet?*

Several studies show that college students are more likely to address male professors by titles and female professors by first names. This is *not* due to the fact that female and male professors request different forms of address. What are the implications of calling your professor Dr. Smith or Janet, Dr. Jones or Jim? Several studies have shown that people associate a teacher who is referred to by a title as opposed to a first name with higher status (Stewart et al., 2003). In one of these, college students read a transcript of a class session in which the male or female instructor was addressed by first name or title by the students (Takiff, Sanchez, & Stewart, 2001). Students perceived the professor as having a higher status (i.e., higher salary, more likely to have tenure) when addressed by title rather than by first name. However, the title was associated with perceiving the female professor as less accessible to students and the male professor as more accessible to students. Thus female professors may have to choose between status and accessibility.

than low-status people (Mast, Jonas, & Hall, 2009). In a second study, the same authors included a control condition and found that high status increased interpersonal sensitivity rather than low status decreasing interpersonal sensitivity. Because women are of a lower status than men and women are typically better at decoding than men, the findings from this study cannot explain why women would be better at decoding.

Status clearly cannot account for the sex difference in smiling (Hall, Horgan, & Carter, 2002). In experimental studies where status is manipulated, there is no effect of status manipulations or people's perceptions of status on smiling. Interestingly, people have stereotypes that low-status people smile more than high-status people, but this stereotype has not been confirmed by the data. Hecht and LaFrance (1998) assigned undergraduates to interact in dyads in which members were either equal or unequal in power. The status of the person did not predict smiling. There was more total smiling in the equal power condition than in the unequal power condition. In terms of sex differences, females engaged in more smiling than males, but only in the equal power condition. Status was related to the *freedom to smile* rather than the tendency to smile, meaning that the high-status person could smile whenever he or she was in a good mood but the low-status person could not. The investigators suggested that people in positions of low power have constraints imposed on them in terms of how they behave; they are not as free as those in higher-power positions to express their feelings.

The relation of status to touch is not clear, partly because there are different kinds of touch. In an observational study of people at an academic conference, high-status people (measured by number of publications and job rank) were observed to engage in more affectionate touching, such as touching an arm or shoulder, whereas low-status people were more likely to engage in formal touching, such as a handshake (Hall, 1996). Hall concluded that high- and low-status persons may be equally likely to engage in touching, but that they initiate touch for different reasons: High-status people may touch to display their power, whereas low-status people may touch to gain power.

From these and other studies, there is growing evidence that status cannot account for sex differences in nonverbal behavior. A meta-analytic review of the literature examined whether status was related to perceptions of nonverbal behavior as well as to actual nonverbal behavior (Hall, Coats, & LeBeau, 2005). Status was described as the "vertical dimension of relationships" and included power, dominance, and hierarchy. Although people perceived a relation between the vertical dimension of relationships and less smiling, more gazing, more touch, more interruptions, less interpersonal distance, and more expressive faces, in actuality there was little relation between the vertical dimension of relationships and nonverbal behavior.

TAKE HOME POINTS

- Status theory suggests that sex differences in communication are due to the status differences between men and women.

- The best tests of this theory have been laboratory studies in which women and men are randomly assigned to high- and low-status positions.

- Status theory is most viable as an explanation for sex differences in interaction styles and some aspects of language.

- Status theory does not seem to be a good explanation for sex differences in nonverbal behavior.

Social Role Theory

Social role theory suggests that our expectations about female and male behavior stem from our stereotypes about the different social roles women and men hold in society. Women are more likely than men to hold domestic roles, for example. Even within the work setting, men and women are likely to hold different roles; for example, men are more likely to be the leaders and the supervisors, whereas women are more likely to be the subordinates. Gender role is an important social role that men and women hold, leading men to behave in agentic or instrumental ways and women to behave in communal or relationship-maintaining ways. To the extent that other roles become more salient than gender roles, people's behavior will be more influenced by other roles than gender roles.

Interaction Styles.   Parsons and Bales (1955) applied social role theory to sex differences in interaction style. They first observed that small group interactions were characterized by two forms of group behavior: task behavior and social behavior. They argued that both kinds of behavior were important to the viability of the group, but that the two were incompatible. In other words, different people were needed to serve the two distinct functions. This idea was confirmed by Bales and Slater (1955), who observed that the best liked person in the group was not the person considered to have the best ideas. The person with the best ideas gave suggestions and opinions: task-oriented behavior. The person who was best liked made statements indicating group solidarity, made statements that relieved group tension, and asked for opinions and suggestions: socioemotional behavior.

Parsons and Bales (1955) suggested that families were small groups, and that husbands and wives held different roles within the family. The father is responsible for task behavior, such as providing for the family, whereas the mother is responsible for socioemotional behavior, such as raising children. Parsons and Bales linked women's and men's traditional family roles to group interactions. They suggested that all groups had two functions: to accomplish the goals of the group and to preserve the group as a unit. They suggested that the first function fit with men's instrumental roles and the second fit with women's socioemotional roles.

Other people have argued more directly that men and women display different interaction styles because of the way they are socialized in our society (Wood & Rhodes, 1992). Females are socialized to be communal, whereas males are socialized to be agentic. A communal person is likely to engage in positive social behavior during group interactions, whereas an agentic person is likely to engage in instrumental social behavior during group interactions.

The study previously described by Carli (1989) supports a social role rather than a status interpretation of interaction styles. Carli found that men displayed the most task behavior and women displayed the most social behavior when men and women were compared in same-sex dyads rather than in mixed-sex dyads. If sex differences in interaction style were due to status, we would find larger differences in interaction styles in mixed-sex or unequal status dyads as opposed to same-sex dyads.

Language.   The differences in the language that men and women use may be considered to reflect different emphases on relationships. Women are said to talk in ways that maintain relationships; they encourage others to communicate by asking questions and making responses that encourage conversation. Men's language is less facilitative of relationships. Men interrupt others, challenge others, disagree, ignore others' comments by delayed use of the minimal response or giving no response, and make declarations of fact and opinion.

However, research has shown that it is not clear whether women's language is related to their lower status or to their gender role's greater emphasis on relationships. Some aspects of women's language are related to status and some are related to relationship maintenance. For example, hedges and disclaimers may reflect women's lower status compared to men, but intensifiers and verbal reinforcers may reflect women's socioemotional orientation. These ideas were examined in a study of same-sex and mixed-sex dyads' discussions of a topic on which the partners disagreed (Carli, 1990). Women used more disclaimers and hedges in mixed-sex than in same-sex dyads, which suggests that status played a role in the behavior. However, women used more intensifiers and verbal reinforcers compared to men in same-sex dyads, which is the kind of language that serves to maintain relationships.

Nonverbal Behavior. Many of the nonverbal behaviors in which women engage can be viewed as behaviors that promote and foster good relationships. Smiling at others, gazing at others, and standing close to others can all be viewed as affiliative behavior. A study of social interactions among groups of college students showed that smiling was unrelated to each person's status in the group but was related to the likability of group members (Cashdan, 1998).

Emotion. Dominance and affiliation have been shown to account for sex differences in displays of emotion. Specifically, males' greater displays of anger relative to females' have been linked to dominance, and females' greater displays of happiness relative to males' have been linked to affiliation (Hess, Adams, & Kleck, 2005). When dominance was manipulated in one of the studies, both high-dominant females and males reacted with anger to a vignette describing the destruction of someone's personal property. However, low-dominant men and women reacted differently—and in accord with gender-role stereotypes—women with sadness and men with anger.

TAKE HOME POINTS

- Social role theory states that the differences in men's and women's communication styles have to do with the different social roles men and women hold in our society, the male role being agentic and the female role being communal.

- Men's task behavior and women's positive social behavior fit their social roles.

- Some aspects of language fit men's goal of gaining control over the interaction (e.g., directives), and some aspects fit women's goal of encouraging communication (e.g., emotion language).

- Social role theory is most helpful in explaining sex differences in nonverbal behavior. Women's smiling, touching (in some contexts), decoding ability, and expressions of emotions are all aimed at fostering relationships.

- Sex differences in emotion can be explained in part by social roles and in part by status.

SUMMARY

Boys and girls clearly have different styles of interacting with one another. Boys play in groups that are loud, boisterous, and hierarchical, whereas girls play in dyads that are quiet, conversational, and egalitarian. A strong preference to play with same-sex peers likely exacerbates the difference in play styles. The source of the different styles is not clear. The distinct play styles map onto the differences in adult interaction styles. In general, studies of small groups show that women are more socioemotional and men are more task oriented. However, these findings are qualified by a number of variables: the nature of the task, the sex of the interaction partner, and the length of the interaction. Sex differences are strongest for gender-typed tasks, for interactions with same-sex people, and when interactions are brief.

Women and men differ in their use of some features of language. Men's language is more instrumental, succinct, and directive, whereas women's language is more affective, elaborative, and indirect. Women's language has been described as promoting relationships but also as being unassertive. Women's style of speaking appears to have negative implications when used by women but not men. In particular, men like—but view as less competent—a woman who uses feminine rather than masculine language.

There are a number of sex differences in nonverbal behavior: Women smile more, gaze more, are better at conveying emotion, and are better at decoding others' emotions compared to men. Sex differences in touch are more complicated. Among children, touch is more frequent among same-sex peers than cross-sex peers. Among adults, touch is more frequent among cross-sex dyads than same-sex dyads. Within adult cross-sex dyads, touch is determined by relationship status: Men initiate touch during the early stages of a relationship, and women initiate touch during the later stages. In general, sex differences in nonverbal behavior are more frequently observed among same-sex dyads than cross-sex dyads.

Research on social influence generally shows that men are more influential and more likely to emerge as leaders than women. Women are more easily influenced, largely because people are nicer and more agreeable to women. Agreement leads to influence, but disagreement does not. Despite the fact that men are more likely than women to be leaders, women leaders are more likely than men leaders to use the transformational style of leadership, which has been determined to be the most effective style.

Women who adopt agentic styles of leadership are viewed negatively—especially by men. This bias stems in part from the inference that agentic women lack communal characteristics. Women are more influential and viewed more positively as leaders when they are perceived to have both agentic and communal qualities.

In general, men and women seem to experience emotion similarly, although women are more emotionally expressive than men. Sex differences in emotional expression depend on the specific emotion: Women are more likely to express sadness, love, and fear, whereas men are more likely to express anger and pride. In terms of physiological reactivity, either men are more reactive than women or there is no sex difference in physiological reactivity to emotion. People attribute women's emotional states to internal causes and men's emotional states to external factors.

There are two primary explanations for sex differences in communication: status and social role. According to status theory, men's communication is a function of their higher status, and women's communication is a function of their lower status. A number of compelling studies show that men and women behave the same when status is held constant. Evidence for status theory is especially strong in studies of group interactions. According to social role theory, men's communication is a function of their instrumental orientation, and women's communication is a function of their expressive orientation. Support for this theory comes largely from studies showing that nonverbal differences between men and women persist across situations, including different statuses.

DISCUSSION QUESTIONS

1. Compare laboratory and field research on sex differences in communication. In which areas of communication do you expect laboratory research and field research to come to different conclusions?
2. Discuss girls' and boys' different play styles and explanations of their origins.
3. From what you have learned in this chapter, in what ways do you expect girls' and boys' online behavior to be similar? To be different?
4. What are some of the factors that affect men's and women's interaction styles?
5. What are some of the moderator variables of sex comparisons in language?
6. Which sex differences in language and nonverbal behavior are best explained by status theory, and which are best explained by social role theory?
7. Imagine you are studying patient–physician communication. What other variables would be important to know besides the sex of the participants?
8. Why are women more easily influenced than men? Is this an advantage or a disadvantage for women?
9. What is the best leadership style for women to adopt? Under what circumstances?
10. How would you determine whether men or women are more emotional?
11. What are the implications of the different attributions people make for women's and men's emotions?

SUGGESTED READING

Brody, L. R., & Hall, J. A. (2008). Gender and emotion in context. In M. Lewis, J. M. Haviland, & L. Barrett (Eds.), *Handbook of emotions*. New York: Guildford Press.

Dindia, K., & Canary, D. J. (2006) (Eds.). *Sex differences and similarities in communication: Critical essays and empirical investigations of sex and gender in interaction* (2nd ed.). Mahwah, NJ: Erlbaum.

Eagly, A. H., & Carli, L. L. (2007). *Through the labyrinth: The truth about how women become leaders.* Boston, MA: Harvard University School Press.

Maccoby, E. E. (1998). *The two sexes: Growing up apart, coming together.* Cambridge, MA: Harvard University Press.

Underwood, M. K. (2003). *Social aggression among girls.* New York: Guilford Press.

Key Terms

Egoistic dominance—Interaction style characterized by verbal aggression that intends to demonstrate superiority over other participants in the interaction.

Expectations states theory—States that group members form expectations about their own and others' abilities, which influence the nature of interactions.

Minimal response—Response that encourages the speaker to continue, such as "uh-huh" or "okay."

Negative social behavior—Behavior during group interaction that could harm a relationship, such as disagreement and provoking conflict.

Positive social behavior—Social behaviors engaged in during group interactions that are intended to maintain group harmony.

Prosocial dominance—Interaction style characterized by providing instruction or assistance that intends to foster connection between those involved in the interaction.

Relational aggression—Aggressive interaction behavior usually expressed by girls that is characterized by social alienation tactics such as excluding someone from an activity or threatening not to be a person's friend anymore.

Task behavior—Social behavior, such as asking questions and offering suggestions, that is directed toward achieving a specific goal.

CHAPTER 8

Friendship

Batman and Robin, Sherlock Holmes and Watson, Tom Sawyer and Huckleberry Finn, Butch Cassidy and the Sundance Kid, the Lone Ranger and Tonto. Who symbolizes friendship to you? What are some famous pairs of friends? What do all these pairs of friends have in common? They are men (see Figure 8.1). When I asked some students if they could think of a famous pair of female friends, the best anyone could come up with was Laverne and Shirley—or maybe Thelma and Louise. Does the bond between two men epitomize friendship? As you will see in this chapter, it depends on what constitutes friendship.

Much of this chapter focuses on friendships between women and friendships between men, or same-sex friends. Although romantic partners can certainly be friends (in fact, I hope they are!), studies on friendship typically focus on platonic, nonromantic relationships. Platonic friendship does exist between men and women; these relationships are referred to as cross-sex friendship. One arena in which cross-sex friendships are likely to form is in the workplace. Because women are increasingly working outside the home and because women are more likely to work in jobs once held exclusively by men, women and men are more likely to come into contact with one another at work. In this chapter, I examine a variety of friendships—same-sex friendship, cross-sex friendship, cross-race friendship, gay and lesbian friendship, and friendship at work.

There are at least two levels of analyses to the study of gender and friendship (Wright, 2006). First, there is the **dispositional level of analysis**, which emphasizes the characteristics of the person as a determinant of friendship. What characteristics of a person predict friendship? One attribute of a person is his or her sex; another is his or her gender role. An example of a dispositional analysis is the research showing that women's relationships are more intimate than those of men because women are more likely than men to self-disclose. The analysis focuses on a characteristic of women as a determinant of friendship

FIGURE 8.1   Batman and Robin are a famous pair of same-sex friends.

closeness: their tendency to self-disclose. There is also a **structural level of analysis** that emphasizes the different positions of women and men in society. One position or role in society that men traditionally have held more than women is the paid employee role. An example of a structural level of analysis is the research showing that men have more cross-sex friendships than women because men are more likely than women to work outside the home. The structural level of analysis also calls attention to the impact of situational variables on gender and friendship.

In reviewing research on friendship, I begin with an examination of the quantity of friendships and then describe in more detail the quality of friendship. *Quantity* refers to the number of friends or the size of the network. *Quality* refers to the nature of the friendship. Is it close? Is it intimate? What functions does the friendship serve? I discuss specific aspects of friendship such as intimacy, self-disclosure, and conflict. After reviewing the different kinds of friendship, I conclude by using the structural level of analysis to describe how friendship changes across the life span.

NETWORK SIZE

Most studies show that boys and girls have a similar number of friends (Baines & Blatchford, 2009). However, boys may have larger social networks compared to girls due to the structural differences in boys' play versus girls' play described in the previous chapter. Girls are more likely to interact in dyads and to spend time talking to one another, whereas boys are more likely to spend time in large groups that are focused on some activity. In an observational study of play among 7- and 8-year-olds, boys' social networks (defined as children who were seen frequently playing together) were nearly twice the size of that of girls', largely because boys were more likely than girls to be playing team games (Baines & Blatchford, 2009). In addition, girls' primary social network consisted of friends, whereas boys' primary social network consisted of both friends and non-friends. This difference may contribute to the greater intimacy that characterizes girls' friendships discussed later in this chapter.

Among adults, some studies show that women have more friends, some studies show that men have more friends, and other studies show no sex difference in number of friends (Wright, 1999). One reason that it is difficult to determine if there are sex differences in the size of friendship networks is that the *concept* of friend may differ for women and men. Now, we discuss the nature of women's and men's friendship.

TAKE HOME POINTS

- It is unlikely that network size differs vastly between girls and boys or between women and men.

- It may appear at times that boys have more friends than girls, because boys play in larger groups than girls.

THE NATURE OF FRIENDSHIP

Friendship is an area of research where the differences between females and males are overemphasized compared to the similarities. There are numerous ways in which men's and women's friendships are quite similar. Yet it is true that women's friendships are closer than those of men, and friendships with women are closer than friendships with men. There are some differences in the nature of men's and women's friendship that may explain these sex differences. First, I review the differences and then I turn to the similarities.

Sex Differences

During childhood, the nature of female and male friendship becomes increasingly distinct. By adolescence, girls spend time talking with their friends, and boys spend time sharing activities with their friends (McNelles & Connolly, 1999). Boys view friendship as instrumental: A friend is someone with whom you do things. Girls view friendship as more emotional: A friend is someone with whom you connect.

The female emphasis on self-disclosure and the male emphasis on shared activities persist in adulthood. Studies of college students show that females find more intimacy in their friendships compared to males, whereas males find more companionship in their friendships compared to females (Singleton & Vacca, 2007). In a study of college students from the United States and Russia (Sheets & Lugar, 2005), females shared more personal information with friends compared to males, and males shared more activities with friends compared to females, as shown in Figure 8.2.

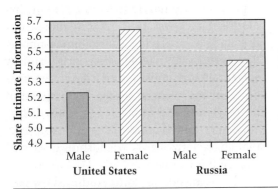
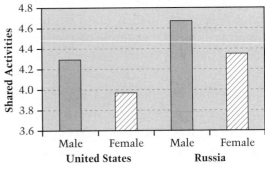

FIGURE 8.2 Sex differences in sharing intimate information and shared activities appeared for both U.S. and Russian college students. Females shared more personal information than males, and males shared more activities with friends than females.
Source: Adapted from Sheets and Lugar (2005).

In addition, college students from the United States shared more intimate information with their friends compared to Russian students, and Russian students shared more activities with friends than U.S. students.

The research is clear in indicating that women's friendships are more communal than those of men, largely due to the emphasis on self-disclosure. However, the sex difference in agency or instrumentality has been more heavily debated (Wright, 2006). The issue may not be whether one sex engages in more shared activities than the other sex but whether the nature of the shared activities varies for females and males. Some shared activities may be considered more intimate than others. For example, going to a movie may be considered to be a less-intimate activity than going out to dinner because there is more opportunity for self-disclosure in the latter than the former activity. It also is the case that people can perform the same activity differently. For example, I play racquetball once a week with a very good friend. This may not sound like an intimate shared activity. However, we play racquetball for 45 of the 60 minutes and talk about family, friends, and politics in between games while we are catching our breath—not to mention the time we spend walking over to and from the court. There are a lot of activities—golf, biking, hiking—that may or may not include more intimate exchanges.

The expressive/instrumental distinction in the nature of female and male friendship also has been linked to potential differences in the ways females and males provide support. A popular book by Deborah Tannen (1990), titled *You Just Don't Understand: Women and Men in Conversation,* argues that women are more likely to respond to others' problems by offering sympathy and men are more likely to respond to others' problems by offering advice. Is there evidence behind Tannen's (1990)

thinking? Modest. A study that asked men and women how they would respond to a series of hypothetical problems found that men were more likely than women to change the subject, and women were more likely than men to express sympathy (Basow & Rubenfeld, 2003). However, the similarities in how women and men responded vastly outweighed these differences (MacGeorge et al., 2004). As shown in Figure 8.3, there were no sex differences in offering advice, sharing similar experiences, or trying to cheer up one another. Even more important, the relative ranking of responses is the same for women and men. Both women and men are much more likely to offer sympathy than joke around or change the subject. In another study, adult women and men were asked what they would say in response to a series of hypothetical same-sex friend problems, and responses were coded into different categories (MacGeorge et al., 2004). Similar proportions of women's and men's responses were coded as sympathy, sharing a similar problem, asking questions, or minimization, but proportionally more of men's responses could be classified as advice compared to women. Again, the similarities in support provision greatly outweighed the differences.

These self-report studies suffer from demand characteristics. Women and men may be confirming gender-role stereotypes. Observational studies in which women and men respond to problems in the laboratory may partly address this problem. These studies have shown some sex differences and some sex similarities—specifically, no sex differences in the provision of advice, modest support for the idea that women provide more emotional support than men, and clear evidence that the sex of the target influences negative responses (Fritz, Nagurney, & Helgeson, 2003; Leaper et al., 1995; Mickelson, Helgeson, & Weiner, 1995; Pasch, Bradbury, & Davila, 1997).

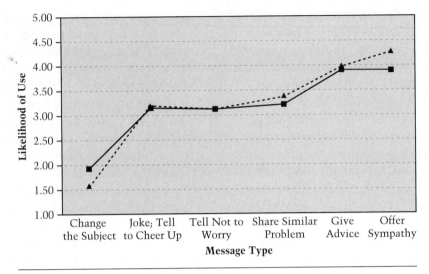

FIGURE 8.3   Men's and women's responses to a friend's problems in the Basow & Rubenfeld (2003) study.

Both men and women are more likely to respond negatively to men compared to women sharing a problem. Hmmm ... and we wonder why it is that men are less likely to self-disclose?

Much of the research on the nature of friendship in the United States has focused on White middle-class children, college students, and adults. Sex differences seem to be larger among White men's and women's friendships compared to those of other races (Way, Becker, & Greene, 2006).

Sex Similarities

Despite these differences, there are important similarities between women's and men's friendships. One way in which women's and men's friendships are similar is in terms of what women and men want from a friend. Both men and women want a friend who is trustworthy, a source of support, and a source of fun and relaxation (Fehr, 2000). Men and women are equally likely to perceive themselves as similar to their friends (Linden-Andersen,

Markiewicz, & Doyle, 2009). Despite the fact that women engage in more self-disclosure with friends compared to men (a sex difference that will be discussed in more depth in a few pages), both women and men spend a substantial amount of time in casual conversation with their friends (Wright, 2006).

Women and men may differ in how important they perceive a feature of a friendship to be, but they often agree on which attributes of a relationship are more or less important. One study asked men and women to rate the importance of affective skills (comforting one another, making a person feel good about himself or herself) and instrumental skills (entertaining one another, casual conversations, conveying information) for a high quality same-sex friendship (Burleson et al., 1996). Women rated the affective aspects as more important than men did, and men rated the instrumental aspects as more important than women did. Aha, differences again! But both men and women agreed that the affective aspects of friendship were more important than the instrumental aspects of friendship. Other research shows that the same features of friendship are associated with satisfaction for women and men. For example, perceived similarity is equally related to friendship satisfaction for females and males (Linden-Andersen et al., 2009). Although men's same-sex friendships are less intimate and less supportive than women's, intimacy and support are equally associated with friendship satisfaction for women and men (Bank & Hansford, 2000).

Egalitarianism is another important feature of friendship for both men and women. Friendship by definition implies equal status. It stands to reason that people would find friendships more satisfying when they are of equal rather than unequal status. Female and male college students perceive an egalitarian friendship more favorably than a friendship in which the power distribution is unequal (Veniegas & Peplau, 1997).

TAKE HOME POINTS

- The primary difference in the nature of men's and women's friendships is that an activity is the focus of men's interactions and conversation is the focus of women's interactions. This difference first appears during childhood and then persists through adolescence and adulthood.

- It is clear that female friendships are more communal than those of males, but the sex difference in the instrumentality of friendship is less clear. Regardless of whether there is a sex difference in shared activities, men and women may spend time sharing activities in different ways so that shared activities are more intimate for women than for men.

- Although some of these findings generalize to different cultures, there are ethnic differences in friendship within the United States. The female emphasis on self-disclosure and the male lack of self-disclosure are more characteristic of White people's friendships than the friendships of other ethnic groups.

- Both men and women want the same things from friendship and view self-disclosure, empathy, trust, and expressions of support as the most important features of a friendship.

- Both women and men engage in casual conversation with friends, view egalitarianism and similarity as central to friendship, and believe fun and relaxation are important aspects of friendship.

CLOSENESS OF FRIENDSHIP

At one time, men's friendships were regarded as stronger than women's friendships. In 1969, Lionel Tiger maintained that men were biologically predisposed to develop superior friendships compared to women. Tiger suggested the male-male bond was as important to the survival of the species as the male-female bond was for reproduction. Men depended on other men for defense of their territory, for gathering food, and for maintaining social order in the community. These ideas may be why friendships that have been depicted in the media (identified at the beginning of this chapter) involve men.

The more recent consensus has been that female friendships are closer than those of males. Starting in middle school, girls begin to report that their friendships are closer and more satisfying than boys do (Bauminger et al., 2008; Linden-Andersen et al., 2009; Swenson & Rose, 2009). Girls report greater validation, support, security, caring, and self-disclosure in same-sex friendships compared to boys. In a study of adolescents in the Netherlands, Turkey, and Morocco, girls placed more trust in their friends compared to boys (Wissink, Dekovic, & Meijer, 2009). Adolescent and adult females rate their same-sex friendships as closer and more cohesive than those of males (Johnson, 2004). Women report greater nurturance, affection, intimacy, and support from friends than men (Barry et al., 2009). Women even receive more supportive comments from friends on their personal Web pages compared to men (Mikami et al., 2010).

Most of these studies arrive at these conclusions via self-report surveys. One way that researchers have been able to get a better sense of the closeness of women's and men's friendships is with a method called the Rochester Interaction Record (RIR). Researchers from the University of Rochester developed the RIR to describe the nature of social interactions on a day-to-day or moment-to-moment basis (Wheeler, Reis, & Nezlek, 1983). Participants complete an RIR for every 10-minute interaction they have over the course of a day. This may seem quite cumbersome, but many of our daily interactions are much briefer, lasting only a minute or two. People typically report about seven or eight 10-minute interactions during an average day. The RIR, shown in Figure 8.4, contains questions about who was

involved in the interaction as well as rating scales of the quality of the interaction. Although the RIR was initially administered via paper, today similar types of instruments have been developed for electronic devices.

In a now classic study, college students completed the RIR for every 10-minute interaction they had every day for 2 consecutive weeks (Wheeler et al., 1983). As shown in Figure 8.5a, researchers found a consistent sex difference in the meaningfulness of interactions, measured as the average of each interaction's intimacy, self-disclosure, other disclosure, pleasantness, and satisfaction (i.e., the first five ratings scales shown in Figure 8.4). Men's same-sex interactions were significantly less meaningful than women's, even when interactions with a best friend were examined. All interactions involving at least one female (female-female, male-female) were equally meaningful and were more meaningful than those involving only males. This study showed

LONELINESS

Date _____	Time _____ AM ____ Length ____ Hrs ____ Mins ____	
	PM ____	
Initials _____	If More Than 3 Others:	
Sex _____	# Of Females _____ # Of Males _____	
Intimacy:	Superficial 1 2 3 4 5 6 7	Meaningful
I Disclosed:	Very Little 1 2 3 4 5 6 7	A Great Deal
Other Disclosed:	Very Little 1 2 3 4 5 6 7	A Great Deal
Quality:	Unpleasant 1 2 3 4 5 6 7	Pleasant
Satisfaction:	Less Than Expected 1 2 3 4 5 6 7	More Than Expected
Initiation:	I Initiated 1 2 3 4 5 6 7	Other Initiated
Influence:	I Influenced More 1 2 3 4 5 6 7	Other Influenced More
Nature: Work	Task Pastime	Conversation Date

FIGURE 8.4 Rochester Interaction Record.

Source: L. Wheeler, H. Reis, and J. Nezlek (1983). Loneliness, social interaction, and sex roles. Journal of Personality and Social Psychology, 45, 943–953.

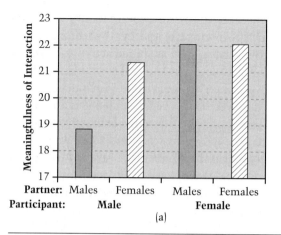 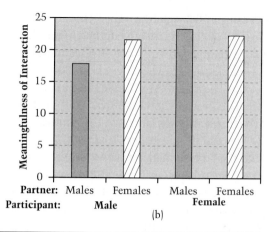

FIGURE 8.5 Meaningfulness of interactions with men and women. A daily diary study showed that men's interactions with men were rated as less meaningful than men's interactions with women or women's interactions with men or women. The results of the study by Wheeler et al. (1983) are depicted in Figure 8.5a. The results were replicated by Reis et al. (1985) and are shown in Figure 8.5b. *Source*: Adapted from Wheeler et al. (1983) and Reis et al. (1985).

that friendship closeness is due not only to a dispositional variable, sex of the person, but also to a structural difference, the sex of the friend with whom one is interacting. Men do not always display less intimacy than women in their interactions with friends. In fact, when men's interactions involve a woman, they can be just as intimate as women's interactions.

The finding that men's interactions with other men are the least meaningful was replicated by a study that explored several explanations for it (see Figure 8.5b; Reis, Senchak, & Solomon, 1985). First, the investigators examined whether men were simply more selective than women about the people with whom they are intimate. Here, RIR interactions with the best friend were examined. Women rated their interactions with their best friend as more meaningful compared to men. Students also provided a written account of their most recent meaningful conversation with their same-sex best friend. Judges reviewed the narratives and determined that women's

accounts were more intimate than those of men. Because these findings held for a best friend, it did not appear that men were being more selective than women.

Second, Reis and colleagues (1985) asked whether men's friendships lacked intimacy because men were not *capable* of intimacy or because men *preferred* not to behave in intimate ways. Students and their best same-sex friends were asked to engage spontaneously in a conversation about something that was important to them. A female graduate student rated videotapes of these interactions and found that men's interactions were as intimate as those of women, as demonstrated by similar levels of self-disclosure. However, a panel of undergraduates found that males discussed less intimate topics than females did. The authors concluded that women and men are equally capable of intimacy, but men *prefer* not to behave as intimately as women.

Cross-cultural research suggests that some of the sex differences in intimacy are a

Western phenomenon. The intimacy of college students' friendships in the United States were compared to those in Germany, the Netherlands, Hong Kong, and Jordan (Reis, 1998). The size of the sex difference in intimacy (female greater than male) varied by culture. The difference was largest in the United States ($d = -.95$), followed by Germany ($d = -.70$) and then the Netherlands ($d = -.39$) and Hong Kong ($d = -.34$). In Jordan, there was no sex difference in intimacy ($d = +.12$). In the three Western cultures, men were more intimate with women than with men. In Jordan and Hong Kong, men were equally intimate with men and women. Thus the link of intimacy to women appears to be a facet of Western culture.

One problem with the conclusion that women's relationships are closer than those of men in the United States has to do with the way that closeness or intimacy is measured. Intimacy is often measured by self-disclosure, and women self-disclose more than men. Some researchers have suggested that self-disclosure is a "feminine" definition of intimacy and that women and men may define intimacy differently. Women may be more likely to express intimacy through self-disclosure, and men may be more likely to express intimacy through participation in shared activities. If this is the case, there would be less evidence for women's friendships being more intimate than those of men.

Do women and men define intimacy differently? One way to address this question is to examine women's and men's conceptions of intimacy or closeness. Radmacher and Azmitia (2006) asked seventh and eighth graders as well as a group of college students to describe a time in which they felt close to someone. A content analysis of these descriptions revealed more similarities than differences between women's and men's conceptions of closeness. Males and females were equally likely to

mention expressive avenues to intimacy, such as self-disclosure, and instrumental avenues to intimacy, such as shared activities—among both adolescents and college students. However, when expressive and instrumental pathways were compared, both females and males were more likely to name expressive than instrumental pathways—and there was an increased emphasis on expressive pathways and a decreased emphasis on shared activities with age. Thus, the authors concluded that intimacy is best conceptualized in terms of expressive pathways, such as self-disclosure, and that the pathway to intimacy for females and males converges between adolescence and adulthood. These findings are consistent with a study of college students and community residents that showed both men and women identified intimate interactions as containing more self-disclosure and emotional support than shared activities and practical support (Fehr, 2004).

In a second study, college students were surveyed about the expressive and instrumental features of their relationships and asked to rate the relationship's closeness (Radmacher & Azmitia, 2006). Self-disclosure predicted relationship closeness for both women and men, but shared activities also predicted relationship closeness for men. These findings replicate those of an earlier study of eighth graders that showed self-disclosure and shared activities predicted closeness to friends for boys, but only self-disclosure predicted closeness to friends for girls (Camarena, Sarigiani, & Petersen, 1990). Even among boys, the relation of self-disclosure to emotional closeness was much stronger than the relation of shared experiences to emotional closeness.

To conclude, men and women have different experiences of intimacy (women's being more affective and men's being more instrumental), but the two sexes seem to agree on the definition of intimacy. As shown in Figure 8.6,

Conceptions of Intimacy

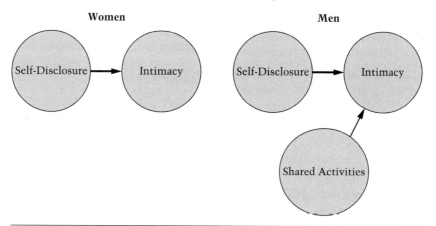

FIGURE 8.6   Self-disclosure is the most important determinant of intimacy for women and men. However, self-disclosure is relatively more important to women than men, and men's definitions of intimacy include shared activities.

self-disclosure is an important, if not the most important, feature of intimacy for both men and women. However, men are more likely than women to incorporate shared experiences into their conceptualizations of intimacy. Studies of intimacy have neglected the fact that we can be engaged in self-disclosure and shared activities simultaneously. Two men may be discussing problems with their girlfriends while fixing a car: How are these episodes classified—as self-disclosure or as shared activities? According to Reis and Shaver (1988), intimacy involves revealing one's innermost self, which can be accomplished via self-disclosure or shared activities. Intimacy is not a static state but a process. This means that self-disclosure alone is not sufficient to establish intimacy. The partner's response to the self-disclosure is just as important as the self-disclosure itself to the intimacy of an interaction. Reis and Shaver suggest that intimate interactions are ones that lead to feeling understood, validated, and cared for. Both self-disclosure and shared activities could accomplish this.

TAKE HOME POINTS

- Females have closer same-sex friendships than males.

- The lack of closeness in male same-sex friendships is not due to men being incapable of intimacy; instead, men prefer not to behave intimately with their same-sex friends.

- The similarities in women's and men's definitions of intimacy greatly outweigh the differences.

SELF-DISCLOSURE

The primary reason that women's friendships are viewed as closer than men's friendships is because women self-disclose more than men. Let's take a more in-depth look at the literature on self-disclosure. Do women self-disclose more than men about everything? To whom do people self-disclose—women or men? Are there any situational factors that influence self-disclosure?

Sex of Discloser

Dindia and Allen (1992) conducted a meta-analysis on sex differences in self-disclosure. They found a small effect ($d = -.18$) indicating that women self-disclose more than men. The size of the sex difference was similar across self-report ($d = -.17$) and observational ($d = -.22$) studies. Subsequent research showed that the sex difference in self-disclosure appears to be larger in the context of close relationships than among acquaintances or strangers (Consedine, Sabag-Cohen, & Krivoshekova, 2007; Derlega, Winstead, & Greene, 2008). Sex differences in self-disclosure may be more apparent when the nature of the topic is examined. Several studies show that women are especially more likely than men to self-disclose about personal issues, such as relationship problems or areas of personal weakness.

Females also engage in a form of self-disclosure with friends that is referred to as **co-rumination** (Rose, 2002): repeatedly discussing problems, including the causes, the consequences, and negative feelings, with a friend. Co-rumination is related to higher friendship quality but also to greater anxiety and depression. Does co-rumination lead to closer relationships, or does co-rumination lead to depression? Or, are people who are depressed more likely to engage in co-rumination? A longitudinal study of third through ninth graders disentangled the direction of these relations (Rose, Carlson, & Waller, 2007). The relation was reciprocal for females: that is, co-rumination was associated with increases in friendship quality as well as increases in anxiety/depression over time, and friendship quality and anxiety/depression predicted increases in co-rumination over time. However, for males, friendship quality and depression/anxiety predicted increases in co-rumination, but co-rumination only predicted

increases in friendship quality. Thus, co-rumination may have more psychological costs for females than males. It appears to be a pathway to closer relationships for males.

Sex of Recipient

When we say that females self-disclose more than males, we are typically considering same-sex friendships. Who is more likely to be on the receiving end of self-disclosure? Dindia and Allen's (1992) meta-analytic review showed two target effects. One indicated that people are more likely to self-disclose to women than to men. The other effect showed that people are more likely to self-disclose to the same sex than to the other sex. Thus, predictions for women are clear. Women are more likely to disclose to a woman than a man because a female target meets both of the above conditions. For men, the prediction is less clear. Do men disclose to women or to the same sex? There may be some topics that men discuss with men and others that men discuss with women. Explore this issue with Do Gender 8.1.

DO GENDER 8.1
What Do Men and Women Tell Each Other?

Come up with a list of topics. Ask a group of men and women to report how frequently they discuss each topic with their same-sex friends and cross-sex friends. You could have them pick their best same-sex friend and best cross-sex friend. Divide the topics into two groups: more intimate and less intimate. Is there a sex of participant difference in self-disclosure? Is there a sex of target difference? Does it depend on the topic?

Situational Variables

Situational variables also affect self-disclosure. Studies have shown that men's levels of self-disclosure can be increased if they are motivated to self-disclose. In one study, researchers manipulated whether participants believed there was the possibility of a future interaction with the other person in the experiment (Shaffer, Pegalis, & Bazzini, 1996). The investigators predicted that men would be especially likely to self-disclose to women if they believed there was the possibility of a future interaction. They also expected this effect would be strongest for traditionally masculine men.

Shaffer and colleagues (1996) had undergraduates work on a first task with a partner and then led them to believe they would be working on a second task with or without their partner. This was the manipulation of future interaction. The initial task was discussing four different topics (the most important decision I ever made, sacrifices I made for others, aspects of personality I dislike, past and present things of which I am ashamed) with a stranger who was really a confederate. Conversations were audiotaped and evaluated by two raters for intimacy of self-disclosure. Women were more intimate when they disclosed to female than male targets. Men's self-disclosure was influenced by their masculinity scores, the sex of the target, and the possibility of future interaction. As shown in the right panel of Figure 8.7, men who scored high on masculinity self-disclosed more to female than male targets when there was the possibility of a future interaction (PFI). When there was no possibility of a future interaction (NPFI; left panel

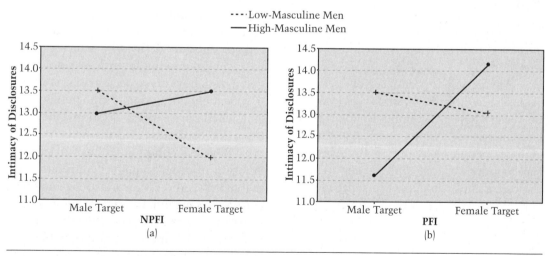

FIGURE 8.7 Men who score high on masculinity are motivated to self-disclose to a female they have just met and with whom they have the possibility of forming a relationship. High-masculine men self-disclosed more intimately to a female than a male target, only when there was the possibility of a future interaction (PFI). Where there was no possibility of a future interaction (NPFI), high-masculine men's disclosures were equally intimate toward a male or female target.
Source: Shaffer, Pegalis, and Bazzini (1996).

of Figure 8.7), high-masculine men self-disclosed equally to male and female targets.

Are highly masculine men increasing their self-disclosure to female targets when they expect to interact with them again? Or are highly masculine men decreasing their self-disclosure to male targets when they expect to interact with them again? Highly masculine men may be especially uncomfortable disclosing to other men if they think they will see them again. Indeed, comfort level did explain the results from this study. High-masculine men reported greater comfort and were more interested in establishing a relationship with the female than the male target when there was the potential for future interaction. In general, female respondents were more comfortable and more interested in establishing a relationship with the female than the male target. Thus it appears both women and masculine men self-disclosed most to female targets when there was the possibility of a future interaction because they felt comfortable and wanted to establish a relationship.

Another moderator of sex differences in disclosure could be the forum for disclosure. As we saw in Chapter 7, communication is taking place increasingly online—especially among younger people. A study of disclosure via Facebook showed that adult women and men disclosed a similar amount of personal information (Nosko, Wood, & Molema, 2010). Perhaps men feel more comfortable disclosing online without the pressure of face-to-face interaction.

TAKE HOME POINTS

- Women engage in more self-disclosure than men.

- Women are especially likely to disclose to women over men. It is unclear whether men disclose more to women or men; it may depend on the topic of disclosure.

- Men are clearly capable of self-disclosure (just as they are capable of intimacy) but seem to prefer not to engage in it. Men can be motivated to self-disclose to women when they are interested in establishing a relationship.

BARRIERS TO CLOSENESS IN MALE FRIENDSHIP

Why are male same-sex friendships less intimate, less disclosing, and sometimes less satisfying than female same-sex friendships? Research with high school boys has shown that there are several characteristics of upholding masculinity during adolescence that have implications for male friendship (Oransky & Fisher, 2009; Oransky & Marecek, 2009). First, boys' interactions with one another seem to be characterized by teasing, taunting, and mocking. Boys make fun of each other and have to learn to stand up to ridicule. Second, boys' identities and relationships are defined by heterosexism—that is, by *not* being feminine or not being gay. Third, boys are expected to be stoic and to hide their emotions and vulnerabilities. In fact, when boys express emotions, they may be mocked or ridiculed for behaving like girls. Boys will cut off other boys' displays of emotion in order to help them retain their masculinity. And, in general, other boys perceive this as helpful. Let's take a closer look at three barriers to closeness in men's same-sex friendships: competition, homophobia, and emotional inexpressiveness.

Competition

One barrier to male friendship is competition. Men's friendships are more overtly competitive than women's friendships. Competition limits intimacy because it is difficult to be close to someone with whom you are in competition; we would not reveal weaknesses, inadequacies, or difficulties to a competitor. And, competition in friendship has been related to less friendship satisfaction for both women and men (Singleton & Vacca, 2007). Competition among men makes them feel threatened by one another's achievements. In general, men are more sensitive than women to status features in relationships.

Note that I said that male friendships were more *overtly* competitive than female friendships. Competition, however, is not limited to male friendship. Female friendships can be competitive but the competition is not as direct or overt. Females are more uncomfortable than males with overt competition (Benenson et al., 2002). In a laboratory study in which a confederate behaved poorly, males were more overtly competitive by making negative remarks about the confederate, whereas females displayed more subtle behavior in the form of mean faces and gestures (Underwood & Buhrmester, 2007). The overt expression of competition in relationships is viewed as unfeminine, so women resort to more subtle tactics. A friend of mine told me of an occasion when her aunt was so concerned about being the best dressed person at a party that she refused to tell her friends what she intended to wear. This is covert competition. My mother was once accused of leaving out a key ingredient of a dessert recipe she passed on to a friend, another example of covert competition. Thus competition may undermine friendships for both women and men but in different ways. Investigate this issue with Do Gender 8.2.

Aside from direct versus indirect, there are other distinctions that can be made in regard to competition. Table 8.1 shows a number of different kinds of competition. One study of seventh graders from Canada, Costa Rica, and Cuba examined the first

DO GENDER 8.2
Female Versus
Male Competition

Interview your friends to find out how competition manifests itself in their friendships. Ask for examples of competitive behavior in their friendships with men and their friendships with women. Over what things do people compete: Money? Status? Physical attractiveness? Grades? Romantic partners? Are the behaviors that men identify different from the behaviors that women identify? Are the behaviors that people identify about women different from the behaviors that people identify about men?

three kinds of competition: hypercompetition, nonhostile social comparison, and enjoyment of competition (Schneider et al., 2005). Hypercompetition involves an intense desire to win at all costs, without any regard to the effects on the opponent. Nonhostile social comparison occurs when we compare our achievement to that of another, but without anger, hostility, or jealousy. Enjoyment of competition reflects an intense engagement in a competitive activity. Overall, boys' friendships contained more competition than girls' friendships. However, the implications of competition for the friendship depended on the nature of the competition. Hypercompetition was related to more conflict and less closeness in friendships for both girls and boys. Enjoyment of competition was unrelated to friendship closeness but was related to more companionship in boys' friendship. Finally, nonhostile social comparison was related to more friendship closeness for boys. Thus the distinctions

TABLE 8.1   THE NATURE OF COMPETITION

Hypercompetition	intense desire to win, associated with hostility; disregard for opponent "I get upset when X wins." "Winning makes me feel powerful."
Nonhostile social comparison	comparison of achievement without hostility "I like to play X to see who is better."
Enjoyment of competition	intense involvement in activity "I like to play X for the fun of it."
Personal development competition	competition for self-improvement "Competition helps me to be the best I can be."

among the different kinds of competition mattered more for boys' than girls' friendships. Another kind of competition that has been studied is personal development competition, which is aimed at using competition for self-improvement. Personal development competition appears to be a healthy kind of competition for both males and females (Burckle et al., 1999; Ryckman et al., 1997).

Homophobia

Another reason men are uncomfortable with closeness in their same-sex friendships is **homophobia**, defined as the fear of homosexuality or the fear of appearing homosexual. Because men do not want to appear to be homosexual, they limit their physical contact and their emotional closeness with other men, reserving those kinds of contacts for romantic relationships with women. Homophobia seems to be tied to men's identities. Men who have higher gender self-esteem, meaning that they are more likely to endorse statements such as "I am proud to be a male," have more negative attitudes toward homosexuals (Falomir-Pichastor & Mugny, 2009). Interestingly, when the threat of homosexuality is removed by convincing men that homosexuality has a biological basis, homophobia is reduced. Apparently, upon hearing that homosexuality is due to biology, heterosexual men no longer have a need to differentiate themselves from homosexuals.

Emotional Inexpressiveness

A third barrier to closeness in men's same-sex relationships is emotional inexpressiveness. Men tend to express less emotion in relationships compared to women. Inexpressiveness may help to maintain power, but at the expense of closeness. Men may avoid expressing their emotions because doing so would appear feminine. Revealing weaknesses and vulnerabilities is inconsistent with the male role. However, failing to reveal one's emotions and problems makes it difficult for others to provide support when needed. Indeed, restricted emotions have been linked to reduced social support, which has been linked to increased psychological distress (Wester et al., 2007). One way in which men are able to be expressive in the context of relationships is by compensating with increased masculine behavior in other arenas, such as more instrumental behavior (Migliaccio, 2009). In fact, self-disclosure between men usually takes place in the context of shared activities (Radmacher & Azmitia, 2006). Having something to do during the interaction may make men feel more comfortable self-disclosing.

Another reason men may not self-disclose as much as women has nothing to do with men's personalities but has to do with society's expectations of men. This would be a structural level of analysis. Men are not viewed as favorably as women when they self-disclose. A meta-analysis of the studies that examined the relation of self-disclosure to liking showed the relation was stronger for female disclosers ($d = +.30$) than male disclosers ($d = +.11$) (Collins & Miller, 1994). This finding held for both female and male respondents. In other words, both women and men liked a woman who disclosed more than a man who disclosed.

Men who self-disclose might be viewed as having more problems than women who self-disclose. This idea was supported by a study conducted a very long time ago in which college students read several vignettes in which one person either did or did not disclose a personal problem (a mental illness or a car accident; Derlega & Chaikin, 1976). The sex of the discloser and the sex of the recipient were varied. Men were rated as better adjusted under nondisclosure than disclosure conditions, whereas women were rated as better adjusted under disclosure than nondisclosure conditions. The sex of the disclosure recipient did not influence the results. In addition, participants liked the female discloser better than the female nondiscloser but liked the male discloser and nondiscloser equally. Regardless of sex, the discloser was rated as more feminine than the nondiscloser. Thus self-disclosure was viewed as part of the female gender role. Try Do Gender 8.3 to see if men are still viewed less favorably than women when they self-disclose.

TAKE HOME POINTS

- Male friendship is more overtly competitive than female friendship. Competition among females is more likely to be covert.

- There are different kinds of competition, only some of which may be barriers to intimacy among men. Hyper-competitiveness is one such form of competition.

DO GENDER 8.3
Do You Want to Be Friends with a Guy Who Discloses a Personal Problem?

Create two vignettes that contain a story about someone disclosing a problem. In one vignette, make the disclosure more personal than the other vignette. Now, vary the sex of the person engaging in self-disclosure across the two vignettes so that you have two versions of each vignette. Randomly assign a group of college students to read one of the vignettes and then answer some questions about how they viewed the person in the story. Did they view female and male disclosures differently in terms of personality traits? in terms of likeability and desirability for friendship? in mental health?

If you want to make the design more complicated, you can also take the opportunity to vary the recipient of disclosure. Are people more accepting of a male who reveals a personal problem to a female than a male?

- Males may score higher than females on other kinds of competition, such as competition for social comparison or personal development competition, but these kinds of competition are not likely to inhibit intimacy.

- Homophobia limits intimacy among men's same-sex friendships. Men do not want to appear to be homosexual and infer homosexuality from expressions of affection between men.

- Men refrain from expressing emotion in their relationships with other men, because expressing emotion is viewed as weakness and as feminine. It is difficult to be close to someone when you hide your feelings from them.

- Another reason that men do not disclose as much as women is because people do not respond as favorably to self-disclosure by men compared to women. If people have negative views of men who disclose their problems, it is not surprising that men are reluctant to ask for help.

CONFLICT IN FRIENDSHIP

Thus far, I have focused on the positive aspects of friendships. But relationships do not always run smoothly. Do women or men have more conflict in their relationships? Despite their greater closeness—and, perhaps, because of it, girls say that they spend more time resolving conflicts with friends (Thomas & Daubman, 2001). It also has been suggested that females' friendships are more fragile than those of males. In a study of sixth graders making the transition to seventh grade, males were more likely than females to maintain the same friends over the transition (Hardy, Bukowski, & Sippola, 2002). Seventh grade males and females had the same number of friends, but proportionally more of the females' friends were new and not the same as those they had in sixth grade. Even among 7- and 8-year-olds, greater stability was observed among boys' than girls' social networks over the course of a year (Baines & Blatchford, 2009). In studies of college students, females' closest friendship seems to be of shorter duration than males' closest friendship (Benenson & Christakos, 2003; Johnson, 2004). In one study, females were more likely than males to say that their closest friends had done something to hurt the friendship, and females had more friendships that had ended compared to males (Benenson & Christakos, 2003). Even among older adults, women are less tolerant than men of friends who betray them, violate their trust, or fail to confide in them (Felmlee & Muraco, 2009). It seems that women have higher expectations of friendship than men.

One reason that there may be more conflict in female than male friendship is that females have more difficulty resolving conflict compared to males (Benenson & Christakos, 2003). Because females are more concerned with directly hurting a relationship, they may express their distress in more subtle ways. A study of fourth and fifth graders showed that girls and boys reported they would respond to hypothetical conflicts quite differently (Rose & Asher, 1999). Girls were more likely to say they would accommodate and compromise, whereas boys were more likely to say they would assert their own interest, walk away from the situation, and use verbal aggression. Studies of adults show that women are more likely than men to bring up the subject of conflict within a same-sex friendship, but that men are more likely than women to be direct in terms of how they discuss the conflict. (As you will see in Chapter 9, this finding also holds for romantic relationships.) For example, men are more likely than women to express anger to their friends. Women may be more concerned than men with the threat that such expressions bring to relationships—which is ironic, because it is women's friendships that seem to be less stable than those of men.

TAKE HOME POINTS

- Although women's relationships are closer than those of men, women may experience more conflict and less stability in their relationships.

- Women and men may respond to conflict in different ways. Women may be more likely than men to confront conflict in their relationships, but women may be more indirect than men in expressing their relationship concerns.

CROSS-SEX FRIENDSHIP

Can men and women be friends? This is the question taken up by the characters played by Meg Ryan and Billy Crystal in the movie *When Harry Met Sally.* Sally told Harry they would just be friends. Harry, however, insisted they could not be friends because men and women can never be friends—sex always gets in the way. Even when Sally said she had a number of male friends, Harry argued that sex is somehow involved in the relationship—if not on her part, then on the part of the men. Of course, as you might imagine, a friendship emerges between Harry and Sally that then blossoms into a romantic relationship, confirming the stereotype that women and men cannot be *just* friends.

Many people today would disagree with Harry. The majority of children (grades 3 through 12) agree that it is possible to have a cross-sex friend, and 93% said that they have or have had a cross-sex friend (McDougall & Hymel, 2007). The number of cross-sex friends increases with age. When college students in the United States and Russia were asked to identify up to their eight closest friends, 27% of those friends were of the other sex for U.S. men and women, 26% were of the other sex for Russian women, and 17% were of the other sex for Russian men (Sheets & Lugar, 2005). In a study of adults ages 25–44 in Greece, three-quarters said that they believed cross-sex friendship was possible and most had or had had a cross-sex friend (Halatsis & Christakis, 2009). However, like the study of Russians, more women thought cross-sex friendship was possible compared to men (81% vs. 69%).

Most relationship research focuses on same-sex friendship or romantic relationships. Cross-sex friendship is a relatively new area of research. A cross-sex friendship is typically defined as a friendship with someone of the other sex that is not romantic, sexual, or familial. Cross-sex friendships are not uncommon, but they are much less common than same-sex friendships. Historically, cross-sex friendships among adults were rare; the traditional division of labor in society did not provide many opportunities for women and men to interact with one another. The changing nature of female and male roles in society has made members of the other sex more available as potential friends.

Comparisons to Same-Sex Friendship

The first studies of cross-sex friendship appeared in the 1980s. Not surprisingly, one of the first questions that researchers asked was how cross-sex friends compared to same-sex friends.

In many ways, cross-sex friendships are similar to same-sex friendships. They are characterized by intimacy, loyalty, and shared activities. As in our selection of same-sex friends, the similarity principle of attraction applies. That is, "Birds of a feather flock together." Cross-sex friends, like same-sex friends, have a great deal of demographic similarity. They are similar in age, education, marital status, and parental status. They also are similar in terms of personality traits (e.g., locus of control), behaviors (e.g., self-disclosure), and relationship beliefs (e.g., how to resolve conflicts; Morry, 2007). And, greater similarity predicts more satisfying friendships.

However, cross-sex friendships are less intimate than same-sex friendships—at least for women. Women are typically closer to their same-sex than cross-sex friends, but it is not clear if men are closer to their same-sex or cross-sex friends. Studies of adolescents show that males receive more support and find more rewards in cross-sex than same-sex friendship (Thomas & Daubman, 2001). There is some evidence that both women and men find their friendships with women to be more rewarding than their friendships with men. High school students report receiving more help from female friends than male friends (Poulin & Pedersen, 2007), and college students are closer to their female friends than their male friends (Reeder, 2003). Although females are more satisfied than males with their same-sex friends, females and males are equally satisfied with cross-sex friendships (Cheung & McBride-Chang, 2007; Singleton & Vacca, 2007).

Do we expect our cross-sex friends to behave like our same-sex friends? Among children, boys and girls prefer that their cross-sex friends act the same way as their same-sex friends (Dijkstra, Lindenberg, & Veenstra, 2007). That is, boys preferred female classmates who were more aggressive than helpful, and girls preferred male classmates who were more helpful than aggressive. With age, however, there seems to be some accommodation of female and male friendship styles in cross-sex friendships. Men reduce their focus on shared activities in cross-sex compared to same-sex friendships, and women increase their focus on shared activities in cross-sex compared to same-sex friendships (Fuhrman, Flannagan, & Matamoros, 2009; McDougall & Hymel, 2007).

Cross-sex friends might serve different functions for women and men compared to same-sex friends. As described in Chapter 7, having cross-sex friends during childhood provides opportunities to learn new styles of play and decreases sex-typed behavior (Fabes, Martin, & Hanish, 2004). Children who have cross-sex friends also may find it easier to interact with the other sex during adolescence, when such encounters are more frequent. Cross-sex friends can give insight into the other sex and avoid the competitiveness and jealousy that sometimes characterizes same-sex friendship (Halatsis & Christakis, 2007; McDougall & Humel, 2007). Cross-sex friendship also can compensate for what is lacking in same-sex friendship. Men may derive more emotional support from cross-sex friends than same-sex friends, whereas women may find more companionship from cross-sex friends and obtain a sense of relief from the intensity of their same-sex friendships (Werking, 1997b). Women have less conflict with their cross-sex friends than their same-sex friends (Werking, 1997b). Women also suggest cross-sex friends provide a resource for physical protection (Bleske-Rechek & Buss, 2001).

Obstacles

In the early research on this topic, O'Meara (1989) identified five challenges that cross-sex friendships face; these are listed in Table 8.2. First is the **emotional bond challenge**, in which friends question the nature of the relationship. Is the closeness called friendship or romantic love? This is the question that was taken up by the movie *When Harry Met Sally*. According to the movie, cross-sex friendship cannot really exist; even their friendship ultimately evolved into a romantic relationship. Second is the **sexual challenge**. We are socialized to view members of the other sex as potential romantic and sexual partners. Is there sexual attraction? This is the issue with which Harry was initially most concerned. Third is the **equality challenge**. Equality is central to friendship, and men

TABLE 8.2 CHALLENGES OF CROSS-SEX FRIENDSHIP

Emotional bond	Is this friendship or romantic love?
Sexual	Is there sexual attraction?
Equality	Is this relationship equal?
Audience	How is this relationship viewed by others—and do I care?
Opportunity	Are there cross-sex people in my life available as friends?

Source: O'Meara (1989).

and women have an unequal status. Will the relationship be equal? Fourth is the **audience challenge**. Friends may be concerned with the public's perception of their relationship. In fact, people often view cross-sex friendships with suspicion and wonder if they are not in fact romantic relationships. Fifth is the **opportunity challenge**. Cross-sex friendships are less common and more difficult to establish than same-sex friendships because women and men are somewhat segregated in school, play, and work.

The prevalence of these challenges in college students' good and casual cross-sex friendships was examined with a series of open-ended questions and closed-ended questions that reflected these challenges (Monsour et al., 1994). The primary conclusion was that the majority of relationships did not suffer from any of these strains. The greatest challenge was the emotional bond challenge, and it was more of a problem with good relationships than with casual relationships. There were no sex differences in the sexual challenge, although more men than women admitted they thought about sex. The sexual challenge was mentioned more often by students who were single compared to students who were involved in a romantic relationship. The fewest problems were reported regarding the equality challenge. Theoretically, the equality challenge should be a major issue for cross-sex friends, because friendship by definition is based on equality, and there may be an imbalance of power in cross-sex friendship.

Although there was little support for the audience challenge, another study did show that women are more concerned with how people view their cross-sex friendships than their same-sex friendships (Wright & Scanlon, 1991). Monsour and colleagues (1994) found that the audience challenge was related to students' scores on a personality variable known as self-monitoring. Recall from Chapter 5 that high self-monitors are very aware of their environment and concerned about the impression they make on others. High self-monitors reported more audience challenge problems.

The authors concluded that researchers have overestimated the degree to which cross-sex friendships face these challenges. However, it is also possible that respondents described only the cross-sex friendships that did not suffer from these challenges. A cross-sex friendship facing any one of these challenges might not be the one that comes to mind when researchers ask about friendship. Cross-sex friendships that face these challenges may be less close than ones that do not. Future research should obtain both persons' perceptions of a cross-sex friendship; one person may not be facing the emotional bond challenge or sexual challenge, but the other may.

Since the development of these ideas about cross-sex challenges, the challenge that has received the most research attention is the sexual challenge. Despite Monsour and colleagues' (1994) results, evidence indicates that sexual tension is a problem in cross-sex friendship, especially for men. A study of adults in Greece showed that 69% of men and 47% of women had experienced sexual attraction to a cross-sex friend (Halatsis & Christakis, 2009). Research with college students has shown that 28% reported that they were currently sexually attracted to a cross-sex friend (Reeder, 2000), and that half (51%) had had sex in the past with a platonic cross-sex friend whom they were not dating nor had any intention of dating (Afifi & Faulkner, 2000). Of those, 56% had sex with more than one cross-sex friend. Men are more likely than women to report sexual attraction and a desire for sex with cross-sex friends compared to women (Bleske & Buss, 2000; Bleske-Rechek & Buss, 2001). Sexual attraction can emerge at any time during a cross-sex friendship, and when it does, it gets in the way of the authenticity of the relationship.

One might ask, "What keeps cross-sex friendships from developing into romantic relationships?" The number one reason for keeping a cross-sex friendship platonic seems to be the desire to preserve the relationship and avoid any kind of breakup (Messman, Canary, & Hause, 2000). People perceive that romantic relationships have the potential to end. By keeping a relationship as a friendship, we can feel more secure in maintaining that relationship.

How does one manage sexual attraction in a cross-sex friendship? Oftentimes, one tries to keep the attraction under control by avoiding discussions of the relationship and by discussing other romantic relationships (Guerrero & Chavez, 2005). At other times, the sexual attraction is acted upon. In some cases, the couple has sex and the relationship reverts

back to friendship. In other cases, a sexual relationship coexists with a friendship. In a survey of adults who disclosed sexual attraction to their partner in a cross-sex friendship, nearly a quarter (22%) evolved into romantic relationships and the friendship ended in 16% of the cases (Halatsis & Christakis, 2009). However, the future course of the relationship also depended on the sex of the discloser. As shown in Figure 8.8, when males disclosed sexual attraction, the most likely outcomes were the coexistence of friendship and sex or friendship without reciprocal attraction. When females disclosed sexual attraction, the most likely outcomes were evolution into a romantic relationship or acting on sexual attraction with a return to friendship. According to Baumgarter (2002), we lack a cultural script for cross-sex friendship. We shouldn't assume sex is bad for

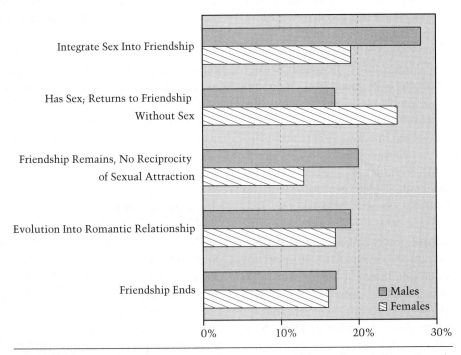

FIGURE 8.8   Future Course of Cross-Sex Friendship After Male or Female Discloses Sexual Attraction.

Source: Adapted from Halatsis & Christakis (2009).

a friendship—it depends on how sex is interpreted by both partners.

In fact, the coexistence of friendship and sex has been referred to as "friends with benefits" (Guerrero & Mongeau, 2008). Friends with benefits are two people who are friends, have sex with one another, but do not label their relationship romantic. It turns out that over half of college students have or have had friends with benefits relationship. With the increased prevalence of group dating—an environment in which a group of friends go out together, some of whom may be coupled and some of whom may not—the potential for friends with benefits increases. To keep the friendship from becoming a romantic relationship, the couple has several implicit rules—remain emotionally detached, minimize jealousy, and do not fall in love (Hughes et al., 2005). These rules are equally endorsed by females and males. Violation of these rules may lead to the development of a romantic relationship or may lead to the termination of a friendship.

Little longitudinal data exists on the outcome of cross-sex friendships. Are they more or less stable than same-sex relationships? What percentage develop into romantic relationships, and, of those, how viable are they? Does getting married or becoming involved in a romantic relationship interfere with cross-sex friendship? Research shows that people who are involved in romantic relationships have lower expectations for closeness in a cross-sex friend (Fuhrman et al., 2009). A local radio station in Pittsburgh invited listeners to call in and share how they would feel if a future husband or wife had a cross-sex friend stand up for them at their wedding. Listeners, especially women, were appalled. However, the listeners to this radio station were hardly a representative sample. Although rare, men do stand up for women

as the "man of honor" or "person of honor," and women do stand up for men as the "best woman" or "best person." These people are sometimes friends and sometimes siblings. Explore the future of cross-sex friendship in Do Gender 8.4.

> ### DO GENDER 8.4
> ### What Happens When
> ### Women and Men Become Friends?
>
> Interview 10 of your fellow students about their current and past cross-sex friendships. Find out what happened to the past relationships: Did they end? Did any of them evolve into romantic relationships? Examine the reasons for the relationship ending, including O'Meara's (1989) challenges.
>
> Examine how certain life events influenced these friendships, such as the development of a romantic relationship. In other words, when one person developed a romantic relationship, did that alter the cross-sex friendship? How did the romantic partner view the cross-sex friendship? Are men and women equally accepting of their partner's cross-sex friends?

TAKE HOME POINTS

- For women, same-sex friendships are closer than cross-sex friendships.

- Men, by contrast, seem to gain more from cross-sex friendships than same-sex friends in terms of emotional support and intimacy.

- Cross-sex friendships serve some important functions that same-sex friendships do not, such as emotional support for men, companionship for women, and the perspective of the other sex for both women and men.

■ Cross-sex friendships face a number of challenges: emotional bond, sexual, equality, audience, and opportunity.

■ The greatest challenges seem to be the emotional bond and sexual challenges. Sexual attraction is not uncommon in cross-sex friendship and seems to be more common among men than women.

CROSS-RACE FRIENDSHIP

Race is a powerful determinant of friendship. The tendency to form friendships with persons of the same ethnic group is called **homophily**. Race/ethnicity is one of the demographic variables upon which friends tend to match. Interestingly, among children, race segregation is not as prevalent as gender segregation. In a study of first through sixth graders, only 11% of children had a person of the other sex in their social network whereas 92% had a person of another race in their social network (Lee, Howes, & Chamberlain, 2007). Cross-race friendship appears to be more common among children than adults. However, among children cross-race friendship declines with age and is less stable than same-race friendships (Aboud, Mendelson, & Purdy, 2003; Lee et al., 2007). Why do cross-race friendships decline with age? Although children do not express overt prejudice—that is, they do not identify race as a factor in selecting a friend—more subtle forms of prejudice may begin to emerge. The **outgroup homogeneity effect** begins to emerge with age (McGlothlin, Killen, & Edmonds, 2005). That is, with increased age, children began to perceive people of other races as more similar to one another—and thus more different from themselves.

One source of homophily is the opportunity to interact with persons of another race. Schools, neighborhoods, and

work are often segregated informally, if not formally, by race. Cross-race friendships are more common among racially diverse schools (Quillian & Campbell, 2003), in part because the racial diversity of a school influences children's perceptions of similarity and feelings toward cross-race friends. In a study of first through fourth graders, children who attended more racially diverse schools evaluated same-race and cross-race peers as equally likely to become friends (McGlothlin & Killen, 2005). However, White children who attended more racially homogenous schools viewed cross-race peers as less likely to become friends than same-race peers—unless cross-race peers shared the same activity interests. Thus, children judged friendship as most likely to occur between two people when there were shared activity interests—regardless of the racial composition of the dyad.

The development of cross-race friendships also has been studied among adolescents transitioning from high school to college (Stearns, Buchmann, & Bonneau, 2009). The number of cross-race friendships increased for Whites, decreased for Blacks, and was unaltered for Asians and Latinos. The increase among Whites can be attributed to increased opportunities. Although Blacks also would have experienced increased opportunities, being a minority race at college may have led them to bond with other African Americans.

Opportunity structure is not the only determinant of cross-race friendship. Another factor is preference, which may reflect prejudice. Prejudice is associated with fewer cross-race friendships (Aboud et al., 2003). Friendship by definition involves an equal-status relationship. If one group perceived the other group as having a different status, either lower or higher, this may inhibit friendship formation. It is difficult to assess preference, however, because people do not want to appear prejudiced. To disentangle preference from opportunity, some researchers inferred the preference of Whites, Blacks, Asians, and Hispanics from the friendships they formed given the racial composition of their schools (Currarini, Jackson, & Pin, 2010). That is, in a sense, they controlled for opportunity structure. Using this method, they determined that Black students had the least preference for cross-race friends, Asians the most, with Whites and Hispanics falling between the two groups. In terms of opportunities to meet persons of other races, Whites had the most opportunities and Asians and Blacks had the fewest opportunities.

Which children have cross-race friends? One study showed that boys have more cross-race friends than girls (Scott, 2004), and another study showed that girls have more cross-race friends than boys (Lee et al., 2007). Social status may be associated with cross-race friendships. In a study of Black and White children, those who were well-liked, popular in school, perceived to be smart, and leaders had more cross-race friends (Lease & Blake, 2005). The authors concluded that the same set of social skills that leads to friendship also leads to crossing racial barriers. The findings of that study did not hold as well for Black boys. In the case of Black boys, those with cross-race friends were perceived to be nice and good listeners, but not leaders or outstanding athletes.

Cross-race friendships are more problematic between Blacks and Whites than between two people of other races (Scott, 2004). White people are more likely to have cross-race friends who are Hispanic or Asian than Black (Quillian & Campbell, 2003). Cross-race friendships also are less common among Whites than among African Americans, largely because African Americans are more likely to be in the minority in their environment, which means more Whites are available for friendship. The increasing racial and ethnic diversity that is occurring in the United States means that future research will need to examine the nature of cross-race friendship more closely.

TAKE HOME POINTS

- Children have more cross-race friendships than adults.

- Barriers to cross-race friendship are both dispositional, for example prejudice, and structural, for example opportunity structure.

FRIENDSHIPS OF LESBIANS AND GAY MEN

The nature of friendship as typically defined by heterosexuals is similar for homosexuals. However, friendship holds a different place in the lives of homosexuals. Friendships often replace or take greater precedence over familial relationships among homosexuals because homosexuals have less support from family than heterosexuals do. Friends are often more accepting of one's sexual orientation than family (Beals & Peplau, 2006). A study of older gay men (ages 50 to 87) showed that men maintain contact with their biological families but call upon friends for assistance (Shippy, Cantor, & Brennan, 2004). There is surprisingly little research on friendships among homosexuals.

In terms of the sheer number of friends, it appears that there is no difference across heterosexuals, lesbians, gay men, and bisexuals (Galupo, 2009). Like heterosexuals, the friendships of gay men and lesbians match on an array of demographic variables. That is, gay men and lesbians are likely to be friends with people who share the same sex, race, age, relationship status, and parental status. Matching on sex may be more difficult for gay men, however, because friendship among men in Western culture is based on norms of heterosexuality. It may be easier for gay men to be friends with women. A study of 15- to 24-year-olds and a study of adults ages 18–80 showed that the majority of heterosexuals' and lesbians' friends were of the same sex but that a smaller percentage of gay men's friends were of the same sex (Diamond & Dube, 2002; Gallupo, 2009). Lesbians had the largest percentage of same-sex friends despite the fact that lesbians have the most difficulty with boundaries between friendship and romantic relationships.

Matching on sexual orientation may be more difficult for gays, lesbians, and bisexuals compared to heterosexuals, in part due to accessibility. Whereas 95% of heterosexual men's and women's friends are of the same sexual orientation, this is the case for only 48% of lesbians, 43% of gay men, and 20% of bisexuals (Galupo, 2009). However, sexual orientation may not affect the quality of the friendship. When female friend dyads were interviewed, friendships between a lesbian or bisexual and a heterosexual were similar to same sexual orientation friendships (Galupo, 2007). Among dyads that included a bisexual woman, however, friends noted that the nature of the friendship changed depending on the sex of the bisexual woman's partner. Other research has shown that there are no differences in closeness, hassles, or frequency of contact between friends who are gay/lesbian/bisexual or straight (Ueno et al., 2009). And, support from gay/lesbian/bisexual and support from straight friends are equally associated with reduced distress and higher self-esteem.

Given the sex difference in the nature of male and female friendship among heterosexuals, one can ask whether these findings generalize to gay and lesbian friendship. Do gay men focus on shared activities? Do lesbians focus on self-disclosure? The question has rarely been explored. When gay and lesbians evaluated their casual, close, and best friends, there were

no sex differences in self-disclosure, activities shared over the previous 2 months, or social support (Nardi & Sherrod, 1994). Thus, unlike studies of friendship among heterosexuals, homosexual men's and women's friendships were more similar in terms of how they spent their time together. These data suggest that the agentic/communal distinction that characterizes sex differences in the heterosexual friendship literature does not reflect sex alone. There were no differences in the amount of conflict gay men and lesbians reported in their friendships, but there were sex differences in how important it was to resolve conflict. Lesbians were more bothered by conflict, said it was more important to resolve the conflict, and expressed more emotion when resolving the conflict compared to gay men. These differences are consistent with the differences between heterosexual women's and men's friendship.

One way in which gay and lesbian friendship differs from heterosexual friendship—at least heterosexual same-sex friendship—is that the potential for romantic or sexual involvement is present. There is more difficulty with the boundary between friendship and romantic relationships among gay men and lesbians compared to heterosexuals (Peplau & Fingerhut, 2007). Because homosexuals' romantic partners are of the same sex as their friends, homosexual same-sex friendship may be more similar to heterosexual cross-sex friendship. Thus homosexual friendship may face some of the same challenges as heterosexual cross-sex friendship. For bisexuals, the issue is even more complicated. Their same-sex and cross-sex friendships present the possibility of romantic attraction. Because men are more likely than women to use sex to achieve intimacy (see Chapter 9), one possibility is that gay men's friendships will be more likely than other friendships to involve sex. One study showed that the majority of gay men had had sex with one or more of their casual friends (62%) and even more had had sex with one or more of their close friends (76%; Nardi, 1992). Fewer lesbians had had sex with one or more of their casual friends (34%) but slightly over half had had sex with one or more of their close friends (59%). The author concluded that sex is likely to precede friendship for gay men, but friendship precedes sex for lesbians. This is parallel to the findings on the relation between sex and intimacy among heterosexual men and women, discussed in Chapter 9.

TAKE HOME POINTS

- Friendship may be especially important in the lives of gay men and lesbians to the extent that they have less available support from family.

- Similarity is an important guiding principle in the development of friendship among gays and lesbians as it is with heterosexuals — with the exception of matching on sex, which may be more difficult for gay men and matching on sexual orientation, which may be more difficult for gay men, lesbians, and bisexuals due to reduced availability.

- Friendships with gay/lesbian/bisexual persons and friendships with heterosexual persons are similar in closeness and conflict.

- The agentic/communal distinction that characterizes friendship among heterosexuals does not seem to characterize friendship among gay men or lesbians.

- The lines between friendship and romantic relationships may be more blurred for gay men, lesbians, and bisexuals because same-sex friends have the potential to be romantic partners.

FRIENDSHIP AT WORK

Because men and women spend so much time at work and because work is so central to our lives, it is not surprising that some of our friendships are based at work. Friendships at work serve multiple functions, all of which can help one to make work more successful (Elsesser & Peplau, 2006). Same-level friendships can provide access to information and assistance with work, promote team building, and provide emotional support. Friendships with mentors can provide advice, protection, and access to promotion. Despite companies' concerns that friendships at work can be disruptive and distracting, there is evidence that having friends at work enhances performance. A 2007 survey reported that 57% of executives and two-thirds of employees believe that having friends at work increases productivity ("Survey: Befriending," 2007). People who have a best friend at work are more likely to be engaged in their work, and people with friends at work are more satisfied with their job and more satisfied with their life (Rath, 2006). A study of a telecommunications company found that workers who developed reciprocal relations at work, in which they did favors for and received favors from one another at work, were more productive (Flynn, 2003). One study showed that a greater number of friends at work were associated with lower rates of turnover (Feeley, Hwang, & Barnett, 2008). Although friendships with a boss are rare, those friendships are associated with job satisfaction (Rath, 2006).

Friendships at work are common. In a recent survey, 95% of adults said that they had people at work whom they considered to be friends ("Nearly half," 2010). Over a third (38%) said that they had personal friends at work whom they interacted with both at work and outside of work. Women were more likely than men to say that they had personal friends at work with whom they shared time outside of work. Older adults were slightly less supportive of interacting with workplace friends outside of work than younger adults.

Work is a good setting to study cross-sex friendships. Although the workplace is still sex segregated, there is increasing opportunity for women and men to work together. Men and women are more likely to develop cross-sex friendships at work if they perform similar jobs. However, there are barriers to cross-sex friendship at work (Elsesser & Peplau, 2006). Men and women may be concerned that friendliness at work will be misinterpreted as romantic or sexual interest—or, worse yet, as sexual harassment. Even if the recipient of the friendly overture does not misinterpret the behavior, women and men may be concerned that coworkers will! In other words, the audience challenge of cross-sex friendship may be especially relevant in the work environment. In a study of men and women professionals at work, men and women were equally likely to voice these concerns about cross-sex friendship at work (Elsesser & Peplau, 2006). However, married employees expressed fewer concerns about cross-sex friendship than unmarried employees, and more concerns were expressed about cross-sex friendships with supervisors or subordinates than peers.

Unlike friendships outside of work, women may be less desirable as friends at work. According to Ibarra (1993), women may not be selected as friends because (1) they are in the minority in terms of numbers at the upper level, (2) they are in lower-status positions at work, and (3) sex-role stereotypes lead to unfavorable attributions for their performance. In a study of friendships at work among information technologists, lawyers, and middle managers, the quality of friendships with men but not women predicted work outcomes (Markiewicz, Devine, & Kausilas, 2000). For example, a stronger relationship with a male friend was associated with a higher salary, and greater conflict with the closest male friend was associated with less job satisfaction. Of course, the study is cross-sectional, so it is not clear whether relationships with men influenced the job outcomes or the job outcomes influenced the relationships.

Friendships at work are usually formed among peers, people who are working at similar job levels. In fact, the promotion of one person in a friendship may present problems for the relationship. However, friendships also form among people who have unequal work statuses. Friendships between supervisors and supervisees have benefits and costs. On the downside, such friendships make disciplinary action more difficult for the supervisor; on the upside, such friendships may encourage greater cooperation and facilitate getting the job done. If the subordinate is female and the supervisor is male, people are often suspicious of the friendship.

There has been little research on how gay men and lesbians form friendships at work. One study of gay men showed that it was difficult for men to find friends at work, in part because the work environment is predominantly heterosexual and it is difficult to identify gay men (Rumens, 2008). Gay men find it difficult to be friends with men because others may be suspicious that the relationship is more than a friendship.

Because a friendship at work involves the merging of two roles—coworker and friend, it is vulnerable to **role conflict**, which occurs when the demands of one role are inconsistent with the demands of another role. You might have found yourself suffering from role conflict when your role as student required that you study for an upcoming exam and your role as a member of some organization (band, fraternity/sorority) required that you work on the upcoming festivities at your school. Bridge and Baxter (1992) outlined four different kinds of role conflict among friends at work. They did not examine the issue of gender, however, so I will speculate as

DO GENDER 8.5
Role Conflict at Work

Develop items to measure the forms of role conflict discussed by Bridge and Baxter (1992). Administer the items to men and women who have a close friend at work. Determine if there are sex differences. Also, develop a set of open-ended questions to assess role conflict at work.

to whether gender ought to be an important factor in these kinds of conflicts. You can test these ideas in Do Gender 8.5.

Impartiality versus favoritism: As a friend, we expect special treatment and favoritism, but the workplace typically requires treating people equally. Is there any reason to believe men or women would be more likely to suffer from this role conflict?

Openness versus closedness: Friendships require open, honest communication. At work, we may be expected to hold confidences. Because women self-disclose to friends more than men do, women might be more likely than men to suffer from this role conflict. However, sex differences in self-disclosure are clearer when the topic is a personal one. It is not clear if a work-related topic is considered personal.

Autonomy versus connectedness: Work provides a way of connecting to one another, which should foster friendship. Difficulties arise when we feel a lack of autonomy in a friendship because we spend so much time with a friend (i.e., seeing the person daily at work). Because autonomy is central to

the male gender role, we might expect that men are more likely than women to suffer from this form of role conflict.

Judgment versus acceptance: An important attribute of friendship is mutual acceptance. The work role might require one person to critically evaluate the other, which creates a differential status between the two people. Because men are more sensitive to the status aspects of relationships, this challenge may be especially hard on men's friendships. However, we also learned that women are more likely to make internal attributions for criticism—to take feedback to heart. Thus, criticism from friends at work may jeopardize women's friendships.

TAKE HOME POINTS

- Friendship at work is increasingly common and tends to be associated with enhanced work productivity and job satisfaction.

- Work presents opportunities for the development of cross-sex friendships. Cross-sex friendships may present more advantages to work for women than men.

- Friendships at work can present conflict between the friendship role and the worker role.

CHANGES OVER THE LIFE SPAN

Friendship changes throughout childhood, adolescence, and adulthood. Friendship takes on increasing importance in adolescence—especially for girls. During adolescence, girls begin to spend more time with friends than boys, and girls' friendships become more intimate and self-disclosing than those of boys (Swenson & Rose, 2009).

Cross-sex friendship increases from childhood to adolescence. In childhood, cross-sex friendship is rare, perhaps because children do not have the opportunity to make friends with members of the other sex. At times, girls and boys are pitted against each other. In school, there may be the boys' lunch line and the girls' lunch line. Often, teams are formed by having the girls compete against the boys. In addition, children, especially boys, are often teased if they play with the other sex. During adolescence, girls and boys begin to interact more with each other and to form friendships with the other sex. Some of those friendships will evolve into romantic relationships, and some will remain platonic. Cross-sex friendship increases during adolescence and peaks in later adolescence and young adulthood. A longitudinal study of sixth graders showed that the number of cross-sex friends increased over the next four years, but more so for girls than boys (Poulin & Pedersen, 2007). As shown in Figure 8.9, girls and boys had a similar number of cross-sex friends in sixth grade but girls had more cross-sex friends than boys in grades 7 through 10. In college, there is more opportunity for cross-sex friendships due to the availability of potential friends and the similar status that men and women hold in college.

More than chronological age, life events affect friendship. Getting married, becoming a parent, building a career, retiring, and widowhood are all examples of structural issues that may influence friendships for women and men. Some of these life events are more likely to be experienced by one sex than the other or are more likely to have an effect on the friendships of one sex than the other. For

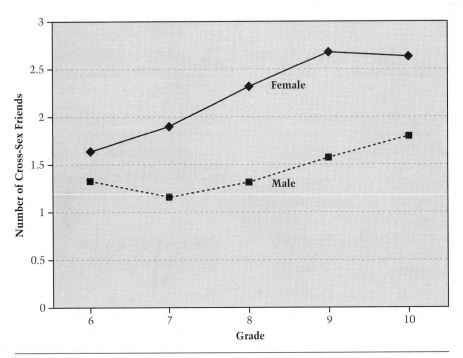

FIGURE 8.9   Boys and girls have the same number of cross-sex friends in 6th grade but girls have more cross-sex friends than boys in grades 7 through 10. *Source*: Adapted from Poulin and Pedersen (2007).

example, widowhood is more likely to affect women than men because women live longer than men. However, widowhood may have a stronger effect on men's friendships than women's friendships because wives are often the link to other relationships for men. Retirement may have a stronger impact on men's friendships than women's friendships because men's friends are more likely than women's to be found in the workplace. Here, I examine some of the structural factors that influence women's and men's friendships in early and later adulthood.

Early Adulthood: Marriage and Family

Historically, women's friendships were based at home and men's friendships were based at work. Women were the social organizers of the couple's friendships, often arranging social activities with other couples. Years ago, young married men had a larger social network than young married women because men had opportunities to meet people at work, whereas women's opportunities to meet people were restricted by having to stay home with children (Fischer, 1979). Women who became parents had even fewer friendships than men, because child care took up a larger portion of women's than men's free time.

However, today the majority of women work outside the home, even when they have children. Would you predict that these earlier findings hold today? Are men's friends at work and women's at home? Are men more likely than women to have friends during the early years of marriage and parenthood? One reason that the earlier findings may hold today is that women who work outside the home are often responsible for housework and child care, which would leave little time for friends. Work also is less likely to lead to friendships

for women who work in male-dominated professions because there would be fewer potential female friends available. Contemporary research shows that the number of friends and the frequency of interaction with friends decreases for both women and men during adulthood due to career development and increased time spent with family. Men spend less time with friends after they get married, in part because they have more familial obligations and in part because friends perceive they should not spend time with them now that they are married (Cohen, 1992). Thus both family and work obligations limit friendship.

Marital status specifically influences cross-sex friendship. Marriage may be a deterrent from friendly relations with the other sex. A number of studies have shown that married people are less likely than unmarried people to have cross-sex friends (Werking, 1997a).

Late Adulthood: Retirement and Empty Nest

The elderly value the same things from friendship as do younger people—similar beliefs, similar lifestyles, and similar demographics, such as sex, race, and marital status (Rawlins, 2004). Similarity is based less on age and more on capabilities. A major barrier to friendship among the elderly is increased health problems (Rawlins, 2004). Health problems may reduce mobility, may prevent reciprocity of support (a key component of friendship), may pose difficulties for communication, and can lead to increased health complaints, which often drive network members away. Although friends are a major source of companionship for the elderly, friends are less likely than family to provide assistance with health problems. Friends do not have the same obligations as family to provide that kind of support.

With advancing age, friendships may increase for women and decrease for men due to differences in the opportunities for friendship. As women get older, they experience the departure of their children from home, which leads to a decrease in household responsibilities. Thus older women are left with more time for friends. For men, increased age brings retirement, which may be associated with a loss of friends if many of their connections are made through work. With retirement, the number of friends often decreases for men, and men's dependence on wives for support and social contacts increases. In addition, women are more likely than men to maintain friendships from their youth in old age (Rawlins, 2004).

A major source of friendship for the elderly, especially women, is the senior center. Elderly women who live alone are more likely than married women to use senior centers, and participation in senior centers is related to better mental health and good health behavior for these women (Aday, Kehoe, & Farney, 2006).

Marital status has a great impact on friendship among the elderly (Akiyama, Elliott, & Antonucci, 1996), especially elderly men. Married men have more people in their social network compared to unmarried men. For men, women are often their link to social relationships. Marital status has no effect on the number of friends that women have because women maintain a network of friends outside their marital relationship. Among the elderly, both women and men have more women friends than men friends (Akiyama et al., 1996). Because men die younger than women, elderly women are more available as friends (see Figure 8.10).

The elderly are the least likely to have friends of the other sex. Elderly people are more likely than younger people to associate cross-sex friendship with romantic interest (Rawlins, 2004), and there is a strong norm

FIGURE 8.10   Partly because women outlive men, and partly because women maintain friendships from youth more than men, friendships among elderly women are strong.

among the elderly against dating. Thus cross-sex friendships are most likely to occur among the elderly in the context of an organized social event involving a lot of other people. Elderly women, in particular, avoid cross-sex friendships. The following example illustrates just how foreign the concept of cross-sex friendship is to an elderly woman. After she was widowed, my mother-in-law lived in an apartment building that housed mostly senior citizens. I often saw a single elderly man sitting by himself at a picnic table outside the building. Even though my mother-in-law was an extremely friendly and sociable person, she did not feel comfortable talking to a man unless she was in the company of other women. If the person at the picnic table were a woman, I have no doubt my mother-in-law would have been sitting right beside her in a minute. It's especially unfortunate for men that the norms against cross-sex interaction are so strong because older men tend to have lost more of their same-sex friends.

The question is whether the norm prohibiting cross-sex friendship is an age effect or a cohort effect. When today's college students reach senior citizen status, will they also find strong norms against cross-sex friendships?

TAKE HOME POINTS

■ Friendship takes on an increasingly important role in the lives of adolescents compared to children — especially for females.

■ Cross-sex friendships are rare among children, peak during adolescence and young adulthood, and diminish substantially among the elderly.

■ The role of friendship in men's and women's lives decreases during early adulthood because family and work roles take up much of people's free time.

■ With the departure of children from the home and retirement, friendship takes on an increasingly important role in women's lives.

■ Elderly men have difficulty maintaining social ties if their friendships are tied to work.

■ Widowhood poses more of a problem for men than women because social connections are often maintained by wives, there are fewer men than women available as friends, and there is a norm against cross-sex friendship.

SUMMARY

Studies on children and adult friendship do not reveal consistent differences in the number of friends that females and males have. However, females' friendships seem to be closer than those of males. One reason for this is the nature of male and female friendship: Men's relationships are agentic— activity focused—and women's relationships are communal—emotion focused. Sex differences in the nature of friendship emerge with age. Boys emphasize the instrumental aspects of friendship (shared activities), and girls emphasize the emotional aspects of friendship (self-disclosure). These differences persist into adulthood.

Girls' and women's friendships are closer or more intimate than those of males. Traditionally, intimacy has been defined by self-disclosure, but this has been a subject of contention. Some people maintain that self-disclosure is a feminine version of intimacy and men define intimacy through shared experiences. Research shows that self-disclosure is important to both men's and women's conceptions of

intimacy, but men's conceptions may also include shared activities. For both women and men, an intimate interaction is one in which they feel understood, cared for, and appreciated. These feelings may come from self-disclosure, shared activities, or some combination of the two. The closeness of male friendships is restricted by competition, homophobia, and emotional inhibition.

Women self-disclose more than men, and women receive more self-disclosure than men. However, it is not the case that men are not capable of self-disclosure. Men simply prefer not to disclose. One reason for sex differences in disclosure is that both women and men view self-disclosure as a feminine activity and view men who self-disclose less favorably than women who self-disclose.

Friendships are not only a source of affection, intimacy, and support but also are a source of conflict. Although women's friendships are closer than those of men, they also may be characterized by more conflict. Women and men handle conflict somewhat differently in their friendships. Women are more likely to confront conflict directly with the intent of resolution and in a way that does not harm the relationship; men raise the issue of conflict, but with less concern about its effect on the relationship.

An emerging area of research is cross-sex friendship. Although cross-sex friends are not as common as same-sex friends, cross-sex friendship is not unusual. Cross-sex friendship is most common among young adults and least common among children and older adults. Social norms and structural barriers discourage children from playing with the other sex, discourage married adults from spending time with the other sex, and inhibit the elderly from developing relationships with the other sex. Women rate same-sex friends as closer than cross-sex friends. However, men are sometimes closer to cross-sex friends than same-sex friends. Cross-sex friendship can serve important functions for women and men, such as insight into the other sex, a source of emotional support for men, and relief from the intensity and conflict of same-sex friendship for women. A number of barriers to cross-sex friendship have been postulated, but little empirical evidence indicates these barriers actually pose serious difficulties with the exception of romantic/sexual attraction. Some evidence suggests this is more of a problem for men than for women. Data are meager on the outcome of cross-sex friendships: Do they last, dissolve, or evolve into romantic relationships?

Cross-race friendships are more common among children than adults. Prejudice and school diversity are related to cross-race friendship.

Friendship is especially important to gay/lesbian/bisexual persons because they receive less support from family members. Gay/lesbian/bisexual persons value the same qualities in a friendship as do heterosexuals. And, friendships with gay/lesbian/bisexual persons are similar to friendships with heterosexuals. The communal/agentic dimensions of friendship used to evaluate heterosexual friendship do not apply to homosexual friendship. Sexuality plays a greater role among the friendships of gay men. Because of the potential for sexual attraction, studies of friendship among gay men and lesbians may benefit from comparisons to cross-sex friendship among heterosexuals.

Friendships at work are increasingly common. Despite the concerns that organizations often have about fraternization among employees, there is evidence that friendship at work is good for productivity. Work presents opportunities for cross-sex friendships but the challenges of cross-sex friendship remain. Friendships at work face some difficulties due to the inherent conflict between the roles of friend and coworker.

The study of friendship is greatly limited by its focus on middle-class White people. Interesting differences appear in the nature of friendship due to ethnicity, social class, and cultural ideology. Friendship also is affected by age and by stage in the life cycle—being married, having children, working. All these factors influence the availability of friends as well as the place of friendship in life.

DISCUSSION QUESTIONS

1. Whose relationships are closer: men's or women's? Why?
2. How should we determine the answer to the previous question? How would you define a friend?
3. What role do self-disclosure and shared activities play in men's and women's friendships?
4. What person and situation variables influence self-disclosure?
5. What inhibits men's self-disclosure to other men?
6. Why are females' relationships considered to be more fragile than those of males?
7. Discuss competition in the context of friendship. Do you believe that it is healthy or unhealthy?
8. Describe how the way a culture construes the roles of women and men could affect their friendships.
9. In what ways are cross-sex friendships similar to and different from same-sex friendships?
10. What are the challenges that cross-sex friendships face?
11. What does the research on same-sex friendship and cross-sex friendship lead you to predict about friendship among gay men and lesbians?
12. What are some critical normative life events that affect friendship? Are the effects for women and men the same?
13. How do marriage and work affect men's and women's friendships?

SUGGESTED READING

Elsesser, K., & Peplau, L. A. (2006). The glass partition: Obstacles to cross-sex friendships at work. *Human Relations, 59,* 1077–1100.

Galupo, M. P. (2009). Cross-category friendship patterns: Comparison of heterosexual and sexual minority adults. *Journal of Social and Personal Relationships, 26,* 811–831.

Rose, A. J. (2007). Structure, content, and socioemotional correlates of girls' and boy's friendships. *Merrill-Palmer Quarterly, 53,* 489–506. Special Issue on Gender and Friendship.

Wright, P. H. (2006). Toward an expanded orientation to the comparative study of women's and men's same-sex friendships. In K. Dindia & D. J. Canary (Eds.), *Sex differences and similarities in communication* (2nd Ed.) (pp. 37–57). Mahwah, NJ: Erlbaum.

KEY TERMS

Audience challenge—Concern that cross-sex friends have about how their relationship is viewed by others.

Autonomy versus connectedness—Conflict encountered by friends at work when the regular exposure to one another required by the work relationship begins to interfere with individual feelings of autonomy.

Co-rumination—Discussing problems repeatedly in the context of a relationship.

Dispositional level of analysis—Emphasizes the characteristics of the person as a determinant of friendship.

Emotional bond challenge—Challenge faced by cross-sex friendship whereby the friends must decide if the closeness they feel toward one another is friendship or romantic love.

Equality challenge—Challenge faced by cross-sex friendships because the equality central to friendship conflicts with the status hierarchy typically associated with male/female relationships.

Homophily—The tendency to form friendships with persons of the same race or ethnicity.

Homophobia—Fear of homosexuality or fear of appearing homosexual.

Impartiality versus favoritism—Situation encountered by friends at work when the desire to give a friend special treatment conflicts with the necessity to treat all workers the same.

Judgment versus acceptance—Difficulty experienced by friends at work when the mutual acceptance expected of friendship conflicts with the requirement that one friend critically evaluate the other.

Openness versus closedness—Situation encountered by friends at work when the expectation of the honest communication central to friendship conflicts with the necessity to keep professional confidences.

Opportunity challenge—Difficulty experienced when attempting to establish a cross-sex friendship that results from the fact that members of the same sex are generally more accessible.

Outgroup homogeneity effect—The tendency to see members of the outgroup as all alike, more similar than different, as compared to the ingroup to which one attributes greater diversity.

Role conflict—Situation that occurs when the demands of one role are inconsistent with the demands of another role.

Sexual challenge—Challenge faced by cross-sex friendship whereby the friends must ask themselves if there is a sexual attraction between them that could lead to a romantic relationship.

Structural level of analysis—Emphasizes the different positions or roles men and women hold in society as a determinant of friendship.

CHAPTER 9

Romantic Relationships

My husband had a number of friends from work with whom we occasionally got together. One of these friends was Bill. My husband had known Bill for about a year, and to his knowledge (or anyone else's), Bill was not romantically involved with anyone. Bill was from India and had gone home for a two-week vacation. When Bill returned, he was married.

This was an arranged marriage, a concept foreign to people in the Western world. Marriage without love? Without romance? It may surprise you to know that romantic relationships are a relatively recent phenomenon even in the United States (Murstein, 1974). Historically, people turned to friends and relatives rather than a spouse for love and emotional support. The functions of marriage were specific: economic security and procreation. Love was not among these functions. One reason love did not play a significant role in marriage is that it was thought to threaten family bonds, which were more important for position in society at that time.

Even a few hundred years ago, love was largely independent of and antithetical to marriage. When two people fell in love, it was regarded as a problem. Parents were concerned about controlling this "dangerous passion." In the 19th century, spouses were polite to one another and, ideally, compatible, but they led largely separate lives. Even by the mid-19th century, love was not a prerequisite to marriage. Love was expected to follow rather than precede marriage. When individual choice did emerge in the 19th century, people generally chose their partner based on character, health, religious morals, and financial stability. These were the same factors that guided parents' choices. Choosing a partner based on physical passion was not at all acceptable.

During the latter part of the 19th century and in the 20th century, the idea of marriage based on love developed. This coincided with American women's increase in freedom and status. The 20th century became known as the century of the "love marriage." Today, the practical functions of marriage have been replaced with more emotional functions. We have very high expectations of marriage. Marriage is expected to be a "SuperRelationship" that fulfills spiritual, sexual, romantic, and emotional needs rather than social, economic, or religious requirements (Whitehead & Popenoe, 2001).

This chapter focuses on romantic relationships, what women and men want from relationships, and how women and men behave in relationships. I discuss how men and women construe the positive aspects of romantic relationships, such as intimacy, love, and sexuality, and also how men and women manage the conflict in their relationships. Research focuses on dating couples, often college students, as well as married couples—both heterosexual and homosexual relationships. One caveat with the research on heterosexuals and sexual minorities is that a large portion of it focuses on White middle-class persons.

There is a growing literature on homosexual relationships, as the issue of same-sex marriage is a contentious political issue in the United States (see Sidebar 9.1 for a discussion of the status of same-sex marriage). Figure 9.1 shows the status of sex-same marriage in the United States (NPR, 2009; State of Hawaii, 1998, State of Washington, 1998).

Studying homosexual relationships is important in its own right, as any theory of relationships ought to be tested on a variety of relationships. However, studying homosexual relationships is particularly interesting from a gender perspective. As Kurdek (2003) describes, gay and lesbian couples are "natural experiments" of relationships without men's paternalistic power and women's maternalistic care. Sex and status are confounded in heterosexual relationships. Research on homosexual relationships can help to tease apart sex from status. To the extent that differences between women's and men's behavior in heterosexual romantic relationships disappears in homosexual relationships, the structure of the heterosexual relationship must contribute to those differences. To the extent that differences in women's and men's behavior appear in both heterosexual and homosexual relationships, those differences must have to do with sex or psychological gender.

RELATIONSHIP DEVELOPMENT

Men and women are definitely interested in romantic relationships. The vast majority of adults want to get married, although the desire is slightly less in women than men (Mahay & Lewin, 2007). Among seventh, ninth, and eleventh graders, 76% say that they probably or definitely will get married; only 5% say that they expect not to marry (Manning, Longmore, & Giordano, 2007).

Characteristics Desired in a Mate

Review the personal ads shown in Table 9.1. In some ways, women and men are looking for different characteristics in a mate. The women seeking men are providing information about their physical attractiveness and seeking men with education and a good work ethic. The men seeking women are interested in finding an attractive mate and providing information about their financial status and work ethic. In the two ads of "women seeking men," we see that both

Sidebar 9.1: *Support for Same-Sex Marriage*

Gay and lesbian relationships have received more recent attention over the past few years in the United States as the subject of same-sex marriage has become pivotal in political elections. Historically, Denmark was the first country in the world to allow same-sex partnerships in 1989. In 1998, the Netherlands was the first country to legalize same-sex marriage. Today, other countries have followed suit, such as Belgium, Spain, Canada, and South Africa. In the United States, Vermont became the first state in the nation to permit civil unions between gay men and lesbians in 2000. These civil unions provide most of the rights and responsibilities of marriage. Connecticut and New Jersey also allow civil unions. In 2004, Massachusetts became the first state to allow same-sex marriage, and in 2005, Canada legalized same-sex marriage. These recent actions have aroused a furor in many states, leading the vast majority of states to develop laws or constitutional amendments to ban same-sex marriage. To date, every state except nine (Connecticut, Iowa, Massachusetts, New Jersey, New Mexico, New Hampshire, New York, Rhode Island, and Vermont) has prohibited same-sex marriage (NPR, 2009; State of Hawaii, 1998; State of Washington, 1998). Thus legal certificates that allow same-sex marriage or civil unions in other states or countries will not be recognized by the majority of the United States. See each state's position on same-sex marriage in Figure 9.1.

Without the right to marriage, many gay men and lesbian women opt for commitment ceremonies. However, the commitment ceremony does not seem to have the same meaning as marriage—in part because it is not accompanied by the same legal rights. Interviews with gays and lesbians in long-term relationships showed that the vast majority would opt for marriage if they had the opportunity (Reczek, Elliott, & Umberson, 2009).

One of the primary objections people raise with respect to gay and lesbian marriage is that it will have an adverse effect on "family values." One study examined this claim and found no relation of a state's same-sex marriage policies to marriage rates, divorce rates, number of abortions, or the number of children born to single women (Langbein & Yost, 2009). Over the past 20 years, attitudes toward homosexuality have changed from being mostly negative to mostly positive (Lubbers, Jaspers, & Ultee, 2009). Acceptance of homosexual relationships also has gathered increasing support. In 2001, 40% of Americans approved of homosexual relations; by 2010, the rate had increased to 52% (Saad, 2010). Likewise, support for same-sex marriage is gradually increasing—especially among younger people. Although the majority of Americans oppose same-sex marriage, the opposition number has decreased from 68% in 1996 to 53% in 2010 (Jones, 2010). People who are opposed to same-sex marriage tend to be Republican, evangelical, and less educated (Fleischmann & Moyer, 2009). The majority of younger people (ages 18–29) support gay marriage (Teixeira, 2009).

women advertise their physical attractiveness and are looking for a stable man with a job, who can handle finances. On the other hand, we also see that both women are educated and independent.

The similarity principle also prevails— the first woman is a huge sports fan and is looking for a sports fan. The second woman likes spending time with family and is looking for someone who is family oriented. The first man emphasizes his interest in sports and music and wanting someone with the same interests. As you will see later, there are important qualities desired by both women

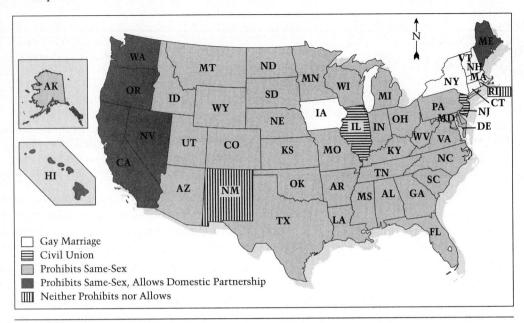

FIGURE 9.1 The status of same-sex marriage in the United States.

TABLE 9.1 PERSONAL ADS

Women Seeking Men

1. A little about me: 35-year-old white female; thick/curvy and very attractive; professional, highly educated; independent; great sense of humor; huge sports fan; consider myself loyal, honest, caring person.

   A little about what I'm looking for: SINGLE male between 29-43; open to all races, ethnicities; has a steady job, own place; good sense of humor; sports fan; a man who can handle an independent woman with a career.

2. Interested in meeting a down to earth Caucasian fellow, age 35-45; looking for qualities such as stability, responsibility, class, good parent to their kids if they have any, able to manage their finances, likes to travel and have fun; would prefer someone who is family oriented. I'm attractive, educated, down to earth, own my home, enjoy cooking; like spending time with family.

Men Seeking Women

1. I'm 28, black, employed and a student, sports fan, honest, very talented, tall; have my own everything (car, apartment, etc); love music, dining out, travel. Hopefully you are: I prefer white or Latina/Hispanic, love sports, music; like to travel, dress well, attractive.

2. I'm a 27 year old guy wanting to meet a petite lady; I'm hardworking, smart, and passionate; great sense of humor; please be 5'3" and under, very thin to medium build.

Source: pittsburgh.craigslist.org 7/28/10.

and men such as a good sense of humor, honesty, and caring.

Evidence.   In general, men and women have similar reasons for entering romantic relationships. Support and companionship are the primary motivating factors. Women and men desire partners who are honest, warm, affectionate, kind, and share their interests. However, some sex differences in desires also appear that are consistent with stereotypes. As indicated in the personal ads, men desire physical attractiveness in a partner, whereas women desire intelligence or occupational status.

In a meta-analysis conducted 20 years ago that compared the characteristics that women and men desired in a mate, results showed that females were substantially more likely than males to emphasize socioeconomic status ($d = -.69$) and ambition ($d = -.67$), but only somewhat more likely to emphasize intelligence ($d = -.30$) and character ($d = -.35$; Feingold, 1992). There was no sex difference in the value attached to personality. In a meta-analysis that was focused only on the importance of a mate's physical attractiveness, men emphasized physical attractiveness in a mate more than women with the size of the difference being larger in self-report studies (ds in the $+.50$ range) than observational studies (ds in the $+.30$ range; Feingold, 1990).

However, these meta-analyses were conducted a long time ago. Do these sex differences still hold? A more recent review of the literature showed that the differences not only still exist but are consistent across a variety of cultures (Shackelford, Schmitt, & Buss, 2005). Women are more likely than men to prefer a mate who has money, ambition, and high social status in 27 of the 37 cultures examined, including the United States, whereas men are more likely than women to prefer a physically attractive mate in 30 of the 37 cultures, also including the United States. A study of single men and women, one-third of whom were Asian and half of whom were European, showed that men were more likely than women to value physical attractiveness in selecting a long-term mate, whereas women were more likely to value intelligence (Furnham, 2009).

Because it is more socially acceptable for men than women to emphasize the physical appearance of a potential mate, demand characteristics that may be exaggerating these differences. A study using fMRI methodology avoided the problems of self-report by having young adult community members rate a series of other-sex faces while in a scanner (Cloutier et al., 2008). More attractive faces were associated with the activation of areas in the brain associated with reward for both men and women. However, one of these areas in particular—the orbitofrontal cortex—was particularly active in response to attractive faces for men. The authors concluded that physical attractiveness has more reward value for men than women.

Women and men are well aware of the fact that they have some different preferences. When college students in the United States, the Netherlands, and Korea were asked how distressed they would be if their partner became interested in someone else who outperformed them on a number of dimensions, males said they would be more distressed than females at rivals who outperformed them in terms of job prospects, physical strength, and financial prospects (Buss et al., 2000). By contrast, females said they would be more distressed than males at rivals who were physically more attractive. These findings held across the three countries.

All of these studies seem to accentuate differences and overlook similarities. Studies that have evaluated the importance of a variety of characteristics show physical attractiveness and status to be relatively *unimportant*. For example, a 2001 national survey of 20- to 29-year-old women showed that 80% believe it is more important that a husband communicate his innermost feelings than make a good living (Whitehead & Popenoe, 2001). The study of single men and women noted above (Furnham, 2009) found that the most important characteristics desired in a mate were caring/loving, funny, and loyal/honest. That study also showed that women rated the importance of 8 of 14 characteristics as more important compared to men, suggesting that women have higher relationship standards than men. A nationally representative sample of seventh through twelfth graders revealed that romantic love, faithfulness, and commitment were the most important values of heterosexuals, gay men, lesbians, and bisexuals (Meier, Hull & Ortyl, 2009).

In general, gay men and lesbians look for the same characteristics in a mate as do heterosexuals—affection, shared interests, similarity, and dependability (Peplau & Fingerhut, 2007). Do gay men and lesbians show the same differences in mate preferences as heterosexual men and women? Unlike heterosexual women, there is no evidence that lesbians value a mate's resources. Having a mate with enough money is viewed as more important to both heterosexual males and females than to gays, lesbians, or bisexuals, suggesting that status is less important to relationships among sexual minorities (Meier et al., 2009). Like heterosexual men, homosexual men seem to value a mate's physical attractiveness, whereas lesbians do not (Hatala & Prehodka, 1996). A study of personal advertisements placed by women showed that lesbians placed the least importance on physical appearance and bisexuals the most

importance, with heterosexual women falling between the two groups (Smith & Stillman, 2002). One study showed that romantic love and commitment were valued more by women than men among heterosexuals, but there were no sex differences when gay men, lesbians, and bisexuals were compared to each other (Meier et al., 2009).

Like heterosexuals, homosexuals may prefer mates who are similar to them. Because the pool of possible mates is smaller for homosexuals, matching may be less possible. Having a mate of the same race (racial homogamy) was viewed as less important to gays, lesbians, and bisexuals compared to heterosexual females and males (Meier et al., 2009). One study showed a striking degree of correspondence between homosexual partners on demographic characteristics, but less correspondence on personality traits (Kurdek, 2003). Lesbians were more likely than gay men to have similar personality traits.

One concern with the research on mate selection is that people are asked to evaluate a single characteristic at a time, which is not how mates are selected in the real world. In real relationships, potential mates possess a number of characteristics, all of which are evaluated simultaneously. Trade-offs may be made depending on the trait's importance and the degree to which it is possessed in a mate. For example, you may prefer a mate who is very nice and very attractive but, if given the choice, you would prefer a very nice average-looking mate to a hostile attractive mate. In a study that examined tradeoffs, women's and men's choices depended on whether the relationship was short term or long term (Fletcher et al., 2004). Given the choice between an attractive mate or a warm mate, men were more likely than women to choose attractiveness in short-term encounters but warmth in long-term relationships.

Given the choice between status and warmth, both women and men chose warmth in short-term and long-term relationships. Another study examined the trade-off issue by giving men and women varying "budgets" for mate selection (Li & Kenrick, 2006). That is, participants were asked to design the ideal mate and given various amounts of "mate dollars" to purchase these characteristics. With a small budget, the typical sex differences prevailed, with women emphasizing a mate's resources and men emphasizing a mate's physical attractiveness. With a larger budget, women's and men's preferences became more similar—especially in long-term relationships.

In conclusion, it appears that women and men agree on the most important characteristics a partner should possess, especially for serious long-term relationships. Physical attractiveness and earning potential are less important characteristics in a mate but ones that heterosexual men and women emphasize differentially—especially in the context of short-term relationships.

Explanations.   What is the explanation for men's preference for physically attractive women and women's preference for financially secure men? Here I review three explanations; the central components of each are highlighted in Table 9.2.

One explanation comes from **evolutionary theory**, which states that women and men behave in ways that will maximize the survival of their genes. Men value physical attractiveness and youth in their mates because these are indicators of fertility. The fact that people are better able to recall attractive than unattractive female faces has been considered evidence that physical attractiveness has evolved as a cue to fertility in women (Becker et al., 2005). There is no difference in the recall of attractive and unattractive male faces. Women prefer mates who have a high occupational status because financial resources will help ensure the survival of their offspring. These ideas are based on the parental investment model, which states that women will invest more in their offspring than will men because they have less opportunity than men to reproduce.

If evolutionary theory can account for sex differences in mate preferences, women who are physically attractive should be more likely than women who are physically unattractive to be paired with mates who are financially stable. Because women's reproductive resources diminish with age, and men's financial resources generally increase with age, evolutionary theory also would predict that younger women would be paired with older men. Indeed, there are vivid instances of young attractive women paired with wealthy older men; Hugh Hefner and Donald Trump are examples of wealthy men who have attracted numerous younger and attractive women. Anna Nicole Smith is an example of an attractive woman who at age 26 married a 90-year-old wealthy oil tycoon, J. Howard Marshall. However, the young beautiful woman coupled with the older wealthy man is the exception rather than the rule. The idea that attractive women will be linked to wealthy, high-status men is known as the "potentials-attract hypothesis." This hypothesis was refuted in a study of young adults who rated themselves on 10 attributes and then rated how much they desired those attributes in a mate (Buston & Emlen, 2003). There was no correspondence between attractiveness in women and desire for status in men or between status in men and desire for attractiveness in women. Instead, the similarity hypothesis prevailed. The higher respondents rated themselves on an attribute, the greater their desire for that

TABLE 9.2   EXPLANATIONS FOR SEX DIFFERENCES IN MATE PREFERENCES

	Supporting Evidence	*Counter-Evidence*
Evolutionary Theory	• cross-cultural evidence men rate attractiveness as more important than women • cross-cultural evidence women rate status as more important than men • men's preference for physical attractiveness in a mate is not affected by the gender traditionality of the culture or by time	• attractive women are not paired with high status men • cross-cultural evidence that men rate domestic skills as more important than women
Social Role Theory	• cross-cultural evidence that women rate status as more important than men • cross-cultural evidence that men rate domestic skills as more important than women • greater sex differences in mate preferences in cultures with distinct female and male roles • sex differences in mate preferences reduced when men and women have less traditional gender-role attitudes • sex differences in mate preferences reduced over time as women's and men's roles have become more similar	• cross-cultural evidence men rate attractiveness as more important than women
Social Construction Theory	• cultural differences in mate preferences • greater sex differences in mate preferences in cultures with distinct male and female roles	

attribute in a mate. When examining who people actually end up with as mates, there also does not appear to be any support for the potentials-attract hypothesis. A study of 129 newlywed couples showed no evidence that physically attractive women were more likely than physically unattractive women to be paired with a financially well-off mate (Stevens, Owens, & Schaefer, 1990). Instead, there was strong support that mates matched on physical attractiveness and education.

Eagly and Wood (1999) have argued that **social role theory** provides a better explanation than evolutionary theory for sex differences in mate selection. They suggest that a society's emphasis on a distinct division of labor between the sexes will be directly linked to sex differences in mate selection. In other words, females will value a mate with high earning capacity and males will value a mate with domestic skills in societies where men's role is to work outside the home and women's role is to work inside the home. Eagly and Wood tested this hypothesis by linking the gender equality of a culture to the size of the sex difference in mate preferences. They reanalyzed the data that Buss and colleagues (1990) had collected on mate selection preferences from 37 cultures around the world. First, they confirmed Buss and colleagues' finding that women were more likely than men to value a mate with high earning capacity and men were more likely than women to value a mate who was physically attractive. However, they also found that men were more likely than women to value a mate who was a good cook and a good housekeeper. This sex difference was as large as the previous two. Evolutionary theory would not lead to this prediction, but social role theory would. Second, sex differences in preferences for a mate with high earning capacity were highly correlated with sex differences in preferences for a mate with good domestic skills. Therefore, cultures in which high earning capacity is valued more by women are the same cultures in which domestic skills are valued more by men. Finally, the gender equality of a culture (as measured by the percentage of women in administrative, technical, and professional positions; the percentage of women in political office; and the percentage of men's salary the average woman earns) was inversely related to the size of the sex difference in earning capacity preference and domestic skill preference, but not physical attractiveness preference. That is, sex differences in earning capacity and domestic skill preference were higher in more traditional cultures. The traditionality of a culture did not have anything to do with the sex difference in the value attached to physical attractiveness.

A more recent study of nine nations has examined an individual's gender-role traditionality rather than the traditionality of the culture and found that sex differences in mate preferences were more common among individuals with traditional gender-role ideologies (Eastwick et al., 2006). Men with more traditional gender-role beliefs showed a greater preference for younger mates with domestic skills, and women with more traditional gender-role beliefs showed a greater preference for older mates with financial resources.

Social role theory would predict that sex differences in mate preferences ought to decrease as women's and men's roles become more similar. Because women are less dependent on men for financial resources today than they were several decades ago, perhaps women's preferences for a high status mate have declined. Changes in mate preferences between 1936 and 1996 show that women have decreased the value they attached to a mate's ambition, men have increased the value they attach to a mate's education and financial assets, and men have decreased the value they place on a mate's domestic skills (Buss et al., 2001). Both men and women have increased their value of physical attractiveness in a mate. In general, men's and women's mate preferences have become more similar over time. Compare mate preferences at your college with the research reviewed here in Do Gender 9.1.

DO GENDER 9.1
Mate Preferences

Identify 10 characteristics of a potential mate. Make sure some of the characteristics are the ones that both women and men rate as important. Also include physical attractiveness and earning potential. Have 10 female and 10 male friends rate how important each characteristic is in a potential mate. Rank the characteristics in terms of relative importance and examine whether there are differences in the value that women and men attach to each characteristic. You might also compare the responses of people who are and are not currently in a romantic relationship. Does being in a relationship alter what people view as important?

A third theory of mate preferences is **social construction theory**, which argues that social norms dictate what is desirable in a mate. A study of American and Israeli college students supported this theory (Pines, 2001). Students were interviewed about their most significant romantic relationship and asked why they had fallen in love. Consistent with evolutionary theory, 80% of men and 53% of women mentioned physical appearance. However, 89% of men and 97% of women mentioned personality, so physical appearance was not the most important feature named. Only 4% of men and women mentioned status, contradicting evolutionary theory. The primary finding of the study, however, was that there were more cultural differences than sex differences in mate preferences, emphasizing how norms shape what is attractive in a mate. Americans were more influenced by status and similarity than Israelis. A study of mate preferences in the United States and the People's Republic of China also supported social construction theory (Toro-Morn & Sprecher, 2003). The most important preferences in a mate were the same for both countries: honest, trustworthy, warm, kind, healthy, sense of humor. The least important preferences also were the same: age, popularity, wealth, and social status. There were more sex differences in China than in the United States. In both countries, men preferred a younger mate and a physically attractive mate compared to women, whereas women preferred a mate with high social status compared to men. These differences, however, were larger in China than in the United States. In addition, only in China did men value a mate who was a good housekeeper more than women. It is not a surprise that the sex differences in mate preferences were larger in a culture where women's and men's roles are more distinct

and there is a greater status differential between women and men. When women have less access to economic resources, it is not surprising that they value a mate's access to economic resources.

Relationship Initiation

Do you remember your first date? How did it come about? Who contacted whom? Who decided what to do? How do women and men become involved in romantic relationships?

Traditionally, the male has taken the initiative in romantic relationships. Today, it is more acceptable for women to invite men on a date, and there are more forums set up for female initiation; there are dances in high school and parties in college where females are intended to initiate. Yet these forums are distinct because they focus on the female as the initiator. Female initiation is not normative. There is evidence that when females initiate first dates, men expect greater sexual involvement—although, in actuality, there is no evidence that more sexual behavior occurs when females initiate (Mongeau et al., 2006).

One way to examine how relationships develop is to examine first date **scripts**. A *script* is a schema or cognitive representation of a sequence of events. These scripts are gender based. In essence, the male is proactive and the female is reactive (Mongeau et al., 2006). The male initiates the date, decides what to do on the date, arranges transportation, pays for the date, and initiates sexual contact. By contrast, the female accepts or rejects the invitation, the plans for the date, and sexual advances (Honeycutt & Cantrill, 2001). Men's first date scripts consist of more gender-stereotypical behavior (e.g., asking for date, initiating sex) than women's first date scripts, which may indicate that the script for a first date is more rigid for men than for women. There is quite a bit of agreement between women and men about how the course of a first date unfolds. College students today still say that men are more likely than women to initiate sex (Dworkin & O'Sullivan, 2007). However, the majority of males also say that they wish women would initiate sex more frequently—in part to share the work of sex and in part because it makes men feel like they are more desirable.

It is interesting that the burden of initiation rests on males when adolescent males today report more awkward communication in romantic relationships, say they are less confident in romantic relationships, and more influenced by their partners compared to females (Giordano, Longmore, & Manning, 2006). Thus, compared to the discussion of self-esteem and self-confidence in Chapter 6, the early stages of romantic relationships may be one arena in which men are less confident and influential than women.

The initiation of a relationship may be more awkward for homosexuals than heterosexuals. One way that a homosexual relationship may develop is out of friendship. Lesbian relationships, in particular, are likely to develop out of friendship (Rose, Zand, & Cini, 1993). However, the progression from friendship to romantic relationship may be difficult for lesbians (Rose et al., 1993). Traditionally, women are not used to taking the initiative in the development of romantic relationships. Thus it may take time for the relationship to move beyond friendship to a romantic relationship. Lesbian friendships may face the emotional bond challenge that confronts cross-sex friendship among heterosexuals: When does the relationship cross over from friendship to romantic love, and are the feelings mutual?

First date scripts have been examined among homosexuals (Klinkenberg & Rose, 1994; Rose & Frieze, 1993). There are some ways in which the first date scripts of homosexuals are similar to those of heterosexuals. Common features included grooming for the date, discussing plans for the date, initiating physical contact, the actual date activity (movie, dinner), and feelings of nervousness. Several differences in the way heterosexual men and women behave also appear in the way gay men and lesbians behave. For example, gay men place a greater emphasis on the physical aspects of intimacy (sex) and lesbians place a greater emphasis on the emotional aspects of intimacy, suggesting that the sex differences observed among heterosexuals is related to being male versus female rather than status. In addition, gay men were more likely than lesbians to discuss making arrangements for the date, suggesting that both homosexual and heterosexual men are more proactive than their female counterparts. With the exception of men being more proactive than women, homosexual scripts did not have stereotypical gender roles; the features of the first date were equally likely to be tied to either partner in the couple.

TAKE HOME POINTS

- Women and men agree on the most important characteristics of a mate—kind, understanding, honest, trustworthy, sense of humor, open and expressive.

- There are consistent sex differences on traits that are relatively unimportant in choosing a mate: Men weigh physical attractiveness more heavily than do women, and women weigh economic resources more heavily than do men.

- The nature of the relationship influences mate preferences. Sex differences are more likely to appear when the relationship is less serious; men's and women's preferences are most similar in serious relationships.

- Gay men and lesbians are attracted to a similar set of characteristics in potential mates as heterosexuals. Gay men, like heterosexual men, are interested in a mate's physical attractiveness — more than lesbians are. However, lesbians, unlike heterosexual women, are not attracted to a potential mate's financial resources.

- People make trade-offs when choosing mates. When trade-offs have to be made, sex differences are minimized, and women and men choose more similar mates.

- Sex differences in mate preferences can be explained by evolutionary theory, social role theory, and social construction theory.

- The weakness of evolutionary theory is that it cannot explain men's preferences for women with domestic skills; the weakness of social role theory is that it cannot explain men's preferences for attractive mates. Both theories, however, can explain why women prefer a mate with greater economic resources.

- Social construction theory of mate preferences is supported by cultural differences in mate preferences. Sex differences in mate preferences may be larger in more traditional cultures where men's and women's roles are distinct and women have less access to economic resources.

- Historically, and still today, society expects men to initiate romantic relationships. Despite this expectation, men may be relatively uncomfortable having this responsibility.

- First date scripts for relationship initiation among heterosexuals and homosexuals contain similar components. Just as heterosexual men take the proactive role in relationships more than heterosexual women, gay men are more proactive than lesbians. However, other aspects of the first date script are not divided by sex in homosexual relationships in the way that they are in heterosexual relationships.

THE NATURE OF ROMANTIC RELATIONSHIPS

Romantic relationships are expected to provide closeness or intimacy, love, and sexual exclusivity. I examine each of these aspects of romantic relationships.

Intimacy

I remember interviewing an elderly couple several months after the husband had suffered a heart attack. I spoke to the two individually. During the course of the separate conversations, I learned that each person had a different conceptualization of "closeness." The wife told me of an occasion when the two of them were sitting together in the living room and watching television. She was not very interested in the television program and he was not talking to her. Because he wasn't paying any attention to her, she went into the other room and called a friend. The husband told me about the same interaction, but it held a different meaning for him. He told me that the two of them were sitting comfortably together watching television, something he defined as a *moment of closeness*. Then, all of a sudden, she disrupted this moment by leaving the room and calling a friend. They were both upset by the sequence of events, but for different reasons. These two people had different definitions of intimacy. She defined *intimacy* by talking or self-disclosure; because the two of them were not talking, she didn't consider the interaction very meaningful, so she called a friend. He defined *intimacy* more as a feeling of comfort in the other's presence and physical proximity. She disrupted this connection by leaving the room.

Although my anecdote suggests differences in women's and men's conceptualizations of intimacy, empirical research has suggested that women's and men's overall conceptualizations are quite similar. One feature of intimacy that seems to be central to women's and men's definitions is self-disclosure. When European and Chinese Canadian dating couples were asked to describe intimacy, the most frequent response was self-disclosure (Marshall, 2008). The Chinese Canadians scored lower on self-disclosure, lower on relationship satisfaction, and higher on traditional gender roles than the European Canadians. And, traditional gender roles accounted for part of the group difference in self-disclosure and relationship satisfaction.

The role of self-disclosure in intimacy is evolving as our access to one another has exponentially increased due to online communications and technologies. For younger people, disclosure increasingly takes place via cell phone, via text, and via personal pages, such as Facebook. A 2007 survey showed that 25% of teens communicate with a boyfriend or girlfriend by cell phone or text message between midnight and 5 A.M. (Subrahmanyam & Greenfield, 2008). Teens both initiate and terminate relationships with these methods. When my daughter started middle school in sixth grade, I was amazed to learn that some of her friends were "going out" with one another. I naively asked exactly what this involved. It typically involved a text-related initiation of a relationship, a text-maintained relationship, and a text-related breakup. I remember agonizing for hours about how to break up with a guy when I was 14 years old. If only text messaging had been available! Another convenient way to break up with someone today is to change one's status from "in a relationship" to "single" on one's Facebook page.

There is some evidence that the relation between intimacy and sex differs for women and men (Vohs & Baumeister, 2004). An increase in intimacy is associated with a greater increase in passion among males than females. And, females seem to require greater intimacy than males to develop passion. Expressing feelings, such as saying "I love you," prior to sex is more strongly associated with positive feelings about the relationship and about having had sex among females than males (Metts, 2004). Even among teens, males are more likely than females to incorporate sex into their notions of an intimate relationship (Cavanagh, 2007).

Both females and males are likely to include romance in their conceptions of an intimate relationship (e.g., We would hold hands; think of ourselves as a couple).

If men are more likely than women to define intimacy through sexuality, we would expect the most sexual behavior to occur among two gay men and the least to occur among two lesbians. This turns out to be true (Herek, 2006; Peplau & Fingerhut, 2007). It is not clear why lesbians have the least sex. It may be because lesbians are less interested in sex, the traditional concept of sex as intercourse does not apply, or females have difficulty initiating sex. Like heterosexual males, the same level of intimacy is not required for the development of passion among gay men compared to women (Vohs & Baumeister, 2004). Gay men develop passion more quickly than heterosexual females and lesbians.

If women's friendships are closer than those of men and women are more relationship focused than men, it seems likely that a romantic relationship between two women will be closer or more intimate than a romantic relationship that involves at least one man. This turned out not to be the case in a comparison of the intimacy level of cohabiting lesbians, cohabiting gay men, and heterosexual married people (Kurdek, 1998). Instead, lesbians and gay men reported greater intimacy than heterosexual married people. Despite the higher intimacy, lesbians and gay men also reported a greater sense of autonomy than heterosexual married couples (e.g., having separate friends from partner, making decisions without checking with partner).

Love

What is love? Many people have shared poetic thoughts ("Beauty and Love Quotes," 2000):

"To love a thing means wanting it to live." (Confucius, *Analects*, 6th century B.C., 12.10, translated by Ch'u Chai and Winberg Chai)

"As selfishness and complaint pervert and cloud the mind, so love with its joy clears and sharpens the vision." (Helen Keller, *My Religion*, 1927)

"The simple lack of her is more to me than others' presence." (Edward Thomas, 1878–1917, English poet)

Even second graders have strong opinions about love. Here are a few comments they made (Noel, 1997):

"When someone comes over, or you're hanging around someone, you know when you're in love. After you love someone, you play with the person you love for a long time." (male)

"When you're in love, you're very nervous. When he or she is very nice and sweet to you for a long time and you are never fighting, you know you're going to be in love and hope it will last a long time." (female)

"When a girl hugs you or kisses you, you know when you're in love. When the girl gives a ring to a boy and the girl says 'I love you.' Then you go out to dinner." (male)

"When you meet someone who likes you, and you like them, then you know you're in love. Then you go on dates. Then it's marriage time, and you might have a baby." (female)

From distinguished poets to second graders, the ideas of love for women and men have been adequately captured. All the elements are there: wanting to spend time together (a very long time), feeling nervous, showing affection, and putting the other person first.

When it comes to matters of the heart, who is more romantic: men or women? One way this question was first addressed was to ask people whether they would marry someone with whom they were not in love. In a study conducted several decades ago, Kephart (1967) asked over 1,000 college students, "If a boy (girl) had all the other qualities you desired, would you marry this person if you were not in love with him (her)?" The majority of the men (65%) but only a small portion of the women (24%) said no. In fact, one of the women remarked, "I'm undecided. It's rather hard to give a 'yes' or 'no' answer to this question. If a boy had all the other qualities I desired, and I was not in love with him—well, I think I could talk myself into falling in love!" (p. 473). This study concluded that men view love as more central to marriage than women do. In this sense, men could be considered the more romantic sex.

One reason men were more romantic than women had to do with the historical relationship between the sexes. Women were marrying not just a man, but a way of life; thus women were taught to be practical in mate selection. Men could "afford" to fall in love. Today, women are more likely to be economically independent than they were 30 years ago. Do Kephart's findings still apply?

More recent studies of the Kephart question have suggested that men and women are equally romantic when it comes to marriage. In a study of college students in the United States, Japan, and Russia, women's and men's responses were similar in the United States and Japan (Sprecher et al., 1994). As shown in Figure 9.2, over 80% of both men and women said they would *not* marry the person if they were not in love with him or her; that is, love was necessary for marriage. In Russia, the sex difference appeared. Women were less likely than men to view love as a basis for marriage. Russians, in general, had less romantic ideals than the Japanese or Americans. Do Gender 9.2 at your college to see if the findings hold.

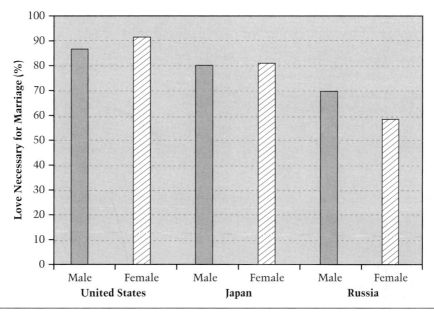

FIGURE 9.2   Students in the United States, Japan, and Russia were asked the "Kephart question" (whether they would marry someone who had all the qualities they desired in a mate but they were not in love with the person). Men and women in the United States and Japan were equally likely to say they would not marry the person, that love was the basis for marriage. Only in Russia were women less likely than men to view love as necessary for marriage.
Source: Adapted from Sprecher, Aron, et al. (1994).

DO GENDER 9.2
Who Is More
Romantic in Love?

Ask 10 women and 10 men the following question: "If a man (woman) had all the other qualities you desired, would you marry this person if you were not in love with him (her)?"

Either have a scale of response options (yes, no, unsure) or create a 5-point scale ranging from 1, definitely no, to 5, definitely yes. What other variables besides sex might be associated with responses? Does age matter? Does ethnicity matter? What about parents' marital status? Gender roles?

Despite the fact that we view women as more relationship oriented than men, research suggests that men are more likely than women to have romantic notions about love. Men score higher than women on the romantic beliefs shown in Table 9.3: (a) love finds a way or conquers all; (b) there is only one true love for a person; (c) one's partner is perfect; and (d) one can fall in love at first sight (Hendrick & Hendrick, 2002). Men fall in love more quickly compared to women. Women are more likely to have a practical view of relationships, believing that it is possible to love more than one person and that economic security is more important than passion to a relationship (Frazier & Esterly, 1990). Thus men may still hold more romantic ideals than women. Although women have achieved greater

TABLE 9.3 Romantic Beliefs Scale

Love Finds a Way

1. If I love someone, I will find a way for us to be together regardless of the opposition to the relationship, physical distance, or any other barrier.
2. If a relationship I have was meant to be, any obstacle (e.g., lack of money, physical distance, career conflicts) can be overcome.
3. I expect that in my relationship, romantic love will really last; it won't fade with time.
4. I believe if another person and I love each other we can overcome any differences and problems that may arise.

One and Only True Love

1. Once I experience "true love," I could never experience it again, to the same degree, with another person.
2. I believe that to be truly in love is to be in love forever.
3. There will be only one real love for me.

Idealization of Partner

1. I'm sure that every new thing I learn about the person I choose for a long-term commitment will please me.
2. The relationship I will have with my "true love" will be nearly perfect.
3. The person I love will make a perfect romantic partner; for example, he or she will be completely accepting, loving, and understanding.

Love at First Sight

1. I am likely to fall in love almost immediately if I meet the right person.
2. When I find my "true love" I will probably know it soon after we meet.
3. I need to know someone for a period of time before I fall in love with him or her.

Source: Adapted from Sprecher and Metts (1989).

economic independence over the past several decades, most women expect that they will not be the sole income provider. Thus women may still have some reason to be more practical when it comes to love.

Another way that men's and women's approaches to love have been addressed is by examining "styles" of loving. According to Lee's (1973) theory of love, there are three primary love styles: **eros**, or romantic love; **storge**, or friendship love; and **ludus**, or game-playing love. There are also three blends of these love styles: **mania**, or manic love, is a blend of eros and ludus; **pragma**, or practical love, is a blend of storge and ludus; **agape**, or pure love, is a blend of eros and storge. The

love styles are depicted in Figure 9.3, and sample items are shown in Table 9.4.

Sex differences appear on some of these love styles. Women typically score higher than men on pragma and storge, and men score higher than women on ludus (Hendrick & Hendrick, 2009). The sex difference in pragma is consistent with the previously reviewed research showing women are more practical than men when it comes to love. The sex difference in ludus is certainly consistent with our stereotypes that men are less willing than women to commit to a relationship. Ludus is associated with lower relationship satisfaction, and storge and pragma are unrelated to relationship satisfaction. Women and men score similarly

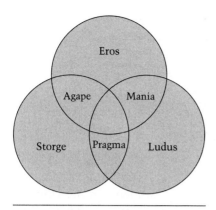

FIGURE 9.3 Love styles.
Source: J. A. Lee (1973).

on eros, which is associated with higher re-lationship satisfaction. One limitation of this research is that most of it has been conducted with college students. It would be interesting to see how people's love styles change with age.

Emotional investment is a concept that includes some of these notions about love.

Specifically, it reflects one's self-perception of being loving, lovable, romantic, affectionate, cuddlesome, compassionate, and passionate. A study of 48 nations showed that women scored higher than men on emotional invest-ment in all but three nations—with the differ-ence being significant in 34 nations (Schmitt et al., 2009). Unexpectedly, the gender-equality of the nation was associated with *larger* sex differences. For example, the largest sex dif-ferences in emotional investment were found in Switzerland, Australia, and Germany and smaller sex differences were found in Turkey, South Korea, and Bolivia. The authors sug-gested that women and men are more likely to make within-sex comparisons in nations where female and male roles are more distinct, making it appear that women and men are similar to one another. By contrast women and men may be more likely to make between-sex comparisons in nations where there is greater

TABLE 9.4 LOVE STYLES

Eros

My lover and I have the right physical "chemistry" between us.
I feel that my lover and I were meant for each other.

Ludus

I try to keep my lover a little uncertain about my commitment to him or her.
I enjoy playing the "game of love" with a number of different partners.

Storge

It is hard to say exactly where friendship ends and love begins.
The best kind of love grows out of a long friendship.

Pragma

I consider what a person is going to become in life before I commit myself to him or her.
An important factor in choosing a partner is whether or not he or she will be a good parent.

Mania

When my lover doesn't pay attention to me, I feel sick all over.
When I am in love, I have trouble concentrating on anything else.

Agape

I would endure all things for the sake of my lover.
I cannot be happy unless I place my lover's happiness before my own.

Source: Hendrick and Hendrick (1986).

variability in female and male roles leading to the perception of larger sex differences.

Sexuality

Men seem to be more satisfied with their sexual relationships than women. Across 29 countries, men reported higher sexual well-being compared to women (Laumann et al., 2006). The sex difference was larger in male-centered countries, such as Brazil, Korea, and Morocco, where there is a greater status differential between men and women. Men may be more satisfied with sex than women because men are more likely to initiate sex or because men are more likely to disclose their sexual desires. In a study of college dating couples, males were more likely than females to discuss sex, including their sexual desires, while females were more likely than males to report that they had difficulty getting their partner to do what they wanted during sex (Greene & Faulkner, 2005). Thus, here is one arena where men seem to communicate more effectively than women.

Attitudes Toward Sex. Sexual attitudes and behaviors have become more permissive over the years. In 1940, two-thirds of college women and one-third of college men said that premarital sex was wrong (Lance, 2007). Those numbers have decreased dramatically. Today, the majority of women and men find sex between an unmarried woman and man acceptable, men slightly more so than women—63% of men compared to 56% of women said that premarital sex was morally acceptable (Saad, 2010).

There are some differences between women's and men's attitudes about sex. First, women have more negative attitudes toward sex compared to men (Geer & Robertson, 2005). Even at younger ages, this seems to be true. A study of adolescents showed that males identified more benefits from having sex compared to females (e.g., physical pleasure, reduced loneliness, respect from friends), whereas females identified more costs associated with sex compared to males (e.g., lose respect from friends, guilt, embarrassment; Deptula et al., 2006).

Second, men have more permissive standards compared to women, meaning men find sex to be more acceptable in general. However, sex differences in attitudes toward sex depend on the degree of commitment in the relationship. College students in the United States, Russia, and Japan were asked how acceptable it was to have intercourse on a first date, a casual date, when seriously dating, when preengaged, and when engaged (Sprecher & Hatfield, 1996). Students rated acceptability for themselves, for a typical male, and for a typical female. Not surprisingly, students in all three countries rated sexual intercourse as more acceptable as the commitment of the relationship increased. People in all three cultures agreed sexual intercourse was not acceptable during the early stages of a relationship. As shown in Figure 9.4, in all countries, men viewed sexual intercourse as more acceptable than women did during the early stages of the relationship, but there were no sex differences in acceptability during the later stages of the relationship. When engaged, about 90% of respondents gave at least some approval to sexual intercourse. Americans were more permissive than the Japanese, and Russians fell between the two groups. These cultural differences were strongest among the more committed relationships. Overall, men place greater emphasis on sex compared to women in both homosexual and heterosexual relationships (Peplau & Fingerhut, 2007), suggesting that this is a domain of behavior that is more strongly related to sex than status.

Women and men tend to believe there is a double standard in regard to sex—that it is more acceptable for men than women to engage in sex. However, laboratory research is not

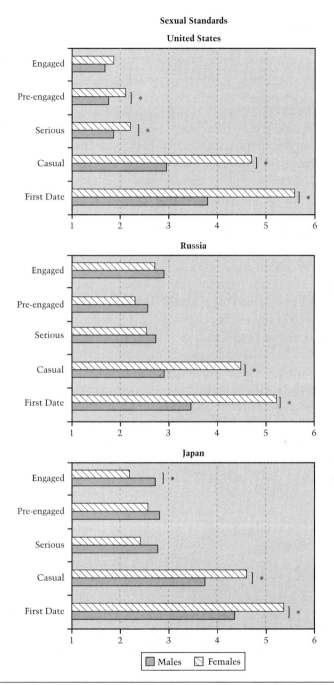

FIGURE 9.4   Sexual standards. Among students from the United States, Russia, and Japan, men have more permissive standards for sexual intercourse than women do when the relationship is more casual. In serious relationships, men and women view sexual intercourse as equally acceptable. Note: Higher numbers mean less permissive; *indicates a sex difference.
Source: Adapted from Sprecher and Hatfield (1996).

clear on this issue. A study of college students and Internet participants were asked to evaluate a female and a male target who had a varying number of sexual partners. Both female and male participants evaluated targets with more sexual partners more negatively—regardless of whether the target was female or male (Marks & Fraley, 2005). Subsequent research showed that the double standard is a stereotype and that stereotypes are more likely to be applied when attention is limited. College students were asked to evaluate a female or a male target who had 1, 7, or 19 sexual partners (Marks, 2008). Half of the students were asked to read the vignette and answer the questions while rehearsing an eight-digit number throughout the experiment, and the other half were not. The double standard appeared only when people were distracted by the rehearsal task. This condition is shown in Figure 9.5. Male and female targets with 1 and 7 partners were evaluated similarly but female targets with 17 partners were viewed more negatively and male targets with 17 partners were viewed more positively.

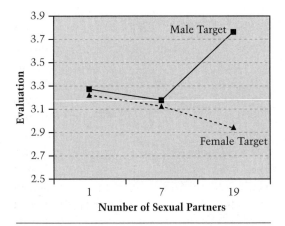

FIGURE 9.5   When attention was divided, participants evaluated male and female targets with 1 and 7 partners similarly. Evaluations of male targets with 19 partners increased, and evaluations of female targets with 19 partners decreased.
Source: Adapted from Marks (2008).

Outside of these vignette studies, the double standard was evaluated among seventh through twelfth graders by linking a student's popularity to number of sexual partners (Kreager & Staff, 2009). Popularity was measured by having each student nominate their five best female friends and five best male friends. Number of nominations received was the measure of popularity. As shown in Figure 9.6, females' popularity was unaffected by whether they had 0 to 8 sexual partners, but was dramatically reduced if they had more than 8 partners. By contrast, the more sexual partners a male had, the more popular he was. In fact, males with no sexual partners were viewed as less popular than females with no sexual partners.

Taken collectively, the double standard seems to be alive and well, but it operates in the more extreme cases. The double standard is also the product of a confirmation bias—that is, people tend to notice information that confirms the double standard but fail to notice information that disconfirms the double standard (Marks & Fraley, 2006). When respondents were provided with a vignette with equal positive and negative statements about a person's sexuality, they were more likely to recall the negative statements when the target was female and more likely to recall the positive statements when the target was male. See if a double standard exists in your school with Do Gender 9.3.

Men not only have more permissive attitudes toward sex, but men also find it more acceptable to try to attract someone else's mate, a phenomenon referred to as "mate poaching." In a study of nearly 17,000 people across 53 countries, more men than women admitted to engaging in mate poaching and to succumbing to mate poaching—meaning that they became involved with other women when they were in a committed relationship (Schmitt et al., 2004). Consistent with social

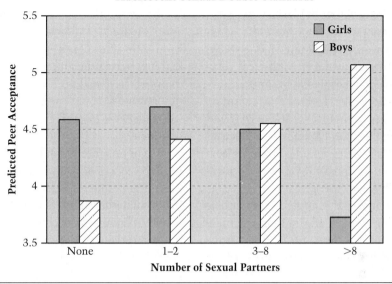

Adolescent Sexual Double Standards

FIGURE 9.6 There is a linear relation between number of sexual partners and peer acceptance for male targets. Acceptance for female targets did not differ between 0, 1-2, and 3-8 sexual partners but dramatically decreased for more than 8 sexual partners.
Source: Kreager & Staff, 2009

role theory, the sex difference in mate-poaching was reduced in countries that provided greater access to resources for women.

Men seem to draw the line at sex when the mate is already married. That is, the vast majority of both women and men in the United States as well as many other countries

disapprove of extramarital affairs (Sprecher, 2006). Although attitudes toward sex in general and sex before marriage have become more liberal over the past few decades, attitudes toward extramarital affairs have not changed and remain negative. Among women, 93% believe that extramarital sex is wrong or almost always wrong, whereas the corresponding figure for men is nearly as high—89% (Thornton & Young-DeMarco, 2001). Nearly two-thirds (64%) of both men and women say that they would not forgive their spouse for having an affair and would likely divorce (Jones, 2008). However, research also shows that the relationship is more likely to end after women than men have affairs (Brand et al., 2007; Fisher et al., 2008). Although both college women and men equally value monogamy in a mate and believe that it is important for a relationship, men are more likely than women to view monogamy as a sacrifice (Schmookler & Bursik, 2007).

DO GENDER 9.3
Sexual Double Standard

Ask a group of men and women to rate the acceptability of sexual intercourse for a man and a woman involved in various levels of relationship commitment (e.g., met at a party, dating for six months, engaged). Do women or men hold a double standard (i.e., believe sex is more acceptable for women than for men) at any particular stage of a relationship?

Because of the way we view the connection between sex and love in women and men, we view extramarital affairs differently when committed by women and men. In one study, college students viewed a hypothetical relationship between a single friend and a married person (Sprecher, Regan, & McKinney, 1998). Students' perception of the married person having the affair depended on whether the person was male or female. Students perceived the female married person as more committed to the affair, as more in love, as more likely to marry the single friend, and as less likely to have other affairs than the male married person. Women and men had similar views on this issue. Thus, people seem to believe that women have affairs only when they are in love with another person but that men have affairs without being in love. It is also possible that people perceive male extramarital affairs as more common than female extramarital affairs and, thus, less meaningful.

First Sexual Experiences.   Given the more permissive attitudes toward sex, it is not a surprise that the age of first intercourse has declined over the years (Wells & Twenge, 2005). The decline is larger among women compared to men. In the late 1960s, the average age of first intercourse was 19 for women and 18 for men. By the 2000s, the median age of first intercourse was 17 (Ott & Santelli, 2007). By 2009, 29% of females and 34% of males in ninth grade had had sex, and 65% of females and 60% of males in twelfth grade had had sex (Centers for Disease Control and Prevention, 2010a). Thus, the majority of youth have had sex by the time that they are 18 years old. The onset of sexual intercourse is earlier in Black boys than White boys but the same among Black and White girls (Zimmer-Gembeck & Helfand, 2008). The onset is similar among Hispanics and Whites and is later among Asian Americans compared

to Whites. These differences remain even when socioeconomic status is taken into consideration. Figure 9.7 shows the percentage of youth in middle school and high school who have had sex. Across the different grades, more boys than girls have had sex. I would have to say that the "abstinence only" campaign is not working. (See Sidebar 9.2 for an expanded discussion of that issue.)

Not only are youth having their first sexual experiences at younger ages but people are marrying at older ages, which means that the first sexual intercourse is much less likely to be with the person who becomes one's spouse. This is not surprising as the median age at first intercourse is almost 10 years earlier than the age at which people marry! Among today's 18- to 19-year-olds, the first sexual partner is likely to become the spouse in 6% of the cases, whereas among today's 50- to 59-year-olds, the first sexual partner was the spouse nearly half the time (45%; Laumann, Mahay, & Youm, 2007).

What predicts the onset of sex? A review of 35 longitudinal studies showed that

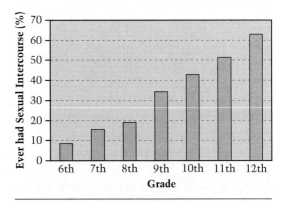

FIGURE 9.7   Percentage of students who have ever had sexual intercourse. Note that the figures for middle school reflect median rather than mean. *Source*: Middle school figures taken from U.S. Department of Health and Human Services (2005); High school figures taken from Centers for Disease Control and Prevention (2006b).

Sidebar 9.2: *Does Abstinence Only Work?*

During the last decade, the federal government has spent more than $1.5 billion on abstinence-only-until-marriage education among upper elementary and middle-school children (Young, 2009). There are a number of tenets of abstinence only education, the most notable of which are (1) abstinence of sex until marriage is the expected standard, and (2) sexual intercourse outside of marriage is associated with harmful psychological and physical consequences. There is no mention made of contraception or condoms, except with respect to failure rates.

In 2005 to 2006, four- to six-year follow-up data were evaluated from programs in Virginia, Florida, Wisconsin, and Mississippi that had randomized students to abstinence only education or a control group that did not receive this program (Trenholm et al., 2007). Results showed no group differences in sexual behavior—49% of students in both groups had remained abstinent. The age of sexual initiation was the same in both groups. There was also no group difference in unprotected sex, which was surprising given that other research has shown that those who pledge abstinence are less likely to use contraception when they break their pledges. Another study in which teens were randomly assigned to an abstinence-only program or not had similar findings—no difference in age at first sexual activity, no difference in unprotected sex, and no difference in the number of sexual partners (Trenholm et al., 2008). A small study of African American students contrasted abstinence only and comprehensive sex education with a control group and showed a modest effect for abstinence only programs to delay sex but only comprehensive sex education programs reduced the number of sexual partners (Jemmott, Jemmott, & Fong, 2010). A study of over 12,000 15- to 19-year-olds showed that those who had had comprehensive sex education were less likely to get pregnant than those who had received abstinence only or no formal sex education (Kohler, Manhart, & Lafferty, 2008). Those who had had comprehensive sex education also were slightly less likely to have engaged in sex than the other two groups. A review of the literature has shown that there is little evidence for the effectiveness of abstinence-only programs and some evidence for potential harm (Ott & Santelli, 2007). By contrast comprehensive sex education programs delay the initiation of sex and reduce risky sexual behaviors.

In terms of the negative consequences of sexual intercourse among adolescents, it is noteworthy that there is little evidence that premarital sex is associated with poor health outcomes, unless the sex was forced, prepubertal, or with a relative (Else-Quest, Hyde, & DeLamater, 2005). For females, negative consequences are more likely if the relationship dissolves soon after sex and if the relationship lacks any kind of emotional commitment (Meier, 2007). However, in the vast majority of cases, sexual intercourse among adolescents is not associated with negative mental health outcomes. It seems unreasonable to have a program aimed at teaching that sexual intercourse is reserved for marriage when the vast majority of Americans have had premarital sex. By age 44, 95% of people have had sex before marriage (Finer, 2007). Given the high rates of sexual activity before marriage and the fact that the United States has the highest rates of teen pregnancy among developed countries, abstinence only education without information on effective contraceptive use seems to be a fairly irresponsible approach. Ott and Santelli (2007) suggest that abstinence only education programs violate the human rights of adolescents by withholding important information on contraception.

Sex education in schools is more likely to be opposed by people who are religious and Hispanic (Chappell & Maggard, 2010). Yet, formal sex education seems to be associated with delaying sex and using birth control when youth first have sex—and this is especially the case among African American women (Mueller, Gavin, & Kulkarni, 2008).

early onset of sexual intercourse is associated with alcohol use, delinquency, and for females, depression (Zimmer-Gembeck & Helfand, 2008). Religiosity predicts girls waiting until they are 18 or older to have sex, and anxiety predicts the same in boys. Familial factors are more strongly associated with the onset of sexual intercourse among Black and Hispanic families than White families. A study of African American girls ages 15–17 showed that closer relationships to mothers were associated with a lower likelihood of having had sex (Usher-Seriki, Bynum, & Callands, 2008). African Americans talk with their parents more about sex and receive more education from parents about sex compared to Whites and Latinos, whereas Asian Americans talk less with their parents about sex than Whites and Latinos (Calzo & Ward, 2009; Epstein & Ward, 2008; Sprecher, Harris, & Meyers, 2008).

Perhaps in response to the abstinence only campaign, some young people have taken a pledge of virginity. Does it work? Yes, and no. Yes, it works in the sense that people who make a public or written commitment to refrain from sex until marriage delay sex compared to those who do not make a pledge. (In this case, *sex* is defined as sexual intercourse. It turns out that pledgers are more likely to have oral and anal sex than nonpledgers.) No, it does not work in that the vast majority of people who make this pledge have sex before marriage. One study followed seventh through twelfth grade pledgers and nonpledgers for five to six years and showed that 88% of pledgers had sex before marriage compared to 99% of nonpledgers (Bruckner & Bearman, 2005). One cause for concern is that pledgers were less likely than nonpledgers to use condoms during the first sexual intercourse. Although the rate of sexually transmitted diseases (STD) was the same for the two groups, pledgers were less likely than nonpledgers to be tested for STDs. There are important differences between virginity

pledge studies and abstinence only programs. People are choosing to engage in a virginity pledge rather than being randomly assigned to take such as pledge, as is the case with research on abstinence only programs.

Motives for Sex. There are both similarities and differences in the reasons that males and females choose to have sex and choose to refrain from sex. Girls' and boys' reasons for having sex are similar: love for their partner, curiosity, and sexual desire (Albert, Brown, & Flanigan, 2003). Boys and girls also agreed that having sex increases a boy's—but not a girl's—popularity.

Research, largely based on college students, also suggests that men have a recreational orientation toward sex in which physical gratification is the goal and a relationship is not required, whereas women have a relational orientation toward sex in which sex is integrated into the relationship as a way to convey intimacy (Regan & Berscheid, 1999). When college women and men were asked what caused sexual desire, love was cited as a cause of women's sexual desire by 42% of respondents and of men's sexual desire by 10% of respondents. Instead, 66% of respondents identified personal causes of sexual desire in men, such as physical need, hormones, and alcohol, whereas 33% identified these factors as causes of sexual desire in women. Respondents also thought the physical environment, such as a romantic setting, was more likely to lead to sexual desire in women than in men.

These sex differences have been replicated among homosexuals. In one study, heterosexual and homosexual men were more interested in having sex for pure pleasure, to relieve sexual tension, and to please their partner than heterosexual and homosexual women (Leigh, 1989). Heterosexual and homosexual women were more interested than men in having sex to express emotional closeness. Thus the difference in motives for sex is a function of people's sex rather than sexual orientation.

Women's and men's motives for sex also can be examined in their motives for infidelity. College students who had been in an exclusive relationship and reported being emotionally or sexually unfaithful to their partner identified a number of reasons for the infidelity (Barta & Kiene, 2005). The number one reason for both men and women was being dissatisfied with the current relationship, although women endorsed this option more than men. The second and third reasons were partner neglect and revenge, for which there were no sex differences. The least endorsed reason was interest in sex and sexual variety, which men endorsed more than women—again supporting the idea that men (at least college-age) have a more recreational view of sex than women. Another study of college students suggested that the primary reason for infidelity for both women and men was attraction to the person (Brand et al., 2007). After that, women were more likely than men to report being unhappy in the current relationship and both were likely to report being bored with the current relationship.

TAKE HOME POINTS

- On the whole, men and women conceptualize intimacy in the same ways. Intimacy includes expressions of love and appreciation, feelings of happiness and contentment, and self-disclosure.

- Sex may be a more important component of intimacy for both heterosexual and homosexual men than women, but it is still not the most important feature of intimacy for men.

- Historically, women had a more practical view of love and men had a more romantic view. Today, the sex differences are smaller, but men still tend to hold more romantic ideals than women.

- Men and women are equally accepting of sex in serious relationships. In more casual relationships, men are more accepting of sex.

- A double standard exists regarding sex in casual relationships, such that it is more acceptable for a man than a woman to engage in premarital sex.

- Both men and women are disapproving of extramarital sex, but women show stronger disapproval than men do.

- There is some evidence that sex may have different meanings for men and women, especially among younger people. Men have a more recreational view of sex and women a more relational view.

- This difference may explain why both women and men perceive that a woman who has an extramarital affair is more serious about the relationship partner than a man who has an extramarital affair.

- The age of first sexual experience is lowering, and the majority of young people have sex before marriage despite abstinence only education and pledges of virginity.

- Abstinence only education and pledges of virginity seem to delay sex but do not postpone sex to marriage and may be associated with less contraceptive use.

Maintaining Relationships

Consider the following book titles that appeared in the past decade:

Creating a Healthy Life and Marriage: A Holistic Approach: Body, Mind, Emotions and Spirit (Desjardins, 2010)

Getting the Love You Want: A Guide for Couples (Hendrix, 2007)

Ten Lessons to Transform Your Marriage: America's Love Lab Experts Share Their Strategies for Strengthening Your Relationship (Gottman, Gottman, & Declaire, 2006)

Couple Skills: Making Your Relationship Work (McKay, Fanning, & Paleg, 2006)

What do these books have in common? First and foremost, they are all geared toward the preservation or maintenance of relationships. Second, toward whom are these books directed? Survey the sex of the people browsing through this section of your local bookstore. As you will see in this section of the chapter, women are typically regarded as the caretakers of relationships.

Maintenance Strategies

What do people do to keep a relationship going? One way that couples maintain relationships is via a series of cognitive mechanisms that reflect both accuracy and bias (Luo & Snider, 2009). In terms of accuracy, couples who have an accurate perception of each other are happier. In terms of bias, couples who view each other more positively than they really are (positivity bias) and couples who perceive each other as more similar than they really are (similarity bias) are happier. Although women show more biases than men, the biases are equally associated with marital satisfaction for both women and men.

Another way relationships are maintained is through accommodation. *Gender-role attitudes* is one such domain. In both married and cohabiting couples, when one partner is traditional, the other partner is more likely to become traditional and when one partner is egalitarian, the other partner is more likely to become egalitarian (Kalmijn, 2005). The effect of men on women is similar to the effect of women on men, but the effects partly depend on the nature of the view. Wives' egalitarian views have a stronger effect on husbands than wives' traditional views. And, husbands' traditional views have a stronger effect on wives than husbands' egalitarian views.

There are some maintenance behaviors that wives are especially more likely to engage in than husbands. First, wives maintain relationships by taking on more than their share of the division of labor in the family. This topic will be discussed in more depth in Chapter 11. Second, wives sacrifice personal leisure time (Canary & Wahba, 2006). For example, at the end of the day when both husband and wife are sitting down watching television, the wife is likely to be folding laundry or creating a grocery list at the same time.

Emotion skills are another way of maintaining relationships. *Emotion skills* refer to the management of one's own and one's partner's emotions during interactions. Softening the delivery of a negative message, being open and receptive to others' communication, anger directed at the behavior rather than the person are examples of emotion skills. In a study of married couples discussing an area of disagreement, the display of emotion skills was associated with marital satisfaction for both women and men (Mirgain & Cordova, 2007). Women scored higher than men on some—but not all—domains of emotion skills.

In married couples, sexual activity can be construed as a maintenance behavior. Sexual activity is both a source of marriage vitality and a source of marriage conflict. Interviews with couples who had been married for over seven years revealed that sexual activity was a barometer of a healthy marriage (Elliott & Umberson, 2008). Couples agreed that the main conflict over sex was in terms of frequency and that husbands desired sex more than wives. In response to this problem, both wives and husbands made attempts to address this problem. Wives said that they purposely tried to become more interested in sex, whereas husbands said that they sometimes tried to inhibit their sexual desires. Sexual desire also was tied to the division of labor. Men participated in household labor in an attempt to reduce their wives' workload and enhance their wives' sexual desire; and wives said that this was effective!

Relationship maintenance behaviors may differ somewhat in dating couples and newly married couples. One study examined both heterosexual and homosexual dating relationships and asked couples what they did to maintain their relationship. Heterosexual women reported being more likely to engage in a variety of strategies than their male counterparts, including monopolizing the mate's time, derogating competition, providing sexual inducements, and enhancing one's appearance (VanderLann & Vasey, 2008). By contrast, there was only one strategy in which heterosexual men engaged more than women—displaying resources. Homosexual men generally behaved like heterosexual men, with one exception. Homosexual men were less likely to display resources than heterosexual men. Homosexual women, however, did not behave like heterosexual women. Lesbians were less likely to use all of the above-mentioned strategies than heterosexual women. In a study of newlywed couples, all of these kinds of mate retention strategies decreased over the first four years of marriage (Kaighobadi, Shackelford, & Buss, 2010). However, some sex differences persisted. Men were more likely than women to display resources, whereas women were more likely than men to enhance their appearance. In addition, men were more likely than women to use submissive behavior—that is, state they were willing to change to accommodate their partner.

It is not only women who maintain relationships but partners of either sex who score high on expressivity or psychological femininity are likely to be concerned with relationship maintenance. Both wives and husbands who score higher on expressivity put more effort into improving the relationship and engage in more maintenance strategies (Canary & Wahba, 2006).

Not surprisingly, couples are more likely to engage in relationship maintenance behaviors when they are in love with their spouse, satisfied with the relationship, and committed to the relationship. It turns out that relationship feelings are a better predictor of maintenance behaviors for wives than husbands (Canary & Wahba, 2006). The most maintenance behaviors occur in a relationship that the wife perceives as equitable, and the least maintenance behaviors occur in a relationship in which the wife feels underbenefited—that she receives less from the relationship than her partner. The husband's perception of relationship equity seems to be less related to maintenance behavior.

Relationship Satisfaction

What predicts how satisfied men and women are with their romantic relationships? One predictor is relationship talk—the extent to which the couple talks about the state of the relationship. Relationship talk is more strongly related to women's than men's marital satisfaction (Badr & Acitelli, 2005). The distribution of power within a couple is a predictor of marital satisfaction. Overall, characteristics of marriage seem to be more strongly linked to women's than men's marital satisfaction (Schmitt, Kliegel, & Shapiro, 2007). People also speculate as to whether homosexual relationships are as satisfying as heterosexual relationships. Here I discuss each of these issues.

Power Distribution. One determinant of relationship satisfaction is in how power is distributed between women and men. One would expect that younger women and men should have more equal power in relationships because they are less likely to adhere to traditional roles. College women and men, in particular, have a similar status and similar access to resources. Thus there is reason to predict that power will be distributed equally in college relationships. However, most dating couples report an imbalance of power in their relationship, usually in the direction of the male having more power (Sprecher & Felmlee, 1997).

One way that power has been assessed in relationships is by the "principle of least interest" (Waller, 1938). The principle of least interest is that the more emotionally uninvolved person in the relationship influences the quality and stability of the relationship. In a longitudinal study of heterosexual dating couples, the majority of couples reported relatively equal involvement but when involvement was unequal, both women and men agreed that the female was more emotionally involved than the male (Sprecher, Schmeeckle, & Felmlee, 2006). Equal emotional involvement was associated with greater relationship satisfaction. Unequal emotional involvement predicted relationship breakup—especially so for females.

One of the difficulties with studies of the distribution of power in relationships is that they are based on self-report. A more creative methodology to assess power in relationships was developed in an older study and applied to several cultures (Wagner et al., 1990). The investigators asked women and men in Austria, the United States, India, and Turkey to imagine they bought a fairly expensive product and their spouse either approved or disapproved of the purchase. Respondents were asked to rate how good or bad they would feel in each situation. The discrepancy between how the person felt when the spouse disapproved versus approved represented "dependence on the other's agreement," which would reflect low power. In other words, if you feel really good when you buy something of which your spouse approves and really bad when you buy something of which your spouse disapproves, you have low power in the relationship. By contrast, if your feelings are relatively unaffected by whether your spouse approves or disapproves of your purchase, you have high power in the relationship.

As expected, in families in which the husband was dominant, men were less dependent than women. This means that men were less affected than women by whether their spouse approved or disapproved of their purchase. In egalitarian families, men and women were equally dependent. Interestingly, these findings held for only the two Western cultures, Austria and the United States. There was actually less dependence in the traditional patriarchal cultures of India and Turkey. If the families are more patriarchal, meaning husbands are dominant, why aren't wives more affected by their husband's approval versus disapproval? The authors explain that the traditional gender roles in India and Turkey are independent roles: Men's and women's roles are distinct from one another and they function in those roles independent of one another. This means that each person has great control over her or his domain but little control over the spouse's domain. They grant each other this power. If one person makes a purchase, the other would have little to say about it. Determine the level of "dependence" in your own and your peers' relationships with Do Gender 9.4.

One reason that it is difficult to evaluate whether power is equitable is that people can report an equal power relationship in two ways. First, power can be equal because the two people share responsibility for all domains; this is the definition of a true egalitarian relationship. Second, power can be equal such that one person has exclusive power in some domains and the other person has exclusive power in other domains; thus there is

DO GENDER 9.4
Economic Independence

One way to determine whether your relationship is *egalitarian* is to examine economic independence. How much can you spend without asking your partner? How much can your partner spend without asking you? What is the most you have ever spent without asking your partner? What is the most your partner has ever spent without asking you?

Now try the Wagner and colleagues' (1990) experiment. Ask each member of a couple to imagine making a fairly expensive purchase. Ask them to imagine that their spouse approves and to rate how they would feel: 1 = Feel very bad and 5 = Feel very good. Then ask them to imagine that their spouse disapproves and to rate how they would feel: 1 = Feel very bad and 5 = Feel very good. To determine power, evaluate the discrepancy in ratings for spouse approval versus disapproval (higher discrepancies equal less power).

an *average* balance of power. This is the situation that characterized the Turkish and Indian marriages. But, are these egalitarian relationships? They can be, but often they are not. If the domains of power are divided along traditional gender-role lines, such that women have power over child care matters and men have power over economic resources, it is unlikely the relationship is truly egalitarian.

One determinant of relationship satisfaction for both women and women is **equity** (Cahn, 1992). An equitable relationship is one in which a person feels that what she or he puts into and gets out of a relationship is equal to what the partner puts into and gets out of the relationship. People who report they are overbenefited (receive more from the relationship than their partner) or underbenefited (receive less from the relationship than their partner) are dissatisfied in relationships, whether male or female (Cahn, 1992). Women who are overbenefited feel guilty, whereas women who are underbenefited feel angry (Pillemer, Hatfield, & Sprecher, 2008). One study showed that women—but not men—being underbenefited predicts divorce (DeMaris, 2007), whereas another study showed that women—but not men—being overbenefited predicts lower marital satisfaction (Goodman, 1999). Thus, it appears that equity is a stronger determinant of relationship quality for women than men. See Sidebar 9.3 for an interesting view of equity and egalitarianism in relationships by Hugh Hefner.

Equality may be more central to gay and lesbian relationships than heterosexual relationships. Same-sex couples have a more egalitarian division of labor in the home than heterosexuals (Herek, 2006). Equality may be especially important to lesbian couples. One study showed that lesbian couples had more shared decision making and equal power compared to gay male or heterosexual couples (Kurdek, 2003). Equality also seems to be strongly linked to relationship satisfaction among lesbians (Peplau & Beals, 2001). These findings are interesting because we know women are more focused than men on equality in heterosexual relationships. Thus equality may have more to do with being female than with being female in the context of a heterosexual relationship.

Social Exchange Theory. According to **social exchange theory**, relationship satisfaction is partly determined by the benefits gained and costs incurred in a relationship. Benefits may be love and support as well as the partner's income. Costs may

SIDEBAR 9.3: *Equity in Relationships According to Hugh Hefner*

In 1999, Hugh Hefner claimed his relationships with his four girlfriends are equal. Here is an excerpt from an interview with Hugh Hefner (by Terry Gross) on National Public Radio (November 29, 1999):

GROSS: Now, here's something I sometimes wonder about couples in which there is a really big age disparity between them.... Like, if you're 52 years older than the woman you're seeing, she ... In some ways, she couldn't possibly be your equal because you've lived a long time, you've been very successful, you've amassed a fortune, and published this world-renowned magazine, whereas they're not even out of college yet. So, it just wouldn't be possible for them to function as your equal.

HEFNER: Is that of some importance?

GROSS: Well, if I was the woman in the relationship, it would be important to me.

HEFNER: Well, I think—quite frankly—that people are attracted to one another for a variety of reasons. There is more than one kind of equality. And in my relationship with the women that I am seeing right now, there is a very real equality in terms of who makes the decisions in the relationship in what we do and how we spend our time, etc. But, I would say that the relationships are more complementary than equal. Each of us brings something different to the relationship. I bring the experience and the years and the wisdom and whatever. And they bring a very special joy, [they] relate to life that is not so sophisticated, not so cynical, and very refreshing.

be time, money, and effort in maintaining the relationship. One prediction from social exchange theory is that the person more dependent on the relationship will have less power in the relationship; the person who has greater personal resources (education, income) will have more power in the relationship. Because women are often more economically dependent on relationships than men, this theory may explain why women are less satisfied than men. Social exchange theory predicts relationship satisfaction for heterosexual and gay men's relationships but less so for lesbian relationships (Peplau & Fingerhut, 2007). The link of resources to power among lesbians is less clear.

Characteristics of Him but Not Her.

Although there are common determinants of relationship satisfaction for women and men, there also is evidence that characteristics of

men are more likely than characteristics of women to predict a partner's or spouse's satisfaction. For example, men's emotional communication skills are associated with wives' marital satisfaction, but women's emotional communication skills are not related to husbands' marital satisfaction (Cordova, Gee, & Warren, 2005). Wives are also more influenced than husbands by their spouse's psychological state. In a study where husbands and wives recorded their emotions periodically throughout the day, the husband's emotions influenced the wife's emotions, but the wife's emotions had no impact on the husband's emotions (Larson & Pleck, 1999). In general, there is more evidence of **emotional transmission** from husbands to wives than wives to husbands (Larson & Almeida, 1999).

Research on gay and lesbian couples can help us determine whether the finding that women are more strongly affected by men than men are by women is due to something about women or something about men. One such study showed that one partner's emotion during a conflict discussion was related to the other partner's relationship satisfaction among lesbian couples but not gay male couples (Gottman Levenson, Gross, et al., 2003). Similarly, one partner's sadness while discussing the events of the day was related to lower relationship satisfaction for the other partner among lesbian couples, but not gay male couples. Thus, it appears that all of these findings suggest that women are more strongly affected than men by their partners.

Why are women more affected than men by what is happening with their partner? Aspects of the female and male gender roles provide some clues. Women are socialized to focus on others, which may explain why others' feelings and behavior influence women's feelings and behavior. By contrast, men are socialized to focus on the self, which may explain why it is only attributes of the self that determine men's feelings and behavior. In addition, women are more skilled than men in detecting another's emotions,

which may make them more responsive to others' emotions (Larson & Pleck, 1999).

Sexual Orientation.   There is a stereotype that gay men and lesbians have less well-functioning relationships. However, the research does not support this claim (Peplau & Fingerhut, 2007). The vast majority of studies shows that gay men and lesbians are as committed and satisfied with their relationships as heterosexuals (Herek, 2006; Peplau & Fingerhut, 2007). Laboratory research has shown that gay and lesbian relationships are similar to that of married individuals in terms of self-reports of the quality of the relationship, observations of interactions, and physiological reactivity to those interactions (Roisman et al., 2008). In a 10-year longitudinal study of the relationships of gay men, lesbians, and heterosexuals with and without children, relationship satisfaction remained the same over the 10 years for lesbians, declined and then returned to the initial state among gay men, declined somewhat and then leveled off for heterosexuals without children, and steadily declined among heterosexuals with children, as shown in Figure 9.8

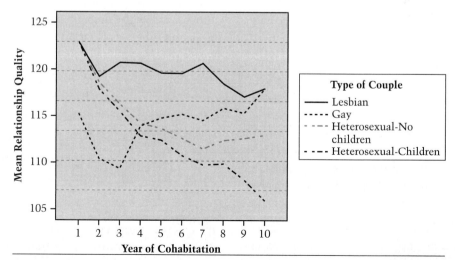

FIGURE 9.8   Relationship Quality over 10 Years of Cohabitation Among Lesbians, Gay Men, Heterosexuals without Children, and Heterosexuals with Children.
Source: Kurdek, 2008a

(Kurdek, 2008a). Note that at the end of the 10 years, relationship satisfaction was highest among lesbians and gay men. Thus the sex difference in marital satisfaction among heterosexuals (male more than female) pertains more to the nature of heterosexual male-female relationships than to sex (i.e., being male or female).

In general, the same kinds of variables that are associated with relationship satisfaction among heterosexuals also are associated with relationship satisfaction and commitment among homosexuals (Herek, 2006; Kurdek, 2006; Kurdek, 2008b). Commitment to a relationship is typically a function of the positive forces that attract one to a relationship and the barriers to leaving a relationship. This commitment process functions the same among heterosexuals and homosexuals although homosexuals face fewer barriers to relationship dissolution than heterosexuals. Homosexual marriage is typically not recognized by the law, and homosexuals are less likely to have children. Although homosexuals are less likely to have family support to maintain the relationship, they are more likely to have friend support (Herek, 2006). Overall, homosexuals face fewer barriers to leaving a relationship.

TAKE HOME POINTS

- Women engage in more relationship maintenance than do men.

- Women's maintenance behaviors are more strongly related to relationship outcomes than men's maintenance behaviors.

- One factor that influences relationship satisfaction is the power balance of the relationship. In general, more egalitarian relationships are associated with relationship satisfaction for both women and men.

- There are different ways of conceptualizing egalitarianism: joint participation or separate but equal participation. The latter may not be a truly egalitarian philosophy.

- Social exchange theory predicts relationship satisfaction for heterosexuals and gay men but is less applicable to lesbian relationships.

- Women's relationship satisfaction is more affected by characteristics of their partner than is men's relationship satisfaction.

- Homosexual relationships are not inferior in quality to heterosexual relationships.

- The same variables that predict relationship satisfaction among heterosexuals predict relationship satisfaction among homosexuals. In terms of commitment, homosexuals face fewer barriers to leaving a relationship than heterosexuals.

CONFLICT

Popular books suggest that men and women experience a good deal of conflict. The title of Lillian Rubin's (1983) popular book *Intimate Strangers* implies that men and women face considerable conflict. In my opinion, this book and others exaggerate the difference between women and men as well as their potential for conflict. However, women and men may approach conflict in different ways.

Conflict Management

When conflict arises, how do men and women handle it? A meta-analysis on conflict resolution strategies in business showed that women are more likely than men to compromise across most cultures (Holt & DeVore, 2005). Men are more likely than women to use a forceful style, which means being goal oriented rather than concerned with the effect on relationships—but only in individualistic cultures. However, women and men may approach conflict in their personal relationships somewhat differently than they approach conflict at work. When Israeli couples were asked about the conflict tactics that they and their partners employed, both women and men were more likely to say that they used soft tactics (e.g., express disappointment, express appreciation for compliance) rather than harsh tactics (e.g., threaten, get angry, emphasize obligation; Schwarzwald, Koslowsky, & Ishak-Nir, 2008). However, men were more likely than women to say that their partner used harsh tactics. Use of harsh tactics was associated with lower marital satisfaction.

One way conflict management has been studied is by observing couples' behavior in the laboratory as they discuss a relationship problem. Distressed spouses in general display more disagreement and more criticism than nondistressed spouses, but this difference is more apparent among women than men. Women display more emotion, in particular more negative affect, than men during conflict discussions (Heyman et al., 2009)—and this is especially the case among distressed couples (Carstensen, Gottman, & Levenson, 2004). However, cultural factors can override this tendency. In a study of U.S. and Pakistani couples, U.S. wives were more negative than Pakistani wives in low satisfaction couples likely because Pakistani culture inhibits the expression of emotion in women (Rehman & Holtzworth-Munroe, 2007). And, negative communication was more strongly related to marital dissatisfaction among U.S. than Pakistani couples. This explains why women in the United States are referred to as the "emotional barometer" of relationships (Floyd & Markman, 1983): If the woman is displaying high negativity, the relationship is likely to be in distress.

The display of negative affect in women may not reflect distress as much as their approach to managing the conflict. Whereas women are more likely to confront the conflict, men are more likely to withdraw or be defensive (Carstensen et al., 2004). When distressed couples come into the laboratory, the wife sees it as an opportunity to resolve a conflict. Thus, she confronts the conflict, which includes displays of negative affect. The husband's goal, by contrast, is to keep the conflict from escalating; thus he responds to her negative affect with displays of either neutral or positive affect. That is, he tries to smooth things over. Rather than perceiving his response as a positive one, she is frustrated that he is not becoming engaged in this conflict. In other words, she perceives her husband's lack of negative affect as a sign that he is not engaged in the interaction. Women then respond by intensifying their negative behavior, which is referred to as *negative reciprocity*. Then, the conflict escalates.

The following exchange illustrates this sequence of events:

WIFE: Let's talk about why you don't help out more with the children. (confrontation of conflict with negative affect)

HUSBAND: You do such a good job with the children that it doesn't seem like this is really an issue of conflict. (attempt to neutralize the affect with positive statement)

WIFE: : You just don't get it, do you? If you spent more time with the children, you could do a good job too. (more negative affect, reciprocity of negative affect, escalation of conflict)

There is some evidence that gay and lesbian couples may be more effective in addressing conflict than heterosexual couples. In a relationship interaction study, lesbian, gay, and heterosexual couples were videotaped discussing a problem (Gottman, Levenson, Swanson, et al., 2003). Homosexual couples were less belligerent, less dominant, and more likely to maintain a positive tone throughout the interaction compared to their heterosexual counterparts. Homosexual couples also used more affection and humor throughout the interaction compared to heterosexual couples.

Demand/Withdraw Pattern

Here's another interaction between a wife and a husband. Read this and decide what is going on here.

PERSON A : Why don't you spend a little more time working inside the house?

PERSON B : What? What do you mean?

PERSON A : You are never at home and when you are at home, you don't even clean up after yourself. I have to clean up everything.

(silence)

PERSON A : You could at least read Mandy a bedtime story.

(still no response; in fact, the sound of a newspaper opening up can be heard)

Links to Gender. Woman or man? Who do you believe is more likely to be Person A? Person B? This episode is an example of the **demand/withdraw pattern** (Christensen & Heavey, 1993). It is characterized by one person demanding, if not nagging, and the other person not responding, or withdrawing. The demander is more likely to initiate problem discussion, whereas the withdrawer is more likely to avoid problem discussion. Among distressed and nondistressed couples, the demander is more likely to be a woman and the withdrawer to be a man (Christensen & Heavey, 1993; Gottman, 1994). In public, women are more likely to appear deferential and polite, but in the private sphere of marriage, women confront

and demand (Gottman & Carrere, 1994). This demand/withdraw pattern has been present in marriage since the early part of the 20th century (Gottman & Carrere, 1994).

Numerous studies of married couples have been conducted that rely on couples' self-reports of demand and withdraw behavior as well as on coders' observations of such behavior while couples discuss problems. There is a great deal of agreement between the two measures of demand and withdraw behavior. Apparently couples know who demands and who withdraws. Across these studies, Christensen and Heavey conclude that about 60% of couples are characterized by wife demand/husband withdraw, 30% by husband demand/wife withdraw, and 10% by an equal proportion of both demanding and withdrawing.

Explanations. Why do wives tend to be the demanders and husbands tend to be the withdrawers? There are three explanations. Christensen and Heavey (1993) suggest that wives and husbands have a fundamental conflict: Women prefer closeness and men prefer independence. This is the basic dilemma identified by Rubin (1983) and Chodorow (1978). Men can achieve independence on their own, but women require the support of their partner to achieve closeness. This fundamental conflict leads women and men to employ different strategies in relationships. Women need to demand to obtain closeness, whereas men can withdraw to achieve independence. Christensen and Heavey measured conflict over closeness versus independence and found this type of conflict is associated with greater demand/withdraw behavior. In addition, the person who wanted greater closeness (usually the woman) was more likely to be the demander, and the person who wanted greater independence (usually the man) was more likely to be the withdrawer.

Another explanation for the wife demand/husband withdraw pattern is that it is wives who most often want change in the relationship. A study that asked couples about the changes that they would like to see in their spouse showed that women desired more change than men (Heyman et al., 2009). Women wanted spouses to participate more in household chores, be more involved in parenting, express more emotion, and spend more time with them. Men, by contrast, requested change in only one area—increased sex.

If this explanation is true, one should observe more husband demanding when the husband wants change in the relationship. In the first test of this idea, Christensen and Heavey (1993) had married couples with children talk about an area in which the mother wanted a change and an area in which the father wanted a change. The two interactions were videotaped. Self-reports and observer ratings of demand/withdraw behavior showed that the typical wife demand/husband withdraw pattern was found when the issue was one in which the mother desired a change (shown on the left side of each of the figures in Figure 9.9). When the issue was one in which the father desired a change (the right half of the figures), there was less mother demanding and more father demanding. However, the pattern did not completely reverse itself. When the couple discussed the father's issue, there was no sex difference in the demand/withdraw pattern.

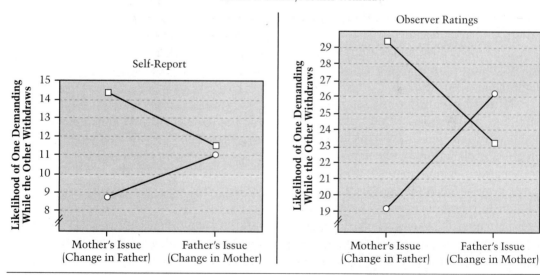

FIGURE 9.9 Demand/withdraw pattern. When the issue being discussed is one in which mothers are concerned, the typical wife demand/husband withdraw pattern is observed. There is little husband demand/wife withdrawal. When the issue being discussed is one in which fathers are concerned, wife demand/husband withdrawal decreases and husband demand/wife withdrawal increases. However, the pattern does not completely reverse itself. Thus the wife demand/husband withdraw pattern is not only a function of wives having more concerns in the relationship.

Source: A. Christensen and C. L. Heavy (1993). Gender differences in marital conflict: The demand/withdraw interaction pattern. In S. Oskamp and M. Constanzo (Eds.), Gender issues in contemporary society (Vol. 6, pp. 113–141). Beverly Hills, CA: Sage.

These findings have been replicated by more recent research on heterosexual, gay, and lesbian couples (Eldridge et al., 2007; McGinn, McFarland, & Christensen, 2009). When the woman wants the change, there is greater female demand and male withdrawal; the pattern changes but does not reverse itself when the male wants the change. In addition, the level of distress in the relationship influences these findings (Eldridge et al., 2007). The findings shown in Figure 9.9 apply more to distressed couples. The expected cross-over pattern (wife demand/husband withdraw for her topic; husband demand/wife withdraw for his topic) is more likely to be found among nondistressed couples. Thus, the idea that demand behavior is linked to the person in the relationship who wants the most change is a good explanation for behavior in non-distressed couples. There must be additional explanations as to why the demand/withdraw pattern is linked to gender in distressed couples. Examine the demand/withdraw pattern and predictors of this pattern in couples you know in Do Gender 9.5.

When husbands want change, why isn't there more evidence that husbands demand and wives withdraw? This bring us to the third explanation for the demand/withdraw pattern. The demand/withdraw pattern may be related to the power structure in relationships and the lower status of women relative to men. Demanding behavior may be an attempt to improve one's status, whereas withdraw behavior may be an attempt to maintain the status quo. Couples may have a history of resolving men's issues compared to women's issues in marriage because men desire less change in relationships and because men have greater power in relationships (Christensen & Heavey, 1993). Thus, men's issues are addressed, meaning that there is less probability of getting into any

DO GENDER 9.5
Who Demands
and Who Withdraws?

Come up with your own self-report measure of demand and withdraw behavior. Some sample items adapted from Christensen and Heavey (1993) are shown here. Measure the frequency with which such behavior occurs among dating couples you know by asking them to complete your survey. Is there evidence that women demand more? Men withdraw more? Is relationship satisfaction related to demand/withdraw? Do you find that the less satisfied person engages in more demand behavior? What other predictions would you make based on the literature reviewed in this chapter?

Sample Demand/Withdraw Items

One person nags and the other person refuses to discuss the topic.
One person makes demands and the other person is silent.
One person criticizes and the other person withdraws.
One person tries to start a conversation about a problem and the other person tries to avoid the topic.

kind of demand/withdraw cycle. The fact that there are no sex differences in demand or withdraw behavior in gay and lesbian relationships (Holley, Sturm, & Levenson, 2010) suggests that the demand/withdraw pattern found in heterosexual relationships is due to the status differences between men and women rather than sex. However, the differential power hypothesis was explored in one study by measuring indicators of power and linking these indicators to demand and withdraw behavior (Vogel et al., 2007). This hypothesis was refuted, as demand and withdraw behaviors were unrelated to occupational status differences between wives and husbands and influenceability by partner. However, there may be other ways of assessing power that could be linked to demand and withdraw behavior.

Cultural differences in demand and withdraw behavior show the linkage to power. Although demand behavior has been linked to being female and withdraw behavior has been linked to being male in Brazil, Italy, and Taiwan (Christensen et al., 2006), other cross-cultural research has shown that demand and withdraw behavior have different meanings in some cultures. In a study of American and Pakistani couples, female demand/male withdraw was greater among Americans than Pakistanis, and male demand/female withdraw was greater among Pakistanis than Americans (Rehman & Holtzworth-Munroe, 2006). The nature of demand and withdraw behavior, however, differed between the two countries. Whereas Americans conceptualize withdraw behavior as reflecting resistance to change, withdraw behavior in Pakistan may reflect a less powerful position—resigned acceptance. Demands on the part of American women were more dominant and aggressive, whereas demands of Pakistani women were more unassertive and pleading. Thus, withdraw behavior among Pakistani women reflected a lack of power and their demand behavior was more passive.

A fourth argument as to why women demand and men withdraw is that women have a greater tolerance for the physiological arousal that conflict produces (Gottman, 1994; Levenson, Carstensen, & Gottman, 1994). Gottman has suggested that men may avoid situations that produce physiological arousal because their bodies recover more slowly from arousal than women's bodies.

Thus men may find the physiological arousal that conflict produces more aversive than women do and withdraw from it. One problem with this explanation is that numerous studies show that women become more physiologically aroused than men during discussion of conflict, as you will see in Chapter 11. Gottman (1994) argues that men's lack of physiological arousal is due to their withdraw behavior being effective.

Thus, the female demand/male withdraw pattern observed in the United States can be explained partly in terms of women's and men's personalities, partly in terms of the structure of marriage (e.g., women perceive more problems, women have less power), and partly in terms of culture.

Implications for Relationships.   What are the implications of the demand/withdraw pattern for relationships? Not surprisingly, high rates of demand/withdraw behavior are associated with poor conflict resolution (McGinn et al., 2009) and low marital satisfaction across a variety of cultures (Christensen et al., 2006; Rehman & Holtzworth Munroe, 2006). However, the negative effect of demand/withdrawal behavior is buffered by the expression of affection (Caughlin & Huston, 2002). In other words, demanding and withdrawing are less likely to be linked to low marital satisfaction if couples are affectionate toward one another.

The effect of the demand/withdraw pattern on marital satisfaction also appears to depend on who is demanding and who is withdrawing. An older study showed that wife demand/husband withdraw behavior was associated with declines in wife satisfaction over time, but husband demand/wife withdraw behavior was associated with *improvements* in wife satisfaction over time (Heavey, Christensen, & Malamuth, 1995).

Why would husband demand behavior be associated with an improvement in wife marital satisfaction? One theory is that demanding behavior reflects engagement in the relationship, and wives are happy that husbands are engaged. In both studies, demand/withdraw behavior did not predict changes in husbands' marital satisfaction, which is consistent with previous research on the predictors of marital satisfaction. Characteristics of the spouse or relationship affect wives more than husbands.

Jealousy

In the context of romantic relationships, jealousy is the concern that there is a rival for the other's affections. There is little evidence for sex differences in jealousy (Wright, 1999). When a difference is found, it is usually in the direction of women being more jealous than men. One concern with this research is that men may be less likely than women to admit jealousy.

Different events may inspire jealousy in men and women. According to evolutionary theory, different situations should provoke jealousy in women and men. Because men are uncertain of the paternity of their offspring, they should be extremely upset by sexual infidelity: Sexual infidelity not only jeopardizes the chance of a man's genes surviving but also means that a man could be investing his resources into raising a child that is not genetically related to him. Sexual infidelity should be less disturbing to women because it does not threaten their genetic link to offspring. Instead, women should be more upset by their partner falling in love with someone else, or emotional infidelity. Emotional infidelity could lead the husband to take his resources elsewhere and invest in children with someone else; thus in that sense emotional infidelity threatens the viability of the female's offspring.

In a now classic study, Buss and colleagues (1992) tested this idea by asking college students whether they would be more disturbed by sexual or emotional infidelity. The exact wording of the questions is contained in Table 9.5. They found that women were more distressed by emotional than sexual infidelity, and men were more distressed by sexual than emotional infidelity. In a subsequent experiment, the investigators also found physiological effects that paralleled the self-reports of distress. Men were more physiologically reactive when they imagined their partner being sexually unfaithful rather than emotionally unfaithful, whereas women were more physiologically reactive when they imagined their partner being emotionally rather than sexually unfaithful. These findings have been confirmed by more recent studies (Schmookler & Bursik, 2007)—with one notable exception. The majority of both men and

TABLE 9.5 **EMOTIONAL VERSUS SEXUAL INFIDELITY**

Imagine you discover that the person with whom you've been seriously involved became interested in someone else. What would upset or distress you more (please circle only one in each set):

Set A

(A) Imagining your partner forming a deep emotional attachment to that person.

(B) Imagining your partner enjoying passionate sexual intercourse with that other person.

Set B

(A) Imagining your partner trying different sexual positions with that other person.

(B) Imagining your partner falling in love with that other person.

Source: Buss et al. (1992).

women are more distressed by emotional infidelity than sexual infidelity (Fernandez et al., 2007). As shown in Figure 9.10, both men and women are more upset by emotional infidelity than sexual infidelity, but men are more upset than women by sexual infidelity and women are more upset than men by emotional infidelity. It also appears that the sex differences are not necessarily borne out when more unobtrusive measures are used. When the Implicit Association Test was used to determine how negatively females and males viewed emotional and sexual infidelity, there was no sex difference in reaction time to linking either emotional or sexual infidelity to positive or negative words (Thomson et al., 2007). However, men did make more mistakes than women when classifying sexual infidelity words in the presence of the positive prime. The authors labeled these mistakes *cognitive interference* and concluded that men are more attentive than women to sexual infidelity.

Findings for homosexual couples are similar to those for heterosexual couples.

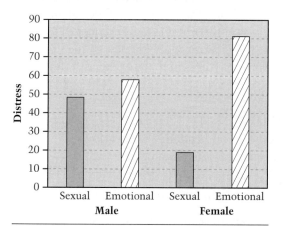

FIGURE 9.10   Men are more upset by sexual infidelity than women, and women are more upset by emotional infidelity than men. However, both men and women are more upset by emotional infidelity than sexual infidelity.

Source: Adapted from Fernandez et al. (2007)

When both heterosexual and homosexual women and men were asked the questions shown in Table 9.5, heterosexual women, gay men, and lesbians all said emotional infidelity was more distressing than sexual infidelity (Sheets & Wolfe, 2001). Heterosexual men said the two kinds of infidelity were equally distressing. Thus heterosexual men were relatively more upset by sexual infidelity than gay men, lesbians, and heterosexual women.

If men—at least heterosexual men—are more distressed than women by sexual infidelity, it would make sense that men may be more likely than women to monitor their partner's fidelity. Men report more suspicion about infidelity and are more likely to discover that a partner has cheated on them compared to women (Andrews et al., 2008; Brand et al., 2007). This was demonstrated in a study of heterosexual dating college students in which both partners completed questionnaires that asked whether they had had sex with someone else during their relationship, whether they thought their partner had had sex with someone else, and how confident they were in the latter assessment (Brand et al., 2007). Confidentiality and anonymity were assured. Men were fairly certain that their partner either did or did not have sex with someone else, whereas women expressed more uncertainty about whether their partners were unfaithful. When the two partners' responses were compared (see Table 9.6), men were much more accurate than women in detecting infidelity (75% compared to 41%). However, men were slightly less accurate than women in detecting fidelity (i.e., estimating that their partner had been faithful when in fact their partner had been faithful; 93% vs. 96%). Men are more likely to detect infidelity than women for two reasons (Andrews et al., 2008; Brand et al., 2007). First, women are more likely than men to disclose their infidelity. Second,

TABLE 9.6   PERCEPTION OF PARTNER BEHAVIOR

		Actual Male Partner Behavior			
		Faithful		Unfaithful	
Female Perception	Faithful	134	96%	34	59%
	Unfaithful	6	4%	24	41%
		140		58	⌐198

		Actual Female Partner Behavior			
		Faithful		Unfaithful	
Male Perception	Faithful	148	93%	9	25%
	Unfaithful	11	7%	27	75%
		159		36	⌐195

Source: Adapted from Andrews et al. (2008).

men are more likely than women to confront their partners with suspicions.

One difficulty with this area of research is the extent to which sexual infidelity and emotional infidelity are intertwined. Perhaps men view sexual infidelity as implying emotional infidelity. Men might think, "If my wife was unfaithful, she must *really* be in love with someone else." Recall that both women and men perceive that women connect sex with love. If that is the case, men are comparing the combination of sexual and emotional infidelity to emotional infidelity alone. Women, by contrast, may perceive that emotional infidelity implies sexual infidelity. They may believe that if their husbands are emotionally unfaithful, they must also be having sex with the person. In other words, wives are comparing sexual infidelity to the combination of emotional and sexual infidelity. These ideas are summarized in Figure 9.11. Explore the link between emotional and sexual infidelity in Do Gender 9.6.

Thus although there are patterns of jealousy that are consistent with evolutionary theory, the evidence in favor of an evolutionary theory of sex differences in jealousy is not clear. A recent review of the literature found little evidence for sex differences in

Relation Between Sexual + Emotional Infidelity

Men are thinking: Female partner emotional infidelity → emotion
Female partner sexual infidelity → emotion + sex

*Conclusion: Males more upset by sexual
infidelity than emotional infidelity*

Women are thinking: Male partner emotional infidelity → emotion + sex
Male partner sexual infidelity → sex

*Conclusion: Females more upset by emotional
infidelity than sexual infidelity*

FIGURE 9.11   Relation between Sexual and Emotional Infidelity.

DO GENDER 9.6
Relations Between
Sexual and Emotional Infidelity

Ask a group of people who are in a steady dating relationship to imagine their partner has become interested in someone else. Read the first item under Set A in Table 9.5 (the item that indicates emotional infidelity). Now have these people rate how likely they would be to think their partner had sexual relations with the other person.

Similarly, have another group of people read the second item under Set A in Table 9.5 (the item that indicates sexual infidelity). Have the people rate how likely they would be to think their partner had fallen in love with the other person.

1. Is sexual infidelity linked to emotional infidelity?

2. Is emotional infidelity linked to sexual infidelity?

3. Do the answers to these questions depend on the sex of the respondent?

■ The demand/withdraw behavior pattern has been linked to gender. Women are more likely to demand, and husbands are more likely to withdraw.

■ There are several explanations for this pattern:

a. Men and women have a basic conflict in that women want connection, which requires cooperation from a partner, and men want autonomy, which they can achieve on their own.

b. Women identify more problems in a relationship than men do. To resolve problems, confrontation or demanding behavior may be necessary.

c. The demand/withdraw pattern may be related to the power structure in relationships and the lower status of women.

d. Men are less tolerant of physiological arousal than women so they withdraw to avoid arousal.

■ The demand/withdraw pattern is associated with lower levels of marital satisfaction.

■ Evolutionary theory predicts that men will be distressed by sexual infidelity, whereas women will be distressed by emotional infidelity. Research shows that both women and men are more distressed by emotional infidelity than sexual infidelity but men are relatively more distressed than women by sexual infidelity.

sexual jealousy (Harris, 2003). Sex differences are reduced under cognitive load; the majority of studies show that men are more upset by emotional than sexual infidelity; and fewer sex differences appear on continuous measures of distress compared to forced-choice measures (i.e., which scenario is more distressing; Green & Sabini, 2006).

TAKE HOME POINTS

■ In marital interaction studies, women display more negative affect than men and are more likely to reciprocate negative affect than men in distressed couples—leading to the suggestion that women are the emotional barometers in relationships.

COHABITING RELATIONSHIPS

Cohabitation is becoming increasingly common, and attitudes toward cohabitation are becoming increasingly favorable. In 2007, 10% of all couples were cohabiting (Popenoe, 2008). In the 2004 Census, just over 5 million men and women cohabited, whereas in 1980 the figure was just over 1.5 million (U.S. Census Bureau, 2004). Cohabitation has even increased among the elderly (Brown, Lee, & Bulanda, 2006). Cohabitation is especially accepted among younger people. Half of seventh, ninth, and eleventh graders say they expect to cohabit before they marry (Manning et al., 2007). The most frequent reason for cohabitation is to spend time together, but people also cohabit as a matter of convenience and as a way to test their relationship before marriage (Rhoades, Stanley, & Markman, 2009).

There are a number of factors that have given rise to the increase in cohabitation, including the sexual revolution of the 1960s, the women's movement, the increase in women's education, the delay in marriage and childbearing, and the increase in the acceptability of premarital sex (Popenoe, 2008). Women may associate marriage with traditional gender roles and view a cohabiting relationship as an egalitarian alternative. In addition, the increase in the divorce rate has made people more leery about the stability of marriage. With the increase in cohabitation, the rate of divorce leveled off and has slowly declined in the past 20 years. However, the divorce rate does not take into account the breakup of cohabiting relationships, and an increasing number of those involve children.

Several conceptualizations of cohabitation have been identified across Europe, New Zealand, and the United States, as shown in Table 9.7 (Heuveline & Timberlake, 2004).

The highest rates of cohabitation are in Scandinavia. In Scandinavia, marriage and cohabitation are almost indistinguishable. The rate of cohabitation is high, the duration is long, and the incidence of having children is high. In France, cohabitation is considered an "alternative to marriage" because of the high rates of cohabitation, the long duration of cohabitation, and the relative low likelihood of getting married even if children are born. The United States is quite variable in terms of its pattern of cohabitation. It is described as an "alternative to being single" because the rate is moderate, the duration relatively short, the proportion ending in marriage moderate, and the incidence of children relatively low. Cohabitation is construed as a "stage in the marriage process" for a number of countries, of which Austria is a good example. Here the rates of cohabitation are moderate, the duration relatively short, the proportion ending in marriage high, and the likelihood of having children while cohabiting low. For Belgium, cohabitation was viewed as a "prelude to marriage" as the frequency of cohabitation is relatively low, the duration is relatively short and the proportion ending in marriage high. Cohabitation played a "marginal role" in

TABLE 9.7   PATTERNS OF COHABITATION

	Example Country	Rate	Duration	End in Marriage	Incidence of Children
Indistinguishable from marriage	Sweden	High	Long	High	High
Alternative to marriage	France	High	Long	Low	Low
Alternative to single	United States	Moderate	Short	Moderate	Low
Stage in marriage	Austria	Moderate	Short	High	Low
Prelude to marriage	Belgium	Relatively Low	Short	High	Very Low
Marginal	Italy	Lowest			

Source: Adapted Heuveline and Timerlake (2004).

relation to marriage in several countries, including Italy where the frequency of cohabitation is extremely low (9%).

The increase in cohabitation accounts for most of the decline in marriage rates in the United States. However, cohabitation has merely delayed rather than replaced marriage. In 1970, the median age of marriage was 23 for men and 21 for women. Today, the median age of marriage is 28 for men and 26 for women (U.S. Census Bureau, 2009a). When first cohabitation and first marriage are conceptualized as first unions, the age at first union has not changed much (Bumpass, Sweet, & Cherlin, 1991).

Who Cohabits

People often associate cohabitation with the college experience. However, cohabitation is more common among less educated people, poorer people, and African Americans and Hispanics compared to Whites (Laumann et al., 2007; Seltzer, 2000). A common reason for cohabiting is to share living expenses; people who have financial constraints may view cohabitation as an alternative to marriage. Economic reasons are undoubtedly responsible for the increase in cohabitation among the elderly (Chevan, 1996). Marriage increases income taxes and reduces social security payments. Elderly people, who are often on a fixed income, do not want to become involved in an arrangement that will reduce their income. Cohabitation is more common among previously married persons than never-married persons and among people whose parents have divorced (Cunningham & Thornton, 2007). People assume cohabiting couples are childless. This is not the case, as rates of having children are almost as high for cohabiting women as married women (U.S. Census Bureau, 2008).

A minority of people are serial cohabitors, meaning that they have cohabited with multiple people over their lives. Serial cohabitors are more likely to have lower income, lower education, and less likely to have a relationship end in marriage (Lichter & Qian, 2008). When serial cohabitors do marry, they are twice as likely to divorce as someone who has cohabited with a future spouse.

Outcomes of Cohabitation

Cohabiting relationships are usually of short duration; most cohabiting couples either marry or terminate their relationship rather than remain in a long-term cohabiting relationship. Thirty percent of cohabiting relationships end in marriage after 1 year, 58% after 3 years, and 70% after 5 years (Bramlett & Mosher, 2002). These figures are higher for Hispanics and considerably lower for Blacks. High income and religious affiliation predict marriage following cohabitation (Bramlett & Mosher, 2002).

We said that people view cohabitation as a way to test the relationship before marriage. Does it work? Is cohabitation the solution to the rising divorce rates? Almost half of Americans (49%) believe that cohabitation makes couples less likely to divorce (Saad, 2008). However, the evidence suggests otherwise. A meta-analytic review of the literature showed that those who cohabited with someone before marrying had lower marital quality and were more likely to divorce than those who had not cohabited before marrying (Jose, O'Leary, & Moyer, 2010). Even cohabitation after divorce is associated with lower happiness upon remarriage and less stable remarriage relationships (Xu, Hudspeth, & Bartkowski, 2006). And, people who say that they are cohabiting in order to test the relationship are the ones with the greatest relationship problems (Rhoades et al., 2009). However, the negative effects of cohabitation on marital quality and divorce disappear if one examines only cohabitation with the eventual marriage partner (Jose et al., 2010).

The negative effects of cohabitation are not limited to the United States. Despite its increase in prevalence in Scandinavia, cohabitation relationships are still less serious, less satisfying, and more likely to break up than marital relationships—even when couples have children (Popenoe, 2008). Cohabitation seems to have negative outcomes for children in the United States but not in Sweden (Bjorklund, Ginther, & Sundstrom, 2007). One reason may be that cohabiting couples spend less time with children than married couples in the United States but the same amount of time with children as married couples in Sweden (Ono & Yeilding, 2009).

What are the reasons for the negative outcomes associated with cohabitation? One answer lies in the kind of people who choose to cohabit. There is a selection bias in comparing marriages among people who did and did not cohabit; after all, people are not randomly assigned to cohabit or not. The kind of person who cohabits has less traditional views of gender roles, less traditional views of marriage, is more accepting of divorce, and is less religious. Each of these factors is associated with divorce.

Cohabitation also may be construed differently by women and men. Men may be less likely than women to perceive cohabitation as a prelude to marriage. One study showed that men who had cohabited prior to marriage were less committed to the marital relationship than men who had not, whereas there was no difference in women's commitment based on cohabitation history (Stanley, Whitton, & Markman, 2004). In another study, men who had cohabited prior to engagement were less committed during marriage than men who had cohabited after engagement or had not cohabited at all, whereas no commitment differences appeared among the groups of women (Rhoades, Stanley, & Markman, 2006).

In addition to the difference in the kinds of people who enter into cohabiting relationships, the marital relationships of people who have cohabited may differ from the marital relationships of people who have not. People may enter cohabiting relationships instead of marriage because they are more tentative about the relationship; that tentativeness could be a sign of a less well-functioning relationship. A great deal of evidence suggests cohabiting relationships are not as healthy as marital relationships (Stanley, Rhoades, & Markman, 2006). Cohabiting heterosexual couples are less committed to their relationship, less satisfied with their relationship, and report more problems in their relationship compared to married couples. A marital interaction study showed that couples who had cohabited prior to engagement displayed more negative interactions, less supportive behavior, and poorer problem-solving skills compared to those who had cohabited after engagement or those who had not cohabited at all (Kline et al., 2004). There is also a higher incidence of domestic violence and child abuse in cohabiting compared to marital relationships (Popenoe & Whitehead, 1999). The lower quality of cohabiting relationships may extend into marriage. Cohabiting couples may drift into marriage without making a serious commitment to the relationship, an effect that has been referred to as "sliding versus deciding" (Popanoe, 2008; Stanley et al., 2006).

A third reason cohabitation may have adverse effects on marriage is the possibility that the cohabitation experience alters the people or the relationship in ways that make it less viable after marriage. People who cohabit have a more egalitarian division of labor –and that egalitarian division of labor extends to marriage (Batalova & Cohen, 2002). A more egalitarian division of labor should be viewed as a benefit but egalitarian expectations are often violated by the pressure to enact traditional roles when marrying (Seltzer, 2000). Similarly, people who cohabit have a greater degree of freedom in their activities than people who are married (Popenoe & Whitehead, 1999). When cohabiting couples extend this freedom to marriage, difficulties may follow.

TAKE HOME POINTS

■ Cohabitation is becoming more widely accepted, especially among younger people but even among the elderly.

■ Despite the rise in cohabitation, cohabitation is associated with poor marital outcomes. That is, those who cohabit prior to marriage are less satisfied and more likely to break up after marriage than those who did not cohabit. There are three explanations for this finding:

1. There is a selection bias; that is, the kind of people who enter into cohabiting relationships are the kind of people who are more prone to divorce.
2. Cohabiting relationships are qualitatively different from marital relationships, especially in terms of commitment level.
3. Cohabitation may change the nature of a relationship in a way that makes it less viable upon marriage.

■ Cohabitation is less likely to be associated with poor marital outcomes if one cohabited with the eventual marital partner.

SUMMARY

Men and women are equally interested in romantic relationships and generally expect to get the same things out of a romantic relationship: love, companionship, intimacy, and sex. Men and women also desire similar characteristics in a partner, such as trustworthiness and kindness. There is an overall sex difference such that women attach more importance to most characteristics compared to men, which implies that women are choosier. There also are consistent sex differences in preferences for some of the less important characteristics; across cultures, men attach greater importance to the physical appearance of their partner and women attach greater importance to the financial status of their partner. Evolutionary theory and social role theory provide explanations for these differences.

Romantic relationships are characterized by intimacy, expressions of love and caring, self-disclosure, and sexuality for both women and men. There is little evidence that women and men define intimacy in their relationship differently. Some evidence suggests that men hold more romantic beliefs about relationships compared to women, and there are some sex differences in styles of love. Men tend to adopt a more game-playing strategy of love, whereas women tend to adopt a more practical and friendship-based approach.

Men have more permissive attitudes toward sex, but these differences are limited to less serious relationships. Men can separate sex from love, but women are more likely to see the two as co-occurring. In fact, men are more likely to seek sex for physical pleasure, whereas women are more likely to seek sex for emotional intimacy.

Who are the happiest couples? Couples who share power seem to be the happiest. Regardless of what one puts into a relationship, women and men are most happy when they perceive their contributions as equitable. It also turns out that characteristics of men (gender roles, personality traits, well-being) are related to women's relationship satisfaction, whereas characteristics of women have less impact on men's relationship satisfaction.

Women and men manage conflict somewhat differently. In laboratory studies of conflict discussions, women are more negative than men and remain engaged in the conflict, whereas men withdraw from the conflict and try to de-escalate it with positive behavior. Because the behavior of women is different in distressed versus nondistressed couples, women have been referred to as the "emotional barometers" of relationships. Much research has focused on a particular pattern of conflict behavior known as the demand/withdraw pattern. Research suggests that women are more likely to demand and men to withdraw, largely because women desire more change in relationships than men do.

Jealousy is equally likely to be evoked in women and men. Evolutionary psychologists have suggested that men are more upset by sexual infidelity and women are more upset by emotional infidelity. The evidence for this proposition is mixed. Men are more likely than women to monitor their partner's fidelity.

Finally, the chapter concludes with a discussion of cohabiting relationships. Cohabiting relationships are of a lower quality than marital relationships, and cohabitation prior to marriage is predictive of divorce. The negative outcomes of cohabitation may be due to the kinds of people who enter into cohabitation, the nature of the cohabiting relationship itself, or to actual adverse effects of cohabitation on people's relationships.

DISCUSSION QUESTIONS

1. What are the similarities and differences in women's and men's mate preferences?
2. How do men and women view the relation of sex to love?
3. Which sex is more romantic? Why?
4. Why do women demand and men withdraw?
5. Knowing what you do about gender roles in relationships, how would you predict that gay men's relationships would differ from lesbians' relationships?
6. What kinds of problems might be unique to homosexual couples? Heterosexual couples?
7. If the majority of men held the male gender role and the majority of women held the female gender role, describe the nature of lesbian relationships, gay relationships, and heterosexual relationships.
8. What are the differences in the way men and women interact when discussing conflict?
9. What does it mean that women are the "emotional barometer" in a relationship?
10. In what ways is the demand/withdraw pattern influenced by culture?
11. What is the evidence for and against the proposition that men are more upset by sexual than emotional infidelity?
12. What are the reasons that people who cohabit before marriage are more likely to divorce than people who did not cohabit before marriage?

SUGGESTED READING

(Classic) Christensen, A., & Heavy, C. L. (1993). Gender differences in marital conflict: The demand/withdraw interaction pattern. In S. Oskamp & M. Constanzo (Eds.), *Gender issues in contemporary society* (Vol. 6, pp. 113–141). New York: Sage.

Gottman, J. M. (1994). *What predicts divorce? The relationship between marital processes and marital outcomes.* Hillsdale, NJ: Erlbaum.

Peplau, L., & Fingerhut, A. (2007). The close relationships of lesbians and gay men. *Annual Review of Psychology, 58,* 405–424.

Popenoe, D. (2008). Cohabitation, marriage, and child well-being. *The National Marriage Project at Rutgers University* (pp. 1–22). Piscataway, NJ: Rutgers University.

Wells, B. E., & Twenge, J. M. (2005). Changes in young people's sexual behavior and attitudes, 1943–1999: A cross-temporal meta-analysis. *Review of General Psychology, 9,* 249–261.

KEY TERMS

Agape—Pure love, a blend of eros and storge.

Demand/withdraw pattern—Interaction episode characterized by one person demanding and the other person not responding or withdrawing.

Equity—State of a relationship in which the ratio of what one puts in and gets out of a relationship equals that of the partner.

Emotional transmission—Situation in which one person's emotions influence another person's emotions.

Evolutionary theory—theory which states that social behavior is shaped by survival of genes.

Eros—Romantic love.

Ludus—Game-playing love.

Mania—Manic love, a blend of eros and ludus.

Pragma—Practical love, a blend of storge and ludus.

Script—Schema or cognitive representation for a sequence of events.

Social constructionist theory—Theory states that women's and men's behavior is determined by the context in which they are in, which includes the norms or rules of a society.

Social exchange theory—Theory that relationship satisfaction is partly a function of the rewards and costs in the relationship.

Social role theory—Theory that states men's and women's behavior is a function of the roles that they hold in society.

Storge—Friendship love.

CHAPTER 10

Sex Differences in Health: Evidence and Explanations

Women are sicker than men. They report spending more days in bed during the year due to illness compared to men, report more pain, are more depressed, perceive their health as less good, and report more physical symptoms than men. Yet women live longer than men! In fact, men are more likely than women to die from 9 of the 10 leading causes of death in the United States. This is the great paradox of gender and health. Women have higher rates of **morbidity** (i.e., illness), but men have higher rates of **mortality**.

This chapter begins the final section of the book, which focuses on the implications of gender for health, one domain in which there are pervasive and sizable sex differences, such as those just described. I construe health broadly, as both emotional well-being (psychological distress, life satisfaction, happiness) and physical problems (physical symptoms, coronary heart disease). This chapter provides an overview of sex differences in health as well as the common classes of explanations for these sex differences. First, I describe the sex differences in mortality rates and then sex differences in morbidity rates. Then, I review numerous explanations for these differences.

SEX DIFFERENCES IN MORTALITY

Life Span

Men die younger than women throughout the life span. Although 105 boys are born for every 100 girls in the United States (Matthews & Hamilton, 2005), more boys than girls die at every age. There is not an equal number of males and females in the United States until age 18. After that, there is a greater number of females than males. The ratio of male to female mortality for each age group is shown in Table 10.1. For every 26 girls who die between the ages of 1 and 4,

TABLE 10.1   NUMBER OF DEATHS PER 100,000 IN 2007

Age	Male	Female	Male:Female Ratio
01–4	32	26	1.23
05–14	17	13	1.31
15–24	116	42	2.76
25–34	145	64	2.27
35–44	232	136	1.71
45–54	529	314	1.68
55–64	1,099	668	1.65
65–74	2,452	1,629	1.51
75–84	6,046	4,309	1.40
85 and over	14,031	12,165	1.13

Source: Adapted from U.S. Department of Health and Human Services (2009a).

32 boys die, resulting in a male to female ratio of 1.23. You can see that the sex difference peaks during adolescence and young adulthood.

Some claim that males are more likely than females to die even before birth. Researchers have suggested that 120 to 160 boys are conceived for every 100 girls (Stillion, 1995), which would imply a high death rate for males in utero if only 105 boys to 100 girls are actually born. However, Waldron (1998) contends that the number of females and males conceived is unknown because we do not have any idea of the number of females and males who die during the first eight weeks after conception.

After birth, males have higher death rates than females at all ages. Thus it comes as no surprise that women live longer than men. In 2006, people in the United States reached a record long life expectancy of 78 years. However, men did not live as long as women. Life expectancy at birth for White women was 81, and for White men, it was 76. Life expectancies at birth for Black people lagged behind, but the sex difference persisted: 77 for Black women and 70 for Black men. The 2000 census showed that the life

expectancies for Hispanics in the United States exceeded those for Blacks and Whites, with Latina women outliving men by six years (women 83.7; men 77.2; Andalo, 2004). On average, women outlive men by five years in the United States.

Sex differences in longevity have existed throughout the 20th century, but their size has varied. The average length of life for women and men during each decade of the 20th century is shown in Table 10.2. In 1900, the average man lived to be 46 and the average woman 48; the sex difference in mortality was only two years. Life spans lengthened for both men and women over the course of the century due to better nutrition, better health care, and the development of vaccines. The sex difference in longevity widened during the middle of the century, peaking in 1979, when women outlived men by nearly 7.8 years. The increased sex difference was due to the reduction in women's mortality during childbirth and the increase in men's mortality from heart disease and lung cancer. The increase in men's lung cancer can be directly tied to smoking.

More recently, the sex gap in mortality has narrowed. In the 1980s and 1990s, sex

TABLE 10.2   LIFE EXPECTANCIES OVER THE 20TH CENTURY TO DATE

	Men	Women	White Men	White Women	Black Men	Black Women
2006	75.1	80.2	75.7	80.6	69.7	76.5
2000	74.1	79.5	74.8	80.0	67.2	74.7
1990	71.8	78.8	72.7	79.4	64.5	73.6
1980	70.0	77.5	70.7	78.1	63.8	72.5
1970	67.1	74.7	68.0	75.6	60.0	68.3
1960	66.6	73.1	67.4	74.1	61.1	66.3
1950	65.6	71.1	66.5	72.2	59.1	62.9
1940	60.8	65.2	62.1	66.6	51.5	54.9
1930	58.1	61.6	59.7	63.5	47.3	49.2
1920	53.6	54.6	54.4	55.6	45.5	45.2
1910	48.4	51.8	48.6	52.0	33.8	37.5
1900	46.3	48.3	46.6	48.7	32.5	33.5

Source: Adapted from U.S. National Center for Health Statistics (2009a).
Note: The figures from 1900 to 1960 for Black people reflect "Black and other" people.

differences in life expectancy grew smaller. In 2010, the gap became the smallest it has been since 1948. The narrowing has been attributed to a greater proportionate decrease in heart disease and cancer mortality among men than women and to a greater increase in the incidence of lung cancer among women than men (Rieker & Bird, 2005). Between 1979 and 1986, lung cancer increased by 7% for men and 44% for women (Rodin & Ickovics, 1990). These statistics can be directly tied to changes in smoking patterns. Women's smoking rates increased during the second half of the 20th century, and women were less likely than men to quit smoking (Waldron, 1995).

As you can see in Table 10.2, there also are large race differences in mortality, and the size of the sex difference in mortality is greater for Black than White people. This is largely due to the high mortality rate of Black men. The poor health of Black men is partly a function of education and partly a function of their minority status. Sex differences in mortality are largest for those with less

education. The rate of male to female mortality is 1.84 for those with less than 12 years of education and 1.56 for those with 13 or more years of education (Williams, 2003). There are large differences in pay and employment between college-educated White and Black men, and this difference has increased over the past 20 years (Williams, 2003). I remember the famous tennis player Arthur Ashe—who was Black and had HIV from a blood transfusion—saying it was more difficult being Black than having AIDS (Deford, 1993). Although this was an era in which HIV was highly stigmatized, Ashe suffered much greater discrimination due to his race than his HIV status, even as a famous athlete. In addition, Black people are six times more likely than White people to become victims of murder (Bureau of Justice Statistics, 2010).

Sex differences in life expectancy exist in other nations of the world. Table 10.3 shows sex differences in life expectancies in Western and Eastern Europe and developing countries. The sex difference is larger in

TABLE 10.3   ESTIMATES OF 2010 LIFE EXPECTANCIES AROUND THE WORLD

	Male	Female	F:M Difference
East			
Bulgaria	69.7	77.2	7.5
Poland	71.9	80.1	8.2
Romania	69.2	76.4	7.2
Russia	59.5	73.2	13.7
West			
Denmark	76.1	81	4.9
France	77.9	84.4	6.5
Ireland	75.8	81.2	5.4
Netherlands	76.9	82.3	5.4
Portugal	75.1	81.9	6.8
Developing Countries			
Botswana	61.1	60.8	−.3
Cambodia	60.4	64.7	4.3
Haiti	59.7	63.1	3.4
Laos	54.8	59.2	4.4
Madagascar	61.3	65.3	4
Nepal	64.6	67.1	2.5
Rwanda	56.1	58.9	2.8
Somalia	48.1	51.9	3.8
Zimbabwe	48	47.1	−.9

Source: The World Factbook: 2010.

Eastern than in Western Europe. The sex difference is more variable in developing countries where the life span is much shorter. In developing countries, the status differential between women and men is even greater, leading to high rates of female infanticide, pregnancy-related deaths, and poverty-related mortality (Murphy, 2003).

Leading Causes of Death

At the turn of the 20th century, women and men were most likely to die from infectious diseases, such as tuberculosis, influenza, pneumonia, and diphtheria. Today, with the exception of AIDS and some recent infection epidemics (e.g., H1N1), people are less likely to die from communicable diseases. Instead, people die from diseases in which lifestyle factors play a role. The leading causes of death in the United States are shown in Table 10.4. The top-most leading cause of death for both men and women—White, Black, and Hispanic—is coronary heart disease. See Sidebar 10.1 for an elaboration on the role of sex and gender in heart disease. The second leading cause of death is cancer, followed by cerebrovascular disease (i.e., stroke), and chronic lower respiratory disease (i.e., emphysema), and then accidents. The etiology of these diseases is much more complicated than the etiology of an infectious disease. There are a variety of factors that play a role in the top five leading causes of death, many of which include behavioral factors, such as smoking, diet, drinking, and driving while intoxicated. The most noteworthy feature of Table 10.4 is that the death rate for 12 of the top 15 causes is higher in males than females. Alzheimer's disease is the only cause of death that has a higher mortality rate for women, and this extends across Whites, Blacks, and Hispanics. The largest sex differences appear for accidents, suicide, liver disease, Parkinson's disease, and homicide. In the case of diabetes, the direction of the sex difference depends on race: Men have higher rates of diabetes than women among Whites, but women have higher rates than men among Blacks and Hispanics. This is likely due to the high rate of obesity among Black and Hispanic women.

The leading causes of death are influenced by a combination of age, race, and sex. The leading cause of death for Hispanic men and women, White men and women, and Black women ages 15 to 24 is accidents. For Black men of age

TABLE 10.4 AGE-ADJUSTED DEATH RATES (PER 100,000) FOR THE LEADING CAUSES OF DEATH IN 2007

Cause of Death	All	M/F	B/W	H/W
Heart disease	190.9	1.5	1.3	.7
Cancer	178.4	1.4	1.2	.6
Cerebrovascular disease	42.2	1.0	1.5	.8
Chronic lower respiratory disease	40.8	1.3	.7	.4
Accidents	40.0	2.1	.9	.7
Alzheimer's disease	22.7	.7	.8	.6
Diabetes mellitus	22.5	1.4	2.1	1.5
Pneumonia and influenza	16.2	1.4	1.2	.8
Kidney disease	14.5	1.4	2.2	.9
Suicide	11.3	3.9	.4	.4
Septicemia	11.0	1.2	2.2	.8
Liver disease	9.1	2.2	.8	1.6
Hypertension and renal disease	7.4	1.0	2.5	1.0
Parkinson's disease	6.4	2.2	.5	.6
Homicide	6.1	3.8	5.7	2.5

Source: Xu, Kochanek, Murphy, and Tejada-Vera (2010). M/F = Male to female ratio; B/W = Black to White ratio; H/W = Hispanic to non-Hispanic White ratio.

15 to 24, the leading cause of death is homicide. Although HIV is not in the top 10 causes of overall mortality, it is among the top 5 for some subgroups of people: Black men and women between the ages of 25 and 44 and Hispanic women between the ages of 35 and 44. Sex differences in accidents, suicide, and homicide account for most of the sex difference in mortality among younger people. Among older people, heart disease and cancer account for most of the sex difference in mortality.

Another noteworthy feature of Table 10.4 is that the mortality rate for Black people is higher than that for White people for 9 of the 15 leading causes of death. The largest differences appear for homicide, hypertension, kidney disease, septicemia, and diabetes. Black people have less than half the rate of suicide and Parkinson's disease as White

people. By contrast, the mortality rate for Hispanics is less than that of non-Hispanic Whites, with the exception of diabetes, homicide, liver disease, and hypertension.

Crime Statistics

Men are more likely than women to commit violent crimes, and men are more likely than women to be the victims of violent crimes, with the exception of rape. That is, men are more likely than women to be assaulted, robbed, threatened with violence, and killed. For homicide, both perpetrator and victim are male in 65% of the cases (U.S. Department of Justice, Federal Bureau of Investigation, 2009). In the year 2008, men comprised 72% of murder victims and 90% of murder perpetrators. It is rare that women commit murder. Imagine

SIDEBAR 10.1: *Is Heart Disease Only for Men?*

Cardiovascular disease is the top-most leading cause of death in the United States. In 2006, 831,272 people died from heart disease, and heart disease accounted for 34% of the deaths in the United States (American Heart Association, 2010). In fact, there were more deaths from heart disease than from the next five leading causes of death combined. Death rates from heart disease have declined since 1980, which greatly contributed to the overall increase in life expectancy. Between 1996 and 2006, death rates have declined 29%.

Heart disease is often viewed as a disease of men. There is good reason for this. Under age 45, White men have six times the risk of heart disease as White women, and Black men have twice the risk of heart disease as Black women (Ho, Paultre, & Mosca, 2005). The risk of heart disease rises with age in both women and men, but rates of heart disease occur on average 10 years later in women (American Heart Association, 2010). Men have higher rates of heart disease than women until age 75. However, heart disease is not limited to men. It is the leading cause of death for *both* men and women. In fact, because women live longer than men, more women than men ultimately die of heart disease (Rieker & Bird, 2005). The death rate from heart disease has declined in recent years, but the decline has been greater for men than women, greatest for White males, and least for Black females (National Institutes of Health, 2006). In terms of absolute numbers, more women than men die from heart disease in a given year, which has been the case since 1984. This fact is due to a greater number of women than men in the population, especially among the elderly—and heart disease is a disease of the elderly.

how society would have reacted if the two teenagers at Columbine High School were girls instead of boys or the college student at Virginia Tech was female instead of male. When women are victims, they are almost 10 times as likely to be killed by a male as a female. However, women are almost four times as likely to kill men as to kill women. The female perpetrator/female victim category is a rare one.

We often imagine murder as involving a stranger. Many of the mass killings we hear about in the media involve a person killing strangers, and these accounts draw a great deal of publicity. However, 2009 statistics show that only 12% of victims were murdered by strangers, 44% knew the perpetrator, and the relationship was unknown in 44% of the cases (U.S. Department of Justice, Federal Bureau of Investigation, 2009). The perpetrator's relationship to the victim differs for men and women. Women are more likely than men to be killed by someone they know across all age groups.

Although men are more likely than women to be victims of violence, the association of violence with poor health seems to be stronger for women than men (Sundaram et al., 2004). In a national survey in Denmark, a history of violence was more strongly associated with self-ratings of poor health, anxiety, depression, and stomach problems in women than men. This may be due to the fact that violence is more likely to take place in the context of relationships for women compared to men.

- Males die younger than females at all ages.

- The sex difference in longevity increased over the 20th century to a record 7.8 years in 1979 but more recently has decreased. Today, women outlive men by five years.

- The leading causes of death are heart disease, cancer, cerebrovascular disease, chronic lower respiratory disease, and accidents—all causes for which lifestyle factors play a role.

- Men are more likely than women to die of most of the leading causes of death.

- Men are more likely than women to commit violent crimes and to be victims of violent crimes, including homicide.

- Women are more likely than men to be killed by someone they know.

SEX DIFFERENCES IN MORBIDITY

Morbidity reflects illness. Whereas mortality rates have decreased and the life span has lengthened, morbidity rates have increased. People are living longer, but partly because they are living with diseases rather than dying from them. During the early part of the 20th century, the leading causes of death were from infectious diseases. The causes of these diseases were relatively simple to understand; typically, there was a single causal agent, the germ. With the development of penicillin and vaccinations, people began to live longer; thus they had more time to develop and subsequently die from chronic diseases. Whereas an acute illness lasts a short time and is either fatal (a possibility in the case of tuberculosis or pneumonia) or nonfatal (the common cold), a **chronic illness** is long lasting and typically does not disappear. A chronic illness can be fatal or nonfatal;

rheumatoid arthritis is an example of a non-fatal chronic illness, and cancer and heart disease are examples of chronic illnesses that can be fatal—in fact, they are the top two leading causes of death. The increase in chronic diseases accounts for the increase in morbidity, that is, the increase in illness, disability, and activity restriction among the U.S. population.

Women have higher morbidity rates than men. In fact, the morbidity-free life expectancy (i.e., life without chronic disease) has declined for both women and men but more so for women than men (Perenboom et al., 2005). In 1989, women and men could expect 55 morbidity-free years. By 2000, women's morbidity-free years had declined to 51, and men's had declined to 54. Although men have higher incident rates (i.e., men contract diseases more than women do) and death rates from the top two leading causes of death (heart disease and cancer), women suffer from more acute illnesses and more nonfatal chronic illnesses compared to men (Case & Paxson, 2005). Women suffer higher rates of arthritis, immune disorders, and digestive conditions compared to men. Women suffer from more painful disorders compared to men, such as migraines, tension headaches, musculoskeletal pain, back pain, abdominal pain, carpal tunnel syndrome, irritable bowel syndrome, rheumatoid arthritis, multiple sclerosis, and Raynaud's disease. Thus at any given point in time, women are more likely than men to be ill and to be living with a chronic disease.

Not surprisingly, women perceive their health to be worse than men do, although the sex difference decreases with age (Gorman & Read, 2006). Subjective health perceptions are typically measured by a single question that asks respondents to rate their health as poor, fair, good, very good, or excellent. Because women have a higher rate of nonfatal chronic diseases causing daily symptoms, pain, and distress, women's ratings of their health are lowered.

Women also report more **illness behavior** than men, that is, behaviors that signify illness. For example, women report more days in bed due to illness, more days in which they restricted their activities due to illness, and greater physical limitations (Pleis & Lethbridge-Cejku, 2007). Among employed persons, women take more sick days from work (Smeby, Bruusgaard, & Claussen, 2009). Women report greater disability and greater functional limitations than men, and this difference persists throughout adulthood and increases with age (Gorman & Read, 2006).

One aspect of illness behavior is seeking medical care. Women report a greater use of health services compared to men (Koopmans & Lamers, 2007), which is often taken as an indication of women being sicker than men. Sex differences in the use of health care services peak during women's childbearing years. When reproductive-related reasons are taken into consideration, sex differences in hospitalization become more similar, but women still receive greater outpatient care than men. One reason women use more health care is that women have a greater number of chronic conditions. Some of women's higher morbidity rates are related to gynecological problems, but even when these problems are taken into consideration, women have higher rates of morbidity than men.

Interestingly, sex differences in morbidity do not appear until adolescence. For example, chronic illnesses, such as asthma and migraine headaches, are more prevalent among boys than girls during childhood, but by early adolescence, this sex difference reverses itself (Sweeting, 1995). Not only does depression increase among girls during adolescence (discussed in Chapter 13), but physical symptoms such as stomach problems and

headache also increase among adolescent girls (Sweeting & West, 2003). In a study of 11- to 15-year-olds across 29 European and North American countries, girls reported more health complaints (e.g., headache, stomachache, depression, dizziness) than boys (Torsheim et al., 2006). The difference appeared in all countries and for each of the nine health complaints. As shown in Table 10.5, the sex difference (i.e., odds ratio, such that higher numbers mean more females than males) increased with age and decreased in countries where women had more education and income (i.e., higher gender development index).

Health care utilization rates reflect the changes in female and male morbidity over adolescence. During childhood, boys visit health care professionals more frequently than girls, but during adolescence, girls visit health care professionals more than boys. Health care utilization in childhood, however, does not reflect children's behavior alone; adults are more likely to be making the decision to seek health care. Thus it may be that parents, in particular mothers, are more likely to take boys than girls to see a doctor when they are young. Parents might take boys' complaints more seriously because they expect boys to be less likely than girls to complain of symptoms; admitting illness violates gender-role norms for boys.

TABLE 10.5 ODDS RATIO OF WOMEN HAVING MORE HEALTH SYMPTOMS THAN MEN

	Low GDI	Medium GDI	High GDI
11-year-olds	1.56	1.17	1.18
13-year-olds	1.88	1.70	1.56
15-year-olds	2.27	1.91	1.88

Note: GDI = Gender Development Index, high GDI signifies women have higher education and income. Source: Torsheim (2006).

- Women have higher rates of morbidity than men.

- Whereas men are more likely to suffer from fatal chronic illnesses, women are more likely than men to suffer from nonfatal chronic illnesses and painful disorders—meaning that at any point in time women are more likely than men to be ill.

- Women report more symptoms, perceive their health to be worse, restrict their activities due to illness, and seek medical care more than men.

- Sex differences in morbidity first appear during adolescence.

EXPLANATIONS FOR SEX DIFFERENCES IN HEALTH

Next, I examine six classes of explanations for sex differences in morbidity and mortality. First, I examine biological factors that might contribute to sex differences in health. Second, I consider the role of artifacts in sex differences in health. **Artifacts** are factors that cause sex differences to appear that do not really exist. For example, men have a higher socioeconomic status (SES) than women, and SES is related to health. Is women's poor health a function of their lower income? Physician bias is another example of an artifact; perhaps physicians treat women and men differently so it appears women are sicker, but women and men are actually equally healthy or unhealthy. Third, I consider the role of health behaviors, such as preventive health care, smoking, drinking, drug use, diet, and exercise; there are sex differences for most of these behaviors. Fourth, I consider aspects of the female and male gender roles that might influence health. Aspects of the male gender role can be linked to specific health behaviors and to general risk-taking behavior; aspects of the female gender role can be related to greater concerns with health, but also to risks associated with involvement in relationships. Fifth, I discuss whether men and women perceive symptoms similarly or whether women have a lower threshold for symptoms, which makes it appear women are sicker than men. Finally, I consider whether men and women respond to symptoms in similar ways in terms of taking care of themselves and seeking medical attention.

BIOLOGY

Genes

Women may have a greater genetic resistance to some diseases compared to men. Women may be genetically predisposed to better health because they have a second X chromosome. The X chromosome carries more information on it than the Y chromosome. In females, an abnormality on an X chromosome is not necessarily a problem because a second X chromosome is there to suppress it; the abnormality is usually recessive. Thus a female will simply be a carrier of the abnormality but will not manifest it. The male, however, has a Y chromosome, which cannot override an abnormality of an X chromosome. This may explain why more males than females suffer some congenital disorders, such as hemophilia, meningitis, muscular dystrophy, and mental retardation.

Hormones

Estrogen plays a significant role in women's health. One reason women have a lower incidence of heart disease than men at younger ages is that women are protected from heart disease by estrogen. The sex difference in rates of heart disease is much larger at younger ages before women reach menopause. After menopause, women's rates of heart disease increase dramatically.

Why does heart disease increase in women after menopause? One theory is that women are protected from heart disease before menopause because of their higher levels of estrogen. With menopause, estrogen levels drop. Although the decline in estrogen that accompanies menopause does not influence blood pressure, diabetes, or body mass index, it may lead to changes in cholesterol (i.e., decreasing the good cholesterol and increasing the bad cholesterol), and it may alter the blood clotting process (Fetters et al., 1996).

In the 1980s and 1990s, researchers were so confident of the link between estrogen and heart disease that many women were put on hormone replacement therapy (HRT) after menopause to reduce their risk of heart disease. However, most of studies linking HRT to lower rates of heart disease were correlational, meaning it was unclear whether HRT caused a reduction in heart disease or whether there was a third confounding variable, like SES, that influenced rates of heart disease. That is, women of a higher SES could have been more likely to use HRT, and women with a higher SES have better health. Finally, a randomized trial of over 16,000 postmenopausal women was conducted to determine the effect of HRT on the prevention of heart disease (Writing Group for the Women's Health Initiative Investigators, 2002). The trial was stopped early in 2002 because the effects of HRT were so dramatic. Unfortunately, the effects were not as predicted. Women on HRT had a significant increased risk of breast cancer and an increased risk of heart attack. Subsequent trials have linked HRT with an increased risk of heart disease and stroke (Lowe, 2004). This is a significant example of how important it is to conduct experimental research to test theories developed from correlational data. We also have learned that higher SES women were, in fact, more likely to use HRT (Lawlor, Smith, & Ebrahim, 2004). More recent studies suggest that the picture may be even more complicated, such that the effect of HRT depends on timing. There is the possibility that HRT used by younger women or used closer to menopause may be associated with reduced risk (Rossouw et al., 2007).

Thus, a clear link between high levels of estrogen and low levels of heart disease has not been established. Another problem for the theory is that oral contraceptives, which often contain estrogen, increase risk factors for heart disease. Oral contraceptives increase blood pressure, cholesterol levels, and blood glucose levels. In the past, using oral contraceptives in combination with smoking was a particularly lethal combination, increasing the risk of a heart attack by a magnitude of 30, but the synergy among more recent classes of contraceptives has been reduced (Chasan-Taber & Stampfer, 2001).

Estrogen also plays a hazardous role in the development of some cancers (breast cancer, endometrial cancer) and may be linked to osteoarthritis. Estrogens may play a role in autoimmune diseases, but whether the links are protective or harmful is not clear. Thus hormones certainly play a role in women's and men's health, but which hormones are responsible for the effects and the direction of the effects are not certain.

Immune System

It has been suggested that the nature of men's and women's immune systems differ (Bouman et al., 2004), but the effects seem to be paradoxical. Women's immune systems may respond to viruses better than men's (Whitacre et al., 1999), and women seem to have a greater immune response to infection than men (Rieker & Bird, 2005). However, this immune response could explain why women's immune systems end up attacking their own bodies resulting in a higher rate of autoimmune diseases. Women are more vulnerable than men to diseases specific to the immune system, such as lupus and rheumatoid arthritis. Among humans, men have lower rates of immunoglobulin M (a protein involved in immune function), which may be a source of men's greater vulnerability to disease (Schuurs & Verheul, 1990). Immune function is likely to be associated with sex hormones (Choudhry, Bland, & Chaudry, 2007).

Cardiovascular Reactivity

Cardiovascular reactivity refers to the increase in blood pressure and heart rate that occurs when engaging in a challenging or stressful task. You may experience cardiovascular reactivity when taking an exam, when thinking about an exam, or when receiving a graded exam. You are also likely to experience cardiovascular reactivity during an argument, during a traffic jam, or when your computer screen freezes. Yet we all do not experience the same level of reactivity to the same stressors. One theory is that people who exhibit heightened physiological responses to stressful events might be damaging their arteries on a daily basis, making them more vulnerable to heart disease. There is some evidence that cardiovascular reactivity is related to indicators of heart disease (Treiber et al., 2003).

To the extent that cardiovascular reactivity is linked to heart disease, sex differences in reactivity become an important topic. Numerous studies have shown that men exhibit greater cardiovascular reactivity than women, which could explain a portion of men's higher rates of heart disease. Cardiovascular reactivity is typically studied in the laboratory by exposing participants to a stressful or challenging task and observing changes in blood pressure or heart rate. Men are more reactive than women to a majority

of stressors studied in the lab (Matthews, Gump, & Owens, 2001).

However, researchers soon realized that men may show greater reactivity than women to laboratory tasks because the tasks are more relevant to men than women. Laboratory tasks that reveal men to be more reactive than women are often achievement oriented. The real-world stressors that show men to be more reactive than women are typically exams and work, which are also achievement oriented. Perhaps women would exhibit greater reactivity than men when the domain is more relevant to women. As you will see in Chapter 11, women exhibit greater cardiovascular, neuroendocrine, and immune reactivity than men when discussing a relationship conflict.

Several studies have examined the idea that men react to stressors relevant to the male gender role and women react to stressors relevant to the female gender role. In one study, men were more reactive than women to two masculine tasks, serial subtraction and a handgrip squeeze, whereas women were more reactive than men to a feminine task, giving a speech on the likes and dislikes about one's physical appearance (Stroud, Niaura, & Salovey, 2000). In another study, college males' and females' reactions to either an achievement (math, verbal memorization) or an interpersonal (rejection) challenge were examined (Stroud, Salovey, & Epel, 2002). As shown in Figure 10.1, men exhibited greater cortisol increases than women in response to the achievement stressor, and women exhibited greater cortisol increases than men in response to the interpersonal stressor.

However, one study found just the opposite pattern of results when examining gender-related traits rather than sex. Masculine people were more reactive to a feminine stressor, and feminine people were more reactive to a masculine stressor (Davis &

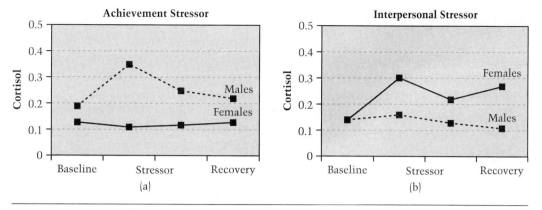

FIGURE 10.1   (a) Men show elevated cortisol reactivity to an achievement stressor compared to women; (b) Women show elevated cortisol reactivity to an interpersonal stressor compared to men. *Source*: Adapted from Stroud et al. (2002).

Matthews, 1996). Participants who scored high on masculinity or femininity were randomly assigned to either persuade or empathize with their partners. Masculine people were more reactive when they had to empathize with rather than persuade their partners, whereas feminine people were more reactive when they had to persuade rather than empathize with their partners.

How do we make sense of these contradictory findings? Are women and men more reactive to gender-congruent or gender-incongruent tasks? One resolution to this issue involves determining whether the task is perceived as a challenge or a threat, which may influence whether the tasks are low or high in difficulty. Wright and colleagues (1997) predicted that people would evidence greater reactivity to a gender-congruent task only when difficulty was high. In that case, the thought of not performing well on a task consistent with one's gender role might be perceived as a threat. When the task is easy, people whose gender role is congruent with the task expect to perform well and are not threatened by the task. People whose gender role is incongruent with the task are likely to

perceive the task as more of a challenge—in a sense, a higher difficulty level. These people feel less capable and expend more effort. In a test of this hypothesis, college students participated in a memory task in which good performance would allow them to avoid a noise stressor. The experimenter told half of the participants that men have greater ability on the task and typically outperform women and the other half that women have greater ability and typically outperform men. The difficulty of the task was also manipulated. The investigators' predictions were confirmed. When the task was low in difficulty, women showed greater reactivity than men to the masculine task, and men showed greater reactivity than women to the feminine task. When the task was high in difficulty, women showed greater reactivity than men to the feminine task, and men showed greater reactivity than women to the masculine task. Thus sex differences in reactivity not only depend on the relevance of the task to gender roles but also on the difficulty of the task. The difficulty of a gender-role congruent task may determine whether the person feels comfortable and competent or threatened by the possibility of failure.

TAKE HOME POINTS

- The fact that women have a second X chromosome may protect women from some genetically based diseases.

- Estrogens clearly play a role in women's greater resistance and vulnerability to disease. The nature of this relation is complicated.

- There is a paradox in immune function for women and men. It appears that women's immune systems may be more responsive to infection, but also more vulnerable to autoimmune disease.

- Historically, research showed that men exhibited greater cardiovascular reactivity to stressful tasks compared to women, which was thought to provide an explanation for men's greater vulnerability to heart disease.

- More recent research has shown that sex differences in cardiovascular reactivity are dependent on the nature of the stressor. Women's and men's reactivity may be quite similar when they feel similarly challenged or threatened.

ARTIFACTS

One class of explanations for sex differences in health is that the differences are not real but are due to artifacts. Recall that artifacts are methodological variables that might lead to the appearance of sex differences in health even when differences do not exist. A confounding variable, such as SES, could be an artifact of the relation between gender and health. Other artifactual explanations have to do with the way that health is measured. Although mortality is an objective index of health, many of the indexes of morbidity are subjective and may be influenced by the way they are assessed. Thus sex differences in morbidity may be especially vulnerable to artifacts.

Socioeconomic Status

Socioeconomic status clearly is related to health. With every increase in income, health improves—even among people who are middle to upper class. If SES is measured by earnings, men have a higher status than women. If SES is measured by education, women and men have a roughly equal status. It does not appear that differences in men's and women's SES can explain sex differences in either mortality or morbidity in the United States. However, in countries where women lack substantially more resources compared to men, such as India, women's health suffers (Roy & Chaudhuri, 2008). Unlike women from wealthier countries, such as the United States, these women do not practice primary prevention.

Another question is whether SES shows the same relation to health for men and women. Data from 2002 suggest that the relation of education to mortality is the same for White men and women and the same for Black men and women (Zajacova & Hummer, 2009). Education is similarly associated with decreased mortality from cancer for women and men (Menvielle et al., 2008). However, one study showed that education was more strongly related to physical functioning in women than in men (Ross & Mirowsky, 2010). Among people with a low level of education, women's physical functioning was much worse than that of men. However, among people with a college education, the sex difference in physical functioning disappeared. Ross and Mirowsky suggested that "resource substitution" explained this effect. Resource substitution implies that one resource will have a stronger effect when other resources are lacking. Because women have fewer socioeconomic resources than men, education has a stronger effect on their health. It also appears that a spouse's SES influences one's health (Skalicka & Kunst, 2008). In a study in Norway, husbands' occupation, income, and education each were related to a decrease in wives' mortality, with relations being stronger for occupation and income. However, it was only wives' education that was related to a reduction in husbands' mortality. Skalicka and Kunst suggested that the traditional female role involves taking care of the family's health—a role that would benefit from women's education.

Physician Bias

Physicians may respond to women and men differently, contributing to sex differences in health. Two areas in which this issue has been well investigated are heart disease and mental health. Physician bias in the context of mental health will be discussed in Chapter 13. Here we examine physician bias in the context of heart disease.

Heart Disease.   Women have a worse prognosis from heart disease compared to men (Berger et al., 2009; Vitale, Miceli, & Rosano, 2007), in part because women are older when heart disease is diagnosed but also in part because women are treated less aggressively than men for heart disease, described in the following paragraphs and summarized in Table 10.6. Why would this be?

One reason women are disadvantaged compared to men is that diagnostic tests and treatments have largely been developed on men. Major clinical trials that have made important contributions to the treatment of heart disease have historically included only men. For example, the Multiple Risk Factor Intervention Trial Research Group (1983) was conducted to reduce risk factors of heart disease. The study included 12,866 men and 0 women. In the Physicians Health Study, physicians were randomly assigned to receive aspirin or placebo to see if aspirin protected against heart disease (Steering Committee,

TABLE 10.6   STAGES OF TREATMENT FOR CORONARY HEART DISEASE

	Women are less likely than men to:
Prevention	have cholesterol checked
	receive cholesterol lowering drugs
Response to symptoms	be referred to a cardiologist
	receive diagnostic tests for heart disease
Treatment	be treated with drugs that dissolve clots
	be treated with angioplasty
	be treated with bypass surgery

1988). The study was terminated early because the benefits of aspirin were so large that it was unethical to withhold this information from the public. No female physicians were included in the study. In response to this concern, the National Institutes of Health made a major commitment to women's health in the 1990s, first by requiring clinical trials to report the number of women and men in studies and second by developing the Women's Health Initiative in 1991. The Women's Health Initiative was a 15-year longitudinal study of about 164,000 women to evaluate the effects of diet, vitamins, and HRT on heart disease, cancer, and osteoporosis.

The fact that diagnostic tests and treatments were developed on men poses two problems for women. First, because women's and men's anatomy differs, it is quite likely that a test developed on men's bodies is not as accurate in detecting disease in women's bodies. Second, a treatment developed for men may not be as effective for women.

Substantial evidence indicates that women and men are treated differently by the health care system with respect to heart disease. Despite the fact that heart disease is the leading cause of death of women as well as men, women are less likely than men to receive information from their physician about the risks of heart disease (Grunau et al., 2009). In terms of prevention, women are less likely than men to have a fasting cholesterol test taken and are less likely than men to be placed on lipid-lowering drugs (Hippisley-Cox et al., 2001). However, these drugs appear to be more effective in preventing heart disease in men than in women (Petretta et al., 2010).

Women are less likely than men to receive each of the three major treatments for heart disease (Kattainen et al., 2005; Sacco, Cerone, & Carolei, 2009; Vitale et al., 2007). One treatment is a type of drug therapy, referred to as **thrombolytic therapy**. Thrombolytic drugs are administered during the course of a heart attack with the hope of opening the arteries, increasing blood flow, and reducing the amount of heart damage. Despite the fact that thrombolytic therapy has been shown to be more effective in women than men (Sacco et al., 2009), it is used less often in women than in men. A second treatment for heart disease is **percutaneous transluminal coronary angioplasty (PTCA)**. With PTCA, a balloon is placed on the tip of a catheter, which is then threaded through the coronary arteries. At the site of the blockage, the balloon is inflated in an effort to increase the diameter of the artery and thus increase blood flow. Women are less likely than men to be referred for coronary angioplasty. A similar procedure is used to insert a coronary stent to help keep the artery open. The third major treatment for heart disease is **coronary artery bypass surgery**. Arteries are taken from the person's leg or chest wall and used to bypass the blockages of the arteries that supply blood to the heart. This is a major surgical procedure. Women are less likely than men to be referred for

bypass surgery even when they have comparable medical profiles (Travis, 2005). Women also are only half as likely as men to receive implantable cardioverter-defibrillators to prevent life-threatening arrhythmias (i.e., irregular heartbeats; Curtis et al., 2007). Although earlier studies showed that women have poorer outcomes from some of these procedures compared to men, more recent studies suggest that the sex difference in mortality following the insertion of a coronary stent or bypass surgery may be disappearing (Ishihara et al., 2008; Travis, 2005).

One reason that women are less likely to be referred for some of these treatments than men is that disease is more advanced in women than men when it is detected. Why is that the case? It turns out that heart disease is more difficult to detect in women than men. Men are more likely to have classic chest pain, and women are more likely to have a variety of ambiguous symptoms, such as nausea, shortness of breath, and back pain (Vitale et al., 2007). This could partly explain why one study showed that women with heart problems were more likely than men with heart problems to be mistakenly discharged from hospital emergency rooms (Pope et al., 2000). When heart damage was assessed 24 to 72 hours later, missed diagnoses were more common in women than men.

However, even when symptoms are the same, physicians appear less likely to diagnose heart disease in women than men. In an experimental study, a videotape of a patient with key symptoms of heart disease (chest pain, stress, heartburn, low energy) was presented to family physicians who were asked to indicate the nature of the problem and the certainty of their opinion (Maserejian et al., 2009). The patient was either male or female and either 55 or 75 years old. Regardless of the diagnosis physicians made, they

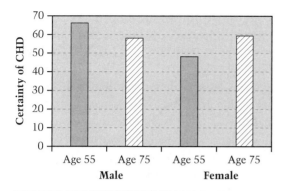

FIGURE 10.2   Physicians were more certain of coronary heart disease diagnoses in males than females, and especially uncertain in the case of younger females.

Source: Adapted from Maserejian et al. (2009).

were more confident in assessing the male than the female. When heart disease was diagnosed, physicians were the least confident in diagnosing a younger female as shown in Figure 10.2. Physicians were more likely to diagnose mental health problems in younger females compared to all other groups.

Women's complaints of cardiac symptoms may be mistaken for signs of psychological distress. Because women are more depressed than men, women's symptoms may more likely be interpreted as depression or anxiety. In fact, chest pain can signify stress and anxiety. When patients report feelings of psychological distress along with cardiac symptoms, the psychosocial complaints may distract the physician from the cardiac symptoms—at least when the patient is female. In one study, medical students and residents were provided with a vignette of a person with clear cardiac symptoms (e.g., chest pain, shortness of breath) who was or was not experiencing stress (Chiaramonte & Friend, 2006). Women and men were treated differently only under conditions of high stress. Coronary heart disease was equally

likely to be diagnosed among women and men in the no-stress condition but less likely to be diagnosed among women than men in the high-stress condition. In addition, women and men in the no-stress condition were equally likely to be referred to a cardiologist, but women were less likely than men to be referred to a cardiologist in the high-stress condition. Chiaramonte and Friend found that symptoms of women in the high-stress condition were less likely to be attributed to a physiological cause compared to the symptoms of the targets in the other three conditions. Thus, stress may distract physicians from diagnosing heart disease in women.

Taken collectively, heart disease in women may not be diagnosed as quickly as it is in men because women's signs of heart disease are more ambiguous and because health care professionals associate heart disease with being male rather than female. See if the men and women with heart disease you encounter have different experiences with the health care system with Do Gender 10.1.

DO GENDER 10.1
Women's and Men's
Experiences with Heart Problems

Interview 10 adult men and 10 adult women who have had a heart problem, such as a heart attack. Ask them what their symptoms of the heart problem were, when they first noticed symptoms, and how they responded to those symptoms. How long did they wait before going to the doctor? How did the physician respond? Did the physician know right away the symptoms were cardiac in nature? How were they treated for their heart problem? Are there any differences between women's and men's responses?

TAKE HOME POINTS

■ Artifactual explanations for sex differences in health include men's higher SES compared to women and physicians' differential treatment of women and men.

■ Although men have a higher SES than women and SES is clearly related to health, SES does not appear to account for sex differences in health in the United States.

■ Men have higher rates of heart disease than women, but women's disease is more advanced at diagnosis compared to men.

■ Women are treated less aggressively than men for cardiac disease, in part because some treatments are less effective and riskier for women than men, in part because symptoms of heart disease are more ambiguous among women than men, and in part because physicians attribute cardiac symptoms to psychological causes in the presence of stress among women.

HEALTH BEHAVIORS

One class of variables that may explain sex differences in mortality and morbidity are **health behaviors**. These include risky behaviors, such as smoking, alcohol abuse, and drug abuse, as well as healthy behaviors, such as preventive health care, exercise, and diet. These behavioral factors contribute to sex differences in the leading causes of death—heart disease, lung cancer, chronic lower respiratory disease, accidents, suicides, homicides, and liver disease. Now that people are living longer and dying of chronic diseases, behavioral factors may play a larger role than biology in sex differences in mortality.

Preventive Health Care

Women are more likely than men to believe in the value of preventive health care. Women attach greater importance to healthy eating than men (Wardle et al., 2004). Across 23 different countries, women were more likely than men to report that they avoided high-fat foods, ate more fruit, ate more fiber, and limited salt. Among college students in the United States, females report a better diet than males among all ethnic groups except Hispanics, in which case there is no sex difference (Courtenay, McCreary, & Merighi, 2002). Among children, the picture is more complicated. One-third of high school girls and boys eat fruit or drink 100% fruit juice; boys are over twice as likely as girls to drink three or more glasses of milk a day, but boys are also more likely than girls to drink soda each day (Centers for Disease Control and Prevention, 2010a).

Women are more likely to perform regular self-exams, to have a regular physician, and to have regular checkups (Courtenay et al., 2002). Women are also more likely to take prescriptions as recommended and to return to the doctor's office for follow-up care. Among adults, more men than women do not see their physician on an annual basis (Pleis & Lethbridge-Cejku, 2007).

One reason women have a regular physician and have better preventive care habits centers on reproductive issues. Women regularly visit the doctor for pap smears, mammograms, birth control, pregnancy, and postmenopausal symptoms. Men do not have the same regular life events or health issues early in life that require establishing a regular physician or routine physician visits. However, even when reproductive visits are excluded from analyses, women still visit the doctor more frequently than do men. In a sense, it is difficult to account completely for reproductive reasons when examining sex differences in the use of health care services. We can certainly count the number of visits attributed to reproductive issues, such as pregnancy or contraception, but we must consider that women are more likely than men to become involved in the health care system in the first place because of reproductive issues. Thus, when it comes to getting a flu shot, getting a regular physical, and seeking medical attention in response to a complaint, women are more likely to have a resource available and to be familiar with turning to that resource. Conduct Do Gender 10.2 to find out if your female and male peers have a physician and examine their reasons.

One group of women do not receive greater health care compared to men: lesbians. Both lesbians and gay men are underserved by the health care system, in part due to a lack of health insurance (Johnson, Miamiaga, & Bradford, 2008). Lesbians are less likely than heterosexual women to have health insurance from a spouse's employment, and lesbian households have lower income. Although rates of screening have increased in recent years for lesbians, screening rates are still lower than rates for heterosexual women (Roberts et al., 2004). Both lesbians and gay men report feeling uncomfortable dealing

with a health care system that is not sensitive to homosexuality. Over the last decade, lesbians have become more likely to disclose their sexual orientation to health care providers (Roberts et al., 2004). However, the health care of older sexual minorities is an issue because older people are less likely to disclose their sexual orientation (Addis et al., 2009).

What are the implications of heterosexual women's greater use of medical services for prevention compared to men? Theoretically, if women visit the doctor more frequently than men do, women's illnesses should be diagnosed at an earlier stage than men's. Early intervention may keep minor illnesses from developing into fatal ones. Routine office visits provide physicians with an opportunity to detect disease and provide patients with an opportunity to disclose problems. Although this is a compelling explanation for sex differences in mortality, there is no evidence to show that women's greater use of health services leads to earlier detection of disease. In fact, heart disease is detected later in women than men, and women delay longer in seeking treatment for symptoms of heart disease.

Smoking

Smoking has been referred to as the single most preventable cause of death (American Cancer Society, 2009). Tobacco accounts for almost one in five deaths in the United States and 30% of cancer-related deaths. Smoking is a major cause of heart disease, stroke, and emphysema. It is also a contributor to at least 15 different kinds of cancer, including lung, lip, oral, esophagus, pancreas, kidney, and stomach. Among men, smoking is associated with slightly less than a one in two chance of developing cancer at some point in life; among women, the rate is slightly more than one in three. There also are some other chronic conditions associated with smoking

---

DO GENDER 10.2
Do You Have a Doctor?

Interview 10 female and 10 male college students to find out if they have a regular doctor. You might ask, "If you become sick, is there a specific doctor you would call?" To really be certain that people have a physician, you might even ask for the physician's name. If a person does not have a physician, ask why.

Then, interview 20 older adults (10 female, 10 male) and ask the same question. You might interview the same students' parents, university staff, or faculty.

Are there sex differences in having a physician? Does it depend on age? What are the reasons for not having a physician? Do men and women provide different reasons?

such as chronic bronchitis and osteoporosis. Among women, smoking is related to early menopause, decreased fertility, and complications during pregnancy.

Smoking is related to heart disease, and this link is stronger in women than men (Grundtvig et al., 2009; Tan, Gast, & van der Schouw, 2010). Smoking reveals a dose-response relation to heart disease, meaning the more one smokes, the greater her or his risk of heart disease (Rich-Edwards et al., 1995). When people quit smoking, their risk of heart disease decreases dramatically. Within three to five years of quitting, their heart disease rates are similar to those of a nonsmoker.

Smoking is most strongly linked to lung cancer. The risk of lung cancer is 23 times higher in men who smoke and 13 times higher among women who smoke (American Cancer Society, 2009). The risk of lung cancer decreases as the length of smoking cessation increases (U.S. Department of Health and Human Services, 2004). However, the risk of lung cancer remains higher among former smokers than nonsmokers, no matter how long the cessation period. The increased rates of men smoking in the middle of the 20th century can be directly tied to the dramatic rise in lung cancer and heart disease among men and the subsequent widening of the sex difference in mortality at that time (Hyams & Johnson, 2010). The increased rates of smoking among women in the 1960s and 1970s can be directly tied to the increased rate of lung cancer that emerged among women 20 to 30 years later. In 1987, lung cancer surpassed breast cancer as the leading cause of cancer death among women. The increase in smoking among women and the lower quit rates among women contributed to the recent narrowing of the sex gap in longevity. Since the 1960s, the number of male smokers decreased by about 50%; the number of women decreased by only 25%. Although rates of lung cancer have decreased since 1984 in men, rates of lung cancer have increased among women until leveling off over the past few years. It is not clear whether smoking is riskier for women or men in terms of lung cancer. Some studies argue that when the amount of smoking is taken into consideration, there are no sex differences in vulnerability to smoking, whereas other studies suggest that women are more vulnerable to lung cancer at every level of smoking. If women are more vulnerable, both hormonal and genetic factors may play a role. Women are clearly more vulnerable to lung cancer than men among nonsmokers.

Prevalence Among Adults. The most recent data from the Centers for Disease Control and Prevention (2009a) show that 21% of adults in the United States smoke. This is down from 42% in 1965 (American Cancer Society, 2009). As shown in Figure 10.3, men are more likely than women to smoke across ethnic groups in the United States, with the largest sex differences appearing among American Indians/Alaska Natives, Asians, and Hispanics and the smallest sex difference occurring in Whites. The state with the lowest rate of smoking is Utah (10%), and the state with the highest rate of smoking is Kentucky (26%; Centers for Disease Control and Prevention, 2009b).

Sex differences in smoking changed over the latter half of the 20th century. In the early part of the century, men smoked more than women because smoking was not viewed as socially acceptable for women. In 1955, 25% of women smoked compared to 52% of men (Chesney & Nealey, 1996). In the 1960s and 1970s, the health hazards of smoking became publicized, but smoking also became more socially acceptable for women. Smoking among women increased during the women's

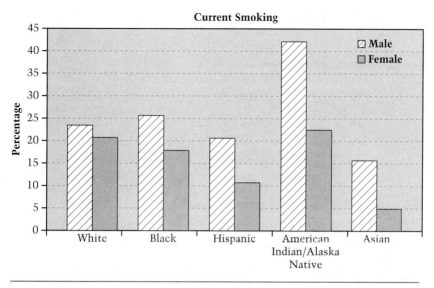

FIGURE 10.3   Percentages of adults in the United States who report they currently smoke. In all ethnic groups, more men than women smoke.
Source: Adapted from Centers for Disease Control and Prevention (2009a).

movement and came to be associated with women's fight for equality. Thus, in the 1960s and 1970s, more women than men started smoking, and more men than women began to quit smoking. Today, men still have higher quit rates than women. The sex difference in smoking has decreased over time.

Along with the sex difference in smoking patterns, the sex difference in lung cancer shifted. In 1950, the male–female ratio of lung cancer was 4.6; in 1960, it was 6.7; in 1990, it was 2.3; and in 2009, it was estimated to be 1.2 (American Cancer Society, 2009). Since the 1980s, the incidence of lung cancer has declined among men but increased among women. Only recently has the rate in women started to level off. Because lung cancer develops over the two to three decades following smoking, the changes in women's and men's rates of lung cancer can be directly tied to the changes in their rates of smoking.

Prevalence Among Adolescents and Children.   Smoking is particularly important to study among children and adolescents. First, a majority of smokers begin to smoke during adolescence or early adulthood (Substance Abuse and Mental Health Services Administration, 2010). By twelfth grade, 44% of youth have tried cigarettes. Second, some evidence suggests that smoking slows lung development among adolescents (Gold et al., 1996). These effects are stronger among females than males.

Among high school students in 2009, 19% of girls and 20% of boys reported that they currently smoked, which was defined as having smoked one or more cigarettes in the past 30 days. As shown in Figure 10.4, the rate of smoking increased among children in the early 1990s, decreased since 1997, and now appears to have leveled off. In the 1990s, smoking among Black males increased dramatically, but those rates have decreased substantially in recent years. Black males and

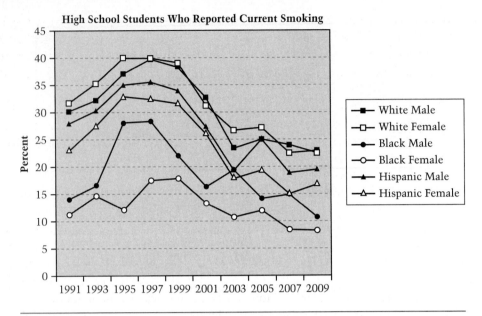

FIGURE 10.4 Prevalence of current cigarette smoking among high school students over time. Smoking rates increased among White, Black, and Hispanic high school students in the early 1990s, decreased since 1997, and seem to have leveled off.
Source: Adapted from Centers for Disease Control and Prevention (2010c).

females have the lowest rates of smoking. Among Whites, a similar percentage of girls and boys smoke, whereas among Blacks and Hispanics, more boys than girls smoke. Data collected on middle school students (sixth through eighth grade) show that more boys than girls smoke (11% vs. 8%), Hispanics smoke the most (11%), Asians the least (5%), with Whites and Blacks in the middle (9% and 10%, respectively; Centers for Disease Control and Prevention, 2007a).

Smoking Cessation. Smoking is more difficult in the United States than it was 10 and 20 years ago, as it has been banned from many public buildings, restaurants, ballparks, and even some beaches. As of 2010, smoking was banned from all public places in 32 states (Kaiser Family Foundation, 2010). With these smoking restrictions, the increased awareness of health risks, and

the increased cost of cigarettes, many people have attempted to quit smoking. Over half of all high school smokers have said that they have tried to quit (Centers for Disease Control and Prevention, 2010a). Among adults, more men than women have quit smoking. There is also evidence that when both women and men try to quit smoking, men's attempts are more often successful (Piper et al., 2010). Both hypnosis (Green, Lynn, & Montgomery, 2008) and nicotine replacement therapy (Perkins & Scott, 2008) are less effective in helping women than men to quit smoking. Perhaps physicians are aware of this difference, as physicians are less likely to prescribe smoking cessation medication to women than men (Steinberg et al., 2006).

Several theories attempt to explain why it is more difficult for women to quit smoking. One theory is that smoking is associated with negative affect and depression, and women are more likely than men to be depressed. People with a history of depression or anxiety disorders are more likely to smoke than are people without such histories (Morrell, Cohen, & McChargue, 2010). Even depressed adolescent females are more likely to start smoking than their male counterparts (Whitbeck et al., 2009). And, the relation of smoking to depression is stronger among women than men (Husky et al., 2008; Massak & Graham, 2008; Morrell et al., 2010). Women smokers, in particular, are likely to believe that smoking enhances their mood and helps them to cope with stress (Hazen, Mannino, & Clayton, 2008; Reid et al., 2009). It also turns out that quitting smoking is associated with an increase in negative mood—and more so for women than men (Morrell et al., 2010). One study of smokers showed that anxiety and hostility increased when smokers abstained, and the increase was greater among women than men (Xu et al., 2008). In addition, when participants were allowed to resume smoking, women experienced more relief from anxiety than men. To recap, one reason women are less able to quit smoking than men is that depression interferes with cessation, women are more likely than men to be depressed, and smoking is more strongly associated with mood enhancement in women than men.

Another theory as to why women have more difficulty quitting smoking is that women are more likely to be physiologically addicted to smoking. Women become addicted to smoking at lower nicotine levels and with fewer cigarettes compared to men (Tuchman, 2010). Female smokers are more likely than male smokers to report behaviors indicative of physiological addiction, including smoking a cigarette within 10 minutes of waking, smoking when sick, being upset about having to go a whole day without a cigarette, and reporting "not feeling right" if one goes too long without smoking (Royce et al., 1997;

Sussman et al., 1998). The Fagerstrom Tolerance Questionnaire, shown in Table 10.7, is a widely used measure of physiological addiction to nicotine (Heatherton et al., 1991). If you have friends who smoke, conduct Do Gender 10.3 to see who is more strongly addicted to smoking. Also see Sidebar 10.2 for a discussion of how methodology affects reporting of withdrawal symptoms.

Perkins (2009), however, has argued that women are *less* likely than men to be physiologically addicted to nicotine. This argument is based on research that shows nicotine replacement therapies are less effective for women. A meta-analytic review of the literature showed that women receive about half the benefit of men from the nicotine patch (Perkins & Scott, 2008). One illustrative study showed that nicotine replacement therapy influenced a physiological recording of sleep quality—an objective measure of withdrawal symptoms—among men but not women (Wetter et al., 1999a). Men and women who had quit smoking were randomly assigned to receive a nicotine patch or a placebo patch, and their sleep quality was measured physiologically. Men who received the nicotine patch had better sleep quality, as indicated by physiological recordings of sleep duration and sleep awakenings, than men who did not receive the patch. The patch did not influence women's sleep quality. Thus, the nicotine patch was effective in helping men sleep but had no effect on women's sleep quality. This research suggests that men are more physiologically addicted to nicotine.

If women are not as physiologically addicted to nicotine, what is the basis of women's addiction? Perkins (2009) suggests that smoking is more of a sensory experience for women than for men. Women enjoy the visual and olfactory experiences of smoking more than men do.

TABLE 10.7   REVISED FAGERSTROM TOLERANCE QUESTIONNAIRE

1. How soon after you wake up do you smoke your first cigarette?
   a. After 60 minutes.
   b. 31–60 minutes.
   c. 6–30 minutes.
   d. Within 5 minutes.

2. Do you find it difficult to refrain from smoking in places where it is forbidden?
   No   Yes

3. Which cigarette would you hate to give up?
   a. The first one in the morning.
   b. Any other.

4. How many cigarettes per day do you smoke?
   a. 10 or fewer
   b. 11–20
   c. 21–30
   d. 31 or more

5. Do you smoke more frequently during the first hours after waking than during the rest of the day?
   No   Yes

6. Do you smoke if you are so ill that you are in bed most of the day?
   No   Yes

Source: T. F. Heatherton et al. (1991). Copyright 1991. Reprinted by permission of Taylor and Francis.

A third theory as to why women have greater difficulty quitting smoking is that women are more concerned with the potential for weight gain. Women around the world are more likely than men to say that they smoke to suppress their appetite (Reid et al., 2009), and women are concerned about gaining

---

DO GENDER 10.3
Who Is More Physiologically Addicted to Smoking?

Administer the Fagerstrom Tolerance Questionnaire shown in Table 10.7 to 10 male and 10 female smokers. Is one sex more addicted than the other? Can you predict addiction from any other variables, such as age or depression?

---

weight if they quit smoking (Larsen, Otten, & Engels, 2009). One reason that depressed women smoke is concern about weight gain (Larsen et al., 2009). Among adults, both underweight and overweight women are more likely to smoke than normal weight women, whereas overweight men are less likely to smoke than normal weight men (Park, 2009). However, after quitting, no evidence indicates that weight gain predicts relapse in women (Borrelli et al., 2001; Perkins et al., 2001).

Quitting smoking does lead to weight gain, but not as much as people think, partly because people underestimate how much they weighed before they quit smoking (Peterson, 1999). According to the U.S. Surgeon General (Centers for Disease Control and Prevention, 2007b), women gain between 6 and 12 pounds during the first year after they quit smoking. In subsequent years, the weight gain diminishes. The weight gain

SIDEBAR 10.2: *How Methodology Affects Self-Report of Withdrawal Symptoms*

One way physiological addiction is measured is by self-reports of withdrawal symptoms when quitting smoking. Withdrawal symptoms include depressed mood, insomnia, irritability, anxiety, difficulty concentrating, restlessness, decreased heart rate, and increased appetite (American Psychiatric Association, 2000). It is not clear whether women or men report more withdrawal symptoms. The methodology of a study appears to influence whether sex differences in withdrawal symptoms emerge. Prospective studies (conducted during cessation) show no sex differences, whereas retrospective studies (conducted after cessation) show that women recall more symptoms than men. What is the source of this discrepancy? Is it that women recall more symptoms than they actually experience or that men recall fewer symptoms? The latter seems to be the case. Pomerleau and colleagues (1994) compared prospective and retrospective reports of withdrawal symptoms. They asked men and women first to recall their experience of four common withdrawal symptoms (anxiety, anger/irritation, difficulty in concentrating, hunger) from previous attempts to quit smoking and then to report prospectively their experience of these symptoms over the first few days that they quit smoking. Men recalled fewer symptoms in the past than they actually experienced during their present attempt; in other words, men's recall of symptoms underestimated the extent to which they actually experienced symptoms. For example, only 5% of men said they experienced difficulty concentrating during past attempts to quit smoking, but 58% reported this symptom during the present attempt. Women's retrospective reports of difficulty concentrating were more similar to their prospective reports (40% vs. 56%). There were no sex differences in any of the prospective reports of symptoms. Thus, retrospective methodologies may suggest that women experience more withdrawal symptoms due to men's tendency to recall fewer symptoms than they actually experienced. According to self-reports of current withdrawal symptoms, women and men experience similar withdrawal symptoms, which means similar levels of physiological addiction.

associated with smoking cessation is far less hazardous to health than the hazards associated with smoking.

One motivator for women to quit smoking is pregnancy. Between 23% and 43% of women quit smoking when they become pregnant in the United States (Schneider et al., 2010). Women who are of a lower SES, have partners who smoke, are more addicted, and have more children are less likely to quit smoking while pregnant. However, most women who quit when they become pregnant subsequently resume smoking after childbirth. Half of women resume smoking within six months of delivery and over two-thirds

resume smoking by one year (Centers for Disease Control and Prevention, 2007b).

Thus, various theories have been put forth to explain why women have more difficulty than men when they try to quit smoking. One theory is that women are more depressed and depression interferes with smoking cessation. Some evidence supports this. Another theory is that women are more physiologically addicted to smoking, but the evidence in support of this theory is completely contradictory. On some self-report measures of physiological addiction, women appear more dependent than men on nicotine; yet another group of investigators suggests men are more physiologically addicted because nicotine patches are more effective in relieving men's withdrawal symptoms than those of women. A third theory is that women are more concerned than men with the weight gain that follows smoking cessation. This concern may interfere with initial cessation efforts but does not predict relapse. People do gain weight when they quit smoking but probably not as much as they expect.

Alcohol

The relation of moderate alcohol intake to health is mixed. On the one hand, alcohol in moderation is protective against heart disease and appears to provide immunity from the common cold (Rich-Edwards et al., 1995). However, alcohol in moderation may also be associated with breast cancer (American Cancer Society, 2009).

Large quantities of alcohol are clearly harmful to health. Heavy use of alcohol is associated with a variety of health risks, including injury, violence, poisoning, and birth defects/miscarriage in the short-term and cardiovascular disease, cancer, and liver disease in the long term (Centers for Disease Control and Prevention, 2008). Alcohol is linked to accidents in general and to motor vehicle accidents in particular. Of fatal crashes, 25% of men and 13% of women were driving under the influence of alcohol (U.S. Department of Transportation, 2008a).

Alcohol has different consequences for women and men (Nolen-Hoeksema & Hilt, 2006). Although women have a lower genetic risk for alcohol-use disorders, the physiological consequences of alcohol are more damaging to women. It takes proportionally less alcohol to have the same effect on a woman as a man; even if a woman and a man of similar weight drink the same amount of alcohol, the woman will have a higher blood-alcohol level.

The ratio of fat to water in a woman's body is greater than that in a man's body; in other words, men have more water available in their systems to dilute consumed alcohol. In addition, more of the alcohol is metabolized by enzymes in the stomachs of men compared to women. Thus, men and women who drink the same amount of alcohol in proportion to their body weight will not have the same blood-alcohol levels. This may be one reason why alcohol is more strongly associated with cirrhosis of the liver in women than in men. The progression from the first drink to an alcohol-related problem is faster among women than men, a process referred to as "telescoping." Thus, women are more vulnerable than men to both acute and chronic (long-lasting) effects of alcohol. Alcohol also seems to be more strongly related to depression in women than men (Harrell & Karim, 2008; Tuchman, 2010).

Prevalence. Alcohol usage and alcohol-related problems are higher among men than women. The prevalence of alcohol usage was examined in the 2008 National Survey of Drug Abuse, which is a national survey of over 8,000 persons of age 12 and above (Substance Abuse and Mental Health Services Administration, 2009). This representative survey revealed that 58% of males and 46% of females have used alcohol in the past month. Binge drinking in the past month, which is defined as five or more drinks on a single occasion for males and four or more drinks on a single occasion for females, is three times as prevalent among men than women over the age of 18 (24% vs. 8%; Centers for Disease Control and Prevention, 2009c). The rate is highest among Whites and lowest among Blacks. There is cross-cultural support for these sex differences. In a study of 10 countries (Australia, Canada, Czech Republic, Estonia, Finland, Israel, Russia, Sweden, Netherlands, and United States), men drank alcohol more frequently, consumed higher amounts of alcohol at one time, had more episodes of heavy drinking, and were more likely to suffer adverse consequences of drinking compared to women (e.g., health problems, criticism by others, losing control; Wilsnack et al., 2000). Studies of college students also show that males drink more alcohol, have more alcohol-related problems, and are more likely to binge drink than females (Harrell & Karim, 2008). The sex difference in alcohol usage holds among sexual minorities. Gay men drink more alcohol than lesbians, but there is no difference between the two groups in alcohol-related problems (Amadio, Adam, & Buletza, 2008). Lesbians drink more than heterosexual women (Fassinger & Arseneau, 2007).

The relation of gender to alcohol among high school students is quite different. Here, the picture is one of similarity. Among ninth through twelfth graders, 43% of females and 41% of males drink alcohol, defined as having one drink during the past 30 days (Centers for Disease Control and Prevention, 2010a). Rates are comparable for females and males among Whites, Blacks, and Hispanics, although overall usage is lower among Blacks than Whites or Hispanics. Binge drinking is also comparable between females and males (23% vs. 25%) among Whites, Blacks, and Hispanics, but again, overall binge drinking (defined as five or more drinks in a row) is lower among Blacks than Whites and Hispanics.

One reason adult women drink less heavily than men has to do with society's attitudes toward drinking (Nolen-Hoeksema & Hilt, 2006). Society disapproves of heavy drinking in women, which is thought to interfere with the female role of being responsible for children. Another reason women drink less than men is that women are more involved in religion, which deters drinking. Sex differences in drinking have decreased over

the last 50 years, such that today there are no sex differences in alcohol usage among youth. Is this because society now views drinking as equally acceptable in women and men? Find out about your peers' attitudes toward men and women drinking in Do Gender 10.4.

Drugs

The health consequences of substance abuse can be severe; the most severe consequence is death. However, substance abuse can also lead to other problems, such as complications with pregnancy, health problems in children born to addicted mothers and fathers, sexual difficulties, and, in the case of intravenous drug use, HIV. Women are quicker to develop physical health problems following drug usage compared to men, such as liver problems, hypertension, and gastrointestinal problems (Tuchman, 2010). Women are less likely to seek treatment than men, because women are poorer, are more likely to have a drug-using

DO GENDER 10.4
Attitudes Toward Men and Women Drinking

Create several scenarios of a person at a party drinking varying amounts of alcohol, ranging from none to moderate to a lot (i.e., so much that he or she gets sick or blacks out). Create two versions of these scenarios by using a female name and a male name. Develop a set of items to measure people's attitudes toward the person in the scenario. Are women and men who do not use alcohol viewed similarly? Are men and women who drink alcohol viewed similarly? Does it depend on the level? Finally, do the answers to these questions depend on the sex of the respondent?

partner, and, in the case of children, lack childcare and fear losing custody of children.

Prevalence. Men use more drugs than women do. According to findings from the 2008 National Household Survey on Drug Abuse, the rate of drug use has declined for both men and women since the late 1970s, stabilized in the 1990s, and shown a slight increase recently (Substance Abuse and Mental Health Services Administration, 2009). These findings are based on persons aged 12 and above using illicit drugs within the prior month. Figure 10.5 shows the rates of drug use for males and females in different age groups in 2008. Males have nearly twice the rate of drug use as females except between the ages of 12 and 17, when rates are similar. The sex difference holds for Whites, Blacks, and Hispanics. Men are also twice as likely as women to be classified as dependent on drugs or alcohol (11.5% vs. 6.4%), although

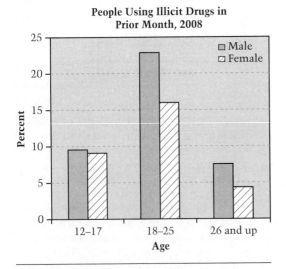

FIGURE 10.5 Percentage of people using illicit drugs in the prior month in 2008.
Source: Adapted from Substance Abuse and Mental Health Services Administration (2009).

the rate among 12- to 17-year-olds is higher among females (8.2%) than males (7.0%). A meta-analytic review of the relation of sexual orientation to substance use showed that sexual minorities engage in more substance usage than heterosexuals ($d = +.59$; Marshal et al., 2008). The effect was especially high for lesbians and bisexuals. The largest effects were for hard drugs, and the smallest effects were for more commonly used drugs, such as marijuana and alcohol.

A study that provides substantial information about drug usage among adolescents is the Monitoring the Future Study (Johnston et al., 2009, 2010). This study has tracked drug use among thousands of high school seniors since 1975 and among thousands of eighth and tenth grade students since 1991. Between the late 1970s and 1990, drug usage declined dramatically among adolescents, but drug usage increased during the 1990s. Since the late 1990s, drug usage has leveled off and more recently shown a slight decline. For example, the percentage of twelfth graders who had used marijuana over the past year increased in the 1970s, peaked at 51% in 1979, decreased to 22% in 1992, rose in the 1990s to near 40% and has declined in recent years to 32%. Similar trends were observed for other illicit drugs. There has been a very slight decline during the past few years. Sex differences in illicit drug use appear to increase with age. There are no sex differences in illicit drug use over the past year among eighth graders, very small sex differences in drug use among tenth graders, and a larger sex difference among twelfth graders in the direction of boys more than girls (39% vs. 34%). Males are more likely than females to use marijuana among eighth, tenth, and twelfth graders, but the size of this sex difference also increases with age.

Males use more of almost all kinds of drugs compared to females—in particular illegal drugs. The only drugs that females tend to use more than males are prescription tranquilizers and sedatives; this finding holds for all age groups. Among high school students, males are more likely to have used cocaine, ecstasy, heroin, and methamphetamines than females (Centers for Disease Control and Prevention, 2010a). Averaging across studies, sex differences in the use of specific drugs are shown in Table 10.8.

Overweight and Obesity

Obesity is a risk factor for all causes of mortality, heart disease, Type 2 diabetes, hypertension (high blood pressure), high cholesterol, and some cancers. Obesity takes different forms in women and men. Men are more likely to have **android obesity**: the apple shape, which consists of extra weight collected around the abdomen. Android obesity is measured by the ratio of waist to hip size. A ratio of more than 1.0 is a significant risk factor for men and a ratio of more than .8 is a significant risk for women (Wing & Klem, 1997). Women are more likely to have **gynoid obesity**: the pear shape, which consists of extra weight around the hips. In

general, android obesity poses greater risks to health than gynoid obesity. Among those 45 years old and younger, obesity has a stronger relation to mortality for men, but among those over 45, overweight and obesity have a stronger relation to hospitalizations and mortality for women (Han, Truesdale et al., 2009; Muennig et al., 2006).

Aside from physical health problems, there are implications of obesity for quality of life. The social, psychological, and economic consequences of obesity are more severe for women than for men (Muennig et al., 2006). Whereas obese women are less likely than non-obese women to go to college, there is no relation of obesity to higher education among men (Crosnoe, 2007). Obesity is also more clearly related to depression in White, Black, and Hispanic women than men (Heo et al., 2006).

Definition. Obesity is typically determined by a combination of height and weight, or the **body mass index (BMI)**, the calculation for which is shown in Table 10.9. A BMI between 25.0 and 29.9 is classified as overweight, and a BMI over 30.0 is classified as obese.

Prevalence. As first indicated by the surgeon general's call to action in 2001, obesity has become an epidemic in the United States. In the 2007–2008 National Health and Nutrition Examination Survey, 34% of adults over 20 years old were overweight and an additional 34% were obese (Flegal et al., 2010). The rate of obesity has doubled since the 1976–1980 survey. The increase in overweight and obesity is due in part to an increase in weight among the most obese (i.e., the heaviest people

TABLE 10.8 SEX DIFFERENCES IN SUBSTANCE ABUSE

Substance	Abuse Ratio
Alcohol	Males higher (5:1)
Amphetamine	Males higher (3–4:1)
Caffeine	Males higher
Cannabis	Males higher
Cocaine	Males higher (1.5–2.0:1)
Hallucinogens	Males higher (3:1)
Heroin	Males higher (3:1)
Inhalants	Males higher
Nicotine	Males higher
Sedatives	Females higher

Source: Adapted from the American Psychiatric Association (2000).

TABLE 10.9 BODY MASS INDEX (BMI)

$$\text{BMI calculation:} \frac{\text{Weight (kilograms)}}{\text{Height}^2 \text{ (meters)}}$$

are becoming heavier) and in part to an increase in weight for all age and sex groups (i.e., the entire distribution of weight has shifted). Men are more likely than women to be overweight, but women are more likely than men to be obese. Among Whites, the rate of obesity is the same for women and men (33% women; 32% men), whereas the rate of obesity is much higher among females than males among Blacks (50% vs. 37%) and Hispanics (45% vs. 36%).

In the vast majority of the countries in the world, women are more likely than men to be obese (Case & Menendez, 2009). For example, in South Africa, women are five times as likely as men to be obese. In Morocco, women are nearly three times as likely as men to be obese (Batnitzky, 2008). Traditional gender roles partly explain these findings. In cultures where women and men have traditional roles, women gain weight due to childbearing; they also lack time for leisure exercise due to the burden of household chores. In addition, women traditionally serve men their meals first, which means that men eat the healthiest food.

Obesity has also increased dramatically among children, although rates appear to have leveled off in recent years. The rates of obesity for children of ages 12 to 19 are shown in Figure 10.6. Obesity among children is defined as a BMI at or above the 95th percentile for one's age and sex. The percentage of obese children in the 2007–2008 survey was 19% for boys and 17% for girls (Ogden & Carroll, 2010). The size and direction of the sex difference depend on race. Among Hispanics, more males are obese compared to females (27% vs. 17%); among Whites, slightly more males are obese compared to females (17% vs. 15%); but among Blacks, more females are obese compared to males (29% vs. 20%). The risk of obesity appears to increase during the transition from adolescence to early adulthood when youth begin to establish independent living situations, but the increase is especially high in some subgroups—specifically, females, immigrants, Blacks, and Hispanics (Harris, Perreira, & Lee, 2009).

Obesity is especially problematic in children because dietary and exercise habits

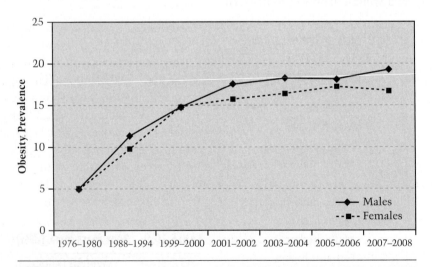

FIGURE 10.6 The rate of obese children and adolescents has dramatically risen over the past 30 years.
Source: Adapted from Ogden and Carroll (2010).

instilled in childhood are difficult to change. In addition, obesity is accompanied by metabolic changes in children that are difficult to reverse (Centers for Disease Control and Prevention, 2000). One result of the increase in obesity among children—especially minority children—is the increase in Type 2 diabetes—formerly a disease thought to characterize older people (Dabelea, 2007). Type 2 diabetes is an endocrine disorder in which the body is not as capable of using insulin to metabolize food. Children who are obese often have risk factors for cardiovascular diseases, such as high blood pressure, high cholesterol, and diabetes (Centers for Disease Control and Prevention, 2011).

Obesity is more common among those with a lower SES (Zhang & Wang, 2004), partly because low SES is associated with poorer diets and less exercise. However, obesity is not clearly related to SES among all ethnic groups. Obesity is related to higher SES among White men, White women, and Black women; lower SES among Black and Hispanic men; and unrelated to SES among Hispanic women.

Views of obesity differ across gender and race. Overweight and obese men are less likely than women to perceive their weight to be a health problem (Gregory et al., 2008). Minority groups may have a less negative view of being overweight because weight symbolized wealth historically. White women are more dissatisfied with their bodies than Black and Hispanic women (Grabe & Hyde, 2006). Among adolescents and adults, Black, Hispanic, and White girls say that they wish that they were thinner but this desire occurs at a lower BMI for White girls than Black and Hispanic girls (Banitt et al., 2008; Fitzgibbon, Blackman, & Avellone, 2000). Among college students, Black women say that being thin is less important to them than White women—especially when race is central to their identity (Fujioka et al., 2009).

Etiology.   There are genetic predispositions to obesity, but societal and behavioral factors also are involved. Because the increase in obesity has been so dramatic and has affected the entire population of people, some explanations must focus on societal changes. Among these are the increased availability of food, the increase in food consumption, and the decrease in physical activity (Flegal & Troiano, 2000). During the 1970s, 1980s, and 1990s, people started consuming more food away from home and a greater proportion of calories started coming from salty snacks, soft drinks, and pizza (Nielsen, Siega-Riz, & Popkin, 2002).

The increase in obesity among children has been attributed to poor diet and lack of physical activity—both of which are influenced by heavy television viewing. Studies have found links of television and computer usage to obesity. In a study of 9- to 14-year-olds, television watching and video and computer game usage were associated with increases in BMI over a one-year period (Berkey et al., 2000). A 28-year longitudinal study of children showed that television viewing as a child predicted increased BMI and lower levels of fitness as adults (Landhuis et al., 2008).

Why are women more likely than men to be obese? First, as described next, women engage in a lower level of physical activity than men. Second, there are life events associated with obesity in women: Women are most likely to gain weight when they get married, when they have a child, and during menopause (Wing & Klem, 1997).

Exercise

Physical activity has been related to lower rates of mortality and morbidity (Centers for Disease Control and Prevention, 2010d), and lack of physical activity is clearly linked to the increase in obesity. Specifically, physical activity is associated with reduced heart disease, hypertension, some cancers (e.g., colon cancer), Type 2 diabetes, osteoporosis, and depression.

The recommended guidelines for physical activity are to engage in moderate-intensity exercise, such as brisk walking, bicycling, gardening, vacuuming, or anything that causes a small increase in breathing or heart rate, for 30 minutes five days per week (Centers for Disease Control and Prevention, 2010e). In 2007, just under half of adults met these guidelines. More men than women exercise (see Figure 10.7 for an exception), but the size of the sex difference depends on race. Slightly more White men than women exercise (54% vs. 50%), more Black men than women exercised (45% vs. 36%), and a similar percentage of Hispanic men and women exercise (43% vs. 42%).

FIGURE 10.7   Adult women exercising. Adult women are less likely than adult men to exercise, and even less likely to be involved in competitive exercise.

Rates of physical activity among children have decreased dramatically. In 2009, 46% of high school boys and 28% of high school girls said that they had been physically active for five of the past seven days (Centers for Disease Control and Prevention, 2010a). Similarly, the percentage of girls who said that they had not engaged in any physical activity in the past seven days was higher (30%) than that of boys (17%). The rate was especially high among Black girls (44%).

The kind of exercise in which females and males engage differs (Jacobs et al., 2005). Females are more likely to be involved in individual sports and noncompetitive exercise, whereas males are more likely to be involved in team sports. In fact, one reason boys get more exercise than girls is that boys are more likely to participate in sports, especially team sports. In 2009, 64% of boys and 52% of girls in grades 9 through 12 participated in team sports. The sex difference was smaller for Whites (64% vs. 58%) than Blacks (68% vs. 47%) and Hispanics (62% vs. 45%). However, the number of girls who participated in high school athletic programs has dramatically increased over the past 30 years (see Figure 10.8). In college, the four sports that had the most male participants were football, baseball, track, and soccer; the leading sports for girls were soccer, track, softball, and basketball. Soccer, in particular, has skyrocketed among girls. Twice as many girls play soccer today as they did 15 years ago.

The motives for exercise also differ (Waldron, 1997); men are motivated by competition, whereas women are motivated by concerns about appearance and weight control. Unfortunately, body shape motives are associated with *lower* levels of physical activity compared to other motives for exercise, such as health and intrinsic interest

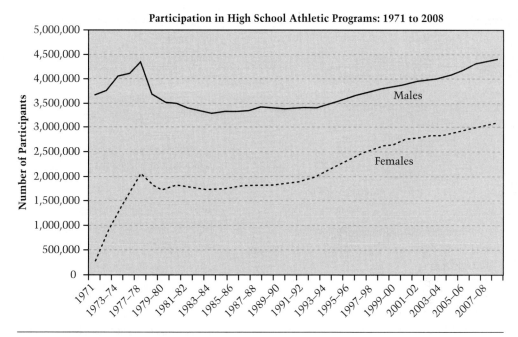

FIGURE 10.8 The number of high school female and male students who participated in team sports between 1971 and 2008. Female participation has dramatically increased.
Source: Adapted from National Federation of State High School Associations (2010).

in exercise (Segar, Spruijt-Metz, & Nolen-Hoeksema, 2006).

One reason for the reduced rates of physical activity among children is that technological advances have made sedentary activities more appealing; these include television, video games, computers, and cell phones. Meyering (2005) refers to the current children as Generation M with the "M" standing for media. Today's children and teenagers are simultaneously surfing the Internet, listening to music, and texting with the television on in the background. One study reported that children spend an average of 6.5 hours per day with media. Two-thirds of children have televisions in their bedrooms (Meyering, 2005). Researchers have suggested that it is not only that television viewing promotes sedentary activity but

also it exposes children to low-nutritional foods via advertising (Jenvey, 2007).

Physical activity in childhood is important because a pattern is set in motion that persists into adulthood. Physical activity is also important because it appears to be a deterrent to risk behavior. Participation in athletics seems to be associated with lower drug usage although the relations to alcohol are contradictory (Connor, 2009; Fredricks & Eccles, 2006). In other ways, physical activity is especially important to adolescent girls. First, physical activity is related to a healthy body image. One study showed that adolescent girls who were physically active and involved in sports were less depressed, in part because they had a more positive view of their bodies (Dishman et al., 2006). Second, physical activity is a deterrent to sexual behavior among girls. A study of college women found that those who participated in team sports during high school engaged in less sexual risk taking and had better sexual and reproductive health (Lehman & Koerner, 2004). A sense of empowerment appeared to explain these relations.

TAKE HOME POINTS

■ Women practice better preventive health care than men by watching their diet and visiting the physician on a regular basis. Reproductive issues do not account for this sex difference.

■ Smoking is the health behavior that can be most strongly tied to the leading causes of death, and smoking contributes greatly to sex differences in mortality.

■ Among adults, men smoke more than women but are quitting at higher rates; among children and adolescents, sex differences in smoking are smaller.

■ Lung cancer is the best illustration of how changes in smoking have influenced changes in mortality rates. Men smoke more than women, have higher rates of lung cancer than women, and die younger than women. However, more men also have quit smoking, and women's rates of smoking have not decreased to the extent that men's have, resulting in an increase in lung cancer among women and a reduction in the sex difference in longevity.

■ There are a variety of reasons why women have more difficulty with smoking cessation compared to men: links of smoking to depression, greater physiological addiction in women (a hotly debated issue), and a concern with weight gain after smoking cessation.

■ Men drink more than women, but the same amount of alcohol per body weight has more hazardous health consequences for women than men.

■ Men use more drugs than women, and the sex difference increases with age during adolescence.

■ The increase in obesity in the United States is now considered an epidemic. Women have higher rates of obesity than men among African Americans and Hispanics, but the same rate among Whites.

■ There are socioeconomic and cultural explanations for ethnic differences in obesity. Black and Hispanic groups have lower incomes, and low income is generally associated with obesity. Culturally, however, being thin is not as valued among the African American as the White community.

■ Physical activity is related to health in general, including obesity. The decline in physical activity is one contributor to the increase in obesity.

■ Television, video games, and computers have been linked to both the decline in physical activity and the increase in obesity.

■ Boys are more active than girls, but the sex difference has decreased in recent years as athletics have become more available to girls.

MEN'S AND WOMEN'S SOCIAL ROLES

If gender roles contribute to sex differences in health, fewer sex differences should exist when roles are more similar. Two older, now classic, studies have tested this hypothesis. First, Leviatan and Cohen (1985) studied men and women on a kibbutz where their roles were more equal. A kibbutz is a community in Israel characterized by a collective lifestyle whereby everyone contributes to the welfare of the community. On a kibbutz, there is equal access to health care, all men and women work inside and outside of the home, and all participate in community decisions. However, roles are not perfectly equal even on a kibbutz. It is still true that women tend to take care of household chores more than men, and the kinds of jobs men and women hold are different and sex-stereotypical. Women are more likely to be employed in education and service industries, whereas men are more likely to be employed in agriculture and industry. Nonetheless, Leviatan and Cohen found that sex differences in life expectancies on the kibbutz were smaller than those in the general population, largely due to an increase in men's life expectancy. Leviatan and Cohen suggest men may have had more social support on the kibbutz and may have been faced with fewer sources of male gender-role strain.

In a second study of people on a kibbutz (Anson, Levenson, & Bonneh, 1990), an array of health outcomes were examined, and sex differences appeared on only two of them—in the direction opposite to that previously discussed in this chapter. Women rated their subjective health as higher than men, and women were less disabled than men. There were no sex differences in psychological distress, physical symptoms, health behaviors, chronic illnesses, restricted activity days, doctor visits, or use of medication. These two studies suggest that when women's and men's social roles are more similar, sex differences in health diminish.

What are some specific features of women's and men's social roles that might be linked to health? Men's social roles include risky behavior, such as working at hazardous jobs and driving. Risk-taking behavior, in general, is part of the male gender role. The female social role includes attending to one's own health concerns. However, the female gender role is also associated with taking care of others, which could have negative implications for health. In this next section, I review some aspects of the female and male social roles, including gender-related traits, that have implications for health.

Job Characteristics

One social role that men and women occupy is their work role. Men work at more hazardous jobs compared to women. According to the U.S. Department of Labor (2010a), men account for 57% of the hours worked but 93% of fatal work injuries. The sex difference in fatalities likely reflects men working in riskier jobs than women. Fatal work injuries are most likely to occur in jobs having to do with agriculture/forestry, mining, transportation, and construction—industries in which more men than women work. Men, especially Black men, are more likely to be exposed to hazardous substances at work, such as asbestos that has been linked to lung cancer (Waldron, 1995). A study of adults in England and Wales found that the sex difference in life expectancy was smaller for professionals and managerial workers than manual unskilled workers (Donkin, Goldblatt, & Lynch, 2002).

Men's labor at home also includes more risks than women's labor at home. For example, men are more likely to be the ones who repair electrical problems and climb on the roof to fix a leak.

Driving

Driving is part of men's social role. Men drive more than women, and when men and women are together, men typically drive. Men drive faster and take more risks while driving. A study of twelfth graders showed that men engage in riskier driving, are more likely to be cited for traffic offenses, and are more likely to get in accidents than women (Elliott et al., 2006). Thus it is not surprising that men have a higher rate of fatal automobile accidents than women at all ages (U.S. Department of Transportation, 2008b). Women also are more likely than men to wear a seat belt (86% vs. 79%), although this sex difference has decreased over the past decade, largely due to increased usage of seat belts among men (U.S. Department of Transportation, 2008c). Among ninth through twelfth graders, it also is the case that girls are more likely than boys to wear a seat belt (92% vs. 88%; Centers for Disease Control and Prevention, 2010a). One risky driving behavior that is on the rise is texting while driving, and this seems to be a larger concern among females than males. One-third of teens of ages 16–17 say that they have texted while driving (Lenhart et al., 2010). Over 50% of girls compared to 38% of boys said that they talked or texted on a phone while driving (White & Athavaley, 2010).

One link to motor vehicle fatalities and an explanation for the sex difference in fatalities is alcohol. Of fatal crashes, 25% of men compared to 13% of women were driving under the influence of alcohol (U.S. Department of Transportation, 2008a). Although there are nearly six times as many males as females involved in alcohol-related fatal crashes (U.S. Department of Transportation, 2009), the rate of women drinking and driving has increased. Between 1999 and 2008, the percentage of women arrested for driving under the influence (DUI) increased 35%, whereas the percentage of men arrested for DUI decreased by 7% (U.S. Department of Justice, 2009). However, men are still 3.5 times as likely as women to be arrested for DUI. Among ninth through twelfth graders, 12% of boys and 8% of girls admit to drinking and driving (Centers for Disease Control and Prevention, 2010a).

Risky Behavior

Many differences in health can be explained by a single aspect of the male gender role: risk-taking behavior. Men's activities are inherently riskier than women's, and men take more risks than women during these activities. Because of men's risk-taking behavior, men have higher rates of all kinds of accidents compared to women, including driving, work, and recreational (Waldron, 1997). We have seen that men's jobs are more hazardous than those of women. We have also seen that men are more likely to find themselves in the driver's seat of a car and to take more risks when driving. Men also are more likely to engage in risky leisure activities such as downhill skiing, skydiving, and mountain climbing. Men are more likely to drown from swimming and boating; men are more likely to own guns and the greater use of guns contributes to a greater number of fatal gun accidents (Waldron, 1995). Until recently, only men participated in the armed services, risking death from combat. Men engage in riskier sexual behavior than women, in terms of inconsistent condom use and sex with multiple partners (Beadnell et al., 2005). See Sidebar 10.3 for a discussion of this issue.

A meta-analysis of 150 risk-taking behavior studies revealed that men were greater risk takers than women ($d = +.13$; Byrnes, Miller, & Schafer, 1999). This effect held across a range of behaviors that included sex, drinking, using drugs, risky driving, risky physical activities, and gambling. Byrnes and colleagues also found that the size of the sex difference had decreased over time. More recent research substantiated that claim, by showing that the sex difference in risk-taking behavior is getting smaller due to an increase in risky behavior among females (Abbott-Chapman, Denholm, &Wyld, 2008). In a study in Australia, high school boys reported a similar level of risky activities as high school girls, whereas fathers recalled more risky activities as teens compared to mothers. Risky activities include body piercing, use of drugs and alcohol, smoking, skipping class, and shoplifting. Among parents, the sex difference was larger for those who were in their teens in

SIDEBAR 10.3: *Condom Use*

Condoms are used to prevent the spread of HIV and other sexually transmitted diseases (STDs) as well as provide a form of contraception to prevent pregnancy. The number of women in the United States who use condoms during sexual intercourse has risen sharply over the past 30 years since the onset of the AIDS epidemic. In 1982, just over half (52%) of women of ages 15–44 had ever used a condom during sex, whereas the corresponding figure from the 2006–2008 survey was 93% (U.S. Department of Health and Human Services, 2010). The figures are highest for Whites and African Americans (96% and 95%) and lowest among Hispanics (81%). Among sexually active teens, 45% report that they consistently use a condom (Manning et al., 2009). The rate is lower for Hispanics and higher for African Americans compared to Whites (Manlove, Ikramullah, & Terry-Humen, 2008). Unfortunately, some studies have shown that adolescents and adults are less likely to use condoms when engaging in casual sex than sex with a more serious romantic partner (Corbett et al., 2009; Manlove et al., 2008).

Condom usage among high-risk individuals is low. In a study of illicit drug users, partners of IV drug users, homeless and poor people, and commercial sex workers, a majority of persons reported that they never used a condom (Corbett et al., 2009). People purposefully refrained from using a condom to try to communicate to their partners that they are interested in establishing a serious relationship. They try to establish trust in the relationship by not using a condom—a behavior they think communicates that they are not having sex with someone else. Thus, the people who are at most risk are least likely to take precautions to protect themselves.

College students who use condoms are more likely to believe in the effectiveness of condoms in preventing pregnancy, HIV, and STDs (Ma et al., 2009; Sturges et al., 2009). They also believe that they are vulnerable to these problems without the use of a condom. Earlier age at first sexual intercourse is a predictor of lower condom usage for men but not women. When men and women believe that condoms have a negative effect on men's sexual experience, they are less likely to use condoms.

The nature of condom usage presents different challenges for heterosexual females and males. Whereas men are deciding whether or not to use a condom, women are deciding whether or not to persuade their partner to use a condom. A study of Mexican adolescents revealed that both women and men believe that the male should initiate condom use (Martinez-Donate et al., 2004). The nature of female and male roles may make the behavior required of women more difficult. Women are more concerned than men that asking a partner to use a condom raises issues of trust and fidelity (Williams et al., 2001). When relationships are troubled, women are less likely to ensure that condoms are used during sex (Manning et al., 2009). Women also have less power in their relationships compared to men, making them less assertive in sexual matters. Both males and females report that they would have more difficulty using a condom when they felt they had less power over the sexual situation (Woolf & Maisto, 2008). The most effective strategy to get one's partner to use a condom is direct communication (Tschann et al., 2010). Among Latino youth, males are more likely than females to employ a direct strategy. Women are also socialized to be the more passive sexual partner. These aspects of the female gender role may make it more difficult for women to ensure their partners use a condom.

the 1950s compared to the teens of the 1960s or 1970s. The diminishing sex difference may be due to greater opportunities for girls to engage in risky activities today.

Risk-taking behavior has been evaluated in children. Numerous studies show that boys engage in riskier behavior than girls, whether this is documented by self-report, parent report, or observation (Morrongiello & Lasenby-Lessard, 2007). There are a number of reasons for this difference. Some reasons have to do with characteristics of girls and boys. Girls perceive situations as riskier than boys (Hillier & Morrongiello, 1998). When facing a risky situation, girls are more likely to ask themselves "Will I get hurt?" and boys are more likely to ask themselves "How hurt will I get?" Emotions also play a role in these sex differences. Boys are more likely than girls to associate risk-taking behavior with excitement (Morrongiello & Mattheis, 2007). When girls and boys were asked to select the highest height at which they would cross a balance beam, boys not only selected a higher height but expressed more excitement, whereas girls expressed more fear. And, excitement predicted greater risk-taking behavior, whereas fear predicted less risk-taking behavior. When asked to choose which path they would take to a destination, with paths varying in the risky activity required, boys chose riskier paths than girls because they found the paths more fun and more convenient (Morrongiello & Dawber, 2004). Girls were more likely to choose paths that they viewed as safe. Boys are also more likely than girls to attribute an injury to bad luck rather than their own behavior (Morrongiello & Lasenby-Lessard, 2007), which means that injuries will not necessarily deter them from repeating the behavior. Interestingly, parents make those same sex-specific attributions (Morrongiello & Hogg, 2004).

Parents—both mothers and fathers—also are more likely to encourage risk-taking behavior in boys than girls (Morrongiello & Lasenby-Lessard, 2007). In one study, parents were shown a video of children on a playground and asked what they would say (Morrongiello & Dawber, 2000). Mothers of girls were more likely to warn of injury risk

and were more likely to intervene and to do so quickly. Parents are less likely to supervise boys than girls (Morrongiello, Klemencic, & Corbett, 2008), and report being more willing to leave boys alone for a few minutes at a younger age compared to girls (Morrongiello, Walpole, & McArthur, 2009). When mothers were presented with hypothetical scenarios in which their children misbehaved in a way that could pose a risk for injury (e.g., climbing on the counters), mothers focused on discipline more than safety for boys and safety more than discipline for girls (Morrongiello & Hogg, 2004). These results are shown in Figure 10.9. Mothers also reacted to boys' behavior with anger and to girls' behavior with disappointment, believing that there was little that they could do to change boys' behavior.

For all of these reasons, it is not a surprise that boys sustain more injuries than girls. Boys are more likely than girls to suffer nonfatal and fatal injuries during childhood (Borse et al., 2008). The sex difference is similar across Whites, Blacks, Asians, and American

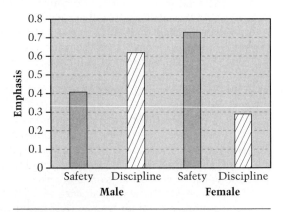

FIGURE 10.9   Parents were more likely to emphasize concerns with safety than discipline for girls' risky behavior but more likely to emphasize discipline than concerns with safety for boys' risky behavior.
Source: Adapted from Morrongiello and Hogg (2004).

Indian/Alaska Natives—although the rate of injury is highest for the latter group.

Risky activities may be linked to the male gender role. Participation in sports while in pain or while injured is an example of a risky behavior with strong connections to traditional masculinity. Playing while injured is a sign of emotional toughness and physical strength; in fact, taking care of oneself after an injury is viewed as weak behavior that undermines masculinity. The athlete who continues to play while injured is afforded high status.

There are a number of studies that have tied male risk-taking behavior to the male gender role. One study measured aspects of masculinity and femininity and showed that masculinity accounted for the sex difference, meaning that males' risk-taking behavior was due to their higher masculinity scores (Meier-Pesti & Penz, 2008). Male risk-taking behavior also seems to be influenced by the presence of the other sex. An observational study of pedestrian risk-taking behavior (i.e., crossing dangerous intersections) showed that males' risk behavior increased when there was a female across the street whereas females' risk behavior was not affected by the presence of a male or female across the street (Pawlowski, Atwal, & Dunbar, 2008). Pawlowski and colleagues concluded that male risk taking is a mate attraction strategy. Try Do Gender 10.5 to see if there are sex differences in risky leisure activities among your peers and if risky activities can be linked to gender roles.

Despite the links of risky behavior to gender roles, fMRI (functional magnetic resonance imaging) research has shown that there may be a neural basis for the sex difference in risk-taking behavior. Females and males show a different pattern of brain activation in response to risky activity (Lee et al., 2009). This does not necessarily imply a biological basis for the sex difference, however,

DO GENDER 10.5
Risky Leisure Activities

Develop a list of leisure activities that vary in their level of risk. Ask a group of women and men if they have ever engaged in the activity and, if so, how often. You might also ask respondents how willing they would be to engage in each activity. Also administer a measure of gender roles. Agency, communion, unmitigated agency, and traditional gender-role attitudes are good candidates.

Is there a sex difference in willingness to engage in risky activities? Is there a sex difference in having engaged in risky activities? Are differences in risky behavior linked to gender-related traits or gender-role attitudes?

as different experiences with risk could lead to the altered pattern of brain activation.

Concerns with Health

So far, we have discussed a number of characteristics of the male gender role that might account for men's higher mortality rates: hazardous jobs, driving, and risky behavior in general. What aspects of the female gender role relate to women's lower mortality rates and higher morbidity rates? One aspect of the female gender role that may be related to both is women's concern with health. More frequent visits to the physician might be counted as higher morbidity, but—if effective—could reduce mortality.

Studies have shown that women are more interested than men in health matters (Green & Pope, 1999). For example, women report they think about health and read about health in newspapers and magazines more often than men do. Women are more likely than men to search the Internet for health information. Women are designated as the persons responsible for the family's health care. However, it is not the case that women's concerns with health lead them to engage in all health promoting behaviors; for example, women exercise less than men and have been more reluctant than men to quit smoking.

By contrast, men are typically unconcerned with health matters and associate preventive health care with undermining masculinity (Courtenay, 2000a). In fact, men may brag about not having seen a doctor, about not taking time off from work when sick, and about engaging in risky activities that undermine health. At times, there can be serious health consequences for adhering to the male gender role. For example, men are less likely to use sunscreen than women and more likely than women to get skin cancer. Men may be especially less likely than women to seek help for mental health problems due to concerns that doing so undermines traditional masculinity. Men are more likely than women to attach a stigma to mental health problems, and men are less likely than women to seek help even when they have more problems (Addis & Mahilik, 2003; Ojeda & Bergstresser, 2008). This difference is larger among White people than African Americans or Latinos. One culture in which the sex difference is larger is Asian Americans. Asian American men not only have concerns about maintaining their male gender role but also have cultural concerns revolved around how they are viewed by others (Chang & Subramaniam, 2008). Asian American men are less likely than European American men to seek help for mental illness.

Nurturant Roles

One aspect of the female gender role poses a risk to women's health and may account for some of women's higher morbidity rates compared to men: women's nurturant role (see

FIGURE 10.10 Women traditionally hold more nurturant roles than men.

Figure 10.10). Women are socialized to take care of others, and taking care of others has its costs. Although there are obvious health benefits to involvement in social networks, reviewed in detail in Chapter 11, there is a downside to such involvement for women. For one, social networks increase exposure to infectious disease; thus women may sustain more minor illnesses than men, such as colds and flu, because they spend more time around people, in particular children, compared to men.

A specific hypothesis about how women's involvement in relationships could be hazardous to their health is the **nurturant role hypothesis** (Gove, 1984; Gove & Hughes, 1979). According to the nurturant role hypothesis, women's roles require them to attend to the needs of others, and taking care of others interferes with taking care of oneself. First, the nurturant role leads to caretaking behavior, which results in fatigue and vulnerability to illness. Second, the nurturant role leads to greater exposure to communicable diseases. Finally, once sick, the nurturant role prevents one from taking care of oneself.

In a classic study, Gove and Hughes (1979) found that women suffered greater health problems than men due to their nurturant roles. Specifically, women were more likely than men to say they did not get enough sleep and did not eat properly when taking care of others. Women also reported they were more likely to catch others' illnesses and did not take care of themselves when they were ill (i.e., continued with chores, did not get proper rest). Married women suffered more of these problems than married men, and the differences were even greater when the people had children. This is because married women, especially mothers, have greater nurturant role obligations. Among married couples without children, 14% of men and 21% of women said they were unable to rest when they were sick; among married couples with children, 16% of men and 44% of women said they were unable to rest when they were sick. Among unmarried individuals who lived alone, there were no sex differences in these nurturant role problems. Nurturant role problems, in particular the inability to rest when ill, were associated with poor physical health and accounted for most of the sex differences in physical health.

The nurturant role hypothesis has not gone without criticism. For example, as you will see in Chapter 11, married women are healthier than single women, which would seem to contradict the nurturant role hypothesis because married women have more nurturant roles. Women with seemingly more role obligations, such as women who work and women who have children, report less illness and less disability.

How can these contradictory ideas be reconciled? Are nurturant roles related to less illness or more illness among women? One possibility is that nurturant roles lead to more illness but also to less *reporting* of illness. People who have more nurturant role responsibilities may be sick more often but seek health care less often. Thus the nurturant role hypothesis is a viable explanation for women's higher rates of morbidity compared to men. As you will see in Chapter 11, marriage and social networks confer fewer

health benefits to women than to men, and one reason is that there are health costs to involvement in social networks for women.

Gender-Related Traits

The last social role explanation for sex differences in morbidity and mortality involves gender-related traits. Gender-related traits include agency, unmitigated agency, communion, and unmitigated communion. These traits could be linked to some of the previously mentioned social role explanations. For example, unmitigated agency is related to feelings of superiority and invulnerability, which would promote risky behavior, whereas unmitigated communion would be related to having overly nurturant roles.

A body of research has linked gender-related traits to health (Helgeson, 1994c). Although the hope was that androgyny, the combination of agency and communion, would be the best predictor of health, research has shown that agency alone is the best predictor of psychological well-being. Overall, agency has been associated with greater perceived health, fewer physical symptoms, reduced psychological distress, reduced psychiatric problems, and better physical health (Ghaed & Gallo, 2006; Helgeson, 1994c). Agency also has been linked to a variety of good health practices, including physical activity, healthy eating, and good dental hygiene (Danoff-Burg, Mosher, & Grant, 2006). By contrast, communion is typically unrelated to psychological or physical health (Ghaed & Gallo, 2006; Helgeson, 1994c). Thus, some of men's lower morbidity rates compared to women may be explained by the male gender-related trait of agency, but women's higher morbidity rates cannot be linked to the female gender-related trait of communion.

The distinctions between agency and unmitigated agency and between communion and unmitigated communion are important. When I first became interested in these issues in my dissertation research, I distinguished agency from unmitigated agency in a group of heart attack survivors and found that unmitigated agency was associated with more severe heart attacks, whereas agency was associated with less severe heart attacks (Helgeson, 1990). Since that time, unmitigated agency has been associated with reckless driving, substance use, binge eating, psychological distress, and overall lower levels of well-being (Danoff-Burg et al., 2006; Ghaed & Gallo, 2006; Yu & Xie, 2008). Although communion is typically unrelated to health, unmitigated communion is associated with poor health, especially greater psychological distress, disturbed eating behavior, and poor health behavior (Ghaed & Gallo, 2006; Helgeson & Fritz, 1996, 1998; Helgeson et al., 2007; Yu & Xie, 2008).

TAKE HOME POINTS

- When women's and men's social roles become more equal, sex differences in health diminish.

- One reason for men's higher mortality rates compared to women—especially from accidents—is men's greater job hazards, greater number of miles driven, and greater risk-taking behavior. Men take greater risks during work, driving, and leisure activities. And, risk-taking behavior is encouraged among males.

- One reason for women's greater morbidity rates compared to men is that women are more concerned with health and more likely to seek the care of a physician.

- A second reason for women's greater morbidity rates compared to men is that women are socialized to take care of others—or to have nurturant roles. Nurturant roles lead to exposure to illness, to fatigue, and to taking care of others instead of the self.

- Among the gender-related traits, agency is related to good health behavior and less psychological distress,

whereas unmitigated agency is related to risk-taking behavior. Communion is unrelated to health, but unmitigated communion is related to poor health behavior and psychological distress, possibly due to nurturant roles.

SYMPTOM PERCEPTION

One explanation of why women suffer greater morbidity compared to men is that women are more sensitive to changes within their body. That is, women have a lower threshold for noticing and reporting symptoms.

Evidence

There is no hard evidence indicating women are more able than men to perceive symptoms. It is important, though difficult, to distinguish symptom perception from symptom reporting. Women may be more likely to report a symptom once it is perceived. During childhood, girls are socialized to report symptoms and boys are socialized to withhold symptoms.

One area of research aimed at addressing symptom perception is pain research. There are sex differences in pain perception. The sex differences are most clear in response to experimentally induced pain. In laboratory studies, a pain stimulus is applied to the respondent at a very low level, and intensity is gradually increased. These studies tend to show that women have lower thresholds of pain, report greater intensity of pain, have lower tolerance levels for pain, and are better able to discriminate different levels of pain compared to men (Defrin, Shramm, & Eli, 2009; Fillingim et al., 2009). Another piece of evidence that pain is linked to sex is the fact that so many pain disorders are more prevalent in women than men—fibromyalgia, rheumatoid arthritis, musculoskeletal pain, and migraines (Fillingim et al., 2009). Across

17 countries—developing and developed—women report more chronic pain conditions than men (Tsang et al., 2008). When women and men present with these disorders, women report more severe pain, longer-lasting pain, and more frequent pain than men (Hurley & Adams, 2008). Even among adolescents (ages 11 to 19) who seek treatment for pain, females reported more severe pain than males without reporting any more depression or disability than males (Keogh & Eccleston, 2006).

Explanations

Although sex differences in pain perception are far from clear, this has not stopped investigators from speculating about the cause of differences. Biological factors have been thought to play a role because women suffer from more painful disorders than men and because women are more responsive than men to some classes of painkillers. Women obtain greater relief than men from some opiates, such as morphine (Cairns & Gazerani, 2009). Sex differences in pain also have been linked to different parts of the brain being activated in women and men (Derbyshire et al., 2002). Hormones may play a role in the pain conditions to which women are more vulnerable (e.g., rheumatoid arthritis) and may play a role in why women respond differently from men to some analgesics.

Psychological factors also have been linked to sex differences in pain. Women report more negative emotions, such as anxiety and depression, which have been shown to influence pain reports (Keogh, 2009). There also appear to be sex differences in coping with pain. Women are more likely than men to seek support when in pain, whereas men are more likely than women to distract themselves from pain (Keogh & Eccleston, 2006). Women also are more likely than men to think catastrophically

or magnify the problem in response to pain, and catastrophic thinking (i.e., feeling helpless, pessimistic) has accounted for some sex differences in pain reports (Hurley & Adams, 2008).

Social factors, too, may influence reports of pain. Family members who experience and frequently express pain may serve as "pain models" for children. In one study, women reported a greater number of pain models than men, and pain models were associated with reports of greater pain symptoms (Koutantji, Pearce, & Oakley, 1998). Reports of pain are also vulnerable to demand characteristics. When college students were exposed to an inert substance and led to believe that they would experience physical symptoms, physical symptoms increased for women and men only when a same-sex confederate displayed those symptoms (Mazzoni et al., 2010).

Gender roles affect pain reports. The male gender role is associated with strength and emotional inhibition, both of which are consistent with minimizing reports of pain. During childhood, boys learn they should be tough and not admit pain. We applaud the male athlete who "plays through the pain." Greater identification with the male role has been associated with higher pain tolerance (Pool et al., 2007; Reidy et al, 2009), whereas feminine traits have been associated with greater pain reports (Bernardes, Keogh, & Lima, 2008). One study showed that gender stereotypes regarding men's and women's willingness to express pain (i.e., the idea that men are less willing than women) accounted for women's greater reports of pain compared to men in response to a laboratory pain stimulus (Robinson et al., 2004). Reports of pain are also vulnerable to the demand characteristics of the situation. In one study, the sex of the experimenter was manipulated and influenced pain reports (Gijsbers & Nicholson, 2005). Men had higher pain thresholds in the presence of a female experimenter than a male experimenter, whereas women had similar pain thresholds in the presence of female and male experimenters. Gender roles also may explain why women's pain reports are associated with their facial expressions of pain, whereas men's are not (Kunz, Gruber, & Lautenbacher, 2006). The male gender role encourages the inhibition of emotion, whereas the female gender role encourages the expression of emotion.

TAKE HOME POINTS

- There is no evidence that women suffer greater morbidity than men because they over-report symptoms or are in greater touch with their bodies compared to men.

- One symptom that is more common among women than men is pain. Women have a lower threshold and tolerance for pain, report more pain, report more severe pain, and suffer from more painful disorders than men.

- Explanations for sex differences in pain include biology, psychological factors such as coping, and social factors such as gender-role norms.

ILLNESS BEHAVIOR

Illness behavior is often referred to as adopting the "sick role," or labeling a symptom as illness and responding to it. Sick role behavior includes restricting activities, getting bed rest, taking medication, and seeking the help of health care professionals. These are all activities that women do more than men.

Implications for Morbidity

These sick role behaviors are frequently included in indices of morbidity. Thus one reason women have higher rates of morbidity compared to men is that women are more likely to adopt the sick role. The **sick role hypothesis** suggests that sex differences in medical care utilization are due to women's greater tendency to adopt the sick role (Nathanson, 1978). If women and men are equally ill, but women are more likely to seek help for symptoms, sex differences in morbidity are really artifactual. It may be more socially acceptable for women than men to reduce their activities when ill.

One reason women may be more willing to adopt the sick role is that women have fewer **fixed role obligations** than men (Marcus & Seeman, 1981). A fixed role is one that is structured and difficult to reschedule. Men are likely to have two fixed roles: worker and head of household. Performance in these roles is visible. Historically, women were likely to have only one role, that of housewife, a role relatively unstructured and invisible. A housewife has few deadlines and can put chores off from one day to the next; thus, women had fewer constraints on their time and were freer to restrict their activities and take care of themselves when ill. In other words, women's social role could accommodate illness. Another tenet of the fixed role obligations hypothesis is that men's fixed roles keep them task focused, whereas women's lack of fixed roles allows them time to ruminate about their problems. This would explain why women perceive their health as worse than men and why women report more symptoms than men.

In an initial test of the fixed role hypothesis, Marcus and Seeman (1981) examined the relation of role obligations to health problems. Fixed role obligations were measured in terms of financial responsibility (how much the person contributes to family income), status as head of household, and employment status. They found that men had greater fixed role obligations than women, and women had greater restricted activity days and more chronic illnesses than men. In addition, fixed role obligations were associated with fewer restricted activity days and fewer chronic illnesses. Thus, women had more restricted activities than men because they had fewer fixed roles, and men were less likely to adopt the sick role because they had more fixed roles. There are alternative interpretations of these data, however. Perhaps men's good health allowed them to have more fixed roles. Because the study is correlational, the causal relation between fixed roles and health cannot be determined.

Today, however, it is not the case that men necessarily have more fixed roles than women. The implication of the fixed role hypothesis is that women who have a large number of role obligations, such as women with children or women who work, would be less likely to adopt the sick role. Are changes in women's roles associated with changes in their health? If women now have more fixed roles, there should be fewer sex differences in morbidity. To some extent this is true, as will be shown in Chapter 12 when we focus on the relation of paid employment to health.

Implications for Mortality

Just as women's illness behaviors may account for their greater morbidity compared to men, these same illness behaviors may account for women's longer life span. Perhaps women respond to acute symptoms of illness more quickly, which makes it appear at a given point in time that women are sicker than men. However, women's early response to symptoms could prevent a minor illness from developing into a more serious one.

Once a symptom is perceived, is there evidence that women and men respond to the symptom differently? Admitting illness may be construed as admitting weakness or vulnerability. Thus, men may be less likely than women to seek help when ill because help-seeking behavior is inconsistent with the male gender role.

Studies show that there are some similarities and some differences in how men and women respond to symptoms. One study found that women reported more physical symptoms than men did, but that women and men were equally likely to have visited a physician in the prior month in response to each symptom (Wyke, Hunt, & Ford, 1998). Women's and men's help-seeking responses seem to be similar when symptoms are severe. Women are more likely than men to visit the doctor for minor conditions, but there are no sex differences in visits to the doctor for serious illness (Dracup et al., 1995; Waldron, 1995, 1997). Women may visit the physician more frequently than men for minor symptoms because they have a lower tolerance for symptoms or feel more comfortable seeking help for minor illness.

It is not clear whether women or men delay longer before seeking help for symptoms of a serious illness. Studies of people who have had heart attacks find there is a tendency for women to delay longer than men before seeking help for symptoms (Dracup et al., 1995; Moscucci et al., 2004). By contrast, men appear to delay longer than women before seeking help for symptoms of cancer (Evans et al., 2005). The findings from both of these studies may be explained by men's and women's lack of knowledge about specific diseases. Women may associate heart disease with being male and be less sensitive to heart disease symptoms. The study of people with cancer showed that men were less knowledgeable than women about cancer and its warning signs. Find out if your female and male peers respond similarly to symptoms in Do Gender 10.6.

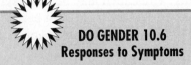

DO GENDER 10.6
Responses to Symptoms

Develop a list of responses to illness. Your list should include visiting a physician, taking medication, and restricting activities. Ask 10 women and 10 men to recall the last time they were ill and have them indicate how they responded to their illness by checking the responses that apply from your list. Also, ask them to state the nature of the illness or injury so you can determine its severity. Do men and women respond to illness in similar ways? Do their responses depend on the severity of the illness or symptom?

TAKE HOME POINTS

- One reason that women have higher morbidity rates than men is that women are more likely than men to adopt the sick role.

- Women are more likely to adopt the sick role because illness is more inconsistent with the male than the female gender role and because women's traditional social roles are more flexible than those of men; in other words, women have fewer "fixed role" obligations that provide them with time to take care of themselves and seek help for symptoms.

- Women's lower mortality rates compared to those of men could be explained by women seeking help for symptoms, which may keep a minor illness from developing into a serious one.

- The evidence that women and men respond differently to symptoms, however, is not clear. Women may be more likely than men to respond to minor symptoms, but there are fewer sex differences in response to severe symptoms. Yet, the sex difference in the time it takes to seek help for symptoms of serious disease, such as cancer and heart disease, is not clear.

CONCLUSIONS

I have reviewed a number of classes of explanations for sex differences in morbidity and mortality. Which has the greatest explanatory power? A number of investigators have reviewed the literature and compared different classes of explanations. Nearly two decades ago, Verbrugge (1985) came to the conclusion that sex differences in health behaviors are a major—if not the major—cause of sex differences in mortality. Courtenay (2000b) certainly agreed; he compiled a list of 30 behaviors—ranging from diet, sleep, and substance abuse to weapon use—that are linked to men's greater mortality than women.

Health behaviors are limited in their ability to explain sex differences in morbidity (Verbrugge, 1989). Men have worse health behaviors than women, yet women have higher morbidity rates. When health behaviors are taken into consideration, sex differences in morbidity actually increase (Verbrugge, 1985). Health behaviors also cannot account in total for the sex difference in mortality. Men may smoke and drink more than women, but women exercise less and are more likely to be obese than men.

It may be that different classes of explanations affect men's and women's health. Denton and Walters (1999) argued that health behaviors play a greater role in men's health, whereas social structural factors play a greater role in women's health. In terms of subjective health status and physical functioning, behavioral factors, such as smoking and drinking, contribute to men's poor health. Social structural factors, such as support from network members and caretaking responsibilities, contribute to women's health. Support is an advantage, whereas caretaking responsibilities are a disadvantage for women. Thus the class of explanations that describe men's health and women's health may differ.

SUMMARY

Men have higher mortality rates than women, but women have higher morbidity rates than men. In this chapter, I have reviewed the different classes of explanations for this paradox. Although biological factors certainly contribute to health, biology alone cannot explain the increase in the size of the sex difference in life expectancy that occurred over the 20th century and the changes in the size of the sex difference in life expectancy that have occurred more recently. SES factors contribute to health but are unable to explain sex differences in health. Although heart disease is the leading cause of death for women as well as men, women are not treated as aggressively as men for heart disease and have poorer outcomes.

A major contributor to sex differences in morbidity and mortality is health behavior. Women engage in more preventive health care compared to men. Although this difference should theoretically lead to women's lower mortality rates, no evidence supports this conjecture. Instead, women's preventive behavior gets counted as physician visits in indexes of morbidity. Smoking is a major contributor to mortality. That men smoke more than women accounts for a portion of the sex difference in mortality as well as the sex difference in specific diseases (e.g., coronary heart disease, lung cancer). That women have increased their rates of smoking during the last half of the 20th century accounts for the fact that the sex difference in life expectancy has narrowed. Men also have higher rates of alcohol and drug usage compared to women.

Other health behaviors pose greater risks to women's than men's health: obesity and lack of exercise. More women than men are obese in the United States, and the sex difference is particularly striking among Blacks and Hispanics. Women also exercise less than men, although more girls are becoming involved in sports.

Another explanation for sex differences in mortality and morbidity focused on the contribution of women's and men's social roles. One of men's social roles is working outside the home, and men are exposed to more hazards at work compared to women. It is also men's social role to drive: Men drive more than women, drive less safely, and are involved in more driving accidents. In general, many of the behaviors that pose dangers for men's health can be conceptualized as general risk-taking behavior. Men's work, home, and leisure activities are riskier than those of women, which undoubtedly contribute to men's higher death rates from accidents.

The female social role has the advantage of making women more concerned with health matters, but the disadvantage of making women the caretakers of other people's health. The nurturant role exposes women to more illness, is a source of fatigue among women, makes them more susceptible to illness, and prevents women from taking care of themselves when they are ill.

Other explanations for sex differences in morbidity have to do with women being more sensitive than men to symptoms, more likely to enact the sick role, and more likely to seek medical care. Women appear to have a lower threshold and tolerance for pain in experimental studies of pain perception. The explanation for this sex difference is not clear. It does not appear that women are more sensitive than men to changes within their bodies. However, women are more likely to respond to symptoms by restricting their activities and taking care of themselves, in other words, enacting the sick role. One explanation for this sex difference is that women have fewer fixed role obligations than men, and fewer role obligations are associated with a greater willingness to respond to health problems. Women use health services more frequently than men, but the sex difference is limited to minor symptoms. In the case of serious illness, there is less evidence that either women or men are more likely to seek the attention of a health care professional.

Taken collectively, different explanations are more and less relevant to men and women. A few health behaviors explain a good portion of men's higher mortality rates compared to women. These health behaviors can be construed in terms of a larger framework reflecting men's risk-taking behavior. Women's higher morbidity rates are more likely to reflect women's social roles than their health behaviors.

DISCUSSION QUESTIONS

1. How do sex and race influence the leading causes of death?
2. Under what conditions do you believe physicians are more or less likely to make a similar diagnosis in a male and a female who present with the same symptoms of heart disease?
3. Which health behaviors pose greater risks to women's health, and which health behaviors pose greater risk to men's health?
4. What are the reasons that women are less successful than men in quitting smoking?
5. Discuss how sex differences in smoking, drinking alcohol, and drug usage have changed over time.
6. Given our culture's increasing health consciousness, in particular, the emphasis on diet and exercise, why do you think rates of obesity have increased?
7. What are some of the reasons that women report more pain than men?
8. Why are nurturant roles hazardous to health?
9. How could you test the fixed role obligations hypothesis today?
10. Discuss how to determine if men and women actually perceive symptoms differently.
11. In what ways are men's and women's responses to illness similar and different?

SUGGESTED READING

Addis, M. E., & Mahalik, J. R. (2003). Men, masculinity, and the contexts of help seeking. *American Psychologist, 58,* 5–14.

Addis, S., Davies, M, Greene, G., MacBride-Stewart, S., & Shepherd, M. (2009). The health, social care, and housing needs of lesbian, gay, bisexual and transgender older people: A review of the literature. *Health and Social Care in the Community, 17,* 647–658.

Courtenay, W. H. (2000a). Constructions of masculinity and their influence on men's well-being. A theory of gender and health. *Social Science and Medicine, 50,* 1385–1401.

Fillingim, R., King, C., Ribeiro-Dasilva, M., Rahim-Williams, B., & Riley, J. (2009). Sex, gender, and pain: A review of recent clinical and experimental findings. *The Journal of Pain, 10,* 447–485.

(Classic) Gove, W. R., & Hughes, M. (1979). Possible causes of the apparent sex differences in physical health: An empirical investigation. *American Sociological Review, 44,* 126–146.

Helgeson, V. S. (1994c). Relation of agency and communion to well-being: Evidence and potential explanations. *Psychological Bulletin, 116,* 412–428.

(Classic) Verbrugge, L. M. (1989). The twain meet: Empirical explanations of sex differences in health and mortality. *Journal of Health and Social Behavior, 30,* 282–304.

KEY TERMS

Android obesity—Extra weight around the abdomen.

Artifacts—Confounding variables that lead sex differences to appear that do not really exist.

Body mass index (BMI)—Measure of obesity that takes into consideration the ratio of weight to height.

Cardiovascular reactivity—Increase in blood pressure and heart rate that occurs when engaging in a challenging or stressful task.

Chronic illness—Disease or condition characterized by persistent health problems that may be treated or controlled but not cured.

Coronary artery bypass surgery—Treatment for heart disease in which arteries taken from a person's leg or chest are used to bypass blockages in the arteries that supply blood to the heart.

Fixed role obligations—Responsibilities specific to one's defining role that are structured and difficult to reschedule.

Gynoid obesity—Extra weight around the hips.

Health behaviors—Activities that either promote good health (e.g., preventive health care, exercise, healthy diet) or contribute to bad health (e.g., smoking, alcohol, and drug use).

Illness behavior—Condition of labeling a symptom as illness and responding to it as such; adopting the "sick role."

Morbidity—Presence of illness or disease.

Mortality—Death rate.

Nurturant role hypothesis—Supposition that women's roles require them to attend to the needs of others, which results in fatigue, exposure to illness, and not taking care of oneself when sick.

Percutaneous transluminal coronary angioplasty (PTCA)—Procedure in which a catheter with a balloon attached to it is inserted into a diseased blood vessel. As the balloon is inflated, the plaque is pressed against the walls of the artery allowing for improved blood flow.

Sick role hypothesis—Suggestion that sex differences in using medical care are due to women's greater tendency than men to adopt the "sick role."

Thrombolytic therapy—Treatment of heart disease employing drugs that dissolve blood clots and reestablish blood flow.

CHAPTER 11

Relationships and Health

In 1977, James Lynch wrote *The Broken Heart.* The title was a metaphor for the effects of relationships on health, specifically coronary heart disease. Lynch claimed there are

> few conditions in life that do not involve some type of human contact, and so in one sense it would be remarkable if human contact did not influence our hearts. Like the air we breathe, it envelops every aspect of our lives. A simple visit to your doctor, arguments, reassurance and praise, sexual activity, social gatherings, competitive sports, the loss of a friend or loved one, jealousies, humiliations, human triumphs, the cuddling of a child in your lap, the silent hand-holding between two lovers, the quiet comforting of a dying patient—all these affect the heart. (p. 12)

Lynch noted an association between markers of social isolation (e.g., high mobility) and high mortality rates from heart disease. Since then, numerous studies have demonstrated links between aspects of social relationships and health.

This chapter examines the implications of relationships for women's and men's health. We know the female gender role involves a relationship orientation. Does this mean women benefit more than men from social relationships? Or does men's lack of a relationship orientation make relationships all the more important to their health? In the first part of the chapter, I describe the influence of relationships more generally on health—a body of work referred to as social support. Next, I focus on the implications of a primary social relationship for health: marriage. I focus on marriage because quite a bit of evidence suggests that marriage affects men's and women's health in different ways. I also focus on marriage because it is one of the most important relationships (if not the most important relationship) to men and women. I explore the health implications of the loss of this relationship through death and relationship dissolution (e.g., divorce). Next, I examine the health implications of the quality of marriage for women's and men's health. One central aspect of quality is how household chores and child care are divided in the family. Thus I describe the division of labor, examine predictors of the division of labor, and discuss the implications of the division of labor for relationship satisfaction and well-being. Then, I discuss another primary relationship—parenthood. I examine how women and men construe parenthood as well as its links to health. Finally, relationships also can go awry. I briefly describe the research on intimate partner violence and on rape, and then examine their implications for health.

EFFECT OF SOCIAL SUPPORT ON HEALTH

We have relationships with family, friends, neighbors, and coworkers. These relationships have the potential to act as sources of social support, which can influence health. Do women and men differ in the amount of support they receive from network members? Does support from network members lead to the same health benefits for women and men? First, I review the literature that compares the nature of men's and women's social support. Then, I turn to the question of how support is related to health for men and women.

Sex Comparisons

There are quantitative and qualitative dimensions of support. Quantitative dimensions are referred to as **structural measures (of support)**; these measures typically assess the size of a social network or the number of social relations. Qualitative dimensions are referred to as **functional measures**

(of support) because they address the question of what functions networks serve. Network members may provide emotional support (love, caring, concern), instrumental support (concrete assistance, such as running an errand), or informational support (guidance, advice). In an early review of the literature on gender and support, Belle (1987) concluded that women's networks were more "intensive" but men's networks were more "extensive." This would suggest that women come out ahead on the functional aspects of support, but men come out ahead on the structural aspects of support.

It is unclear whether there are sex differences in structural measures of support. Some studies show that men have larger social networks compared to women (Berkman, Vaccarino, & Seeman, 1993), but other studies show just the opposite (Pugliesi & Shook, 1998). Sex differences in support functions are more clear. Women are more likely than men to perceive that support is available from network members (Kendler, Myers, & Prescott, 2005) starting in early adolescence (Rueger, Malecki, & Demaray, 2010), and this is especially the case for emotional support. Women are more likely than men to have someone available to talk to when they are distressed (Matthews, Stansfeld, & Power, 1999). These findings generalize across many cultures (Okamoto & Tanaka, 2004). These sex differences may have more to do with the female gender role than female sex. Femininity, or communion, is related to perceived support more than sex (Helgeson & Fritz, 1998; Reevy & Maslach, 2001).

There are a number of reasons why men lack support compared to women. One reason is that men are more reluctant than women to ask for help. The male gender role's emphasis on independence and invulnerability inhibits men from asking for help

DO GENDER 11.1
Social Support Seeking

Is it true that men are less likely than women to seek support when they are having problems? If so, why? Have a group of women and men recall the last time they experienced a stressful event. Then ask them to rate how much they sought the help of others. If they check a response that indicates they did not seek help or did not seek much help, ask them why. Tally your responses to see if women's and men's reasons for not seeking help differ.

when they need it. Another reason has to do with the perceptions others hold about women's and men's needs for support. People assume that men do not want or need support and may be less likely to offer support to men. Men also may not be as skilled as women in activating support. Because men have been reluctant to ask for help in the past, they may be unsure about how to obtain help when they really need it. Determine why men and women at your school do not seek support in Do Gender 11.1.

Evidence: Relations to Health

Structural Indices.   A number of large epidemiological studies have evaluated the relation of social network indices to health. These studies typically evaluate women's and men's initial health status, measure aspects of their social networks (group membership, church attendance, frequency of contact with neighbors, and, sometimes, marital status), and then measure physical health years later. A number of these studies show stronger health benefits of social networks for men than women. For

example, in a study of 2,754 men and women from Tecumseh County, Michigan, men who reported more social relationships and more activities (e.g., attending voluntary associations and going out to social events) were less likely to die 9 to 12 years later (House, Robbins, & Metzner, 1982). There were weak trends in the same direction for women, but they were not significant. Other studies have found social network indices predict mortality among men but not women (Kaplan et al., 1988; Schoenbach et al., 1986).

Some studies even show adverse effects of social networks on women's health. For example, Schoenbach and colleagues (1986) found that their social network index was associated with *greater* mortality among White women under the age of 60. In a study in Sweden, a social network index was related to reduced mortality for both men and women with one exception: For women between the ages of 65 and 74, the social network index was associated with heightened mortality (Orth-Gomer & Johnson, 1987).

The explanations for the lack of effects and adverse effects of structural support on women's health often revolve around women's social roles. The presence of a social network for women is a double-edged sword (Belle, 1982): It means more people are available to help women but also that more people will turn to women for help. For example, what happens in marriage when one person has a chronic illness? Women are expected to take care of the family whether they are the caregiver or the patient. Social networks may also expose women to additional sources of stress, an issue that will be discussed in more depth in Chapter 13. However, women also may benefit from their role as support providers. A nine-year longitudinal study of employees showed that men who received more support than they provided had fewer sick days nine years later, whereas women who provided more support than they received had fewer sick days nine years later (Vaananen et al., 2005).

Thus it appears that women are more likely than men to reap the benefits of a social network but also to suffer the costs of network involvement. Women are more likely to have social support available but also more likely to have problematic social relations and conflict. The positive and negative effects of social networks for women may cancel each other out in terms of health: Supportive relations decrease depression, but unsupportive relations and caregiver burden increase depression.

Functional Indices.   Some evidence—but not all—suggests the functional aspects of support are more strongly related to health among women than men. Support has been more strongly related to better perceived health and less functional disability (Denton & Walters, 1999), good health practices (Jackson, 2006), and positive health perceptions (Cheng & Chan, 2006) among women than men. A study of opposite-sex dizygotic twins showed that social support predicted a reduction in the onset of major depression over the next year among females but not males (Kendler et al., 2005). By contrast, a study of people with heart disease showed social support was equally related to life satisfaction and mood for women and men (Rueda & Perez-Garcia, 2006), and a study of elderly people in Japan showed that social support was more strongly related to positive health perceptions among men than women (Okamoto & Tanaka, 2004). One way that the effect of functional support on health has been examined is in the context of stressor reactivity studies. See Sidebar 11.1 for a discussion of how support buffers one from laboratory stressors.

Why would the qualitative dimensions of support be more strongly related to women's than men's health? One explanation is that women's identities are more strongly tied than men's identities to their connection to others. Variability in an identity-relevant domain is more likely to have implications for health. It may also be that supportive networks benefit women more than men because they facilitate women's coping with distress. Women are more likely to seek support during times of stress; thus if others are supportive, women's needs are met.

TAKE HOME POINTS

- Women have more support available to them compared to men, and women provide more support to others than men.

- Quantitative, or structural, measures of relationships seem to have a stronger effect on men's than women's health.

- One reason for these findings is that relationships are a double-edged sword for women—a source of support and a source of stress.

- Qualitative, or functional, measures of relationships may have a stronger effect on women's than men's health.

EFFECT OF MARRIAGE ON HEALTH

"I now pronounce you man and wife." Those are the words of the traditional marriage ceremony. Historically, marriage for women meant they became defined by their relationship to their husband; marriage for men meant they had someone to take care of the home and the children. Today, however, marriage may have a more similar meaning for women and men: gaining a partner, a

SIDEBAR 11.1: *Manipulation of Social Support In The Laboratory*

Because survey studies on support and health cannot distinguish cause and effect, a number of laboratory studies have been conducted in which social support is manipulated while the participant undergoes some kind of stressor, such as giving a speech or performing a difficult math task. Health is measured in terms of cardiovascular reactivity (e.g., change in blood pressure and heart rate), immune function, or the production of stress hormones (e.g., cortisol). A meta-analytic review of the literature showed that the experimental manipulation of support during a stressful task performed in the laboratory had beneficial effects on heart rate, blood pressure, and cortisol (Thorsteinsson & James, 1999). Most studies only involved female participants. One study that examined both males and females found stronger effects of support on reactivity for females than males (Smith, Ruiz, & Uchino, 2004).

The sex of the support provider also might influence how males and females respond. One study manipulated the sex of the support provider and found that support provided by a female confederate was effective in reducing blood pressure for both male and female participants, but support from a male confederate was ineffective for both male and female participants (Glynn et al., 1999). In fact, there was a slight tendency for male participants to show increased reactivity in response to support from a male confederate. The difference between male and female confederates is interesting, given that the support manipulation was standardized. Thus it is not only that women may provide more support than men, but also that support from women may be more health beneficial. The same behavior may be interpreted differently when displayed by a female than by a male.

The kind of support manipulated in the vast majority of these laboratory studies, including the last one, is emotional support. Thus the extent to which other kinds of support may be effective in reducing reactivity to stress is unknown. It is also not known whether men and women benefit from different kinds of support in terms of reduced reactivity to stress. Dawn Wilson and her colleagues have examined both emotional support and instrumental support (e.g., advice, concrete assistance) in several studies of African American adolescents. In a study that aimed to enhance a low-sodium diet to prevent hypertension, Black boys did not benefit as much from family emotional support as Black girls in terms of dietary compliance (Wilson & Ampey-Thornhill, 2001). In a laboratory study in which Black boys and girls were asked to role-play several stressful encounters, boys showed higher levels of reactivity when provided with emotional support and lower reactivity in response to instrumental support (Wilson et al., 1999).

Thus the laboratory studies of social support leave several questions unanswered. Is support provided by women more effective than support provided by men, or does this pertain only to emotional support? Do women and men benefit more from emotional support compared to other kinds of support, or does the kind of support that is beneficial depend on the sex of the support provider? For example, it may be that instrumental support from men is effective and emotional support from women is effective.

person with whom to share one's life. Today, the minister or officiator is more likely to say, "I now pronounce you husband and wife," reflecting the similarity of marriage for men and women.

There has been a shift in cultural values toward marriage over the last several decades. Today, there is a greater emphasis on individual and personal fulfillment, which means people may be less likely to tolerate unsatisfying relationships. There also are greater expectations for relationships: Marriage is expected to provide a source of intimacy, sexuality, and companionship. Thus people have increasing expectations of marriage, and marriage may be less likely to meet those expectations. It is also much easier to dissolve a marriage today than it was in the middle of the 20th century, and society is more tolerant of marital breakups.

Thus, one characteristic of modern marriage is that it is less likely to last. In 2004, 23% of women and 21% of women had been divorced at least one time (U.S. Census Bureau, 2007b). The rates were higher among Whites (24%) than Blacks (19%), Hispanics (13%), and Asians (9%). See Table 11.1 for a list of factors that decrease one's risk of divorce.

Although the divorce rate increased over much of the 20th century, peaking in 1981, it has steadily decreased since that time (Centers for Disease Control and Prevention, 2005, 2009d). One reason that divorce rates have stabilized is that women and men wait longer before they marry, and older age at first marriage is less likely to result in divorce. Today, the median age of marriage is 28 for men and 26 for women (U.S. Census Bureau, 2010a).

The marriage rate also has declined in recent years, in part due to increased cohabitation and in part due to people waiting longer before getting married. In 2008, 59% of males and 56% of females over 18 in the United States were married, although the rate was much lower among Blacks (44% male; 37% female) than Asians (65% male and female), Whites (55% male; 54% female), and Hispanics (56% male; 58% female; U.S. Census Bureau, 2009a). The percentage of the population marrying has decreased while the percentage of people who are divorced and never married has increased. In 2009, 30% of men and 23% of adult women had never married (U.S. Census Bureau, 2010b), but these numbers varied greatly by race. Figures for never-married males and females were comparable among Whites and Asians (White: 26% male; 19% female; Asian: 28% male; 19% female) but much larger for Blacks (43% male; 41% female) and much lower for Hispanics (4% male; 5% female).

Nonetheless, most young adults say that they want to get married (Pew Research, 2007), although African American adolescents have lower expectations than their White and Mexican American counterparts (Crissey, 2005). African Americans are less likely to marry than other groups in part due to socioeconomic factors (Bulanda & Brown, 2007). There are proportionally fewer African American men with stable jobs, and economic problems lead to family conflict. Although Hispanics share some of the same economic problems, Hispanic culture attaches greater value to marriage whereas African American culture emphasizes the importance of the extended family.

Evidence

In 1957, Hannah Lees wrote the book *Help Your Husband Stay Alive*. She expressed concern over the fact that men die younger than women and the sex difference in longevity was widening. She suggested that women were not living up to their duty of helping

TABLE 11.1 FACTORS THAT PROTECT AGAINST DIVORCE DURING THE FIRST 10 YEARS OF MARRIAGE

- higher income
- having a baby seven months or more after marriage (as compared to before marriage)
- at least age 25 at marriage
- parents married (rather than divorced)
- religious affiliation
- higher education

Source: Bramlett and Mosher (2002).

to lengthen the life span of their husbands. Lees said wives should provide support to husbands, make husbands' lives easier, help husbands cope with the pressures and frustrations they face in the working world, provide opportunities for husbands to relax, and help husbands take care of their health.

Lees (1957) may have been too critical of wives. It turns out that women do help men live longer. Numerous studies have shown that being married is advantageous to psychological and physical health for both women and men but that men reap greater rewards from marriage than women do. These findings come from large epidemiological studies in which women's and men's marital status and health status are measured and then followed for many years. In three such studies, men who were married were less likely to die than men who were unmarried over the 9 to 15 years they were followed (Berkman & Syme, 1979; House et al., 1982; Shye et al., 1995). Marital status did not predict mortality among women in any of these studies. A more recent eight-year longitudinal study showed that never-married persons had a 158% increase in mortality compared to married persons, but the difference between the two groups was larger for men than women (Kaplan & Kronick, 2006). Never-married men had especially high rates of mortality from infectious disease and accidents if younger and heart disease if older. Two other studies showed that being never married was more hazardous to men's than women's health (Molloy et al., 2009; Pizzetti & Manfredini, 2008).

On health parameters other than mortality, married people also fare better and the benefits seem to be stronger for men. Four studies—in Japan, Korea, the United States, and Canada—showed that married people had less depression than unmarried people, but the difference was greater for men than women (Hughes & Waite, 2009; Inaba et al., 2005; Jang et al., 2009; St. John & Montgomery, 2009). A study of Hispanic older adults found that living alone was associated with depression but more so for men than women (Russell & Taylor, 2009). A study of cancer survivors showed that married men were less distressed than unmarried men, but married women were more distressed than unmarried women (Goldzweig et al., 2009). Another study examined C-reactive protein, a marker of inflammation that predicts cardiovascular disease, in older adults and found that married men had lower levels of C-reactive protein than unmarried men, but there were no differences in C-reactive protein among married and unmarried women (Sbarra, 2009). Married people also have a reduced risk of stroke compared to unmarried persons, and the relation is stronger in men than women (Maselko et al., 2009). Taken collectively, it appears that marriage has stronger benefits on men's than women's health.

Is marriage less beneficial for women than men because marriage is associated with relatively more distress for women or because being unmarried is associated with relatively more distress for men? There is some support for both ideas. One study showed that the rate of psychiatric disorders was higher among married women than married men, but similar among unmarried women and men (Sachs-Ericsson & Ciarlo, 2000). However, another study showed that the state of being unmarried was more distressing for men. In a study of over 4,000 adults in Germany, the three groups of unmarried men were more lonely than the three groups of unmarried women (divorced, widowed, and never married), whereas there was no sex difference in loneliness among the married (see Figure 11.1; Pinquart, 2003).

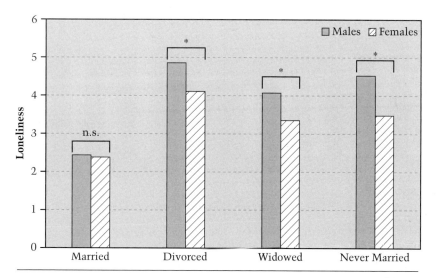

FIGURE 11.1   Among married people, men and women report equal levels of loneliness. Among divorced, widowed, and never-married people, men report more loneliness than women.
Source: Adapted from Pinquart (2003).

Is it marriage per se that leads to health benefits, or is it the presence of a partner in the household? Several studies have examined the effects of cohabitation on health. A study of people over 50 years of age showed that cohabitation did not provide the same benefits as marriage (Brown, Bulanda, & Lee, 2005). Those in cohabiting relationships were more depressed than those who were married but had better mental health than those who were widowed and divorced. A study that examined life satisfaction in married and cohabiting heterosexual couples in 30 countries showed that married people were more satisfied than cohabiting couples in most countries (Soons & Kalmijn, 2009). However, married people were also more religious and more likely to be employed than cohabiting people, which accounted for some of the marital status differences in life satisfaction. Another study examined the drinking behavior of young adults (ages 24 to 34) in 10

European countries (Plant et al., 2008). Cohabiting people were similar to married people in terms of the frequency with which they drank alcohol, but those who were cohabiting drank more alcohol per occasion than those who were married. An epidemiological study showed that unmarried people had 1.25 times the risk of mortality as married people, but unpartnered (which included unmarried) people had 1.31 times the risk of mortality as married people (Lund et al., 2002). In general, it appears cohabitation has benefits on health—effects that are similar for women and men—but the benefits are not as strong as the benefits from marriage.

Do the benefits of marriage extend to same-sex cohabiting relationships? One study compared partnered gays and lesbians to married people, heterosexual cohabitors, heterosexual dating couples, unattached persons, and single gays and lesbians (Wienke & Hill, 2009). As shown in Figure 11.2, married

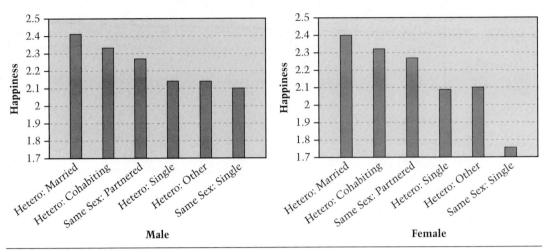

FIGURE 11.2 Married men and women are happier than unmarried groups. Among the unmarried groups, partnered gays and lesbians are similar in happiness to cohabiting heterosexuals, both of which are happier than the remaining groups.
Source: Adapted from Wienke and Hill (2009).

people were happier than all other groups but partnered gays and lesbians were similar in happiness to heterosexual cohabitors and happier than the rest of the groups. The effects were similar for women and men.

Explanations

Many theories address why marriage benefits health. Marriage is presumed to affect health through a set of physiological processes. Two categories of variables might affect physiology: psychological and behavioral. Marriage may provide one with a sense of identity, a source of self-esteem, and a companion to share activities, all of which should promote a positive psychological state. Marriage may also promote good health behavior (e.g., exercising), decrease risk behavior (e.g., smoking), and promote early detection of disease (e.g., routine physical exam). These effects of marriage on health are referred to as direct effects, or **main effects** (Cohen & Wills, 1985). In each case, marriage is directly linked to a psychological state or behavior that influences health.

An alternative hypothesis is that marriage indirectly affects health by providing resources to cope with stress. These effects are referred to as **buffering effects**; marriage is buffering one against the negative effects of stressors (Cohen & Wills, 1985). During times of stress, marriage may help us perceive a stressful event as less troublesome and may provide resources to cope with stress (e.g., emotional support, financial support). In the face of an illness, marriage may help us make the health behavior changes necessary for a successful recovery.

The distinction between the main effects and buffering effects hypotheses is shown in Figure 11.3. In Figure 11.3a, the main effects hypothesis shows that married people are less distressed than unmarried people, regardless of the level of stress. The magnitude of the difference between the two lines is the same across low- and high-stress groups. Of course, stress leads to an increase in distress among both married and unmarried people. In Figure 11.3b, the stress-buffering hypothesis

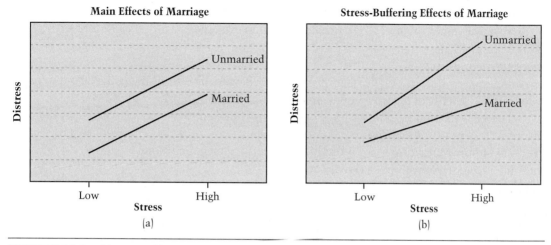

FIGURE 11.3 (a) Main effects of marriage: Married people are less distressed than unmarried people, regardless of their levels of stress. (b) Stress-buffering effects of marriage: Married people are especially less distressed than unmarried people when they face high levels of stress. In other words, marriage buffers people from the deleterious effects of stress.

shows that stress is associated with a larger increase in distress among unmarried people than married people. That is, married people who face high levels of stress are protected from the large increase in distress that unmarried people suffer. Here, the magnitude of the difference between the two lines is greater under high levels of stress. Next, I review some of the research on these psychological and behavioral links of marriage to health.

Social Support. One explanation for the effects of marriage on health involves social support. Married women and men report higher levels of support than unmarried persons, but men may have more of an advantage than women. Husbands receive more support from their spouses than do wives (Goldzweig et al., 2009; Verhofstadt, Buysee, & Ickes, 2007). This is especially the case for emotional support. Wives, by contrast, receive more support than husbands from their broader network of friends. One study showed that the reason men who lived alone were more

depressed than men who lived with someone else, typically a spouse, was due to a lack of social support (Russell & Taylor, 2009). There were fewer differences in support between women who lived alone and women who lived with someone else because women have access to support from other network members.

However, observational studies of marital interactions and daily diary studies in which men and women record their behavior on a more momentary basis seem to show that men and women are equally likely to provide their spouses with social support (Neff & Karney, 2005). Yet all support is not the same. Women may provide more effective support than men. Neff and Karney's study showed that men and women provided the same amount of support, but women's support was better timed than men's. At the end of each day for seven days, husbands and wives reported their levels of stress, the support they provided, and the support they received. Wives were more likely than husbands to provide support when their partners were stressed. In an observational portion of the study where each spouse took turns describing a personal problem, wives provided more support when husbands were describing more severe problems. However, there was no relation between the support husbands provided and the severity of the wives' problems.

The kind of support that we have been discussing is emotional support. The one kind of support that women are more likely than men to receive from marriage is financial support.

Stressful Life Events.   Another reason for the differences in distress among people of different marital statuses has to do with the occurrence of negative life events. Some states of being unmarried—separation, divorce, widowhood—can be stressful life events in and of themselves. They can also lead to other negative life events, such as changes in one's social network or financial situation. Thus, it may be that unmarried states are associated with more stress rather than the married state being associated with less stress. However, it also is possible that marriage provides resources that buffer individuals against negative life events as shown in Figure 11.3b.

Health Behavior.   Marriage has a positive effect on both men's and women's health behavior, but the effects are more pronounced among men. Wives take more responsibility for their husbands' health than husbands take for their wives' health. Married men are more likely to endorse proactive health beliefs, including preventive health care and the tendency to take care of oneself when sick, compared to single men, whereas there are no differences in proactive health beliefs between married and single women (Markey et al., 2005). Unmarried men drink more alcohol than married men, and both unmarried men and women smoke more than married men and women (Molloy et al., 2009). Differences in these health behaviors explained part of the effect of marital status on heart disease mortality. Another study examined the effects of marital status on health behaviors by examining twins who differed in marital status (Osler et al., 2008). The divorced or widowed twin smoked more than the married twin, with the difference being larger among men than women.

Marital Satisfaction.   Another reason marriage may be more health beneficial for men than women is that women are more dissatisfied with their marriages. Women report more problems in marriage, more negative feelings about marriage, and more frequent thoughts of divorce. In one study, marital satisfaction decreased over the first four years of marriage for both women and men, but the decrease was larger for women than men (Kurdek, 2005). Men also are more optimistic about marriage than women. A study of college students in Taiwan showed that both women and men perceived that they were more likely than other people to have a happy marriage but the difference between self and others was larger for men than women as shown in Figure 11.4a (Lin & Raghubir, 2005). Men and women also rated their chances of getting divorced as lower than that of other people but again the difference between self and others was larger for men than women (see Figure 11.4b).

One reason marriage may present more problems for women is that women's roles change more after marriage compared to those of men. Historically, women conformed more than men to what their spouses expected of them upon marriage. Because women were more dependent than men on marriage for financial security, women had more at stake in maintaining the marriage. Thus women were more motivated to accommodate to their spouses' wishes.

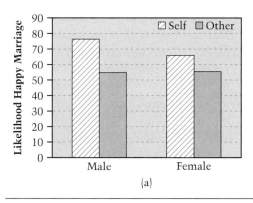
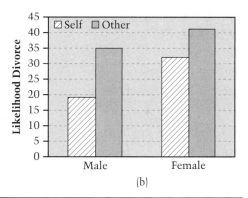

FIGURE 11.4 (a) College students estimated that they would be more likely to have a happy marriage than others, but the difference for males was greater than females. (b) College students also estimated that they would be less likely to get divorced than others, but this difference was greater for males than females.
Source: Adapted from Lin and Raghubir (2005).

In addition, the traditional housewife role lacks status, structure, and recognition because "accomplishments" often go unnoticed (Gove & Tudor, 1973). Today, however, women are more likely to take on other roles besides housewife and are better equipped to take care of themselves financially. Thus women's and men's roles are now more similar in marriage. If the difference in roles is the explanation for why marriage is more health beneficial for men, we should see more similar effects of marriage on women's and men's health in the future.

Selection Hypothesis. I have been discussing ways in which marriage could influence health, but it also is possible that health influences marriage. This is the **marital selection hypothesis**, the idea that healthier people are "selected" into marriage. Individuals tend to match in terms of health when they marry (Wilson, 2002). To examine the marital selection hypothesis, a longitudinal study must be conducted to determine whether initial health influences subsequent marital status and whether initial marital status

influences subsequent health. One such study showed that persons who married over a six-year period started out less depressed than those who did not marry (Frech & Williams, 2007). Thus, psychological health predicted marital status. However, those who married benefited in terms of reduced psychological distress six years later compared to those who did not. Thus, there was a reciprocal relation between marriage and health.

TAKE HOME POINTS

- The benefits of marriage to health are stronger for men than women.

- There are a number of reasons for this: Marriage is a greater source of emotional support, is more likely to alleviate stress, and encourages better health behavior for men than for women. In addition, men are more satisfied with marriage compared to women, partly due to the receipt of more social support resources.

- The relation between marriage and health is bidirectional. Healthier people are more likely to get married, and married people have better health over time.

EFFECT OF BEREAVEMENT ON HEALTH

If marriage is good for health, presumably losing a spouse has negative effects on health. These negative effects could stem from the loss of resources that the deceased spouse provided as well as the general experience of bereavement. Determining the effects of bereavement on health is not easy. Two kinds of studies have been conducted to address this issue: cross-sectional and longitudinal. Cross-sectional studies evaluate people who are widowed at a single point in time. The advantage of this methodology is that large representative samples can be studied. There are three disadvantages. First, people are widowed for varying lengths of time, and the length of time since widowhood is bound to influence health. Second, the healthiest people are more likely to remarry after widowhood. Thus the people who remain widowed are not representative of all widowed people and may be more unhealthy than the widowed who have remarried. Third, causality cannot be inferred. In other words, we will not know if widowhood caused the decline in health or if unhealthy people were more likely to be widowed. At first glance, this latter possibility may seem unlikely. However, recall that people are attracted to similar others and marry people who are similar to themselves. One characteristic on which matching could occur is health. It is possible, then, that less healthy people are more likely to lose a spouse.

An important methodological issue to keep in mind when evaluating cross-sectional studies of the effect of widowhood on health is whether an appropriate comparison group of nonwidowed persons was used. This is especially important when evaluating sex differences in the effects of widowhood on health. Why? If widowed women and widowed men show equal health profiles, can we conclude that widowhood has the same effects on the health of women and men? No, because women and men who are not widowed differ in health. For example, married women are more depressed than married men. A study that shows no sex differences in depression among widowed women and men could imply that widowhood increased men's distress levels to those of women or lowered women's distress levels to those of men. In other words, widowhood could have very different effects on women's and men's distress. Let's take another example. In general, men have higher suicide rates compared to women. A study that shows no sex differences in suicide rates among the widowed could imply that widowhood increased women's suicide rates to those of men or decreased men's suicide rates to those of women. The most appropriate comparison group to use in a study of widowhood is married women and men because both widowed and married people share the experience of having entered into marriage. It would not be appropriate to compare widowed persons to never-married persons because we know there are differences between the kinds of people who do and do not get married.

The second way to examine the effects of widowhood on health is to conduct a longitudinal study. Longitudinal studies typically examine people shortly after widowhood and then follow them over time to assess changes in their health. The disadvantage of this methodology is that we do not know people's level of health before widowhood. The advantage, however, is that we know people's initial health status immediately after widowhood so we can truly examine changes in health over time.

The ideal study of widowhood would use a **prospective design** in which people's health is examined before and after widowhood. Imagine how difficult it would be to conduct such a study. One would have to enroll a large number of people into a study and then follow them for a long time so a sufficient number of people lose a spouse. Thus you can imagine there are few prospective studies on widowhood. One way in which a prospective study can be conducted is to follow couples in which a spouse is at high risk for death. However, the caregiver spouse's health might already be impacted if a spouse is ill.

Evidence

Widowhood seems to have a more negative effect on men's health than women's health (Stroebe, Schut, & Stroebe, 2007). A seven-year prospective study showed that widowed men had higher mortality rates compared to married people but widowed women did not (Molloy et al., 2009). Another study showed that men's mortality was higher if widowed than married but women's mortality was lower if widowed than married (Pizzetti & Manfredini, 2008). A study of stroke showed that widowed persons were at increased risk relative to married persons, but the risk was greater for men (Maselko et al., 2009).

Men also appear to be more distressed following widowhood compared to women. In a prospective study that followed couples before and after a spouse died from severe renal disease, men reported greater grief six months following the loss of their spouses than women (Pruchno, Cartwright, & Wilson-Genderson, 2009). A nationally representative survey showed that the transition to widowhood was associated with a decline in self-reported health for men but not women (Williams & Umberson, 2004). However, the negative effects were short-lived. Within three to five years, these men's health had substantially improved. By contrast, another study showed that small sex differences in distress appeared among recently widowed persons, but large sex differences emerged among those who had been widowed for more than four years (van Grootheest et al., 1999). Finally, one study found that widowed women initially had worse mental health than married women (Wilcox et al., 2003), but with time, the mental health of widowed women improved and ended up exceeding that of the married women. Thus women may recover more easily from widowhood than men.

Explanations

Strains.   One explanation for sex differences in health following the loss of a spouse is that women and men face different strains or stressors from widowhood. Traditionally, women suffered financial strains, whereas men suffered strains from having to keep up with household chores. The strain of keeping up with household chores is an immediate strain and a daily strain, which may explain why men suffer more than women immediately following widowhood. Alternatively, caring for an ill spouse is a strain that is removed by widowhood. Because women are traditionally more involved in caregiving than men—whether the spouse is ill or not—one reason that women might not suffer as much as men following the loss of a spouse is that some of the burden associated with support provision has been removed. In an interview study with recently widowed men and women, women mentioned a freedom from having to look after someone as a deterrent to remarriage, whereas men did not express this concern (Davidson, 2001).

Social Support.   A major loss associated with widowhood is the loss of social support. *Interpersonal protection theory* has been used to explain why men suffer more than women upon widowhood (Stroebe & Stroebe, 1983). Interpersonal protection theory implies there are differences in social support across the marital statuses, and social support provides a buffer against distress. There are four support-related explanations for greater negative effects of widowhood on men than women. First, because marriage increases men's more than women's social support, widowhood results in a greater loss of support among men than women, especially emotional support. Recall that men are more likely than women to rely on their spouses as the sole source of emotional support; women, by contrast, receive less support from marriage compared to men and often obtain support from other network members. Second, family and friends provide more support to women than men following widowhood (Lee, Willetts, & Seccombe, 1998; van Groot-heest et al., 1999), in part because women are more likely than men to seek help from others. Third, men suffer a greater loss of support from other network members after widowhood because it is typically the wife who arranges social affairs and maintains contacts with friends and family. Fourth, widowed men have a smaller reference group compared to widowed women. Because women outlive men, widowed women have a larger peer group available than widowed men do. Thus men lose more in terms of receiving support from a spouse and support from other network members following widowhood. One study that provided evidence for this social support explanation showed that men are more interested in remarriage after widowhood *only* when they lack social support from friends (Carr, 2004). Six months post loss, more men than women expressed interest in remarrying (30% vs. 16%). However, when support from friends was taken into consideration, few women or

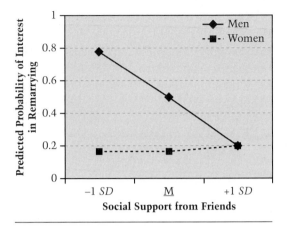

FIGURE 11.5 Among those with low support, men are more interested in remarriage compared to women. Among those with high support, men and women are equally uninterested in remarriage. *Source*: Carr (2004).

men expressed interest in remarriage when they had high levels of support but more men than women expressed interest in the absence of support. These results are shown in Figure 11.5.

Selection. Selection might not seem like an obvious explanation for why widowhood is associated with poor health. However, there is evidence that people who become widowed over a three-year period differ from those who were already widowed or people who were married. Researchers followed a group of older adults over three years, measuring their marital status and health at the beginning and end of the study (Williams et al., 2008). The group of people who would eventually become widowed was similar to the already widowed in terms of self-rated health, anxiety, and energy levels but similar to the married in terms of age, income, mobility, and health problems. The point is that these people were distinct in terms of some health parameters from the married and distinct in terms of other parameters from the already widowed. Because widowhood can be a longer process for some people, the events leading up to widowhood may take their toll on health.

- There are a number of methodological difficulties when studying the effects of widowhood on health:

  - An appropriate comparison group must be selected as women and men have different health prior to widowhood. The most appropriate group is married people, as both married and widowed people have selected into marriage.

  - Cross-sectional studies, while easy to conduct, pose several difficulties, including the inability to determine causation, the fact that the healthiest people might have remarried, and the varying time frames since widowhood.

- Studies generally show that widowhood is associated with greater adverse effects on men's than women's health across an array of health indicators.

- Reasons for this sex difference have to do with the different strains men and women face and the greater loss of support that a spouse's death poses for men compared to women.

EFFECT OF RELATIONSHIP DISSOLUTION ON HEALTH

Evidence clearly suggests that marriage is associated with greater health benefits for men than for women and that the loss of marriage through widowhood is associated with greater harm to men's than women's health. Can we conclude that the breakup of marriage or other significant relationships has more adverse effects on men's than women's health? The answer is not as clear.

Relationship Breakup

There is some evidence that women adjust better than men to the breakup of dating relationships (Choo, Levine, & Hatfield, 1996). In a study of long-distance college student dating relationships, women adjusted better than men to the breakup (Helgeson, 1994a). Just over 100 students were enrolled in the study at the beginning of the school year and were followed for one semester. At the end of the semester, 36% of the couples had broken up. As shown in Figure 11.6, at the beginning of the study, when the couples were together (Time 1), women were more distressed than

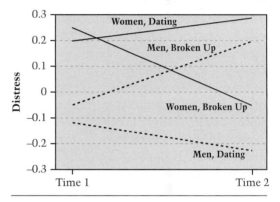

FIGURE 11.6   At the beginning of the semester, when relationships were intact (Time 1), women were more distressed than men. By the end of the semester, when a third of couples had broken up (Time 2), women's distress levels did not significantly differ from those of men. This is because women were more distressed than men among couples who remained together but were less distressed than men among couples who had broken up. Women's distress level decreased following breakup, whereas men's distress level increased following breakup.

Source: V. S. Helgeson (1994). Long distance romantic relationships: Sex differences in adjustment and breakup. Personality and Social Psychology Bulletin, 20, 254–265.

men. At the end of the semester, when a third of the couples had broken up (Time 2), there was no sex difference in distress among people who had broken up, but women were more distressed than men when the relationship still existed. An alternative way of viewing these findings is that men who broke up became more distressed, whereas women who broke up became less distressed. Women also reported better adjustment to the breakup than men did.

In terms of the breakup of marital relationships, findings are contradictory. One indicator that women may adjust better to the breakup of a marriage is that women are less likely than men to remarry after divorce. In 2001, 55% of men compared to 44% of women who had divorced were currently remarried (U.S. Census Bureau, 2005). However, the research findings are not clear as to whether one sex suffers more than the other following separation and divorce. Three studies showed that people who were separated/divorced had worse health than married people but the effects were stronger for women than men—in terms of mortality from heart disease (Molloy et al., 2009) and self-reported health (Lindstrom, 2009; Liu & Umberson, 2008). However, two others studies showed stronger adverse effects of separation/divorce on men than women—in terms of mortality (Sbarra & Nietert, 2009) and psychological distress (Hope, Rodgers, & Power, 1999). An older cross-cultural study (United States, Canada, Puerto Rico, Germany, Taiwan, Korea, Lebanon, France, and New Zealand) showed that separated and divorced individuals were two to four times more likely to have major depression than married individuals, but the difference was greater for men than women in all of the countries except Canada and Taiwan (Weissman et al., 1996).

There are a number of factors that might influence the sex difference in response to separation and divorce. One is the presence of children. If there are no children, women suffer fewer ill effects of separation and divorce (Elliott & Umberson, 2004). When children are involved, strains associated with raising children alone arise. Thus, income and parenthood are important moderators of the effects of divorce on women and men.

Explanations

Strains.   Separation and divorce are associated with a number of strains, including the change in roles that accompanies divorce, single parenthood if children are involved, and the potential for conflict with an ex-spouse (Whisman, Weinstock, & Tolejko, 2006). These strains may differ for women and men. Relationship dissolution may be associated with greater social strains for men and greater economic strains for women. Marital dissolution results in a loss of men's primary confidant. For women, the economic strain associated with marital dissolution is especially large if they retain custody of children. Even in cohabiting relationships, the economic strains associated with relationship dissolution are greater for women than men. One study showed that men's income declined by 10%, whereas women's declined by 33% after the relationships dissolved (Avellar & Smock, 2005). In that study, the greater strains for women partly had to do with the presence of children.

If differential strains experienced by women and men following separation/divorce explain the effects of relationship dissolution on health, one would expect the dissolution of traditional marriages to have stronger negative effects on women and men than the dissolution of egalitarian marriages.

In egalitarian marriages, women are less likely to depend on their spouses for financial support and men are less likely to depend on their spouses to take care of the house and to be the sole source of emotional support. Research has yet to investigate this possibility.

The strain explanation for the negative health effects of separation and divorce is most appealing when studies emerge that show there are greater differences in health between married people and divorced/separated people than married people and unmarried people (Whisman et al., 2006). To the extent that this is the case, the health benefits of marriage have less to do with the benefits of marriage per se, but more to do with the strains associated with the breakup of a relationship. If the health advantage of marriage was due to marriage per se, married people should have better health than all other groups.

Social Selection. The social selection hypothesis could also explain why those who separate and divorce have worse health than those who remain married. Perhaps, poor health precedes rather than follows relationship dissolution. Two studies support this possibility. A nine-year longitudinal study of adults in England showed that separation and divorce were associated with poor mental health but also that poor mental health was associated with marital dissolution (Wade & Pevalin, 2004). A longitudinal study of twins found that those whose marriages dissolved had poorer health prior to the breakup compared to those whose marriages remained in tact (Osler et al., 2008).

Women Initiate Breakup. One reason the health costs of relationship dissolution could be stronger for men than women is that women are more likely than men to initiate the breakup of a relationship. About two-thirds of those who file for divorce are women (Brinig & Allen, 2000). In some ways, this is not a surprise as women are less satisfied than men with marriage. Because women are less satisfied with marriage, women also might be more aware of problems in the relationship than men, which would lead them to be better prepared for the relationship to end. In the study of dating couples shown in Figure 11.6, women reported that they had thought about and talked about the possibility of a breakup more than men, regardless of who ultimately initiated it (Helgeson, 1994a). Men thought about and talked about the possibility of a breakup only when they ended up initiating it. Thus women may have been more psychologically prepared for the breakup than men. These findings are consistent with a study of distressed couples seeking marital therapy that showed women were more aware of problems in the relationship than men (Doss, Atkins, & Christensen, 2003). In that study, both men and women agreed that women were the first to recognize that there was a problem in the relationship, the first to consider seeking help, and the first to initiate treatment. Thus women may adjust better than men to the dissolution of a relationship because they are more aware of relationship problems and the potential for the relationship to end.

TAKE HOME POINTS

- It is not clear whether relationship dissolution has stronger adverse effects on women or men. Inconsistencies in effects may have to do with the phase of the dissolution evaluated, the presence of children, and the socioeconomic status of the couple.

- In traditional couples, men and women face different strains following separation and divorce—men's strains have to do with having to care for the house and a loss of support, whereas women's strains are largely financial.

■ To the extent that women adjust better than men to relationship dissolution, reasons might be that women are more likely to initiate the breakup, are more aware of problems in the relationship, and more prepared for a breakup.

MARITAL TRANSITIONS AND HEALTH

Most of the research on the relation of marital status to health implicitly adopts the "resource model," implying that marriage is a resource that promotes health or protects health. However, an alternative model is the "crisis model," which suggests that the dissolution of a relationship through divorce or widowhood causes declines in health (Williams & Umberson, 2004). The only way to disentangle the two models is to conduct a longitudinal study in which one not only compares people of different marital statuses but also examines the effects of changes in marital statuses on health. One such study examined the effects of marital transitions rather than marital status on weight loss (Umberson, Liu, & Powers, 2009), considering that weight loss is a risk factor for mortality. Umberson and colleagues found that the continuously married, never married, and divorced showed a small increase in weight over time—with the exception of African American women who showed a larger weight gain. Weight loss, however, was tied to the loss of a spouse through divorce or widowhood. The transition to divorce was associated with a short-term weight loss that was later regained, but the transition to widowhood was associated with a substantial weight loss that remained—more so among African Americans. Thus, this study concluded that marital dissolution was more important than marital formations in predicting health in terms of weight loss.

Three other studies showed that changes in marital status or marital transitions are associated with more health problems rather than marital status per se. An eight-year longitudinal study showed that the health of the continually divorced and never married was the same as the continually married (Williams & Umberson, 2004). Transitions out of marriage through divorce or widowhood were associated with adverse effects on health, and these effects were stronger for men than women. The negative effects were also stronger for older men, which supports the role strain argument as older men are probably less prepared to assume household chores than younger men. Another longitudinal study showed that never-married women had the same health as continuously married women and that both groups had better health than women whose marital status had changed over the course of the study (Hughes & Waite, 2009). However, this was not the case for men, as never-married men had worse health and more depression than continuously married men. Finally, a two-year longitudinal study showed that the consistently married had the same level of distress as the consistently widowed (Strohschein et al., 2005) but distress increased among those who were widowed during the two years. These findings support the crisis model rather than the resource model of marriage.

TAKE HOME POINT

■ Transitions out of marriage seem to have stronger adverse health consequences than the specific unmarried states, supporting the crisis rather than the resource model of marriage.

EFFECT OF MARITAL QUALITY ON HEALTH

I have been discussing the effects of marital status—whether one is single, married, widowed, or divorced—on health. Does marital status alone determine our health? Surely, all marriages are not the same or provide the same health benefits. Is a distressed marriage better for health than no marriage at all? Research suggests that the answer is no. For example, a study of the elderly showed that married people were less distressed than unmarried people, but married people who were not happy with the way their spouse treated them were more distressed than unmarried people (Hagedoorn et al., 2006). Thus it is important to consider the quality of the relationship when evaluating the health implications of marriage.

Many of the explanations of why marriage benefits men's health more than women's pertain to the quality of the marital relationship. For example, a primary explanation for sex differences in the effects of marriage and widowhood on health has to do with marriage providing relatively more social support to men. This explanation suggests the quality of the marital relationship is different for women and men. Perhaps marriage benefits men's health more than women's health because the relationship is more satisfying to men. In fact, we know men are more satisfied in marriage than women are. To understand thoroughly the effects of marriage on health, we need to examine the quality of the relationship.

Two types of studies examine the nature of marital relationships. In survey studies, women and men complete various marital satisfaction or marital strain inventories. The relation of these self-report measures of marital quality to women's and men's health is then examined. In laboratory studies, men and women engage in some sort of marital interaction (usually, a discussion of a conflict) that is videotaped, recorded, and analyzed. The relation of specific interaction patterns to health is examined. I review both kinds of studies.

Evidence

Survey Studies.   It is clear that the benefits of marriage depend on its quality. One study showed that happily married men were less depressed than unmarried men but there was no difference between the two groups for women (St. John & Montgomery, 2009). However, unhappily married men and women were more depressed than their unmarried counterparts, as shown in Figure 11.7. Other research has confirmed that the benefits of marriage depend on the quality (Frech & Williams, 2007). Some studies indicate that the quality of the marital relationship is more strongly related to women's than men's psychological well-being (Walker & Luszcz, 2009). Marital quality is more strongly related to women's than men's physical health in studies that span periodontal disease, rheumatoid arthritis, blood pressure, and cardiac problems (Kiecolt-Glaser & Newton, 2001). In terms of psychological distress, relationship satisfaction among cohabiting and married couples has been more strongly associated with reduced distress for women than men (Whisman & Uebelacker, 2006). In a longitudinal study of newlywed couples, marital dissatisfaction predicted an increase in depression 18 months later for women but not men (Fincham et al., 1997). Conflict has been associated with psychological distress among lesbian couples (Otis, Riggle, & Rostosky, 2006).

However, other studies find similar effects on women's and men's health. Two

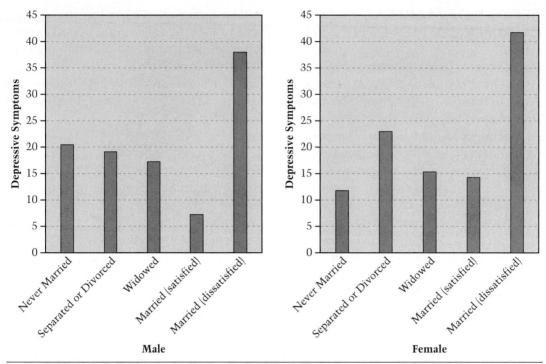

FIGURE 11.7   Happily married men are less depressed than unmarried men, whereas there is no difference in depression between happily married women and unmarried women. However, unhappily married men and women are more depressed than their unmarried counterparts. In addition, separated and divorced men and women were more depressed than married men and women.
Source: Adapted from St. John and Montgomery (2009).

studies showed that marital quality was associated with better subjective health perceptions among both women and men (Umberson & Williams, 2005; Umberson et al., 2006), and one study showed that unhappily married people had higher blood pressure during the day than either happily married people or single people, with similar effects for women and men (Holt-Lunstad, Birmingham, & Jones, 2008).

Laboratory Studies.   The studies I reviewed on marital quality and health rely on people's self-reports of marital satisfaction or distress. Another way to examine the link between features of the marital relationship and

health is to examine the health consequences of specific behaviors that occur during marital interactions. Because communication is central to the quality of a relationship, numerous studies have couples come into the laboratory and observe how they communicate. Topics of relationship conflict are usually the subject matter. Health is measured in terms of physiological responses to the interactions, such as blood pressure, heart rate, hormone production, and immune function.

These studies tend to show that women are more physiologically reactive to conflict discussions than men are. In a study of 90 newlywed couples, negative and hostile behavior during a 30-minute conflict

Relationships and Health 411

discussion was associated with changes in immune function and elevations in blood pressure in both women and men, but women showed more negative immune changes than men (Kiecolt-Glaser et al., 1993). Endocrine function was later examined in these same couples (Kiecolt-Glaser et al., 1996). Husbands' behavior during the interaction influenced the production of hormones in wives; for example, when husbands withdrew from conflict, wives' cortisol increased, and when husbands provided validation, wives' stress hormones decreased. The behavior of wives was not related to men's hormone levels. These findings are consistent with Floyd and Markman's (1983) idea that women are the emotional barometers of relationships. Women's bodies respond physiologically to the nature of marital interactions, whereas men's do not.

The greater physiological responsiveness of women compared to men in these studies directly contradicts Gottman's (1994) explanation for why men withdraw from discussions of conflict. Recall from Chapter 9 that he argued men withdraw because they are more physiologically reactive to stress and less able than women to tolerate such physiological changes. These studies suggest it is women who are more physiologically reactive.

One reason that discussions about conflict produce greater physiological changes in women compared to men is that such discussions may be more threatening to women. Relationships are central to the female gender role, and conflict is a threat to relationships. As women's and men's roles become more equal, we might expect future studies to show similar effects of marital quality on men's and women's health.

To summarize, it appears that what is important for men is the mere presence of a spouse, but what is important for women is the support of the spouse or the quality of the relationship. This may be because women are more adept than men at providing the features of social interactions that benefit health. In particular, women may be more effective support providers. A laboratory study supported this conclusion (Glynn, Christenfeld, & Gerin, 1999). College students underwent a stressful task (giving a speech) in the presence of either a supportive or nonsupportive confederate. The confederate was either male or female. Support from a female decreased both men's and women's cardiovascular reactivities (i.e., increases in blood pressure), whereas support from a male had no effect. Thus the mere existence of a relationship with a woman is health protective, whereas the nature of the relationship with a man must be considered for women to reap health benefits.

TAKE HOME POINTS

- Whereas simply being married influences men's more than women's health, the quality of marriage has a greater effect on women's health.

- The evidence that supports this claim is stronger for studies of marital interactions than for surveys of self-reported marital quality.

- The nature of marital interactions is more strongly associated with physiological changes in women than men.

DIVISION OF LABOR

Who does what in the family, or the division of labor, is an important aspect of marital relationships that has effects on psychological and physical health. A sex-segregated division of labor consists of men working outside the home and women working inside the home. The way work is divided affects the quality of the marital relationship as well as general psychological distress. I examine the literature on who does what in the family and show how the division of labor is associated with marital satisfaction and well-being.

Who Does What?

"A man may work from sun to sun, but a woman's work is never done." Is there any truth to this old adage? According to Hochschild (1989), there is. She refers to employed women's work at home as "the second shift": Women work one shift at work and a second shift at home. Hochschild interviewed 50 couples and found that women worked on average 15 hours a week longer than men, including paid employment, household chores, and child care. Over the course of a year, she remarked this extra time added up to a full month.

Household labor includes preparing meals, cleaning, yard work, household repairs, grocery shopping, washing clothes, paying bills, automobile maintenance, and running errands. A 2007 Gallop Poll revealed that women do more household chores than men, with the exception of the stereotypical masculine chores, such as car maintenance and yard work (Newport, 2008). Household chores are shown in Figure 11.8.

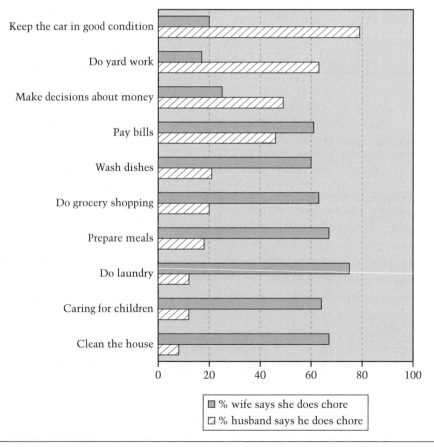

FIGURE 11.8   Women perform more of most household tasks compared to men, although both women and men estimate that they do more than their partner credits them. *Source*: Adapted from Newport (2008).

Even when women are employed full time, women contribute more to household labor than men do (Gager, 2008). A survey of U.S. couples who each worked at least 30 hours outside of the home showed that wives spent 34 hours on household labor and husbands spent 21 hours on household labor per week (Bartley, Blanton, & Gilliard, 2005). Even a study of self-proclaimed feminists married to transgendered men showed that women do more household labor than men (Pfeffer, 2010). Because the majority (93%) of these women identify themselves as feminists, they typically rationalized the unequal arrangement by stating that they were more skilled at household labor or that they were choosing to engage in these activities. In a cross-cultural study of 25 European countries, women spent three times the amount of time on domestic work as men—19 hours compared to 6 (Boye, 2009). However, when men and women engaged in paid employment were compared, the difference was smaller—14.5 compared to 6.

Sex differences in household labor are larger among married than cohabiting individuals. Marriage leads women and men to enact traditional roles (Judge & Livingston, 2008). Whereas cohabiting women perform fewer household chores than married women, cohabiting men perform more household chores than married men (Coltrane, 2000). Parenthood also leads to a decrease in egalitarian beliefs (Corrigall & Konrad, 2007) and an increase in a more traditional division of labor—especially for women (Katz-Wise, Priess, & Hyde, 2010).

Admittedly, the size of the sex difference in household labor and child care has decreased over the past four decades, mostly due to women spending less time on such activities and partly due to men spending more time on such activities (Coltrane, 2000). In 2008, men participated in 30% of household labor, compared to 15% in the 1960s (Sullivan & Coltrane, 2008). In 2008, men said that they shared or did most of the cooking in 56% of households (Galinsky, Aumann, & Bond, 2009). In 1992, the figure was 34%. In a study of six countries across Europe and North America, women's domestic labor decreased by one hour per day between 1960 and 1997, whereas men's increased by 20 minutes (Sullivan, 2004).

One way to examine the influence of gender roles on the division of labor is to explore how gay and lesbian couples divide household labor. Is it always the case that one person performs the traditionally masculine chores (e.g., mow the lawn, take out the garbage) and one person performs the traditionally feminine chores (e.g., prepare the meal, wash the dishes)? The answer is "no." The traditional male–female roles in regard to the division of labor do not apply to homosexual couples. There is a more equal division of labor in gay and lesbian couples compared to heterosexuals (Peplau & Fingerhut, 2007), in part due to the more egalitarian division of labor outside the home. Whereas men are more likely than women to work full time in traditional heterosexual marriages, both partners are likely to work full time in gay and lesbian relationships. In gay and lesbian relationships, personal preference rather than gender roles dictates who does what in the household.

How does parenthood affect the division of labor in same-sex relationships? One study showed that household labor was divided equally between two lesbian partners but the biological mother spent more time on childcare than the nonbiological mother (Goldberg & Perry-Jenkins, 2007). Another study of Black lesbian relationships showed that biological mothers performed more household chores than nonbiological mothers

(Moore, 2008). Thus, parenthood may alter the division of labor in homosexual families.

What Determines Who Does What?

Gender-Role Attitudes. We would expect that whether the couple endorses traditional versus egalitarian views of marriage would influence the household division of labor. Husbands' gender-role attitudes are more predictive of the division of labor than wives' gender-role attitudes (Cunningham, 2005; Stevens et al., 2006). When the husband has an egalitarian view of marriage, he contributes more and the wife contributes less compared to other couples. Wives' egalitarian views seem to be unrelated to either husbands' or wives' household contributions.

Rabin (1998) points out that women's and men's gender-role attitudes are changing and undergoing some negotiation. She refers to the **gender tension line** as the point at which people feel uncomfortable with further change: "The gender tension line is that point beyond which the person can no longer change in terms of gender role and still feel masculine or feminine enough" (p. 182). For example, a man may have egalitarian views and believe both mothers and fathers should change a child's diapers. When at home, the man may be willing to change the child's diaper; when in public, however, the man may not be willing to take the child into the men's room to change the diaper. Public displays of such behavior cross the line for this man. Similarly, a woman may have egalitarian views of her marriage and work full time; however, when it comes to deciding who retrieves a sick child from school, the woman feels more comfortable having the school contact her than her husband. See if you can determine what your own gender tension lines are in Do Gender 11.2.

DO GENDER 11.2
Determine Your Gender Tension Line

This exercise involves some in-depth self-analysis. First, think carefully about the behaviors that characterize the other sex in which you would be willing to engage. Start with a domain of behavior, such as appearance. For example, "I am a woman and I would be willing to wear a suit." Then, keep upping the stakes until you find a domain of behavior that "crosses the line" for you. For example, "I would be unwilling to be a stay-at-home parent." Do the same for at least two other domains, such as leisure interests, how you behave in relationships with friends or with a romantic partner, how you would divide the household chores in your family, and so on.

Power/Status. Because the division of labor is more equal in homosexual couples, the differential status between women and men in heterosexual couples may contribute to the uneven division of labor. In homosexual couples, there is no differential status based on gender and the division of labor is more evenly divided. In lesbian relationships, performing household chores may not even be viewed as a low-status role. One study of lesbian families showed that the woman who performed more household chores had more rather than less authority in the family (Moore, 2008). The person in charge of household labor had more decision power in terms of how the family spent money, how children were raised, and how the household was organized. Even income, a traditional measure of status, was not related to time on household labor.

In heterosexual couples, education and income—indicators of power and status—are related to the division of labor. Husbands contribute more to household labor when either they have lower incomes or wives have higher incomes (Erickson, 2005). As the income gap increases (men earning more than women), women spend more time on child care and household chores (Stevens et al., 2006). The income gap influences men's participation rates more than women's. In other words, high-income men are especially unlikely to spend time on household labor. One study showed that women's income was a better predictor of her household labor than her husband's income (Gupta, 2006). When her income increases, her housework decreases. Women's income may provide her with greater power in the relationship to negotiate household labor and also may provide her with the resources to "buy out of household labor" by going out to eat or hiring a housekeeper.

Further evidence that power underlies the division of labor among heterosexuals comes from a study that examined the implications of men's status at work for household labor. When women's and men's earnings were similar, men who held subordinate positions at work were especially unlikely to participate in household chores (Arrighi & Maume, 2000). Arrighi and Maume suggested that men may be reluctant to perform tasks at home which they construe as feminine when their jobs threaten their masculinity. However, when men had a much higher income than women (affirming their masculinity), the nature of the job had less effect on participation in household chores.

The effect of the differential status between women and men on household labor was also examined in a cross-cultural study of 22 countries (Fuwa, 2004). As predicted, countries in which women had made greater achievements (e.g., Canada, United States), as measured by income and political and economic representation in the country, had a more egalitarian division of labor than countries in which women had made fewer achievements (e.g., Japan, Italy).

Work Outside the Home.   Who does what inside the home is bound to be influenced by who does what outside the home. If one partner works full time (usually the husband) and one works part time or not at all (usually the wife), would a 50:50 split on household chores really be an equitable arrangement? Several studies have found that the number of hours people work outside the home influences the division of labor at home. The more hours husbands work outside the home, the fewer hours they work inside the home and the more hours wives work inside the home (Coltrane, 2000; Erickson, 2005). In addition, the more hours wives work outside the home, the more hours husbands work inside the home and the fewer hours wives work inside the home. Wives' employment, however, is a better predictor of the division of labor in the family than husbands' employment (Coltrane, 2000). That is, a wife's employment most definitely decreases her contributions to household labor and often increases the husband's contributions to household labor. The number of hours that husbands are employed outside the home is not a consistent predictor of men's contribution to household labor.

Relationship Commitment.   Some have suggested that men's commitment to the relationship is associated with their contribution to the division of labor. A study of cohabiting couples showed that men who had planned to marry their partners spent more time on household chores than men who did not have marriage plans (Ciabattari, 2004). Women's relationship commitment was unrelated to their contribution to household chores. A study of married couples showed that men's dedication to the relationship was associated with wives being more satisfied with the division of labor (Rhoades, Petralla et al., 2006).

Satisfaction

Are women and women satisfied with an inequitable division of labor? Not surprisingly, women are less satisfied than men with this state of affairs (Erickson, 2005; Stevens et al., 2006). A wife's perception of inequity in the division of labor is associated with divorce (Frisco & Williams, 2003) as well as the breakup of relationships among cohabiting couples (Hohmann-Marriott, 2006).

However, not all women value an equal division of labor. Socioeconomic status, egalitarian attitudes, and women's employment status all influence how an inequitable division of labor is perceived. One study of working-class women showed that those who spent less time on child care than they expected and whose husbands spent more time on child care than they expected were more rather than less distressed (Goldberg & Perry-Jenkins, 2004). This was especially the case for women with a traditional gender-role ideology.

Among women who value equity in the division of labor, men do not have to perform half of the chores for women to be satisfied. In fact, rarely is household labor divided 50:50, even when women and men work equally outside the home. Why are women satisfied with a less-than-equitable division of labor? One answer has to do with to whom women compare themselves, that is, their comparison referents. As will

be discussed in more depth in Chapter 12, women and men make same-sex comparisons. That is, women compare what they do at home to what other women do at home but not to what their husbands do at home. Women compare their husbands' involvement in household labor to that of other men. A woman may be satisfied that her husband performs 25% of household chores because the neighbor's husband does not participate in any household chores. Wives' evaluations of husbands' assistance at home may be even more favorable if the comparison referents become men of previous generations: fathers or grandfathers. Thus one reason women are not as dissatisfied with the division of labor as we would expect is that they do not directly compare themselves to men. However, the comparison referent may be starting to change for women. One study showed that women compared their contribution to the division of labor to that of their husbands as well as other women, whereas men only compared their contribution to that of other

DO GENDER 11.3
Is It Fair? To Whom
Do You Compare?

Interview a few college students who are involved in a romantic relationship and living with a partner. These people can be married or cohabiting. First, try to find out who does what in the relationship. Second, try to find out the rationale for this division of labor. Third, ask about their perceptions of fairness: Is the division of labor fair? How do they decide if it is fair? Ask about comparison referents; that is, to whom do they compare themselves when judging the fairness of how much time they spend on household tasks?

men (Gager & Hohmann-Marriott, 2006). Thus women may be more unsatisfied with the division of labor in the future because they are using different comparison referents to evaluate fairness. Find out to whom your peers compare their contributions to household labor in Do Gender 11.3.

TAKE HOME POINTS

■ The sex difference in the division of labor has decreased over the past 40 years, largely due to the increase of women in the employed labor force.

■ Even when women hold full-time jobs outside the home, they spend more time than men on household labor and child care.

■ One determinant of the division of labor is people's gender-role attitudes; the husband's attitude is a stronger predictor than the wife's. For the division of labor to be more equal, the husband must have an egalitarian gender-role attitude.

■ Power is a major determinant of the division of labor in heterosexual relationships. The person who makes more money, works more hours outside the home, and has a higher education typically participates less in household labor — except in gay and lesbian relationships.

■ Homosexual couples adopt a more egalitarian division of labor and do not divide tasks in terms of female and male gender roles.

■ The inequity in the division of labor is a prominent source of marital distress for women. Yet, women are not as dissatisfied with the unequal division of labor as one might expect. One reason is that women do not compare their own contributions to those of their husbands; instead women compare themselves to other women and compare their husbands to other men. This kind of comparison usually results in a more favorable view of husbands and leaves women more satisfied.

PARENTING AND HEALTH

During the 18th and 19th centuries, men were regarded as the ultimate source of moral influence on children (Pleck, 1987). If marriages dissolved, men retained custody of the children. Fathers' custody of children was partly due to the fact that fathers were in greater proximity to work and children were involved in work. This connection was especially strong with sons. During the 19th and 20th centuries, the role of mother in the family expanded. Women were regarded as pure and innocent, thus possessing the ideal qualities to raise children. In addition, society began to regard infancy and childhood as critical times of development, times in which a mother's role was especially important. It was at this time that it became the norm to award mothers custody of children in the event of divorce. Fathers were still regarded as the moral authority but became far removed from children, in part due to industrialization shifting fathers' work farther from home.

Family roles again shifted in the middle of the 20th century, specifically after World War II, when women moved into the workforce. The roles of mothers and fathers in the family were not as distinct as they once were. Partly as a result of the women's movement and partly as a result of women's participation in the paid workforce, in the 1970s and 1980s a new father role emerged that was more involved and more nurturing (Levant & Wimer, 2009; see Figure 11.9). Fathers, today, however, do not completely embrace this role. Even when women work outside the home, fathers typically think of themselves as economic providers rather than family caretakers. For example, the arrival of children in the family is more likely to bring maternity leave than paternity leave. The parenting role is still

FIGURE 11.9 Photograph of father and child spending time together at the beach.

more central to women's than men's identities (Katz-Wise et al., 2010).

The traditional family has changed quite a lot over the years. The increased divorce rate and the increased tendency to have children outside of marriage have led to a decline in the two-parent family. In 1970, 81% of children lived with two parents who were married to each other, whereas the figure was 67% in 2009 (U.S. Census Bureau, 2010c). The percentage for African Americans is much lower (35%) than Whites (73%). Even among two-parent families, the notion that the man works outside the home and the woman stays home and takes care of the family has changed dramatically. This notion characterized 45% of couples in 1975 but only 20% of couples today (Harrington, Deusen, & Ladge, 2010).

Single parenting is also more common. In 2008, 41% of births in the United States were to unmarried women compared to 28% in 1990 (Taylor et al., 2010). These numbers are highest for African American (72%) and Hispanic (53%) compared to White (29%) and Asian (17%) women. These numbers

occur despite the fact that nearly half of Whites and Blacks believe it is immoral to have a child without being married (Taylor, Funk, & Clark, 2007). Younger people, however, are more accepting of this arrangement than older people.

It is also the case that fewer women are having children today. In 1976, only 10% of women between the ages of 40 and 44 did not have children; in 2008, the figure was 18% (Livingston & Cohn, 2010). The rate is similar across ethnic groups. In the late 1950s, there were 3.5 births per woman. In the middle of the 1970s, the rate had declined to 1.8. During the past decade, the rate has hovered around 2. Childlessness has increased with improved contraception, the increased participation of women in the paid workforce, and some reduction in the stigma associated with choosing not to have children. The most common reasons for not having children are valuing freedom, placing high importance on education/careers, and believing that children detract from marriage. As you will see in a subsequent section, there is some truth to the latter point.

With more women working outside the home, some people fear that parents do not spend as much time with children today as they did years ago. This turns out not to be true. Parents are spending just as much time with children as they did 20 years ago (Galinsky, 2005). But today, there is less of a separation between work and family, as more parents work at home and bring work home. Children perceive parents today as stressed and fatigued.

Another change in the traditional family is the increased involvement of fathers in childcare. Today, fathers spend more time with children. In 1977, fathers spent on average two hours per day with children (Galinsky et al., 2009). The figure increased to three hours per day by 2008. Most women say that they have primary responsibility for childcare (67%) but 31% say that childcare is shared. The shared figure is up from 21% in 1992. Although the number of stay-at-home dads has increased, the overall figure is relatively low. Among married couples with children at home, 23% of mothers and less than 1% of fathers stayed home to care for children (U.S. Census Bureau, 2009b).

In this section, I examine the implications of the parent role for health—research that is largely based on heterosexual couples. Parenting has been a subject of controversy in the gay and lesbian community. Some of these issues are discussed in Sidebar 11.2.

SIDEBAR 11.2: *Parenting Among Homosexuals*

More and more children are being raised by gay and lesbian parents. It is difficult to determine the exact number of children because it is difficult to estimate the number of gay and lesbian people. Parents who are homosexual may also be less likely to report their sexual orientation because they are concerned about losing custody or contact with their children. A national poll showed that nearly half of gay men and lesbians who did not have children said that they would like to have children (Kaiser Family Foundation, 2001).

There are two groups of homosexual parents. The first and largest group consists of homosexual persons who were once married, had children, and then divorced, often due to the discovery or acceptance of homosexuality. A second growing group of parents consists of homosexual couples who choose to have children. In the case of lesbian couples, one partner may become pregnant through the use of a sperm donor. In the case of a gay couple, the most likely avenue is adoption. Alternatively, a lesbian and gay man may decide to have a child together. States are mostly silent on whether gays and lesbians can adopt children. Only two states explicitly prohibit it—Florida and Mississippi (U.S. Department of Health and Human Services, 2009b).

Issues about parenting have arisen for homosexuals that do not arise for heterosexuals. The first issue concerns whether homosexual persons are fit to be parents. The second issue concerns the effects of a parent's homosexuality on children: effects on the children's psychological adjustment, gender-role development, and sexual orientation. Each of these issues has been raised during custody disputes over whether children should be allowed to reside with a homosexual parent. As you will see, there is no evidence to support any of these concerns.

Are homosexuals any less fit to be parents? Lesbian and gay men are equally good as parents as heterosexuals (Goldberg, 2010). No evidence suggests that homosexual parents differ from heterosexual parents in levels of self-esteem, psychological distress, or emotional stability (Golombok et al., 2003; Patterson, 2000). Among people who have divorced, one advantage that homosexual parents seem to have over heterosexual parents is that they have fewer difficulties with their divorced partners. This means children of a homosexual parent have more contact with both parents than children whose parents have divorced. In terms of parenting skills, one study found that lesbian parents were better than heterosexual mothers at coming up with solutions to hypothetical child difficulties (Flaks et al., 1995). Another study showed that lesbian mothers were less likely to hit their children and more likely to engage in imaginative play with children (Golombok et al., 2003). Few studies have compared gay fathers to heterosexual fathers; one reason may be that custody disputes typically revolve around whether a lesbian mother rather than a gay father is a fit parent. The woman's sexual orientation is more in question because the norm is for women to retain custody of children.

Are there any adverse effects of homosexual parents on children's psychological well-being? The answer appears to be "no" (Patterson, 2009). A meta-analytic review of 19 studies concluded that there were no effects on cognitive development, gender-role behavior, gender identity, sexual preference, psychological adjustment, or relationships with parents (Crowl, Ahn, & Baker, 2008). One concern that people raise is that children of same-sex couples will be teased by peers. There is evidence that children of homosexual parents are teased at some point because of their family structure (Goldberg, 2010). However, there does not seem to be any difference in the quality of peer relations, as assessed by either self-report and peer report (Wainright & Patterson, 2008). One of the greatest concerns people have expressed is that children raised by gay and lesbian parents will become homosexual. The meta-analytic review revealed no effect on sexual preferences (Crowl et al., 2008). Most of the research involves children who were born to parents who divorced and were then raised by homosexual couples. There is much less research on children who are adopted by same-sex couples or gay couples.

Thus there seems to be no evidence that heterosexual and homosexual parents differ in their adjustment levels or parenting abilities. There is also no evidence that a parent's sexual orientation influences children's psychological adjustment, relationships with peers, gender-role development, or sexual orientation. This field of research challenges psychoanalytic theory and social learning theory, which maintain it is important for children to be raised by both a male and a female. Psychoanalytic theory would suggest that children's gender-role development will be impeded without a mother and father in the home because both parents are necessary for the successful resolution of the Oedipal conflict. Social learning theory suggests that children model their parents' sexual orientation, which does not appear to be true; otherwise, there would be no homosexual children with heterosexual parents.

Effects of the Parent Role on Health

In general, we tend to believe having children is good for our overall life satisfaction and well-being. However, the data are not so clear-cut. One study of working women and men (Bond, Galinsky, & Swanberg, 1998) concluded that parental status is unrelated to psychological well-being. Another study in which women and men wore ambulatory blood pressure cuffs for 24 hours showed that parents had lower systolic and diastolic blood pressure than nonparents but that the benefit of parenthood was observed only for women, as shown in Figure 11.10 (Holt-Lunstad et al., 2009). These effects remained even when employment was taken into consideration, so it was not that mothers benefitted only because they were less likely than fathers to be employed.

The effect of parental status on health may differ across cultures. In a cross-cultural study of 17 nations around the world, being a parent was associated with less loneliness but was unrelated to health (Stack, 1998). The effects on loneliness were stronger for men than for women. In a comparison of the United States and India, the presence of children in the home was associated with lower satisfaction with home life among U.S. women but higher satisfaction with home life among Indian women (Sastry, 1999). Sastry suggested that having children is more closely tied to a woman's identity in India than in the United States. In the United States, the presence of children is more likely to lead to role conflict for women because they assume other roles.

The reason for the contradictory findings regarding parenthood and health is that

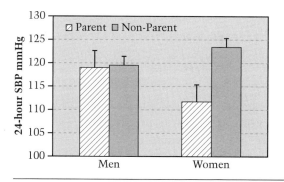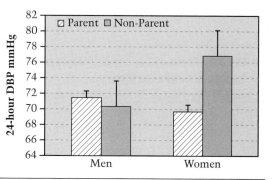

FIGURE 11.10   Parents have lower systolic and diastolic blood pressure than nonparents but the benefit is larger for women than men.

Source: Holt-Lunstad, Birmingham, Howard, and Thoman (2009).

there are a host of moderator variables that influence whether being a parent detracts from or adds to health. One moderator variable is the health of the child. Parents of children with disabilities have poorer psychological and physical health than parents of children without disabilities—and this difference is the same for women and men (Ha et al., 2008). Another moderator variable is marital status. Single parents have poorer mental and physical health than married parents (Cunningham & Knoester, 2007; Evenson & Simon, 2005). Single mothers are more depressed than married mothers, whereas single fathers have more alcohol problems than married fathers.

Another reason for the contradictory findings regarding parenthood and health is that parents are a heterogeneous group, consisting of those with children at home; those whose children have left home; those who live with biological children, step-children, or a combination of the two; and those who do not have custody of their children. The different kinds of parents were distinguished from one another in a survey on depression (Evenson & Simon, 2005). Overall, parents were more depressed than nonparents. However,

there were differences within the categories of parents. First, there was no group of parents who were better off than nonparents. However, parents who had children at home were more depressed than nonparents but parents whose children had left home had similar levels of depression as nonparents. Second, noncustodial parents and parents with adult children living at home were more depressed than parents with minor children at home. In general, these findings were similar for both women and men.

What are some of the reasons that having children could negatively affect health? First, children are a financial strain. Second, children detract from the emotional support available to a spouse, a point I turn to next. Third, there are selection effect issues to consider. Healthier people are more likely to become parents than are less healthy people.

There also is the potential for parenthood to improve aspects of health. Becoming a parent may provide people with a sense of identity and meaning in life. In addition, being a parent discourages poor health behavior. People are less likely to engage in substance abuse when they become parents.

Effect of Parenthood on Marriage

A meta-analytic review of 90 studies revealed that parents have lower levels of marital satisfaction than nonparents ($d = -.19$; Twenge, Campbell, & Foster, 2003). The association seems to be stronger for women ($d = -.19$) than men ($d = -.13$). Marital satisfaction is inversely related to the number of children couples have, such that more children translates into lower marital satisfaction. There are a number of variables that moderate the relation of parenthood to marital satisfaction. One is the age of the child—at least for women. The difference in marital satisfaction between women with infants and women without children was large ($d = -.50$), whereas the difference between women with older children and women without children was small ($d = -.14$). The age of the child had no influence on the relation of parental status to men's marital satisfaction. In addition, the negative effects of parenthood on marital satisfaction were stronger among higher SES (socioeconomic status) couples and higher in more recent years.

There are several explanations for the association of parenthood to a decline in marital satisfaction. First, there are economic costs associated with children, which could translate into financial problems in marriages. However, if that were the primary explanation, the parent status difference in marital satisfaction would be smaller rather than larger in high SES couples. One also would have predicted the parent status difference in marital satisfaction to be higher among couples with older children because older children cost more money; as noted earlier, this was not the case.

A second possibility is that the presence of children contributes to a decline in opportunities for sex, which leads to a decline in sexual satisfaction. If that were the case, one would probably expect larger parent status differences for men than women. Just the opposite was the case.

The third explanation has to do with the restriction on freedom associated with parenting and the role conflict that parenthood brings. This explanation provides a good fit for the data from the meta-analysis. The finding that parenthood has more adverse effects among higher SES families is consistent with the restriction of freedom theory as higher SES families would be more distressed at having to give up the freedom that money can buy (e.g., extensive travel and expensive leisure activities). The finding that parenting effects were stronger for women than men, and especially in the case of women with small children, also fits the restriction of freedom and role conflict hypothesis. Parenthood leads to greater changes in women's than men's roles as women take on more of the responsibility associated with the parent role. Child care is a greater restriction on women's than men's freedom in the family. The fact that the parenthood status findings are larger in more recent years also fits with the role conflict explanation as women face more conflict in juggling family and work roles today than ever before.

Part of the reason that women suffer more role conflict than men with the arrival of children is that the division of labor becomes more traditional with the arrival of children (Katz-Wise et al., 2010). Regardless of the division of labor prior to the arrival of children, women increase their contributions to household tasks when they become parents. This change may increase marital conflict and decrease women's marital satisfaction. When fathers become involved in child care, there seem to be fewer negative consequences for marital satisfaction (Ozer et al., 1998).

Most of the studies that have linked parenthood to marital satisfaction are cross-sectional. This creates two problems for interpretation. First, there may be a selection bias. Perhaps people who are less happy with their marriage are more likely to have children (or people who are more happy with their marriage refrain from becoming parents). Second, it may be that couples who have children are less likely to divorce, meaning that the parenting couples contain a greater number of unhappy marriages than the nonparenting couples.

TAKE HOME POINTS

- The effects of the parent role on women's and men's health are not completely clear but there is little research that shows benefits.

- The mixed effects are due to the fact that so many factors qualify the effect of parenthood on health: ages and number of children, whether the children live in the home, income, and other roles that parents possess.

- Parenthood is associated with a decline in marital satisfaction, and the decline is larger among women than men.

- The negative effects of parenting on marital satisfaction are due to restrictions on freedom, to a move toward a more traditional division of labor, and to less time that spouses spend together in non–child-focused activities.

INTIMATE PARTNER VIOLENCE

In this section of the chapter, I discuss how marriage or romantic relationships influence health when the relationship becomes violent. Intimate partner violence (IPV) refers to psychological and physical violence that takes place in the context of intimate relationships—marital relationships, cohabiting relationships, and dating relationships. In the past, this area of research was referred to as *domestic abuse*, referring to violence that occurs within married couples. The subject of violence within marriage came to the public's attention in the 1970s with the development of the women's movement. Shelters for battered women appeared in the 1970s and 1980s. In 1985, Surgeon General C. Everett Koop proclaimed that violence against women was the number-one health problem afflicting women. More attention was brought to the subject of battered women by the 1994 to 1995 trial of O. J. Simpson for the murder of his wife, Nicole Brown Simpson. Although Simpson was acquitted of the murder, the evidence was clear there had been a history of IPV in the relationship.

In an effort to recognize IPV as a crime, a number of states have enacted mandatory arrest laws that require the police to arrest the perpetrator when a violent incident is reported (American Bar Association, 2007). Unfortunately, there is some data that suggest mandatory arrest laws increase rather than reduce violence (Iyengar, 2008). Mandatory arrest laws may inhibit people from reporting violence and may provoke perpetrators. To date, the law is controversial.

I begin this section by examining the incidence of IPV. Then I examine characteristics of both perpetrators and victims of IPV. I conclude by reviewing theories of IPV. Some common myths about IPV are shown in Table 11.2.

Incidence

It is difficult to calculate the incidence of IPV, in part because abuse can be physical or psychological. Researchers have relied on both surveys as well as police and physician

TABLE 11.2   MYTHS ABOUT IPV

1. "A woman is beaten every _____seconds in the United States. "
   Fill in the blank with the statistic that you have heard. Regardless, there is no governmental agency that keeps records of domestic abuse.
2. "_____ million women are abused each year in the United States."
   Same limitation as number 1.
3. "Women who kill their abusers receive more severe sentences than men who kill their abusers."
   The Bureau of Justice Statistics shows just the opposite.
4. "Domestic abuse always escalates."
   As you will see in this section of the text, escalation occurs in only a small subset of domestic abuse.
5. "Only men are the perpetrators of domestic abuse."
   Again, as you will see in this section of the text, this is not at all the case. The most common cases of domestic abuse involve both partners.

Source: Gelles (2007).

reports to estimate abuse. Obviously, police and physicians underestimate the incidence of abuse because they will be aware of only the most extreme cases. In a phone survey of 16,000 people, only one-fourth of physical assaults by former or current partners were reported to the police (Tjaden & Thoennes, 2000). However, even surveys may underestimate abuse because poor people and non–English-speaking people are underrepresented in surveys.

The first national survey of IPV was conducted in 1976 and involved 2,143 families (Straus, Gelles, & Steinmetz, 1980). Rates of violence were so high that the phrase "the marriage license as a hitting license" was coined. The investigators found that 28% of families had engaged in at least one incident of violence over the course of their relationship, and 16% of families had done so in the prior year. Violent acts include punching, kicking, biting, hitting, beating, shooting, and stabbing. The items used to measure violence in this study are from the Conflict Tactics Scale, a revised version of which is shown in Table 11.3. This definition of violence has been used in many subsequent studies.

TABLE 11.3   INDICATORS OF PHYSICAL ASSAULT FROM THE REVISED CONFLICT TACTICS SCALE

- threw something that could hurt
- grabbed
- slapped
- kicked, bit, or punched
- hit with something
- beat up
- twisted arm or hair
- pushed or shoved
- slammed against wall
- choked
- burned or scalded on purpose
- used knife or gun.

Source: Adapted from Straus et al. (1996).

One of the great controversies in the field has to do with whether males are more likely than females to perpetrate IPV. In the study reported earlier, men were violent 25% of the time, women were violent 25% of the time, and violence was mutual half of the time (Straus et al., 1980). Numerous studies have been conducted in the intervening 30 years. The conclusion is the same—the literature is quite clear that males are not more likely than females to perpetrate IPV (Archer, 2002; Carney, Buttell, & Dutton, 2007; Dutton, 2007; Godbout et al., 2009).

Women initiate as much as or more IPV compared to men. A nationally representative survey showed that women reported receiving and perpetrating more violence than men, but the violence was mutual in half the relationships (Williams & Frieze, 2005). In the past, when similar rates of IPV were found between females and males, researchers suggested that female IPV was more likely to be characterized as self-defense than male IPV. However, this is not true (Carney et al., 2007; Dutton, 2007). There is no evidence that female perpetration of violence is more likely to be characterized by self-defense, and females are just as likely as males if not more likely to strike first (Felson & Cares, 2005).

A meta-analysis of physical aggression in heterosexual couples showed that females were more likely to throw, slap, kick/bite/punch, and hit their partners with an object compared to males—as reported by both females and males (Archer, 2002). Males were more likely to beat up and choke or strangle their partners. The overall sex difference in rates of perpetration, favoring females, was even stronger in younger samples, in particular high school and college groups.

IPV among dating couples appears to be similar to research on adult married and cohabiting couples. A five-year longitudinal study of over 2,000 college students in the United States showed that 26% of college students experienced physical IPV in their freshman year (Nabors & Jasinski, 2009). Again, females reported that they perpetrated more violence than males (30% vs. 18%). Over the course of the study, women were 2.5 times more likely than men to say they engaged in IPV. In two smaller studies of college students, there was no sex difference in perpetration of IPV (Gratz et al., 2009; Katz, Kuffel, & Coblentz, 2002). Again, the majority of IPV in college student

relationships seems to be mutual (Prospero & Kim, 2009). A study that examined physical assault among students from 31 colleges that spanned 16 countries showed that the median (50th percentile) percentage of physical assaults among dating couples over the last year was 29%, ranging from a low of 17% to a high of 45%, which was detected in a university in the United States (Straus, 2004). The incidence of physical assault in some of the countries is shown in Figure 11.11. Female perpetration rates were higher than male perpetration rates in 21 of the 31 universities. A meta-analytic review of sex differences in physical aggression in heterosexual romantic relationships showed a small effect in the direction of females being more aggressive than males ($d = -.05$; Archer, 2000). However, the age of the sample was an important moderator, such that females perpetrated more aggression than males in younger samples (age 22 and younger, $d = -.12$), and males perpetrated more aggression than females in older samples (age over 22, $d = +.12$).

Findings are similar among high school students and middle school students. In a study of a racially diverse group of high school students, women and men were equally likely to report being victims of violence (about 30%), and women reported that they perpetrated violence more than men (40% vs. 24%; O'Leary et al., 2008). However, two-thirds of the violence was mutual. Unilateral violence was more likely to occur in the instance of female than male perpetrators (27% vs. 5%), as reported by both females and males. The rate of injury was the same for women and men. The least physical aggression occurred among Asians compared to Whites, Hispanics, and African Americans. A study of sixth graders showed that females were more likely than males to initiate violence in relationships with

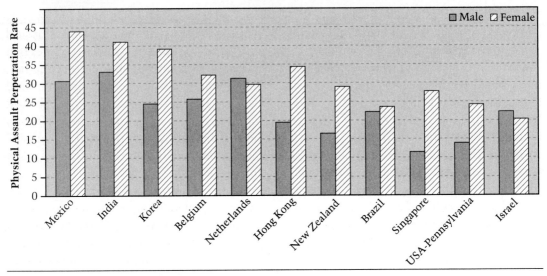

FIGURE 11.11   Sample of countries in which rates of physical assault were examined among dating couples. In most countries, the rate of female perpetration exceeded the rate of male perpetration. *Source*: Adapted from Straus (2004).

boyfriends/girlfriends and that violence was typically mutual (Miller et al., 2009). One reason for this finding is that both girls and boys believed that it was more acceptable for females than males to hit their partners (Simon et al., 2010). Over half (53%) said it was okay for a girl to hit a boy but only 28% said it was okay for a boy to hit a girl. Not surprisingly, those who were more accepting of violence in their relationships were more likely to be either a perpetrator or a victim of violence.

Violence in gay and lesbian relationships has also been studied. A nationally representative study of adolescents in same-sex relationships revealed an overall violence rate of 24% using the Conflict Tactics Scale, with slightly higher rates for female than male relationships (Halpern et al., 2004). Violence in same-sex romantic relationships was half the rate of violence in opposite-sex romantic relationships for males, but rates were comparable across same-sex and opposite-sex

relationships for females. A study of lesbian couples showed that 44% experienced either physical or psychological IPV (Eaton et al., 2008).

There are several explanations as to why the data do not support people's intuition that men are more likely than women to be perpetrators of IPV. One possibility is that men inflict more severe violence than women. The meta-analytic review revealed that females sustain more injuries than males ($d = +.15$; Archer, 2000). This conclusion was confirmed by a more recent study of married adults (Bookwala, Sobin, & Zdaniuk, 2005) but refuted by the cross-cultural study of college students (Straus, 2004). Males reported higher rates of injury infliction than females in 18 of the 31 universities. However, a nationally representative sample of adults showed that females are more likely to be injured than males but males' injuries were more serious than those of females' (Felson &

Cares, 2005). Overall, then, severity is not the likely explanation for why the data suggest similar rates of violence by women and men.

Another reason for the higher than expected rates of female perpetration of violence has to do with less public disapproval of this kind of violence. Female–male violence is judged less serious than male–female violence (Seelau & Seelau, 2005). A cross-cultural survey of dating couples showed that students were more approving of women slapping men than men slapping women in all 31 universities (Straus, 2004). Across the universities, 76% found it acceptable for a woman to slap a man, whereas only 42% found it acceptable for a man to slap a woman.

However, the primary reason that the data do not support people's views of IPV is that there are different kinds of IPV. Johnson (2008) distinguishes between three kinds of IPV: (1) **intimate terrorism**, (2) violent resistance, and (3) **situational couple violence.** The first two are connected. Intimate terrorism differs from other kinds of violence in that it is rooted in control. Violent resistance involves violent efforts on the part of the victim to resist this control. Intimate terrorism involves the systematic repetition of violence and the use of the control tactics shown in Figure 11.12. Situational couple violence, by contrast, refers to the occasional episodes of violent behavior on the part of husbands and wives precipitated by stressful events; it is not linked to the power imbalance between men and women or to efforts on the part of one person to control the other. Surveys do not distinguish among these kinds of violence. Men are likely to perpetrate intimate terrorism, whereas women and men are equally likely to engage in situational couple violence. And, situational couple violence is more common than intimate terrorism.

Some studies have tried to distinguish intimate terrorism from situational couple violence. Although the majority of violence is situational couple violence, there are more severe consequences associated with intimate terrorism (Johnson, 2008). Intimate terrorism is more likely to be associated with injury, missed work, distress, doctor visits, and overall poorer health (Johnson, 2008; Johnson & Leone, 2005). These findings may explain why IPV is more strongly related to distress and poor health among female than male victims (Afifi et al., 2009; Williams & Frieze, 2005). It is because females are more likely than males to be victims of the more severe form of IPV-intimate terrorism.

Characteristics of Perpetrator and Victim

The characteristics of female and male perpetrators are quite similar. Many have a history of aggression and substance use (Carney et al., 2007). Both women and men who engage in IPV as adults are often exposed to violence as a child, as either the subject of or a witness to violence (Afifi et al., 2009; Godbout et al., 2009; Gratz et al., 2009; Nabors & Jasinski, 2009). However, that link seems to be stronger for those who engage in intimate terrorism rather than situational couple violence (Johnson, 2009). Lower education also seems to be associated with both the perpetration and being a victim of IPV (Leone et al., 2004).

IPV is associated with more traditional gender-role attitudes. One longitudinal study showed that this relation was largely due to violence leading to changes in gender-role attitudes rather gender-role attitudes leading to violence (Nabors & Jasinski, 2009). In this study, engaging in IPV was associated with greater acceptance of gender-role stereotypes in women and men and an increase in acceptance of

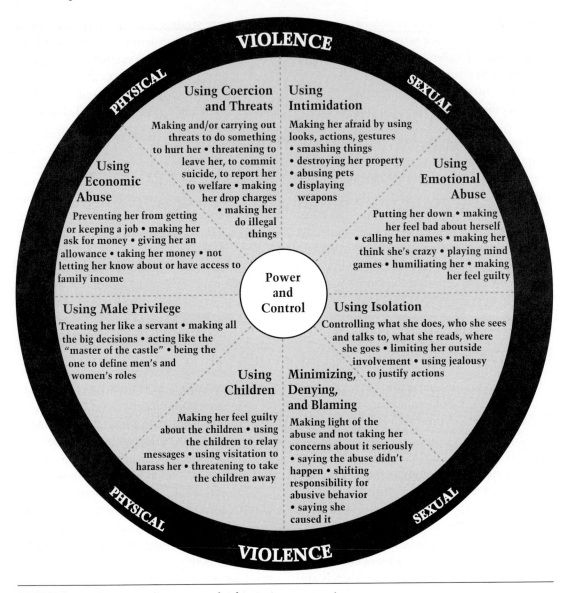

FIGURE 11.12 Control tactics involved in intimate terrorism.

Source: E. Pence and M. Paymar (1993). Education groups for men who batter: The Duluth model. Copyright 1993. Reprinted by permission of Springer Publishing Co.

violence among men five years later. Men who engage in IPV or tolerate IPV also score higher on hostile sexism (Glick et al., 2002), masculine gender-role stress (Copenhaver, Lash, & Eisler, 2000), and unmitigated agency (Mosher & Danoff-Burg, 2005).

IPV is more common among younger couples (Capaldi, Kim, & Shortt, 2004). In one study, 46% of male victims and 49% of female victims were under the age of 35, despite the fact that this age group comprised only 20%–23% of the population (Laroche,

2005). Recall that the meta-analysis noted that the sex difference in abuse (female greater than male) was limited to younger couples.

An often asked question is why women who are victims of intimate terrorism remain in the relationship. The answer depends more on features of the situation than characteristics of the victim. A good predictor of whether someone stays in or leaves a relationship is not how satisfied the person is with the relationship but whether the person has alternatives to that relationship. In one study, women who had experienced violence from their husbands said they stayed in the relationship because they did not have anywhere to go and did not have a job (Kurz, 1998). Women who are more financially dependent on their husbands and have less support from other network members may be less likely to leave the relationship.

Theories

Some researchers view men's abuse of women as a reflection of the imbalance of power in the relationship. Spousal abuse is viewed as men's attempt to control women and establish dominance in their relationships with women. Thus control and dominance seem to be the primary motivations behind abuse. This theory fits one kind of IPV—intimate terrorism (Johnson, 2009). However, establishing control and power on a more momentary basis may be related to situational couple violence. A study of lesbian couples showed that IPV was related to an imbalance of power in the relationship (Eaton et al., 2008). Women who lacked decision-making power in the relationship were more likely to be victims of IPV.

IPV also could be linked to a distorted perception of male–female interactions.

In one study, married men watched three videotapes of women discussing personal problems with a therapist (these were actual sessions) and were asked to rate at various points in the videotape whether the women were critical and/or rejecting of their husbands (Schweinle, Ickes, & Bernstein, 2002). In comparison to a panel of neutral judges, the men who scored higher on a measure of tendency toward IPV were more likely to infer critical/rejecting feelings. Thus men who engage in violence toward women may be more likely to perceive interactions with women in negative terms. These findings suggest that violence in men is not necessarily linked to features or behavior of a particular woman because all women are perceived in more negative terms.

A personality characteristic, Masculine Gender Role Stress (MGRS), has been linked to this biased perception of interactions between women and men. Men who score high on MGRS are more likely to perceive situations that challenge traditional male–female roles as stressful. In one study, men listened to vignettes of male–female dating partners having a conflict and were asked to imagine themselves in each situation (Eisler et al., 2000). Men who scored higher on MGRS became angrier, perceived their partners more negatively, and said they would respond to the conflict with greater verbal and physical aggression.

Difficulties regulating emotions may also play a role in IPV. One study showed that adults who had been exposed to violence as children had maladaptive ways of responding to emotions, which included the inability to control one's behavior when upset (Gratz et al., 2009). Gratz and colleagues reasoned that children who are exposed to violence experience extreme emotions without being taught how to respond appropriately.

Difficulties regulating emotions explained the link of childhood violence to adult violence for men but not women. The inability to regulate emotions may be particularly troublesome for men because society has communicated to men that they should inhibit their emotions.

Research also has linked male-perpetrated IPV to lower levels of empathy. In a laboratory study of adult couples in which a relationship problem was discussed, males who had perpetrated IPV in the past scored lower in empathic accuracy than males who had not perpetrated IPV (Clements et al., 2007). Empathic accuracy is measured by comparing how partner A actually feels to how partner B estimates partner A to feel. However, empathic accuracy did not distinguish between violent and nonviolent females.

We may know less about how it is that females become violent in the context of intimate relationships because we do not pay much attention to aggression among females during childhood and adolescence. Because girls are less physically aggressive than boys, we take less notice of aggression in girls.

TAKE HOME POINTS

- The majority of research shows that women and men are equally likely to engage in physical violence in the context of intimate relationships—that is, IPV.

- People are more accepting of female violence toward men than male violence toward women.

- Violence is associated with more negative consequences for women than men.

- There are three different kinds of IPV: intimate terrorism, violent resistance, and situational couple violence.

- Intimate terrorism is violence that stems from a need to control and typically targets women.

- Situational couple violence is the kind of violence that erupts in families in response to stress, does not escalate, and characterizes both women and men.

- IPV has been linked to the imbalance in power in female–male relationships, distorted perceptions of male–female interactions, difficulties with emotion regulation, and lack of empathy. These theories are more relevant to male than female perpetration of IPV.

RAPE AND OTHER FORMS OF SEXUAL COERCION

In 2009, a woman filed a complaint against the Pittsburgh Steelers two-time Super Bowl winning quarterback, Ben Roethlisberger, alleging that he sexually assaulted her in a hotel room and that hotel officials covered up the incident. A coworker said the sex was consensual and that the woman bragged about wanting to get pregnant by Roethlisberger. The case is not yet resolved. Less than one year later in 2010, Roethlisberger was accused of sexually assaulting a woman in a restroom of a nightclub. Although the district attorney did not file charges against Roethlisberger, the NFL (National Football League) took action and suspended him from the first six games of the season—a penalty that was later reduced to four games.

Sexual coercion, sexual assault, and rape are acts of violence with numerous physical and mental health consequences. Physical injuries range from minor bruises to life-threatening injuries to death. Mental health consequences range from fear, anxiety, and depression, to posttraumatic stress syndrome (Koss et al., 2003). A history of sexual assault, especially repeated assault, has been linked to physical disease (Stein & Barrett-Connor, 2000). The consequences can be long-lasting. One study found greater symptoms of anxiety, depression, and sexual concerns among people who

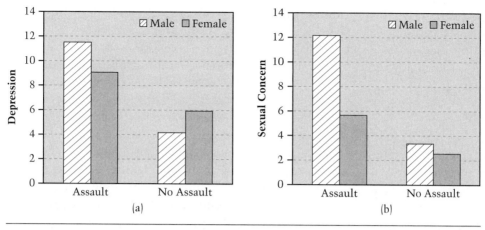

FIGURE 11.13   Sexual assault victims reported more symptoms of depression (a) and sexual concerns (b) than nonvictims 14 years after the assault. Male victims reported more symptoms than female victims.
Source: Adapted from Elliott et al. (2004).

experienced a sexual assault even 14 years ago compared to people who had not experienced a sexual assault (Elliott, Mok, & Briere, 2004). The consequences were more severe for men than women (see Figure 11.13).

In this section, I first define rape and then report studies that examine the incidence of rape and other forms of sexual coercion. I examine rape myths and then discuss characteristics of the perpetrator and victim: Who rapes and who is likely to be raped? Finally, I discuss theories of rape.

Definitions

You might expect that rape is a straightforward concept with a straightforward definition. However, there are many definitions of *rape*. Definitions vary regarding the specific behavior that distinguishes rape from other sexual acts. The most conservative definition of rape restricts the behavior to penile–vaginal penetration. More liberal definitions include other forms of sexual contact, such as kissing, fondling, oral sex, and anal sex.

Definitions also vary in how *nonconsent* to engage in sexual behavior is determined. What is an adequate indicator of nonconsent? Some definitions refer to rape as sexual behaviors that are undesired by the victim. Other definitions require evidence of victim resistance. There are other situations in which a person is unable to give informed consent, such as being under age, mentally ill, or intoxicated. Consent also may be obtained under duress. Many definitions refer to the sexual behavior as being forced on the recipient, but defining *force* is difficult. Does there have to be evidence of physical injury? Are verbal threats sufficient?

One kind of rape that especially suffers from definitional issues is spousal rape. It used to be believed that spousal rape could not occur in marriage, because sexual intercourse between husband and wife is a right of marriage. Historically, rape laws in the United States contained what is known as the **marital rape exemption clause** in their definitions of rape. That is, rape was defined as "the forcible penetration of the body of a woman, not the wife of the perpetrator"

(Russell, 1990, p. 17). It was not until 1993 that all 50 states had deleted the marital rape exemption clause. However, some other countries still employ some form of marital rape exemption.

Incidence

In 2008, 203,830 cases of rape/sexual assault were reported (Bureau of Justice Statistics, 2009). Of these, 81% of victims were female. Estimates from a variety of studies show that between 15% and 30% of women have experienced attempted or completed sexual assault (Russell & Bolen, 2000). Estimating the prevalence of rape is difficult because it is underreported. Many victims do not report rape because they feel guilty, feel a sense of shame, do not want to share their personal sexual history with strangers, and/or doubt that people will believe them (Ullman, 2010). Thus, very few victims report rape to the police. Among the cases reported to the police, the conviction rate is only 6% (Horvath & Brown, 2009).

Even surveys of rape may underestimate its incidence. A majority of surveys ask individuals a single question about whether they have been raped and use only the term *rape*. However, some individuals do not apply the label of rape to experiences that would qualify as rape; people often do not include oral sex or anal penetration when thinking of rape. In addition, people may not include rape attempts as rape.

Studies of college students report higher incidences of sexual assault, but definitions are often more liberal. In a national survey of female college students, 54% of the 3,187 women reported some form of sexual victimization: 16% rape, 12% attempted rape, 11% sexual coercion, and 15% sexual contact (Ullman, Karabatsos, & Koss, 1999). In over half of the cases (53%), women said

the offender used alcohol; in 42% of the cases, the women reported using alcohol. Use of alcohol was not only common during sexual assault but was also associated with the severity of the assault. The more severe cases of assault (i.e., rape, attempted rape) were associated with alcohol usage by both offender and victim. Forty percent of the sexual assaults occurred during a date. Despite the media highlighting the potential for men to administer "date rape" drugs to women, alcohol is by far the most widely used drug during rape (Lovett & Horvath, 2009).

We typically think of women as the victims of rape and sexual assault; in fact, criminal statistics define rape as something that happens only to women. Although rape may be rare among men, sexual coercion may not. Men may find it difficult to refuse sex because the expectation of the male gender role is that men are always ready and willing to have sex. However, sexual coercion seems to mean something different to men and women. Men feel less able to refuse sex, so they don't—but they also typically do not suffer serious consequences; women feel more able to refuse, so when victimization occurs, they suffer more serious consequences.

Rape Myths

One reason that women do not report rape is that there are widely shared myths about rape that reflect unfavorably on the victim. There are myths about how rape occurs, about the behavior of the perpetrator and the victim, as well as about the consequences of rape. As early as 1975, Brownmiller identified four basic rape myths: (1) All women want to be raped; (2) a woman cannot be raped against her will; (3) a woman who is raped is asking for it; and (4) if a woman is going to be raped, she might as well enjoy it. Numerous scales have emerged to measure acceptance of

TABLE 11.4   SAMPLE ITEMS FROM RAPE MYTH ACCEPTANCE SCALE

1. Any healthy woman can successfully resist a rapist if she really wants to.

2. When women go around braless or wearing short skirts and tight tops, they are just asking for trouble.

3. In the majority of rapes, the victim is promiscuous or has a bad reputation.

4. Women who get raped while hitchhiking get what they deserve.

5. Many women have an unconscious wish to be raped and may then unconsciously set up a situation in which they are likely to be attacked.

Source: Burt (1980).

DO GENDER 11.4
Endorsement
of Rape Myths

Administer the items in Table 11.4 to a group of women and men to establish the prevalence of female rape myths. Then develop a few items of your own to measure male rape myths. What variables do you expect to be associated with female or male rape myths: traditional attitudes toward gender roles, gender-related traits (agency, communion, unmitigated agency, unmitigated communion), socioeconomic status? Measure one of these other variables and see if it is associated with either female or male rape myths.

rape myths. Items from one of the most widely used scales (Burt, 1980) are shown in Table 11.4. Rape myths seem to revolve around several themes, including the victim is to blame, claims of rape are false or exaggerated, perpetrators are responding to an overactive sex drive, and only certain kinds of women are raped (Bohner et al., 2009). Not only does a large proportion of the general population endorse some of these rape myths but the victims themselves often endorse them—in which case they are reluctant to contact the police. Men are more likely than women to endorse rape myths, and older people are more likely than younger people to endorse rape myths (Ullman, 2010).

Just as there are myths about female rape victims, there also are myths about male rape victims (Chapleau, Oswald, & Russell, 2008). Men are more likely than women to endorse these myths—especially the myth that male rape victims are responsible for the rape. In addition, benevolent sexism toward men is associated with male rape myths. See how many people today endorse rape myths with Do Gender 11.4.

Characteristics of Perpetrator

Most of us tend to perceive rape as occurring by a stranger, but in a majority of cases, the two people know each other. In 2008, only 32% of women and 0% of men reported being raped or sexually assaulted by a stranger (Bureau of Justice Statistics, 2009). One reason rape is underreported and not given more serious attention is that people have more sympathy for victims who do not know their attackers. Gender-related attitudes affect whether people make a distinction between acquaintance rape and stranger rape. People who score high on benevolent sexism are especially unsympathetic to victims of acquaintance rape compared to stranger rape (Abrams et al., 2003; Viki, Abrams, & Masser, 2004). Benevolent sexism includes the belief that women should be protected by men but also the belief that women should behave in ways to elicit men's protection. With acquaintance rape, the closeness of the relationship between perpetrator and

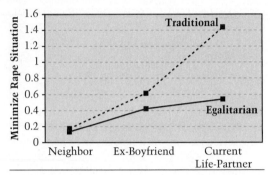

FIGURE 11.14   College students who held more traditional gender-role attitudes were more likely than those with egalitarian attitudes to minimize the severity of rape when committed by an ex-boyfriend or a current life-partner than a neighbor.

Source: Adapted from Ben-David and Schneider (2005).

victim influences how people perceive the rape. As shown in Figure 11.14, people who have traditional gender-role attitudes are more likely to minimize the severity of rape when it is committed by an ex-boyfriend or a current partner compared to a neighbor, whereas people with egalitarian attitudes do not make this distinction (Ben-David & Schneider, 2005).

We also perceive rape as involving physical force, but rape often involves verbal threats. We have less sympathy for victims who do not show physical signs of abuse. To make matters worse, strangers are more likely to use physical force, and known others are more likely to use verbal threats (Cleveland, Koss, & Lyons, 1999). Thus the most common occurrence of rape—committed by a known other who uses verbal threats—evokes the least sympathy from the community.

Traditional masculine beliefs have been directly linked to sexual aggression. In a meta-analytic review of the literature,

11 different measures of masculine ideology were linked to sexual aggression (Murnen, Wright, & Kaluzny, 2002). The strongest relations appeared with measures that reflected acceptance of violence and dominance over women.

Perpetrators often hold myths about women and rape. On average, men are more likely than women to endorse these rape myths. However, women also subscribe to some rape myths, and the extent to which they endorse these myths influences their likelihood of admitting to rape. College women who met the legal definition of rape but did not define themselves as having been raped were more likely to endorse rape myths (Peterson & Muehlenhard, 2004). For example, women who did not physically fight off the person who raped them and who subscribed to the rape myth that "it can't be rape if a woman doesn't fight back" were less likely to acknowledge that they had been raped.

Characteristics of Victim

In general, victims of rape and sexual assault span all age ranges and all educational backgrounds. However, rape and sexual assault are more likely to occur among younger people (i.e., ages 13 to 24), Black people, people of a lower SES, and people who have been sexually abused as a child (Elliott et al., 2004; Ullman, 2010). Victimization also may be associated with one's orientation toward relationships. In one study, college women who were more anxious about their relationships and feared losing their partners reported being more willing to engage in unwanted sex (Impett & Peplau, 2002).

The strategies a victim employs to resist rape affects how victims are viewed (Ullman, 1997). Evidence of resistance may be used as proof of the rape. There is an upside and a downside to focusing on rape resistance strategies. The upside is that resistance reduces the likelihood of a completed rape. The downside is that focusing on resistance strategies places the burden on victims—typically women. Some people are concerned that employing rape resistance strategies threatens one's life. However, a review of the literature has shown that forceful physical resistance strategies are associated with a slight increase in physical injury but decrease the likelihood of a completed rape; nonforceful physical strategies (fleeing, shielding oneself) decrease the likelihood of a completed rape and are not associated with an increase in physical injury; and forceful verbal strategies (screaming) decrease the likelihood of a completed rape (Ullman, 1997). Nonforceful resistance strategies (pleading) were ineffective with respect to rape completion. See Sidebar 11.3 for a discussion of rape prevention strategies.

Theories

The early theories of rape focused on characteristics of the perpetrator (Donat & D'Emilio, 1992). The rapist was considered to be mentally ill and sexually perverted. Thus, in a sense, researchers focused on the plight of the perpetrator rather than the plight of the victim. In addition, rape was considered

SIDEBAR 11.3: *Rape Prevention Strategies*

Rozee and Koss (2001) developed a strategy for women to resist rape, referred to as the AAA strategy: assess, acknowledge, and act:

1. After saying "no" to sex, ASSESS the situation to see if it is dangerous.

2. If dangerous, ACKNOWLEDGE this and label the situation as a dangerous one.

3. ACT, employ rape resistance strategies:

   a. Leave the situation if possible.

   b. If not, use verbal strategies.

   c. If verbal strategies are not effective, employ physical tactics (self-defense).

People commonly perceive that resisting rape will increase the likelihood of further injury. However, no evidence supports this belief. Attempts to resist rape are more likely to prevent a rape from occurring. In addition, rape resistance strategies increase women's sense of empowerment.

In recognition of the fact that rape is as much a man's problem as a woman's problem, Rozee and Koss (2001) also developed a comparable rape prevention strategy for men, also referred to as the AAA strategy: ask, acknowledge, and act. The strategy is depicted as follows:

1: ASK oneself if the woman is capable of consenting

If yes → ask if she wants to have sex.	If no → ACKNOWLEDGE the fact and ACT (stop).
↓	↓
If yes → ACT (sex is OK).	If no → ACKNOWLEDGE the fact and ACT (stop).

a form of sexually deviant behavior and thus tied to sex rather than aggression. Later, theorists began to focus on characteristics of the victim. As women's sexuality became more accepted during the middle of the 20th century, people came to wonder what role women played in rape. People asked what the woman could have done to cause or prevent the rape: What was she wearing? Did she fight back? Was there evidence of physical harm? Even today, certain characteristics of women are associated with more blame for rape. Women and men assign greater blame to women who wear more revealing clothing, are walking alone at night, and have sexually promiscuous backgrounds.

The next phase in history appeared with the development of the women's movement. Rape was reconceptualized as an act of violence rather than an act of sex. Feminists maintained that rape was a "means of enforcing gender roles in society and maintaining the hierarchy in which men retained control" (Donat & D'Emilio, 1992, p. 14). In her best-selling book *Against Our Will: Men, Women, and Rape,* Susan Brownmiller (1975) defined rape as "a conscious process of intimidation by which all men keep all women in a state of fear" (p. 15). Today, people generally regard rape as an act of violence rather than sex. Men are socialized to be aggressive, to be dominant over women, and to view women as sexual conquests.

Laboratory studies consistently show that males are more likely than females to blame the victim in response to rape vignettes (Grubb & Harrower 2008). One reason may have to do with the fact that females can relate more than males to a female victim. People who perceive themselves as similar to the victim are more likely to blame the perpetrator. In a study of college students that manipulated perceived similarity by noting the victim either attended

the same school or a nearby school, both female and male students blamed the perpetrator more when the victim attended the same school than a nearby school (Harrison et al., 2008).

Yet, rape also may be related to an important situational variable: misperceptions of sexual intentions and behavior. Men interpret sexual behavior differently than women, perhaps because men are more likely than women to assume others are interested in sex. Several studies of college students have demonstrated that men are more likely than women to interpret neutral behavior in more sexual terms (Bondurant & Donat, 1999).

Our culture's scripts for heterosexual dating set up these kinds of opportunities for miscommunication (Krahé, 2000). Despite changes in women's and men's roles, dating scripts have retained traditional male and female relations. It is still the case that women are not supposed to initiate sexual interactions and that men have the burden of deciphering the subtle cues of sexual interest that women convey. The expectation is that sexual interest is conveyed with implicit nonverbal behavior rather than explicit verbal behavior. Another feature of the heterosexual dating script is that women should initially reject sexual advances, even when desired. This is referred to as *token resistance.* Studies of undergraduates reveal that 40% have used token resistance at least once in a relationship. Thus, the heterosexual dating script sets the stage for miscommunication about sexual interest.

We are also more likely to infer sexual assault when an act is committed by a male rather than a female because our stereotype of sexual assault involves a male perpetrator and a female victim. Male college students were asked to rate the extent to which fourteen behaviors were indicative of sexual assault when the perpetrator was male and female (Lev-Wiesel & Besser, 2006). The list contained eight sexual assault behaviors and six neutral behaviors. Students were more likely to rate the sexual assault behaviors as indicative of sexual assault if the perpetrator was male than female.

Thus rape and sexual coercion may be a function of both the person and the situation. Sexual violence may be more likely to occur in certain situations among people who have predisposing characteristics.

TAKE HOME POINTS

- It is difficult to measure the frequency of rape and sexual coercion due to a variety of definitional issues, including the specific act and the determination of consent.

- Although women are more likely than men to be victims of rape, studies of college students report similar levels of sexual coercion among females and males.

- Being a victim of heterosexual sexual coercion is associated with more negative consequences for females than males.

- People are less sympathetic to victims of rape when the rape is committed by a known other and there is no evidence of physical injury, which is unfortunate because it is the most typical rape scenario. Rape is most often committed by someone who is known and with the use of verbal rather than physical threats.

- Perpetrators of rape are more likely to hold rape myths. People who hold rape myths express less sympathy for victims.

- Most recent theories conceptualize rape as an act of violence rather than an act of sex.

- Situational forces contribute to rape and sexual coercion. Men are more likely than women to perceive neutral behaviors in sexual terms.

- Sexual scripts for male–female relationships contribute to these misperceptions, as men are expected to initiate sexual interactions and women are expected to dismiss men's advances.

SUMMARY

It is not clear if there are sex differences in the structural dimensions of support, but women perceive and receive greater support functions. Supportive relations are a double-edged sword for women: The mere existence of social relationships means women have more support available to them but also that women have greater caregiving burdens. This is a likely explanation for why structural measures of support are more consistently related to men's health than women's health. However, the functional aspects of support seem to be more strongly related to women's than men's health.

Marriage is associated with better health for both women and men, but men accrue more benefits than women. Longitudinal research shows that initial health also influences the likelihood of getting married; however, even adjusting for these selection effects, marriage benefits health. Marriage is more beneficial for men because it provides greater support and promotes better health behavior, and because men are more satisfied with marriage compared to women.

The loss of marriage through widowhood seems to have more adverse effects on men's than women's health. The effects of widowhood on health can be understood in terms of the different strains women and men suffer when they lose their spouse. The primary reason widowhood has stronger effects on men's health has to do with men's loss of support; women have alternative sources of support available after widowhood. Men are more likely than women to remarry after widowhood and to do so sooner, and remarriage is associated with health benefits for men.

Both women's and men's health suffers upon relationship dissolution. It is not clear whether men suffer greater ill effects compared to women. Marital dissolution seems to be associated with different strains for women and men and to have different consequences for women's and men's social networks. Women are more likely to initiate the breakup of relationships, and women may be better prepared than men for relationships to end.

Although the state of being married seems to have more benefits for men's than women's health, when the quality of marriage is examined, women are more strongly affected than men. Marital interaction studies show that communication patterns influence women's more than men's physiology, especially when those communications have to do with discussing a marital conflict.

One important aspect of the marital relationship that has implications for relationship satisfaction as well as health is how labor is divided in the family. In general, women contribute more to household labor than men regardless of their employment status. Sex differences in the division of labor are greatest among married couples. Factors that influence how labor is divided are based on power and status, such as gender, income, education, and hours worked outside the home. Gender-role attitudes also influence the division of labor within the family. Further evidence that status and power influence the division of labor in the heterosexual family comes from studies of homosexual couples, where household labor is divided more equally.

In general, the more men contribute to household labor, the more satisfied women are. In fact, the division of labor in the family has a stronger effect on women's than men's marital satisfaction and well-being. However, men do not have to participate equally in household chores for women to be satisfied. It is perhaps remarkable that more women are not dissatisfied with the current state of affairs. A primary reason has to do with the fact that women make within-sex rather than between-sex social comparisons.

Aside from marriage, the other important relationship role held by many adults is the parent role. Unlike the marital role, there is no clear evidence that the parent role benefits women's and men's health. The mixed effects are due to the fact that so many factors qualify the effect of parenthood on health: ages and number of children, whether the children live in the home, income, and other roles that parents possess. Women report more strains in the parent role than men do. The quality of this role influences both women's and men's health, but the relation may be stronger among women. Parenthood has a negative effect on marital satisfaction. These effects are stronger for women than men, largely due to the greater restrictions on freedom and the greater role changes that women face when they become parents. The quality of parenting has become an important issue for homosexuals, especially lesbian mothers. However, research shows heterosexual and homosexual parents are similar, and there are few differences among the children they raise.

Serious threats to relationships include IPV and rape. Surprisingly, women are more likely than men to perpetrate IPV—although most IPV is mutual. There are different kinds of IPV. Women are more likely than men to be victims of intimate terrorism, but women and men are equally likely to be victims to the more common situational couple violence. Intimate terrorism is the kind of violence that is characterized by domination and control on the part of males over females. Intimate terrorism escalates and poses serious threats to women's health. Situational couple violence is the kind of violence that erupts from stress and does not escalate.

Rape and *sexual coercion* are difficult to define. Although women are more likely than men to be victims of rape, reports of sexual coercion are more similar between women and men. Yet, like IPV, women report more severe consequences of sexual coercion compared to men. Perpetrators of rape are more likely to hold rape myths. Both rape and sexual coercion are influenced by situational factors, such as the tendency to interpret neutral behaviors in sexual terms.

DISCUSSION QUESTIONS

1. Why are structural indexes of support more strongly related to men's health than women's health?
2. What is the marital selection hypothesis?
3. Why does marriage have a stronger effect on men's than women's health?
4. What are some of the methodological issues to consider when examining the effect of widowhood on women's and men's health?
5. Given what you know about how women and men behave in marriage and what women and men get out of marriage, what predictions would you make about how women and men should adjust to separation and divorce?
6. What determines household division of labor?
7. What is the gender tension line, and how has it changed over the past 20 years?
8. To the extent that parenthood has a negative effect on marriage, what are the explanations?
9. What are some of the variables that moderate the relation of parenthood to health?
10. Are men and women equally likely to be victims of IPV? Why or why not?
11. What are the differences between intimate terrorism and situational couple violence?
12. What do you think would be the best way to measure the prevalence of sexual coercion? How would you define it?

Suggested Reading

(Classic) Brownmiller, S. (1975). *Against our will: Men, women, and rape.* New York: Bantam Books.

Gager, C. T., & Hohmann-Marriott, B. (2006). Distributive justice in the household: A comparison of alternative models. *Marriage and Family Review, 40,* 5–42.

Gerson, K. (2010). *The unfinished revolution: How a new generation is reshaping family, work, and gender in America.* New York: Oxford University Press.

(Classic) Hochschild, A. R. (1989). *The second shift.* New York: Avon Books.

Horvath, M., & Brown, J. (Eds.), (2009). *Rape: Challenging contemporary thinking.* Portland, OR: Willan Publishing.

Johnson, M. P. (2009). Differentiating among types of domestic violence. In H. E. Peters & C. M. K. Dush (Eds.), *Marriage and families: Perspectives and complexities* (pp. 281–297). New York: Columbia University Press.

Patterson, C. J. (2009). Children of lesbian and gay parents: Psychology, Law, and Policy. *American Psychologist, 64,* 727–736.

Key Terms

Buffering effects—Link of social support to health only under conditions of high stress.

Functional measures (of support)—Qualitative dimensions of support, such as the type of support offered by network members.

Gender tension line—Point at which one feels uncomfortable with the adoption of some aspect of the other gender role.

Intimate terrorism—Violence on the part of men that stems from their attempts to control women.

Main effects—Direct link of social support to health, regardless of level of stress.

Marital rape exemption clause—Clause that once appeared in state definitions of rape that excluded forced intercourse with one's wife.

Marital selection hypothesis—Suggestion that healthier people are "selected" into marriage.

Prospective design—Research method in which the dependent variable (e.g., health) is measured before and after exposure to the independent variable (e.g., widowhood).

Situational couple violence—Occasional episodes of violent behavior on the part of husbands and wives that are precipitated by stressful events.

Structural measures (of support)—Quantitative dimensions of support, such as the size of a social network or the number of social relations.

CHAPTER 12

Paid Worker Role and Health

Life was pretty simple for June and Ward Cleaver of *Leave It to Beaver*. Every morning, Ward, dressed in a suit, kissed his wife and left for work. June, in a dress, took care of the children and had a hot meal waiting for Ward's return from work. The routine was the same for Margaret and Jim Anderson, the married couple on *Father Knows Best*. These two popular television shows from the late 1950s depicted the traditional nuclear family, where men worked outside the home and women worked inside the home.

Contrast that scenario with today's single-parent families where a woman might be responsible for the emotional, practical, and economic support of her children. More recent television shows reflect this changing state of the family by offering alternatives to the traditional families of the 1950s, such as *Parenthood*, a show about a single mother raising two children, or *Modern Family*, a show about two gay men raising an adopted girl. Even the media images of two-parent families reflect a move from the traditional. Consider the show *Friday Night Lights*, a show about a mother who is the high school principal and a father who is the football coach, both of whom are involved with raising children. Today, more families are sharing responsibilities. Women, even mothers, often work outside the home, and men are more involved in parenting. There are societal signs of this shift. For example, public places have "family restrooms" where both women and men can change children's diapers.

Today, both women and men juggle multiple roles, in particular the roles of spouse, parent, and paid employee. A **role** is defined as a position in society governed by a set of **norms**, which are expectations for behavior. Having multiple roles means that there are many norms to which you are expected to adhere, posing the potential for role conflict. On the other hand, access to multiple roles provides many resources—resources that can be used to offset stressors arising from any one role.

The focus of this chapter is on the role of paid worker. Because this role does not typically exist by itself, I also examine how women and men combine the role of paid worker with family roles. First, I discuss how the paid worker role influences health. Then I examine how the paid worker role affects family roles, how family roles affect the paid worker role, and whether people are better off if they have fewer or more roles. I also discuss how the quality of the paid worker role affects health. One important aspect of this role that is relevant to gender is discrimination, including the pay disparity between men and women. I discuss a variety of factors that contribute to the pay disparity. Another gender-related aspect of the paid worker role is sexual harassment. I define sexual harassment, discuss its incidence and effects on the worker, and describe theories of sexual harassment.

One important reason for studying the effects of different roles on women's and men's health is that sex differences in the possession of roles may explain some of the sex differences in health discussed in Chapter 10. Are women more depressed than men because they hold fewer roles, hold different roles, or value different roles? The **differential exposure hypothesis** states that differences in the kinds of roles women and men possess explain sex differences in health. For example, to the extent that men are more likely than women to possess the paid worker role, and the paid worker role is associated with good mental health,

women may suffer poorer mental health compared to men. The **differential vulnerability hypothesis** states that roles have different effects on health for women and men. For example, if parenthood is more central to women's than men's self-concepts, difficulties with children may be more strongly related to women's than men's health.

PAID WORKER ROLE

The traditional belief that it is better for men to earn the money in the family and women to take care of the home and children has changed over time. As shown in Figure 12.1, whereas 52% of women and 74% of men endorsed this belief in 1977, the numbers decreased to 39% of women and 42% of men by 2008 (Galinsky, Aumann, & Bond, 2009). The numbers not only changed but the sex difference greatly decreased. On the other hand, it is remarkable that over a third of

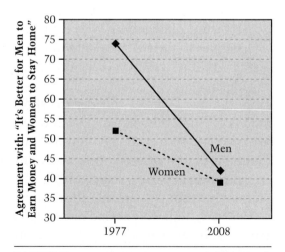

FIGURE 12.1   The traditional belief that men should earn the money and women should take care of the home and children has decreased over time. *Source*: Adapted from Galinsky et al. (2009).

women and even more men maintain this belief even today. The figures are somewhat lower for younger people, suggesting that there will be further change.

Over the course of the 20th century, women made great progress in terms of education and participation in the labor force. In 1970, 43% of women age 16 and over worked outside the home, and in 2009, the rate was 59% (see Figure 12.2; U.S. Department of Labor, 2010b). Among whites, the percentages were 73% women versus 59% men; among blacks, 65% versus 60%; and among Asians, 75% versus 58%. Both women and men may work outside the home due to choice but also due to economic necessity. There has been a change in women's desire to work outside the home. A 2007 Gallup Poll showed that 50% of women and 68% of men prefer to work outside the home (Saad, 2007a). In 1974, 36% of women preferred to work outside the home, which rose to 49% in 1978. Interestingly, this number has not changed much but fluctuated between 49% and 53% over the past 30 years!

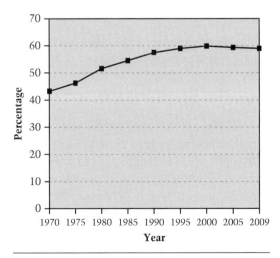

FIGURE 12.2 Percentage of women age 16 and over who participate in the civilian labor force. *Source*: Adapted from U.S. Department of Labor (2010b).

Whereas women's labor force participation has increased since 1975, the participation rate for men has decreased. The reason is unemployment. Historically, women had higher unemployment rates than men, but the recent economic turndown has led to a greater increase in unemployment among men than women (Galinsky et al., 2009). Men are employed in industries that have suffered the greatest job loss. In June of 2010, the unemployment rates for White men and women were 9% and 7%, respectively. The corresponding figures for Black men and women were higher—17% and 12%, respectively.

What is the effect of paid employment on men's and women's health? There is reason to assume that both the differential exposure and differential vulnerability hypotheses explain sex differences in the effects of the paid worker role on health. Men are more likely to possess this role than women, especially if the paid worker role is limited to those who are employed full time. To the extent the paid worker role is associated with good health, men are more likely than women to reap the benefits. This is the differential exposure hypothesis. As a society, we attach greater importance to men working outside the home compared to women; thus the effect of the paid worker role on health may be stronger for men. This is the differential vulnerability hypothesis.

Strong evidence suggests that the paid worker role influences the health of both women and men. As you will see next, paid employment is generally associated with better health for women and men. It is difficult to compare the effects of the paid worker role on women's and men's health because it is more normative for men than women to work outside the home. When we compare men who do and do not work outside the home, we are typically studying the effect of unemployment on health. When we compare women who do and do not work outside the home, we are comparing employed women to two groups of nonemployed women—unemployed women and women who choose not to work outside the home. The two groups are not the same.

The effect of employment on health is a topic that necessarily focuses on women because there is more variability in women's than men's employment. In this first section of the chapter, I focus on the effects of women's employment on their health. Then, I examine the effects of multiple roles on women's and men's health and how work and family roles influence one another. I also evaluate the effect of work on health by briefly describing the literature on retirement. After evaluating the effects of the mere possession of the paid worker role on health, I turn to the implications of the more qualitative aspects of the paid worker role for health.

Women's Employment

A historical explanation of why women were more distressed and had worse health than men was that women were less likely to possess the paid worker role (Gove & Tudor, 1973). Work was associated with a number of resources, not the least of which was economic, and women had less access to this resource than men. However, when women entered the paid workforce, people began to consider the negative effects of employment on health. People were concerned that women who combined work and family roles would suffer role strain and role overload. People were also concerned that women working outside the home would detract from the time women spent taking care of their husbands and family. Thus, in this section, I examine the implications of women working for their own health and the implications of women working for the family.

Effects on Health. A cross-cultural study of 25 European countries showed that women's lower well-being compared to that of men was due in part to the fact that women engaged in less paid work and more domestic work compared to men (Boye, 2009). The more hours worked outside the home was associated with higher well-being for women, and the more hours of domestic work was associated with lower well-being for women.

When women who work outside the home are compared to women who work inside the home, a wealth of evidence indicates that employed women report better psychological and physical health (Fokkema, 2002; Khlat, Sermet, & Le Pape, 2000), even in traditional societies like Spain (Artazcoz, Borrell et al., 2004). Even among women with children, the weight of the evidence is that employed mothers are healthier than nonemployed mothers, and more so if children are older (Fokkema, 2002).

One problem with studies that compare the health of employed women to housewives is that they are often cross-sectional, meaning the people are studied at a single point in time. Thus we do not know if employment leads to an improvement in health or if healthier people are more likely to be employed. This is the basis of the **selection effect**. Longitudinal studies in which both employment and health are tracked over time enable us to determine whether health leads to employment or employment leads to health. There is evidence for both. Physically healthier people are more likely to be employed (Christ et al., 2007), and employment leads to better health for women (Klumb & Lampert, 2004).

Explanations. The employee role benefits women's health for a number of reasons. Employment increases self-esteem, instills a sense of accomplishment, and provides more social contacts—for both women and men. Employment also can affect one's sense of control (Rosenfield, 1989). To the extent that employment increases one's sense of control, it should be helpful. However, if employment decreases one's sense of control, it may be harmful. Employment may enhance women's feelings of control by increasing women's economic resources and thus power within the family. However, employment may detract from women's sense of control by making it more difficult for women to manage household responsibilities. Thus paid work has the potential to increase resources for women in one area but decrease resources in another. Each of these resources has implications for control. This model is shown in Figure 12.3.

This model has been supported by three different studies (Rosenfield, 1989). In all three, women who were susceptible to high family demands (i.e., women employed full time with children) were more distressed than men, whereas women with fewer demands (women employed part time with children or women employed full time without children) had levels of distress similar to men's. If demands were low, employed women were less distressed than housewives. Employment also increased women's perceptions of control when it increased their relative income in the family. Women with higher relative incomes had a heightened sense of control and, subsequently, reduced distress. In total, the healthiest women in this study were those who had children and were employed part time. These women gained some advantage from an increase in relative income that was not offset by an increase in demands.

Currently, there is debate between the effects of part-time and full-time paid work on women's health. The model is useful for understanding this issue, as the effects of

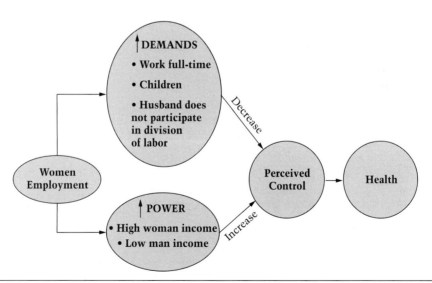

FIGURE 12.3 Model of how employment influences women's health. To the extent that employment increases women's household demands, employment reduces perceptions of control and harms health. To the extent that employment increases women's relative income in the family, employment increases perceptions of control and benefits health.
Source: Adapted from Rosenfield (1989).

part-time and full-time work on women's health are undoubtedly a function of demands and power in the family. Full-time employment contributes much more to economic resources than part-time employment and should be more beneficial to women's health *if* household demands can be met. If demands cannot be met, part-time employment may be more adaptive for women's health.

According to this model, the best way for full-time employed women to manage their psychological health is to offset the increase in family demands by having husbands involved in household labor. Alternatively, full-time employed women may be able to pay someone to perform household chores. One study showed that the paid worker role was beneficial to women's health only when they could afford services to assist them with child care and household labor (Khlat et al., 2000). Thus the paid worker role may be more beneficial to middle-class than lower-class women

because middle-class women are more able to pay for such services. In addition, lower-class women are more likely to be married to husbands who are unwilling to participate in household labor (Arrighi & Maume, 2000).

Effects on the Family

The control theory depicted in Figure 12.3 that was used to explain the effect of work on women's health also can be used to explain the effect of women working on men's health (Rosenfield, 1992). Unfortunately, the benefits to wives translate into costs for husbands. A wife working will increase a husband's distress to the extent it decreases his resources (relative income) and increases his family demands (household responsibilities). According to this theory, a wife working presents a two-fold dilemma for men and women, depicted in Figure 12.4. If a wife's employment increases the husband's family demands and decreases

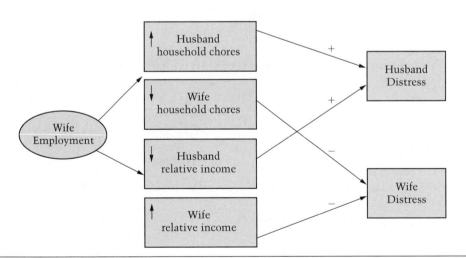

FIGURE 12.4   The dilemma behind women's employment. At the same time that women's employment reduces household demands for women, it increases them for men. Because household demands are associated with increased distress, women benefit and men suffer. At the same time that women's employment increases women's relative income in the family, it decreases men's relative income and power. Because relative income is associated with a decrease in distress, women benefit and men suffer.

the wife's family demands, the husband will be more distressed and the wife will be less distressed—because family demands are associated with increased distress. To the extent that wife's employment decreases the husband's relative income and increases the wife's relative income, the husband will be more distressed and the wife will be less distressed—because relative income is associated with reduced distress.

To test the theoretical model shown in Figure 12.4, Rosenfield (1992) examined psychological distress in 172 married couples. Women were more distressed than men. There were no differences in the distress levels of husbands whose wives worked versus husbands whose wives did not work. Thus, wives' employment per se did not affect men's distress. However, to the extent that wives' employment decreased husbands' relative income, men's distress levels increased. Men's distress levels also increased if they shared household chores. The effect of family demands was greater than the effect of reduced relative income on men's distress. Thus, wives' employment alone did not influence husbands' distress, but husbands' distress increased to the extent that wives' employment decreased husbands' relative income and increased husbands' family demands. Rosenfield also noted that relative income and household demands were inversely related, meaning that those who had more power (i.e., higher relative income) probably used that power to avoid household tasks. Another study supported the relative income aspect of the model: An increase in women's relative income over time was associated with an increase in women's psychological well-being, but a decrease in men's psychological well-being (Rogers & DeBoer, 2001).

Thus, one feature of women's employment that has implications for the family just as it had implications for women's and men's health is the wife's income—especially

relative to the husband's income. Although men are still more likely than women to be the sole wage earner or to earn more money than women, it is no longer unusual for women to make more money than men. In the year 2000, 11% of wives were the primary income providers, 27% made equal contributions to family incomes, and 60% contributed less than 40% to the family income (Winslow-Bowe, 2009). Among dual-earner couples in 2008, 26% of women and 60% of men earned more than 10% more than their spouses (Galinsky et al., 2009). Women are less likely to be major contributors to family income when there are children in the home. These figures largely characterize White women, as African American women are more likely to be primary income providers or co-providers. The race differences stem in part from the fact that African American women have a longer history of participating in the paid labor force and in part from the fact that African American men face great difficulties entering the paid labor force.

What is the effect of women's rise in relative income on family relationships? One study showed that the changes in income disparity between husband and wife over a two-year period had no implications for wives' marital satisfaction but strong implications for husbands' marital satisfaction (Brennan, Barnett, & Gareis, 2001). A decrease in the disparity in income (men's higher than women's) was associated with a decrease in men's marital satisfaction, especially among men who said they valued the monetary aspects of their jobs. Thus an increase in women's relative income compared to that of men may be most problematic for men who have traditional gender-role attitudes and define the male role as the breadwinner.

Another feature of women's paid work that has implications for the family is how many hours a week women work. One study showed that there were negative effects on marriage when women worked more than 40 hours a week (Hyde, DeLamater, & Hewitt, 1998). By contrast, a study of female physicians showed that more hours of paid employment was associated with higher marital quality (Barnett & Gareis, 2002). The reason seemed to be that husbands were more involved in household labor when women worked longer hours. Thus, again, the effects of women working outside the home and how many hours they work outside the home are related to the control models shown in Figures 12.3 and 12.4. To understand the full effect of women working outside the home, one has to take into consideration the effects on domestic labor and relative income.

It is also important to consider whether the couple wants the woman to be working. Women may be working due to choice or due to economic necessity. When women are employed out of economic necessity rather than choice, they are less happy with their marriages (Perry-Jenkins, Seery, & Crouter, 1992). Women and men with traditional values also may be less happy when women are engaged in paid employment. There also may be problems when women and men do not agree as to whether women should be working outside the home. Conduct Do Gender 12.1 to find out college students' attitudes toward married women's paid employment.

Retirement

Imagine you are 55 years old, work full time, and make $100,000 a year. Your boss calls you into her office and says you can stop working, keep your salary for two years, and then earn two-thirds of your salary for the rest of your life. Would you retire? The incentives to retire can be strong in some industries.

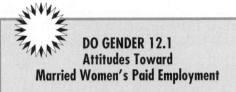

DO GENDER 12.1
Attitudes Toward
Married Women's Paid Employment

Interview a group of women and men about whether they would be in favor of a married woman working outside the home. Start out by asking women the very simple question, "If you get married, how much would you want to work outside the home?" For men, ask how much they would want their wife to work outside the home. Use a scale such as 1 = not at all to 5 = very much.

Then, see if you can figure out what conditions influence women's and men's responses. Are there personality characteristics that influence support for married women working, such as whether their mothers worked or whether they have traditional gender-role attitudes? Are there characteristics of the situation that influence support, such as the presence of children, the number of children, and the age of children? What if the woman worked more than 40 hours per week? What if she made more money than her husband did? Come up with some of your own qualifications. The goal is to try to describe how supportive women and men are today of married women working outside the home and what limitations there are to people's support.

As a greater portion of our population moves into retirement, this period of life is receiving more attention. Retirement can take a variety of forms. Some people phase in their retirement by reducing the hours they work, whereas others opt for an abrupt retirement. Because people are living longer, elderly people can consider working after age 65. A greater proportion of the elderly in the workforce, however, reduces the number of jobs available to younger people. This is one reason many organizations are offering incentives to retire early. In 1930, 5.4% of the population was over 65; in 2008, 12% of the population was over 65.

If work is associated with good health, what is the effect of retirement on health? One determinant will be whether the person chooses to retire or feels forced to retire. People who are forced to retire and retire early due to health reasons do not benefit from retirement as much as people who choose to retire (Brockmann, Muller, & Helmert, 2009; van Solinge, 2007). Longitudinal studies have linked retirement to improved mental health in both women and men in the United States (Mandal & Roe, 2008), in France (Westerlund et al., 2009), and in Switzerland (Mojon-Azzi, Sousa-Poza, & Widmer, 2007).

Who benefits the most from retirement? One study showed that people with higher incomes benefit the most from retirement (Price & Balaswamy, 2009). This is likely due to the fact that high income can be translated into more discretionary money to spend on leisure activities during retirement. However, another study showed that people benefited more from retirement when they had low job satisfaction, low occupational status, or worked in poor environmental conditions (Westerlund et al., 2009). These people would have more to gain from retirement because retirement would signify the removal of sources of stress.

Given these facts, do women and men benefit equally from retirement? The evidence here is contradictory. Retired women show better psychological and physical health than women who did not work outside the home (Silver, 2010), but a selection effect could explain these findings. If healthier people select into the paid workforce, they may still have better health when they

retire than those who did not select into the paid workforce. Research that compares the effect of retirement on women and men has revealed inconsistent findings: One study showed women benefited more from retirement than men (Mandal & Roe, 2008), one study showed that retirement is a greater risk for mortality for men than women (Pizzetti & Manfredini, 2008), some studies showed no differences (Mojon-Azzi et al., 2007; Westerlund et al., 2009), and one study showed women gained more weight following retirement compared to men because men were more active than women after retirement (Forman-Hoffman et al., 2008).

What are the reasons for these contradictory findings? The effects of retirement not only depend upon whether one chooses to retire, the income available after retirement, and the centrality of paid work to one's sense of self, but also on the context in which retirement occurs. Retirement is more likely to take place in the context of other life events for women. Women are more likely than men to retire due to family obligations—caring for an ill spouse, a parent, or a relative. These life events have a stronger effect on women's than men's adjustment to retirement because the life events are more strongly linked to caregiving responsibilities for women.

TAKE HOME POINTS

- Paid employment has a positive effect on both women's and men's health.

- The effects may be stronger among men, supporting the differential vulnerability hypothesis, but this difference may be due to the fact that men and women who are not in the paid labor force are not the same. Men who are not in the paid labor force are likely to be unemployed, whereas women who are not in the paid labor force are likely to have opted out of paid labor to work inside the home.

- Although there is a selection effect, meaning that the healthiest people are likely to become employed, longitudinal studies show that employment leads to good health for women and men.

- Control theory explains how women's paid employment can influence both women's and men's health: Increased relative income has a positive effect on health, whereas increased family demands have a negative effect on health.

- The effect of retirement on health depends on whether the person chooses to retire and the circumstances surrounding retirement. Retirement takes place in the context of other life stressors that entail caregiving responsibilities for women.

COMBINING PAID LABOR WITH FAMILY ROLES

Historically, men have easily combined the roles of paid worker, spouse, and parent. Today, more women are combining all three of these roles. The labor force participation rates of married women are as high as, or even higher than, those of unmarried women. In 2007, 69% of married women with children were employed; 75% of women with children between the ages of 6 and 13 and 62% of women with children under 6 (Bureau of Labor Statistics, 2010). Women with children are not necessarily employed full time, however. More married than unmarried women work part time, especially if they have children. Many reasons account for the sharp increase in the number of married working women since 1960. Desire for more income is one reason, but there are other important factors, such as

birth control, women's increase in education, and the decline in the wage gap. In fact, the increase in employment among married women is larger among those whose husbands are in the top half rather than the bottom half of the income distribution.

The question is, are combining work and family roles good for health? This is the "multiple roles question." There are two theories about the effects of multiple roles on health, each of which makes opposing predictions. The **role scarcity hypothesis** suggests multiple roles have a negative effect on health because time and resources are limited and additional roles tap resources. This is also referred to as *role strain*. The scarcity hypothesis predicts two kinds of strain that stem from the possession of multiple roles: **Role overload** refers to the difficulties in fulfilling obligations for all of one's roles because time is limited; **role conflict** refers to the demands of one role conflicting with the demands from another role. You are suffering from role overload when you feel stressed because you have three exams on Monday, a party to plan for Saturday, and a fund-raising event to attend on Sunday. You suffer from role conflict when your grandmother turns 90 and your best friend turns 21 on the same Saturday, and family obligations prevent you from celebrating the occasion with your best friend. In either case, having more roles is problematic because it is difficult to meet all the demands of multiple roles.

By contrast, the **role expansion hypothesis** (also known as the *role enhancement hypothesis*) suggests benefits are to be gained from having diverse roles. The additional resources gained by multiple roles outweigh the increase in strains that might arise from more roles. Resources from one role can be

Role Expansion
> Family Role Provides Resources to Employee Role
>> Ex: Spouse gives me advice about how to solve problems at work
> Employee Role Provides Resources to Family Role
>> Ex: Having a fulfilling job makes me a happier person at home

Role Scarcity
> Family Roles Overburden Employee Roles
>> Ex: Taking care of children reduces the time I can spend at work
> Employee Roles Overburden Family Roles
>> Ex: Working long hours means I miss some family activities

---

FIGURE 12.5   Examples of Role Scarcity and Role Enhancement with Respect to Employee and Family Roles.

used to buffer strains arising from another role, which has been referred to as stress buffering (recall Figure 11.3b). For example, social support from coworkers may help alleviate distress arising from family problems. Examples of the role scarcity and role expansion hypotheses regarding employment and family roles are shown in Figure 12.5.

What is the evidence for the scarcity and expansion hypotheses? Are multiple roles healthful or harmful? The preponderance of evidence shows that multiple roles are good for women's and men's health (Barnett, 2004). A number of studies have shown that the healthiest people, men or women, are the ones who possess all three roles: spouse, parent, and paid worker (McMunn, Bartley, & Kuh, 2006). The most distressed people possess none of these roles. A longitudinal study of Swedish adults supported the role expansion hypothesis by showing that the greater number of roles was associated with less physical illness, and an increase in roles over an eight-year period reduced the risk of health problems (Nordenmark, 2004).

It may not be the mere accumulation of roles but the particular combination of roles

that is beneficial. One role may enhance the effects of another role; for example, the parent role may be adaptive only if we possess the worker role. The worker role is critical in the presence of children because financial needs are greater. The parent role also appears to be beneficial to health only if one possesses the spouse role, at least for women (Fokkema, 2002; Khlat et al., 2000). A wealth of evidence suggests that unmarried mothers have the worst psychological and physical health (Lahelma et al., 2002; Sachs-Ericsson & Ciarlo, 2000). Unmarried mothers may feel overwhelmed with raising children because they lack the emotional and financial support of a spouse.

Thus far, all fingers point to role enhancement. Is there any evidence for the role scarcity hypothesis? There is, in terms of exercise. Among employed persons, married men and women exercise less than those who are unmarried, and the effects are stronger for men than women (Nomaguchi & Bianchi, 2004). As shown in Figure 12.6, marriage reduces exercise more for men than women (a), as does the presence of children (b). Simply examining whether more or fewer roles are beneficial to women's and

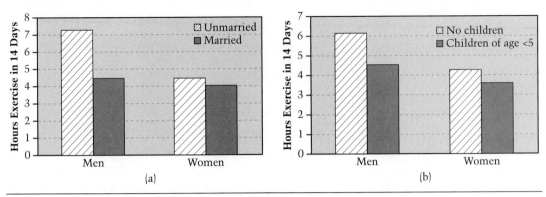

FIGURE 12.6   (a) Employed married men and women exercise less than their unmarried counterparts, but the effects are stronger for men. (b) The presence of children under age 5 is associated with less exercise for employed men and women, but the effects are stronger for men.
Source: Adapted from Nomaguchi and Bianchi (2004).

men's health does not tell us much about how combining roles influences health. Roles cannot be viewed as resources or sources of stress that are combined in an additive way because they interact with one another. For example, taking on the parent role may affect how one views and enacts the paid worker role. And, taking on the paid worker role may affect how one views and enacts the parent role. Roles are enacted in a mutually exclusive way but affect one another—a phenomenon known as **role spillover.** Next we examine the specific ways that employee and family roles affect one another.

Effects of the Paid Worker Role on Family Roles

It is not clear whether the paid worker role conflicts with family roles more for women or men. A meta-analysis revealed that job stress detracts from family satisfaction for both women and men but that the relation is stronger for men (Ford, Heinen, & Langkamer, 2007). Is this because men face

more job stress, or is this because men's work is more likely to interfere with family life? By contrast, a study examined the extent to which the paid worker role created conflicts for family roles and the extent to which family roles created conflicts for the paid worker role and found that women scored higher than men on both (Innstrand et al., 2009). A study of dual-earner couples showed that men and women were equally likely to perceive that job demands interfered with their marital relationship, but women were more likely than men to perceive that their spouses' job demands interfered with their relationship (Matthews et al., 2006). Although there was greater spillover from the paid worker role to the spouse role for men than women, the spillover had greater negative consequences to the marital relationship for women. It may be that it is more normative for men's than women's paid work to spill over into the family so it is more noteworthy when women's work affects family life. From my own experiences, women are more likely to attend children's school and sports activities that take place during the day than are men. However, when fathers show up, they are praised. When mothers are absent, people are concerned.

There are features of the paid worker role that seem to have specific consequences for family roles. More hours worked outside the home and greater job pressures are associated with greater work–family conflict (Galinsky et al., 2009)—but more so for women (Pedersen et al., 2009). Job flexibility is associated with higher quality family roles for women but not men (Pedersen et al., 2009). There are also aspects of family roles that may influence work spillover. When both wives and husbands work full time and have children, greater inequity in the division of labor leads to greater work–family conflict for women (Edwards, 2006).

Features of the paid worker role can also benefit family roles. For example, a supportive job is associated with greater family satisfaction for both women and men (Ford et al., 2007). The paid worker role also buffers one from the distress associated with caregiving roles at home. One study showed that caregivers' health declined more if they were not employed than if they were employed (Pavalko & Woodbury, 2000). Employment may provide one with a needed respite from caregiving, which in the end could enable one to be a more effective caregiver.

Thus, it appears that the paid worker role can have negative and positive effects on family roles. Stressors in one's job can cause or exacerbate strains in the family. However, the paid worker role can also buffer one against family stressors. When work conflicts with family, work may be more likely to win out for men, and family may be more likely to win out for women. In that sense, work conflicts with family more for men than women.

Women are more likely to have flexible jobs, to work part time, or not to be paid workers compared to men. This makes it easier for women than men to prioritize family.

Effects of Family Roles on the Paid Worker Role

Features of family roles can influence the quality of the paid worker role. Family stress and conflict are associated with lower job satisfaction, and family support is associated with higher job satisfaction among both women and men (Ford et al., 2007). Family roles can enhance the paid worker role—especially when the quality of family roles is high (Pedersen et al., 2009). People who have spouses who help with child care and people who have good relationships with their children seem to be able to benefit more from the paid worker role (Gareis & Barnett, 2002; Pederson et al., 2009). Thus family roles can buffer as well as exacerbate strains at work for women and men.

Difficulties in Combining Roles

Combining the paid worker role with family roles is a newer challenge for women than it is for men. To understand how work and family roles are combined, one needs to examine what the individual roles have meant to women and men historically (Simon, 1995). The paid worker role has been more closely intertwined with family roles for men than women. Historically, a man's family role has been to provide economic support, an obligation he can fulfill through paid employment. However, a woman's family role has been to take care of the home and children, functions not served by paid employment. The paid worker role for women does not facilitate the function of her family role and may even detract her from it. See Sidebar 12.1 for an elaboration of the difficulties women face as employees and mothers.

A number of difficulties arise in families where both women and men work. In 1989, Hochschild identified three kinds of tension in dual-earner couples that still apply today. The first tension exists when women and men have different views about who should do what work outside the home and inside the home. I discussed in Chapter 11 how disagreement about the division of labor in the family is associated with marital unhappiness, especially for women. The second tension occurs when women and men have the desire for traditional roles but their economic status does not permit them to enact those roles. In other words, both husband and wife prefer that the wife takes care of the home and the husband is employed outside of the home, but lack of financial resources requires the woman to be employed outside the home. In this instance, the husband may contribute to household chores, but neither the husband nor the wife is satisfied with this arrangement.

SIDEBAR 12.1: *Paid Workers and Mothers*

Society provides women with mixed messages about whether they should be paid workers when they have children. Employed mothers receive the message that it is acceptable to work outside the home and to be a parent—as long as parenting is the number one priority. That is, paid work should never interfere with parenting. In fact, women are more likely than men to take time off from paid work to take care of children. This means the parenting role has the potential to interfere with the paid worker role more for women than men. Women who opt not to work outside the home while raising children, however, may receive a different message from society. Today, these mothers often feel the need to justify why they are not working outside the home. Here, I examine whether paid employment benefits mothers.

Whether working outside the home is beneficial for women with children depends on a number of factors, including characteristics of the job such as salary, hours worked, nature of the work, job control and flexibility as well as characteristics of the home environment, such as number of children, availability of child care, and husband's participation in household and child care activities (Elgar & Chester, 2007). A greater number of children in the home may detract from the benefits of employment, but this depends on what resources are available to assist the woman in caring for her children. Access to resources, such as income, child care, or a supportive husband, influences whether mothers benefit from work.

Another factor that may influence the effect of combining paid work and family roles on women's health is the traditionality of the field in which women work. It may be easier for women to combine paid work with family roles if they are employed in a field that by tradition is inhabited by women rather than men. However, traditional jobs for women, such as nurses, secretaries, and teachers, may have less flexibility than higher-status positions to accommodate family needs. One of the attributes of a high-status position is that the person often sets her or his own hours.

Thus the optimal conditions for paid work to benefit mothers' health include a husband who helps out at home, an income that can provide for high-quality child care, and a job that accommodates family responsibilities.

The third tension is one that pervades egalitarian couples who are heavily involved in work outside the home. Husbands and wives in these couples jointly devalue family responsibilities to justify spending more time on their careers. The egalitarian philosophy leads such couples to share responsibilities such that less time is devoted to home and family—less time on housework, less time with children, less time with each other—and someone is hired to take care of most household tasks (cooking, cleaning, and child care). The ideas about what a family needs change to accommodate the couple's egalitarian focus on careers. This issue reminds me of a dual-earner couple I know who adopted two children. After the first child was in preschool, the husband proudly remarked to me that he had never even met the preschool teacher or attended any of the preschool programs for parents because the nanny took care of all of these chores. After the second child, the couple asked the nanny to move in with them. The husband shared that he and his wife slept downstairs while the nanny slept in a room upstairs with the children, which was wonderful because the nanny could console the children at night. Hochschild (1989) calls it a hollow victory "if the work of raising a family becomes devalued because women have become equal to men on traditionally male terms" (p. 211). The homemaker role is now being devalued by both women and men. One way to increase the value of this role is for men to become more involved in household labor and child care.

Although a great many changes have been made over the past several decades in terms of work and family roles, in some ways our fundamental way of thinking about men and women has not changed. According to Valian (1998), "... the usual solutions proffered to solve 'women's' problems are

DO GENDER 12.2
Combining Roles

Interview a group of women and men who have combined the paid worker role with family roles—preferably, people who have children. Ask specific questions about the challenges that they have faced in combining roles.

higher-quality, more affordable, more widely available childcare; flexible work hours; and family-leave policies. All those improvements are needed, but they fail to question the way the problem is framed. They do not ask why combining work and family is a female problem rather than a human problem, and thus do not address it as a human problem" (p. 45).

Conduct Do Gender 12.2 to find out for yourself what difficulties women and men face when combining the paid worker role with family roles.

TAKE HOME POINTS

- Multiple roles are good for both women's and men's health.

- There is greater support for the role expansion hypothesis than for the role scarcity hypothesis. Roles provide resources, and having more roles buffers us from the strains that arise in any one role. The fewer roles we have, the greater the effect that strain in any one role will have on health.

- The paid worker role and family role can both buffer one from the distress associated with the other role as well as exacerbate stressors that are associated with other roles.

- Employment benefits women's health even in the presence of children, but the presence of children adds to the complexity of understanding the conditions under which paid work is beneficial to women.

- To understand the interactive effects among roles, we need to consider what roles mean to women and men and what the demands are in each of the roles.

QUALITY OF PAID WORKER ROLE

One reason it is difficult to evaluate the effects of paid work on men's and women's health is that the nature of the paid worker role differs for men and women. For example, women and men are not employed in the same kinds of jobs. Table 12.1 shows the percentage of women employed in a variety of jobs in 1983 and 25 years later in 2008 (U.S. Department of Labor, 2009b). Although women today are more likely to be found in professions such as accountant, architect, dentist, financial manager, lawyer, and physician, some professions remain sex segregated; for example, auto mechanic, carpenter, dental assistant, and elementary school teacher.

Women also are more likely than men to be employed in part-time positions. In 2007, 72% of employed women held full-time jobs compared to 87% of men (U.S. Department of Labor, 2009c). However, this figure really represents a comparison of White and Hispanic women to White and Hispanic men, as Black women are almost equally likely to be employed full time as Black men. Women and men also report different job conditions. Thus to compare employed women and men, we need to know more about the characteristics of their jobs to see if the two groups are really comparable. In the following section, I examine the characteristics of paid work that men and women value as well as face.

TABLE 12.1 PERCENTAGE OF WOMEN WORKERS IN SELECTED OCCUPATIONS IN 1983 AND 2008

Occupation	1983	2008
Accountants/Auditors	38.7	61.1
Airplane pilots and flight engineers	2.1	2.6
Architects	12.7	24.8
Auto service technicians and mechanics	0.5	1.6
Carpenters	1.4	1.5
Clergies	5.6	14.8
Computer programmers	32.5	22.4
Dental assistants	98.1	96.3
Dentists	6.7	27.2
Financial managers	38.6	54.8
Firefighters	1.0	4.8
Lawyers	15.3	34.4
Mail carriers	17.1	33
Photographers	20.7	44.1
Physicians and surgeons	15.8	30.5
Psychologists	57.1	66.9
Registered nurses	95.8	91.7
Social workers	64.3	79.4
Teachers—college and university	36.3	46.1
Teachers—elementary and middle school	83.3	81.2
Word processors and typists	95.6	92.9

Source: Adapted from U.S. Department of Labor (2009b).

Characteristics of Paid Work

Do men and women value the same characteristics of work? A meta-analytic review of studies that included all age groups, ranging from children to adults, revealed that males value a high income, autonomy, challenge, recognition, and power more than females (see Figure 12.7; Konrad et al., 2000; Lips & Lawson, 2009). By contrast, females value an easy commute, the physical environment,

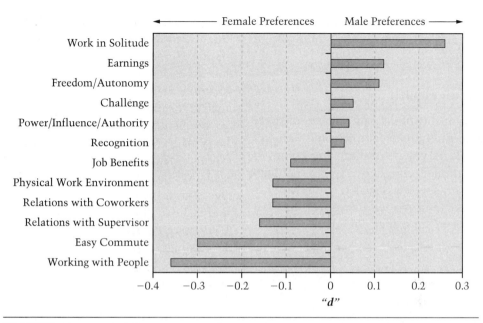

FIGURE 12.7   Sex differences in preferences for a number of job characteristics. The effect sizes ("*d*" statistic) are shown here.

Source: Adapted from Konrad et al. (2000).

relations with coworkers and supervisor, job benefits, and the opportunity to work with people more than males. A study of managers and executives in a variety of industries showed that both rated the agentic aspects of work (i.e., strategy, motivation, task focus) as more important than the communal aspects of work (communication, interpersonal skills), but that men valued the agentic aspects more than women and women valued the communal aspects more than men (Frame et al., 2010). In addition, people in higher-level positions valued agency over communion. A meta-analysis of vocational interests revealed that men prefer to work with things and women prefer to work with people (Su, Rounds, & Armstrong, 2009). In the meta-analysis shown in Figure 12.7, the largest sex difference in the direction of men is working in solitude. Although these differences in vocational interests have decreased over time, they persist and explain why men

are attracted to engineering and science and women are attracted to creative arts, nursing, teaching, and social work.

The work environments of men and women differ, and status plays a role in these differences. Men seem to receive more instrumental support at work, in terms of advice and collaboration with colleagues, compared to women (van Emmerik, 2006). Women are less likely than men to have mentoring relationships at work, and mentors can lead to career advancement (Nelson & Burke, 2000). Women also complain of sexual harassment and discrimination (Bond et al., 2004), both of which are reviewed in more detail later in this chapter. Women are especially likely to report these latter sources of strain in work environments that are predominately male (Gardiner & Tiggemann, 1999). Women also report greater job monotony than men (Matthews & Power, 2002). Yet work provides women with a resource that it does not equally provide men: Women receive more support at work compared to men (Bond et al., 2004).

Effects on Health

Does the quality of the paid worker role have the same implications for men's and women's health? It may depend upon the aspect of work examined. One study showed that high job demands were associated with lower job satisfaction and greater distress for men but not women (Bond et al., 2004), and another study linked job stress to depression in men but not women (Godin et al., 2009). Yet interpersonal conflict at work (Appelberg et al., 1996) and perceptions of control at work (Muhonen & Torkelson, 2004) seem to be more strongly related to job and health outcomes for women than men. It is difficult to compare the impact of job quality on women's and men's health because the women and men being compared to one another may differ in the other roles they possess. Perhaps paid work is less related to women's than men's health because more of the women in the study work part time compared to the men. Or the women in the study are more likely than the men to have family roles (spouse, parent). Even studies of dual-earner couples may find that one person is more involved or less involved in family roles.

DISCRIMINATION

An important aspect of paid work that has implications for women's and men's psychological and physical well-being is discrimination. There are two kinds of discrimination: **access discrimination** and **treatment discrimination**.

Access discrimination occurs when hiring decisions are made. If women or men are not offered a job or are offered a lesser job because of their sex, this is access discrimination. Some high-status jobs are certainly less accessible to women than to men. For example, women are less represented than men in the judicial and legislative branches of government, although important strides have been made. Nancy Pelosi was elected the first woman speaker of the U.S. House of Representatives in 2006. Sonia Sotomayor became a member of the U.S. Supreme Court in 2009, and is currently one of three females on the Court (see Figure 12.8). In 1979, 3% of the U.S. Congress was female. Over 30 years later in 2010, the figure was 16.5%: 17 of 100 U.S. senators were female, and 72 of 439 (16%) U.S. representatives were female. Six of the 50 state governors (12%) are women. In 2008, New Hampshire became the first state to have a majority of women in the state senate. There are a variety of reasons as to why there are a small number of women in some occupations, one of which is access discrimination.

Access discrimination was the subject of a 2002 nationwide sex discrimination case against Rent-A-Center (Grossman, 2002). The case resulted in the awarding of a

FIGURE 12.8 Sonia Sotomayor was elected to the U.S. Supreme Court in 2009. Of the nine Supreme Court Justices, she is one of three women.

$47 million settlement. This was the largest national sex discrimination case in the history of the United States for a company of this size (13,000 employees; 2,300 stores). Rent-A-Center was charged with not hiring applicants because they were women and firing employees who were female. The class action suit was brought on behalf of 5,300 women and thousands of rejected job applicants.

One approach to access discrimination is affirmative action. However, affirmative action policies are controversial. Proponents argue that affirmative action remedies deficits in the past due to discrimination by giving underrepresented persons more of an opportunity. Opponents are concerned that underqualified persons receive jobs, which then disadvantage more qualified applicants. The issue is far from resolved. Interestingly, a laboratory study showed that affirmative action benefited men more than women (Ng & Wiesner, 2007). When a male applied for a position as a nurse, he was more likely to be hired in the presence of an affirmative action policy even if he was less qualified than the female—people's fears confirmed! By contrast, when a woman applied for a police officer position, she was more likely to be hired only when she was equally or more qualified than the male.

Treatment discrimination occurs after the person has the job and takes the form of reduced salary or reduced opportunities for promotion. In 2004, the largest class action suit regarding treatment discrimination of women was brought against Wal-Mart. Women earned less than men in the same positions and were less likely than men to be promoted, despite the same or better qualifications and service. In 2011, the Supreme Court rejected the class-action lawsuit of the nearly 1.5 million women but did not deny that sex discrimination occurred (Liptak, 2011).

A recent law was passed that closed a corporate loophole in treatment discrimination cases. In 2009, President Obama signed into law the Lilly Ledbetter Fair Pay Restoration Act (CNN Politics, 2009). This legislation was developed in response to a lawsuit filed by Lilly Ledbetter in 1998 claiming that she was paid less than men for comparable work at Goodyear Tire and Rubber. After working for Goodyear for 19 years, Ledbetter learned that she had been paid less than men for comparable work. Although the jury ruled in her favor, the claim was later overturned by a federal appeals court on the basis that she did not file the claim within six months of receipt of the first paycheck showing she was paid less than men. (How it is that people are supposed to learn that they are not receiving fair pay within their first six months of employment is not clear to me!) The 2007 Supreme Court also rejected her claim—again not because they denied she suffered discrimination but because the claim was filed more than six months after the initial discriminatory paycheck. With the Ledbetter Fair Pay Restoration Act, people can sue employers for discrimination as long as the complaint is filed within six months of the most recent discriminatory paycheck.

The **glass ceiling** is a form of treatment discrimination that refers to barriers to the advancement of women and minorities in organizations. The glass ceiling is illustrated by the fact that only 15 Fortune 500 companies were run by women in 2010. The glass ceiling is also illustrated by the fact that we have not had a female president of the United States. When Hillary Clinton realized that Barack Obama would receive the Democratic nomination for the president of the United States, she withdrew from the race by proclaiming that there were 18 million cracks in the "highest, hardest glass ceiling," signifying the 18 million people who had voted for her in the primaries (*New York Times*, 2008).

One reason that women do not advance at the rate of men is that women are less likely than men to have mentors (Gutek, 2001). There are fewer women in high-powered positions available to mentor, and men are uncomfortable mentoring young women. The **glass escalator** is another form of treatment discrimination. It refers to the ability of men to be promoted quickly when they take positions in traditionally female fields, such as nursing, social work, or education (Williams, 1998). Despite the fact that 70% of human resource managers are female, male human resource managers earn 47% more than women (*Wall Street Journal*, 2008).

Another form of treatment discrimination is holding different standards for men's and women's performance. Laboratory studies have shown that women are held to higher standards than men even when their performance is the same—especially when the task is masculine in nature (Foschi, 2000). For masculine jobs, the same performance is evaluated more favorably if people believe the employee is male rather than female (Davison & Burke, 2000). For feminine jobs, performance is evaluated more favorably when the employee is female rather than male. The problem is that high-powered leadership positions are viewed as masculine domains. In field studies, which are far fewer and more difficult to conduct, a bias against women is not as clear (Bowen, Swim, & Jacobs, 2000). The only time that males were evaluated more favorably than females was when all the raters were male. However, men and women are evaluated favorably on different dimensions. Women are judged as more competent than men on interpersonal domains, and men are judged as more competent than women on agentic domains. The question is which domain leads to pay increases and promotions. See Sidebar 12.2 for a humorous essay that illustrates how men's and women's behavior at work may be perceived differently.

SIDEBAR 12.2: *Perceptions of Men and Women Employees*

The family picture is on HIS desk.
Ah, a solid, responsible family man.
   The family picture is on HER desk.
   Umm, her family will come before her career.

HE is talking with his coworkers.
He must be discussing the latest deal.
   SHE is talking with her coworkers.
   She must be gossiping.

HE's not in the office.
He's meeting customers.
   SHE's not in the office.
   She must be out shopping.

HE's having lunch with the boss.
He's on his way up.
  SHE's having lunch with the boss.
  They must be having an affair.

HE got an unfair deal.
Did he get angry?
  SHE got an unfair deal.
  Did she cry?

HE's getting married.
He'll get more settled.
  SHE's getting married.
  She'll get pregnant and leave.

HE's having a baby.
He'll need a raise.
  SHE's having a baby.
  She'll cost the company money in maternity benefits.

HE's leaving for a better job.
He knows how to recognize a good opportunity.
  SHE's leaving for a better job.
  Women are not dependable.

Source: Gardenswartz and Rowe (1994).

Pay Disparity

One form of treatment discrimination that is well studied is **pay disparity**. In 1979, women who worked full time earned 62% of men's median salary (U.S. Department of Labor, 2010c). In 2009, the comparable figure was 80%. The pay disparity is smaller for younger women—93% for women between the ages of 16–24 and 89% for women between the ages of 25–34. The wage gap has historically been and, as shown in Figure 12.9, is still smaller among Blacks (94%) and Hispanics (89%) than Whites (79%) and Asians (82%).

Calculating the wage gap is difficult: Using weekly salaries neglects the fact that women's work week is shorter than men's,

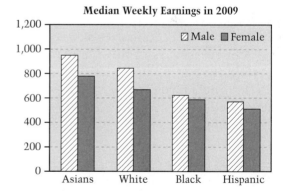

FIGURE 12.9 Men earn more than women across all four ethnic groups, but the gap is larger for Asians and Whites than Blacks and Hispanics. *Source*: Adapted from U.S. Department of Labor (2010c).

and using annual salaries neglects the fact that women work fewer weeks per year than men. In 2009, among those employed full time, men worked on average 40 hours per week and women worked on average 35 hours per week, with a 5-hour discrepancy consistent across Whites, Blacks, Asians, and Hispanics (U.S. Department of Labor, 2010d).

Different theories explain the wage gap. **Supply-side theory**, or human capital theory, emphasizes the difference characteristics of workers that may contribute to the wage gap (Dunn, 1996); thus, the focus is on the person. Today, women and men tend to have more similar job qualifications, such as education and experience. The other explanation for the wage gap is referred to as **demand-side theory**, or discrimination, which emphasizes the different ways women and men are treated (Dunn, 1996); the focus here is on the environment. The effects of discrimination are typically estimated by the proportion of the wage gap that cannot be explained by all the personal characteristics that distinguish women and men (i.e., supply-side theory). Discrimination is difficult to estimate, and its accuracy fully depends on whether all other factors are taken into consideration.

In an analysis of three longitudinal studies, the pay gap that spanned the years 1978 through 2000 was examined to disentangle how much of the gap was due to human capital and how much was due to unequal treatment or discrimination (Joshi, Makepeace, & Dolton, 2007). Because the pay gap decreased over this period of time, people assumed it was due to women's greater education, greater labor force participation, and more equal opportunities—that is, changes in human capital. However, education, experience, and other human capital factors do not explain much of the pay gap. In fact, because women today have more education and more

experience than men, women should be paid more than men. The fact that the pay gap persists suggest discrimination is still operating. Similarly, a cross-cultural study of 28 countries concluded that sex discrimination persists because married men made more money than married women in 26 of the countries when age, number of children, education, hours worked, and nature of occupation were taken into consideration (Stickney & Konrad, 2007). That is, supply-side theory did not account for the pay disparity.

One study in support of supply-side theory involved 16,000 executives (Gayle, Golan, & Miller, 2008). Over 14 years of follow-up, women were found to be promoted at the same rate as men when they had comparable background characteristics and occupational experience. However, females were more likely than males to leave their jobs by taking time off, retiring, or moving to another job, and this difference in behavior contributed to the pay disparity. When turnover history was statistically controlled along with other supply-side variables, women were paid slightly more than men. The reasons that more women than men left their jobs are not known. It could be the case that characteristics of women and/or their family situations were associated with a higher turnover rate, supporting supply-side theory, or it could be that characteristics of the work environment were associated with a higher turnover rate, reflecting discrimination.

There are so many ways in which women's and men's situations may differ that it is difficult to estimate all human capital characteristics. It is easier to distinguish supply-side theory from demand-side theory conceptually than empirically.

Sex Segregation and Comparable Worth.
A primary reason for the pay disparity is that work is segregated by sex. That is, women

and men work in different occupations, and different occupations have different salaries. Many factors contribute to occupational segregation. Traditional gender role is one factor. As shown in Figure 12.10, traditional gender roles are related to more income for men but less income for women (Judge & Livingston, 2008). One reason is that traditional gender roles are related to occupational segregation. Men with traditional gender roles are likely to be in higher-paying occupations inhabited by men, such as technology, and women with traditional gender roles are likely to be in lower-paying occupations inhabited by women, such as service industries. Sex segregation of occupations declined in the 1970s as women moved into occupations that had traditionally been inhabited by men, such as medicine and law. However, there has been less change in occupational segregation in the 1980s and 1990s, and after the turn of the century. Occupational integration does not solve all the problems. Even if similar numbers of women and men are in a particular occupation, they often hold different positions.

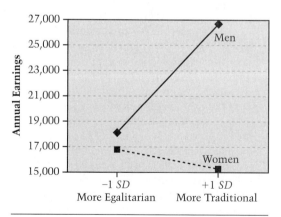

FIGURE 12.10 Traditional gender roles are strongly related to more income for men; traditional gender roles are slightly related to less income for women.

Source: Adapted from Judge and Livingston (2008).

Why do the occupations men enter pay more than the occupations women enter? One theory is that sex is used to determine the wage of an occupation. The proportion of women in a given occupation is directly and inversely related to the wage (Dunn, 1996). In other words, a job is worth less if women are more likely than men to hold it. In fact, people assume that jobs inhabited by men pay more than jobs inhabited by women—a phenomenon referred to as the **salary estimation effect**. Two studies—one of college students and one of community members—showed that when given a series of jobs to which male or female names are randomly assigned, respondents estimate higher salaries for jobs associated with male names than jobs associated with female names (Williams, Paluck, & Spencer-Rodgers, 2010). Male respondents were more likely to show the salary estimation effect than females. Interestingly, the salary estimation effect was unrelated to awareness of the actual pay gap. Instead, implicit stereotypes regarding gender were associated with the salary estimation effect. Using an Implicit Association Test, respondents who linked being male with wealth were more likely to show the salary estimation effect. In another study, college students were provided with job descriptions that contained the same educational qualifications, same skills, and same responsibilities but the gender-related nature of the industry was varied to be masculine (e.g., automotive) or feminine (e.g., gourmet food; Alksnis, Desmarais, & Curtis, 2008). As shown in Figure 12.11, both men and women assigned higher pay to jobs (clerk in Figure 12.11a and editor in 12.11b) assumed to be held by male employees than female employees.

The resolution to this issue is the **comparable worth policy**, which states that men and women in different jobs should be paid the same wage for comparable work. The

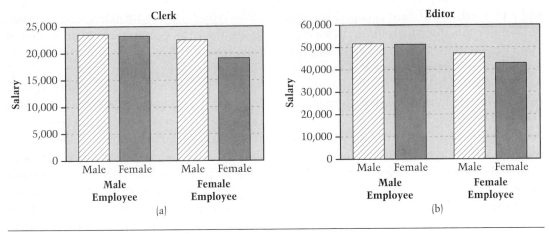

FIGURE 12.11 Female and male respondents assign higher salaries to clerks (a) who are presumed to be male than female and to editors (b) who are presumed to be male than female. *Source*: Adapted from Alksnis et al. (2008).

difficulty comes in identifying comparable work. Some of the factors considered in developing comparable worth standards are job activities, responsibilities, environmental conditions/hazards, knowledge required, education required, skill involved, and experience needed. A comparable worth measure of occupations was developed in the Netherlands (De Ruijter, Schippers, & Van Doorne-Huiskes, 2004). Experts who were job evaluators, vocational advisors, and social scientists evaluated the education, training, responsibility, physical and mental effort, and the cognitive, physical, and social skills required by a number of jobs. They concluded that differences in occupational worth accounted for the pay disparity between male-dominated and female-dominated occupations. However, they also concluded that people in female-dominant occupations are underpaid relative to their worth.

Many of the features of a job used in developing comparable worth policies are quite subjective, making it difficult to develop rigorous guidelines. In addition, it is difficult to determine how to weigh each aspect of a job.

Try to develop your own comparable worth standards in Do Gender 12.3 to see if you can identify comparable jobs.

When jobs are comparable, does the pay gap remain? The statistics in Table 12.2 show

---

DO GENDER 12.3
Development of Comparable Worth Standards

Identify features of a job you think should influence the salary of that job. Then, choose 10 jobs, including some that are sex segregated (e.g., truck drivers, nurses). Rate each of the jobs on the features you have identified. For example, one feature of a job might be education required; rate each of the jobs on this dimension (use a scale such as 1 = no education required; 5 = higher education required). Come up with a score based on your ratings for each job. In the end, you should have a rank order of which jobs should be paid the most and the least. Comment on how you think your rank order fits with the real-world salaries of those jobs.

TABLE 12.2   WEEKLY EARNINGS IN DOLLARS FOR FULL-TIME EMPLOYEES

	Men	*Women*
Accountant/Auditor	1,190	902
Secretary and administrative assistant	666	619
Art designer	956	730
Baker	448	466
College/University teacher	1,342	1,030
Computer programmer	1,267	1,182
Elementary or middle school teacher	1,040	891
Financial manager	1,443	961
Janitor or building cleaner	494	401
Lawyer	1,934	1,449
Mail carrier	944	904
Physician/Surgeon	1,914	1,228
Police detective/Sheriff	971	805
Real estate sales	939	745
Registered nurse	1,090	1,035
Social worker	864	774
Driver/sales worker or truck driver	690	512
Waiter/Waitress	419	363

Source: U.S. Department of Labor (2010c).

that women still receive less money than men when they have similar jobs. A number of studies have directly compared the salaries of men and women with the same jobs. A study of Canadian lawyers found that females earned less than males and that the pay disparity was accounted for by supply-side factors (Robson & Wallace, 2001). Women had less experience practicing law, had shorter work hours, were less likely to be employed by a firm, and were employed in less prestigious areas of law. It is unclear whether these differences in work situations were products of women's choices or environmental constraints. Interestingly, women were also less likely than men to have "family capital," which includes being married and having children; family capital was associated with higher incomes—although you will see later that this is really only the case for men.

A nationally representative sample of women and men who received bachelor's degrees in 1999 to 2000 was followed for the first year after graduation to examine salaries (Dey & Hill, 2007). Among full-time workers, women's salary was 80% of men's salary. However, a major portion of that gap had to do with the different fields that women and men entered. Women were more likely than men to enter lower-paying fields, such as education and health. However, even within the same major, men made more money than women, and the wage gap increased each year following graduation. During the first year after graduation, the proportion of men's salary made by women was 81% for business majors, 75% for biology majors, 76% for math majors, and 95% for engineering majors. The first year after graduation is an important year to examine because both men and women are less likely to be married and have families—thus, their roles are quite similar.

Using census data, one study showed that the wage gap narrowed when women and men in high status management positions were compared (Cohen, 2007). In fact, the extent to which women are represented in the higher management levels of an organization has a beneficial effect for all women in the organization in terms of pay disparity.

The gender pay gap may interact with the race pay gap. A study of women and men who graduated from historically Black compared to historically White institutions showed that the sex difference in pay was smaller among graduates from historically Black than historically White institutions (Renzulli, Grant, & Kathuria, 2006). Is it because there is less sex discrimination among Black people? Probably not. It is not the case that Black women made relatively more than White women. Instead, men from historically Black institutions made less than men from historically White institutions.

Negotiation.   Another reason for the pay disparity is that men negotiate higher starting salaries than women. A meta-analytic review of the literature on negotiation showed that women were more cooperative than men during negotiation and received poorer outcomes ($d = +.09$; Walters, Stuhlmacher, & Meyer, 1998). In a study of over 200 students who had just received MBAs, women and men were equally likely to negotiate for a higher salary when offered a position, but women received less than men from the negotiation (Gerhart & Rynes, 1991). Men's negotiations led to a 4.3% salary increase, whereas women's negotiations led to a 2.7% salary increase. This may not sound like much of a difference to you, but a small difference based on a percentage can become large over time. As shown in Figure 12.12, if a man and a woman were offered an initial salary of $50,000 at age 25 and the above-mentioned difference in salary increase occurred each year, the man's salary would be nearly double the woman's by age 65—a phenomenon Babcock and Laschever (2003) refer to as the "accumulation of disadvantage."

In their book *Women Don't Ask: Negotiation and the Gender Divide*, Babcock and Laschever (2003) point out that women are less likely to negotiate salaries, ask for less when they do negotiate, and concede earlier than men. The fact that men make a larger initial request than women is important

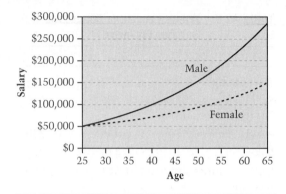

FIGURE 12.12   Hypothetical salary of a male and a female over the ages of 25 through 65 if the male received a 4.3% increase and the female received a 2.7% increase each year.

because the initial request is strongly correlated with the final outcome.

Why don't women ask for higher salaries, raises or promotions, and better jobs compared to men? There are a number of reasons. One reason is that men feel like they deserve more than women. In a study of MBA students negotiating a job offer, men negotiated a higher salary than women and were more likely than women to say that they knew their worth (Barron, 2003). In addition, men were more likely to say that they deserved more than others, whereas women perceived that they were entitled to the same as others. A second reason that women negotiate less than men is that women are more concerned that negotiation will lead to conflict and concerned that conflict will jeopardize the relationship with the negotiator. Third, women are more likely than men to believe in a meritocracy—that hard work will bring success without having to ask for it. Finally, for all these reasons, women are more anxious than men during negotiations, and anxiety is likely to interfere with women's performance.

Is there a situation in which women are more assertive in negotiation? Yes—when they are asking on behalf of others (Babcock & Laschever, 2003). Because seeing that others' needs are met is part of women's gender role, women are actually more assertive on behalf of others than themselves. Laboratory studies have shown that women will make larger requests when they are made on behalf of others than themselves, whereas men make larger requests for themselves than for others. One study showed that women identified a lower salary request as pushy compared to men and negotiated a lower salary than men *only* when they were requesting on behalf of themselves (Amanatullah & Morris, 2010). When the request was on behalf of another person, the differences between women and men disappeared (see Figure 12.13).

Is the solution to teach women to behave more like men during negotiation? Perhaps not. Employers may be more receptive to negotiation among men than women (Wade, 2001). Negotiation takes place in a social context, and women's negotiations are viewed differently from those of men. Recall from Chapter 7 that women who behave in assertive, agentic ways are not liked—especially by men—and thus are not influential. Women may have to find a way to negotiate that does not compromise perceptions of femininity.

Family Ties.   A third reason for the wage gap is related to family ties—what is known as the "mommy tax." Of the relatively few women who have made it to the top in the corporate or noncorporate world, half of those women have no children (Cheung & Halpern, 2010). Only one of the three women who sit on the Supreme Court has children. In her book *The Price of Motherhood: Why the Most Important Job in the World Is Still the Least Valued*, Crittenden (2001) states "motherhood is now the single greatest obstacle left in the path to economic equality for women" (p. 87). The mommy tax refers to the fact that women have primary responsibility for children, which detracts from their wages. When women have

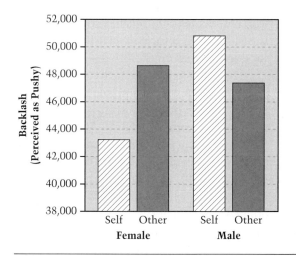
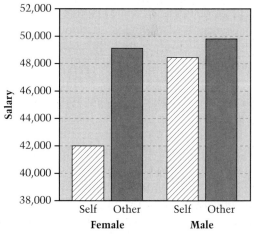

FIGURE 12.13   Women indicate that a lower salary is perceived as pushy compared to men when asking on behalf of themselves but not others. Women also negotiate less salary than men when negotiating on behalf of themselves than others.

Source: Adapted from Amanatullah and Morris (2010).

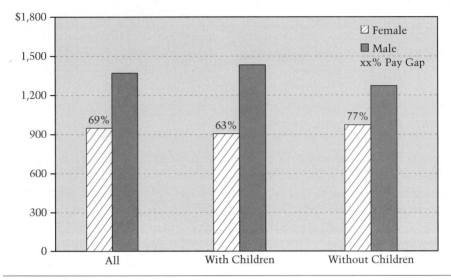

FIGURE 12.14 The difference between men's and women's pay is larger for parents than nonparents.
Source: Dey and Hill (2007).

children, they may experience the **maternal wall**, which means that employers view them as less desirable employees and provide them with fewer resources and opportunities (Williams, 1999). A 10-year follow-up study of college graduates in 2003 showed that the pay gap between men and women was much larger for those with children than those without children (see Figure 12.14; Dey & Hill, 2007).

Some of the effects of parental status on women's salaries are tangible, in that women lose experience and time from paid work when they have children. A study of currently employed adults examined the extent to which women and men made concessions in their employment to address child care responsibilities (Carr, 2002). Of nearly 2,500 surveyed, more women (53%) than men (14%) reported they had made concessions, such as taking time off from employment to care for children, reducing work hours to care for children, or switching to less demanding or more flexible jobs to accommodate

children. Among men, those who were younger were more likely to have made trade-offs than those who were older. Interestingly, whether or not men made trade-offs was unrelated to their incomes, but women who had made trade-offs had lower incomes. See Sidebar 12.3 for a discussion of family-supportive work environments.

Another reason that the pay disparity increases when women and men become parents is that life priorities shift—especially for women. One longitudinal study followed top math and science graduate students between the ages of 25 and 35 (Ferriman, Lubinski, & Benbow, 2009). Although both women and men said that job flexibility and limited work hours were a priority at age 25, these issues became more important over the next 10 years to women than men—especially among those who became parents. There is an economic cost to job flexibility and limited work hours.

The fact that women value aspects of work that have implications for family roles

Sidebar 12.3: *Family-Supportive Work Environment*

Because there is the potential for both role overload and role conflict when the paid work role is combined with family roles, many employers have taken action to support families. There are ways that employment can provide resources to cope with family issues. First, employers can provide child care support, in terms of on-site day care or monetary subsidies. Second, employers can provide flexible work hours.

A third policy that employers can institute is family leave. Most developed countries provide some kind of leave for parents with children and hold their job until they return. Mothers and fathers receive paid entitlement to parental leave in 66 countries (O'Brien, Brandth, & Kvande, 2007). The most extensive leave policies are found in the Nordic countries. Iceland has a nine-month leave: three months maternity, three months paternity, and three months to be shared, with up to 80% of salary paid (O'Brien et al., 2007). In Sweden, national paternity leave has been in existence since 1974 (Klinth, 2008). In 1992, corporations in Sweden were required to file an "action plan for equality" in which they outlined their policy to recruit, retain, and promote women. Although paternity leave facilitates this, few corporations have any kind of formal programs. Today in Sweden, both parents are provided with a total of 16 months leave, 13 for which they receive 80% of their salary and 3 for which they receive a fixed amount. They can take this leave at any time until the child reaches 8 years old. Mothers and fathers can distribute the leave between themselves in any way that they wish. Typically, mothers take the first part of the leave and fathers take the second part.

In the United States, there is no national paternity leave policy; in fact, there is no national paid leave. However, in 1993, President Clinton signed into law the Family and Medical Leave Act (FMLA). The FMLA allows employees to take a 12-week unpaid leave of absence from employment to care for a child or an ill relative without fear of losing their jobs. In 2002, California became the first state to provide paid family leave, with six weeks of leave at 55% of one's salary (O'Brien et al., 2007). Although there is no national policy for paid paternity leave, many fathers do take time off from paid work when they have children. In a nationally representative sample of 10,000 fathers, 89% took some time off (Nepomnyaschy & Waldfogel, 2007). However, a majority do not take off much time—64% took off one week or less.

Fathers are five times more likely to take parental leave if their employers offer it (Tanaka & Waldfogel, 2007). A major difference between the policies in the United States and other countries, such as Sweden, is that the leave is unpaid in the United States but paid in other countries. In the United States, men typically use their vacation days or personal days for child care. Because state and federal legislation in the United States has increased opportunities for parental leave, more women and men have taken advantage of it (Han, Ruhm, & Waldfogel, 2009). Even in Sweden, 90% of fathers take` paternity leave but they only use 20% of the days to which they are entitled (Haas & Hwang, 2008; Klinth, 2008). This means that there are other reasons why men in the United States and men elsewhere do not take paternity leave.

One obstacle is the connection of work to the male gender role. Some men believe that employers and coworkers have a negative attitude toward paternity leave and that taking leave would be viewed as unmasculine and as lacking a commitment to work. Although organizations provide for paternity leave to avoid sex discrimination charges, they do not necessarily encourage men to take advantage of it. In fact, after the FMLA became law in 1993, two lawsuits were filed by fathers who said they were discriminated against when they tried to take a family leave to care for a newborn. In 1999, Kevin Knussman, a former Maryland state trooper, was awarded

$375,000 in the first sex discrimination case associated with the act (Morse, 1999). Knussman requested an extended leave because his wife had a complicated pregnancy and was not able to take care of the baby. Knussman claimed his request was denied. In 1999, a second suit was filed by David Roberts, a former South Carolina state trooper, who complained he was fired for requesting family leave to care for his newborn daughter (American Civil Liberties Union, 2000). He requested family leave because his wife had not worked long enough to accrue paid leave and he wanted to offer her the opportunity to advance in her position. His supervisor responded by telling him it was a mother's duty to take care of the children. The sharp criticism he received from his supervisors made him withdraw the request, but three months later, he was terminated. In 2003, the U.S. Supreme Court held that state government employees are protected by the FMLA (American Civil Liberties Union, 2003).

may have implications for the wage gap. Recall that female managers value communion more than male managers and that higher-level managers valued agentic characteristics as more important to their jobs than managers in lower-level positions (Frame et al., 2010). A study of undergraduates revealed that women value the implications of work for family (i.e., accommodations for family) more than men and that these values are linked to the expectation to work fewer hours and to the expectation of a lower salary (Lips & Lawson, 2009). By contrast, men valued the status aspects of a job more than women, and status values were related to the expectations to work longer hours and to have higher salaries.

Yet, even when the money lost from taking time off work is taken into consideration, parenthood still has a negative effect on women's salaries. Other effects of motherhood on the pay gap are not so tangible. Motherhood is conceived as a low-status characteristic, meaning that it undermines perceptions of women's competence and commitment in the workforce (Ridgeway & Correll, 2004). A number of laboratory studies have shown the negative effect motherhood has on perceptions of women's competence. When college

students read applications from two females, the labeling of one applicant as a parent influenced perceptions of competence and job commitment and allocation of salary (Correll, Benard, & Paik, 2007). Mothers were judged as less competent and less committed than nonmothers, and salary recommendations were $11,000 less for mothers than nonmothers. Whereas 84% of nonmothers were recommended for hire, only 47% of mothers were recommended for hire. The bias was demonstrated for both White and African American applicants and by both female and male participants. Interestingly, fathers were rated as more committed and given a higher salary than men who were not fathers.

This pattern of findings is not limited to vignette studies. Field experiments have shown similar results. When fictitious job applications were sent to employers with the sex and parental status of the applicant manipulated, employers were more likely to call women who were not mothers than mothers for an interview and were more likely to call fathers than men who were not fathers for an interview (Correll et al., 2007). When retail store employers were confronted with pregnant or nonpregnant female applicants, they were equally likely to tell both applicants that jobs were available but showed greater hostility toward pregnant than nonpregnant applicants according to audiotapes of the interactions (Hebl et al., 2007).

Employers may have different beliefs about mothers and fathers as workers. Employers may perceive that they can pay women less than men because they are less likely to leave their position for more money; family ties will keep them in the area. Employers also may believe that mothers are less dedicated to their work than fathers. A study of professors in academia showed that senior faculty perceived that junior faculty mothers were less involved with work than fathers despite the fact that junior faculty mothers reported being more involved with work than fathers (King, 2008). Although mothers and fathers reported equal interest in career advancement, senior faculty perceived that fathers were more interested than mothers. The concern is that employers' stereotypes could influence how they behave toward mothers and fathers. Employers may believe it is more worthwhile to reward single women than married women because single women are less likely to let family obligations interfere with work and are more likely to seek a job elsewhere that pays more money. Employers may also believe it is more worthwhile to reward fathers than men without families because fathers have a family to support. Recall the study of Canadian lawyers in which family capital was associated with higher incomes for men (Robson & Wallace, 2001). This phenomenon has been referred to as the **marital bonus** for men.

The marital bonus is also alive and well in China. In a study that examined job advertisements in China, 40% of the ads were directly discriminatory in specifying the sex of the applicant, and a substantial number referred to the preferred marital status (Woodhams, Lupton, & Xian, 2009). There was greater concern with the marital status of women than men. When marital status was mentioned in the ad, women were preferred if they were unmarried and men were preferred if they were married. For women, being married means that they have domestic responsibilities that could detract from work. For men, being married means that they can be more committed to work because they have someone at home to take care of domestic responsibilities.

What can women do to escape the "mommy tax"? One way that women have resolved this problem is to delay childbearing until they are established in their careers. These women earn more money and have greater job opportunities (Crittenden, 2001). However, this is a choice that is not appealing to all women—and a choice that men do not have to make.

One group of women who may not suffer from the wage gap is lesbians. One might expect that gay men and lesbians earn less money for comparable work than their heterosexual counterparts because of sexual orientation discrimination. This is true in the case of gay men, but lesbians earn more than heterosexual women (Black et al., 2003; Peplau & Fingerhut, 2004). One explanation is based on **human capital accumulation theory** (Black et al., 2003). Heterosexual women limit their market skills more than lesbians because they expect to be part of a traditional family where a second income will exist. Lesbians do not limit their market skills because they are less certain of a second income. Lesbians are more educated than heterosexual women and more likely than heterosexual women to have full-time jobs. Lesbians are also more likely than heterosexual women to have nontraditional jobs, which are associated with higher salaries. Lesbians have greater freedom

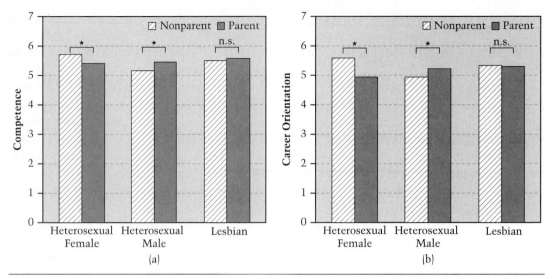

FIGURE 12.15 Heterosexual women were rated as less competent and less career oriented when they were a parent compared to a nonparent; heterosexual men were rated as more competent and more career oriented when they were a parent compared to a nonparent. Lesbians were rated as equally competent (a) and equally career oriented (b) regardless of parental status * = difference is significant; n.s. = difference is not significant.
Source: Adapted from Peplau and Fingerhut (2004).

to pursue their careers because they do not have the constraints of a husband and are less likely to have children. However, even when lesbians have children (which is increasingly common), motherhood does not detract from perceptions of competence as it does for heterosexual women. As shown in Figure 12.15, heterosexual college students rated a heterosexual woman as less competent and less career oriented when she was a parent than a nonparent, rated a heterosexual man as more competent and more career oriented when he was a parent than a nonparent, and rated a lesbian as equally competent and career oriented regardless of whether she was a parent or not. Just because lesbians have higher incomes than heterosexual women does not mean that they do not suffer from access or treatment discrimination, however. To the extent that discrimination does exist, the difference

in salaries between lesbians and heterosexual women should be even larger.

Denial of Discrimination

A 2007 Gallup Poll revealed that 49% of women and 37% of men said that women and men do not have equal job opportunities (Saad, 2007b). Women, on average, perceive that other women are victims of discrimination—but they are not. Many years ago, Faye Crosby (1984) asked women the following three questions in several studies (p. 371):

1. Do you currently receive the benefits from your job that you deserve to receive?

2. Are you at present the victim of sex discrimination?

3. Are women discriminated against?

The vast majority of women said yes to questions 1 and 3, but no to question 2. They believed they receive the benefits they deserve, that they do not suffer personal discrimination, but that other women are victims of discrimination. Crosby refers to this phenomenon as the **denial of disadvantage**. That is, women (and men) are more likely to agree that women in general are subject to discrimination and that women do not receive the same salary as men for comparable work, but women deny any personal disadvantage. See if this phenomenon appears at your school in Do Gender 12.4.

DO GENDER 12.4
Denial of Personal
Discrimination

You probably will not be able to measure actual discrimination in this exercise, but you can determine the extent to which women perceive that others compared to themselves are subject to discrimination. Ask a group of men and women Crosby's (1984) three questions:

1. Do you currently receive the benefits from your job that you deserve to receive?

2. Are you at present the victim of sex discrimination?

3. Are women discriminated against?

For interest, ask an additional question:

4. Are men discriminated against?

What percentage of women and men perceive that women are victims of discrimination? That men are victims of discrimination? What percentage of men and women perceive they are victims of sex discrimination?

Why do women deny personal discrimination? There are a couple of explanations (Crosby, 1984; Sechrist & Swim, 2008). First, it is difficult for a person to infer discrimination on the basis of a single case. We can always find another reason why we did not receive the job, the promotion, or the salary increase: Other people had more experience, education, or knowledge. It is difficult for a single person to compare himself or herself to a group of individuals. Second, perceiving discrimination arouses discomfort. If an individual suffers discrimination, someone specific is to blame. Perceiving that a group of people suffer discrimination (i.e., all women) does not cause as much discomfort because the source of the discrimination is more diffuse: society as a whole.

Third, even if one personally acknowledges discrimination, there may be consequences to the self and the perpetrator if a public announcement is made. A study of college students showed that both women and men are less inclined to perceive discrimination when the source is a person than a rule and when there are negative consequences to that person. When students were discriminated against (i.e., received less credit than another person for a superior performance) due to either a sexist experimenter or a sexist rule, people were more inclined to perceive discrimination if the cause was a rule than a person (i.e., the experimenter; Sechrist & Delmar, 2009). Females were especially unlikely to perceive discrimination when the source of the behavior was the person than the rule. A follow-up study showed that students were especially unlikely to perceive discrimination due to a sexist experimenter when the possibility existed for the experimenter's supervisor to know about the person's behavior. Both males and females may be concerned about consequences to themselves as well as consequences to the perpetrators.

Another reason women do not perceive personal discrimination is that women feel entitled to less pay than men. In two laboratory studies, female college students paid themselves less for the same task than male college students (Desmarais & Curtis, 1997). One reason women feel less entitled to equal pay is because they compare their earnings to those of other women rather than those of other men (Bylsma & Major, 1994). Because work is often segregated by sex, women find other women more suitable sources of comparison. A basic principle of social comparison theory is that we compare ourselves with "similar others." Women perceive similar others to be women in general rather than men—even if they are working along side men. Thus, members of disadvantaged groups—in this case, women—will be satisfied with unfair treatment and may even judge they deserve it. A study of college students showed that women expected lower pay than men, and this expectation accounted for about a third of the difference in the actual salaries of the jobs students aimed to find (Heckert et al., 2002). Heckert and colleagues argued that women's expectations of a lower salary become self-fulfilling prophecies. Women expect lower pay and are thus satisfied with lower pay. For women to be dissatisfied with less pay than men, comparisons to men need to be made salient and relevant. When women compare themselves to men, they become less satisfied. Recall from Chapter 11 that the tendency of women to compare themselves to women rather than men was also used to explain why women are satisfied with an unequal division of household responsibilities.

TAKE HOME POINTS

- Women suffer from both access discrimination and treatment discrimination.

- Treatment discrimination can take the form of the glass ceiling, the glass escalator, and pay disparity.

- The pay disparity between women and men can be accounted for by factors that distinguish women and men workers (supply-side theory) and the differences in the ways that women and men are treated (demand-side theory).

- One factor that distinguishes male and female workers and accounts for a large portion of the pay disparity is that men enter occupations associated with higher salaries than women. In addition, jobs held by men are associated with higher pay than jobs held by women, reflecting the salary estimation effect.

- Sex differences in wages appear among women and men in the same occupation, although the size of the disparity is smaller.

- The fact that women negotiate less than men and women's negotiations are less successful than those of men also contributes to the pay gap.

- Another factor that contributes to the pay gap is children. Women take more time off from paid work for children, and this differential work experience accounts for a sizable difference in earnings. The presence of children also indirectly contributes to the pay gap as it undermines perceptions of competence for women but not men. In fact, men's salaries seem to benefit from the presence of children, whereas women's suffer.

- Women are not as dissatisfied with the pay disparity as one might expect. Part of the reason is that women do not perceive themselves as victims of discrimination, although they perceive that *other women* are victims of discrimination.

- One reason that women do not recognize a personal pay disparity is that women compare their salary to that of other women rather than that of men. When comparisons to men are made salient, women become less satisfied with their pay.

SEXUAL HARASSMENT

In 1991, the Tailhook Association, an organization for Navy aviators, convened at the Hilton Hotel in Las Vegas for their annual convention. The convention was known for its memorable parties and rowdy behavior, but this year, things got out of hand—or this year, people got caught. Women who were on vacation, as well as women who were members of the association, walked in on the third-floor party to find the halls lined with men (known as the "Banister") who proceeded to grab and fondle various body parts and remove clothing despite the women's screams and attempts to fight the men off. The final report sent to the Navy contained incidents of verbal abuse, physical abuse, and sexual molestation (Ballingrud, 1992).

Not nearly as famous as Tailhook, but equally as devastating, was the Eveleth Mines case (Tevlin, 1998). In 1993, 16 female mine workers successfully sued Oglebay Norton Corp. in the first ever hostile sexual work environment class-action lawsuit in the United States. The mine was decorated with pornography, obscene graffiti, and sexual objects. One woman went to discuss these issues with her supervisor but found a picture of a vagina on his desk. The women were subjected to dirty jokes, sexual propositions, fondling, and groping on a daily basis. One woman even found semen on the clothes in her locker. Although the courts agreed the women suffered sexual harassment, it took five years to settle the case. Monetary awards were provided to the women, but the company did not apologize.

In this section of the chapter, I define sexual harassment, examine its incidence, and describe characteristics of perpetrators and victims. Then, I review some theories of sexual harassment.

Definitions

The following is the U.S. Equal Employment Opportunity Commission's (EEOC, 1980, p. 74677) definition of sexual harassment:

> Unwelcome sexual advances, requests for sexual favors, and other verbal or physical conduct of a sexual nature constitute sexual harassment when (1) submission to such conduct is made either explicitly or implicitly a term or condition of an individual's employment, (2) submission to or rejection of such conduct by an individual is used as the basis for employment decisions affecting such individual, or (3) such conduct has the purpose or effect of unreasonably interfering with an individual's work performance or creating an intimidating, hostile, or offensive working environment.

The EEOC defines two types of sexual harassment: (1) **quid pro quo**, which means one person offers work benefits (e.g., promotion) or threatens work repercussions (e.g., loss of job) in exchange for sexual favors, and (2) **hostile environment**, which means the person is faced with a hostile, intimidating work environment. Quid pro quo, which can be translated as "this for that," is likely to occur among two people of different statuses. Hostile environment sexual harassment, which frequently consists of pervasive pornographic material, sexual language, and displays of sexual behavior, is more likely to occur among coworkers; this type of harassment was the subject of the Eveleth Mines case.

It is difficult to define *sexual harassment* exclusively in terms of behavior because a given behavior can be construed as harassment in some instances and not others. Although some behaviors can clearly be defined as sexual harassment, such as a sexual bribe, others cannot be objectively classified as harassment in an absolute sense. How can you tell whether a comment or a look is flirting or harassment? Paludi and Barickman (1998) have suggested that one way to determine whether a behavior is harassment is to examine whether the recipient has the freedom to pursue the relationship. If the person feels free to pursue or not pursue the relationship, the behavior is not harassment; if the person feels she or he has no choice, the behavior is harassment. A second way to determine whether a behavior is harassment is to examine the effect of the behavior on the person. If the behavior makes one feel good and even attractive, the behavior is not harassment; if the behavior makes one feel uncomfortable, the behavior is harassment. These definitional distinctions are problematic because they rely on the recipient's interpretation of the behavior. One recipient may feel uncomfortable when a person whistles at her, whereas another recipient may feel attractive.

Much of this discussion has focused on the psychological rather than the legal definition of *sexual harassment*. In defining *hostile environment sexual harassment*, the U.S. Supreme Court has set forth guidelines that both the alleged victim and a "reasonable person" must perceive the behavior as hostile (Weiner & Gutek, 1999). Not surprisingly, this standard has been difficult to implement.

There is consensus across studies of undergraduates and adult populations that some behaviors are clearly sexual harassment and some are not (Frazier, Cochran, & Olson, 1995). Sexual propositions, sexual coercion, and sexual touching are viewed as sexual harassment by almost everyone. Sexist comments, jokes, coarse language, flirting, and staring, however, are typically not viewed as harassment. There is more agreement that harassment has occurred when behaviors are physical (e.g., petting, pinching) rather than verbal (e.g., sexual comments, innuendoes). Undergraduates are less likely than other adults to view behaviors as sexual harassment.

There are three levels of sexual harassment (Fitzgerald, Gelfand, & Drasgow, 1995). They are shown in Table 12.3, in order from least to most severe. The first two levels are more similar to hostile environment sexual harassment, whereas the third reflects quid pro quo sexual harassment. There is more agreement that harassment has occurred at the most severe levels. One common instrument used to measure sexual harassment,

---

TABLE 12.3 LEVELS OF SEXUAL HARASSMENT

1.	Gender harassment	sexist comments suggestive stories
2.	Unwanted sexual attention	leering attempts at touching repeated requests for dates
3.	Sexual coercion	bribes and threats involving sex negative consequences for refusals to have sex

Source: Fitzgerald et al. (1995).

TABLE 12.4   SAMPLE ITEMS FROM THE SEXUAL EXPERIENCES QUESTIONNAIRE

Gender harassment	Crude sexist remarks
Seductive behavior	Propositions
Sexual bribery	Direct offers of reward
Sexual coercion	Direct threats
Sexual imposition	Unwanted attempts to touch or fondle

Source: Fitzgerald et al. (1988).

TABLE 12.5   SEXUAL HARASSMENT MYTHS

Fabrication/Exaggeration:
- Women often file frivolous charges of sexual harassment.
- Women who wait weeks or months to report sexual harassment are probably just making it up.

Ulterior Motives:
- Sometimes, women make up allegations of sexual harassment to extort money from their employers.
- Women sometimes file charges of sexual harassment for no apparent reason.

Natural Heterosexuality:
- Most women are flattered when they get sexual attention from men with whom they work.
- It's inevitable that men will "hit on" women.

Woman's Responsibility:
- Women can usually stop unwanted sexual attention by simply telling their supervisors about it.
- Nearly all instances of sexual harassment would end if the woman simply told the man to stop.

especially in college students, is the Sexual Experiences Survey (Fitzgerald et al., 1995; Fitzgerald, Shullman et al., 1988). Sample items are shown in Table 12.4.

Women and men differ in their definitions of sexual harassment. Women are more likely than men to label the same behavior as harassment, according to a meta-analytic review of 62 studies (Rotundo, Nguyen, & Sackett, 2001). Sex differences in perception were larger for hostile environment harassment than quid pro quo harassment. Differences between women's and men's interpretations of a behavior are most likely to emerge for more ambiguous behaviors, such as staring or sexist remarks. Women and men clearly agree that a sexual proposition is sexual harassment. Men are more likely than women to endorse the different domains of sexual harassment myths shown in Table 12.5 (Lonsway, Cortina, & Magley, 2008). Men who endorse these myths have more hostile attitudes toward women.

Perceptions of sexual harassment also vary by culture. In a cross-cultural study of college students, those from individualistic cultures (e.g., United States, Germany) were more likely to perceive a behavior as sexual harassment, to assign more responsibility to the perpetrator, and to assign less responsibility to the victim than those from collectivist cultures (e.g., India, Taiwan; Sigal et al., 2005).

A given behavior also may be more likely to be labeled harassment if the perpetrator is male than female. Both women and men assign harsher penalties for the same behavior if the perpetrator is male than female (Cummings & Armenta, 2002). One reason is that males have a higher status than females, and status is related to whether a behavior is interpreted as sexual harassment. A meta-analysis showed that a behavior was more likely to be labeled harassment when there was a status difference between the perpetrator and the target ($d = +.65$; Blumenthal, 1998).

However, one study showed that status has a more complicated relation to perceptions of harassment. Although status is associated with power, which leads to a behavior being interpreted as harassment, status is also associated with perceiving the person in more favorable terms, which leads to a behavior not being interpreted as harassment (Sheets & Braver, 1999). Thus if a high-status person engages in an ambiguous behavior, such as making sexual innuendoes, we will be less likely to interpret the behavior as harassment if we know and like the person than if we do not know and/or do not like the person. This fits with other research that shows we judge harassment by attractive men less harshly than harassment by unattractive men (Golden, Johnson, & Lopez, 2001). Thus, if we like the person due to his or her status or physical attractiveness, we will be less likely to infer sexual harassment.

Incidence

In 2009, 12,696 charges of sexual harassment were filed with the EEOC (U.S. Equal Employment Opportunity Commission, 2010). A majority of charges were filed by women; 16% were filed by men.

How many people have experienced sexual harassment during their working history? The prevalence of sexual harassment is typically measured with surveys. One methodological difficulty with the survey method is that only a subset of people complete them. The people who complete the survey differ from the people who do not complete the survey. The kind of person who responds to a survey is likely to be interested in the topic, and it makes sense that the people who will be most interested in the topic of sexual harassment are those who have experienced it. There is evidence that such a response bias exists.

A meta-analytic review of the literature showed that the sampling technique influenced reports of sexual harassment (Ilies et al., 2003). Reports of sexual harassment were higher in convenience samples than representative random samples. This finding suggests that the people who volunteer to be in studies of sexual harassment are more likely to have been harassed. Thus to obtain a good estimate of the frequency of sexual harassment, it is very important to have a representative sample of participants and a high response rate.

Good studies with representative samples show that about half of women and a substantial number of men experience unwanted sexual harassment at work (Stockdale & Bhattacharya, 2009). The meta-analytic review reached similar conclusions but also noted that the incidence of harassment depended on how it is assessed (Ilies et al., 2003). When people are explicitly asked in a survey if they have been sexually harassed, fewer people report harassment than when they are asked if any of a series of behaviors such as those shown in Table 12.4 have occurred. Representative samples using the first method revealed that 24% of people reported harassment; the second method yielded an estimate of 58%. Higher percentages of harassment occur for milder forms, such as sexual remarks (Stockdale & Bhattacharya, 2009). Of all types of organizations, harassment rates were highest among military samples (Ilies et al., 2003).

What is the incidence of sexual harassment on college campuses? A 2005 nationally representative survey of undergraduates showed that sexual harassment is prevalent, with two-thirds of students reporting some kind of harassment (Hill & Silva, 2005), which is consistent with another recent report of 57% (Huerta et al., 2006). A majority of harassment incidents consist of verbal behaviors, such as lewd comments, jokes, sexual innuendoes, and remarks about body parts. Female and male students are equally likely to be harassed, but females are more bothered than males by the harassment. Lesbian, gay, and bisexual students were more likely than heterosexuals to experience harassment. Interestingly, when students were asked why they engaged in sexual harassment, the most common response was because they thought it was funny. Only 17% did so because they wanted to date the person. Conduct your own study of sexual harassment on campus with Do Gender 12.5.

Sexual harassment has been studied among high school students. In one such study, nearly all students (96% female, 88% male) said that they had experienced at least one sexually harassing behavior from peers when completing an adapted version of the Sexual Experiences Questionnaire, shown in Table 12.4 (Ormerod, Collinsworth, & Perry, 2008). Just over half of females (53%) and 38% of males said that they had been sexually harassed by an adult. Females reported more frequent and more severe harassment.

One reason that the problem of sexual harassment is underestimated is that victims do not always report sexual harassment.

✺ DO GENDER 12.5
Prevalence of Sexual
Harassment on Campus

First, you must decide on a definition of *sexual harassment*. Then, you must decide on the behaviors that constitute sexual harassment. Administer a survey to 10 men and 10 women on campus and ask them how frequently they have experienced each behavior. After the frequency ratings are made, you might ask the respondents to evaluate whether they perceive each of these behaviors as sexual harassment.

Unfortunately, the failure to file a complaint makes victims less credible and less successful in court (Gutek, 2008). Why don't victims report harassment? There are a number of reasons. Victims may be embarrassed, may fear for their jobs—especially in a situation in which the person's income is essential to the family—or may fear that they won't be believed and will be further victimized. Laboratory studies on sexual harassment have compounded this problem by overestimating the extent to which victims would confront a perpetrator. One group of researchers compared what people said they would do in response to harassment via a vignette study to how people actually responded to harassment in an experimental study (Woodzicka & LaFrance, 2001). In the vignette study, women were asked how they would respond to a job interviewer who asked harassing questions, such as if they had a boyfriend and if they thought women should wear a bra to work. In the laboratory study, women were asked these questions during a mock interview. Although 68% of the women in the vignette study said that they would refuse to answer one or more questions and 25% said they would tell the interviewer off or leave, none of the women in the laboratory study refused to answer the questions, none of the women confronted the interviewer, and none of the women left.

Men may be even less likely than women to report sexual harassment. Men are expected to handle these kinds of situations on their own; admitting to harassment means admitting to victim status, which is inconsistent with the male gender role. Being the subject of harassment by another man would be especially threatening to men. Thus it is not surprising that men are even less likely to report sexual harassment by other men (Dziech & Hawkins, 1998).

Interestingly, people seem to be harsher in judging male compared to female victims. Male victims are less likely to be believed, are liked less, and punished more compared to female victims (Madera et al., 2007). Female victims are liked more than male victims—especially if they are attractive.

Outcomes of Sexual Harassment

Sexual harassment is associated with negative job outcomes, increased psychological distress, and poorer physical health (Chan et al., 2008; Stockdale & Bhattacharya, 2009). In terms of work quality, people who are harassed are unhappy with their jobs, have more difficulty performing their jobs, and are less committed to their jobs. People who are harassed may quit their jobs, be fired, or lose career opportunities. Among college students, sexual harassment has been related to academic disengagement and poor academic performance (Huerta et al., 2006). Health outcomes range from psychological distress, such as loss of self-esteem, anxiety, and depression, to physical symptoms, such as headaches and gastrointestinal problems, and even eating disturbances. Sexual harassment also may affect people's ability to trust others. People who are harassed may withdraw from social interactions. The links to outcomes are generally the same for women and men. However, there are fewer studies of harassment among men, leaving open the possibility that there could be sex differences in the relation of harassment to health and well-being. Sexual harassment is more strongly related to poor outcomes among younger than older people. The more frequent and the more severe the harassment, the more severe the consequences (Collinsworth, Fitzgerald, & Drasgow, 2009). There also are negative effects of witnessing sexual harassment, referred to as *ambient sexual harassment* (Glomb et al., 1997). Witnesses realize that they work in a culture in which they are neither supported nor protected from sexual harassment.

There is no indication that reporting sexual harassment leads to better outcomes (Bergman et al., 2002). The outcome depends on the organization's response, and a typical response is retaliation of some sort. Retaliation and minimization of sexual harassment lead to lower job satisfaction.

Most research on the outcomes of sexual harassment come from survey studies. The problem with survey studies is that both the independent variable (sexual harassment) and the dependent variable (distress) rely on self-report. Laboratory studies in which sexual harassment is manipulated can provide more definitive evidence of its effects. One such study showed that sexual harassment during the interview process impaired women's performance (Woodzicka & LaFrance, 2005). Young adult females were interviewed for a job by a male and randomly assigned to receive one of two sets of interviewer questions. Both sets of questions were out of the ordinary (to control for the surprise element of the questions), but only one set of questions could be construed as sexual harassment. For example, in the control condition, women were asked if they had a best friend and if they thought it was important for people to believe in God. Like the previous study, in the sexual harassment condition, women were asked if they had a boyfriend and if they thought it was important for women to wear a bra to work. The interview was videotaped and transcribed and rated by coders who were blind to condition. Women in the sexual harassment condition spoke less fluently, gave lower-quality answers to questions, and asked fewer relevant questions during the interview than women in the control condition. Interestingly, women's perception of being harassed was not related to these outcomes. Thus, the objective measure of harassment hurt performance, whereas the subjective perception of harassment did not.

Characteristics of the victim also influence responses to sexual harassment. A study of college students showed that nontraditional/feminist attitudes buffered the effects of sexual harassment for White women but exacerbated the effects of sexual harassment for Black women (Rederstorff, Buchanan, & Settles, 2007). Rederstorff and colleagues argued that feminist attitudes provided White women with an external attribution for the harassment—societal problems at large. Black women, however, face oppression from both race and gender, and sexual harassment may make this double victimization salient, leading to psychological distress.

Characteristics of Perpetrator

There are few distinctive demographic characteristics of men who sexually harass women. Sexual harassment is usually not related to a man's age, marital status, physical attractiveness, or occupation (Paludi & Barickman, 1998). Harassers are more likely to be coworkers than supervisors (Bondurant & White, 1996), in part because people have more coworkers than supervisors, which means hostile environment harassment is more common than quid pro quo harassment.

Although male harassers cannot be distinguished by demographic characteristics, psychological characteristics are linked to those who may harass. People who score higher on hostile and benevolent sexism are more tolerant of sexual harassment (Russell & Trigg, 2004). Pryor (1998) developed the Likelihood to Sexually Harass (LSH) scale to identify the person most likely to engage in sexual harassment. This scale consists of a series of situations that create the opportunity for quid pro quo sexual harassment to occur. Following each scenario, respondents are asked how likely they would be to engage in a number of behaviors. A sample scenario is shown in Table 12.6. Men who score high on this scale say they would respond to the series of scenarios by engaging in sexual behavior. These men endorse stereotypical masculine beliefs and have traditional attitudes toward women (Paludi & Barickman, 1998; Pryor, Giedd, & Williams, 1995). These men equate masculinity with high status, appearing tough, and being dominant.

Characteristics of Victim

Younger and unmarried women are more likely to be harassed than older and married women (Gutek & Done, 2000). Ethnicity is related to sexual harassment, but it depends on assimilation into American culture. A study of women working in a food processing company showed that 23% of low-acculturated Hispanic women had been sexually harassed, in contrast to 61% of high-acculturated Hispanic women and 77% of non-Hispanic White women (Shupe et al., 2002). The investigators suggested that the higher rate of sexual harassment among high-acculturated women had to do with the greater threat they posed to traditional roles compared to low-acculturated women. Low-acculturated women retained the traditional male/female roles that are rooted in Hispanic culture.

Women's occupations also are linked to sexual harassment. Women employed in male-dominated positions are more likely to be harassed than women employed in traditional occupations (Bondurant & White, 1996), in part because these women have greater contact with men. Women's occupations also influence the type of sexual harassment. Women in

TABLE 12.6   LIKELIHOOD TO SEXUALLY HARASS SCENARIO

Imagine you are a college professor. You are 38 years old; you teach in a large Midwestern university; you are a full professor with tenure; you are renowned in your field (abnormal psychology) and have numerous offers for other jobs. One day, following the return of an examination to a class, a female student stops in your office. She tells you that her score is one point away from an A and asks you if she can do an extra credit project to raise her score. She tells you that she may not have a sufficient grade to get into graduate school without the A. Several other students have asked you to do extra credit assignments and you have declined to let them. This particular woman is a stunning blonde. She sits in the front row of the class every day and always wears short skirts. You find her extremely sexy. How likely are you to do the following things in this situation?

a. Would you let her carry out a project for extra credit (e.g., write a paper)?

   Not at all likely   1   2   3   4   5   Very likely

b. Assuming that you are very secure in your job and the university has always tolerated professors who make passes at students, would you offer the student a chance to earn extra credit in return for sexual favors?

   Not at all likely   1   2   3   4   5   Very likely

c. Given the same assumptions as in the question above, would you ask her to join you for dinner to discuss the possible extra credit assignments?

   Not at all likely   1   2   3   4   5   Very likely

Source: Pryor (1998).

traditional occupations are likely to suffer quid pro quo sexual harassment, whereas women in nontraditional occupations are likely to suffer from hostile environment sexual harassment (Lach & Gwartney-Gibbs, 1993). When women are in nontraditional jobs, they are perceived by male peers as a threat to their jobs. Sexual harassment is most likely to occur in situations where women reject the traditional female role. According to Burgess and Borgida (1999), sexual harassment is a way of punishing women who do not adhere to the prescriptive component of stereotypes. Sexual harassment is used to maintain the status differential between women who threaten the status quo and men.

Theories

One theory of sexual harassment is that it is a natural and normal part of male–female relationships (Tangri & Hayes, 1997). Sexual harassment may be viewed as the product of male hormones or as a normal part of male courting behavior. One motive for sexual harassment may be to seek sexual intimacy. The behavior becomes a problem, however, when it is not desired on the part of the female.

Another theory of sexual harassment is that it is a manifestation of patriarchy—men's dominance over women. According to this view, harassment is a form of men asserting their power over women and has more to do with power than sex (Sandler & Shoop, 1997; Tangri & Hayes, 1997). With quid pro quo harassment, power is certainly an important factor. However, even with hostile environment harassment between coworkers, some would argue that assertion of power is the underlying motivation. Sexual harassment is a way for men to reinforce gender-role norms of men having power over women (Stockdale & Bhattacharya, 2009). The fact that women who violate gender-role norms are more likely to be victims of sexual harassment supports this theory.

A social psychological perspective conceptualizes sexual harassment as the product of both personality factors and situational factors. Sexual harassment is a behavior that occurs among some of the people some of the time (Pryor et al., 1995). Characteristics of people who harass are addressed with Pryor's (1998) LSH scale. What are the environmental conditions that foster sexual harassment? In one study, priming men with a sexist film was associated with sexual harassment (i.e., number of sexist questions asked of a female during a mock job interview; Pryor et al., 2000). In another study, men whose masculinity was threatened by being outperformed by a female on a masculine task were more likely to engage in the same form of sexual harassment; that is, ask sexist questions (Pryor et al., 2000).

Sexual harassment is most likely to occur in situations where it is perceived as acceptable or tolerated (Pryor et al., 1995). In organizations where management condones sexual harassment, the frequency increases. Attending a school with a climate that condones harassment is associated with lower self-esteem, higher distress, and feelings of unsafety at school for both females and males (Ormerod et al., 2008).

Another theory of sexual harassment that emphasizes the contribution of situational variables is **sex-role spillover theory**, which suggests that expectations about women's and men's roles carry over to the workplace when they are not appropriate or relevant (Tangri & Hayes, 1997). This theory implies that sexual harassment is more likely to occur when gender is salient (Gutek & Done, 2000). Gender is salient when women work in male-dominated occupations. This theory also applies to men: Men who work with a large number of women are more likely to experience sexual harassment (Gutek & Done, 2000). Gender roles also can be made salient when an occupation highlights one's gender role. For example, waitresses and secretaries may suffer higher rates of sexual harassment because their sex is salient (Gutek & Done, 2000).

TAKE HOME POINTS

- There are two kinds of sexual harassment: quid pro quo and hostile environment.

- *Sexual harassment* is difficult to define because it rests in part on how the recipient perceives the behavior.

- Sexual harassment ranges in severity from lewd comments to sexual coercion; there is more agreement that a behavior constitutes harassment when it is more severe.

- Women are more likely than men to perceive a behavior as harassment. There is more agreement between women and men on the more severe forms of sexual harassment.

- Sexual harassment appears to be fairly common; the most common forms are the less severe forms.

- A psychological instrument, the LSH scale, has been developed to distinguish between men who are more and less likely to harass.

- Women in traditionally male occupations are more likely to be harassed, perhaps because their presence represents a threat to men.

- Social psychological theories of sexual harassment emphasize that the behavior is a product of both individual difference variables (such as the LSH scale) and situational variables (when the male role is threatened, when women's sex is made salient).

SUMMARY

In this chapter, I evaluated the effect of paid worker roles on women's and men's health. The paid worker role is associated with health benefits for both women and men. The effect of the paid worker role on women's and men's health is largely due to its influence on resources and demands. To the extent that women's employment increases women's economic resources and detracts from men's economic resources, women benefit and men suffer. To the extent that women's employment increases men's participation in household chores and decreases women's, women benefit and men suffer. This presents a challenge for couples in which wives and husbands both work outside the home.

Having multiple roles, such as the roles of paid worker, spouse, and parent, has the potential to provide resources that can be used to buffer strains arising from any one role. This is referred to as the *role expansion hypothesis*. However, multiple roles also can lead to role strain or role conflict, which is known as the *role scarcity hypothesis*. That is, stress from one role can exacerbate problems in another role. Taken collectively, more evidence supports the role expansion hypothesis than the role scarcity hypothesis. More roles seem to be associated with better health for women and men, but this does not mean role strains do not occur. Women, in particular, face difficulties combining work and family roles when children are at home. These women do not necessarily suffer, however, when they have resources to cope with the increased demands—resources in terms of a high income or a husband who shares household responsibilities.

One reason it is difficult to compare the effect of paid work on health for men and women is that men and women have different employment experiences. One aspect of the paid worker role with consequences for women's well-being is discrimination. I distinguished between access and treatment discrimination: Access discrimination reflects the differential opportunities women and men have to hold certain jobs; once hired, treatment discrimination occurs in the form of the glass ceiling and pay disparity. Women make less money than men even when characteristics of women and men such as education and experience are taken into consideration. However, the wage gap is closing. Factors that contribute to the wage gap include sex segregation of occupations and parenthood. Women with children earn less than women without children, and both concrete and abstract explanations account for this difference. Interestingly, women are not as dissatisfied with pay disparity as we would expect. Although women believe other women suffer discrimination, a majority of women deny any personal discrimination; this phenomenon is referred to as the *denial of personal disadvantage*. One theory of why women deny disadvantage involves social comparison theory: Women compare themselves to other women rather than to men.

Another aspect of work that has consequences for well-being is sexual harassment. Women are more likely to be harassed than men, and sexual harassment is associated with an array of adverse outcomes. There are a variety of forms of sexual harassment. Women are more likely than men to label a given behavior as harassment, but both women and men agree on the more severe forms of harassment. Both person factors and situational factors combine to produce sexual harassment.

DISCUSSION QUESTIONS

1. Under what conditions is employment most strongly related to good health for women? To poor health for women?
2. Distinguish between the role expansion and role scarcity hypotheses.
3. What are some of the difficulties women and men face when combining paid work and family roles? How could these be alleviated?
4. Give an example of how family roles can exacerbate or buffer the stress associated with work roles.
5. What is the difference between access discrimination and treatment discrimination?
6. Why do women deny personal discrimination?
7. What is the difference between supply-side theory and demand-side theory accounts of discrimination?
8. What are some of the reasons for the pay disparity?
9. To what does the "mommy tax" refer? What are the explanations for it? Are these explanations about personality variables or situational variables?
10. Do women and men define sexual harassment differently?
11. Describe sexual harassment from a social psychological perspective. Offer an explanation that takes into consideration both dispositional and situational factors.

SUGGESTED READING

Babcock, L., & Laschever, S. (2003). *Women don't ask: Negotiation and the gender divide.* Princeton, NJ: Princeton University Press.

Biernat, M., Crosby, F., & Williams, J. (Eds.). (2004). The maternal wall: Research and policy perspectives on discrimination against mothers. *Journal of Social Issues, 60,* 675–682.

Crittenden, A. (2001). *The price of motherhood: Why the most important job in the world is still the least valued.* New York: Henry Holt and Company.

Eagly, A. H., & Carli, L. L. (2007). *Through the labyrinth: The truth about how women become leaders.* Boston, MA: Harvard University School Press.

Gerson, K. (2010). *The unfinished revolution: How a new generation is reshaping family, work, and gender in America.* New York: Oxford University Press.

Gutek, B. A., & Done, R. S. (2000). Sexual harassment. In R. K. Unger (Ed.), *Handbook of the psychology of women and gender* (pp. 1–61). New York: Wiley.

Klumb, P. L., & Lampert, T. (2004). Women, work, and well-being 1950–2000: A review and methodological critique. *Social Science and Medicine, 58,* 1007–1024.

KEY TERMS

Access discrimination—Situation in which an individual is not offered a given job or is offered a lesser job because of some defining characteristic (e.g., sex).

Comparable worth policy—States that men and women in different jobs should be paid the same wage for comparable work.

Demand-side theory—Explanation for the wage gap that emphasizes the different ways men and women are treated.

Denial of disadvantage—Condition in which women perceive that discrimination exists but deny that they personally are victims of it.

Differential exposure hypothesis—Proposition that men and women possess different roles, which are associated with different stressors and different resources.

Differential vulnerability hypothesis—Proposition that a specific role has different effects on men's and women's health.

Glass ceiling—Label applied to barriers to the advancement of women and minorities in organizations.

Glass escalator—Term referring to the ability of men to be promoted quickly when they take positions in traditionally female fields.

Hostile environment—Type of sexual harassment in which one person is creating a hostile, intimidating work environment for another.

Human capital accumulation theory—A job and the salary associated with the job are functions of the person's characteristics or "human capital," such as skills, experience, and education (see supply-side theory).

Marital bonus—Increase in income granted to men who are married and/or have children compared to men who are single.

Maternal wall—Employer's devaluation and limitation of job opportunities of female employees when they become parents.

Norms—Expectations for behavior.

Pay disparity—Type of treatment discrimination in which women are paid less than men for doing comparable work.

Quid pro quo—Type of sexual harassment in which one person offers work benefits or threatens work repercussions in exchange for sexual favors.

Role—Position in society governed by a set of norms.

Role conflict—Condition in which the demands of one role are at odds with the demands of another role.

Role expansion hypothesis—Idea that benefits are to be gained from having diverse roles.

Role overload—Condition that arises when time limitations create difficulties in fulfilling obligations for one's roles.

Role scarcity hypothesis—Idea that multiple roles will have a negative effect on health because time and resources are limited and additional roles tap resources.

Role spillover—The idea that the effects of enacting one role spill over or affect how one enacts another role.

Salary estimation effect—The assumption that jobs inhabited by men pay more than jobs inhabited by women.

Selection effect—Potential for healthier people to choose certain roles, which then leads to difficulties in determining whether those roles influence health.

Sex-role spillover theory—Suggestion that expectations about men's and women's roles carry over to the workplace when they are not appropriate or are irrelevant.

Supply-side theory—Explanation for the wage gap that emphasizes the different characteristics of male and female workers.

Treatment discrimination—Situation in which an individual receives a reduced salary or reduced opportunities for promotion compared to other individuals having the same job.

CHAPTER 13

Mental Health

I n 2005, 118 million prescriptions for antidepressants were written, making antide-pressants the most commonly prescribed drugs in the United States (Cohen, 2007). In 10 years (1996 to 2005), the use of antidepressants doubled; 10% of Americans now take antidepressants (Olfson & Marcus, 2009). And, women are twice as likely as men to use antidepressants (National Center for Health Statistics, 2009b).

Mental health, in particular depression, is clearly an important problem in our country. Depression is not only related to mortality (Collins, Glei, & Goldman, 2009; Ryan et al., 2008) as well as specific diseases (e.g., heart disease; Haukkala et al., 2009) and risk factors for disease (Toker, Shirom, & Melamed, 2008), but is an important problem in and of itself. Some important public figures have brought attention to men-tal health problems, with the effect of reducing their stigma and permitting more people to seek help for them. Richard Dreyfuss and Mel Gibson have bipolar disorder, and each has appeared in a documentary about the disorder. Great Britain's Princess Diana acknowledged depression and an eating disorder before her death. Tina Turner (1986) admitted in her autobiography that she tried to kill herself with an overdose of Valium. Mental health problems afflict women and men somewhat differently. Substantial evi-dence indicates that women are more likely than men to suffer from depression and to have an eating disorder, whereas men are more likely than women to commit suicide.

I begin this chapter by reviewing the evidence for sex differences in depression. There seems to be a large and pervasive sex difference in depression, such that women suffer more depression than men. Critics, however, argue that definitional and methodological problems make this difference less clear. Thus, I examine the extent to which methodologi-cal artifacts can account for this difference. The rest of the discussion is devoted to the-oretical explanations for the sex difference in depression. These theories have biological, psychological, social, and cultural underpinnings. No one theory can completely account for women being more depressed than men. It is most likely a combination of theories that synergistically interact to explain the sex difference in depression. Many theories have female gender-role socialization at their cores. Theories differentially emphasize the following ideas: (1) women are led to perceive less control over their environment than men; (2) women and men cope differently with stress; (3) women and men face different stressors; and (4) women are more vulnerable to different classes of stressors. One reason gender-role explanations are so viable is that sex differences in depression emerge during adolescence when gender-role norms become salient. Thus I conclude with some remarks about the challenges of adolescence and how they might spark the sex difference in depression. In addition to reviewing research on depression, I also examine how men and women respond to the onset of a chronic illness, because it is a major stressful life event that often evokes depression.

Aside from depression, I examine two other mental health problems relevant to gender: eating disorders and suicide. Suicide has a paradoxical link to gender; although women attempt suicide more often than men, more men kill themselves than women.

SEX DIFFERENCES IN DEPRESSION

Before we examine the incidence of depression in women and men, we must distinguish between depressive symptoms, which all of us experience to some extent at one time or another, and major depressive disorder or clinical depression, which is a diagnosable mental health problem. Instruments that measure depressive symptoms include

TABLE 13.1 CENTER FOR EPIDEMIOLOGICAL STUDIES IN DEPRESSION SCALE (CES-D)

1. I was bothered by things that usually don't bother me.
2. I did not feel like eating; my appetite was poor.
3. I felt that I could not shake off the blues even with the help of my family or friends.
4. I felt that I was just as good as other people.*
5. I had trouble keeping my mind on what I was doing.
6. I felt depressed.
7. I felt that everything I did was an effort.
8. I felt hopeful about the future.*
9. I thought my life had been a failure.
10. I felt fearful.
11. My sleep was restless.
12. I was happy.*
13. I talked less than usual.
14. I felt lonely.
15. People were unfriendly.
16. I enjoyed life.*
17. I had crying spells.
18. I felt sad.
19. I felt that people disliked me.
20. I could not get "going."

These items are reverse scored so that lower endorsement indicates more depression.
Source: Radloff (1977).

feeling sad or blue, feeling depressed, having crying spells, difficulty concentrating, and loss of interest in activities. Perhaps you have completed such an instrument during college. A widely used self-report measure of depression, the Center for Epidemiological Studies in Depression scale (CES-D; Radloff, 1977), is shown in Table 13.1.

The criteria for a major depressive disorder, as diagnosed by the *Diagnostic and Statistical Manual of Mental Disorders (DSM-IV-TR)* (American Psychiatric Association, 2000), are shown in Table 13.2. The critical feature of a major depressive disorder is the experience of a set of depressive symptoms for a period no

TABLE 13.2   **MAJOR DEPRESSIVE EPISODE CRITERIA FROM *DSM-IV-TR***

Five or more of these symptoms present for two weeks:

- Depressed mood most of the day, nearly every day. *
- Markedly diminished interests in activities. *
- Significant weight loss.
- Insomnia.
- Psychomotor agitation or retardation.
- Fatigue or loss of energy.
- Feelings of worthlessness.
- Diminished ability to think or concentrate or indecisiveness.
- Recurrent thoughts of death.

One of the five symptoms must include one of these.
Source: American Psychiatric Association (2000).

shorter than two weeks. Major depressive disorder is often referred to as **clinical depression**.

How do we determine the frequency of depressive symptoms or the incidence of clinical depression? Two different methods are used. Depressive symptoms are typically evaluated with community surveys. The strength of this methodology is that large representative samples of women and men can be obtained to identify the frequency of depression. The weakness of this methodology is that depression is measured by self-report instruments, which are vulnerable to demand characteristics. If men are less willing than women to report depression, community surveys may underestimate men's levels of depression. Information on clinical depression is typically obtained from treatment facilities. The strength of this methodology is that depression can be evaluated with more sophisticated measures employed by trained clinicians. The weakness is that respondents are not representative of the population. To the extent that men are less likely than women to seek help for depression, studies of people in clinics also may underestimate men's rates of depression.

These two methodologies have provided a wealth of evidence that women experience more depressive symptoms than men in the general population, and women are more likely than men to be diagnosed with clinical depression. In a study that combined the two methods described here by conducting face-to-face clinical interviews with members of the community in 15 countries, females were between 1.3 and 2.6 times more likely than males to be depressed across the 15 countries (Seedat et al., 2009). You can see from Figure 13.1

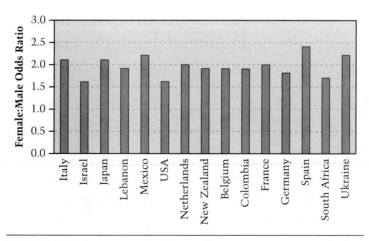

FIGURE 13.1   Ratio of female to male depression in 15 countries.
Source: Adapted from Seedat et al. (2009).

that the female to male odds ratio exceeds 1.0 in all cases, signifying higher rates in women than men. In the United States, women were 1.6 times as likely as men to be clinically depressed. This study also showed that countries in which the female gender role has become less traditional (as measured by female education and participation in the labor force) showed a decrease in the sex difference in depression over time. However, it is not clear if the smaller sex difference is due to a lowered rate of depression in females or an elevated rate of depression in males. Interestingly, there is no overall sex difference in bipolar disorder (more commonly known as manic-depressive illness). See Sidebar 13.1 for a brief discussion.

There is other cross-cultural support for sex differences in depression. Women are two to three times more likely than men to be depressed in the majority of Islamic countries (Alansari, 2006). In some populations, sex differences in depression are less likely to be found. For example, sex differences in depression are often not found in homogeneous populations, such as college students (Grant et al., 2002). Another population that shows no sex difference in depression is the

widowed. As discussed in Chapter 11, this is largely because rates of depression increase among men more than women following widowhood.

The sex difference in depression emerges during adolescence and is fairly consistent across the life span. A meta-analysis of sex differences in depression showed that girls are slightly less likely than boys to be depressed prior to age 13 but that girls' depression increases after age 13, creating the sex difference, as shown in Figure 13.2 (Twenge & Nolen-Hoeksema, 2002). After this, the sex difference in depression remains stable over the life span.

We may wonder whether the same women and men remain depressed throughout their lives or if, at any given point, women are twice as likely as men to become depressed. No evidence suggests that depression is more chronic in women or that depression is more likely to recur in women than men (Kessler, 2000; Nolen-Hoeksema, 2004). Once women and men sustain an episode of major depression, they are equally likely to experience a recurrence. In a large-scale study of adults ages 48 to 79, 60% of both women and men who had had one

Sidebar 13.1: *Bipolar Disorder*

Bipolar disorder includes both manic and depressive symptoms. The disorder takes different forms in women and men. Depressive symptoms predominate in women, whereas manic symptoms predominate in men (Kawa et al., 2005). Men are more likely than women to have mania at the onset of disorder. Bipolar disorder is also more likely to take place in the context of alcohol abuse, drug abuse, and conduct disorders among males, and more likely to take place in the context of eating disorders and panic disorder among females (Baldassano et al., 2005; Benedetti et al., 2007; Carter et al., 2005). The incidence of bipolar disorder peaks during the ages of 16 to 25, during which time it is more common among males than females (Kennedy et al., 2005). After age 25, bipolar disorder decreases among both males and females, but the decrease is larger for males. Thus, throughout adulthood, females have higher rates of bipolar disorder than males.

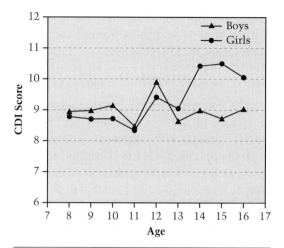

FIGURE 13.2 CDI (depression) scores for girls and boys. Prior to age 13, boys have slightly higher scores than girls. After age 13, females' rates of depression substantially increase leading to a sex difference in depression that persists across the lifespan.

Source: Twenge and Nolen-Hoeksema (2002).

episode of depression experienced a recurrence (Wainwright & Surtees, 2002). Thus among those without a history of depression, women are more likely than men to become depressed at any given point in time, but no evidence indicates that depression is more likely to recur among women than men among those with a history of depression.

There is a higher prevalence of some mental health problems among gay and lesbian people compared to heterosexuals. A meta-analytic review of the literature showed that sexual minorities have more anxiety, depression, and substance abuse problems than heterosexuals (Meyer, 2003). More recent studies have confirmed these findings (Coker, Austin, & Schuster, 2010). However, a majority of studies in this area focus on younger samples—adolescents and college students. Because adults have more time to adjust to their sexual orientation, fewer differences may be found. Among adults, the difference in mental health problems between sexual minorities and heterosexuals is less clear. It also is not clear whether the difference is larger for males or females. One study of mood disorders (anxiety and depression) indicated that the difference between gay men and heterosexual men is larger than the difference between lesbians and heterosexual women (Bostwick et al., 2010), whereas two other studies found just the opposite (Bybee et al., 2009; Cochran et al., 2007).

There are several reasons why sexual minorities have elevated mental health problems compared to heterosexuals. One is the impact of discrimination. A second, and related, reason is lack of social support (Spencer & Patrick, 2009). Finally, sexual minorities may internalize society's negative attitudes toward them. One study showed that explicit measures of antigay attitudes were not related to mental health problems among sexual minorities, but implicit attitudes were (Hatzenbuehler et al., 2009). Over a 10-day period, stigma-related stress was associated with more distress but only among sexual minorities who held implicit antigay attitudes.

TAKE HOME POINTS

- Females are more likely than males to report depressive symptoms as well as major depressive disorder.

- Sex differences persist across a variety of cultures but are not observed in some homogenous populations, such as college students and the widowed.

- The sex difference in depression is related to the onset of depression—not recurrence.

- There are elevated rates of mental health problems among sexual minorities.

METHODOLOGICAL ARTIFACTS

Some investigators have contested these seemingly indisputable data that a sex difference in depression exists. Three sets of methodological problems or artifacts could explain why women "appear" to be more depressed. First, there may be a bias on the part of clinicians, such that depression is overdiagnosed among women and underdiagnosed among men. Second, there may be a response bias on the part of depressed persons; men may be less likely than women to admit depression or to seek help for depression. Third, women and men may manifest depression in different ways, and instruments are biased in the direction of tapping female depression.

Clinician Bias

One source of bias is the clinician's judgment. Perhaps clinicians are more likely to interpret a set of symptoms as depression when the patient is female than male. Why might this be? First, clinicians are undoubtedly aware of the sex difference in depression. Thus clinicians' mental illness schema for a female patient is more likely to contain depression than their mental illness schema for a male patient. When a female patient comes into the office, depression-related schemas are more likely to be activated. Ambiguous symptoms such as feeling tired or lacking energy can be indicators of a variety of health problems. Clinicians may be more likely to interpret such symptoms as depression in a female patient and cardiac disease in a male patient.

The evidence for clinician bias is equivocal. In a study that compared primary care physicians' detection of mental health problems among over 19,000 patients to an independent screening, physicians were less likely

to detect depression in men compared to women, and in African Americans and Hispanics compared to Caucasians (Borowsky et al., 2000). That is, more of men's than women's depression went undetected by physicians. However, another study asked primary care physicians to review vignettes of elderly patients with depression and showed that physicians correctly classified the patients as depressed in 85% of the cases, and equally so for males and females (Kales et al., 2005). Although physicians are more likely to prescribe antidepressants and antianxiety drugs to women than to men, even when they have similar diagnoses (Simoni-Wastila, 1998), this may not be the case among physicians who specialize in mental illness—psychiatrists. Psychiatrists may be less vulnerable than primary care physicians to biases. One study showed that psychiatrists were equally likely to diagnose similar symptoms as depression in women and men and prescribed drugs and psychotherapy with equal frequency to women and men (Olfson et al., 2001). Conduct Do Gender 13.1 to see if your

DO GENDER 13.1
Is This Depression?

Create a description of a depressed person. Make the symptoms subtle. Do not say the person is depressed. Use items from Tables 13.1 and 13.2 to help you. Create two versions of this description, one with a female name and one with a male name. Randomly distribute one of the two versions to 20 people. Ask each respondent to identify the person's problem.

Compare the percentages of people who identify depression in the female and male vignettes.

peers are predisposed to identify depression in a female more than a male.

Response Bias

Because depression is diagnosed based on the information people provide about themselves, there may be a response bias on the part of women and men that contributes to the sex difference in depression. A common concern is that men are less likely than women to report depression because depression is inconsistent with the male gender role. The term *depression* has feminine connotations; it implies a lack of self-confidence, a lack of control, and passivity—all of which contradict the traditional male gender role. Sex differences in attitudes toward depression appear by early adolescence. A study of eighth graders showed that boys said that they would be less willing than girls to use mental health services for emotional problems and viewed people who sought mental health services as weird and weak (Chandra & Minkovitz, 2006). Attitudes toward the use of mental health services becomes more positive with age, but the sex difference remains (Gonzales, Alegria, & Prihoda, 2005; MacKenzie, Gekoski, & Knox, 2006). In a study of nearly 5,000 people in Israel, women were more likely than men to seek the help of a mental health care professional for mental health problems (Levinson & Ifrah, 2010). The sex difference among adults also seems to be limited to Whites; Hispanic and African American males and females have more similar attitudes to mental health problems.

One reason that men might be less willing than women to report depression is that they are concerned that others will view them negatively. This concern has some basis in fact. In a national survey, both women and men reported they were less willing to interact with a male than a female with mental health problems, including depression (Schnittker, 2000).

I have suggested a couple of reasons why men might want to deny being depressed. Is there evidence that men do, in fact, underreport depression? An older experimental study showed that men are leery of admitting depressive symptoms. As shown in Figure 13.3, men were more likely to endorse depressive items on an instrument labeled "hassles" than an instrument labeled "depression" (Page & Bennesch, 1993). The label did not affect women's reports of depression.

A more subtle response bias on the part of men is that they may be less likely than women to realize they are depressed or to interpret their symptoms as depression. In other words, men may fall victim to the same kind of clinician bias just discussed. Men might perceive depression as a female problem and

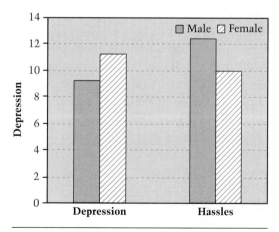

FIGURE 13.3 Effects of questionnaire label on self-report of depression. Men were more likely to report symptoms of depression on a questionnaire that was labeled "hassles" rather than "depression." The label attached to the questionnaire did not influence women's reports of depressive symptoms. *Source*: Adapted from S. Page and Bennesch (1993).

be unlikely to associate ambiguous symptoms with depression. I once interviewed a man following coronary bypass surgery who complained of a lack of energy, a loss of interest in leisure activities, and a desire to stay in bed all day. He was perplexed by these symptoms but completely denied any feelings of depression on a questionnaire I administered. Thus men may underreport their depression because they do not recognize depressive symptoms.

Different Manifestations of Depression

One difficulty in examining sex differences in depression, or any other disorder, is that symptoms of depression may differ for women and men. This is a general problem associated with the classification of many mental illnesses (Winstead & Sanchez, 2005). Most mental health problems seem to be more prevalent in one sex than the other, raising concerns about whether there is an actual sex difference in prevalence or if the disorder is described in ways that make it seem one sex is more likely to experience it than the other. If one eliminated disorders from the *DSM-IV-TR* for which there are sex differences in prevalence, the majority of the disorders would be removed. For example, histrionic personality disorder is more common among women than men. In an earlier version of the manual used to diagnosis this disorder (the *DSM-III-R*), a feature of the disorder was "overconcern with physical attractiveness." There was some concern that this feature biased the disorder in favor of women. In the most recent version of the manual (*DSM-IV-TR*), this feature was changed to "physical appearance draws attention to the self." Undoubtedly, this change in wording reduced the extent to which the disorder was linked to women. However, the change in wording also altered

the actual feature of the disorder. If a feature of a disorder is linked to gender roles, should it be altered so it is equally endorsed by both sexes? We certainly would not change the features of medical illnesses such as prostate cancer or breast cancer so they are equally represented among both men and women. You may recall from Chapter 10 that heart disease is manifested differently among women and men. Men are more likely than women to experience classic chest pain, and women are more likely than men to experience shortness of breath. However, as Winstead and Sanchez (2005) point out, in this case, the underlying disease—heart disease—is the same among men and women. With psychiatric disorders there is no underlying disease (to date!) that can be objectively measured independently of symptom reports.

With respect to depression, some people argue that women and men are equally "distressed" but manifest it in different ways. A study of male and female twins showed differences in symptoms of depression (Khan et al., 2002). Females reported more fatigue, excessive sleepiness, and slowed speech and body movements, and males reported more insomnia and agitation. A study of depressed adolescents showed that females reported more guilt, body dissatisfaction, self-blame, feelings of failure, and difficulties concentrating compared to males (Bennett et al., 2005). The latter items could be linked to rumination (discussed later in the chapter), whereas the other items seem to reflect greater links to self-esteem difficulties in females. Find out if your peers perceive depression differently among women and men in Do Gender 13.2.

The idea that some items are more likely to be associated with a trait, such as depression, among men versus women is referred to as **differential item functioning**. For example, crying is a depression item

DO GENDER 13.2
Perceptions of
Depression in Women and Men

Interview five people. Ask each of them to describe how they identify depression in a series of people, for example, their partner, a parent, a sibling, a friend, a work associate, and a stranger. Be sure to record the sex of each of these target people. On average, do people perceive depression differently when it is displayed by a female versus a male?

that may be susceptible to differential item functioning. That is, crying is a symptom of depression that characterizes women more than men, even when women and men are equally depressed. This item could cause depression to be overdiagnosed in women. Recent research, however, argues against differential item functioning, noting that the items on depression inventories seem to be related to each other in similar ways for females and males (Leach, Christensen, & Mackinnon, 2008).

Other investigators argue that women and men manifest depressive symptoms in completely different ways and that male depression is not tapped by existing instruments. Supporters of this view argue that women display symptoms of depression, such as sadness, lethargy, and crying, whereas men are more likely to turn to alcohol when depressed. Depression is more likely to be related to alcohol problems in males than females (Marcus et al., 2008).

The idea that alcohol and drug problems are manifestations of depression in men is not easily refuted. In some sense, the reasoning is circular because depression ends up being defined as whatever mental health problems that women and men exhibit. Even if men and women do manifest distress in different ways, we can still ask why women are more depressed than men and why men have more problems with alcohol than women. I now turn to the different theories that have been developed to account for sex differences in depression.

TAKE HOME POINTS

■ Sex differences in depression among clinic populations may be exaggerated to the extent that physicians overdiagnose depression in women and underdiagnose depression in men.

■ Sex differences in depression among community populations may be exaggerated to the extent that men are less willing than women to admit or recognize symptoms of depression.

■ There is some evidence that people respond more negatively to depression in men than in women.

■ It is possible that women and men are equally distressed, but that they manifest distress in different ways. Women may show symptoms of depression, and men may have alcohol problems.

THEORIES OF DEPRESSION

Sex differences in depression can be understood by distinguishing between two sets of factors: susceptibility factors and precipitating factors (Radloff & Rae, 1979). **Susceptibility factors** are innate, usually biological, factors that place women at greater risk for depression than men. Hormones or genes unique to women would be susceptibility factors. Gender-role socialization, however, also could be a susceptibility factor. If we learn women are socialized in different ways than men that make them more at risk for depression, their learning history would be a susceptibility factor. **Precipitating factors** are environmental events that trigger depression. If certain environmental factors induce depression—and women face them more than men—such as poverty or high relationship strain, depression might be triggered more in women than in men.

One fact that any theory of sex differences in depression must take into consideration is that sex differences in depression do not appear until adolescence. Before age 13 or 14, boys and girls are equally depressed or boys are more likely than girls to be depressed (Twenge & Nolen-Hoeksema, 2002). This fact suggests that any theory of sex differences in depression must take one of three forms

(Nolen-Hoeksema & Girgus, 1994): (1) same cause but cause activated in females during adolescence, (2) different causes but female cause activated in adolescence, or (3) interactive theory, in which females have more of the cause than males and the cause is activated in adolescence. These three perspectives are shown in Figure 13.4, and there is some evidence for each (Seiffge-Krenke & Stemmler, 2002).

The **same cause theory** suggests that the same factor causes depression in both females and males, but that factor must increase during adolescence for females only. For example, imagine that a poor body image was equally associated with depression in girls and boys, but a poor body image increased among girls but not boys during adolescence.

The **different cause theory** says there are different causes of girls' and boys' depression, and only the cause of girls' depression

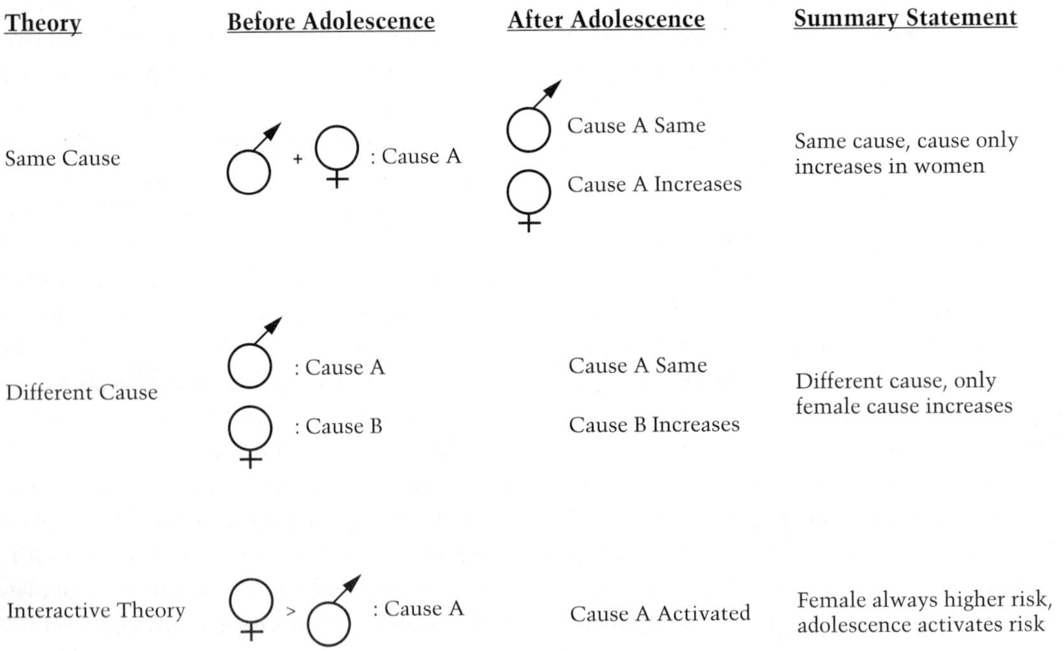

Theory	Before Adolescence	After Adolescence	Summary Statement
Same Cause	♂ + ♀ : Cause A	♂ Cause A Same ♀ Cause A Increases	Same cause, cause only increases in women
Different Cause	♂ : Cause A ♀ : Cause B	Cause A Same Cause B Increases	Different cause, only female cause increases
Interactive Theory	♀ > ♂ : Cause A	Cause A Activated	Female always higher risk, adolescence activates risk

FIGURE 13.4   The same cause, different cause, and interactive theories of depression.
Source: Adapted from Nolen-Hoeksema and Girgus (1994).

increases during adolescence. For example, imagine a poor body image is associated with depression among girls and being a poor athlete is associated with depression among boys. This theory could explain the emergence of sex differences in depression during adolescence if it were true that a negative body image (i.e., women's risk factor for depression) becomes more prevalent during adolescence, but poor athletic ability (i.e., men's risk factor for depression) does not change over time.

The **interactive theory** suggests being female always poses a risk for depression, but the events of adolescence activate that risk factor. For example, imagine females are more concerned than males with their relationships—before and after adolescence—and that unsatisfying relationships are more strongly related to girls' than boys' distress. Concern with relationships would be the "female risk factor." This concern could interact with events likely to occur during adolescence such as interpersonal conflict. Because females are more relationship focused than males, girls will be more likely than boys to react to interpersonal conflict with depression.

In sum, these theories suggest either that the cause of depression is the same for men and women, that there are different causes for male and female depression, or that environmental factors interact with predisposing factors to predict depression. Each of the theories that follow supports one of these perspectives.

Biology

Genes.   There is undoubtedly a genetic influence on depression (Mosing et al., 2009). The question is whether this genetic risk accounts for the sex difference. If there is a genetic explanation for the sex difference in depression, we would expect the depression risk factor to lie on the X chromosome. That being the case, we would predict that depressed fathers would be more likely to pass on their depressive gene to daughters than sons because fathers give daughters their X chromosome and sons their Y chromosome. However, more father–son pairs are depressed than father–daughter pairs (Nolen-Hoeksema, 1987). It is also the case that females have higher rates of depression than males among other-sex twins (Takkinen et al., 2004). Thus, sex-linked genes alone cannot explain depression.

Because genes are present at birth, a genetic theory of depression has difficulty explaining the emergence of depression in females during adolescence. Genetic theories would have to suggest that women are at risk for depression and the events of adolescence interact with that risk. One study that evaluated 8- to 20-year-old monozygotic and dizygotic twins showed that some genetic effects are activated around the age of puberty, partly supporting this theory (Kendler, Gardner, & Lichtenstein, 2008). However, other genetic effects seemed to wane over time. Genetic factors may interact with psychological variables to increase depression. A five-day study in which female twins were prompted throughout the day to complete measures of stress and negative affect showed that the relation of stress to negative affect was stronger for monozygotic twins than dizygotic twins, especially if there was a history of depression (Wichers et al., 2007). Wichers and colleagues concluded that there was a genetic contribution to reactions to daily stressors.

Hormones.   In contrast to genes, hormones change over the life span, and there is a great deal of hormonal fluctuation during adolescence when sex differences in depression emerge. Thus hormones would seem to be an ideal explanation for the sex difference in depression. However, no consistent evidence supports the theory that the changes in hormones during puberty are associated with the onset of depression in adolescent females (Nolen-Hoeksema & Girgus, 1994). Hormones may interact with other environmental factors, supporting the interactive theory of depression. For example, some research suggests that hormonal changes during puberty alter the way the body responds to stress in females (Stroud et al., 2004).

Aside from the hormonal changes that occur during puberty, researchers have attempted to link hormonal changes at other times in women's lives to depression. Fluctuations in women's hormones, in particular estrogen, prior to menstruation and after the birth of a child are related to depression, but these effects are not nearly large enough to account for the sex difference in depression. One study observed that depression increased as women transitioned through menopause and then decreased after menopause (Freeman et al., 2006). These changes in hormones were associated with the increase in depression that occurred during menopause. However, another study was unable to link the decline in estrogen in the elderly to depression (Erdincler et al., 2004). In sum, it has been difficult to link increases in female hormones to depression. It seems more likely that a general pattern of hormonal fluctuation is related to depression.

Some research has focused on the protective effects of male hormones, specifically testosterone, in regard to depression. However, even that relation is not a simple one. In one study, testosterone showed a curvilinear relation to depression, such that people with extremely low or extremely high levels of testosterone were depressed (Booth, Johnson, & Granger, 1999). The relation of high testosterone to depression appeared to be accounted for by its relation to antisocial behavior. High-testosterone men were more likely to engage in antisocial behavior, which was linked to depression. This research is consistent with the idea that men and women manifest depression in different ways. In this study, low testosterone levels were associated with the more stereotypical female form of depression, whereas high levels were associated with the more stereotypical male form of distress—acting-out behavior.

A more recent theory of hormonal influences on depression has focused on oxytocin. Oxytocin increases during puberty and has been shown to promote affiliative behavior (Campbell, 2010). In experimental research, the administration of intranasal oxytocin increased trust during a game with a stranger (Kosfeld et al., 2005), maintained trust when it was violated (Baumgartner et al., 2008), increased generosity (Zak, Stanton, & Ahmadi, 2007), and improved the recognition of happy faces (Marsh et al., 2010). Likewise, displays of affiliative behavior, such as touch, have been associated with the release of oxytocin (Holt-Lunstad, Birmingham, & Light, 2008).

Affiliative behavior, however, should not lead to depression. But, affiliative behavior could interact with some of the events during adolescence to place women at risk for depression. Specifically, changes in oxytocin regulation during puberty may cause females to be more reactive to interpersonal stressors (Klein, Corwin, & Ceballos, 2006). Research has linked oxytocin to relationship difficulties (Taylor et al., 2006; Taylor, Saphire-Bernstein, & Seeman, 2010). However, the direction of the relation is not clear. Do high levels of oxytocin cause greater relationship difficulties, or do relationship difficulties lead to elevated levels of oxytocin?

Thus, it appears that interpersonal stress increases oxytocin, which then promotes affiliative behavior and prosocial behavior, both of which could reduce distress. So, how does oxytocin enter into the relation to depression? More recently, it has been found that dysregulated patterns of oxytocin are associated with depression. When levels of oxytocin in the blood were measured in depressed and nondepressed women during two tasks, depressed women showed greater variability in oxytocin than nondepressed women (Cyranowski et al., 2008).

The Brain.   More recently, researchers have examined whether structural or functional differences in women's and men's brains contribute to sex differences in depression. There is some evidence that women and men use different regions of the brain to process emotional stimuli (Robison & Shankman, 2008). When a sad mood was induced among men and women, brain scans revealed greater specificity in brain activation for males than females (Schneider et al., 2000), suggesting that negative emotions might be processed in a more diffuse way among females.

Taken collectively, biological factors alone are not sufficient to explain sex differences in depression. However, more research is needed on this issue. Hormones, in particular, may play a role, but their effect is not a direct one. The role of oxytocin in depression is a promising avenue of research. Hormones probably have their greatest explanatory power when they are examined within the context of environmental events. Research on the brain is relatively new and also may help to identify biological underpinnings of depression in women and men.

Learned Helplessness

Learned helplessness is the sense of giving up because we perceive that nothing can be done to alter a situation. If you have ever studied long hours for a class without improving your grade, you might have experienced learned helplessness. Learned helplessness is the product of three events (Seligman, 1992). First, we learn an outcome is beyond our control; second, we respond by giving up or ceasing to respond; third, we generalize this response to new situations—perceive that future responses cannot influence future outcomes. A model of learned helplessness is shown in Figure 13.5. According to the model, the chain of events is set into motion by an environmental event rather than by a characteristic of the perceiver. That is, something happens to lead to the perception of uncontrollability. For example, you exercise daily and eat a healthy diet for six months without losing any weight. Or, with each passing quiz, you increase your studying but your grade declines. After the

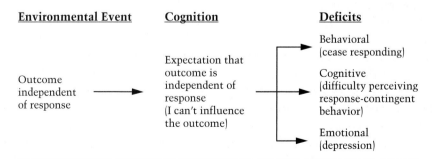

FIGURE 13.5   A model of learned helplessness. An environmental event leads to a cognition, which produces behavioral, cognitive, and emotional deficits. *Source*: Adapted from Seligman (1992).

environmental event occurs, you develop the expectation that future responses will not influence the outcome. This leads to the behavior of giving up. Recall your own experiences of learned helplessness in Do Gender 13.3.

Is there any evidence that women are more susceptible than men to learned helplessness? Some evidence suggests women receive more "helplessness training" than men. Women are more likely to find themselves in situations in which they do not have control, partly due to their lower status. During childhood, girls learn they cannot influence boys, which is one reason girls play with other girls rather than with boys (Maccoby, 1998). As discussed in Chapter 6, girls receive less attention from teachers, which may teach them that they can do little to influence their environment. The power differential in heterosexual relationships undermines females' sense of control (Chonody & Siebert, 2008). In a study of 1,000 community residents, women scored lower on feelings of control than men did, and reduced feelings of control were associated with depression (Nolen-Hoeksema, Larson, & Grayson, 1999). The female stereotype

---

DO GENDER 13.3
Personal Experience of
Learned Helplessness

Review the model of learned helplessness in Figure 13.5. Think about a time when you exerted a response over and over again and found it had no effect on the outcome. Did you give up? After how long? Why? What were the effects of this experience? Specifically, did this lead you to give up on subsequent tasks—related or unrelated to the present one? What were the short-term effects? The long-term effects?

---

includes passivity, dependence, and needing others' protection, all of which undermine feelings of personal control.

The learned helplessness theory of depression is supported by the fact that other demographic variables associated with a lack of control are associated with depression, such as education. The relation of low education to higher depression is stronger among women than men (Ross & Mirowsky, 2006), possibly due to the fact that women with low education suffer from two sources of low status and lack of control—being female and lacking education. As shown in Figure 13.6, the sex difference in depression is much larger among those with lower levels of education and disappears among those with a college degree and higher. Thus, one reason that increased education decreases women's rates of depression is that it enhances their sense of control.

Overall, the learned helplessness theory of depression is appealing, but there are not good studies that directly test whether this theory accounts for sex differences in depression. The evidence is largely circumstantial.

Coping

Coping refers to the different strategies that we use to manage stressful events and the accompanying distress associated with them. If your girlfriend breaks up with you, you may go talk to a friend about it, you may wallow in self-pity, you may try to figure out what happened, or you may decide to go swimming to take your mind off things. All of these represent different ways of coping.

One distinction that has been made in the literature is between emotion-focused coping and problem-focused coping (Lazarus & Folkman, 1984). **Problem-focused coping** refers to attempts to alter the stressor itself. Finding a solution to the problem, seeking the advice of others as to how to solve the

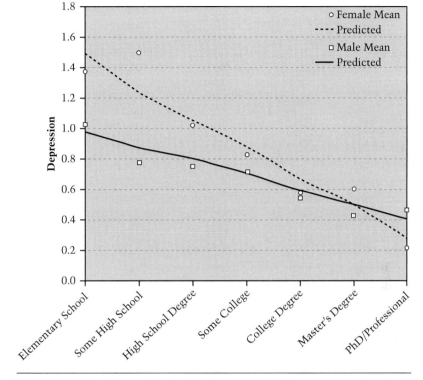

FIGURE 13.6   Rates of depression for women and men across educational level. The figure depicts the actual means for females and males at each education level as well as the regression lines showing the predicted means. The sex difference in depression is large among those with lower levels of education and disappears among those with a college degree and higher.
Source: Ross and Mirowsky (2006).

problem, and coming up with a plan to approach the problem are all problem-solving methods. **Emotion-focused coping** refers to ways in which we accommodate ourselves to the stressor. There are a variety of emotion-focused coping strategies that are quite distinct from one another. Distracting oneself from the stressor, avoiding the problem, and denying the problem's existence are all ways we change our reaction to the stressor rather than altering the stressor itself. Talking about the problem to relieve distress, accepting the problem, and putting a positive spin on the problem are also emotion-focused ways of coping.

Investigators frequently suggest that women cope with stressful events by engaging in emotion-focused strategies and men cope by engaging in problem-focused strategies. Although the conceptual distinction between problem-focused coping and emotion-focusing coping is a useful one, this distinction may be less useful when studying gender. When coping strategies are placed into these two broad categories, sometimes expected sex differences appear (i.e., women are more emotion focused, men are more problem focused), sometimes no sex differences appear, and sometimes sex differences appear in the opposite direction (i.e., women are more problem focused). The broad categories of emotion-focused coping and problem-focused coping average across distinct coping strategies, and only some of these may show sex differences. For example, researchers hypothesize that men are more likely than women to engage in problem-focused coping but one primary problem-focused coping strategy is to seek the advice of others. And, we know women are more likely than men to seek out others for help. People can seek different kinds of help, however. If people seek others' advice, they are engaging in problem-focused coping; if people seek out others in order to express feelings, they are engaging in emotion-focused coping. In the latter case, the person is trying to reduce distress rather than alter the stressor. Researchers do not always distinguish between these two kinds of support-seeking strategies. However, it is possible that women are more likely than men to do both.

Thus to evaluate sex differences in coping, it is important to turn to specific coping strategies. Examples of specific kinds of coping are shown in Table 13.3.

Specific Coping Strategies. Partly in response to the issues raised earlier—specifically that people seem to think men engaged in problem-focused coping and women engaged in emotion-focused coping—my colleagues and I conducted a meta-analytic review of the literature on sex comparisons in coping (Tamres, Janicki, & Helgeson, 2002). We showed that women were more likely than men to engage in nearly all the coping strategies, both problem focused and emotion focused. The sizes of these sex differences were small, however. The largest differences appeared for positive self-talk (i.e., encouraging oneself), seeking support, and

TABLE 13.3   SAMPLES OF COPING STRATEGIES

Distraction	I read a book or watch TV to take my mind off the problem.
Self-blame	I blame myself for what happened.
Denial	I pretend the problem does not exist.
Wishful thinking	I wish the problem would go away.
Seek social support	I find someone to talk to about the problem.
Positive reappraisal	I try to look on the bright side of things.
Problem-focused or Active coping	I figure out what to do to solve the problem.
Planning	I make a plan of action to approach the problem.

rumination—all in the direction of women more than men. Notice that each of these strategies involves the expression of feelings, either to oneself or to someone else.

One difficulty in interpreting the literature on gender and coping is that women may report more of all kinds of coping simply because women are more distressed than men, and more distressed people try a greater range of strategies. We found some support for this idea in the meta-analysis. We argued that sex differences in coping would be better understood by an examination of **relative coping**, which refers to how likely men or women are to use one strategy compared to another. Instead of comparing the frequency with which women and men engage in a specific kind of coping, we compare the frequency with which women engage in one coping strategy compared to another strategy and the frequency with which men engage in one coping strategy compared to another strategy. Within the range of coping responses, are men relatively more likely to use a strategy compared to women? For example, imagine both women and men report engaging in problem-focused coping with equal frequency: "some of the time." For men, this may be the most frequently employed strategy, whereas women may report engaging in other strategies "almost all of the time." In that case, men would engage in problem-focused coping relatively more often than women. Our meta-analysis showed that men engage in *relatively* more active coping strategies, and women engage in *relatively* more support seeking strategies.

More recent research has shown that females and males tend to engage in a similar amount of most coping strategies with a couple of exceptions consistent with the research mentioned earlier. A study of couples coping with cancer showed that women were more likely than men to engage in only one coping strategy—seeking emotional support (Ptacek, Pierce, & Ptacek, 2007). A study of elderly hemodialysis patients showed that women were more likely to seek support and to express emotions than men, whereas men were more likely than women to engage in avoidant coping (Yeh et al., 2009). A study of coping in nearly 2,000 children and adolescents showed that girls were more likely to seek support and problem-solve than boys (Eschenbeck, Kohlmann, & Lohaus, 2007). The sex difference in support seeking was larger among older than younger students, largely because support seeking declined in males with increased age. One study of children and adolescents showed that boys were more likely than girls to engage in avoidant coping (Eschenbeck et al., 2007), whereas another study showed that girls were more likely than boys to engage in avoidant coping (Kort-Butler, 2009). An examination of relative coping might reconcile these disparate findings. Thus, the sex difference in

support seeking seems to be clear and robust, whereas the sex difference in avoidant coping is open to debate.

Moving beyond self-reports of coping strategies, brain imaging research has shown that coping strategies may operate differently for females and males. One study examined how women's and men's brains respond during positive reappraisal (McRae et al., 2008). Positive reappraisal is a common coping strategy in which one tries to find something good in the bad. Women and men were shown a series of negative pictures and asked to engage in positive reappraisal while in a brain scanner. Although both women and men reported a reduction in negative affect when engaging in positive reappraisal, their brains responded somewhat differently. Women had greater increases in activity in areas of the brain associated with reappraisal (prefrontal region) and reward (ventral striatal region) than men, suggesting that women engage in more effort when reappraising than men. These findings may suggest that women engage in greater coping effort than men or that the specific coping strategy of positive reappraisal is more difficult for women than men. We will learn much about gender and coping with future studies like this one.

Tend and Befriend. Historically, the general response to stress has been described as "fight or flight." However, Taylor and colleagues (2000) argued that this response may apply only to men, and that women's response to stress may be better understood as "tend and befriend." What is the evidence for this hypothesis? We have seen that one of the most consistent sex differences in coping is that women seek the support of others, which is consistent with the tend and befriend idea. We also have some evidence that men may engage in more avoidant coping or distraction, consistent with "flight," and it is clear that men are more physically aggressive than women, consistent with "fight."

Taylor and colleagues (2000) argue that women's response to stress may have biological underpinnings. In particular, they emphasize the role of oxytocin, which may inhibit the flight response and encourage the tending to relationships in women. As discussed earlier in the chapter, oxytocin promotes affiliative behavior and may calm us down during times of stress.

Although this theory explains why women may cope differently with stress than men, it does not explain why women are more depressed than men. The tend and befriend idea, however, does suggest women will be more involved in relationships than men. To the extent that relationships are a source of stress (an idea expanded on later in this chapter), women's tendency to tend and befriend may have some negative outcomes.

Rumination.   A large program of research on sex differences in depression has focused on two specific kinds of coping strategies: rumination and distraction. Susan Nolen-Hoeksema (1987, 1994) has argued that women are more depressed than men because women respond to environmental stressors or to negative affect by talking about and trying to figure out their feelings—that is, rumination, whereas men respond by playing sports and by avoiding thoughts about the reasons for their feelings, that is, distraction. Nolen-Hoeksema and her colleagues argue (Nolen-Hoeksema, Wisco, & Lyubomirsky, 2008) that rumination increases depression in three ways, each of which is depicted in Figure 13.7. First, rumination impairs problem-solving, which inhibits instrumental behavior that could reduce depression. For example, if you are dwelling on a poor grade from a first exam, your distress may keep you from studying for the next exam, which ultimately will lead to another failure experience and further

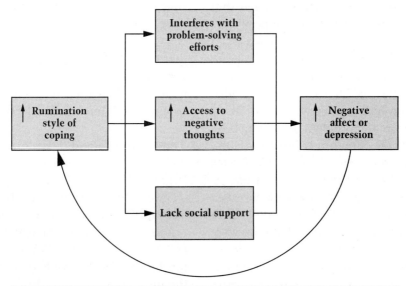

FIGURE 13.7   Model of Rumination and Depression. A ruminative style of coping leads to interference with problem-solving efforts, increased access to negative thoughts, and a lack of social support—all of which increase negative affect or depressive symptoms. Negative affect or depressive symptoms also lead to more ruminative coping.

depression. Second, rumination about negative feelings makes other negative feelings and negative memories more salient, which reinforces depression. After failing an exam, other failure experiences may become increasingly vivid. Third, rumination is associated with a lack of social support, which is associated with elevated rates of depression. Those who ruminate have difficulties with social network members and are perceived negatively by others, possibly because others become annoyed or frustrated with the person's perseverance on the problem. If the person then responds to increased depression by further rumination, the cycle is difficult to break. Sample rumination and distraction items from Nolen-Hoeksema's Responses to Depression Questionnaire are shown in Table 13.4.

Nolen-Hoeksema (1987) originally hypothesized that women were more likely than men to ruminate about their feelings and men were more likely than women to distract themselves. To date, the sex difference in rumination is well established but the sex difference in distraction is not (Rood et al., 2009). It is not

DO GENDER 13.4
Sex Differences in
Rumination and Distraction

Ask 10 women and 10 men to think about how they respond when they are depressed about an achievement-related failure (e.g., failing an exam) and a relationship-related failure (e.g., relationship breakup). You choose the two specific failure experiences. Then ask people how they responded to each failure experience by having them answer the items in Table 13.4.

Is there a sex difference in rumination and distraction? Does it depend on the situation? Is there another personality variable related to sex that is linked to rumination and distraction?

clear whether men are more likely than women to engage in distraction. See if there are sex differences in rumination and distraction at your school with Do Gender 13.4.

TABLE 13.4   NOLEN-HOEKSEMA'S RESPONSES TO DEPRESSION QUESTIONNAIRE

Sample Rumination Scale Items
 1. Think about how alone you feel.
 2. Think "I won't be able to do my job/work because I feel so badly."
 3. Think about your feelings of fatigue and achiness.
 4. Think about how sad you feel.
 5. Go away by yourself and think about why you feel this way.
 6. Write down what you are thinking about and analyze it.
 7. Analyze your personality and try to understand why you are depressed.
 8. Think "Why do I have problems other people don't have?"
 9. Think "What am I doing to deserve this?"
10. Think "Why do I always react this way?"

Sample Distraction Scale Items
 1. Help someone else with something in order to distract yourself.
 2. Remind yourself that these feelings won't last.
 3. Go to a favorite place to get your mind off your feelings.
 4. Concentrate on your work.
 5. Do something you enjoy.

Source: Nolen-Hoeksema and Morrow (1991).

What is the evidence that rumination leads to more depression, and distraction leads to less depression? A meta-analytic review of the literature showed that rumination is associated with current depression and predicts future depression (Rood et al., 2009). When baseline levels of depression are taken into consideration to see if rumination predicts changes in depression over time, the effect is smaller but remains significant. Rumination is more strongly linked to the onset of depression than the duration of depression (Nolen-Hoeksema et al., 2008). As for distraction, there is a small effect for distraction to be associated with lower levels of current depression but distraction does not predict changes in depression over time.

One concern that has been raised about the relation of rumination to depression is that some of the rumination items are confounded with depression. If you review the items in Table 13.4, you will see that the first four items involve ruminating about depression. That is, you are thinking about how depressed you feel. This makes the theory somewhat circular because in order to think about negative feelings, you have to have those negative feelings. When the items that overlapped with depression were removed from the scale, the remaining items formed two sets of traits: (1) reflective pondering (as indicated by items 5, 6, and 7) and (2) brooding (as indicated by items 8, 9, and 10; Treynor, Gonzales, & Nolen-Hoeksema, 2003). The brooding items were more predictive of depression than the reflective items, and brooding appears to explain the sex difference in depression. Females are more likely than males to brood, and brooding is associated with depression (Aldao, Nolen-Hoeksema, & Schweizer, 2010; Lopez, Driscoll, & Kistner, 2009).

Much of this research is quite compelling because it has been conducted in the field with people facing actual stressful life events; thus the research has good external validity. However, recall that the cost of field research is often a loss of internal validity. Is rumination an actual cause of depression? The reciprocal nature of the relation between rumination and depression shows that depression also causes rumination. One way to address the causal issue is to conduct an experiment in a controlled laboratory setting.

Just such an experiment was conducted and showed that inducing depressed people to ruminate increases their depression and inducing depressed people to distract reduces their depression (Lyubomirsky & Nolen-Hoeksema, 1993). Rumination and distraction were manipulated in the laboratory by having depressed and nondepressed college students either think about their feelings and why they are the kind of person they are (rumination condition) or think about external events (distraction condition). Among depressed students, rumination increased depressed mood and distraction reduced depressed mood. However, rumination and distraction had no effect on nondepressed students' moods. There was also evidence that the rumination manipulation interfered with the potential for instrumental behavior among depressed students. Depressed students who were induced to ruminate about themselves reported they were less likely to engage in a list of pleasant activities (e.g., go to dinner with friends, play favorite sport) than the other students.

Why are women more likely than men to ruminate in response to stressful events? One possibility is that people encourage women to ruminate. A behavioral observation study of adolescents and their mothers showed that mothers were more likely to encourage their 11-year-old girls than boys to engage in emotional expression when discussing a stressor (Cox, Mezulis, & Hyde, 2010).

This differential encouragement of emotional expression predicted greater female than male rumination four years later. In another study, sixth, seventh, and eighth graders responded to vignettes of men and women ruminating or distracting (Broderick & Korteland, 2002). Distraction was viewed as more appropriate for males than females, and rumination was viewed as more appropriate for females than males. People might encourage women to ruminate because they do not believe it is maladaptive—at least for women. When I ask students in my classes why they think that women live longer than men, one of the first responses (usually from a female) is that women think about their feelings and talk about their feelings while men keep their emotions bottled up inside. This answer may be partly correct, but it is also partly incorrect in a very important way. When thinking about their feelings becomes brooding, there are costs to health for women.

Given that women are more likely than men to ruminate and rumination is related to depression, does rumination explain the sex difference in depression? The causal sequence between rumination and depression was identified in a study of over 1,200 adolescents (Jose & Brown, 2008). The sex difference in rumination appeared at age 12 and the sex difference in depression appeared at age 13, suggesting that rumination precedes depression. A study of 11- to 13-year-olds showed that rumination predicted an increase in depression over seven months and accounted for the sex difference in depression (Hilt, McLaughlin, & Nolen-Hoeksema, 2010).

Rumination appears to be an interactive cause of sex differences in depression, as Nolen-Hoeksema (1994) originally suggested. Females are more likely than males to ruminate even before adolescence, but the negative events that occur to females during adolescence make their ruminative response more detrimental. These negative events include troublesome body changes, difficulties in relationships, and awareness of the limits of the female gender role (i.e., role inconsistent with independence and achievement). These difficulties are addressed in the section on adolescence and depression.

A related construct that we addressed in Chapter 8 is co-rumination—a repetitive and ruminative discussion of a problem with a friend. Like rumination, females engage in co-rumination more than males. One study of college students showed that co-rumination with the closest friend explained part of the reason that females were more depressed than males but also part of the reason females were more satisfied with their friendships than males (Calmes & Roberts, 2008). Similarly, a study of urban African American adolescents showed that this coping style explained part of why girls were more distressed than boys (Carlson & Grant, 2008). Thus, co-rumination is a double-edged sword for females—it draws them closer to their friends but at the expense of increase in psychological distress.

Private Self-Consciousness.   Private self-consciousness, or attending to one's inner thoughts and feelings, is typically considered a personality trait rather than a way of coping. Because self-awareness or self-consciousness is so closely linked to rumination, I discuss it here. Sample items from the private self-consciousness scale are "I'm always trying to figure myself out" and "I generally pay attention to my inner feelings" (Fenigstein, Scheier, & Buss, 1975).

There is no strong evidence for a sex difference in private self-consciousness. Early studies in this area showed no sex differences in private self-consciousness (Fenigstein et al.,

1975), one more recent study showed a sex difference (Sethi & Nolen-Hoeksema, 1997), and one did not (Flory et al., 2000). However, even if there is not an overall sex difference in private self-consciousness, there could be a sex difference in the tendency to react to environmental events by engaging in private self-consciousness. That is, private self-consciousness could be an interactive theory of depression. In an experience sampling study where women and men were beeped periodically via palm pilots, private self-consciousness was more strongly associated with negative affect after negative social interactions for women than men (Flory et al., 2000).

Other research has shown that women may be more vulnerable than men to situational cues that evoke private self-consciousness. A meta-analysis of self-report studies of private self-consciousness and mirror manipulations to induce private self-consciousness showed that the link of private self-consciousness to negative affect and self-blame was stronger for women than men (Fejfar & Hoyle, 2000). In sum, the tendency to engage in private self-consciousness provides an explanation for sex differences in depression, partly due to its overlap with rumination. It is also an interactive theory of depression because it predicts that women are more likely than men to respond to certain cues by becoming introspective.

Stressful Life Events

One reason that women may be more depressed than men is that women experience more traumatic or stressful life events. Although women suffer higher rates of post-traumatic stress disorder than men (Olff et al., 2007), this does not mean that women face more trauma than men. A meta-analysis of sex differences in traumatic events found that men experienced more trauma than women (Tolin & Foa, 2006). This sex difference depended greatly on the nature of the trauma. Whereas women were 6 times as likely as men to report adult sexual assault and 2.5 times as likely as men to report child sexual assault, men were 3.5 times as likely to experience combat/war/terrorism and over 1.5 times as likely to experience nonsexual assault.

Just as we distinguished between major depressive disorder and depressive symptoms, we can also distinguish between traumatic life events (e.g., sexual assault, disaster) and stressful life events (e.g., job loss, divorce, relationship problems, financial difficulties). A meta-analytic review of the literature on sex differences in stressful life events showed that across 119 studies there was a small tendency for females to report more stressful events than males ($d = +.12$; Davis, Matthews, & Twamley, 1999). The size of this effect is extremely small, and a number of variables influenced the size of the relation. One factor that influenced the effect size was how stress was measured. Researchers who study stressful life events typically ask respondents to indicate whether an event happened and/or to rate the level of stress associated with an event. That is, ratings are made of *stress exposure* and *stress impact*. When these two kinds of ratings were distinguished from one another in the meta-analysis, the sex difference in exposure was smaller than the sex difference in impact ($d = +.08$ vs. $d = +.18$). Thus, women may appraise stressors as more severe than men, but women and men do not necessarily experience a different number of stressors. The age of the sample also influenced the size of the relation. The sex difference in stress was larger among adolescent samples compared to children and adult samples, supporting Nolen-Hoeksema's (1994) claim that adolescent females face more stress than adolescent males.

One reason the overall sex difference in exposure to stress is small may be that women and men experience stressors in different domains, just as they experience trauma in different domains. The meta-analysis examined whether sex differences appeared for different kinds of stressors. The sex difference for interpersonal stressors was larger than the sex difference for noninterpersonal stressors ($d = +.17$ vs. $d = +.07$). There was no category of stressor on which men scored higher than women.

A great deal of research on adolescents supports the meta-analysis finding that females report greater interpersonal stress than males. Females are exposed to more social stressors during adolescence than males (Rudolph, 2009). In a study of preadolescent (ages 8 to 12) and adolescent (ages 13 to 18) boys and girls, there was no sex difference in the total number of stressful events reported, but females reported greater interpersonal stress and males reported greater noninterpersonal stress—only among the older age group (Rudolph & Hammen, 1999). As shown in the left half of Figure 13.8, adolescent girls reported higher levels of interpersonal stress than preadolescent girls, preadolescent boys, or adolescent boys. As shown in the right half of Figure 13.8, adolescent boys experienced greater noninterpersonal stress than the other three groups. Other studies have shown that adolescent females report more relationship stressors, and adolescent males report more personal stressors (Murberg & Bru, 2004; Shih et al., 2006).

Thus it appears that the link of gender to trauma and stress has more to do with women and men experiencing different kinds

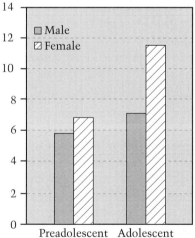
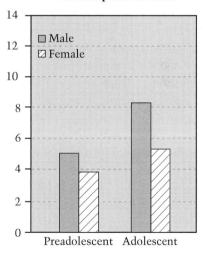

FIGURE 13.8 Sex comparisons of interpersonal and noninterpersonal stress among preadolescents and adolescents. Adolescent females reported higher levels of interpersonal stress compared to adolescent males and either group of preadolescents. Adolescent males reported higher noninterpersonal stress compared to adolescent females and either group of preadolescents. *Source*: Adapted from Rudolph and Hammen (1999).

of traumas and stressors rather than one sex experiencing more trauma or stress than the other. Women are more likely than men to report stressful events that involve relationships and actually occur to others. Although both of these events are sometimes referred to as relationship stressors, there is a difference. In the first case, investigators are finding that women are more likely to report problems within relationships, such as conflicts, breakups, or losses. In the second case, research is showing that women are more likely than men to perceive stressful events that occur to others as their own personal stressors. Further investigate the distinction between these two kinds of stressors with Do Gender 13.5.

Investigators have asked whether sex differences in depression are due to **differential exposure** to stressful events or **differential vulnerability** to stressful events. Differential exposure suggests that women are more depressed than men because they experience more of a certain kind of stressful event. We discussed the idea that females report more interpersonal stressors than males. Some major stressors that women experience more than men, such as poverty and sexual abuse, are associated with depression (Nolen-Hoeksema & Keita, 2003). Controlling for these events reduces the sex difference in depression, but does not eliminate it (Kessler, 2000). In fact, if all the stressful events were statistically controlled (not just the ones that affect women more than men), the sex difference in depression would be unchanged. Thus women are not more depressed than men because they simply experience more stressful events—or more of a certain kind of stressor.

Differential vulnerability implies that certain stressful events are more strongly associated with distress among women than men. There is a great deal of evidence to

DO GENDER 13.5
Sex Differences in
Stressful Life Events

Develop a list of stressful life events that are relevant to the population you are sampling. Classify these events into categories, such as personal events and relationship events. Have 10 women and 10 men:

1. Indicate if the event occurred to them in the previous year.

2. If the event occurred, have them rate how much the event affected them (none, a little bit, a lot).

3. Indicate if the event happened to someone they know in the previous year.

4. If the event occurred to someone else, rate how much the event personally affected them (none, a little bit, a lot).

Are there sex differences in exposure to different kinds of life events? Are there sex differences in exposure to events that occur to others? Are there sex differences in the magnitude of response to (impact of) personal events? Others' events?

support differential vulnerability on the part of females—especially in the case of interpersonal stressors. Studies of adolescents have shown that females respond more negatively than males to social stressors (Rudolph, 2009; Shih et al., 2006). A longitudinal study of 11-year-olds showed that relationship losses were associated with increases in depression three years later for both males and females but the associations were stronger for females (Bakker et al., 2010). Even a study of third graders showed that relationship problems were associated with an increase in depression three years later among girls but not boys (Rudolph, Ladd, & Dinella, 2007).

Better tests of this hypothesis have come from studies that use ecological momentary assessment (EMA) methods. EMA methods involve having respondents complete measures of stress at specified intervals or random intervals over the course of the day for several days or weeks. A study of eighth and tenth graders who completed measures of daily stress for a week showed that females reported more interpersonal stress and males reported more achievement stress (Hankin, Mermelstein, & Roesch, 2007). The relation of daily stress to depression one year later was stronger for females than males. It was interpersonal stress, however, that accounted for the sex difference in depression, providing evidence for differential vulnerability. A study of college students who completed measures of stress and depressed mood several times a day for a week showed that women were more reactive to stress than men—but only those without a history of depression (Husky et al., 2009). Among those with a history, men and women were equally reactive to stress.

Taken collectively, these studies show that the reason women are more depressed than men has less to do with the stressful events they face and more to do with how strongly they respond to those events. Women are especially affected by stressors that involve others. Why? This question is addressed next, when I examine the female gender role as an explanation of sex differences in depression.

The Female Gender Role

Communion and Agency. Trait measures of the female gender role are typically measured with communion scales of the BSRI (Bem Sex Role Inventory) or PAQ (Personal Attributes Questionnaire), which reflect a positive focus on others. These scales include traits such as being helpful, kind, and caring. Communion, however, is unrelated to depression (Hirokawa & Dohi, 2007). By contrast, agency, which includes traits such as independent, self-confident, and persistent, is related to lower levels of depression. Agency reflects a positive focus on and regard for the self. Increases in agency over adolescence are associated with decreases in depression (Priess, Lindberg, & Hyde, 2009). In addition, agency seems to influence the relation of communion to depression. Communion is associated with less depression among individuals who are high in agency, whereas communion is associated with more depression among individuals who are low in agency (Lam & McBride-Chang, 2007). The combination of high communion and low agency is similar to the construct of unmitigated communion, discussed in more detail next.

Thus there appears to be no data linking the female gender role trait of communion to depression. Instead, it seems that features of the male gender role (agency) protect against depression. However, gender roles are multifaceted. I argue there is an aspect of the female gender role related to depression: unmitigated communion.

Unmitigated Communion. Recall that *unmitigated communion* is defined as a focus on others to the exclusion of the self (Helgeson, 1994c; Helgeson & Fritz, 1998). Unmitigated communion has been associated with depression in studies of college students, cardiac patients, healthy adolescents, adolescents with diabetes, and healthy adults (Aube, 2008; Helgeson & Fritz, 1998; Hirokawa & Dohi, 2007; Jin et al., 2010). In addition, unmitigated communion can account for the sex difference in depression.

For example, in a study of adolescents with diabetes, unmitigated communion was more strongly related to depression than respondent's sex, and no sex differences in depression were noted once levels of unmitigated communion were considered (Helgeson & Fritz, 1996).

People who score high on unmitigated communion rely on others for self-esteem and internalize others' views of themselves. This makes the self-esteem of the unmitigated communion individual quite unstable and vulnerable. This external focus is critical to the link of unmitigated communion to depression (Dear & Roberts, 2002; Fritz & Helgeson, 1998). Consistent with this line of thinking, other research has shown that women are more likely to have "interpersonal contingent self-esteem," which means that they base their self-esteem on the quality of their relationships (Cambron, Acitelli, & Pettit, 2008). This instability appears to be a risk factor for depression in females but not males.

As shown in Figure 13.9, there are two explanations for the link of unmitigated communion to depression: self-neglect and overinvolvement in others' problems—both of which may stem from low self-esteem and an externalized self-perception (Fritz & Helgeson, 1998). Individuals who score high on unmitigated communion are afraid to assert their own needs, inhibit self-expression to avoid conflict, and don't take care of themselves when they are ill—all indicators of self-neglect. Second, people characterized by unmitigated communion become overly involved in others' problems and take on others' problems as their own. Unmitigated communion has been linked to reporting more interpersonal stressors (Helgeson & Fritz, 1996) and more stressful events that occurred to others (Fritz & Helgeson, 1998). There are several reasons for the connection of unmitigated communion to interpersonal stressors. First, unmitigated communion may be associated with exposure to more interpersonal stressors because such individuals seek out others to help. Second, the person who scores high on unmitigated communion may be more likely than other people to interpret another person's problem as his or her own. For example, two people may both be exposed to a neighbor going through a divorce, but only the unmitigated communion person defines this stressful event as her or his own personal stressor. Third, the intrusive behavior of the unmitigated communion person may lead to relationship difficulties, meaning that the personality creates the interpersonal stressors.

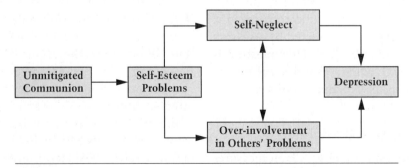

FIGURE 13.9   Model of the relation between unmitigated communion and depression.
Source: Adapted from Fritz and Helgeson (1998).

Unmitigated communion is also associated with rumination (Nolen-Hoeksema et al., 2008). However, the nature of the rumination may be more about other people's problems than one's own. Two laboratory studies showed that people high in unmitigated communion ruminate about others' problems (Fritz & Helgeson, 1998). In one study, a confederate disclosed a problem to the participant. In the second study, a friend disclosed a problem to the participant. Participants who scored high on unmitigated communion reported more intrusive thoughts about the discloser's problem two days later, whether the discloser was a friend or a stranger.

Consistent with the differential vulnerability hypothesis, some evidence suggests that people who score high on unmitigated communion are more reactive to interpersonal stress. Two studies of college students and one study of women with fibromyalgia have shown that interpersonal stress is more strongly related to distress among individuals high rather than low in unmitigated communion (Nagurney, 2007, 2008; Reynolds et al., 2006). Similar findings appeared in a study that measured a construct related to unmitigated communion, interpersonal sensitivity (how much feelings and behavior of others affect the self). In a study that involved 12 weekly phone calls with adult women who had osteoarthritis or rheumatoid arthritis, the relation of interpersonal stress to negative affect was stronger for those who scored high on interpersonal sensitivity (Smith & Zautra, 2002).

The vulnerability to interpersonal stress has implications for the self-neglect aspect of unmitigated communion. In a study of adolescents with diabetes, older adolescents (ages 15 to 18) who scored high on unmitigated communion reported being more upset by stressful events that involved others, more depression, and worse diabetes control (Helgeson & Fritz, 1996). Interpersonal stressors explained the link of unmitigated communion to increased depression and poor control over diabetes. Presumably, those characterized by unmitigated communion were taking care of others at the expense of taking care of themselves.

Caregiving

Aside from the personality trait of unmitigated communion, the caregiving aspect of the female gender role may be linked to depression. People characterized by unmitigated communion may be more likely to be caregivers; however, people can end up in the caregiver role regardless of their level of unmitigated communion. Events such as a spouse becoming ill, parents growing older and needing care, and children becoming sick can happen to anyone. A review of the literature on parents of children with cancer shows that mothers are more distressed than fathers (Clarke et al., 2009). It is not clear if these differences are due to a general sex difference in distress or to women being more distressed than men when they are caregivers. Women traditionally shoulder more of the burden of caregiving responsibilities than men. Caregiving is also more likely to lead to distress in women than in men. A longitudinal study of dual-earner couples who transitioned into caregiving showed that the transition led to a greater increase in distress among men than women (Chesley & Moen, 2006). One reason may be that some women decrease or cease employment when they become caregivers (Pavalko & Woodbury, 2000), whereas men are more likely to obtain assistance with caregiving (Yee & Schulz, 2000). In a meta-analytic review of the caregiving literature, women reported greater burden than men ($d = +.34$), greater depression than men ($d = +.34$), and a greater number of caregiving tasks than men ($d=+.20$; Pinquart & Sorensen, 2006). The sex difference in depression among caregivers was larger than the sex difference found in noncaregiving populations. In a more recent study of spouses of patients with Parkinson's disease, female spouses reported greater role strain and greater increases in role strain over 10 years than male spouses (Lyons et al., 2009).

It is the caregiving role that may explain why social ties are not as protective against depression among women as they are among men. Recall from Chapter 11 that social relations are a double-edged sword for women. Social ties are not only a source of support, but also a source of stress for women. One study showed that the number of social roles was directly related to fewer mental health problems among men but showed a curvilinear relation to mental health problems among women (Weich, Sloggett, & Lewis, 1998). That is, women with the fewest social roles and women with the most social roles had higher levels of mental distress. Women who have many social roles may find that the stressors to which they are exposed outweigh the support they receive.

- Women's tendency to ruminate interferes with instrumental behavior, increases access to other negative cognitions, and decreases social support, all of which have been linked to depression.

- Women may be more likely than men to respond to stressful events by becoming introspective — that is, privately self-conscious, a construct related to rumination.

- Women are more likely than men to experience relationship events and more vulnerable than men to the negative effects of relationship stressors. It is the latter that is most strongly linked to sex differences in depression.

- There are multiple aspects of the female gender role. Although communion is not related to depression, unmitigated communion is.

- People who score high on unmitigated communion become involved in others' problems to the neglect of themselves, both of which may increase women's risk for depression.

- Aside from unmitigated communion, women are more likely than men to find themselves in the caregiving role. Women report greater caregiver burden than men, increasing their risk of depression.

TAKE HOME POINTS

- Biological factors, including genes and hormones, most certainly contribute to depression but cannot alone explain the sex difference in depression.

- Females' low status in society may lead to lower perceptions of control. A lack of control could contribute to perceptions of helplessness, a precipitant of depression.

- It is not the case that men exhibit more problem-focused coping, and women exhibit more emotion-focused coping. Instead, there are specific coping styles related to sex. Women seek support and ruminate in response to stress more than men.

CHALLENGES OF ADOLESCENCE

Sex differences in depression begin to appear at around age 13, the time of transition from middle school to high school. Recall Figure 13.2 which showed that boys had slightly higher depression scores than girls below age 13, but that girls had higher scores than boys at age 13 and over (Twenge & Nolen-Hoeksema, 2002). Thus something must occur during adolescence to spark this sex difference in depression. Cyranowski and colleagues (2000) state, "Pubertal maturation sensitizes females to the depressogenic effects of negative life events" (p. 22). In this section of the chapter, I examine some of the challenges of adolescence that might lead to an increase in depression among young women.

Gender Intensification

Adolescence has been referred to as a time of **gender intensification** (Hill & Lynch, 1983), which means that gender roles and their associated norms become salient to females and males. During adolescence, girls become increasingly concerned with adhering to the female gender role and boys become increasingly concerned with adhering to the male gender role. These concerns arise in part from outside forces: Adolescents feel increasing pressure from society to adhere to their gender roles. I watched this happen before my very eyes as my t-shirt and blue jeans daughter (who scolded me for wearing makeup for years) started shaving her legs and had her ears pierced three weeks before her twelfth birthday and received makeup, perfume, and nail polish from friends as presents. The message is clear—it is time to look like a girl.

However, the evidence for gender intensification is not clear. A study that examined changes in masculinity (or agency) and femininity (or communion) among 11-, 13-, and 15-year-olds showed that girls scored higher than boys on communion at all assessments but neither communion scores nor the sex difference in communion changed over time (Priess et al., 2009). There was no sex difference in agency at any assessment. However, there may be other ways to measure gender intensification aside from tracking these traits. It may be more informative to examine specific behaviors, such as how girls and boys spend their time or how they interact with one another. A study of fifth, eighth, and twelfth graders showed that boys found it more difficult to share their feelings with others as age increased, whereas girls found it easier to share their feelings with others as age increased (Polce-Lynch et al., 1998). Here there is some evidence for gender intensification during adolescence.

Why would gender intensification lead to depression? Depression might be heightened among women who realize the limiting value of the female gender role. Although intelligence and achievement orientation in childhood or adolescence exert protective effects on men's mental health, these qualities may pose risks for women's mental health. Two older studies suggested that this was the case. IQ scores were associated with ambition, productivity, persistence, and self-satisfaction in young adult men (ages 18 and 23), but with introspection, anxiety, rumination, and guilt among young adult women (Block & Kremen, 1996). A longitudinal study showed that higher IQ scores during preschool predicted greater depression among female 23-year-olds, but less depression among males of the same age (Gjerde, 1995). These studies were conducted quite some time ago, however. It is important to determine whether high achievement still poses risks to mental health among adolescent females.

Puberty

Because the emergence of sex differences in depression coincides with puberty, researchers have investigated whether the physical changes that accompany puberty are associated with depression in women. Some research has shown that reaching puberty is associated with the sex difference in depression (Angold, Costello, & Worthman, 1998), whereas other research has shown that it is the timing of puberty. Reaching puberty early for one's age has been associated with depression in girls (Graber, Brooks-Gunn, & Warren, 2006). One way in which pubertal changes may be associated with depression is through their impact on adolescents' body image.

Body Image

Both differential exposure and differential vulnerability are relevant to the link between gender, body image, and depression. Adolescent and college-age females have a more negative body image than males (Ambwani & Strauss, 2007; Ata, Ludden, & Lally, 2007), and a negative body image predicts the onset of depression in females but not in males (Bearman & Stice, 2008). The nature of body concerns during adolescence differs for females and males. Females are concerned with losing weight, and males are concerned with gaining weight—especially in their upper body.

Girls not only are more dissatisfied with their bodies than boys, but also have a more distorted body image compared to boys. One study showed that boys were accurate in identifying the size of the male figure desired by girls, whereas girls identified a thinner female figure than what was actually desired by boys (Safir, Flaisher-Kellner, & Rosenmann, 2005).

Body image is not only influenced by sex but also by race and ethnicity. A meta-analysis of ethnic differences in body image revealed that White females are more dissatisfied with their bodies than females from other ethnic groups ($d = +.29$; Grabe & Hyde, 2006). However, the difference in body image depended upon which ethnic group was the subject of comparison. White and Hispanic women are more dissatisfied with their bodies than African American women, with Asian women falling in between. The sex difference in body dissatisfaction is smaller in Chinese than American children (Marsh et al., 2007).

It is not only body image but **body objectification** that is related to depression. Objectification theory states that there are social and cultural forces that sexually objectify

women, which lead women to continually monitor their bodies and evaluate themselves based on their appearance (Fredrickson & Roberts, 1997). Body objectification has been associated with depression among adolescent females and males but the relation is stronger in females (Grabe, Hyde, & Lindberg, 2007). In addition, the sex difference in body objectification seems to precede the sex difference in depression suggesting that body objectification may play a causal role in the increase in depression among girls.

The negative effects of body objectification have been demonstrated in experimental research. For example, in one study, college students were asked to unscramble a series of words to form sentences under one of three conditions (Roberts & Gettman, 2004). In one condition, some of the words reflected body competence (e.g., fitness, health, stamina); in a second condition, some of the words reflected body objectification (e.g., attractive, shapely, sexy); and in the last condition, the words were neutral (e.g., honesty, music, interesting). As shown in Figure 13.10,

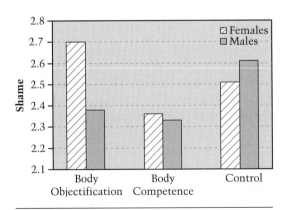

FIGURE 13.10   Women's feelings of shame increased relative to those of men in response to the body objectification prime compared to the body competence prime.

Source: Adapted from Roberts and Gettman (2004).

women's feelings of shame increased in the body objectification condition relative to the control condition and decreased in the body competence condition relative to the control condition. In another study, female college students completed brief questionnaires on hand-held computers multiple times a day for two weeks to assess the relation between body objectification and affect (Breines, Crocker, & Garcia, 2008). Daily self-objectification was related to greater negative affect—but this effect was limited to those whose self-esteem was linked to their appearance. Interestingly, one way to reduce body objectification in young women is to expose them to images of female athletes (Daniels, 2009). Assuming the female athlete is not sexually objectified, these images should enhance women's sense of confidence and competence. Unfortunately, there are times when women athletes are depicted as sexual objects. The depiction of Lindsey Vonn, a 2010 gold medalist skier, on the cover of *Sports Illustrated*, raised a furor as some viewers thought the picture was sexually provocative whereas others did not.

Among African Americans, body objectification may occur in relation to skin tone. Because darker skin tones are associated with more discrimination, African American females may be sensitive to their skin tone and monitor their body's skin tone. One study showed that the habitual monitoring of skin tone—a reflection of body objectification—was associated with body dissatisfaction among African American adults (Buchanan et al., 2008).

TAKE HOME POINTS

- Gender intensification suggests that gender-role norms become salient during adolescence. One reason that girls' depression may increase during adolescence is that they become aware of the limitations of the female gender role.

- A variety of events occur during adolescence—body image changes, challenges to relationships with parents and peers—that may pose a greater risk for depression among girls than boys.

- Girls not only have a poorer body image than boys but body image is more strongly related to depression among girls than boys. Girls are also more likely than boys to suffer from body objectification, a related cause of depression.

This concludes our examination of the theories of depression. There are a variety of other mental illnesses that are relevant to gender either because they afflict one sex more than another or because the characteristics of the disorder are relevant to gender roles. See Sidebar 13.2 for a discussion of some of these mental illnesses and Table 13.5 for a list of their gender-related features. Because there is a large sex difference in attention deficit hyperactivity disorder, I elaborate on it in Sidebar 13.3.

SIDEBAR 13.2: *Gender and Other Mental Illnesses*

In general, women are more likely to have higher rates of histrionic and dependent personality disorders, whereas men are more likely to have higher rates of schizoid, antisocial, and compulsive personality disorders (Winstead & Sanchez, 2005). Women have higher rates of what are referred to as *internalizing problems* (e.g., depression, anxiety), whereas men have higher rates of what are referred to as *externalizing problems* (e.g., substance abuse, antisocial disorders; Rosenfield & Smith, 2010). These differences hold across most cultures (Seedat et al., 2009). Here I review some of the specific mental illnesses for which gender plays a role. Most of the information described here is taken from the *Diagnostic and Statistical Manual of Mental Disorders* (4th ed. text revised; American Psychological Association, 2000).

Schizophrenia is a form of psychopathology. It is a form of psychosis that includes paranoia, delusions, hallucinations, disorganized speech, and flattened affect. There is a slightly higher incidence among men than women. Major symptoms differ for women and men. Women are more likely to show affective disturbances, paranoia, and hallucinations, whereas men are more likely to show flat affect and social withdrawal. The age of onset also differs. Men are at highest risk for schizophrenia between the ages of 18 and 25, whereas women are at highest risk between 25 and 35. The role of hormones may be implicated in female schizophrenia, as there is an increase in late-onset schizophrenia (after menopause) in women (Lewine & Seeman, 1995). The genetic component of schizophrenia is also stronger in women than men. A great deal of attention has focused on the brain to understand sex differences in schizophrenia. Some research shows that different hemispheres of the brain are affected in women and men (Purcell et al., 1998), and other research shows that there are differences in the brain structure of women and men (Guerguerian & Lewine, 1998).

Antisocial personality disorder is characterized by a disregard for others, breaking the law, aggression, deceit, manipulation, and lack of empathy. It is a diagnosis made among adults, and one feature of the disorder is that the individual must have a history of conduct disorder as a child. Conduct disorder includes aggression toward people or animals, destruction of property, and serious violation of rules. Both antisocial personality disorder and conduct disorder are much more common in men than women. The emphasis on aggression may account for some of its lower prevalence among women. The psychological and behavioral correlates of antisocial personality disorder are similar for women and men (Cale & Lilienfeld, 2002a, 2002b). For example, a history of sexual and physical abuse is predictive for both sexes.

Borderline personality disorder is characterized by unstable interpersonal relationships and maladaptive interpersonal functioning. Symptoms include fear of abandonment, low self-esteem, and impulsivity, including suicide attempts. About three quarters of the people diagnosed with this disorder are women. Among patients with borderline personality disorder, men and women show equal levels of impairment (Zlotnick, Rothschild, & Zimmerman, 2002).

Histrionic personality disorder includes excessive emotionality and attention seeking. People with this disorder may be dramatic, inappropriately sexually seductive, and use physical appearance to draw attention to themselves. Women are diagnosed with this disorder more than men. Clearly, gender-role stereotypes may play a role in this differential diagnosis. The same behavior in men may not be viewed as pathological. There is some support that among personality disorders, histrionic personality disorder is the female version and antisocial personality disorder is the male version. In a study of actors, psychopathology was more strongly correlated with histrionic personality disorder in females and antisocial personality disorder in males (Cale & Lilienfeld, 2002a, 2002b).

Dependent personality disorder is a disorder related to interpersonal functioning. People with this disorder are passive, indecisive without reassurance from others, and clingy and insecure in relationships, and want to be taken care of by others. Women are diagnosed with this disorder more than men. It is also one of the most frequently diagnosed personality disorders.

Narcissistic personality disorder is characterized by feelings of self-importance and superiority, inflation of abilities, entitlement, and a lack of empathy. More men than women are diagnosed with this disorder.

Panic disorder is characterized by recurrent panic attacks and concerns about future panic attacks. A panic attack is the presence of an intense fear without a basis in reality. Females are more likely than males to suffer from panic disorder. Sex role stereotypes could play a role here as women are encouraged to express their emotions more than men. When an experimental procedure was applied to induce symptoms of panic (i.e., inhalation of carbon dioxide), females and males had similar physiological responses but females reported less control, greater panic, and more fear during the task and shortly after the task than males (Kelly, Forsyth, & Karekla, 2006).

One concern with the sex differences in some of these disorders is that features of a particular disorder are perceived as more maladaptive in one sex than another. Borderline personality disorder is a good example. Being overly dependent, demanding, and having high rates of sexual activity may be viewed as more pathological among females than males (Nehls, 1998). To determine the validity of this concern, one study surveyed clinicians from the American Psychological Association (Anderson, Sankis, & Widiger, 2001). Clinicians were provided with a list of features of antisocial personality, borderline personality, histrionic personality, and narcissistic personality disorders and asked to rate either how rare each feature was in a particular person or how maladaptive the feature was in a particular person. Clinicians were randomly assigned to rate a male, a female, or a person whose sex was not specified. Although there were differences in the frequency with which clinicians ascribed features of personality disorders to females and males, there was no difference in the pathology of a given feature for females and males for any of the disorders. A similar study was performed with college students and showed that students rated dependent, depressive, and borderline symptoms as more maladaptive in females than males (Sprock, Crosby, & Nielsen, 2001). However, of 105 symptoms, only 8 were rated as differentially maladaptive in females versus males. Furthermore, it is probably more important that clinicians rather than college students do not perceive symptoms differently.

SIDEBAR 13.3: *Attention Deficit Hyperactivity Disorder—A Problem for Males Only?*

Males have higher rates of attention deficit hyperactivity disorder (ADHD) than females. The size of the difference depends on how it is measured (Cassidy, 2007). Among clinic samples, the male to female ratio ranges from 9:1 to 6:1. Among community samples, the difference is smaller but still sizable, on the order of 3:1. There are some sex similarities and differences in ADHD. ADHD is equally likely to be associated with mood disorders and family difficulties in girls and boys (Bauermeister et al., 2007). However, ADHD is more likely to be associated with school suspensions in boys than girls. This may be due to the fact that ADHD manifests itself differently in males and females. A meta-analytic review of the literature showed that females with ADHD have more intellectual impairment than males, but males with ADHD have more hyperactivity, externalizing behavior, and aggression (Gaub & Carlson, 1997). Boys with ADHD are more likely than girls to have problems at school and to have conduct disorders (Biederman et al., 2002). Three types of ADHD have been delineated: (1) inattentive, (2) hyperactive, and (3) combined—inattentive plus hyperactive. Some studies have shown that females are more likely than males to have the inattentive type (Cassidy, 2007), but other studies showed no sex differences (Ghanizadeh, 2009). If true, this would explain why boys are more likely than girls to be referred to clinics for ADHD—their behavior is more disruptive and attracts attention. Among adults, there does not seem to be a sex difference in subtypes (Rasmussen & Levander, 2009). ADHD in young children (ages 4–6) predicts subsequent mental health problems, such as anxiety and depression, in adolescence—more so for females than males (Lahey et al., 2007).

TABLE 13.5 PERSONALITY DISORDERS

Antisocial	Men more than women
—disregard for others	
—breaking the law	
—aggression	
—lack of empathy	
—deceitful	
—impulsive	
—irresponsible	
Borderline	Women more than men
—unstable interpersonal relationships	
—maladaptive interpersonal functioning	
—fear of abandonment	
—low self-esteem	
—impulsivity	
—suicidal behavior	
Histrionic	Women more than men
—excessive emotionality	
—needs to be the center of attention	
—uses physical appearance to get attention	
—overly dramatic	
—inappropriate sexual behavior in interactions with others	
Dependent	Women more than men
—passive	
—can't make decisions without reassurance	
—difficulty doing things on one's own	
—clingy in relationships	
—desire to be taken care of by others	
—high fear of abandonment	
Narcissistic	Men more than women
—feelings of self-importance	
—feelings of superiority	
—high need for admiration	
—inflation of abilities	
—sense of entitlement	
—exploits others	
—lack of empathy	

Source: DSM-IV-TR (American Psychiatric Association, 2000).

ADJUSTMENT TO CHRONIC ILLNESS

This man, let's call him Bill, was 38 years old and had suffered a heart attack. He had a strong family history of heart disease. His father had died of heart disease when he was in his thirties, his mother had recently undergone bypass surgery, and he had already lost a brother to heart disease. Bill smoked two packs of cigarettes a day. He did not have time for exercise or to really think about what he was eating. Bill owned a business and was struggling—not to make ends meet, but to make the business an overwhelming success. He was very stressed by the business. Bill was married and had two young children. How did he respond to his heart attack? He was angry but resigned. He had no intention of changing any of his behaviors. He would continue to smoke, continue to work long hours at work and get little sleep, and had no intention of spending more time with family. The heart attack convinced him he might not live as long as he had hoped, but his response to this fact was to work even harder to ensure the financial security of his family when he passed away. He told me this was the responsibility he had as the "man of the family."

A few days later, I interviewed a woman, let's call her Marie. Marie reluctantly agreed to let me interview her while she was in the hospital recovering from a heart attack. She said she doubted she would have time for the 90-minute interview because she was certain her physician would be in soon to discharge her. (Having experience with the hospital discharge process, I knew we would probably have at least 90 minutes before the physician arrived and the paperwork would be finished!) Marie was anxious to leave the hospital to take care of her husband, who was dying of lung cancer. I asked Marie to recall the earliest signs of her heart problem. She recalled having symptoms of chest pain over a year ago. Her physician had wanted to hospitalize her for some tests, but she refused to leave her ill husband. Instead, she used a nitroglycerin spray daily for the past year to alleviate chest pain. Marie had difficulty answering the questions I asked because she could not keep her mind focused on the interview. She asked me why I was asking so many questions about her when it was her husband who had the real problem. I wondered when Marie left the hospital if she would take care of herself. Somehow, I doubted it.

These two people are among the hundreds of people I have interviewed with a chronic illness, in this case heart disease. I present these two cases, one by a man and one by a woman, to illustrate two very different responses I believe can be tied to traditional gender roles—the man as the breadwinner and the woman as the family caretaker.

In this section of the chapter, I describe how people adjust to chronic illness, with an emphasis on the implications of gender roles. Studies of heart disease show that women adjust more poorly than men (Boutin-Foster & Charlson, 2007; Ford et al., 2008; Hunt-Shanks, Blanchard, & Reid, 2009). However, many of these studies suffer from an important methodological flaw. They fail to consider differences between women's and men's functioning before the onset of the illness. For example, one investigator found that women were more depressed than men one year after bypass surgery. However, women were also older, were more likely to be widowed, had less income, and had more other health problems compared to men (Ai et al., 1997). When these factors were taken into consideration, the sex difference in depression disappeared. Sex differences in depression following the onset of a chronic illness are especially suspect because of the research just reviewed showing women are more depressed than men among physically healthy samples.

One reason that women might have more difficulty than men adjusting to chronic illness is that they continue to assume caregiving responsibilities and their spouses are not as skilled as caregivers. Husbands may not be as supportive as wives when their spouses are ill because they are less familiar with the caregiver role. Women who are ill continue to provide support to their spouses, whereas men who are ill focus more on themselves (Revenson et al., 2005). A study of men and women with heart disease showed that women were less likely than men to have help with household chores when they returned home from the hospital (Boutin-Foster & Charlson, 2007). This lack of instrumental assistance was associated with an elevated rate of depression in women compared to men. A study of elderly women with osteoarthritis showed that husbands were less likely to provide support when the women expressed symptoms of pain—suggesting that men may be more likely than women to withdraw from the caregiver role (Stephens et al., 2006). A meta-analytic review of couples with cancer showed that women are more distressed than men whether they are the patient or the spouse (Hagedoorn et al., 2008).

Are there sex differences in how children adjust to chronic illness? Williams (2000) found that adolescent girls with diabetes and asthma adapted better to their illness than adolescent boys. The girls incorporated their illness into their social identities, whereas the boys did not. Girls shared their illness with friends, whereas boys hid their illness from friends because they viewed the illness as a threat to their identity. The boys compartmentalized the illness so it had little effect on other aspects of their lives.

One framework that can be used to understand how women and men adjust to chronic illness is a gender-role perspective. Chronic illness poses different challenges for men and women, in terms of traditional roles. Both the traditional male gender role and the traditional female gender role may make it more difficult to adjust to chronic

DO GENDER 13.6
Gender Roles and
Chronic Illness

Interview two female and two male college students who had a chronic illness as a child. Common chronic illnesses during childhood are diabetes, asthma, and cancer. Ask them a series of open-ended questions to find out how the illness affected their lives—relationships with parents, relationships with friends, leisure activities, schoolwork, self-esteem. After the interview, view the participants' responses from a gender-role perspective. Did any of the effects of the illness seem to be related to gender roles?

illness. The reasons for these adverse associations, however, differ. After reading this section, use Do Gender 13.6 to see if a gender-role framework helps you understand how someone adjusts to chronic illness.

Male Gender Role

A number of years ago, an episode of a news program was aired that depicted a man who had been diagnosed with a chronic illness—heart disease. The man with heart disease suffered a heart attack but resisted his physician's instructions to reduce his stress, to slow down, and to take life a little easier. Instead, this man reacted against the physician's instructions and against his newfound vulnerability, heart disease, by proving he was just as strong as before and worked even longer hours to maintain his business. He was very concerned about maintaining a macho image. The man suffered a second, more debilitating heart attack. Ironically, he was so impaired by the second heart attack that he lost the business he was trying so hard to save. If he had followed his physician's instructions the first time, he might not have lost the business or suffered the loss of physical functioning caused by the second heart attack.

The traditional male gender role may be an advantage or a disadvantage in adjusting to chronic illness (see Figure 13.11). On the negative side, characteristics of the traditional male gender role, specifically independence and self-control, are inconsistent with chronic illness. People with a traditional masculine orientation may find it difficult to depend on

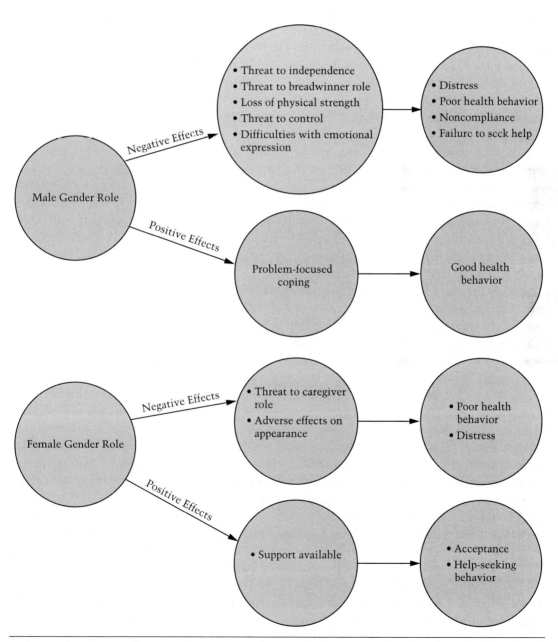

FIGURE 13.11   Implications of Gender Roles for Adjustment to Chronic Illness.

others for assistance or to ask others for help. This will only be problematic if help is needed. For example, a cardiac patient who refuses to ask for assistance with mowing the lawn or shoveling snow is placing himself or herself at risk for a fatal heart attack.

In addition, the mere existence of a chronic illness may be viewed as a weakness, and vulnerability and weakness are inconsistent with the male gender role. Studies have found that adolescent males feel more stigmatized by chronic illness than adolescent females (Williams, 2000). A chronic illness will be especially threatening to men to the extent that it undermines their breadwinner role, which is the case when women go to work, men retire, or men reduce their workloads in response to their illness (Charmaz, 1995).

The male gender role might also impede adjustment by interfering with compliance to physician instructions. For example, among cardiac patients, strong orders by physicians to follow a strict diet, exercise regularly, and refrain from physical exertion could evoke a state of **psychological reactance** (Brehm, 1966). Psychological reactance occurs when you perceive that someone has taken away your freedom or sense of control by telling you what to do. To restore that freedom, you do just the opposite of what was instructed. A more familiar term for this idea is "reverse psychology." Think of the times you told someone to do just the opposite of what you wanted so they would react against your instructions and do what you really want. Psychological reactance may be dangerous in the case of failing to adhere to physician instructions. In this case, patients' noncompliance restores personal control at the expense of taking care of themselves. People who might be most vulnerable to noncompliance as a result of psychological reactance are those who score high on

the gender-related trait unmitigated agency. Unmitigated agency has been associated with poor adjustment to heart disease, in part due to the failure to adhere to physicians' instructions (Helgeson, 1993) and poor health behaviors, in particular smoking (Helgeson & Mickelson, 2000).

Another feature of the male gender role that might impede adjustment to illness is difficulties with emotional expression. The traditional male role requires men to keep feelings and vulnerabilities hidden from others. However, the failure to share feelings and difficulties will keep others from providing needed support. In a study of men with prostate cancer, unmitigated agency was associated with difficulties with emotional expression (Helgeson & Lepore, 1997). It was these emotional expression difficulties that explained the link of unmitigated agency to poor psychological and physical functioning.

On the positive side, characteristics of the male gender role may be quite helpful in coping with chronic illness, when the illness is construed as a problem meant to be solved. To the extent there are clear-cut behaviors that can solve or "control" the problem, men might be especially likely to engage in those behaviors. A study of patients with heart disease showed that men were more likely than women to attribute the cause of their illness to controllable factors (e.g., diet, overworking, alcohol), and less likely than women to attribute the cause of their illness to uncontrollable factors (e.g., heredity; Grace et al., 2005). One behavior that is helpful for managing many illnesses is exercise. Male cardiac patients are more likely than their female counterparts to exercise (Hunt-Shanks et al., 2009). Exercise, in and of itself, is consistent with the male gender role. Exercise can also be construed as a problem-focused coping behavior. Adolescent males with diabetes are more likely than adolescent females to use exercise as a way to control their illness (Williams, 2000). In general, male adolescents with chronic illness are more likely to perceive they can control their illness than female adolescents (Williams, 2000). To the extent that control is possible and control behaviors are helpful in regulating the illness, this perspective is a healthy one. Agency is an aspect of the male gender role that may reflect this problem-solving orientation. Agency has been linked to positive adjustment to chronic illnesses, such as heart disease (Helgeson, 1993; Fritz, 2000; Helgeson & Mickelson, 2000), prostate cancer (Helgeson & Lepore, 1997, 2004), and irritable bowel syndrome (Voci & Cramer, 2009). However, the "chronic" aspect of chronic illness suggests control efforts will be limited in their effects. This aspect of illness could be frustrating to men who focus on control.

Thus the male gender role has links to both successful and problematic adjustment to chronic illness. To the extent the illness threatens masculinity, recovery will be difficult. To the extent it can be used to aid recovery, masculinity will be helpful.

Female Gender Role

When I first started interviewing cardiac patients over 20 years ago, I wondered if the female cardiac patient would have the same "Type A" characteristics as the male cardiac patient—impatience and hostility. The first 20 women I interviewed created quite a different picture of the woman with heart disease. Two of these 20 women had been admitted to the hospital for heart attacks the day after their husbands were admitted for potential heart problems. Interestingly, in each case, the husband did not sustain a heart attack, but the wife did. The most noteworthy case was the woman I described

previously who had put the health care needs of her husband before her own. A common theme that ran throughout the course of my interviews with these 20 women was that their concern with taking care of others and putting others' needs first had adverse consequences for their own health. Some of these women undoubtedly had difficulty with recovery because they continued to take care of others at the expense of taking care of themselves. However, a few women did view their heart attack as a wake-up call—a chance to shift their priorities and put themselves first.

There are a variety of aspects of the female gender role that have implications for adjustment to chronic illness (see Figure 13.11). One issue is the extent to which the illness interferes with caregiving. If the caregiver role is central to one's identity and a chronic illness undermines this role, the person will have difficulty adjusting to the illness. This is the issue that concerned many of the women cardiac patients I first interviewed. When taking care of oneself detracts from taking care of others, these women may neglect their own health. One study of cardiac patients showed that women were more likely than men to resume household responsibilities after they were discharged from the hospital (Rose et al., 1996).

The conflict between receiving assistance and providing assistance to others may be especially difficult for women who are highly invested in the caregiving role, such as those who score high on unmitigated communion. Unmitigated communion has been linked to poor adjustment to chronic illnesses such as heart disease (Helgeson, 1993; Fritz, 2000), breast cancer (Helgeson, 2003), diabetes (Helgeson & Fritz, 1996), and irritable bowel syndrome (Voci & Cramer, 2009). One reason for this relation is that these women neglect their own health in favor of helping others. In a study of heart disease, people who scored high on unmitigated communion were less likely to adhere to physicians' recommended exercise regimens (Fritz, 2000). A study of adolescents with diabetes showed that those who scored high on unmitigated communion had poor control over their diabetes because they were attending to the needs of others instead of themselves (Helgeson & Fritz, 1996).

The female gender role is also implicated in poor adjustment to illnesses that involve alterations in physical appearance. To the extent that concerns with appearance override concerns with physical health, the female gender role is a disadvantage. In one study, adolescent females with diabetes showed particular difficulties following a diabetic diet because of concerns with weight and body image (Williams, 2000). Dieting in the form of restricting food intake can be very dangerous for people with diabetes.

Aspects of the female gender role may facilitate adjustment to chronic illness. The female gender role permits help seeking and reliance on others for support. One aspect of the female gender role, communion, has been associated with the availability of social support (Helgeson, 1994c). Thus the female gender role can be adaptive in terms of acquiring needed support resources.

TAKE HOME POINTS

- Clear-cut sex differences in adjustment to chronic illness are not apparent.

- Gender provides an important framework within which we can understand the issues that women and men with a chronic illness face.

- The male gender role is advantageous to the extent a chronic illness is construed as a problem meant to be

solved, but disadvantageous to the extent it implies weakness and limits men's feelings of control.

- The female gender role can facilitate adjustment to chronic illness by providing support resources but can impede adjustment when physical attractiveness and caregiving issues interfere with taking proper care of oneself.

EATING DISORDERS

Princess Diana, Justine Bateman, Elton John, Paula Abdul, Fiona Apple, Mary-Kate Olsen, Oprah Winfrey, Ana Carolina Reston, Kirsten Haglund—what do they all have in common? They all have had eating disorders or disturbances. However, the outcomes are not all the same. Ana Carolina Reston, a Brazilian model, died in 2006 from the disorder. Kirsten Haglund received the help that she needed and went on to become Miss America in 2008.

Definitions and Prevalence

The three major eating disorders are anorexia nervosa, bulimia nervosa, and binge eating disorder (National Institute of Mental Health, 2007). Potentially 10 million females and 1 million males in the United States have anorexia nervosa or bulimia nervosa and many more have binge eating disorder (National Eating Disorders Association, 2005). Although the three disorders can be clearly defined and distinguished from one another, people can have degrees of any one of them. In fact, various degrees of binge eating exist in the normal population.

Anorexia Nervosa.   Of the three, **anorexia nervosa** is the most life-threatening eating disorder. The primary feature of this disorder is the continual pursuit of thinness.

The anorexic person has a distorted body image and refuses to maintain a normal weight. One of the diagnostic features is that the anorexic person weighs less than 85% of what is considered normal for that person's age and height. A common symptom of anorexia in women is amenorrhea (cessation of menstrual cycling).

Ironically, anorexia is more common in industrialized societies, where food is plentiful (American Psychiatric Association, 2000). A majority of cases of anorexia (90%) are found in women, and the lifetime incidence in the female population is 0.5%. The onset of anorexia typically occurs between the ages of 14 and 18.

Bulimia Nervosa.   **Bulimia nervosa** is characterized by recurrent binge eating followed by inappropriate methods to prevent weight gain, such as vomiting, intense exercising, or the use of laxatives, diuretics, and enemas. By far the most common method of purging is vomiting. Although any food can be consumed during a binge, foods typically consist of sweets and fats. During the binge, the person usually feels a loss of control. This person constantly thinks about food and weight control. The typical person with bulimia is of average weight but may have been overweight prior to the onset of the disorder. The low weight of an anorexic person is a feature that distinguishes her or him from the bulimic.

There are two types of bulimia: (1) purging, which involves vomiting and using laxatives, diuretics, and enemas, and (2) nonpurging, which involves dieting and exercise and not the other, more extreme methods. As with anorexia, about 90% of bulimia cases are found among women, and between 1% and 3% of women have bulimia (Pike & Striegel-Moore, 1997). The onset of bulimia is somewhat later than anorexia, during late adolescence to early adulthood (Pike & Striegel-Moore, 1997). The incidence of bulimia has increased over the past several decades, whereas the rate of anorexia has stabilized.

Binge Eating Disorder.   **Binge eating disorder** is characterized by recurrent binge eating without purging or fasting. Binge eating is accompanied by eating rapidly, eating large amounts of food in the absence of hunger, eating in isolation from others, and feelings of guilt and disgust with oneself for eating. Unlike anorexia and bulimia, binge eating does not include purging, fasting, or exercise, which means that people with binge eating disorder are likely to be overweight or obese. Of the three, binge eating disorder is the most prevalent, affecting 3.5% of women and 2% of men over their lifetimes (Hudson et al., 2007). Although binge eating disorder is more common among women than men, there is some evidence that binge eating behavior is more common among men than women (Saules et al., 2009). Unlike anorexia and bulimia, which typically occur during adolescence, the typical onset of binge eating disorder is young adulthood.

Disturbed Eating Behavior.   Because the prevalence rate of eating disorders in the general population is so small, investigators often study symptoms of bulimia or anorexia. These symptoms are referred to as *disturbed eating behavior*. One of the most frequently used instruments to assess disturbed eating is the Eating Disorder Inventory (Garner, Olmstead, & Polivy, 1983). Three subscales of this inventory have been linked to eating disorders: drive for thinness, symptoms of bulimia, and body dissatisfaction. The items from each of these scales are shown in Table 13.6. Many of the studies reviewed in this section have used this instrument or a similar one.

TABLE 13.6   EATING DISORDER INVENTORY

Drive for Thinness

1. I eat sweets and carbohydrates without feeling nervous.*
2. I think about dieting.
3. I feel extremely guilty after overeating.
4. I am terrified of gaining weight.
5. I exaggerate or magnify the importance of weight.
6. I am preoccupied with the desire to be thinner.
7. If I gain a pound, I worry that I will keep gaining.

Bulimia

1. I eat when I am upset.
2. I stuff myself with food.
3. I have gone on eating binges where I have felt that I could not stop.
4. I think about bingeing (overeating).
5. I eat moderately in front of others and stuff myself when they are gone.
6. I have thought of trying to vomit in order to lose weight.
7. I eat or drink in secrecy.

Body Dissatisfaction

1. I think that my stomach is too big.
2. I think that my thighs are too large.
3. I think that my stomach is just the right size.*
4. I feel satisfied with the shape of my body.*
5. I like the shape of my buttocks.*
6. I think my hips are too big.
7. I think that my thighs are just the right size.*
8. I think that my buttocks are too large.
9. I think that my hips are just the right size.*

*These items are reverse scored meaning less endorsement is indicative of greater problems.
Source: Garner et al. (1983).

Consequences

The disease course for anorexia is more negative than it is for bulimia (Crow, 2010). Five to ten years after a diagnosis of anorexia nervosa, one-third of people still have the disease, one-third have some symptoms but do not meet diagnostic requirements, and one-third fully recover. Anorexia has the highest death rate of any cause of death among females ages 15–24. In fact, anorexia has the highest mortality rate of any mental health problem (Striegel-Moore & Bulik, 2007). Death results from electrolyte and fluid imbalances, cardiac arrest, and suicide (National Institute of Mental Health, 2007). People are more likely to recover from bulimia than anorexia. Rates of recovery from bulimia range from 31% to 74%, with relapse being quite common (Wilson, Grilo, & Vitousek, 2007).

Other consequences of eating disorders range from minor to severe (National Institute of Mental Health, 2007). Gastrointestinal problems and colon problems may result from repeated use of laxatives. Dental problems may occur from repeated vomiting. Bone problems may occur with anorexia and place one at risk for osteoporosis. Women with eating disorders are likely to have problems getting pregnant. People with anorexia are likely to suffer from hypotension (low blood pressure), which could cause cardiovascular problems. One study reported possible long-term effects of anorexia on the structure of the brain, some of which may not be reversible (Katzman et al., 1997).

Etiology

The etiology of eating disorders is unclear. Eating disorders often co-occur with other mental health problems, such as depression, anxiety, and substance abuse (Hudson et al., 2007). Researchers have examined genetic links, demographic factors that may predispose one to eating disorders, social factors, and a variety of psychological factors, including difficulties with achievement and lack of control.

Biology.   It is clear that there is a genetic component to eating disorders from studies of twins and from studies of genotypes (Striegel-Moore & Bulik, 2007). There appears to be greater heritability of anorexia nervosa than bulimia (Keel & Klump, 2003). There are greater cultural differences in bulimia than anorexia. Whereas rates of bulimia dramatically increased over the last half of the 20th century, rates of anorexia have been stable. Bulimia appears to be a largely Western phenomenon, whereas anorexia is not limited to Western cultures. Given the onset of eating disorders in adolescence, any biological theory would necessarily have to be an interactive one. Eating disorders are more common among women who come from families with a female member who has an eating disorder. This overlap could be due to shared genes or shared environment.

Hormones also may play a role in eating behavior. Prenatal exposure to testosterone has been linked to a reduced incidence of eating disturbances, which may partly account for why females seem to be at greater risk than males. The relation of eating disorders to testosterone was examined in a study of same-sex and other-sex twins, reasoning that female other-sex twins have greater exposure to testosterone than female same-sex twins (Culbert et al., 2008). Results supported the theory. The highest rate of eating disorders was found in female same-sex twins, followed by female other-sex twins, followed by male other-sex twins, and then male same-sex twins.

Demographics.   Females are more likely than males to have eating disorders and disturbed eating behavior, but the sex difference is smaller for binge eating disorder and disturbed eating behavior (Striegel-Moore & Bulik, 2007). Overall, the effect sizes are smaller than one would think, so it is important to realize that men also can suffer from eating disturbances (Striegel-Moore et al., 2009). Historically, higher socioeconomic status was viewed as a risk factor for eating disorders, and minority persons were less vulnerable to eating disorders than Caucasians. Today, it is no longer the case that eating disorders are limited to upper class Caucasian girls (Crow, 2010; Harrison & Hefner, 2008).

Females and males with eating disorders have a similar age of onset and similar symptoms (Woodside et al., 2001). One difference is that homosexuality is a risk factor for eating disorders among men but not women. Eating disorders are more common among gay men than heterosexual men but not among lesbians compared to heterosexual women (Peplau et al., 2009), perhaps because of a greater preference for thinness and higher body dissatisfaction among gay men (Boroughs & Thompson, 2002).

Female Gender Role.   Eating disorders have been linked to features of the female gender role. First, the female gender role places a high value on physical attractiveness. Second, women are interpersonally oriented, so others' opinions are important to them. Both of these concerns play a role in eating disorders.

Gender intensification could provide a framework for understanding eating disorders as it does for depression. Eating disorders first appear during adolescence when gender roles become salient. But, have gender roles been linked to eating disorders? A meta-analytic review of the literature found a small positive relation between psychological femininity, or communion, and disturbed eating behavior ($d = +.14$; Murnen & Smolak, 1997). However, more recent studies have failed to find a relation (e.g., Hepp, Spindler, & Milos, 2005).

There may be other aspects of the female gender role that are more strongly linked to eating disturbances. *Negative femininity* seems to play a role in the development of eating disorders. Negative femininity includes being dependent, weak, timid, and needing others' approval. In studies that examine the positive and negative aspects of femininity, only negative femininity has emerged as a predictor of disordered eating behavior—among both heterosexuals and homosexuals (Lakkis, Ricciardelli, & Williams, 1999; Paxton & Sculthorpe, 1991). Unmitigated communion is another gender-related trait that has been implicated in problematic eating behavior (Helgeson et al., 2007; Mosher & Danoff-Burg, 2008). Unmitigated communion individuals have low self-esteem and evaluate themselves based on others' views. Thus, they may be more vulnerable to societal pressures to be thin. Unmitigated communion is also related to a poor body image (Helgeson, 2003).

Societal Factors.   One perspective on eating disorders places the blame on society's obsession with dieting and the pressure for thinness among women. Not surprisingly, dieting appears to be an antecedent to eating disorders (Cogan & Ernsberger, 1999). A nationwide survey of ninth through twelfth graders showed that 59% of females and 31% of males were trying to lose weight (Centers for Disease Control and Prevention, 2010d). A sizable number had gone without eating for 24 hours in the past 30 days to lose weight: 15% females and 7% males. A 2005 Gallup Poll showed that 46% of American women and 31% of American men had made three or more serious attempts to lose weight (Gallup, 2010). One problem with dieting is that it causes metabolism to decrease over time, making it increasingly difficult to lose weight. Thus, after initial pounds are shed, more extreme methods are required to achieve the same rate of weight loss.

U.S. society's image of the ideal woman is an extremely thin form, really without shape. Toy models such as Barbie display unrealistic body shapes. When the measurements of Barbie were compared to the actual measurements of a sample of 18- to 35-year-old women, the chances of finding Barbie's measurements in this population were estimated to be less than 1 in 100,000 (Norton et al., 1996). The standards for thinness have grown increasingly strict and have become more unrealistic over the past three to four decades (Siever, 1996). The standards of the ideal male body also have changed. One group of investigators examined changes in male action figures over the previous 30 years, in particular, G. I. Joe and Star Wars characters (Pope et al., 1999). Over time, the figures have grown more muscular. Again, if the dimensions of these figures were translated into human beings, only the rare adult male would meet these specifications. Pope and colleagues contend that changes in these action toys reflect changing standards of the male body image. These changes could be linked to eating disturbances in men.

Today, young women are surrounded by media exposure to thinness through magazines and television, which undoubtedly influence their body image and their eating behavior (Harrison & Hefner, 2008). The media normalizes dieting and excessive thinness and also encourages people to evaluate their bodies and to use extreme measures to improve them. A longitudinal study showed that frequent magazine reading was associated with an increase in unhealthy weight control measures (e.g., fasting, skipping meals, smoking cigarettes) among female adolescents five years later (van den Berg et al., 2007). Even among men, media exposure has been related to greater body concerns. College men who read more magazines about fitness and muscularity spent more time thinking about their appearance and seemed to be more dissatisfied with their bodies (Hatoum & Belle, 2004). However, much of the research in this area is correlational, meaning that cause and effect cannot be determined.

Laboratory studies can disentangle cause from effect by observing the effects of brief media exposure on body image. A meta-analysis of these kinds of studies showed a clear adverse effect of exposure to slender female body image ideals on body satisfaction ($d = -.31$; Groesz, Levine, & Murnen, 2002). After exposure to these images, females estimated their bodies to be larger, wished they were thinner, and were unhappy with their bodies. Effects were stronger for adolescents than adults. An experimental field study randomly assigned adolescent girls to receive a 15-month subscription to a fashion magazine or not (Stice, Spangler, & Agras, 2001). Although the magazine subscription did not have an overall adverse effect on girls, the subscription affected girls who were more vulnerable to body image problems. Among those who started the study with more body image concerns, magazine exposure was associated with an increase in negative affect.

Concerns about thinness also come from sources other than the media, such as family and friends, who are often dieting themselves. Girls receive more pressure from family and friends to lose weight than boys, whereas boys receive more pressure from family and friends to gain muscle (Ata et al., 2007). These kinds of pressure have been associated with disturbed eating behavior in both females and males (Ata et al., 2007). Eating disorders are associated with families who express concerns about weight and with families in which parents are overly critical of weight and appearance (American Psychological Association, 2007).

Peers also can influence eating behavior. One study showed an association between peers dieting and eating disturbances in both women and men (Gravener et al., 2008). The previously mentioned study of eighth and ninth graders showed girls engage in "fat talk" with one another (Nichter, 2000). Fat talk begins with one girl stating, "I'm so fat!" and may be followed up with a friend replying, "No, you're not fat." A dialogue begins in which body weight is the focus of attention. When one person begins engaging in unhealthy eating behavior, friends may follow. A study of female college students showed that exposure to two female confederates who complained about their bodies led to a decrease in body satisfaction (Shomaker & Furman, 2007). However, these effects were only observed among women who tended to compare themselves to others and were highly invested in their appearance.

Psychological Factors. A general psychological theory of eating disorders is that they stem from feelings of a lack of autonomy, a lack of control, and a lack of a sense of self in combination with a striving for perfection and achievement. Weight loss is one way to fulfill these needs: Losing weight is a way to gain control over one's body and has the potential to enhance self-esteem. In a longitudinal study of 12- to 16-year-olds, perfectionism predicted anorexia over the next two to eight years (Tyrka et al., 2002). Another study showed that feelings of control and autonomy were related to a lower incidence of disturbed eating behavior in college women (Peterson, Grippo, & Tantleff-Dunn, 2008). Many investigators have argued that eating disorders emerge in women during adolescence because it is during this time that girls feel a loss of control, become concerned with others' views of them, and become aware of the limitations of the female gender role with respect to achievement (Silverstein & Perlick, 1995). One way of responding to these challenges is to exert control over weight. Consistent with this theory, feelings of autonomy, control, and empowerment are associated with a more positive body image and less disturbed eating in college women (Peterson et al., 2008).

Not surprisingly, a negative body image is associated with eating disturbances (Peterson et al., 2008). What is interesting though is that it is the perception of being overweight rather than actual weight that is associated with eating disturbances (Saules et al., 2009). Eating disorders have been linked to a host of other problems that female adolescents suffer, such as anxiety and depression. Eating disorders are one way that distress manifests itself among these girls. However, the sex ratio of eating disorders is much larger than the sex difference in depression; thus eating disorders must be more than a manifestation of psychological distress.

TAKE HOME POINTS

- There are three major kinds of eating disorders: anorexia nervosa, bulimia nervosa, and binge eating disorder. Anorexia is the most lethal of the three.

- Eating disorders tend to emerge during adolescence.

- It is during adolescence that girls experience body changes (in particular, an increase in body fat), become dissatisfied with their bodies, and become increasingly concerned with their appearance and how others view them. During adolescence, girls also recognize limiting factors associated with the female gender role.

- Contributing factors to eating disorders include genes, gender roles, psychological factors (e.g., need for control and perfectionism), and the social environment.

- Media exposure has been implicated in eating disorders for both women and men. Experimental studies have shown that media exposure affects girls' views of their bodies.

SUICIDE

In 1994, Kurt Cobain, 27 years old and lead singer of the popular alternative rock band Nirvana, committed suicide by shooting himself. In 2005, Hunter S. Thompson, famous journalist and author, killed himself with a gun outside his home at the age of 67. Mark Madoff, the son of Bernie Madoff who was convicted of the largest Ponzi scheme in history, hung himself on the second anniversary of his father's arrest at age 46.

Despite the fact that women are more depressed than men, men actually commit suicide more frequently than women. There is an even more interesting paradox: Men commit suicide more frequently than women, but women attempt suicide more frequently than men. In this section of the chapter, I provide statistical information on suicide rates and attempts and then discuss some of the factors associated with suicide and suicide attempts in men and women.

Incidence

Suicide is more common than people think. Did you know more people die from suicide than homicide? In 2007, 34,592 people committed suicide. Suicide is the third leading cause of death for people between the ages of 15 and 24. The suicide rate is twice as high among Whites as Blacks, Asians, and Hispanics, but equally high among American Indians/Alaska Natives (National Center for Health Statistics, 2009b). As shown in Figure 13.12, the size of the sex difference is relatively stable across the life span until old age. The sex difference also persists across ethnic groups, although it is smaller among Asian Americans than other groups (Langhinrichsen-Rohling, Friend, & Powell, 2009). Among the elderly, there is a dramatic increase in men's suicide rates, which increases the magnitude of the sex difference. Among persons 65 years and older, men have seven times the rate of suicide as women. The sex difference is also a bit larger among the younger cohorts: Among 20- to 24-year-olds, men are nearly six times as likely as women to commit suicide.

Sex differences in suicide extend across cultures. The sex difference (male–female

ratio) in suicide rates for 20 countries is shown in Table 13.7. Historically, men have had higher rates of suicide compared to women for some time. Over the last few decades of the 20th century, the sex difference in suicide rates worldwide has increased, largely due to an increase in suicide among men (World Health Organization, 2010b).

As shown in Table 13.7, the size of the sex difference in suicide is smaller in Asian cultures. China is an exception to the sex difference in suicide rates. Here suicide is the leading cause of death among those aged 15 to 34 years but rates are higher among females than males (Mitra & Shroff, 2008; Phillips, Li, & Zhang, 2002). There are a variety of reasons for the sex reversal. A major reason is the low status of women. Women suffer high rates of physical and sexual abuse, are more likely to live in poverty and lack economic resources than men, and are unable to express themselves freely. Second, there are no religious sanctions against suicide. Third, suicide rates are higher in rural

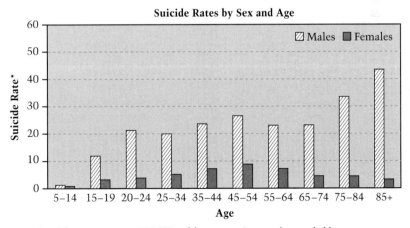

*Note: These rates are per 100,000 and for persons 5 years of age and older.

FIGURE 13.12   Suicide rates by sex and age. Men have higher suicide rates than women at all ages. The sex difference is particularly high among young people and the elderly.
Source: Adapted from National Center for Health Statistics (2009b).

TABLE 13.7   Sex Differences in Suicide

Nation	Male–Female Suicide Ratio
Australia	3.8
Austria	3.22
Belize	8.38
Canada	3.20
Chile	5.12
China	0.88
Denmark	2.73
France	2.83
Germany	2.98
India	1.34
Ireland	4.58
Italy	3.54
Japan	2.61
Luxembourg	4.12
Mexico	5.23
New Zealand	3.00
Sweden	2.18
Thailand	3.16
United Kingdom	3.61
United States	3.93

Source: World Health Organization (2010a).

areas where levels of social support are lower, and there are a large number of rural woman. Although the rate of suicide for women is not higher than men in India, the sex difference is smaller. An examination of the different regions of India showed that regions in which women have greater restrictions are regions in which there was a relatively higher rate of female to male suicide (Mitra & Shroff, 2008).

One reason for the sex difference in suicide rates is that men use more violent methods than women (Payne, Swami, & Stanistreet, 2008). Men are more likely to use guns and to hang themselves, whereas women are more likely to use poisons. However, the most common method of suicide for both women and men is the use of a gun. Interestingly, more deaths by gun are due to suicide than homicide. However, the difference in methods does not account for the sex difference in suicide rates entirely. Even within a given method, suicide attempts are more likely to be fatal among men compared to women.

Suicide rates are not as easy to estimate as you might think. The official statistics on suicide rates are likely to be underestimates because some suicides are mistakenly classified as other causes of death. This misclassification may lead to a greater underestimation of female suicide because women are more likely to use ambiguous methods, such as poisoning. Men, by contrast, are more likely to use guns; it is easier to determine that a self-inflicted gunshot was a suicide.

Attempts

Although men commit suicide more frequently than women, women are more likely than men to attempt suicide and to express more suicidal thoughts than men. This paradox holds across most Western societies. A study of 15 European countries showed that females are more likely than males to attempt suicide in 14 of the countries and that the highest rates are among 25- to 34-year-olds (Platt et al., 1992). A more recent study of adults across 17 countries showed that women were more likely than men to report suicidal thinking (Nock et al., 2008). Among adolescents, females also report more suicidal thinking and more suicide attempts than males. A nationwide survey of ninth through twelfth graders revealed that 8.1% of girls and 4.6% of boys had attempted suicide during the past year, with higher overall rates but similar sex ratios among Blacks and Hispanics compared to Whites (Centers for Disease Control and Prevention, 2010d). Suicidal ideation was higher but the sex difference remained: 17% of females and 10% of males reported seriously considering suicide in the past year.

Suicide attempts are difficult to estimate, however. For example, an overdose of drugs can be interpreted as a suicide attempt or as an accident. Here, men's suicide attempts may be underreported because attempting suicide and not succeeding are considered weak behaviors inconsistent with the strength and decisiveness of the male gender role. Thus, men may be less likely than women to admit making a suicide attempt, and clinicians may be less likely to consider the possibility that a drug overdose in a man was a suicide attempt.

The Gender Paradox

A theoretical explanation for the gender paradox is gender-role socialization (Payne et al., 2008). Suicide is not viewed as acceptable but it is viewed as less unacceptable among men than women. Suicide is considered masculine behavior. However, suicide attempts are considered feminine behavior. Among men, committing suicide is considered to be a powerful response to some kind of failure; attempting but not completing a suicide is construed as weak behavior and viewed negatively, especially in men. The gender paradox in suicide attempts and suicide rates is most prominent among adolescents and young adults, the very people who are most concerned with adhering to gender roles.

Gender roles also influence the method used to commit suicide. Men are more likely than women to be familiar with guns, and men may be more willing to use violent methods to commit suicide because they are less likely than women to be concerned with the appearance of their body following suicide (Payne et al., 2008).

As alluded to earlier, there is also a methodological explanation for the paradox of men's higher suicide rates and women's higher suicide attempts. Women's suicide

rates may be underestimated, and men's suicide attempts may be underestimated. Because women use more ambiguous methods than men to commit suicide, women's actual suicides may be underestimated as some are classified as other causes of death (e.g., accidental). Because attempting suicide is inconsistent with the strength of the male gender role, men may be less likely than women to admit to a suicide attempt, leading to a greater underestimation of men's than women's suicide attempts. Women also are more likely than men to express their emotions, which might include reports of thinking about suicide and suicide attempts. To the extent that is the case, it will be more difficult to identify men than women who are at risk for suicide (Langhinrichsen-Rohling et al., 2009).

Factors Associated with Suicide Among Adults

Among adults, suicide and suicide attempts have been linked to substance abuse and depression. The link of suicide to depression is problematic, however, because a suicide attempt might lead to a diagnosis of depression. One study of suicide attempters found that depression predicted subsequent suicide within the next six years for both men and women (Skogman, Alsen, & Ojehagen, 2004). The link of mental illness to suicide is stronger in women than men, but this could be an artifact of women being more likely than men to seek help for mental illness (Payne et al., 2008). Men who commit suicide are less likely than women who commit suicide to have used mental health services. By contrast, alcohol use and abuse are more strongly related to suicide in men than women, perhaps because drinking alcohol is a more socially acceptable way for men to respond to mental illness.

One antecedent to suicide is the breakup of a relationship. The risk of suicide is higher among unmarried, divorced, and widowed persons than married persons but this risk is larger for men than women (Payne et al., 2008), consistent with the research on marital status in Chapter 11. Thus suicide rates in men are linked, in part, to the absence of marriage, which may signify the absence of emotional support. Women's greater integration into social relationships may protect them from suicide. Women not only receive support from network members but provide support to them as well. The fact that women have people to take care of, such as a husband and children, may make them less likely to commit suicide. An in-depth analysis of suicides in the United Kingdom showed that relationship difficulties were equally likely to be present in male and female suicides but relationship difficulties were more likely to be the primary trigger in the case of males than females (Shiner et al., 2009).

Suicide rates are higher among those of a lower socioeconomic status and have been linked to unemployment and financial problems (Payne et al., 2008; Shiner et al., 2009). These associations are stronger among men than women. The recent economic turndown has been associated with a number of high-profile male suicides, including a former executive of Enron and a French investment manager who lost substantial sums of money in the Madoff scandal. Gender roles may explain this relation, as unemployment is a threat to the traditional male provider role. In a study of 34 European nations, the per capita income of the country was related to the suicide rate of the country's men but not women (Sher, 2006).

Suicidal thinking and suicide attempts are more common among sexual minority persons than heterosexuals (Cochran & Mays, 2006; Payne et al., 2008). This is especially the case for men, perhaps because there is a greater stigma attached to homosexuality in males than females. Homosexuality is viewed as more inconsistent with the male role than the female role.

Gender roles have been implicated in suicide. In a study of the elderly in the United States, the suicide rate of women and men in each state was examined in relation to agentic variables (indicators of financial and social status, such as income and education) and communal variables (indicators of social stability, such as moving, and social environment stress, such as living in a crowded area; Coren & Hewitt, 1999). The investigators found that agentic variables more strongly predicted suicide among elderly men than women, and communal variables more strongly predicted suicide among elderly women than men. The agentic personality trait is associated with less suicidal thinking among adults, and high levels of agency buffer the relation between depression and suicidal thinking (Hobbs & McLaren, 2009). That is, the relation of depression to suicidal ideation is weaker among high agency persons.

Factors Associated with Suicide Among Adolescents

Like adults, suicide and suicide attempts in adolescents are associated with other mental disorders, in particular, depression and substance abuse (Langhinrichsen-Rohling et al., 2009). It is not clear whether suicide and suicidal behavior are more strongly associated with depression in males or females. One longitudinal study of 14- to 18-year-olds showed that a previous suicide attempt predicted a subsequent suicide attempt by age 24 in women but not men (Lewinsohn, Rohde, & Seeley, 2001), suggesting more of a history of suicidal problems in females. One study suggested that depression may be directly linked to suicide in females but indirectly linked to suicide in males through substance abuse (Metha et al., 1998). However, the literature is not clear as to whether alcohol use is more strongly linked to suicidal behavior in males or females and whether antisocial behavior is more strongly linked to suicidal behavior in males or females. In one study, investigators examined suicidal thinking in a high-risk group: adolescents who had a friend commit suicide in the prior six years. Aggressive behavior predicted suicidal thinking among adolescent boys, and depression predicted suicidal thinking among adolescent girls (Prigerson & Slimack, 1999).

Social isolation and problematic social relationships also play a role in adolescent suicide (Langhinrichsen-Rohling et al., 2009). Lack of support from and troubled relationships with family and friends have been associated with greater suicidal ideation and more frequent suicide attempts (Wannan & Fombonne, 1998). Suicide among adolescents has also been associated with the breakup of romantic relationships. In one study, investigators interviewed family members of adolescents who had committed suicide to find out what kinds of life events occurred in the prior year. Compared to a control group of adolescents, family members

of suicide victims reported that the adolescents were more likely to have experienced problems in romantic relationships, including breakups (Brent et al., 1993).

TAKE HOME POINTS

- Men commit suicide more than women. This sex difference appears across the life span and persists across cultures.

- Women attempt suicide more than men.

- This gender paradox is partly explained by methodological issues. Suicide in women may be underestimated because women are more likely to use ambiguous methods (e.g., overdose of pills) than men, which may be misclassified as accidents. Men's suicide attempts may be underestimated because men are less likely than women to admit to a failed suicide attempt.

- Suicide in both women and men—adults and adolescents—is likely to be associated with other mental health problems, such as depression and substance abuse.

- Among adults, marital breakup and unemployment are linked to suicide—especially in men.

- Among both adolescents and adults, relationship difficulties have been linked to suicide.

SUMMARY

There is a consistent and pervasive sex difference in depression in the United States that extends to other cultures. Sex differences in depression emerge during adolescence and persist over the life span. Sex differences in depression may be affected by a response bias on the part of clinicians and respondents; clinicians may be more

likely to recognize or interpret symptoms as depression in women than in men, and men may be more reluctant than women to admit, report, or seek help for depression.

There are numerous theories of sex differences in depression, tapping biological, psychological, and social factors. Little evidence indicates that genes can explain sex differences in depression. Although hormonal changes have been associated with mood changes, the evidence is inconsistent as to which hormone is protective or harmful at what time. It is more likely that hormonal fluctuation rather than a level of a particular hormone is involved in depression.

Psychological theories of depression suggest women are socialized in ways that lead them to perceive less control than men over their environment. Thus, women are more vulnerable to learned helplessness, which can lead to depression. Other theories of sex differences in depression focus on the stressors that women and men face and how they cope with them. The coping literature suggests that women may be more likely than men to engage in most coping strategies, which may be a result rather than a cause of women's distress. One promising theory of sex differences in depression focuses on a particular maladaptive form of coping, rumination. A great deal of evidence suggests women are more likely than men to respond to stressful events by ruminating about them, and rumination is linked to depression.

There is little evidence that women experience more trauma or stressful life events than men, but women do experience more of a specific kind of trauma or stressor—those that involve relationships. Women report more stressful events that involve relationships, and the association of relationship stressors to distress is stronger for women than for men. It is women's differential vulnerability to stress rather than differential exposure to stress that best explains depression.

There are characteristics of the female gender role implicated in depression. Whereas communion is unrelated to depression, unmitigated communion is consistently associated with depression. People characterized by unmitigated communion take on others' problems as their own and become overly involved in helping others. Aside from this specific personality trait, caregiving has been linked more broadly to the female gender role and may be linked to depression.

Regardless of which theory best explains sex difference in depression, the onset during adolescence must be addressed. Several challenges of adolescence were reviewed that might explain this onset, including body image changes and strains in relationships. These events might activate depression in girls who are at risk for depression.

In terms of adjustment to chronic illness, it is not clear if there are sex differences. However, gender provides an important framework within which we can understand the issues that women and men with a chronic illness face. The male gender role is advantageous to the extent a chronic illness is construed as a problem meant to be solved, but disadvantageous to the extent it implies weakness and limits men's feelings of control. The female gender role can facilitate adjustment to chronic illness by providing support resources but can impede adjustment when physical attractiveness and caregiving issues interfere with taking proper care of oneself.

Another mental health problem discussed in this chapter was eating disorders, which are more common in women than in men and more likely to arise during adolescence than at any other time in life. Many of the theories of eating disorders are linked to adolescence. During adolescence, girls' bodies change and girls become more aware of societal pressures to be thin. It is also during adolescence that women recognize the limitations placed on the female gender role and on their control more generally. Eating disorders may be a manifestation of attempts to exert control.

The last mental health problem reviewed was suicide. Men commit suicide more frequently than women at all ages and across most cultures, but women contemplate suicide and attempt suicide more frequently than men. Substance abuse, depression, and impaired social relations all play a role in suicidal behavior among adolescents and adults.

DISCUSSION QUESTIONS

1. Which methodological bias do you believe is most likely to undermine sex differences in depression?
2. What kind of experiences during childhood, adolescence, and adulthood do females face compared to males that might instill learned helplessness?
3. Debate the following statement: Men engage in problem-focused coping and women engage in emotion-focused coping.
4. Explain how rumination leads to depression.
5. What is the difference between the differential exposure and the differential vulnerability hypotheses concerning the relation of stressful events to depression?
6. Which aspects of gender roles are related to depression?
7. What are some of the reasons that sex differences in depression emerge during adolescence?
8. Describe the aspects of the male gender role and the female gender role that hinder and facilitate adjustment to chronic illness.
9. Considering the traits of agency and communion, characterize the couple that would adapt the best to chronic illness.
10. How does society contribute to the development of eating disorders in women? In men?
11. Discuss how the difficulties in documenting suicide rates and suicide attempts might alter the sex difference in suicide and suicide attempts.
12. What social factors are associated with suicide in females and males?

SUGGESTED READING

Groesz, L. M., Levine, M. P., & Murnen, S. K. (2002). The effect of experimental presentation of thin media images on body satisfaction: A meta-analytic review. *International Journal of Eating Disorders, 31*, 1–16.

Helgeson, V. S., & Fritz, H. L. (1998). A theory of unmitigated communion. *Personality and Social Psychology Review, 2*, 173–183.

Hughes, T. L., Smith, C., & Dan, A. (Eds.). (2003). *Mental health issues for sexual minority women: Redefining women's mental health.* New York: Harrington Park Press.

Nolen-Hoeksema, S., & Hilt, L. M. (2009). *Handbook of depression in adolescents.* New York: Routledge.

Payne, S., Swami, V., & Stanistreet, D. (2008). The social construction of gender and its influence on suicide: A review of the literature. *Journal of Men's Health & Gender, 5,* 23–35.

Rudolph, K. D. (2009). The interpersonal context of adolescent depression. In S. Nolen-Hoeksema & L. M. Hilt (Eds.),

Handbook of depression in adolescents (pp. 377–418). New York: Routledge/Taylor Francis Group.

Special Issue of *American Psychologist* (2007). Special Issue: Eating Disorders, Vol. 62.

KEY TERMS

Anorexia nervosa—Eating disorder characterized by the continual pursuit of thinness, a distorted body image, and refusal to maintain a weight that is more than 85% of what is considered normal for the person's age and height.

Binge eating disorder—Eating disorder characterized by recurrent binge eating without purging or fasting.

Body objectification—The experience of one's body being treated as an object to be evaluated and used by others.

Bulimia nervosa—Eating disorder characterized by recurrent binge eating followed by purging via vomiting, laxatives, diuretics, enemas, and/or exercising.

Clinical depression—Another name for major depressive disorder, the critical feature of which is that the person must have experienced a set of depressive symptoms for a period no shorter than two weeks.

Different cause theory—Suggestion that there are different causes of girls' and boys' depression and the cause of girls' depression increases during adolescence.

Differential exposure—Idea that men and women are exposed to a different number of or kinds of stressors.

Differential item functioning—Idea that some items are more likely to be associated with a trait, such as depression, among men versus women.

Differential vulnerability—Idea that certain stressors are more strongly linked to distress in one sex than the other.

Emotion-focused coping—Approach to stressful situations in which individuals attempt to accommodate themselves to the stressor.

Gender intensification—Gender roles becoming salient during adolescence, causing boys and girls to adhere more strongly to these roles.

Interactive theory—Suggestion that being female always poses a risk for depression and the events of adolescence activate that risk.

Learned helplessness—Learning that our actions are independent of outcomes, which then leads us to stop responding (give up) in other situations.

Precipitating factors—Environmental events that trigger the emergence of a disorder (e.g., depression).

Problem-focused coping—Approach to stressful situations in which we attempt to alter the stressor itself.

Psychological reactance—Reaction to a perceived threat to control that involves doing the opposite of what is demanded.

Relative coping—Likelihood that men or women use one coping strategy compared to another strategy.

Same cause theory—Suggestion that the same factor could cause depression in both men and women, but the factor increases during adolescence only for girls.

Susceptibility factors—Innate, usually biological, factors that place one group (e.g., women) at greater risk for a disorder (e.g., depression) than another group.

REFERENCES

Abbott-Chapman, J., Denholm, C., & Wyld, C. (2008). Gender differences in adolescent risk taking: Are they diminishing? An Australian intergenerational study. *Youth and Society, 40,* 131–154.

Abel, M. II., & Meltzer, A. L. (2007). Student ratings of a male and female professors' lecture on sex discrimination in the workforce. *Sex Roles, 57,* 173–180.

Aboud, F. E., Mendelson, M. J., & Purdy, K. T. (2003). Cross-race peer relations and friendship quality. *International Journal of Behavioral Development, 27,* 165–173.

Abrams, D., Viki, G. T., Masser, B., & Bohner, G. (2003). Perceptions of stranger and acquaintance rape: The role of benevolent and hostile sexism in victim blame and rape proclivity. *Journal of Personality and Social Psychology, 84,* 111–125.

Aday, R. H., Kehoe, G. C., & Farney, L. A. (2006). Impact of senior center friendships on aging women who live alone. *Journal of Women & Aging, 18,* 57–73.

Addis, M. E., & Mahalik, J. R. (2003). Men, masculinity, and the context of help seeking. *American Psychologist, 58,* 5–14.

Addis, S., Davies, M., Greene, G., MacBride-Stewart, S., & Shepherd, M. (2009). The health, social care and housing needs of lesbian, gay, bisexual, and transgender older people: A review of the literature. *Health and Social Care in the Community, 17,* 647–658.

Afifi, T. O., MacMillan, H., Cox, B. J., Asmundson, G. J. G., Stein, M. B., & Sareen, J. (2009). Mental health correlates of intimate partner violence in marital relationships in a nationally representative sample of males and females. *Journal of Interpersonal Violence, 24,* 1398–1417.

Afifi, W. A., & Faulkner, S. L. (2000). On being "just friends": The frequency and impact of sexual activity in cross-sex friendships. *Journal of Social and Personal Relationships, 17,* 205–222.

Ai, A. L., Peterson, C., Dunkle, R. E., Saunders, D. G., Bolling, S. F., & Buchtel, H. A. (1997). How gender affects psychological adjustment one year after coronary artery bypass graft surgery. *Women and Health, 26*(4), 45–65.

Akiyama, H., Elliott, K., & Antonucci, T. C. (1996). Same-sex and cross-sex relationships. *Journal of Gerontology, 51B*(6), 374–382.

Akman, I., & Mishra, A. (2010). Gender, age, and income differences in Internet usage among employees in organizations. *Computers in Human Behavior, 26,* 482–490.

Alansari, B. M. (2006). Gender differences in depression among undergraduates from seventeen Islamic countries. *Social Behavior and Personality, 34,* 729–738.

Albert, B., Brown, S., & Flanigan, C. (Eds.). (2003). *14 and younger: The sexual behavior of young adolescents (summary).* Washington, DC: National Campaign to Prevent Teen Pregnancy.

Aldao, A., Nolen-Hoeksema, S., & Schweizer, S. (2010). Emotion-regulation strategies across psychopathology: A meta-analytic review. *Clinical Psychology Review, 30,* 217–237.

Aleman, A., Bronk, E., Kessels, R. P. C., Koppeschaar, H. P. F., & Van Honk, J. (2004). A single administration of testosterone improves visuospatial ability in young women. *Psychoneuroendocrinology, 29,* 612–617.

Alexander, M. G., & Fisher, T. D. (2003). Truth and consequences: Using the bogus pipeline to examine sex differences in self-reported sexuality. *Journal of Sex Research, 40*(1), 27–35.

Algars, M., Santtila, P., Varjonen, M., Witting, K., Johansson, A., Jern, P., et al. (2009). The adult body: How age, gender, and body mass index are related to body image. *Journal of Aging and Health, 21,* 1112–1132.

Alksnis, C., Desmarais, S., & Curtis, J. (2008). Workforce segregation and the gender wage gap: Is "women's" work valued as highly as "men's"? *Journal of Applied Social Psychology, 38,* 1416–1441.

Allen, N., & Bloxham, A. (2009). Fort Hood shooting: 13 killed and 30 injured at U.S. army base. *Telegraph.* Retrieved May 26, 2010, from http://www.telegraph.co.uk/news/worldnews/northamerica/usa/65123

Almeida, J., Johnson, R. M., Corliss, H. L., Molnar, B. E., & Azrael, D. (2009). Emotional distress among LGBT youth: The influence of perceived discrimination based on sexual orientation. *Journal of Youth and Adolescence, 38,* 1001–1014.

Altermatt, E. R., Jovanovic, J., & Perry, M. (1998). Bias or responsivity? Sex and achievement-level effects on teachers' classroom questioning practices. *Journal of Educational Psychology, 90,* 516–527.

Amadio, D. M., Adam, T., & Buletza, K. (2008). Gender differences in alcohol use and alcohol-related problems: Do they hold for lesbians and gay men? *Journal of Gay and Lesbian Social Services, 20,* 315–327.

Amanatullah, E. T., & Morris, M. W. (2010). Negotiation gender roles: Gender differences in assertive negotiating are mediated by women's fear of backlash and attenuated when negotiating on behalf of others. *Journal of Personality and Social Psychology, 98,* 256–267.

Ambwani, A., & Strauss, J. (2007). Love thyself before loving others? A qualitative and quantitative analysis of gender differences in body image and romantic love. *Sex Roles, 56,* 13–21.

American Association of University Women. (2000). *Tech-savvy: Educated girls in the new computer age.* Washington, DC: Author.

American Bar Association. (2007). *Domestic violence arrest policies by state.* Retrieved August 16, 2010, from http://www.abanet.org/domviol

American Cancer Society. (2009). *Cancer facts and figures 2009.* Retrieved July 28, 2010, from http://www.cancer.org/Research/CancerFactsFigures/cancer-facts-figures-2009

American Civil Liberties Union. (2000, March 8). *In blocking father's time off to care for first-born, South Carolina is the "deadbeat," ACLU charges* [news release]. Retrieved July 24, 2003, from www.aclu.org/news/ewsPrint.cfm?D= 7860&c=182

American Civil Liberties Union. (2003). *In victory for working family, high court says states must comply with family and medical leave act* [news release]. Retrieved July 24, 2003, from www.aclu.org/news/NewsPrint.cfm?D= 12736&c=175

American Congress of Obstetricians and Gynecologists. (2009). *ACOG statement on single-dose EC reformulation.* Retrieved May 7, 2010, from http://www.acog.org/from_home/publications/press_releases/nr07-15

American Heart Association. (2010). *Heart disease and stroke statistics – 2010 update.* Retrieved September 23, 2010, from http://www.americanheart.org/presenter.jhtml?dentifier=3000090

American Psychiatric Association. (2000). *Diagnostic and statistical manual of mental disorders* (4th ed.). Washington, DC: American Psychiatric Association.

American Psychological Association. (2007). *Report of the APA task force on the sexualization of girls.* Retrieved November 8, 2007, from www.apa.org/pi/wpo/sexualization.html

Andalo, P. (2004). *Health for one and all: Latinos in the USA.* Retrieved February 26, 2007, from www.paho.org/English/DD/PIN/Number19_article01.htm

Andersen, P. A. (2006). The evolution of biological sex differences in communication. In K. Dindia & D. J. Canary (Eds.), *Sex differences and similarities in communication* (2nd ed., pp. 117–135). Mahwah, NJ: Lawrence Erlbaum Associates.

Anderson, K. G., Sankis, L. M., & Widiger, T. A. (2001). Pathology versus statistical infrequency: Potential sources of gender bias in personality disorder criteria. *Journal of Nervous and Mental Disease, 189,* 661–667.

Anderson, K. J., Kanner, M., & Elsayegh, N. (2009). Are feminists man haters? Feminists' and nonfeminists' attitudes toward men. *Psychology of Women Quarterly, 33,* 216–224.

Andreou, E. (2006). Social preference, perceived popularity, and social intelligence: Relations to overt and relational aggression. *School Psychology International, 27,* 339–351.

Andrews, P. W., Gangestad, S. W., Miller, G. F., Haselton, M. G., Thornhill, R., & Neale, M. C. (2008). Sex differences in detecting sexual infidelity: Results of a maximum likelihood method for analyzing the sensitivity of sex differences to underreporting. *Human Nature, 19,* 347–373.

Angold, A., Costello, E. J., & Worthman, C. M. (1998). Puberty and depression: The roles of age, pubertal status and pubertal timing. *Psychological Medicine, 28,* 51–61.

Anson, O., Levenson, A., & Bonneh, D. Y. (1990). Gender and health on the kibbutz. *Sex Roles, 22,* 213–231.

Appelberg, K., Romanov, K., Heikkila, K., Honkasalo, M.-L., & Koskenvou, M. (1996). Interpersonal conflict as a predictor of work disability: A follow-up study of 15,348 Finnish employees. *Journal of Psychosomatic Research, 40,* 157–167.

Archer, J. (2000). Sex differences in aggression between heterosexual partners: A meta-analytic review. *Psychological Bulletin, 126,* 651–680.

Archer, J. (2002). Sex differences in physically aggressive acts between heterosexual partners: A meta-analytic review. *Aggression and Violent Behavior, 7,* 313–351.

Archer, J. (2004). Sex differences in aggression in real-world settings: A meta-analytic review. *Review of General Psychology, 8*(4), 291–322.

Archer, J. (2009). Does sexual selection explain human sex differences in aggression? *Behavioral and Brain Sciences, 32,* 249–311.

Archer, J., & Cote, S. (2005). Sex differences in aggressive behavior. In R. E. Tremblay, W. W. Hartup, &

J. Archer (Eds.), *Developmental origins of aggression* (pp. 425–443). New York: Guilford Press.

Archer, J., & Coyne, S. M. (2005). An integrated review of indirect, relational, and social aggression. *Personality and Social Psychology Review, 9,* 212–230.

Aries, E. (2006). Sex differences in interaction: A reexamination. In K. Dindia & D. J. Canary (Eds.), *Sex differences and similarities in communication* (2nd ed., pp. 21–36). Mahwah, NJ: Lawrence Erlbaum Associates.

Aristotle. (1963). *Generation of animals* (Rev. ed.). (A. L. Peck, Trans.). Cambridge, MA: Harvard University Press.

Arrighi, B. A., & Maume, D. J., Jr. (2000). Workplace subordination and men's avoidance of housework. *Journal of Family Issues, 21*(4), 464–487.

Artazcoz, L., Borrell, C., Benach, J., Cortes, I., & Rohlfs, I. (2004). Women, family demands and health: The importance of employment status and socio-economic position. *Social Science & Medicine, 59,* 263–274.

Ashmore, R. D. (1990). Sex, gender, and the individual. In L. A. Pervin (Ed.), *Handbook of personality: Theory and research* (pp. 486–526). New York: Guilford Press.

Ata, R. N., Ludden, A. B., & Lally, M. M. (2007). The effects of gender and family, friend, and media influences on eating behaviors and body image during adolescence. *Journal of Youth and Adolescence, 36,* 1024–1037.

Atencio, M., & Wright, J. (2008). "We be killin' them": Hierarchies of Black masculinity in urban basketball spaces. *Sociology of Sport Journal, 25,* 263–280.

Aube, J. (2008). Balancing concern for other with concern for self: Links between unmitigated communion, communion, and psychological well-being. *Journal of Personality, 76,* 101–133.

Ault, A., & Brzuzy, S. (2009). Removing gender identity disorder from the *Diagnostic and Statistical Manual of Mental Disorders*: A call for action. *Social Work, 54*(2), 187–189.

Auster, C. J., & Ohm, S. C. (2000). Masculinity and femininity in contemporary American society: A reevaluation using the Bem Sex-Role Inventory. *Sex Roles, 43*(7/8), 499–528.

Auyeung, B., Baron-Cohen, S., Ashwin, E., Knickmeyer, R., Taylor, K., Hackett, G., et al. (2009). Fetal testosterone predicts sexually differentiated childhood behavior in girls and in boys. *Psychological Science, 20,* 144–148.

Avellar, S., & Smock, P. J. (2005). The economic consequences of the dissolution of cohabiting unions. *Journal of Marriage and Family, 67,* 315–327.

Ayman, R., & Korabik, K. (2010). Leadership: Why gender and culture matter. *American Psychologist, 65,* 157–170.

Babcock, L., & Laschever, S. (2003). *Women don't ask: Negotiation and the gender divide.* Princeton, NJ: Princeton University Press.

Badr, H., & Acitelli, L. K. (2005). Dyadic adjustment in chronic illness: Does relationship talk matter? *Journal of Family Psychology, 19,* 465–469.

Baenninger, M., & Newcombe, N. (1989). The role of experience in spatial test performance: A meta-analysis. *Sex Roles, 20,* 327–344.

Baillargeon, R. H., Keenan, K., Wu, H. X., Zoccolillo, M., Cote, S., Perusse, D., et al. (2007). Gender differences in physical aggression: A prospective population-based survey of children before and after 2 years of age. *Developmental Psychology, 43,* 13–26.

Baines, E., & Blatchford, P. (2009). Sex differences in the structure and stability of children's playground social networks and their overlap with friendship relations. *British Journal of Developmental Psychology, 27,* 743–760.

Bakan, D. (1966). *The duality of human existence.* Chicago: Rand McNally.

Baker, N. L. (2006). Feminist psychology in the service of women: Staying engaged without getting married. *Psychology of Women Quarterly, 30,* 1–14.

Bakker, M. P., Ormel, J., Verhulst, F. C., & Oldehinkel, A. J. (2010). Peer stressors and gender differences in adolescents' mental health: The TRAILS study. *Journal of Adolescent Health, 46,* 444–450.

Baldassano, C. F., Marangell, L. B., Gyulai, L., Ghaemi, S. N., Joffe, H., Kim, D. R., et al. (2005). Gender differences in bipolar disorder: Retrospective data from the first 500 STEP-BD participants. *Bipolar Disorders, 7,* 465–470.

Bales, R. F., & Slater, P. E. (1955). Role differentiation in small decision-making groups. In T. Parsons & R. F. Bales (Eds.), *Family, socialization, and interaction process* (pp. 259–306). Glencoe, IL: Free Press.

Ballingrud, D. (1992). Assaults tarnish navy group [Electronic Version]. *St. Petersburg Times.* Retrieved June 6, 2011, from http://proquest.umi.com/pqdweb?did= 54181879&sid=1&Fmt=3&clientId=3259&RQT=309& VName=PQD

Bandura, A., & Walters, R. (1963). *Social learning and personality development.* New York: Holt, Rinehart & Winston.

Banitt, A. A., Kaur, H., Pulvers, K. M., Nollen, N. L., Ireland, M., & Fitzgibbon, M. L. (2008). BMI percentiles and body image discrepancy in Black and White adolescents. *Obesity, 16,* 987–991.

Bank, B. J., & Hansford, S. L. (2000). Gender and friendship: Why are men's best same-sex friendships less intimate and supportive? *Personal Relationships, 7,* 63–78.

Barnett, R. C. (2004). Women and multiple roles: Myths and reality. *Harvard Review of Psychiatry, 12,* 158–164.

Barnett, R. C., & Gareis, K. C. (2002). Full-time and reduced-hours work schedules and marital quality. *Work and Occupations, 29,* 364–379.

Barreto, M., & Ellemers, N. (2005). The burden of benevolent sexism: How it contributes to the maintenance of gender inequalities. *European Journal of Social Psychology, 35,* 633–642.

Barrett, L., & Bliss-Moreau, E. (2009). She's emotional. He's having a bad day: Attributional explanations for emotion stereotypes. *Emotion, 9,* 649–658.

Barron, L. A. (2003). Ask and you shall receive? Gender differences in negotiators' beliefs about requests for a higher salary. *Human Relations, 56,* 635–662.

Barry, C. M., Madsen, S. D., Nelson, L. J., Carroll, J. S., & Badger, S. (2009). Friendship and romantic relationship qualities in emerging adulthood: Differential associations with identity development and achieved adulthood criteria. *Journal of Adult Development, 16,* 209–222.

Barta, W. D., & Kiene, S. M. (2005). Motivations for infidelity in heterosexual dating couples: The roles of gender, personality differences, and sociosexual orientation. *Journal of Social and Personal Relationships, 22,* 339–360.

Bartley, S. J., Blanton, P. W., & Gilliard, J. L. (2005). Husbands and wives in dual-earner marriages: Decision-making, gender role attitudes, division of household labor, and equity. *Marriage and Family Review, 37,* 69–94.

Basow, S. A., & Rubenfeld, K. (2003). "Troubles talk": Effects of gender and gender-typing. *Sex Roles, 48,* 183–187.

Batalova, J. A., & Cohen, P. N. (2002). Premarital cohabitation and housework: Couples in cross-national perspective. *Journal of Marriage and Family, 64,* 743–755.

Batnitzky, A. (2008). Obesity and household roles: Gender and social class in Morocco. *Sociology of Health and Illness, 30,* 445–462.

Bauermeister, J. J., Shrout, P. E., Chavez, L., Rubio-Stipec, M., Ramirez, R., Padilla, L., et al. (2007). ADHD and gender: Are risks and sequela of ADHD the same for boys and girls? *Journal of Child Psychology and Psychiatry, 48,* 831–839.

Baumeister, R. F., & Sommer, K. L. (1997). What do men want? Gender differences and two spheres of belongingness: Comment on Cross and Madson (1997). *Psychological Bulletin, 122,* 38–44.

Baumgarter, R. (2002). Cross-gender friendship: The troublesome relationship. In R. Goodwin (Ed.), *Inappropriate relationships: The unconventional, the disapproved, and the forbidden* (pp. 103–124). Mahwah, NJ: Erlbaum.

Baumgartner, T., Heinrichs, M., Vonlanthen, A., Fischbacher, U., & Fehr, E. (2008). Oxytocin shapes the neural circuitry of trust and trust adaptation in humans. *Neuron, 58,* 639–650.

Bauminger, N., Finzi-Dottan, R., Chason, S., & Har-Even, D. (2008). Intimacy in adolescent friendship: The roles of attachment, coherence, and self-disclosure. *Journal of Social and Personal Relationships, 25,* 409–428.

Beadnell, B., Morrison, D. M., Wilsdon, A., Wells, E. A., Murowchick, E., Hoppe, M., et al. (2005). Condom use, frequency of sex, and number of partners: Multidimensional characterization of adolescent sexual risk-taking. *Journal of Sex Research, 42,* 192–202.

Beals, K. P., & Peplau, L. A. (2006). Disclosure patterns within social networks of gay men and lesbians. *Journal of Homosexuality, 51,* 101–120.

Bearman, S. K., & Stice, E. (2008). Testing a gender additive model: The role of body image in adolescent depression. *Journal of Abnormal Child Psychology, 36,* 1251–1263.

Beauty and love quotes. (2000). Retrieved June 15, 2000, from www.cc.gatech.edu/grads/b/Gary.N.Boone/beauty_and_love_quotes.html

Becker, D. V., Kenrick, D. T., Guerin, S., & Maner, J. K. (2005). Concentrating on beauty: Sexual selection and sociospatial memory. *Personality and Social Psychology Bulletin, 31,* 1643–1652.

Bell, L. A. (1996). In danger of winning: Consciousness raising strategies for empowering girls in the United States. *Women's Studies International Forum, 19*(4), 419–427.

Belle, D. (1982). Social ties and social support. In D. Belle (Ed.), *Lives in stress: Women and depression* (pp. 133–144). Beverly Hills, CA: Sage.

Belle, D. (1985). Ironies in the contemporary study of gender. *Journal of Personality, 53,* 400–405.

Belle, D. (1987). Gender differences in the social moderators of stress. In R. Barnett, L. Beiner, & G. K. Baruch (Eds.), *Gender and stress* (pp. 257–277). New York: Free Press.

Bem, S. L. (1974). The measurement of psychological androgyny. *Journal of Consulting and Clinical Psychology, 42*(2), 155–162.

Bem, S. L. (1975). Sex role adaptability: One consequence of psychological androgyny. *Journal of Personality and Social Psychology, 31,* 634–643.

Bem, S. L. (1981). Gender schema theory: A cognitive account of sex typing. *Psychological Review, 88,* 354–364.

Bem, S. L. (1984). Androgyny and gender schema theory: A conceptual and empirical integration. In T. B. Sonderegger (Ed.), *Nebraska symposium on motivation 1984: Psychology and gender* (Vol. 32, pp. 179–226). Lincoln, NE: University of Nebraska Press.

Bem, S. L. (1995). Dismantling gender polarization and compulsory heterosexuality: Should we turn the volume down or up? *Journal of Sex Research, 32*(4), 329–334.

Bem, S. L. (1998). *An unconventional family.* New Haven, CT: Yale University Press.

Ben-David, S., & Schneider, O. (2005). Rape perceptions, gender role attitudes, and victim-perpetrator acquaintance. *Sex Roles, 53,* 385–399.

Benedetti, A., Fagiolini, A., Casamassima, F., Mian, M. S., Adamovit, A., Musetti, L., et al. (2007). Gender differences in bipolar disorder type 1: A 48-week prospective follow-up of 72 patients treated in an Italian tertiary care center. *Journal of Nervous and Mental Disease, 195,* 93–96.

Benenson, J. F., & Christakos, A. (2003). The greater fragility of females' versus males' closest same-sex friendships. *Child Development, 74,* 1123–1129.

Benenson, J. F., Roy, R., Waite, A., Goldbaum, S., Linders, L., & Simpson, A. (2002). Greater discomfort as a proximate cause of sex differences in competition. *Merrill-Palmer Quarterly, 48,* 225–247.

Bennett, D. S., Ambrosini, P. J., Kudes, D., Metz, C., & Rabinovich, H. (2005). Gender differences in adolescent depression: Do symptoms differ for boys and girls? *Journal of Affective Disorders, 89,* 35–44.

Berger, J. S., Elliott, L., Gallup, D., Roe, M., Granger, C. B., Armstrong, P. W., et al. (2009). Sex differences in mortality following acute coronary syndromes. *Journal of the American Medical Association, 302,* 874–882.

Bergman, M. E., Langhout, R. D., Palmieri, P. A., Cortina, L. M., & Fitzgerald, L. F. (2002). The (un)reasonableness of reporting: Antecedents and consequences of reporting sexual harassment. *Journal of Applied Psychology, 87,* 230–242.

Berkey, C. S., Rockett, H. R., Field, A. E., Gillman, M. W., Frazier, A. L., Camargo, C. A. J., et al. (2000). Activity, dietary intake, and weight changes in a longitudinal study of preadolescent and adolescent boys and girls. *Pediatrics, 105*(4), E56.

Berkman, L. F., & Syme, S. L. (1979). Social networks, host resistance, and mortality: A nine-year follow-up study of Alameda County residents. *American Journal of Epidemiology, 109*(2), 186–204.

Berkman, L. F., Vaccarino, V., & Seeman, T. (1993). Gender differences in cardiovascular morbidity and mortality: The contribution of social networks and support. *Annals of Behavioral Medicine, 15,* 112–118.

Bernardes, S. F., Keogh, E., & Lima, M. L. (2008). Bridging the gap between pain and gender research: A selective literature review. *European Journal of Pain, 12,* 427–440.

Bertakis, K. D. (2009). The influence of gender on the doctor-patient interaction. *Patient Education and Counseling, 76,* 356–360.

Bettencourt, B. A., & Miller, N. (1996). Gender differences in aggression as a function of provocation: A meta-analysis. *Psychological Bulletin, 119,* 422–447.

Bhanot, R., & Jovanovic, J. (2005). Do parents' academic gender stereotypes influence whether they intrude on their children's homework? *Sex Roles, 52,* 597–607.

Biederman, J., Mick, E., Faraone, S. V., Braaten, E., Doyle, A., Spencer, T., et al. (2002). Influence of gender on attention deficit hyperactivity disorder in children referred to a psychiatric clinic. *American Journal of Psychiatry, 159,* 36–42.

Biernat, M. (2003). Toward a broader view of social stereotyping. *American Psychologist, 58,* 1019–1027.

Biernat, M., & Eidelman, S. (2007). Translating subjective language in letters of recommendation: The case of the sexist professor. *European Journal of Social Psychology, 37,* 1149–1175.

Birkett, M., Espelage, D. L., & Koenig, B. (2009). LGB and questioning students in schools: The moderating effects of homophobic bullying and school climate on negative outcomes. *Journal of Youth and Adolescence, 38,* 989–1000.

Biro, F. M., Striegel-Moore, R. H., Franko, D. L., Padgett, J., & Bean, J. A. (2006). Self-esteem in adolescent females. *Journal of Adolescent Health, 39*(4), 501–507.

Bishop, K. M., & Wahlsten, D. (1997). Sex differences in the human corpus callosum: Myth or reality? *Neuroscience and Biobehavioral Reviews, 21,* 581–601.

Bjorklund, A., Ginther, D. K., & Sundstrom, M. (2007). *Is cohabitation bad for children? Assessing the causal impact of legal marriage on child outcomes* (IZA Discussion Paper Series No. 3189 (pp. 1–37)). Bonn, Germany: Institute for the Study of Labor.

Black, D. A., Makar, H. R., Sanders, S. G., & Taylor, L. J. (2003). "The Earnings Effects of Sexual Orientation," *Industrial & Labor Relations Review*, Vol. 56 (3), 449–469.

Blakemore, J. E. O., & Centers, R. E. (2005). Characteristics of boys' and girls' toys. *Sex Roles, 53,* 619–633.

Blanch, D. C., Hall, J. A., Rote, D. L., & Frankel, R. M. (2008). Medical student gender and issues of confidence. *Patient Education and Counseling, 72,* 374–381.

Blashill, A. J., & Powlishta, K. K. (2009). Gay stereotypes: The use of sexual orientation as a cue for gender-related attributes. *Sex Roles, 61,* 783–793.

Bleske, A. L., & Buss, D. M. (2000). Can men and women be just friends? *Personal Relationships, 7,* 131–151.

Bleske-Rechek, A. L., & Buss, D. M. (2001). Opposite-sex friendship: Sex differences and similarities in initiation, selection, and dissolution. *Personality and Social Psychology Bulletin, 27,* 1310–1323.

Block, J. H. (1976). Issues, problems, and pitfalls in assessing sex differences: A critical review of the psychology of sex differences. *Merrill-Palmer Quarterly, 22*(4), 283–308.

Block, J. H., & Kremen, A. M. (1996). IQ and ego-resiliency: Conceptual and empirical connections and separateness. *Journal of Personality and Social Psychology, 70,* 349–361.

Blumenthal, J. A. (1998). The reasonable woman standard: A meta-analytic review of gender differences in perceptions of sexual harassment. *Law and Human Behavior, 22*(1), 33–57.

Bly, R. (1990). *Iron John: A book about men*. Reading, MA: Addison-Wesley.

Bohanek, J. G., Marin, K. A., & Fivush, R. (2008). Family narratives, self, and gender in early adolescence. *Journal of Early Adolescence, 28,* 153–176.

Bohner, G., Eyssel, F., Pina, A., Siebler, F., & Viki, G. T. (2009). Rape myth acceptance: Cognitive, affective and behavioural effects of beliefs that blame the victim and exonerate the perpetrator. In M. Horvath & J. Brown (Eds.), *Rape: Challenging contemporary thinking* (pp. 17–45). Portland, OR: Willan Publishing.

Bombardieri, M. (2005). Harvard women's group rips Summers. *Boston Globe*. Retrieved January 31, 2007, from www.boston.com/news/education/higher/articles/2005/01/19

Bond, J. T., Galinsky, E., & Swanberg, J. E. (1998). *The 1997 national study of the changing workforce*. New York: Families and Work Institute.

Bond, M. A., Punnett, L., Pyle, J. L., Cazeca, D., & Cooperman, M. (2004). Gendered work conditions, health, and work outcomes. *Journal of Occupational Health Psychology, 9,* 28–45.

Bonds-Raacke, J. M., Cady, E. T., Schlegel, R., Harris, R. J., & Firebaugh, L. (2007). Remembering gay/lesbian media characters: Can Ellen and Will improve attitudes toward homosexuals? *Journal of Homosexuality, 53,* 19–34.

Bondurant, B., & Donat, P. L. N. (1999). Perceptions of women's sexual interest and acquaintance rape: The role of sexual overperception and affective attitudes. *Psychology of Women Quarterly, 23,* 691–705.

Bondurant, B., & White, J. W. (1996). Men who sexually harass: An embedded perspective. In D. K. Shrier (Ed.), *Sexual harassment in the work place and academia* (pp. 59–78). Washington, DC: American Psychiatric Press.

Book, A. S., Starzyk, K. B., & Quinsey, V. L. (2001). The relationship between testosterone and aggression: A meta-analysis. *Aggression and Violent Behavior, 6,* 579–599.

Bookwala, J., Sobin, J., & Zdaniuk, B. (2005). Gender and aggression in marital relationships: A life-span perspective. *Sex Roles, 52,* 797–806.

Booth, A., Johnson, D. R., & Granger, D. A. (1999). Testosterone and men's depression: The role of social behavior. *Journal of Health and Social Behavior, 40,* 130–140.

Boroughs, M., & Thompson, J. K. (2002). Exercise status and sexual orientation as moderators of body image disturbance and eating disorders in males. *International Journal of Eating Disorders, 31,* 307–311.

Borowsky, S. J., Rubenstein, L. V., Meredith, L. S., Camp, P., Jackson-Triche, M., & Wells, K. B. (2000). Who is at risk of nondetection of mental health problems in primary care? *Journal of General Internal Medicine, 15,* 381–388.

Borrelli, B., Niaura, R. S., Hitsman, B., Spring, B., & Papandonatos, G. (2001). Influences of gender and weight gain on short-term relapse to smoking in a cessation trial. *Journal of Consulting and Clinical Psychology, 69,* 511–515.

Borse, N. N., Gilchrist, J., Dellinger, A. M., Rudd, R. A., Ballesteros, M. F., & Sleet, D. A. (2008). *CDC childhood injury report: Patterns of unintentional injuries among 0–19 year olds in the United States, 2000–2006*. Atlanta, GA: Centers for Disease Control and Prevention, National Center for Injury Prevention and Control.

Bosson, J. K., Haymovitz, E. L., & Pinel, E. C. (2004). When saying and doing diverge: The effects of stereotype threat on self-reported versus non-verbal anxiety. *Journal of Experimental Social Psychology, 40,* 247–255.

Bostwick, W. B., Boyd, C. J., Hughes, T. L., & McCabe, S. E. (2010). Dimensions of sexual orientation and the prevalence of mood and anxiety disorders in the United States. *American Journal of Public Health, 100,* 468–475.

Bouman, A., Schipper, M., Heineman, M. J., & Faas, M. M. (2004). Gender difference in the non-specific and specific immune response in humans. *American Journal of Reproductive Immunology, 52,* 19–26.

Boutin-Foster, C., & Charlson, M. E. (2007). Do recent life events and social support explain gender differences in depressive symptoms in patients who had percutaneous transluminal coronary angioplasty? *Journal of Women's Health, 16,* 114–123.

Bowen, C.-C., Swim, J. K., & Jacobs, R. R. (2000). Evaluating gender biases on actual job performance of real people: A meta-analysis. *Journal of Applied Social Psychology, 30,* 2194–2215.

Boye, K. (2009). Relatively different? How do gender differences in well-being depend on paid and unpaid work in Europe? *Social Indicators Research, 93,* 509–525.

Boysen, G. A., Vogel, D. L., Madon, S., & Wester, S. R. (2006). Mental health stereotypes about gay men. *Sex Roles, 54,* 69–82.

Brady, K. L., & Eisler, R. M. (1995). Gender bias in the college classroom: A critical review of the literature and implications for future research. *Journal of Research and Development in Education, 29*(1), 9–19.

Bramlett, M. D., & Mosher, W. D. (2002). Cohabitation, marriage, divorce, and remarriage in the United States. *National Center for Health Statistics: Vital Health Statistics, 23*(22), 1–93.

Brand, R. J., Markey, C. M., Mills, A., & Hodges, S. D. (2007). Sex differences in self-reported infidelity and its correlates. *Sex Roles, 57,* 101–109.

Brehm, J. W. (1966). *A theory of psychological reactance*. New York: Academic Press.

Breines, J. G., Crocker, J., & Garcia, J. A. (2008). Self-objectification and well-being in women's daily lives. *Personality and Social Psychology Bulletin, 34*, 583–598.

Brendgen, M., Girard, A., Dionne, G., Boivin, M., Vitaro, F., & Perusse, D. (2005). Examining genetic and environmental effects on social aggression: A study of 6-year-old twins. *Child Development, 76*, 930–946.

Brennan, R. T., Barnett, R. C., & Gareis, K. C. (2001). When she earns more than he does: A longitudinal study of dual-earner couples. *Journal of Marriage and the Family, 63*, 168–182.

Brent, D. A., Perper, J. A., Moritz, G., Baugher, M., Roth, C., Balach, L., et al. (1993). Stressful life events, psychopathology, and adolescent suicide: A case control study. *Suicide and Life-Threatening Behavior, 23*(3), 179–187.

Brescoll, V. L., & Uhlmann, E. L. (2008). Can an angry woman get ahead? Status conferral, gender, and expression of emotion in the workplace. *Psychological Science, 19*, 268–275.

Brescoll, V., & LaFrance, M. (2004). The correlates and consequences of newspaper reports of research on sex differences. *American Psychological Society, 15*, 515–520.

Bridge, K., & Baxter, L. A. (1992). Blended relationships: Friends as work associates. *Western Journal of Communication, 56*, 200–225.

Brinig, M. F., & Allen, D. W. (2000). "These boots are made for walking": Why most divorce filers are women. *American Law and Economics Review, 2*, 126–169.

Briton, N. J., & Hall, J. A. (1995). Beliefs about female and male nonverbal communication. *Sex Roles, 32*, 79–90.

Brockmann, H., Muller, R., & Helmert, U. (2009). Time to retire-time to die? A prospective cohort study of the effects of early retirement on long-term survival. *Social Science and Medicine, 69*, 160–164.

Broderick, P. C., & Korteland, C. (2002). Coping style and depression in early adolescence: Relationships to gender, gender role, and implicit beliefs. *Sex Roles, 46*(7/8), 201–213.

Brody, L. R., & Hall, J. A. (1993). Gender and emotion. In M. Lewis & J. M. Haviland (Eds.), *Handbook of emotions* (pp. 447–460). New York: Guilford Press.

Brody, L. R., & Hall, J. A. (2008). Gender and emotion in context. In M. Lewis, J. M. Haviland, & L. Barrett (Eds.), *Handbook of emotions* (pp. 395–408). New York: Guilford Press.

Broverman, I. K., Vogel, S. R., Broverman, D. M., Clarkson, F. E., & Rosenkrantz, P. S. (1972). Sex-role stereotypes: A current appraisal. *Journal of Social Issues, 28*, 59–78.

Brown, S. L., Bulanda, J. R., & Lee, G. R. (2005). The significance of nonmarital cohabitation: Marital status and mental health benefits among middle-aged and older adults. *Journals of Gerontology: Series B: Psychological Sciences and Social Sciences, 60B*(1), S21–S29.

Brown, S. L., Lee, G. R., & Bulanda, J. R. (2006). Cohabitation among older adults: A national portrait. *Journal of Gerontology, 61B*, S71–S79.

Browne, B. A. (1998). Gender stereotypes in advertising on children's television in the 1990s: A cross-national analysis. *Journal of Advertising, 27*(1), 83–96.

Brownmiller, S. (1975). *Against our will: Men, women, and rape*. New York: Bantam Books.

Bruckner, H., & Bearman, P. (2005). After the promise: The STD consequences of adolescent virginity pledges. *Journal of Adolescent Health, 36*, 271–278.

Buchanan, T. S., Fischer, A. R., Tokar, D. M., & Yoder, J. D. (2008). Testing a culture-specific extension of objectification theory regarding African American women's body image. *Counseling Psychologist, 36*, 697–718.

Bulanda, J. R., & Brown, S. L. (2007). Race-ethnic differences in marital quality and divorce. *Social Science Research, 36*, 945–967.

Bullock, H. E., & Fernald, J. L. (2003). "Feminism lite?" Feminist identification, speaker appearance, and perceptions of feminist and antifeminist messengers. *Psychology of Women Quarterly, 27*, 291–299.

Bumpass, L. L., Sweet, J. A., & Cherlin, A. (1991). The role of cohabitation in declining rates of marriage. *Journal of Marriage and the Family, 53*, 913–927.

Burckle, M. A., Ryckman, R. M., Gold, J. A., Thornton, B., & Audesse, R. J. (1999). Forms of competitive attitude and achievement orientation in relation to disordered eating. *Sex Roles, 40*, 853–870.

Bureau of Justice Statistics. (2009). *Criminal victimization, 2008*. Retrieved August 25, 2010, from http://bjs.ojp.usdoj.gov/content/pub/pdf/cv08.pdf

Bureau of Justice Statistics. (2010). *Homicide trends in the U.S.* Retrieved July 7, 2010, from http://bjs.ojp.usdoj.gov/content/homicide/race.cfm

Burgess, D., & Borgida, E. (1999). Who women are, who women should be: Descriptive and prescriptive gender stereotyping in sex discrimination. *Psychology, Public Policy and Law, 5*, 665–692.

Burleson, B. R., Kunkel, A. W., Samter, W., & Werking, K. J. (1996). Men's and women's evaluations of communication skills in personal relationships: When sex differences make a difference and when they don't. *Journal of Social and Personal Relationships, 13*, 201–224.

Burt, M. R. (1980). Cultural myths and supports for rape. *Journal of Personality and Social Psychology, 38*, 217–230.

Buss, D. M. (1994). *The evolution of desire*. New York: Basic Books.

Buss, D. M. (1995). Psychological sex differences: Origins through sexual selection. *American Psychologist, 50*, 164–168.

Buss, D. M. (2007). *Evolutionary psychology: The new science of the mind* (3rd ed.). Needham Heights, MA: Allyn & Bacon.

Buss, D. M., Abbott, M., Angleitner, A., & Asherian, A. (1990). International preferences in selecting mates: A study of 37 cultures. *Journal of Cross-Cultural Psychology, 21,* 5–47.

Buss, D. M., Larsen, R. J., Westen, D., & Semmelroth, J. (1992). Sex differences in jealousy: Evolution, physiology, and psychology. *Psychological Science, 3*(4), 251–255.

Buss, D. M., Shackelford, T. K., Choe, J., Buunk, B. P., & Dijkstra, P. (2000). Distress about mating rivals. *Personal Relationships, 7,* 235–243.

Buss, D. M., Shackelford, T. K., Kirkpatrick, L. A., & Larsen, R. J. (2001). A half century of mate preferences: The cultural evolution of values. *Journal of Marriage and the Family, 63,* 491–503.

Bussey, K., & Bandura, A. (1992). Self-regulatory mechanisms governing gender development. *Child Development, 63,* 1236–1250.

Bussey, K., & Bandura, A. (1999). Social cognitive theory of gender development and differentiation. *Psychological Review, 106,* 676–713.

Buston, P. M., & Emlen, S. T. (2003). Cognitive processes underlying human mate choice: The relationship between self-perception and mate preference in Western society. *Proceedings of the National Academy of Sciences, 100,* 8805–8810.

Bybee, J. A., Sullivan, E. L., Zielonka, E., & Moes, E. (2009). Are gay men in worse mental health than heterosexual men? The role of age, shame and guilt, and coming-out. *Journal of Adult Development, 16,* 144–154.

Bylsma, W. H., & Major, B. (1994). Social comparisons and contentment: Exploring the psychological costs of the gender wage gap. *Psychology of Women Quarterly, 18,* 241–249.

Byrnes, J. P., Miller, D. C., & Schafer, W. D. (1999). Gender differences in risk taking: A meta-analysis. *Psychological Bulletin, 125,* 367–383.

Cahn, D. D. (1992). *Conflict in intimate relationships.* New York: Guilford Press.

Cairns, B. E., & Gazerani, P. (2009). Sex-related differences in pain. *Maturitas, 63,* 292–296.

Cale, E. M., & Lilienfeld, S. O. (2002a). Sex differences in psychopathy and antisocial personality disorder: A review and integration. *Clinical Psychology Review, 22,* 1179–1207.

Cale, E. M., & Lilienfeld, S. O. (2002b). Histrionic personality disorder and antisocial personality disorder: Sex-differentiated manifestations of psychopathy? *Journal of Personality Disorders, 16,* 52–72.

Calmes, C. A., & Roberts, J. E. (2008). Rumination in interpersonal relationships: Does co-rumination explain gender differences in emotional distress and relationship satisfaction among college students? *Cognitive Therapy and Research, 32,* 577–590.

Calvert, S. L., Mahler, B. A., Zehnder, S. M., Jenkins, A., & Lee, M. S. (2003). Gender differences in preadolescent children's online interactions: Symbolic modes of self-presentation and self-expression. *Applied Developmental Psychology, 24,* 627–644.

Calzo, J. P., & Ward, L. M. (2009). Contributions of parents, peers, and media to attitudes toward homosexuality: Investigating sex and ethnic differences. *Journal of Homosexuality, 56,* 1101–1116.

Camarena, P. M., Sarigiani, P. A., & Petersen, A. C. (1990). Gender-specific pathways to intimacy in early adolescence. *Journal of Youth and Adolescence, 19,* 19–32.

Cambron, M. J., Acitelli, L. K., & Pettit, J. W. (2008). When women's self-esteem hinges on relationships: A contingent self-esteem model of gender differences in depression. In P. R. Bancroft & L. B. Ardley (Eds.), *Major depression in women* (pp. 123–136). New York: Nova Science Publishers.

Campbell, A. (2006). Sex differences in direct aggression: What are the psychological mediators? *Aggression and Violent Behavior, 11,* 237–264.

Campbell, A. (2010). Oxytocin and human social behavior. *Personality and Social Psychology Bulletin, 14,* 281–295.

Campbell, S. M., & Collaer, M. L. (2009). Stereotype threat and gender differences in performance on a novel visuospatial task. *Psychology of Women Quarterly, 33,* 437–444.

Canary, D. J., & Wahba, J. (2006). Do women work harder than men at maintaining relationships? In K. Dindia & D. J. Canary (Eds.), *Sex differences and similarities in communication* (2nd ed., pp. 359–377). Mahwah, NJ: Lawrence Erlbaum Associates.

Cao, L., Zhang, Y., & He, N. (2008). Carrying weapons to school for protection: An analysis of the 2001 school crime supplement data. *Journal of Criminal Justice, 36,* 154–164.

Capaldi, D. M., Kim, H. K., & Shortt, J. W. (2004). Women's involvement in aggression in young adult romantic relationships: A developmental systems model. In M. Putallaz & K. L. Bierman (Eds.), *Aggression, antisocial behavior and violence among girls: A developmental perspective* (pp. 223–241). New York: Guilford Press.

Card, N. A., Stucky, B. D., Sawalani, G. M., & Little, T. D. (2008). Direct and indirect aggression during childhood and adolescence: A meta-analytic review of gender differences, intercorrelations, and relations to maladjustment. *Child Development, 79,* 1185–1229.

Carli, L. L. (1989). Gender differences in interaction style and influence. *Journal of Personality and Social Psychology, 56,* 565–576.

Carli, L. L. (1990). Gender, language, and influence. *Journal of Personality and Social Psychology, 59,* 941–951.

Carlson, G. A., & Grant, K. E. (2008). The roles of stress and coping in explaining gender differences in risk for psychopathology among African American urban adolescents. *Journal of Early Adolescence, 28,* 375–404.

Carney, M., Buttell, F., & Dutton, D. (2007). Women who perpetrate intimate partner violence: A review of the literature with recommendations for treatment. *Aggression and Violent Behavior, 12,* 108–115.

Carr, D. (2002). The psychological consequences of work-family trade-offs for three cohorts of men and women. *Social Psychology Quarterly, 65,* 103–124.

Carr, D. (2004). The desire to date and remarry among older widows and widowers. *Journal of Marriage and Family, 66,* 1051–1068.

Carroll, J. (2006). *Americans prefer male boss to a female boss.* Retrieved January 30, 2007, from www.galluppoll.com/content/Default.aspx?i=24346&pg =1&VERSION=p

Carstensen, L. L., Gottman, J. M., & Levenson, R. W. (2004). Emotional behavior in long-term marriage. In H. T. Reis & C. E. Rusbult (Eds.), *Close relationships: Key readings* (pp. 457–470). New York: Psychology Press.

Carter, J. S., Corra, M., & Carter, S. K. (2009). The interaction of race and gender: Changing gender-role attitudes, 1974–2006. *Social Science Quarterly, 90*(1), 196–211.

Case, A., & Menendez, A. (2009). Sex differences in obesity rates in poor countries: Evidence from South Africa. *Economics and Human Biology, 7,* 271–282.

Case, A., & Paxson, C. (2005). Sex differences in morbidity and mortality. *Demography, 42,* 189–214.

Cashdan, E. (1998). Smiles, speech, and body posture: How women and men display sociometric status and power. *Journal of Nonverbal Behavior, 22,* 209–228.

Cassidy, K. W. (2007). Gender differences in cognitive ability, attitudes, and behavior. In D. Sadker & E. S. Silber (Eds.), *Gender in the classroom: Foundations, skills, methods, and strategies across the curriculum* (pp. 33–72). Mahwah, NJ: Lawrence Erlbaum Associates.

Caughlin, J. P., & Huston, T. L. (2002). A contextual analysis of the association between demand/withdraw and marital satisfaction. *Personal Relationships, 9,* 95–119.

Cavanagh, S. E. (2007). The social construction of romantic relationships in adolescence: Examining the role of peer networks, gender, and race. *Sociological Inquiry, 77,* 572–600.

Ceci, S. J., Williams, W. M., & Barnett, S. M. (2009). Women's underrepresentation in science: Sociocultural and biological considerations. *Psychological Bulletin, 135,* 218–261.

Centers for Disease Control and Prevention. (2000). Preventing obesity among children. *Chronic Disease Notes and Reports, 13.* Retrieved June 6, 2011, from http://www.cdc.gov/chronicdisease/resources/reports.htm

Centers for Disease Control and Prevention. (2005). Advance report of final divorce statistics, 1989 and 1990. *Monthly Vital Statistics Report, 43*(9), 1–32.

Centers for Disease Control and Prevention. (2007a). *2006 National youth tobacco survey and key prevalence indicators.* Retrieved July 26, 2010, from http://www.cdc.gov/tobacco/data_statistics/surveys/nyts/pdfs/indicators.pdf

Centers for Disease Control and Prevention. (2007b). *Smoking & tobacco use: 2001 surgeon general's report— women and smoking.* Retrieved June 25, 2007, from www.cdc.gov/tobacco/data_statistics/sgr/sgr_2001/sgr_women

Centers for Disease Control and Prevention. (2008). *Quick stats: General information on alcohol use and health.* Retrieved August 19, 2008, from http://www.cdc.gov/alcohol/quickstats/general_info.htm

Centers for Disease Control and Prevention. (2009a). *Cigarette smoking among adults and trends in smoking cessation—United States, 2008.* Retrieved May 20, 2010, from http://www.cdc.gov/mmwr/preview/mmwrhtml/mm5844a2.htm

Centers for Disease Control and Prevention. (2009b). *Prevalence and trends data: Tobacco use – 2009.* Retrieved July 26, 2010, from http://apps.nccd.cdc.gov/brfss/list.asp?at=TU&yr=2009&qkey=4396&state=All

Centers for Disease Control and Prevention. (2009c). Sociodemographic differences in binge drinking among adults – 14 states, 2004. *Morbidity and Mortality Weekly Report, 58,* 301–304.

Centers for Disease Control and Prevention. (2009d). *National marriage and divorce rate trends.* Retrieved July 16, 2010, from http://www.cdc.gov/nchs/nvss/marriage_divorce_tables.htm

Centers for Disease Control and Prevention. (2010a). Youth risk behavior surveillance—United States, 2009. *Morbidity and Mortality Weekly Report, 59,* 1–142.

Centers for Disease Control and Prevention. (2010b). *10 Leading causes of deaths, United States.* Retrieved June 17, 2010, from http://webappa.cdc.gov/sasweb/ncipc/leadcaus10.html

Centers for Disease Control and Prevention. (2010c). *Cigarette use among high school students—United States, 1991–2009.* Retrieved July 20, 2010, from http://www.cdc.gov/mmwr/preview/mmwrhtml/mm5926a1.htm

Centers for Disease Control and Prevention. (2010d). *The link between physical activity and morbidity and mortality.* Retrieved July 26, 2010, from http://www.cdc.gov/nccdphp/sgr/mm.htm

Centers for Disease Control and Prevention. (2010e). *U.S. Physical activity statistics.* Retrieved July 26, 2010, from http://apps.nccd.cdc.gov/PASurveillance/Demo-CompareResultV.asp

Centers for Disease Control and Prevention. (2011). CDC grand rounds: Childhood obesity in the United States. *Morbidity and Mortality Weekly Report, 60*(2), 42–46.

Chalabaev, A., Sarrazin, P., Trouilloud, D., & Jussim, L. (2009). Can sex-undifferentiated teacher expectations mask an influence of sex stereotypes? Alternative forms of sex bias in teacher expectations. *Journal of Applied Social Psychology, 39,* 2469–2498.

Chan, D. K.-S., Lam, C. B., Chow, S. Y., & Cheung, S. F. (2008). Examining the job-related, psychological, and physical outcomes of workplace sexual harassment: A meta-analytic review. *Psychology of Women Quarterly, 32,* 362–376.

Chan, D. W., Ho, C. S-h., Tsang, S-m., Lee, S-h., & Chung, K. K. H. (2007). Prevalence, gender ratio and gender differences in reading-related cognitive abilities among Chinese children with dyslexia in Hong Kong. *Educational Studies, 33,* 249–265.

Chandra, A., & Minkovitz, C. S. (2006). Stigma starts early: Gender differences in teen willingness to use mental health services. *Journal of Adolescent Health, 38,* 754e1–754e8.

Chang, C., & Hitchon, J. C. B. (2004). When does gender count? Further insights into gender schematic processing of female candidates' political advertisements. *Sex Roles, 51,* 197–208.

Chang, T., & Subramaniam, P. R. (2008). Asian and Pacific Islander American men's help-seeking: Cultural values and beliefs, gender roles, and racial stereotypes. *International Journal of Men's Health, 7,* 121–136.

Chapleau, K. M., Oswald, D. L., & Russell, B. L. (2007). How ambivalent sexism toward women and men support rape myth acceptance. *Sex Roles, 57,* 131–136.

Chapleau, K. M., Oswald, D. L., & Russell, B. L. (2008). Male rape myths: The role of gender, violence, and sexism. *Journal of Interpersonal Violence, 23,* 600–615.

Chappell, A. T., & Maggard, S. R. (2010). A theoretical investigation of public attitudes toward sex education. *Sociological Spectrum, 30,* 196–219.

Charmaz, K. (1995). Identity dilemmas of chronically ill men. In D. Sabo & D. F. Gordon (Eds.), *Men's health and illness: Gender, power, and the body* (pp. 266–291). Thousand Oaks, CA: Sage Publications.

Chasan-Taber, L., & Stampfer, M. (2001). Oral contraceptives and myocardial infarction: The search for the smoking gun. *New England Journal of Medicine, 345,* 1841–1843.

Chatard, A., Guimond, S., & Selimbegovic, L. (2007). "How good are you in math?" The effect of gender stereotypes on students' recollection of their school marks. *Journal of Experimental Social Psychology, 43,* 1017–1024.

Chen, Z., Fiske, S. T., & Lee, T. L. (2009). Ambivalent sexism and power-related gender-role ideology in marriage. *Sex Roles, 60,* 765–778.

Cheng, S. T., & Chan, A. C. M. (2006). Social support and self-rated health revisited: Is there a gender difference in later life? *Social Science & Medicine, 63,* 118–122.

Chesley, N., & Moen, P. (2006). When workers care: Dual-earner couples' caregiving strategies, benefit use, and psychological well-being. *American Behavioral Scientist, 49,* 1248–1269.

Chesney, M. A., & Nealey, J. B. (1996). Smoking and cardiovascular disease risk in women: Issues for prevention and women's health. In P. M. Kato & T. Mann (Eds.), *Handbook of diversity issues in health psychology* (pp. 199–218). New York: Plenum Press.

Chesney-Lind, M., & Pasko, L. (2004). *Girls, women, and crime: Selected readings.* Thousand Oaks, CA: Sage.

Cheung, F. M., & Halpern, D. F. (2010). Women at the top: Powerful leaders define success as work + family in a culture of gender. *American Psychologist, 65*(3), 182–193.

Cheung, S. K., & McBride-Chang, C. (2007). Correlates of cross-sex friendship satisfaction in Hong Kong adolescents. *International Journal of Behavioral Development, 31,* 19–27.

Chevan, A. (1996). As cheaply as one: Cohabitation in the older population. *Journal of Marriage and the Family, 58,* 656–667.

Chia, R. C., Allred, L. J., & Jerzak, P. A. (1997). Attitudes toward women in Taiwan and China: Current status, problems, and suggestions for future research. *Psychology of Women Quarterly, 21,* 137–150.

Chia, R. C., Moore, J. L., Lam, K. N., Chuang, C. J., & Cheng, B. S. (1994). Cultural differences in gender role attitudes between Chinese and American students. *Sex Roles, 31*(1/2), 23–29.

Chiaramonte, G. R., & Friend, R. (2006). Medical students' and residents' gender bias in the diagnosis, treatment, and interpretation of coronary heart disease symptoms. *Health Psychology, 25,* 255–266.

Chisholm, J. F. (2000). Culture, ethnicity, race, and class. In F. Denmark, V. Rabinowitz, & J. Sechzer (Eds.), *Engendering psychology* (pp. 107–139). Boston, MA: Allyn & Bacon.

Chodorow, N. (1978). *The reproduction of mothering: Psychoanalysis and the sociology of gender.* London: University of California Press.

Chonody, J. M., & Siebert, D. C. (2008). Gender differences in depression: A theoretical examination of power. *Journal of Women and Social Work, 23,* 338–348.

Choo, P., Levine, T., & Hatfield, E. (1996). Gender, love schemas, and reactions to romantic break-ups. *Journal of Social Behavior and Personality, 11*(5), 143–160.

Choudhry, M. A., Bland, K. I., & Chaudry, I. H. (2007). Trauma and immune response: Effect of gender differences. *Injury: International Journal of the Care of the Injured, 38,* 1382–1391.

Chrisler, J. C. (2008). 2007 presidential address: Fear of losing control: Power, perfectionism, and the psychology of women. *Psychology of Women Quarterly, 32,* 1–12.

Christ, S. L., Lee, D. J., Fleming, L. E., LeBlanc, W. G., Arheart, K. L., Chung-Bridges, K., et al. (2007). Employment and occupation effects on depressive symptoms in older Americans: Does working past age 65 protect against depression? *Journals of Gerontology, 62B,* s399–s403.

Christensen, A., & Heavey, C. L. (1993). Gender differences in marital conflict: The demand/withdraw interaction pattern. In S. Oskamp & M. Constanzo (Eds.), *Gender issues in contemporary society* (Vol. 6, pp. 113–141). New York: Sage.

Christensen, A., Eldridge, K., Catta-Preta, A. B., Lim, V. R., & Santagata, R. (2006). Cross-cultural consistency of the demand/withdraw interaction pattern in couples. *Journal of Marriage and Family, 68,* 1029–1044.

Chung, W. (2007). The relation of son preference and religion to induced abortion: The case of South Korea. *Journal of Biosocial Science, 39,* 707–719.

Church, A. T. (2000). Culture and personality: Toward an integrated cultural trait psychology. *Journal of Personality, 68,* 651–703.

Ciabattari, T. (2004). Cohabitation and housework: The effects of marital intentions. *Journal of Marriage and Family, 66,* 118–125.

Cillessen, A. H. N., & Borch, C. (2006). Developmental trajectories of adolescent popularity: A growth curve modelling analysis. *Journal of Adolescence, 29,* 935–959.

Clarke, N. E., McCarthy, M. C., Downie, P., Ashley, D. M., & Anderson, V. A. (2009). Gender differences in the psychosocial experience of parents of children with cancer: A review of the literature. *Psycho-Oncology, 18,* 907–915.

Clearfield, M. W., & Nelson, N. M. (2006). Sex differences in mothers' speech and play behavior with 6-, 9-, and 14-month-old infants. *Sex Roles, 54,* 127–137.

Clements, K., Holtzworth-Munroe, A., Schweinle, W., & Ickes, W. (2007). Empathic accuracy of intimate partners in violent versus nonviolent relationships. *Personal Relationships, 14,* 369–388.

Cleveland, H. H., Koss, M. P., & Lyons, J. (1999). Rape tactics from the survivors' perspective: Contextual dependence and within-event independence. *Journal of Interpersonal Violence, 14*(5), 532–547.

Cloutier, J., Heatherton, T. F., Whalen, P. J., & Kelley, W. M. (2008). Are attractive people rewarding? Sex differences in the neural substrates of facial attractiveness. *Journal of Cognitive Neurosciences, 20,* 941–951.

CNN Politics. (2009). *Day of vindication for grandma as pay law signed.* Retrieved May 11, 2010, from http://www.cnn.com/2009/POLITICS/01/29/obama.fair.pay/

Cochran, S. D., & Mays, V. M. (2006). Estimating prevalence of mental and substance-using disorders among lesbians and gay men from existing national health data. In A. M. Omoto & H. S. Kurtzman (Eds.), *Sexual orientation and mental health: Examining identity and development in lesbian, gay, and bisexual people* (pp. 143–165). Washington, DC: American Psychological Association.

Cochran, S. D., Mays, V. M., Alegria, M., Ortega, A. N., & Takeuchi, D. (2007). Mental health and substance use disorders among Latino and Asian American lesbian, gay, and bisexual adults. *Journal of Consulting and Clinical Psychology, 75,* 785–794.

Cogan, J. C., & Ernsberger, P. (1999). Dieting, weight, and health: Reconceptualizing research and policy. *Journal of Social Issues, 55*(2), 187–205.

Cohen, E. (2007). *CDC: Antidepressants most prescribed drugs in U.S.* Retrieved August 2, 2007, from www.cnn.com/2007/HEALTH/07/09/antidepressants/index.html

Cohen, J. (1977). *Statistical power analysis for the behavioral sciences.* New York: Academic Press.

Cohen, S., & Wills, T. A. (1985). Stress, social support, and the buffering hypothesis. *Psychological Bulletin, 98,* 310–357.

Cohen, T. F. (1992). Men's families, men's friends: A structural analysis of constraints on men's social ties. In P. M. Nardi (Ed.), *Men's friendships* (pp. 115–131). Newbury Park, CA: Sage.

Coker, T. R., Austin, S. B., & Schuster, M. A. (2010). The health and health care of lesbian, gay, and bisexual adolescents. *Annual Review of Public Health, 31,* 457–477.

Cokley, K., & Moore, P. (2007). Moderating and mediating effects of gender and psychological disengagement on the academic achievement of African American college students. *Journal of Black Psychology, 33,* 169–187.

Colapinto, J. (2000). *As nature made him: The boy who was raised as a girl.* New York: HarperCollins.

Colapinto, J. (2004). Gender gap. *Slate.* Retrieved January 22, 2007, from www.slate.com/id/2101678

Colley, A., Todd, Z., Bland, M., Holmes, M., Khanom, N., & Pike, H. (2004). Style and content in e-mails and letters to male and female friends. *Journal of Language and Social Psychology, 23,* 369–378.

Collins, A. L., Glei, D. A., & Goldman, N. (2009). The role of life satisfaction and depressive symptoms in all-cause mortality. *Psychology and Aging, 24,* 696–702.

Collins, N. L., & Miller, L. C. (1994). Self-disclosure and liking: A meta-analytic review. *Psychological Bulletin, 116,* 457–475.

Collinsworth, L. L., Fitzgerald, L. F., & Drasgow, F. (2009). In harm's way: Factors related to psychological distress following sexual harassment. *Psychology of Women Quarterly, 33,* 475–490.

Collis, B. (1991). Adolescent females and computers: Real and perceived barriers. In J. Gaskell & A. McLaren (Eds.), *Women and education: A Canadian perspective* (pp. 147–161). Calgary, Canada: Detselig.

Coltrane, S. (2000). Research on household labor: Modeling and measuring the social embeddedness of routine family work. *Journal of Marriage and the Family, 62,* 1208–1233.

Confer, J. C., Easton, J. A., Fleischman, D. S., Goetz, C. D., Lewis, D. M. G., Perilloux, C., et al. (2010). Evolutionary psychology: Controversies, questions, prospects, and limitations. *American Psychologist, 65,* 110–126.

Connell, R. W., & Messerschmidt, J. W. (2005). Hegemonic masculinity: Rethinking the concept. *Gender & Society, 19,* 829–859.

Connor, S. M. (2009). *Participation increases some unhealthy behaviors in male teens; positive associations seen for females.* Paper presented at the American Public Health Association's 137th Annual Meeting and Exposition.

Consedine, N. S., Sabag-Cohen, S., & Krivoshekova, Y. S. (2007). Ethnic, gender, and socioeconomic differences in young adults' self-disclosure: Who discloses what and to whom? *Cultural Diversity and Ethnic Minority Psychology, 13,* 254–263.

Constantinople, A. (1973). Masculinity–femininity: An exception to a famous dictum? *Psychological Bulletin, 80,* 389–407.

Copenhaver, M. M., Lash, S. J., & Eisler, R. M. (2000). Masculine gender-role stress, anger, and male intimate abusiveness: Implications for men's relationships. *Sex Roles, 42,* 405–414.

Corbett, A. M., Dickson-Gomez, J., Hilario, H., & Weeks, M. R. (2009). A little thing called love: Condom use in high-risk primary heterosexual relationships. *Perspectives on Sexual and Reproductive Health, 41,* 218–224.

Corby, B. C., Hodges, E. V. E., & Perry, D. G. (2007). Gender identity and adjustment in Black, Hispanic, and White preadolescents. *Developmental Psychology, 43,* 261–266.

Cordova, J. V., Gee, C. B., & Warren, L. Z. (2005). Emotional skillfulness in marriage: Intimacy as a mediator of the relationship between emotional skillfulness and marital satisfaction. *Journal of Social and Clinical Psychology, 24,* 218–235.

Coren, S., & Hewitt, P. L. (1999). Sex differences in elderly suicide rates: Some predictive factors. *Aging and Mental Health, 3*(2), 112–118.

Correll, S. (2004). Constraints into preferences: Gender, status, and emerging career aspirations. *American Sociological Review, 69,* 93–113.

Correll, S. J. (2001). Gender and the career choice process: The role of biased self-assessments. *American Journal of Sociology, 106,* 1691–1730.

Correll, S. J., Benard, S., & Paik, I. (2007). Getting a job: Is there a motherhood penalty? *American Journal of Sociology, 112,* 1297–1338.

Corrigall, E. A., & Konrad, A. M. (2007). Gender role attitudes and careers: A longitudinal study. *Sex Roles, 56,* 847–855.

Costa, P. T., Jr., Terracciano, A., & McCrae, R. R. (2001). Gender differences in personality traits across cultures: Robust and surprising findings. *Journal of Personality and Social Psychology, 81,* 322–331.

Cotliar, S. (1996). Buss gets death in child slaying. *Chicago Sun-Times.* Retrieved June 6, 2011, from http://proquest. umi.com/pqdweb?did=16874531&sid=1&Fmt=2&clie ntId=3259&RQT=309&VName=PQD

Courtenay, W. H. (2000a). Constructions of masculinity and their influence on men's well-being: A theory of gender and health. *Social Science & Medicine, 50,* 1385–1401.

Courtenay, W. H. (2000b). Behavioral factors associated with disease, injury, and death among men: Evidence and implications for prevention.*Journal of Men's Studies, 9,* 81–142.

Courtenay, W. H., McCreary, D. R., & Merighi, J. R. (2002). Gender and ethnic differences in health beliefs and behaviors. *Journal of Health Psychology, 7,* 219–231.

Cox, S. J., Mezulis, A. H., & Hyde, J. S. (2010). The influence of child gender role and maternal feedback to child stress on the emergence of the gender difference in depressive rumination in adolescence. *Developmental Psychology, 46,* 842–852.

Crick, N. R., Ostrov, J. M., Appleyard, K., Jansen, E. A., & Casas, J. F. (2004). Relational aggression in early childhood: "you can't come to my birthday party unless. . ." In M. Putallaz & K. L. Bierman (Eds.), *Aggression, antisocial behavior, and violence among girls* (pp. 71–89). New York: Guilford Press.

Crick, N. R., Werner, N. E., Casas, J. F., O'Brien, K. M., Nelson, D. A., Grotpeter, J. K., et al. (1999). Childhood aggression and gender: A new look at an old problem. In D. Bernstein (Ed.), *Nebraska symposium on motivation and gender* (pp. 75–141). Lincoln, NE: University of Nebraska Press.

Crissey, S. R. (2005). Race/ethnic differences in the marital expectations of adolescents: The role of romantic relationships. *Journal of Marriage and Family, 67,* 697–709.

Crittenden, A. (2001). *The price of motherhood: Why the most important job in the world is still the least valued.* New York: Henry Holt and Company.

Crombie, G., Sinclair, N., Silverthorn, N., Byrne, B. M., DuBois, D. L., & Trinneer, A. (2005). Predictors of young adolescents' math grades and course enrollment intentions: Gender similarities and differences. *Sex Roles, 52*, 351–367.

Crosby, F. (1984). The denial of personal discrimination. *American Behavioral Scientist, 27*(3), 371–386.

Crosnoe, R. (2007). Gender, obesity, and education. *Sociology of Education, 80*, 241–260.

Cross, S. E., Bacon, P. L., & Morris, M. L. (2000). The relational-interdependent self-construal and relationships. *Journal of Personality and Social Psychology, 78*, 791–808.

Cross, S. E., & Madson, L. (1997). Models of the self: Self-construals and gender. *Psychological Bulletin, 122*, 5–37.

Cross, S. E., & Morris, M. L. (2003). Getting to know you: The relational self-construal, relational cognition, and well-being. *Personality and Social Psychology Bulletin, 29*, 512–523.

Crow, S. J. (2010). Eating disorders in young adults. In J. E. Grant & M. N. Potenza (Eds.), *Young adult mental health* (pp. 397–405). New York: Oxford University Press.

Crowl, A., Ahn, S., & Baker, J. (2008). A meta-analysis of developmental outcomes for children of same-sex and heterosexual parents. *Journal of GLBT Family Studies, 4*, 385–407.

Culbert, K. M., Breedlove, S. M., Burt, S. A., & Klump, K. L. (2008). Prenatal hormone exposure and risk for eating disorders: A comparison of opposite-sex and same-sex twins. *Archives of General Psychiatry, 65*, 329–336.

Cummings, K. M., & Armenta, M. (2002). Penalties for peer sexual harassment in an academic context: The influence of harasser gender, participant gender, severity of harassment, and the presence of bystanders. *Sex Roles, 47*, 273–280.

Cunningham, A.-M., & Knoester, C. (2007). Marital status, gender, and parents' psychological well-being. *Sociological Inquiry, 77*, 264–287.

Cunningham, M. (2005). Gender in cohabitation and marriage: The influence of gender ideology on housework allocation over the life course. *Journal of Family Issues, 26*, 1037–1061.

Cunningham, M., & Thornton, A. (2007). Direct and indirect influences of parents' marital instability on children's attitudes toward cohabitation in young adulthood. *Journal of Divorce and Remarriage, 46*, 125–143.

Currarini, S., Jackson, M. O., & Pin, P. (2010). Identifying the roles of race-based choice and chance in high school friendship network formation. *Proceedings of the National Academy of Sciences, 107*, 4857–4861.

Curtis, L. H., Al-Khatib, S. M., Shea, A. M., Hammill, B. G., Hernandez, A. F., & Schulman, K. A. (2007). Sex differences in the use of implantable cardioverter-defibrillators for primary and secondary prevention of sudden cardiac death. *Journal of the American Medical Association, 298*, 1517–1524.

Cyranowski, J. M., Frank, E., Young, E., & Shear, M. K. (2000). Adolescent onset of the gender difference in lifetime rates of major depression. *Archives of General Psychiatry, 57*, 21–27.

Cyranowski, J. M., Hofkens, T. L., Frank, E., Seltman, H., Cai, H.-M., & Amico, J. A. (2008). Evidence of dysregulated peripheral oxytocin release among depressed women. *Psychosomatic Medicine, 70*, 967–975.

Dabbs, J. M., Jr., Carr, T. S., Frady, R. L., & Riad, J. K. (1995). Testosterone, crime, and misbehavior among 692 male prison inmates. *Personality and Individual Differences, 18*, 627–633.

Dabbs, J. M., Jr., Chang, E.-L., Strong, R. A., & Milun, R. (1998). Spatial ability, navigation strategy, and geographic knowledge among men and women. *Evolution and Human Behavior, 19*, 89–98.

Dabbs, J. M., Jr., Riad, J. K., & Chance, S. E. (2001). Testosterone and ruthless homicide. *Personality and Individual Differences, 31*, 599–603.

Dabelea, D. (2007). Incidence of diabetes in youth in the United States. *Journal of the American Medical Association, 297*, 2716–2724.

Dahl, G. B., & Moretti, E. (2008). The demand for sons. *Review of Economic Studies, 75*, 1085–1120.

Daly, M., & Wilson, M. (1999). An evolutionary perspective on homicide. In M. Smith & M. A. Zahn (Eds.), *Homicide: A sourcebook of social research* (pp. 58–71). Thousand Oaks, CA: Sage.

Daly, M., & Wilson, M. (2001). Risk-taking, intrasexual competition and homicide. In J. A. French, A. C. Kamil, & D. W. Legen (Eds.), *Evolutionary psychology and motivation* (pp. 1–36). Lincoln, NE: University of Nebraska Press.

Daniels, E. A. (2009). Sex objects, athletes, and sexy athletes: How media representations of women athletes can impact adolescent girls and college women. *Journal of Adolescent Research, 24*, 399–422.

Danoff-Burg, S., Mosher, C. E., & Grant, C. A. (2006). Relations of agentic and communal personality traits to health behavior and substance use among college students. *Personality and Individual Differences, 40*, 353–363.

Davidson, K. (2001). Late life widowhood, selfishness and new partnership choices: A gendered perspective. *Ageing and Society, 21*, 297–317.

Davis, B. M., & Gilbert, L. A. (1989). Effect of dispositional and situational influences on women's dominance expression in mixed-sex dyads. *Journal of Personality and Social Psychology, 57*, 294–300.

Davis, M. C., & Matthews, K. A. (1996). Do gender-relevant characteristics determine cardiovascular reactivity? Match versus mismatch of traits and situation. *Journal of Personality and Social Psychology, 71,* 527–535.

Davis, M. C., Matthews, K. A., & Twamley, E. W. (1999). Is life more difficult on Mars or Venus? A meta-analytic review of sex differences in major and minor life events. *Annals of Behavioral Medicine, 21,* 83–97.

Davison, H. K., & Burke, M. J. (2000). Sex discrimination in simulated employment contexts: A meta-analytic investigation. *Journal of Vocational Behavior, 56,* 225–248.

De Ruijter, J. M. P., Schippers, J. J., & Van Doorne-Huiskes, A. (2004). Comparable worth: Policy and measures. *Netherlands' Journal of Social Sciences, 40,* 41–67.

de Vries, G. J., & Sodersten, P. (2009). Sex differences in the brain: The relation between structure and function. *Hormones and Behavior, 55,* 589–596.

Dear, G. E., & Roberts, C. M. (2002). The relationships between codependency and femininity and masculinity. *Sex Roles, 46,* 159–165.

Deaux, K. (1984). From individual differences to social categories: Analysis of a decade's research on gender. *American Psychologist, 39,* 105–116.

Deaux, K., & Major, B. (1987). Putting gender into context: An interactive model of gender-related behavior. *Psychological Review, 94,* 369–389.

Deford, F. (1993, February 22). Lessons from a friend. *Newsweek,* pp. 60–61.

Defrin, R., Shramm, L., & Eli, I. (2009). Gender role expectations of pain is associated with pain tolerance limit but not with pain threshold. *Pain, 145,* 230–236.

DeMaris, A. (2007). The role of relationship inequity in marital disruption. *Journal of Social and Personal Relationships, 24,* 177–195.

Denissen, J. J. A., & Zarrett, N. R. (2007). I like to do it, I'm able, and I know I am: Longitudinal couplings between domain-specific achievement, self-concept, and interest. *Child Development, 78,* 430–447.

Denton, M., & Walters, V. (1999). Gender differences in structural and behavioral determinants of health: An analysis of the social production of health. *Social Science and Medicine, 48,* 1221–1235.

Department of Education. (2006). Nondiscrimination on the basis of sex in education programs or activities receiving federal financial assistance; final rule. *Federal Register, 71*(206), 62530–62543.

Deptula, D. P., Henry, D. B., Shoeny, M. E., & Slavick, J. T. (2006). Adolescent sexual behavior and attitudes: A costs and benefits approach. *Journal of Adolescent Health, 38,* 35–43.

Derbyshire, S. W. G., Nichols, T. E., Firestone, L., Townsend, D. W., & Jones, A. K. P. (2002). Gender differences in patterns of cerebral activation during equal experience of painful laser stimulation. *Journal of Pain, 3,* 401–411.

Derlega, V. J., & Chaikin, A. L. (1976). Norms affecting self-disclosure in men and women. *Journal of Consulting and Clinical Psychology, 44,* 376–380.

Derlega, V. J., Winstead, B. A., & Greene, K. (2008). Self-disclosure and starting a close relationship. In S. Sprecher, A. Wenzel, & J. Harvey (Eds.), *Handbook of relationship initiation* (pp. 153–174). New York: Psychology Press.

Desmarais, S., & Curtis, J. (1997). Gender and perceived pay entitlement: Testing for effects of experience with income. *Journal of Personality and Social Psychology, 72,* 141–150.

Dessens, A. B., Slijper, F. M. E., & Drop, S. L. S. (2005). Gender dysphoria and gender change in chromosomal females with congenital adrenal hyperplasia. *Archives of Sexual Behavior, 34,* 389–397.

Dey, J. G., & Hill, C. (2007). *Behind the pay gap.* Washington, DC: American Association of University Women Educational Foundation.

Diamond, L. M., & Dube, E. M. (2002). Friendship and attachment among heterosexual and sexual-minority youths: Does the gender of your friend matter? *Journal of Youth and Adolescence, 31,* 155–166.

Diamond, M., & Sigmundson, H. K. (1997). Sex reassignment at birth: Long-term review and clinical implications. *Archives of Pediatric and Adolescent Medicine, 151,* 298–304.

Dickhauser, O., & Meyer, W. U. (2006). Gender differences in young children's math ability attributions. *Psychological Science, 48,* 3–16.

Diekman, A. B., & Murnen, S. K. (2004). Learning to be little women and little men: The inequitable gender equality of nonsexist children's literature. *Sex Roles, 50,* 373–385.

Diekman, A. B., Eagly, A. H., Mladinic, A., & Ferreira, M. C. (2005). Dynamic stereotypes about women and men in Latin America and the United States. *Journal of Cross-Cultural Psychology, 36,* 209–226.

Dijkstra, J. K., Lindenberg, S., & Veenstra, R. (2007). Same-gender and cross-gender peer acceptance and peer rejection and their relation to bullying and helping among preadolescents: Comparing predictions from gender-homophily and goal-framing approaches. *Developmental Psychology, 43,* 1377–1389.

Dill, K. E., & Thill, K. P. (2007). Video game characters and the socialization of gender roles: Young people's perceptions mirror sexist media depictions. *Sex Roles, 57,* 851–864.

DiMatteo, M. R., Murray, C. B., & Williams, S. L. (2009). Gender disparities in physician–patient communication among African American patients in primary care. *Journal of Black Psychology, 35,* 204–227.

Dindia, K. (2006). Men are from North Dakota, women are from South Dakota. In K. Dindia & D. J. Canary

(Eds.), *Sex differences and similarities in communi-cation* (2nd ed., pp. 3–20). Mahwah, NJ: Lawrence Erlbaum Associates.

Dindia, K., & Allen, M. (1992). Sex differences in self-disclosure: A meta-analysis. *Psychological Bulletin, 112,* 106–124.

Dishman, R. K., Hales, D. P., Pfeiffer, K. A., Felton, G., Saunders, R., Ward, D. S., et al. (2006). Physical self-concept and self-esteem mediate cross-sectional relations of physical activity and sport participation with depression symptoms among adolescent girls. *Health Psychology, 25,* 396–407.

Dodd, D. K., Russell, B. L., & Jenkins, C. (1999). Smiling in school yearbook photos: Gender differences from kindergarten to adulthood. *Psychological Record, 49,* 543–554.

Donat, P. L. N., & D'Emilio, J. (1992). A feminist redefinition of rape and sexual assault: Historical foundation and change. *Journal of Social Issues, 48*(1), 9–22.

Donkin, A., Goldblatt, P., & Lynch, K. (2002). Inequalities in life expectancy by social class, 1972–1999. *Health Statistics Quarterly, 15,* 5–15.

Doss, B. D., Atkins, D. C., & Christensen, A. (2003). Who's dragging their feet? Husbands and wives seeking marital therapy. *Journal of Marital and Family Therapy, 29,* 165–177.

Douvan, E., & Adelson, J. (1966). *The adolescent experience.* New York: Wiley.

Dovidio, J. F., & Penner, L. A. (2001). Helping and altruism. In G. Fletcher & M. S. Clark (Eds.), *Blackwell handbook of social psychology: Interpersonal processes* (pp. 162–195). Oxford, UK: Blackwell.

Dracup, K., Moser, D. K., Eisenberg, M., Meischke, H., Alonzo, A. A., & Braslow, A. (1995). Causes of delay in seeking treatment for heart attack symptoms. *Social Science & Medicine, 40*(3), 379–392.

Draganski, B., Winkler, J., Flugel, D., & May, A. (2004). Selective activation of ectopic grey matter during motor task. *NeuroReport, 15*(2), 251–253.

Droogsma, R. A. (2007). Redefining hijab: American Muslim women's standpoints on veiling. *Journal of Applied Communication Research, 35,* 294–319.

Duffy, J., Warren, K., & Walsh, M. (2001). Classroom interactions: Gender of teacher, gender of student, and classroom subject. *Sex Roles, 45,* 579–593.

Duncan, G. J., & Hoffman, S. D. (1985). A reconsideration of the economic consequences of marital dissolution. *Demography, 22,* 485–497.

Dunn, D. (1996). Gender and earnings. In P. J. Dubeck & K. Borman (Eds.), *Women and work: A handbook* (pp. 61–63). New York: Garland.

Dutton, D. (2007). Female intimate partner violence and developmental trajectories of abusive females. *International Journal of Men's Health, 6,* 54–71.

Dweck, C. (2008). Mindsets and math/science achievement. *The Opportunity Equation.* Retrieved June 24, 2010, from www.opportunityequation.org

Dweck, C. S., Davidson, W., Nelson, S., & Enna, B. (1978). Sex differences in learned helplessness. II: The contingencies of evaluative feedback in the classroom, and III: An experimental analysis. *Developmental Psychology, 14,* 268–276.

Dworkin, S. L., & O'Sullivan, L. F. (2007). "It's less work for us and it shows us she has good taste": Masculinity, sexual initiation, and contemporary sexual scripts. In M. Kimmel (Ed.), *The sexual self: Construction of sexual scripts* (pp. 105–121). Nashville, TN: Vanderbilt Press.

Dziech, B. W., & Hawkins, M. W. (1998). *Sexual harassment in higher education: Reflection and new perspectives.* New York: Garland Press.

Eagly, A. H. (1987). *Sex differences in social behavior: A social role interpretation.* Hillsdale, NJ: Erlbaum.

Eagly, A. H. (2009). The his and hers of prosocial behavior: An examination of the social psychology of gender. *American Psychologist, 64,* 644–658.

Eagly, A. H., & Crowley, M. (1986). Gender and helping behavior: A meta-analytic review of the social psychological literature. *Psychological Bulletin, 100,* 283–308.

Eagly, A. H., & Johannesen-Schmidt, M. C. (2001). The leadership styles of women and men. *Journal of Social Issues, 57,* 781–797.

Eagly, A. H., & Karau, S. J. (1991). Gender and the emergence of leaders: A meta-analysis. *Journal of Personality and Social Psychology, 60,* 685–710.

Eagly, A. H., & Karau, S. J. (2002). Role congruity theory of prejudice toward female leaders. *Psychological Review, 109,* 573–598.

Eagly, A. H., & Wood, W. (1999). The origins of sex differences in human behavior: Evolved dispositions versus social roles. *American Psychologist, 54,* 408–423.

Eagly, A. H., Diekman, A. B., Johannesen-Schmidt, & Koenig, A. M. (2004). Gender gaps in sociopolitical attitudes: A social psychological analysis. *Journal of Personality and Social Psychology, 87,* 796–816.

Eagly, A. H., Johannesen-Schmidt, M. C., & van Engen, M. L. (2003). Transformational, transactional, and laissez-faire leadership styles: A meta-analysis comparing women and men. *Psychological Bulletin, 129,* 569–591.

Eagly, A. H., Wood, W., & Diekman, A. B. (2000). Social role theory of sex differences and similarities: A current appraisal. In T. Eckes & H. M. Trautner (Eds.), *The developmental social psychology of gender* (pp. 123–174). Mahwah, NJ: Erlbaum.

Eastwick, P. W., Eagly, A. H., Glick, P., Johannesen-Schmidt, M. C., Fiske, S. T., Freiburger, P., et al. (2006). Is traditional gender ideology associated with sex-typed mate preferences? A test in nine nations. *Sex Roles, 54,* 603–614.

Eaton, L., Kaufman, M., Fuhrel, A., Cain, D., Cherry, C., Pope, H., et al. (2008). Examining factors co-existing with interpersonal violence in lesbian relationships. *Journal of Family Violence, 23,* 697–705.

Eccles, J. S., Barber, B., Jozefowicz, D., Malenchuk, O., & Vida, M. (1999). Self-evaluations of competence, task values, and self-esteem. In N. Johnson, G. Roberts, & M. C. Roberts (Eds.), *Beyond appearance: A new look at adolescent girls* (pp. 53–83). Washington, DC: American Psychological Association.

Eccles, J. S., Freedman-Doan, C., Frome, P., Jacobs, J. E., & Yoon, K. S. (2000). Gender-role socialization in the family: A longitudinal approach. In T. Eckes & H. M. Trautner (Eds.), *The developmental social psychology of gender* (pp. 333–360). Mahwah, NJ: Lawrence Erlbaum Associates.

Ecuyer-Dab, I., & Robert, M. (2004). Have sex differences in spatial ability evolved from male competition for mating and female concern for survival? *Cognition, 91,* 221–257.

Edwards, M. R. (2006). The role of husbands' supportive communication practices in the lives of employed mothers. *Marriage and Family Review, 40,* 23–46.

Eisenberg, N., & Fabes, R. A. (1998). Prosocial development. In W. Damon & N. Eisenberg (Eds.), *Handbook of child psychology* (Vol. 3, pp. 701–757). New York: John Wiley & Sons, Inc.

Eisler, R. M., Franchina, J. J., Moore, T. M., Honeycutt, H. G., & Rhatigan, D. L. (2000). Masculine gender role stress and intimate abuse: Effects of gender relevance of conflict situations on men's attributions and affective responses. *Psychology of Men and Masculinity, 1*(1), 30–36.

Ekman, P. (1992). An argument for basic emotion. *Cognition and Emotion, 6,* 169–200.

Eldridge, K. A., Sevier, M., Jones, J., Atkins, D. C., & Christensen, A. (2007). Demand-withdraw communication in severely distressed, moderately distressed, and nondistressed couples: Rigidity and polarity during relationship and personal problem discussions. *Journal of Family Psychology, 21,* 218–226.

Elgar, K., & Chester, A. (2007). The mental health implications of maternal employment: Working versus at-home mothering identities. *Australian E-Journal for the Advancement of Mental Health, 6,* 1–9.

Elliott, D. M., Mok, D. S., & Briere, J. (2004). Adult sexual assault: Prevalence, symptomatology, and sex differences in the general population. *Journal of Traumatic Stress, 17,* 203–211.

Elliott, M. R., Shope, J. T., Raghunathan, T. E., & Waller, P. F. (2006). Gender differences among young drivers in the association between high-risk driving and substance use/environmental influences. *Journal of Studies on Alcohol, 67,* 252–260.

Elliott, S., & Umberson, D. (2004). Recent demographic trends in the US and implications for well-being. In J. Scott & J. Treas (Eds.), *The Blackwell companion to the sociology of families* (pp. 34–53). Malden, MA: Blackwell Publishing.

Elliott, S., & Umberson, D. (2008). The performance of desire: Gender and sexual negotiation in long-term marriages. *Journal of Marriage and Family, 70*(2), 391–406.

Ellis, H. (1894). *Man and woman.* London: Scott.

Ellis, L. (2006). Gender differences in smiling: An evolutionary neuroandrogenic theory. *Physiology & Behavior, 88,* 303–308.

Else-Quest, N. M., Hyde, J. S., & DeLamater, J. D. (2005). Context counts: Long-term sequelae of premarital intercourse or abstinence. *Journal of Sex Research, 42,* 102–112.

Else-Quest, N. M., Hyde, J. S., & Linn, M. C. (2010). Cross-national patterns of gender differences in mathematics: A meta-analysis. *Psychological Bulletin, 136,* 103–127.

Elsesser, K., & Peplau, L. A. (2006). The glass partition: Obstacles to cross-sex friendships at work. *Human Relations, 59,* 1077–1100.

Embry, A., Padgett, M. Y., & Caldwell, C. B. (2008). Can leaders step outside of the gender box? An examination of leadership and gender role stereotypes. *Journal of Leadership and Organizational Studies, 15,* 30–45.

Endres, M. L., Chowdhury, S. K., & Alam, I. (2008). Gender effects on bias in complex financial decisions. *Journal of Managerial Issues, 20,* 238–254.

Epstein, M., & Ward, L. M. (2008). "Always use protection": Communication boys receive about sex from parents, peers, and the media. *Journal of Youth and Adolescence, 37,* 113–126.

Erdincler, D., Bugay, G., Ertan, T., & Eker, E. (2004). Depression and sex hormones in elderly women. *Archives of Gerontology and Geriatrics, 39,* 239–244.

Erickson, R. J. (2005). Why emotion work matters: Sex, gender, and the division of household labor. *Journal of Marriage and Family, 67,* 337–351.

Erikson, E. H. (1950). *Childhood and society.* New York: Norton.

Ernst, M., Maheu, F. S., Schroth, E., Hardin, J., Golan, L. G., Cameron, J., et al. (2007). Amygdala function in adolescents with congenital adrenal hyperplasia: A model for the study of early steroid abnormalities. *Neuropsychologia, 45,* 2104–2113.

Eschenbeck, H., Kohlmann, C.-W., & Lohaus, A. (2007). Gender differences in coping strategies in children and adolescents. *Journal of Individual Differences, 28,* 18–26.

Evans, R. E. C., Brotherstone, H., Miles, A., & Wardle, J. (2005). Gender differences in early detection of cancer. *Journal of Men's Health & Gender, 2,* 209–217.

Evenson, R. J., & Simon, R. W. (2005). Clarifying the relationship between parenthood and depression. *Journal of Health and Social Behavior, 46,* 341–358.

Fabes, R. A., Martin, C. L., & Hanish, L. D. (2003). Young children's play qualities in same-, other-, and mixed-sex peer groups. *Child Development, 74,* 921–932.

Fabes, R. A., Martin, C. L., & Hanish, L. D. (2004). The next 50 years: Considering gender as a context for understanding young children's peer relationships. *Merrill-Palmer Quarterly, 50,* 260–273.

Falomir-Pichastor, J. M., & Mugny, G. (2009). "I'm not gay. I'm a real man!": Heterosexual men's gender self-esteem and sexual prejudice. *Personality and Social Psychology Bulletin, 35,* 1233–1243.

Faludi, S. (1991). *Backlash: The undeclared war against American women.* New York: Crown.

Fassinger, R. E., & Arseneau, J. R. (2007). "I'd rather get wet than be under that umbrella": Differentiating the experiences and identities of lesbian, gay, bisexual, and transgender people. In K. J. Bieschke, R. M. Perez, & K. A. DeBord (Eds.), *Handbook of counseling and psychotherapy with lesbian, gay, bisexual, and transgender clients* (pp. 19–49). Washington, DC: American Psychological Association.

Fassinger, R. E., Shullman, S. L., & Stevenson, M. R. (2010). Toward an affirmative lesbian, gay, bisexual, and transgender leadership paradigm. *American Psychologist, 65,* 201–215.

Feder, J., Levant, R. F., & Dean, J. (2007). Boys and violence: A gender-informed analysis. *Professional Psychology: Research and Practice, 38,* 385–391.

Federal Bureau of Investigation. (2008). *Uniform crime reports (1998-2008).* Retrieved September 10, 2010, from http://www.fbi.gov/ucr/cius2008/data/table_40.html

Feeley, T. H., Hwang, J., & Barnett, G. A. (2008). Predicting employee turnover from friendship networks. *Journal of Applied Communication Research, 36,* 56–73.

Fehr, B. (2000). The life cycle of friendship. In C. H. Hendrick & S. S. Hendrick (Eds.), *Close relationships: A sourcebook* (pp. 71–82). Thousand Oaks, CA: Sage Publications Inc.

Fehr, B. (2004). Intimacy expectations in same-sex friendships: A prototype interaction-pattern model. *Journal of Personality and Social Psychology, 86,* 265–284.

Feingold, A. (1990). Gender differences in effects of physical attractiveness on romantic attraction: A comparison across five research paradigms. *Journal of Personality and Social Psychology, 59,* 981–993.

Feingold, A. (1992). Gender differences in mate selection preferences: A test of the parental investment model. *Psychological Bulletin, 112,* 125–139.

Fejfar, M. C., & Hoyle, R. H. (2000). Effect of private self-awareness on negative affect and self-referent attribution: A quantitative review. *Personality and Social Psychology Review, 4,* 132–142.

Felmlee, D., & Muraco, A. (2009). Gender and friendship norms among older adults. *Research and Aging, 31,* 318–344.

Felson, R. B., & Cares, A. C. (2005). Gender and the seriousness of assaults on intimate partners and other victims. *Journal of Marriage and Family, 67,* 1182–1195.

Fenigstein, A., Scheier, M. F., & Buss, A. H. (1975). Public and private self-consciousness: Assessment and theory. *Journal of Consulting and Clinical Psychology, 43,* 522–527.

Fernandez, A. M., Vera-Villarroel, P., Sierra, J. C., & Zubeidat, I. (2007). Distress in response to emotional and sexual infidelity: Evidence of evolved gender differences in Spanish students. *Journal of Psychology: Interdisciplinary and Applied, 141*(1), 17–24.

Ferriman, K., Lubinski, D., & Benbow, C. P. (2009). Work preferences, life values, and personal views of top math/science graduate students and the profoundly gifted: Developmental changes and gender differences during emerging adulthood and parenthood. *Journal of Personality and Social Psychology, 97,* 517–532.

Feshbach, S. (1989). The bases and development of individual aggression. In J. Groebel & R. A. Hinde (Eds.), *Aggression and war: Their biological and social bases* (pp. 78–90). New York: Cambridge University Press.

Fetters, J. K., Peterson, E. D., Shaw, L. J., Newby, K., & Califf, R. M. (1996). Sex-specific differences in coronary artery disease risk factors, evaluation, and treatment: Have they been adequately evaluated? *American Heart Journal, 131*(4), 796–813.

Fifth girl dies. (2006). Fifth girl dies after Amish school shooting. *CNN.com* [Electronic Version]. Retrieved January 22, 2007, from www.cnn.com/2006/US/10/02/amish.shooting/ index.html

Fillingim, R. B., King, C. D., Ribeiro-Dasilva, M. C., Rahim-Williams, B., & Riley, J. L. (2009). Sex, gender, and pain: A review of recent clinical and experimental findings. *Journal of Pain, 10,* 447–485.

Fincham, F. D., Beach, S. R. H., Harold, G. T., & Osborne, L. N. (1997). Marital satisfaction and depression: Different causal relationships for men and women? *Psychological Science, 8*(5), 351–357.

Finer, L. B. (2007). Trends in premarital sex in the United States, 1954–2003. *Public Health Reports, 122,* 73–78.

Fischer, A. H., & Manstead, A. S. R. (2000). The relation between gender and emotions in different cultures. In A. H. Fischer (Ed.), *Gender and emotion: Social psychological perspectives* (pp. 71–94). New York: Cambridge University Press.

Fischer, A. H., Mosquera, P. M. R., van Vianen, A. E. M., & Manstead, A. S. R. (2004). Gender and culture differences in emotion. *Emotion, 4,* 87–94.

Fischer, A. R. (2006). Women's benevolent sexism as reaction to hostility. *Psychology of Women Quarterly, 30,* 410–416.

Fischer, C. S. (1979). *Friendship, gender and the life cycle.* Unpublished manuscript. University of California, Berkeley.

Fisher, T. D. (2007). Sex of experimenter and social norm effects on reports of sexual behavior in young men and women. *Archives of Sexual Behavior, 36,* 89–100.

Fiske, S. T., & Stevens, L. E. (1993). What's so special about sex? Gender stereotyping and discrimination. In S. Oskamp & M. Costanzo (Eds.), *Gender issues in contemporary society* (pp. 173–196). Newbury Park, CA: Sage.

Fiske, S. T., Bersoff, D. N., Borgida, E., Deaux, K., & Heilman, M. E. (1991). Social science research on trial: Use of sex stereotyping research in *Price Waterhouse v. Hopkins. American Psychologist, 46,* 1049–1060.

Fitzgerald, L. F., Gelfand, M. J., & Drasgow, F. (1995). Measuring sexual harassment: Theoretical and psychometric advances. *Basic and Applied Social Psychology, 17*(4), 425–445.

Fitzgerald, L. F., Shullman, S. L., Bailey, N., Richards, M., Swecker, J., Gold, Y., et al. (1988). The incidence and dimensions of sexual harassment in academia and the workplace. *Journal of Vocational Behavior, 32,* 152–175.

Fitzgibbon, M. L., Blackman, L. R., & Avellone, M. E. (2000). The relationship between body image discrepancy and body mass index across ethnic groups. *Obesity Research, 8,* 582–589.

Fitzpatrick, M. J., & McPherson, B. J. (2010). Coloring within the lines: Gender stereotypes in contemporary coloring books. *Sex Roles, 62,* 127–137.

Flaks, D. K., Ficher, I., Masterpasqua, F., & Joseph, G. (1995). Lesbians choosing motherhood: A comparative study of lesbian and heterosexual parents and their children. *Developmental Psychology, 31,* 105–114.

Flegal, K. M., & Troiano, R. P. (2000). Changes in the distribution of body mass index of adults and children in the US population. *International Journal of Obesity, 24,* 807–818.

Flegal, K. M., Carroll, M. D., Ogden, C. L., & Curtin, L. R. (2010). Prevalence and trends in obesity among U.S. adults, 1999–2008. *Journal of the American Medical Association, 303,* 235–241.

Fleischmann, A., & Moyer, L. (2009). Competing social movements and local political culture: Voting on ballot propositions to ban same-sex marriage in the U.S. states. *Social Science Quarterly, 90,* 134–149.

Fletcher, G. J. O., Tither, J. M., O'Loughlin, C., Friesen, M., & Overall, N. (2004). Warm and homely or cold and beautiful? Sex differences in trading off traits in mate selection. *Personality and Social Psychology Bulletin, 30,* 659–672.

Flory, J. D., Raikkonen, K., Matthews, K. A., & Owens, J. F. (2000). Self-focused attention and mood during everyday social interactions. *Personality and Social Psychology Bulletin, 26,* 875–883.

Floyd, F. J., & Markman, H. J. (1983). Observational biases in spouse observation: Toward a cognitive/behavioral model of marriage. *Journal of Consulting and Clinical Psychology, 51,* 450–457.

Flynn, F. J. (2003). How much should I give and how often? The effects of generosity and frequency of favor exchange on social status and productivity. *Academy of Management Journal, 46,* 539–553.

Fokkema, T. (2002). Combining a job and children: Contrasting the health of married and divorced women in the Netherlands? *Social Science & Medicine, 54,* 741–752.

Ford, E. S., Mokdad, A. H., Li, C., McGuire, L. C., Strine, T. W., Okoro, C. A., et al. (2008). Gender differences in coronary heart disease and health-related quality of life: Findings from 10 states from the 2004 behavioral risk factor surveillance system. *Journal of Women's Health, 17,* 757–768.

Ford, M. T., Heinen, B. A., & Langkamer, K. L. (2007). Work and family satisfaction and conflict: A meta-analysis of cross-domain relations. *Journal of Applied Psychology, 92,* 57–80.

Forman-Hoffman, V. L., Richardson, K. K., Yankey, J. W., Hillis, S. L., Wallace, R. B., & Wolinsky, F. D. (2008). Retirement and weight changes among men and women in the health and retirement study. *Journal of Gerontology, 63b,* s146–s153.

Forrest, J. A., & Feldman, R. S. (2000). Detecting deception and judge's involvement: Lower task involvement leads to better lie detection. *Personality and Social Psychology Bulletin, 26,* 118–125.

Forsterlee, L., Fox, G. B., Forsterlee, R., & Ho, R. (2004). The effects of a victim impact statement and gender on juror information processing in a criminal trial: Does the punishment fit the crime? *Australian Psychologist, 39,* 57–67.

Foschi, M. (2000). Double standards for competence: Theory and research. *Annual Review of Sociology, 26,* 21–42.

Four dead in fitness center shooting. (2009). Four dead in fitness center shooting: Among the dead, gunman had note in gym bag. *Pittsburgh Post Gazette.* Retrieved May 26, 2010, from http://www.post-gazette.com/pg/09217/988669-55.stm

FOX News. (2006, May 25). *Hasbro halts plans for doll based on Pussycat dolls.* Retrieved January 23, 2007, from www.foxnews.com/printer_friendly_story/0,3566,196943,00.Html

Fox, A. B., Bukatko, D., Hallahan, M., & Crawford, M. (2007). The medium makes a difference: Gender similarities and differences in instant messaging. *Journal of Language and Social Psychology, 26,* 389–397.

Frame, M. C., Roberto, K. J., Schwab, A. E., & Harris, C. T. (2010). What is important on the job? Differences across gender, perspective, and job level. *Journal of Applied Social Psychology, 40,* 36–56.

Franck, K., & Rosen, E. (1949). A projective test of masculinity–femininity. *Journal of Consulting Psychology, 13,* 247–256.

Frazier, P. A., & Esterly, E. (1990). Correlates of relationship beliefs: Gender, relationship experience and relationship satisfaction. *Journal of Social and Personal Relationships, 7,* 331–352.

Frazier, P. A., Cochran, C. C., & Olson, A. M. (1995). Social science research on lay definitions of sexual harassment. *Journal of Social Issues, 51*(1), 21–37.

Frech, A., & Williams, K. (2007). Depression and the psychological benefits of entering marriage. *Journal of Health and Social Behavior, 48,* 149–163.

Frederick, D. A., Forbes, G. B., Grigorian, K. E., & Jarcho, J. M. (2007). The UCLA body project 1: Gender and ethnic differences in self-objectification and body satisfaction among 2,206 undergraduates. *Sex Roles, 57,* 317–327.

Fredricks, J. A., & Eccles, J. S. (2006). Is extracurricular participation associated with beneficial outcomes? Concurrent and longitudinal relations. *Developmental Psychology, 42,* 698–713.

Fredricks, J. A., Simpkins, S., & Eccles, J. S. (2005). Family socialization, gender, and participation in sports and instrumental music. In C. R. Cooper, C. T. G. Coll, W. T. Bartko, H. Davis, & C. Chatman (Eds.), *Developmental pathways through middle childhood* (pp. 41–62). Mahwah, NJ: Lawrence Erlbaum Associates.

Fredrickson, B. L., & Roberts, T.-A. (1997). Objectification theory: Toward understanding women's lived experiences and mental health risks. *Psychology of Women Quarterly, 21,* 173–206.

Freedman-Doan, C., Wigfield, A., Eccles, J. S., Blumenfeld, P., Arbreton, A., & Harold, R. D. (2000). What am I best at? Grade and gender differences in children's beliefs about ability improvement. *Journal of Applied Developmental Psychology, 21,* 379–402.

Freeman, E. W., Sammel, M. D., Lin, H., & Nelson, D. B. (2006). Associations of hormones and menopausal status with depressed mood in women with no history of depression. *Archives of General Psychiatry, 63,* 375–382.

Freeman, N. K. (2007). Preschoolers' perception of gender appropriate toys and their parents' beliefs about genderized behaviors: Miscommunication, mixed messages, or hidden truths? *Early Childhood Education Journal, 34,* 357–366.

French, D. C., Jansen, E. A., & Pidada, S. (2002). United States and Indonesian children's and adolescents'

reports of relational aggression by disliked peers. *Child Development, 73,* 1143–1150.

Freud, S. (1924). The dissolution of the Oedipus complex. *Standard Edition, 19,* 172–179.

Freud, S. (1925). Some physical consequences of the anatomical distinction between the sexes. *Standard Edition, 19,* 243–258.

Friedan, B. (1963). *The feminine mystique.* New York: Norton.

Fried-Buchalter, S. (1997). Fear of success, fear of failure, and the imposter phenomenon among male and female marketing managers. *Sex Roles, 37,* 847–859.

Frisco, M. L., & Williams, K. (2003). Perceived housework equity, marital happiness, and divorce in dual-earner households. *Journal of Family Issues, 24,* 51–73.

Fritz, H. L. (2000). Gender-linked personality traits predict mental health and functional status following a first coronary event. *Health Psychology, 19,* 420–428.

Fritz, H. L., & Helgeson, V. S. (1998). Distinctions of unmitigated communion from communion: Self-neglect and overinvolvement with others. *Journal of Personality and Social Psychology, 75,* 121–140.

Fritz, H. L., Nagurney, A., & Helgeson, V. S. (2003). The effects of partner sex, gender-related personality traits, and social support on cardiovascular reactivity during problem disclosure. *Personality and Social Psychology Bulletin, 29,* 713–725.

Frome, P. M., Alfeld, C. J., Eccles, J. S., & Barber, B. L. (2006). Why don't they want a male-dominated job? An investigation of young women who changed their occupational aspirations. *Educational Research and Evaluation, 12,* 359–372.

Fuhrman, R. W., Flannagan, D., & Matamoros, M. (2009). Behavior expectations in cross-sex friendships, same-sex friendships, and romantic relationships. *Personal Relationships, 16,* 575–596.

Fujioka, Y., Ryan, E., Agle, M., Legaspi, M., & Toohey, R. (2009). The role of racial identity in responses to thin media ideals: Differences between White and Black college women. *Communication Research, 36,* 451–474.

Furnham, A. (2009). Sex differences in mate selection preferences. *Personality and Individual Differences, 47,* 262–267.

Fuwa, M. (2004). Macro-level gender inequality and the division of household labor in 22 countries. *American Sociological Review, 69,* 751–767.

Gadassi, R., & Gati, I. (2009). The effect of gender stereotypes on explicit and implicit career preferences. *Counseling Psychologist, 37,* 902–922.

Gager, C. T. (2008). What's fair is fair? Role of justice in family labor allocation decisions. *Marriage and Family Review, 44,* 511–545.

Gager, C. T., & Hohmann-Marriott, B. (2006). Distributive justice in the household: A comparison of alternative models. *Marriage and Family Review, 40,* 5–42.

Galinsky, E. (2005). Children's perspectives of employed mothers and fathers: Closing the gap between public debates and research findings. In D. F. Halpern & S. E. Murphy (Eds.), *From work-family balance to work-family interaction* (pp. 219–236). Mahwah, NJ: Lawrence Erlbaum Associates.

Galinsky, E., Aumann, K., & Bond, J. T. (2009). *Times are changing: Gender and generation at work and at home.* Retrieved August 25, 2010, from http://familiesandwork. org/site/research/reports/Times_Are_Changing.pdf

Gallace, A., & Spence, C. (2010). The science of interpersonal touch: An overview. *Neuroscience and Biobehavioral Reviews, 34,* 246–259.

Gallagher, A., Levin, J., & Cahalan, C. (2002). *GRE research—cognitive patterns of gender differences on mathematics admissions tests* (No. 02-19 ETS Research Report). Princeton, NJ: Educational Testing Service.

Gallup. (2010). *Personal weight situation.* Retrieved August 24, 2010, from http://www.gallup.com/poll/7264/ personal-weight-situation.aspx

Gallup Poll. (2005). *Math problematic for U.S. teens: More girls than boys find math, science toughest classes.* Retrieved January 30, 2007, from www.galluppoll.com/content/ Default.aspx?i=16360&pg=1&VERSION=p

Galupo, M. P. (2007). Women's close friendships across sexual orientation: A comparative analysis of lesbian-heterosexual and bisexual-heterosexual women's friendships. *Sex Roles, 56,* 473–482.

Galupo, M. P. (2009). Cross-category friendship patterns: Comparison of heterosexual and sexual minority adults. *Journal of Social and Personal Relationships, 26,* 811–831.

Garaigordobil, M., Magnanto, C., Perez, J. I., & Sansinenea, E. (2009). Gender differences in socioemotional factors during adolescence and effects of a violence prevention program. *Journal of Adolescent Health, 44,* 468–477.

Garbarino, J. (1999). *Lost boys: Why our sons turn violent and how we can save them.* New York: Free Press.

Garcia-Falgueras, A., & Swaab, D. F. (2008). A sex difference in the hypothalamic uncinate nucleus: Relationship to gender identity. *Brain, 2008,* 3132–3146.

Gard, M. G., & Kring, A. M. (2007). Sex differences in the time course of emotion. *Emotion, 7,* 429–437.

Gardenswartz, L., & Rowe, A. (1994). *Diverse teams at work: Capitalizing on the power of diversity.* Homewood, IL: Irwin.

Gardiner, M., & Tiggemann, M. (1999). Gender differences in leadership style, job stress and mental health in male- and female-dominated industries. *Journal of Occupational and Organizational Psychology, 72,* 301–315.

Garn, C. L., Allen, M. D., & Larsen, J. D. (2009). An fMRI study of sex differences in brain activation during object naming. *Cortex, 45,* 610–618.

Garner, D. M., Olmstead, M. P., & Polivy, J. (1983). Development and validation of a multidimensional eating disorder inventory for anorexia nervosa and bulimia. *International Journal of Eating Disorders, 2*(2), 15–34.

Gaub, M., & Carlson, C. L. (1997). Gender differences in ADHD: A meta-analysis and critical review. *Journal of the American Academy of Child and Adolescent Psychiatry, 36,* 1036–1045.

Gayle, G.-L., Golan, L., & Miller, R. (2008). *Are there glass ceilings for female executives?* GSIA Working Papers. Retrieved August 30, 2010, from http://ideas. repec.org/p/cmu/gsiawp/-1969975920.html

Geer, J. H., & Robertson, G. G. (2005). Implicit attitudes in sexuality: Gender differences. *Archives of Sexual Behavior, 34,* 671–677.

Gelles, R. J. (2007). The politics of research: The use, abuse, and misuse of social science data—the cases of intimate partner abuse. *Family Court Review, 45,* 42–51.

Gentile, B., Grabe, S., Dolan-Pascoe, B., Twenge, J. M., Wells, B. E., & Maitino, A. (2009). Gender differences in domain-specific self-esteem: A meta-analysis. *Review of General Psychology, 13,* 34–45.

Gerber, G. L. (2009). Status and the gender stereotyped personality traits: Toward an integration. *Sex Roles, 61,* 297–316.

Gerhart, B., & Rynes, S. (1991). Determinants and consequences of salary negotiations by male and female MBA graduates. *Journal of Applied Psychology, 76*(2), 256–262.

Ghaed, S. G., & Gallo, L. C. (2006). Distinctions among agency, communion, and unmitigated agency and communion according to the interpersonal circumplex, five-factor model, and social-emotional correlates. *Journal of Personality Assessment, 86,* 77–88.

Ghanizadeh, A. (2009). Psychiatric comorbidity differences in clinic-referred children and adolescents with ADHD according to the subtypes and gender. *Journal of Child Neurology, 24,* 679–684.

Gijsbers, K., & Nicholson, F. (2005). Experimental pain thresholds influenced by sex of experimenter. *Perceptual and Motor Skills, 101,* 803–807.

Gillespie, B. L., & Eisler, R. M. (1992). Development of the feminine gender role stress scale: A cognitive-behavioral measure of stress, appraisal, and coping for women. *Behavior Modification, 16*(3), 426–438.

Gilligan, C. (1982). *In a different voice.* Cambridge, MA: Harvard University Press.

Gillum, T. L. (2007). "How do I view my sister?" Stereotypic views of African American women and their potential to impact intimate partnerships. *Journal of Human Behavior in the Social Environment, 15,* 347–366.

Gilmore, D. D. (1990). *Manhood in the making: Cultural concepts of masculinity.* New Haven, CT: Yale University Press.

Giordano, P. C., Longmore, M. A., & Manning, W. D. (2006). Gender and meanings of adolescent romantic relationships: A focus on boys. *American Sociological Review, 71,* 260–287.

Gjerberg, E. (2002). Gender similarities in doctors' preferences—and gender differences in final specialisation. *Social Science & Medicine, 54,* 591–605.

Gjerde, P. F. (1995). Alternative pathways to chronic depressive symptoms in young adults: Gender differences in developmental trajectories.*Child Development, 66,* 1277–1300.

Glick, P., & Fiske, S. T. (1996). The ambivalent sexism inventory: Differentiating hostile and benevolent sexism. *Journal of Personality and Social Psychology, 70,* 491–512.

Glick, P., & Fiske, S. T. (1999a). The ambivalence toward men inventory. *Psychology of Women Quarterly, 23,* 519–536.

Glick, P., & Fiske, S. T. (1999b). Gender, power dynamics, and social interaction. In M. M. Ferree, J. Lorber, & B. B. Hess (Eds.), *Revisioning gender* (Vol. 5, pp. 365–398). Thousand Oaks, CA: Sage Publications.

Glick, P., & Fiske, S. T. (2001). An ambivalent alliance: Hostile and benevolent sexism as complementary justifications for gender inequality. *American Psychologist, 56*(2), 109–118.

Glick, P., Fiske, S. T., Masser, B., Manganelli, A. M., Huang, L., Castro, Y. R., et al. (2004). Bad but bold: Ambivalent attitudes toward men predict gender inequality in 16 nations. *Journal of Personality and Social Psychology, 86,* 713–728.

Glick, P., Fiske, S. T., Mladinic, A., Saiz, J. L., Abrams, D., Masser, B., et al. (2000). Beyond prejudice as simple antipathy: Hostile and benevolent sexism across cultures. *Journal of Personality and Social Psychology, 79*(5), 763–775.

Glick, P., Sakalli-Ugurlu, N., Gerreira, M. C., & de Souza, M. A. (2002). Ambivalent sexism and attitudes toward wife abuse in Turkey and Brazil. *Psychology of Women Quarterly, 26,* 292–297.

Glomb, T. M., Richman, W. L., Hulin, C. L., Dragsow, F., Schneider, K. T., & Fitzgerald, L. F. (1997). Ambient sexual harassment: An integrated model of antecedents and consequences. *Organizational Behavior and Human Decision Processes, 71,* 309–328.

Glynn, L. M., Christenfeld, N., & Gerin, W. (1999). Gender, social support, and cardiovascular responses to stress. *Psychosomatic Medicine, 61,* 234–242.

Godbout, N., Dutton, D., Lussier, Y., & Sabourin, S. (2009). Early exposure to violence, domestic violence, attachment representations, and marital adjustment. *Personal Relationships, 16,* 365–384.

Godin, I., Kornitzer, M., Clumeck, N., Linkowski, P., Valente, F., & Kittel, F. (2009). Gender specificity in the prediction of clinically diagnosed depression: Results of a large cohort of Belgian workers. *Social Psychiatry and Psychiatric Epidemiology, 44,* 592–600.

Gold, D. R., Wang, X., Wypij, D., Speizer, F. E., Ware, J. H., & Dockery, D. W. (1996). Effects of cigarette smoking on lung function in adolescent boys and girls. *New England Journal of Medicine, 335,* 931–937.

Goldberg, A. E. (2010). *Lesbian and gay parents and their children: Research on the family life cycle.* Washington, DC: American Psychological Association.

Goldberg, A. E., & Perry-Jenkins, M. (2004). Division of labor and working-class women's well-being across the transition to parenthood. *Journal of Family Psychology, 18,* 225–236.

Goldberg, A. E., & Perry-Jenkins, M. (2007). The division of labor and perceptions of parental roles: Lesbian couples across the transition to parenthood. *Journal of Social and Personal Relationships, 24,* 297–318.

Goldberg, H. (1976). *The hazards of being male.* New York: New American Library.

Golden, J. H., Johnson, C. A., & Lopez, R. A. (2001). Sexual harassment in the workplace: Exploring the effects of physical attractiveness on perception of harassment. *Sex Roles, 45,* 767–784.

Goldzweig, G., Andritsch, E., Hubert, A., Walach, N., Perry, S., Brenner, B., et al. (2009). How relevant is marital status and gender variables in coping with colorectal cancer? A sample of middle-aged and older cancer survivors. *Psycho-Oncology, 18,* 866–874.

Golombok, S., Perry, B., Burston, A., Murray, C., Mooney-Somers, J., Stevens, M., et al. (2003). Children with lesbian parents: A community study. *Developmental Psychology, 39,* 20–33.

Golombok, S., Rust, J., Zervoulis, K., Croudace, T., Golding, J., & Hines, M. (2008). Developmental trajectories of sex-typed behavior in boys and girls: A longitudinal general population study of children aged 2.5–8 years. *Child Development, 79,* 1583–1593.

Gonzalez, J. M., Alegria, M., & Prihoda, T. J. (2005). How do attitudes toward mental health treatment vary by age, gender, and ethnicity/race in young adults? *Journal of Community Psychology, 33,* 611–629.

Good, C., Aronson, J., & Harder, J. A. (2008). Problems in the pipeline: Stereotype threat and women's achievement in high-level math courses. *Journal of Applied Developmental Psychology, 29*(1), 17–28.

Gooden, A. M., & Gooden, M. A. (2001). Gender representation in notable children's picture books: 1995–1999. *Sex Roles, 45,* 89–101.

Goodman, C. C. (1999). Reciprocity of social support in long-term marriage. *Journal of Mental Health and Aging, 5,* 341–357.

Goodman, M. J., Griffin, P. B., Estioko-Griffen, A. A., & Grove, J. S. (1985). The compatibility of hunting among the Agta hunter-gatherers of the Philippines. *Sex Roles, 12,* 1199–1209.

Gorman, B. K., & Read, J. G. (2006). Gender disparities in adult health: An examination of three measures of morbidity. *Journal of Health and Social Behavior, 47,* 95–110.

Gorman, E. H. (2005). Gender stereotypes, same-gender preferences, and organizational variation in the hiring of women: Evidence from law firms. *American Sociological Review, 70,* 702–728.

Gottman, J. M. (1994). *What predicts divorce? The relationship between marital processes and marital outcomes.* Hillsdale, NJ: Erlbaum.

Gottman, J. M., & Carrere, S. (1994). Why can't men and women get along? Developmental roots and marital inequities. In D. J. Canary & L. Stafford (Eds.), *Communication and relational maintenance* (pp. 203–229). London: Academic Press.

Gottman, J. M., Levenson, R. W., Gross, J., Frederickson, B. L., McCoy, K., Rosenthal, et al. (2003). Correlates of gay and lesbian couples' relationship satisfaction and relationship dissolution. *Journal of Homosexuality, 45,* 23–43.

Gottman, J. M., Levenson, R. W., Swanson, C., Swanson, K., Tyson, R., & Yoshimoto, D. (2003). Observing gay, lesbian and heterosexual couples' relationships: Mathematical modeling of conflict interaction. *Journal of Homosexuality, 45,* 65–90.

Gove, W. R. (1984). Gender differences in mental and physical illness: The effects of fixed roles and nurturant roles. *Social Science & Medicine, 19*(2), 77–91.

Gove, W. R., & Hughes, M. (1979). Possible causes of the apparent sex differences in physical health: An empirical investigation. *American Sociological Review, 44,* 126–146.

Gove, W. R., & Tudor, J. F. (1973). Adult sex roles and mental illness. *American Journal of Sociology, 78,* 812–835.

Grabe, M. E., Trager, K. D., Lear, M., & Rauch, J. (2006). Gender in crime news: A case study test of the chivalry hypothesis. *Mass Communication & Society, 9,* 137–163.

Grabe, S., & Hyde, J. S. (2006). Ethnicity and body dissatisfaction among women in the United States: A meta-analysis. *Psychological Bulletin, 132,* 622–640.

Grabe, S., Hyde, J. S., & Lindberg, S. M. (2007). Body objectification and depression in adolescents: The role of gender, shame, and rumination. *Psychology of Women Quarterly, 31,* 164–175.

Graber, J. A., Brooks-Gunn, J., & Warren, M. P. (2006). Pubertal effects on adjustment in girls: Moving from demonstrating effects to identifying pathways. *Journal of Youth and Adolescence, 35,* 413–423.

Grace, S. L., Krepostman, S., Brooks, D., Arthur, H., Scholey, P., Suskin, N., et al. (2005). Illness perceptions among cardiac patients: Relation to depressive symptomatology and sex. *Journal of Psychosomatic Research, 59,* 153–160.

Grant, K., Marsh, P., Syniar, G., Williams, M., Addlesperger, E., Kinzler, M. H., et al. (2002). Gender differences in rates of depression among undergraduates: Measurement matters. *Journal of Adolescence, 25,* 613–617.

Gratz, K. L., Paulson, A., Jakupcak, M., & Tull, M. T. (2009). Exploring the relationship between childhood maltreatment and intimate partner abuse: Gender differences in the mediating role of emotion dysregulation. *Violence and Victims, 24,* 68–82.

Gravener, J. A., Haedt, A. A., Heatherton, T. F., & Keel, P. K. (2008). Gender and age differences in associations between peer dieting and drive for thinness. *International Journal of Eating Disorders, 41,* 57–63.

Gray, J. (1992). *Men are from Mars, women are from Venus.* New York: HarperCollins.

Green, C. A., & Pope, C. R. (1999). Gender, psychosocial factors and the use of medical services: A longitudinal analysis. *Social Science and Medicine, 48,* 1363–1372.

Green, J. P., Lynn, S. J., & Montgomery, G. H. (2008). Gender-related differences in hypnosis-based treatments for smoking: A follow-up meta-analysis. *American Journal of Clinical Hypnosis, 50,* 259–271.

Green, M. C., & Sabini, J. (2006). Gender, socioeconomic status, age, and jealousy: Emotional responses to infidelity in a national sample. *Emotion, 6,* 330–334.

Greene, K., & Faulkner, S. L. (2005). Gender, belief in the sexual double standard, and sexual talk in heterosexual dating relationships. *Sex Roles, 53,* 239–251.

Greenwald, A. G., & Farnham, S. D. (2000). Using the implicit association test to measure self-esteem and self-concept. *Journal of Personality and Social Psychology, 79,* 1022–1038.

Gregory, C. O., Blanck, H. M., Gillespie, C., Maynard, L. M., & Serdula, M. K. (2008). Perceived health risk of excess body weight among overweight and obese men and women: Differences by sex. *Preventive Medicine, 47,* 46–52.

Groesz, L. M., Levine, M. P., & Murnen, S. K. (2002). The effect of experimental presentation of thin media images on body satisfaction: A meta-analytic review. *International Journal of Eating Disorders, 31,* 1–16.

Grossman, J. (2008). Court's decision is a victory for transsexuals' right not to face employment discrimination. Retrieved May 26, 2010, from http://www.sldn.

org/news/archives/courts-decision-is-a-victory-for-transsexuals-right-not-to-face-employment-/

Grossman, R. J. (2002). Paying the price. *Human Resources Magazine*. Retrieved May 8, 2003, from proquest.umi.com/pqdweb?S=1052408275&RQT=309&CC=2&Dtp=1&Did=0000001

Grubb, A., & Harrower, J. (2008). Attribution of blame in cases of rape: An analysis of participant gender, type of rape and perceived similarity to the victim. *Aggression and Violent Behavior, 13,* 396–405.

Grunau, G. L., Ratner, P. A., Galdas, P. M., & Hossain, S. (2009). Ethnic and gender differences in patient education about heart disease risk and prevention. *Patient Education and Counseling, 76,* 181–188.

Grundtvig, M., Hagen, T. P., German, M., & Reikvam, A. (2009). Sex-based differences in premature first myocardial infarction caused by smoking: Twice as many years lost by women as by men. *European Journal of Cardiovascular Prevention and Rehabilitation, 16,* 174–179.

Guerguerian, R., & Lewine, R. R. J. (1998). Brain torque and sex differences in schizophrenia. *Schizophrenia Research, 30,* 175–181.

Guerrero, L. K., & Chavez, A. M. (2005). Relational maintenance in cross-sex friendships characterized by different types of romantic intent: An exploratory study. *Western Journal of Communication, 69,* 339–358.

Guerrero, L. K., & Mongeau, P. A. (2008). On becoming "more than friends": The transition from friendship to romantic relationship. In S. Sprecher, A. Wenzel, & J. Harvey (Eds.), *Handbook of relationship initiation* (pp. 175–194). New York: Psychology Press.

Guiller, J., & Durndell, A. (2006). "I totally agree with you": Gender interactions in educational online discussion groups. *Journal of Computer Assisted Learning, 22,* 368–381.

Guimond, S., Brunot, S., Chatard, A., Garcia, D. M., Martinot, D., Branscombe, N. R., et al. (2007). Culture, gender, and the self: Variations and impact of social comparison processes. *Journal of Personality and Social Psychology, 92,* 1118–1134.

Guimond, S., Chatard, A., Martinot, D., Crisp, R. J., & Redersdorff, S. (2006). Social comparison, self-stereotyping, and gender differences in self-construals. *Journal of Personality and Social Psychology, 90,* 221–242.

Gupta, S. (2006). Her money, her time: Women's earnings and their housework hours. *Social Science Research, 35,* 975–999.

Gurian, M. (2009). *The purpose of boys: Helping our sons find meaning, significance, and direction in their lives.* San Francisco, CA: Jossey-Bass.

Gurian, M., & Stevens, K. (2007). *The minds of boys: Saving our sons from falling behind in school and life.* San Francisco, CA: Jossey-Bass.

Gutek, B. A. (2001). Women and paid work. *Psychology of Women Quarterly, 25,* 379–393.

Gutek, B. A. (2008). Commentary on research relevant to sex discrimination and sexual harassment. In E. Borgida & S. T. Fiske (Eds.), *Beyond common sense: Psychological science in the courtroom* (pp. 327–339). Malden, MA: Wiley-Blackwell.

Gutek, B. A., & Done, R. S. (2000). Sexual harassment. In R. K. Unger (Ed.), *Handbook of the psychology of women and gender* (pp. 1–61). New York: Wiley.

Ha, J.-H., Hong, J., Seltzer, M. M., & Greenberg, J. S. (2008). Age and gender differences in the well-being of midlife and aging parents with children with mental health or developmental problems: Report of a national study. *Journal of Health and Social Behavior, 49,* 301–316.

Haas, L., & Hwang, C. P. (2008). The impact of taking parental leave on fathers' participation in childcare and relationships with children: Lessons from Sweden. *Community, Work & Family, 11*(1), 85–104.

Hagedoorn, M., Sanderman, R., Bolks, H. N., Tuinstra, J., & Coyne, J. C. (2008). Distress in couples coping with cancer: A meta-analysis and critical review of role and gender effects. *Psychological Bulletin, 134,* 1–30.

Hagedoorn, M., Van Yperen, N. W., Coyne, J. C., van Jaarsveld, C. H. M., Ranchor, A. V., van Sonderen, E., et al. (2006). Does marriage protect older people from distress? The role of equity and recency of bereavement. *Psychology and Aging, 21,* 611–620.

Halatsis, P., & Christakis, N. (2009). The challenge of sexual attraction within heterosexuals' cross-sex friendship. *Journal of Social and Personal Relationships, 26*(6–7), 919–937.

Hall, C. C. I. (2009). Asian American women: The nail that sticks out is hammered down. In N. Tewari & A. N. Alvarez (Eds.), *Asian American psychology: Current perspectives* (pp. 193–209). New York: Routledge/Taylor & Francis Group.

Hall, J. A. (1996). Touch, status, and gender at professional meetings. *Journal of Nonverbal Behavior, 20*(1), 23–44.

Hall, J. A. (1998). How big are nonverbal sex differences? The case of smiling and sensitivity to nonverbal cues. In D. J. Canary & K. Dindia (Eds.), *Sex differences and similarities in communication* (pp. 155–177). Mahwah, NJ: Erlbaum.

Hall, J. A. (2006). How big are nonverbal sex differences? The case of smiling and nonverbal sensitivity. In K. Dindia & D. J. Canary (Eds.), *Sex differences and similarities in communication* (2nd ed., pp. 59–81). Mahwah, NJ: Lawrence Erlbaum Associates.

Hall, J. A., & Carter, J. D. (1999). Gender-stereotype accuracy as an individual difference. *Journal of Personality and Social Psychology, 77,* 350–359.

Hall, J. A., & Mast, M. S. (2008). Are women always more interpersonally sensitive than men? Impact of goals and content domain. *Personality and Social Psychology Bulletin, 34,* 144–155.

Hall, J. A., & Roter, D. L. (2002). Do patients talk differently to male and female physicians? A meta-analytic review. *Patient Education and Counseling, 48,* 217–224.

Hall, J. A., & Veccia, E. M. (1990). More "touching" observations: New insights on men, women, and interpersonal touch. *Journal of Personality and Social Psychology, 59,* 1155–1162.

Hall, J. A., Carter, J. D., & Horgan, T. G. (2000). Gender differences in nonverbal communication of emotion. In A. H. Fischer (Ed.), *Gender and emotion: Social and psychological perspectives* (pp. 97–117). New York: Cambridge University Press.

Hall, J. A., Coats, E. J., & LeBeau, L. S. (2005). Nonverbal behavior and the vertical dimension of social relations: A meta-analysis. *Psychological Bulletin, 131,* 898–924.

Hall, J. A., Horgan, T. G., & Carter, J. D. (2002). Assigned and felt status in relation to observer-coded and participant-reported smiling. *Journal of Nonverbal Behavior, 26*(2), 63–81.

Halpern, C. T., Young, M. L., Waller, M. W., Martin, S. L., & Kupper, L. L. (2004). Prevalence of partner violence in same-sex romantic and sexual relationships in a national sample of adolescents. *Journal of Adolescent Health, 35,* 124–131.

Halpern, D. F. (2000). *Sex differences in cognitive abilities* (3rd ed.). Mahwah, NJ: Erlbaum.

Halpern, D. F., & Collaer, M. L. (2005). Sex differences in visuospatial abilities: More than meets the eye. In P. Shah & A. Miyake (Eds.), *The Cambridge handbook of visuospatial thinking* (pp. 170–212). New York: Cambridge University Press.

Halpern, D. F., Benbow, C. P., Geary, D. C., Gur, R. C., Shibley Hyde, J., & Gernsbacher, M. A. (2007). The science of sex differences in science and mathematics. *Psychological Science in the Public Interest, 8,* 1–51.

Halpern, D. F., Wai, J., & Saw, A. (2005). A psychobiosocial model: Why females are sometimes greater than and sometimes less than males in math achievement. In A. M. Gallagher & J. C. Kaufman (Eds.), *Gender differences in mathematics: An integrative psychological approach* (pp. 48–72). New York: Cambridge University Press.

Hamilton, L. (2007). Trading on heterosexuality. *Gender and Society, 21,* 145–172.

Han, E., Truesdale, K. P., Taber, D. R., Cai, J., Juhaeri, J., & Stevens, J. (2009). Impact of overweight and obesity on hospitalization: Race and gender differences. *International Journal of Obesity, 33,* 249–256.

Han, W.-J., Ruhm, C., & Waldfogel, J. (2009). Parental leave policies and parents' employment and leave-taking. *Journal of Policy Analysis and Management, 28,* 29–54.

Hankin, B. L., Mermelstein, R., & Roesch, L. (2007). Sex differences in adolescent depression: Stress exposure and reactivity models. *Child Development, 78,* 279–295.

Hardy, C. L., Bukowski, W. M., & Sippola, L. K. (2002). Stability and change in peer relationships during the transition to middle-level school. *Journal of Early Adolescence, 22,* 117–142.

Harrell, Z. A. T., & Karim, N. M. (2008). Is gender relevant only for problem alcohol behaviors? An examination of correlates of alcohol use among college students. *Addictive Behaviors, 33,* 359–365.

Harrington, B., Van Deusen, F., & Ladge, J. (2010). *The new dad: Exploring fatherhood within a career context.* Boston College: Center for Work and Family.

Harris, C. R. (2003). A review of sex differences in sexual jealousy, including self-report data, psychophysiological responses, interpersonal violence, and morbid jealousy. *Personality and Social Psychology Review, 7,* 102–128.

Harris, J. A. (1999). Review and methodological considerations in research on testosterone and aggression. *Aggression and Violent Behavior, 4,* 273–291.

Harris, J. R. (1998). *The nurture assumption: Why children turn out the way they do: Parents matter less than you think and peers matter more.* New York: Free Press.

Harris, K. M., Perreira, K. M., & Lee, D. (2009). Obesity in the transition to adulthood: Predictions across race/ethnicity, immigrant generation, and sex. *Archives of Pediatrics & Adolescent Medicine, 163,* 1022–1028.

Harris, M. B. (1996). Aggressive experiences and aggressiveness: Relationship to ethnicity, gender, and age. *Journal of Applied Social Psychology, 26*(10), 843–870.

Harrison, K., & Hefner, V. (2008). Media, body image, and eating disorders. In S. L. Calvert & B. J. Wilson (Eds.), *The handbook of children, media, and development* (pp. 381–406). Malden, MA: Blackwell Publishing.

Harrison, L. A., Howerton, D. M., Secarea, A. M., & Nguyen, C. Q. (2008). Effects of ingroup bias and gender role violations of acquaintance rape attributions. *Sex Roles, 59,* 713–725.

Hartman, H., & Hartman, M. (2008). How undergraduate engineering students perceive women's (and men's) problems in science, math, and engineering. *Sex Roles, 58,* 251–265.

Hatala, M. N., & Prehodka, J. (1996). Content analysis of gay male and lesbian personal advertisements. *Psychological Reports, 78,* 371–374.

Hathaway, S. R., & McKinley, J. C. (1940). A multiphasic personality schedule (Minnesota): Construction of the schedule. *Journal of Psychology, 10,* 249–254.

Hatoum, I. J., & Belle, D. (2004). Mags and abs: Media consumption and bodily concerns in men. *Sex Roles, 51*(7–8), 397–407.

Hatzenbuehler, M. L., Dovidio, J. F., Nolen-Hoeksema, S., & Phills, C. E. (2009). An implicit measure of anti-gay attitudes: Prospective associations with emotion regulation strategies and psychological distress. *Journal of Adult Development, 45,* 1316–1320.

Haukkala, A., Konttinen, H., Uutela, A., Kawachi, I., & Laatikainen, T. (2009). Gender differences in the associations between depressive symptoms, cardiovascular diseases, and all-cause mortality. *Annals of Epidemiology, 19,* 623–629.

Hazen, D. A., Mannino, D. M., & Clayton, R. (2008). Gender specific differences in the pros and cons of smoking among current smokers in Eastern Kentucky: Implications for future smoking cessation interventions. *International Journal of Environmental Research and Public Health, 5,* 230–242.

Heatherton, T. F., Kozlowski, L. T., Frecker, R. C., & Fagerstrom, K.-O. (1991). The Fagerström test for nicotine dependence: A revision of the Fagerström tolerance questionnaire. *British Journal of Addiction, 86,* 1119–1127.

Heaven, P., & Ciarrochi, J. (2008). Parental styles, gender and the development of hope and self-esteem. *European Journal of Personality, 22,* 707–724.

Heavey, C. L., Christensen, A., & Malamuth, N. M. (1995). The longitudinal impact of demand and withdrawal during marital conflict. *Journal of Consulting and Clinical Psychology, 63,* 797–801.

Hebl, M. R., King, E. B., Glick, P., Singletary, S. L., & Kazama, S. (2007). Hostile and benevolent reactions toward pregnant women: Complementary interpersonal punishments and rewards that maintain traditional roles. *Journal of Applied Psychology, 92,* 1499–1511.

Hecht, M. A., & LaFrance, M. (1998). License or obligation to smile: The effect of power and sex on amount and type of smiling. *Personality and Social Psychology Bulletin, 24,* 1332–1342.

Heckert, T. M., Droste, H. E., Adams, P. J., Griffin, C. M., Roberts, L. L., Mueller, M. A., et al. (2002). Gender differences in anticipated salary: Role of salary estimates for others, job characteristics, career paths, and job inputs. *Sex Roles, 47,* 139–151.

Hedges, L. V., & Nowell, A. (1995). Sex differences in mental test scores, variability, and numbers of high-scoring individuals. *Science, 269,* 41–45.

Heilman, M. E., & Okimoto, T. G. (2007). Why are women penalized for success at male tasks? The implied communality deficit. *Journal of Applied Psychology, 92,* 81–92.

Helgeson, V. S. (1990). The role of masculinity in a prognostic predictor of heart attack severity. *Sex Roles, 22,* 755–774.

Helgeson, V. S. (1993). Implications of agency and communion for patient and spouse adjustment to a first coronary event. *Journal of Personality and Social Psychology, 64,* 807–816.

Helgeson, V. S. (1994a). Long-distance romantic relationships: Sex differences in adjustment and breakup. *Personality and Social Psychology Bulletin, 20,* 254–265.

Helgeson, V. S. (1994b). Prototypes and dimensions of masculinity and femininity. *Sex Roles, 31,* 653–682.

Helgeson, V. S. (1994c). Relation of agency and communion to well-being: Evidence and potential explanations. *Psychological Bulletin, 116,* 412–428.

Helgeson, V. S. (2003). Unmitigated communion and adjustment to breast cancer: Associations and explanations. *Journal of Applied Social Psychology, 33,* 1643–1661.

Helgeson, V. S., & Fritz, H. L. (1996). Implications of communion and unmitigated communion for adolescent adjustment to Type I diabetes. *Women's Health: Research on Gender, Behavior, and Policy, 2*(3), 169–194.

Helgeson, V. S., & Fritz, H. L. (1998). A theory of unmitigated communion. *Personality and Social Psychology Review, 2,* 173–183.

Helgeson, V. S., & Fritz, H. L. (1999). Unmitigated agency and unmitigated communion: Distinctions from agency and communion. *Journal of Research in Personality, 33,* 131–158.

Helgeson, V. S., & Lepore, S. J. (1997). Men's adjustment to prostate cancer: The role of agency and unmitigated agency. *Sex Roles, 37,* 251–267.

Helgeson, V. S., & Lepore, S. J. (2004). Quality of life following prostate cancer: The role of agency and unmitigated agency. *Journal of Applied Social Psychology, 34,* 2559–2585.

Helgeson, V. S., & Mickelson, K. D. (2000). Coping with chronic illness among the elderly. In S. B. Manuck, R. Jennings, B. S. Rabin, & A. Baum (Eds.), *Behavior, health, and aging* (pp. 153–178). Mahwah, NJ: Lawrence Erlbaum.

Helgeson, V. S., Escobar, O., Siminerio, L., & Becker, D. (2007). Unmitigated communion and health among adolescents with and without diabetes: The mediating role of eating disturbances. *Personality and Social Psychology Bulletin, 33,* 519–536.

Hendrick, C., & Hendrick, S. (1986). A theory and method of love. *Journal of Personality and Social Psychology, 50,* 392–402.

Hendrick, C., & Hendrick, S. S. (2009). Love. In C. R. Snyder & S. J. Lopez (Eds.), *Oxford handbook of positive psychology* (pp. 447–454). New York: Oxford University Press.

Hendrick, S. S., & Hendrick, C. (2002). Linking romantic love with sex: Development of the perceptions of love and sex scale. *Journal of Social and Personal Relationships, 19,* 361–378.

Henley, N. M. (1977). *Body politics: Power, sex, and nonverbal communication.* Upper Saddle River, NJ: Prentice-Hall.

Heo, M., Pietrobelli, A., Fontaine, K. R., Sirey, J. A., & Faith, M. S. (2006). Depressive mood and obesity in US adults: Comparison and moderation by sex, age, and race. *International Journal of Obesity, 30,* 513–519.

Hepp, U., Spindler, A., & Milos, G. (2005). Eating disorder symptomatology and gender role orientation. *International Journal of Eating Disorders, 37,* 227–233.

Herbert, J., & Stipek, D. (2005). The emergence of gender differences in children's perceptions of their academic competence. *Applied Developmental Psychology, 26,* 276–295.

Herek, G. M. (2006). Legal recognition of same-sex relationships in the United States: A social science perspective. *American Psychologist, 61,* 607–621.

Hess, U., Adams, R. B., & Kleck, R. E. (2005). Who may frown and who should smile? Dominance, affiliation, and the display of happiness and anger. *Cognition and Emotion, 19,* 515–536.

Hessini, L. (1994). Wearing the hijab in contemporary Morocco: Choice and identity. In F. M. Gocek & S. Balaghi (Eds.), *Reconstructing gender in the Middle East* (pp. 40–56). New York: Columbia University Press.

Heuveline, P., & Timberlake, J. M. (2004). The role of cohabitation in family formation: The United States in comparative perspective. *Journal of Marriage and Family, 66,* 1214–1230.

Heyman, R. E., Hunt-Martorano, A. N., Malik, J., & Smith Slep, A. M. (2009). Desired change in couples: Gender differences and effects on communication. *Journal of Family Psychology, 23,* 474–484.

Hicks, B. M., Johnson, W., Iacono, W. G., & McGue, M. (2008). Moderating effects of personality on the genetic and environmental influences of school grades helps to explain sex differences in scholastic achievement. *European Journal of Personality, 22,* 247–268.

Hill, C., & Silva, E. (2005). *Drawing the line: Sexual harassment on campus.* Washington, DC: American Association of University Women Educational Foundation.

Hill, C., Corbett, C., & St. Rose, A. (2010). *Why so few? Women in science, technology, engineering, and mathematics.* Washington, DC: American Association of University Women.

Hill, D. B., Rozanski, C., Carfagnini, J., & Willoughby, B. (2007). Gender identity disorders in childhood and adolescence: A critical inquiry. *International Journal of Sexual Health, 19,* 57–75.

Hill, J. P., & Lynch, M. E. (1983). The intensification of gender-related role expectations during early adolescence. In J. Brooks-Gunn & A. C. Petersen (Eds.), *Girls at puberty* (pp. 201–228). New York: Plenum Press.

Hilt, L. M., McLaughlin, K. A., & Nolen-Hoeksema, S. (2010). Examination of the response styles theory in a community sample of young adolescents. *Journal of Abnormal Child Psychology, 38,* 545–556.

Hines, M., Ahmed, S. F., & Hughes, I. A. (2003). Psychological outcomes and gender-related development in complete androgen insensitivity syndrome. *Archives of Sexual Behavior, 32,* 93–101.

Hines, M., Brook, C., & Conway, G. S. (2004). Androgen and psychosexual development: Core gender identity, sexual orientation, and recalled childhood gender role behavior in women and men with congenital adrenal hyperplasia (CAH). *Journal of Sex Research, 41,* 75–81.

Hippisley-Cox, J., Pringle, M., Crown, N., Meal, A., & Wynn, A. (2001). Sex inequalities in ischaemic heart disease in general practice: Cross sectional survey. *British Medical Journal, 322,* 832–834.

Hirnstein, M., Bayer, U., & Hausmann, M. (2009). Sex-specific response strategies in mental rotation. *Learning and Individual Differences, 19,* 225–228.

Hirokawa, K., & Dohi, I. (2007). Agency and communion related to mental health in Japanese young adults. *Sex Roles, 56,* 517–524.

Hiscock, M., Israelian, M., Inch, R., Jacek, C., & Hiscock-Kalil, C. (1995). Is there a sex difference in human laterality? II: An exhaustive survey of visual laterality studies from six neuropsychology journals. *Journal of Clinical and Experimental Neuropsychology, 17,* 590–610.

Ho, J. E., Paultre, F., & Mosca, L. (2005). The gender gap in coronary heart disease mortality: Is there a difference between Blacks and Whites? *Journal of Women's Health, 14,* 117–127.

Hobbs, M., & McLaren, S. (2009). The interrelations of agency, depression and suicidal ideation among older adults. *Suicide and Life-Threatening Behavior, 39,* 161–171.

Hochschild, A. R. (1989). *The second shift.* New York: Avon Books.

Hoffmann, M. L., & Powlishta, K. K. (2001). Gender segregation in childhood: A test of the interaction style theory. *Journal of Genetic Psychology, 162*(3), 298–313.

Hohmann-Marriott, B. E. (2006). Shared beliefs and the union stability of married and cohabiting couples. *Journal of Marriage and Family, 68,* 1015–1028.

Holley, S. R., Sturm, V. E., & Levenson, R. W. (2010). Exploring the basis for gender differences in the demand-withdraw pattern. *Journal of Homosexuality, 57,* 666–684.

Holmes-Lonergan, H. A. (2003). Preschool children's collaborative problem-solving interactions: The role of gender, pair type, and task. *Sex Roles, 48,* 505–517.

Holt, J. L., & DeVore, C. J. (2005). Culture, gender, organizational role, and styles of conflict resolution: A meta-analysis. *International Journal of Intercultural Relations, 29,* 165–196.

Holt-Lunstad, J., Birmingham, W., & Jones, B. Q. (2008). Is there something unique about marriage? The relative impact of marital status, relationship quality, and network social support on ambulatory blood pressure and mental health. *Annals of Behavioral Medicine, 35,* 239–244.

Holt-Lunstad, J., Birmingham, W., Howard, A. M., & Thoman, D. (2009). Married with children: The influence of parental status and gender on ambulatory blood pressure. *Annals of Behavioral Medicine, 38,* 170–179.

Homan, K. J., & Boyatzis, C. J. (2009). Body image in older adults: Links with religion and gender. *Journal of Adult Development, 16,* 230–238.

Honeycutt, J. M., & Cantrill, J. G. (2001). *Cognition, communication, and romantic relationships.* Mahwah, NJ: Lawrence Erlbaum Associates.

Hope, S., Rodgers, B., & Power, C. (1999). Marital status transitions and psychological distress: Longitudinal evidence from a national population sample. *Psychological Medicine, 29,* 381–389.

Horn, S. S., Kosciw, J. G., & Russell, S. T. (2009). Special issue introduction: New research on lesbian, gay, bisexual, and transgender youth: Studying lives in context. *Journal of Youth and Adolescence, 38,* 863–866.

Horner, M. S. (1972). Toward an understanding of achievement-related conflicts in women. *Journal of Social Issues, 28,* 157–175.

Horney, K. (1926). The flight from womanhood: The masculinity-complex in women, as viewed by men and by women. *International Journal of Psycho-Analysis, 7,* 324–339.

Horney, K. (1973). The flight from womanhood. In J. B. Miller (Ed.), *Psychoanalysis and women* (pp. 5–20). Baltimore, MD: Penguin Books.

Horvath, M. A. H., & Brown, J. M. (2009). Setting the scene: Introduction to understanding rape. In M. Horvath & J. Brown (Eds.), *Rape: Challenging contemporary thinking* (pp. 1–16). Portland, OR: Willan Publishing.

House, J. S., Robbins, C., & Metzner, H. L. (1982). The association of social relationships and activities with mortality: Prospective evidence from the Tecumseh community health study. *American Journal of Epidemiology, 116*(1), 123–140.

Hubbard, J. A., McAuliffe, M., Morrow, M. T., & Romano, L. J. (2010). Reactive and proactive aggression in childhood and adolescence: Precursors, outcomes, processes, experiences, and measurement. *Journal of Personality, 78,* 95–118.

Hudson, J. I., Hiripi, E., Pope, H. G., Jr., & Kessler, R. C. (2007). The prevalence and correlates of eating disorders in the national comorbidity survey replication. *Biological Psychiatry, 61,* 348–358.

Huerta, M., Cortina, L. M., Pang, J. S., Torges, C. M., & Magley, V. J. (2006). Sex and power in the academy: Modeling sexual harassment in the lives of college women. *Personality and Social Psychology Bulletin, 32,* 616–628.

Hughes, M. E., & Waite, L. J. (2009). Marital biography and health at mid-life. *Journal of Health and Social Behavior, 50,* 344–358.

Hughes, M., Morrison, K., & Asada, K. J. K. (2005). What's love got to do with it? Exploring the impact of maintenance rules, love attitudes, and network support on friends with benefits relationships. *Western Journal of Communication, 69,* 49–66.

Hunt-Shanks, T., Blanchard, C., & Reid, R. D. (2009). Gender differences in cardiac patients: A longitudinal investigation of exercise, autonomic anxiety, negative affect and depression. *Psychology, Health and Medicine, 14,* 375–385.

Hurley, R. W., & Adams, M. C. B. (2008). Sex, gender, and pain: An overview of a complex field. *Pain Mechanisms, 107,* 309–317.

Husky, M. M., Mazure, C. M., Maciejewski, P. K., & Swendsen, J. D. (2009). Past depression and gender interact to influence emotional reactivity to daily life stress. *Cognitive Therapy and Research, 33,* 264–271.

Husky, M. M., Mazure, C. M., Paliwal, P., & McKee, S. A. (2008). Gender differences in the comorbidity of smoking behavior and major depression. *Drug and Alcohol Dependence, 93,* 176–179.

Hutson-Comeaux, S. L., & Kelly, J. R. (1996). Sex differences in interaction style and group task performance: The process-performance relationship. *Journal of Social Behavior and Personality, 11*(5), 255–275.

Hyams, T., & Johnson, P. A. (2010). *Out of the shadows: Women and lung cancer.* Washington, DC: Lung Cancer Alliance. Retrieved October 4, 2010, from http://www.lungcanceralliance.org/shadows

Hyde, J. S. (2005a). The gender similarities hypothesis. *American Psychologist, 60,* 581–592.

Hyde, J. S. (2005b). The genetics of sexual orientation. In J. Shibley Hyde (Ed.), *Biological substrates of human sexuality* (pp. 9–20). Washington, DC: American Psychological Association.

Hyde, J. S., & Linn, M. C. (1988). Gender differences in verbal ability: A meta-analysis. *Psychological Bulletin, 104,* 53–69.

Hyde, J. S., & McKinley, N. M. (1997). Gender differences in cognition: Results from meta-analysis. In P. J. Caplan, M. Crawford, J. S. Hyde, & J. T. E. Richardson (Eds.), *Gender differences in human cognition* (pp. 30–51). New York: Oxford University Press.

Hyde, J. S., DeLamater, J. D., & Hewitt, E. C. (1998). Sexuality and the dual-earner couple: Multiple roles and sexual functioning. *Journal of Family Psychology, 12*(3), 1–15.

Hyde, J. S., Fennema, E., & Lamon, S. J. (1990). Gender differences in mathematics performance: A meta-analysis. *Psychological Bulletin, 107,* 139–155.

Hyde, J. S., Lindberg, S. M., Linn, M. C., Ellis, A. B., & Williams, C. C. (2008). Gender similarities characterize math performance. *Science, 321,* 494–495.

Ibarra, H. (1993). Personal networks of women and minorities in management: A conceptual framework. *Academy of Management Review, 18,* 56–87.

Ibroscheva, E. (2007). Caught between East and West? Portrayals of gender in Bulgarian television advertisements. *Sex Roles, 57,* 409–418.

Iervolino, A. C., Hines, M., Golombok, S. E., Rust, J., & Plomin, R. (2005). Genetic and environmental influences on sex-typed behavior during the preschool years. *Child Development, 76,* 826–840.

Ilies, R., Hauserman, N., Schwochau, S., & Stibal, J. (2003). Reported incidence rates of work-related sexual harassment in the United States using meta-analysis to explain reported rate disparities. *Personnel Psychology, 56,* 607–631.

Impett, E. A., & Peplau, L. A. (2002). Why some women consent to unwanted sex with a dating partner: Insights from attachment theory. *Psychology of Women Quarterly, 26,* 360–370.

Inaba, A., Thoits, P. A., Ueno, K., Gove, W. R., Evenson, R. J., & Sloan, M. (2005). Depression in the United States and Japan: Gender, marital status, and SES patterns. *Social Science & Medicine, 61,* 2280–2292.

Innstrand, S. T., Langballe, E. M., Falkum, E., Espnes, G. A., & Aasland, O. G. (2009). Gender-specific perceptions of four dimensions of the work/family interaction. *Journal of Career Assessment, 17,* 402–416.

Ishihara, M., Inoue, I., Kawagoe, T., Shimatani, Y., Kurisu, S., Nakama, Y., et al. (2008). Trends in gender difference in mortality after acute myocardial infarction. *Journal of Cardiology, 52,* 232–238.

Iwamoto, D. K., & Liu, W. M. (2009). Asian American men and Asianized attribution: Intersections of masculinity, race, and sexuality. In N. Tewari & A. Alvarez (Eds.), *Asian American psychology: Current perspectives* (pp. 210–232). New York: Lawrence Erlbaum Associates.

Iyengar, R. (2009). Does the certainty of arrest reduce domestic violence? Evidence from mandatory and recommended arrest laws. *Journal of Public Economics, 93,* 85–98.

Jacklin, C. N. (1989). Female and male: Issues of gender. *American Psychologist, 44,* 127–133.

Jackman, M. R. (1994). *The velvet glove: Paternalism and conflict in gender, class, and race relations.* Berkeley and Los Angeles: University of California Press.

Jackson, L. A., von Eye, A., Fitzgerald, H. E., Zhao, Y., & Witt, E. A. (2010). Self-concept, self-esteem, gender, race and information technology use. *Computers in Human Behavior, 26,* 323–328.

Jackson, L. A., Zhao, Y., Kolenic, A., Fitzgerald, H. E., Harold, R., & von Eye, A. (2008). Race, gender, and information technology use: The new digital divide. *Cyberpsychology and Behavior, 11,* 437–442.

Jackson, L. A., Zhao, Y., Qiu, W., Kolenic, A., Fitzgerald, H. E., Harold, R., et al. (2008). Culture, gender and information technology use: A comparison of Chinese and US children. *Computers in Human Behavior, 24,* 2817–2829.

Jackson, L. A., Zhao, Y., Witt, E. A., Fitzgerald, H. E., & von Eye, A. (2009). Gender, race and morality in the virtual world and its relationship to morality in the real world. *Sex Roles, 60,* 859–869.

Jackson, T. (2006). Relationships between perceived close social support and health practices within community samples of American women and men. *Journal of Psychology, 140,* 229–246.

Jacobs, J. E., Vernon, M. K., & Eccles, J. (2005). Activity choices in middle childhood: The roles of gender, self-beliefs, and parents' influence. In J. L. Mahoney, R. W. Larson, & J. S. Eccles (Eds.), *Organized activities as contexts of development* (pp. 235–254). Mahwah, NJ: Lawrence Erlbaum Associates.

Jang, S.-N., Kawachi, I., Chang, J., Boo, K., Shin, H.-G., Lee, H., et al. (2009). Marital status, gender, and depression: Analysis of the baseline survey of the Korean longitudinal study of ageing (KLoSA). *Social Science and Medicine, 69,* 1608–1615.

Jemmott, J. B., Jemmott, L. S., & Fong, G. T. (2010). Efficacy of a theory-based abstinence-only intervention over 24 months. *Archives of Pediatrics & Adolescent Medicine, 164,* 152–159.

Jenvey, V. B. (2007). The relationship between television viewing and obesity in young children: A review of existing explanations. *Early Child Development and Care, 177,* 809–820.

Jin, L., Van Yperen, N. W., Sanderman, R., & Hagedoorn, M. (2010). Depressive symptoms and unmitigated communion in support providers. *European Journal of Personality, 24,* 56–70.

Johns, M., Schmader, T., & Martens, A. (2005). Knowing is half the battle: Teaching stereotype threat as a means of improving women's math performance. *Psychological Science, 16,* 175–179.

Johnson, C. V., Mimiaga, M. J., & Bradford, J. (2008). Health care issues among lesbian, gay, bisexual, transgender and intersex (LGBTI) populations in the United States: Introduction. *Journal of Homosexuality, 54,* 213–224.

Johnson, M. P. (2004). Patriarchal terrorism and common couple violence: Two forms of violence against women. In H. T. Reis & C. E. Rusbult (Eds.), *Close relationships: Key readings* (pp. 471–482). New York: Psychology Press.

Johnson, M. P. (2008). *A typology of domestic violence: Intimate terrorism, violent resistance, and situational couple violence.* Lebanon, NH: Northeastern University Press.

Johnson, M. P. (2009). Differentiating among types of domestic violence. In H. E. Peters & C. M. K. Dush (Eds.), *Marriage and families: Perspective and complexities* (pp. 281–297). New York: Columbia University Press.

Johnson, M., & Helgeson, V. S. (2002). Sex differences in response to evaluative feedback. A field study. *Psychology of Women Quarterly, 26,* 242–251.

Johnson, M. P., & Leone, J. M. (2005). The differential effects of intimate terrorism and situational couple violence: Findings from the national violence against women survey. *Journal of Family Issues, 26,* 322–349.

Johnson, S. K., Murphy, S. E., Zewdie, S., & Reichard, R. J. (2008). The strong, sensitive type: Effects of gender stereotypes and leadership prototypes on the evaluation of male and female leaders. *Organizational Behavior and Human Decision Processes, 106,* 39–60.

Johnson, W., & Bouchard, T. J. (2007). Sex differences in mental ability: A proposed means to link them to brain structure and function. *Intelligence, 35,* 197–209.

Johnston, L. D., O'Malley, P. M., Bachman, J. G., & Schulenberg, J. E. (2009). *Monitoring the future national survey results on drug use, 1975–2008: Volume I, Secondary school students* (NIH Publication No. 09-7402). Bethesda, MD: National Institute on Drug Abuse.

Johnston, L. D., O'Malley, P. M., Bachman, J. G., & Schulenberg, J. E. (2010). *Monitoring the future national results on adolescent drug use: Overview of key findings 2009* (NIH Publication No. 10-7583). Bethesda, MD: National Institute on Drug Abuse.

Jones, E. E., & Davis, K. E. (1965). From acts to dispositions: The attribution process in social psychology. In L. Berkowitz (Ed.), *Advances in experimental social psychology* (Vol. 2, pp. 219–266). New York: Academic Press.

Jones, J. M. (2008). Most Americans not willing to forgive unfaithful spouse: Six in 10 would tell unfaithful spouse to face media alone. *Gallup, Inc.* Retrieved July 1, 2010, from http://www.gallup.com/poll/105682/most-Americans-willing-forgive-unfaithful-spouse.aspx

Jones, J. M. (2010). Americans' opposition to gay marriage eases slightly: Forty-four percent favor legal recognition; 53% are opposed. *Gallup, Inc.* Retrieved June 29, 2010, from http://www.gallup.com/poll/128291/Americans-opposition-gay-marriage-eases-slightly.aspx

Jordan, K., Wustenberg, T., Heinze, H.-J., Peters, M., & Jancke, L. (2002). Women and men exhibit different cortical activation patters during mental rotation tasks. *Neuropsychologia, 40,* 2397–2408.

Jose, A., O'Leary, K. D., & Moyer, A. (2010). Does premarital cohabitation predict subsequent marital stability and marital quality? A meta-analysis. *Journal of Marriage and Family, 72,* 105–116.

Jose, P. E., & Brown, I. (2008). When does the gender difference in rumination begin? Gender and age differences in the use of rumination by adolescents. *Journal of Youth and Adolescence, 37,* 180–192.

Joshi, H., Makepeace, G., & Dolton, P. (2007). More or less unequal? Evidence on the pay of men and women from the British birth cohort studies. *Gender, Work, and Organization, 14,* 37–55.

Judge, T. A., & Livingston, B. A. (2008). Is the gap more than gender? A longitudinal analysis of gender, gender role orientation, and earnings. *Journal of Applied Psychology, 93,* 994–1012.

Judge, T. A., & Piccolo, R. F. (2004). Transformational and transactional leadership: A meta-analytic test of their relative validity. *Journal of Applied Psychology, 89,* 755–768.

Jussim, L., & Eccles, J. S. (1992). Teacher expectations. II: Construction and reflection of student achievement. *Journal of Personality and Social Psychology, 63,* 947–961.

Kaighobadi, F., Shackelford, T. K., & Buss, D. M. (2010). Spousal mate retention in the newlywed year and three years later. *Personality and Individual Differences, 48,* 414–418.

Kaiser Family Foundation. (2001). *Inside-out: A report on the experiences of lesbians, gays and bisexuals in America and the public's views on issues and policies related to sexual orientation.* Menlo Park, CA: Kaiser Foundation. Retrieved November 19, 2007, from www.kff.org/Kaiserpolls/3193-index.cfm

Kaiser Family Foundation. (2010). *States with public place smoking bans, 2010.* Retrieved July 7, 2010, from http://www.statehealthfacts.org/comparetable.jsp

Kalbfleisch, P. J., & Herold, A. L. (2006). Sex, power, and communication. In K. Dindia & D. J. Canary (Eds.), *Sex differences and similarities in communication* (2nd ed., pp. 299–313). Mahwah, NJ: Lawrence Erlbaum Associates.

Kales, H. C., Neighbors, H. W., Valenstein, M., Blow, F. C., McCarthy, J. F., Ignacio, R. V., et al. (2005). Effect of race and sex on primary care physicians' diagnosis and treatment of late-life depression. *Journal of American Geriatrics, 53,* 777–784.

Kalmijn, M. (2005). Attitude alignment in marriage and cohabitation: The case of sex-role attitudes. *Personal Relationships, 12,* 521–535.

Kaplan, G. A., Salonen, J. T., Cohen, R. D., Brand, R. J., Syme, S. L., & Puska, P. (1988). Social connections and mortality from all causes and from cardiovascular disease: Prospective evidence from Eastern Finland. *American Journal of Epidemiology, 128*(2), 370–380.

Kaplan, R. M., & Kronick, R. G. (2006). Marital status and longevity in the United States. *Journal of Epidemiology and Community Health, 60,* 760–765.

Karniol, R., Gabay, R., Ochion, Y., & Harai, Y. (1998). Is gender or gender-role orientation a better predictor of empathy in adolescence? *Sex Roles, 39,* 45–59.

Kattainen, A., Salomaa, V., Jula, A., Kesaniemi, Y. A., Kukkonen-Harjula, K., Kahonen, M., et al. (2005). Gender differences in the treatment and secondary prevention of CHD at population level. *Scandinavian Cardiovascular Journal, 39,* 327–333.

Katz, J., Kuffel, S. W., & Coblentz, A. (2002). Are there gender differences in sustaining dating violence? An examination of frequency, severity, and relationship satisfaction. *Journal of Family Violence, 17,* 247–271.

Katzman, D. K., Zipursky, R. B., Lambe, E. K., & Mikulis, D. J. (1997). A longitudinal magnetic resonance imaging study of brain changes in adolescents with anorexia nervosa. *Archives of Pediatric Adolescent Medicine, 151,* 793–797.

Katz-Wise, S. L., Priess, H. A., & Hyde, J. S. (2010). Gender-role attitudes and behavior across the transition to parenthood. *Developmental Psychology, 46,* 18–28.

Kaufman, S. B. (2007). Sex differences in mental rotation and spatial visualization ability: Can they be accounted for by differences in working memory capacity? *Intelligence, 35,* 211–223.

Keel, P. K., & Klump, K. L. (2003). Are eating disorders culture-bound syndromes? Implications for conceptualizing their etiology. *Psychological Bulletin, 129,* 747–769.

Keller, J. (2002). Blatant stereotype threat and women's math performance: Self-handicapping as a strategic means to cope with obtrusive negative performance expectations. *Sex Roles, 47,* 193–198.

Kelly, M. M., Forsyth, J. P., & Karekla, M. (2006). Sex differences in response to a panicogenic challenge procedure: An experimental evaluation of panic vulnerability in a non-clinical sample. *Behaviour Research and Therapy, 44,* 1421–1430.

Kendler, K. S., Gardner, C. O., & Lichtenstein, P. (2008). A developmental twin study of symptoms of anxiety and depression: Evidence for genetic innovation and attenuation. *Psychological Medicine, 38,* 1567–1575.

Kendler, K. S., Myers, J., & Prescott, C. A. (2005). Sex differences in the relationship between social support and risk for major depression: A longitudinal study of opposite-sex twin pairs. *American Journal of Psychiatry, 162,* 250–256.

Kennedy, M. A., Templeton, L., Gandhi, A., & Gorzalka, B. B. (2004). Asian body image satisfaction: Ethnic and gender differences across Chinese, Indo-Asian, and European-descent students. *Eating Disorders, 12,* 321–336.

Kennedy, N., Boydell, J., Kalidindi, S., Fearon, P., Jones, P. B., van Os, J., et al. (2005). Gender differences in incidence and age at onset of mania and bipolar disorder over a 35-year period in Camberwell, England. *American Journal of Psychiatry, 162,* 257–262.

Kenney-Benson, G. A., Pomerantz, E. M., Ryan, A. M., & Patrick, H. (2006). Sex differences in math performance: The role of children's approach to schoolwork. *Developmental Psychology, 42,* 11–26.

Keogh, E. (2009). Sex differences in pain. In R. J. Moore (Ed.), *Biobehavioral approaches to pain* (pp. 125–148). New York: Springer Science + Business Media.

Keogh, E., & Eccleston, C. (2006). Sex differences in adolescent chronic pain and pain-related coping. *Pain, 123,* 275–284.

Kephart, W. M. (1967). Some correlates of romantic love. *Journal of Marriage and the Family, 29,* 470–474.

Kessler, R. C. (2000). Gender differences in major depression. In E. Frank (Ed.), *Gender and its effects on psychopathology* (pp. 61–84). Washington, DC: American Psychiatric Press, Inc.

Khan, A. A., Gardner, C. O., Prescott, C. A., & Kendler, K. S. (2002). Gender differences in the symptoms of major depression in opposite-sex dizygotic twin pairs. *American Journal of Psychiatry, 159,* 1427–1429.

Khlat, M., Sermet, C., & Le Pape, A. (2000). Women's health in relation with their family and work roles: France in the early 1900s. *Social Science & Medicine, 50,* 1807–1825.

Kiecolt-Glaser, J. K., & Newton, T. L. (2001). Marriage and health: His and hers. *Psychological Bulletin, 127,* 472–503.

Kiecolt-Glaser, J. K., Malarkey, W. B., Chee, M., Newton, T., Cacioppo, J. T., Mao, H.-Y., et al. (1993). Negative behavior during marital conflict is associated with immunological down-regulation. *Psychosomatic Medicine, 55,* 395–409.

Kiecolt-Glaser, J. K., Newton, T., Cacioppo, J. T., MacCallum, R. C., Glaser, R., & Malarkey, W. B. (1996). Marital conflict and endocrine function: Are men really more physiologically affected than women? *Journal of Consulting and Clinical Psychology, 64*(2), 324–332.

Killeen, L. A., Lopez-Zafra, E., & Eagly, A. H. (2006). Envisioning oneself as a leader: Comparisons of women and men in Spain and the United States. *Psychology of Women Quarterly, 30,* 312–322.

Kim, J. L., Sorsoli, L., Collins, K., Zylbergold, B. A., Schooler, D., & Tolman, D. L. (2007). From sex to sexuality: Exposing the heterosexual script on prime-time network television. *Journal of Sex Research, 44,* 145–158.

Kimura, D. (1999). *Sex and cognition.* Cambridge, MA: MIT Press.

King, E. B. (2008). The effect of bias on the advancement of working mothers: Disentangling legitimate concerns from inaccurate stereotypes as predictors of advancement in academe. *Human Relations, 61,* 1677–1711.

Kippen, R., Evans, A., & Gray, E. (2007). Parental preference for sons and daughters in a Western industrial setting: Evidence and implications. *Journal of Biosocial Science, 39,* 583–597.

Kite, M. E., & Whitley, B. E., Jr. (2003). Do heterosexual women and men differ in their attitudes toward homosexuality? A conceptual and methodological analysis. In L. D. Garnets & D. C. Kimmel (Eds.), *Psychological perspectives on lesbian, gay, and bisexual experiences* (2nd ed., pp. 165–187). New York: Columbia University Press.

Kite, M. E., Stockdale, G. D., Whitley, B. E., Jr., & Johnson, B. T. (2005). Attitudes toward younger and older adults: An updated meta-analytic review. *Journal of Social Issues, 61,* 241–266.

Klein, L. C., Corwin, E. J., & Ceballos, R. M. (2006). The social costs of stress: How sex differences in stress responses can lead to social stress vulnerability and depression in women. In C. L. M. Keyes & S. H. Goodman (Eds.), *Women and depression: A handbook for the social, behavioral, and biomedical sciences* (pp. 199–218). New York: Cambridge University Press.

Klimes-Dougan, B., Brand, A. E., Zahn-Waxler, C., Usher, B., Hastings, P. D., Kendziora, K., et al. (2007). Parental emotion socialization in adolescence: Differences in sex, age and problem status. *Social Development, 16,* 326–342.

Kline, G. H., Stanley, S. M., Markman, H. J., Olmos-Gallo, P. A., St. Peters, M., Whitton, S. W., et al. (2004). Timing is everything: Pre-engagement cohabitation and increased risk for poor marital outcomes. *Journal of Family Psychology, 18,* 311–318.

Kling, K. C., Hyde, J. S., Showers, C. J., & Buswell, B. N. (1999). Gender differences in self-esteem: A meta-analysis. *Psychological Bulletin, 125,* 470–500.

Klinger, L. J., Hamilton, J. A., & Cantrell, P. J. (2001). Children's perception of aggressive and gender-specific content in toy commercials. *Social Behavior and Personality, 29*(1), 11–20.

Klinkenberg, D., & Rose, S. (1994). Dating scripts of gay men and lesbians. *Journal of Homosexuality, 26*(4), 23–35.

Klinth, R. (2008). The best of both worlds? Fatherhood and gender equality in Swedish paternity leave campaigns, 1976–2006. *Fathering, 6*(1), 20–38.

Klumb, P. L., & Lampert, T. (2004). Women, work, and well-being 1950–2000: A review and methodological critique. *Social Science & Medicine, 58,* 1007–1024.

Knafo, A., Iervolino, A. C., & Plomin, R. (2005). Masculine girls and feminine boys: Genetic and environmental contributions to atypical gender development in early childhood. *Journal of Personality and Social Psychology, 88,* 400–412.

Kneidinger, L. M., Maple, T. L., & Tross, S. A. (2001). Touching behavior in sport: Functional components, analysis of sex differences, and ethological considerations. *Journal of Nonverbal Behavior, 25*(1), 43–62.

Knickmeyer, R., Baron-Cohen, S., Raggatt, P., Taylor, K., & Hackett, G. (2006). Fetal testosterone and empathy. *Hormones and Behavior, 49,* 282–292.

Knight, G. P., Fabes, R. A., & Higgins, D. A. (1996). Concerns about drawing causal inferences from meta-analyses: An example in the study of gender differences in aggression. *Psychological Bulletin, 119,* 410–421.

Knight, G. P., Guthrie, I. K., Page, M. C., & Fabes, R. A. (2002). Emotional arousal and gender differences in aggression: A meta-analysis. *Aggressive Behavior, 28,* 366–393.

Knofler, T., & Imhof, M. (2007). Does sexual orientation have an impact on nonverbal behavior in interpersonal communication? *Journal of Nonverbal Behavior, 31,* 189–204.

Koch, S. C. (2004). Constructing gender: A lens-model inspired gender communication approach. *Sex Roles, 51,* 171–186.

Koenig, A. M., & Eagly, A. H. (2005). Stereotype threat in men on a test of social sensitivity. *Sex Roles, 52,* 489–496.

Kohlberg, L. (1963). The development of children's orientations toward a moral order: Sequence in the development of moral thought. *Vita Humana, 6,* 11–33.

Kohlberg, L. (1966). A cognitive-developmental analysis of children's sex-role concepts and attitudes. In E. E. Maccoby (Ed.), *The development of sex differences* (pp. 82–173). Stanford, CA: Stanford University Press.

Kohlberg, L. (Eds.). (1981). *The psychology of moral development* (Vol. 2). San Francisco, CA: Harper & Row.

Kohler, P. K., Manhart, L. E., & Lafferty, W. E. (2008). Abstinence-only and comprehensive sex education and the initiation of sexual activity and teen pregnancy. *Journal of Adolescent Health, 42,* 344–351.

Kolaric, G. C., & Galambos, N. L. (1995). Face-to-face interactions in unacquainted female–male adolescent dyads: How do girls and boys behave? *Journal of Early Adolescence, 15*(3), 363–382.

Konrad, A. M., & Harris, C. (2002). Desirability of the Bem Sex-Role Inventory items for women and men: A comparison between African Americans and European Americans. *Sex Roles, 47,* 259–271.

Konrad, A. M., Ritchie, J., J. E., Lieb, P., & Corrigall, E. (2000). Sex differences and similarities in job attribute preferences: A meta-analysis. *Psychological Bulletin, 126,* 593–641.

Koopmans, G. T., & Lamers, L. M. (2007). Gender and health care utilization: The role of mental distress and help-seeking propensity. *Social Science & Medicine, 64,* 1216–1230.

Kort-Butler, L. A. (2009). Coping styles and sex differences in depressive symptoms and delinquent behavior. *Journal of Youth and Adolescence, 38,* 122–136.

Kosciw, J. G., Greytak, E. A., & Diaz, E. M. (2009). Who, what, where, when, and why: Demographic and ecological factors contributing to hostile school climate for lesbian, gay, bisexual, and transgender youth. *Journal of Youth and Adolescence, 38,* 976–988.

Kosfeld, M., Heinrichs, M., Zak, P. J., Fischbacher, U., & Fehr, E. (2005). Oxytocin increases trust in humans. *Nature, 435,* 673–676.

Koss, M. P., Bailey, J. A., Yuan, N. P., Herrera, V. M., & Lichter, E. L. (2003). Depression and PTSD in survivors of male violence: Research and training initiatives to facilitate recovery. *Psychology of Women Quarterly, 27,* 130–142.

Koutantji, M., Pearce, S. A., & Oakley, D. A. (1998). The relationship between gender and family history of pain with current pain experience and awareness of pain in others. *Pain, 77,* 25–31.

Krahe, B. (2000). Sexual scripts and heterosexual aggression. In T. Eckes & H. M. Trautner (Eds.), *The developmental social psychology of gender* (pp. 273–292). Mahwah, NJ: Erlbaum.

Kreager, D. A., & Staff, J. (2009). The sexual double standard and adolescent peer acceptance. *Social Psychology Quarterly, 72,* 143–164.

Krendl, A. C., Richeson, J. A., Kelley, W. M., & Heatherton, T. F. (2008). The negative consequences of threat: A functional magnetic resonance imaging investigation of the neural mechanisms underlying women's underperformance in math. *Psychological Science, 19,* 168–175.

Kring, A. M., & Gordon, A. H. (1998). Sex differences in emotion: Expression, experience, and physiology. *Journal of Personality and Social Psychology, 74,* 686–703.

Kristjansson, A. L., & Sigfusdottir, I. D. (2009). The role of parental support, parental monitoring, and time spent with parents in adolescent academic achievement in Iceland: A structural model of gender differences. *Scandinavian Journal of Educational Research, 53,* 481–496.

Kunz, M., Gruber, A., & Lautenbacher, S. (2006). Sex differences in facial encoding of pain. *Journal of Pain, 7,* 915–928.

Kurdek, L. A. (1998). Relationship outcomes and their predictors: Longitudinal evidence from heterosexual married, gay cohabiting, and lesbian cohabiting couples. *Journal of Marriage and the Family, 60,* 553–568.

Kurdek, L. A. (2003). Differences between gay and lesbian cohabiting couples. *Journal of Social and Personal Relationships, 20,* 411–436.

Kurdek, L. A. (2005). Gender and marital satisfaction early in marriage: A growth curve approach. *Journal of Marriage and Family, 67,* 68–84.

Kurdek, L. A. (2006). Differences between partners from heterosexual, gay, and lesbian cohabiting couples. *Journal of Marriage and Family, 68,* 509–528.

Kurdek, L. A. (2008a). Change in relationship quality for partners from lesbian, gay male, and heterosexual couples. *Journal of Family Psychology, 22,* 701–711.

Kurdek, L. A. (2008b). A general model of relationship commitment: Evidence from same-sex partners. *Personal Relationships, 15,* 391–405.

Kurtz-Costes, B., Rowley, S. J., Harris-Britt, A., & Woods, T. A. (2008). Gender stereotypes about mathematics and science and self-perceptions of ability in late childhood and early adolescence. *Merrill-Palmer Quarterly, 54,* 386–410.

Kurz, D. (1998). Old problems and new directions in the study of violence against women. In R. K. Bergen (Ed.), *Issues in intimate violence* (pp. 197–208). Thousand Oaks, CA: Sage.

Lach, D. H., & Gwartney-Gibbs, P. A. (1993). Sociological perspectives on sexual harassment and workplace dispute recognition. *Journal of Vocational Behavior, 42*(1), 102–115.

Lacombe, A. C., & Gay, J. (1998). The role of gender in adolescent identity and intimacy decisions. *Journal of Youth and Adolescence, 27*(6), 795–802.

LaFrance, M., & Banaji, M. (1992). Toward a reconsideration of the gender-emotion relationship. In M. S. Clark (Ed.), *Review of personality and social psychology* (Vol. 14, pp. 178–201). Newbury Park, CA: Sage.

LaFrance, M., & Hecht, M. A. (2000). Gender and smiling: A meta-analysis. In A. H. Fischer (Ed.), *Gender and emotion: Social psychological perspectives* (pp. 118–142). New York: Cambridge University Press.

LaFrance, M., Hecht, M. A., & Paluck, E. L. (2003). The contingent smile: A meta-analysis of sex differences in smiling. *Psychological Bulletin, 129,* 305–334.

Lahelma, E., Arber, S., Kivelä, K., & Roos, E. (2002). Multiple roles and health among British and Finnish women: The influence of socioeconomic circumstances. *Social Science & Medicine, 54,* 727–740.

Lahey, B. B., Hartung, C. M., Loney, J., Pelham, W. E., Chronis, A. M., & Lee, S. S. (2007). Are there sex differences in the predictive validity of DSM-IV ADHD among younger children? *Journal of Clinical Child and Adolescent Psychology, 36,* 113–126.

Lakkis, J., Ricciardelli, L. A., & Williams, R. J. (1999). Role of sexual orientation and gender-related traits in disordered eating. *Sex Roles, 41,* 1–16.

Lam, C. B., & McBride-Chang, C. A. (2007). Resilience in young adulthood: The moderating influences of gender-related personality traits and coping flexibility. *Sex Roles, 56,* 159–172.

Lance, L. M. (2007). College student sexual morality revisited: A consideration of pre-marital sex, extra-marital sex and childlessness between 1940 and 2000–2005. *College Student Journal, 41,* 727–733.

Landhuis, C. E., Poulton, R., Welch, D., & Hancox, R. J. (2008). Programming obesity and poor fitness: The long-term impact of childhood television. *Obesity, 16,* 1457–1459.

Langbein, L., & Yost, M. A. (2009). Same-sex marriage and negative externalities. *Social Science Quarterly, 90,* 292–308.

Langhinrichsen-Rohling, J., Friend, J., & Powell, A. (2009). Adolescent suicide, gender, and culture: A rate and risk factor analysis. *Aggression and Violent Behavior, 14,* 402–414.

Larche, D. W. (1985). *Father gander nursery rhymes.* Santa Barbara, CA: Advocacy Press.

Laroche, D. (2005). *Aspects of the context and consequences of domestic violence: Situational couple violence and intimate terrorism in Canada in 1999.* Retrieved August 12, 2010, from http://www.stat.gouv.qc.ca/publications/conditions/pdf/AspectViolen_an.pdf

Larsen, J. K., Otten, R., & Engels, R. C. M. E. (2009). Adolescent depressive symptoms and smoking behavior: The gender-specific role of weight concern and dieting. *Journal of Psychosomatic Research, 66,* 305–308.

Larson, R. W., & Almeida, D. M. (1999). Emotional transmission in the daily lives of families: A new paradigm for studying family process. *Journal of Marriage and the Family, 61,* 5–20.

Larson, R., & Pleck, J. (1999). Hidden feelings: Emotionality in boys and men. In D. Bernstein (Ed.), *Gender and motivation* (Vol. 45, pp. 25–74). Lincoln, NE: University of Nebraska Press.

Larson, R., & Wilson, S. (2004). Adolescence across place and time: Globalization and the changing pathways to adulthood. In R. M. Lerner & L. Steinberg (Eds.), *Handbook of adolescent psychology* (2nd ed., pp. 299–330). Hoboken, NJ: John Wiley & Sons.

Laumann, E. O., Mahay, J., & Youm, Y. (2007). Sex, intimacy, and family life in the United States. In M. Kimmel (Ed.), *The sexual self: Construction of sexual scripts* (pp. 165–190). Nashville, TN: Vanderbilt Press.

Laumann, E. O., Paik, A., Glasser, D. B., Kang, J. H., Wang, T., Levinson, B., et al. (2006). A cross-national study of subjective sexual well-being among older women and men: Findings from the global study of sexual attitudes and behaviors. *Archives of Sexual Behavior, 35,* 145–161.

Lauzen, M. M., Dozier, D. M., & Horan, N. (2008). Constructing gender stereotypes through social roles in prime-time television. *Journal of Broadcasting and Electronic Media, 52,* 200–215.

Lawlor, D. A., Smith, G. D., & Ebrahim, S. (2004). Socioeconomic position and hormone replacement therapy use: Explaining the discrepancy in evidence from observational and randomized controlled trials. *American Journal of Public Health, 94,* 2149–2154.

Lawrence, A. A. (2008). Gender identity disorders in adults: Diagnosis and treatment. In D. L. Rowland & L. Incrocci (Eds.), *Handbook of sexual and gender identity disorders* (pp. 423–456). Hoboken, NJ: John Wiley and Sons, Inc.

Lawton, C. A. (2001). Gender and regional differences in spatial referents used in direction giving. *Sex Roles, 44,* 321–337.

Lazarus, R. S., & Folkman, S. (1984). Stress, appraisal and coping. *Journal of Adolescence, 14,* 119–133.

Leach, L. S., Christensen, H., & Mackinnon, A. J. (2008). Gender differences in the endorsement of symptoms for depression and anxiety. Are gender-biased items responsible? *Journal of Nervous and Mental Disease, 196,* 128–135.

Leaper, C., & Ayres, M. M. (2007). A meta-analytic review of gender variations in adults' language use: Talkativeness, affiliative speech, and assertive speech. *Personality and Social Psychology Review, 11,* 328–363.

Leaper, C., & Smith, T. E. (2004). A meta-analytic review of gender variations in children's language use: Talkativeness, affiliative speech, and assertive speech. *Developmental Psychology, 40,* 993–1027.

Leaper, C., Carson, M., Baker, C., Holliday, H., & Myers, S. (1995). Self-disclosure and listener verbal support in same-gender and cross-gender friends' conversations. *Sex Roles, 33,* 387–404.

Leary, M. R., Tambor, E. S., Terdal, S. K., & Downs, D. L. (1995). Self-esteem as an interpersonal monitor: The sociometer hypothesis. *Journal of Personality and Social Psychology, 68,* 518–530.

Lease, A. M., & Blake, J. J. (2005). A comparison of majority-race children with and without a minority-race friend. *Social Development, 14,* 20–41.

Ledbetter, A. M., & Larson, K. A. (2008). Nonverbal cues in e-mail supportive communication: Associations with sender sex, recipient sex, and support satisfaction. *Information, Communication, and Society, 11,* 1089–1110.

Lee, E. (2009). The relationship of aggression and bullying to social preference: Differences in gender and types of aggression. *International Journal of Behavioral Development, 33,* 323–330.

Lee, G. R., Willetts, M. C., & Seccombe, K. (1998). Widowhood and depression: Gender differences. *Research on Aging, 20,* 611–630.

Lee, J. A. (1973). *The colors of love: An exploration of the ways of loving.* Don Mills, Ontario: New Press.

Lee, L., Howes, C., & Chamberlain, B. (2007). Ethnic heterogeneity of social networks and cross-ethnic friendships of elementary school boys and girls. *Merrill-Palmer Quarterly: Journal of Developmental Psychology, 53*(3), 325–346.

Lee, T. M. C., Chan, C. C. H., Leung, A. W. S., Fox, P. T., & Gao, J.-H. (2009). Sex-related differences in neural activity during risk taking: An fMRI study. *Cerebral Cortex, 19,* 1303–1312.

Lees, H. (1957). *Help your husband stay alive!* New York: Appleton-Century-Crofts.

Leff, S. S., Kupersmidt, J. B., & Power, T. J. (2003). An initial examination of girls' cognitions of their relationally aggressive peers as a function of their own social standing. *Merrill-Palmer Quarterly, 49,* 28–54.

Lehman, S. J., & Koerner, S. S. (2004). Adolescent women's sports involvement and sexual behavior/health: A process-level investigation. *Journal of Youth and Adolescence, 33,* 443–455.

Leigh, B. C. (1989). Reasons for having and avoiding sex: Gender, sexual orientation, and relationship to sexual behavior. *Journal of Sex Research, 26*(2), 199–209.

Lenhart, A. (2009). *Teens and mobile phones over the past five years: Pew Internet looks back.* Retrieved July 20, 2010, from http://pewinternet.org/Reports/2009/14--Teens-and-Mobile-Phones-Data-Memo/1-Data-Memo.aspx

Lenhart, A., & Madden, M. (2007). *Social networking websites and teens: An overview.* Retrieved July 20, 2010, from http://pewinternet.org/Reports/2007/Social-Networking-Websites-and-Teens.aspx

Lenhart, A., Ling, R., Campbell, S., & Purcell, K. (2010). *Teens and mobile phones: Text messaging explodes as teens embrace it as the centerpiece of their communication strategies with friends.* Retrieved July 20, 2010, from http://pewinternet.org/Reports/2010/Teens-and-Mobile-Phones/Summary-of-findings.aspx

Lenroot, R. K., & Giedd, J. N. (2010). Sex differences in the adolescent brain. *Brain and Cognition, 72,* 46–55.

Leone, J. M., Johnson, M. P., Cohan, C. L., & Lloyd, S. E. (2004). Consequences of male partner violence for low-income minority women. *Journal of Marriage and Family, 66,* 472–490.

Levant, R. F., & Fischer, J. (1998). The male role norms inventory. In C. M. Davis, W. H. Yarber, R. Bauserman, G. Schreer, & S. L. Davis (Eds.), *Sexuality-related measures: A compendium* (2nd ed., pp. 469–472). Newbury Park, CA: Sage.

Levant, R. F., & Richmond, K. (2007). A review of research on masculinity ideologies using the male role norms inventory. *Journal of Men's Studies, 15,* 130–146.

Levant, R. F., & Wimer, D. J. (2009). The new fathering movement. In C. Z. Oren & D. C. Oren (Eds.), *Counseling fathers* (pp. 3–21). New York: Routledge/Taylor & Francis Group.

Leviatan, U., & Cohen, J. (1985). Gender differences in life expectancy among kibbutz members. *Social Science and Medicine, 21*(5), 545–551.

Levinson, D., & Ifrah, A. (2010). The robustness of the gender effect on help seeking for mental health needs in three subcultures in Israel. *Social Psychiatry and Psychiatric Epidemiology, 45,* 337–344.

Lev-Wiesel, R., & Besser, A. (2006). Male definitions of sexual assault: The role of the perpetrator's gender. *Individual Differences Research, 4,* 47–50.

Lewine, R. R. J., & Seeman, M. V. (1995). Gender, brain, and schizophrenia: Anatomy of differences/differences of anatomy. In M. V. Seeman (Ed.), *Gender and psychopathology* (pp. 131–158). Washington, DC: American Psychiatric Press, Inc.

Lewinsohn, P. M., Rohde, P., & Seeley, J. R. (2001). Gender differences in suicide attempts from adolescence to young adulthood. *Journal of the American Academy of Child and Adolescent Psychiatry, 40,* 427–434.

Li, N., & Kirkup, G. (2007). Gender and cultural differences in Internet use: A study of China and the UK. *Computers & Education, 48*(2), 301–317.

Li, N. P., & Kenrick, D. T. (2006). Sex similarities and differences in preferences for short-term mates: What, whether, and why. *Journal of Personality and Social Psychology, 90,* 468–489.

Lichter, D. T., & Qian, Z. (2008). Serial cohabitation and the marital life course. *Journal of Marriage and Family, 70,* 861–878.

Lin, Y. C., & Raghubir, P. (2005). Gender differences in unrealistic optimism about marriage and divorce: Are men more optimistic and women more realistic? *Personality and Social Psychology Bulletin, 31,* 198–207.

Linden-Andersen, S., Markiewicz, D., & Doyle, A.-B. (2009). Perceived similarity among adolescent friends: The role of reciprocity, friendship quality, and gender. *Journal of Early Adolescence, 29,* 617–637.

Lindstrom, M. (2009). Marital status, social capital, material conditions and self-rated health: A population-based study. *Health Policy, 93,* 172–179.

Linn, M. C., & Petersen, A. C. (1985). Emergence and characterization of sex differences in spatial ability: A meta-analysis. *Child Development, 56,* 1479–1498.

Lips, H., & Lawson, K. (2009). Work values, gender, and expectations about work commitment and pay: Laying the groundwork for the "motherhood penalty"? *Sex Roles, 61,* 667–676.

Liptak, A. (2011). Justice rules for Wal-Mart in class action bias case. *The New York Times,* June 20, 2011. http://www.nytimes.com/2011/06/21/business/21bizcourt.html?

Liss, M., Crawford, M., & Popp, D. (2004). Predictors and correlates of collective action. *Sex Roles, 11/12,* 771–779.

Liu, H., & Umberson, D. (2008). The times they are a changin': Marital status and health differentials from 1972 to 2003. *Journal of Health and Social Behavior, 49,* 239–253.

Livingston, G., & Cohn, D. V. (2010). *More women without children.* Retrieved June 30, 2010, from http://pewresearch.org/pubs/1642/more-women-without-children

Lloyd, J. E. V., Walsh, J., & Yailagh, M. S. (2005). Sex differences in performance attributions, self-efficacy, and achievement in mathematics: If I'm so smart, why don't I know it? *Canadian Journal of Education, 28,* 384–408.

Longman, J. (2009). For all the wrong reason, women's soccer is noticed. *New York Times*. Retrieved May 27, 2010, from http://www.nytimes.com/2009/11/11/sports/soccer/11violence.html

Lonsway, K. A., Cortina, L. M., & Magley, V. J. (2008). Sexual harassment mythology: Definition, conceptualization, and measurement. *Sex Roles, 58*, 599–615.

Lopez, C. M., Driscoll, K. A., & Kistner, J. M. (2009). Sex differences and response styles: Subtypes of rumination and associations with depressive symptoms. *Journal of Clinical Child and Adolescent Psychology, 38*, 27–35.

Lovett, J., & Horvath, M. (2009). Alcohol and drugs in rape and sexual assault. In M. Horvath & J. Brown (Eds.), *Rape: Challenging contemporary thinking* (pp. 125–159). Portland, OR: Willan Publishing.

Lowe, G. D. O. (2004). Hormone replacement therapy and cardiovascular disease: Increased risks of venous thromboembolism and stroke, and no protection from coronary heart disease. *Journal of Internal Medicine, 256*, 361–374.

Lubbers, M., Jaspers, E., & Ultee, W. (2009). Primary and secondary socialization impacts on support for same-sex marriage after legalization in the Netherlands. *Journal of Family Issues, 30*, 1714–1745.

Lubinski, D., & Benbow, C. P. (2006). Study of mathematically precocious youth after 35 years: Uncovering antecedents for the development of math-science expertise. *Perspectives on Psychological Science, 1*, 316–345.

Lueptow, L. B., Garovich-Szabo, L., & Lueptow, M. B. (2001). Social change and the persistence of sex typing: 1974–1997. *Social Forces, 80*, 1–36.

Lund, R., Due, P., Modvig, J., Holstein, B. E., Damsgaard, M. T., & Andersen, P. K. (2002). Cohabitation and marital status as predictors of mortality: An eight year follow-up study. *Social Science & Medicine, 55*, 673–679.

Lundeberg, M. A., Fox, P. W., Brown, A. C., & Elbedour, S. (2000). Cultural influences on confidence: Country and gender. *Journal of Educational Psychology, 92*, 152–159.

Luo, S., & Snider, A. G. (2009). Accuracy and biases in newlyweds' perceptions of each other: Not mutually exclusive but mutually beneficial. *Psychological Science, 20*, 1332–1339.

Lupart, J. L., Cannon, E., & Telfer, J. A. (2004). Gender differences in adolescent academic achievement, interests, values and life-role expectations. *High Ability Studies, 15*, 25–42.

Lust, J. M., Geuze, R. H., Van de Beek, C., Cohen-Kettenis, P. T., Groothuis, A. G. G., & Bouma, A. (2010). Sex specific effect of prenatal testosterone on language lateralization in children. *Neuropsychologia, 48*, 536–540.

Lynch, J. J. (1977). *The broken heart*. New York: Basic Books.

Lyons, K. S., Stewart, B. J., Archbold, P. G., & Carter, J. H. (2009). Optimism, pessimism, mutuality, and gender: Predicting 10-year role strain in Parkinson's disease spouses. *Gerontologist, 49*(3), 378–387.

Lytton, H., & Romney, D. M. (1991). Parents' differential socialization of boys and girls: A meta-analysis. *Psychological Bulletin, 109*, 267–296.

Lyubomirsky, S., & Nolen-Hoeksema, S. (1993). Self-perpetuating properties of dysphoric rumination. *Journal of Personality and Social Psychology, 65*, 339–349.

Ma, Q., Ono-Kihara, M., Cong, L., Pan, X., Xu, G., Zamani, S., et al. (2009). Behavioral and psychosocial predictors of condom use among university students in Eastern china. *AIDS Care, 21*, 249–259.

Maccoby, E. E. (1966). Sex differences in intellectual functioning. In E. E. Maccoby (Ed.), *The development of sex differences* (pp. 25–55). Stanford, CA: Stanford University Press.

Maccoby, E. E. (1998). *The two sexes: Growing up apart, coming together*. Cambridge, MA: Harvard University Press.

Maccoby, E. E., & Jacklin, C. N. (1974). *The psychology of sex differences*. Stanford, CA: Stanford University Press.

MacGeorge, E. L., Graves, A. R., Feng, B., Gillihan, S. J., & Burleson, B. R. (2004). The myth of gender cultures: Similarities outweigh differences in men's and women's provision of and responses to supportive communication. *Sex Roles, 50*, 143–175.

Mackenzie, C. S., Gekoski, W. L., & Knox, V. J. (2006). Age, gender, and the underutilization of mental health services: The influence of help-seeking attitudes. *Aging & Mental Health, 10*, 574–582.

Madera, J. M., Hebl, M. R., & Martin, R. C. (2009). Gender and letters of recommendation for academia: Agentic and communal differences. *Journal of Applied Psychology, 94*, 1591–1599.

Madera, J. M., Podratz, K. E., King, E. B., & Hebl, M. R. (2007). Schematic responses to sexual harassment complainants: The influence of gender and physical attractiveness. *Sex Roles, 56*, 223–230.

Mael, F., Alonso, A., Gibson, D., Rogers, K., & Smith, M. (2005). *Single-sex versus coeducational schooling: A systematic review, U.S. Department of education office of planning, evaluation and policy development*. Washington, DC: American Institutes for Research.

Mahay, J., & Lewin, A. C. (2007). Age and the desire to marry. *Journal of Family Issues, 28*, 706–723.

Mainiero, L. A., Gibson, D. E., & Sullivan, S. E. (2008). Retrospective analysis of gender differences in reaction to media coverage of crisis events: New insights on the justice and care orientations. *Sex Roles, 58*, 556–566.

Major, B., Schmidlin, A. M., & Williams, L. (1990). Gender patterns in social touch: The impact of setting and age. *Journal of Personality and Social Psychology, 58*, 634–643.

Malcolmson, K. A., & Sinclair, L. (2007). The Ms. stereotype revisited: Implicit and explicit facets. *Psychology of Women Quarterly, 31*(3), 305–310.

Manago, A. M., Brown, C. S., & Leaper, C. (2009). Feminist identity among Latina adolescents. *Journal of Adolescent Research, 24,* 750–776.

Manago, A. M., Graham, M. B., Greenfield, P. M., & Salimkhan, G. (2008). Self-presentation and gender on MySpace. *Journal of Applied Developmental Psychology, 29,* 446–458.

Mandal, B., & Roe, B. (2008). Job loss, retirement and the mental health of older Americans. *Journal of Mental Health Policy and Economics, 11,* 167–176.

Manlove, J., Ikramullah, E., & Terry-Humen, E. (2008). Condom use and consistency among male adolescents in the United States. *Journal of Adolescent Health, 43,* 325–333.

Mann, J. (1985a, October 4). Poverty after divorce. *Washington Post.* Retrieved May 21, 2007, from web.lexis-nexis.com/universe/printdoc

Mann, J. (1985b, October 2). Disastrous divorce results. *Washington Post.* Retrieved May 21, 2007, from web.lexis-nexis.com/universe/printdoc

Manner, P. J. (2009). Gender identity disorder in adolescence: A review of the literature. *Child and Adolescent Mental Health, 14,* 62–68.

Manning, A. (1989). The genetic bases of aggression. In J. Groebel & R. A. Hinde (Eds.), *Aggression and war: Their biological and social bases* (pp. 48–57). New York: Cambridge University Press.

Manning, W. D., Flanigan, C. M., Giordano, P. C., & Longmore, M. A. (2009). Relationship dynamics and consistency of condom use among adolescents. *Perspectives on Sexual and Reproductive Health, 41,* 181–190.

Manning, W. D., Longmore, M. A., & Giordano, P. C. (2007). The changing institution of marriage: Adolescents' expectations to cohabit and marry. *Journal of Marriage and Family, 69,* 559–575.

Marcia, J. E. (1993). The status of the statuses: Research review. In J. E. Marcia, D. R. Matteson, J. L. Orlofsky, A. S. Waterman, & S. L. Archer (Eds.), *Ego identity: A handbook for psychosocial research* (pp. 22–41). New York: Springer-Verlag.

Marcus, A. C., & Seeman, T. E. (1981). Sex differences in reports of illness and disability: A preliminary test of the fixed role obligations hypothesis. *Journal of Health and Social Behavior, 22,* 174–182.

Marcus, S. M., Kerber, K. B., Rush, A. J., Wisniewski, S. R., Nierenberg, A., Balasubramani, G. K., et al. (2008). Sex differences in depression symptoms in treatment-seeking adults: Confirmatory analyses from the sequenced treatment alternatives to relieve depression study. *Comprehensive Psychiatry, 49*(3), 238–246.

Marecek, J., Crawford, M., & Popp, D. (2004). On the construction of gender, sex, and sexualities. In A. H. Eagly, A. E. Beall, & R. J. Sternberg (Eds.), *The psychology of gender* (2nd ed., pp. 192–216). New York: Guilford Press.

Markey, C. N., Markey, P. M., Schneider, C., & Brownlee, S. (2005). Marital status and health benefits: Different relations for men and women. *Sex Roles, 53,* 443–451.

Markiewicz, D., Devine, I., & Kausilas, D. (2000). Friendships of women and men at work: Job satisfaction and resource implications. *Journal of Managerial Psychology, 15*(2), 161–184.

Marks, M. J. (2008). Evaluations of sexually active men and women under divided attention: A social cognitive approach to the sexual double standard. *Basic and Applied Social Psychology, 30,* 84–91.

Marks, M. J., & Fraley, R. C. (2005). The sexual double standard: Fact or fiction? *Sex Roles, 52,* 175–186.

Marsh, A. A., Yu, H. H., Pine, D. S., & Blair, R. J. R. (2010). Oxytocin improves specific recognition of positive facial expressions. *Psychopharmacology, 209,* 225–232.

Marsh, H. W., Hau, K. T., Sung, R. Y. T., & Yu, C. W. (2007). Childhood obesity, gender, actual-ideal body image discrepancies, and physical self-concept in Hong Kong children: Cultural differences in the value of moderation. *Developmental Psychology, 43,* 647–662.

Marshal, M. P., Friedman, M. S., Stall, R., King, K. M., Miles, J., & Gold, M. A. (2008). Sexual orientation and adolescent substance use: A meta-analysis and methodological review. *Addiction, 103,* 546–556.

Marshall, T. C. (2008). Cultural differences in intimacy: The influence of gender-role ideology and individualism-collectivism. *Journal of Social and Personal Relationships, 25,* 143–168.

Martell, R. F., Lane, D. M., & Emrich, C. (1996). Male-female differences: A computer simulation. *American Psychologist, 51,* 157–158.

Martin, C. L., & Fabes, R. A. (2001). The stability and consequences of young children's same-sex peer interactions. *Developmental Psychology, 37,* 431–446.

Martin, C. L., & Ruble, D. N. (2004). Children's search for gender cues. *Current Directions in Psychological Science, 13,* 67–70.

Martin, C. L., & Ruble, D. N. (2009). Patterns of gender development. *Annual Review of Psychology, 61,* 353–381.

Martin, C. L., Fabes, R. A., Evans, S. M., & Wyman, H. (1999). Social cognition on the playground: Children's beliefs about playing with girls versus boys and their relations to sex segregated play. *Journal of Social and Personal Relationships, 16,* 751–771.

Martin, R. (1997). "Girls don't talk about garages!": Perceptions of conversation in same- and cross-sex friendships. *Personal Relationships, 4,* 115–130.

Martinez-Donate, A. P., Hovell, M. F., Blumberg, E. J., Zellner, J. A., Sipan, C. L., Shillington, A. M., et al. (2004). Gender differences in condom-related behaviors and attitudes among Mexican adolescents living on the U.S.-Mexico border. *AIDS Education and Prevention, 16,* 172–186.

Maselko, J., Bates, L. M., Avendano, M., & Glymour, M. M. (2009). The intersection of sex, marital status, and cardiovascular risk factors in shaping stroke incidence: Results from the health and retirement study. *Journal of the American Geriatric Society, 57,* 2293–2299.

Maserejian, N. N., Link, C. L., Lutfey, K. L., Marceau, L. D., & McKinlay, J. B. (2009). Disparities in physicians' interpretations of heart disease symptoms by patient gender: Results of a video vignette factorial experiment. *Journal of Women's Health, 18,* 1661–1667.

Massa, L. J., Mayer, R. E., & Bohon, L. M. (2005). Individual differences in gender role beliefs influence spatial ability test performance. *Learning and Individual Differences, 15,* 99–111.

Massak, A., & Graham, K. (2008). Is the smoking-depression relationship confounded by alcohol consumption? An analysis by gender. *Nicotine and Tobacco Research, 10,* 1231–1243.

Mast, M. S., Jonas, K., & Hall, J. A. (2009). Give a person power and he or she will show interpersonal sensitivity: The phenomenon and its why and when. *Journal of Personality and Social Psychology, 97,* 835–850.

Matthews, K. A., Gump, B. B., & Owens, J. F. (2001). Chronic stress influences cardiovascular and neuroendocrine responses during acute stress and recovery, especially in men. *Health Psychology, 20,* 403–410.

Matthews, R. A., Del Priore, R. E., Acitelli, L. K., & Barnes-Farrell, J. L. (2006). Work-to-relationship conflict: Crossover effects in dual-earner couples. *Journal of Occupational Health Psychology, 11,* 228–240.

Matthews, S., & Power, C. (2002). Socio-economic gradients in psychological distress: A focus on women, social roles and work-home characteristics. *Social Science & Medicine, 54,* 799–810.

Matthews, S., Stansfeld, S., & Power, C. (1999). Social support at age 33: The influence of gender, employment status and social class. *Social Science & Medicine, 49,* 133–142.

Matthews, T. J., & Hamilton, B. E. (2005). Trend analysis of the sex ratio at birth in the United States. *National Vital Statistics Reports, 53*(20), 1–20.

Mau, W. C. (2003). Factors that influence persistence in science and engineering career aspirations. *Career Development Quarterly, 51,* 234–243.

McAndrew, F. T. (2009). The interacting roles of testosterone and challenges to status in human male aggression. *Aggression and Violent Behavior, 14,* 330–335.

McClelland, D. C., Atkinson, J. W., Clark, R. A., & Lowell, E. L. (1953). *The achievement motive.* New York: Appleton-Century-Crofts.

McCloskey, L. A. (1996). Gender and the expression of status in children's mixed-age conversations. *Journal of Applied Developmental Psychology, 17,* 117–133.

McClure, E. B. (2000). A meta-analytic review of sex differences in facial expression processing and their development in infants, children and adolescents. *Psychological Bulletin, 126,* 424–453.

McDermott, E., Roen, K., & Scourfield, J. (2008). Avoiding shame: Young LGBT people, homophobia, and self-destructive behaviours. *Culture, Health and Sexuality, 10,* 815–829.

McDermott, R., Johnson, D., Cowden, J., & Rosen, S. (2007). Testosterone and aggression in a simulated crisis game. *Annals of the American Academy of Political and Social Science, 614,* 15–33.

McDougall, P., & Hymel, S. (2007). Same-gender versus cross-gender friendship conceptions. *Merrill-Palmer Quarterly, 53,* 347–380.

McGinn, M. M., McFarland, P. T., & Christensen, A. (2009). Antecedents and consequences of demand/withdraw. *Journal of Family Psychology, 23,* 749–757.

McGlone, M. S., Aronson, J., & Kobrynowicz, D. (2006). Stereotype threat and the gender gap in political knowledge. *Psychology of Women Quarterly, 30,* 392–398.

McGlothlin, H., & Killen, M. (2005). Children's perceptions of intergroup and intragroup similarity and the role of social experience. *Applied Developmental Psychology, 26,* 680–698.

McGlothlin, H., Killen, M., & Edmonds, C. (2005). European–American children's intergroup attitudes about peer relationships. *British Journal of Developmental Psychology, 23,* 227–249.

McHale, S. M., Kim, J. Y., Whiteman, S., & Crouter, A. C. (2004). Links between sex-typed time use in middle childhood and gender development in early adolescence. *Developmental Psychology, 40,* 868–881.

McIntosh, D. N., Keywell, J., Reifman, A., & Ellsworth, P. C. (1994). Stress and health in first-year law students: Women fare worse? *Journal of Applied Social Psychology, 24*(16), 1474–1499.

McKinnon, D. H., McLeod, S., & Reilly, S. (2007). The prevalence of stuttering, voice, and speech-sound disorders in primary school students in Australia. *Language, Speech, and Hearing Services in Schools, 38,* 5–15.

McMunn, A., Bartley, M., & Kuh, D. (2006). Women's health in mid-life: Life course social roles and agency as quality. *Social Science & Medicine, 63,* 1561–1572.

McNelles, L. R., & Connolly, J. A. (1999). Intimacy between adolescent friends: Age and gender differences in intimate affect and intimate behaviors. *Journal of Research on Adolescence, 9*(2), 143–159.

McRae, K., Ochsner, K. N., Mauss, I. B., Gabrieli, J. J. D., & Gross, J. J. (2008). Gender differences in emotion regulation: An fMRI study of cognitive reappraisal. *Group Processes and Intergroup Relations, 11,* 143–162.

Medicine, B. (2002, May 6). Directions in gender research in American Indian societies: Two spirits and other categories. *Online Readings in Psychology and Culture.* Retrieved September 9, 2010, from http://www.ac.wwu.edu/~culture/medicine.htm

Mehta, C. M., & Strough, J. (2009). Sex segregation in friendships and normative contexts across the life span. *Developmental Review, 29,* 201–220.

Meier, A. (2007). Adolescent first sex and subsequent mental health. *American Journal of Sociology, 112,* 1811–1847.

Meier-Pesti, K., & Penz, E. (2008). Sex or gender? Expanding the sex-based view by introducing masculinity and femininity as predictors of financial risk taking. *Journal of Economic Psychology, 29,* 180–196.

Menvielle, G., Kunst, A. E., Stirbu, I., Strand, B. H., Borrell, C., & Regidor, E. (2008). Educational differences in cancer mortality among women and men: A gender pattern that differs across Europe. *British Journal of Cancer, 98,* 1012–1019.

Messman, S. J., Canary, D. J., & Hause, K. S. (2000). Motives to remain platonic, equity, and the use of maintenance strategies in opposite-sex friendships. *Journal of Social and Personal Relationships, 17,* 67–94.

Messner, M. A., & Cooky, C. (2010). *Gender in televised sports: News and highlights shows, 1989–2009.* Los Angeles, CA: University of Southern California, Center for Feminist Research.

Metha, A., Chen, E., Mulvenon, S., & Dode, I. (1998). A theoretical model of adolescent suicide risk. *Archives of Suicide Research, 4,* 115–133.

Metts, S. (2004). First sexual involvement in romantic relationships: An empirical investigation of communicative framing, romantic beliefs, and attachment orientation in the passion turning point. In J. H. Harvey, A. Wenzel, & S. Sprecher (Eds.), *The handbook of sexuality in close relationships* (pp. 135–158). Mahwah, NJ: Lawrence Erlbaum Associates.

Meyer, I. H. (2003). Prejudice, social stress, and mental health in lesbian, gay, and bisexual populations: Conceptual issues and research evidence. *Psychological Bulletin, 129*(5), 674–697.

Meyer-Bahlburg, H. F. L., Dolezal, C., Baker, S. W., & New, M. I. (2008). Sexual orientation in women with classical or non-classical congenital adrenal hyperplasia as a function of degree of prenatal androgen excess. *Archives of Sexual Behavior, 37,* 85–99.

Meyering, K. (2005). Meet generation M. *Kaiser Youth Media Study.* Retrieved August 4, 2010, from http://www.frankwbaker.com/kids_media_report.htm

Mezulis, A. H., Abramson, L. Y., Hyde, J. S., & Hankin, B. L. (2004). Is there a universal positivity bias in attributions? A meta-analytic review of individual, developmental, and cultural differences in the self-serving attributional bias. *Psychological Bulletin, 130*(5), 711–747.

Mickelson, K. D., Helgeson, V. S., & Weiner, E. (1995). Gender effects on social support provision and receipt. *Personal Relationships, 2,* 221–224.

Miedzian, M. (1991). *Boys will be boys: Breaking the link between masculinity and violence.* Thousand Oaks, CA: Sage.

Migliaccio, T. (2009). Men's friendships: Performances of masculinity. *Journal of Men's Studies, 17,* 226–241.

Mikami, A. Y., Szwedo, D. E., Allen, J. P., Evans, M. A., & Hare, A. L. (2010). Adolescent peer relationships and behavior problems predict young adults' communication on social networking websites. *Developmental Psychology, 46,* 46–56.

Miller, C. F., Lurye, L. E., Zosuls, K. M., & Ruble, D. N. (2009). Accessibility of gender stereotype domains: Developmental and gender differences in children. *Sex Roles, 60,* 870–881.

Miller, C., & Swift, K. (1980). *The handbook of nonsexist writing.* New York: Harper & Row.

Miller, C., Swift, K., & Maggio, R. (1997, September/October). Liberating language. *Ms.,* 51–54.

Miller, S., Gorman-Smith, D., Sullivan, T., Orpinas, P., & Simon, T. R. (2009). Parent and peer predictors of physical dating violence perpetration in early adolescence: Test of moderation and gender differences. *Journal of Clinical Child & Adolescent Psychology, 38,* 538–550.

Mirgain, S. A., & Cordova, J. V. (2007). Emotion skills and marital health: The association between observed and self-reported emotion skills, intimacy, and marital satisfaction. *Journal of Social and Clinical Psychology, 26,* 983–1009.

Mischel, W. (1966). A social-learning view of sex differences in behavior. In E. E. Maccoby (Ed.), *The development of sex differences* (pp. 56–81). Stanford, CA: Stanford University Press.

Mitra, S., & Shroff, S. (2008). What suicides reveal about gender bias. *Journal of Socio-Economics, 37,* 1713–1723.

Mo, P. K. H., Malik, S. H., & Coulson, N. S. (2009). Gender differences in computer-mediated communication: A systematic literature review of online health-related support groups. *Patient Education and Counseling, 75,* 16–24.

Mojon-Azzi, S., Sousa-Poza, A., & Widmer, R. (2007). The effect of retirement on health: A panel analysis using data from the Swiss household panel. *Swiss Medicine Weekly, 137,* 581–585.

Molloy, G. J., Stamatakis, E., Randall, G., & Hamer, M. (2009). Marital status, gender and cardiovascular mortality: Behavioural, psychological distress and metabolic explanations.*Social Science & Medicine, 69,* 223–228.

Mongeau, P. A., Serewicz, M. C. M., Henningsen, M. L. M., & Davis, K. L. (2006). Sex differences in the transition to a heterosexual romantic relationship. In K. Dindia & D. J. Canary (Eds.), *Sex differences and similarities in communication* (2nd ed., pp. 337–358). Mahwah, NJ: Lawrence Erlbaum Associates.

Monk-Turner, E., Kouts, T., Parris, K., & Webb, C. (2007). Gender role stereotyping in advertisements on three radio stations: Does musical genre make a difference? *Journal of Gender Studies, 16,* 173–182.

Monsour, M., Harris, B., Kurzweil, N., & Beard, C. (1994). Challenges confronting cross-sex friendships: Much ado about nothing? *Sex Roles, 31,* 55–77.

Montgomery, M. J. (2005). Psychosocial intimacy and identity: From early adolescence to emerging adulthood. *Journal of Adolescent Research, 20,* 346–374.

Moore, D. J. (2007). Emotion as a mediator of the influence of gender on advertising effectiveness: Gender differences in online self-reports. *Basic and Applied Social Psychology, 29,* 203–211.

Moore, M. R. (2008). Gendered power relations among women: A study of household decision making in Black, lesbian stepfamilies. *American Sociological Review, 73,* 335–356.

Morgan, C. (2001). The effects of negative managerial feedback on student motivation: Implications for gender differences in teacher–student relations. *Sex Roles, 44,* 513–535.

Morrell, H. E. R., Cohen, L. M., & McChargue, D. E. (2010). Depression vulnerability predicts cigarette smoking among college students: Gender and negative reinforcement expectancies as contributing factors. *Addictive Behaviors, 35,* 607–611.

Morrongiello, B. A., & Dawber, T. (2000). Mothers' responses to sons and daughters engaging in injury-risk behaviors on a playground: Implications for sex differences in injury rates. *Journal of Experimental Child Psychology, 76,* 89–103.

Morrongiello, B. A., & Dawber, T. (2004). Identifying factors that relate to children's risk-taking decisions. *Canadian Journal of Behavioural Science, 36,* 255–266.

Morrongiello, B. A., & Hogg, K. (2004). Mothers' reactions to children misbehaving in ways that can lead to injury: Implications for gender differences in children's risk taking and injuries. *Sex Roles, 50,* 103–118.

Morrongiello, B. A., & Lasenby-Lessard, J. (2007). Psychological determinants of risk taking by children: An integrative model and implications for interventions. *Injury Prevention, 13,* 20–25.

Morrongiello, B. A., & Matheis, S. (2007). Understanding children's injury-risk behaviors: The independent contributions of cognitions and emotions. *Journal of Pediatric Psychology, 32,* 926–937.

Morrongiello, B. A., Klemencic, N., & Corbett, M. (2008). Interactions between child behavior patterns and parental supervision: Implications for children's risk of unintentional injury. *Child Development, 79,* 627–638.

Morrongiello, B. A., Walpole, B., & McArthur, B. A. (2009). Young children's risk of unintentional injury: A comparison of mothers' and fathers' supervision beliefs and reported practices. *Journal of Pediatric Psychology, 34,* 1063–1068.

Morry, M. M. (2007). The attraction-similarity hypothesis among cross-sex friends: Relationship satisfaction, perceived similarities, and self-serving perceptions. *Journal of Social and Personal Relationships, 24,* 117–138.

Morse, J. (1999). Make time for daddy. *Time.* Retrieved November 13, 2007, from www.time.com/t?ine/article/0,9171,990197,00.html

Moscucci, M., Smith, D. E., Jani, S. M., Montoye, C. K., Defranco, A. C., Chandra, H., et al. (2004). *Gender differences in time to treatment for patients undergoing primary percutaneous coronary intervention for acute ST segment elevation myocardial infarction: An important target for quality improvement.* Paper presented at the American Heart Association's Scientific Sessions, New Orleans.

Mosher, C. E., & Danoff-Burg, S. (2005). Agentic and communal personality traits: Relations to attitudes toward sex and sexual experiences. *Sex Roles, 52,* 121–129.

Mosher, C. E., & Danoff-Burg, S. (2008). Agentic and communal personality traits: Relations to disordered eating behavior, body shape concern, and depressive symptoms. *Eating Behaviors, 9,* 497–500.

Mosing, M. A., Gordon, S. D., Medland, S. E., Statham, D. J., Nelson, E. C., Heath, A. C., et al. (2009). Genetic and environmental influences on the co-morbidity between depression, panic disorder, agoraphobia, and social phobia: A twin study. *Depression and Anxiety, 26,* 1004–1011.

Moskowitz, D. S., Suh, E. J., & Desaulniers, J. (1994). Situational influences on gender differences in agency and communion. *Journal of Personality and Social Psychology, 66,* 753–761.

Moya, M., Glick, P., Exposito, F., de Lemus, S., & Hart, J. (2007). It's for your own good: Benevolent sexism and women's reactions to protectively justified restrictions. *Personality and Social Psychology Bulletin, 33,* 1421–1434.

Mueller, T. E., Gavin, L. E., & Kulkarni, A. (2008). The association between sex education and youth's engagement in sexual intercourse, age at first intercourse, and birth control use at first sex. *Journal of Adolescent Health, 42,* 89–96.

Muennig, P., Lubetkin, E., Jia, H., & Franks, P. (2006). Gender and the burden of disease attributable to obesity. *American Journal of Public Health, 96,* 1662–1668.

Muhonen, T., & Torkelson, E. (2004). Work locus of control and its relationship to health and job satisfaction from a gender perspective. *Stress and Health, 20,* 21–28.

Mulac, A. (2006). The gender-linked language effect: Do language differences really make a difference? In K. Dindia & D. J. Canary (Eds.), *Sex differences and similarities in communication* (2nd ed., pp. 195–215). Mahwah, NJ: Lawrence Erlbaum Associates.

Mulac, A., Bradac, J. J., & Gibbons, P. (2001). Empirical support for the gender-as-culture hypothesis: An intercultural analysis of male/female language differences. *Human Communication Research, 27,* 121–152.

Mullis, I. V. S., Martin, M. O., Gonzalez, E. J., & Kennedy, A. M. (2003). *PIRLS 2001 international report: IEA's study of reading literacy achievement in primary school in 35 countries.* Retrieved from http://timss.bc.edu/pirls2001i/pdf/p1_ir_book.pdf

Multiple Risk Factor Intervention Trial Research Group. (1983). Multiple risk factor intervention trial: Risk factor changes and mortality results. *Journal of the American Medical Association, 248,* 1465–1477.

Munroe, R. L., & Romney, A. K. (2006). Gender and age differences in same-sex aggregation and social behavior: A four-culture study. *Journal of Cross-Cultural Psychology, 37,* 3–19.

Munroe, R. L., Hulefeld, R., Rodgers, J. M., Tomeo, D. L., & Yamazaki, S. K. (2000). Aggression among children in four cultures. *Cross-Cultural Research, 34,* 3–25.

Murberg, T. A., & Bru, E. (2004). Social support, negative life events and emotional problems among Norwegian adolescents. *School Psychology International, 25,* 387–403.

Murnen, S. K., & Smolak, L. (1997). Femininity, masculinity, and disordered eating: A meta-analytic review. *International Journal of Eating Disorders, 22,* 231–242.

Murnen, S. K., Wright, C., & Kaluzny, G. (2002). If "boys will be boys," then girls will be victims? A meta-analytic review of the research that relates masculine ideology to sexual aggression. *Sex Roles, 46,* 359–375.

Murphy, E. M. (2003). Being born female is dangerous for your health. *American Psychologist, 58,* 205–210.

Murphy, K. (2003). States balance he's and she's. *Stateline.* Retrieved May 10, 2010, from http://www.stateline.org/live/ViewPage.action?iteNodeId=136&languageId=1&contentId=15208

Murray-Close, D., Crick, N. R., & Galotti, K. M. (2006). Children's moral reasoning regarding physical and relational aggression. *Social Development, 15,* 345–372.

Murray-Close, D., Ostrov, J. M., & Crick, N. R. (2007). A short-term longitudinal study of growth of relational aggression during middle childhood: Associations with gender, friendship intimacy, and internalizing problems. *Development and Psychopathology, 19,* 187–203.

Murstein, B. I. (1974). *Love, sex, and marriage through the ages.* New York: Springer.

Muzzatti, B., & Agnoli, F. (2007). Gender and mathematics: Attitudes and stereotype threat susceptibility in Italian children. *Developmental Psychology, 43,* 747–759.

Myhill, D., & Jones, S. (2006). "She doesn't shout at no girls": Pupils' perceptions of gender equity in the classroom. *Cambridge Journal of Education, 36,* 99–113.

Nabors, E. L., & Jasinski, J. L. (2009). Intimate partner violence perpetration among college students: The role of gender role and gendered violence attitudes. *Feminist Criminology, 4,* 57–82.

Nagoshi, J. L., Adams, K. A., Terrell, H. K., Hill, E. D., Brzuzy, S., & Nagoshi, C. T. (2008). Gender differences in correlates of homophobia and transphobia. *Sex Roles, 59,* 521–531.

Nagurney, A. J. (2007). The effects of relationship stress and unmitigated communion on physical and mental health outcomes. *Stress and Health, 23,* 267–273.

Nagurney, A. J. (2008). The effects of unmitigated communion and life events among women with fibromyalgia syndrome. *Journal of Health Psychology, 13,* 520–528.

Naifeh, S., & Smith, G. W. (1984). *Why can't men open up?* New York: Warner Books.

Nansel, T. R., Overpeck, M. D., Haynie, D. L., Ruan, W. J., & Scheidt, P. C. (2003). Relationships between bullying and violence among US youth. *Archives of Pediatrics and Adolescent Medicine, 157,* 348–352.

Nardi, P. M. (1992). Sex, friendship, and gender roles among gay men. In P. M. Nardi (Ed.), *Men's friendships* (pp. 173–185). Newbury Park, CA: Sage.

Nardi, P. M., & Sherrod, D. (1994). Friendship in the lives of gay men and lesbians. *Journal of Social and Personal Relationships, 11,* 185–199.

Nathanson, C. A. (1978). Sex roles as variables in the interpretation of morbidity data: A methodological critique. *International Journal of Epidemiology, 7*(3), 253–262.

National Association for Single-Sex Public Education. (2010). *Single-sex schools/schools with single-sex classrooms/ what's the difference?* Retrieved June 25, 2010, from http://www.singlesexschools.org/schools-schools.htm

National Center for Education Statistics. (2007). *Status and trends in the education of racial and ethnic minorities.* Retrieved June 24, 2010, from http://nces.ed.gov/pubs2007/minoritytrends/tables/table_16.asp

National Center for Education Statistics. (2008a). *Enrollment rates of 18- to 24-year-olds in degree-granting institutions by type of institution and sex and race/ethnicity of student: 1967 through 2007.* Retrieved June 8, 2010, from http://nces.ed.gov/programs/digest/d08/tables/dt08_204.asp

National Center for Education Statistics. (2008b). *Postsecondary institutions in the United States: Fall 2007, degrees and other awards conferred: 2006–2007, and 12-month enrollment: 2006–2007.* Retrieved June 8, 2010.

National Center for Education Statistics. (2008c). *First-professional degrees conferred by degree-granting institutions, by sex, race/ethnicity, and field of study: 2006–07.* Retrieved June 28, 2010, from http://nces.ed.gov/programs/digest/d08/tables/dt08_294.asp

National Center for Education Statistics. (2009a). *Bachelor's, master's, and doctor's degrees conferred by degree-granting institutions, by sex of student and discipline division: 2007–2008.* Retrieved June 9, 2010, from http://nces.ed.gov/programs/digest/d09/tables/dt09_275.asp

National Center for Education Statistics. (2009b). *Percentage of high school dropouts among persons 16 through 24 years old (status dropout rate), by sex and race/ethnicity: Selected years, 1960 through 2008.* Retrieved June 24, 2010, from http://nces.ed.gov/programs/digest/d09/tables/dt09_108.asp

National Center for Health Statistics. (2009a). Expectation of life at birth, 1970–2006, and projections, 2010–2020. *National Vital Statistics Reports (NVSR), Deaths: Final Data for 2006, 57,* Retrieved June 6, 2011, from http://www.cdc.gov/nchs/data/nvsr/nvsr57/nvsr57_14.pdf

National Center for Health Statistics. (2009b). *Health, United States, 2009: With special feature on medical technology.* Retrieved June 6, 2011, from http://www.cdc.gov/nchs/data/hus/hus09.pdf

National Eating Disorders Association. (2005). *Eating disorders and their precursors.* Retrieved August 31, 2010, from www.nationaleatingdisorders.org/uploads/statistics_tmp.pdf

National Federation of State High School Associations. (2010). *2008–09 High school athletics participation survey.* Retrieved July 27, 2010, from www.nfhs.org/WorkArea/linkit.aspx?inkIdentifier=id&ItemID=3506

National Institute of Mental Health. (2007). *Eating disorders.* Retrieved August 31, 2010, from www.nimh.nih.gov/health/./eating-disorders/nimheatingdisorders.pdf

National Institutes of Health. (2006). *Fact book fiscal year 2005* (pp. 37–55). National Institutes of Health. National Heart, Lung, and Blood Institute. Washington, DC: U.S. Department of Health & Human Service.

National Organization for Men Against Sexism. (2010). *Statement of principles.* Retrieved May 3, 2010, from www.nomas.org

National Organization for Women. (2004). *NOW acts: March for women's lives inspired a flurry of activity.* Retrieved January 12, 2007, from www.now.org/organization/conference/resolutions/2006.html

National Public Radio. (1999, November 29). *Fresh air.* Interview with Hugh Hefner by Terry Gross.

National Public Radio Morning Edition. (2001). *Money in marriage and divorce.* Retrieved January 15, 2007, from www.equalityinmarriage.org/d/Pressroom/art_6.html

Nearly half. (2010). *Nearly half of working adults socialize with colleagues: More see benefits than risks of having workplace friendships.* Retrieved July 13, 2010, from http://www.ipsos-na.com/news-polls/pressrelease.aspx?d=4690

Neff, L. A., & Karney, B. R. (2005). Gender differences in social support: A question of skill or responsiveness? *Journal of Personality and Social Psychology, 88,* 79–90.

Nehls, N. (1998). Borderline personality disorder: Gender stereotypes, stigma, and limited system of care. *Issues in Mental Health Nursing, 19,* 97–112.

Nelson, D. L., & Burke, R. J. (2000). Women executives: Health, stress and success. *Academy of Management Executive, 14,* 107–121.

Nepomnyaschy, L., & Waldfogel, J. (2007). Paternity leave and fathers' involvement with their young children: Evidence from the American ECLS-B. *Community, Work & Family, 10*(4), 427–453.

Neuenschwander, M. P., Vida, M., Garrett, J. L., & Eccles, J. S. (2007). Parents' expectations and students' achievement in two Western nations. *International Journal of Behavioral Development, 31,* 594–602.

Neuville, E., & Croizet, J.-C. (2007). Can salience of gender identity impair math performance among 7-8 years old girls? The moderating role of task difficulty. *European Journal of Psychology of Education, 22,* 307–316.

New York Times. (1980). *Are boys better at math?.* Retrieved July 6, 2000, from web.lexis-nexis.com/universe/docu

New York Times. (2008). *Hillary Clinton endorses Barack Obama.* Retrieved August 16, 2010, from http://www.nytimes.com/2008/06/07/us/politics/07text-clinton.html

Newman, M. L., Groom, C. J., Handelman, L. D., & Pennebaker, J. W. (2008). Gender differences in language use: An analysis of 14,000 text samples. *Discourse Processes, 45,* 211–236.

Newport, F. (2007). *Americans continue to express slight preference for boys: Little changed since 1941.* Retrieved May 3, 2010, from http://www.gallup.com/poll/28045/Americans-continue-express-slight-preference-boys.aspx

Newport, F. (2008). *Wives still do laundry, men do yard work.* Retrieved July 1, 2010, from http://www.gallup.com/poll/106249/wives-still-laundry-men-yard-work.aspx

Ng, E. S., & Wiesner, W. H. (2007). Are men always picked over women? The effects of employment equity directives on selection decisions. *Journal of Business Ethics, 76,* 177–187.

Nichols, J. (1975). *Men's liberation: A new definition of masculinity.* New York: Penguin.

Nichter, M. (2000). *Fat talk: What girls and their parents say about dieting.* Cambridge, MA: Harvard University Press.

Nicolai, J., & Demmel, R. (2007). The impact of gender stereotypes on the evaluation of general practitioners' communication skills: An experimental study using transcripts of physician–patient encounters. *Patient Education and Counseling, 69,* 200–205.

Nielsen, S. J., Siega-Riz, A. M., & Popkin, B. M. (2002). Trends in energy intake in U.S. Between 1977 and 1996: Similar shifts seen across age groups. *Obesity Research, 10,* 370–378.

Niemann, Y. F., Jennings, L., Rozelle, R. M., Baxter, J. C., & Sullivan, E. (1994). Use of free responses and cluster analysis to determine stereotypes of eight groups. *Personality and Social Psychology Bulletin, 20,* 379–390.

Nock, M. K., Borges, G., Bromet, E. J., Alonso, J., Angermeyer, M., Beautrais, A., et al. (2008). Cross-national prevalence and risk factors for suicidal ideation, plans and attempts. *British Journal of Psychiatry, 192,* 98–105.

Noel, C. (1997, February 12). Springer school students offer definitions of love. *Los Altos Town Crier,* 26.

Nokelainen, P., Tirri, K., & Merenti-Valimaki, H.-L. (2007). Investigating the influence of attribution styles on development of mathematical talent. *Gifted Child Quarterly, 51,* 64–81.

Nolen-Hoeksema, S. (1987). Sex differences in unipolar depression: Evidence and theory. *Psychological Bulletin, 101,* 259–282.

Nolen-Hoeksema, S. (1994). An interactive model for the emergence of gender differences in depression in adolescence. *Journal of Research on Adolescence, 4,* 519–534.

Nolen-Hoeksema, S. (2004). The etiology of gender: Differences in depression. In C. M. Mazure & G. Puryear (Eds.), *Understanding depression in women: Applying empirical research to practice and policy* (pp. 9–43). Washington, DC: American Psychological Association.

Nolen-Hoeksema, S., & Girgus, J. S. (1994). The emergence of gender differences in depression during adolescence. *Psychological Bulletin, 115,* 424–443.

Nolen-Hoeksema, S., & Hilt, L. (2006). Possible contributors to the gender differences in alcohol use and problems. *Journal of General Psychology, 133,* 357–374.

Nolen-Hoeksema, S., & Keita, G. P. (2003). Women and depression: Introduction. *Psychology of Women Quarterly, 27,* 89–90.

Nolen-Hoeksema, S., Larson, J., & Grayson, C. (1999). Explaining the gender difference in depressive symptoms. *Journal of Personality and Social Psychology, 77,* 1061–1072.

Nolen-Hoeksema, S., & Morrow, J. (1991). A prospective study of depression and distress following a natural disaster: The 1989 Loma Prieta earthquake. *Journal of Personality and Social Psychology, 61,* 105–121.

Nolen-Hoeksema, S., Wisco, B. E., & Lyubomirsky, S. (2008). Rethinking rumination. *Perspectives on Psychological Science, 3,* 400–424.

Nomaguchi, K. M., & Bianchi, S. M. (2004). Exercise time: Gender differences in the effects of marriage, parenthood, and employment. *Journal of Marriage and Family, 66,* 413–430.

Nordenmark, M. (2004). Multiple social roles and well-being: A longitudinal test of the role stress theory and the role expansion theory. *Acta Sociologica, 47,* 115–126.

Nordvik, H., & Amponsah, B. (1998). Gender differences in spatial abilities and spatial activity among university students in an egalitarian educational system. *Sex Roles, 38,* 1009–1023.

Norton, K. I., Olds, T. S., Olive, S., & Dank, S. (1996). Ken and Barbie at life size. *Sex Roles, 34,* 287–294.

Nosek, B. A., Smyth, F. L., Sriram, N., Linder, N. M., Devos, T., Ayala, A., et al. (2009). National differences in gender-science stereotypes predict national sex differences in science and math achievement. *Proceedings of the National Academy of Sciences, 106,* 10593–10597.

Nosko, A., Wood, E., & Molema, S. (2010). All about me: Disclosure in online social networking profiles: The case of Facebook. *Computers in Human Behavior, 26,* 406–418.

NPR. (December 15, 2009). *State by state: The legal battle over gay marriage.* Retrieved May 17, 2011, from http://www.npr.org/templates/story/story.php?storyId=112448663

Nunner-Winkler, G., Meyer-Nikele, M., & Wohlrab, D. (2007). Gender differences in moral motivation. *Merrill-Palmer Quarterly, 53,* 26–52.

Nuttall, R. L., Casey, M. B., & Pezaris, E. (2005). Spatial ability as a mediator of gender differences on mathematics tests. In A. M. Gallagher & J. C. Kaufman (Eds.), *Gender differences in mathematics: An integrative psychological approach* (pp. 121–142). New York: Cambridge University Press.

Nuttbrock, L., Hwahng, S., Bockting, W., Rosenblum, A., Mason, M., Macri, M., et al. (2010). Psychiatric impact of gender-related abuse across the life course of male-to-female transgender persons. *Journal of Sex Research, 47,* 12–23.

Nyquist, L. V., & Spence, J. T. (1986). Effects of dispositional dominance and sex role expectations on leadership behaviors. *Journal of Personality and Social Psychology, 50,* 87–93.

O'Barr, W. M. (2006). Representations of masculinity and femininity in advertisements. *Advertising & Society Review.* Retrieved November 12, 2007, from www.aef.com/on-campus/asr/contents

O'Brien, M., Brandth, B., & Kvande, E. (2007). Fathers, work and family life: Global perspectives and new insights. *Community, Work & Family, 10*(4), 375–386.

O'Brien, M., Peyton, V., Mistry, R., Hruda, L., Jacobs, A., Caldera, Y., et al. (2000). Gender-role cognition in three-year-old boys and girls. *Sex Roles, 42,* 1007–1025.

O'Meara, J. D. (1989). Cross-sex friendship: Four basic challenges of an ignored relationship. *Sex Roles, 21,* 525–543.

Ogden, C., & Carroll, M. (2010). Prevalence of obesity among children and adolescents: United States, trends 1963–1965 through 2007–2008. *National Center for Health Statistics: Health E-Stats.*

Ohannessian, C. M. (2009). Media use and adolescent psychological adjustment: An examination of gender differences. *Journal of Child Family Studies, 18,* 582–593.

Ojeda, V. D., & Bergstresser, S. M. (2008). Gender, race-ethnicity, and psychosocial barriers to mental health care: An examination of perceptions and attitudes among adults reporting unmet need. *Journal of Health and Social Behavior, 49,* 317–334.

Okamoto, K., & Tanaka, Y. (2004). Gender differences in the relationship between social support and subjective health among elderly persons in Japan. *Preventive Medicine, 38,* 318–322.

O'Leary, K. D., Slep, A. M. S., Avery-Leaf, S., & Cascardi, M. (2008). Gender differences in dating aggression among multiethnic high school students. *Journal of Adolescent Health, 42,* 473–479.

Olff, M., Langeland, W., Draijer, N., & Gersons, B. P. R. (2007). Gender differences in posttraumatic stress disorder. *Psychological Bulletin, 133,* 183–204.

Olfson, M., & Marcus, S. C. (2009). National patterns in antidepressant medication treatment. *Archives of General Psychiatry, 66,* 848–856.

Olfson, M., Zarin, D. A., Mittman, B. S., & McIntyre, J. S. (2001). Is gender a factor in psychiatrists' evaluation and treatment of patients with major depression? *Journal of Affective Disorders, 63,* 149–157.

Ono, H., & Yeilding, R. (2009). Marriage, cohabitation and childcare: The US and Sweden. *Social Indicators Research, 93,* 137–140.

Oransky, M., & Fisher, C. (2009). The development and validation of the meanings of adolescent masculinity scale. *Psychology of Men and Masculinity, 10,* 57–72.

Oransky, M., & Marecek, J. (2009). "I'm not going to be a girl." Masculinity and emotions in boys' friendships and peer groups. *Journal of Adolescent Research, 24,* 218–241.

Orlofsky, J. L. (1993). Intimacy status: Theory and research. In E. Marcia, D. R. Matteson, J. L. Orlofsky, A. S. Waterman, & S. L. Archer (Eds.), *Ego identity: A handbook for psychosocial research* (pp. 111–133). New York: Springer-Verlag.

Orth-Gomer, K., & Johnson, J. (1987). Social network interaction and mortality: A six-year follow-up of a random sample of the Swedish population. *Journal of Chronic Diseases, 4,* 944–957.

Osborne, D., & Wagner, W. E. (2007). Exploring the relationship between homophobia and participation in core sports among high school students. *Sociological Perspectives, 50,* 597–613.

Osler, M., McGue, M., Lund, R., & Christensen, K. (2008). Marital status and twins' health and behavior: An analysis of middle-aged Danish twins. *Psychosomatic Medicine, 70,* 482–487.

Ostrov, J. M., Crick, N. R., & Stauffacher, K. (2006). Relational aggression in sibling and peer relationships during early childhood. *Applied Developmental Psychology, 27,* 241–253.

Otis, M. D., Riggle, E. D. B., & Rostosky, S. S. (2006). Impact of mental health on perceptions of relationship satisfaction and quality among female same-sex couples. *Journal of Lesbian Studies, 10,* 267–283.

Ott, M. A., & Santelli, J. S. (2007). Abstinence and abstinence-only education. *Current Opinion in Obstetrics and Gynecology, 19,* 446–452.

Owens, T. E., Allen, M. D., & Spangler, D. L. (2010). An fMRI study of self-reflection about body image: Sex differences. *Personality and Individual Differences, 48,* 849–854.

Oyserman, D., Gant, L., & Ager, J. (1995). A socially contextualized model of African American identity: Possible selves and school persistence. *Journal of Personality and Social Psychology, 69,* 1216–1232.

Ozer, E. M., Barnett, R. C., Brennan, R. T., & Sperling, J. (1998). Does child care involvement increase or decrease distress among dual-earner couples? *Women's Health: Research on Gender, Behavior, and Policy, 4*(4), 285–311.

Page, S., & Bennesch, S. (1993). Gender and reporting differences in measures of depression. *Canadian Journal of Behavioural Science, 25,* 579–589.

Pajares, F. (2005). Gender differences in mathematics self-efficacy beliefs. In A. M. Gallagher & J. C. Kaufman (Eds.), *Gender differences in mathematics: An integrative psychological approach* (pp. 294–315). New York: Cambridge University Press.

Palomares, N. A. (2004). Gender schematicity, gender identity salience, and gender-linked language use. *Human Communication Research, 30,* 556–588.

Palomares, N. A. (2008). Explaining gender-based language use: Effects of gender identity salience on references to emotion and tentative language in intra- and intergroup contexts. *Human Communication Research, 34,* 263–286.

Palomares, N. A. (2009). Women are sort of more tentative than men, aren't they? How men and women use tentative language differently, similarly, and counterstereotypically as a function of gender salience. *Communication Research, 36,* 538–560.

Paludi, M. A., & Barickman, R. B. (1998). *Sexual harassment, work, and education.* New York: State University of New York Press.

Park, E. (2009). Gender as a moderator in the association of body weight to smoking and mental health. *American Journal of Public Health, 99,* 146–151.

Parks, J. B., & Roberton, M. A. (2008). Generation gaps in attitudes toward sexist/nonsexist language. *Journal of Language and Social Psychology, 27,* 276–283.

Parmley, M., & Cunningham, J. G. (2008). Children's gender-emotion stereotypes in the relationship of anger to sadness and fear. *Sex Roles, 58,* 358–370.

Parrott, D. J. (2009). Aggression toward gay men as gender role enforcement: Effects of male role norms, sexual prejudice, and masculine gender role stress. *Journal of Personality, 77,* 1137–1166.

Parsons, T., & Bales, R. F. (1955). *Family, socialization and interaction process.* Glencoe, IL: Free Press.

Pasch, L. A., Bradbury, T. N., & Davila, J. (1997). Gender, negative affectivity, and observed social support behavior in marital interaction. *Personal Relationships, 4,* 361–378.

Pasterski, V., Hindmarsh, P., Geffner, M., Brook, C., Brain, C., & Hines, M. (2007). Increased aggression and activity level in 3- to 11-year-old girls with congenital adrenal hyperplasia (CAH). *Hormones and Behavior, 52,* 368–374.

Patterson, C. J. (2000). Family relationships of lesbians and gay men. *Journal of Marriage and the Family, 62,* 1052–1069.

Patterson, C. J. (2009). Children of lesbian and gay parents: Psychology, law, and policy. *American Psychologist, 64,* 727–736.

Pavalko, E. K., & Woodbury, S. (2000). Social roles as process: Caregiving careers and women's health. *Journal of Health and Social Behavior, 41,* 91–105.

Pawlowski, B., & Atwal, R. (2008). Sex differences in everyday risk-taking behavior in humans. *Evolutionary Psychology, 6,* 29–42.

Paxton, S. J., & Sculthorpe, A. (1991). Disordered eating and sex role characteristics in young women: Implications for sociocultural theories of disturbed eating. *Sex Roles, 24,* 587–598.

Payne, S., Swami, V., & Stanistreet, D. L. (2008). The social construction of gender and its influence on suicide: A review of the literature. *Journal of Men's Health & Gender, 5,* 23–35.

Pedersen, D. E., Minnotte, K. L., Kiger, G., & Mannon, S. E. (2009). Workplace policy and environment, family role quality, and positive family-to-work spillover. *Journal of Family Economic Issues, 30,* 80–89.

Pedersen, W. C., Miller, L. C., & Putcha-Bhagavatula, A. D. (2002). Evolved sex differences in the number of partners desired? The long and the short of it. *Psychological Science, 13,* 157–160.

Pelak, C. F. (2008). The relationship between sexist naming practices and athletic opportunities at colleges and universities in the Southern United States. *Sociology of Education, 81,* 189–210.

Pence, E., & Paymar, M. (1993). *Education groups for men who batter: The Duluth model.* New York: Springer.

Peplau, L. A., & Beals, K. P. (2001). Lesbians, gay men, and bisexuals in relationships. In J. Worrell (Ed.), *Encyclopedia of women and gender: Sex similarities and differences and the impact of society on gender* (pp. 657–666). San Diego, CA: Academic.

Peplau, L. A., & Fingerhut, A. (2004). The paradox of the lesbian worker. *Journal of Social Issues, 60,* 719–735.

Peplau, L. A., & Fingerhut, A. W. (2007). The close relationships of lesbians and gay men. *Annual Review of Psychology, 58,* 405–424.

Peplau, L. A., Frederick, D. A., Yee, C., Maisel, N., Lever, J., & Ghavami, N. (2009). Body image satisfaction in heterosexual, gay, and lesbian adults. *Archives of Sexual Behavior, 38,* 713–725.

Peralta, R. L. (2007). College alcohol use and the embodiment of hegemonic masculinity among European American men. *Sex Roles, 56,* 741–756.

Perenboom, R. J. M., van Herten, L. M., Boshuizen, H. C., & van den Bos, G. A. M. (2005). Life expectancy without chronic morbidity: Trends in gender and socioeconomic disparities. *Public Health Reports, 120,* 46–54.

Perkins, K. A. (2009). Sex differences in nicotine reinforcement and reward: Influences on the persistence of tobacco smoking. In R. A. Bevins & A. R. Caggiula (Eds.), *The motivational impact of nicotine and its role in tobacco use* (pp. 143–169). New York: Springer Science + Business Media.

Perkins, K. A., & Scott, J. (2008). Sex differences in long-term smoking cessation rates due to nicotine patch. *Nicotine and Tobacco Research, 10,* 1245–1251.

Perkins, K. A., Marcus, M. D., Levine, M. D., D'Amico, D., Miller, A., Broge, M., et al. (2001). Cognitive-behavioral therapy to reduce weight concerns improves smoking cessation outcome in weight-concerned women. *Journal of Consulting and Clinical Psychology, 69,* 604–613.

Perry, D. G., & Bussey, K. (1979). The social learning theory of sex differences: Imitation is alive and well. *Journal of Personality and Social Psychology, 37,* 1699–1712.

Perry-Jenkins, M., Seery, B., & Crouter, A. C. (1992). Linkages between women's provider-role attitudes, psychological well-being, and family relationships. *Psychology of Women Quarterly, 16,* 311–329.

Petersen, J. L., & Hyde, J. S. (2010). A meta-analytic review of research on gender differences in sexuality, 1993–2007. *Psychological Bulletin, 136,* 21–38.

Peterson, A. L. (1999). Inaccurate estimation of body weight prior to smoking cessation: Implications for quitting and weight gain. *Journal of Applied Biobehavioral Research, 4*(2), 79–84.

Peterson, R. D., Grippo, K. P., & Tantleff-Dunn, S. (2008). Empowerment and powerlessness: A closer look at the relationship between feminism, body image and eating disturbance. *Sex Roles, 58,* 639–648.

Peterson, Z. D., & Muehlenhard, C. L. (2004). Was it rape? The function of women's rape myth acceptance and definitions of sex in labeling their own experiences. *Sex Roles, 51,* 129–144.

Petretta, M., Costanzo, P., Perrone-Filardi, P., & Chiariello, M. (2010). Impact of gender in primary prevention of coronary heart disease with statin therapy: A meta-analysis. *International Journal of Cardiology, 138,* 25–31.

Pew. (2009a). *The stronger sex: Spiritually speaking.* Retrieved June 6, 2011, from http://pewresearch.org/pubs/1135/religious-fervor-sex-differences

Pew. (2009b). *Pew Internet project data: Adults and social network websites.* Retrieved June 29, 2010, from http://www.pewinternet.org/~/media/files/reports/2009/pip_adult_social_networking_data_memo_final.pdf

Pew. (2010). *Internet, broadband, and cell phone statistics.* Retrieved May 11, 2011, from http://www.pewinternet.org/Reports/2010/Internet-broadband-and-cell-phone-statistics.aspx

Pew Research. (2007). *How young people view their lives, futures, and politics: A portrait of "generation next."* Retrieved August 26, 2010, from http://people-press.org/reports/pdf/300.pdf

Pfeffer, C. A. (2010). "Women's work"? Women partners of transgender men doing housework and emotion work. *Journal of Marriage and Family, 72,* 165–183.

Phelan, J. E., Sanchez, D. T., & Broccoli, T. L. (2010). The danger in sexism: The links among fear of crime, benevolent sexism, and well-being. *Sex Roles, 62,* 35–47.

Phillips, M. R., Li, X., & Zhang, Y. (2002). Suicides rates in China, 1995–99. *Lancet, 359,* 835–840.

Pike, J. J., & Jennings, N. A. (2005). The effects of commercials on children's perceptions of gender appropriate toy use. *Sex Roles, 52,* 83–91.

Pike, K. M., & Striegel-Moore, R. H. (1997). Disordered eating and eating disorders. In S. J. Gallant, G. P. Keita, & R. Royak-Schaler (Eds.), *Health care for women: Psychological, social, and behavioral influences* (pp. 97–114). Washington, DC: American Psychological Association.

Pillemer, J., Hatfield, E., & Sprecher, S. (2008). The importance of fairness and equity for marital satisfaction of older women. *Journal of Women and Aging, 20,* 215–229.

Pines, A. M. (2001). The role of gender and culture in romantic attraction. *European Psychologist, 6,* 96–102.

Pinquart, M. (2003). Loneliness in married, widowed, divorced, and never-married older adults. *Journal of Social and Personal Relationships, 20,* 31–53.

Pinquart, M., & Sorensen, S. (2006). Gender differences in caregiver stressors, social resources, and health: An updated meta-analysis. *Journal of Gerontology, 61B,* 33–45.

Piper, M. E., Cook, J. W., Schlam, T. R., Jorenby, D. E., Smith, S. S., Bolt, D. M., et al. (2010). Gender, race, and education differences in abstinence rates among participants in two randomized smoking cessation trials. *Nicotine and Tobacco Research, 12,* 647–657.

Pizzetti, P., & Manfredini, M. (2008). "The shock of widowhood"? Evidence from an Italian population (Parma, 1989–2000). *Social Indicators Research, 85,* 499–513.

Plant, M., Miller, P., Plant, M., Kuntsche, S., & Gmel, G. (2008). Marriage, cohabitation and alcohol consumption in young adults: An international exploration. *Journal of Substance Use, 13,* 83–98.

Platt, S., Bille-Brahe, U., Kerkhof, A., Schmidtke, A., Bjerke, T., Crepet, P., et al. (1992). Parasuicide in Europe: The WHO/EURO multicentre study on parasuicide. I. Introduction and preliminary analysis for 1989. *Acta Psychiatrica Scandinavica, 85,* 97–104.

Pleck, J. H. (1987). Men in domestic settings: American fathering in historical perspective. In M. S. Kimmel (Ed.), *Changing men: New directions in research on men and masculinity* (pp. 83–97). Newbury Park, CA: Sage.

Pleck, J. H. (1995). The gender role strain paradigm: An update. In R. F. Levant & W. S. Pollack (Eds.), *A new psychology of men* (pp. 11–32). New York: Basic Books.

Plumm, K. M. (2008). Technology in the classroom: Burning the bridges to the gaps in gender-biased education? *Computers and Education, 50,* 1052–1068.

Polce-Lynch, M., Myers, B. J., Kilmartin, C. T., Forssmann-Falck, R., & Kliewer, W. (1998). Gender and age patterns in emotional expression, body image, and self-esteem: A qualitative analysis. *Sex Roles, 38,* 1025–1048.

Pollack, W. S. (1998). *Real boys: Rescuing our sons from the myths of boyhood.* New York: Henry Holt.

Pollack, W. S. (2000). *Real boys' voices.* New York: Random House.

Pollack, W. S. (2006). The "war" for boys: Hearing "real boys" voices, healing their pain. *Professional Psychology: Research and Practice, 37,* 190–195.

Pomerantz, E. M., Altermatt, E. R., & Saxon, J. L. (2002). Making the grade but feeling distressed: Gender differences in academic performance and internal distress. *Journal of Educational Psychology, 94*(2), 396–404.

Pomerantz, E. M., & Dong, W. (2006). Effects of mothers' perceptions of children's competence: The moderation role of mothers' theories of competence. *Developmental Psychology, 42,* 950–961.

Pomerantz, E. M., & Ruble, D. N. (1998). The multidimensional nature of control: Implications for the development of sex differences in self-evaluation. In J. Heckhausen & C. S. Dweck (Eds.), *Motivation and self-regulation across the life span* (pp. 159–184). Cambridge, MA: Cambridge University Press.

Pomerantz, E. M., Ng, F. F.-Y., & Wang, Q. (2004). Gender socialization: A parent × child model. In A. H. Eagly, A. E. Beall, & R. J. Sternberg (Eds.), *The psychology of gender* (2nd ed., pp. 120–144). New York: Guilford Press.

Pomerleau, C. S., Tate, J. C., Lumley, M. A., & Pomerleau, O. F. (1994). Gender differences in prospectively versus retrospectively assessed smoking withdrawal symptoms. *Journal of Substance Abuse, 6,* 433–440.

Pool, G. J., Schwegler, A. F., Theodore, B. R., & Fuchs, P. N. (2007). Role of gender norms and group identification on hypothetical and experimental pain tolerance. *Pain, 129,* 122–129.

Pope, H. G., Jr., Olivardia, R., Gruber, A., & Borowiecki, J. (1999). Evolving ideals of male body image as seen through action toys. *International Journal of Eating Disorders, 26*(1), 65–72.

Pope, J. H., Aufderheide, T. P., Ruthazer, R., Woolard, R. H., Feldman, J. A., Beshansky, J. R., et al. (2000). Missed diagnoses of acute cardiac ischemia in the emergency department. *New England Journal of Medicine, 16,* 1163–1170.

Popenoe, D. (2008). Cohabitation, marriage and child wellbeing. In *The national marriage project at Rutgers University* (pp. 1–22). Piscataway, NJ: Rutgers University.

Popenoe, D., & Whitehead, B. D. (1999). *The state of our unions. The social health of marriage in America.* Retrieved November 12, 2007, from marriage.rutgers.edu

Poulin Dubois, D., Serbin, L. A., Eichstedt, J. A., & Sen, M. G. (2002). Men don't put on make-up: Toddlers' knowledge of the gender stereotyping of household activities. *Social Development, 11,* 166–181.

Poulin, F., & Boivin, M. (2000). Reactive and proactive aggression: Evidence of a two-factor model. *Psychological Assessment, 12*(2), 115–122.

Poulin, F., & Pedersen, S. (2007). Developmental changes in gender composition of friendship networks in adolescent girls and boys. *Developmental Psychology, 43,* 1484–1496.

Powell, G. N., & Graves, L. M. (2006). Gender and leadership: Perceptions and realities. In K. Dindia & D. J. Canary (Eds.), *Sex differences and similarities in communication* (2nd ed., pp. 83–97). Mahwah, NJ: Lawrence Erlbaum Associates.

Preckel, F., Goetz, T., Pekrun, R., & Kleine, M. (2008). Gender differences in gifted and average-ability students. *Gifted Child Quarterly, 52,* 146–159.

Price, C. A., & Balaswamy, S. (2009). Beyond health and wealth: Predictors of women's retirement satisfaction. *International Journal of Aging and Human Development, 68,* 195–214.

Priess, H. A., Lindberg, S. M., & Hyde, J. S. (2009). Adolescent gender-role identity and mental health: Gender intensification revisited. *Child Development, 80,* 1531–1544.

Prigerson, H. G., & Slimack, M. J. (1999). Gender differences in clinical correlates of suicidality among young adults. *Journal of Nervous and Mental Disease, 187*(1), 23–31.

Proctor, A., Yairi, E., Duff, M. C., & Zhang, J. (2008). Prevalence of stuttering in African American preschoolers. *Journal of Speech, Language, and Hearing Research, 51*(6), 1465–1479.

Pronk, R. E., & Zimmer-Gembeck, M. J. (2010). It's "mean," but what does it mean to adolescents? Relational aggression described by victims, aggressors, and their peers. *Journal of Adolescent Research, 25,* 175–204.

Prospero, M., & Kim, M. (2009). Mutual partner violence: Mental health symptoms among female and male victims in four racial/ethnic groups. *Journal of Interpersonal Violence, 24,* 2039–2056.

Pruchno, R. A., Cartwright, F. P., & Wilson-Genderson, M. (2009). Effects of marital closeness on the transition from caregiving to widowhood. *Aging and Mental Health, 13,* 808–817.

Pryor, J. B. (1998). The likelihood to sexually harass scale. In C. M. Davis, W. H. Yarber, R. Bauserman, G. Schreer, & S. L. Davis (Eds.), *Sexuality-related measures: A compendium* (pp. 295–298). Beverly Hills, CA: Sage.

Pryor, J. B., Giedd, J. L., & Williams, K. B. (1995). A social psychological model for predicting sexual harassment. *Journal of Social Issues, 51*(1), 69–84.

Pryor, J. B., Hesson-McInnis, M. S., Hitlan, R. T., Olson, M., & Hahn, E. J. (2000). *Antecedents of gender harassment: An analysis of person and situation factors.* Unpublished manuscript.

Ptacek, J. T., Pierce, G. R., & Ptacek, J. J. (2007). Coping, distress, and marital adjustment in couples with cancer: An examination of the personal and social context. *Journal of Psychosocial Oncology, 25,* 37–58.

Pugliesi, K., & Shook, S. L. (1998). Gender, ethnicity, and network characteristics: Variation in social support resources. *Sex Roles, 38,* 215–238.

Purcell, D. W., Lewine, R. R. J., Caudle, J., & Price, L. R. (1998). Sex differences in verbal IQ-performance IQ discrepancies among patients with schizophrenia and normal volunteers. *Journal of Abnormal Psychology, 107,* 161–165.

Puts, D. A., McDaniel, M. A., Jordan, C. L., & Breedlove, S. M. (2008). Spatial ability and prenatal androgens: Meta-analyses of congenital adrenal hyperplasia and digit ratio (2d:4d) studies. *Archives of Sexual Behavior, 37,* 100–111.

Quillian, L., & Campbell, M. E. (2003). Beyond Black and White: The present and future of multiracial friendship segregation. *American Sociological Review, 68,* 540–566.

Quinn, P. C., & Liben, L. S. (2008). A sex difference in mental rotation in young infants. *Psychological Science, 19,* 1067–1070.

Rabin, C. (1998). Gender and intimacy in the treatment of couples in the 1990s. *Sexual and Marital Therapy, 13*(2), 179–190.

Radloff, L. S. (1977). The CES-D scale: A self-report depression scale for research in the general population. *Journal of Applied Psychological Measurement, 1,* 385–401.

Radloff, L. S., & Rae, D. S. (1979). Susceptibility and precipitating factors in depression: Sex differences and similarities. *Journal of Abnormal Psychology, 88,* 174–181.

Radmacher, K., & Azmitia, M. (2006). Are there gendered pathways to intimacy in early adolescents' and emerging adults' friendships? *Journal of Adolescent Research, 21,* 415–448.

Ragland, D., & West, D. (2009). Pharmacy students' knowledge, attitudes, and behaviors regarding emergency contraception. *American Journal of Pharmaceutical Education, 73*(2), 26.

Ramet, S. P. (1996). *Gender reversals and gender cultures.* New York: Pointing-Green.

Rasmussen, K., & Levander, S. (2009). Untreated ADHD in adults. *Journal of Attention Disorders, 12,* 353–360.

Rath, T. (2006). *Vital friends: The people you can't afford to live without.* New York: Gallup Press.

Räty, H., Vänskä, J., Kasanen, K., & Kärkkäinen, R. (2002). Parents' explanations of their child's performance in mathematics and reading: A replication and extension of Yee and Eccles. *Sex Roles, 46,* 121–128.

Rawlins, W. K. (2004). Friendships in later life. In J. F. Nussbaum (Ed.), *Handbook of communication and aging research* (2nd ed., pp. 273–299). Mahwah, NJ: Lawrence Erlbaum Associates Publishers.

Reczek, C., Elliott, S., & Umberson, D. (2009). Commitment without marriage: Union formation among long-term same-sex couples. *Journal of Family Issues, 30,* 738–756.

Rederstorff, J. C., Buchanan, N. T., & Settles, I. H. (2007). The moderating roles of race and gender-role attitudes in the relationship between sexual harassment and psychological well-being. *Psychology of Women Quarterly, 31,* 50–61.

Reeder, H. M. (2003). The effect of gender role orientation on same- and cross-sex friendship formation. *Sex Roles, 49,* 143–152.

Reevy, G. M., & Maslach, C. (2001). Use of social support: Gender and personality differences. *Sex Roles, 44,* 437–459.

Regan, P. C., & Berscheid, E. (1999). *Lust: What we know about human sexual desire.* Thousand Oaks, CA: Sage.

Rehman, U. S., & Holtzworth-Munroe, A. (2006). A cross-cultural analysis of the demand-withdraw marital interaction: Observing couples from a developing country. *Journal of Consulting and Clinical Psychology, 74,* 755–766.

Rehman, U. S., & Holtzworth-Munroe, A. (2007). A cross-cultural examination of the relation of marital communication behavior to marital satisfaction. *Journal of Family Psychology, 21,* 759–763.

Reid, R. D., Pipe, A. L., Riley, D. L., & Sorensen, M. (2009). Sex differences in attitudes and experiences concerning smoking and cessation: Results from an international survey. *Patient Education and Counseling, 76,* 99–105.

Reid, S. A., Keerie, N., & Palomares, N. A. (2003). Language, gender salience, and social influence. *Journal of Language and Social Psychology, 22,* 210–233.

Reidy, D. E., Dimmick, K., MacDonald, K., & Zeichner, A. (2009). The relationship between pain tolerance and trait aggression: Effects of sex and gender role. *Aggressive Behavior, 35,* 422–429.

Reidy, D. E., Shirk, S. D., Sloan, C. A., & Zeichner, A. (2009). Men who aggress against women: Effects of feminine gender role violation on physical aggression in hypermasculine men. *Psychology of Men and Masculinity, 10,* 1–12.

Reis, H. T. (1998). Gender differences in intimacy and related behaviors: Context and process. In D. J. Canary & K. Dindia (Eds.), *Sex differences and similarities in communication* (pp. 203–231). Mahwah, NJ: Erlbaum.

Reis, H. T., & Shaver, P. (1988). Intimacy as an interpersonal process. In S. Duck (Ed.), *Handbook of personal relationships: Theory, relationships, and interventions* (pp. 367–389). Chichester, England: Wiley.

Reis, H. T., Senchak, M., & Solomon, B. (1985). Sex differences in the intimacy of social interaction: Further examination of potential explanations. *Journal of Personality and Social Psychology, 48,* 1204–1217.

Rejeski, W. J., Parker, P. E., Gagne, M., & Koritnik, D. R. (1990). Cardiovascular and testosterone responses to contested dominance in women. *Health Psychology, 9,* 35–47.

Renzulli, L. A., Grant, L., & Kathuria, S. (2006). Race, gender, and the wage gap: Comparing faculty salaries in predominately White and historically Black colleges and universities. *Gender & Society, 20,* 491–510.

Reuss, P., & Erickson, J. (2006). Access for all? Reclaiming women's contraceptive options one pharmacy at a time. *National Organization for Women* [Electronic Version]. Retrieved January 12, 2007, from ww.now.org/issues/reproductive/ec_action_plan.html

Reuvers, M., van Engen, M. L., Vinkenburg, C. J., & Wilson-Evered, E. (2008). Transformational leadership and innovative work behaviour: Exploring the relevance of gender differences. *Leadership and Innovation, 17,* 227–243.

Revenson, T. A., Abraido-Lanza, A. F., Majerovitz, S. D., & Jordan, C. (2005). Couples coping with chronic illness: What's gender got to do with it? In T. A. Revenson, K. Kayser, & G. Bodenmann (Eds.), *Couples coping with stress: Emerging perspectives on dyadic coping* (pp. 137–156). Washington, DC: American Psychological Association.

Reynolds, K. A., Helgeson, V. S., Seltman, H., Janicki, D., Page-Gould, E., & Wardle, M. (2006). Impact of interpersonal conflict on individuals high in unmitigated communion. *Journal of Applied Social Psychology, 36,* 1595–1616.

Reznik, S. (2010). Plan B: How it works. *Health Progress, 91,* 59–61.

Rhee, S. H., & Waldman, I. D. (2002). Genetic and environmental influences on antisocial behavior: A meta-analysis of twin and adoption studies. *Psychological Bulletin, 128,* 490–529.

Rhoades, G. K., Petralla, J. N., Stanley, S. M., & Markman, H. J. (2006). Premarital cohabitation, husbands' commitment, and wives' satisfaction with the division of household contributions. *Marriage and Family Review, 40,* 5–22.

Rhoades, G. K., Stanley, S. M., & Markman, H. J. (2006). Pre-engagement cohabitation and gender asymmetry in marital commitment. *Journal of Family Psychology, 20,* 553–560.

Rhoades, G. K., Stanley, S. M., & Markman, H. J. (2009). Couples' reasons for cohabitation associations with individual well-being and relationship quality. *Journal of Family Issues, 30,* 233–258.

Richards, J. M., & Gross, J. J. (2000). Emotion regulation and memory: The cognitive costs of keeping one's cool. *Journal of Personality and Social Psychology, 79,* 410–424.

Rich-Edwards, J. W., Manson, J. E., Hennekens, C. H., & Buring, J. E. (1995). Medical progress: The primary prevention of coronary heart disease in women. *New England Journal of Medicine, 332*(26), 1758–1766.

Rideout, V. J., Foehr, U. G., & Roberts, D. F. (2010). Generation M2: Media in the lives of 8- to 18-year-olds. *Kaiser Family Foundation Study.* Retrieved July 20, 2010, from http://www.kff.org/entmedia/upload/8010.pdf

Ridgeway, C. L., & Correll, S. J. (2004). Motherhood as a status characteristic. *Journal of Social Issues, 60,* 683–700.

Rieker, P. P., & Bird, C. E. (2005). Rethinking gender differences in health: Why we need to integrate social and biological perspectives. *Journal of Gerontology, 60B,* 40–47.

Rivadeneyra, R., & Ward, L. M. (2005). From Ally McBeal to Sábado Gigante: Contributions of television viewing to the gender role attitudes of Latino adolescents. *Journal of Adolescent Research, 20,* 453–475.

Roberts, L. R., & Petersen, A. C. (1992). The relationship between academic achievement and social self-image during early adolescence. *Journal of Early Adolescence, 12,* 197–219.

Roberts, S. J., Patsdaughter, C. A., Grindel, C. G., & Tarmina, M. S. (2004). Health related behaviors and cancer screening of lesbians: Results of the Boston Lesbian Health Project II. *Women & Health, 39,* 41–55.

Roberts, T.-A., & Gettman, J. Y. (2004). Mere exposure: Gender differences in the negative effects of priming a state of self-objectification. *Sex Roles, 51,* 17–27.

Roberts, T.-A., & Nolen-Hoeksema, S. (1994). Gender comparisons in responsiveness to others' evaluations in achievement settings. *Psychology of Women Quarterly, 18,* 221–240.

Robinson, M. E., Wise, E. A., Gagnon, C., Fillingim, R. B., & Price, D. D. (2004). Influences of gender role and anxiety on sex differences in temporal summation of pain. *Journal of Pain, 5,* 77–82.

Robison, E. J., & Shankman, S. A. (2008). The role of emotion and personality in gender differences in depression. In P. R. Bancroft & L. B. Ardley (Eds.), *Major depression in women* (pp. 1–9). New York: Nova Science Publishers.

Robson, K., & Wallace, J. E. (2001). Gendered inequalities in earnings: A study of Canadian lawyers. *Canadian Review of Sociology and Anthropology, 38,* 75–95.

Rodin, J., & Ickovics, J. R. (1990). Women's health: Review and research agenda as we approach the 21st century. *American Psychologist, 45,* 1018–1034.

Rogers, S. J., & DeBoer, D. D. (2001). Changes in wives' income: Effects on marital happiness, psychological well-being, and the risk of divorce. *Journal of Marriage and the Family, 63,* 458–472.

Roisman, G. I., Clausell, E., Holland, A., Fortuna, K., & Elieff, C. (2008). Adult romantic relationships as contexts of human development: A multimethod comparison of same-sex couples with opposite-sex dating, engaged, and married dyads. *Developmental Psychology, 44,* 91–101.

Rood, L., Roelofs, J., Bogels, S. M., Nolen-Hoeksema, S., & Schouten, E. (2009). The influence of emotion-focused rumination and distraction on depressive symptoms in non-clinical youth: A meta-analytic review. *Clinical Psychology Review, 29,* 607–616.

Rose, A. J. (2002). Co-rumination in the friendships of girls and boys. *Child Development, 73,* 1830–1843.

Rose, A. J., & Asher, S. R. (1999). Children's goals and strategies in response to conflicts within a friendship. *Developmental Psychology, 35,* 69–79.

Rose, A. J., & Rudolph, K. D. (2006). A review of sex differences in peer relationship processes: Potential trade-offs for the emotional and behavioral development of girls and boys. *Psychological Bulletin, 132,* 98–131.

Rose, A. J., Carlson, W., & Waller, E. M. (2007). Prospective associations of co-rumination with friendship and emotional adjustment: Considering the socioemotional trade-offs of co-rumination. *Developmental Psychology, 43,* 1019–1031.

Rose, G. L., Suls, J., Green, P. J., Lounsbury, P., & Gordon, E. (1996). Comparison of adjustment, activity, and tangible social support in men and women patients and their spouses during the six months post-myocardial infarction. *Annals of Behavioral Medicine, 18*(4), 264–272.

Rose, S., & Frieze, I. H. (1993). Young singles' contemporary dating scripts. *Sex Roles, 28,* 499–509.

Rose, S., Zand, D., & Cini, M. A. (1993). Lesbian courtships scripts. In E. D. Rothblum & K. A. Brehony (Eds.), *Boston marriages* (pp. 70–85). Amherst, MA: University of Massachusetts Press.

Rosenbloom, A. (2000, April 16). Only a generation ago, the marathon banned women. *Boston Globe,* p. D1.

Rosenfield, S. (1989). The effects of women's employment: Personal control and sex differences in mental health. *Journal of Health and Social Behavior, 30,* 77–91.

Rosenfield, S. (1992). The costs of sharing: Wives' employment and husbands' mental health. *Journal of Health and Social Behavior, 33,* 213–225.

Rosenfield, S., & Smith, D. (2010). Gender and mental health: Do men and women have different amounts or types of problems? In T. L. Scheid & T. N. Brown (Eds.), *A handbook for the study of mental health: Social contexts, theories, and systems* (pp. 256–267). New York: Cambridge University Press.

Rosenthal, R. (1966). *Experimenter effects in behavioral research.* New York: Appleton-Century-Crofts.

Rosenthal, R. (1994). Parametric measures of effect size. In H. Cooper & L. V. Hedges (Eds.), *The handbook of research synthesis* (pp. 231–244). New York: Russell Sage Foundation.

Rosip, J. C., & Hall, J. A. (2004). Knowledge of nonverbal cues, gender, and nonverbal decoding accuracy. *Journal of Nonverbal Behavior, 28,* 267–286.

Ross, C., & Mirowsky, J. (2006). Sex differences in the effect of education on depression: Resource multiplication or resource substitution? *Social Science & Medicine, 63,* 1400–1413.

Ross, C. E., & Mirowsky, J. (2010). Gender and the health benefits of education. *Sociological Quarterly, 51,* 1–19.

Rossouw, J. E., Prentice, R. L., Manson, J. E., Wu, L., Barad, D., Barnabei, V. M., et al. (2007). Postmenopausal hormone therapy and risk of cardiovascular disease by age and years since menopause. *Journal of the American Medical Association, 297,* 1465–1477.

Roter, D. L., Hall, J. A., & Aoki, Y. (2002). Physician gender effects in medical communication: A meta-analytic review. *Journal of the American Medical Association, 288,* 756–764.

Rothbart, M., & John, O. P. (1985). Social categorization and behavior episodes: A cognitive analysis of the effects of intergroup contact. *Journal of Social Issues, 41*(3), 81–104.

Rotundo, M., Nguyen, D.-H., & Sackett, P. R. (2001). A meta-analytic review of gender differences in perceptions of sexual harassment. *Journal of Applied Psychology, 86,* 914–922.

Roy, K., & Chaudhuri, A. (2008). Influence of socioeconomic status, wealth and financial empowerment on gender differences in health and healthcare utilization in later life: Evidence from India. *Social Science & Medicine, 66,* 1951–1962.

Roy, R. E., Weibust, K. S., & Miller, C. T. (2007). Effects of stereotypes about feminists on feminist self-identification. *Psychology of Women Quarterly, 31,* 146–156.

Royce, J. M., Corbett, K., Sorensen, G., & Ockene, J. (1997). Gender, social pressure, and smoking cessations: The community intervention trial for smoking cessation (commit) at baseline. *Social Science & Medicine, 44*(3), 359–370.

Royer, J. M., & Garofoli, L. M. (2005). Cognitive contributions to sex differences in math performance. In A. M. Gallagher & J. C. Kaufman (Eds.), *Gender differences in mathematics* (pp. 99–120). New York: Cambridge University Press.

Royster, D. A. (2007). What happens to potential discouraged? Masculinity norms and the contrasting institutional and labor market experiences of less affluent Black and White men. *Annals of the American Academy, 609,* 153–180.

Rozee, P. D., & Koss, M. P. (2001). Rape: A century of resistance. *Psychology of Women Quarterly, 25,* 295–311.

Rubin, L. B. (1983). *Intimate strangers.* New York: Harper & Row.

Rudman, L. A., & Fairchild, K. (2004). Reactions to counterstereotypic behavior: The role of backlash in cultural stereotype maintenance. *Journal of Personality and Social Psychology, 87,* 157–176.

Rudman, L. A., & Fairchild, K. (2007). The F word: Is feminism incompatible with beauty and romance? *Psychology of Women Quarterly, 31,* 125–136.

Rudman, L. A., & Glick, P. (2001). Prescriptive gender stereotypes and backlash toward agentic women. *Journal of Social Issues, 57,* 743–762.

Rudman, L. A., & Phelan, J. E. (2007). The interpersonal power of feminism: Is feminism good for romantic relationships? *Sex Roles, 57,* 787–799.

Rudman, L. A., Glick, P., & Phelan, J. E. (2008). From the laboratory to the bench: Gender stereotyping research in the courtroom. In E. Borgida & S. T. Fiske (Eds.), *Beyond common sense: Psychological science in the courtroom* (pp. 83–101). Malden, MA: Blackwell Publishing.

Rudolph, K. D. (2009). The interpersonal context of adolescent depression. In S. Nolen-Hoeksema & L. M. Hilt (Eds.), *Handbook of depression in adolescents* (pp. 377–418). New York: Routledge/Taylor Francis Group.

Rudolph, K. D., & Hammen, C. (1999). Age and gender as determinants of stress exposure, generation, and reactions in youngsters: A transactional perspective. *Child Development, 70,* 660–677.

Rudolph, K. D., Ladd, G., & Dinella, L. (2007). Gender differences in the interpersonal consequences of early-onset depressive symptoms. *Merrill-Palmer Quarterly, 53,* 461–488.

Rueda, B., & Perez-Garcia, A. M. (2006). Gender and social support in the context of cardiovascular disease. *Women & Health, 43,* 59–73.

Rueger, S. Y., Malecki, C. K., & Demaray, M. K. (2010). Relationship between multiple sources of perceived social support and psychological and academic adjustment in early adolescence: Comparisons across gender. *Journal of Youth and Adolescence, 39,* 47–61.

Rumens, N. (2008). Working at intimacy: Gay men's workplace friendships. *Gender, Work, and Organization, 15,* 9–30.

Russell, A., & Owens, L. (1999). Peer estimates of school-aged boys' and girls' aggression to same- and cross-sex targets. *Social Development, 8*(3), 364–379.

Russell, B. L., & Trigg, K. Y. (2004). Tolerance of sexual harassment: An examination of gender differences, ambivalent sexism, social dominance, and gender roles. *Sex Roles, 50,* 565–573.

Russell, D. (1990). *Rape in marriage.* Bloomington, IN: Indiana University Press.

Russell, D., & Taylor, J. (2009). Living alone and depressive symptoms: The influence of gender, physical disability, and social support among Hispanic and non-Hispanic older adults. *Journal of Gerontology: Social Sciences, 64B,* 95–104.

Russell, D. E. H., & Bolen, R. M. (2000). *The epidemic of rape and child sexual abuse in the United States.* Thousand Oaks, CA: Sage Publications.

Rust, J., Golombok, S., Hines, M., Johnston, K., & Golding, J. (2000). The role of brothers and sisters in the gender development of preschool children. *Journal of Experimental Child Psychology, 77*(4), 292–303.

Ryan, J., Carriere, I., Ritchie, K., Stewart, R., Toulemonde, G., Dartigues, J.-F., et al. (2008). Late-life depression and mortality: Influence of gender and antidepressant use. *British Journal of Psychiatry, 192,* 12–18.

Ryckman, R. M., Libby, C. R., van den Borne, B., Gold, J. A., & Lindner, M. A. (1997). Values of hyper-competitive and personal development competitive individuals. *Journal of Personality Assessment, 69,* 271–283.

Saad, L. (2007a). *Women slightly more likely to prefer working to homemaking: After a recent slide, more women again opt for holding a job outside the home.* Retrieved August 31, 2007, from http://www.gallup.com/poll/28567/women-slightly-more-likely-prefer-working-homemaking.aspx

Saad, L. (2007b). *Democrats are encouraged about women's job rights.* Retrieved August 16, 2010, from http://www.gallup.com/poll/28117/democrats-encouraged-about-womens-job-rights.aspx

Saad, L. (2008). *By age 24, marriage wins out.* Retrieved June 29, 2010, from http://www.gallup.com/poll/109402/age-24-marriage-wins.aspx

Saad, L. (2010). Four moral issues sharply divide Americans. *Gallup Poll.* Retrieved June 29, 2010, from http://www.gallup.com/poll/137357/four-moral-issues-sharply-divide-Americans.aspx

Sacco, S., Cerone, D., & Carolei, A. (2009). Gender and stroke: Acute phase treatment and prevention. *Functional Neurology, 24,* 45–52.

Sachs-Ericsson, N., & Ciarlo, J. A. (2000). Gender, social roles, and mental health: An epidemiological perspective. *Sex Roles, 43,* 605–628.

Sadker, D. M., & Zittleman, K. R. (2007). *Teachers, schools, and society: A brief introduction to education.* New York: McGraw Hill.

Sadker, M., & Sadker, D. (1994). *Failing at fairness: How America's schools cheat girls.* New York: Charles Scribner's Sons.

Safir, M. P., Flaisher-Kellner, S., & Rosenmann, A. (2005). When gender differences surpass cultural differences in personal satisfaction with body shape in Israeli college students. *Sex Roles, 52,* 369–378.

Sainz, M., & Lopez-Saez, M. (2010). Gender differences in computer attitudes and the choice of technology-related occupations in a sample of secondary students in Spain. *Computers and Education, 54,* 578–587.

Sandhu, H., Adams, A., Singleton, L., Clark-Carter, D., & Kidd, J. (2009). The impact of gender dyads on doctor–patient communication: A systematic review. *Patient Education and Counseling, 76,* 348–355.

Sandler, B. R., & Shoop, R. J. (1997). What is sexual harassment? In B. R. Sandler & R. J. Shoop (Eds.), *Sexual harassment on campus: A guide for administrators, faculty, and students* (pp. 1–21). Boston, MA: Allyn & Bacon.

Sastry, J. (1999). Household structure, satisfaction and distress in India and the United States: A comparative cultural examination.*Journal of Comparative Family Studies, 30*(1), 135–152.

SAT Data Tables. (2010). *Total group writing subscore report*. Retrieved June 7, 2010, from http://www.collegeboard.com/prod_downloads/highered/ra/sat/2006-total-group-writing-subscore-report.pdf

Saules, K. K., Collings, A. S., Angelella, N. E., Alschuler, K., Ivezaj, V., Saunders-Scott, D., et al. (2009). The contributions of weight problem perception, BMI, gender, mood, and smoking status to binge eating among college students. *Eating Behaviors, 10,* 1–9.

Sbarra, D. A. (2009). Marriage protects men from clinically meaningful elevations in C-reactive protein: Results from the national social life, health, and aging project (NSHAP). *Psychosomatic Medicine, 71,* 828–835.

Sbarra, D. A., & Nietert, P. J. (2009). Divorce and death: Forty years of the Charleston heart study. *Psychological Science, 20,* 107–113.

Schmitt, D. P., & 121 Members of the International Sexuality Description Project. (2004). Patterns and universals of mate poaching across 53 nations: The effects of sex, culture, and personality on romantically attracting another person's partner. *Journal of Personality and Social Psychology, 86,* 560–584.

Schmitt, D. P., Realo, A., Voracek, M., & Allik, J. (2008). Why can't a man be more like a woman? Sex differences in big five personality traits across 55 cultures. *Journal of Personality and Social Psychology, 94,* 168–182.

Schmitt, D. P., Youn, G., Bond, B., Brooks, S., Frye, H., Johnson, S., et al. (2009). When will I feel love? The effects of culture, personality, and gender on the psychological tendency to love. *Journal of Research in Personality, 43,* 830–846.

Schmitt, M., Kliegel, M., & Shapiro, A. (2007). Marital interaction in middle and old age: A predictor of marital satisfaction? *International Journal of Aging and Human Development, 65,* 283–300.

Schmookler, T., & Bursik, K. (2007). The value of monogamy in emerging adulthood: A gendered perspective. *Journal of Social and Personal Relationships, 24,* 819–835.

Schneider, B. H., Woodburn, S., del Toro, M., & Udvari, S. J. (2005). Cultural and gender differences in the implications of competition for early adolescent friendship. *Merrill-Palmer Quarterly, 51,* 163–191.

Schneider, F., Habel, U., Kessler, C., Salloum, J. B., & Posse, S. (2000). Gender differences in regional cerebral activity during sadness. *Human Brain Mapping, 9*(4), 226–238.

Schneider, S., Huy, C., Schutz, J., & Diehl, K. (2010). Smoking cessation during pregnancy: A systematic literature review. *Drug and Alcohol Review, 29,* 81–90.

Schnittker, J. (2000). Gender and reactions to psychological problems: An examination of social tolerance and perceived dangerousness. *Journal of Health and Social Behavior, 44,* 224–240.

Schoenbach, V. J., Kaplan, B. H., Fredman, L., & Kleinbaum, D. G. (1986). Social ties and mortality in Evans County, Georgia. *American Journal of Epidemiology, 123*(4), 577–591.

Schuurs, A. H., & Verheul, H. A. (1990). Effects of gender and sex steroids on the immune response. *Journal of Steroid and Biochemistry, 35*(2), 157–172.

Schwarzwald, J., Koslowsky, M., & Izhak-Nir, E. B. (2008). Gender role ideology as a moderator of the relationship between social power tactics and marital satisfaction. *Sex Roles, 59,* 657–669.

Schweinle, W. E., Ickes, W., & Bernstein, I. H. (2002). Empathic inaccuracy in husband to wife aggression: The overattribution bias. *Personal Relationships, 9,* 141–158.

Scott, K. A. (2004). African-American-White girls' friendships. *Feminism & Psychology, 14,* 383–388.

Sechrist, G. B., & Delmar, C. (2009). When do men and women make attribution to gender discrimination? The role of discrimination source. *Sex Roles, 61,* 607–620.

Sechrist, G. B., & Swim, J. K. (2008). Psychological consequences of failing to attribute negative outcomes to discrimination. *Sex Roles, 59,* 21–38.

Seedat, S., Scott, K. M., Angermeyer, M. C., Berglund, P., Bromet, E. J., & Brugha, T. S. (2009). Cross-national associations between gender and mental disorders in the world health organization world mental health surveys. *Archives of General Psychiatry, 66,* 785–795.

Seelau, S. M., & Seelau, E. P. (2005). Gender-role stereotypes and perceptions of heterosexual, gay and lesbian domestic violence. *Journal of Family Violence, 20,* 363–371.

Segar, M., Spruijt-Metz, D., & Nolen-Hoeksema, S. (2006). Go figure? Body-shape motives are associated with decreased physical activity participation among midlife women. *Sex Roles, 54,* 175–187.

Seiffge-Krenke, I., & Stemmler, M. (2002). Factors contributing to gender differences in depressive symptoms: A test of three developmental models. *Journal of Youth and Adolescence, 31,* 405–417.

Seligman, M. E. P. (1992). *Helplessness: On depression, development, and death.* New York: Freeman.

Seltzer, J. A. (2000). Families formed outside of marriage. *Journal of Marriage and the Family, 62,* 1247–1268.

Serbin, L. A., Poulin-Dubois, D., Colburne, K. A., Sen, M. G., & Eichstedt, J. A. (2001). Gender stereotyping in infancy: Visual preferences for and knowledge of gender-stereotyped toys in the second year. *International Journal of Behavioral Development, 25,* 7–15.

Sethi, S., & Nolen-Hoeksema, S. (1997). Gender differences in internal and external focusing among adolescents. *Sex Roles, 37,* 687–700.

Sevcik, K. (2007). She's turning him into a girl. *Marie Claire,* 121–127.

Shackelford, T. K., Schmitt, D. P., & Buss, D. M. (2005). Universal dimensions of human mate preferences. *Personality and Individual Differences, 39,* 447–458.

Shaffer, D. R., Pegalis, L. J., & Bazzini, D. G. (1996). When boy meets girl (revisited): Gender, gender-role orientation, and prospect of future interaction as determinants of self-disclosure among same- and opposite-sex acquaintances. *Personality and Social Psychology Bulletin, 22,* 495–506.

Shah, S., & Conchar, C. (2009). Why single-sex schools? Discourses of culture/faith and achievement. *Cambridge Journal of Education, 39,* 191–204.

Sharma, A. R., McGue, M. K., & Benson, P. L. (1996). The emotional and behavioral adjustment of United States adopted adolescents: Part I. An overview. *Children and Youth Services Review, 18*(1–2), 83–100.

Shaywitz, S. E., Shaywitz, B. A., Fletcher, J. M., & Escobar, M. D. (1990). Prevalence of reading disability in boys and girls: Results of the Connecticut Longitudinal Study. *Journal of the American Medical Association, 264,* 998–1002.

Sheets, V. L., & Braver, S. L. (1999). Organizational status and perceived sexual harassment: Detecting the mediators of a null effect. *Personality and Social Psychology Bulletin, 25,* 1159–1171.

Sheets, V. L., & Lugar, R. (2005). Friendship and gender in Russia and the United States. *Sex Roles, 52,* 131–140.

Sheets, V. L., & Wolfe, M. D. (2001). Sexual jealousy in heterosexuals, lesbians, and gays. *Sex Roles, 44,* 255–276.

Sher, L. (2006). Per capita income is related to suicide rates in men but not in women. *Journal of Men's Health & Gender, 3,* 39–42.

Shields, S. A. (1975). Functionalism, Darwinism, and the psychology of women: A study in social myth. *American Psychologist, 30,* 739–754.

Shih, J. H., Eberhart, N. K., Hammen, C. L., & Brennan, P. A. (2006). Differential exposure and reactivity to interpersonal stress predict sex differences in adolescent depression. *Journal of Clinical Child and Adolescent Psychology, 35,* 103–115.

Shih, M., Pittinsky, T. L., & Ambady, N. (1999). Stereotype susceptibility: Identity salience and shifts in quantitative performance. *Psychological Science, 10*(1), 80–83.

Shiner, M., Scourfield, J., Fincham, B., & Langer, S. (2009). When things fall apart: Gender and suicide across the life-course. *Social Science & Medicine, 69,* 738–746.

Shippy, R. A., Cantor, M. H., & Brennan, M. (2004). Social networks of aging gay men. *Journal of Men's Studies, 13,* 107–120.

Shomaker, L. B., & Furman, W. (2007). Same-sex peers' influence on young women's body image: An experimental manipulation. *Journal of Social and Clinical Psychology, 26,* 871–895.

Shupe, E. I., Cortina, L. M., Ramos, A., Fitzgerald, L. F., & Salisbury, J. (2002). The incidence and outcomes of sexual harassment among Hispanic and non-Hispanic White women: A comparison across levels of cultural affiliation. *Psychology of Women Quarterly, 26,* 298–308.

Shye, D., Mullooly, J. P., Freeborn, D. K., & Pope, C. R. (1995). Gender differences in the relationship between social network support and mortality: A longitudinal study of an elderly cohort. *Social Science & Medicine, 41*(7), 935–947.

Sibley, C. G., Overall, N. C., & Duckitt, J. (2007). When women become more hostilely sexist toward their gender: The system-justifying effect of benevolent sexism. *Sex Roles, 57,* 743–754.

Sibley, C. G., Wilson, M. S., & Duckitt, J. (2007). Antecedents of men's hostile and benevolent sexism: The dual roles of social dominance orientation and right-wing authoritarianism. *Personality and Social Psychology Bulletin, 33,* 160–172.

Siever, M. D. (1996). The perils of sexual objectification: Sexual orientation, gender, and socioculturally acquired vulnerability to body dissatisfaction and eating disorders. In C. J. Alexander (Ed.), *Gay and lesbian mental health: A sourcebook for practitioners* (pp. 223–247). New York: Harrington Park Press.

Sigal, J., Gibbs, M. S., Goodrich, C., Rashid, T., Anjum, A., Hsu, D., et al. (2005). Cross-cultural reactions to academic sexual harassment: Effects of individualist vs. Collectivist culture and gender of participants. *Sex Roles, 52,* 201–215.

Silver, M. P. (2010). Women's retirement and self-assessed well-being: An analysis of three measures of well-being among recent and long-term retirees relative to homemakers. *Women and Health, 50,* 1–19.

Silverstein, B., & Perlick, D. (1995). *The cost of competence: Why inequality causes depression, eating disorders, and illness in women.* New York: Oxford University Press.

Simms, K. B., Knight, D. M., Jr., & Dawes, K. I. (1993). Institutional factors that influence the academic success of African-American men. *Journal of Men's Studies, 1*(3), 253–266.

Simon, R. W. (1995). Gender, multiple roles, role meaning, and mental health. *Journal of Health and Social Behavior, 36,* 182–194.

Simon, R. W., & Nath, L. E. (2004). Gender and emotion in the United States: Do men and women differ in self-reports of feelings and expressive behavior? *American Journal of Sociology, 109,* 1137–1176.

Simon, T. R., Miller, S., Gorman-Smith, D., Orpinas, P., & Sullivan, T. (2010). Physical dating violence norms and behavior among sixth-grade students from four U.S. sites. *Journal of Early Adolescents, 30,* 395–409.

Simoni-Wastila, L. (1998). Gender and psychotropic drug use. *Medical Care, 36*(1), 88–94.

Simpkins, S. D., Davis-Kean, P. E., & Eccles, J. S. (2005). Parents' socializing behavior and children's participation in math, science, and computer out-of-school activities. *Applied Developmental Science, 9,* 14–30.

Simpkins, S. D., Davis-Kean, P. E., & Eccles, J. S. (2006). Math and science motivation: A longitudinal examination of the links between choices and beliefs. *Developmental Psychology, 42,* 70–3.

Singh, K., Allen, K. R., Scheckler, R., & Darlington, L. (2007). Women in computer-related majors: A critical synthesis of research and theory from 1994–2005. *Review of Educational Research, 77,* 500–533.

Singleton, R. A., & Vacca, J. (2007). Interpersonal competition in friendships. *Sex Roles, 57,* 617–627.

Skalicka, V., & Kunst, A. E. (2008). Effects of spouses' socioeconomic characteristics on mortality among men and women in a Norwegian longitudinal study. *Social Science & Medicine, 66,* 2035–2047.

Skogman, K., Alsen, M., & Ojehagen, A. (2004). Sex differences in risk factors for suicide after attempted suicide: A follow-up study of 1052 suicide attempters. *Social Psychiatry and Psychiatric Epidemiology, 39,* 113–120.

Smeby, L., Bruusgaard, D., & Claussen, B. (2009). Sickness absence: Could gender divide be explained by occupation, income, mental distress and health? *Scandinavian Journal of Public Health, 37,* 674–681.

Smith, B. W., & Zautra, A. J. (2002). The role of personality in exposure and reactivity to interpersonal stress in relation to arthritis disease activity and negative affect in women. *Health Psychology, 21,* 81–88.

Smith, C. A., & Stillman, S. (2002). What do women want? The effects of gender and sexual orientation on the desirability of physical attributes in the personal ads of women. *Sex Roles, 46,* 337–341.

Smith, T. W., Ruiz, J. M., & Uchino, B. N. (2004). Mental activation of supportive ties, hostility, and cardiovascular reactivity to laboratory stress in young men and women. *Health Psychology, 23,* 476–485.

Smithers, A., & Robinson, P. (2006, July). *The paradox of single-sex and co-educational schooling.* Paper presented at the Headmasters' and Headmistresses' Conference Centre for Education and Employment Research, University of Buckingham, Buckingham, UK.

Smith-Lovin, L., & Robinson, D. T. (1992). Gender and conversational dynamics. In C. Ridgeway (Ed.), *Gender, interaction, and inequality* (pp. 122–156). New York: Springer-Verlag.

Snyder, M. (1979). Self-monitoring processes. In L. Berkowitz (Ed.), *Advances in experimental social psychology* (Vol. 12, pp. 85–128). New York: Academic Press.

Snyder, M., Tanke, E. D., & Berscheid, E. (1977). Social perception and interpersonal behavior: On the self-fulfilling nature of social stereotypes. *Journal of Personality and Social Psychology, 35,* 656–666.

Sobieraj, S. (1998). Taking control: Toy commercials and the social construction of patriarchy. In L. H. Bowker (Ed.), *Masculinities and violence* (pp. 15–28). Thousand Oaks, CA: Sage.

Sommer, I. E. C., Aleman, A., Bouma, A., & Kahn, R. S. (2004). Do women really have more bilateral language representation than men? A meta-analysis of functional imaging studies. *Brain, 127,* 1845–1852.

Soons, J. P. M., & Kalmijn, M. (2009). Is marriage more than cohabitation? Well-being differences in 30 European countries. *Journal of Marriage and Family, 71,* 1141–1157.

Special Issue of American Psychologist. (2007). Special Issue: Eating Disorders. *62(3), 158–262.*

Spelke, E. S. (2005). Sex differences in intrinsic aptitude for mathematics and science? *American Psychologist, 60,* 950–958.

Spence, J. T., & Buckner, C. E. (2000). Instrumental and expressive traits, trait stereotypes, and sexist attitudes: What do they signify? *Psychology of Women Quarterly, 24,* 44–62.

Spence, J. T., & Helmreich, R. L. (1972). The attitudes toward women scale: An objective instrument to measure attitudes toward the rights and roles of women in contemporary society. *JSAS Catalog of Selected Documents in Psychology, 2,* 667–668.

Spence, J. T., & Sawin, L. L. (1985). Images of masculinity and femininity: A reconceptualization. In V. E. O'Leary, R. K. Unger, & B. S. Wallston (Eds.), *Women, gender, and social psychology* (pp. 35–66). Hillsdale, NJ: Lawrence Erlbaum.

Spence, J. T., Helmreich, R. L., & Holahan, C. K. (1979). Negative and positive components of psychological masculinity and femininity and their relationships to self-reports of neurotic and acting out behaviors. *Journal of Personality and Social Psychology, 37,* 1673–1682.

Spence, J. T., Helmreich, R. L., & Stapp, J. (1974). The Personal Attributes Questionnaire: A measure of sex role stereotypes and masculinity–femininity. *Journal Supplement Abstract Service Catalog of Selected Documents in Psychology, 4(43)* (Ms. No. 617).

Spencer, S. M., & Patrick, J. H. (2009). Social support and personal mastery as protective resources during emerging adulthood. *Journal of Adult Development, 16,* 191–198.

Sprecher, S. (2006). Sexuality in close relationships. In P. Noller & J. A. Feeney (Eds.), *Close relationships: Functions, forms and processes* (pp. 267–284). New York: Psychology Press.

Sprecher, S., & Felmlee, D. (1997). The balance of power in romantic heterosexual couples over time from "his" and "her" perspectives. *Sex Roles, 37,* 361–379.

Sprecher, S., & Hatfield, E. (1996). Premarital sexual standards among U.S. college students: Comparison with Russian and Japanese students. *Archives of Sexual Behavior, 25*(3), 261–288.

Sprecher, S., & Metts, S. (1989). Development of the romantic beliefs scale and examination of the effects of gender and gender-role orientation. *Journal of Social and Personal Relationships, 6,* 387–411.

Sprecher, S., Aron, A., Hatfield, E., Cortese, A., Potapova, E., & Levitskaya, A. (1994). Love: American style, Russian style, and Japanese style. *Personal Relationships, 1,* 349–369.

Sprecher, S., Harris, G., & Meyers, A. (2008). Perceptions of sources of sex education and targets of sex communication: Sociodemographic and cohort effects. *Journal of Sex Research, 45*(1), 17–26.

Sprecher, S., Regan, P. C., & McKinney, K. (1998). Beliefs about the outcomes of extramarital sexual relationships as a function of the gender of the cheating spouse. *Sex Roles, 38,* 301–311.

Sprecher, S., Schmeeckle, M., & Felmlee, D. (2006). The principle of least interest: Inequality in emotional involvement in romantic relationships. *Journal of Family Issues, 27,* 1255–1280.

Sprock, J., Crosby, J. P., & Nielsen, B. A. (2001). Effects of sex and sex roles on the perceived maladaptiveness of DSM-IV personality disorder symptoms. *Journal of Personality Disorders, 15,* 41–59.

St. John, P. D., & Montgomery, P. R. (2009). Marital status, partner satisfaction, and depressive symptoms in older men and women. *Canadian Journal of Psychiatry, 54,* 487–492.

Stack, S. (1998). Marriage, family, and loneliness: A cross-national study. *Sociological Perspectives, 41*(2), 415–432.

Stader, D. L., & Graca, T. J. (2007). Student-on-student sexual orientation harassment: Legal protections for sexual minority youth. *The Clearing House: A Journal of Educational Strategies; Issues and Ideas, 80,* 117–122.

Stahlberg, D., Braun, F., Irmen, L., & Sczesny, S. (2007). Representation of the sexes in language. In K. Fielder (Ed.), *Social communication: The sexes in language* (pp. 163–187). New York: Psychology Press.

Stangor, C., & McMillan, D. (1992). Memory for expectancy-congruent and expectancy-incongruent information: A review of the social and social developmental literatures. *Psychological Bulletin, 111,* 42–61.

Stankiewicz, J. M., & Rosselli, F. (2008). Women as sex objects and victims in print advertisements. *Sex Roles, 58,* 579–589.

Stanley, S. M., Rhoades, G. K., & Markman, H. J. (2006). Sliding versus deciding: Inertia and the premarital cohabitation effect. *Family Relations,* 499–509.

Stanley, S. M., Whitton, S. W., & Markman, H. J. (2004). Maybe I do. *Journal of Family Issues, 25,* 496–519.

Staples, R. (1995). Health among Afro-American males. In D. F. Sabo & D. F. Gordon (Eds.), *Research on men and masculinities series* (Vol. 8, pp. 121–138). Thousand Oaks, CA: Sage Publications, Inc.

Star Tribune. (2000, May 16). Sheriff releases time line of columbine shooting: The report from the 13-month investigation seems to counter claims that police officers could have saved lives had they acted more quickly. *Star Tribune,* Minneapolis, MN, 06A.

State of Hawaii. (1998). *The Hawaii Marriage Amendment.* Retrieved May 17, 2011, from http://www.capitol. hawaii.gov/hrscurrent/Vol01_Ch0001-0042F/05-Const/CONST_0001-0023.htm

State of Washington. (1998). *RCW 26.04.020: Prohibited marriages.* Retrieved May 17, 2011, from http://apps. leg.wa.gov/rcw/default.aspx?cite=26.04.02

Stateline. (2007). *State policies on same-sex marriage.* Retrieved February 1, 2007, from www.stateline.org/live/ digitalassets/4883_social_policy.pdf

Stearns, E., Buchmann, C., & Bonneau, K. (2009). Interracial friendships in the transition to college: Do birds of a feather flock together once they leave the nest? *Sociology of Education, 82,* 173–195.

Steering Committee of the Physicians' Health Study Research Group. (1988). Preliminary report: Findings from the aspirin component of the ongoing physicians' health study. *New England Journal of Medicine, 318*(4), 262–264.

Stein, M. B., & Barrett-Connor, E. (2000). Sexual assault and physical health: Findings from a population-based study of older adults. *Psychosomatic Medicine, 62,* 838–843.

Steinberg, M. B., Akincigil, A., Delnevo, C. D., Crystal, S., & Carson, J. L. (2006). Gender and age disparities for smoking-cessation treatment. *American Journal of Preventive Medicine, 30,* 405–412.

Steinmayr, R., & Spinath, B. (2008). Sex differences in school achievement: What are the roles of personality and achievement motivation? *European Journal of Personality, 22,* 185–209.

Stephens, M. A. P., Martire, L. M., Cremeans-Smith, J. K., Druley, J. A., & Wojno, W. C. (2006). Older women with osteoarthritis and their caregiving husbands: Effects of pain and pain expression on husbands' well-being and support. *Rehabilitation Psychology, 51,* 3–12.

Stevens, D. P., Minnotte, K. L., Mannon, S. E., & Kiger, G. (2006). Family work performance and satisfaction: Gender ideology, relative resources, and emotion work. *Marriage and Family Review, 40,* 47–74.

Stevens, G., Owens, D., & Schaefer, E. C. (1990). Education and attractiveness in marriage choices. *Social Psychology Quarterly, 53*(1), 62–70.

Stewart, T. L., Berkvens, M., Engels, W. A. E. W., & Pass, J. A. (2003). Status and likability: Can the "mindful" woman have it all? *Journal of Applied Social Psychology, 33,* 2040–2059.

Stice, E., Spangler, D., & Agras, W. S. (2001). Exposure to media-portrayed thin-ideal images adversely affects vulnerable girls: A longitudinal experiment. *Journal of Social and Clinical Psychology, 20,* 270–288.

Stickney, L. T., & Konrad, A. M. (2007). Gender-role attitudes and earnings: A multinational study of married women and men. *Sex Roles, 57,* 801–811.

Stillion, J. M. (1995). Premature death among males. In D. Sabo & D. F. Gordon (Eds.), *Men's health and illness: Gender, power, and the body* (pp. 46–67). Thousand Oaks, CA: Sage.

Stockdale, M. S., & Bhattacharya, G. (2009). Sexual harassment and the glass ceiling. In M. Barreto, M. K. Ryan, & M. T. Schmitt (Eds.), *The glass ceiling in the 21st century: Understanding barriers to gender equality* (pp. 171–199). Washington, DC: American Psychological Association.

Stotzer, R. L. (2009). Violence against transgender people: A review of United States data. *Aggression and Violent Behavior, 14,* 170–179.

Straus, M. A. (2004). Prevalence of violence against dating partners by male and female university students worldwide. *Violence against Women, 10,* 790–811.

Straus, M. A., Gelles, R. J., & Steinmetz, S. K. (1980). *Behind closed doors: Violence in the American family.* Garden City, NY: Anchor Books.

Straus, M. A., Hamby, S. L., Boney-McCoy, S., & Sugarman, D. B. (1996). The revised conflict tactics scales (CTS2): Development and preliminary psychometric data. *Journal of Family Issues, 17,* 283–316.

Streigel-Moore, R. H., & Bulik, C. M. (2007). Risk factors for eating disorders. *American Psychologist, 62,* 181–198.

Streigel-Moore, R. H., Rosselli, F., Perrin, N., DeBar, L., Wilson, G. T., & May, A. (2009). Gender difference in the prevalence of eating disorder symptoms. *International Journal of Eating Disorders, 42,* 471–474.

Strober, M. H. (2002). What's a wife worth? In M. Yalom & L. L. Carstensen (Eds.), *Inside the American couple* (pp. 174–188). Berkeley, CA: University of California Press.

Stroebe, M. S., & Stroebe, W. (1983). Who suffers more? Sex differences in health risks of the widowed. *Psychological Bulletin, 93,* 279–301.

Stroebe, M. S., Schut, H., & Stroebe, W. (2007). Health outcomes of bereavement. *Lancet, 370,* 1960–1973.

Strohschein, L., McDonough, P., Monette, G., & Shao, Q. (2005). Marital transitions and mental health: Are there gender differences in the short-term effects of marital status change? *Social Science & Medicine, 61,* 2293–2303.

Stroud, L. R., Niaura, R. S., & Salovey, P. (2000, March). *Stressor type and oral contraceptive use influence males' and females' cardiovascular responses to stress.* Paper presented at the American Psychosomatic Society, Savannah, Georgia.

Stroud, L. R., Salovey, P., & Epel, E. S. (2002). Sex differences in stress responses: Social rejection versus achievement stress. *Biological Psychiatry, 52,* 318–327.

Stroud, L. R., Papandonatos, G. D., Williamson, D. E., & Dahl, R. E. (2004). Sex differences in the effects of pubertal development on responses to a corticotropin-releasing hormone challenge: The Pittsburgh psychobiologic studies. *Annals of the New York Academy of the Sciences, 1021,* 348–351.

Sturges, J. W., Sims, J. M., Omar, K., Balian, R., Angell, C., & Davenport, J. (2009). It doesn't feel good: The biggest obstacle to condom use among college students. *Behavior Therapist, 32,* 36–40.

Su, R., Rounds, J., & Armstrong, P. I. (2009). Men and things, women and people: A meta-analysis of sex differences in interests. *Psychological Bulletin, 135,* 859–884.

Subrahmanyam, K., & Greenfield, P. (2008). Online communication and adolescent relationships. *Future of Children, 18,* 119–146.

Substance Abuse and Mental Health Services Administration. (2009). *Results from the 2008 national survey on drug use and health: National findings* (Office of Applied Studies, NSDUH Series H-36, HHS Publication N0. SMA 09-4434). Rockville, MD.

Substance Abuse and Mental Health Services Administration. (2010). *Results from the 2009 national survey on drug use and health: Volume I. Summary of national findings* (Office of Applied Studies, NSDUH Series H-38A, HHS Publication No. SMA 10-4586Findings). Rockville, MD.

Suh, S. H. (2007). Too maternal and not womanly enough: Asian-American women's gender identity conflict. *Women and Therapy, 30,* 35–50.

Sullivan, O. (2004). Changing gender practices within the household: A theoretical perspective. *Gender & Society, 18,* 207–222.

Sullivan, O., & Coltrane, S. (2008). *USA: Men's changing contribution to housework and child care.* Retrieved August 10, 2010, from http://www.contemporaryfamilies. org/subtemplate.php?=briefingPapers&ext=mens housework

Summers, L. H. (2005). *Remarks at NBER conference on diversifying the science & engineering workforce.* Retrieved January 31, 2007, from www.president.harvard. edu/speeches/ 2005/nber.html

Sundaram, V., Helweg-Larsen, K., Laursen, B., & Bjerregaard, P. (2004). Physical violence, self rated health, and morbidity: Is gender significant for victimisation? *Journal of Epidemiology and Community Health, 58,* 65–70.

Survey: Befriending. (2007). *Survey: Befriending coworkers increases job productivity.* Retrieved July 7, 2010, from http://findarticles.com/p/articles/mi_qa3718/ is_20070727/ai_n19487646/

Sussman, S., Dent, C. W., Nezami, E., Stacy, A. W., Burton, D., & Flay, B. R. (1998). Reasons for quitting and smoking temptation among adolescent smokers: Gender differences. *Substance Use and Misuse, 33*(14), 2703–2720.

Suter, E. A., & Toller, P. W. (2006). Gender role and feminism revisited: A follow-up study. *Sex Roles, 55,* 135–146.

Sweeting, H. (1995). Reversals of fortune? Sex differences in health in childhood and adolescence. *Social Science & Medicine, 40*(1), 77–90.

Sweeting, H., & West, P. (2003). Sex differences in health at ages 11, 13 and 15. *Social Science & Medicine, 56,* 31–39.

Swenson, L. P., & Rose, A. J. (2009). Friends' knowledge of youth internalizing and externalizing adjustment: Accuracy, bias, and the influences of gender, grade, positive friendship quality, and self-disclosure. *Journal of Abnormal Child Psychology, 37,* 887–901.

Swim, J. K., & Sanna, L. J. (1996). He's skilled, she's lucky: A meta-analysis of observers' attributions for women's and men's successes and failures. *Personality and Social Psychology Bulletin, 22,* 507–519.

Swim, J. K., Aikin, K. J., Hall, W. S., & Hunter, B. A. (1995). Sexism and racism: Old-fashioned and modern prejudices. *Journal of Personality and Social Psychology, 68,* 199–214.

Swim, J. K., Johnston, K., & Pearson, N. B. (2009). Daily experiences with heterosexism: Relations between heterosexist hassles and psychological well-being. *Journal of Social and Clinical Psychology, 28,* 597–629.

Swim, J. K., Mallett, R., & Stangor, C. (2004). Understanding subtle sexism: Detection and use of sexist language. *Sex Roles, 51,* 117–128.

Tafoya, T. (2007). Native American culture and sex. In M. S. Tepper & A. F. Owens (Eds.), *Sexual health: Moral and cultural foundations* (pp. 203–227). Westport, CT: Praeger Publishers/Greenwood Publishing Group.

Takiff, H. A., Sanchez, D. T., & Stewart, T. L. (2001). What's in a name? The status implications of students' terms of address for male and female professors. *Psychology of Women Quarterly, 25,* 134–144.

Takkinen, S., Gold, C., Pedersen, N. L., Malmberg, B., Nilsson, S., & Rovine, M. (2004). Gender differences in depression: A study of older unlike-sex twins. *Aging & Mental Health, 8,* 187–195.

Tamres, L. K., Janicki, D., & Helgeson, V. S. (2002). Sex difference in coping behavior: A meta-analytic review. *Personality and Social Psychology Review, 6,* 2–30.

Tan, Y. Y., Gast, G.-C. M., & van der Schouw, Y. T. (2010). Gender differences in risk factors for coronary heart disease. *Maturitas, 65,* 149–160.

Tanaka, S., & Waldfogel, J. (2007). Effects of parental leave and work hours on fathers' involvement with their babies: Evidence from the millennium cohort study. *Community, Work & Family, 10*(4), 409–426.

Tangri, S. S., & Hayes, S. M. (1997). Theories of sexual harassment. In W. O'Donohue (Ed.), *Sexual harassment: Theory, research, and treatment* (pp. 112–128). Needham Heights, MA: Allyn & Bacon.

Tannen, D. (1990). *You just don't understand: Women and men in conversation.* New York: William Morrow.

Taylor, P., Cohn, D. V., Livingston, G., Wang, W., & Dockterman, D. (2010). *The new demography of American motherhood.* Retrieved August 16, 2010, from http://pewsocialtrends.org

Taylor, P., Funk, C., & Clark, A. (2007). *Generation gap in values, behaviors: As marriage and parenthood drift apart, public is concerned about social impact.* Retrieved August 16, 2010, from http://pewresearch.org

Taylor, S. E., Gonzaga, G. C., Klein, L. C., Hu, P., Greendale, G. A., & Seeman, T. E. (2006). Relation of oxytocin to psychological stress responses and hypothalamic-pituitary-adrenocortical axis activity in older women. *Psychosomatic Medicine, 68,* 238–245.

Taylor, S. E., Klein, L. C., Lewis, B. P., Gruenewald, T. L., Gurung, R. A. R., & Updegraff, J. A. (2000). Biobehavioral responses to stress in females: Tend-and-befriend, not fight-or-flight. *Psychological Review, 107,* 411–429.

Taylor, S. E., Saphire-Bernstein, S., & Seeman, T. E. (2010). Are plasma oxytocin in women and plasma vasopressin in men biomarkers of distressed pair-bond relationships? *Psychological Science, 21,* 3–7.

Teixeira, R. (2009). The coming end of the culture wars. *Center for American Progress.* Retrieved September 30, 2010, from http://www.americanprogress.org

Tenenbaum, H. R., & Leaper, C. (2002). Are parents' gender schemas related to their children's gender-related cognitions? A meta-analysis. *Developmental Psychology, 38,* 615–630.

Tenenbaum, H. R., & Leaper, C. (2003). Parent-child conversations about science: The socialization of gender inequities? *Developmental Psychology, 39,* 34–47.

Terburg, D., Morgan, B., & van Honk, J. (2009). The testosterone-cortisol ratio: A hormonal marker for proneness to social aggression. *International Journal of Law and Psychiatry, 32,* 216–223.

Terman, L. M., & Miles, C. C. (1936). *Sex and personality: Studies in masculinity and femininity.* New York: McGraw-Hill.

Terrell, H. K., Hill, E. D., & Nagoshi, C. T. (2008). Gender differences in aggression: The role of status and personality in competitive interactions. *Sex Roles, 59,* 814–826.

Tevlin, J. (1998). The Eveleth Mines case. *Star Tribune.* Retrieved August 8, 2007, from web.lexis-nexis.com/universe/docu

Tharinger, D. J. (2008). Maintaining the hegemonic masculinity through selective attachment, homophobia, and gay-baiting in schools: Challenges to intervention. *School Psychology Review, 37*(2), 221–227.

The worldwide. (2010). The worldwide war on baby girls. *Economist.* Retrieved May 11, 2010, from http://www.economist.com/world/international/displaystory.cfm?tory_id=15636231

Thoman, D. B., White, P. H., Yamawaki, N., & Koishi, H. (2008). Variations of gender-math stereotype content affect women's vulnerability to stereotype threat. *Sex Roles, 58,* 702–712.

Thomas, J. J., & Daubman, K. A. (2001). The relationship between friendship quality and self-esteem in adolescent girls and boys. *Sex Roles, 45,* 53–65.

Thomas-Hunt, M. C., & Phillips, K. W. (2004). When what you know is not enough: Expertise and gender dynamics in task groups. *Personality and Social Psychology Bulletin, 30,* 1585–1598.

Thompson, C. A., Klopf, D. W., & Ishii, S. (1991). A comparison of social style between Japanese and Americans. *Communication Research Reports, 8,* 165–172.

Thomson, J. W., Patel, S., Platek, S. M., & Shackelford, T. K. (2007). Sex differences in implicit association and attentional demands for information about infidelity. *Evolutionary Psychology, 5,* 569–583.

Thomson, R., Murachver, T., & Green, J. (2001). Where is the gender in gendered language? *Psychological Science, 12,* 171–175.

Thornton, A., & Young-DeMarco, L. (2001). Four decades of trends in attitudes toward family issues in the United States: The 1960s through the 1990s. *Journal of Marriage and Family, 63,* 1009–1037.

Thorsteinsson, E. B., & James, J. E. (1999). A meta-analysis of the effects of experimental manipulations of social support during laboratory stress. *Psychology and Health, 14,* 869–886.

Thunberg, M., & Dimberg, U. (2000). Gender differences in facial reactions to fear-relevant stimuli. *Journal of Nonverbal Behavior, 24,* 45–51.

Tiger, L. (1969). *Men in groups.* New York: Random House.

Time. (1973, January 8). Biological imperatives, p. 34.

Timmers, M., Fischer, A. H., & Manstead, A. S. R. (1998). Gender differences in motives for regulating emotions. *Personality and Social Psychology Bulletin, 24*(9), 974–985.

Titus-Ernstoff, L., Perez, K., Hatch, E. E., Troisi, R., Palmer, J. R., & Hartge, P. (2003). Psychosexual characteristics of men and women exposed prenatally to diethylstilbestrol. *Epidemiology, 14,* 155–160.

Tjaden, P., & Thoennes, N. (2000). *Extent, nature, and consequences of intimate partner violence: Findings from the national violence against women survey.* Retrieved November 12, 2007, from www.ojp.usdoj.gov/nij

Toker, S., Shirom, A., & Melamed, S. (2008). Depression and the metabolic syndrome: Gender-dependent associations. *Depression and Anxiety, 25,* 661–669.

Tolin, D. F., & Foa, E. B. (2006). Sex differences in trauma and posttraumatic stress disorder: A quantitative review of 25 years of research. *Psychological Bulletin, 132,* 959–992.

Tolman, D. L., Kim, J. L., Schooler, D., & Sorsoli, L. (2007). Rethinking the associations between television viewing and adolescent sexuality development: Bringing gender into focus. *Journal of Adolescent Health, 40,* 84.e89–84.e16.

Toro-Morn, M., & Sprecher, S. (2003). A cross-cultural comparison of mate preferences among university students: The United States vs. the People's Republic of China (PRC). *Journal of Comparative Family Studies, 34,* 151–170.

Torsheim, T., Ravens-Sieberer, U., Hetland, J., Valimaa, R., Danielson, M., & Overpeck, M. (2006). Cross-national variation of gender differences in adolescent subjective health in Europe and North America. *Social Science & Medicine, 62,* 815–827.

Toys "R" Us scolded. (2009). *Toys "R" Us scolded for gender discrimination.* Retrieved June 3, 2010, from http://www.thelocal.se/22504/20091006

Trautner, H. M., Ruble, D. N., Cyphers, L., Kirsten, B., Behrendt, R., & Hartmann, P. (2005). Rigidity and flexibility of gender stereotypes in childhood: Developmental or differential? *Infant and Child Development, 14,* 365–381.

Travis, C. B. (2005). 2004 Carolyn Sherif award address: Heart disease and gender inequity. *Psychology of Women Quarterly, 29,* 15–23.

Treiber, F. A., Kamarck, T., Schneiderman, N., Sheffield, D., Kapuku, G., & Taylor, T. (2003). Cardiovascular reactivity and development of preclinical and clinical disease states. *Psychosomatic Medicine, 65,* 46–62.

Trenholm, C., Devaney, B., Fortson, K., Clark, M., Quay, L., & Wheeler, J. (2008). Impacts of abstinence education on teen sexual activity, risk of pregnancy, and risk of sexually transmitted diseases. *Journal of Policy Analysis and Management, 27,* 255–276.

Trenholm, C., Devaney, B., Fortson, K., Quay, L., Wheeler, J., & Clark, M. (2007). *Impacts of four title V, section 510 abstinence education programs.* Retrieved June 7, 2007, from aspe.hhs.gov/hsp/abstinence07/

Treynor, W., Gonzalez, R., & Nolen-Hoeksema, S. (2003). Rumination reconsidered: A psychometric analysis. *Cognitive Therapy and Research, 27,* 247–259.

Tsang, A., Von Korff, M., Lee, S., Alonso, J., Karam, E., & Angermeyer, M. C. (2008). Common chronic pain conditions in developed and developing countries: Gender and age differences and comorbidity with depression-anxiety disorders. *Journal of Pain, 9,* 883–891.

Tschann, J. M., Flores, E., de Groat, C. L., Deardorff, J., & Wibbelsman, C. J. (2010). Condom negotiation strategies and actual condom use among Latino youth. *Journal of Adolescent Health, 47*(3), 254–262.

Tuchman, E. (2010). Women and addiction: The importance of gender issues in substance abuse research. *Journal of Addictive Diseases, 29,* 127–138.

Turner, T., & with Loder, K. (1986). *I, Tina: My life story.* New York: Morrow.

Twenge, J. M. (1997). Attitudes toward women, 1970–1995. *Psychology of Women Quarterly, 21,* 35–51.

Twenge, J. M., & Campbell, W. K. (2001). Age and birth cohort differences in self-esteem: A cross-temporal meta-analysis. *Personality and Social Psychology Review, 5,* 321–344.

Twenge, J. M., & Crocker, J. (2002). Race and self-esteem: Meta-analyses comparing Whites, Blacks, Hispanics, Asians, and American Indians and comment on Gray-Little and Hafdahl (2000). *Psychological Bulletin, 128,* 371–408.

Twenge, J. M., & Nolen-Hoeksema, S. (2002). Age, gender, race, socioeconomic status, and birth cohort differences on the children's depression inventory: A meta-analysis. *Journal of Abnormal Psychology, 11,* 578–588.

Twenge, J. M., Campbell, W. K., & Foster, C. A. (2003). Parenthood and marital satisfaction: A meta-analytic review. *Journal of Marriage and Family, 65,* 574–583.

Tyrka, A. R., Waldron, I., Graber, J. A., & Brooks-Gunn, J. (2002). Prospective predictors of the onset of anorexic and bulimic syndromes. *International Journal of Eating Disorders, 32,* 282–290.

U.S. Bureau of Labor Statistics. (2010). *Labor force statistics from the current population survey.* Retrieved August 24, 2010, from http://www.bls.gov/cps/tables.html

U.S. Census Bureau. (1991). *Current population reports, series P-70, no.23, family division and economic hardship: The short-run picture for children.* Washington, DC: U.S. Government Printing Office.

U.S. Census Bureau. (2004). *Unmarried-partner households by sex of partners: 2004.* Retrieved February 21, 2007, from www.census.gov/prod/2006pubs/07status/pop.pdf

U.S. Census Bureau. (2005). *Number, timing, and duration of marriages and divorces: 2001* (Current population reports (P70-97)). Retrieved November 12, 2007, from www.sipp.census.gov/sipp/

U.S. Census Bureau. (2007a). *Participation in NCAA sports: 2004 to 2005.* Retrieved November 12, 2007, from www.census.gov/compendia/statab/2007edition.html

U.S. Census Bureau. (2007b). *Marital history for people 15 years and over, by age and sex: 2004.* Retrieved September 30, 2010, from www.census.gov/population/socdemo/marital-hist/2004/Table3.2004.xls

U.S. Census Bureau. (2008). *Fertility of American women: 2006.* Retrieved August 19, 2010, from www.census.gov/prod/2008pubs/p20-558.pdf

U.S. Census Bureau. (2009a). *Current population reports, p20-537 and earlier reports; and families and living arrangements.* Retrieved September 30, 2010, from http://www.census.gov/population/www/socdemo/hh-fam.html

U.S. Census Bureau. (2009b). *Parents and children in stay-at-home parent family groups: 1994 to present.* Retrieved August 25, 2010, from http://www.census.gov/population/socdemo/hh-fam/shp1.xls

U.S. Census Bureau. (2010a). *Current population survey, March and annual social and economic supplements, 2006 and earlier. Estimated median age at first marriage, by sex: 1980 to the present.* Retrieved August 12, 2010, from http://www.census.gov/population/socdemo/hh-fam/ms2.csv

U.S. Census Bureau. (2010b). *Marital status of people 15 years and over, by age, sex, personal earnings, race, and Hispanic origin, 2009.* Retrieved September 30, 2010, from www.census.gov/population/www/socdemo/marr-div.html

U.S. Census Bureau. (2010c). *Living arrangements of children under 18 years and marital status of parents by age, sex, race, and Hispanic origin and selected characteristics of the child for all children.* Retrieved August 12, 2010, from http://www.census.gov/populations/www/socdemo/hh-fam/cps2009.html

U.S. Department of Health and Human Services. (2004). *The health consequences of smoking: A report of the surgeon general.* Atlanta, GA: Department of Health and Human Services.

U.S. Department of Health and Human Services. (2005). *Middle school youth risk behavior survey 2003.* Retrieved

November 12, 2007, from www.cdc.gov/HealthyYouth/yrbs/middleschool2003/pdf/fullreport.pdf

U.S. Department of Health and Human Services. (2009a). *Deaths: Preliminary data for 2007.* Retrieved July 27, 2010, from www.cdc.gov/nchs/data/nvsr/nvsr58/nvsr58_01.pdf

U.S. Department of Health and Human Services. (2009b). *Who may adopt, be adopted, or place a child for adoption? Summary of state laws.* Retrieved August 12, 2010, from http://www.childwelfare.gov/systemwide/laws_policies/statutes/partiesall.pdf

U.S. Department of Health and Human Services. (2010). Use of contraception in the United States: 1982–2008. *Vital and Health Statistics, 23*(29). Retrieved June 6, 2011, from http://www.cdc.gov/nchs/data/series/sr_23/sr23_029.pdf

U.S. Department of Justice. (2008). *Hate crime statistics.* Retrieved 5 7, 2010, from http://www.fbi.gov/ucr/hc2008/data/table_01.html

U.S. Department of Justice. (2009). *Ten-year arrest trends by sex, 1999–2008.* Retrieved July 19, 2010, from http://www.fbi.gov/ucr/cius2008/data/table_33.html

U.S. Department of Justice Federal Bureau of Investigation. (2009). *Crime in the United States, 2008.* Retrieved July 26, 2010, from http://www.fbi.gov/ucr/cius2008/about/index.html

U.S. Department of Labor. (2009a). *Volunteering in the United States, 2009.* Retrieved June 30, 2010, from http://www.bls.gov/news.release/volun.nr0.htm

U.S. Department of Labor. (2009b). *Women in the labor force: A databook.* Retrieved August 17, 2010, from www.bls.gov/cps/wlf-databook2009.htm

U.S. Department of Labor. (2009c). *Work experience of the population by sex and full- and part-time status, selected years, 1970–2007.* Retrieved August 26, 2010, from http://www.bls.gov/cps/eetech_methods.pdf

U.S. Department of Labor. (2010a). *Hours worked and fatal work injuries, by gender of worker, 2008.* Retrieved September 23, 2010, from http://www.bls.gov/iif/oshcfoi1.htm

U.S. Department of Labor. (2010b). *Employment status of civilian noninstitutional population by age, sex, and race.* Retrieved August 26, 2010, from http://www.bls.gov/cps/cps_over.htm

U.S. Department of Labor. (2010c). *Highlights of women's earnings in 2009.* Retrieved August 17, 2010, from www.bls.gov/cps/cpswom2009.pdf

U.S. Department of Labor. (2010d). *Persons at work in nonagricultural industries by age, sex, race, Hispanic or Latino ethnicity, marital status, and usual full- or part-time status.* Retrieved August 26, 2010, from http://www.bls.gov/cps/cps_over.htm

U.S. Department of Transportation. (2008a). *Alcohol-impaired driving.* Retrieved July 26, 2010, from http://www-nrd.nhtsa.dot.gov/Pubs/811155.PDF

U.S. Department of Transportation. (2008b). *Comparison of crash fatalities by sex and age group.* Retrieved September 23, 2010, from http://www-nrd.nhtsa.dot.gov/Pubs/810853.PDF

U.S. Department of Transportation. (2008c). *Seat belt use in 2007—Demographic results.* Retrieved September 22, 2010, from www-nrd.nhtsa.dot.gov/pubs/810932.pdf

U.S. Department of Transportation. (2009). *Alcohol-impaired drivers involved in fatal crashes, by gender and state, 2007–2008.* Retrieved July 26, 2010, from http://www.nhtsa.gov/DOT/NHTSA/reports/811095.pdf

U.S. Equal Employment Opportunity Commission. (1980). Guidelines on discrimination because of sex (sec. 1604.11). *Federal Register, 45,* 74676–74677.

U.S. Equal Employment Opportunity Commission. (2010). *Sexual harassment charges EEOC & FEPAs combined: FY 1997– FY 2009.* Retrieved August 16, 2010, from http://www.eeoc.gov/eeoc/statistics/enforcement/sexual_harassment.cfm

U.S. Open 2009. (2009). U.S. Open 2009: Serena Williams unrepentant for rant after Kim Clijsters defeat. *Telegraph.* Retrieved June 7, 2010, from http://www.telegraph.co.uk/sport/tennis/usopen/6182175/US-Open-20

Ueno, K., Gayman, M. D., Wright, E. R., & Quantz, S. D. (2009). Friends' sexual orientation, relational quality, and mental health among gay, lesbian, and bisexual youth. *Personal Relationships, 16,* 659–670.

Ullman, S. E. (1997). Review and critique of empirical studies of rape avoidance. *Criminal Justice and Behavior, 24*(2), 177–204.

Ullman, S. E. (2010). *Talking about sexual assault: Society's response to survivors.* Washington, DC: American Psychological Association.

Ullman, S. E., Karabatsos, G., & Koss, M. P. (1999). Alcohol and sexual assault in a national sample of college women. *Journal of Interpersonal Violence, 14*(6), 603–625.

Umberson, D., & Williams, K. (2005). Marital quality, health, and aging: Gender equity? *Journals of Gerontology, 60B,* 109–112.

Umberson, D., Liu, H., & Powers, D. (2009). Marital status, marital transitions, and body weight. *Journal of Health and Social Behavior, 50,* 327–343.

Umberson, D., Williams, K., Powers, D. A., Liu, H., & Needham, B. (2006). You make me sick: Marital quality and health over the life course. *Journal of Health and Social Behavior, 47,* 1–16.

Underwood, M. K. (2003). *Social aggression among girls.* New York: Guilford Press.

Underwood, M. K., & Buhrmester, D. (2007). Friendship features and social exclusion: An observational study examining gender and social context. *Merrill-Palmer Quarterly, 53,* 412–438.

Usher-Seriki, K. K., Bynum, M. S., & Callands, T. A. (2008). Mother-daughter communication about sex and sexual intercourse among middle to upper class African American girls. *Journal of Family Issues, 29,* 901–917.

Vaananen, A., Buunk, B. P., Kivimaki, M., Pentti, J., & Vahtera, J. (2005). When it is better to give than to receive: Long-term health effects of perceived reciprocity in support exchange. *Journal of Personality and Social Psychology, 89,* 176–193.

Valian, V. (1998). *Why so slow? The advancement of women.* Cambridge, MA: MIT Press.

van den Berg, P., Neumark-Sztainer, D., Hannan, P. J., & Haines, J. (2007). Is dieting advice from magazines helpful or harmful? Five-year associations with weight-control behaviors and psychological outcomes in adolescents. *Pediatrics, 119,* e30–e37.

van Emmerik, I. H. (2006). Gender differences in the creation of different types of social capital: A multilevel study. *Social Networks, 28,* 24–37.

van Engen, M. L., & Willemsen, T. M. (2004). Sex and leadership styles: A meta-analysis of research published in the 1990's. *Psychological Reports, 94,* 3–18.

van Grootheest, D. S., Beekman, A. T. F., van Groenou, M. I. B., & Deeg, D. J. H. (1999). Sex differences in depression after widowhood: Do men suffer more? *Social Psychiatry and Psychiatric Epidemiology, 34,* 391–398.

van Middendorp, H., Geenen, R., Sorbi, M. J., Hox, J. J., Vingerhoets, A. J. J. M., & Doornen, L. J. P. (2005). Gender differences in emotion regulation and relationships with perceived health in patients with rheumatoid arthritis. *Women & Health, 42,* 75–97.

van Solinge, H. (2007). Health change in retirement: A longitudinal study among older workers in the Netherlands. *Research on Aging, 29,* 225–256.

Vekiri, I., & Chronaki, A. (2008). Gender issues in technology use: Perceived social support, computer self-efficacy and value beliefs, and computer use beyond school. *Computers and Education, 51,* 1392–1404.

Veniegas, R. C., & Peplau, L. A. (1997). Power and the quality of same-sex friendships. *Psychology of Women Quarterly, 21,* 279–297.

Verbrugge, L. M. (1985). Gender and health: An update on hypotheses and evidence. *Journal of Health and Social Behavior, 26,* 156–182.

Verbrugge, L. M. (1989). The twain meet: Empirical explanations of sex differences in health and mortality. *Journal of Health and Social Behavior, 30,* 282–304.

Verhofstadt, L. L., Buysse, A., & Ickes, W. (2007). Social support in couples: An examination of gender differences using self-report and observational methods. *Sex Roles, 57,* 267–282.

Viki, G. T., Abrams, D., & Masser, B. (2004). Evaluating stranger and acquaintance rape: The role of benevolent sexism in perpetrator blame and recommended sentence length. *Law and Human Behavior, 28,* 295–303.

Viki, G. T., Massey, K., & Masser, B. (2005). When chivalry backfires: Benevolent sexism and attitudes toward Myra Hindley. *Legal and Criminological Psychology, 10,* 109–120.

Vitale, C., Miceli, M., & Rosano, G. M. C. (2007). Gender-specific characteristics of atherosclerosis in menopausal women: Risk factors, clinical course and strategies for prevention. *Climacteric, 10,* 16–20.

Voci, S. C., & Cramer, K. M. (2009). Gender-related traits, quality of life, and psychological adjustment among women with irritable bowel syndrome. *Quality of Life Research, 18,* 1169–1176.

Vogel, J. J., Bowers, C. A., & Vogel, D. S. (2003). Cerebral lateralization of spatial abilities: A meta-analysis. *Brain and Cognition, 52*(2), 197–204.

Vogel, D. L., Murphy, M. J., Werner-Wilson, R. J., Cutrona, C. E., & Seeman, J. (2007). Sex differences in the use of demand and withdraw behavior in marriage: Examining the social structure hypothesis. *Journal of Counseling Psychology, 54,* 165–177.

Vohs, K. D., & Baumeister, R. F. (2004). Sexual passion, intimacy, and gender. In D. J. Mashek & A. Aron (Eds.), *Handbook of closeness and intimacy* (pp. 189–199). Mahwah, NJ: Lawrence Erlbaum Associates.

Voyer, D., Postma, A., Brake, B., & Imperato-McGinley, J. (2007). Gender differences in object location memory: A meta-analysis. *Psychonomic Bulletin and Review, 14,* 23–38.

Voyer, D., Voyer, S., & Bryden, M. P. (1995). Magnitude of sex differences in spatial abilities: A meta-analysis and consideration of critical variables. *Psychological Bulletin, 117,* 250–270.

Wade, M. E. (2001). Women and salary negotiation: The costs of self-advocacy. *Psychology of Women Quarterly, 25,* 65–76.

Wade, T. J., & Pevalin, D. J. (2004). Marital transitions and mental health. *Journal of Health and Social Behavior, 45,* 155–170.

Wager, T. D., Phan, K. L., Liberzon, I., & Taylor, S. F. (2003). Valence, gender, and lateralization of functional brain anatomy in emotion: A meta-analysis of findings from neuroimaging. *Neuroimage, 19,* 513–531.

Wagner, W., Kirchler, E., Clack, F., Tekarslan, E., & Verma, J. (1990). Male dominance, role segregation, and spouses' interdependence in conflict. *Journal of Cross-Cultural Psychology, 21*(1), 48–70.

Wai, J., Lubinski, D., & Benbow, C. P. (2009). Spatial ability for STEM domains: Aligning over 50 years of cumulative psychological knowledge solidifies its importance.*Journal of Educational Psychology, 101,* 817–835.

Wainwright, J. L., & Patterson, C. J. (2008). Peer relations among adolescents with female same-sex parents. *Sex Roles, 44,* 117–126.

Wainwright, N. W. J., & Surtees, P. G. (2002). Childhood adversity, gender and depression over the life-course. *Journal of Affective Disorders, 72,* 33–44.

Waldron, I. (1995). Contributions of changing gender differences in behavior and social roles to changing gender differences in mortality. In D. Sabo (Ed.), *Men's health and illness: Gender, power, and the body* (pp. 22–45). Thousand Oaks, CA: Sage.

Waldron, I. (1997). Changing gender roles and gender differences in health behavior. In D. S. Gochman (Ed.), *Handbook of health behavior research: I. Personal and social determinants* (pp. 303–328). New York: Plenum Press.

Waldron, I. (1998). Factors determining the sex ratio at birth. In *Too young to die: Genes or gender?* (pp. 53–63). New York: United Nations.

Waldron, V. R., & DiMare, L. (1998). Gender as a culturally determined construct: Communication styles in Japan and the United States. In D. J. Canary & K. Dindia (Eds.), *Sex differences and similarities in communication* (pp. 179–201). Mahwah, NJ: Erlbaum.

Walker, R. B., & Luszcz, M. A. (2009). The health and relationship dynamics of late-life couples: A systematic review of the literature. *Ageing and Society, 29,* 455–480.

Wall Street Journal. (2008). *Even in HR, women's pay lags men's.* Retrieved November 10, 2008, from http://bx.businessweek.com/executive-compensation/even-in-hr-womens-pay-lags-mens---wsjcom/12168987941385187144-ebe38ef-4cb51092172612d58d1f5b7d6/

Walters, A. E., Stuhlmacher, A. F., & Meyer, L. L. (1998). Gender and negotiator competitiveness: A meta-analysis. *Organizational Behavior and Human Decision Processes, 76,* 1–29.

Walton, G. M., & Spencer, S. J. (2009). Latent ability: Grades and test scores systematically underestimate the intellectual ability of negatively stereotyped students. *Psychological Science, 20,* 1132–1139.

Wannan, G., & Fombonne, E. (1998). Gender differences in rates and correlates of suicidal behavior amongst child psychiatric outpatients. *Journal of Adolescence, 21,* 371–381.

Wardle, J., Haase, A. M., Steptoe, A., Nillapun, M., Jonwutiwes, K., & Bellisle, F. (2004). Gender differences in food choice: The contribution of health beliefs and dieting. *Annals of Behavioral Medicine, 27,* 107–116.

Wasserman, B. D., & Weseley, A. J. (2009). ¿Qué? Quoi? Do languages with grammatical gender promote sexist attitudes? *Sex Roles, 61*(9–10), 634–643.

Way, N., Becker, B. E., & Greene, M. L. (2006). Friendships among Black, Latino, and Asian American adolescents in an urban context. In L. Balter & C. S. Tamis-LeMonda (Eds.), *Child psychology: A handbook of contemporary issues* (pp. 415–443). New York: Psychology Press.

Weich, S., Sloggett, A., & Lewis, G. (1998). Social roles and gender difference in the prevalence of common mental disorders. *British Journal of Psychiatry, 173,* 489–493.

Weiner, B., Frieze, I. H., Kukla, A., Reed, L., Rest, & Rosenbaum, R. M. (1971). *Perceiving the causes of success and failure.* Morristown, NJ: General Learning Press.

Weiner, R. L., & Gutek, B. A. (1999). Advances in sexual harassment research, theory, and policy. *Psychology, Public Policy and Law, 5,* 507–518.

Weissman, M. M., Bland, R. C., Canino, G. J., Faravelli, C., Greenwald, S., & Hwu, H.-G. (1996). Cross-national epidemiology of major depression and bipolar disorder. *Journal of the American Medical Association, 276,* 293–299.

Weitzman, L. J. (1985). *The divorce revolution: The unexpected social and economic consequences for women and children in America.* New York: Free Press.

Wells, B. E., & Twenge, J. M. (2005). Changes in young people's sexual behavior and attitudes, 1943–1999: A cross-temporal meta-analysis. *Review of General Psychology, 9,* 249–261.

Werking, K. J. (1997a). Cross-sex friendship research as ideological practice. In S. Duck (Ed.), *Handbook of personal relationships: Theory, research, and interventions* (2nd ed., pp. 391–410). West Sussex, England: Wiley.

Werking, K. J. (1997b). *We're just good friends: Women and men in nonromantic relationships.* New York: Guilford Press.

Werner, N. E., & Crick, N. R. (1999). Relational aggression and social-psychological adjustment in a college sample. *Journal of Abnormal Psychology, 108,* 615–623.

Wester, S. R., Christianson, H. F., Vogel, D. L., & Wei, M. (2007). Gender role conflict and psychological distress: The role of social support. *Psychology of Men and Masculinity, 8,* 215–224.

Westerlund, H., Kivimaki, M., Singh-Manoux, A., Melchior, M., Ferrie, J. E., & Pentti, J. (2009). Self-rated health before and after retirement in France (GAZEL): A cohort study. *Lancet, 374,* 1889–1896.

Wetter, D. W., Fiore, M. C., Young, T. B., McClure, J. B., de Moor, C. A., & Baker, T. B. (1999). Gender differences in response to nicotine replacement therapy: Objective and subjective indexes of tobacco withdrawal. *Experimental and Clinical Psychopharmacology, 7*(2), 135–144.

Wetzel, P. J. (1988). Are powerless communication strategies the Japanese norm? *Language and Society, 17,* 555–564.

Wheeler, L., Reis, H., & Nezlek, J. (1983). Loneliness, social interaction, and sex roles. *Journal of Personality and Social Psychology, 45*, 943–953.

Whisman, M. A., & Uebelacker, L. A. (2006). Impairment and distress associated with relationship discord in a national sample of married or cohabiting adults. *Journal of Family Psychology, 20*, 369–377.

Whisman, M. A., Weinstock, L. M., & Tolejko, N. (2006). Marriage and depression. In C. L. Keyes & S. H. Goodman (Eds.), *Women and depression: A handbook for the social, behavioral, and biomedical sciences* (pp. 219–240). New York: Cambridge University Press.

Whitacre, C. C., Reingold, S. C., O'Looney, P. A., & the Task Force on Gender, M. S. A. A. (1999). Biomedicine: A gender gap in autoimmunity. *Science, 283*, 1277–1278.

Whitbeck, L. B., Yu, M., McChargue, D. E., & Crawford, D. M. (2009). Depressive symptoms, gender, and growth in cigarette smoking among indigenous adolescents. *Addictive Behaviors, 34*, 421–426.

White, J. B., & Athavaley, A. (2010). Do girls speed more than boys? Survey says girls drive more aggressively; insurers up rates. *Wall Street Journal*. Retrieved June 15, 2010, from http://online.wsj.com/article/SB10001424052748704866204575224110235731780.html

Whitehead, B. D., & Popenoe, D. (2001, June 27). Singles seek soul mates for marriage. *Gallup News Service*. Retrieved June 6, 2011, from http://www.gallup.com/poll/4552/singles-seek-soul-mates-marriage.aspx.

Whiting, B. B., & Edwards, C. P. (1988). *Children of different worlds*. Cambridge, MA: Harvard University Press.

Whitley, B. E., Jr. (2001). Gender-role variables and attitudes toward homosexuality. *Sex Roles, 45*, 691–721.

Whitley, J., B. E., & Egisdottir, S. (2000). The gender belief system, authoritarianism, social dominance orientation, and heterosexuals' attitudes toward lesbians and gay men. *Sex Roles, (42)*, 947–967.

Wichers, M., Myin-Germeys, I., Jacobs, N., Peeters, F., Kenis, G., & Derom, C. (2007). Genetic risk of depression and stress-induced negative affect in daily life. *British Journal of Psychiatry, 191*, 218–223.

Wiener, R. L., & Gutek, B. A. (1999). Advances in sexual harassment research, theory, and policy. *Psychology, Public Policy and Law, 5*(3), 507–518.

Wienke, C., & Hill, G. J. (2009). Does the "marriage benefit" extend to partners in gay and lesbian relationships? *Journal of Family Issues, 30*, 259–289.

Wigfield, A., & Eccles, J. S. (2002). The development of competence beliefs, expectancies for success, and achievement values from childhood through adolescence. In A. Wigfield & J. S. Eccles (Eds.), *Development of achievement motivation* (pp. 91–120). San Diego, CA: Academic Press.

Wilcox, S., Aragaki, A., Mouton, C. P., Evenson, K. R., Wassertheil-Smoller, S., & Loevinger, B. L. (2003). The effects of widowhood on physical and mental health, health behaviors, and health outcomes: The women's health initiative. *Health Psychology, 22*, 513–522.

Williams, B. R., Sawyer, P., Roseman, J. M., & Allman, R. M. (2008). Marital status and health: Exploring pre-widowhood. *Journal of Palliative Medicine, 11*, 848–856.

Williams, C. (2000). Doing health, doing gender: Teenagers, diabetes and asthma. *Social Science & Medicine, 50*, 387–396.

Williams, C. L. (1998). The glass escalator: Hidden advantages for men in the female professions. In M. S. Kimmel & M. A. Messner (Eds.), *Men's lives* (pp. 285–299). Boston, MA: Allyn & Bacon.

Williams, D. R. (2003). The health of men: Structured inequalities and opportunities. *American Journal of Public Health, 93*, 724–731.

Williams, J. (1999). *Unbending gender: Why family and work conflict and what to do about it*. New York: Oxford University Press.

Williams, K., & Umberson, D. (2004). Marital status, marital transitions, and health: A gendered life course perspective. *Journal of Health and Social Behavior, 45*, 81–98.

Williams, M. J., Paluck, E. L., & Spencer-Rodgers, J. (2010). The masculinity of money: Automatic stereotypes predict gender differences in estimated salaries. *Psychology of Women Quarterly, 34*, 7–20.

Williams, S. L., & Frieze, I. H. (2005). Patterns of violent relationships, psychological distress, and marital satisfaction in a national sample of men and women. *Sex Roles, 52*, 771–784.

Williams, S. P., Gardos, P. S., Ortiz-Torres, B., Tross, S., & Ehrhardt, A. A. (2001). Urban women's negotiation strategies for safer sex with their male partners. *Women & Health, 33*, 133–148.

Williams, W. L. (1993). Persistence and change in the Berdache tradition among contemporary Lakota Indians. In L. D. Garnets & D. C. Kimmel (Eds.), *Psychological perspectives on lesbian and gay male experiences* (pp. 339–347). New York: Columbia University Press.

Williamson, B. F. (1985, October 13). Victims of reform. *New York Times*. Sunday, Late City Final Edition. Retrieved May 21, 2007, from web.lexis-nexis.com/universe/printdoc

Wilsnack, R. W., Vogeltanz, N. D., Wilsnack, S. C., & Harris, T. R. (2000). Gender differences in alcohol consumption and adverse drinking consequences: Cross-cultural patterns. *Addiction, 95*(2), 251–265.

Wilson, D. K., & Ampey-Thornhill, G. (2001). The role of gender and family support on dietary compliance in an African American adolescent hypertension prevention study. *Annals of Behavioral Medicine, 23*, 59–67.

Wilson, D. K., Kliewer, W., Bayer, L., Jones, D., Welleford, A., & Heiney, M. (1999). The influence of gender and emotional versus instrumental support on cardiovascular reactivity in African-American adolescents. *Annals of Behavioral Medicine, 21,* 235–243.

Wilson, G. T., Grilo, C. M., & Vitousek, K. M. (2007). Psychological treatment of eating disorders. *American Psychologist, 62*(3), 199–216.

Wilson, S. E. (2002). The health capital of families: An investigation of the inter-spousal correlation in health status. *Social Science & Medicine, 55,* 1157–1172.

Wing, R. R., & Klem, M. L. (1997). Obesity. In S. J. Gallant, G. P. Keita, & R. Royak-Schaler (Eds.), *Health care for women: Psychological, social, and behavioral influences* (pp. 115–131). Washington, DC: American Psychological Association.

Winslow-Bowe, S. (2009). Husbands' and wives' relative earnings: Exploring variation by race, human capital, labor supply, and life stage. *Journal of Family Issues, 30*(10), 1405–1432.

Winstead, B., & Sanchez, J. (2005). Gender and psychopathology. In J. E. Maddux & B. A. Winstead (Eds.), *Psychopathology: Foundations for a contemporary understanding* (pp. 39–61). Mahwah, NJ: Lawrence Erlbaum Associates.

Wissink, I. B., Dekovic, M., & Meijer, A. M. (2009). Adolescent friendship relations and developmental outcomes. *Journal of Early Adolescence, 29,* 405–425.

Women and Girls Foundation. (2006). *The girlcott story.* Retrieved January 23, 2007, from www.girl12girlgrants.com/girlsOurVoices/girlcott.htm

Woo, M., & Oei, T. P. S. (2006). The MMPI-2 gender-masculine and gender-feminine scales: Gender roles as predictors of psychological health in clinical patients. *International Journal of Psychology, 41,* 413–422.

Wood, W., & Eagly, A. H. (2002). A cross-cultural analysis of the behavior of women and men: Implications for the origins of sex differences. *Psychological Bulletin, 128,* 699–727.

Wood, W., & Eagly, A. H. (2009). Gender identity. In M. R. Leary & R. H. Hoyle (Eds.), *Handbook of individual differences in social behavior* (pp. 109–125). New York: Guilford Press.

Wood, W., & Rhodes, N. (1992). Sex differences in interaction style in task groups. In C. L. Ridgeway (Ed.), *Gender, interaction, and inequality* (pp. 97–121). New York: Springer-Verlag.

Woodhams, C., Lupton, B., & Xian, H. (2009). The persistence of gender discrimination in China: Evidence from recruitment advertisements. *International Journal of Human Resource Management, 20,* 2084–2109.

Woodside, D. B., Garfinkel, P. E., Lin, E., Goering, P., Kaplan, A. S., & Goldbloom, D. S. (2001). Comparisons of men with full or partial eating disorders, men without eating disorders, and women with eating disorders in the community. *American Journal of Psychiatry, 158,* 570–574.

Woodzicka, J. A. (2008). Sex differences in self-awareness of smiling during a mock job interview. *Journal of Nonverbal Behavior, 32,* 109–121.

Woodzicka, J. A., & LaFrance, M. (2001). Real versus imagined gender harassment. *Journal of Social Issues, 57,* 15–30.

Woodzicka, J. A., & LaFrance, M. (2005). The effects of subtle sexual harassment on women's performance in a job interview. *Sex Roles, 53,* 67–77.

Woolf, S. E., & Maisto, S. A. (2008). Gender differences in condom use behavior? The role of power and partner-type. *Sex Roles, 58,* 689–701.

World Factbook. (2010). *Field listing: Life expectancy at birth.* Retrieved July 7, 2010, from https://www.cia.gov/library/publications/the-world-factbook/fields/2102.html

World Health Organization. (2010a). *Suicide rates per 100,000 by country, year and sex.* Retrieved August 3, 2010, from http://www.who.int/mental_health/prevention/suicide_rates/en/index.html

World Health Organization. (2010b). *Evolution of global suicide rates 1950–2000 (per 100,000).* Retrieved August 31, 2010, from http://www.who.int/mental_health/prevention/suicide/evolution/en/index.html

Wright, D. E. (1999). *Personal relationships: An interdisciplinary approach.* Mountain View, CA: Mayfield.

Wright, P. H. (2006). Toward an expanded orientation to the comparative study of women's and men's same-sex friendships. In K. Dindia & D. J. Canary (Eds.), *Sex differences and similarities in communication* (2nd ed., pp. 37–57). Mahwah, NJ: Lawrence Erlbaum Associates Publishers.

Wright, P. H., & Scanlon, M. B. (1991). Gender role orientation and friendship: Some attenuation, but gender differences abound. *Sex Roles, 24,* 551–566.

Wright, R. A., Murray, J. B., Storey, P. L., & Williams, B. J. (1997). Ability analysis of gender relevance and sex differences in cardiovascular response to behavioral challenge. *Journal of Personality and Social Psychology, 73,* 405–417.

Writing Group for the Women's Health Initiative Investigators. (2002). Risks and benefits of estrogen plus progestin in healthy postmenopausal women: Principal results from the women's health initiative randomized controlled trial. *Journal of the American Medical Association, 288,* 321–333.

Wyke, S., Hunt, K., & Ford, G. (1998). Gender differences in consulting a general practitioner for common symptoms of minor illness. *Social Science & Medicine, 46*(7), 901–906.

Xu, J., Azizian, A., Monterosso, J., Domier, C. P., Brody, A. L., & London, E. D. (2008). Gender effects on mood and cigarette craving during early abstinence and resumption of smoking. *Nicotine and Tobacco Research, 10,* 1653–1661.

Xu, J., Kochanek, K. D., Murphy, S. L., & Tejada-Vera, B. (2010). Deaths: Final data for 2007. *National Vital Statistics Reports, 58*(19). Retrieved June 6, 2011, from http://www.cdc.gov/nchs/data/nvsr/nvsr58/nvsr58_01.pdf

Xu, X., Hudspeth, C. D., & Bartkowski, J. P. (2006). The role of cohabitation in remarriage. *Journal of Marriage and Family, 68,* 261–274.

Yee, J. L., & Schulz, R. (2000). Gender differences in psychiatric morbidity among family caregivers: A review and analysis. *Gerontologist, 40*(2), 147–164.

Yeh, S.-C. J., Huang, C.-H., Chou, H.-C., & Wan, T. T. H. (2009). Gender differences in stress and coping among elderly patients on hemodialysis. *Sex Roles, 60,* 44–56.

Young, M. (2009). Federal involvement in abstinence-only education: Has the buck been passed too far? In E. Schroeder & J. Kuriansky (Eds.), *Sexuality education: Past, present, and future, vol 1: History and foundations* (pp. 136–149). Westport, CT: Praeger Publishers/Greenwood Publishing Group.

Yu, L., & Xie, D. (2008). The relationship between desirable and undesirable gender role traits, and their implications for psychological well-being in Chinese culture. *Personality and Individual Differences, 44,* 1517–1527.

Yu, L., & Xie, D. (2010). Multidimensional gender identity and psychological adjustment in middle childhood: A study in China. *Sex Roles, 62,* 100–113.

Zahn-Waxler, C., & Polanichka, N. (2004). All things interpersonal. In M. Putallaz & K. L. Bierman (Eds.), *Aggression, antisocial behavior, and violence among girls: A developmental perspective* (pp. 48–70). New York: Guilford Publications.

Zajacova, A., & Hummer, R. A. (2009). Gender differences in education effects on all-cause mortality for White and Black adults in the United States. *Social Science and Medicine, 69,* 529–537.

Zak, P. J., Kurzban, R., Ahmadi, S., Swerdloff, R. S., Park, J., & Efremidze, L. (2009). Testosterone administration decreases generosity in the ultimatum game. *PLoS ONE, 4,* e8330.

Zak, P. J., Stanton, A. A., & Ahmadi, S. (2007). Oxytocin increases generosity in humans. *PLoS ONE, 2*(11), e1128.

Zemore, S. E., Fiske, S. T., & Kim, H.-J. (2000). Gender stereotypes and the dynamics of social interaction. In T. Eckes & Trautner H. M (Eds.), *The developmental social psychology of gender* (pp. 207–241). Mahwah, NJ: Erlbaum.

Zhang, Q., & Wang, Y. (2004). Socioeconomic inequality of obesity in the United States: Do gender, age, and ethnicity matter? *Social Science & Medicine, 58,* 1171–1180.

Zimmer-Gembeck, M. J., & Helfand, M. (2008). Ten years of longitudinal research on U.S. adolescent sexual behavior: Developmental correlates of sexual intercourse, and the importance of age, gender and ethnic background. *Developmental Review, 28,* 153–224.

Zlotnick, C., Rothschild, L., & Zimmerman, M. (2002). The role of gender in the clinical presentation of patients with borderline personality disorder. *Journal of Personality Disorders, 16,* 277–282.

Zucker, K. J. (2010). Gender identity and sexual orientation. In M. K. Dulcan (Ed.), *Dulcan's textbook of child and adolescent psychiatry* (pp. 543–552). Arlington, VA: American Psychiatric Publishing.

Zucker, K. J., & Cohen-Kettenis, P. T. (2008). Gender identity disorder in children and adolescents. In D. L. Rowland & L. Incrocci (Eds.), *Handbook of sexual and gender identity disorders* (pp. 376–422). Hoboken, NJ: John Wiley and Sons, Inc.

Zurbriggen, E. L., & Morgan, E. M. (2006). Who wants to marry a millionaire? Reality dating television programs, attitudes toward sex, and sexual behaviors. *Sex Roles, 54,* 1–17.

NAME INDEX

SUBJECT INDEX